UNITED NATIONS CONFERENCE ON TRADE AND DEVELOPMENT
CONFERENCE DES NATIONS UNIES SUR LE COMMERCE ET LE DÉVELOPPEMENT

CNUCED

UNCTAD

UNCTAD
HANDBOOK
OF STATISTICS

2011

MANUEL
DE STATISTIQUES
DE LA CNUCED

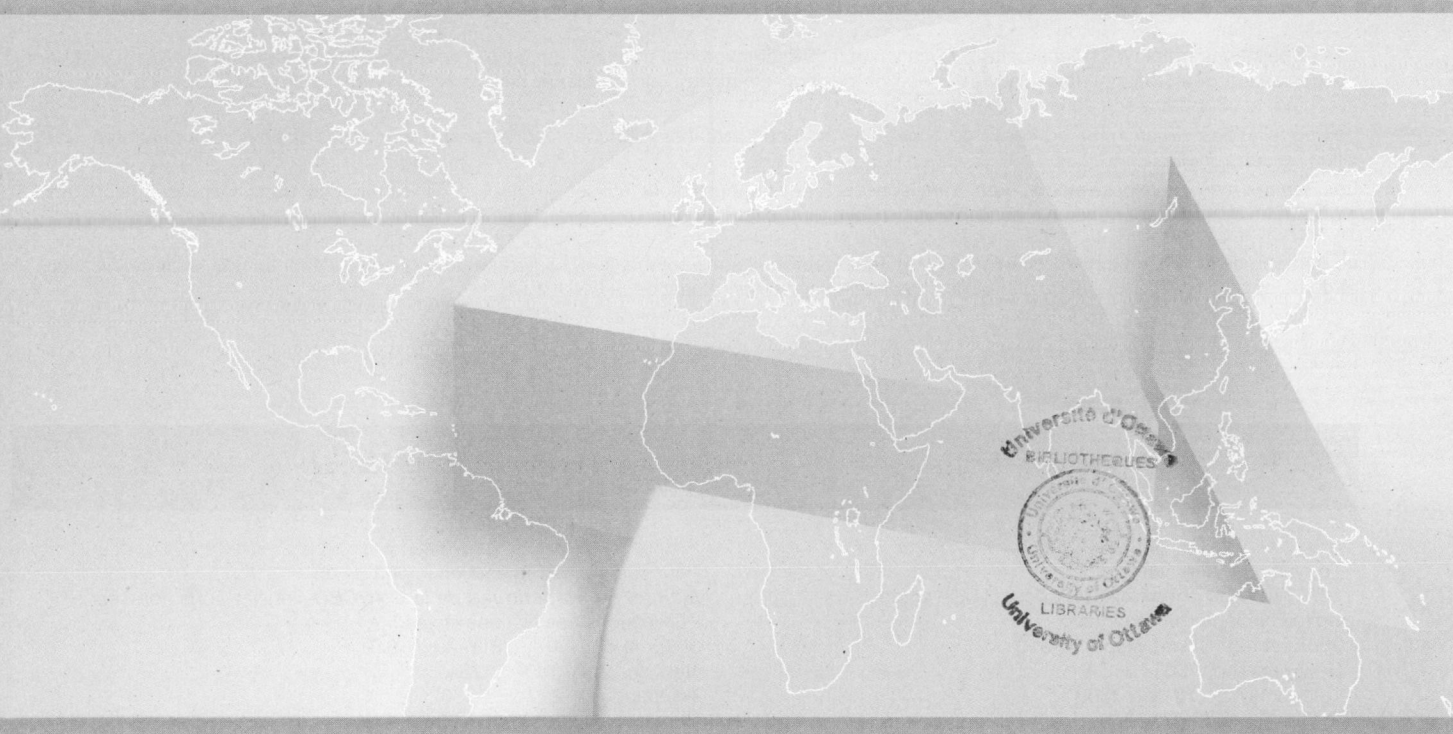

UNITED NATIONS
New York and Geneva

NATIONS UNIES
New York et Genève

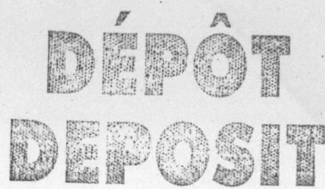

NOTE

Symbols of United Nations documents are composed of capital letters combined with figures. Mention of such a symbol indicates a reference to a United Nations document.

General disclaimer

The designations employed and the presentation of the material in this publication do not imply the expression of any opinion whatsoever on the part of the secretariat of the United Nations concerning the legal status of any country, territory, city or area, or of its authorities, or concerning the delimitation of its frontiers or boundaries.

Where the designations "economy" or "country or area" appear in tables, they cover countries, territories, cities and areas.

The designations "developing", "transition" and "developed" are intended for statistical convenience and do not necessarily express a judgement about the stage reached by a particular country or area in the development process.

Material in this publication may be freely quoted or reprinted, but acknowledgement is obligatory, together with a reference to the document number (TD/STAT.36). A copy of the publication containing the quotation or reprint should be sent to the UNCTAD secretariat.

*
* *

La cote des documents de l'Organisation des Nations Unies se compose de lettres majuscules et de chiffres. La mention d'une telle cote indique qu'il est fait référence à un document de l'Organisation.

Déni de responsabilité

Les appellations employées dans cette publication et la présentation des données qui y figurent n'impliquent, de la part du secrétariat de l'Organisation des Nations Unies, aucune prise de position quant au statut juridique des pays, territoires, villes ou zones, ou de leurs autorités, ni quant au tracé de leurs frontières ou limites.

Les appellations «économie» ou «pays ou zone» figurant dans certaines rubriques des tableaux désignent des pays, des territoires, des villes ou des zones.

Les termes «en développement», «en transition» et «développés» sont utilisés pour plus de commodité dans la présentation des statistiques et n'impliquent pas nécessairement un jugement quant au stade de développement atteint par un pays ou une zone donnée.

Le contenu de la présente publication peut être cité ou reproduit sans autorisation, sous réserve qu'il soit fait mention de ladite publication et de sa cote (TD/STAT.36) et qu'un justificatif soit adressé au secrétariat de la CNUCED.

How to order the *Handbook*

To order the print version of the
UNCTAD Handbook of Statistics, please contact:
United Nations Publications
300East 42nd Street, Room IN-919
New York, NY 10017, USA
Telephone: 1-212-963-8302
Toll free: 1-800-253-9646
Fax: 1-212-963-3489
Internet: https://unp.un.org

Comment commander le *Manuel*

Pour commander la version imprimée du
Manuel de Statistiques de la CNUCED, veuillez vous adresser à :
Publications des Nations Unies
300East 42nd Street, Bureau IN-919
New York, NY 10017, USA
Téléphone : 1-212-963-8302
Numéro vert : 1-800-253-9646
Fax : 1-212-963-3489
Internet : https://unp.un.org

TD/STAT. 36
UNITED NATIONS PUBLICATION – PUBLICATION DES NATIONS UNIES
Sales number / Numéro de vente : B.11.II.D.1
ISBN 978-92-1-112829-1
e-ISBN 978-92-1-054993-6
ISSN 0251-9461

The *UNCTAD Handbook of Statistics* provides essential data for analysing and measuring world trade, investment, international financial flows and development. Reliable statistical information is often considered as the first step during the preparation of making recommendations or taking decisions that countries will commit for many years as they strive to integrate into the world economy and improve the living standards of their citizens. Whether it is for research, consultation or technical cooperation, UNCTAD requires comparable, often detailed economic, demographic and social data, over several decades and for as many countries as possible.

In addition to facilitating the work of the secretariat's economists, the *UNCTAD Handbook of Statistics* also enables other users, such as policymakers, research specialists, academics, officials from national governments or international organizations, executive managers or members of nongovernmental organizations (NGOs) from developing, transition or developed countries to have access to this rich statistical information. The *Handbook* further offers journalists comprehensive information in a presentation that meets their needs.

This publication is available in printed copy and DVD. Moreover, the underlying data of the *Handbook* are available online at *UNCTADstat* (http://unctadstat.unctad.org). Unlike the *Handbook* which captures statistics at one point of time, *UNCTADstat* is continuously updated, enriched and providing users with the latest available data. In this regard, users should use caution when comparing data between the *Handbook* and *UNCTADstat*, as the date of update may differ.

User should be aware that, in this edition, the scope and definition of some country groups have changed compared to previous edition of *Handbook*. In addition, the presentation of tables 7.3 and 7.4 Remittances and table 7.1 Current account net was improved by the addition of all countries and country groups. Furthermore, the following tables prior to this edition - table 5.3 Tourism indicators, table 7.2 Balance of payments: capital and financial account summaries and table 8.5 Demographic indicators - are discontinued and no longer available.

To provide better and more relevant statistics to users, you are invited to fill up the feedback questionnaire on the last page or you can send your comments directly to statistics@unctad.org

Particular acknowledgement is due to the Statistics Division of the Department of Economic and Social Affairs of the United Nations, as well as to other international organizations, for its help in preparing this publication.

Le but du *Manuel de statistiques de la CNUCED* est de fournir les données statistiques essentielles à l'analyse du commerce mondial, de l'investissement, des flux financiers internationaux et du développement. Une information statistique fiable est souvent le préalable à la formulation de recommandations et à la prise de décisions qui engageront les pays pour de longues années dans leur processus d'intégration dans l'économie mondiale et l'amélioration des conditions de leurs peuples. Que ce soit pour la recherche, la concertation ou la coopération technique, la CNUCED a besoin de données économiques, démographiques et sociales comparables et souvent détaillées, disponibles si possible sur plusieurs décennies et pour un maximum de pays.

Au-delà de la mobilisation et de la vérification des données, du calcul d'indicateurs dérivés qui alimentent les travaux des économistes du secrétariat, le *Manuel de statistiques de la CNUCED* est l'occasion de partager une base statistique riche avec les décideurs et les chercheurs, qu'ils soient universitaires, fonctionnaires d'administrations nationales ou d'organisations internationales, cadres d'entreprises ou membres d'organisations non gouvernementales de pays en développement, en transition ou développés. Les journalistes trouvent aussi dans ce manuel une information synthétique dans une présentation bien adaptée à leurs préoccupations.

Le *Manuel* est disponible en version imprimée et DVD. Les données présentées dans le *Manuel* sont disponibles en ligne, dans *UNCTADstat* (http://unctadstat.unctad.org). À la différence du *Manuel* qui présente des statistiques figées à un moment donné, *UNCTADstat* est actualisé et enrichi régulièrement pour mettre à la disposition des utilisateurs les données les plus récentes. À cet égard, il est important de signaler que les données d'*UNCTADstat* et du *Manuel* ne pourront être comparées systématiquement en raison de la différence de date de leur mise à jour et de publication.

La couverture et la définition des groupements présentés dans cette nouvelle édition du *Manuel* ont changé. Cette année, la table des matières a également été revue. En effet, les indicateurs du tourisme, le sommaire des comptes de capital et d'opérations financières de la balance des paiements ainsi que les indicateurs démographiques (tableaux 5.3, 7.2 et 8.5 des précédentes éditions) ont été retirés tandis que les tableaux de la balance du compte courant (7.1) et des envois de fonds des travailleurs (7.3 et 7.4) ont été améliorés grâce à la présentation des données pour tous les pays et groupements de pays.

Pour mieux nous adapter aux besoins de nos utilisateurs et mettre à leur disposition des statistiques pertinentes, nous vous invitons à remplir le questionnaire qui se trouve en fin de publication. Vous pouvez également nous faire part de vos commentaires en nous écrivant à statistics@unctad.org

Le secrétariat de la CNUCED tient à remercier la Division de statistique du Département des affaires économiques et sociales de l'ONU et diverses organisations internationales du concours qu'elles ont apporté à la préparation de cette publication.

TABLE OF CONTENTS	TABLE DES MATIÈRES

PART ONE	PREMIÈRE PARTIE
International merchandise trade	**Commerce international des marchandises**

TABLE OF CONTENTS

TABLE DES MATIÈRES

TABLE OF CONTENTS

TABLE DES MATIÈRES

PART EIGHT
Development indicators

EXPLANATION OF SYMBOLS

0   Zero means that the amount is nil or negligible.

_   The symbol underscore indicates that the item is not applicable

..   Two dots indicate that the data are not available or are not separately reported.

-   The use of a hyphen on data area means that data is estimated and included in the aggregation but not to be shown. A hyphen between years (e.g. 1985-1990) signifies the full period involved, including the initial and final years.

(b)   Break in the series

(e)   Estimate

(f)   Forecast

(p)   Provisional data

(r)   Revised data

Some exceptions are indicated in footnotes.

TABLE DES MATIÈRES

7.6.1. Flux financiers publics bilatéraux et multilatéraux par pays et régions géographiques 376

7.6.2 Flux financiers publics bilatéraux et multilatéraux à destination des économies en développement par groupements économiques 391

7.7 Dette extérieure à long terme par catégories de prêt
A. Économies en développement 395
B. Économies en développement : Afrique 396
C. Économies en développement : Amérique 397
D. Économies en développement : Asie 398
E. Économies en développement : Océanie 399
F. Économies en développement : principaux exportateurs de pétrole et de gaz 400
G. Économies en développement : principaux exportateurs d'articles manufacturés 401

HUITIÈME PARTIE
Indicateurs du développement

8.1.1 Produit intérieur brut nominal : total et par habitant des pays et des régions géographiques 404

8.1.2 Produit intérieur brut nominal : total et par habitant des groupements économiques 412

8.2.1 Taux de croissance annuels moyens du produit intérieur brut réel total et par habitant des pays et des régions géographiques 414

8.2.2 Taux de croissance annuels moyens du produit intérieur brut réel total et par habitant des groupements économiques 422

8.3.1 Produit intérieur brut nominal par catégories de dépenses et par branches d'activité économique des pays et des régions géographiques 424

8.3.2 Produit intérieur brut nominal par catégories de dépenses et par branches d'activité économique des groupements économiques 442

8.4.1 Population et main-d'œuvre des pays et des régions géographiques 446

8.4.2 Population et main-d'œuvre des groupements économiques 465

SIGNIFICATION DES SYMBOLES

0   Un zéro signifie que le montant est nul ou négligeable.

_   Un tiret signifie que la rubrique est sans objet.

..   Deux points signifient que les données ne sont pas disponibles ou ne sont pas communiquées séparément.

-   Le trait d'union dans le champ des données indique que le chiffre est estimé et inclus dans l'agrégation mais n'est pas publié. Le trait d'union entre deux millésimes (par exemple 1985-1990) indique qu'il s'agit de la période tout entière, y compris la première et la dernière année mentionnées.

(b)   Interruption de la série

(e)   Estimation

(f)   Prévision

(p)   Donnée provisoire

(r)   Donnée révisée

Les exceptions sont indiquées dans les notes en bas de page.

These notes summarize the content of each part of the *Handbook* according to the revised Table of Contents of the present issue of the *Handbook of Statistics*.

The tables included in this book represent analytical summaries of the full time series contained in the *UNCTAD Handbook of Statistics 2011* on DVD.

PART ONE
International merchandise trade

Table 1.1 shows the value of total exports (f.o.b.) and imports (c.i.f.), expressed in millions of dollars and percentages of the world total, of individual countries and geographical regions (1.1.1), economic groupings (1.1.2), and trade groups (1.1.3). The trade flows shown in table 1.1.1 refer to the General Trade System except for the countries which employ the Special Trade System and which are marked with an asterisk. The General Trade System is used when the statistical territory of a compiling country coincides with its economic territory. Consequently, imports include all goods entering the economic territory of a compiling country and exports include all goods leaving the economic territory of the compiling country. The Special Trade System is used when the statistical territory comprises only a particular part of the economic territory within which "goods may be disposed of without customs restriction". In such a case, imports include all goods entering the free circulation area of the compiling country, which means cleared through customs for home use, and exports include all goods leaving the free circulation area of a compiling country.

Average annual growth rates of international trade derived from table 1.1 are presented in table 1.2.

Table 1.3 contains trade balances (exports f.o.b. minus imports c.i.f.) and these balances, as a percentage of imports of individual countries, geographical regions and economic groupings.

Table 1.4 shows the relative importance of trade among group members as compared to the regional or total trade of that group.

PART TWO
International merchandise trade by region

Table 2.1 shows the export and import structure of individual countries by main regions of origin and destination. Data are presented for as many individual countries as possible, while trade partners are grouped in 14 major clusters.

Table 2.2 (A to L) presents the structure of exports by destination and imports by origin by major commodity groups for 12 selected country groups. The table provides detailed information on the world trade network for 19 regions of origin and destination and six commodity groups.

Totals of international merchandise trade presented in the tables found in parts one and two are not strictly comparable due to complementary but different sources and remaining unallocated trade flows, despite efforts to distribute trade flows by destination, origin and commodity group.

Exports by destination may differ considerably in some cases from data on imports as reported by countries of destination for a variety of factors, among which the following may be of particular importance:
- Most import data are reported on a c.i.f. rather than an f.o.b. basis;
- There is a time lag between the date on which goods are recorded as exports and their arrival at their destination;
- There may be considerable differences between the recorded destination of exports and the actual destination as shown in import statistics.

PART THREE
International merchandise trade by product

Table 3.1 shows the export and import structure of individual economies by commodity groups for selected years for nine commodity groups (total, all food items, agricultural raw materials, fuels, ores and metals, manufactured goods, including chemical products, machinery and transport equipment and other manufactured goods).

Table 3.2 (A, B and C, respectively) presents the structure of exports for the world, for developing and developed economies, by product, at the SITC group (Revision 3, 3-digit) level. Each product share of world exports is calculated for each economic grouping as well as the average annual growth rate and the latter's deviation in relation to the world growth rate.

Table 3.2D establishes for each economy the list of main products exported (SITC group, Revision 3, 3-digit level). Each product's share of total exports of individual countries, geographical regions and the world is also indicated.

Table 3.2E lists major exporters of 70 leading products among developing economies at the SITC group (Revision 3, 3-digit) level as well as corresponding shares in world trade.

Table 3.3 provides concentration indices and structural change indices for exports and imports by product group at SITC (Revision 3, 3-digit) level. The first indicator shows how a product market is concentrated in a few countries or homogeneously distributed among several countries. The structural change indicator shows whether the market share for a given product among export countries has changed significantly when compared with a reference year.

Totals of international merchandise trade presented in the tables of this third part may also differ from the data contained in the first and second parts for the above reasons, to which must be added margins of exports and imports not distributed by commodity group or the use of different product nomenclatures by the exporting and importing countries.

PART FOUR
International merchandise trade indicators

Table 4.1 includes calculation results of concentration and diversification indices for individual countries, geographical regions and economic groupings. This concentration index specifically shows how exports and imports of individual countries or country groupings are concentrated on several products or otherwise distributed in a more homogeneous manner among a series of products. The diversification indicator signals whether the structure of exports or imports by product of a given country or country grouping differs from the structure by product shown for the world.

Table 4.2 contains volume indices of exports and imports, rounding out trade value available in tables 1.1 and 1.2, unit value indices of exports and imports and derived terms of trade and purchasing power of exports presented at the level of individual countries and geographical regions (4.2.1) and economic groupings (4.2.2).

To improve data coverage, especially for the latest periods, the following procedure was used in the calculation of unit value indices:
- A set of average prices indices at SITC (Revision 3, 3-digit) group level was constructed using *UNCTADstat* Commodity Price Statistics, international and national sources and UNCTAD secretariat estimates;
- At the country level, unit value indices were calculated using current year's trade values as weights at the SITC (Revision 3, 3-digit) level. Trade values are available in table 3.2.

In some instances these indices may differ from the estimates published in official sources, since the main aim is to provide tentative estimates for most developing countries on a comparable basis.

Table 4.3 presents average applied import MFN tariff rates for major categories of non-agricultural and non-fuel products by individual markets.

PART FIVE
International trade in services

Tables 5.1.1, 5.1.2 and 5.1.3 present the value of total trade in services by individual country, geographical region, economic grouping and trade group. The tables show values of exports (credits) and imports (debits) of services that were derived from statistics on international service transactions as presented in the International Monetary Fund's (IMF's) *Balance of Payments Statistics*. Services are defined as the economic output of intangible commodities that may be produced, transferred and consumed at the same time. However, services cover a heterogeneous range of intangible products and activities that are difficult to capture within a single definition and are sometimes hard to separate from goods. Services are outputs produced to order, and they typically include changes in the condition of the consumers realized through the activities of the producers at the demand of customers. By the time production of a service is completed, it must have been provided to a consumer.

Services figures shown here comprise 11 principal services categories according to the concepts and definitions of the IMF *Balance of Payments Manual (BPM5, 1993)*. These categories cover transport; travel; communications; construction; insurance; financial services; computer and information services; royalties and license fees; other business services; personal, cultural and recreational services; and government services n.i.e. Given the general difficulties involved in statistically capturing certain aspects of the trade in services, the balance-of-payments figures presented here may be somewhat downward-biased as compared with the actual value of the international trade in services. The aggregate data from tables 5.1 include the UNCTAD secretariat's estimates of missing values that are not shown separately.

Table 5.2 indicates 20 major exporters and importers, among developing economies, for each of the 10 principal services sectors as defined in the IMF *Balance of Payments Manual (BPM5, 1993)*, which are transport; travel; communication; construction; computer and information services; insurance; financial services; royalties and licence fees; other business services; and personal, cultural and recreational services. Government services n.i.e. are not included.

Table 5.3 concerns international maritime transport. It contains data on the world merchant fleet by flag of registration and by type of ship by region and economy, highlighting the group of major open-registry countries. A ship owner who registers his or her vessel in an open-registry country does not need to have any connection with a country of registry. The number of open-registry countries has varied over the years. The group in this table includes 10 countries. Table 5.3 contains consolidated time series from various issues of the UNCTAD *Review of Maritime Transport*. The Review reports on the worldwide evolution of shipping, ports and multimodal transport related to the major traffics of liquid bulk, dry bulk and containers.

PART SIX
Commodities

Table 6.1 includes aggregated price indices for primary commodity groups such as food, tropical beverages, vegetable oilseeds and oils, agricultural raw materials and minerals, ores and metals, as well as an all groups price index in current United States dollars. Also included are the annual and quarterly free-market price indices for selected commodities exported by developing economies. The weight of price indices for the above mentioned commodity groups (2000=100) are based on the value of exports of developing countries from 1999 to 2001.

Table 6.2 presents instability indices and trends in free-market prices for selected primary commodities that are of particular interest to developing economies.

PART SEVEN
International finance

Tables 7.1.1, 7.1.2 and 7.1.3 present values of the current account net in millions of dollars and as percentages of GDP for individual countries, geographical regions, and trade and economic groupings. Balance-of-payments current account data cover all transactions between residents and non-residents of a reporting economy. In general, the current account balance describes the difference between current receipts and expenditures for internationally traded goods, services and income payments. At the same time, from a national perspective, the current account balance would equal the gap between national savings and domestic investment.

Tables 7.2.1, 7.2.2 and 7.2.3 contain information on foreign direct investment (FDI) inflows and outflows by individual country, geographical region, economic grouping and trade group. These figures correspond to the Statistical Annexes of the UNCTAD *World Investment Report 2011*. FDI is defined as an investment involving a long-term relationship and reflecting a lasting interest in and control by a resident entity in one economy (foreign direct investor or parent enterprise) of an enterprise resident in a different economy (FDI enterprise or affiliate enterprise or foreign affiliate). Such investment involves both the initial transaction between the two entities and all subsequent transactions between them and among foreign affiliates. A direct investment enterprise is defined as an incorporated or unincorporated enterprise in which the direct investor, resident in another economy, owns 10 percent or more of the ordinary shares or voting power (or the equivalent).

Tables 7.3.1 and 7.3.2 present values of receipts (credits) of total migrants' remittances, in millions of dollars, for individual economies and regional and economic groupings. They also show total remittances receipts as percentage of GDP and international trade. The *Balance of Payments Manual (BPM5, 1993)* classifies workers' remittances, compensation of employees and migrants' transfers separately. In this table, their sum is given in order to present a clearer picture of the flows that enter economies via transactions by migrants and temporary or cross-border workers. BPM5 defines workers' remittances as goods and financial instruments transferred by migrants living and working (being residents) in a new economy to residents of the economy in which the migrants formerly resided. A migrant must live and work in the new economy for more than one year to be considered a resident there. Compensation of employees includes wages, salaries and other benefits, in cash or in kind, earned by individuals – in economies where they are not residents – for work performed for residents of those economies. It covers seasonal and other short-term workers and border workers. Migrants' transfers cover flows of goods and changes in financial items that arise from migration (change of residence for at least one year).

Tables 7.4.1 and 7.4.2 include data on payments (debits) of total migrants' remittances, based on the same approach used for tables 7.3.1 and 7.3.2.

Tables 7.5.1 and 7.5.2 present statistics on total international reserves (including gold) of developing countries by country, region and economic grouping, in millions of dollars. Other calculations included show months of imports that these reserves could finance at current import levels, as well as the annual change in total reserves. According to the IMF definition, international reserves consist of the sum of the country's foreign exchange, its reserve position in the IMF, the monetary gold reserves, and the United States dollar value of SDR holdings by its monetary authorities.

Tables 7.6 give a summary of official financial flows by type of flow, country, region and economic grouping. Flows from bilateral and multilateral sources are shown, as recorded by the Organization for Economic Cooperation and Development (OECD) Development Assistance Committee (DAC).

Tables 7.7 present time series on the external long-term indebtedness of developing economies. They also provide a detailed breakdown of public and publicly guaranteed debt by source of lending. External debt data in this table are based on the Debtor Reporting System (DRS) maintained by the World Bank.

PART EIGHT
Development indicators

Table **8.1** provides information on total and per capita nominal gross domestic product (GDP) (in United States dollars) by individual country, geographical region and economic grouping. The GDP figures in dollars are derived from GDP data provided in national currencies. The prevailing annual average market exchange rates, as reported by IMF, have been used for the conversion from national currencies to dollars.

Table **8.2** contains annual average growth rates of total and per capita real GDP by individual country, geographical region and economic grouping. The growth rates are based on GDP in United States dollars at constant 2005 prices.

Table **8.3** provides data on GDP by type of expenditure and kind of economic activity by country, geographical region and economic grouping.

Tables **8.4.1** and **8.4.2** provide some estimates on population and labour force: total population, urban population (as a percentage of total population), total labour force, female labour force (as a percentage of total labour force), total agriculture labour force and female labour force (as a percentage of total agriculture labour force). The figures for certain groups may be different from those published by the sources cited when the UNCTAD definitions for those groups are different.

OTHER NOTES

Unless otherwise specified, country aggregates are the sums of the relevant country data by group. Calculations of aggregates may in some cases include data estimated by the UNCTAD secretariat that are not necessarily all reported separately.

Because of rounding, details and percentages in tables do not necessarily add up to totals.

Data were collected and checked to ensure that they matched the geographical coverage of the countries, as described at the beginning of the *Handbook*. However, some gaps could not be avoided due to data unavailability and are described in the notes at the end tables.

Unless otherwise stated, dollars ($) refer to United States dollars and data in dollars are expressed in current United States dollars of the year to which they refer.

Average annual growth rates are defined as the coefficient b in the exponential trend function $y = ae^{bt}$ where t stands for time. This method takes all observations in a period into account. Therefore, the resulting growth rates reflect trends that are not unduly influenced by exceptional values

The country distributions presented are for statistical convenience only and follow those used by the Statistics Division, Department of Economic and Social Affairs (DESA), of the United Nations. They are grouped by economic criteria or by adhesion to commercial agreements for the purpose of statistical analysis and research.

The term "economies", as used in this publication, refers to regions, countries and territories.

Country-level data are included where statistics have been reported or where it was possible to make an estimate.

The composition of country and product groups is evolving in order to provide relevant statistics for research and analysis. In this regard, UNCTAD reviews and updates the definition and composition of groups every year. User should be aware that the changes may impact significantly the figures from one given release to the other. The detailed changes in the groups are thoroughly outlined in the section Classifications at *UNCTADstat* website.

1. Geographical regions

There is no established convention for the designation of "developed" and "developing" countries or areas in the United Nations system. In common practice, Israel and Japan in Asia, Bermuda, Canada, Greenland, Saint Pierre et Miquelon, and the United States in North America, Australia and New Zealand in Oceania, and Europe are considered "developed" regions or areas. This section includes all countries and territories divided into three major categories: developing countries, transition economies and developed economies. Each category is further divided by geographical regions.

1) Developing economies:
This category includes countries and territories in America, Africa, Asia and Oceania not specified below. The geographical regions are further subdivided into subregions in order to present more detailed statistics. Exceptions are specified in table footnotes.

2) Transition economies
This group includes countries in transition from centrally planned to market economies.

3) Developed economies:
This category is subdivided into four geographical regions: America, Asia, Europe and Oceania.

World' total represents the sum of the figures of the three above-mentioned groups plus the figures of a group of territories and partners not elsewhere classified, whose composition is detailed below. Data of these territories are included in the world total if they have been reported but are not presented individually or in any group, either by geography, economy or trade.

The composition of the group "not elsewhere classified" is as follows:
- Territories: Antarctica, Bouvet Island, British Antarctic Territory, British Indian Ocean Territory, Christmas Island, Cocos (Keeling) Islands, French Southern Territories, Heard and McDonald Islands, Norfolk Island, Pitcairn, Saint Barthélemy, Saint Martin (French part), South Georgia and South Sandwich Islands, United States Minor Outlying Islands, and United States Miscellaneous Pacific Islands.
- Partners: "Confidential information and differences", "Neutral zone", "Free zones", "Bunkers", and "Ship stores". These specific partners are only used in the merchandise trade tables.

The total of each group presented in the *Handbook* is also completed, should the case arise, with data that have not been allocated to the different elements composing the group.

2. Economic groupings of developing countries

The *Handbook* provides numerous and varied groups of countries and territories in order to provide easy access to the statistics necessary for socio-economic analysis and development research.

Developing economies are presented at three levels of aggregation: the total group, the group excluding China (referring to continental China) and the group excluding the least developed countries.

The category of heavily indebted poor countries includes those economies benefiting from the HIPC debt reduction initiative of the World Bank and the International Monetary Fund.

LDCs and landlocked developing countries (LLDCs) are recognized by the United Nations as categories that require special attention from the international community.

Since 1994, the United Nations has recognized the particular problems of the Small Island Developing States (SIDS), even though the criteria for drawing up an official list of SIDS have not yet been determined. The unofficial list is used by UNCTAD for analytical purposes only.

The developing economies are also categorized into three subgroups according to their average 2004-2006 per capita GDP: high-income (above $4,500), middle-income (between $1,000 and $4,500) and low-income (below $1,000).

The group of major petroleum and gas exporters consists of countries whose share of petroleum and gas (SITC code 33 plus 34) was not less than 50 per cent of their total exports, and whose exports of these products amounted to at least one per cent of petroleum and gas world share for the period 2004–2006. This group is divided into three geographical zones: Africa, America and Asia.

The group of major manufactured goods exporters consists of economies whose share of manufactured products (SITC 5 to 8, excluding 667 and 68) was not less than 50 per cent of their total exports, and whose exports of these products amounted to at least one per cent of manufactured goods world share for the period 2004–2006.The group comprises countries in America and Asia.

The composition of the groups of emerging economies (in America and Asia) and newly industrialized Asian economies (composed of first and second tier) corresponds to UNCTAD's *Trade and Development Report*.

The different geographical regions are also presented at various levels of aggregation:

- Africa: Northern Africa excluding Sudan, sub-Saharan Africa, including Sudan, including and excluding South Africa.

- America: Central America and Greater Caribbean Islands excluding Puerto Rico, including and excluding Mexico, South America and Central America, and South America excluding Brazil.

- Asia: Eastern and South-Eastern Asia excluding China, and Southern Asia excluding India.

3. Trade groups and interregional groupings

Statistics of trade groups with special analytic interest are presented according to their pertinence. These groupings include all relevant economies and are subclassified by geographical regions, with the exception of following interregional groups: African, Caribbean and Pacific Group of States; Asia–Pacific Economic Cooperation; Black Sea Economic Cooperation; and Commonwealth of Independent States.
Two groups have been added in this edition: the East African Community and the Organization of American States.

DISTRIBUTION BY GEOGRAPHICAL REGION

DEVELOPING ECONOMIES

AFRICA

Eastern Africa

Burundi	Malawi	Uganda
Comoros	Mauritius	United Republic of Tanzania
Djibouti	Mayotte	Zambia
Eritrea	Mozambique	Zimbabwe
Ethiopia	Rwanda	
Kenya	Seychelles	
Madagascar	Somalia	

Middle Africa

Angola	Congo	Sao Tome and Principe
Cameroon	Democratic Republic of the Congo	
Central African Republic	Equatorial Guinea	
Chad	Gabon	

Northern Africa

Algeria	Morocco	Western Sahara
Egypt	Sudan	
Libyan Arab Jamahiriya	Tunisia	

Southern Africa

Botswana	Namibia	Swaziland
Lesotho	South Africa	

Western Africa

Benin	Guinea	Nigeria
Burkina Faso	Guinea-Bissau	Saint Helena
Cape Verde	Liberia	Senegal
Côte d'Ivoire	Mali	Sierra Leone
Gambia	Mauritania	Togo
Ghana	Niger	

AMERICA

Caribbean islands

Greater Caribbean	**Small Caribbean islands**	
Cuba	Anguilla	Grenada
Dominican Republic	Antigua and Barbuda	Montserrat
Haiti	Aruba	Netherlands Antilles
Jamaica	Bahamas	Saint Kitts and Nevis
	Barbados	Saint Lucia
	British Virgin Islands	Saint Vincent and the Grenadines
	Cayman Islands	Trinidad and Tobago
	Dominica	Turks and Caicos Islands

Central America

Belize	Guatemala	Nicaragua
Costa Rica	Honduras	Panama
El Salvador	Mexico	

South America

Argentina	Ecuador	Suriname
Bolivia (Plurinational State of)	Falkland Islands (Malvinas)	Uruguay
Brazil	Guyana	Venezuela (Bolivarian Republic of)
Chile	Paraguay	
Colombia	Peru	

DISTRIBUTION BY GEOGRAPHICAL REGION

DEVELOPING ECONOMIES (concluded)

ASIA

Eastern Asia

China
Democratic People's Republic
  of Korea
Hong Kong, Special Administrative
  Region of China

Macao, Special Administrative
  Region of China
Mongolia
Republic of Korea
Taiwan Province of China

Southern Asia

Afghanistan
Bangladesh
Bhutan

India
Iran (Islamic Republic of)
Maldives

Nepal
Pakistan
Sri Lanka

South-Eastern Asia

Brunei Darussalam
Cambodia
Indonesia
Lao People's Democratic Republic

Malaysia
Myanmar
Philippines
Singapore

Thailand
Timor-Leste
Viet Nam

Western Asia

Bahrain
Iraq
Jordan
Kuwait
Lebanon

Occupied Palestinian territory
Oman
Qatar
Saudi Arabia
Syrian Arab Republic

Turkey
United Arab Emirates
Yemen

OCEANIA

American Samoa
Cook Islands
Fiji
French Polynesia
Guam
Kiribati
Marshall Islands

Micronesia (Federated States of)
Nauru
New Caledonia
Niue
Northern Mariana Islands
Palau
Papua New Guinea

Samoa
Solomon Islands
Tokelau
Tonga
Tuvalu
Vanuatu
Wallis and Futuna Islands

DISTRIBUTION BY GEOGRAPHICAL REGION

TRANSITION ECONOMIES

Albania

Armenia

Azerbaijan

Belarus

Bosnia and Herzegovina

Croatia

Georgia

Kazakhstan

Kyrgyzstan

Montenegro

Republic of Moldova

Russian Federation

Serbia

Tajikistan

The former Yugoslav Republic
   of Macedonia

Turkmenistan

Ukraine

Uzbekistan

DEVELOPED ECONOMIES

AMERICA

Bermuda

Canada

Greenland

Saint Pierre and Miquelon

United States of America
   including Puerto Rico and
   United States Virgin Islands

ASIA

Israel

Japan

EUROPE

Andorra

Austria

Belgium

Bulgaria

Cyprus

Czech Republic

Denmark

Estonia

Faeroe Islands

Finland including Åland Islands

France including French Guyana,
   Guadeloupe, Martinique,
   Monaco and Réunion

Germany

Gibraltar

Greece

Holy See

Hungary

Iceland

Ireland

Italy

Latvia

Lithuania

Luxembourg

Malta

Netherlands

Norway including Svalbard
   and Jan Mayen

Poland

Portugal

Romania

San Marino

Slovakia

Slovenia

Spain

Sweden

Switzerland including Liechtenstein

United Kingdom of Great Britain and
   Northern Ireland including Channel
   Islands and Isle of Man

OCEANIA

Australia

New Zealand

DISTRIBUTION OF DEVELOPING ECONOMIES BY ECONOMIC GROUPING

Heavily indebted poor countries (40)

Afghanistan	Gambia	Nicaragua
Benin	Ghana	Niger
Bolivia (Plurinational State of)	Guinea	Rwanda
Burkina Faso	Guinea-Bissau	Sao Tome and Principe
Burundi	Guyana	Senegal
Cameroon	Haiti	Sierra Leone
Central African Republic	Honduras	Somalia
Chad	Kyrgyzstan	Sudan
Comoros	Liberia	Togo
Congo	Madagascar	Uganda
Côte d'Ivoire	Malawi	United Republic of Tanzania
Democratic Republic of the Congo	Mali	Zambia
Eritrea	Mauritania	
Ethiopia	Mozambique	

Landlocked developing countries (31)

Afghanistan	Kazakhstan*	Rwanda
Armenia*	Kyrgyzstan*	Swaziland
Azerbaijan*	Lao People's Democratic Republic	Tajikistan*
Bhutan	Lesotho	The former Yugoslav Republic
Bolivia (Plurinational State of)	Malawi	of Macedonia*
Botswana	Mali	Turkmenistan*
Burkina Faso	Mongolia	Uganda
Burundi	Nepal	Uzbekistan*
Central African Republic	Niger	Zambia
Chad	Paraguay	Zimbabwe
Ethiopia	Republic of Moldova*	

* These countries are classified as economies in transition (neither developed nor developing).
  However, as they are landlocked States, they are also members of this group.

Small island developing States (29)

Antigua and Barbuda	Maldives	Samoa
Bahamas	Marshall Islands	Sao Tome and Principe
Barbados	Mauritius	Seychelles
Cape Verde	Micronesia (Federated States of)	Solomon Islands
Comoros	Nauru	Timor-Leste
Dominica	Palau	Tonga
Fiji	Papua New Guinea	Trinidad and Tobago
Grenada	Saint Kitts and Nevis	Tuvalu
Jamaica	Saint Lucia	Vanuatu
Kiribati	Saint Vincent and the Grenadines	

Least developed countries (48)

Africa and Haiti	Year of inclusion in the group		Year of inclusion in the group	*Asia*	Year of inclusion in the group
Angola	1994	Malawi	1971	Afghanistan	1971
Benin	1971	Mali	1971	Bangladesh	1975
Burkina Faso	1971	Mauritania	1986	Bhutan	1971
Burundi	1971	Mozambique	1988	Cambodia	1991
Central African Republic	1975	Niger	1971	Lao People's Democratic Republic	1971
Chad	1971	Rwanda	1971	Myanmar	1987
Democratic Republic of the Congo	1991	Senegal	2000	Nepal	1971
Djibouti	1982	Sierra Leone	1982	Yemen	1971
Equatorial Guinea	1982	Somalia	1971		
Eritrea	1994	Sudan	1971	*Islands*	
Ethiopia	1971	Togo	1982	Comoros	1977
Gambia	1975	Uganda	1971	Kiribati	1986
Guinea	1971	United Republic of Tanzania	1971	Samoa	1971
Guinea-Bissau	1981	Zambia	1991	Sao Tome and Principe	1982
Haiti	1971			Solomon Islands	1991
Lesotho	1971			Timor-Leste	2003
Liberia	1990			Tuvalu	1986
Madagascar	1991			Vanuatu	1985

DISTRIBUTION OF DEVELOPING ECONOMIES BY ECONOMIC GROUPING

UNCTAD ECONOMIC GROUPINGS

2004-2006 average per capita current GDP above $4,500: High-income (46)

American Samoa
Anguilla
Antigua and Barbuda
Argentina
Aruba
Bahamas
Bahrain
Barbados
British Virgin Islands
Brunei Darussalam
Cayman Islands
Chile
Cook Islands
Costa Rica
Equatorial Guinea
Falkland Islands (Malvinas)
French Polynesia

Guam
Hong Kong, Special Administrative
    Region of China
Kuwait
Lebanon
Libyan Arab Jamahiriya
Macao, Special Administrative
    Region of China
Malaysia
Mexico
Montserrat
Netherlands Antilles
New Caledonia
Niue
Northern Mariana Islands
Oman
Palau

Qatar
Republic of Korea
Saint Kitts and Nevis
Saint Lucia
Saudi Arabia
Seychelles
Singapore
Taiwan Province of China
Trinidad and Tobago
Turkey
Turks and Caicos Islands
United Arab Emirates
Uruguay
Venezuela (Bolivarian Republic of)

2004-2006 average per capita current GDP between $1,000 and $4,500: Middle-income (50)

Algeria
Belize
Bolivia (Plurinational State of)
Botswana
Brazil
Cape Verde
China
Colombia
Congo
Cuba
Dominica
Dominican Republic
Ecuador
Egypt
El Salvador
Fiji
Gabon

Grenada
Guatemala
Honduras
Iran (Islamic Republic of)
Jamaica
Jordan
Maldives
Marshall Islands
Mauritius
Micronesia (Federated States of)
Morocco
Namibia
Nauru
Occupied Palestinian territory
Panama
Paraguay
Peru

Philippines
Saint Helena
Saint Vincent and the Grenadines
Samoa
South Africa
Sri Lanka
Suriname
Swaziland
Syrian Arab Republic
Thailand
Tokelau
Tonga
Tunisia
Tuvalu
Vanuatu
Wallis and Futuna Islands

2004-2006 average per capita current GDP below $1,000: Low-income (60)

Afghanistan
Angola
Bangladesh
Benin
Bhutan
Burkina Faso
Burundi
Cambodia
Cameroon
Central African Republic
Chad
Comoros
Côte d'Ivoire
Democratic People's Republic of Korea
Democratic Republic of the Congo
Djibouti
Eritrea
Ethiopia
Gambia
Ghana
Guinea

Guinea-Bissau
Guyana
Haiti
India
Indonesia
Iraq
Kenya
Kiribati
Lao People's Democratic Republic
Lesotho
Liberia
Madagascar
Malawi
Mali
Mauritania
Mongolia
Mozambique
Myanmar
Nepal
Nicaragua
Niger

Nigeria
Pakistan
Papua New Guinea
Rwanda
Sao Tome and Principe
Senegal
Sierra Leone
Solomon Islands
Somalia
Sudan
Timor-Leste
Togo
Uganda
United Republic of Tanzania
Viet Nam
Yemen
Zambia
Zimbabwe

DISTRIBUTION OF DEVELOPING ECONOMIES BY ECONOMIC GROUPING

Major petroleum and gas exporters (12)

Africa	*America*	*Asia*
Algeria	Venezuela (Bolivarian Republic of)	Iran (Islamic Republic of)
Angola		Iraq
Libyan Arab Jamahiriya		Kuwait
Nigeria		Oman
		Qatar
		Saudi Arabia
		United Arab Emirates

Major manufactured goods exporters (8)

America	*Asia*
Mexico	China
	Hong Kong, Special Administrative Region of China
	Malaysia
	Republic of Korea
	Singapore
	Taiwan Province of China
	Thailand

Emerging economies (10)

America	*Asia*
Argentina	Malaysia
Brazil	Republic of Korea
Chile	Singapore
Mexico	Taiwan Province of China
Peru	Thailand

Newly industrialized Asian economies (8)

First tier	*Second tier*
Hong Kong, Special Administrative Region of China	Indonesia
Republic of Korea	Malaysia
Singapore	Philippines
Taiwan Province of China	Thailand

DISTRIBUTION OF ECONOMIES BY TRADE GROUP

AFRICA

Arab Maghreb Union – UMA (5) — Year of accession
Algeria	1989
Libyan Arab Jamahiriya	1989
Mauritania	1989
Morocco	1989
Tunisia	1989

Common Market for Eastern and Southern Africa (19) - COMESA
Burundi	1994
Comoros	1994
Democratic Republic of the Congo	1994
Djibouti	1994
Egypt	1994
Eritrea	1994
Ethiopia	1994
Kenya	1994
Libyan Arab Jamahiriya	2005
Madagascar	1994
Malawi	1994
Mauritius	1994
Rwanda	1994
Seychelles	1994
Sudan	1994
Swaziland	1994
Uganda	1994
Zambia	1994
Zimbabwe	1994

East African Community (5) - EAC
Burundi	2007
Kenya	2001
Rwanda	2007
Uganda	2001
United Republic of Tanzania	2001

Economic Community of Central African States (10) - ECCAS — Year of accession
Angola	1999
Burundi	1983
Cameroon	1983
Central African Republic	1983
Chad	1983
Congo	1983
Democratic Republic of the Congo	1983
Equatorial Guinea	1983
Gabon	1983
Sao Tome and Principe	1983

Economic Community of the Great Lakes Countries (3) - CEPGL
Burundi	1970
Democratic Republic of the Congo	1976
Rwanda	1976

Economic Community of West African States (15) - ECOWAS
Benin	1975
Burkina Faso	1975
Cape Verde	1977
Côte d'Ivoire	1975
Gambia	1975
Ghana	1975
Guinea	1975
Guinea-Bissau	1975
Liberia	1975
Mali	1975
Niger	1975
Nigeria	1975
Senegal	1975
Sierra Leone	1975
Togo	1975

Economic and Monetary Community of Central Africa (6) - CEMAC — Year of accession
Cameroon	1994
Central African Republic	1994
Chad	1994
Congo	1994
Equatorial Guinea	1994
Gabon	1994

Mano River Union (4) - MRU
Côte d'Ivoire	2008
Guinea	1980
Liberia	1973
Sierra Leone	1973

Southern African Development Community (15) - SADC
Angola	1992
Botswana	1992
Democratic Republic of the Congo	1992
Lesotho	1992
Madagascar	2005
Malawi	1992
Mauritius	1992
Mozambique	1992
Namibia	1992
Seychelles	2007
South Africa	1994
Swaziland	1992
United Republic of Tanzania	1992
Zambia	1992
Zimbabwe	1992

West African Economic and Monetary Union (8) - UEMOA
Benin	1994
Burkina Faso	1994
Côte d'Ivoire	1994
Guinea-Bissau	1997
Mali	1994
Niger	1994
Senegal	1994
Togo	1994

AMERICA

Andean Community (4) - ANCOM — Year of accession
Bolivia (Plurinational State of)	1996
Colombia	1996
Ecuador	1996
Peru	1996

Caribbean Community (15) - CARICOM
Antigua and Barbuda	1974
Bahamas	1983
Barbados	1973
Belize	1974
Dominica	1974
Grenada	1974
Guyana	1973
Haiti	2002
Jamaica	1973
Montserrat	1974
Saint Kitts and Nevis	1974
Saint Lucia	1974
Saint Vincent and the Grenadines	1974
Suriname	1995
Trinidad and Tobago	1973

Central American Common Market (5) - CACM — Year of accession
Costa Rica	1962
El Salvador	1961
Guatemala	1961
Honduras	1961
Nicaragua	1961

Free Trade Area of the Americas (34) - FTAA
Antigua and Barbuda	1994
Argentina	1994
Bahamas	1994
Barbados	1994
Belize	1994
Bolivia (Plurinational State of)	1994
Brazil	1994
Canada	1994
Chile	1994
Colombia	1994
Costa Rica	1994
Dominica	1994

Year of accession
Dominican Republic	1994
Ecuador	1994
El Salvador	1994
Grenada	1994
Guatemala	1994
Guyana	1994
Haiti	1994
Honduras	1994
Jamaica	1994
Mexico	1994
Nicaragua	1994
Panama	1994
Paraguay	1994
Peru	1994
Saint Kitts and Nevis	1994
Saint Lucia	1994
Saint Vincent and the Grenadines	1994
Suriname	1994
Trinidad and Tobago	1994
United States of America	1994
Uruguay	1994
Venezuela (Bolivarian Republic of)	1994

DISTRIBUTION OF ECONOMIES BY TRADE GROUP

AMERICA (concluded)

Latin American Integration Association (12) - LAIA	Year of accession
Argentina	1980
Bolivia (Plurinational State of)	1980
Brazil	1980
Chile	1980
Colombia	1980
Cuba	1999
Ecuador	1980
Mexico	1980
Paraguay	1980
Peru	1980
Uruguay	1980
Venezuela (Bolivarian Republic of)	1980

Mercado Común del Sur (4) - MERCOSUR	
Argentina	1994
Brazil	1994
Paraguay	1994
Uruguay	1994

North American Free Trade Agreement (3) - NAFTA	
Canada	1994
Mexico	1994
United States of America	1994

Organization of American States (34) - OAS	Year of accession
Antigua and Barbuda	1981
Argentina	1948
Bahamas	1982
Barbados	1967
Belize	1991
Bolivia (Plurinational State of)	1948
Brazil	1948
Canada	1990
Chile	1948
Colombia	1948
Costa Rica	1948
Cuba	2009
Dominica	1979
Dominican Republic	1948
Ecuador	1948
El Salvador	1948
Grenada	1975
Guatemala	1948
Guyana	1948
Haiti	1948
Jamaica	1969
Mexico	1948
Nicaragua	1948
Panama	1948
Paraguay	1948

	Year of accession
Peru	1951
Saint Kitts and Nevis	1984
Saint Lucia	1979
Saint Vincent and the Grenadines	1981
Suriname	1977
Trinidad and Tobago	1967
United States of America	1951
Uruguay	1951
Venezuela (Bolivarian Republic of)	1951

Organization of Eastern Caribbean States (7) - OECS	
Antigua and Barbuda	1981
Dominica	1981
Grenada	1981
Montserrat	1981
Saint Kitts and Nevis	1981
Saint Lucia	1981
Saint Vincent and the Grenadines	1981

ASIA

Asia-Pacific Trade Agreement (6) - APTA	Year of accession
Bangladesh	1975
China	2001
India	1975
Lao People's Democratic Republic	1975
Republic of Korea	1975
Sri Lanka	1975

Association of South-East Asian Nations (10) - ASEAN	
Brunei Darussalam	1984
Cambodia	1999
Indonesia	1967
Lao People's Democratic Republic	1997
Malaysia	1967
Myanmar	1997

	Year of accession
Philippines	1967
Singapore	1967
Thailand	1967
Viet Nam	1995

Economic Cooperation Organization (10) - ECO	
Afghanistan	1992
Azerbaijan	1992
Iran (Islamic Republic of)	1985
Kazakhstan	1992
Kyrgyzstan	1992
Pakistan	1985
Tajikistan	1992
Turkey	1985
Turkmenistan	1992
Uzbekistan	1992

Gulf Cooperation Council (6) - GCC	Year of accession
Bahrain	1981
Kuwait	1981
Oman	1981
Qatar	1981
Saudi Arabia	1981
United Arab Emirates	1981

South Asian Association for Regional Cooperation (8) - SAARC	
Afghanistan	2007
Bangladesh	1985
Bhutan	1985
India	1985
Maldives	1985
Nepal	1985
Pakistan	1985
Sri Lanka	1985

EUROPE

European Free Trade Association (3) - EFTA	Year of accession
Iceland	1970
Norway	1960
Switzerland	1960

European Union (27) - EU	
Austria	1995
Belgium	1957
Bulgaria	2008
Cyprus	2004
Czech Republic	2004
Denmark	1973
Estonia	2004
Finland	1995
France	1957
Germany	1957
Greece	1981

	Year of accession
Hungary	2004
Ireland	1973
Italy	1957
Latvia	2004
Lithuania	2004
Luxembourg	1957
Malta	2004
Netherlands	1957
Poland	2004
Portugal	1986
Romania	2008
Slovakia	2004
Slovenia	2004
Spain	1986
Sweden	1995
United Kingdom	1973

Euro area (17)	Year of accession
Austria	2002
Belgium	2002
Cyprus	2008
Estonia	2011
Finland	2002
France	2002
Germany	2002
Greece	2002
Ireland	2002
Italy	2002
Luxembourg	2002
Malta	2008
Netherlands	2002
Portugal	2002
Slovakia	2009
Slovenia	2007
Spain	2002

DISTRIBUTION OF ECONOMIES BY TRADE GROUP

OCEANIA

Year of accession

Melanesia Spearhead Group (4) - MSG

Fiji	1998
Papua New Guinea	1993
Solomon Islands	1993
Vanuatu	1993

DISTRIBUTION OF ECONOMIES BY INTERREGIONAL GROUPING

African, Caribbean and Pacific Group of States (79) - ACP

Angola	Gambia	Rwanda
Antigua and Barbuda	Ghana	Saint Kitts and Nevis
Bahamas	Grenada	Saint Lucia
Barbados	Guinea	Saint Vincent and the Grenadines
Belize	Guinea-Bissau	Samoa
Benin	Guyana	Sao Tome and Principe
Botswana	Haiti	Senegal
Burkina Faso	Jamaica	Seychelles
Burundi	Kenya	Sierra Leone
Cameroon	Kiribati	Solomon Islands
Cape Verde	Lesotho	Somalia
Central African Republic	Liberia	South Africa
Chad	Madagascar	Sudan
Comoros	Malawi	Suriname
Congo	Mali	Swaziland
Cook Islands	Marshall Islands	Timor-Leste
Côte d'Ivoire	Mauritania	Togo
Cuba	Mauritius	Tonga
Democratic Republic of the Congo	Micronesia (Federated States of)	Trinidad and Tobago
Djibouti	Mozambique	Uganda
Dominica	Namibia	United Republic of Tanzania
Dominican Republic	Nauru	Vanuatu
Equatorial Guinea	Niger	Zambia
Eritrea	Nigeria	Zimbabwe
Ethiopia	Niue	
Fiji	Palau	
Gabon	Papua New Guinea	

Year of accession		*Year of accession*		*Year of accession*	
Asia-Pacific Economic Cooperation (21) - APEC		**Black Sea Economic Cooperation (12) - BSEC**		**Commonwealth of Independent States (11) - CIS**	
Australia	1989	Albania	1992	Armenia	1991
Brunei Darussalam	1989	Armenia	1992	Azerbaijan	1991
Canada	1989	Azerbaijan	1992	Belarus	1991
Chile	1994	Bulgaria	1992	Kazakhstan	1991
China	1991	Georgia	1992	Kyrgyzstan	1991
Hong Kong, Special		Greece	1992	Republic of Moldova	1991
Administrative Region of China	1991	Republic of Moldova	1992	Russian Federation	1991
Indonesia	1989	Romania	1992	Tajikistan	1991
Japan	1989	Russian Federation	1992	Turkmenistan	1991
Malaysia	1989	Serbia	2004	Ukraine	1991
Mexico	1993	Turkey	1992	Uzbekistan	1991
New Zealand	1989	Ukraine	1992		
Papua New Guinea	1993				
Peru	1998				
Philippines	1989				
Republic of Korea	1989				
Russian Federation	1998				
Singapore	1989				
Taiwan Province of China	1991				
Thailand	1989				
United States of America	1989				
Viet Nam	1998				

ABBREVIATIONS AND ACRONYMS

ACP	African, Caribbean and Pacific Group of States
ANCOM	Andean Community
APEC	Asia–Pacific Economic Cooperation
APTA	Asia-Pacific Trade Agreement (former Bangkok Agreement)
ASEAN	Association of South-East Asian Nations
BPM	*Balance of Payments Manual* (IMF)
BSEC	Black Sea Economic Cooperation
CACM	Central American Common Market
CARICOM	Caribbean Community
CCSA	Committee for the Coordination of Statistical Activities
CEMAC	Economic and Monetary Community of Central Africa
CEPGL	Economic Community of the Great Lakes Countries
c.i.f.	cost, insurance and freight
CIS	Commonwealth of Independent States
COMESA	Common Market for Eastern and Southern Africa
DAC	Development Assistance Committee (of OECD)
DRS	Debtor Reporting System
EAC	East African Community
ECCAS	Economic Community of Central African States
ECE	Economic Commission for Europe
ECLAC	Economic Commission for Latin America and the Caribbean
ECO	Economic Cooperation Organization
ECOWAS	Economic Community of West African States
EFTA	European Free Trade Association
EIU	Economic Intelligence Unit
ESCAP	Economic and Social Commission for Asia and the Pacific
ESCWA	Economic and Social Commission for Western Asia
EU	European Union
excl.	excluding
FAO	Food and Agriculture Organization of the United Nations
FDI	foreign direct investment
f.o.b.	free on board
FTAA	Free Trade Area of the Americas
GATS	General Agreement on Trade in Services
GCC	Gulf Cooperation Council
GDP	gross domestic product
GFCF	gross fixed capital formation
GNP	gross national product
HIPC	heavily indebted poor countries
HS	Harmonized System
ILO	International Labour Organization
IMF	International Monetary Fund
LAIA	Latin American Integration Association
LDC	least developed country
MERCOSUR	Mercado Común del Sur
MFN	most favoured nation
MRU	Mano River Union
MSG	Melanesia Spearhead Group
NAFTA	North American Free Trade Agreement
n.e.s.	not elsewhere specified
NIE	newly industrialized economies
n.i.e.	not included elsewhere
NPISHs	non-profit institutions serving households
OA	official aid
OAS	Organization of American States
ODA	official development assistance
OECD	Organization for Economic Cooperation and Development
OECS	Organization of Eastern Caribbean States
OOF	other official flows
OPEC	Organization of the Petroleum Exporting Countries
SAARC	South Asian Association for Regional Cooperation
SADC	Southern African Development Community
SAR	Special Administrative Region
SDR	special drawing right
SFR	Socialist Federative Republic of Yugoslavia (former)
SIDS	Small Island Developing States
SITC	Standard International Trade Classification
TFYR	The former Yugoslav Republic of Macedonia
TNC	transnational corporation
TRAINS	Trade Analysis and Information System
UMA	Arab Maghreb Union
UN/DESA/SD	United Nations Department of Economic and Social Affairs, Statistics Division
UNDP	United Nations Development Programme
UNESCO	United Nations Educational, Scientific and Cultural Organization
UNICEF	United Nations Children's Fund
USSR	Union of Soviet Socialist Republics
WAEMU	West African Economic and Monetary Union
WITS	World Integrated Trade Solution
WTO	World Trade Organization

Ces notes générales présentent le contenu de chaque tableau du *Manuel de statistiques* ainsi que les modifications introduites dans cette nouvelle édition, s'il y a lieu.

Les tableaux inclus dans cette publication constituent un résumé analytique des séries chronologiques complètes publiées dans le *Manuel de statistiques 2011 de la CNUCED* sur DVD.

PREMIÈRE PARTIE
Commerce international des marchandises

Les tableaux **1.1** donnent la valeur des exportations (f.a.b.) et des importations (c.a.f.) totales de marchandises, exprimée en millions de dollars et en pourcentage du monde, des pays et régions géographiques (1.1.1), groupements économiques (1.1.2) et groupements commerciaux (1.1.3). Les flux du commerce présentés dans le tableau 1.1.1 se réfèrent au Système du Commerce Général, à l'exception des pays et territoires qui utilisent le Système du Commerce Spécial et qui sont munis d'un astérisque. Le Système du Commerce Général est utilisé lorsque le territoire statistique d'un pays coïncide avec son territoire économique, et en conséquence, les importations comprennent tous les biens admis sur le territoire du pays déclarant et les exportations tous les biens qui le quittent. Le Système du Commerce Spécial est utilisé lorsque le territoire statistique ne comprend qu'une partie du territoire économique à l'intérieur de laquelle « les biens peuvent être écoulés librement sans restriction douanière ». Dans ce cas, les importations comprennent tous les biens qui entrent dans la zone de libre circulation du pays déclarant, c'est-à-dire qui ont été dédouanés pour mise à la consommation et les exportations comprennent tous les biens qui quittent la zone de libre circulation du pays déclarant.

Les taux d'évolution annuels moyens du commerce international des marchandises, calculés à partir des valeurs des tableaux 1.1, figurent dans les tableaux **1. 2**.

Les tableaux **1.3** présentent les balances commerciales (exportations f.a.b. moins importations c.a.f.), ainsi que ces mêmes balances en pourcentage des importations des pays, régions géographiques et groupements économiques.

Le tableau **1.4** indique l'importance des échanges entre pays membres de groupements commerciaux par rapport aux exportations régionales et totales de ces groupements.

DEUXIÈME PARTIE
Commerce international des marchandises par régions

Le tableau **2.1** présente la structure des exportations et des importations des pays par régions de destination et d'origine. Le plus grand nombre possible de pays en développement sont inclus tandis que les partenaires commerciaux sont regroupés en 14 groupes considérés comme particulièrement importants pour l'analyse du commerce international.

Les tableaux **2.2 (A à L)** indiquent la structure des exportations par destination ainsi que des importations par origine et par groupes de produits pour le monde et une sélection de 12 groupements de pays. Le tableau fournit une information détaillée sur le réseau du commerce international avec le monde, 19 régions d'origine et de destination, et pour six différents groupes de produits.

Les totaux du commerce international des marchandises présentés dans les tableaux des première et deuxième parties ne sont pas strictement comparables en raison de sources complémentaires mais différentes et d'une marge d'exportations et d'importations non distribuées, en dépit des efforts déployés pour répartir les flux commerciaux par destinations et origines.

Les exportations ventilées par destinations peuvent accuser un écart parfois considérable par rapport aux importations déclarées par les pays destinataires en raison de divers facteurs dont les plus importants sont les suivants :

- Les importations sont déclarées en principe "valeur c.a.f." plutôt que "valeur f.a.b".;
- Les importations de marchandises peuvent arriver à destination et être enregistrées longtemps après la date de leur enregistrement à l'exportation ;

- D'importantes différences peuvent exister entre la destination des exportations déclarée par les pays exportateurs et la destination réelle telle qu'indiquée dans les statistiques d'importation.

TROISIÈME PARTIE
Commerce international des marchandises par produits

Le tableau **3.1** fournit la structure des exportations et des importations des pays par produits classés en 9 groupes (total, produits alimentaires, matières premières d'origine agricole, combustibles, minerais et métaux, produits manufacturés, dont produits chimiques, machines et matériel de transport, articles manufacturés divers) pour plusieurs années.

Les tableaux **3.2A**, **B** et **C** présentent respectivement les exportations par produits du monde, des économies en développement et développées, à un niveau très détaillé (CTCI révision 3, position à trois chiffres). Les parts que représente chaque produit dans les exportations du monde et de la région, sont calculées pour chaque groupe d'économies, ainsi que le taux annuel de croissance et l'écart de ce dernier par rapport au taux de croissance mondial.

Le tableau **3.2D** établit, pour chaque économie, la liste des principaux produits qu'elle exporte (CTCI révision 3, position à trois chiffres). La part de chaque produit dans le total des exportations du pays, de la région et du monde est également indiquée.

Le tableau **3.2E** liste les plus gros exportateurs de 70 produits parmi les produits les plus exportés par les économies en développement (CTCI révision 3, position à trois chiffres), ainsi que les parts correspondantes dans le commerce mondial.

Le tableau **3.3** fournit les indices de concentration et de changements structurels des exportations et des importations des produits au niveau de la CTCI (révision 3, position à trois chiffres). Le premier indicateur a vocation à montrer comment le marché d'un produit est concentré sur quelques pays ou réparti de façon plus homogène entre les pays. L'indicateur de changement structurel indique si la répartition du commerce d'un produit entre les pays exportateurs ou importateurs a connu une évolution importante par rapport à une année de référence.

Les totaux du commerce international des marchandises présentés dans les tableaux de cette troisième partie peuvent aussi être différents des données des première et deuxième parties pour les raisons précédemment citées, auxquelles il convient d'ajouter des marges d'exportations et d'importations non distribuées par groupes de produits ou l'utilisation de nomenclatures différentes de produits par le pays exportateur et le pays importateur.

QUATRIÈME PARTIE
Indicateurs du commerce international des marchandises

Les tableaux **4.1** contiennent les résultats du calcul des indices de concentration et de diversification des pays, régions géographiques et groupements économiques. Cet indice de concentration a vocation à montrer comment les exportations et importations d'un pays ou groupe de pays sont concentrées sur quelques produits ou réparties de façon plus homogène sur une gamme de produits. L'indicateur de diversification indique si la structure par produits des exportations ou importations d'un pays ou groupe de pays diverge de la structure par produits observée au niveau du monde.

Les tableaux **4.2** fournissent les indices de volume des exportations et des importations complétant ainsi l'information en valeur disponible dans les tableaux 1.1 et 1.2, les indices de la valeur unitaire des exportations et importations ainsi que les indices de termes de l'échange et le pouvoir d'achat des exportations dérivés des indices de valeur unitaire. Ces indices sont calculés au niveau des pays et régions géographiques (4.2.1) et des groupements économiques (4.2.2).

Afin d'améliorer la couverture des données et spécialement pour les années récentes, la méthode suivante a été utilisée pour le calcul des valeurs unitaires :

- Un ensemble d'indices de prix moyens au niveau des groupes de la CTCI (révision 3, position à 3 chiffres) a été construit en utilisant des données provenant de *UNCTADstat* Statistiques des produits

de base, des sources internationales et nationales ainsi que des estimations du secrétariat de la CNUCED.

- Au niveau des pays individuels, les indices de la valeur unitaire ont été calculés en utilisant comme pondération les valeurs des exportations et des importations de l'année courante disponibles dans la table 3.2 au niveau de la CTCI (révision 3, position à 3 chiffres).

Dans certains cas ces indices peuvent différer des estimations publiées dans les sources officielles, le but principal étant de fournir des estimations approximatives et comparables pour la plupart des pays en développement.

Le tableau 4.3 contient les données sur les droits de douane NPF moyens appliqués à l'importation des principales catégories de produits non-agricoles et non-pétroliers, par marchés individuels.

CINQUIÈME PARTIE
Commerce international des services

Les tableaux 5.1.1, 5.1.2 et 5.1.3 présentent la valeur des exportations et des importations totales des services par pays, par régions géographiques, groupements économiques et groupements commerciaux. Les tableaux incluent les valeurs des exportations (crédits) et des importations (débits) des services qui proviennent des statistiques sur les transactions internationales de services, telles qu'elles sont présentées dans les Statistiques de la balance des paiements du FMI. Les services sont définis comme rendements économiques de produits intangibles qui peuvent être produits, transférés et consommés au même moment. Cependant, les services recouvrent un groupe large et hétérogène de produits et d'activités que l'on peut difficilement englober dans une définition. Parfois, la démarcation entre services et marchandises n'est pas aisée. Les services sont produits sur commande et ont généralement pour résultat un changement des conditions des consommateurs qui ont demandé ces services. Pour que la production d'un service soit terminée, il doit être fourni au consommateur.

Les chiffres couvrent les 11 catégories principales de services conformément à la définition du *Manuel de la balance des paiements* du FMI (*MBP5, 1993*). Ces catégories comprennent : les transports; les voyages; les communications; le bâtiment et les travaux publics; les assurances; les services financiers; l'informatique et l'information; les redevances et droits de licence; les autres services aux entreprises; les services personnels, culturels et relatifs aux loisirs; et les services fournis ou reçus par les administrations publiques. De manière générale, les difficultés à mesurer statistiquement la valeur du commerce des services persistent et les données de la balance des paiements sur les services peuvent être inférieures à la valeur des transactions réelles. Les agrégats inclus dans le tableau 5.1 comprennent les valeurs manquantes, estimées par le secrétariat de la CNUCED, qui ne sont pas présentées séparément.

Le tableau 5.2 liste, parmi les économies en développement, les 20 plus gros exportateurs et importateurs pour chacun des 10 secteurs principaux du commerce des services, c'est-à-dire les transports; les voyages; les communications; le bâtiment et les travaux publics; l'informatique et l'information; les assurances; les services financiers; les redevances et droits de licence; autres services aux entreprises; et les services personnels, culturels et relatifs aux loisirs. Les services fournis ou reçus par les administrations publiques ne sont pas inclus.

Le tableau 5.3 concerne le transport maritime international. Il contient des données sur la flotte marchande mondiale par pavillons d'immatriculation et par types de navires et fait spécialement ressortir le groupe des principaux pays de libre immatriculation. Un propriétaire qui enregistre son navire dans un pays "libre d'immatriculation" ne doit avoir aucune relation avec ce pays. Le nombre de pays de libre immatriculation a changé au cours des années. Dans le tableau 5.3, le groupe comprend 10 pays. Le tableau incorpore les informations consolidées provenant des différentes éditions de la publication *Review of Maritime Transport*. Elle rend compte de l'évolution mondiale du transport multimodal, portuaire et maritime concernant les principaux trafics de vracs liquides, de vracs secs et de conteneurs.

SIXIÈME PARTIE
Produits de base

Le tableau 6.1 donne les indices annuels et trimestriels de prix en dollars courants sur le marché libre d'une sélection de produits de base exportés par les économies en développement. Ces indices sont aussi disponibles au niveau des groupes de produits de base suivants : produits alimentaires, boissons tropicales, huiles et graines oléagineuses, matières premières d'origine agricole, minéraux, minerais et métaux ainsi qu'un indice de l'ensemble. Les pondérations ont été calculées à partir de la valeur des exportations des pays en développement de 1999 à 2001 et les indices en utilisant 2000=100 comme année de base.

Le tableau 6.2 complète l'information sur les prix des produits de base par les indices d'instabilité et les tendances de prix sur le marché libre d'une sélection de produits de base ayant une importance particulière pour les économies en développement.

SEPTIÈME PARTIE
Finance internationale

Les tableaux 7.1.1, 7.1.2 et 7.1.3 fournissent les valeurs de compte courant net par pays, par régions et par groupements économiques et commerciaux. Les chiffres sont présentés en millions de dollars, ainsi qu'en pourcentage du produit intérieur brut. Le compte des transactions courantes de la balance des paiements recouvre toutes les transactions entre entités résidentes et non-résidentes de l'économie déclarante. En général, la balance du compte courant indique la différence entre les recettes et les paiements pour les biens, les services et les revenus faisant partie des transactions internationales. De même, de la perspective nationale, la balance du compte courant représente l'écart entre les épargnes nationales et l'investissement intérieur.

Les tableaux 7.2.1, 7.2.2 et 7.2.3 sont consacrés aux investissements directs en provenance de l'étranger (IED). Ils représentent les flux entrants et sortants de l'IED par pays et régions géographiques, groupements économiques et groupements commerciaux. Les chiffres correspondent aux données contenues dans l'Annexe statistique du *World Investment Report 2011* de la CNUCED. L'investissement étranger direct (IED) est un investissement impliquant une relation à long terme et témoignant de l'intérêt durable d'une entité résidant dans un pays (investisseur étranger direct ou société mère) à l'égard d'une entreprise résidant dans un autre pays (entreprise bénéficiaire, entreprise affiliée, ou encore filiale étrangère). Cet investissement englobe à la fois la transaction initiale entre les deux entités et toutes les transactions ultérieures entre elles et entre filiales étrangères, qu'elles soient constituées ou non en sociétés. L'entreprise d'investissement direct est définie comme une entreprise dotée ou non de la personnalité morale, dans laquelle un investisseur direct qui est résident d'une autre économie détient au moins 10% des actions ordinaires ou des droits de vote (ou l'équivalent).

Les tableaux 7.3.1 et 7.3.2 fournissent les informations sur les recettes (crédits) des envois de fonds des travailleurs et migrants – en millions de dollars - par pays, par régions et par groupements économiques. Ces données sont également communiquées en pourcentage du PIB et du commerce international. Le *Manuel de la balance des paiements* du FMI (*MBP5, 1993*) classe séparément les envois de fonds des travailleurs, la rémunération des salariés et les transferts des migrants. Dans ce tableau leur somme est présentée afin de mieux cerner les flux entrant une économie à travers les transferts liés aux travailleurs migrants ou autres travailleurs employés à l'étranger à court-terme. Selon la définition du *MBP5* les envois de fonds des travailleurs sont les transferts de biens ou d'actifs financiers effectués par les migrants qui vivent et travaillent (considérés comme résidents) dans une économie en faveur des résidents de leur ancien pays de résidence. Un migrant doit vivre et travailler dans une nouvelle économie durant plus d'une année pour y être considéré résident. La rémunération des salariés comprend les salaires, traitements et autres prestations, en numéraire ou nature, gagnés par les particuliers, dans une économie où ils ne sont pas résidents, pour un travail exécuté au profit d'un résident de cette économie.

Les salariés peuvent être des travailleurs saisonniers ou d'autres travailleurs à temps limité ou encore des travailleurs frontaliers. Les transferts des migrants couvrent les flux de biens et les variations des actifs financiers qui résultent de la migration (changement de résidence pour une durée d'un an au moins).

Les tableaux 7.4.1 et 7.4.2 font apparaître les statistiques sur les paiements (débits) des envois des travailleurs et migrants, suivant la même approche utilisée dans les tableaux 7.3.1 et 7.3.2.

Les tableaux 7.5.1 et 7.5.2 incluent les données relatives aux réserves internationales (y compris l'or) des économies en développement par pays, par régions et par groupements économiques. Les mois d'importation que ces réserves peuvent financer, dans la situation actuelle du commerce international du pays, sont également indiqués, ainsi que la variation annuelle des réserves totales. Selon la définition du FMI, les réserves totales représentent la somme des avoirs du pays en devises, la position de ses réserves au FMI, les réserves de l'or monétaire, et la valeur en dollars des États-Unis des avoirs en DTS de ses autorités monétaires.

Les flux financiers publics sont présentés dans les tableaux 7.6 par catégories de flux, pays, régions géographiques et groupements économiques. La définition des flux bilatéraux et multilatéraux est conforme aux publications du Comité d'aide au développement (CAD) de l'OCDE.

Les tableaux 7.7 contiennent les données sur la dette extérieure à long terme des principaux groupes d'économies en développement, en particulier la ventilation détaillée de la dette publique ou garantie par l'État par sources d'emprunt. Les données de la dette extérieure présentées dans ces tableaux se basent sur le Système de notification des pays débiteurs (SNPD), géré par la Banque mondiale.

HUITIÈME PARTIE
Indicateurs du développement

Les tableaux 8.1 fournissent le produit intérieur brut (PIB) nominal total et par habitant des pays, régions géographiques et groupements économiques. Les données de PIB en dollars ont été obtenues à partir des valeurs de PIB exprimées à l'origine en monnaies nationales. Les taux de change moyens annuels sur le marché libre, obtenus des séries statistiques du FMI, ont été utilisés pour la plupart des pays lors de la conversion en dollars.

Les taux annuels moyens de variation du PIB réel total et du PIB réel par habitant des pays, régions géographiques et groupements économiques sont disponibles dans les tableaux 8.2. Les taux de croissance se basent sur le PIB aux prix constants en dollars de l'année 2005.

Le PIB total est décomposé par catégories de dépenses et la valeur ajoutée totale par branches d'activité économique dans les tableaux 8.3 pour les pays, régions géographiques et groupements économiques.

Les tableaux 8.4.1 et 8.4.2 présentent des estimations sur la population et la main-d'œuvre : population totale, population urbaine (en pourcentage de la population totale), main-d'œuvre totale, main-d'œuvre féminine (en pourcentage de la main-d'œuvre totale), main-d'œuvre dans l'agriculture, main-d'œuvre féminine (en pourcentage de la main-d'œuvre totale dans l'agriculture). Les chiffres pour certains groupes peuvent être différents de ceux publiés par la Division de la population lorsque les définitions de la CNUCED de ces groupes sont différentes.

AUTRES NOTES

Sauf indication contraire, les agrégats de pays sont obtenus en sommant les données des pays composant le groupe. Les calculs d'agrégats peuvent dans certains cas inclure des données estimées par le secrétariat de la CNUCED qui ne sont pas nécessairement toutes rapportées séparément.

Par ailleurs, la somme des chiffres et des pourcentages indiqués dans les tableaux ne correspond pas nécessairement aux totaux en raison des arrondis.

Les données ont été collectées et vérifiées pour qu'elles correspondent à la couverture géographique des pays, telle qu'elle est décrite en début de *Manuel*. Toutefois certains écarts n'ont pu être évités en fonction de la disponibilité des données. Ils sont alors décrits dans les notes de fin de tableau.

Sauf indication contraire, le terme «dollar» s'entend du dollar des États-Unis d'Amérique et les données en dollars sont exprimées en dollars courants de l'année à laquelle elles se réfèrent.

Les taux moyens d'évolution annuelle sont définis par le coefficient b de la fonction exponentielle de tendance $y = ae^{bt}$, où t représente le temps. Cette méthode permet de prendre en compte toutes les observations concernant une période donnée sans que le taux de croissance obtenu ne soit trop affecté par des valeurs exceptionnelles.

Les pays et territoires sont présentés suivant des critères géographiques conformes à ceux de la Division de statistique, Département des affaires économiques et sociales (DAES) de l'ONU. Les pays et territoires sont aussi regroupés suivant des critères économiques ou d'adhésion à des accords commerciaux à des fins d'analyse statistique et de recherche.

Dans cette publication, le terme «économie» couvre les régions, les pays et les territoires.

Les pays sont présentés dans les tableaux s'ils ont communiqué des données ou si des estimations ont pu être calculées.

La composition des groupements de pays et produits évolue constamment pour mettre des statistiques pertinentes à la disposition de la recherche et de l'analyse. C'est pourquoi la CNUCED révise et met à jour la définition et la composition des groupes chaque année. Ces changements peuvent affecter de manière significative les chiffres d'une année de publication à l'autre. Le détail des changements est disponible dans la section Nomenclatures sur le site web de *UNCTADstat*.

1. Régions géographiques

La distinction entre pays ou régions "développés" et "en développement" ne correspond à aucune nomenclature officielle à l'échelle du système des Nations Unies. Dans la pratique, on considère généralement comme développés Israël et Japon pour l'Asie, Bermudes, Canada, États-Unis, Groenland et Saint-Pierre-et-Miquelon pour l'Amérique septentrionale, Australie et Nouvelle-Zélande pour l'Océanie et l'Europe. Les pays et territoires sont répartis en trois grandes catégories, les économies en développement, les économies en transition et les économies développées, elles-mêmes subdivisées suivant des critères géographiques.

1) Économies en développement :
Ces économies sont réparties entre quatre grandes régions géographiques : Afrique, Amérique, Asie et Océanie elles-mêmes subdivisées en sous-régions pour permettre la présentation de statistiques plus détaillées. Les exceptions à ce classement que l'on retrouve dans certains tableaux sont indiquées dans des notes.

2) Économies en transition
Il s'agit des pays opérant la transition d'une économie planifiée à une économie de marché.

3) Économies développées :
Ces économies sont réparties entre quatre grandes régions géographiques : Amérique, Asie, Europe et Océanie.

Le total 'Monde' inclut la somme des données de ces trois groupes à laquelle s'ajoutent les données d'un groupement 'Autres territoires' (territoires ou partenaires non classés ailleurs), dont la composition est détaillée ci-dessous. Lorsqu'elles sont rapportées, les données relatives à ces territoires ne sont pas présentées individuellement.
La composition du groupement 'Autres territoires' est la suivante:
   -Territoires non-classés ailleurs : Antarctique, île Bouvet, Territoire britannique de l'Antarctique, Territoire britannique de l'océan Indien, île Christmas, îles des Cocos (Keeling), Terres australes et antarctiques françaises, îles Heard et McDonald, île Norfolk, Pitcairn, Saint-Barthélemy, Saint Martin (partie française), Géorgie du Sud et îles Sandwich méridionales, îles mineures éloignées des États-Unis et îles du Pacifique sous administration des États-Unis.
   - Partenaires non classés ailleurs : 'combustibles de soute et provisions de bord', 'informations confidentielles et différences', 'zone neutre', 'zones franches' qui sont utilisés exclusivement dans les tableaux du commerce de marchandises.
   Les statistiques présentées au niveau de chacun des groupements précédemment décrits sont calculées à partir des valeurs des économies qui entrent dans la composition du groupement et complétées le cas échéant par un reliquat qu'il n'a pas été possible de répartir entre les éléments du groupement.

2. Groupements économiques des économies en développement

Dans le *Manuel de statistiques de la CNUCED*, les regroupements des pays et territoires en développement sont nombreux et variés afin de disposer facilement des données statistiques nécessaires à l'analyse socio-économique et aux recherches sur le développement.

Les économies en développement sont présentées à trois niveaux d'agrégation : le groupe dans son intégralité, puis sans la Chine continentale et enfin sans les pays les moins avancés.

Le groupe des pays pauvres très endettés inclut les pays bénéficiant de l'initiative de désendettement de la Banque mondiale et du Fonds monétaire international.

Les PMA et les pays en développement sans littoral sont des groupes de pays qui requièrent une attention particulière de la communauté internationale. Les PMA sont présentés aux niveaux d'agrégation suivants : Afrique et Haïti, Asie et les îles. Depuis 1994, les Nations Unies ont également pris en compte les problèmes particuliers des petits États insulaires en développement mais n'ont pas établi de liste officielle de ces États. La liste présentée dans le *Manuel de statistiques* est utilisée par la CNUCED à des fins analytiques uniquement.

Les économies en développement sont également réparties en trois groupes de revenu en fonction du PIB par habitant pour la moyenne des années de 2004 à 2006 : revenu élevé (supérieur à 4500 dollars), revenu intermédiaire (compris entre 1000 et 4500 dollars) et revenu faible (inférieur à 1000 dollars).

Le groupement des principaux exportateurs de pétrole et de gaz comprend les pays, dont la part de pétrole et de gaz (CTCI codes 33 plus 34), ne représentait 1) pas moins de 50 % de leurs exportations totales, et les exportations de ces produits s'élevaient à 2) au moins 1 % de la part mondiale pour la période 2004-2006. Les pays composant ce groupement sont répartis en trois zones géographiques : Afrique, Amérique et Asie.

Le groupement des principaux exportateurs d'articles manufacturés (CTCI 5 à 8 moins 667 et 68), répartis entre Amérique et Asie, comprend les économies dont la part d'articles manufacturés ne représentait 1) pas moins de 50 % de leurs exportations totales, et 2) leurs exportations d'articles manufacturés représentait au moins 1 % de la part mondiale pour la période 2004-2006.

La composition des groupements des économies émergentes (réparties entre Amérique et Asie) et des économies nouvellement industrialisées d'Asie (première et deuxième génération) correspond à celle utilisée dans le *Rapport sur le commerce et le développement* de la CNUCED.

Les différentes régions géographiques sont également présentées à différents niveaux d'agrégation :
   - Afrique : Afrique septentrionale sans le Soudan, Afrique subsaharienne, Soudan compris, avec et sans l'Afrique du Sud.
   - Amérique : Amérique centrale et Grandes Antilles sans Porto Rico, avec et sans le Mexique, Amérique du Sud et centrale, Amérique du Sud sans le Brésil.
   - Asie : Asie orientale et du Sud-Est sans la Chine et Asie méridionale sans l'Inde.

3. Groupements commerciaux et interrégionaux

Les statistiques des groupements régionaux et commerciaux sont présentées dès lors qu'elles sont pertinentes et présentent un intérêt analytique. Ces groupements englobent toutes les économies concernées et sont classés selon les grandes régions géographiques utilisées précédemment, à l'exception des groupements interrégionaux suivants : le groupe des États d'Afrique, des Caraïbes et du Pacifique, le groupe de Coopération économique de l'Asie et du Pacifique, le groupe de Coopération économique de la mer Noire et la Communauté des États indépendants. Dans cette édition du *Manuel*, deux groupes ont été ajoutés: la Communauté de l'Afrique de l'Est ainsi que l'Organisation des États américains.

RÉPARTITION PAR RÉGIONS GÉOGRAPHIQUES

ÉCONOMIES EN DÉVELOPPEMENT

AFRIQUE

Afrique orientale

Burundi	Malawi	Seychelles
Comores	Maurice	Somalie
Djibouti	Mayotte	Zambie
Érythrée	Mozambique	Zimbabwe
Éthiopie	Ouganda	
Kenya	République-Unie de Tanzanie	
Madagascar	Rwanda	

Afrique centrale

Angola	Gabon	République démocratique du Congo
Cameroun	Guinée équatoriale	Sao Tomé-et-Principe
Congo	République centrafricaine	Tchad

Afrique septentrionale

Algérie	Maroc	Tunisie
Égypte	Sahara occidental	
Jamahiriya arabe libyenne	Soudan	

Afrique australe

Afrique du Sud	Lesotho	Swaziland
Botswana	Namibie	

Afrique occidentale

Bénin	Guinée	Nigéria
Burkina Faso	Guinée-Bissau	Sainte-Hélène
Cap-Vert	Libéria	Sénégal
Côte d'Ivoire	Mali	Sierra Leone
Gambie	Mauritanie	Togo
Ghana	Niger	

AMÉRIQUE

Amérique centrale

Belize	Guatemala	Nicaragua
Costa Rica	Honduras	Panama
El Salvador	Mexique	

Amérique du Sud

Argentine	Équateur	Suriname
Bolivie (État plurinational de)	Guyana	Uruguay
Brésil	Îles Falkland (Malvinas)	Venezuela (République bolivarienne du)
Chili	Paraguay	
Colombie	Pérou	

Caraïbes

Grandes Antilles	**Petites Antilles**	
Cuba	Anguilla	Îles Caïmanes
Haïti	Antigua-et-Barbuda	Îles Turques et Caïques
Jamaïque	Antilles néerlandaises	Îles Vierges britanniques
République dominicaine	Aruba	Montserrat
	Bahamas	Sainte-Lucie
	Barbade	Saint-Kitts-et-Nevis
	Dominique	Saint-Vincent-et-les Grenadines
	Grenade	Trinité-et-Tobago

RÉPARTITION PAR RÉGIONS GÉOGRAPHIQUES

ÉCONOMIES EN DÉVELOPPEMENT (fin)

ASIE

Asie orientale

Chine
Hong Kong, région administrative
   spéciale de Chine
Macao, région administrative
   spéciale de Chine

Mongolie
Province chinoise de Taiwan
République de Corée
République populaire démocratique
   de Corée

Asie méridionale

Afghanistan
Bangladesh
Bhoutan

Inde
Iran (République islamique d')
Maldives

Népal
Pakistan
Sri Lanka

Asie du Sud-Est

Brunéi Darussalam
Cambodge
Indonésie
Malaisie

Myanmar
Philippines
République démocratique populaire lao
Singapour

Thaïlande
Timor-Leste
Viet Nam

Asie occidentale

Arabie saoudite
Bahreïn
Émirats arabes unis
Iraq
Jordanie

Koweït
Liban
Oman
Qatar
République arabe syrienne

Territoire palestinien occupé
Turquie
Yémen

OCÉANIE

Fidji
Guam
Îles Cook
Îles Mariannes septentrionales
Îles Marshall
Îles Salomon
Îles Wallis-et-Futuna

Kiribati
Micronésie (États fédérés de)
Nauru
Nioué
Nouvelle-Calédonie
Palaos
Papouasie-Nouvelle-Guinée

Polynésie française
Samoa
Samoa américaines
Tokélaou
Tonga
Tuvalu
Vanuatu

RÉPARTITION PAR RÉGIONS GÉOGRAPHIQUES

ÉCONOMIES EN TRANSITION

Albanie
Arménie
Azerbaïdjan
Bélarus
Bosnie-Herzégovine
Croatie
ex-République yougoslave
de Macédoine

Fédération de Russie
Géorgie
Kazakhstan
Kirghizistan
Monténégro
Ouzbékistan
République de Moldova
Serbie

Tadjikistan
Turkménistan
Ukraine

ÉCONOMIES DÉVELOPÉES

AMÉRIQUE

Bermudes
Canada

États-Unis d'Amérique, y compris
Porto Rico et les îles Vierges
américaines

Groenland
Saint-Pierre-et-Miquelon

ASIE

Israël
Japon

EUROPE

Allemagne
Andorre
Autriche
Belgique
Bulgarie
Chypre
Danemark
Espagne
Estonie
Finlande, y compris les îles d'Åland
France, y compris la Guadeloupe,
la Guyane française, la Martinique,
Monaco et la Réunion
Gibraltar

Grèce
Hongrie
Îles Féroé
Irlande
Islande
Italie
Lettonie
Lituanie
Luxembourg
Malte
Norvège, y compris les îles Svalbard
et Jan Mayen
Pays-Bas
Pologne

Portugal
République tchèque
Roumanie
Royaume-Uni de Grande-Bretagne
et d'Irlande du Nord, y compris les îles
Anglo-Normandes et l'île de Man
Saint-Marin
Saint-Siège
Slovaquie
Slovénie
Suède
Suisse, y compris le Liechtenstein

OCÉANIE

Australie
Nouvelle-Zélande

RÉPARTITION DES ÉCONOMIES EN DÉVELOPPEMENT PAR GROUPEMENTS ÉCONOMIQUES

Pays pauvres très endettés (40)

Afghanistan	Guinée-Bissau	République centrafricaine
Bénin	Guyana	République démocratique du Congo
Bolivie (État plurinational de)	Haïti	République-Unie de Tanzanie
Burkina Faso	Honduras	Rwanda
Burundi	Kirghizistan	Sao Tomé-et-Principe
Cameroun	Libéria	Sénégal
Comores	Madagascar	Sierra Leone
Congo	Malawi	Somalie
Côte d'Ivoire	Mali	Soudan
Érythrée	Mauritanie	Tchad
Éthiopie	Mozambique	Togo
Gambie	Nicaragua	Zambie
Ghana	Niger	
Guinée	Ouganda	

Pays en développement sans littoral (31)

Afghanistan	Kirghizistan*	République de Moldova*
Arménie*	Lesotho	Rwanda
Azerbaïdjan*	Malawi	Swaziland
Bhoutan	Mali	Tadjikistan*
Bolivie (État plurinational de)	Mongolie	Tchad
Botswana	Népal	Turkménistan*
Burkina Faso	Niger	Zambie
Burundi	Ouganda	Zimbabwe
Éthiopie	Ouzbékistan*	
ex-République yougoslave de Macédoine*	Paraguay	
	République centrafricaine	
Kazakhstan*	République démocratique populaire lao	

* Ces pays font partie du groupement des économies en transition (ni développées ni en développement). Cependant, comme ce sont des pays sans littoral, ils appartiennent aussi à ce groupement.

Petits États insulaires en développement (29)

Antigua-et-Barbuda	Jamaïque	Saint-Vincent-et-les Grenadines
Bahamas	Kiribati	Samoa
Barbade	Maldives	Sao Tomé-et-Principe
Cap-Vert	Maurice	Seychelles
Comores	Micronésie (États fédérés de)	Timor-Leste
Dominique	Nauru	Tonga
Fidji	Palaos	Trinité-et-Tobago
Grenade	Papouasie-Nouvelle-Guinée	Tuvalu
Îles Marshall	Sainte-Lucie	Vanuatu
Îles Salomon	Saint-Kitts-et-Nevis	

Pays les moins avancés (48)

Afrique et Haïti	Année d'inclusion dans le groupe		Année d'inclusion dans le groupe		Année d'inclusion dans le groupe
Angola	1994	Mozambique	1988	**Asie**	
Bénin	1971	Niger	1971	Afghanistan	1971
Burkina Faso	1971	Ouganda	1971	Bangladesh	1975
Burundi	1971	République centrafricaine	1975	Bhoutan	1971
Djibouti	1982	République démocratique du Congo	1991	Cambodge	1991
Érythrée	1994	République-Unie de Tanzanie	1971	Myanmar	1987
Éthiopie	1971	Rwanda	1971	Népal	1971
Gambie	1975	Sénégal	2000	République démocratique populaire lao	1971
Guinée	1971	Sierra Leone	1982	Yémen	1971
Guinée-Bissau	1981	Somalie	1971	**Îles**	
Guinée Équatoriale	1982	Soudan	1971	Comores	1977
Haïti	1971	Tchad	1971	Îles Salomon	1991
Lesotho	1971	Togo	1982	Kiribati	1986
Libéria	1990	Zambie	1991	Samoa	1971
Madagascar	1991			Sao Tomé-et-Principe	1982
Malawi	1971			Timor-Leste	2003
Mali	1971			Tuvalu	1986
Mauritanie	1986			Vanuatu	1985

RÉPARTITION DES ÉCONOMIES EN DÉVELOPPEMENT PAR GROUPEMENTS ÉCONOMIQUES

GROUPEMENTS ÉCONOMIQUES DE LA CNUCED

PIB courant par habitant supérieur à 4500 dollars pour la moyenne 2004-2006 : Revenu élevé (46)

Anguilla
Antigua-et-Barbuda
Antilles néerlandaises
Arabie saoudite
Argentine
Aruba
Bahamas
Bahreïn
Barbade
Brunéi Darussalam
Chili
Costa Rica
Émirats arabes unis
Guam
Guinée équatoriale
Hong-Kong, région administrative
    spéciale de Chine

Îles Caïmanes
Îles Cook
Îles Falkland (Malvinas)
Îles Mariannes du Nord
Îles Turques et Caïques
Îles Vierges britanniques
Jamahiriya arabe libyenne
Koweït
Liban
Macao, région administrative
    spéciale de Chine
Malaisie
Mexique
Montserrat
Nioué
Nouvelle-Calédonie
Oman

Palaos
Polynésie française
Province chinoise de Taiwan
Qatar
République de Corée
Sainte-Lucie
Saint-Kitts-et-Nevis
Samoa américaines
Seychelles
Singapour
Trinité-et-Tobago
Turquie
Uruguay
Venezuela (République bolivarienne du)

PIB courant par habitant compris entre 1000 et 4500 dollars pour la moyenne 2004-2006 : Revenu intermédiaire (50)

Afrique du Sud
Algérie
Belize
Bolivie (État plurinational de)
Botswana
Brésil
Cap-Vert
Chine
Colombie
Congo
Cuba
Dominique
Égypte
El Salvador
Équateur
Fidji
Gabon

Grenade
Guatemala
Honduras
Îles Marshall
Îles Wallis-et-Futuna
Iran (République islamique d')
Jamaïque
Jordanie
Maldives
Maroc
Maurice
Micronésie (États fédérés de)
Namibie
Nauru
Panama
Paraguay
Pérou

Philippines
République arabe syrienne
République dominicaine
Sainte-Hélène
Saint-Vincent-et-les Grenadines
Samoa
Sri Lanka
Suriname
Swaziland
Territoire palestinien occupé
Thaïlande
Tokélaou
Tonga
Tunisie
Tuvalu
Vanuatu

PIB courant par habitant inférieur à 1000 dollars pour la moyenne 2004-2006 : Revenu faible (60)

Afghanistan
Angola
Bangladesh
Bénin
Bhoutan
Burkina Faso
Burundi
Cambodge
Cameroun
Comores
Côte d'Ivoire
Djibouti
Érythrée
Éthiopie
Gambie
Ghana
Guinée
Guinée-Bissau
Guyana
Haïti
Îles Salomon

Inde
Indonésie
Iraq
Kenya
Kiribati
Lesotho
Libéria
Madagascar
Malawi
Mali
Mauritanie
Mongolie
Mozambique
Myanmar
Népal
Nicaragua
Niger
Nigéria
Ouganda
Pakistan
Papouasie-Nouvelle-Guinée

République centrafricaine
République démocratique du Congo
République populaire démocratique
    de Corée
République démocratique populaire lao
République-Unie de Tanzanie
Rwanda
Sao Tomé-et-Principe
Sénégal
Sierra Leone
Somalie
Soudan
Tchad
Timor-Leste
Togo
Viet Nam
Yémen
Zambie
Zimbabwe

RÉPARTITION DES ÉCONOMIES EN DÉVELOPPEMENT PAR GROUPEMENTS ÉCONOMIQUES

Principaux pays exportateurs de pétrole et de gaz (12)

Afrique
Algérie
Angola
Jamahiriya arabe libyenne
Nigéria

Amérique
Venezuela
   (République bolivarienne du)

Asie
Arabie saoudite
Émirats arabes unis
Iran (République islamique d')
Iraq
Koweït
Oman
Qatar

Principaux pays exportateurs d'articles manufacturés (8)

Amérique
Mexique

Asie
Chine
Hong Kong, région administrative
   spéciale de Chine
Malaisie
Province chinoise de Taiwan
République de Corée
Singapour
Thaïlande

Économies émergentes (10)

Amérique
Argentine
Brésil
Chili
Mexique
Pérou

Asie
Malaisie
Province chinoise de Taiwan
République de Corée
Singapour
Thaïlande

Économies nouvellement industrialisées d'Asie (8)

Première génération
Hong Kong, région administrative
   spéciale de Chine
Province chinoise de Taiwan
République de Corée
Singapour

Deuxième génération
Indonésie
Malaisie
Philippines
Thaïlande

RÉPARTITION DES ÉCONOMIES PAR GROUPEMENTS COMMERCIAUX

AFRIQUE

	Année d'adhésion
Communauté de l'Afrique de l'Est (5) - CAE	
Burundi	2007
Kenya	2001
Ouganda	2001
République-Unie de Tanzanie	2001
Rwanda	2007
Communauté de développement de l'Afrique australe (15) - CDAA	
Afrique du Sud	1994
Angola	1992
Botswana	1992
Lesotho	1992
Madagascar	2005
Malawi	1992
Maurice	1992
Mozambique	1992
Namibie	1992
République démocratique du Congo	1992
République-Unie de Tanzanie	1992
Seychelles	2007
Swaziland	1992
Zambie	1992
Zimbabwe	1994
Communauté économique des États de l'Afrique centrale (10) - CEEAC	
Angola	1999
Burundi	1983
Cameroun	1983
Congo	1983
Gabon	1983
Guinée équatoriale	1983
République centrafricaine	1983
République démocratique du Congo	1983
Sao Tomé-et-Principe	1983
Tchad	1983

	Année d'adhésion
Communauté économique et monétaire de l'Afrique centrale (6) - CEMAC	
Cameroun	1994
Congo	1994
Gabon	1994
Guinée équatoriale	1994
République centrafricaine	1994
Tchad	1994
Communauté économique des États de l'Afrique de l'Ouest (15) - CEDEAO	
Bénin	1975
Burkina Faso	1975
Cap-Vert	1977
Côte d'Ivoire	1976
Gambie	1975
Ghana	1975
Guinée	1975
Guinée-Bissau	1975
Libéria	1975
Mali	1975
Niger	1975
Nigéria	1975
Sénégal	1975
Sierra Leone	1975
Togo	1975
Communauté économique des pays des Grands Lacs (3) - CEPGL	
Burundi	1976
République démocratique du Congo	1976
Rwanda	1976
Marché commun des États de l'Afrique de l'Est et du Sud (19) - COMESA	
Burundi	1994
Comores	1994
Djibouti	1994
Égypte	1994
Érythrée	1994
Éthiopie	1994
Kenya	1994
Jamahiriya arabe libyenne	2005

	Année d'adhésion
Madagascar	1994
Malawi	1994
Maurice	1994
Ouganda	1994
République démocratique du Congo	1994
Rwanda	1994
Seychelles	1994
Soudan	1994
Swaziland	1994
Zambie	1994
Zimbabwe	1994
Union du fleuve Mano (4) - UFM	
Côte d'Ivoire	2000
Guinée	1980
Libéria	1973
Sierra Leone	1973
Union du Maghreb arabe (5) - UMA	
Algérie	1989
Jamahiriya arabe libyenne	1989
Maroc	1989
Mauritanie	1989
Tunisie	1989
Union économique et monétaire ouest-africaine (8) - UEMOA	
Bénin	1994
Burkina Faso	1994
Côte d'Ivoire	1994
Guinée-Bissau	1997
Mali	1994
Niger	1994
Sénégal	1994
Togo	1994

AMÉRIQUE

	Année d'adhésion
Accord de libre-échange nord-américain (3) - ALENA	
Canada	1994
États-Unis d'Amérique	1994
Mexique	1994
Association latino-américaine d'intégration (12) - ALADI	
Argentine	1980
Bolivie (État plurinational de)	1980
Brésil	1980
Chili	1980
Colombie	1980
Cuba	1999
Équateur	1980
Mexique	1980
Paraguay	1980
Pérou	1980
Uruguay	1980
Venezuela (République bolivarienne du)	1980

	Année d'adhésion
Communauté andine (4) - ANCOM	
Bolivie (État plurinational de)	1996
Colombie	1996
Équateur	1996
Pérou	1996
Communauté des Caraïbes (15) - CARICOM	
Antigua-et-Barbuda	1974
Bahamas	1983
Barbade	1973
Belize	1974
Dominique	1974
Grenade	1974
Guyana	1973
Haïti	2002
Jamaïque	1973
Montserrat	1974
Sainte Lucie	1974
Saint-Kitts-et-Nevis	1974
Saint-Vincent-et-les- Grenadines	1974
Suriname	1995
Trinité-et-Tobago	1973

	Année d'adhésion
Marché commun d'Amérique centrale (5) - MCAC	
Costa Rica	1962
El Salvador	1961
Guatemala	1961
Honduras	1961
Nicaragua	1961
Marché commun sud-américain (4) - MERCOSUR	
Argentine	1994
Brésil	1994
Paraguay	1994
Uruguay	1994

RÉPARTITION DES ÉCONOMIES PAR GROUPEMENTS COMMERCIAUX

AMÉRIQUE (fin)

Organisation des États américains (34) - OEA	Année d'adhésion
Antigua-et-Barbuda	1981
Argentine	1948
Bahamas	1982
Barbade	1967
Belize	1991
Bolivie (État plurinational de)	1948
Brésil	1948
Canada	1990
Chili	1948
Colombie	1948
Costa Rica	1948
Cuba	2009
Dominique	1979
El Salvador	1948
Équateur	1948
États-Unis d'Amérique	1948
Grenade	1975
Guatemala	1948
Guyana	1948
Haïti	1948
Jamaïque	1969
Mexique	1948
Nicaragua	1948
Panama	1948
Paraguay	1948
Pérou	1948
République dominicaine	1948
Sainte-Lucie	1979
Saint-Kitts-et-Nevis	1984
Saint-Vincent-et-les Grenadines	1981
Suriname	1977
Trinité-et-Tobago	1967
Uruguay	1948
Venezuela (République bolivarienne du)	1948

Organisation des États des Caraïbes orientales (7) - OECO	Année d'adhésion
Antigua-et-Barbuda	1981
Dominique	1981
Grenade	1981
Montserrat	1981
Sainte-Lucie	1981
Saint-Kitts-et-Nevis	1981
Saint-Vincent-et-les Grenadines	1981

Zone de libre-échange des Amériques (34) - ZLEA	Année d'adhésion
Antigua-et-Barbuda	1994
Argentine	1994
Bahamas	1994
Barbade	1994
Belize	1994
Bolivie (État plurinational de)	1994
Brésil	1994
Canada	1994
Chili	1994
Colombie	1994
Costa Rica	1994
Dominique	1994
El Salvador	1994
Équateur	1994
États-Unis d'Amérique	1994
Grenade	1994
Guatemala	1994
Guyana	1994
Haïti	1994
Honduras	1994
Jamaïque	1994
Mexique	1994
Nicaragua	1994
Panama	1994
Paraguay	1994
Pérou	1994
République dominicaine	1994
Sainte-Lucie	1994
Saint-Kitts-et-Nevis	1994
Saint-Vincent-et-les Grenadines	1994
Suriname	1994
Trinité-et-Tobago	1994
Uruguay	1994
Venezuela (République bolivarienne du)	1994

ASIE

Accord commercial de l'Asie et du Pacifique (6) - ACAP	Année d'adhésion
Bangladesh	1975
Chine	2001
Inde	1975
République de Corée	1975
République démocratique populaire lao	1975
Sri Lanka	1975

Association de l'Asie du Sud pour la coopération régionale (8) - SAARC	Année d'adhésion
Afghanistan	2007
Bangladesh	1985
Bhoutan	1985
Inde	1985
Maldives	1985
Népal	1985
Pakistan	1985
Sri Lanka	1985

Association des nations de l'Asie du Sud-Est (10) - ANASE	Année d'adhésion
Brunéi Darussalam	1984
Cambodge	1999
Indonésie	1967
Malaisie	1967
Myanmar	1997
Philippines	1967
République démocratique populaire lao	1997
Singapour	1967
Thaïlande	1967
Viet Nam	1995

Conseil de coopération du Golfe (6) - CCG	Année d'adhésion
Arabie saoudite	1981
Bahreïn	1981
Émirats arabes unis	1981
Koweït	1981
Oman	1981
Qatar	1981

Organisation de coopération économique (10) - ECO	Année d'adhésion
Afghanistan	1992
Azerbaïdjan	1992
Iran (République islamique d')	1985
Kazakhstan	1992
Kirghizistan	1992
Ouzbékistan	1992
Pakistan	1985
Tadjikistan	1992
Turkménistan	1992
Turquie	1985

EUROPE

Association européenne de libre-échange (3) - AELE	Année d'adhésion
Islande	1970
Norvège	1960
Suisse	1960

Union européenne (27) - EU	Année d'adhésion
Allemagne	1957
Autriche	1995
Belgique	1957
Bulgarie	2008
Chypre	2004
Danemark	1973
Espagne	1986
Estonie	2004
Finlande	1995
France	1957
Grèce	1981
Hongrie	2004
Irlande	1973
Italie	1957
Lettonie	2004
Lituanie	2004
Luxembourg	1957
Malte	2004
Pays-Bas	1957
Pologne	2004
Portugal	1986
République tchèque	2004
Roumanie	2008
Royaume-Uni	1973
Slovaquie	2004
Slovénie	2004
Suède	1995

Zone euro (17)	Année d'adhésion
Allemagne	2002
Autriche	2002
Belgique	2002
Chypre	2008
Espagne	2002
Estonie	2011
Finlande	2002
France	2002
Grèce	2002
Irlande	2002
Italie	2002
Luxembourg	2002
Malte	2008
Pays-Bas	2002
Portugal	2002
Slovaquie	2009
Slovénie	2007

RÉPARTITION DES ÉCONOMIES PAR GROUPEMENTS COMMERCIAUX

OCÉANIE

Année d'adhésion

Groupe Fer de lance mélanésien (4)

Fidji	1998
Îles Salomon	1993
Papouasie-Nouvelle-Guinée	1993
Vanuatu	1993

RÉPARTITION DES ÉCONOMIES PAR GROUPEMENTS INTERRÉGIONAUX

Groupe des États d'Afrique, des Caraïbes et du Pacifique (79) - ACP

Afrique du Sud	Guinée équatoriale	République démocratique du Congo
Angola	Guyana	République dominicaine
Antigua et Barbuda	Haïti	République-Unie de Tanzanie
Bahamas	Îles Cook	Rwanda
Barbade	Îles Marshall	Sainte-Lucie
Belize	Îles Salomon	Saint-Kitts-et-Nevis
Bénin	Jamaïque	Saint-Vincent-et-les Grenadines
Botswana	Kenya	Samoa
Burkina Faso	Kiribati	Sao Tomé-et-Principe
Burundi	Lesotho	Sénégal
Cameroun	Libéria	Seychelles
Cap-Vert	Madagascar	Sierra Leone
Comores	Malawi	Somalie
Congo	Mali	Soudan
Côte d'Ivoire	Maurice	Suriname
Cuba	Mauritanie	Swaziland
Djibouti	Micronésie (États fédérés de)	Tchad
Dominique	Mozambique	Timor-Leste
Érythrée	Namibie	Togo
Éthiopie	Nauru	Tonga
Fidji	Niger	Trinité-et-Tobago
Gabon	Nigéria	Tuvalu
Gambie	Nioué	Vanuatu
Ghana	Ouganda	Zambie
Grenade	Palaos	Zimbabwe
Guinée	Papouasie-Nouvelle-Guinée	
Guinée-Bissau	République centrafricaine	

Coopération économique de l'Asie et du Pacifique (21) - CEAP	*Année d'adhésion*	Coopération économique de la mer Noire (12) - CEMN	*Année d'adhésion*	Communauté des États indépendants (11) - CEI	*Année d'adhésion*
Australie	1989	Albanie	1992	Arménie	1991
Brunéi Darussalam	1989	Arménie	1992	Azerbaïdjan	1991
Canada	1989	Azerbaïdjan	1992	Bélarus	1991
Chili	1994	Bulgarie	1992	Fédération de Russie	1991
Chine	1991	Fédération de Russie	1992	Kazakhstan	1991
États-Unis d'Amérique	1989	Géorgie	1992	Kirghizistan	1991
Fédération de Russie	1998	Grèce	1992	Ouzbékistan	1991
Hong Kong, région administrative spéciale	1991	République de Moldova	1992	République de Moldova	1991
Indonésie	1989	Roumanie	1992	Tadjikistan	1991
Japon	1989	Serbie	2004	Turkménistan	1991
Malaisie	1989	Turquie	1992	Ukraine	1991
Mexique	1993	Ukraine	1992		
Nouvelle-Zélande	1989				
Papouasie-Nouvelle-Guinée	1993				
Pérou	1998				
Philippines	1989				
Province chinoise de Taiwan	1991				
République de Corée	1989				
Singapour	1989				
Thaïlande	1989				
Viet Nam	1998				

AASP	autres apports du secteur public
ACAP	Accord commercial de l'Asie et du Pacifique (ex-Accord de Bangkok)
ACP	Groupe des États d'Afrique, des Caraïbes et du Pacifique
AELE	Association européenne de libre-échange
AGCS	Accord général sur le commerce des services
ALADI	Association latino-américaine d'intégration
ALENA	Accord de libre-échange nord-américain
ANASE	Association des nations de l'Asie du Sud-Est
ANCOM	Communauté andine
anc.	ancien, ancienne, anciennement
AP	aide publique
APD	aide publique au développement
CAD	Comité d'aide au développement (OCDE)
CARICOM	Communauté des Caraïbes
CCG	Conseil de coopération du Golfe
CCSA	Comité de coordination des activités statistiques
CAE	Communauté de l'Afrique de l'Est
CDAA	Communauté de développement de l'Afrique australe
CEAP	Coopération économique de l'Asie et du Pacifique
CEDEAO	Communauté économique des États de l'Afrique de l'Ouest
CEE	Commission économique pour l'Europe
CEEAC	Communauté économique des États de l'Afrique centrale
CEI	Communauté des États indépendants
CEMAC	Communauté économique et monétaire de l'Afrique centrale
CEMN	Coopération économique de la mer Noire
CEPALC	Commission économique pour l'Amérique Latine et les Caraïbes
CEPGL	Communauté économique des pays des Grands Lacs
CESAP	Commission économique et sociale pour l'Asie et le Pacifique
CESAO	Commission économique et sociale pour l'Asie occidentale
c.a.f.	coût, assurance, fret
COMESA	Marché commun d'Afrique de l'Est et du Sud
CTCI	Classification type pour le commerce international
DTS	droit de tirage spécial
EIU	Economic Intelligence Unit
f.a.b.	franco à bord
FAO	Organisation des Nations Unies pour l'alimentation et l'agriculture
FBCF	formation brute de capital fixe
FMI	Fonds monétaire international
IED	Investissement étranger direct
ISBLM	institutions sans but lucratif au service des ménages
LERY	L'ex-République yougoslave de Macédoine
MBP	Manuel de la balance des paiements (FMI)
MCAC	Marché commun d'Amérique centrale
MERCOSUR	Marché commun sud-américain
MSG	Groupe Fer de lance mélanésien
n.c.a.	non classé ailleurs
n.d.a.	non dénommé ailleurs
NEI	nouvelles économies industrialisées
NPF	nation la plus favorisée
OCDE	Organisation de coopération et de développement économiques
OCE	Organisation de coopération économique
OEA	Organisation des États américains
OECO	Organisation des États des Caraïbes orientales
OIT	Organisation internationale du travail
OMC	Organisation mondiale du commerce
ONU/DAES/DS	Organisation des Nations Unies, Département des affaires économiques et sociales, Division de statistique
OPEP	Organisation des pays exportateurs de pétrole
PIB	produit intérieur brut
PMA	pays les moins avancés
PNB	produit national brut
PNUD	Programme des Nations Unies pour le développement
PPTE	pays pauvres très endettés
RAS	région administrative spéciale
RSF	République socialiste fédérative de Yougoslavie (anc.)
SAARC	Association de l'Asie du Sud pour la coopération régionale
SH	Système harmonisé
SNPD	Système de notification des pays débiteurs
STN	société transnationale
UE	Union européenne
UEMOA	Union économique et monétaire des États de l'Afrique de l'Ouest
UFM	Union du fleuve Mano
UMA	Union du Maghreb arabe
UNESCO	Organisation des Nations Unies pour l'éducation, la science et la culture
UNICEF	Fonds des Nations Unies pour l'enfance
URSS	Union des Républiques socialistes soviétiques
ZLEA	Zone de libre échange des Amériques

The *Handbook of Statistics* refers to the Standard International Trade Classification (SITC) Revision 3 detailed below.

Depending on the table, nomenclature of statistics is detailed at the 3-digit level or by broad product groupings as follows:

Le *Manuel de statistiques* se réfère à la Classification type pour le commerce international (CTCI) révision 3 détaillée ci-dessous.

Selon les tableaux, les statistiques sont présentées, au niveau détaillé de la nomenclature (position à trois chiffres) ou par groupements de produits dont la composition est la suivante :

SITC Codes – Codes CTCI	Product groupings	Groupements de produits
0 to 9 – 0 à 9	All products	Total tous produits
0 + 1 + 22 + 4	All food items	Produits alimentaires
2 - (22 + 27 + 28)	Agricultural raw materials	Matières premières d'origine agricole
27 + 28 + 68 + 667 + 971	Ores, metals, precious stones and non-monetary gold	Minerais, métaux, pierres précieuses et or à usage non monétaire
3	Fuels	Combustibles
5 + 6 + 7+ 8 - (667 + 68)	Manufactured goods:	Articles manufacturés :
5	- Chemical products	- Produits chimiques
7	- Machinery and transport equipment	- Machines et matériel de transport
6 + 8 - (667 + 68)	- Other manufactured goods	- Articles manufacturés divers

Codes	Standard International Trade Classification (SITC) Revision 3 (1 to 3 digits)	Classification type pour le commerce international (CTCI) Révision 3 (positions de un à trois chiffres)
0	**Food and live animals**	**Produits alimentaires et animaux vivants**
00	**Live animals other than animals of division 03**	**Animaux vivants autres que ceux figurant dans la division 03**
001	Live animals other than animals of division 03	Animaux vivants autres que ceux figurant dans la division 03
01	**Meat and meat preparations**	**Viandes et préparations de viande**
011	Meat of bovine animals, fresh, chilled or frozen	Viande des animaux de l'espèce bovine, fraîche, réfrigérée/congel.
012	Other meat and edible meat offal	Autres viandes et abats comestibles
016	Meat, edible meat offal, salted, dried; flours, meals	Viandes et abats comestibles salés, fumés; farines et poudres
017	Meat, edible meat offal, prepared, preserved, n.e.s.	Préparations de viandes et d'abats, n.d.a.
02	**Dairy products and birds' eggs**	**Produits laitiers et oeufs d'oiseaux**
022	Milk, cream and milk products (excluding butter, cheese)	Lait et produits laitiers (sauf beurre, fromages)
023	Butter and other fats and oils derived from milk	Beurre et autres matières grasses du lait
024	Cheese and curd	Fromages et caillebotte
025	Birds' eggs, and eggs' yolks; egg albumin	Oeufs d'oiseaux et jaunes d'oeufs frais, blanc d'oeuf
03	**Fish (not marine mammals), crustaceans, molluscs and aquatic invertebrates and preparations thereof**	**Poissons (sauf mammifères marins), crustacés, mollusques et autres invertébrés aquatiques et préparations**
034	Fish, fresh (live or dead), chilled or frozen	Poissons frais, vivants ou morts, réfrigérés ou congelés
035	Fish, dried, salted or in brine; smoked fish	Poissons séchés, salés, fumés
036	Crustaceans, molluscs and aquatic invertebrates	Crustacés, mollusques et invertébrés aquatiques
037	Fish, aqua. invertebrates, prepared, preserved, n.e.s.	Poissons, crustacés, mollusques, préparés ou conservés, n.d.a.
04	**Cereals and cereal preparations**	**Céréales et préparations à base de céréales**
041	Wheat (including spelt) and meslin, unmilled	Froment (dont épeautre) et méteil non moulus
042	Rice	Riz
043	Barley, unmilled	Orge non mondée
044	Maize (not including sweet corn), unmilled	Maïs non moulu
045	Cereals, unmilled (excluding wheat, rice, barley, maize)	Céréales non moulues (sauf froment, riz, orge, maïs)
046	Meal and flour of wheat and flour of meslin	Semoules et farines de froment et farines de méteil
047	Other cereal meals and flour	Autres semoules et farines de céréales
048	Cereal preparations, flour of fruits or vegetables	Préparations à base de céréales, de farines, de fécules
05	**Vegetables and fruit**	**Légumes et fruits**
054	Vegetables, fresh, chilled, frozen or simply preserved; roots tubers and other edible vegetable products, n.e.s. fresh, dried	Légumes et plantes potagères, frais, réfrigérés, congelés ou simplement conservés; autres produits végétaux n.d.a. frais, séchés
056	Vegetables, roots, tubers, prepared, preserved, n.e.s.	Préparations ou conserves de légumes, n.d.a.
057	Fruits and nuts (excluding oil nuts), fresh or dried	Fruits (sauf oléagineux), frais ou secs
058	Fruit, preserved, and fruit preparations (no juice)	Préparations et conserves de fruits (sauf jus)
059	Fruit and vegetable juices, unfermented, no spirit	Jus de fruits, non fermentés, sans alcool
06	**Sugars, sugar preparations and honey**	**Sucres, préparations à base de sucre et miel**
061	Sugars, molasses and honey	Sucres, mélasses et miel
062	Sugar confectionery	Sucreries
07	**Coffee, tea, cocoa, spices and manufactures thereof**	**Café, thé, cacao, épices, et produits dérivés**
071	Coffee and coffee substitutes	Café et succédanés du café
072	Cocoa	Cacao
073	Chocolate, food preparations with cocoa, n.e.s.	Chocolat et autres préparations du cacao, n.d.a.
074	Tea and mate	Thé et maté
075	Spices	Épices

08	**Feeding stuff for animals (excluding unmilled cereals)**	**Nourriture destinée aux animaux (sauf céréales non moulues)**
081	Feeding stuff for animals (excluding unmilled cereals)	Nourriture destinée aux animaux (sauf céréales non moulues)
09	**Miscellaneous edible products and preparations**	**Produits et préparations alimentaires divers**
091	Margarine and shortening	Margarine et graisses culinaires
098	Edible products and preparations, n.e.s.	Produits et préparations alimentaires, n.d.a.
1	**Beverages and tobacco**	**Boissons et tabacs**
11	**Beverages**	**Boissons**
111	Non-alcoholic beverages, n.e.s.	Boissons non alcooliques, n.d.a.
112	Alcoholic beverages	Boissons alcooliques
12	**Tobacco and tobacco manufactures**	**Tabacs bruts et fabriqués**
121	Tobacco, unmanufactured; tobacco refuse	Tabacs bruts ou non fabriqués; déchets de tabac
122	Tobacco, manufactured (whether or not containing tobacco substitutes)	Tabacs fabriqués (même contenant des succédanés de tabac)
2	**Crude materials, inedible, except fuels**	**Matières brutes non comestibles, sauf carburants**
21	**Hides, skins and furskins, raw**	**Cuirs, peaux et pelleteries, bruts**
211	Hides and skins (except furskins), raw	Cuirs et peaux (sauf pelleteries), bruts
212	Furskins, raw, other than hides and skins of group 211	Pelleteries brutes autres que ceux du groupe 211
22	**Oil seeds and oleaginous fruits**	**Graines et fruits oléagineux**
222	Oil seeds and oleaginous fruits (excluding flour) of a kind used for the extraction of soft' oils	Graines et fruits oléagineux (sauf farines) servant normalement à l'extraction d'huiles végétales fixes douces
223	Oil seeds and oleaginous fruits (incl. flour, n.e.s.) of a kind used for the extraction of other fixed vegetable oils	Graines et fruits oléagineux (y compris les farines) servant normalement à l'extraction d'autres huiles végétales fixes
23	**Crude rubber (including synthetic and reclaimed)**	**Caoutchouc brut (y compris synthétique et régénéré)**
231	Natural rubber, balata, gutta percha, guayule, chicle and similar natural gums, in primary forms	Caoutchouc naturel, balata, gutta-percha, guayule, chicle et gommes naturelles analogues sous formes primaires
232	Synthetic rubber; reclaimed rubber; waste and scrap	Caoutchouc synthétique; caoutchouc régénéré; déchets et débris
24	**Cork and wood**	**Liège et bois**
244	Cork, natural, raw and waste (incl. blocks, sheets)	Liège naturel brut et déchets (dont blocs, feuilles)
245	Fuel wood (excluding wood waste) and wood charcoal	Bois de chauffage (sauf déchets), charbon de bois
246	Wood in chips or particles and wood waste	Bois en plaquettes, particules, déchets de bois
247	Wood in the rough or roughly squared	Bois bruts ou équarris
248	Wood, simply worked, and railway sleepers of wood	Bois simplement travaillés, traverses de bois pour voies ferrées
25	**Pulp and waste paper**	**Pâtes à papier et déchets de papier**
251	Pulp and waste paper	Pâtes à papier et déchets de papier
26	**Textiles fibres and their wastes**	**Fibres textiles et leurs déchets**
261	Silk	Soie
263	Cotton	Coton
264	Jute and other textile bast fibre, n.e.s., not spun; tow, waste	Jute et autres fibres textiles libériennes, n.d.a.; déchets
265	Vegetable textile fibres, not spun; waste of them	Fibres textiles végétales (sauf coton, jute); déchets
266	Synthetic fibres suitable for spinning	Fibres synthétiques discontinues, pour filature
267	Other man-made fibres suitable for spinning and waste	Autres fibres synthétiques/artificielles pouvant être filées; déchets
268	Wool and other animal hair (including wool tops)	Laines et autres poils (dont rubans de laine)
269	Worn clothing and other worn textile articles, rags	Friperie, drilles et chiffons
27	**Crude fertilizers, other than those of division 56, & crude minerals (excluding coal, petroleum & precious stones)**	**Engrais bruts, autres que ceux de la division 56 et minéraux bruts (à l'exclusion du charbon, pétrole et pierres précieuses)**
272	Crude fertilizers (excluding those of division 56)	Engrais bruts (sauf ceux de la division 56)
273	Stone, sand and gravel	Pierres, sables et graviers
274	Sulphur and unroasted iron pyrites	Soufre et pyrites de fer non grillées
277	Natural abrasives, n.e.s. (including industrial diamonds)	Abrasifs naturels, n.d.a. (dont diamants industriels)
278	Other crude minerals	Autre minéraux bruts
28	**Metalliferous ores and metal scrap**	**Minerais métallifères et déchets de métaux**
281	Iron ore and concentrates	Minerais de fer et leurs concentrés
282	Ferrous waste and scrap; remelting ingots, iron, steel	Déchets et débris de fer, fonte, acier; lingots
283	Copper ores and concentrates; copper mattes, cement copper	Minerais de cuivre, concentrés; mattes de cuivre; cuivre de cément
284	Nickel ores and concentrates; nickel mattes, etc.	Minerais de nickel et concentrés; mattes, etc.
285	Aluminium ores and concentrates (including alumina)	Minerais d'aluminium et concentrés (dont alumine)
286	Ores and concentrates of uranium or thorium	Minerais d'uranium ou de thorium et concentrés
287	Ores and concentrates of base metals, n.e.s.	Minerais de métaux communs et concentrés, n.d.a.
288	Non-ferrous base metal waste and scrap, n.e.s.	Déchets et débris de métaux communs non ferreux, n.d.a.

289	Ores and concentrates of precious metals; waste, scrap	Minerais de métaux précieux et concentrés; débris et déchets
29	**Crude animal and vegetable materials, n.e.s.**	**Matières brutes d'origine animale ou végétale, n.d.a.**
291	Crude animal materials, n.e.s.	Matières brutes d'origine animale, n.d.a.
292	Crude vegetable materials, n.e.s.	Matières brutes d'origine végétale, n.d.a.
3	**Mineral fuels, lubricants and related materials**	**Combustibles minéraux, lubrifiants et produits connexes**
32	**Coal, coke and briquettes**	**Houilles, cokes et briquettes**
321	Coal, whether or not pulverized, not agglomerated	Houilles, même pulvérisées, mais non agglomérées
322	Briquettes, lignites and peat	Briquettes, lignite et tourbe
325	Coke and semi-cokes of coal, lignite or peat; retort carbon	Cokes, semi-cokes de houille, lignite ou tourbe; charbon de cornue
33	**Petroleum, petroleum products and related materials**	**Pétrole et produits dérivés du pétrole et produits connexes**
333	Petroleum oils, oils from bituminous materials, crude	Huiles brutes de pétrole ou de minéraux bitumineux
334	Petroleum oils or bituminous minerals > 70 % oil	Huiles de pétrole ou minéraux bitumineux > 70% huile
335	Residual petroleum products, n.e.s., related materials	Produits résiduels du pétrole, n.d.a., produits connexes
34	**Gas, natural and manufactured**	**Gaz naturel et gaz manufacturé**
342	Liquefied propane and butane	Propane et butane liquéfiés
343	Natural gas, whether or not liquefied	Gaz naturel, même liquéfié
344	Petroleum gases, other gaseous hydrocarbons, n.e.s.	Gaz de pétrole et autres hydrocarbures gazeux, n.d.a.
345	Coal gas, water gas and similar gases (excl. hydrocarbons)	Gaz de houille, pauvre et similaires (sauf hydrocarbures)
35	**Electric current**	**Énergie électrique**
351	Electric current	Énergie électrique
4	**Animal and vegetable oils, fats and waxes**	**Huiles, graisses et cires d'origine animale ou végétale**
41	**Animal oils and fats**	**Huiles et graisses d'origine animale**
411	Animal oils and fats	Huiles et graisses d'origine animale
42	**Fixed vegetable fats and oils, crude, refined or fractionated**	**Graisses et huiles végétales fixes, brutes, raffinées ou fractionnées**
421	Fixed vegetable oils & fats, 'soft', crude, refined or fractionated	Huiles végétales fixes, douces, brutes, épurées ou raffinées
422	Fixed vegetable fats and oils, crude, refined, fractionated, other than 'soft'	Huiles végétales fixes, brutes, épurées ou raffinées, autres que douces
43	**Animal and vegetable fats and oils, processed; waxes of animal or vegetable origin; inedible mixtures**	**Huiles et graisses animales ou végétales, préparées ; cires d'origine animale et végétale; mélanges non alimentaires**
431	Animal or veg. oils and fats, processed, n.e.s.; waxes, mixt.	Huiles et graisses animales ou végétales, préparées, n.d.a.; cires
5	**Chemicals and related products, n.e.s.**	**Produits chimiques et produits connexes, n.d.a.**
51	**Organic chemicals**	**Produits chimiques organiques**
511	Hydrocarbons, n.e.s., and halogenated, nitr. derivatives	Hydrocarbures, n.d.a., dérivés halogènes, nitrosés, sulfonés, nitrés
512	Alcohols, phenols, and their derivatives	Alcools, phénols, et leurs dérivés halogénés
513	Carboxylic acids, anhydrides, halides, peroxides; derivatives	Acides carboxyliques, anhydrides, halogénures, péroxydes; dérivés
514	Nitrogen-function compounds	Composés à fonctions azotées
515	Organo-inorganic, heterocyclic compounds, nucl. acids	Composés organo-inorganiques et composés hétérocycliques; sels
516	Other organic chemicals	Autres produits chimiques organiques
52	**Inorganic chemicals**	**Produits chimiques inorganiques**
522	Inorganic chemical elements, oxides and halogen salts	Produits chimiques inorganiques : éléments, oxydes, sels
523	Metallic salts and peroxysalts, of inorganic acids	Sels et persels métalliques des acides inorganiques
524	Other inorganic chemicals; organic and inorganic compounds of precious metals	Autres produits chimiques inorganiques, composés organiques ou inorganiques de métaux précieux
525	Radioactive and associated materials	Matières radioactives et produits associés
53	**Dyeing, tanning and colouring materials**	**Produits pour teinture et tannage et colorants**
531	Synthetic organic colouring matter and colouring lakes	Matières colorantes organiques synthétiques; préparations, laques
532	Dyeing and tanning extracts, synthetic tanning materials	Extraits pour teinture et tannage
533	Pigments, paints, varnishes and related materials	Pigments, peintures, vernis et produits connexes
54	**Medical and pharmaceutical products**	**Produits médicinaux et pharmaceutiques**
541	Medicinal and pharmaceutical products, excluding 542	Produits médicinaux et pharmaceutiques (sauf 542)
542	Medicaments (including veterinary medicaments)	Médicaments pour médecine humaine ou vétérinaire
55	**Essential oils and resinoids and perfume materials; toilet, polishing and cleaning preparations**	**Huiles essentielles, résinoïdes et produits de parfumerie; préparations pour la toilette; produits d'entretien et détersifs**
551	Essential oils, perfume and flavour materials	Huiles essentielles, produits utilisés en parfumerie et en confiserie
553	Perfumery, cosmetics or toilet preparations (excluding soaps)	Produits de parfumerie ou de toilette préparés et préparations cosmétiques (à l'exclusion des savons)
554	Soaps, cleansing and polishing preparations	Savons, produits d'entretien et détersifs
56	**Fertilizers (other than those of group 272)**	**Engrais (autres que ceux du groupe 272)**

562	Fertilizers (other than those of group 272)	Engrais (autres que ceux du groupe 272)
57	**Plastics in primary forms**	**Matières plastiques sous formes primaires**
571	Polymers of ethylene, in primary forms	Polymères de l'éthylène, sous formes primaires
572	Polymers of styrene, in primary forms	Polymères du styrène, sous formes primaires
573	Polymers of vinyl chloride or of halogenated olefins	Polymères du chlorure de vinyle ou d'autres oléfines halogènes
574	Polyeacetals, other polyethers and epoxide resins, polyesters	Polyacetals, autres polyéthers et résines époxydes, polyesters
575	Other plastics, in primary forms	Autres matières plastiques, sous formes primaires
579	Waste, parings and scrap, of plastics	Déchets, rognures et débris de matières plastiques
58	**Plastics in non-primary forms**	**Matières plastiques sous formes autres que primaires**
581	Tubes, pipes and hoses of plastics	Tubes et tuyaux en matières plastiques
582	Plates, sheets, films, foil and strip, of plastics	Plaques, feuilles, rubans en matières plastiques
583	Monofilament, cross-sectional dimension > 1 mm, rods, sticks, profile shapes, of plastics	Monofilaments, coupe transversale > 1mm (monofils), joncs, bâtons et profiles, en matières plastiques
59	**Chemical materials and products, n.e.s.**	**Matières et produits chimiques, n.d.a.**
591	Insecticides and similar products, for retail sale	Insecticides, produits similaires, pour la vente au détail
592	Starches, wheat gluten; albuminoidal substances; glues	Amidons, fécules, gluten de froment; matières albuminoïdes; colles
593	Explosives and pyrotechnic products	Explosifs et articles de pyrotechnie
597	Prepared additives for mineral oils; lubricating preparations;	Additifs pour huiles minérales
598	Miscellaneous chemical products, n.e.s.	Produits chimiques divers, n.d.a.
6	**Manufactured goods classified chiefly by material**	**Articles manufacturés classés principalement d'après la matière première**
61	**Leather, leather manufactures, n.e.s. and dressed furskins**	**Cuirs et peaux, préparés et ouvrages en cuir, n.d.a.; et pelleteries apprêtées**
611	Leather	Cuirs et peaux préparés
612	Manufactures of leather, n.e.s.; saddlery and harness	Ouvrages en cuir, n.d.a.; articles de bourrellerie ou de sellerie
613	Furskins, tanned or dressed, excluding those of 8483	Pelleteries tannées ou apprêtées (sauf 8483)
62	**Rubber manufactures, n.e.s.**	**Caoutchouc manufacturé, n.d.a.**
621	Materials of rubber (e.g. pastes, plates, sheets, bods, etc.)	Produits en caoutchouc (pâtes, plaques, feuilles, fils, tubes, etc.)
625	Rubber tyres, interchangeable tyre treads, tyre flaps and inner tubes for wheels of all kinds	Pneumatiques, en caoutchouc; bandes de roulement amoviles pour pneumatiques, "flaps" et chambres à air pour tous types de roues
629	Articles of rubber, n.e.s.	Ouvrages en caoutchouc, n.d.a.
63	**Cork and wood manufactures (excluding furniture)**	**Ouvrages en liège et en bois (à l'exclusion des meubles)**
633	Cork manufactures	Ouvrages en liège
634	Veneers, plywood, and other wood, worked, n.e.s.	Placage, contre-plaqué et autres bois travaillés, n.d.a.
635	Wood manufacture, n.e.s.	Ouvrages en bois, n.d.a.
64	**Paper, paperboard, aricles of paper pulp, of paper, or of paperboard**	**Papiers, cartons et ouvrages en pâte de cellulose, en papier ou en carton**
641	Paper and paperboard	Papiers et cartons
642	Paper and paperboard, cut to shape or size, and articles of paper or paperboard	Papiers et cartons découpés en vue d'un usage déterminé; ouvrages en papier ou carton
65	**Textile yarn, fabrics, made-up articles, n.e.s., and related products**	**Fils, tissus, articles textiles façonnés, n.d.a. et produits connexes**
651	Textile yarn	Fils textiles
652	Cotton fabrics, woven (excluded narrow or special fabrics)	Tissus de coton (sauf petites largeurs ou spéciaux)
653	Fabrics, woven, of man-made fabrics	Tissus en matières textiles synthétiques ou artificielles
654	Other textile fabrics, woven	Autres tissus
655	Knitted or crocheted fabrics, n.e.s.	Étoffes de bonneterie (dont velours), n.d.a.
656	Tulles, trimmings, lace, ribbons and other small wares	Tulles, dentelles et autres articles de mercerie
657	Special yarn, special textile fabrics and related	Fils spéciaux, tissus spéciaux et produits connexes
658	Made-up articles, wholly or chiefly of textile materials, n.e.s	Articles confectionnés entièrement ou principalement en matières textiles, n.d.a.
659	Floor coverings, etc.	Revêtements de sols, etc.
66	**Non metallic mineral manufactures, n.e.s.**	**Articles minéraux non métalliques manufacturés, n.d.a.**
661	Lime, cement and fabricated construction materials (excluding glass and clay materials)	Chaux, ciments et matériaux de construction fabriqués (sauf argile et verre)
662	Clay construction and refractory construction materials	Matériaux de construction réfractaires, en argile
663	Mineral manufactures, n.e.s.	Articles minéraux manufacturés, n.d.a.
664	Glass	Verre
665	Glassware	Ouvrages en verre
666	Pottery	Poterie

667	Pearls, precious and semi-precious stones	Perles fines ou de culture, pierres gemmes et similaires
67	**Iron and steel**	**Fer et acier**
671	Pig iron and spiegeleisen, sponge iron, powder and granules	Fonte, fer spongieux, poudres de fer et d'acier
672	Ingots, primary forms, of iron or steel; semi-finished products	Lingots et autres formes primaires en fer ou acier;
673	Flat-rolled prod., iron, non-alloy steel, not coated	Produits laminés plats, en fer ou aciers non alliés
674	Flat-rolled prod., iron, non-alloy steel, coated, clad	Produits laminés plats, fer, aciers non alliés, zingués
675	Flat-rolled products of alloy steel	Produits laminés plats, en aciers alliés
676	Iron and steel bars, rods, angles, shapes and sections	Barres et profilés en fer ou acier (y compris les palplanches)
677	Rails and railway track construction mat., iron, steel	Rails et autres éléments de voies ferrées, en fonte, fer ou acier
678	Wire of iron or steel	Fils de fer ou d'acier
679	Tubes, pipes and hollow profiles, fittings, iron, steel	Tubes, profilés creux et accessoires, fer ou acier
68	**Non-ferrous metals**	**Métaux non ferreux**
681	Silver, platinum, other metals of the platinum group	Argent, platine et métaux de la mine du platine
682	Copper	Cuivre
683	Nickel	Nickel
684	Aluminium	Aluminium
685	Lead	Plomb
686	Zinc	Zinc
687	Tin	Étain
689	Miscellaneous non-ferrous base metals for metallurgy	Autres métaux communs non ferreux utilisés en métallurgie
69	**Manufactures of metal, n.e.s.**	**Articles manufacturés en métal, n.d.a.**
691	Structures and parts, n.e.s., of iron, steel, aluminium	Constructions et parties, n.d.a. en fonte, fer, acier ou aluminium
692	Metal containers for storage or transport	Récipients métalliques pour le stockage ou le transport
693	Wire products (excluding electrical) and fencing grills	Ouvrages en fils métalliques (sauf électriques), grillages
694	Nails, screws, nuts, bolts, rivets and the like, of iron, steel, copper or aluminium	Pointes, clous, vis, écrous, boulons, rondelles, rivets et aricles similaires, en fer, en acier, en cuivre ou en aluminium
695	Tools for use in the hand or in machine	Outils à main et outils pour machines
696	Cutlery	Coutellerie
697	Household equipment of base metal, n.e.s.	Articles d'économie domestique en métaux communs, n.d.a.
699	Manufactures of base metal, n.e.s.	Articles manufacturés en métaux communs, n.d.a.
7	**Machinery and transport equipment**	**Machines et matériel de transport**
71	**Power generating machinery and equipment**	**Machines génératrices, moteurs et leur équipement**
711	Steam or other vapour generating boilers, super-heated water boilers and auxiliary plant for use therewith; parts	Chaudières à vapeur, chaudières dites "à eau surchauffée", et leurs appareils auxiliaires, leurs parties et pièces détachées
712	Steam turbines and other vapour turbines, parts thereof, n.e.s.	Turbines à vapeur, leurs parties et pièces détachées, n.d.a.
713	Internal combustion piston engines and parts thereof, n.e.s.	Moteurs à explosion ou à combustion interne, n.d.a.
714	Engines and motors, non-electric; parts, n.e.s.	Moteurs et machines motrices, non électrique; leurs parties n.d.a.
716	Rotating electric plant and parts thereof, n.e.s.	Appareils électriques rotatifs, leurs pièces détachées, n.d.a.
718	Other power generating machinery and parts thereof, n.e.s.	Moteurs et machines motrices, leurs parties et pièces, n.d.a.
72	**Machinery specialized for particular industries**	**Machines et appareils spécialisés pour industries particulières**
721	Agricultural machinery (excluding tractors) and parts	Machines agricoles (sauf tracteurs), parties, pièces
722	Tractors (excluding those of 71414 and 74415)	Tracteurs (sauf 74414 et 74415)
723	Civil ingineering and contractors' plant and equipment	Appareils et matériel de génie civil et de construction; parties
724	Textile and leather machinery, and parts thereof, n.e.s.	Machines pour l'industrie textile, cuir et peaux, n.d.a.
725	Paper mill and pulp mill machinery; paper cutting machines and other machinery; parts thereof	Machines et appareils pour la fabrication de la pâte à papier et du papier; coupeuses et autres appareils; leurs parties et pièces
726	Printing and bookbinding machinery, and parts thereof	Machines pour imprimerie, brochage, reliure; parties
727	Food-processing machines (excluding domestic)	Machines pour industrie alimentaire (appareils ménagers exclus)
728	Other machinery and equipment specialized for particular industries, and parts thereof, n.e.s.	Autres machines et appareils spécialisées pour industries particulières, et leurs parties et pièces détachées, n.d.a.
73	**Metal working machinery**	**Machines et appareils pour le travail des métaux**
731	Machine-tools working by removing metal or other material	Machines-outils travaillant par enlèvement de métal/autres matières
733	Machine.-tools for working metal (without removing material)	Machines pour travail des métaux (sans enlèvement de matière)
735	Parts, n.e.s., and accessories for machines of 731, 733	Pièces et accessoires, n.d.a., des machines des groupes 731, 733
737	Metalworking machinery (excluding machine tools) and parts	Machines pour travail des métaux, n.d.a.; pièces détachées
74	**General industrial machinery and equipment, n.e.s. and machine parts, n.e.s.**	**Machines et appareils industriels d'application générale, n.d.a.; parties et pièces détachées de machines, d'appareils, d'engins**
741	Heating and cooling equipment and parts thereof, n.e.s.	Appareils de chauffage et de réfrigération, n.d.a.; pièces détachées
742	Pumps for liquids; liquid elevators; parts for such pumps	Pompes pour liquides; élévateurs à liquides; parties et pièces

743	Pumps (excluding liquid), air and gas compressors, and fans; centrifuges; filtering or purifying apparatus; parts	Pompes (sauf pour liquides), compresseurs; ventilateurs; hottes aspirantes; centrifugeuses; appareils pour la filration, l'épuration
744	Mechanical handling equipment, and parts, n.e.s.	Équipement mécanique de manutention, pièces, n.d.a.
745	Other non-electrical machinery, tools and mechanical apparatus, and parts thereof, n.e.s.	Machines, appareils et outils non électriques et leurs parties et pièces détachées, n.d.a.
746	Ball or roller bearings	Roulements à billes, à galets, à rouleaux ou à aiguilles
747	Taps, cocks, valves and similar appliances, for pipes, boiler shells, tanks, vats and the like	Articles de robinetterie, oragnes similaires pour tuyauteries, chaudières, réservoirs, cubes ou contenants similaires
748	Transmission shafts and cranks; bearings housings; gears and gearing; flywheels and pulleys; clutches, shaft couplings	Arbres de transmission et manivelles; engrenages et roues de friction; volants et poulies; embrayages, organes d'accouplement
749	Non-electric parts and accessories. of machinery, n.e.s.	Parties, non électriques d'appareils mécaniques, n.d.a.
75	**Office machines and automatic data processing machines**	**Machines et appareils de bureau ou pour le traitement automatique de l'information**
751	Office machines	Machines et appareils de bureau
752	Automatic data processing machines and units thereof; magnetic or optical readers	Machines automatiques de traitement de l'information et leurs unités; lecteurs magnétiques ou optiques
759	Parts, accessories for machines of groups 751, 752	Parties et pièces détachées pour groupes 751, 752
76	**Telecommunications and sound recording apparatus and reproducing apparatus and equipment**	**Appareils et équipements de télécommunication et pour l'enregistrement et la reproduction du son**
761	Television receivers, whether or not combined	Téléviseurs, même combinés à d'autres appareils
762	Radio-broadcast receivers, whether or not combined	Appareils de radiodiffusion, même combinés à d'autres appareils
763	Sound recorders or reproducers; television image and sound recorders or reproducers, prepared unrecorded media	Appareils d'enregistrement ou de reproduction du son; appareils d'enregistrement/reproduction de l'image et du son en télévision
764	Telecommunication equipment, n.e.s.; and parts, n.e.s.	Équipements de télécommunication, n.d.a. et parties
77	**Electrical machinery, apparatus and appliances, n.e.s. and electrical parts thereof**	**Machines et appareils électriques, n.d.a.; et leurs parties et pièces détachées électriques**
771	Electric power machinery, and parts thereof	Appareils pour production, transformation de l'électricité
772	Apparatus for switching or protecting electrical circuits or for making connections; switchboard, control panels	Appareils pour la coupure, la protection, le branchement la connexion des circuits électriques; tableaux de commande
773	Equipment for distributing electricity, n.e.s.	Équipement pour la distribution d'électricité, n.d.a.
774	Electro-diagnostic apparatus for medical or veterinary sciences and radiological apparatus	Appareils d'électrodiagnostic à usage médical ou vétérinaire et appareils de radiologie
775	Household type, electrical and non-electrical equipment, n.e.s.	Machines et appareils, électriques ou non, à usage domestique, n.d.a.
776	Thermionic, cold cathode or photo-cathode valves and tubes; diodes, transistors and similar;	Lampes, tubes, valves électroniques à cathode chaude, froide ou à photocathode; diodes, transistors et dispositifs similaires
778	Electrical machinery and apparatus, n.e.s.	Machines et appareils électriques, n.d.a.
78	**Road vehicles (including air-cushion vehicles)**	**Véhicules routiers (y compris les véhicules à coussin d'air)**
781	Motor cars and other motor vehicles principally designed for the transport of persons	Véhicules de tourisme et autres véhicules automobiles principalement conçus pour le transport de personnes
782	Motor vehicles for the transport of goods and special purposes	Véhicules automobiles pour le transport de marchandises et pour usages spéciaux
783	Road motor vehicles, n.e.s.	Véhicules routiers, n.d.a.
784	Parts and accessories of the motor vehicles of groups 722, 781, 782, and 783	Parties, pièces détachées et accessoires des véhicules automobiles des groupes 722, 781, 782 et 783
785	Motorcycles and cycles, motorized or not; invalid carriages	Motocycles et cycles, avec ou sans moteur; fauteuils roulants
786	Trailers and semi-trailers; other vehicles, not mechanically propelled; specially designed & equiped transport containers	Remorques et semi-remorques; autres véhicules non automobiles; cadres et conteneurs conçus et équipés pour le transport
79	**Other transport equipment**	**Autres matériels de transport**
791	Railway vehicles and associated equipment	Véhicules et matériel pour chemin de fer
792	Aircraft and associated equipment; spacecraft and spacecraft launch vehicles, parts thereof	Aéronefs et matériels connexes; véhicules spatiaux et leurs véhicules lanceurs; leurs parties et pièces détachées
793	Ships, boats (including hovercrafts) and floating structures	Navires, bateaux (y compris les aéroglisseurs) et engins flottants
8	**Miscellaneous manufactured articles**	**Articles manufacturés divers**
81	**Prefabricated buildings, sanitary plumbing, heating and lighting fixtures and fittings, n.e.s.**	**Constructions préfabriquées, appareils sanitaires et appareillage de plomberie, de chauffage et d'éclairage, n.d.a.**
811	Prefabricated buildings	Constructions préfabriquées
812	Sanitary, plumbing and heating fixtures, and fittings, n.e.s.	Appareils sanitaires et appareillage de plomberie, chauffage, n.d.a.
813	Lighting fixtures and fittings, n.e.s.	Appareillages d'éclairage, n.d.a.
82	**Furniture and parts thereof; bedding, mattresses, mattress supports, cushions and similar stuffed furnishings**	**Meubles et leurs parties; articles de literie; matelas, sommiers coussins, articles similaires rembourrés/garnis intérieurement**

821	Furniture and parts thereof; bedding, mattresses, mattress supports, cushions and similar stuffed furnishings	Meubles et leurs parties; articles de literie; matelas, sommiers, coussins et articles similaires rembourrés ou garnis intérieurement
83	**Travel goods, handbags and similar containers**	**Articles de voyage, sacs à mains et contenants similaires**
831	Travel goods, handbags and similar containers	Articles de voyage, sacs à mains et contenants similaires
84	**Articles of apparel, and clothing accessories**	**Vêtements et accessoires du vêtement**
841	Men's or boy's clothing of textile fabrics, not knitted or crocheted	Articles d'habillement en matières textiles pour hommes et garçonnets, autres que de bonneterie
842	Women's and girl's clothing, of textile fabrics, not knitted or crocheted	Articles d'habillement en matières textiles pour femmes ou fillettes, autres que de bonneterie
843	Men's or boy's clothing, of textile, knitted, crocheted	Articles d'habillement, en bonneterie pour hommes et garçonnets
844	Women's and girl's clothing, of textile, knitted or crocheted	Articles d'habillement, en bonneterie pour femmes ou fillettes
845	Articles of apparel, of textile fabrics, n.e.s.	Vêtements en matières textiles, même en bonneterie, n.d.a.
846	Clothing accessories, of textile fabrics	Accessoires du vêtement en matières textiles
848	Articles of apparel, clothing access., excluding textile	Vêtements et accessoires en matières non textiles
85	**Footwear**	**Chaussures**
851	Footwear	Chaussures
87	**Professional, scientific, and controlling instruments and apparatus, n.e.s.**	**Instruments et appareils professionnels, scientifiques et de contrôle, n.d.a.**
871	Optical instruments and apparatus, n.e.s.	Appareils et instruments d'optique, n.d.a.
872	Instruments and appliances, n.e.s., for medical, surgical, dental or veterinary purposes	Instruments et appareils, n.d.a. pour la médecine, la chirurgie, l'art dentaire ou l'art vétérinaire
873	Meters and counters, n.e.s.	Compteurs et instruments de mesure, n.d.a.
874	Measuring, checking, analysing and controlling instruements and apparatus, n.e.s.	Appareils et instruments de mesure, de vérification, d'analyse et de contrôle, n.d.a.
88	**Photographic apparatus, equipment and supplies and optical goods, n.e.s.; watches and clocks**	**Appareils et fournitures de photographie et d'optique, n.d.a.; montres et horloges**
881	Photographic apparatus and equipment, n.e.s.	Appareils et équipement photographiques, n.d.a.
882	Cinematographic and photographic supplies	Fournitures cinématographiques et photographiques
883	Cinematograph films, exposed and developed, whether or not incorporating sound track	Films cinématographiques, impressionnés, développés, comportant ou non l'enregistrement du son
884	Optical goods, n.e.s.	Éléments d'optique et articles de lunetterie, n.d.a.
885	Watches and clocks	Horlogerie
89	**Miscellaneous manufactured articles, n.e.s.**	**Articles manufacturés divers, n.d.a.**
891	Arms and ammunition	Armes et munitions
892	Printed matter	Imprimés
893	Articles, n.e.s., of plastics	Ouvrages, n.d.a. en matières plastiques
894	Baby carriages, toys, games and sporting goods	Voitures pour le transport des enfants, jouets, jeux et articles pour divertissements et pour sports
895	Office and stationery supplies, n.e.s.	Articles de papeterie et fournitures de bureau, n.d.a.
896	Works of art, collectors' pieces and antiques	Objets d'art, de collection et d'antiquité
897	Jewellery and articles of precious material., n.e.s.	Articles de bijouterie et d'orfèvrerie, n.d.a.
898	Musical instruments, parts and accessories therof; records, tapes and other sound or similar recordings	Instruments de musique et leurs parties; disques, bandes et autres supports pour l'enregistrement du son
899	Miscellaneous manufactured articles, n.e.s.	Autres articles manufacturés divers
9	**Commodities and transactions, not classified elsewhere in the SITC**	**Articles et transactions, non classés ailleurs dans la CTCI**
91	**Postal packages not classified according to kind**	**Colis postaux non classés par catégorie**
911	Postal packages not classified according to kind	Colis postaux non classés par catégorie
93	**Special transactions and commodities not classified according to kind**	**Transactions spéciales et articles spéciaux non classés par catégorie**
931	Special transactions and commodities not classified according to kind	Transactions spéciales et articles spéciaux non classés par catégorie
96	**Coin (other than gold coin), not being legal tender**	**Monnaies (autres que les pièces d'or) n'ayant pas cours légal**
961	Coin (other than gold coin), not being legal tender	Monnaies (autres que les pièces d'or) n'ayant pas cours légal
97	**Gold, non-monetary (excluding ores and concentrates)**	**Or, à usage non monétaire (sauf minerais et concentrés d'or)**
971	Gold, non-monetary (excluding gold ores and concentrates)	Or, à usage non monétaire (sauf minerais et concentrés d'or)

1

INTERNATIONAL **MERCHANDISE** TRADE

COMMERCE INTERNATIONAL DES **MARCHANDISES**

1.1.1 Exports and imports of countries and geographical regions
Value

Region, country or territory	Exports (f.o.b.) - Exportations (f.a.b.) Millions of dollars							
	1980	1990	2000	2005	2007	2008	2009	2010
WORLD	2 035 542	3 479 906	6 448 571	10 495 704	13 996 644	16 122 770	12 511 198	15 174 439
DEVELOPING ECONOMIES	599 757	842 125	2 056 072	3 797 426	5 274 070	6 290 288	4 977 192	6 339 389
TRANSITION ECONOMIES	85 426	118 709	154 524	363 057	550 679	739 536	478 857	617 544
DEVELOPED ECONOMIES	1 350 359	2 519 072	4 237 975	6 335 222	8 171 895	9 092 947	7 055 149	8 217 505
Developing economies: Africa	121 876	105 100	149 402	317 869	434 492	569 739	393 401	493 243
Eastern Africa	1 019	7 827	10 190	16 646	24 269	27 965	25 523	31 626
Burundi*(1)	65	75	50	56	62	54	62	100
Comoros*	11	18	14	12	14	7	12	(e)13
Djibouti (2)	13	25	32	40	58	69	77	(e)70
Eritrea			19	11	13	(e)11	(e)11	(e)12
Ethiopia	–	–	486	926	1 277	1 602	1 618	2 580
Ethiopia (former)	425	298	–	–	–	–	–	–
Kenya	1 245	1 032	1 734	3 293	4 080	4 972	4 463	5 151
Madagascar*	401	318	862	836	1 343	1 667	1 096	1 082
Malawi	295	417	379	508	869	879	1 188	1 066
Mauritius	435	1 194	1 810	2 138	2 238	2 384	1 942	2 239
Mayotte	..	..	3	6	8	8	7	-
Mozambique	281	126	364	1 745	2 412	2 653	2 147	2 243
Rwanda	121	109	53	125	177	268	193	297
Seychelles	21	57	194	340	360	430	395	400
Somalia	141	(e)150	(e)193	(e)251	(e)346	(e)415	(e)422	(e)450
Uganda	345	152	450	1 016	1 776	2 208	2 327	2 164
United Republic of Tanzania	511	331	734	1 684	2 219	3 040	2 982	4 051
Zambia (3)	1 305	1 309	892	1 810	4 617	5 099	4 312	7 200
Zimbabwe	1 396	1 711	1 923	1 850	2 400	2 200	2 269	(e)2 500
Middle Africa	8 856	11 818	17 078	49 522	76 163	118 129	70 305	88 624
Angola*(4)	1 902	3 884	7 887	24 105	43 452	72 179	40 080	49 259
Cameroon*(5)	1 384	2 002	1 833	2 861	3 604	4 300	3 370	3 878
Central African Republic*(5)	116	120	161	129	178	150	(e)124	(e)139
Chad*(4)	71	234	183	3 144	3 668	4 328	2 636	(e)3 411
Congo*(5)	911	981	2 489	4 745	5 635	8 324	6 123	(e)8 192
Dem. Rep. of the Congo*	2 269	2 326	824	2 403	3 100	4 400	3 500	(e)5 400
Equatorial Guinea (4)	14	62	1 097	7 064	10 210	14 930	9 108	(e)9 964
Gabon*(6)	2 173	2 204	2 602	5 065	6 309	9 506	5 356	(e)8 374
Sao Tome and Principe*	17	4	3	7	7	11	8	6
Northern Africa	44 042	36 856	54 264	114 109	159 317	218 644	141 648	174 284
Algeria*	13 871	12 880	22 031	46 002	60 163	79 298	45 194	57 051
Egypt	3 046	2 585	4 675	10 652	16 200	26 246	23 062	26 438
Libyan Arab Jamahiriya	21 910	13 225	12 716	30 948	43 571	61 766	37 055	46 310
Morocco*	2 441	4 265	7 185	11 190	15 340	20 345	14 054	17 559
Sudan (7)	543	374	1 807	4 824	8 879	11 671	7 834	(e)10 500
Tunisia (8)	2 231	3 527	5 850	10 494	15 163	19 319	14 449	16 427
Southern Africa	28 433	27 242	37 168	65 181	87 180	96 874	75 296	96 858
Botswana*	504	1 785	2 763	4 425	5 174	4 951	3 456	4 693
Lesotho	58	62	221	651	770	894	726	801
Namibia	1 459	1 086	1 320	2 070	2 919	3 188	3 101	4 111
South Africa	(b)26 039	23 753	31 950	56 261	76 435	86 118	66 542	85 700
Swaziland	373	557	914	1 774	1 881	1 723	1 471	1 552
Western Africa	33 532	21 862	30 703	72 411	87 562	108 126	80 629	101 851
Benin*	63	288	392	578	1 047	1 282	1 225	1 388
Burkina Faso	90	152	206	468	623	693	900	1 288
Cape Verde (9)	4	6	11	18	19	32	35	45
Côte d'Ivoire*	3 135	3 072	3 888	7 697	8 669	10 390	10 996	(e)10 323
Gambia (10)	31	31	15	8	13	14	(e)15	(e)15
Ghana	1 258	897	1 671	2 802	4 321	5 270	5 840	7 960
Guinea*	401	671	666	846	1 203	1 342	1 050	1 471
Guinea-Bissau	11	19	62	89	107	128	122	(e)120
Liberia*	600	(e)868	(e)329	131	187	234	155	(e)200
Mali*	205	359	545	1 101	1 556	2 097	1 774	1 958
Mauritania*	194	447	355	625	1 402	1 811	1 364	2 044
Niger*	566	283	283	489	663	912	997	1 040
Nigeria	25 934	13 596	20 975	55 145	65 133	80 615	53 000	70 579
Saint Helena	(e)1	(e)6	(e)8	(e)20	(e)23	(e)31	(e)28	(e)26
Senegal (11)	477	762	920	1 575	1 652	2 206	2 017	2 161
Sierra Leone*	224	138	13	159	245	216	208	340
Togo*	338	268	364	659	700	853	903	(e)893

For sources and notes, see end of table 1.1.1.

1.1.1 Exportations et importations des pays et des régions géographiques
Valeur

1980	1990	2000	2005	2007	2008	2009	2010	Régions, pays ou territoires
Imports (c.i.f.) - Importations (c.a.f.) Millions de dollars								
2 078 123	3 588 082	6 662 891	10 800 151	14 252 228	16 464 800	12 670 083	15 353 255	MONDE
496 880	797 007	1 919 794	3 424 536	4 729 574	5 749 263	4 668 601	6 001 415	ÉCONOMIES EN DÉVELOPPEMENT
83 598	139 945	104 699	271 901	468 154	610 954	409 820	490 873	ÉCONOMIES EN TRANSITION
1 497 645	2 651 129	4 638 399	7 103 715	9 054 500	10 104 584	7 591 662	8 860 968	ÉCONOMIES DÉVELOPPÉES
96 856	94 372	130 215	262 230	375 966	480 629	422 235	488 151	Économies en développement : Afrique
10 706	12 698	16 983	32 128	45 378	59 804	53 248	61 533	Afrique orientale
168	231	148	267	319	402	402	509	Burundi*(1)
29	52	43	99	138	176	170	(e)185	Comores*
213	215	207	277	473	574	451	(e)417	Djibouti (2)
–	–	471	(e)495	(e)510	(e)602	(e)587	(e)690	Érythrée
–	–	1 262	4 095	5 809	8 680	7 974	9 692	Éthiopie
722	1 081	–	–	–	–	–	–	Éthiopie (anc.)
2 125	2 223	3 105	6 149	8 989	11 074	10 207	12 090	Kenya
764	566	997	1 686	2 445	3 851	3 159	2 546	Madagascar*
439	575	532	1 164	1 380	2 204	2 022	2 173	Malawi
614	1 618	2 207	3 157	3 894	4 651	3 728	4 402	Maurice
..	..	139	309	499	606	502	-	Mayotte
800	878	1 162	2 408	3 050	4 008	3 764	3 564	Mozambique
262	287	213	471	737	1 174	1 308	1 431	Rwanda
99	187	342	675	859	1 053	807	989	Seychelles
435	(e)81	(e)343	(e)626	(e)887	(e)1 131	(e)931	(e)955	Somalie
293	288	1 538	2 054	3 493	4 526	4 247	4 664	Ouganda
1 258	1 364	1 524	3 287	5 337	7 081	6 296	7 702	République-Unie de Tanzanie
1 088	1 220	888	2 558	4 007	5 060	3 793	5 321	Zambie (3)
1 396	1 833	1 861	2 350	2 550	2 950	2 900	(e)3 700	Zimbabwe
5 884	6 992	7 619	19 073	30 836	42 392	44 113	48 681	Afrique centrale
1 328	1 578	3 040	8 353	13 662	20 982	22 660	24 926	Angola*(4)
1 602	1 400	1 484	2 735	4 200	5 400	4 300	5 133	Cameroun*(5)
81	154	117	173	249	300	(e)271	(e)341	République centrafricaine*(5)
74	499	317	949	1 797	1 906	2 289	(e)2 507	Tchad*(4)
562	621	479	1 343	2 532	3 053	2 984	(e)2 990	Congo*(5)
1 519	1 739	697	2 690	3 400	4 300	3 800	(e)4 500	Rép. dém. du Congo*
26	61	504	1 310	2 760	3 746	5 205	(e)5 680	Guinée équatoriale (4)
674	918	952	1 471	2 157	2 591	2 501	(c)2 492	Gabon*(6)
19	21	30	50	79	114	103	112	Sao Tomé-et-Principe*
31 553	37 374	48 786	92 084	127 560	184 295	167 185	186 270	Afrique septentrionale
10 559	9 770	9 152	20 357	27 631	39 475	39 258	41 000	Algérie*
4 860	9 216	13 963	19 816	27 063	48 775	44 946	52 923	Égypte
6 777	5 336	4 018	11 188	12 979	19 706	21 168	24 647	Jamahiriya arabe libyenne
4 255	6 922	11 534	20 790	32 010	42 366	32 881	35 522	Maroc*
1 576	619	1 553	6 757	8 775	9 352	9 691	(e)9 960	Soudan (7)
3 526	5 513	8 567	13 177	19 101	24 622	19 241	22 218	Tunisie (8)
22 807	23 053	35 704	73 316	101 700	110 009	88 956	111 460	Afrique australe
693	1 947	2 082	3 232	4 067	5 211	4 728	5 657	Botswana*
427	673	809	1 410	1 739	2 032	1 978	2 203	Lesotho
1 156	1 163	1 550	2 577	3 520	4 340	4 980	(e)5 648	Namibie
(e,b)19 906	(e)18 606	(e)30 211	(e)64 192	(e)90 527	(e)96 704	(e)75 647	(e)96 249	Afrique du Sud
625	664	1 052	1 904	1 846	1 723	1 623	1 703	Swaziland
25 906	14 255	21 123	45 629	70 493	84 129	68 733	80 207	Afrique occidentale
331	265	613	1 018	2 037	2 289	2 064	(e)2 161	Bénin*
359	536	611	1 251	1 678	2 211	1 870	2 048	Burkina Faso
68	136	230	438	750	825	709	742	Cap-Vert (9)
2 991	2 098	2 482	5 865	6 683	7 884	6 960	(e)6 898	Côte d'Ivoire*
165	188	187	260	321	322	305	276	Gambie (10)
1 129	1 205	2 976	5 347	8 061	10 269	8 046	10 922	Ghana
270	723	612	820	1 218	1 366	1 060	1 405	Guinée*
55	86	60	123	191	227	235	(e)229	Guinée-Bissau
535	210	(e)668	324	530	849	563	(e)650	Libéria*
439	602	806	1 544	2 185	3 339	2 431	(e)2 781	Mali*
286	220	454	1 424	1 443	1 966	1 425	1 823	Mauritanie*
594	389	395	943	1 149	1 575	2 364	(e)2 399	Niger*
16 643	5 627	8 721	21 314	37 576	42 378	33 906	40 760	Nigéria
(e)13	(e)21	(e)42	(e)61	(e)117	(e)59	(e)52	(e)63	Sainte-Hélène
1 052	1 220	1 553	3 498	4 871	6 528	4 713	4 782	Sénégal (11)
427	149	149	345	446	533	521	773	Sierra Leone*
551	581	562	1 054	1 237	1 509	1 509	(e)1 496	Togo*

Pour les sources et les notes, se reporter à la fin du tableau 1.1.1.

1.1.1 Exports and imports of countries and geographical regions
Value

Region, country or territory	Exports (f.o.b.) - Exportations (f.a.b.) Millions of dollars							
	1980	1990	2000	2005	2007	2008	2009	2010
Developing economies: America	**111 352**	**143 934**	**366 507**	**576 636**	**771 611**	**901 287**	**688 097**	**872 612**
Caribbean	*22 368*	*11 666*	*19 000*	*25 756*	*32 318*	*38 981*	*23 366*	*25 095*
Anguilla	..	..	4	15	9	11	23	12
Antigua and Barbuda	26	21	81	83	59	58	35	35
Aruba (12)	..	155	2 524	3 483	2 691	3 705	1 434	266
Bahamas (13)	5 009	238	576	549	802	956	711	702
Barbados	228	215	272	359	490	488	379	429
Cayman Islands	..	..	..	60	27	17	19	16
Cuba*	5 677	1 010	1 676	2 010	2 991	3 074	2 100	(e)2 000
Dominica*	10	66	61	41	38	40	36	31
Dominican Republic (14)	962	735	5 737	6 145	7 160	6 748	5 483	6 598
Grenada*	17	26	48	28	33	31	29	24
Haiti	226	160	318	470	522	480	576	579
Jamaica	963	1 158	1 296	1 600	2 234	2 490	1 316	1 378
Montserrat*	1	2	1	1	3	4	3	1
Netherlands Antilles*(15)	5 162	1 790	2 009	608	676	1 088	810	811
Saint Kitts and Nevis*	24	24	29	34	39	51	43	45
Saint Lucia*	70	134	43	64	107	164	163	165
Saint Vincent and the Grenadines*	15	83	51	40	48	52	49	42
Trinidad and Tobago*	4 077	1 960	4 274	9 941	13 394	18 650	9 126	10 188
Turks and Caicos Islands	..	..	9	15	16	25	21	-
Central America	*23 379*	*45 703*	*182 934*	*236 849*	*300 707*	*322 912*	*256 794*	*329 145*
Belize	111	133	218	208	254	290	224	280
Costa Rica*	1 002	1 448	5 850	7 026	9 376	9 575	8 711	9 343
El Salvador	1 075	644	2 941	3 418	3 984	4 549	3 797	4 499
Guatemala (16)	1 520	1 163	2 711	5 381	6 898	7 737	7 214	8 466
Honduras (17)	829	934	3 343	5 048	5 784	6 199	4 825	5 742
Mexico	18 031	40 711	166 368	213 891	272 055	291 827	229 683	298 138
Nicaragua	451	331	643	858	1 194	1 489	1 393	1 845
Panama, excl. Canal Zone (former)	361							
Panama*	–	340	859	1 018	1 164	1 247	948	832
South America	*65 605*	*86 564*	*164 573*	*314 032*	*438 585*	*539 394*	*407 938*	*518 371*
Argentina*	8 021	12 353	26 341	40 351	55 779	70 588	56 065	68 500
Bolivia (Plurinational State of)	942	926	1 230	2 791	4 458	7 058	4 918	6 179
Brazil	20 132	31 414	55 119	118 529	160 649	197 942	152 995	201 915
Chile*	4 705	8 373	19 210	41 267	67 666	66 456	51 963	68 996
Colombia	3 924	6 721	13 043	21 146	29 786	38 265	32 784	39 710
Ecuador	2 481	2 714	4 927	10 100	13 852	18 818	13 863	17 415
Falkland Islands (Malvinas)	(e)8	(e)15	(e)85	(e)154	(e)164	(e)178	(e)131	(e)162
Guyana*	389	251	502	553	679	795	763	877
Paraguay	310	959	869	1 655	2 817	4 463	3 167	4 534
Peru*	3 898	3 231	7 028	17 368	27 882	31 529	26 885	35 565
Suriname	514	472	396	997	1 359	1 743	1 393	2 026
Uruguay	1 059	1 693	2 295	3 405	4 485	6 421	5 417	6 707
Venezuela (Bolivarian Rep. of)	19 221	17 444	33 529	55 716	69 010	95 138	57 595	65 786
Developing economies: Asia	**364 287**	**590 380**	**1 535 072**	**2 896 260**	**4 058 969**	**4 809 702**	**3 888 563**	**4 964 751**
Eastern Asia	*76 165*	*280 556*	*774 891*	*1 538 367*	*2 186 282*	*2 475 001*	*2 090 464*	*2 716 238*
China	18 099	62 091	249 203	761 953	1 217 790	1 428 660	1 201 790	1 578 270
China, Hong Kong SAR	19 752	82 151	201 860	289 337	344 509	362 675	318 510	390 174
China, Macao SAR	613	1 701	2 539	2 476	2 543	1 997	961	870
China, Taiwan Province of	19 786	67 079	147 777	197 779	246 377	255 062	203 691	274 641
Korea, Dem. People's Rep. of	..	1 857	708	1 338	1 685	2 060	1 995	(e)3 000
Korea, Republic of (18)	17 512	65 016	172 268	284 419	371 489	422 007	361 614	466 384
Mongolia	403	661	536	1 065	1 889	2 539	1 903	2 899
Southern Asia	*26 127*	*47 005*	*92 725*	*189 233*	*278 982*	*354 368*	*285 323*	*373 325*
Afghanistan	670	235	137	384	497	540	403	388
Bangladesh	759	1 671	6 389	9 297	12 453	15 380	15 073	19 239
Bhutan	17	70	103	258	674	519	496	641
India (19)	8 586	17 969	42 379	99 620	149 951	194 531	164 921	221 406
Iran (Islamic Rep. of)*	12 328	19 305	28 345	56 252	88 733	113 668	78 830	100 900
Maldives	8	78	109	162	228	331	169	200
Nepal	80	175	804	863	868	939	823	834
Pakistan	2 618	5 589	9 028	16 051	17 838	20 323	17 523	21 410
Sri Lanka	1 062	1 912	5 430	6 347	7 740	8 137	7 085	8 307
South-Eastern Asia	*73 957*	*145 284*	*431 901*	*652 731*	*865 721*	*998 771*	*813 634*	*1 052 127*
Brunei Darussalam*	4 581	2 213	3 903	6 249	7 668	10 721	7 203	9 160
Cambodia (4)	16	86	1 389	2 910	4 088	4 708	4 302	(e)5 500

For sources and notes, see end of table 1.1.1.

1.1.1 Exportations et importations des pays et des régions géographiques
Valeur

Imports (c.i.f.) - Importations (c.a.f.) Millions de dollars								Régions, pays ou territoires
1980	1990	2000	2005	2007	2008	2009	2010	
123 594	126 635	391 895	533 987	756 005	923 464	689 494	891 129	Économies en développement : Amérique
27 362	18 701	32 414	42 779	55 199	68 804	48 546	53 710	*Caraïbes*
..	..	95	130	248	272	169	157	Anguilla
88	255	407	550	727	742	650	520	Antigua-et-Barbuda
..	581	2 584	3 462	2 853	4 201	1 911	1 343	Aruba (12)
7 546	1 112	2 074	2 567	3 103	3 230	2 699	2 863	Bahamas (13)
525	704	1 156	1 604	1 709	1 879	1 471	1 562	Barbade
..	..	..	1 191	1 032	1 052	883	991	Îles Caïmanes
6 505	6 746	4 813	8 084	10 886	15 300	9 620	(e)11 000	Cuba*
48	118	148	165	196	247	233	224	Dominique*
1 964	3 006	9 479	9 869	13 597	15 993	12 296	15 299	République dominicaine (14)
50	105	239	334	365	363	283	317	Grenade*
375	332	1 036	1 454	1 682	2 315	2 124	3 146	Haïti
1 171	1 928	3 301	4 460	6 748	8 465	5 064	5 225	Jamaïque
12	48	22	30	30	38	30	(e)30	Montserrat*
5 676	2 141	2 862	1 950	2 549	3 079	2 607	(e)2 687	Antilles néerlandaises*(15)
45	110	196	210	272	325	302	228	Saint-Kitts-et-Névis*
124	271	355	479	635	657	539	581	Sainte-Lucie*
57	136	162	240	327	373	333	379	Saint-Vincent-et-les Grenadines*
3 178	1 109	3 308	5 694	7 662	9 591	6 955	6 483	Trinité-et-Tobago*
..	..	149	304	581	591	375	-	Îles Turques et Caïques
29 743	51 774	208 906	272 734	351 846	389 502	295 557	375 067	*Amérique centrale*
150	211	524	593	684	837	669	709	Belize
1 540	1 990	6 389	9 812	12 957	15 366	11 460	13 557	Costa Rica*
966	1 263	4 948	6 690	8 712	9 754	7 255	8 485	El Salvador
1 598	1 649	5 171	10 499	13 576	14 547	11 531	13 836	Guatemala (16)
1 009	938	3 988	6 545	8 888	10 453	7 299	8 550	Honduras (17)
22 144	43 548	182 702	231 821	296 578	325 157	246 104	316 556	Mexique
887	637	1 805	2 595	3 579	4 338	3 438	4 229	Nicaragua
1 449								Panama, sans la zone du canal (anc.)
–	1 539	3 379	4 180	6 872	9 050	7 801	9 145	Panama*
66 489	56 160	150 575	218 475	348 959	465 158	345 392	462 351	*Amérique du Sud*
10 545	4 078	25 154	28 693	44 707	57 413	39 105	56 443	Argentine*
665	687	1 830	2 341	3 457	5 081	4 434	5 182	Bolivie (État plurinational de)
24 961	22 522	58 643	77 628	126 645	182 377	133 673	191 464	Brésil
5 797	7 940	18 507	32 735	47 164	61 903	41 364	57 928	Chili*
4 739	5 589	11 539	21 204	33 164	39 320	32 898	40 683	Colombie
2 253	1 862	3 721	10 287	13 565	18 852	15 090	20 591	Équateur
(e)6	(e)36	(e)67	(e)66	(e)103	(e)64	(e)59	(e)112	Îles Falkland (Malvinas)
396	311	582	788	1 059	1 312	1 161	1 400	Guyana*
615	1 352	2 260	3 274	5 859	9 033	6 940	10 040	Paraguay
2 499	2 634	7 415	12 502	20 368	29 953	21 870	29 880	Pérou*
504	472	526	1 050	1 044	1 304	1 296	1 397	Suriname
1 680	1 343	3 466	3 879	5 726	8 943	6 907	8 619	Uruguay
11 827	7 335	16 865	24 027	46 097	49 602	40 597	38 613	Venezuela (Rép. bolivarienne du)
272 880	570 906	1 391 359	2 618 575	3 584 962	4 330 558	3 544 902	4 608 458	Économies en développement : Asie
85 536	265 898	742 792	1 411 364	1 910 913	2 208 651	1 858 754	2 517 894	*Asie orientale*
19 941	53 345	225 024	660 206	956 233	1 131 620	1 004 170	1 396 200	Chine
22 447	82 492	212 805	299 533	367 647	388 505	347 311	433 193	Chine (RAS de Hong Kong)
543	1 533	2 255	3 913	5 366	5 365	4 622	5 513	Chine (RAS de Macao)
19 764	54 831	139 927	182 571	219 649	240 690	174 582	251 498	Province chinoise de Taiwan
..	2 930	1 686	2 718	3 055	3 580	3 095	(e)3 000	Corée, Rép. populaire dém. de
22 292	69 844	160 481	261 238	356 846	435 275	322 843	425 212	Corée, République de (18)
548	924	615	1 184	2 117	3 616	2 131	3 278	Mongolie
39 540	57 368	96 071	236 847	343 676	466 845	380 422	482 350	*Asie méridionale*
841	936	1 176	2 470	2 819	3 020	3 336	5 154	Afghanistan
2 599	3 618	8 883	13 889	18 595	23 840	21 851	27 794	Bangladesh
50	81	175	386	526	540	530	855	Bhoutan
14 864	23 580	51 523	142 842	228 686	320 785	257 187	328 360	Inde (19)
13 427	18 330	15 207	40 041	44 942	57 401	50 469	62 670	Iran (Rép. islamique d')*
29	137	389	745	1 096	1 388	967	1 095	Maldives
342	624	1 573	2 283	3 122	3 590	4 384	5 128	Népal
5 350	7 376	10 864	25 357	32 590	42 329	31 648	37 783	Pakistan
2 037	2 685	6 281	8 834	11 301	13 953	10 049	13 512	Sri Lanka
65 641	162 349	380 151	602 824	776 769	946 542	728 224	952 146	*Asie du Sud-Est*
572	1 001	1 107	1 491	2 101	2 543	2 454	3 359	Brunéi Darussalam*
180	164	1 936	3 918	5 439	6 508	5 876	(e)7 400	Cambodge (4)

Pour les sources et les notes, se reporter à la fin du tableau 1.1.1.

1.1.1 Exports and imports of countries and geographical regions
Value

Region, country or territory	Exports (f.o.b.) - Exportations (f.a.b.) Millions of dollars							
	1980	1990	2000	2005	2007	2008	2009	2010
Indonesia including East Timor	23 950	26 807	65 407	–	–	–	–	–
Indonesia	–	–	–	86 179	118 728	139 605	119 646	157 823
Lao People's Dem. Rep.*	28	79	330	553	923	1 092	1 005	1 746
Malaysia (20)	12 945	29 452	98 229	140 870	176 028	209 719	157 516	198 800
Myanmar	477	328	1 646	3 813	6 317	6 950	6 731	8 749
Philippines	5 741	8 117	39 783	39 879	50 270	49 205	38 308	51 432
Singapore (21)	19 375	52 730	137 804	229 649	299 272	338 176	269 832	351 867
Thailand*	6 505	23 068	68 963	110 178	153 858	175 897	151 986	195 375
Timor-Leste (22)	–	–	–	8	7	13	8	17
Viet Nam	339	2 404	14 447	32 442	48 561	62 685	57 096	71 658
Western Asia	**188 038**	**117 536**	**235 556**	**515 929**	**727 984**	**981 563**	**699 143**	**823 061**
Bahrain (4)	3 606	3 761	6 194	10 242	13 634	17 316	11 874	13 647
Iraq*	26 349	10 314	20 380	23 697	39 516	63 726	44 275	52 084
Jordan	574	1 064	1 899	4 302	5 725	7 788	6 531	7 023
Kuwait†	10 012	7 042	10 126	11 060	62 109	87 427	61 679	65 984
Lebanon (23)	955	494	715	2 337	3 574	4 454	4 187	5 021
Occupied Palestinian territory	..	..	401	335	513	558	518	563
Oman	2 387	5 508	11 319	18 692	24 136	37 719	28 053	36 601
Qatar*	5 680	3 529	11 409	25 339	41 491	54 912	48 306	72 054
Saudi Arabia*(24)	101 577	44 416	77 481	180 572	233 174	313 462	192 296	235 342
Syrian Arab Republic*	2 108	4 212	4 633	9 174	11 546	15 410	10 855	(e)14 000
Turkey*	2 910	12 959	27 775	73 476	107 272	132 027	102 143	113 883
United Arab Emirates	21 967	23 544	49 835	117 287	178 606	239 180	192 167	198 362
Yemen (former Arab Republic)	23	–	–	–	–	–	–	–
Yemen (former Democratic)	60	–	–	–	–	–	–	–
Yemen*	–	692	4 079	5 608	6 299	7 584	6 259	8 497
Developing economies: Oceania	**2 242**	**2 710**	**5 091**	**6 660**	**8 998**	**9 560**	**7 131**	**8 783**
American Samoa*(25)	127	311	346	374	(e)450	(e)570	(e)470	(e)480
Cook Islands	4	5	9	5	5	4	3	5
Fiji	377	398	538	700	758	923	628	613
French Polynesia*	30	111	244	210	196	273	167	(e)173
Guam	61	82	74	52	91	105	51	46
Kiribati	3	3	4	4	10	15	20	(e)15
Marshall Islands	–	3	9	25	22	(e)20	(e)21	(e)20
Micronesia (Federated States of)	–	4	17	13	22	27	(e)27	(e)27
Nauru	65	60	28	4	(e)15	(e)100	(e)21	(e)35
New Caledonia*	409	480	606	1 093	2 104	1 300	1 029	1 268
Niue	..	0	0	0	3	0	(e)0	(e)0
Northern Mariana Islands	–	..	1 017	651	308	149	3	(e)10
Palau	–	..	12	14	11	12	12	12
Papua New Guinea	1 031	1 144	2 070	3 276	4 683	5 714	4 404	5 736
Samoa (23)	17	9	14	87	97	72	46	60
Solomon Islands*	74	70	69	103	165	210	165	227
Tokelau	..	..	..	(e)0	(e)0	-	-	-
Tonga	7	11	9	10	9	9	8	8
Tuvalu	..	1	0	0	0	(e)0	(e)0	(e)0
Vanuatu	36	19	26	38	50	56	57	49
Wallis and Futuna Islands	..	..	-	(e)0	-	-	-	-
Transition economies	**85 426**	**118 709**	**154 524**	**363 057**	**550 679**	**739 536**	**478 857**	**617 544**
Albania	..	224	261	658	1 078	1 355	1 091	1 550
Armenia*	–	–	294	950	1 219	1 057	698	1 011
Azerbaijan (26)	–	–	1 745	7 649	21 269	30 586	21 097	26 476
Belarus	–	–	7 326	15 979	24 275	32 571	21 304	25 284
Bosnia and Herzegovina*(27)	–	–	1 069	2 406	4 154	5 029	3 954	4 803
Croatia*	–	–	4 432	8 773	12 364	14 112	10 474	11 806
Georgia (28)	–	–	323	865	1 240	1 507	1 140	1 581
Kazakhstan*(28)	–	–	8 812	28 301	48 351	71 971	43 196	57 244
Kyrgyzstan	–	–	511	674	1 321	1 856	1 673	1 760
Montenegro	–	–	–	–	–	659	403	437
Republic of Moldova	–	–	472	1 091	1 340	1 597	1 283	1 542
Russian Federation (29)	–	–	105 565	243 799	354 403	471 765	303 388	400 424
Serbia and Montenegro*	–	–	1 711	5 058	9 648			
Serbia	–	–	–	–	–	10 972	8 345	9 795
SFR of Yugoslavia (former)	8 978	14 308						
Tajikistan (28)	–	–	784	891	1 468	1 406	1 010	1 206
TFYR of Macedonia*	–	–	1 323	2 041	3 302	3 920	2 691	3 291
Turkmenistan (28)	–	–	2 506	4 944	7 920	11 920	6 595	(e)6 000
Ukraine (28)	–	–	14 573	34 228	49 296	66 954	39 782	51 478
USSR (former)	76 449	104 177						
Uzbekistan (28)	–	–	2 817	4 749	8 029	10 298	10 735	11 857

For sources and notes, see end of table 1.1.1.

		Imports (c.i.f.) - Importations (c.a.f.) Millions de dollars						Régions, pays ou territoires
1980	1990	2000	2005	2007	2008	2009	2010	
10 834	21 768	43 075	–	–	–	–	–	Indonésie, y compris le Timor oriental
			75 631	93 101	127 454	93 802	132 099	Indonésie
92	185	535	882	1 067	1 405	1 414	2 060	Rép. dém. populaire lao*
10 779	29 258	81 963	114 410	146 767	164 406	123 695	164 733	Malaisie (20)
357	273	2 401	1 927	3 280	4 299	4 393	4 807	Myanmar
8 291	13 004	37 027	49 487	57 708	60 485	45 735	58 229	Philippines
24 007	60 899	134 545	200 047	263 155	319 780	245 785	310 791	Singapour (21)
9 214	33 045	61 923	118 158	141 294	178 680	134 827	184 590	Thaïlande*
			112	176	269	295	298	Timor-Leste (22)
1 314	2 752	15 638	36 761	62 682	80 714	69 949	83 779	Viet Nam
82 164	*85 291*	*172 345*	*367 539*	*553 604*	*708 520*	*577 502*	*656 068*	*Asie occidentale*
3 483	3 712	4 633	9 393	10 926	14 246	9 613	11 190	Bahreïn (4)
8 707	6 526	13 210	23 532	19 556	35 496	38 437	44 203	Iraq*
2 402	2 600	4 597	10 506	13 511	16 764	14 534	15 085	Jordanie
6 533	3 972	7 156	15 801	21 319	24 866	20 336	22 423	Koweït*
3 650	2 525	6 230	9 633	12 251	16 754	16 574	18 460	Liban (23)
..	..	2 383	2 667	3 141	3 569	3 601	4 385	Territoire palestinien occupé
1 732	2 681	5 040	8 827	15 978	22 925	17 865	19 775	Oman
1 447	1 695	3 248	10 061	23 430	27 900	24 922	22 000	Qatar*
30 165	24 107	30 197	59 463	90 157	115 134	95 567	103 651	Arabie saoudite*(24)
4 124	2 400	3 815	10 862	14 655	18 150	15 443	(e)18 880	République arabe syrienne*
7 910	22 303	54 503	116 774	170 063	201 964	140 928	185 544	Turquie*
8 631	11 199	35 009	84 642	150 103	200 300	170 497	180 726	Émirats arabes unis
1 853	–	–	–	–	–	–	–	Yémen (anc. République arabe du)
1 527								Yémen (anc. démocratique)
–	1 571	2 324	5 378	8 514	10 452	9 185	9 746	Yémen*
3 550	*5 094*	*6 324*	*9 743*	*12 641*	*14 611*	*11 969*	*13 677*	*Économies en développement : Océanie*
95	360	506	506	650	680	600	(e)550	Samoa américaines*(25)
23	52	51	81	106	150	181	(e)314	Îles Cook
562	754	856	1 607	1 801	2 259	1 434	1 271	Fidji
547	928	1 072	1 723	1 863	2 187	1 732	(e)1 740	Polynésie française*
400	401	421	533	688	649	635	698	Guam
17	27	40	76	70	74	68	73	Kiribati
–	56	55	94	95	(e)100	(e)90	(e)120	Îles Marshall
–	84	107	130	143	155	172	(e)155	Micronésie (États fédérés de)
12	34	27	26	(e)55	(e)87	(e)99	(e)131	Nauru
456	883	922	1 774	2 809	3 233	2 574	3 303	Nouvelle-Calédonie*
..	4	2	8	7	8	(e)5	(e)5	Nioué
..	..	–	–	–	–	–	–	Îles Mariannes du Nord
–	..	127	108	108	130	104	113	Palaos
1 176	1 118	1 151	1 728	2 950	3 560	3 200	(e)3 883	Papouasie-Nouvelle-Guinée
63	81	90	239	266	288	231	310	Samoa (23)
89	91	92	185	287	329	268	405	Îles Salomon*
..	..	1	(e)0	(e)0	–	–	–	Tokélaou
38	62	69	120	143	166	145	159	Tonga
..	4	5	13	15	26	(e)14	(e)16	Tuvalu
73	96	87	149	229	313	291	284	Vanuatu
..	..	37	51	–	–	–	–	Îles Wallis-et-Futuna
83 598	*139 945*	*104 699*	*271 901*	*468 154*	*610 954*	*409 820*	*490 873*	*Économies en transition*
..	423	1 091	2 618	4 188	5 251	4 550	4 601	Albanie
–	–	882	1 768	3 282	4 427	3 303	3 783	Arménie*
–	–	1 172	4 211	5 714	7 170	6 123	6 599	Azerbaïdjan (26)
–	–	8 646	16 708	28 693	39 381	28 569	34 884	Bélarus
–	–	3 894	7 122	9 719	12 155	8 754	9 223	Bosnie-Herzégovine*(27)
–	–	7 887	18 560	25 830	30 728	21 203	20 051	Croatie*
–	–	709	2 490	5 217	6 066	4 386	5 097	Géorgie (28)
–	–	5 040	17 979	33 260	38 452	28 409	24 024	Kazakhstan*(28)
–	–	558	1 189	2 789	4 072	3 040	3 223	Kirghizistan
–	–	–	–	–	3 731	2 313	2 182	Monténégro
–	–	776	2 293	3 690	4 899	3 278	3 855	République de Moldova
–	–	49 125	137 977	245 837	321 170	210 984	273 614	Fédération de Russie (29)
–	–	3 711	11 679	21 729	–	–	–	Serbie-et-Monténégro*
					22 875	16 047	16 734	Serbie
15 076	18 871	–	–	–				RSF de Yougoslavie (anc.)
–	–	675	1 330	2 455	3 270	2 569	2 658	Tadjikistan (28)
–	–	2 094	3 228	5 177	6 844	5 032	5 449	LERY de Macédoine*
–	–	1 786	2 947	3 620	5 650	6 750	(e)5 600	Turkménistan (28)
–	–	13 956	36 136	60 618	85 535	45 487	60 911	Ukraine (28)
68 522	120 651	–	–	–	–	–	–	URSS (anc.)
–	–	2 697	3 666	6 338	9 277	9 023	8 384	Ouzbékistan (28)

Pour les sources et les notes, se reporter à la fin du tableau 1.1.1.

1.1.1 Exports and imports of countries and geographical regions
Value

Region, country or territory	Exports (f.o.b.) - Exportations (f.a.b.) Millions of dollars							
	1980	1990	2000	2005	2007	2008	2009	2010
Developed economies: America	**293 549**	**521 758**	**1 058 872**	**1 267 050**	**1 580 098**	**1 753 793**	**1 373 187**	**1 664 019**
Bermuda (4)	37	60	51	49	25	24	29	26
Canada	67 734	127 629	276 617	359 430	416 654	452 162	316 043	386 026
Greenland	211	452	271	402	428	486	359	382
Saint Pierre and Miquelon	1	26	(e)14	(e)11	(e)11	(e)10	(e)6	(e)5
United States (30)	225 566	393 592	781 918	907 158	1 162 980	1 301 110	1 056 750	1 277 580
Developed economies: Asia	**135 979**	**299 157**	**510 653**	**637 675**	**768 276**	**842 874**	**628 653**	**828 230**
Israel*	5 538	11 579	31 404	42 770	54 065	60 825	47 934	58 392
Japan	130 441	287 581	479 249	594 905	714 211	782 049	580 719	769 838
Developed economies: Europe	**893 466**	**1 649 011**	**2 590 701**	**4 302 738**	**5 654 300**	**6 278 410**	**4 874 565**	**5 481 495**
Andorra*	..	..	45	142	127	96	63	54
Austria	17 409	41 195	67 540	126 101	160 102	180 663	126 428	152 413
Belgium*	-	-	187 906	334 265	430 375	469 924	368 357	411 826
Bulgaria*	10 372	4 822	4 809	11 739	18 494	22 271	16 253	20 646
Cyprus*	532	957	951	1 464	1 392	1 626	1 252	1 411
Czechoslovakia (former) (31)	14 891	11 906						
Czech Republic*(32)	–	–	28 996	78 079	122 334	146 203	112 501	132 708
Denmark*(33)	16 749	37 037	51 166	85 086	103 033	116 448	93 538	97 568
Estonia*(28)	–	–	3 830	7 713	10 995	12 407	9 015	11 593
Faeroe Islands	187	400	477	602	746	852	762	817
Finland*	14 150	26 571	45 989	65 471	89 904	96 064	62 602	69 958
France*	116 409	217 265	326 802	463 240	558 863	613 737	482 832	520 902
Germany (former Dem. Rep.)	17 312	–	–	–	–	–	–	–
Germany (former Federal Rep.)	192 860	–	–	–	–	–	–	–
Germany*	–	410 104	550 447	970 521	1 319 447	1 440 297	1 115 537	1 267 653
Gibraltar (34)	10	83	127	200	304	283	264	-
Greece*	5 153	8 105	11 722	17 271	23 547	26 275	20 387	21 545
Hungary*(35)	8 671	9 598	28 016	62 911	95 272	108 063	82 674	95 345
Iceland	918	1 592	1 892	3 091	4 772	5 355	4 057	4 604
Ireland*	8 398	23 747	77 222	109 613	121 381	125 209	115 462	116 608
Italy*	78 104	170 486	239 924	372 983	499 213	540 544	405 273	446 870
Latvia*	–	–	1 865	5 159	8 297	10 103	7 671	9 518
Lithuania*(28)	–	–	3 548	11 802	17 121	23 550	10 388	20 015
Luxembourg*	3 005	6 305	8 357	18 790	22 360	25 433	21 134	19 592
Malta	483	1 130	2 443	2 398	3 073	2 976	2 233	2 519
Netherlands*	84 948	131 775	232 554	406 208	550 018	635 327	495 889	572 808
Norway	18 543	34 049	60 058	103 752	136 371	172 621	120 880	131 395
Poland*	14 191	13 627	31 651	89 401	139 959	169 766	135 954	155 602
Portugal*	4 640	16 422	24 303	38 134	52 433	56 905	44 033	48 689
Romania*	11 209	5 775	10 367	27 730	40 434	49 334	40 404	49 353
Slovakia*	–	–	11 889	31 876	58 437	70 853	55 856	65 150
Slovenia*	–	–	8 732	19 240	30 061	33 989	26 072	29 418
Spain*	20 720	55 521	114 966	192 566	252 959	280 350	226 424	245 401
Sweden*	30 906	57 538	86 917	130 909	168 591	182 583	130 431	158 161
Switzerland*	29 634	63 794	80 467	130 930	172 078	200 615	172 474	195 000
United Kingdom*	110 137	185 107	284 720	384 321	438 504	457 799	351 454	405 290
Developed economies: Oceania	**27 365**	**49 146**	**77 749**	**127 759**	**169 221**	**217 870**	**178 744**	**243 761**
Australia	21 944	39 752	63 870	105 832	141 099	186 965	153 884	212 362
New Zealand	5 421	9 394	13 879	21 927	28 122	30 905	24 860	31 399

For sources and notes, see end of table 1.1.1.

Imports (c.i.f.) - Importations (c.a.f.) Millions de dollars								Régions, pays ou territoires
1980	1990	2000	2005	2007	2008	2009	2010	
320 210	**641 358**	**1 505 270**	**2 068 247**	**2 411 614**	**2 588 937**	**1 937 040**	**2 361 820**	**Économies développées : Amérique**
343	595	719	985	1 167	1 160	1 065	967	Bermudes (4)
62 544	123 244	244 778	331 553	389 314	417 364	329 907	391 257	Canada
328	445	365	599	687	872	699	777	Groenland
10	86	(e)108	(e)50	(e)45	(e)51	(e)68	(e)59	Saint-Pierre-et-Miquelon
256 985	516 987	1 259 300	1 735 060	2 020 400	2 169 490	1 605 300	1 968 760	États-Unis (30)
151 080	**252 162**	**417 197**	**562 064**	**678 776**	**830 287**	**599 808**	**753 642**	**Économies développées : Asie**
9 784	16 794	37 686	47 142	59 039	67 656	49 278	61 200	Israël*
141 296	235 368	379 511	514 922	619 737	762 631	550 530	692 433	Japon
998 484	**1 700 124**	**2 000 100**	**1 231 260**	**5 767 299**	**6 451 051**	**4 864 084**	**5 513 251**	**Économies développées : Europe**
..	..	1 019	1 802	1 913	1 932	1 681	1 514	Andorre*
24 444	49 088	72 215	127 275	162 819	183 545	142 488	158 856	Autriche*
-	-	177 073	318 571	411 007	464 413	350 529	390 068	Belgique*
9 650	4 710	6 505	18 163	29 921	36 758	23 444	25 378	Bulgarie*
1 202	2 568	3 846	6 313	8 603	10 600	7 803	8 490	Chypre*
12 774	13 106							Tchécoslovaquie (anc.) (31)
–	–	33 852	76 481	118 011	141 461	104 626	126 073	République tchèque*(32)
19 340	33 248	45 445	75 551	97 896	108 918	82 318	84 793	Danemark*(33)
–	–	5 052	10 234	15 656	15 961	10 102	12 240	Estonie*(28)
219	333	533	747	1 016	988	783	775	Îles Féroé
15 635	27 001	34 358	58 742	81 594	91 409	60 645	68 601	Finlande*
137 554	240 753	338 103	503 920	630 018	713 883	558 618	606 624	France*
19 082	–	–	–	–	–	–	–	Allemagne (anc. Rép. dém. d')
188 002	–	–	–	–	–	–	–	Allemagne (anc. Rép. fédérale d')
–	346 153	495 970	776 758	1 053 572	1 180 253	922 622	1 065 813	Allemagne*
110	362	482	551	852	827	747	-	Gibraltar (34)
10 548	19 777	33 397	54 414	78 427	92 204	69 169	63 416	Grèce*
9 245	8 671	31 955	66 525	95 437	108 498	77 448	88 035	Hongrie*(35)
999	1 000	2 591	4 557	6 690	6 166	3 604	3 920	Islande
11 153	20 682	50 915	68 537	83 710	83 624	62 452	60 090	Irlande*
100 741	181 968	238 167	384 634	510 978	559 637	413 436	484 713	Italie*
–	–	3 184	8 694	15 301	16 077	9 772	11 666	Lettonie*
–	–	5 219	15 542	24 380	30 972	18 230	23 376	Lituanie*(28)
3 612	7 596	11 250	21 884	27 529	31 889	24 800	23 960	Luxembourg*
938	1 961	3 400	3 679	4 754	5 137	4 110	4 172	Malte
88 419	126 475	217 728	363 675	491 957	578 577	441 371	516 429	Pays-Bas*
16 926	27 221	34 392	55 480	80 378	90 293	69 292	77 252	Norvège
16 690	8 413	48 940	101 598	165 488	207 956	148 858	173 481	Pologne*
9 309	25 264	39 854	61 159	82 019	94 033	71 375	75 563	Portugal*
13 843	9 843	13 055	40 463	70 220	83 712	54 106	61 935	Roumanie*
–	–	13 412	34 635	60 535	73 611	55 426	66 323	Slovaquie*
–	–	10 116	20 328	31 517	36 884	26 401	30 008	Slovénie*
34 078	87 554	155 757	288 669	388 781	419 094	292 039	314 017	Espagne*
33 438	54 245	72 700	111 652	153 021	167 818	119 594	148 573	Suède*
36 356	69 691	82 487	126 574	161 180	183 516	155 378	176 000	Suisse*
115 545	224 416	347 198	513 464	622 119	630 404	480 911	560 350	Royaume-Uni*
27 871	**51 486**	**85 763**	**152 135**	**196 812**	**234 309**	**190 730**	**232 255**	**Économies développées : Océanie**
22 399	41 985	71 529	125 281	165 336	200 273	165 471	201 639	Australie
5 472	9 501	14 235	26 854	31 476	34 036	25 259	30 616	Nouvelle-Zélande

Pour les sources et les notes, se reporter à la fin du tableau 1.1.1.

1.1.1 Exports and imports of countries and geographical regions
Share

Region, country or territory	Exports (f.o.b.) - Exportations (f.a.b.) Percentage - En pourcentage										
	1980	1990	1995	2000	2004	2005	2006	2007	2008	2009	2010
WORLD	100.000	100.000	100.000	100.000	100.000	100.000	100.000	100.000	100.000	100.000	100.000
DEVELOPING ECONOMIES	29.464	24.200	27.712	31.884	33.819	36.181	37.424	37.681	39.015	39.782	41.777
TRANSITION ECONOMIES	4.197	3.411	2.354	2.396	3.072	3.459	3.759	3.934	4.587	3.827	4.070
DEVELOPED ECONOMIES	66.339	72.389	69.934	65.720	63.109	60.360	58.816	58.385	56.398	56.391	54.154
Developing economies: Africa	5.987	3.020	2.188	2.317	2.537	3.029	3.073	3.104	3.534	3.144	3.250
Eastern Africa	0.011	0.213	0.161	0.158	0.160	0.159	0.171	0.173	0.173	0.204	0.208
Burundi*(1)	0.003	0.002	0.002	0.001	0.001	0.001	0.000	0.000	0.000	0.000	0.001
Comoros*	0.001	0.001	0.000	0.000	0.000	0.000	0.000	0.000	0.000	0.000	(e)0.000
Djibouti (2)	0.001	0.001	0.000	0.000	0.000	0.000	0.000	0.000	0.000	0.001	(e)0.000
Eritrea	–	–	0.002	0.000	0.000	0.000	0.000	0.000	(e)0.000	(e)0.000	(e)0.000
Ethiopia	–	–	0.008	0.008	0.007	0.009	0.009	0.009	0.010	0.013	0.017
Ethiopia (former)	0.021	0.009	–	–	–	–	–	–	–	–	–
Kenya	0.061	0.030	0.036	0.027	0.029	0.031	0.028	0.029	0.031	0.036	0.034
Madagascar*	0.020	0.009	0.010	0.013	0.011	0.008	0.008	0.010	0.010	0.009	0.007
Malawi	0.015	0.012	0.008	0.006	0.005	0.005	0.005	0.006	0.005	0.009	0.007
Mauritius	0.021	0.034	0.030	0.028	0.022	0.020	0.019	0.016	0.015	0.016	0.015
Mayotte	..	..	..	0.000	0.000	0.000	0.000	0.000	0.000	0.000	-
Mozambique	0.014	0.004	0.003	0.006	0.016	0.017	0.020	0.017	0.016	0.017	0.015
Rwanda	0.006	0.003	0.001	0.001	0.001	0.001	0.001	0.001	0.002	0.002	0.002
Seychelles	0.001	0.002	0.001	0.003	0.003	0.003	0.003	0.003	0.003	0.003	0.003
Somalia	0.007	(e)0.004	(e)0.003	(e)0.003	(e)0.002	(e)0.002	(e)0.002	(e)0.002	(e)0.003	(e)0.003	(e)0.003
Uganda	0.017	0.004	0.009	0.007	0.008	0.010	0.010	0.013	0.014	0.019	0.014
United Republic of Tanzania	0.025	0.010	0.013	0.011	0.016	0.016	0.016	0.016	0.019	0.024	0.027
Zambia (3)	0.064	0.038	0.020	0.014	0.017	0.017	0.031	0.033	0.032	0.034	0.047
Zimbabwe	0.069	0.049	0.041	0.030	0.021	0.018	0.016	0.017	0.014	0.018	(e)0.016
Middle Africa	0.435	0.340	0.220	0.265	0.348	0.472	0.500	0.544	0.733	0.562	0.584
Angola*(4)	0.093	0.112	0.072	0.122	0.147	0.230	0.256	0.310	0.448	0.320	0.325
Cameroon*(5)	0.068	0.058	0.031	0.028	0.027	0.027	0.029	0.026	0.027	0.027	0.026
Central African Republic*(5)	0.006	0.003	0.003	0.002	0.001	0.001	0.001	0.001	0.001	(e)0.001	(e)0.001
Chad*(4)	0.003	0.007	0.005	0.003	0.024	0.030	0.028	0.026	0.027	0.021	(e)0.022
Congo*(5)	0.045	0.028	0.023	0.039	0.037	0.045	0.050	0.040	0.052	0.049	(e)0.054
Dem. Rep. of the Congo*	0.111	0.067	0.032	0.013	0.021	0.023	0.022	0.022	0.027	0.028	(e)0.036
Equatorial Guinea (4)	0.001	0.002	0.002	0.017	0.050	0.067	0.068	0.073	0.093	0.073	(e)0.066
Gabon*(6)	0.107	0.063	0.052	0.040	0.041	0.048	0.045	0.045	0.059	0.043	(e)0.055
Sao Tome and Principe*	0.001	0.000	0.000	0.000	0.000	0.000	0.000	0.000	0.000	0.000	0.000
Northern Africa	2.164	1.059	0.678	0.841	0.909	1.087	1.136	1.138	1.356	1.132	1.149
Algeria*	0.681	0.370	0.198	0.342	0.349	0.438	0.450	0.430	0.492	0.361	0.376
Egypt	0.150	0.074	0.066	0.072	0.084	0.101	0.113	0.116	0.163	0.184	0.174
Libyan Arab Jamahiriya	1.076	0.380	0.164	0.197	0.222	0.295	0.325	0.311	0.383	0.296	0.305
Morocco*	0.120	0.123	0.133	0.111	0.108	0.107	0.105	0.110	0.126	0.112	0.116
Sudan (7)	0.027	0.011	0.011	0.028	0.041	0.046	0.047	0.063	0.072	0.063	(e)0.069
Tunisia (8)	0.110	0.101	0.106	0.091	0.105	0.100	0.096	0.108	0.120	0.115	0.108
Southern Africa	1.397	0.783	0.664	0.576	0.612	0.621	0.622	0.623	0.601	0.602	0.638
Botswana*	0.025	0.051	0.041	0.043	0.038	0.042	0.037	0.037	0.031	0.028	0.031
Lesotho	0.003	0.002	0.003	0.003	0.008	0.006	0.006	0.006	0.006	0.006	0.005
Namibia	0.072	0.031	0.027	0.020	0.020	0.020	0.022	0.021	0.020	0.025	0.027
South Africa	(b)1.279	0.683	0.575	0.495	0.525	0.536	0.543	0.546	0.534	0.532	0.565
Swaziland	0.018	0.016	0.017	0.014	0.021	0.017	0.015	0.013	0.011	0.012	0.010
Western Africa	1.647	0.628	0.439	0.476	0.508	0.690	0.644	0.626	0.671	0.644	0.671
Benin*	0.003	0.008	0.008	0.006	0.006	0.006	0.006	0.007	0.008	0.010	0.009
Burkina Faso	0.004	0.004	0.005	0.003	0.005	0.004	0.005	0.004	0.004	0.007	0.008
Cape Verde (9)	0.000	0.000	0.000	0.000	0.000	0.000	0.000	0.000	0.000	0.000	0.000
Côte d'Ivoire*	0.154	0.088	0.072	0.060	0.075	0.073	0.070	0.062	0.064	0.088	(e)0.068
Gambia (10)	0.002	0.001	0.000	0.000	0.000	0.000	0.000	0.000	0.000	(e)0.000	(e)0.000
Ghana	0.062	0.026	0.033	0.026	0.027	0.027	0.031	0.031	0.033	0.047	0.052
Guinea*	0.020	0.019	0.014	0.010	0.008	0.008	0.009	0.009	0.008	0.009	0.010
Guinea-Bissau	0.001	0.001	0.000	0.001	0.001	0.001	0.001	0.001	0.001	0.001	(e)0.001
Liberia*	0.029	(e)0.025	(e)0.016	(e)0.005	0.001	0.001	0.001	0.001	0.001	0.001	(e)0.001
Mali*	0.010	0.010	0.009	0.008	0.011	0.010	0.013	0.011	0.013	0.014	0.013
Mauritania*	0.010	0.013	0.009	0.005	0.005	0.006	0.011	0.010	0.011	0.011	0.013
Niger*	0.028	0.008	0.006	0.004	0.005	0.005	0.004	0.005	0.006	0.008	0.007
Nigeria	1.274	0.391	0.238	0.325	0.339	0.525	0.474	0.465	0.500	0.424	0.465
Saint Helena	(e)0.000	(e)0.000	(e)0.000	(e)0.000	(e)0.000	(e)0.000	(e)0.000	(e)0.000	(e)0.000	(e)0.000	(e)0.000
Senegal (11)	0.023	0.022	0.019	0.014	0.016	0.015	0.013	0.012	0.014	0.016	0.014
Sierra Leone*	0.011	0.004	0.001	0.000	0.002	0.002	0.002	0.002	0.001	0.002	0.002
Togo*	0.017	0.008	0.007	0.006	0.007	0.006	0.005	0.005	0.005	0.007	(e)0.006

For sources and notes, see end of table.

Imports (c.i.f.) - Importations (c.a.f.) Percentage - En pourcentage											Régions, pays ou territoires
1980	1990	1995	2000	2004	2005	2006	2007	2008	2009	2010	
100.000	100.000	100.000	100.000	100.000	100.000	100.000	100.000	100.000	100.000	100.000	MONDE
23.910	22.213	28.610	28.813	30.650	31.708	32.304	33.185	34.919	36.847	39.089	ÉCONOMIES EN DÉVELOPPEMENT
4.023	3.900	2.206	1.571	2.354	2.518	2.811	3.285	3.711	3.235	3.197	ÉCONOMIES EN TRANSITION
72.067	73.887	69.184	69.615	66.997	65.774	64.885	63.530	61.371	59.918	57.714	ÉCONOMIES DÉVELOPPÉES
4.661	2.630	2.374	1.954	2.253	2.428	2.456	2.638	2.919	3.333	3.179	Économies en développement : Afrique
0.515	0.354	0.299	0.255	0.277	0.297	0.308	0.318	0.303	0.420	0.401	Afrique orientale
0.008	0.006	0.004	0.002	0.002	0.002	0.003	0.002	0.002	0.003	0.003	Burundi*(1)
0.001	0.001	0.001	0.001	0.001	0.001	0.001	0.001	0.001	0.001	(e)0.001	Comores*
0.010	0.006	0.003	0.003	0.003	0.003	0.003	0.003	0.003	0.004	(e)0.005	Djibouti (2)
–	–	0.009	0.007	(e)0.005	(e)0.005	(e)0.004	(e)0.004	(e)0.004	(e)0.005	(e)0.004	Érythrée
–	–	0.022	0.019	0.030	0.038	0.042	0.041	0.053	0.063	0.063	Éthiopie
0.035	0.030	–	–	–	–	–	–	–	–	–	Éthiopie (anc.)
0.102	0.062	0.057	0.047	0.040	0.067	0.069	0.063	0.067	0.081	0.079	Kenya
0.037	0.016	0.012	0.015	0.017	0.016	0.014	0.017	0.023	0.025	0.017	Madagascar*
0.021	0.016	0.009	0.008	0.010	0.011	0.010	0.010	0.013	0.016	0.014	Malawi
0.030	0.045	0.038	0.033	0.029	0.029	0.029	0.027	0.028	0.029	0.029	Maurice
..	..	..	0.002	0.003	0.003	0.003	0.004	0.004	0.004	–	Mayotte
0.038	0.024	0.013	0.017	0.021	0.022	0.023	0.021	0.024	0.030	0.023	Mozambique
0.013	0.008	0.005	0.003	0.003	0.004	0.005	0.005	0.007	0.010	0.009	Rwanda
0.005	0.005	0.004	0.005	0.005	0.006	0.006	0.006	0.006	0.006	0.006	Seychelles
0.021	(e)0.002	(e)0.005	(e)0.005	(e)0.006	(e)0.006	(e)0.006	(e)0.006	(e)0.007	(e)0.007	(e)0.006	Somalie
0.014	0.008	0.020	0.023	0.018	0.019	0.021	0.025	0.027	0.034	0.030	Ouganda
0.061	0.038	0.032	0.023	0.029	0.030	0.034	0.037	0.043	0.050	0.050	République-Unie de Tanzanie
0.052	0.034	0.013	0.013	0.023	0.024	0.025	0.028	0.031	0.030	0.035	Zambie (3)
0.067	0.051	0.051	0.028	0.023	0.022	0.019	0.018	0.018	0.023	(e)0.024	Zimbabwe
0.283	0.195	0.114	0.114	0.157	0.177	0.179	0.216	0.257	0.348	0.317	Afrique centrale
0.061	0.044	0.028	0.046	0.061	0.077	0.071	0.096	0.127	0.179	0.162	Angola*(4)
0.077	0.039	0.021	0.022	0.025	0.025	0.025	0.029	0.033	0.034	0.033	Cameroun*(5)
0.004	0.004	0.003	0.002	0.002	0.002	0.002	0.002	0.002	(e)0.002	(e)0.002	République centrafricaine*(5)
0.004	0.014	0.009	0.005	0.010	0.009	0.011	0.013	0.012	0.018	(e)0.016	Tchad*(4)
0.027	0.017	0.013	0.007	0.011	0.012	0.016	0.018	0.019	0.024	(e)0.019	Congo*(5)
0.073	0.048	0.020	0.010	0.022	0.025	0.023	0.024	0.026	0.030	(e)0.029	Rép. dém. du Congo*
0.001	0.002	0.002	0.008	0.012	0.012	0.016	0.019	0.023	0.041	(e)0.037	Guinée équatoriale (4)
0.032	0.026	0.017	0.014	0.014	0.014	0.014	0.015	0.016	0.020	(e)0.016	Gabon*(6)
0.001	0.001	0.001	0.000	0.000	0.000	0.001	0.001	0.001	0.001	0.001	Sao Tomé-et-Principe*
1.518	1.042	0.881	0.732	0.786	0.853	0.805	0.895	1.119	1.320	1.213	Afrique septentrionale
0.508	0.272	0.193	0.137	0.193	0.188	0.173	0.194	0.240	0.310	0.267	Algérie*
0.234	0.257	0.224	0.210	0.135	0.183	0.168	0.190	0.296	0.355	0.345	Égypte
0.326	0.149	0.098	0.060	0.092	0.104	0.083	0.091	0.120	0.167	0.161	Jamahiriya arabe libyenne
0.205	0.193	0.191	0.173	0.188	0.192	0.194	0.225	0.257	0.260	0.231	Maroc*
0.076	0.017	0.023	0.023	0.043	0.063	0.065	0.062	0.057	0.076	(e)0.065	Soudan (7)
0.170	0.154	0.151	0.129	0.135	0.122	0.122	0.134	0.150	0.152	0.145	Tunisie (8)
1.097	0.642	0.699	0.536	0.675	0.679	0.731	0.714	0.668	0.702	0.726	Afrique australe
0.033	0.054	0.037	0.031	0.034	0.030	0.025	0.029	0.032	0.037	0.037	Botswana*
0.021	0.019	0.021	0.012	0.015	0.013	0.012	0.012	0.012	0.016	0.014	Lesotho
0.056	0.032	0.031	0.023	0.025	0.024	0.023	0.025	0.026	0.039	(e)0.037	Namibie
(e,b)0.958	(e)0.519	(e)0.592	(e)0.453	(e)0.580	(e)0.594	(e)0.655	(e)0.635	(e)0.587	(e)0.597	(e)0.627	Afrique du Sud
0.030	0.018	0.019	0.016	0.020	0.018	0.016	0.013	0.010	0.013	0.011	Swaziland
1.247	0.397	0.380	0.317	0.359	0.422	0.433	0.495	0.511	0.542	0.522	Afrique occidentale
0.016	0.007	0.014	0.009	0.009	0.009	0.010	0.014	0.014	0.016	(e)0.014	Bénin*
0.017	0.015	0.009	0.009	0.013	0.012	0.012	0.012	0.013	0.015	0.013	Burkina Faso
0.003	0.004	0.005	0.003	0.005	0.004	0.004	0.005	0.005	0.006	0.005	Cap-Vert (9)
0.144	0.058	0.056	0.037	0.050	0.054	0.047	0.047	0.048	0.055	(e)0.045	Côte d'Ivoire*
0.008	0.005	0.003	0.003	0.002	0.002	0.002	0.002	0.002	0.002	0.002	Gambie (10)
0.054	0.034	0.036	0.045	0.043	0.050	0.055	0.057	0.062	0.064	0.071	Ghana
0.013	0.020	0.016	0.009	0.008	0.008	0.008	0.009	0.008	0.008	0.009	Guinée*
0.003	0.002	0.003	0.001	0.001	0.001	0.001	0.001	0.001	0.002	(e)0.001	Guinée-Bissau
0.026	0.006	(e)0.010	(e)0.010	0.003	0.003	0.004	0.004	0.005	0.004	(e)0.004	Libéria*
0.021	0.017	0.015	0.012	0.014	0.014	0.015	0.015	0.020	0.019	(e)0.018	Mali*
0.014	0.006	0.008	0.007	0.010	0.013	0.009	0.010	0.012	0.011	0.012	Mauritanie*
0.029	0.011	0.007	0.006	0.008	0.009	0.008	0.008	0.010	0.019	(e)0.016	Niger*
0.801	0.157	0.157	0.131	0.149	0.197	0.216	0.264	0.257	0.268	0.265	Nigéria
(e)0.001	(e)0.001	(e)0.000	(e)0.001	(e)0.000	(e)0.001	(e)0.001	(e)0.001	(e)0.000	(e)0.000	(e)0.000	Sainte-Hélène
0.051	0.034	0.027	0.023	0.030	0.032	0.030	0.034	0.040	0.037	0.031	Sénégal (11)
0.021	0.004	0.003	0.002	0.003	0.003	0.003	0.003	0.003	0.004	0.005	Sierra Leone*
0.026	0.016	0.011	0.008	0.009	0.010	0.009	0.009	0.009	0.012	(e)0.010	Togo*

Pour les sources et les notes, se reporter à la fin du tableau.

Region, country or territory	Exports (f.o.b.) - Exportations (f.a.b.) Percentage - En pourcentage										
	1980	1990	1995	2000	2004	2005	2006	2007	2008	2009	2010
Developing economies: America	5.470	4.136	4.442	5.684	5.218	5.494	5.682	5.513	5.590	5.500	5.751
Caribbean	*1.099*	*0.335*	*0.250*	*0.295*	*0.227*	*0.245*	*0.264*	*0.231*	*0.242*	*0.187*	*0.165*
Anguilla	..	..	0.000	0.000	0.000	0.000	0.000	0.000	0.000	0.000	0.000
Antigua and Barbuda	0.001	0.001	0.001	0.001	0.001	0.001	0.001	0.000	0.000	0.000	0.000
Aruba (12)	..	0.004	0.026	0.039	0.030	0.033	0.030	0.019	0.023	0.011	0.002
Bahamas (13)	0.246	0.007	0.003	0.009	0.005	0.005	0.006	0.006	0.006	0.006	0.005
Barbados	0.011	0.006	0.005	0.004	0.003	0.003	0.004	0.004	0.003	0.003	0.003
Cayman Islands				..	..	0.001	0.000	0.000	0.000	0.000	0.000
Cuba	0.274	0.141	0.031	0.026	0.025	0.022	0.025	0.028	0.025	0.025	(e)0.025
Dominica*	0.000	0.002	0.001	0.001	0.000	0.000	0.000	0.000	0.000	0.000	0.000
Dominican Republic (14)	0.047	0.021	0.073	0.089	0.065	0.059	0.054	0.051	0.042	0.044	0.043
Grenada*	0.001	0.001	0.000	0.001	0.000	0.000	0.000	0.000	0.000	0.000	0.000
Haiti	0.011	0.005	0.002	0.006	0.001	0.004	0.004	0.004	0.003	0.005	0.004
Jamaica	0.047	0.033	0.028	0.020	0.015	0.014	0.015	0.016	0.015	0.011	0.009
Montserrat*	0.000	0.000	0.000	0.000	0.000	0.000	0.000	0.000	0.000	0.000	0.000
Netherlands Antilles*(15)	0.254	0.051	0.029	0.031	0.006	0.006	0.006	0.005	0.007	0.006	0.005
Saint Kitts and Nevis*	0.001	0.001	0.000	0.000	0.000	0.000	0.000	0.000	0.000	0.000	0.000
Saint Lucia*	0.003	0.004	0.002	0.001	0.001	0.001	0.001	0.001	0.001	0.001	0.001
Saint Vincent and the Grenadines*	0.001	0.002	0.001	0.001	0.000	0.000	0.000	0.000	0.000	0.000	0.000
Trinidad and Tobago*	0.200	0.056	0.047	0.066	0.071	0.095	0.117	0.096	0.116	0.073	0.067
Turks and Caicos Islands	..	..	..	0.000	0.000	0.000	0.000	0.000	0.000	0.000	-
Central America	*1.149*	*1.313*	*1.732*	*2.837*	*2.287*	*2.257*	*2.276*	*2.148*	*2.003*	*2.053*	*2.169*
Belize	0.005	0.004	0.003	0.003	0.002	0.002	0.002	0.002	0.002	0.002	0.002
Costa Rica*	0.049	0.042	0.067	0.091	0.069	0.067	0.068	0.067	0.059	0.070	0.062
El Salvador	0.053	0.019	0.032	0.046	0.036	0.033	0.031	0.028	0.028	0.030	0.030
Guatemala (16)	0.075	0.033	0.038	0.042	0.055	0.051	0.050	0.049	0.048	0.058	0.056
Honduras (17)	0.041	0.027	0.034	0.052	0.049	0.048	0.041	0.041	0.039	0.039	0.038
Mexico	0.886	1.170	1.536	2.580	2.058	2.038	2.065	1.944	1.810	1.836	1.965
Nicaragua	0.022	0.010	0.009	0.010	0.008	0.008	0.008	0.009	0.009	0.011	0.012
Panama, excl. Canal Zone (former)	0.018	–	–	–	–	–	–	–	–	–	–
Panama*	–	0.010	0.012	0.013	0.010	0.010	0.009	0.008	0.008	0.008	0.005
South America	*3.223*	*2.488*	*2.460*	*2.552*	*2.703*	*2.992*	*3.142*	*3.134*	*3.346*	*3.261*	*3.416*
Argentina*	0.394	0.355	0.405	0.408	0.376	0.384	0.384	0.399	0.438	0.448	0.451
Bolivia (Plurinational State of)	0.046	0.027	0.021	0.019	0.023	0.027	0.032	0.032	0.044	0.039	0.041
Brazil	0.989	0.903	0.898	0.855	1.052	1.129	1.136	1.148	1.228	1.223	1.331
Chile*	0.231	0.241	0.309	0.298	0.354	0.393	0.484	0.483	0.412	0.415	0.455
Colombia	0.193	0.193	0.196	0.202	0.177	0.201	0.201	0.213	0.237	0.262	0.262
Ecuador	0.122	0.078	0.083	0.076	0.084	0.096	0.105	0.099	0.117	0.111	0.115
Falkland Islands (Malvinas)	(e)0.000	(e)0.000	(e)0.001	(e)0.001	(e)0.001	(e)0.001	(e)0.001	(e)0.001	(e)0.001	(e)0.001	(e)0.001
Guyana*	0.019	0.007	0.009	0.008	0.006	0.005	0.005	0.005	0.005	0.006	0.006
Paraguay	0.015	0.028	0.018	0.013	0.017	0.016	0.015	0.020	0.028	0.025	0.030
Peru*	0.192	0.093	0.106	0.109	0.139	0.165	0.196	0.199	0.196	0.215	0.234
Suriname	0.025	0.014	0.009	0.006	0.009	0.010	0.010	0.010	0.011	0.011	0.013
Uruguay	0.052	0.049	0.041	0.036	0.032	0.032	0.033	0.032	0.040	0.043	0.044
Venezuela (Bolivarian Rep. of)	0.944	0.501	0.364	0.520	0.432	0.531	0.541	0.493	0.590	0.460	0.434
Developing economies: Asia	17.896	16.965	20.995	23.805	25.998	27.595	28.606	29.000	29.832	31.081	32.718
Eastern Asia	*3.742*	*8.062*	*10.865*	*12.016*	*13.987*	*14.657*	*15.177*	*15.620*	*15.351*	*16.709*	*17.900*
China	0.889	1.784	2.873	3.864	6.457	7.260	7.992	8.701	8.861	9.606	10.401
China, Hong Kong SAR	0.970	2.361	3.356	3.130	2.821	2.757	2.612	2.461	2.249	2.546	2.571
China, Macao SAR	0.030	0.049	0.039	0.039	0.031	0.024	0.021	0.018	0.012	0.008	0.006
China, Taiwan Province of	0.972	1.928	2.155	2.292	1.893	1.884	1.844	1.760	1.582	1.628	1.810
Korea, Dem. People's Rep. of	..	0.053	0.019	0.011	0.014	0.013	0.012	0.012	0.013	0.016	(e)0.020
Korea, Republic of (18)	0.860	1.868	2.415	2.671	2.762	2.710	2.683	2.654	2.617	2.890	3.073
Mongolia	0.020	0.019	0.009	0.008	0.009	0.010	0.013	0.013	0.016	0.015	0.019
Southern Asia	*1.284*	*1.351*	*1.255*	*1.438*	*1.632*	*1.803*	*1.948*	*1.993*	*2.198*	*2.281*	*2.460*
Afghanistan	0.033	0.007	0.003	0.002	0.003	0.004	0.003	0.004	0.003	0.003	0.003
Bangladesh	0.037	0.048	0.068	0.099	0.090	0.089	0.097	0.089	0.095	0.120	0.127
Bhutan	0.001	0.002	0.002	0.002	0.002	0.002	0.003	0.005	0.003	0.004	0.004
India (19)	0.422	0.516	0.592	0.657	0.834	0.949	1.004	1.071	1.207	1.318	1.459
Iran (Islamic Rep. of)*	0.606	0.555	0.355	0.440	0.483	0.536	0.635	0.634	0.705	0.630	0.665
Maldives	0.000	0.002	0.002	0.002	0.002	0.002	0.002	0.002	0.002	0.001	0.001
Nepal	0.004	0.005	0.007	0.012	0.008	0.008	0.007	0.006	0.006	0.007	0.005
Pakistan	0.129	0.161	0.154	0.140	0.146	0.153	0.140	0.127	0.126	0.140	0.141
Sri Lanka	0.052	0.055	0.073	0.084	0.063	0.060	0.057	0.055	0.050	0.057	0.055
South-Eastern Asia	*3.633*	*4.175*	*6.247*	*6.698*	*6.194*	*6.219*	*6.354*	*6.185*	*6.195*	*6.503*	*6.934*
Brunei Darussalam*	0.225	0.064	0.046	0.061	0.055	0.060	0.063	0.055	0.066	0.058	0.060
Cambodia (4)	0.001	0.002	0.017	0.022	0.030	0.028	0.030	0.029	0.029	0.034	(e)0.036

For sources and notes, see end of table.

1980	1990	1995	2000	2004	2005	2006	2007	2008	2009	2010	Régions, pays ou territoires
											Imports (c.i.f.) - Importations (c.a.f.) Percentage - En pourcentage
5.947	3.529	4.746	5.882	4.755	4.944	5.137	5.304	5.609	5.442	5.804	**Économies en développement : Amérique**
1.317	*0.521*	*0.383*	*0.486*	*0.354*	*0.396*	*0.408*	*0.387*	*0.418*	*0.383*	*0.350*	*Caraïbes*
..	..	0.001	0.001	0.001	0.001	0.002	0.002	0.002	0.001	0.001	Anguilla
0.004	0.007	0.007	0.006	0.005	0.005	0.005	0.005	0.005	0.005	0.003	Antigua-et-Barbuda
..	0.016	0.034	0.039	0.032	0.032	0.031	0.020	0.026	0.015	0.009	Aruba (12)
0.363	0.031	0.024	0.031	0.021	0.024	0.024	0.022	0.020	0.021	0.019	Bahamas (13)
0.025	0.020	0.015	0.017	0.015	0.015	0.013	0.012	0.011	0.012	0.010	Barbade
			..	..	0.011	0.008	0.007	0.006	0.007	0.006	Îles Caïmanes
0.313	0.188	0.054	0.073	0.059	0.075	0.082	0.076	0.093	0.076	(e)0.074	Cuba*
0.002	0.003	0.002	0.002	0.002	0.002	0.001	0.001	0.002	0.002	0.001	Dominique*
0.095	0.084	0.099	0.142	0.083	0.091	0.098	0.095	0.097	0.097	0.100	République dominicaine (14)
0.002	0.003	0.002	0.004	0.003	0.003	0.002	0.003	0.002	0.002	0.002	Grenade
0.018	0.009	0.012	0.016	0.014	0.013	0.014	0.012	0.014	0.017	0.020	Haïti
0.056	0.054	0.054	0.050	0.040	0.041	0.043	0.047	0.051	0.040	0.034	Jamaïque
0.001	0.001	0.001	0.000	0.000	0.000	0.000	0.000	0.000	0.000	(e)0.000	Montserrat*
0.273	0.060	0.035	0.043	0.018	0.018	0.018	0.018	0.019	0.021	(e)0.018	Antilles néerlandaises*(15)
0.002	0.003	0.003	0.003	0.002	0.002	0.002	0.002	0.002	0.002	0.001	Saint-Kitts-et-Nevis*
0.006	0.008	0.006	0.005	0.005	0.004	0.005	0.004	0.004	0.004	0.004	Sainte-Lucie*
0.003	0.004	0.003	0.002	0.002	0.002	0.002	0.002	0.002	0.003	0.002	Saint-Vincent-et-les Grenadines*
0.153	0.031	0.033	0.050	0.051	0.053	0.052	0.054	0.058	0.055	0.042	Trinité-et-Tobago*
..	..	..	0.002	0.002	0.003	0.004	0.004	0.004	0.003	-	Îles Turques et Caïques
1.431	*1.443*	*1.761*	*3.135*	*2.559*	*2.525*	*2.547*	*2.469*	*2.366*	*2.333*	*2.443*	*Amérique centrale*
0.007	0.006	0.005	0.008	0.005	0.005	0.005	0.005	0.005	0.005	0.005	Belize
0.074	0.055	0.078	0.096	0.087	0.091	0.093	0.091	0.093	0.090	0.088	Costa Rica*
0.046	0.035	0.064	0.074	0.067	0.062	0.062	0.061	0.059	0.057	0.055	El Salvador
0.077	0.046	0.063	0.078	0.100	0.097	0.096	0.095	0.088	0.091	0.090	Guatemala (16)
0.049	0.026	0.036	0.060	0.061	0.061	0.059	0.062	0.063	0.058	0.056	Honduras (17)
1.066	1.214	1.449	2.742	2.177	2.146	2.168	2.081	1.975	1.942	2.062	Mexique
0.043	0.018	0.019	0.027	0.023	0.024	0.024	0.025	0.026	0.027	0.028	Nicaragua
0.070											Panama, sans la zone du canal (anc.)
–	0.043	0.048	0.051	0.038	0.039	0.039	0.048	0.055	0.062	0.060	Panama*
3.199	*1.565*	*2.602*	*2.260*	*1.843*	*2.023*	*2.181*	*2.448*	*2.825*	*2.726*	*3.011*	*Amérique du Sud*
0.507	0.114	0.382	0.378	0.236	0.266	0.276	0.314	0.349	0.309	0.368	Argentine*
0.032	0.019	0.027	0.027	0.019	0.022	0.023	0.024	0.031	0.035	0.034	Bolivie (État plurinational de)
1.201	0.628	1.034	0.880	0.700	0.719	0.775	0.889	1.108	1.055	1.247	Brésil
0.279	0.221	0.304	0.278	0.261	0.303	0.311	0.331	0.376	0.326	0.377	Chili*
0.228	0.156	0.265	0.173	0.176	0.196	0.211	0.233	0.239	0.260	0.265	Colombie
0.108	0.052	0.080	0.056	0.087	0.095	0.098	0.095	0.114	0.119	0.134	Équateur
(e)0.000	(e)0.001	(e)0.001	(e)0.001	(e)0.001	(e)0.001	(e)0.001	(e)0.001	(e)0.000	(e)0.000	(e)0.001	Îles Falkland (Malvinas)
0.019	0.009	0.010	0.009	0.007	0.007	0.007	0.007	0.008	0.009	0.009	Guyana*
0.030	0.038	0.060	0.034	0.028	0.030	0.038	0.041	0.055	0.055	0.065	Paraguay
0.120	0.073	0.145	0.111	0.106	0.116	0.124	0.143	0.182	0.173	0.195	Pérou*
0.024	0.013	0.011	0.008	0.008	0.010	0.008	0.007	0.008	0.010	0.009	Suriname
0.081	0.037	0.055	0.052	0.033	0.036	0.038	0.040	0.054	0.055	0.056	Uruguay
0.569	0.204	0.228	0.253	0.179	0.222	0.272	0.323	0.301	0.320	0.251	Venezuela (Rép. bolivarienne du)
13.131	15.911	21.378	20.882	23.545	24.246	24.623	25.154	26.302	27.979	30.016	**Économies en développement : Asie**
4.116	*7.411*	*10.839*	*11.148*	*12.977*	*13.068*	*13.324*	*13.408*	*13.414*	*14.670*	*16.400*	*Asie orientale*
0.960	1.487	2.523	3.377	5.913	6.113	6.402	6.709	6.873	7.926	9.094	Chine
1.080	2.299	3.682	3.194	2.856	2.773	2.706	2.580	2.360	2.741	2.822	Chine (RAS de Hong Kong)
0.026	0.043	0.039	0.034	0.037	0.036	0.037	0.038	0.033	0.036	0.036	Chine (RAS de Macao)
0.951	1.528	1.981	2.100	1.771	1.690	1.641	1.541	1.462	1.378	1.638	Province chinoise de Taiwan
..	0.082	0.026	0.025	0.024	0.025	0.024	0.021	0.022	0.024	(e)0.020	Corée, Rép. populaire dém. de
1.073	1.947	2.581	2.409	2.365	2.419	2.501	2.504	2.644	2.548	2.770	Corée, République de (18)
0.026	0.026	0.008	0.009	0.011	0.011	0.012	0.015	0.022	0.017	0.021	Mongolie
1.903	*1.599*	*1.393*	*1.442*	*1.878*	*2.193*	*2.278*	*2.411*	*2.835*	*3.003*	*3.142*	*Asie méridionale*
0.040	0.026	0.007	0.018	0.023	0.023	0.021	0.020	0.018	0.026	0.034	Afghanistan
0.125	0.101	0.128	0.133	0.127	0.129	0.130	0.130	0.145	0.172	0.181	Bangladesh
0.002	0.002	0.002	0.003	0.004	0.004	0.003	0.004	0.003	0.004	0.006	Bhoutan
0.715	0.657	0.663	0.773	1.051	1.323	1.443	1.605	1.948	2.030	2.139	Inde (19)
0.646	0.511	0.244	0.228	0.373	0.371	0.330	0.315	0.349	0.398	0.408	Iran (Rép. islamique d')*
0.001	0.004	0.005	0.006	0.007	0.007	0.007	0.008	0.008	0.008	0.007	Maldives
0.016	0.017	0.025	0.024	0.020	0.021	0.020	0.022	0.022	0.035	0.033	Népal
0.257	0.206	0.219	0.163	0.189	0.235	0.241	0.229	0.257	0.250	0.246	Pakistan
0.098	0.075	0.099	0.094	0.084	0.082	0.083	0.079	0.085	0.079	0.088	Sri Lanka
3.159	*4.525*	*6.787*	*5.706*	*5.417*	*5.582*	*5.566*	*5.450*	*5.749*	*5.748*	*6.202*	*Asie du Sud-Est*
0.028	0.028	0.040	0.017	0.015	0.014	0.013	0.015	0.015	0.019	0.022	Brunéi Darussalam*
0.009	0.005	0.023	0.029	0.034	0.036	0.039	0.038	0.040	0.046	(e)0.048	Cambodge (4)

Pour les sources et les notes, se reporter à la fin du tableau.

Region, country or territory	Exports (f.o.b.) - Exportations (f.a.b.) Percentage - En pourcentage										
	1980	1990	1995	2000	2004	2005	2006	2007	2008	2009	2010
Indonesia including East Timor	1.177	0.770	0.916	1.014	–	–	–	–	–	–	–
Indonesia	–	–	–	–	0.781	0.821	0.853	0.848	0.866	0.956	1.040
Lao People's Dem. Rep.*	0.001	0.002	0.006	0.005	0.004	0.005	0.007	0.007	0.007	0.008	0.012
Malaysia (20)	0.636	0.846	1.427	1.523	1.368	1.342	1.324	1.258	1.301	1.259	1.310
Myanmar	0.023	0.009	0.017	0.026	0.026	0.036	0.038	0.045	0.043	0.054	0.058
Philippines	0.282	0.233	0.338	0.617	0.432	0.380	0.391	0.359	0.305	0.306	0.339
Singapore (21)	0.952	1.515	2.284	2.137	2.162	2.188	2.241	2.138	2.098	2.157	2.319
Thailand*	0.320	0.663	1.090	1.069	1.047	1.050	1.078	1.099	1.091	1.215	1.288
Timor-Leste (22)	–	–	–	–	0.000	0.000	0.000	0.000	0.000	0.000	0.000
Viet Nam	0.017	0.060	0.195	0.291	0.268	0.005	0.020	0.347	0.389	0.456	0.472
Western Asia	**9.238**	**3.378**	**2.628**	**3.653**	**4.185**	**4.916**	**5.128**	**5.201**	**6.088**	**5.588**	**5.424**
Bahrain (4)	0.177	0.108	0.079	0.096	0.082	0.098	0.101	0.097	0.107	0.095	0.090
Iraq*	1.294	0.296	0.010	0.316	0.201	0.226	0.252	0.282	0.395	0.354	0.343
Jordan	0.028	0.039	0.024	0.020	0.010	0.011	0.040	0.041	0.046	0.052	0.046
Kuwait	0.975	0.202	0.247	0.301	0.311	0.427	0.462	0.447	0.542	0.413	0.435
Lebanon (23)	0.047	0.014	0.013	0.011	0.024	0.022	0.023	0.026	0.028	0.033	0.033
Occupied Palestinian territory	..	..	0.008	0.006	0.003	0.003	0.003	0.004	0.003	0.004	0.004
Oman	0.117	0.158	0.117	0.176	0.145	0.178	0.178	0.172	0.234	0.224	0.241
Qatar*	0.279	0.101	0.067	0.177	0.201	0.241	0.277	0.296	0.341	0.386	0.475
Saudi Arabia*(24)	4.990	1.276	0.966	1.202	1.371	1.720	1.740	1.666	1.944	1.537	1.551
Syrian Arab Republic*	0.104	0.121	0.069	0.072	0.081	0.087	0.090	0.082	0.096	0.087	(e)0.092
Turkey*	0.143	0.372	0.417	0.431	0.687	0.700	0.705	0.766	0.819	0.816	0.750
United Arab Emirates	1.079	0.677	0.563	0.773	0.990	1.117	1.200	1.276	1.483	1.536	1.307
Yemen (former Arab Republic)	0.001	–	–	–	–	–	–	–	–	–	–
Yemen (former Democratic)	0.003	–	–	–	–	–	–	–	–	–	–
Yemen*	–	0.020	0.038	0.063	0.044	0.053	0.055	0.045	0.047	0.050	0.056
Developing economies: Oceania	**0.110**	**0.078**	**0.088**	**0.079**	**0.066**	**0.063**	**0.064**	**0.064**	**0.059**	**0.057**	**0.058**
American Samoa*(25)	0.006	0.009	0.005	0.005	0.005	0.004	0.004	(e)0.003	(e)0.004	(e)0.004	(e)0.003
Cook Islands	0.000	0.000	0.000	0.000	0.000	0.000	0.000	0.000	0.000	0.000	0.000
Fiji	0.019	0.011	0.011	0.008	0.008	0.007	0.006	0.005	0.006	0.005	0.004
French Polynesia*	0.001	0.003	0.004	0.004	0.002	0.002	0.002	0.001	0.002	0.001	(e)0.001
Guam	0.003	0.002	0.002	0.001	0.001	0.000	0.000	0.001	0.001	0.000	0.000
Kiribati	0.000	0.000	0.000	0.000	0.000	0.000	0.000	0.000	0.000	0.000	(e)0.000
Marshall Islands	–	0.000	0.000	0.000	0.000	0.000	0.000	0.000	(e)0.000	(e)0.000	(e)0.000
Micronesia (Federated States of)	–	0.000	0.001	0.000	0.000	0.000	0.000	0.000	0.000	(e)0.000	(e)0.000
Nauru	0.003	0.002	0.001	0.000	0.000	0.000	(e)0.000	(e)0.000	(e)0.001	(e)0.000	(e)0.000
New Caledonia*	0.020	0.014	0.009	0.009	0.011	0.010	0.011	0.015	0.008	0.008	0.008
Niue	..	0.000	0.000	0.000	0.000	0.000	0.000	0.000	(e)0.000	0.000	0.000
Northern Mariana Islands	–	..	..	0.016	0.009	0.006	0.004	0.002	0.001	0.000	(e)0.000
Palau	–	..	0.000	0.000	0.000	0.000	0.000	0.000	0.000	0.000	0.000
Papua New Guinea	0.051	0.033	0.051	0.032	0.028	0.031	0.034	0.033	0.035	0.035	0.038
Samoa (23)	0.001	0.000	0.000	0.000	0.001	0.001	0.001	0.001	0.000	0.000	0.000
Solomon Islands*	0.004	0.002	0.003	0.001	0.001	0.001	0.001	0.001	0.001	0.001	0.001
Tokelau	..	..	..	..	(e)0.000	(e)0.000	(e)0.000	(e)0.000	-	-	-
Tonga	0.000	0.000	0.000	0.000	0.000	0.000	0.000	0.000	0.000	0.000	0.000
Tuvalu	..	0.000	0.000	0.000	0.000	0.000	0.000	0.000	(e)0.000	(e)0.000	(e)0.000
Vanuatu	0.002	0.001	0.001	0.000	0.000	0.000	0.000	0.000	0.000	0.000	0.000
Wallis and Futuna Islands	..	..	..	-	0.000	(e)0.000	(e)0.000	-	-	-	-
Transition economies	**4.197**	**3.411**	**2.354**	**2.396**	**3.072**	**3.459**	**3.759**	**3.934**	**4.587**	**3.827**	**4.070**
Albania	..	0.006	0.004	0.004	0.007	0.006	0.007	0.008	0.008	0.009	0.010
Armenia*	–	–	0.005	0.005	0.008	0.009	0.008	0.009	0.007	0.006	0.007
Azerbaijan (26)	–	–	0.011	0.027	0.039	0.073	0.107	0.152	0.190	0.169	0.174
Belarus	–	–	0.093	0.114	0.150	0.152	0.163	0.173	0.202	0.170	0.167
Bosnia and Herzegovina*(27)	–	–	0.003	0.017	0.021	0.023	0.027	0.030	0.031	0.032	0.032
Croatia*	–	–	0.087	0.069	0.087	0.084	0.086	0.088	0.088	0.084	0.078
Georgia (28)	–	–	0.003	0.005	0.007	0.008	0.008	0.009	0.009	0.009	0.010
Kazakhstan*(28)	–	–	0.101	0.137	0.224	0.270	0.320	0.345	0.446	0.345	0.377
Kyrgyzstan	–	–	0.008	0.008	0.008	0.006	0.007	0.009	0.012	0.013	0.012
Montenegro	–	–	–	–	–	–	–	–	0.004	0.003	0.003
Republic of Moldova	–	–	0.014	0.007	0.011	0.010	0.009	0.010	0.010	0.010	0.010
Russian Federation (29)	–	–	1.601	1.637	1.994	2.323	2.506	2.532	2.926	2.425	2.639
Serbia and Montenegro*	–	–	0.030	0.027	0.044	0.048	0.059	0.069	–	–	–
Serbia	–	–	–	–	–	–	–	–	0.068	0.067	0.065
SFR of Yugoslavia (former)	0.441	0.411	–	–	–	3	–	–	–	–	–
Tajikistan (28)	–	–	0.014	0.012	0.010	0.008	0.012	0.010	0.009	0.008	0.008
TFYR of Macedonia*	–	–	0.023	0.021	0.018	0.019	0.020	0.024	0.024	0.022	0.022
Turkmenistan (28)	–	–	0.036	0.039	0.042	0.047	0.059	0.057	0.074	0.053	(e)0.040
Ukraine (28)	–	–	0.254	0.226	0.355	0.326	0.316	0.352	0.415	0.318	0.339
USSR (former)	3.756	2.994	–	–	–	–	–	–	–	–	–
Uzbekistan (28)	–	–	0.066	0.044	0.047	0.045	0.046	0.057	0.064	0.086	0.078

For sources and notes, see end of table.

1980	1990	1995	2000	2004	2005	2006	2007	2008	2009	2010	Régions, pays ou territoires
					Imports (c.i.f.) - Importations (c.a.f.) Percentage - En pourcentage						
0.521	0.607	0.777	0.646	–	–	–	–	–	–	–	Indonésie, y compris le Timor oriental
–	–	–	–	0.580	0.700	0.652	0.653	0.774	0.740	0.860	Indonésie
0.004	0.005	0.011	0.008	0.008	0.008	0.009	0.007	0.009	0.011	0.013	Rép. dém. populaire lao*
0.519	0.815	1.484	1.230	1.109	1.059	1.060	1.030	0.999	0.976	1.073	Malaisie (20)
0.017	0.008	0.026	0.036	0.023	0.018	0.021	0.023	0.026	0.035	0.031	Myanmar
0.399	0.362	0.541	0.556	0.486	0.458	0.437	0.405	0.367	0.361	0.379	Philippines
1.155	1.697	2.378	2.019	1.829	1.852	1.930	1.846	1.942	1.940	2.024	Singapour (21)
0.443	0.921	1.352	0.929	0.995	1.094	1.041	0.991	1.085	1.064	1.202	Thaïlande*
				0.001	0.001	0.001	0.001	0.002	0.002	0.002	Timor-Leste (22)
0.063	0.077	0.156	0.235	0.337	0.340	0.304	0.440	0.100	0.552	0.546	Viet Nam
3.954	*2.377*	*2.359*	*2.587*	*3.273*	*3.403*	*3.455*	*3.884*	*4.303*	*4.558*	*4.273*	*Asie occidentale*
0.100	0.102	0.071	0.070	0.078	0.087	0.080	0.077	0.087	0.076	0.073	Bahreïn (4)
0.419	0.182	0.013	0.198	0.210	0.218	0.178	0.107	0.216	0.207	0.288	Iraq
0.116	0.072	0.071	0.069	0.086	0.097	0.093	0.095	0.102	0.115	0.098	Jordanie
0.314	0.111	0.149	0.107	0.133	0.146	0.139	0.150	0.151	0.161	0.146	Koweït*
0.176	0.070	0.139	0.094	0.101	0.089	0.078	0.086	0.102	0.131	0.120	Liban (23)
..	..	0.032	0.036	0.025	0.025	0.022	0.022	0.022	0.028	0.029	Territoire palestinien occupé
0.083	0.075	0.081	0.076	0.093	0.082	0.088	0.112	0.139	0.141	0.129	Oman
0.070	0.047	0.065	0.049	0.063	0.093	0.133	0.164	0.169	0.197	0.143	Qatar*
1.452	0.672	0.536	0.453	0.499	0.551	0.564	0.633	0.699	0.754	0.675	Arabie saoudite*(24)
0.198	0.067	0.090	0.057	0.089	0.101	0.093	0.103	0.110	0.122	(e)0.123	République arabe syrienne*
0.381	0.622	0.682	0.818	1.028	1.081	1.129	1.193	1.227	1.112	1.208	Turquie*
0.415	0.312	0.401	0.525	0.826	0.784	0.809	1.053	1.217	1.346	1.177	Émirats arabes unis
0.089	–	–	–	–	–	–	–	–	–	–	Yémen (anc. République arabe du)
0.073	–	–	–	–	–	–	–	–	–	–	Yémen (anc. démocratique)
–	0.044	0.030	0.035	0.042	0.050	0.049	0.060	0.063	0.072	0.063	Yémen*
0.171	*0.142*	*0.113*	*0.095*	*0.096*	*0.090*	*0.088*	*0.089*	*0.089*	*0.094*	*0.089*	*Économies en développement : Océanie*
0.005	0.010	0.008	0.008	0.006	0.005	0.005	0.005	0.004	0.005	(e)0.004	Samoa américaines*(25)
0.001	0.001	0.001	0.001	0.001	0.001	0.001	0.001	0.001	0.001	(e)0.002	Îles Cook
0.027	0.021	0.017	0.013	0.015	0.015	0.015	0.013	0.014	0.011	0.008	Fidji
0.026	0.026	0.019	0.016	0.010	0.010	0.013	0.013	0.013	0.014	(e)0.011	Polynésie française*
0.019	0.013	0.008	0.006	0.005	0.005	0.004	0.005	0.004	0.005	0.005	Guam
0.001	0.001	0.001	0.001	0.001	0.001	0.001	0.000	0.000	0.001	0.000	Kiribati
–	0.002	0.001	0.001	0.001	0.001	0.001	0.001	(e)0.001	(e)0.001	(e)0.001	Îles Marshall
–	0.002	0.002	0.002	0.001	0.001	0.001	0.001	0.001	0.001	(e)0.001	Micronésie (États fédérés de)
0.001	0.001	0.001	0.000	0.000	0.000	(e)0.000	(e)0.000	(e)0.001	(e)0.001	(e)0.001	Nauru
0.022	0.025	0.018	0.014	0.017	0.016	0.017	0.020	0.020	0.020	0.022	Nouvelle-Calédonie*
..	0.000	0.000	0.000	0.000	0.000	0.000	0.000	0.000	(e)0.000	(e)0.000	Nioué
–	..	..	-	(e)0.007	-	-	-	-	-	-	Îles Mariannes du Nord
–	..	0.001	0.002	0.001	0.001	0.001	0.001	0.001	0.001	0.001	Palaos
0.057	0.031	0.028	0.017	0.018	0.016	0.019	0.021	0.022	0.025	(e)0.025	Papouasie-Nouvelle-Guinée
0.003	0.002	0.002	0.001	0.002	0.002	0.002	0.002	0.002	0.002	0.002	Samoa (23)
0.004	0.003	0.003	0.001	0.001	0.002	0.002	0.002	0.002	0.002	0.003	Îles Salomon*
..	..	..	0.000	(e)0.000	(e)0.000	(e)0.000	(e)0.000	-	-	-	Tokélaou
0.002	0.002	0.001	0.001	0.001	0.001	0.001	0.001	0.001	0.001	0.001	Tonga
..	0.000	0.000	0.000	0.000	0.000	0.000	0.000	0.000	(e)0.000	(e)0.000	Tuvalu
0.003	0.003	0.002	0.001	0.001	0.001	0.002	0.002	0.002	0.002	0.002	Vanuatu
..	..	..	0.001	0.001	0.000	0.000	-	-	-	-	Îles Wallis-et-Futuna
4.023	*3.900*	*2.206*	*1.571*	*2.354*	*2.518*	*2.811*	*3.285*	*3.711*	*3.235*	*3.197*	*Économies en transition*
..	0.012	0.014	0.016	0.024	0.024	0.025	0.029	0.032	0.036	0.030	Albanie
–	–	0.013	0.013	0.014	0.016	0.018	0.023	0.027	0.026	0.025	Arménie*
–	–	0.013	0.018	0.037	0.039	0.043	0.040	0.044	0.048	0.043	Azerbaïdjan (26)
–	–	0.106	0.130	0.174	0.155	0.181	0.201	0.239	0.225	0.227	Bélarus
–	–	0.021	0.058	0.063	0.066	0.059	0.068	0.074	0.069	0.060	Bosnie-Herzégovine*(27)
–	–	0.140	0.118	0.175	0.172	0.174	0.181	0.187	0.167	0.131	Croatie*
–	–	0.009	0.011	0.019	0.023	0.030	0.037	0.037	0.035	0.033	Géorgie (28)
–	–	0.073	0.076	0.146	0.166	0.195	0.233	0.234	0.224	0.156	Kazakhstan*(28)
–	–	0.010	0.008	0.010	0.011	0.016	0.020	0.025	0.024	0.021	Kirghizistan
								0.023	0.018	0.014	Monténégro
–	–	0.016	0.012	0.019	0.021	0.022	0.026	0.030	0.026	0.025	République de Moldova
–	–	1.315	0.737	1.129	1.278	1.465	1.725	1.951	1.665	1.782	Fédération de Russie (29)
–	–	0.051	0.056	0.125	0.108	0.121	0.152	–	–	–	Serbie-et-Monténégro*
								0.139	0.127	0.109	Serbie
0.725	0.526	–	–	–	–	–	–	–	–	–	RSF de Yougoslavie (anc.)
–	–	0.015	0.010	0.013	0.012	0.014	0.017	0.020	0.020	0.017	Tadjikistan (28)
–	–	0.033	0.031	0.031	0.030	0.030	0.036	0.042	0.040	0.035	LERY de Macédoine*
–	–	0.026	0.027	0.035	0.027	0.021	0.025	0.034	0.053	(e)0.036	Turkménistan (28)
–	–	0.296	0.209	0.306	0.335	0.364	0.425	0.520	0.359	0.397	Ukraine (28)
3.297	3.363	–	–	–	–	–	–	–	–	–	URSS (anc.)
–	–	0.055	0.040	0.036	0.034	0.035	0.044	0.056	0.071	0.055	Ouzbékistan (28)

Pour les sources et les notes, se reporter à la fin du tableau.

1.1.1 Exports and imports of countries and geographical regions
Share

Region, country or territory	Exports (f.o.b.) - Exportations (f.a.b.) Percentage - En pourcentage										
	1980	1990	1995	2000	2004	2005	2006	2007	2008	2009	2010
Developed economies: America	**14.421**	**14.993**	**15.013**	**16.420**	**12.227**	**12.072**	**11.775**	**11.289**	**10.878**	**10.976**	**10.966**
Bermuda (4)	0.002	0.002	0.001	0.001	0.001	0.000	0.000	0.000	0.000	0.000	0.000
Canada	3.328	3.668	3.712	4.290	3.314	3.425	3.211	2.977	2.804	2.526	2.544
Greenland	0.010	0.013	0.007	0.004	0.004	0.004	0.003	0.003	0.003	0.003	0.003
Saint Pierre and Miquelon	0.000	0.001	0.000	(e)0.000	(e)0.000	(e)0.000	(e)0.000	(e)0.000	(e)0.000	(e)0.000	(e)0.000
United States (30)	11.081	11.310	11.293	12.125	8.908	8.643	8.560	8.309	8.070	8.446	8.419
Developed economies: Asia	**6.680**	**8.597**	**8.925**	**7.919**	**6.576**	**6.076**	**5.744**	**5.489**	**5.228**	**5.025**	**5.458**
Israel*	0.272	0.333	0.368	0.487	0.420	0.408	0.386	0.386	0.377	0.383	0.385
Japan	6.408	8.264	8.558	7.432	6.156	5.668	5.358	5.103	4.851	4.642	5.073
Developed economies: Europe	**43.893**	**47.387**	**44.706**	**40.175**	**43.142**	**40.995**	**40.093**	**40.398**	**38.941**	**38.962**	**36.123**
Andorra*	..	..	0.001	0.001	0.001	0.001	0.001	0.001	0.001	0.001	0.000
Austria*	0.809	1.182	1.115	1.047	1.286	1.192	1.126	1.167	1.120	1.091	1.004
Belgium*	-	-	3.443	2.914	3.334	3.185	3.021	3.075	2.915	2.944	2.714
Bulgaria*	0.510	0.139	0.103	0.075	0.108	0.112	0.124	0.132	0.138	0.130	0.136
Cyprus*	0.026	0.028	0.024	0.015	0.010	0.014	0.011	0.010	0.010	0.010	0.009
Czechoslovakia (former) (31)	0.732	0.342									
Czech Republic*(32)	–	–	0.419	0.450	0.749	0.744	0.782	0.874	0.907	0.899	0.875
Denmark*(33)	0.823	1.064	0.983	0.793	0.837	0.811	0.762	0.736	0.722	0.748	0.643
Estonia*(28)	–	–	0.036	0.059	0.064	0.073	0.080	0.079	0.077	0.072	0.076
Faeroe Islands	0.009	0.011	0.007	0.007	0.007	0.006	0.005	0.005	0.005	0.006	0.005
Finland*	0.695	0.764	0.782	0.713	0.668	0.624	0.636	0.642	0.596	0.500	0.461
France*	5.719	6.243	5.830	5.068	4.911	4.414	4.084	3.993	3.807	3.859	3.433
Germany (former Dem. Rep.)	0.850	–	–	–	–	–	–	–	–	–	–
Germany (former Federal Rep.)	9.475	–	–	–	–	–	–	–	–	–	–
Germany*	–	11.785	10.110	8.536	9.884	9.247	9.127	9.427	8.933	8.916	8.354
Gibraltar (34)	0.000	0.002	0.002	0.002	0.002	0.002	0.002	0.002	0.002	0.002	-
Greece*	0.253	0.233	0.213	0.182	0.166	0.165	0.171	0.168	0.163	0.163	0.142
Hungary*(35)	0.426	0.276	0.247	0.434	0.604	0.599	0.620	0.681	0.670	0.661	0.628
Iceland	0.045	0.046	0.035	0.029	0.032	0.029	0.028	0.034	0.033	0.032	0.030
Ireland*	0.413	0.682	0.863	1.198	1.138	1.044	0.896	0.867	0.777	0.923	0.768
Italy*	3.837	4.899	4.515	3.721	3.843	3.554	3.434	3.567	3.353	3.239	2.945
Latvia*	–	–	0.025	0.029	0.044	0.049	0.051	0.059	0.063	0.061	0.063
Lithuania*(28)	–	–	0.052	0.055	0.101	0.112	0.116	0.122	0.146	0.131	0.137
Luxembourg*	0.148	0.181	0.150	0.130	0.177	0.179	0.189	0.160	0.158	0.169	0.129
Malta	0.024	0.032	0.037	0.038	0.027	0.023	0.023	0.022	0.018	0.018	0.017
Netherlands*	4.173	3.787	3.924	3.606	3.883	3.870	3.819	3.930	3.941	3.964	3.775
Norway	0.911	0.978	0.811	0.931	0.890	0.989	1.007	0.974	1.071	0.966	0.866
Poland*	0.697	0.392	0.442	0.491	0.815	0.852	0.912	1.000	1.053	1.087	1.025
Portugal*	0.228	0.472	0.440	0.377	0.389	0.363	0.369	0.375	0.353	0.352	0.321
Romania*	0.551	0.166	0.153	0.161	0.256	0.264	0.267	0.289	0.306	0.323	0.325
Slovakia*	–	–	0.166	0.184	0.301	0.304	0.345	0.418	0.439	0.446	0.429
Slovenia*	–	–	0.161	0.135	0.178	0.183	0.191	0.215	0.211	0.208	0.194
Spain*	1.018	1.595	1.890	1.783	1.984	1.835	1.760	1.807	1.739	1.810	1.617
Sweden*	1.518	1.653	1.554	1.348	1.339	1.247	1.217	1.205	1.132	1.043	1.042
Switzerland*	1.456	1.833	1.577	1.248	1.339	1.247	1.219	1.229	1.244	1.379	1.285
United Kingdom*	5.411	5.319	4.596	4.415	3.775	3.662	3.695	3.133	2.839	2.809	2.671
Developed economies: Oceania	**1.344**	**1.412**	**1.289**	**1.206**	**1.165**	**1.217**	**1.205**	**1.209**	**1.351**	**1.429**	**1.606**
Australia	1.078	1.142	1.026	0.990	0.940	1.008	1.016	1.008	1.160	1.230	1.399
New Zealand	0.266	0.270	0.264	0.215	0.224	0.209	0.189	0.201	0.192	0.199	0.207

For sources and notes, see next page.

				Imports (c.i.f.) - Importations (c.a.f.) Percentage - En pourcentage							Régions, pays ou territoires
1980	1990	1995	2000	2004	2005	2006	2007	2008	2009	2010	
15.409	**17.875**	**17.952**	**22.592**	**19.038**	**19.150**	**18.415**	**16.921**	**15.724**	**15.288**	**15.383**	**Économies développées : Amérique**
0.016	0.017	0.011	0.011	0.010	0.009	0.009	0.008	0.007	0.008	0.006	Bermudes (4)
3.010	3.435	3.210	3.674	2.949	3.070	2.892	2.732	2.535	2.604	2.548	Canada
0.016	0.012	0.008	0.005	0.006	0.006	0.006	0.005	0.005	0.006	0.005	Groenland
0.000	0.002	0.001	(e)0.002	(e)0.001	(e)0.000	(e)0.001	(e)0.001	(e)0.000	(e)0.001	(e)0.000	Saint-Pierre-et-Miquelon
12.366	14.408	14.723	18.900	16.072	16.065	15.508	14.176	13.177	12.670	12.823	États-Unis (30)
7.270	**7.028**	**6.980**	**6.262**	**5.241**	**5.204**	**5.093**	**4.763**	**5.043**	**4.734**	**4.909**	**Économies développées : Asie**
0.471	0.468	0.565	0.566	0.452	0.436	0.407	0.414	0.411	0.000	0.399	Israël*
6.799	6.560	6.415	5.696	4.789	4.768	4.686	4.348	4.632	4.345	4.510	Japon
46.047	**47.330**	**42.011**	**30.175**	**41.318**	**40.011**	**40.036**	**40.466**	**39.181**	**38.390**	**35.909**	**Économies développées : Europe**
..	..	0.020	0.015	0.018	0.017	0.014	0.013	0.012	0.012	0.010	Andorre*
1.176	1.368	1.265	1.084	1.261	1.178	1.108	1.142	1.115	1.125	1.035	Autriche*
-	-	3.151	2.658	3.004	2.950	2.841	2.884	2.821	2.767	2.541	Belgique*
0.404	0.131	0.108	0.098	0.152	0.168	0.188	0.210	0.223	0.185	0.165	Bulgarie*
0.058	0.072	0.071	0.058	0.058	0.058	0.056	0.060	0.064	0.062	0.055	Chypre*
0.615	0.365										Tchécoslovaquie (anc.) (31)
-	-	0.504	0.508	0.736	0.708	0.753	0.828	0.859	0.826	0.821	République tchèque*(32)
0.931	0.927	0.877	0.682	0.717	0.700	0.691	0.687	0.662	0.650	0.552	Danemark*(33)
-	-	0.049	0.076	0.088	0.095	0.109	0.110	0.097	0.080	0.080	Estonie*(28)
0.011	0.009	0.006	0.008	0.007	0.007	0.006	0.007	0.006	0.006	0.005	Îles Féroé
0.752	0.753	0.563	0.516	0.541	0.544	0.560	0.573	0.555	0.479	0.447	Finlande*
6.619	6.710	5.666	5.074	4.953	4.666	4.378	4.420	4.336	4.409	3.951	France*
0.918	-	-	-	-	-	-	-	-	-	-	Allemagne (anc. Rép. dém. d')
9.047	-	-	-	-	-	-	-	-	-	-	Allemagne (anc. Rép. fédérale d')
	9.647	8.861	7.444	7.528	7.192	7.324	7.392	7.168	7.282	6.942	Allemagne*
0.005	0.010	0.008	0.007	0.006	0.005	0.005	0.006	0.005	0.006	-	Gibraltar (34)
0.508	0.551	0.495	0.501	0.555	0.504	0.514	0.550	0.560	0.546	0.413	Grèce*
0.445	0.242	0.294	0.480	0.637	0.616	0.632	0.670	0.659	0.611	0.573	Hongrie*(35)
0.040	0.047	0.031	0.039	0.037	0.042	0.048	0.047	0.037	0.028	0.026	Islande
0.537	0.576	0.618	0.764	0.650	0.635	0.591	0.587	0.508	0.493	0.391	Irlande*
4.848	5.071	3.935	3.575	3.737	3.561	3.575	3.585	3.399	3.263	3.157	Italie*
-	-	0.035	0.048	0.075	0.080	0.093	0.107	0.098	0.077	0.076	Lettonie*
-	-	0.070	0.078	0.130	0.144	0.156	0.171	0.188	0.144	0.152	Lituanie*(28)
0.174	0.212	0.186	0.169	0.211	0.203	0.215	0.193	0.194	0.196	0.156	Luxembourg*
0.045	0.055	0.056	0.051	0.038	0.034	0.035	0.033	0.031	0.033	0.027	Malte
4.255	3.525	3.538	3.268	3.362	3.367	3.367	3.452	3.514	3.484	3.364	Pays-Bas*
0.814	0.759	0.630	0.516	0.507	0.514	0.520	0.564	0.548	0.547	0.503	Norvège
0.803	0.234	0.555	0.735	0.943	0.941	1.026	1.161	1.263	1.175	1.130	Pologne*
0.448	0.704	0.623	0.598	0.578	0.566	0.571	0.575	0.571	0.563	0.492	Portugal*
0.666	0.274	0.196	0.196	0.344	0.375	0.413	0.493	0.508	0.427	0.403	Roumanie*
-	-	0.176	0.201	0.314	0.321	0.363	0.425	0.447	0.437	0.432	Slovaquie*
-	-	0.181	0.152	0.187	0.188	0.195	0.221	0.224	0.208	0.195	Slovénie*
1.640	2.440	2.169	2.338	2.717	2.673	2.655	2.728	2.545	2.305	2.045	Espagne*
1.609	1.512	1.242	1.091	1.056	1.034	1.030	1.074	1.019	0.944	0.968	Suède*
1.749	1.942	1.531	1.238	1.222	1.172	1.143	1.131	1.115	1.226	1.146	Suisse*
5.560	6.254	5.105	5.211	4.950	4.754	4.858	4.365	3.829	3.796	3.650	Royaume-Uni*
1.341	**1.435**	**1.437**	**1.287**	**1.401**	**1.409**	**1.342**	**1.381**	**1.423**	**1.505**	**1.513**	**Économies développées : Océanie**
1.078	1.170	1.170	1.074	1.152	1.160	1.126	1.160	1.216	1.306	1.313	Australie
0.263	0.265	0.267	0.214	0.248	0.249	0.216	0.221	0.207	0.199	0.199	Nouvelle-Zélande

Pour les sources et les notes, se reporter à la page suivante.

1.1.1 Exports and imports of countries and geographical regions
Share

Sources:
- UN DESA Statistics Division, *Yearbook of International Trade Statistics*
- UN DESA Statistics Division, *Monthly Bulletin of Statistics*
- IMF, *International Financial Statistics* on CD-ROM
- IMF, *Direction of Trade Statistics*
- World Trade Organization
- Other international and national sources
- UNCTAD secretariat estimates

Notes:

(*)	Special Trade System.
(1)	Excluding exports of gold.
(2)	From 1996 onward, imports f.o.b.
(3)	Prior to 2008, special trade.
(4)	Imports f.o.b.
(5)	Trade with other member countries of CEMAC is excluded. Imports f.o.b.
(6)	Trade with other member countries of CEMAC is excluded.
(7)	Prior to 1995, data refer to fiscal year ending June.
(8)	Prior to 1974, special trade.
(9)	Excluding re-exports (oil for bunkering).
(10)	Excluding re-exports.
(11)	Prior to 2005, special trade.
(12)	Prior to 1986, included in Netherlands Antilles. Including exports and imports of crude oil and oil products. Imports f.o.b.
(13)	From 1990 onwards, trade statistics exclude certain oil and chemical products. Imports f.o.b.
(14)	Prior to 1993, excluding free trade processing zones. Imports f.o.b.
(15)	Prior to 1986, including Aruba.
(16)	Prior to 2002, special trade.
(17)	From 1990 onward, including goods for processing. Imports f.o.b.
(18)	Excluding imports of goods financed through foreign aid.
(19)	Excluding military goods, fissionable materials, bunkers, ships and aircraft.
(20)	Inter-trade between the States of Malaysia included. From 1965 onwards, excluding military imports and offshore installations of petroleum industry.
(21)	Including trans-shipments to and from peninsular Malaysia.
(22)	Excluding exports of oil and gas.
(23)	Prior to 2001, special trade.
(24)	Excluding defense imports.
(25)	Data refer to fiscal year ending September.
(26)	Excluding military goods, precious metals and goods procured in foreign ports.
(27)	Prior to 1998, data refer to the Federation of Bosnia and Herzegovina only. The other entity of Bosnia and Herzegovina, Republika Srpska, is not included.
(28)	Prior to 1994, covers only trade with countries outside the CIS.
(29)	Prior to 1994, excluding trade with independent states resulting from the former USSR.
(30)	Prior to 1975, excludes non-monetary gold.
(31)	From 1985 onwards, data are not comparable to those shown for prior periods due to revisions of the koruna-to-US dollar exchange rate.
(32)	From 1995 onward, including goods for processing.
(33)	Prior to 1988, excluding ships.
(34)	Excluding petroleum products.
(35)	Prior to 1996, excluding customs free zones.

Sources :
- ONU DAES Division de statistique, *Annuaire statistique du commerce international*
- ONU DAES Division de statistique, *Bulletin mensuel de statistique*
- FMI, *Statistiques financières internationales* sur CD-ROM
- FMI, *Direction of Trade Statistics*
- Organisation mondiale du commerce
- Autres sources internationales et nationales
- Estimations du secrétariat de la CNUCED

Notes :

(*)   Système du commerce spécial.
(1)   Non-compris les exportations d'or.
(2)   À partir de 1996, importations f.a.b.
(3)   Avant 2008, commerce spécial.
(4)   Importations f.a.b.
(5)   Non-compris le commerce avec les autres pays membres de la CEMAC. Importations f.a.b.
(6)   Non-compris le commerce avec les autres pays membres de la CEMAC.
(7)   Avant 1995, les données se rapportent à l'exercice budgétaire finissant juin.
(8)   Avant 1974, commerce spécial.
(9)   Non-compris les réexportations (huile pour mise en soute).
(10)   Non-compris les réexportations.
(11)   Avant 2005, commerce spécial.
(12)   Avant 1986 compris dans Antilles néerlandaises. Les données comprennent les exportations et importations de pétrole brut et produits dérivés. Importations f.a.b.
(13)   À partir de 1990, certains produits pétroliers et chimiques ne sont plus inclus dans les statistiques du commerce. Importations f.a.b.
(14)   Avant 1993, non-compris les zones franches douanières. Importations f.a.b.
(15)   Avant 1986, y compris Aruba.
(16)   Avant 2002, commerce spécial.
(17)   À partir de 1990, y compris les biens destinés à subir des transformations. Importations f.a.b.
(18)   Non-compris les biens d'importation financés par l'aide à l'étranger.
(19)   Non-compris les biens à usage militaire, le matériel fissile, le combustible de soute et l'avitaillement des navires et aéronefs.
(20)   Y compris le commerce entre les États de la Malaisie. Non-compris les importations militaires et l'installation près des côtes de l'industrie pétrolière.
(21)   Y compris les transbordements vers et en provenance de la Malaisie péninsulaire.
(22)   Non-compris les exportations de pétrole et le gaz.
(23)   Avant 2001, commerce spécial.
(24)   Non-compris les importations de la défense.
(25)   Les données se rapportent à l'exercice budgétaire finissant septembre.
(26)   Non-compris les biens à usage militaire, les métaux précieux et les biens fournis dans les ports étrangers.
(27)   Avant 1998, les données se réfèrent uniquement à la Fédération de la Bosnie-Herzégovine. L'autre entité de la Bosnie-Herzégovine, Republika Srpska, n'est pas incluse.
(28)   Avant 1994, concerne seulement le commerce avec les pays extérieurs à la CEI.
(29)   Avant 1994, non-compris le commerce avec les républiques indépendantes de l'ancienne URSS.
(30)   Avant 1975, non-compris l'or industriel.
(31)   À partir de 1985, les chiffres ne sont pas comparables à ceux des années antérieures à cause des révisions du taux de change de la couronne par rapport au dollar des États-Unis.
(32)   À partir de 1995, y compris les biens destinés à subir des transformations.
(33)   Avant 1988, non-compris les navires.
(34)   Non-compris les produits pétroliers.
(35)   Avant 1996, non-compris les zones franches douanières.

1.1.2 Exports and imports of economic groupings
Value

Economic grouping	Exports (f.o.b.) - Exportations (f.a.b.) Millions of dollars							
	1980	1990	2000	2005	2007	2008	2009	2010
DEVELOPING ECONOMIES	**599 757**	**842 125**	**2 056 072**	**3 797 426**	**5 274 070**	**6 290 288**	**4 977 192**	**6 339 389**
Developing economies excluding China	581 658	780 034	1 806 869	3 035 473	4 056 280	4 861 628	3 775 402	4 761 119
Developing economies excluding LDCs	585 168	823 847	2 019 905	3 714 954	5 146 255	6 113 408	4 850 035	6 179 120
High-income developing countries	342 709	502 504	1 248 358	2 041 367	2 666 427	3 131 792	2 420 655	3 021 779
Middle-income developing countries	144 058	231 797	584 558	1 342 044	2 017 247	2 395 453	1 944 727	2 528 277
Low-income developing countries	112 990	107 823	223 153	414 008	590 388	763 035	611 803	789 326
Heavily indebted poor countries (IMF)	20 313	20 434	28 187	55 098	77 039	96 949	82 081	101 359
Landlocked developing countries	8 386	10 726	32 781	77 331	132 040	179 821	125 742	158 400
Small island developing States	12 546	6 993	11 657	19 598	25 947	33 295	19 865	22 713
Least developed countries	*14 588*	*18 278*	*36 167*	*82 471*	*127 815*	*176 880*	*127 158*	*160 269*
Africa and Haiti	12 301	14 817	21 160	58 525	95 346	138 784	91 749	114 289
Asia	2 129	3 337	14 878	23 687	32 120	37 711	35 092	45 595
Islands	158	124	129	259	349	384	317	386
Major petroleum and gas exporters	*272 968*	*174 688*	*315 343*	*678 622*	*949 483*	*1 299 090*	*868 529*	*1 050 312*
Africa	63 617	43 585	63 609	156 199	212 319	293 858	175 329	223 199
America	19 221	17 444	33 529	55 716	69 010	95 138	57 595	65 786
Asia	190 130	113 658	218 205	466 707	668 154	910 094	635 605	761 327
Major exporters of manufactured goods	*132 006*	*422 299*	*1 242 471*	*2 228 076*	*3 081 378*	*3 484 023*	*2 894 622*	*3 753 649*
America	18 031	40 711	166 368	213 891	272 055	291 827	229 683	298 138
Asia	113 975	381 588	1 076 103	2 014 185	2 809 323	3 192 196	2 664 939	3 455 511
Emerging economies	*130 912*	*333 426*	*899 106*	*1 394 301*	*1 831 054*	*2 059 203*	*1 662 230*	*2 160 180*
America	54 788	96 081	274 066	431 406	584 030	658 342	517 591	673 113
Asia	76 124	237 346	625 040	962 895	1 247 024	1 400 861	1 144 639	1 487 067
Newly industrialized Asian countries	*125 567*	*354 421*	*932 090*	*1 378 290*	*1 760 531*	*1 952 346*	*1 621 103*	*2 086 496*
First tier	76 425	266 976	659 709	1 001 184	1 261 647	1 377 920	1 153 647	1 483 066
Second tier	49 141	87 444	272 381	377 106	498 884	574 426	467 456	603 430
Developing economies: Africa	121 876	105 100	149 402	317 869	434 492	569 739	393 401	493 243
Northern Africa excluding Sudan	43 500	36 482	52 457	109 285	150 438	206 974	133 815	163 784
Sub-Saharan Africa	78 376	68 618	96 946	208 584	284 054	362 765	259 586	329 459
Sub-Saharan Africa excluding South Africa	52 337	44 864	64 996	152 323	207 619	276 647	193 044	243 759
Developing economies: America	111 352	143 934	366 507	576 636	771 611	901 287	688 097	872 612
Central America and Greater Caribbean Islands excluding Puerto Rico	31 107	52 666	191 959	247 282	314 594	336 552	267 279	341 450
Central America and Greater Caribbean Islands excluding Mexico and Puerto Rico	13 076	11 955	25 591	33 391	42 539	44 725	37 596	43 312
South America and Central America	88 984	132 268	347 507	550 880	739 293	862 306	664 732	847 516
South America excluding Brazil	45 473	55 151	109 454	195 503	277 936	341 452	254 943	316 456
Developing economies: Asia	364 287	590 380	1 535 072	2 896 260	4 058 969	4 809 702	3 888 563	4 964 751
Eastern and South-Eastern Asia excluding China	132 023	363 749	957 588	1 429 145	1 834 212	2 045 111	1 702 308	2 190 095
Southern Asia excluding India	17 542	29 035	50 345	89 614	129 031	159 837	120 402	151 919

Sources:
- Data in this table are based on trade figures in table 1.1.1.

Imports (c.i.f.) - Importations (c.a.f.) Millions de dollars								Groupements économiques
1980	1990	2000	2005	2007	2008	2009	2010	
496 880	**797 007**	**1 919 794**	**3 424 536**	**4 729 574**	**5 749 263**	**4 668 601**	**6 001 415**	**ÉCONOMIES EN DÉVELOPPEMENT**
476 939	743 662	1 694 770	2 764 330	3 773 341	4 617 643	3 664 431	4 605 215	Économies en développement sans la Chine
471 838	771 574	1 876 375	3 337 391	4 605 134	5 587 080	4 514 180	5 823 037	Économies en développement sans les PMA
243 111	452 923	1 154 026	1 745 499	2 353 617	2 756 460	2 154 861	2 705 845	Pays en développement à revenu élevé
150 925	236 585	562 118	1 236 396	1 736 852	2 131 248	1 794 191	2 401 463	Pays en développement à revenu intermédiaire
94 844	107 499	200 611	442 331	638 606	860 948	719 048	893 605	Pays en développement à revenu faible
25 048	23 988	36 902	75 104	105 468	134 778	116 992	134 501	Pays pauvres très endettés (FMI)
10 613	13 700	36 176	75 797	118 297	153 639	130 897	142 402	Pays en développement sans littoral
15 717	10 404	17 293	26 055	34 896	41 836	31 422	33 125	Petits Etats Insulaires en développement
25 042	*25 434*	*43 419*	*87 145*	*124 440*	*162 183*	*154 421*	*178 377*	*Pays les moins avancés*
16 912	17 609	24 029	55 088	79 818	106 940	102 013	113 750	Afrique et Haïti
7 841	7 453	19 003	31 134	43 361	53 654	50 969	62 944	Asie
289	372	387	922	1 260	1 588	1 440	1 683	Îles
117 776	*98 156*	*150 863*	*327 606*	*503 429*	*656 165*	*575 682*	*625 393*	*Principaux exportateurs de pétrole et de gaz*
35 307	22 311	24 931	61 212	91 848	122 541	116 993	131 333	Afrique
11 827	7 335	16 865	24 027	46 097	49 602	40 597	38 613	Amérique
70 642	68 510	109 067	242 367	365 485	484 022	418 093	455 448	Asie
150 588	*427 262*	*1 199 370*	*2 067 984*	*2 748 169*	*3 184 113*	*2 599 317*	*3 482 773*	*Principaux exportateurs d'articles manufacturés*
22 144	43 548	182 702	231 821	296 578	325 157	246 104	316 556	Amérique
128 445	383 714	1 016 668	1 836 163	2 451 591	2 858 956	2 353 213	3 166 217	Asie
152 003	*328 599*	*871 261*	*1 259 803*	*1 663 173*	*1 995 634*	*1 483 847*	*1 989 094*	*Économies émergentes*
65 947	80 722	292 421	383 379	535 462	656 803	482 115	652 270	Amérique
86 056	247 877	578 839	876 424	1 127 711	1 338 831	1 001 732	1 336 824	Asie
127 629	*365 140*	*871 747*	*1 301 075*	*1 646 166*	*1 915 275*	*1 488 580*	*1 960 345*	*Économies nouvellement industrialisées d'Asie*
88 511	268 066	647 758	943 389	1 207 297	1 384 250	1 090 521	1 420 694	Première génération
39 118	97 075	223 989	357 686	438 869	531 025	398 059	539 651	Deuxième génération
96 856	**94 372**	**130 215**	**262 230**	**375 966**	**480 629**	**422 235**	**488 151**	**Économies en développement : Afrique**
29 977	36 756	47 234	85 328	118 784	174 944	157 494	176 310	Afrique septentrionale sans le Soudan
66 879	57 616	82 982	176 903	257 182	305 686	264 741	311 841	Afrique subsaharienne
46 973	39 010	52 771	112 711	166 654	208 982	189 094	215 591	Afrique subsaharienne sans l'Afrique du Sud
123 594	**126 635**	**391 895**	**533 987**	**756 005**	**923 464**	**689 494**	**891 129**	**Économies en développement : Amérique**
39 759	63 785	227 565	296 602	384 758	431 665	324 664	410 037	Amérique centrale et Grandes Antilles sans Porto Rico
17 615	20 237	44 863	64 781	88 180	106 508	78 560	93 481	Amérique centrale et Grandes Antilles sans le Mexique et Porto Rico
96 232	107 934	359 481	491 209	700 805	854 660	640 949	837 419	Amérique du Sud et Amérique centrale
41 528	33 638	91 932	140 847	222 314	282 781	211 719	270 887	Amérique du Sud sans le Brésil
272 880	**570 906**	**1 391 359**	**2 618 575**	**3 584 962**	**4 330 558**	**3 544 902**	**4 608 458**	**Économies en développement : Asie**
131 235	374 902	897 920	1 353 982	1 731 449	2 023 573	1 582 808	2 073 840	Asie orientale et Asie du Sud-Est sans la Chine
24 675	33 788	44 548	94 005	114 990	146 060	123 235	153 990	Asie méridionale sans l'Inde

Sources :
- Les données dans ce tableau ont été calculées d'après les chiffres du tableau 1.1.1.

1.1.2 Exports and imports of economic groupings
Share

Economic grouping	Exports (f.o.b.) - Exportations (f.a.b.) Percentage										
	1980	1990	1995	2000	2004	2005	2006	2007	2008	2009	2010
DEVELOPING ECONOMIES	**29.46**	**24.20**	**27.71**	**31.88**	**33.82**	**36.18**	**37.42**	**37.68**	**39.01**	**39.78**	**41.78**
Developing economies excluding China	28.58	22.42	24.84	28.02	27.36	28.92	29.43	28.98	30.15	30.18	31.38
Developing economies excluding LDCs	28.75	23.67	27.25	31.32	33.16	35.39	36.58	36.77	37.92	38.77	40.72
High-income developing countries	16.84	14.44	17.22	19.36	18.65	19.45	19.63	19.05	19.42	19.35	19.91
Middle-income developing countries	7.08	6.66	7.71	9.06	11.73	12.79	13.72	14.41	14.86	15.54	16.66
Low-income developing countries	5.55	3.10	2.79	3.46	3.44	3.04	4.00	4.22	4.73	4.89	5.20
Heavily indebted poor countries (IMF)	1.00	0.59	0.47	0.44	0.51	0.52	0.55	0.55	0.60	0.66	0.67
Landlocked developing countries	0.41	0.31	0.52	0.51	0.65	0.74	0.85	0.94	1.12	1.01	1.04
Small island developing States	0.62	0.20	0.10	0.10	0.16	0.19	0.21	0.19	0.21	0.16	0.16
Least developed countries	*0.72*	*0.53*	*0.46*	*0.56*	*0.66*	*0.79*	*0.85*	*0.91*	*1.10*	*1.02*	*1.06*
Africa and Haiti	0.60	0.43	0.30	0.33	0.45	0.56	0.60	0.68	0.86	0.73	0.75
Asia	0.10	0.10	0.16	0.23	0.21	0.23	0.24	0.23	0.23	0.28	0.30
Islands	0.01	0.00	0.00	0.00	0.00	0.00	0.00	0.00	0.00	0.00	0.00
Major petroleum and gas exporters	*13.41*	*5.02*	*3.36*	*4.89*	*5.19*	*6.47*	*6.79*	*6.78*	*8.06*	*6.94*	*6.92*
Africa	3.13	1.25	0.67	0.99	1.06	1.49	1.50	1.52	1.82	1.40	1.47
America	0.94	0.50	0.36	0.52	0.43	0.53	0.54	0.49	0.59	0.46	0.43
Asia	9.34	3.27	2.33	3.38	3.70	4.45	4.74	4.77	5.64	5.08	5.02
Major exporters of manufactured goods	*6.49*	*12.14*	*17.14*	*19.27*	*20.57*	*21.23*	*21.84*	*22.02*	*21.61*	*23.14*	*24.74*
America	0.89	1.17	1.54	2.58	2.06	2.04	2.06	1.94	1.81	1.84	1.96
Asia	5.60	10.97	15.60	16.69	18.51	19.19	19.77	20.07	19.80	21.30	22.77
Emerging economies	*6.43*	*9.58*	*12.63*	*13.94*	*13.21*	*13.28*	*13.43*	*13.08*	*12.77*	*13.29*	*14.24*
America	2.69	2.76	3.25	4.25	3.98	4.11	4.26	4.17	4.08	4.14	4.44
Asia	3.74	6.82	9.37	9.69	9.23	9.17	9.17	8.91	8.69	9.15	9.80
Newly industrialized Asian countries	*6.17*	*10.18*	*13.98*	*14.45*	*13.27*	*13.13*	*13.03*	*12.58*	*12.11*	*12.96*	*13.75*
First tier	3.75	7.67	10.21	10.23	9.64	9.54	9.38	9.01	8.55	9.22	9.77
Second tier	2.41	2.51	3.77	4.22	3.63	3.59	3.65	3.56	3.56	3.74	3.98
Developing economies: Africa	**5.99**	**3.02**	**2.19**	**2.32**	**2.54**	**3.03**	**3.07**	**3.10**	**3.53**	**3.14**	**3.25**
Northern Africa excluding Sudan	2.14	1.05	0.67	0.81	0.87	1.04	1.09	1.07	1.28	1.07	1.08
Sub-Saharan Africa	3.85	1.97	1.52	1.50	1.67	1.99	1.98	2.03	2.25	2.07	2.17
Sub-Saharan Africa excluding South Africa	2.57	1.29	0.95	1.01	1.14	1.45	1.44	1.48	1.72	1.54	1.61
Developing economies: America	**5.47**	**4.14**	**4.44**	**5.68**	**5.22**	**5.49**	**5.68**	**5.51**	**5.59**	**5.50**	**5.75**
Central America and Greater Caribbean Islands excluding Puerto Rico	1.53	1.51	1.87	2.98	2.40	2.36	2.37	2.25	2.09	2.14	2.25
Central America and Greater Caribbean Islands excluding Mexico and Puerto Rico	0.64	0.34	0.33	0.40	0.34	0.32	0.31	0.30	0.28	0.30	0.29
South America and Central America	4.37	3.80	4.19	5.39	4.99	5.25	5.42	5.28	5.35	5.31	5.59
South America excluding Brazil	2.23	1.58	1.56	1.70	1.65	1.86	2.01	1.99	2.12	2.04	2.09
Developing economies: Asia	**17.90**	**16.97**	**21.00**	**23.80**	**26.00**	**27.59**	**28.61**	**29.00**	**29.83**	**31.08**	**32.72**
Eastern and South-Eastern Asia excluding China	6.49	10.45	14.24	14.85	13.72	13.62	13.54	13.10	12.68	13.61	14.43
Southern Asia excluding India	0.86	0.83	0.66	0.78	0.80	0.85	0.94	0.92	0.99	0.96	1.00

Sources:
- Data in this table are based on trade figures in table 1.1.1.

Imports (c.i.f.) - Importations (c.a.f.) En pourcentage											Groupements économiques
1980	1990	1995	2000	2004	2005	2006	2007	2008	2009	2010	
23.91	**22.21**	**28.61**	**28.81**	**30.65**	**31.71**	**32.30**	**33.18**	**34.92**	**36.85**	**39.09**	**ÉCONOMIES EN DÉVELOPPEMENT**
22.95	20.73	26.09	25.44	24.74	25.60	25.90	26.48	28.05	28.92	30.00	Économies en développement sans la Chine
22.70	21.50	27.96	28.16	29.90	30.90	31.49	32.31	33.93	35.63	37.93	Économies en développement sans les PMA
11.70	12.62	17.12	17.32	16.09	16.16	16.38	16.51	16.74	17.01	17.62	Pays en développement à revenu élevé
7.65	6.59	8.54	8.44	11.03	11.45	11.74	12.19	12.94	14.16	15.64	Pays en développement à revenu intermédiaire
4.56	3.00	2.94	3.05	3.52	4.10	4.18	4.48	5.23	5.68	5.82	Pays en développement à revenu faible
1.21	0.67	0.58	0.55	0.64	0.70	0.71	0.74	0.82	0.92	0.88	Pays pauvres très endettés (FMI)
0.52	0.44	0.64	0.55	0.68	0.70	0.74	0.83	0.93	1.03	0.93	Pays en développement sans littoral
0.76	0.29	0.26	0.26	0.24	0.24	0.24	0.24	0.25	0.25	0.22	Petits États insulaires en développement
1.21	*0.71*	*0.65*	*0.65*	*0.75*	*0.81*	*0.82*	*0.87*	*0.99*	*1.22*	*1.16*	*Pays les moins avancés*
0.81	0.49	0.39	0.36	0.46	0.51	0.52	0.56	0.65	0.81	0.74	Afrique et Haïti
0.38	0.21	0.25	0.29	0.28	0.29	0.29	0.30	0.33	0.40	0.41	Asie
0.01	0.01	0.01	0.01	0.01	0.01	0.01	0.01	0.01	0.01	0.01	Îles
5.67	*2.74*	*2.19*	*2.26*	*2.87*	*3.03*	*3.06*	*3.53*	*3.99*	*4.54*	*4.07*	*Principaux exportateurs de pétrole et de gaz*
1.70	0.62	0.48	0.37	0.50	0.57	0.54	0.64	0.74	0.92	0.86	Afrique
0.57	0.20	0.23	0.25	0.18	0.22	0.27	0.32	0.30	0.32	0.25	Amérique
3.40	1.91	1.49	1.64	2.20	2.24	2.24	2.56	2.94	3.30	2.97	Asie
7.25	*11.91*	*17.43*	*18.00*	*19.02*	*19.15*	*19.45*	*19.28*	*19.34*	*20.52*	*22.68*	*Principaux exportateurs d'articles manufacturés*
1.07	1.21	1.45	2.74	2.18	2.15	2.17	2.08	1.97	1.94	2.06	Amérique
6.18	10.69	15.98	15.26	16.84	17.00	17.28	17.20	17.36	18.57	20.62	Asie
7.31	*9.16*	*13.09*	*13.08*	*11.55*	*11.66*	*11.83*	*11.67*	*12.12*	*11.71*	*12.96*	*Économies émergentes*
3.17	2.25	3.31	4.39	3.48	3.55	3.65	3.76	3.99	3.81	4.25	Amérique
4.14	6.91	9.78	8.69	8.07	8.11	8.17	7.91	8.13	7.91	8.71	Asie
6.14	*10.18*	*14.77*	*13.08*	*11.99*	*12.05*	*11.97*	*11.55*	*11.63*	*11.75*	*12.77*	*Économies nouvellement industrialisées d'Asie*
4.26	7.47	10.62	9.72	8.82	8.73	8.78	8.47	8.41	8.61	9.25	Première génération
1.88	2.71	4.15	3.36	3.17	3.31	3.19	3.08	3.23	3.14	3.51	Deuxième génération
4.66	**2.63**	**2.37**	**1.95**	**2.25**	**2.43**	**2.46**	**2.64**	**2.92**	**3.33**	**3.18**	**Économies en développement : Afrique**
1.44	1.02	0.86	0.71	0.74	0.79	0.74	0.83	1.06	1.24	1.15	Afrique septentrionale sans le Soudan
3.22	1.61	1.52	1.25	1.51	1.64	1.72	1.80	1.86	2.09	2.03	Afrique subsaharienne
2.26	1.09	0.92	0.79	0.93	1.04	1.06	1.17	1.27	1.49	1.40	Afrique subsaharienne sans l'Afrique du Sud
5.95	**3.53**	**4.75**	**5.88**	**4.76**	**4.94**	**5.14**	**5.30**	**5.61**	**5.44**	**5.80**	**Économies en développement : Amérique**
1.91	1.78	1.98	3.42	2.75	2.75	2.79	2.70	2.62	2.56	2.67	Amérique centrale et Grandes Antilles sans Porto Rico
0.85	0.56	0.53	0.67	0.58	0.60	0.62	0.62	0.65	0.62	0.61	Amérique centrale et Grandes Antilles sans le Mexique et Porto Rico
4.63	3.01	4.36	5.40	4.40	4.55	4.73	4.92	5.19	5.06	5.45	Amérique du Sud et Amérique centrale
2.00	0.94	1.57	1.38	1.14	1.30	1.41	1.56	1.72	1.67	1.76	Amérique du Sud sans le Brésil
13.13	**15.91**	**21.38**	**20.88**	**23.55**	**24.25**	**24.62**	**25.15**	**26.30**	**27.98**	**30.02**	**Économies en développement : Asie**
6.32	10.45	15.10	13.48	12.48	12.54	12.49	12.15	12.29	12.49	13.51	Asie orientale et Asie du Sud-Est sans la Chine
1.19	0.94	0.73	0.67	0.83	0.87	0.84	0.81	0.89	0.97	1.00	Asie méridionale sans l'Inde

Sources :
- Les données dans ce tableau ont été calculées d'après les chiffres du tableau 1.1.1.

1.1.3 Exports and imports of trade groups
Value

Trade group	Exports (f.o.b) - Exportations (f.a.b.) Millions of dollars							
	1980	1990	2000	2005	2007	2008	2009	2010
AFRICA								
CEMAC	4 668	5 604	8 365	23 008	29 605	41 539	26 717	33 958
CEPGL	2 455	2 510	927	2 583	3 339	4 722	3 755	5 798
COMESA	34 219	25 781	29 832	63 561	92 917	127 655	92 886	115 076
EAC	2 287	1 699	3 021	6 173	8 314	10 542	10 027	11 763
ECCAS	9 042	12 002	17 181	49 703	76 402	118 451	70 560	89 022
ECOWAS	33 337	21 408	30 340	71 765	86 138	106 284	79 237	99 782
MRU	4 360	4 749	4 896	8 834	10 303	12 181	12 409	12 334
SADC	36 849	38 597	52 174	101 763	148 847	190 139	134 111	171 216
UMA	40 040	04 011	10 107	00 060	106 000	102 630	112 117	120 200
WAEMU	4 884	5 202	6 661	12 657	15 017	18 562	18 934	19 172
AMERICA								
ANCOM	11 246	13 592	26 227	51 405	75 978	95 671	78 449	98 869
CACM	4 877	4 519	15 488	21 731	27 235	29 548	25 939	29 895
CARICOM	11 681	4 932	8 157	14 870	20 049	26 240	14 846	16 754
FTAA	393 904	658 283	1 418 734	1 836 569	2 343 678	2 645 556	2 055 340	2 531 129
LAIA	88 302	131 447	331 634	528 537	712 420	832 479	638 444	817 244
MERCOSUR	29 522	46 418	84 624	163 940	223 730	279 414	217 644	281 656
NAFTA	311 331	561 932	1 224 903	1 480 479	1 851 689	2 045 099	1 602 476	1 961 744
OAS	398 652	662 259	1 417 067	1 833 840	2 341 875	2 643 332	2 053 625	2 529 187
OECS	164	345	307	292	327	400	359	345
ASIA								
APTA	46 045	148 738	476 000	1 102 188	1 700 340	2 009 000	1 751 400	2 295 052
ASEAN	73 957	145 284	431 901	652 723	865 714	998 758	813 625	1 052 110
ECO	18 527	38 088	82 461	193 371	302 699	394 595	283 205	341 124
GCC	155 060	87 800	175 674	397 000	553 539	750 016	524 374	621 990
SAARC	13 799	27 700	64 380	132 981	190 249	240 700	206 493	272 425
EUROPE								
EFTA	49 095	99 434	142 417	237 772	313 221	378 591	297 411	330 999
EU	844 175	1 549 094	2 447 635	4 064 021	5 339 902	5 898 587	4 576 065	5 149 361
Euro area	627 049	1 223 684	1 915 580	3 176 885	4 187 862	4 612 468	3 588 796	4 004 355
OCEANIA								
MSG	1 518	1 631	2 703	4 117	5 656	6 904	5 254	6 625
INTERREGIONAL								
ACP	98 208	80 913	115 308	236 177	321 068	406 860	288 406	363 401
APEC	627 358	1 332 535	3 115 417	4 687 786	6 224 305	7 074 894	5 635 771	7 231 648
BSEC	29 644	31 886	177 905	419 459	619 591	815 701	556 010	699 284
CIS	–	–	145 405	343 256	518 892	701 982	450 760	584 282

Sources:
- Data in this table are based on trade figures in table 1.1.1.

Imports (c.i.f.) - Importations (c.a.f.) Millions de dollars								Groupements commerciaux
1980	1990	2000	2005	2007	2008	2009	2010	
								AFRIQUE
3 018	3 653	3 852	7 980	13 694	16 996	17 550	19 143	CEMAC
1 949	2 256	1 058	3 429	4 456	5 876	5 511	6 440	CEPGL
23 570	27 948	35 098	67 852	89 669	130 833	122 983	142 542	COMESA
4 106	4 392	6 528	12 229	18 876	24 258	22 461	26 397	CAE
0 014	7 600	7 980	19 812	31 892	43 968	45 824	50 622	CEEAC
25 607	14 013	20 626	44 143	68 934	82 103	67 257	78 321	CEDEAO
1 000	2 170	3 912	7 354	8 877	10 632	9 104	9 726	UFM
31 347	34 045	47 958	99 959	139 839	162 299	138 725	168 736	SADC
25 402	27 761	33 725	66 936	93 164	128 135	113 973	125 210	UMA
0 071	5 777	7 082	15 296	20 032	25 561	22 146	22 793	UEMOA
								AMÉRIQUE
10 157	10 772	24 504	46 334	70 555	93 206	74 292	96 335	ANCOM
6 001	6 476	22 301	36 140	47 712	54 458	40 984	48 657	MCAC
14 268	7 222	14 036	20 219	26 242	31 680	23 806	25 064	CARICOM
430 925	757 316	1 885 352	2 585 383	3 147 438	3 485 632	2 609 044	3 234 149	ZLEA
94 231	105 635	336 945	456 476	654 216	803 025	598 603	787 297	ALADI
37 801	29 295	89 523	113 474	182 937	257 766	186 624	266 566	MERCOSUR
341 673	683 779	1 686 780	2 298 434	2 706 292	2 912 011	2 181 311	2 676 573	ALENA
436 421	763 123	1 886 208	2 586 923	3 149 436	3 490 568	2 611 368	3 236 900	OEA
423	1 043	1 528	2 009	2 551	2 746	2 369	2 278	OECO
								ASIE
61 826	153 257	452 727	1 087 891	1 572 727	1 926 877	1 617 514	2 193 138	ACAP
65 641	162 340	380 151	602 712	776 593	946 273	727 929	951 848	ANASE
27 528	48 945	93 678	215 964	304 589	372 605	282 295	341 639	ECO
51 991	47 366	85 283	188 187	311 912	405 371	338 800	359 765	CCG
26 113	39 038	80 864	196 806	298 734	409 444	329 953	419 680	SAARC
								EUROPE
54 281	98 592	119 470	186 611	248 248	279 975	228 274	257 171	AELE
943 874	1 606 837	2 508 665	4 131 559	5 515 271	6 167 329	4 632 700	5 253 044	UE
713 349	1 250 184	1 900 613	3 103 428	4 123 476	4 634 755	3 513 394	3 949 383	Zone euro
								OCÉANIE
1 900	2 059	2 186	3 669	5 267	6 461	5 193	5 843	MSG
								INTERRÉGIONAUX
91 643	76 981	113 895	219 353	313 711	375 958	316 479	370 446	ACP
669 769	1 404 563	3 341 768	5 149 966	6 506 342	7 455 688	5 765 142	7 410 248	CEAP
41 951	57 057	175 171	417 307	677 175	872 031	581 806	711 469	CEMN
–	–	85 314	226 204	396 295	523 304	347 535	427 536	CEI

Sources :
- Les données dans ce tableau ont été calculées d'après les chiffres du tableau 1.1.1.

1.1.3 Exports and imports of trade groups
Share

Trade group	Exports (f.o.b) - Exportations (f.a.b.) Percentage										
	1980	1990	1995	2000	2004	2005	2006	2007	2008	2009	2010
AFRICA											
CEMAC	0.23	0.16	0.12	0.13	0.18	0.22	0.22	0.21	0.26	0.21	0.22
CEPGL	0.12	0.07	0.03	0.01	0.02	0.02	0.02	0.02	0.03	0.03	0.04
COMESA	1.68	0.74	0.46	0.46	0.51	0.61	0.65	0.66	0.79	0.74	0.76
EAC	0.11	0.05	0.06	0.05	0.06	0.06	0.06	0.06	0.07	0.08	0.08
ECCAS	0.44	0.34	0.22	0.27	0.35	0.47	0.50	0.66	0.70	0.50	0.99
ECOWAS	1.64	0.62	0.43	0.47	0.50	0.68	0.63	0.62	0.66	0.63	0.66
MRU	0.21	0.14	0.10	0.08	0.09	0.08	0.08	0.07	0.08	0.10	0.08
SADC	1.81	1.11	0.88	0.01	0.88	0.97	1.01	1.06	1.10	1.07	1.13
UMA	2.00	0.99	0.61	0.75	0.79	0.95	0.99	0.97	1.13	0.90	0.92
WAEMU	0.24	0.15	0.13	0.10	0.13	0.12	0.12	0.11	0.12	0.15	0.13
AMERICA											
ANCOM	0.55	0.39	0.41	0.41	0.42	0.49	0.53	0.54	0.59	0.63	0.65
CACM	0.24	0.13	0.18	0.24	0.22	0.21	0.20	0.19	0.18	0.21	0.20
CARICOM	0.57	0.14	0.11	0.13	0.12	0.14	0.17	0.14	0.16	0.12	0.11
FTAA	19.35	18.92	19.36	22.00	17.38	17.50	17.39	16.74	16.41	16.43	16.68
LAIA	4.34	3.78	4.01	5.14	4.77	5.04	5.22	5.09	5.16	5.10	5.39
MERCOSUR	1.45	1.33	1.36	1.31	1.48	1.56	1.57	1.60	1.73	1.74	1.86
NAFTA	15.29	16.15	16.54	18.99	14.28	14.11	13.84	13.23	12.68	12.81	12.93
OAS	19.58	19.03	19.36	21.97	17.35	17.47	17.37	16.73	16.40	16.41	16.67
OECS	0.01	0.01	0.01	0.00	0.00	0.00	0.00	0.00	0.00	0.00	0.00
ASIA											
APTA	2.26	4.27	6.03	7.38	10.21	11.07	11.84	12.58	12.84	14.00	15.13
ASEAN	3.63	4.17	6.25	6.70	6.19	6.22	6.35	6.19	6.19	6.50	6.93
ECO	0.91	1.09	1.17	1.28	1.69	1.84	2.03	2.16	2.45	2.26	2.25
GCC	7.62	2.52	2.04	2.72	3.10	3.78	3.96	3.95	4.65	4.19	4.10
SAARC	0.68	0.80	0.90	1.00	1.15	1.27	1.31	1.36	1.49	1.65	1.80
EUROPE											
EFTA	2.41	2.86	2.42	2.21	2.26	2.27	2.25	2.24	2.35	2.38	2.18
EU	41.47	44.52	42.27	37.96	40.87	38.72	37.83	38.15	36.59	36.58	33.93
Euro area	30.80	35.16	33.70	29.71	32.24	30.27	29.28	29.92	28.61	28.68	26.39
OCEANIA											
MSG	0.07	0.05	0.07	0.04	0.04	0.04	0.04	0.04	0.04	0.04	0.04
INTERREGIONAL											
ACP	4.82	2.33	1.80	1.79	1.92	2.25	2.27	2.29	2.52	2.31	2.39
APEC	30.82	38.29	45.46	48.31	44.18	44.66	45.03	44.47	43.88	45.05	47.66
BSEC	1.46	0.92	2.78	2.76	3.64	4.00	4.23	4.43	5.06	4.44	4.61
CIS	–	–	2.20	2.25	2.89	3.27	3.55	3.71	4.35	3.60	3.85

Sources:
- Data in this table are based on trade figures in table 1.1.1.

Imports (c.i.f.) - Importations (c.a.f.) En pourcentage											Groupements commerciaux
1980	1990	1995	2000	2004	2005	2006	2007	2008	2009	2010	
											AFRIQUE
0.15	0.10	0.07	0.06	0.07	0.07	0.08	0.10	0.10	0.14	0.12	CEMAC
0.09	0.06	0.03	0.02	0.03	0.03	0.03	0.03	0.04	0.04	0.04	CEPGL
1.13	0.78	0.63	0.53	0.53	0.63	0.60	0.63	0.79	0.97	0.93	COMESA
0.20	0.12	0.12	0.10	0.10	0.11	0.12	0.13	0.15	0.18	0.17	CAE
0.30	0.21	0.12	0.12	0.16	0.18	0.10	0.22	0.27	0.36	0.33	CEEAC
1.23	0.39	0.37	0.31	0.35	0.41	0.42	0.48	0.50	0.53	0.51	CEDEAO
0.20	0.09	0.08	0.06	0.06	0.07	0.06	0.06	0.06	0.07	0.06	UFM
1.51	0.55	0.51	0.73	0.80	0.85	0.87	0.80	0.88	1.09	1.10	SADC
1.22	0.77	0.64	0.51	0.62	0.62	0.58	0.65	0.78	0.90	0.82	UMA
0.31	0.16	0.14	0.11	0.13	0.14	0.13	0.14	0.16	0.17	0.15	UEMOA
											AMÉRIQUE
0.49	0.30	0.52	0.37	0.39	0.43	0.46	0.50	0.57	0.59	0.63	ANCOM
0.29	0.18	0.26	0.33	0.34	0.33	0.33	0.33	0.33	0.32	0.32	MCAC
0.69	0.20	0.19	0.21	0.18	0.19	0.19	0.18	0.19	0.19	0.16	CARICOM
20.74	21.11	22.55	28.30	23.66	23.94	23.39	22.08	21.17	20.59	21.06	ZLEA
4.53	2.94	4.08	5.06	4.06	4.23	4.42	4.59	4.88	4.72	5.13	ALADI
1.82	0.82	1.53	1.34	1.00	1.05	1.13	1.28	1.57	1.47	1.74	MERCOSUR
16.44	19.06	19.38	25.32	21.20	21.28	20.57	18.99	17.69	17.22	17.43	ALENA
21.00	21.27	22.57	28.31	23.66	23.95	23.41	22.10	21.20	20.61	21.08	OEA
0.02	0.03	0.02	0.02	0.02	0.02	0.02	0.02	0.02	0.02	0.01	OECO
											ASIE
2.98	4.27	6.00	6.79	9.55	10.07	10.57	11.03	11.70	12.77	14.28	ACAP
3.16	4.52	6.79	5.71	5.42	5.58	5.57	5.45	5.75	5.75	6.20	ANASE
1.32	1.36	1.34	1.41	1.89	2.00	2.04	2.14	2.26	2.23	2.23	ECO
2.50	1.32	1.30	1.28	1.69	1.74	1.81	2.19	2.46	2.67	2.34	CCG
1.26	1.09	1.15	1.21	1.51	1.82	1.95	2.10	2.49	2.60	2.73	SAARC
											EUROPE
2.61	2.75	2.19	1.79	1.77	1.73	1.71	1.74	1.70	1.80	1.68	AELE
45.42	44.78	40.59	37.65	39.52	38.25	38.30	38.70	37.46	36.56	34.21	UE
34.33	34.84	31.60	28.53	29.78	28.74	28.46	28.93	28.15	27.73	25.72	Zone euro
											OCÉANIE
0.09	0.06	0.05	0.03	0.04	0.03	0.04	0.04	0.04	0.04	0.04	MSG
											INTERRÉGIONAUX
4.41	2.15	1.91	1.71	1.87	2.03	2.12	2.20	2.28	2.50	2.41	ACP
32.23	39.15	46.52	50.15	47.16	47.68	47.26	45.65	45.28	45.50	48.26	CEAP
2.02	1.59	3.16	2.63	3.63	3.86	4.21	4.75	5.30	4.59	4.63	CEMN
–	–	1.94	1.28	1.92	2.09	2.37	2.78	3.18	2.74	2.78	CEI

Sources :
- Les données dans ce tableau ont été calculées d'après les chiffres du tableau 1.1.1.

Region, country or territory	Exports (f.o.b) - Exportations (f.a.b.) Percentage										
	80-00	90-00	00-10	05-08	05-09	05-10	2005	2007	2008	2009	2010
WORLD	7.1	6.8	10.9	15.4	6.6	6.1	14.2	15.4	15.2	-22.4	21.3
DEVELOPING ECONOMIES	7.7	9.1	14.3	18.1	9.1	9.0	22.2	16.2	19.3	-20.9	27.4
TRANSITION ECONOMIES	1.4	6.7	18.3	26.2	10.9	9.3	28.6	20.8	34.3	-35.2	29.0
DEVELOPED ECONOMIES	7.2	5.9	8.5	13.0	4.7	4.0	9.2	14.5	11.3	-22.4	16.5
Developing economies: Africa	1.9	3.3	16.2	21.0	8.9	7.8	36.4	16.6	31.1	-31.0	25.4
Eastern Africa	3.3	4.9	13.2	18.7	12.3	12.0	13.2	17.2	15.2	-8.7	23.9
Burundi*(1)	-2.1	-4.3	7.9	-0.3	1.3	8.9	19.2	6.9	-13.3	14.6	62.0
Comoros*	-3.1	-10.9	(e)-5.9	-14.4	-4.7	(e)0.0	-35.5	32.5	-52.8	83.2	(e)8.0
Djibouti (2)	4.2	7.1	(e)10.3	18.6	16.8	(e)12.2	4.0	3.7	18.5	12.4	(e)-9.1
Eritrea	–	–	(e)-6.7	(e)0.4	(e)-1.7	(e)-0.7	0.1	7.7	(e)-15.3	(e)-2.7	(e)10.1
Ethiopia	..	..	19.2	20.5	18.7	21.0	36.5	22.5	25.4	1.0	59.4
Kenya	3.8	6.3	12.2	15.1	10.3	9.6	22.7	18.7	21.9	-10.2	15.4
Madagascar*	3.8	9.2	4.8	26.6	11.0	5.1	-13.9	33.2	24.1	-34.3	-1.3
Malawi	3.4	0.9	12.2	21.1	21.9	16.9	5.1	30.4	1.2	35.1	-10.2
Mauritius	9.7	4.3	2.9	2.9	-1.7	-0.7	7.3	-3.9	6.5	-18.5	15.3
Mayotte	..	..	-	6.3	1.5	-	31.3	5.6	-0.9	-12.4	-
Mozambique	2.7	10.3	19.1	13.5	5.4	3.0	16.1	1.3	10.0	-19.1	4.5
Rwanda	-5.2	-3.8	18.3	28.0	15.8	17.2	27.1	20.0	51.4	-28.0	54.3
Seychelles	12.6	15.5	8.3	6.8	4.4	3.2	16.8	-5.2	19.5	-8.1	1.2
Somalia	(e)3.8	(e)6.5	(e)7.7	(e)18.6	(e)15.2	(e)13.0	(e)35.7	(e)21.4	(e)19.9	(e)1.7	(e)6.6
Uganda	1.9	15.3	21.7	31.4	25.6	18.8	33.8	49.6	24.3	5.4	-7.0
United Republic of Tanzania	3.3	7.8	18.2	21.1	17.4	18.8	14.1	15.5	37.0	-1.9	35.8
Zambia (3)	0.3	-0.8	25.9	39.2	22.6	23.6	14.9	22.5	10.4	-15.4	67.0
Zimbabwe	3.0	3.4	(e)4.5	7.3	5.2	(e)5.3	-2.0	20.0	-8.3	3.1	(e)10.2
Middle Africa	3.4	3.4	23.1	32.8	14.7	11.4	54.9	25.7	55.1	-40.5	26.1
Angola*(4)	6.6	6.1	27.6	43.7	20.4	14.8	78.9	39.8	66.1	-44.5	22.9
Cameroon*(5)	3.7	-1.3	9.8	13.1	5.3	4.4	15.5	0.9	19.3	-21.6	15.1
Central African Republic*(5)	3.4	3.6	(e)-0.4	6.0	(e)-1.3	(e)-1.5	-3.7	13.1	-15.7	(e)-17.6	(e)12.2
Chad*(4)	7.1	0.3	(e)42.2	11.1	-1.0	(e)-0.4	43.0	9.4	18.0	-39.1	(e)29.4
Congo*(5)	3.7	7.5	(e)15.9	17.5	8.6	(e)9.4	38.2	-7.3	47.7	-26.4	(e)33.8
Dem. Rep. of the Congo*	-3.2	-6.1	(e)20.9	21.5	13.2	(e)15.9	25.3	14.6	41.9	-20.5	(e)54.3
Equatorial Guinea (4)	23.6	41.2	(e)27.5	27.9	11.7	(e)7.1	53.6	24.4	46.2	-39.0	(e)9.4
Gabon*(6)	1.9	1.6	(e)14.4	22.6	6.9	(e)8.6	35.9	15.8	50.7	-43.7	(e)56.3
Sao Tome and Principe*	-6.1	-6.2	11.0	12.8	7.0	0.9	25.9	-12.6	58.0	-23.7	-21.4
Northern Africa	0.8	2.9	16.4	23.3	9.4	7.5	36.6	15.6	37.2	-35.2	23.0
Algeria*	0.3	3.0	14.4	18.9	3.4	2.3	43.4	10.2	31.8	-43.0	26.2
Egypt	0.5	3.8	23.5	33.3	24.5	20.7	38.6	18.3	62.0	-12.1	14.6
Libyan Arab Jamahiriya	-2.7	-2.3	19.4	24.3	8.4	6.4	51.6	10.7	41.8	-40.0	25.0
Morocco*	7.5	7.8	10.9	21.9	9.7	8.4	12.7	20.4	32.6	-30.9	24.9
Sudan (7)	2.1	14.0	(e)23.5	36.4	18.5	(e)15.8	27.7	57.0	31.4	-32.9	(e)34.0
Tunisia (8)	7.1	6.0	12.4	23.3	12.1	9.3	8.4	29.7	27.4	-25.2	13.7
Southern Africa	3.1	3.3	11.8	14.3	5.5	6.1	15.9	15.5	11.1	-22.3	28.6
Botswana*	9.5	5.0	7.1	4.8	-4.0	-1.6	26.0	14.3	-4.3	-30.2	35.8
Lesotho	11.5	12.4	13.5	11.1	4.8	3.9	-8.1	10.8	16.1	-18.8	10.3
Namibia	2.0	0.9	14.5	15.0	10.5	12.1	13.3	10.3	9.2	-2.7	32.6
South Africa	(b)2.7	3.1	12.2	15.3	6.2	6.7	16.6	16.1	12.7	-22.7	28.8
Swaziland	7.6	6.0	5.0	-0.4	-4.1	-3.8	-9.2	4.4	-8.4	-14.6	5.6
Western Africa	1.2	3.5	16.7	14.1	5.5	5.9	55.2	12.1	23.5	-25.4	26.3
Benin*	14.1	3.3	15.5	31.5	22.8	19.1	1.7	42.3	22.5	-4.5	13.4
Burkina Faso	7.2	12.6	19.3	13.2	15.9	20.2	-2.4	5.9	11.3	29.9	43.0
Cape Verde (9)	6.8	11.0	16.4	19.0	20.2	21.4	16.0	-6.7	66.4	10.1	26.4
Côte d'Ivoire*	2.6	5.4	(e)11.6	9.7	9.6	(e)7.2	11.2	2.3	19.9	5.8	(e)-6.1
Gambia (10)	-5.3	-12.5	(e)2.7	18.5	(e)15.4	(e)12.2	-20.2	9.2	9.2	(e)9.7	(e)0.0
Ghana	3.9	9.0	17.2	22.7	19.9	21.3	14.4	16.0	22.0	10.8	36.3
Guinea*	2.7	0.6	8.5	16.6	7.2	8.7	11.4	16.5	11.5	-21.8	40.1
Guinea-Bissau	8.5	13.6	(e)9.0	15.6	12.3	(e)9.4	18.1	44.4	19.8	-5.2	(e)-1.0
Liberia*	(e)0.4	(e)-8.8	(e)0.5	21.3	7.9	(e)7.0	26.5	22.0	25.1	-33.6	(e)28.9
Mali*	8.1	6.1	13.7	21.4	13.4	10.8	12.7	0.4	34.8	-15.4	10.4
Mauritania*	2.9	-2.0	23.6	37.9	20.2	19.3	42.2	2.5	29.2	-24.7	49.8
Niger*	-1.4	0.0	16.4	23.8	22.3	19.1	11.9	30.6	37.5	9.3	4.3
Nigeria	0.4	3.2	18.4	13.5	2.6	3.5	77.0	13.4	23.8	-34.3	33.2
Saint Helena	(e)14.4	(e)2.6	(e)11.6	(e)15.3	(e)11.4	(e)7.3	(e)4.1	(e)10.7	(e)38.1	(e)-10.9	(e)-8.0
Senegal (11)	3.6	4.0	9.3	11.3	8.8	7.9	4.4	6.2	33.5	-8.6	7.1
Sierra Leone*	-12.8	-29.5	32.7	10.3	4.8	10.1	14.4	5.8	-11.8	-3.6	63.7
Togo*	3.8	6.7	(e)10.1	9.2	9.8	(e)8.3	9.6	11.1	21.8	5.9	(e)-1.1

For sources and notes, see end of table.

1.2.1 Taux d'évolution annuels moyens des exportations et importations des pays et des régions géographiques

				Imports (c.i.f.) - Importations (c.a.f.) En pourcentage							Régions, pays ou territoires
80-00	90-00	00-10	05-08	05-09	05-10	2005	2007	2008	2009	2010	
7.0	6.7	10.6	15.1	6.2	5.8	13.8	15.2	15.5	-23.0	21.2	**MONDE**
8.1	8.7	14.1	18.8	10.3	10.4	17.7	18.4	21.6	-18.8	28.5	ÉCONOMIES EN DÉVELOPPEMENT
0.9	3.7	19.4	31.3	14.8	11.2	21.7	34.6	30.5	-32.9	19.8	ÉCONOMIES EN TRANSITION
6.9	6.2	8.5	12.5	3.7	3.0	11.7	12.8	11.6	-24.9	16.7	ÉCONOMIES DÉVELOPPÉES
2.2	4.5	16.5	22.5	15.2	13.2	22.6	23.8	27.8	-12.1	15.6	*Économies en développement : Afrique*
4.0	*4.4*	*15.9*	*22.6*	*15.8*	*13.8*	*22.2*	*19.3*	*31.8*	*-11.0*	*15.6*	*Afrique orientale*
-1.3	-6.9	15.8	9.7	7.8	9.7	51.6	-25.9	26.1	0.0	26.6	Burundi*(1)
3.0	-1.7	(e)17.2	21.1	16.2	(e)13.9	15.3	20.0	27.2	-3.6	(e)9.1	Comores*
-0.8	-1.3	(e)11.2	28.7	16.3	(e)9.3	6.1	41.0	21.3	-21.5	(e)-7.5	Djibouti (2)
_	_	(e)3.6	(e)6.3	(e)5.5	(e)6.9	(e)3.1	(e)3.0	(e)17.9	(e)-2.3	(e)17.5	Érythrée
_	_	23.6	26.7	20.2	18.7	42.5	11.5	49.4	-8.1	21.5	Éthiopie
3.6	6.0	17.1	21.8	15.4	14.0	35.1	23.0	23.2	-7.8	18.5	Kenya
3.3	6.3	15.2	32.4	22.6	13.0	2.1	38.9	57.5	-18.0	-19.4	Madagascar*
4.2	-0.6	16.6	22.7	18.6	15.8	24.8	14.1	59.7	-8.3	7.5	Malawi
9.6	4.1	9.1	13.1	6.0	5.6	13.9	7.4	19.5	-19.8	18.1	Maurice
..	..	-	26.2	15.9	-	9.9	36.8	21.4	-17.2	-	Mayotte
2.1	1.2	14.6	17.2	13.1	9.1	18.4	6.3	31.4	-6.1	-5.3	Mozambique
-1.1	-1.6	23.4	34.4	31.4	27.1	66.1	24.7	59.2	11.5	9.4	Rwanda
8.8	9.6	11.6	15.7	7.1	6.8	35.9	13.4	22.6	-23.4	22.6	Seychelles
(e)-2.7	(e)26.6	(e)11.6	(e)20.8	(e)12.2	(e)8.4	(e)2.6	(e)11.9	(e)27.5	(e)-17.7	(e)2.6	Somalie
8.5	21.0	15.7	30.8	22.4	18.3	19.4	36.6	29.6	-6.2	9.8	Ouganda
3.0	0.1	19.9	28.8	19.9	17.8	20.6	25.7	32.7	-11.1	22.3	République-Unie de Tanzanie
0.2	-0.3	20.8	26.0	13.7	13.8	18.9	30.3	26.3	-25.1	40.3	Zambie (3)
4.7	2.3	(e)7.5	8.2	6.9	(e)9.3	6.6	10.9	15.7	-1.7	(e)27.6	Zimbabwe
1.5	*3.1*	*21.9*	*31.3*	*26.2*	*22.4*	*28.2*	*38.9*	*37.5*	*4.1*	*10.4*	*Afrique centrale*
4.0	7.8	26.4	37.8	33.2	28.4	43.2	55.6	53.6	8.0	10.0	Angola*(4)
-0.2	2.0	13.9	26.2	15.5	13.2	13.7	33.3	28.6	-20.4	19.4	Cameroun*(5)
2.0	0.2	(e)13.1	20.5	(e)13.8	13.9	22.9	20.7	(e)-9.8	(e)25.9	République centrafricaine*(5)
9.0	-1.3	(e)17.4	26.9	23.4	(e)20.4	-0.5	33.2	6.1	20.1	(e)9.5	Tchad*(4)
1.0	2.9	(e)22.4	30.9	22.3	(e)16.6	34.5	25.8	20.6	-2.3	(e)0.2	Congo*(5)
-3.7	-5.7	(e)21.8	17.0	11.5	(e)10.9	31.1	17.6	26.5	-11.6	(e)18.4	Rép. dém. du Congo*
16.5	29.7	(e)29.5	41.4	40.2	(e)34.9	20.0	36.6	35.7	39.0	(e)9.1	Guinée équatoriale (4)
1.3	2.2	(e)11.9	21.2	15.8	(e)11.9	9.2	25.1	20.1	-3.5	(e)-0.4	Gabon*(6)
4.3	0.7	17.3	20.7	21.4	17.2	20.3	11.0	44.2	-9.4	8.0	Sao Tomé-et-Principe*
2.0	*4.3*	*16.8*	*26.2*	*19.8*	*16.8*	*23.5*	*28.1*	*44.5*	*-9.3*	*11.4*	*Afrique septentrionale*
-0.8	0.8	17.9	25.1	21.2	17.6	11.2	28.8	42.9	-0.5	4.4	Algérie*
2.4	7.7	17.9	34.6	28.3	25.0	54.4	30.6	80.2	-7.8	17.7	Égypte
-1.6	-1.6	20.8	21.3	21.2	20.5	28.1	26.0	51.8	7.4	16.4	Jamahiriya arabe libyenne
6.3	5.5	15.4	27.4	16.0	11.8	16.7	33.5	32.4	-22.4	8.0	Maroc*
(e)1.0	9.8	(e)22.1	11.2	9.1	(e)7.6	65.8	8.7	6.6	3.6	(e)2.8	Soudan (7)
6.3	5.2	11.2	23.5	13.3	10.8	2.8	27.0	28.9	-21.9	15.5	Tunisie (8)
3.8	*5.6*	*14.3*	*14.3*	*6.0*	*6.3*	*14.5*	*12.6*	*8.2*	*-19.1*	*25.3*	*Afrique australe*
7.0	1.9	11.6	18.6	13.7	13.2	-0.1	31.8	28.1	-9.3	19.6	Botswana*
5.6	2.0	12.0	13.3	10.3	9.7	-2.8	16.3	16.8	-2.7	11.4	Lesotho
3.3	3.9	(e)15.4	19.3	18.8	(e)17.9	7.6	22.0	23.3	14.7	(e)13.4	Namibie
(e,b)3.6	(e)6.2	(e)14.6	(e)14.4	(e)5.2	(e)5.5	(e)16.6	(e)11.8	(e)6.8	(e)-21.8	(e)27.2	Afrique du Sud
5.1	5.1	5.8	-3.4	-4.3	-3.2	-1.4	-4.5	-6.7	-5.8	4.9	Swaziland
0.1	*3.8*	*17.2*	*23.5*	*13.5*	*11.3*	*34.0*	*31.5*	*19.3*	*-18.3*	*16.7*	*Afrique occidentale*
4.0	9.7	(e)16.2	34.1	22.6	(e)16.8	13.7	65.8	12.4	-9.8	(e)4.7	Bénin*
4.0	3.6	14.5	20.0	12.7	10.2	-1.5	11.7	31.7	-15.4	9.5	Burkina Faso
7.9	6.0	15.0	24.9	14.9	10.6	1.4	38.1	10.1	-14.1	4.7	Cap-Vert (9)
1.5	3.5	(e)13.7	10.8	6.7	(e)4.4	24.4	14.8	18.0	-11.7	(e)-0.9	Côte d'Ivoire*
4.3	0.2	8.4	9.0	5.5	2.3	13.4	23.8	0.4	-5.5	-9.5	Gambie (10)
7.1	9.1	16.3	23.8	13.2	13.2	31.2	19.4	27.4	-21.6	35.7	Ghana
4.8	-3.0	9.6	19.4	9.1	9.3	5.1	27.4	12.2	-22.4	32.5	Guinée*
2.4	-4.1	(e)17.5	23.5	19.0	(e)14.4	28.3	32.2	18.4	3.8	(e)-2.9	Guinée-Bissau
(e)1.8	(e)11.1	(e)10.4	35.2	18.6	(e)13.8	9.9	13.5	60.3	-33.7	(e)15.5	Libéria*
5.2	4.7	(e)14.6	28.4	16.4	(e)12.9	13.1	20.1	52.8	-27.2	(e)14.4	Mali*
3.9	3.1	18.0	12.5	5.4	5.4	53.4	23.6	36.3	-27.5	27.9	Mauritanie*
-0.2	0.8	(e)21.2	18.9	26.4	(e)24.7	25.8	21.0	37.1	50.2	(e)1.5	Niger*
-2.5	3.1	20.3	27.1	14.9	12.3	50.5	40.4	12.8	-20.0	20.2	Nigéria
(e)5.9	(e)8.8	(e)7.1	(e)1.7	(e)-7.2	(e)-5.9	(e)40.8	(e)32.7	(e)-49.4	(e)-12.6	(e)22.7	Sainte-Hélène
2.3	3.9	14.4	24.0	12.4	7.7	23.2	32.7	34.0	-27.8	1.5	Sénégal (11)
-4.4	-4.2	15.2	15.6	12.1	15.7	20.5	14.7	19.5	-2.3	48.4	Sierra Leone*
2.2	5.5	(e)12.4	12.8	11.0	(e)8.8	19.5	14.1	22.0	-0.1	(e)-0.9	Togo*

Pour les sources et les notes, se reporter à la fin du tableau.

Region, country or territory	Exports (f.o.b) - Exportations (f.a.b.) Percentage										
	80-00	90-00	00-10	05-08	05-09	05-10	2005	2007	2008	2009	2010
Developing economies: America	6.4	10.7	11.1	15.6	6.4	6.6	20.3	12.0	16.8	-23.7	26.8
Caribbean	-2.1	6.9	6.2	13.4	0.0	-2.5	23.3	1.0	20.6	-40.1	7.4
Anguilla	-	(e)26.6	18.5	-10.4	8.2	3.4	149.2	-25.0	24.6	101.0	-46.1
Antigua and Barbuda	5.5	2.8	-6.1	-12.2	-17.8	-17.2	44.8	-19.8	-2.9	-38.8	-1.4
Aruba (12)	(e)35.0	16.8	-8.5	-1.2	-16.2	-35.5	27.3	-26.6	37.7	-61.3	-81.5
Bahamas (13)	-17.3	8.5	6.6	19.6	8.6	4.2	15.1	14.0	19.2	-25.6	-1.2
Barbados	-0.2	3.9	7.3	10.7	2.1	1.2	29.2	11.0	-0.4	-22.4	13.3
Cayman Islands	..	..	(e)-20.5	-31.2	-23.9	-20.5	..	3.8	-37.0	11.8	-15.8
Cuba	-9.1	-1.7	(e)11.2	21.0	5.1	(e)7.7	-8.8	58.8	8.2	21.0	(e)22.2
Dominica'	0.1	0.0	-0.2	-2.2	-0.2	-0.0	0.1	-11.0	5.0	0.4	5.1
Dominican Republic (14)	11.7	26.6	2.1	3.7	-2.1	-0.8	3.5	8.3	-5.8	-18.7	20.3
Grenada*	2.5	6.3	-5.4	5.9	3.0	-1.0	-12.4	31.7	-8.6	-4.4	-17.2
Haiti	0.4	12.2	8.2	1.2	3.8	4.1	20.2	5.6	-8.1	20.1	0.5
Jamaica	3.0	2.1	4.0	17.7	0.0	4.4	7.0	10.7	0.7	10.0	0.0
Montserrat*	-0.5	0.3	8.2	46.7	30.9	4.9	-66.0	106.0	50.3	-22.5	-65.1
Netherlands Antilles*(15)	-5.4	-0.4	-9.4	18.8	10.8	7.0	16.6	-2.6	60.9	-25.6	0.1
Saint Kitts and Nevis*	2.0	2.9	4.2	12.5	7.3	5.5	-14.8	-1.8	31.2	-16.0	4.7
Saint Lucia*	0.8	-11.1	15.6	34.2	27.4	21.4	-19.5	13.7	53.9	-0.8	1.2
Saint Vincent and the Grenadines*	2.5	-4.9	0.7	10.9	7.6	3.0	8.9	25.2	9.4	-6.0	-15.4
Trinidad and Tobago*	-0.1	6.8	14.4	20.1	1.0	-2.4	52.5	-5.4	39.2	-51.1	11.6
Turks and Caicos Islands	-	-	-	16.0	10.8	-	20.5	-7.7	52.4	-16.2	-
Central America	10.5	16.0	7.1	10.7	3.2	4.4	12.7	8.9	7.4	-20.5	28.2
Belize	4.3	5.0	4.3	10.0	2.4	3.2	-2.3	-4.6	14.2	-22.8	24.9
Costa Rica*	11.2	17.0	7.0	11.2	6.0	4.7	11.5	14.1	2.1	-9.0	7.3
El Salvador	7.0	19.7	4.8	9.7	4.2	4.6	3.4	7.5	14.2	-16.5	18.5
Guatemala (16)	4.5	10.2	12.4	13.1	8.7	8.7	6.8	14.7	12.2	-6.8	17.4
Honduras (17)	8.2	15.3	6.2	7.3	0.7	1.3	11.3	9.6	7.2	-22.2	19.0
Mexico	11.0	16.1	7.0	10.7	3.0	4.3	13.1	8.6	7.3	-21.3	29.8
Nicaragua	1.7	10.3	12.9	19.8	14.3	15.2	13.5	16.2	24.7	-6.4	32.5
Panama*	_	9.4	1.7	6.9	-0.1	-3.8	7.9	6.4	7.2	-24.0	-12.2
South America	5.5	7.2	14.9	19.3	9.1	8.7	26.4	15.1	23.0	-24.4	27.1
Argentina*	7.6	10.1	11.9	20.4	11.3	10.3	16.7	19.8	26.5	-20.6	22.2
Bolivia (Plurinational State of)	2.3	4.3	21.2	34.0	18.9	15.8	30.1	15.1	58.3	-30.3	25.7
Brazil	5.4	5.9	15.5	18.4	9.1	9.5	22.6	16.6	23.2	-22.7	32.0
Chile*	10.0	9.4	17.1	17.0	6.0	6.4	26.9	15.3	-1.8	-21.8	32.8
Colombia	8.1	7.4	14.7	21.9	14.2	13.0	30.3	22.1	28.5	-14.3	21.1
Ecuador	4.3	6.8	16.4	21.5	10.8	9.8	30.3	8.8	35.8	-26.3	25.6
Falkland Islands (Malvinas)	(e)14.6	(e)27.5	(e)7.7	(e)5.9	(e)-1.0	(e)0.2	(e)19.7	(e)14.6	(e)8.9	(e)-26.4	(e)23.7
Guyana*	4.7	8.7	6.1	13.1	9.9	9.7	-6.8	15.4	17.1	-4.0	15.0
Paraguay	7.7	1.7	19.1	40.5	24.4	22.6	6.5	52.8	58.4	-29.0	43.2
Peru*	4.2	9.0	20.6	21.5	12.2	12.3	35.6	17.0	13.1	-14.7	32.3
Suriname	-0.1	0.4	19.0	20.0	11.2	13.1	23.5	15.7	28.3	-20.1	45.4
Uruguay	5.5	5.2	14.3	22.5	15.2	14.4	16.2	13.5	43.2	-15.6	23.8
Venezuela (Bolivarian Rep. of)	2.3	6.3	12.2	18.0	4.5	2.2	40.5	5.2	37.9	-39.5	14.2
Developing economies: Asia	9.0	9.5	14.8	18.3	9.6	9.6	21.2	17.0	18.5	-19.2	27.7
Eastern Asia	13.1	10.0	15.3	17.3	9.5	10.0	19.7	18.8	13.2	-15.5	29.9
China	14.7	14.5	22.4	23.5	13.9	13.5	28.4	25.6	17.3	-15.9	31.3
China, Hong Kong SAR	14.5	8.3	7.8	7.9	3.3	4.6	11.6	8.7	5.3	-12.2	22.5
China, Macao SAR	7.2	3.9	-8.2	-6.3	-19.3	-21.4	-11.9	-0.6	-21.4	-51.9	-9.5
China, Taiwan Province of	10.8	7.2	8.0	9.0	1.9	4.1	13.7	10.2	3.5	-20.1	34.8
Korea, Dem. People's Rep. of	(e)-9.2	-9.2	(e)13.5	15.4	12.1	(e)15.9	4.7	15.0	22.3	-3.2	(e)50.4
Korea, Republic of (18)	12.2	10.1	12.4	14.1	7.7	8.7	12.0	14.1	13.6	-14.3	29.0
Mongolia	-1.7	0.7	21.2	32.4	18.0	18.5	22.4	22.4	34.4	-25.1	52.4
Southern Asia	6.4	6.5	17.4	22.7	13.0	12.8	26.2	18.1	27.0	-19.5	30.8
Afghanistan	-9.8	-2.0	20.1	13.0	3.9	0.3	25.9	21.8	8.7	-25.3	-3.7
Bangladesh	12.5	15.7	13.0	16.9	13.1	14.0	11.9	5.5	23.5	-2.0	27.6
Bhutan	11.5	7.0	24.3	29.5	16.6	14.8	41.0	62.6	-22.9	-4.5	29.4
India (19)	9.4	9.5	19.9	24.8	15.9	15.9	30.0	23.1	29.7	-15.2	34.2
Iran (Islamic Rep. of)*	2.4	1.2	17.5	25.3	11.2	9.7	26.7	15.2	28.1	-30.6	28.0
Maldives	13.9	4.4	8.1	24.2	4.9	1.7	-10.7	1.2	45.2	-49.0	18.3
Nepal	10.7	13.1	2.5	2.9	0.2	-0.4	11.8	3.6	8.1	-12.4	1.4
Pakistan	7.9	4.3	9.6	7.9	3.6	4.9	20.0	5.4	13.9	-13.8	22.2
Sri Lanka	9.6	11.3	5.9	9.0	3.9	4.3	10.2	12.4	5.1	-12.9	17.3
South-Eastern Asia	11.1	11.1	11.2	14.9	7.3	8.0	14.7	12.3	15.4	-18.5	29.3
Brunei Darussalam*	-1.7	2.4	11.2	17.7	6.5	6.1	23.6	0.8	39.8	-32.8	27.2
Cambodia (4)	32.1	26.8	(e)15.0	16.7	10.8	(e)11.4	4.0	10.7	15.2	-8.6	(e)27.9

For sources and notes, see end of table.

30

1.2.1 Taux d'évolution annuels moyens des exportations et importations des pays et des régions géographiques

80-00	90-00	00-10	05-08	05-09	05-10	2005	2007	2008	2009	2010	Régions, pays ou territoires
7.8	12.0	10.6	19.9	9.3	9.0	18.3	19.0	22.2	-25.3	29.2	**Économies en développement : Amérique**
0.2	7.1	7.8	16.4	5.8	3.6	27.3	9.4	24.6	-29.4	10.6	*Caraïbes*
-	(e)13.0	12.4	26.1	7.5	0.6	26.7	10.7	9.6	-37.8	-6.8	Anguilla
7.8	4.4	6.2	11.1	5.2	-0.4	21.2	16.8	2.0	-12.4	-20.0	Antigua-et-Barbuda
(e)18.8	9.4	-1.2	3.0	-10.3	-16.7	15.2	-24.7	47.3	-54.5	-29.7	Aruba (12)
-8.0	7.7	6.0	7.6	1.8	0.8	29.9	4.0	4.1	-16.5	6.1	Bahamas (13)
3.3	7.2	5.0	5.4	-0.3	-1.0	13.6	4.9	9.9	-21.7	6.2	Barbade
..	..	(e)-3.9	-3.7	-5.7	-3.9	..	-1.0	1.9	-16.1	12.2	Îles Caïmanes
-4.8	2.5	(e)12.4	22.1	7.9	(e)5.4	44.1	7.0	41.4	-37.5	(e)17.4	Cuba*
6.5	3.5	7.2	14.6	11.4	8.2	13.9	17.3	26.2	-5.5	-4.2	Dominique*
9.5	12.0	6.7	16.9	7.4	7.0	25.1	11.7	17.6	-23.1	24.4	République dominicaine (14)
7.8	8.7	4.9	4.6	1.4	1.3	30.1	22.2	0.8	-22.4	17.4	Grenade
3.7	14.4	11.2	14.7	11.1	14.7	11.3	-2.4	37.7	-8.3	48.1	Haïti
5.8	7.1	7.7	24.1	7.5	2.5	18.2	27.0	25.5	-40.2	3.2	Jamaïque
3.9	-6.3	(e)4.3	7.4	2.2	(e)0.6	3.6	-1.9	28.5	-22.2	(e)1.0	Montserrat*
-3.6	1.3	(e)0.4	16.3	9.6	(e)6.8	12.3	15.4	20.8	-15.3	(e)3.1	Antilles néerlandaises*(15)
7.8	5.7	4.7	14.9	10.4	3.3	15.2	8.9	19.6	-7.0	-24.5	Saint-Kitts-et-Nevis*
6.6	2.3	7.2	10.7	3.5	2.1	9.6	7.3	3.5	-18.1	7.8	Sainte-Lucie*
6.1	3.8	9.5	16.2	10.2	9.1	6.7	20.4	14.2	-10.6	13.8	Saint-Vincent-et-les Grenadines*
0.0	12.1	10.1	18.9	8.2	3.1	17.2	18.2	25.2	-27.5	-6.8	Trinité-et-Tobago*
-	-	-	24.0	6.1	-	37.7	16.6	1.8	-36.5	-	Îles Turques et Caïques
12.2	14.0	7.2	12.5	3.8	4.4	12.3	11.7	10.7	-24.1	26.9	*Amérique centrale*
6.3	5.9	4.3	11.0	4.6	3.1	14.1	1.2	22.3	-20.1	6.1	Belize
10.9	13.9	9.2	15.8	6.2	5.2	18.7	12.5	18.6	-25.4	18.3	Costa Rica*
9.9	14.0	6.6	13.4	4.1	3.3	5.7	13.7	12.0	-25.6	17.0	El Salvador
7.6	11.6	10.5	11.7	3.9	3.9	10.8	13.9	7.2	-20.7	20.0	Guatemala (16)
8.0	16.8	9.7	17.4	5.9	4.4	12.3	21.7	17.6	-30.2	17.1	Honduras (17)
13.4	14.2	6.8	11.8	3.2	4.1	12.2	10.6	9.6	-24.3	28.6	Mexique
3.1	11.6	10.7	18.7	9.8	9.1	17.3	19.3	21.2	-20.7	23.0	Nicaragua
_	8.7	13.7	30.6	20.6	17.4	16.3	42.2	31.7	-13.8	17.2	Panama*
7.1	11.1	15.0	20.7	13.7	14.0	24.9	29.3	33.3	-25.7	33.9	*Amérique du Sud*
10.3	16.9	14.6	26.5	12.1	12.2	27.8	30.9	28.4	-31.9	44.3	Argentine*
6.8	9.7	13.7	28.8	20.5	17.8	27.0	22.8	47.0	-12.7	16.9	Bolivie (État plurinational de)
7.2	12.6	14.9	32.9	18.9	18.3	16.9	32.1	44.0	-26.7	43.2	Brésil
9.9	10.2	14.9	23.6	9.9	10.0	32.0	22.8	31.3	-33.2	40.0	Chili*
6.9	9.6	15.3	23.3	13.8	12.5	26.6	27.3	18.6	-16.3	23.7	Colombie
5.0	7.7	17.5	21.3	12.8	13.6	25.0	12.0	39.0	-20.0	36.5	Équateur
(e)12.9	(e)8.2	(e)2.8	(e)2.2	(e)-3.7	(e)4.3	(e)-26.7	(e)37.4	(e)-38.0	(e)-7.2	(e)89.4	Îles Falkland (Malvinas)
5.0	7.3	10.7	18.6	12.3	11.7	21.0	19.1	23.9	-11.5	20.6	Guyana*
10.7	7.0	19.9	38.4	23.9	22.7	22.5	23.2	54.2	-23.2	44.7	Paraguay
6.8	12.2	17.4	33.7	19.6	18.1	23.8	33.0	47.1	-27.0	36.6	Pérou*
1.5	0.9	12.6	7.0	7.0	7.1	41.9	3.1	24.9	-0.7	7.9	Suriname
7.9	10.1	14.3	30.9	19.5	17.2	24.6	20.4	56.2	-22.8	24.8	Uruguay
2.3	5.8	14.3	28.3	15.5	9.0	41.2	37.1	7.6	-18.2	-4.9	Venezuela (Rép. bolivarienne du)
9.4	8.4	14.7	18.2	10.1	10.4	17.2	17.7	20.8	-18.1	30.0	**Économies en développement : Asie**
12.7	9.3	14.5	16.1	8.8	10.2	14.6	16.0	15.6	-15.8	35.5	*Asie orientale*
13.0	13.0	20.9	19.8	12.7	14.1	17.6	20.8	18.3	-11.3	39.0	Chine
14.4	8.8	8.3	9.1	4.6	5.9	10.5	9.8	5.7	-10.6	24.7	Chine (RAS de Hong Kong)
7.5	2.2	10.5	11.7	5.1	5.1	12.5	17.5	0.0	-13.9	19.3	Chine (RAS de Macao)
11.8	8.5	8.0	9.5	0.8	3.6	8.6	8.2	9.6	-27.5	44.1	Province chinoise de Taiwan
(e)-7.0	-7.0	(e)7.5	8.8	4.4	(e)2.1	19.3	1.5	17.2	-13.5	(e)-3.1	Corée, Rép. populaire dém. de
11.1	7.1	12.6	18.2	7.9	8.2	16.4	15.3	22.0	-25.8	31.7	Corée, République de (18)
-4.2	0.5	20.5	44.8	22.9	21.1	16.0	42.5	70.8	-41.1	53.8	Mongolie
4.8	5.2	20.2	25.0	15.6	14.6	32.8	22.0	35.8	-18.5	26.8	*Asie méridionale*
-3.2	5.5	11.0	7.2	7.9	13.8	13.5	9.2	7.1	10.5	54.5	Afghanistan
7.3	11.3	13.3	19.4	13.9	14.2	15.4	16.0	28.2	-8.3	27.2	Bangladesh
4.8	7.9	16.2	13.1	9.2	14.4	-6.0	25.3	2.7	-1.9	61.3	Bhoutan
6.9	10.1	24.2	30.7	19.3	17.3	43.2	28.1	40.3	-19.8	27.7	Inde (19)
0.3	-4.8	14.8	12.5	8.4	9.3	13.1	10.2	27.7	-12.1	24.2	Iran (Rép. islamique d')*
15.1	11.8	14.2	22.6	9.7	6.8	16.1	18.3	26.6	-30.3	13.2	Maldives
8.5	10.7	14.0	17.2	18.2	18.3	17.8	25.3	15.0	22.1	16.9	Népal
4.5	3.1	16.8	17.7	8.3	7.2	41.3	9.3	29.9	-25.2	19.4	Pakistan
7.8	8.9	9.2	15.8	5.8	6.7	10.8	10.2	23.5	-28.0	34.5	Sri Lanka
11.0	8.3	11.5	15.9	7.2	7.9	17.3	12.8	21.9	-23.1	30.7	*Asie du Sud-Est*
6.9	1.6	10.6	20.1	15.2	16.7	4.9	25.9	21.1	-3.5	36.9	Brunéi Darussalam*
14.8	25.2	(e)15.3	18.0	11.9	(e)12.1	19.8	14.0	19.7	-9.7	(e)25.9	Cambodge (4)

Pour les sources et les notes, se reporter à la fin du tableau.

Region, country or territory	Exports (f.o.b) - Exportations (f.a.b.) Percentage										
	80-00	90-00	00-10	05-08	05-09	05-10	2005	2007	2008	2009	2010
Indonesia including East Timor	6.3	8.4	–	–	–	–	–	–	–	–	–
Indonesia	–	–	–	17.2	10.0	10.9	20.1	14.7	17.6	-14.3	31.9
Lao People's Dem. Rep.*	16.1	15.4	19.6	23.2	15.1	19.8	52.2	4.6	18.3	-7.9	73.7
Malaysia (20)	12.7	12.2	9.2	13.7	5.0	5.4	12.0	9.6	19.1	-24.9	26.2
Myanmar	7.4	14.4	17.3	23.6	16.8	16.7	60.2	37.8	10.0	-3.2	30.0
Philippines	11.4	18.8	3.4	7.1	-0.4	1.8	0.5	6.0	-2.1	-22.1	34.3
Singapore (21)	12.2	9.9	12.0	13.4	5.6	6.6	15.6	10.1	13.0	-20.2	30.4
Thailand*	15.2	10.5	12.6	16.9	9.9	10.4	14.5	17.6	14.3	-13.6	28.5
Timor-Leste (22)	–	–	–	12.5	4.9	12.4	0.0	-22.2	84.3	-34.2	96.3
Viet Nam	21.0	22.7	19.4	24.3	17.2	16.3	22.5	21.9	29.1	-8.9	25.5
Western Asia	**2.0**	**6.5**	**17.4**	**23.2**	**11.2**	**8.9**	**34.2**	**17.0**	**34.8**	**-28.8**	**17.7**
Bahrain (4)	2.0	3.5	11.7	18.4	6.7	4.7	35.5	11.8	27.0	-31.4	14.9
Iraq*	-8.6	31.1	16.8	38.1	22.0	17.1	28.2	29.4	61.3	-30.5	17.6
Jordan	8.8	8.0	15.0	22.7	13.2	10.4	9.7	10.6	36.0	-16.1	7.5
Kuwait*	-0.1	10.5	16.7	25.5	7.0	6.0	66.0	11.7	20.0	-40.8	77.7
Lebanon (23)	-0.3	4.1	20.6	24.3	17.7	16.1	6.3	27.0	24.6	-6.0	19.9
Occupied Palestinian territory	-	(e)1.1	7.5	20.5	13.8	11.2	7.3	39.9	8.9	-7.2	8.6
Oman	6.7	5.7	14.8	24.8	14.7	14.0	40.1	11.8	56.3	-25.6	30.5
Qatar*	1.9	10.1	23.3	28.8	19.5	20.7	37.5	23.4	32.3	-12.0	49.2
Saudi Arabia*(24)	-0.1	3.1	16.1	19.2	5.4	3.9	43.3	10.5	34.4	-38.7	22.4
Syrian Arab Republic*	4.8	0.9	(e)12.5	17.5	7.0	(e)7.1	22.6	5.7	33.5	-29.6	(e)29.0
Turkey*	10.8	9.1	17.4	22.0	11.5	8.7	16.3	25.4	23.1	-22.6	11.5
United Arab Emirates	5.1	6.5	19.3	26.4	16.0	11.3	29.0	22.7	33.9	-19.7	3.2
Yemen*	–	20.6	9.7	8.9	3.6	6.1	37.7	-5.3	20.4	-17.5	35.8
Developing economies: Oceania	**5.6**	**4.4**	**7.8**	**13.1**	**3.5**	**3.5**	**9.3**	**16.3**	**6.2**	**-25.4**	**23.2**
American Samoa*(25)	4.3	1.4	(e)4.0	(e)13.8	(e)7.5	(e)5.0	-16.1	(e)2.6	(e)26.7	(e)-17.5	(e)2.1
Cook Islands	0.2	0.0	-7.8	-3.2	-10.7	-3.4	-26.7	47.2	-20.1	-33.6	82.0
Fiji	4.5	5.5	3.0	9.6	0.7	-2.2	0.9	9.2	21.7	-31.9	-2.4
French Polynesia*	14.0	9.6	(e)0.1	6.1	-3.1	(e)-4.7	13.5	-17.0	39.5	-38.8	(e)3.3
Guam	3.8	-0.5	0.6	30.4	6.7	-1.6	-1.8	72.4	14.8	-51.4	-9.8
Kiribati	2.7	6.1	(e)20.9	51.9	48.3	(e)33.6	74.5	55.3	53.4	33.3	(e)-25.0
Marshall Islands	–	4.1	(e)7.3	(e)-6.7	(e)-4.4	(e)-3.8	28.2	1.9	(e)-9.1	(e)5.0	(e)-4.8
Micronesia (Federated States of)	–	-8.1	(e)6.0	27.4	(e)20.9	(e)15.9	-7.3	21.5	27.0	(e)-1.1	(e)0.0
Nauru	-6.3	-5.3	(e)7.0	(e)208.5	(e)95.9	(e)68.7	-73.8	(e)328.6	(e)566.7	(e)-79.5	(e)70.7
New Caledonia*	4.1	1.7	11.7	10.1	-1.6	-1.6	5.8	55.7	-38.2	-20.9	23.2
Niue	(e)9.9	9.9	(e)-13.2	-46.0	(e)-58.1	(e)-55.9	14.1	144.8	-99.3	(e)5.4	(e)0.0
Northern Mariana Islands	–	(e)-38.5	-38.6	-69.4	(e)-65.0	-21.2	-36.8	-51.6	-97.9	(e)218.5	
Palau	–	(e)-8.9	-1.2	-7.1	-5.1	-3.6	137.3	-20.4	4.4	0.0	1.7
Papua New Guinea	6.2	3.6	14.0	19.6	9.5	9.5	28.2	12.4	22.0	-22.9	30.3
Samoa (23)	-1.6	12.0	5.5	-1.7	-11.1	-8.9	2.3	49.6	-26.1	-36.1	29.4
Solomon Islands*	4.1	2.3	16.4	27.6	16.0	15.6	6.3	35.5	27.9	-21.6	37.3
Tokelau	..	..	-	-	-	-	(e)36.4	(e)-59.3	-	-	-
Tonga	3.3	-3.8	-2.6	-3.7	-5.2	-4.2	-34.1	-8.7	2.7	-13.1	5.9
Tuvalu	(e)-4.2	-38.2	(e)28.9	(e)37.7	(e)52.4	(e)47.7	-53.1	78.5	(e)64.5	(e)100.0	(e)0.0
Vanuatu	-0.1	4.8	11.4	13.1	10.2	5.5	1.2	2.1	13.6	0.7	-14.4
Wallis and Futuna Islands	..	..	-	-	-	-	(e)-19.1		-	-	-
Transition economies	**1.4**	**6.7**	**18.3**	**26.2**	**10.9**	**9.3**	**28.6**	**20.8**	**34.3**	**-35.2**	**29.0**
Albania	(e)1.0	7.2	20.2	28.0	16.6	16.8	8.8	35.1	25.7	-19.5	42.1
Armenia*	–	–	12.3	5.3	-5.5	-2.6	32.9	21.4	-13.3	-34.0	45.0
Azerbaijan (26)	–	–	38.6	59.2	33.4	25.8	111.6	63.4	43.8	-31.0	25.5
Belarus	–	–	16.4	26.4	11.4	8.4	16.0	23.0	34.2	-34.6	18.7
Bosnia and Herzegovina*(27)	–	–	20.4	27.6	15.2	12.7	25.8	25.4	21.0	-21.4	21.5
Croatia*	–	–	12.5	17.4	6.8	4.8	9.3	19.2	14.1	-25.8	12.7
Georgia (28)	–	–	19.8	20.8	10.2	10.9	33.8	24.9	21.5	-24.3	38.7
Kazakhstan*(28)	–	–	25.3	35.3	15.8	12.9	37.4	24.7	48.9	-40.0	32.5
Kyrgyzstan	–	–	16.8	40.9	29.1	22.2	-6.5	48.3	40.5	-9.8	5.2
Montenegro	–	–	–	–	–	–	–	–	–	-38.8	8.4
Republic of Moldova	–	–	12.6	14.9	7.7	7.4	11.3	27.4	19.2	-19.7	20.1
Russian Federation	–	–	17.7	23.8	9.2	8.2	33.1	16.6	33.1	-35.7	32.0
Serbia and Montenegro*	–	–	–	–	–	–	23.9	33.8			
Serbia	–	–	–	–	–	–	–	–	–	-23.9	17.4
Tajikistan (28)	–	–	7.0	15.2	2.6	1.4	-2.6	5.0	-4.2	-28.2	19.4
TFYR of Macedonia*	–	–	13.4	25.6	11.0	8.7	21.8	37.7	18.7	-31.4	22.3
Turkmenistan (28)	–	–	(e)14.0	31.5	11.5	(e)3.3	27.8	10.7	50.5	-44.7	(e)-9.0
Ukraine (28)	–	–	15.1	25.4	9.0	7.3	4.8	28.5	35.8	-40.6	29.4
Uzbekistan (28)	–	–	18.9	30.7	25.1	21.3	11.0	43.0	28.3	4.2	10.5

For sources and notes, see end of table.

1.2.1 Taux d'évolution annuels moyens des exportations et importations des pays et des régions géographiques

Imports (c.i.f.) - Importations (c.a.f.) En pourcentage											Régions, pays ou territoires
80-00	90-00	00-10	05-08	05-09	05-10	2005	2007	2008	2009	2010	
7.9	6.2	–				–	–	–	–	–	Indonésie, y compris le Timor oriental
			18.6	9.3	10.7	37.5	15.4	36.9	-26.4	40.8	Indonésie
10.3	12.7	16.0	15.1	13.0	16.6	23.7	0.7	31.7	0.6	45.8	Rép. dém. populaire lao*
12.9	9.5	8.6	12.8	3.9	5.2	8.7	12.0	12.0	-24.8	33.2	Malaisie (20)
12.9	22.6	7.6	30.4	24.2	20.3	-12.3	27.9	31.1	2.2	9.4	Myanmar
10.5	12.5	4.9	6.9	-0.5	1.0	7.3	6.7	4.8	-24.4	27.3	Philippines
10.6	7.8	11.4	16.2	7.3	7.4	15.2	10.2	21.5	-23.1	26.4	Singapour (21)
12.9	5.0	12.7	14.3	6.1	7.7	25.2	9.8	26.5	-24.5	36.9	Thaïlande*
			37.4	33.9	27.6	-8.2	74.3	52.6	9.9	1.0	Timor-Leste (22)
13.6	22.9	20.6	30.9	20.6	17.7	15.0	39.2	28.8	-13.3	19.8	Viet Nam
3.3	**7.1**	**17.4**	**25.0**	**15.1**	**12.3**	**18.3**	**29.6**	**28.0**	**-18.5**	**13.6**	**Asie occidentale**
1.2	0.3	11.9	14.4	4.1	3.0	27.2	9.8	30.4	-32.5	16.4	Bahreïn (4)
-8.5	30.9	15.1	11.8	15.7	16.8	17.9	-11.1	81.5	9.3	15.0	Iraq*
2.4	5.1	15.6	17.0	10.9	8.1	29.3	18.0	24.1	-13.3	3.8	Jordanie
0.9	5.5	13.8	17.0	9.1	7.1	25.1	23.7	16.6	-18.2	10.3	Koweït*
5.5	8.7	12.1	20.9	17.8	16.0	0.2	27.0	36.8	-1.1	11.4	Liban (23)
-	(e)9.2	8.7	10.6	9.0	10.2	12.4	13.9	13.6	0.9	21.8	Territoire palestinien occupé
5.1	0.1	17.1	30.3	24.0	18.3	-0.4	46.4	43.5	-22.1	10.7	Oman
5.2	7.4	27.9	40.7	26.4	16.5	67.8	42.5	19.1	-10.7	-11.7	Qatar*
-0.5	0.8	16.3	25.1	15.6	12.0	25.5	29.3	27.7	-17.0	8.5	Arabie saoudite*(24)
0.4	3.6	(e)19.2	19.5	12.3	(e)11.7	29.1	27.6	23.8	-14.9	(e)22.3	République arabe syrienne*
10.7	10.3	17.0	20.2	7.7	7.5	19.7	21.8	18.8	-30.2	31.7	Turquie*
8.8	10.7	20.2	34.8	23.3	17.6	7.9	50.0	33.4	-14.9	6.0	Émirats arabes unis
–	0.6	18.2	26.2	17.5	13.5	34.8	40.2	22.8	-12.1	6.1	Yémen*
3.9	**1.6**	**9.2**	**14.6**	**7.3**	**6.3**	**6.7**	**16.3**	**15.6**	**-18.1**	**14.3**	**Économies en développement : Océanie**
5.9	3.0	(e)1.8	10.5	5.1	(e)1.6	-16.2	12.3	4.6	-11.8	(e)-8.3	Samoa américaines*(25)
4.9	-3.8	(e)19.0	21.0	22.3	(e)29.0	7.0	6.8	40.7	21.2	(e)73.1	Îles Cook
3.8	3.0	7.2	10.7	0.0	-4.6	11.2	-0.1	25.5	-36.5	-11.4	Fidji
3.9	1.6	(e)6.0	8.7	2.9	(e)1.0	16.4	12.5	17.4	-20.8	(e)0.5	Polynésie française*
3.5	-0.8	4.6	9.5	6.3	5.9	5.8	37.2	-5.7	-2.1	9.9	Guam
6.1	4.1	6.5	-0.1	-0.8	0.1	28.7	10.8	5.1	-7.6	7.2	Kiribati
	0.9	(e)7.1	(e)2.3	(e)0.1	(e)3.6	12.1	4.4	(e)5.3	(e)-10.0	(e)33.3	Îles Marshall
	0.9	(e)4.8	5.8	7.0	(e)4.7	-1.9	3.4	8.8	10.8	(e)-9.9	Micronésie (États fédérés de)
2.6	-11.0	(e)20.0	(e)52.0	(e)44.3	(e)40.6	43.6	(e)68.9	(e)57.6	(e)13.2	(e)33.2	Nauru
6.2	1.1	15.0	23.2	12.4	11.6	8.4	32.7	15.1	-20.4	28.3	Nouvelle-Calédonie*
(e)-6.6	-6.6	(c)14.1	4.1	(e)-2.5	(e)-4.0	5.6	87.0	14.1	(e)-35.1	(e)0.0	Nioué
-		-	-	-	-	-	-	-	-	-	Îles Mariannes du Nord
	(e)17.0	0.8	5.0	0.4	0.3	0.7	-6.7	21.1	-20.6	9.2	Palaos
1.2	-0.8	(e)15.1	27.4	18.2	(e)16.2	2.8	28.9	20.7	-10.1	(e)21.3	Papouasie-Nouvelle-Guinée
4.3	0.9	11.6	5.4	-0.2	2.5	13.7	-3.5	8.4	-19.9	34.4	Samoa (23)
3.1	0.7	19.3	22.3	12.3	14.4	52.3	32.4	14.7	-18.6	51.2	Îles Salomon*
-	-	-	-	-	-	(e)-39.5	(e)0.0	-	-	-	Tokélaou
4.0	1.9	9.2	12.4	7.5	6.4	14.9	22.7	16.2	-12.8	9.8	Tonga
(e)4.8	5.2	(e)14.9	26.4	(e)9.4	(e)5.6	13.0	21.0	72.9	(e)-47.1	(e)14.3	Tuvalu
2.5	0.9	16.1	25.5	18.6	13.5	16.4	5.3	36.7	-6.8	-2.5	Vanuatu
..	..	-	-	-	-	-3.5	-	-	-	-	Îles Wallis-et-Futuna
0.9	**3.7**	**19.4**	**31.3**	**14.8**	**11.2**	**21.7**	**34.6**	**30.5**	**-32.9**	**19.8**	**Économies en transition**
(e)10.0	9.4	17.5	27.1	17.9	12.9	13.4	36.9	25.4	-13.3	1.1	Albanie
–	–	19.4	37.1	21.6	16.4	30.9	49.6	34.9	-25.4	14.5	Arménie*
–	–	20.8	18.3	11.2	8.7	19.8	8.5	25.5	-14.6	7.8	Azerbaïdjan (26)
–	–	18.3	32.6	17.8	14.5	1.3	28.4	37.3	-27.5	22.1	Bélarus
–	–	11.5	20.8	9.7	6.1	19.4	33.1	25.1	-28.0	5.4	Bosnie-Herzégovine*(27)
–	–	12.2	18.5	6.4	1.5	11.9	20.2	19.0	-31.0	-5.4	Croatie*
–	–	27.5	35.3	17.7	12.9	34.9	41.8	16.3	-27.7	16.2	Géorgie (28)
–	–	20.7	29.7	14.8	6.1	30.1	37.9	15.6	-26.1	-15.4	Kazakhstan*(28)
–	–	26.0	50.1	30.0	21.2	25.5	44.4	46.0	-25.3	6.0	Kirghizistan
–	–	–	–	–	–	–	–	–	-38.0	-5.7	Monténégro
–	–	20.2	29.6	14.0	10.4	29.3	37.0	32.8	-33.1	17.6	République de Moldova
–	–	21.1	32.8	15.3	12.6	28.8	35.7	30.6	-34.3	29.7	Fédération de Russie (29)
–	–	–	–	–	–	-1.2	44.6	–			Serbie-et-Monténégro*
–	–	–	–	–	–	–	–	–	-29.8	4.3	Serbie
–	–	18.9	35.7	21.6	15.2	11.7	42.5	33.2	-21.4	3.5	Tadjikistan (28)
–	–	14.3	29.4	16.1	11.4	10.1	38.0	32.2	-26.5	8.3	LERY de Macédoine*
–	–	(e)13.1	25.8	27.8	(e)20.6	-11.2	41.4	56.1	19.5	(e)-17.0	Turkménistan (28)
–	–	18.7	33.4	11.6	8.9	24.6	34.6	41.1	-46.8	33.9	Ukraine (28)
–	–	16.0	37.1	29.1	21.0	8.1	44.7	46.4	-2.7	-7.1	Ouzbékistan (28)

Pour les sources et les notes, se reporter à la fin du tableau.

1.2.1 Annual average growth rates of exports and imports of countries and geographical regions

Region, country or territory	Exports (f.o.b) - Exportations (f.a.b.) Percentage										
	80-00	90-00	00-10	05-08	05-09	05-10	2005	2007	2008	2009	2010
Developed economies: America	**7.5**	**7.5**	**6.2**	**11.4**	**3.7**	**3.9**	**12.8**	**10.6**	**11.0**	**-21.7**	**21.2**
Bermuda (4)	3.9	-0.7	-8.0	-19.6	-10.7	-7.9	-32.9	-3.8	-4.0	20.8	-10.3
Canada	7.2	8.3	4.9	7.9	-1.1	-0.5	18.0	7.0	8.5	-30.1	22.1
Greenland	2.7	-3.6	4.4	6.7	-0.2	-1.2	5.8	8.6	13.5	-26.2	6.5
Saint Pierre and Miquelon	(e)12.9	(e)-3.4	(e)-2.7	(e)-12.8	(e)-23.0	(e)-23.7	(e)57.8	(e)-73.7	(e)-1.5	(e)-46.2	(e)-7.8
United States (30)	7.6	7.2	6.6	12.7	5.5	5.5	10.8	12.0	11.9	-18.8	20.9
Developed economies: Asia	**7.1**	**4.4**	**6.4**	**9.8**	**1.6**	**3.2**	**5.5**	**10.3**	**9.7**	**-25.4**	**31.7**
Israel*	9.8	11.1	8.1	12.8	5.0	5.1	10.8	15.6	12.5	-21.2	21.8
Japan	7.0	4.1	6.3	9.6	1.4	3.0	5.2	9.9	9.5	-25.7	32.6
Developed economies: Europe	**7.1**	**5.6**	**9.5**	**13.7**	**5.2**	**3.9**	**8.5**	**16.3**	**11.0**	**-22.4**	**12.5**
Andorra*	-	(e)1.2	3.6	-12.7	-18.7	-19.8	17.4	-15.6	-24.4	-34.0	-14.6
Austria*	0.0	0.1	0.0	13.6	1.6	0.1	6.0	10.6	10.6	24.4	11.7
Belgium*	-	-	9.7	12.6	4.5	3.3	9.1	17.5	9.2	-21.6	11.8
Bulgaria*	-6.7	2.2	18.0	23.7	11.0	9.7	18.2	22.5	20.4	-27.0	27.0
Cyprus*	5.0	1.3	5.7	3.7	-1.1	-0.6	54.8	4.5	16.8	-23.0	12.6
Czech Republic*(31)	_	_	18.5	23.8	12.3	10.0	13.4	29.0	19.5	-23.1	18.0
Denmark*(32)	7.5	3.7	8.3	11.1	4.3	2.4	10.6	11.4	13.0	-19.7	4.3
Estonia*(28)	_	_	13.3	16.8	5.8	5.7	30.3	13.5	12.8	-27.3	28.6
Faeroe Islands	6.0	1.6	5.7	12.5	7.7	6.3	-3.0	14.8	14.2	-10.6	7.2
Finland*	7.4	8.0	6.7	13.9	1.3	-0.7	6.6	16.6	6.9	-34.8	11.8
France*	7.4	5.0	6.2	10.1	3.0	1.7	2.6	12.8	9.8	-21.3	7.9
Germany*	_	3.9	10.3	14.6	5.6	4.2	6.9	19.2	9.2	-22.5	13.6
Gibraltar (33)	16.5	10.0	-	13.5	7.4	-	1.5	25.3	-6.8	-6.7	-
Greece*	6.0	3.7	9.1	14.9	5.9	3.4	13.0	13.6	11.6	-22.4	5.7
Hungary*(34)	5.4	12.7	15.1	20.4	9.5	7.4	13.4	26.7	13.4	-23.5	15.3
Iceland	5.5	3.2	10.9	21.8	10.3	7.7	6.7	38.2	12.2	-24.3	13.5
Ireland*	13.2	13.8	4.7	5.2	2.5	1.5	4.8	11.7	3.2	-7.8	1.0
Italy*	7.7	4.6	8.1	13.8	4.4	2.6	5.6	19.9	8.3	-25.0	10.3
Latvia*	_	_	20.5	26.1	13.8	11.9	28.9	34.9	21.8	-24.1	24.1
Lithuania*(28)	_	_	21.0	25.4	12.4	10.8	27.1	21.2	37.5	-30.4	27.0
Luxembourg*	7.4	3.3	11.0	9.3	3.5	0.3	15.8	-2.3	13.7	-16.9	-7.3
Malta	10.6	6.3	1.9	7.7	-0.8	-1.3	-4.6	10.0	-3.2	-25.0	12.8
Netherlands*	6.7	7.0	11.5	16.3	7.4	6.1	13.9	10.7	15.5	-21.9	15.5
Norway	6.4	5.2	11.3	17.8	6.7	4.0	26.9	11.7	26.6	-30.0	8.7
Poland*	5.2	9.9	19.8	24.1	13.5	10.8	19.3	26.5	21.3	-19.9	14.5
Portugal*	11.1	5.3	9.0	14.6	5.4	3.7	6.8	17.3	8.5	-22.6	10.6
Romania*	-2.7	8.5	18.5	21.5	12.4	11.3	18.1	24.7	22.0	-18.1	22.2
Slovakia*	_	_	21.7	31.4	17.9	14.2	15.1	39.7	21.2	-21.2	16.6
Slovenia*	_	_	15.5	21.7	10.4	7.7	17.8	29.5	13.1	-23.3	12.8
Spain*	11.0	8.3	9.5	13.8	6.1	4.4	5.6	18.5	10.8	-19.2	8.4
Sweden*	6.8	6.0	8.3	12.0	2.1	1.9	6.4	14.2	8.3	-28.6	21.3
Switzerland*	7.1	3.0	10.4	15.4	8.9	7.7	6.4	16.4	16.6	-14.0	13.1
United Kingdom*	6.6	5.5	4.9	5.2	-1.6	-1.2	10.8	-2.2	4.4	-23.2	15.3
Developed economies: Oceania	**6.6**	**4.8**	**13.3**	**19.1**	**11.3**	**12.4**	**19.4**	**15.8**	**28.7**	**-18.0**	**36.4**
Australia	6.7	5.0	14.0	20.2	12.4	13.5	22.5	14.4	32.5	-17.7	38.0
New Zealand	5.9	4.2	9.5	13.2	5.7	6.3	6.5	23.0	9.9	-19.6	26.3

For sources and notes, see next page.

34

1.2.1 Taux d'évolution annuels moyens des exportations et importations des pays et des régions géographiques

Imports (c.i.f.) - Importations (c.a.f.) En pourcentage											Régions, pays ou territoires
80-00	90-00	00-10	05-08	05-09	05-10	2005	2007	2008	2009	2010	
7.9	**9.1**	**6.0**	**7.6**	**0.0**	**0.7**	**14.5**	**5.9**	**7.4**	**-25.2**	**21.9**	**Économies développées : Amérique**
3.3	2.7	4.8	5.7	2.2	-0.5	-0.3	6.7	-0.6	-8.2	-9.2	Bermudes (4)
7.3	7.5	6.4	8.1	1.5	1.9	18.4	8.9	7.2	-21.0	18.6	Canada
1.8	-1.0	9.8	12.9	6.6	5.5	9.7	9.3	26.9	-19.8	11.2	Groenland
(e)14.4	(e)2.5	(e)-1.2	(e)-5.1	(e)1.7	(e)1.3	(e)-27.8	(e)-43.6	(e)13.3	(e)33.5	(e)-13.4	Saint-Pierre-et-Miquelon
8.1	9.5	5.9	7.5	-0.3	0.5	13.7	5.3	7.4	-26.0	22.6	États-Unis (30)
6.2	**4.9**	**7.9**	**13.3**	**4.1**	**4.4**	**13.0**	**7.8**	**22.3**	**-27.8**	**25.6**	**Économies développées : Asie**
7.0	8.6	6.4	13.2	3.9	4.0	10.0	17.3	14.6	-27.2	24.2	Israël*
6.1	4.6	8.0	13.3	4.2	4.5	13.3	6.9	23.1	-27.8	25.8	Japon
6.6	**5.0**	**9.7**	**14.5**	**5.1**	**3.7**	**10.2**	**16.5**	**11.9**	**-24.6**	**13.3**	**Économies développées : Europe**
-	(e)3.1	5.2	2.9	-1.7	-3.4	3.4	8.0	1.0	-18.2	-4.2	Andorre*
8.0	4.5	9.7	13.5	5.3	3.9	6.3	18.8	12.7	-22.4	11.5	Autriche*
-	-	10.1	13.7	4.8	3.3	11.7	17.0	13.0	-24.5	11.3	Belgique*
-5.6	5.3	18.4	26.7	10.2	5.6	25.5	28.6	22.9	-36.2	8.3	Bulgarie*
7.6	4.3	10.9	19.4	8.9	6.0	15.0	24.3	23.2	-26.4	8.8	Chypre*
_	_	15.7	23.1	11.0	9.0	9.5	26.7	19.9	-26.0	20.5	République tchèque*(31)
6.2	4.2	8.7	13.1	4.2	1.6	11.0	14.6	11.3	-24.4	3.0	Danemark*(32)
_	_	11.4	16.0	1.5	0.2	23.0	16.5	1.9	-36.7	21.2	Estonie*(28)
3.0	5.5	6.2	11.6	3.3	0.5	18.8	29.7	-2.7	-20.7	-1.0	Îles Féroé
5.3	5.1	10.0	16.1	3.5	1.4	14.4	17.7	12.0	-33.7	13.1	Finlande*
6.3	3.8	8.0	12.7	4.9	3.3	7.2	16.4	13.3	-21.7	8.6	France*
_	3.5	9.9	15.1	6.3	5.1	8.7	16.3	12.0	-21.8	15.5	Allemagne*
11.5	1.7	-	15.6	8.4	-	3.8	25.5	-2.9	-9.7	-	Gibraltar (33)
7.5	5.2	10.3	19.6	8.9	3.4	3.3	23.4	17.6	-25.0	-8.3	Grèce*
6.5	13.5	12.8	18.1	6.5	4.4	10.1	22.1	13.7	-28.6	13.7	Hongrie*(34)
5.5	5.5	8.7	10.7	-4.3	-6.5	28.2	11.7	-7.8	-41.6	8.8	Islande
9.4	10.7	3.8	7.6	-0.5	-3.2	11.1	14.6	-0.1	-25.3	-3.8	Irlande*
5.8	3.2	9.1	13.5	3.9	3.0	8.5	15.6	9.5	-26.1	17.2	Italie*
_	_	17.1	23.7	5.8	3.0	22.7	32.7	5.1	-39.2	19.4	Lettonie*
_	_	18.3	25.9	6.2	6.2	23.7	26.0	27.0	-41.1	20.2	Lituanie*(20)
8.2	4.2	10.2	12.4	4.4	1.1	9.4	3.7	15.8	-22.2	-3.4	Luxembourg*
8.7	4.4	4.9	11.6	4.1	1.7	1.2	10.5	8.1	-19.8	1.3	Malte
6.4	6.7	11.3	16.9	7.4	6.2	14.0	18.1	17.6	-23.7	17.0	Pays-Bas*
5.2	4.2	11.1	18.3	8.2	5.9	15.4	25.0	12.3	-23.3	11.5	Norvège
8.1	18.3	16.5	27.3	13.4	10.1	13.5	30.4	25.7	-28.4	16.5	Pologne*
9.8	5.3	9.0	15.5	6.1	3.6	11.5	16.1	14.6	-24.1	5.9	Portugal*
-0.7	6.8	19.9	28.4	11.3	7.3	23.9	37.4	19.2	-35.4	14.5	Roumanie*
_	_	19.6	29.2	15.4	12.3	16.2	34.7	21.6	-24.7	19.7	Slovaquie*
_	_	14.5	22.8	9.9	7.0	14.7	30.7	17.0	-28.4	13.7	Slovénie*
9.7	6.0	9.9	13.7	2.7	0.4	11.9	18.4	7.8	-30.3	7.5	Espagne*
5.5	4.4	9.9	15.1	4.2	3.9	11.4	20.1	9.7	-28.7	24.2	Suède*
6.1	2.5	9.1	13.3	6.9	6.1	9.1	14.0	13.9	-15.3	13.3	Suisse*
7.1	5.6	6.1	6.7	-0.8	-0.6	9.3	3.5	1.3	-23.7	16.5	Royaume-Uni*
6.5	**6.3**	**12.5**	**15.8**	**8.3**	**8.0**	**14.4**	**18.6**	**19.1**	**-18.6**	**21.8**	**Économies développées : Océanie**
6.7	6.4	13.1	17.1	9.6	9.2	14.5	18.7	21.1	-17.4	21.9	Australie
6.0	5.9	9.5	9.2	1.2	1.6	14.0	18.0	8.1	-25.8	21.2	Nouvelle-Zélande

Pour les sources et les notes, se reporter à la page suivante.

1.2.1 Annual average growth rates of exports and imports of countries and geographical regions

Sources:
- UN DESA Statistics Division, *Yearbook of International Trade Statistics*
- UN DESA Statistics Division, *Monthly Bulletin of Statistics*
- IMF, *International Financial Statistics* on CD-ROM
- IMF, *Direction of Trade Statistics*
- World Trade Organization
- Other international and national sources
- UNCTAD secretariat estimates

Notes:
(*)	Special Trade System.
(1)	Excluding exports of gold.
(2)	From 1996 onward, imports f.o.b.
(3)	Prior to 2008, special trade.
(4)	Imports f.o.b.
(5)	Trade with other member countries of CEMAC is excluded. Imports f.o.b.
(6)	Trade with other member countries of CEMAC is excluded.
(7)	Prior to 1995, data refer to fiscal year ending June.
(8)	Prior to 1974, special trade.
(9)	Excluding re-exports (oil for bunkering).
(10)	Excluding re-exports.
(11)	Prior to 2005, special trade.
(12)	Prior to 1986, included in Netherlands Antilles. Including exports and imports of crude oil and oil products. Imports f.o.b.
(13)	From 1990 onwards, trade statistics exclude certain oil and chemical products. Imports f.o.b.
(14)	Prior to 1993, excluding free trade processing zones. Imports f.o.b.
(15)	Prior to 1986, including Aruba.
(16)	Prior to 2002, special trade.
(17)	From 1990 onward, including goods for processing. Imports f.o.b.
(18)	Excluding imports of goods financed through foreign aid.
(19)	Excluding military goods, fissionable materials, bunkers, ships and aircraft.
(20)	Inter-trade between the States of Malaysia included. From 1965 onwards, excluding military imports and offshore installations of petroleum industry.
(21)	Including trans-shipments to and from peninsular Malaysia.
(22)	Excluding exports of oil and gas.
(23)	Prior to 2001, special trade.
(24)	Excluding defense imports.
(25)	Data refer to fiscal year ending September.
(26)	Excluding military goods, precious metals and goods procured in foreign ports.
(27)	Prior to 1998, data refer to the Federation of Bosnia and Herzegovina only. The other entity of Bosnia and Herzegovina, Republika Srpska, is not included.
(28)	Prior to 1994, covers only trade with countries outside the CIS.
(29)	Prior to 1994, excluding trade with independent states resulting from the former USSR.
(30)	Prior to 1975, excludes non-monetary gold.
(31)	From 1995 onward, including goods for processing.
(32)	Prior to 1988, excluding ships.
(33)	Excluding petroleum products.
(34)	Prior to 1996, excluding customs free zones.

Sources :
- ONU DAES Division de statistique, *Annuaire statistique du commerce international*
- ONU DAES Division de statistique, *Bulletin mensuel de statistique*
- FMI, *Statistiques financières internationales* sur CD-ROM
- FMI, *Direction of Trade Statistics*
- Organisation mondiale du commerce .
- Autres sources internationales et nationales
- Estimations du secrétariat de la CNUCED

Notes :
(*)   Système du commerce spécial.
(1)   Non-compris les exportations d'or.
(2)   À partir de 1996, importations f.a.b.
(3)   Avant 2008, commerce spécial.
(4)   Importations f.a.b.
(5)   Non-compris le commerce avec les autres pays membres de la CEMAC. Importations f.a.b.
(6)   Non-compris le commerce avec les autres pays membres de la CEMAC.
(7)   Avant 1995, les données se rapportent à l'exercice budgétaire finissant juin..
(8)   Avant 1974, commerce spécial.
(9)   Non-compris les réexportations (huile pour mise en soute).
(10)   Non-compris les réexportations.
(11)   Avant 2005, commerce spécial.
(12)   Avant 1986 compris dans Antilles néerlandaises. Les données comprennent les exportations et importations de pétrole brut et produits dérivés. Importations f.a.b.
(13)   À partir de 1990, certains produits pétroliers et chimiques ne sont plus inclus dans les statistiques du commerce. Importations f.a.b.
(14)   Avant 1993, non-compris les zones franches douanières. Importations f.a.b.
(15)   Avant 1986, y compris Aruba.
(16)   Avant 2002, commerce spécial.
(17)   À partir de 1990, y compris les biens destinés à subir des transformations. Importations f.a.b.
(18)   Non-compris les biens d'importation financés par l'aide à l'étranger.
(19)   Non-compris les biens à usage militaire, le matériel fissile, le combustible de soute et l'avitaillement des navires et aéronefs.
(20)   Y compris le commerce entre les États de la Malaisie. Non-compris les importations militaires et l'installation près des côtes de l'industrie pétrolière.
(21)   Y compris les transbordements vers et en provenance de la Malaisie péninsulaire.
(22)   Non-compris les exportations de pétrole et le gaz.
(23)   Avant 2001, commerce spécial.
(24)   Non-compris les importations de la défense.
(25)   Les données se rapportent à l'exercice budgétaire finissant septembre.
(26)   Non-compris les biens à usage militaire, les métaux précieux et les biens fournis dans les ports étrangers.
(27)   Avant 1998, les données se réfèrent uniquement à la Fédération de la Bosnie-Herzégovine. L'autre entité de la Bosnie-Herzégovine, Republika Srpska, n'est pas incluse.
(28)   Avant 1994, concerne seulement le commerce avec les pays extérieurs à la CEI.
(29)   Avant 1994, non-compris le commerce avec les républiques indépendants de l'ancienne URSS.
(30)   Avant 1975, non-compris l'or industriel.
(31)   À partir de 1995, y compris les biens destinés à subir des transformations.
(32)   Avant 1998, non-compris les navires.
(33)   Non-compris les produits pétroliers.
(34)   Avant 1996, non-compris les zones franches douanières.

Economic grouping	Exports (f.o.b.) - Exportations (f.a.b.) Percentage										
	80-00	90-00	00-10	05-08	05-09	05-10	2005	2007	2008	2009	2010
DEVELOPING ECONOMIES	**7.7**	**9.1**	**14.3**	**18.1**	**9.1**	**9.0**	**22.2**	**16.2**	**19.3**	**-20.9**	**27.4**
Developing economies excluding China	7.1	8.5	12.5	16.7	7.7	7.7	20.7	13.6	19.9	-22.3	26.1
Developing economies excluding LDCs	7.7	9.1	14.2	17.9	8.9	8.9	21.9	16.0	18.8	-20.7	27.4
High-income developing countries	8.1	9.1	11.6	15.0	6.3	6.4	19.1	12.0	17.5	-22.7	24.8
Middle-income developing countries	8.0	9.6	18.0	21.3	11.7	11.5	24.5	21.2	18.7	-18.8	30.0
Low-income developing countries	4.9	8.0	16.3	22.3	12.9	12.5	30.9	19.4	29.2	-19.8	29.0
Heavily indebted poor countries (IMF)	2.6	4.7	15.5	20.1	12.3	11.7	18.1	14.6	25.8	-15.3	23.5
Landlocked developing countries	9.1	12.0	20.9	32.0	16.5	13.7	30.0	28.0	36.2	-30.1	26.0
Small island developing States	-0.3	4.5	10.6	17.4	2.9	0.6	30.6	1.2	28.3	-40.3	14.3
Least developed countries	*5.0*	*7.6*	*19.4*	*28.5*	*15.1*	*13.0*	*36.2*	*24.2*	*38.4*	*-18.7*	*26.0*
Africa and Haiti	3.0	4.2	22.6	33.0	16.6	13.4	42.3	30.0	45.6	-33.9	24.6
Asia	11.0	16.4	13.1	16.0	11.0	12.0	23.5	9.7	17.4	-6.9	29.9
Islands	1.8	1.8	11.1	15.5	7.8	7.6	2.0	29.9	10.0	-17.6	21.9
Major petroleum and gas exporters	*0.9*	*4.7*	*17.5*	*23.3*	*10.0*	*7.9*	*42.3*	*15.3*	*36.8*	*-33.1*	*20.9*
Africa	-0.1	2.1	18.9	22.7	7.3	5.8	60.8	16.3	38.4	-40.3	27.3
America	2.3	6.3	12.2	18.0	4.5	2.2	40.5	5.2	37.9	-39.5	14.2
Asia	1.1	5.3	17.8	24.0	11.4	9.1	37.2	16.1	36.2	-30.2	19.8
Major exporters of manufactured goods	*12.8*	*10.9*	*13.6*	*16.1*	*8.3*	*8.9*	*17.9*	*16.3*	*13.1*	*-16.9*	*29.7*
America	11.0	16.1	7.0	10.7	3.0	4.3	13.1	8.6	7.3	-21.3	29.8
Asia	13.1	10.3	14.3	16.6	8.8	9.4	18.4	17.1	13.6	-16.5	29.7
Emerging economies	*10.9*	*10.3*	*10.9*	*13.7*	*6.0*	*7.0*	*14.8*	*12.4*	*12.5*	*-19.3*	*30.0*
America	8.5	11.8	11.0	14.9	6.2	6.9	18.0	12.9	12.7	-21.4	30.0
Asia	12.2	9.7	10.9	13.2	5.9	7.0	13.5	12.1	12.3	-18.3	29.9
Newly industrialized Asian countries	*11.9*	*9.5*	*10.0*	*12.2*	*5.5*	*6.7*	*13.1*	*11.4*	*10.9*	*-17.0*	*28.7*
First tier	12.5	8.8	10.1	11.2	4.9	6.2	13.0	10.9	9.2	-16.3	28.6
Second tier	10.8	11.5	10.0	14.8	7.2	7.9	13.1	12.8	15.1	-18.6	29.1
Developing economies: Africa	**1.9**	**3.3**	**16.2**	**21.0**	**8.9**	**7.8**	**36.4**	**16.6**	**31.1**	**-31.0**	**25.4**
Northern Africa excluding Sudan	0.8	2.7	16.1	22.7	8.9	7.0	37.0	13.9	37.6	-35.3	22.4
Sub-Saharan Africa	2.5	3.6	16.2	20.0	8.9	8.2	36.0	18.1	27.7	-28.4	26.9
Sub-Saharan Africa excluding South Africa	2.4	3.9	18.0	21.7	9.8	8.8	44.9	18.8	33.2	-30.2	26.3
Developing economies: America	**6.4**	**10.7**	**11.1**	**15.6**	**6.4**	**6.6**	**20.3**	**12.0**	**16.8**	**-23.7**	**26.8**
Central America and Greater Caribbean Islands excluding Puerto Rico	9.1	15.4	7.0	10.7	3.2	4.3	12.3	9.2	7.0	-20.6	27.8
Central America and Greater Caribbean Islands excluding Mexico and Puerto Rico	3.4	12.0	6.7	10.5	4.2	3.9	7.2	13.3	5.1	-15.9	15.2
South America and Central America	7.4	10.9	11.3	15.7	6.7	6.9	20.1	12.5	16.6	-22.9	27.5
South America excluding Brazil	5.6	8.0	14.6	19.8	9.1	8.2	28.9	14.2	22.9	-25.3	24.1
Developing economies: Asia	**9.0**	**9.5**	**14.8**	**18.3**	**9.6**	**9.6**	**21.2**	**17.0**	**18.5**	**-19.2**	**27.7**
Eastern and South-Eastern Asia excluding China	11.8	9.5	10.3	12.6	5.9	6.9	13.3	11.7	11.5	-16.8	28.7
Southern Asia excluding India	4.6	4.3	14.6	20.4	9.7	9.0	22.3	12.7	23.9	-24.7	26.2

Sources:
- Data in this table are based on trade figures in table 1.1.1.

Imports (c.i.f.) - Importations (c.a.f.) En pourcentage											Groupements économiques
80-00	90-00	00-10	05-08	05-09	05-10	2005	2007	2008	2009	2010	
8.1	8.7	14.1	18.8	10.3	10.4	17.7	18.4	21.6	-18.8	28.5	ÉCONOMIES EN DÉVELOPPEMENT
7.8	8.2	12.7	18.6	9.7	9.4	17.7	17.8	22.4	-20.6	25.7	Économies en développement sans la Chine
8.3	8.7	14.0	18.7	10.1	10.3	17.6	18.2	21.3	-19.2	29.0	Économies en développement sans les PMA
9.7	8.8	11.1	16.4	7.6	7.5	14.3	16.2	17.1	-21.8	25.6	Pays en développement à revenu élevé
7.4	8.8	16.9	19.9	11.9	12.6	18.1	19.6	22.7	-15.8	33.8	Pays en développement à revenu intermédiaire
4.0	7.5	18.8	24.7	16.0	14.7	32.4	23.5	34.8	-16.5	24.3	Pays en développement à revenu faible
3.0	5.7	15.7	21.4	14.1	12.2	23.6	20.5	27.8	-13.2	15.0	Pays pauvres très endettés (FMI)
8.2	10.2	17.1	26.8	17.4	13.6	17.6	28.7	29.9	-14.8	8.8	Pays en développement sans littoral
1.1	0.0	9.3	17.0	7.3	4.4	16.3	16.9	19.9	-24.9	5.4	Petits États insulaires en développement
3.5	6.5	16.9	23.0	17.6	15.8	22.9	23.4	30.3	-4.8	15.5	Pays les moins avancés
2.7	4.3	18.9	24.8	19.1	16.4	26.9	25.2	34.0	-4.6	11.5	Afrique et Haïti
4.8	10.4	13.6	19.9	14.9	14.6	16.5	20.5	23.7	-5.0	23.5	Asie
3.5	0.7	17.4	19.6	13.7	12.5	18.4	17.6	26.0	-9.4	16.9	Îles
0.7	3.5	17.9	26.7	18.3	14.6	20.1	33.2	30.3	-12.3	8.6	Principaux exportateurs de pétrole et de gaz
-1.4	1.6	20.4	27.0	20.9	17.9	30.1	36.5	33.4	-4.5	12.3	Afrique
2.3	5.8	14.3	28.3	15.5	9.0	41.2	37.1	7.6	-18.2	-4.9	Amérique
1.3	3.7	17.8	26.5	17.9	14.3	16.2	31.9	32.4	-13.6	8.9	Asie
12.5	9.5	12.8	15.3	7.7	8.9	14.6	14.2	15.9	-18.4	34.0	Principaux exportateurs d'articles manufacturés
13.4	14.2	6.8	11.8	3.2	4.1	12.2	10.6	9.6	-24.3	28.6	Amérique
12.4	8.9	13.6	15.8	8.2	9.5	14.9	14.7	16.6	-17.7	34.5	Asie
11.3	0.5	10.0	10.0	0.0	7.4	14.5	13.7	20.0	-25.6	34.0	Économies émergentes
10.6	13.7	10.2	19.5	8.7	9.1	16.0	18.5	22.7	-26.6	35.3	Amérique
11.6	7.7	10.8	14.8	5.6	6.7	14.4	11.6	18.7	-25.2	33.5	Asie
11.9	8.1	10.2	13.5	5.4	6.5	14.3	11.2	16.3	-22.3	31.7	Économies nouvellement industrialisées d'Asie
12.1	8.1	10.1	13.4	5.5	6.5	12.7	11.2	14.7	-21.2	30.3	Première génération
11.2	7.9	10.5	13.8	5.2	6.7	18.9	11.2	21.0	-25.0	35.6	Deuxième génération
2.2	4.5	16.5	22.5	15.2	13.2	22.6	23.8	27.8	-12.1	15.6	Économies en développement : Afrique
2.0	4.1	16.5	27.3	20.6	17.5	21.0	29.8	47.3	-10.0	11.9	Afrique septentrionale sans le Soudan
2.4	4.7	16.5	20.1	12.4	11.1	23.4	21.2	18.9	-13.4	17.8	Afrique subsaharienne
1.8	3.9	17.5	23.3	16.2	13.9	27.7	26.9	25.4	-9.5	14.0	Afrique subsaharienne sans l'Afrique du Sud
7.8	12.0	10.6	19.9	9.3	9.0	18.3	19.0	22.2	-25.3	29.2	Économies en développement : Amérique
10.3	13.1	7.3	13.2	4.1	4.5	13.5	11.7	12.2	-24.8	26.3	Amérique centrale et Grandes Antilles sans Porto Rico
4.7	10.0	9.4	17.8	7.5	6.2	18.2	15.6	20.8	-26.2	19.0	Amérique centrale et Grandes Antilles sans le Mexique et Porto Rico
9.2	12.6	10.8	20.2	9.5	9.4	17.6	19.8	22.0	-25.0	30.7	Amérique du Sud et Amérique centrale
7.0	10.4	15.0	26.3	13.9	12.4	29.9	27.8	27.2	-25.1	27.9	Amérique du Sud sans le Brésil
9.4	8.4	14.7	18.2	10.1	10.4	17.2	17.7	20.8	-18.1	30.0	Économies en développement : Asie
11.8	8.2	10.5	14.1	6.0	7.0	14.3	12.1	16.9	-21.8	31.0	Asie orientale et Asie du Sud-Est sans la Chine
3.3	1.5	14.2	15.4	9.3	9.7	19.7	11.3	27.0	-15.6	25.0	Asie méridionale sans l'Inde

Sources :
- Les données dans ce tableau ont été calculées d'après les chiffres du tableau 1.1.1.

1.2.3 Annual average growth rates of exports and imports of trade groups

Trade group	Exports (f.o.b) - Exportations (f.a.b.) Percentage										
	80-00	90-00	00-10	05-08	05-09	05-10	2005	2007	2008	2009	2010
AFRICA											
CEMAC	3.5	3.4	18.4	20.6	7.6	6.7	38.9	10.4	40.3	-35.7	27.1
CEPGL	-3.3	-5.9	20.3	21.5	13.1	15.9	25.3	14.7	41.4	-20.5	54.4
COMESA	-0.3	1.2	18.3	25.2	13.1	11.3	34.4	17.1	37.4	-27.2	23.9
EAC	2.8	7.0	15.6	19.9	15.2	14.2	21.9	23.2	26.8	-4.9	17.3
ECCAS	3.3	3.3	23.1	32.8	14.7	11.5	54.8	25.6	55.0	-40.4	26.2
ECOWAS	1.2	3.6	16.6	13.8	9.4	5.7	33.4	12.2	20.4	20.1	20.0
MRU	2.1	2.4	11.0	10.6	9.3	7.5	11.5	4.1	18.2	1.9	-0.6
SADC	3.2	3.3	15.5	23.0	10.4	9.3	25.9	21.3	27.7	-29.5	27.7
UMA	0.0	7.6	16.7	21.6	6.9	5.1	30.6	13.2	34.0	-30.0	24.9
WAEMU	3.3	5.1	12.2	12.9	11.4	9.5	9.4	6.4	23.6	2.0	1.3
AMERICA											
ANCOM	5.7	7.5	17.2	22.4	13.1	12.3	32.0	17.2	25.9	-18.0	26.0
CACM	7.5	15.2	7.9	10.9	5.7	5.5	9.0	12.4	8.5	-12.2	15.3
CARICOM	-2.7	5.1	11.7	18.6	2.7	-0.1	35.7	0.2	30.9	-43.4	12.9
FTAA	7.4	8.3	7.6	12.8	4.6	4.8	15.0	11.1	12.9	-22.3	23.1
LAIA	7.0	10.6	11.4	16.0	6.7	7.0	20.6	12.6	16.9	-23.3	28.0
MERCOSUR	6.0	7.0	14.5	19.3	10.0	10.0	20.8	17.6	24.9	-22.1	29.4
NAFTA	7.8	8.3	6.3	11.3	3.6	4.0	12.8	10.3	10.4	-21.6	22.4
OAS	7.3	8.2	7.6	12.8	4.6	4.8	15.0	11.1	12.9	-22.3	23.2
OECS	2.8	-2.8	2.8	10.3	6.7	4.2	0.2	3.8	22.4	-10.3	-3.7
ASIA											
APTA	12.9	12.2	10.2	21.3	12.6	12.6	23.9	22.6	17.6	-15.4	31.1
ASEAN	11.1	11.1	11.2	14.9	7.3	8.0	14.7	12.3	15.4	-18.5	29.3
ECO	7.3	7.3	18.6	26.4	13.1	10.6	24.5	22.7	30.4	-28.2	20.5
GCC	1.5	5.3	17.8	22.8	10.5	8.4	39.4	15.3	35.5	-30.1	18.6
SAARC	9.0	9.1	17.3	21.6	13.8	14.0	26.0	19.4	26.5	-14.2	31.9
EUROPE											
EFTA	6.8	3.8	10.8	16.5	8.0	6.2	14.5	14.6	20.9	-21.4	11.3
EU	7.1	5.7	9.4	13.5	5.0	3.7	8.2	16.4	10.5	-22.4	12.5
Euro area	7.5	5.6	9.3	13.7	5.2	3.7	7.2	17.9	10.1	-22.2	11.6
OCEANIA											
MSG	5.6	3.9	12.2	18.2	8.4	8.0	21.7	12.4	22.1	-23.9	26.1
INTERREGIONAL											
ACP	1.8	4.0	15.3	19.5	8.2	7.5	34.1	16.6	26.7	-29.1	26.0
APEC	9.3	8.5	10.6	14.6	6.5	7.1	15.5	14.0	13.7	-20.3	28.3
BSEC	10.4	17.5	17.6	24.4	10.8	9.2	25.5	20.8	31.7	-31.8	25.8
CIS	–	–	18.3	26.3	10.9	9.3	29.4	20.4	35.3	-35.8	29.6

Sources:
- Data in this table are based on trade figures in table 1.1.1.

1.2.3 Taux d'évolution annuels moyens des exportations et importations des groupements commerciaux

Imports (c.i.f.) - Importations (c.a.f.) En pourcentage											Groupements commerciaux
80-00	90-00	00-10	05-08	05-09	05-10	2005	2007	2008	2009	2010	
											AFRIQUE
1.7	3.1	17.9	28.9	22.9	19.2	14.8	30.9	24.1	3.3	9.1	CEMAC
-2.9	-5.2	21.4	19.1	14.5	13.6	36.5	13.9	31.9	-6.2	16.9	CEPGL
1.9	4.6	17.5	24.2	19.3	17.4	35.0	21.7	45.9	-6.0	15.9	COMESA
3.7	5.2	17.8	25.6	18.4	16.3	29.3	24.7	28.5	-7.4	17.5	CAE
1.3	2.7	21.8	31.1	26.1	22.3	29.2	37.3	37.9	4.2	10.5	CEEAC
0.0	3.8	17.2	23.8	13.8	11.4	33.5	31.7	19.1	-18.1	16.5	CEDEAO
1.6	2.8	12.7	13.4	7.9	6.2	21.0	16.3	19.8	-14.4	6.8	UFM
0.7	4.0	15.0	17.4	10.0	9.0	17.2	16.4	16.1	-14.5	21.6	SADC
2.1	2.8	16.1	24.7	17.8	14.8	14.2	29.5	37.5	-11.1	9.9	UMA
2.3	3.9	14.8	19.1	12.7	9.5	19.4	23.5	27.6	-13.4	2.9	UEMOA
											AMÉRIQUE
6.5	10.0	16.2	26.1	15.6	14.6	25.5	25.4	32.1	-20.3	29.7	ANCOM
8.4	13.6	9.2	14.7	5.4	4.6	12.5	15.2	14.1	-24.7	18.7	MCAC
0.0	7.8	8.4	16.0	6.7	4.0	19.2	14.4	20.7	-24.9	5.3	CARICOM
8.0	9.7	7.1	10.3	2.1	2.6	15.1	8.8	10.7	-25.1	24.0	ZLEA
8.7	12.4	10.9	20.6	9.7	9.6	18.4	19.8	22.7	-25.5	31.5	ALADI
8.1	13.1	14.9	31.4	17.5	17.0	19.9	31.1	40.9	-27.6	42.8	MERCOSUR
8.3	9.6	6.1	8.0	0.3	1.1	14.2	6.4	7.6	-25.1	22.7	ALENA
7.9	9.7	7.1	10.3	2.1	2.6	15.2	8.8	10.8	-25.2	24.0	OEA
7.0	4.1	6.6	11.3	5.5	2.6	16.6	14.3	7.6	-13.7	-3.8	OECO
											ASIE
11.0	10.1	18.8	20.9	12.5	13.2	20.1	20.3	22.5	-16.1	35.6	ACAP
11.0	8.3	11.5	15.9	7.2	7.9	17.3	12.8	21.8	-23.1	30.8	ANASE
6.8	6.0	16.8	20.0	9.7	8.4	20.5	20.5	22.3	-24.2	21.0	ECO
2.5	4.8	18.4	30.1	19.3	14.5	17.1	39.1	30.0	-16.4	6.2	CCG
6.4	8.8	21.2	27.3	16.9	15.5	37.7	24.0	37.1	-19.4	27.2	SAARC
											EUROPE
5.8	3.1	9.7	14.8	7.1	5.7	11.3	17.3	12.8	-18.5	12.7	AELE
6.7	5.1	9.7	14.5	5.1	3.6	10.1	16.4	11.8	-24.9	13.4	UE
6.8	4.7	9.7	14.6	5.4	3.8	9.8	17.2	12.4	-24.2	12.4	Zone euro
											OCÉANIE
2.2	0.6	12.7	20.3	11.1	8.8	8.7	16.4	22.7	-19.6	12.5	MSG
											INTERRÉGIONAUX
1.9	5.1	14.9	19.7	11.5	10.1	23.4	19.4	19.8	-15.8	17.1	ACP
9.1	8.7	9.8	12.9	4.8	5.6	15.1	11.3	14.6	-22.7	28.5	CEAP
9.6	12.3	18.3	28.1	12.5	9.7	21.2	30.1	28.8	-33.3	22.3	CEMN
–	–	20.2	32.5	15.5	12.0	24.3	35.1	32.0	-33.6	23.0	CEI

Sources :
- Les données dans ce tableau ont été calculées d'après les chiffres du tableau 1.1.1.

1.3.1 Value of trade balance, and as percentage of imports of countries and geographical regions

Region, country or territory	Trade balance (1) - Balance commerciale (1) Millions of dollars - Millions de dollars								
	1989-91	1994-96	1999-01	2003-05	2004-06	2005-07	2006-08	2007-09	2008-10
WORLD	-107 406	-68 585	-201 392	-277 771	-281 629	-266 109	-278 637	-252 167	-226 577
DEVELOPING ECONOMIES	19 118	-55 251	96 341	247 599	371 879	487 178	543 223	464 704	395 864
TRANSITION ECONOMIES	-8 791	5 140	34 258	61 643	86 119	93 990	106 465	93 381	108 097
DEVELOPED ECONOMIES	-117 733	-18 474	-331 991	-587 012	-739 628	-847 277	-928 325	-810 252	-730 538
Developing economies: Africa	4 081	-5 783	4 033	28 159	47 952	61 037	72 194	39 600	21 789
Eastern Africa	-1 719	-5 989	-7 251	-12 107	-14 806	-17 979	-23 431	-26 891	-29 824
Burundi*(2)	-143	-106	-87	-153	-238	-280	-326	-315	-366
Comoros*	-30	-48	-37	-65	-86	-105	-133	-150	-166
Djibouti (3)	-186	-164	-169	-221	-247	-311	-400	-431	-409
Eritrea	..	-416	-449	-460	-479	-488	-523	-555	-615
Ethiopia	..	-789	-1 062	-2 518	-3 170	-3 900	-5 730	-5 909	-6 049
Ethiopia (former)	-526								
Kenya	-1 080	-832	-1 235	-2 013	-2 866	-3 880	-4 962	-5 585	-6 262
Madagascar*	-119	-112	-155	-623	-761	-901	-1 346	-1 783	-1 903
Malawi	-211	-121	-165	-457	-549	-570	-793	-890	-1 088
Mauritius	-376	-503	-472	-754	-1 031	-1 324	-1 740	-1 903	-2 072
Mayotte	..	..	-146	-263	-313	-384	-483	-528	-547
Mozambique	-731	-646	-671	-634	-561	-596	-827	-1 203	-1 431
Rwanda	-209	-158	-183	-243	-325	-450	-637	-861	-1 052
Seychelles	-128	-191	-233	-227	-306	-404	-500	-511	-541
Somalia	36	-36	-154	-365	-436	-475	-588	-589	-577
Uganda	-94	-555	-1 012	-934	-1 123	-1 375	-1 802	-1 985	-2 246
United Republic of Tanzania	-954	-861	-888	-1 252	-1 727	-2 349	-3 162	-3 491	-3 669
Zambia (4)	264	309	50	-639	-210	186	448	389	812
Zimbabwe	-231	-761	-228	-286	-372	-317	-400	-510	-860
Middle Africa	4 209	5 094	6 993	18 975	28 652	38 063	53 159	49 086	47 290
Angola*(5)	2 028	2 291	3 416	9 141	15 234	22 616	34 431	32 802	30 983
Cameroon*(6)	425	452	178	105	206	-16	-424	-875	-1 095
Central African Republic*(6)	-6	5	31	-17	-35	-53	-89	-123	-166
Chad*(5)	-193	-232	-292	1 082	1 814	2 023	2 099	1 547	1 224
Congo*(6)	338	208	1 359	2 553	3 301	3 523	4 146	3 838	4 537
Dem. Rep. of the Congo*	475	550	154	-180	-203	-258	-129	-167	233
Equatorial Guinea (5)	-14	-42	601	3 718	5 149	6 464	8 274	7 513	6 457
Gabon*(7)	1 175	1 884	1 574	2 610	3 233	3 824	4 931	4 641	5 217
Sao Tome and Principe*	-18	-22	-30	-38	-47	-59	-80	-90	-101
Northern Africa	-3 311	-8 837	-2 042	12 401	23 068	30 662	34 770	13 523	-1 058
Algeria*	2 844	1 352	8 482	16 842	24 192	30 445	35 171	26 097	20 603
Egypt	-7 614	-8 170	-10 125	-6 342	-7 113	-9 018	-13 473	-18 425	-23 633
Libyan Arab Jamahiriya	5 624	3 824	6 439	13 314	20 171	26 477	33 910	29 513	26 537
Morocco*	-2 467	-2 894	-3 768	-7 657	-9 578	-12 502	-16 642	-19 173	-19 604
Sudan (8)	-415	-772	-328	-857	-1 549	-1 415	2	189	334
Tunisia (9)	-1 644	-2 179	-2 742	-2 900	-3 055	-3 323	-4 197	-4 677	-5 295
Southern Africa	3 638	-518	1 307	-6 478	-10 268	-12 503	-14 169	-13 771	-13 799
Botswana*	-112	417	610	610	971	1 248	764	-141	-832
Lesotho	-627	-864	-583	-719	-768	-843	-969	-1 120	-1 264
Namibia	-50	-188	-324	-598	-438	-449	-663	-1 211	-1 522
South Africa	4 533	248	1 669	-5 776	-9 955	-12 383	-13 268	-11 261	-10 080
Swaziland	-105	-133	-64	5	-79	-75	-32	-39	-101
Western Africa	4 263	4 468	5 026	15 368	21 306	22 792	21 864	17 654	19 179
Benin*	41	-162	-266	-379	-420	-641	-830	-946	-873
Burkina Faso	-369	-278	-420	-726	-829	-917	-1 162	-1 181	-1 082
Cape Verde (10)	-125	-223	-226	-392	-453	-558	-682	-733	-722
Côte d'Ivoire*	751	1 059	1 405	2 182	2 231	2 158	2 383	2 843	3 323
Gambia (11)	-146	-193	-159	-206	-239	-269	-288	-302	-287
Ghana	-334	-435	-1 503	-1 685	-2 398	-3 103	-3 921	-3 648	-3 389
Guinea*	-45	-35	88	-8	28	30	13	-16	11
Guinea-Bissau	-62	-82	1	-23	-42	-63	-84	-99	-107
Liberia*	435	225	-164	-148	-233	-283	-424	-455	-491
Mali*	-162	-308	-259	-391	-367	-447	-713	-843	-907
Mauritania*	161	61	-79	-502	-361	-213	1	-86	2
Niger*	-91	-104	-125	-346	-403	-460	-530	-838	-1 130
Nigeria	4 977	5 546	7 732	19 949	27 166	30 691	32 159	28 296	29 050
Saint Helena	-13	-30	-35	-27	-44	-67	-63	-49	-30
Senegal (12)	-486	-366	-644	-1 463	-1 789	-2 419	-3 219	-3 412	-3 213
Sierra Leone*	-25	-97	-121	-182	-164	-182	-226	-278	-355
Togo*	-244	-111	-200	-284	-377	-462	-549	-600	-621

For sources and notes, see end of table.

Percentage of imports (1) Part dans les importations en pourcentage (1)									Régions, pays ou territoires
1989-91	1994-96	1999-01	2003-05	2004-06	2005-07	2006-08	2007-09	2008-10	
-3.10	-1.36	-3.17	-2.97	-2.64	-2.18	-1.93	-1.71	-1.50	**MONDE**
2.51	-3.83	5.32	8.42	10.45	12.01	11.51	9.18	7.22	ÉCONOMIES EN DÉVELOPPEMENT
-5.85	4.82	32.16	26.71	30.35	27.43	23.27	18.51	21.23	ÉCONOMIES EN TRANSITION
-4.62	-0.53	-7.45	-9.24	-10.24	-10.56	-10.29	-8.94	-8.11	ÉCONOMIES DÉVELOPPÉES
4.43	-4.97	3.03	11.97	17.64	19.83	18.93	9.09	4.25	**Économies en développement : Afrique**
-39.89	*-38.11*	*-41.87*	*-44.95*	*-45.95*	*-46.77*	*-48.45*	*-50.61*	*-51.30*	*Afrique orientale*
-63.42	-56.56	-64.18	-76.13	-79.63	-81.99	-84.48	-83.86	-83.80	Burundi*(2)
-59.86	-83.23	-73.07	-75.88	-85.67	-89.59	-92.42	-93.09	-94.09	Comores*
89.20	89.76	84.76	85.20	84.95	85.60	86.25	86.10	84.66	Djibouti (3)
_	-83.37	-95.82	-97.94	-97.62	-97.55	-97.69	-97.90	-98.18	Érythrée
_	-65.75	-68.65	-78.43	-77.92	-78.46	-79.84	-79.76	-78.21	Éthiopie
-62.06	_	_	_	_	_	_	_	_	Éthiopie (anc.)
-50.86	-30.39	-40.52	-40.92	-46.83	-51.35	-54.24	-55.33	-56.26	Kenya
-22.78	-18.63	-16.71	-39.12	-44.78	-46.07	-48.16	-55.69	-59.83	Madagascar*
-36.05	-22.64	-27.50	-46.09	-49.82	-46.11	-47.36	-46.14	-50.76	Malawi
-25.06	-24.56	-21.80	-26.67	-32.04	-36.86	-42.35	-46.40	-48.60	Maurice
..	..	-97.91	-97.96	-98.05	-98.11	-98.38	-98.60	-98.69	Mayotte
-84.86	-77.18	-59.21	-31.36	-23.54	-21.82	-23.91	-32.55	-37.94	Mozambique
-67.65	-76.99	-73.52	-71.52	-71.34	-74.88	-76.10	-79.50	-80.57	Rwanda
-73.45	-71.71	-54.87	-41.59	-46.98	-52.53	-55.69	-56.07	-56.56	Seychelles
52.07	61.54	-41.37	-62.15	-64.54	-61.65	-62.79	-59.66	-56.95	Somalie
-26.87	-53.45	-67.58	-54.94	-53.33	-51.09	-51.31	-48.53	-50.02	Ouganda
-72.25	-56.09	-55.75	-45.71	-49.82	-53.99	-56.75	-56.04	-52.37	République-Unie de Tanzanie
29.36	43.72	7.02	-31.25	-11.13	2.88	12.88	9.90	16.59	Zambie (4)
-11.76	-24.17	-12.49	-12.66	-16.23	-13.40	-14.78	-17.69	-26.54	Zimbabwe
64.80	*81.68*	*86.46*	*115.48*	*149.20*	*159.89*	*166.23*	*128.34*	*106.69*	*Afrique centrale*
142.46	136.93	110.28	131.05	191.25	220.25	238.72	179.64	139.50	Angola*(5)
33.43	40.57	13.29	4.35	6.99	1.28	-7.04	-18.73	-22.15	Cameroun*(6)
1.00	3.52	27.14	-9.81	-19.68	-25.29	-33.52	-44.21	-54.49	République centrafricaine*(6)
-45.99	-51.01	-55.15	112.46	170.07	161.27	126.53	82.12	59.44	Tchad*(5)
50.78	37.94	232.27	236.71	233.10	192.64	165.73	133.48	150.62	Congo*(6)
28.59	62.67	24.07	-8.35	-7.90	-8.66	-4.32	-4.80	4.81	Rép. dém. du Congo*
-22.67	-0.42	99.72	323.04	355.62	338.51	291.61	214.51	149.66	Guinée équatoriale (5)
139.04	217.08	169.93	191.64	212.32	217.59	225.11	191.18	205.70	Gabon*(7)
-77.52	-80.44	-92.00	-85.68	-87.47	-88.98	-90.43	-91.44	-92.38	Sao Tomé-et-Principe*
-7.40	*-20.13*	*-4.09*	*15.51*	*24.77*	*29.06*	*27.30*	*9.42*	*-1.02*	*Afrique septentrionale*
33.29	14.82	89.99	94.41	118.59	132.75	124.38	77.91	51.72	Algérie*
-63.12	-69.86	-70.64	-43.24	-40.09	-40.10	-40.08	-45.01	-48.31	Égypte
106.84	76.34	153.29	149.60	197.56	231.57	243.84	174.73	125.46	Jamahiriya arabe libyenne
-38.43	-31.09	-34.48	-42.96	-45.78	-48.37	-50.30	-53.77	-53.27	Maroc*
-52.63	-57.79	-18.23	-15.90	-21.94	-19.12	-1.32	2.27	3.68	Soudan (8)
-32.65	-29.44	-30.98	-23.74	-22.36	-21.08	-21.47	-22.35	-24.17	Tunisie (9)
15.77	*-0.97*	*3.78*	*-10.17*	*-13.25*	*-13.94*	*-14.22*	*-13.86*	*-13.47*	*Afrique australe*
-5.78	23.98	30.54	20.07	30.74	36.97	23.01	-1.55	-16.31	Botswana*
-90.45	-84.01	-71.80	-54.31	-52.86	-54.38	-55.09	-58.34	-60.97	Lesotho
-3.97	-11.75	-20.65	-26.56	-17.22	-15.00	-17.28	-27.11	-30.49	Namibie
24.37	1.58	5.77	-10.34	-14.47	-15.54	-15.07	-12.85	-11.32	Afrique du Sud
-16.01	-13.19	-6.09	0.75	-4.12	-3.91	-1.62	-2.49	-6.07	Swaziland
30.04	*24.46*	*23.05*	*40.35*	*47.17*	*42.89*	*32.83*	*23.35*	*24.27*	*Afrique occidentale*
16.86	-23.57	-39.90	-40.34	-39.96	-43.99	-44.24	-44.42	-40.14	Bénin*
-75.87	-57.55	-64.89	-63.40	-61.89	-62.10	-64.11	-61.12	-52.54	Burkina Faso
-95.18	-96.22	-95.48	-96.29	-96.23	-96.55	-96.59	-96.20	-95.05	Cap-Vert (10)
35.72	42.48	53.46	51.51	41.22	35.53	35.72	39.83	46.48	Côte d'Ivoire*
-79.04	-88.72	-92.76	-95.88	-96.04	-96.20	-95.81	-95.65	-95.13	Gambie (11)
-29.06	-20.91	-46.70	-38.35	-44.08	-46.26	-46.63	-40.83	-34.41	Ghana
-6.13	-3.89	14.93	-1.41	2.87	3.35	1.69	-1.31	0.66	Guinée*
-77.43	-65.67	2.44	-22.10	-32.41	-40.08	-45.44	-45.28	-46.37	Guinée-Bissau
184.10	53.85	-34.88	-53.42	-63.85	-63.82	-68.15	-69.89	-71.38	Libéria*
-33.34	-43.31	-29.90	-28.04	-23.97	-24.09	-26.92	-31.00	-31.27	Mali*
69.89	14.37	-17.58	-49.93	-30.46	-13.94	2.13	-5.01	-0.02	Mauritanie*
-24.60	-27.22	-30.80	-44.43	-45.46	-45.64	-43.60	-47.38	-52.18	Niger*
88.70	81.13	83.61	120.62	131.10	115.57	92.74	73.29	73.23	Nigéria
-71.32	-86.42	-79.68	-55.72	-66.58	-74.87	-68.13	-57.89	-50.88	Sainte-Hélène
-40.35	-27.83	-39.53	-49.73	-53.15	-59.56	-63.31	-63.16	-59.40	Sénégal (12)
-14.34	-56.45	-89.19	-58.48	-48.71	-46.61	-48.47	-54.97	-58.55	Sierra Leone*
-48.31	-7.35	-35.04	-30.69	-37.09	-40.94	-42.94	-42.36	-41.31	Togo*

Pour les sources et les notes, se reporter à la fin du tableau.

1.3.1 Value of trade balance, and as percentage of imports of countries and geographical regions

Region, country or territory	Trade balance (1) - Balance commerciale (1) Millions of dollars - Millions de dollars								
	1989-91	1994-96	1999-01	2003-05	2004-06	2005-07	2006-08	2007-09	2008-10
Developing economies: America	10 504	-23 519	-30 125	29 321	41 539	37 366	15 758	-2 656	-14 030
Caribbean	*-7 888*	*-7 308*	*-13 122*	*-14 178*	*-16 069*	*-19 460*	*-23 727*	*-25 961*	*-27 873*
Anguilla	..	-55	-85	-95	-141	-188	-237	-215	-184
Antigua and Barbuda	-219	-305	-337	-405	-471	-561	-633	-655	-595
Aruba (13)	-413	-348	-205	-198	-122	-86	-259	-378	-683
Bahamas (14)	-796	-1 047	-1 427	-1 618	-1 932	-2 200	-2 285	-2 188	-2 141
Barbados	-490	-506	-846	-1 108	-1 189	-1 217	-1 266	-1 234	-1 205
Cayman Islands	..	..	..	-1 131	-1 074	-1 051	-1 019	-968	-958
Cuba*	-2 397	-1 151	-3 216	-4 009	-5 412	-6 621	-8 505	-8 278	-8 476
Dominica*	-60	-66	-88	-105	-117	-135	-163	-187	-198
Dominican Republic (15)	-2 320	-1 505	-3 383	-2 611	-3 747	-5 242	-7 082	-7 498	-8 253
Grenada*	-83	-110	-179	-247	-266	-304	-313	-306	-293
Haiti	-184	-429	-716	-913	-1 042	-1 124	-1 408	-1 514	-1 483
Jamaica	-747	-1 328	-1 935	-2 601	-2 927	-3 641	-4 663	-4 766	-4 557
Montserrat*	-38	-27	-20	-26	-27	-28	-30	-29	-30
Netherlands Antilles*(16)	-349	-650	-525	-1 330	-1 353	-1 576	-1 793	-1 887	-1 888
Saint Kitts and Nevis*	-83	-116	-151	-159	-176	-206	-239	-255	-239
Saint Lucia*	-157	-206	-307	-371	-423	-480	-507	-466	-429
Saint Vincent and the Grenadines*	-60	-86	-135	-184	-207	-238	-278	-295	-314
Trinidad and Tobago*	509	609	576	2 397	4 527	5 884	7 488	5 654	4 978
Turks and Caicos Islands	..	..	-143	-219	-326	-444	-537	-495	-461
Central America	*-7 809*	*-11 575*	*-25 100*	*-31 463*	*-35 867*	*-42 021*	*-52 256*	*-52 164*	*-50 425*
Belize	-111	-97	-279	-346	-367	-408	-462	-474	-474
Costa Rica*	-374	-698	-593	-2 104	-2 686	-3 224	-4 226	-4 041	-4 252
El Salvador	-717	-1 478	-1 910	-2 974	-3 418	-3 985	-4 630	-4 463	-4 216
Guatemala (17)	-560	-1 208	-2 556	-4 409	-5 154	-5 899	-6 463	-5 935	-5 499
Honduras (18)	-50	-169	-709	-1 270	-1 606	-2 209	-3 128	-3 179	-3 179
Mexico	-4 565	-5 395	-15 410	-16 192	-17 732	-20 060	-25 194	-24 758	-22 723
Nicaragua	-363	-576	-1 221	-1 490	-1 722	-2 032	-2 403	-2 427	-2 426
Panama*	-1 068	-1 954	-2 422	-2 678	-3 183	-4 203	-5 750	-6 788	-7 657
South America	*26 201*	*-4 637*	*8 097*	*74 962*	*93 476*	*98 848*	*91 740*	*75 469*	*64 267*
Argentina*	5 837	-1 578	1 737	13 174	12 066	11 713	12 219	13 736	14 064
Bolivia (Plurinational State of)	110	-333	-570	245	604	837	1 340	1 154	1 152
Brazil	10 688	-3 171	-2 458	31 156	37 705	38 958	30 513	22 964	15 113
Chile*	683	-887	907	6 200	12 178	16 436	15 110	11 884	8 740
Colombia	1 333	-3 409	626	-463	-746	-1 698	-2 031	-1 516	-714
Ecuador	602	403	652	-380	-15	238	289	-324	-1 479
Falkland Islands (Malvinas)	-20	-11	28	64	65	72	81	82	79
Guyana*	-50	-48	-90	-119	-198	-306	-400	-432	-480
Paraguay	-290	-1 962	-1 249	-1 117	-1 884	-2 525	-3 509	-3 795	-4 616
Peru*	617	-1 788	-471	2 750	5 364	6 966	5 869	4 702	4 092
Suriname	-17	-75	-109	-28	59	141	305	284	388
Uruguay	238	-853	-1 097	-214	-487	-840	-1 523	-1 751	-1 975
Venezuela (Bolivarian Rep. of)	6 471	9 076	10 197	23 694	28 766	28 855	33 470	28 483	29 902
Developing economies: Asia	6 760	-24 584	124 015	193 163	285 473	392 061	459 214	432 270	393 032
Eastern Asia	*10 823*	*-7 172*	*41 451*	*76 065*	*124 556*	*198 458*	*244 906*	*257 809*	*232 134*
China	3 421	11 392	25 289	53 104	103 809	180 296	245 393	252 072	225 577
China, Hong Kong SAR	-347	-15 748	-9 254	-10 048	-13 292	-17 066	-22 278	-25 923	-32 550
China, Macao SAR	62	-37	119	-759	-1 370	-2 089	-2 733	-3 284	-3 891
China, Taiwan Province of	13 007	9 892	11 207	12 524	13 908	20 877	20 599	23 403	22 208
Korea, Dem. People's Rep. of	-937	-353	-846	-1 121	-1 309	-1 432	-1 478	-1 330	-873
Korea, Republic of (19)	-4 524	-12 340	15 020	22 518	22 882	17 969	5 819	13 382	22 225
Mongolia	-173	21	-85	-152	-71	-97	-416	-511	-561
Southern Asia	*-12 217*	*-5 057*	*-8 033*	*-30 585*	*-40 477*	*-52 590*	*-74 211*	*-90 757*	*-105 534*
Afghanistan	-514	-326	-1 171	-1 972	-2 044	-2 194	-2 325	-2 578	-3 393
Bangladesh	-2 005	-2 639	-2 755	-3 922	-4 185	-4 989	-6 278	-7 127	-7 931
Bhutan	-17	-21	-74	-157	-121	5	41	31	-89
India (20)	-4 336	-3 578	-9 162	-26 648	-41 006	-59 542	-87 219	-99 085	-108 491
Iran (Islamic Rep. of)*	-1 974	6 602	8 815	10 873	20 488	32 081	45 433	42 806	40 953
Maldives	-64	-184	-291	-454	-582	-718	-875	-908	-917
Nepal	-434	-885	-775	-1 226	-1 413	-1 776	-2 186	-2 822	-3 502
Pakistan	-2 044	-2 601	-1 524	-4 994	-8 924	-12 318	-16 551	-16 961	-17 501
Sri Lanka	-828	-1 425	-1 095	-2 083	-2 692	-3 140	-4 250	-4 114	-4 662
South-Eastern Asia	*-13 665*	*-28 661*	*47 844*	*54 799*	*62 417*	*73 702*	*74 476*	*75 530*	*79 207*
Brunei Darussalam*	1 237	218	2 171	3 829	4 777	5 421	6 561	6 165	6 243
Cambodia (5)	-67	-338	-534	-677	-853	-1 146	-1 410	-1 575	-1 758

For sources and notes, see end of table.

44

Percentage of imports (1) Part dans les importations en pourcentage (1)									Régions, pays ou territoires
1989-91	1994-96	1999-01	2003-05	2004-06	2005-07	2006-08	2007-09	2008-10	
8.76	-9.74	-8.20	6.28	7.56	6.18	2.71	-0.18	-1.56	Économies en développement : Amérique
-41.95	-36.33	-43.07	-39.71	-38.07	-39.28	-40.47	-45.56	-49.50	Caraïbes
..	-97.39	-96.15	-92.34	-92.36	-93.08	-95.53	-92.80	-91.41	Anguilla
-88.95	-86.99	-84.24	-85.17	-86.83	-88.30	-90.73	-92.88	-93.37	Antigua-et-Barbuda
-61.18	-19.46	-10.18	-7.61	-3.81	-2.73	-6.87	-14.14	-38.99	Aruba (13)
-59.56	-85.62	-74.60	-76.79	-76.96	-76.40	-73.66	-72.74	-73.18	Bahamas (14)
-70.68	-68.60	-76.12	-79.00	-76.94	-73.95	-72.76	-73.21	-73.61	Barbade
..	..	..	-94.96	-96.23	-96.62	-97.76	-97.87	-98.21	Îles Caïmanes
-43.99	-41.55	-66.54	-64.59	66.92	68.40	60.11	60.13	60.41	Cuba*
-53.91	-57.43	-63.53	-71.36	-73.66	-76.73	-79.68	-82.99	-84.31	Dominique*
-75.09	-28.57	-38.50	-30.25	-36.06	-43.59	-50.28	-53.52	-56.70	République dominicaine (15)
-75.48	-83.07	-80.92	-88.04	-90.21	-91.36	-91.37	-90.70	-91.20	Grenade*
-53.54	-78.96	-69.89	-69.51	-69.67	-69.32	-73.19	-73.71	-77.91	Haïti
-40.56	-49.40	-60.56	-65.70	-64.75	-66.05	-67.65	-70.75	-73.27	Jamaïque
-96.01	-90.11	-95.12	-91.39	-92.02	-93.90	-91.96	-89.86	-91.67	Montserrat*
-17.11	-29.56	-20.60	-64.67	-69.04	-70.28	-68.89	-69.01	-67.80	Antilles néerlandaises*(16)
-77.02	-84.59	-83.90	-80.36	-81.92	-84.48	-84.66	-85.22	-83.42	Saint-Kitts-et-Nevis*
-56.14	-66.78	-86.49	-84.27	-84.17	-84.66	-80.81	-76.02	-72.17	Sainte-Lucie*
-44.22	-64.88	-73.39	-82.78	-84.37	-84.92	-85.79	-85.56	-86.79	Saint-Vincent-et-les Grenadines*
41.69	41.48	17.01	47.26	75.71	89.25	95.87	66.82	60.94	Trinité-et-Tobago*
..	..	-94.73	-94.60	-95.36	-96.27	-96.49	-95.83	-95.14	Îles Turques et Caïques
-14.20	-11.78	-12.83	-12.96	-13.00	-13.36	-14.67	-14.92	-14.15	Amérique centrale
-48.62	-37.82	-58.48	-62.26	-61.52	-62.81	-62.95	-64.91	-64.14	Belize
-19.90	-17.39	-9.05	-24.18	-26.95	-28.24	-31.34	-29.77	-30.92	Costa Rica*
-54.10	-48.77	-40.56	-47.44	-49.44	-51.60	-53.09	-51.76	-49.33	El Salvador
-32.51	-39.48	-49.65	-46.91	-48.38	-49.16	-48.51	-44.48	-41.02	Guatemala (17)
-5.16	-9.35	-18.35	-22.14	-24.27	-28.51	-34.46	-36.51	-35.81	Honduras (18)
-9.43	-6.46	-9.07	-7.86	-7.61	-7.54	-8.38	-8.40	-7.58	Mexique
-53.79	-57.73	-67.29	-66.87	-66.18	-66.45	-66.03	-63.94	-60.51	Nicaragua
-74.84	-76.14	-73.48	-73.79	-75.58	-78.69	-82.22	-85.71	-88.33	Panama*
46.41	-3.37	5.41	13.81	13.35	36.00	27.64	19.92	15.09	Amérique du Sud
126.11	-7.21	8.91	69.47	43.67	33.91	28.01	30.36	29.23	Argentine*
18.94	-22.58	-32.56	11.49	24.42	28.62	35.18	26.25	23.02	Bolivie (État plurinational de)
50.06	-3.33	-4.47	47.36	47.34	41.11	26.39	16.61	9.48	Brésil
8.85	-4.81	5.33	23.12	36.67	40.77	34.54	25.48	17.36	Chili*
25.98	-26.06	5.80	-3.07	-3.25	-5.61	-6.41	1.10	1.81	Colombie
30.54	10.26	22.38	-4.91	-0.83	1.79	2.34	-2.06	-7.91	Équateur
-51.97	-25.65	58.33	86.14	88.62	93.98	109.18	119.34	114.48	Îles Falkland (Malvinas)
-16.76	-9.11	-15.18	-16.56	-24.23	-33.23	-36.43	-36.57	-37.03	Guyana*
-15.40	-67.79	-59.09	-41.10	-50.85	-54.21	-54.59	-52.29	-53.27	Paraguay
22.62	-25.00	-6.66	24.59	40.46	43.81	32.60	21.69	15.74	Pérou*
-2.37	-15.82	-21.95	-3.25	6.70	13.69	26.58	23.77	28.71	Suriname
19.01	-28.57	-33.28	-5.80	-11.67	-16.94	-22.26	-23.82	-23.99	Uruguay
80.79	89.88	60.76	141.56	120.01	92.22	78.86	61.13	68.02	Venezuela (Rép. bolivarienne du)
1.32	-2.19	9.72	8.69	10.48	12.59	12.74	11.33	9.50	Économies en développement : Asie
3.98	-1.29	6.41	6.11	8.36	11.71	12.73	12.98	10.80	Asie orientale
5.99	8.67	12.53	9.10	14.52	21.73	25.34	24.43	19.66	Chine
-0.24	-8.42	-4.61	-3.76	-4.37	-5.01	-6.09	-7.08	-8.29	Chine (RAS de Hong Kong)
4.75	-1.67	5.62	-20.74	-33.29	-44.44	-53.12	-64.86	-75.40	Chine (RAS de Macao)
23.05	10.15	9.77	8.26	7.33	10.23	9.45	11.60	10.62	Province chinoise de Taiwan
-32.80	-26.53	-53.06	-47.56	-48.67	-48.98	-46.21	-40.95	-26.00	Corée, Rép. populaire dém. de
-5.76	-9.12	11.32	10.12	9.05	6.06	2.08	4.35	6.21	Corée, République de (19)
-19.05	5.47	-14.16	-16.01	-7.02	-5.67	-12.23	-17.10	-17.35	Mongolie
-21.89	-6.80	-8.69	-15.93	-17.38	-18.35	-19.68	-22.64	-23.90	Asie méridionale
-67.91	-64.91	-89.29	-87.86	-84.88	-83.67	-82.89	-84.13	-87.50	Afghanistan
-56.19	-43.15	-31.56	-32.36	-30.15	-30.83	-31.64	-33.18	-32.43	Bangladesh
-20.30	-19.02	-40.68	-45.09	-29.98	-2.12	7.67	5.93	-11.76	Bhoutan
-19.96	-10.43	-18.59	-24.06	-28.40	-32.15	-35.18	-36.55	-35.94	Inde (20)
-7.78	49.05	58.11	31.25	51.61	75.60	94.78	83.89	71.74	Iran (Rép. islamique d')*
-46.46	-69.26	-73.76	-72.61	-75.27	-77.73	-77.01	-79.29	-80.14	Maldives
-71.05	-69.72	-52.17	-61.54	-62.91	-66.92	-70.80	-75.76	-79.61	Népal
-26.98	-23.52	-14.58	-23.55	-35.13	-41.73	-46.83	-47.30	-46.65	Pakistan
-31.04	-27.99	-18.22	-26.38	-29.61	-30.84	-35.36	-34.23	-36.57	Sri Lanka
-8.26	-8.35	13.94	11.16	10.31	10.56	9.64	9.57	9.25	Asie du Sud-Est
120.77	11.18	186.27	269.30	310.19	313.33	314.15	260.04	229.27	Brunéi Darussalam*
-42.68	-34.01	-28.54	-20.26	-20.92	-24.39	-25.03	-26.43	-26.71	Cambodge (5)

Pour les sources et les notes, se reporter à la fin du tableau.

Region, country or territory	Trade balance (1) - Balance commerciale (1) Millions of dollars - Millions de dollars								
	1989-91	1994-96	1999-01	2003-05	2004-06	2005-07	2006-08	2007-09	2008-10
Indonesia including East Timor	4 790	7 306	19 729	–	–	–	–	–	–
Indonesia	–	–	–	16 622	16 718	19 668	20 202	21 207	21 240
Lao People's Dem. Rep.*	-103	-303	-203	-268	-285	-217	-211	-288	-345
Malaysia (21)	154	-1 541	16 546	21 442	25 464	28 402	34 687	36 132	37 734
Myanmar	-51	-398	-813	821	1 364	2 315	2 570	2 676	2 977
Philippines	-4 117	-11 298	1 502	-7 459	-7 565	-7 904	-8 461	-8 715	-8 501
Singapore (22)	-6 830	-6 136	4 210	26 119	29 252	32 939	29 203	26 187	27 840
Thailand*	-8 270	-13 385	6 040	-547	-1 354	2 221	3 954	8 980	8 387
Timor-Leste (23)	–	–	–	-113	-103	-122	-172	-237	-275
Viet Nam	-406	-2 786	-804	-4 970	-4 997	-7 876	-12 446	-15 001	-14 334
Western Asia	**21 819**	**16 306**	**42 754**	**92 884**	**138 977**	**172 491**	**214 042**	**189 688**	**187 226**
Bahrain (5)	-286	229	1 166	666	1 090	1 935	2 675	2 680	2 596
Iraq*	2 042	-1 005	3 999	-1 081	2 407	9 548	18 903	18 009	13 983
Jordan	-1 311	-2 121	-2 387	-4 357	-5 561	-6 754	-7 678	-8 255	-8 347
Kuwait'	1 601	6 360	8 404	18 242	27 026	36 338	47 513	45 027	45 621
Lebanon (24)	-2 328	-6 296	-5 778	-6 736	-7 180	-7 602	-9 270	-11 122	-12 709
Occupied Palestinian territory	..	-1 470	-2 120	-1 971	-2 261	-2 451	-2 677	-2 907	-3 305
Oman	2 106	2 073	4 706	6 479	8 337	9 564	11 208	11 047	13 937
Qatar*	1 507	729	6 554	11 997	14 965	16 842	20 753	22 819	33 483
Saudi Arabia*(25)	15 378	24 727	35 590	85 353	113 683	135 148	160 887	146 025	142 249
Syrian Arab Republic*	1 127	-1 649	247	-665	-1 061	-1 789	-2 139	-3 479	-4 069
Turkey*	-6 988	-13 219	-16 811	-33 252	-43 904	-53 377	-62 256	-57 171	-60 128
United Arab Emirates	10 207	8 511	8 150	18 085	30 230	35 557	37 636	29 684	26 062
Yemen*	–	-51	1 032	124	298	-469	-1 501	-2 670	-2 348
Developing economies: Oceania	**-2 226**	**-1 365**	**-1 582**	**-3 044**	**-3 085**	**-3 287**	**-3 942**	**-4 511**	**-4 928**
American Samoa*(26)	-55	-183	-155	-152	-144	-158	-150	-147	-103
Cook Islands	-46	-55	-39	-69	-80	-91	-114	-142	-211
Fiji	-280	-321	-329	-732	-922	-1 019	-1 162	-1 062	-933
French Polynesia*	-768	-742	-796	-1 408	-1 409	-1 533	-1 667	-1 715	-1 682
Guam	-321	-298	-346	-471	-460	-508	-529	-575	-593
Kiribati	-22	-27	-35	-59	-62	-63	-59	-56	-55
Marshall Islands	-47	-51	-50	-64	-67	-70	-74	-74	-83
Micronesia (Federated States of)	-76	-61	-94	-112	-119	-120	-123	-131	-134
Nauru	33	6	5	-7	-18	-30	-19	-35	-54
New Caledonia*	-305	-414	-448	-680	-683	-717	-1 135	-1 395	-1 838
Niue	-4	-4	-2	-6	-6	-5	-5	-6	-6
Northern Mariana Islands	..	..	..	162	162	..	..	..	..
Palau	..	-36	-92	-92	-99	-97	-105	-102	-104
Papua New Guinea	-121	1 030	794	1 089	1 433	1 720	1 922	1 697	1 737
Samoa (24)	-74	-85	-81	-113	-162	-177	-198	-190	-217
Solomon Islands*	-29	9	-17	-42	-67	-100	-112	-115	-134
Tokelau	..	..	..	0	0	0	0	0	..
Tonga	-47	-61	-62	-92	-102	-117	-133	-143	-148
Tuvalu	-3	-7	-6	-11	-12	-14	-18	-18	-19
Vanuatu	-64	-66	-68	-93	-123	-153	-201	-223	-242
Wallis and Futuna Islands	..	..	-33	-48	-54	-54	-57	..	..
Transition economies	**-8 791**	**5 140**	**34 258**	**61 643**	**86 119**	**93 990**	**106 465**	**93 381**	**108 097**
Albania	-202	-536	-910	-1 693	-1 975	-2 444	-3 089	-3 488	-3 469
Armenia*	–	-382	-562	-682	-881	-1 357	-2 208	-2 679	-2 916
Azerbaijan (27)	–	-197	482	1 167	3 762	8 914	15 573	17 982	19 422
Belarus	–	-868	-973	-1 686	-2 021	-2 588	-4 615	-6 164	-7 892
Bosnia and Herzegovina*(28)	–	-1 093	-3 089	-4 067	-4 252	-4 756	-5 560	-5 830	-5 449
Croatia*	–	-2 367	-3 811	-8 792	-9 822	-11 455	-13 731	-13 604	-11 863
Georgia (29)	–	-355	-425	-1 168	-1 836	-2 762	-3 740	-3 927	-3 774
Kazakhstan*(29)	–	928	2 324	6 929	10 583	13 352	21 084	21 132	27 176
Kyrgyzstan	–	-141	-63	-293	-593	-1 007	-1 575	-1 684	-1 682
Montenegro	–	–	–	–	–	–	–	–	-2 242
Republic of Moldova	–	-165	-247	-869	-1 212	-1 731	-2 431	-2 549	-2 537
Russian Federation (30)	–	14 021	43 754	78 054	101 558	112 384	127 309	117 188	123 270
Serbia and Montenegro*	–	-1 700	-2 244	-6 520	-7 393	-8 838	–	–	–
Serbia	–	–	–	–	–	–	–	–	-8 848
SFR of Yugoslavia (former)	-2 239	–	–	–	–	–	–	–	–
Tajikistan (29)	–	-55	33	-266	-346	-583	-1 058	-1 470	-1 625
TFYR of Macedonia*	–	-464	-631	-1 127	-1 266	-1 472	-2 051	-2 380	-2 474
Turkmenistan (29)	–	523	293	1 222	2 381	3 631	5 055	3 472	2 172
Ukraine (29)	–	-2 000	281	603	-1 636	-6 633	-12 191	-11 869	-11 240
USSR (former)	-6 351	–	–	–	–	–	–	–	–
Uzbekistan (29)	–	-8	46	833	1 069	1 337	1 316	1 475	2 069

For sources and notes, see end of table.

Percentage of imports (1) Part dans les importations en pourcentage (1)									Régions, pays ou territoires
1989-91	1994-96	1999-01	2003-05	2004-06	2005-07	2006-08	2007-09	2008-10	
24.06	19.50	51.63	–	–	–	–	–	–	Indonésie, y compris le Timor oriental
–	–	–	32.89	24.25	23.26	21.79	21.54	18.85	Indonésie
-56.00	-49.03	-38.82	-37.91	-34.35	-22.52	-17.51	-21.55	-22.13	Rép. dém. populaire lao*
1.94	-2.08	22.80	21.27	21.68	21.85	23.33	24.95	25.19	Malaisie (21)
-1.57	-30.38	-33.27	41.68	61.70	89.78	77.70	69.16	65.63	Myanmar
-33.21	-39.89	4.43	-16.08	-15.22	-14.88	-14.62	-15.93	-15.52	Philippines
-11.51	-5.17	3.55	15.54	14.37	14.13	11.11	9.75	9.58	Singapour (22)
-25.54	-20.04	10.76	0.38	-1.06	1.25	2.98	6.69	5.67	Thaïlande*
–	–	–	-93.38	-92.46	-93.32	-94.10	-96.11	-95.58	Timor-Leste (23)
-15.85	-32.80	-5.12	-16.37	-13.48	-15.27	-18.80	-21.08	-18.39	Viet Nam
25.95	**13.60**	**25.34**	**29.72**	**36.57**	**39.15**	**38.53**	**30.37**	**28.35**	**Asie occidentale**
-7.67	5.67	27.08	9.54	11.32	18.80	22.97	23.28	22.34	Bahreïn (5)
23.75	-37.98	31.11	-8.73	10.69	47.16	73.44	65.60	27.62	Iraq*
-53.99	-55.91	-54.10	-52.38	-55.20	-57.16	-55.32	-55.41	-54.02	Jordanie
27.42	70.07	112.81	132.87	178.47	200.71	223.26	199.62	199.99	Koweït*
-81.44	-91.10	-87.61	-76.02	-74.56	-72.47	-71.69	-72.99	-73.65	Liban (24)
..	-79.70	-85.51	-86.24	-86.98	-85.93	-84.91	-84.54	-85.71	Territoire palestinien occupé
79.41	48.32	90.15	79.93	86.67	86.86	71.12	57.54	68.89	Oman
96.00	32.17	206.23	176.18	154.56	111.16	92.81	89.24	139.39	Qatar*
60.78	93.13	118.55	174.07	190.78	188.34	177.87	144.04	133.51	Arabie saoudite*(25)
47.57	-31.42	5.98	-4.81	-10.50	-13.90	-13.76	-22.01	-23.55	République arabe syrienne*
-34.56	-36.14	-35.75	-34.72	-37.01	-37.57	-36.76	-33.02	-33.59	Turquie*
87.93	39.27	22.43	23.43	33.35	34.35	27.97	17.04	13.96	Émirats arabes unis
–	-0.34	44.64	2.65	5.30	-4.07	-14.64	-28.44	-24.04	Yémen*
-43.14	**-22.71**	**-26.17**	**-33.56**	**-31.25**	**-29.76**	**-30.74**	**-34.60**	**-36.93**	**Économies en développement : Océanie**
-14.74	-39.20	-31.24	-26.23	-25.54	-27.06	-23.74	-22.87	-16.86	Samoa américaines*(26)
-91.39	-92.82	-86.36	-90.62	-93.53	-95.05	-96.28	-96.95	-98.04	Îles Cook
-41.85	-36.18	-36.93	-50.92	-56.64	-58.60	-59.51	-57.75	-55.70	Fidji
-87.60	-76.76	-77.70	-88.54	-87.01	-87.69	-87.60	-89.12	-89.32	Polynésie française*
-80.42	-77.93	-82.30	-90.51	-89.73	-88.80	-86.65	-87.50	-89.74	Guam
-85.36	-82.14	-86.44	-94.86	-93.42	-90.16	-85.26	-78.78	-76.57	Kiribati
-90.19	-70.04	-83.14	-76.41	-75.23	-75.38	-77.70	-77.84	-80.00	Îles Marshall
-93.55	-62.34	-88.64	-88.02	-88.89	-87.38	-84.84	-83.88	-83.10	Micronésie (États fédérés de)
190.92	24.09	47.51	-29.36	-64.50	-82.45	-49.08	-45.71	-45.87	Nauru
-35.38	-43.96	-46.81	-41.43	-37.13	-33.22	-40.35	-48.32	-60.49	Nouvelle-Calédonie*
-98.75	-93.22	-90.32	-96.80	-87.82	-74.62	-75.34	-85.85	-99.65	Nioué
..	..	..	24.40	24.40	..	..	..	..	Îles Mariannes du Nord
..	-69.99	-88.54	-90.68	-89.74	-88.08	-89.38	-89.68	-89.64	Palaos
-7.39	66.85	69.94	67.81	74.52	76.78	67.10	52.30	48.63	Papouasie-Nouvelle-Guinée
-88.35	-92.08	-73.49	-54.98	-66.40	-67.70	-71.54	-72.79	-78.61	Samoa (24)
-27.56	6.09	-19.60	-28.42	-36.03	-43.61	-40.92	-39.09	-39.56	Îles Salomon*
..	..	..	-3.61	42.70	83.19	149.22	44.14	..	Tokélaou
-80.72	-82.21	-87.15	-86.21	-89.76	-92.49	-93.42	-94.36	-94.67	Tonga
-66.23	-94.36	-99.31	-99.02	-99.31	-99.51	-99.48	-98.90	-98.47	Tuvalu
-75.88	-70.39	-73.84	-73.25	-74.37	-76.84	-79.26	-80.22	-81.75	Vanuatu
..	..	-99.87	-99.80	-99.93	-99.94	-99.94	..	..	Îles Wallis-et-Futuna
-5.85	**4.82**	**32.16**	**26.71**	**30.35**	**27.43**	**23.27**	**18.51**	**21.23**	**Économies en transition**
-44.55	-74.63	-76.66	-74.87	-74.19	-74.35	-74.13	-74.83	-72.18	Albanie
–	-57.05	-66.13	-46.58	-49.19	-54.45	-64.41	-72.62	-76.09	Arménie*
–	-23.47	36.53	27.70	77.19	167.00	248.65	281.13	290.78	Azerbaïdjan (27)
–	-16.79	-12.27	-11.60	-10.85	-10.49	-14.80	-19.37	-23.41	Bélarus
–	-85.97	-76.40	-68.39	-62.93	-59.37	-56.84	-56.90	-53.79	Bosnie-Herzégovine*(28)
–	-33.09	-45.88	-53.61	-52.03	-52.19	-52.64	-52.27	-48.60	Croatie*
–	-65.02	-59.27	-63.25	-67.73	-71.49	-74.80	-75.13	-72.71	Géorgie (29)
–	22.67	49.29	48.34	55.74	54.50	64.42	61.53	92.50	Kazakhstan*(29)
–	-17.92	-10.41	-28.80	-40.33	-49.93	-53.64	-50.68	-48.27	Kirghizistan
–	–	–	–	–	–	–	–	-81.63	Monténégro
–	-18.62	-31.58	-46.95	-52.69	-59.02	-64.01	-63.98	-62.76	République de Moldova
–	21.19	86.92	70.06	71.83	62.87	52.94	44.95	45.68	Fédération de Russie (30)
–	-47.27	-56.37	-62.51	-58.06	-54.76	–	–	–	Serbie-et-Monténégro*
–	–	–	–	–	–	–	–	-47.17	Serbie
-12.91	–	–	–	–	–	–	–	–	RSF de Yougoslavie (anc.)
–	-8.43	4.92	-21.90	-24.99	-30.67	-38.66	-52.63	-57.43	Tadjikistan (29)
–	-28.74	-33.81	-40.11	-38.57	-36.36	-38.34	-41.82	-42.95	LERY de Macédoine*
–	37.51	13.54	42.97	87.94	122.01	136.42	75.82	38.61	Turkménistan (29)
–	-12.51	1.76	2.53	-2.48	-12.92	-18.40	-17.65	-16.58	Ukraine (29)
-3.96	–	–	–	–	–	–	–	–	URSS (anc.)
–	1.87	1.57	25.17	27.98	28.15	21.98	18.89	23.80	Ouzbékistan (29)

Pour les sources et les notes, se reporter à la fin du tableau.

1.3.1 Value of trade balance, and as percentage of imports of countries and geographical regions

Region, country or territory	Trade balance (1) - Balance commerciale (1) Millions of dollars - Millions de dollars								
	1989-91	1994-96	1999-01	2003-05	2004-06	2005-07	2006-08	2007-09	2008-10
Developed economies: America	**-110 673**	**-166 799**	**-403 671**	**-678 672**	**-777 955**	**-827 328**	**-838 643**	**-743 504**	**-698 933**
Bermuda (5)	-494	-505	-671	-877	-973	-1 049	-1 115	-1 105	-1 038
Canada	2 935	20 383	27 555	26 757	28 119	29 033	31 340	16 091	5 235
Greenland	-14	-80	-90	-158	-199	-230	-293	-328	-374
Saint Pierre and Miquelon	-55	-48	-98	-50	-48	-38	-39	-46	-53
United States (31)	-113 046	-186 550	-430 368	-704 344	-804 854	-855 044	-868 537	-758 117	-702 703
Developed economies: Asia	**59 551**	**86 952**	**80 743**	**88 956**	**83 104**	**77 308**	**56 300**	**43 644**	**38 673**
Israel*	-5 188	-9 965	-6 674	-4 378	4 054	-4 296	-5 116	-4 383	-3 664
Japan	64 739	96 918	87 417	93 334	87 158	81 605	61 416	48 027	42 337
Developed economies: Europe	**-63 740**	**67 906**	**-1 420**	**26 064**	**-21 426**	**-73 349**	**-124 719**	**-91 720**	**-64 639**
Andorra*	..	-941	-1 005	-1 564	-1 634	-1 689	-1 747	-1 713	-1 604
Austria*	-6 020	-9 001	-4 003	-2 017	-1 077	674	667	2 820	6 162
Belgium*	..	12 326	12 288	19 176	17 333	16 719	13 325	14 236	15 032
Bulgaria*	580	-291	-1 778	-4 774	-6 376	-8 673	-11 361	-11 035	-8 803
Cyprus*	-1 587	-2 368	-2 822	-4 253	-4 995	-5 883	-7 258	-7 579	-7 535
Czechoslovakia (former) (32)	-16								
Czech Republic*(33)	_	-4 726	-4 335	-1 491	785	2 552	3 601	5 647	6 417
Denmark*(34)	3 127	5 576	5 549	9 169	8 496	7 239	6 571	7 963	10 508
Estonia*(29)	_	-728	-1 182	-2 420	-2 893	-3 646	-3 990	-3 101	-1 763
Faeroe Islands	66	61	-11	-98	-95	-183	-180	-142	-39
Finland*	-99	9 036	10 786	9 141	8 204	7 621	6 930	4 974	2 656
France*	-20 505	5 091	-2 246	-22 090	-35 165	-52 615	-72 437	-82 362	-87 218
Germany*	_	56 854	69 830	178 058	196 268	220 294	242 388	239 611	218 266
Gibraltar (35)	-281	-308	-345	-335	-374	-445	-509	-525	-513
Greece*	-11 062	-14 481	-20 598	-35 309	-39 120	-44 951	-54 547	-56 531	-52 194
Hungary*(36)	355	-2 946	-3 369	-4 549	-3 860	-2 261	-1 201	1 542	4 034
Iceland	-105	22	-476	-842	-1 554	-1 974	-1 755	-758	109
Ireland*	3 267	11 584	27 684	40 918	39 850	38 108	38 277	44 089	50 371
Italy*	-12 382	31 308	8 320	-3 786	-12 941	-16 357	-18 838	-13 007	-21 699
Latvia*	_	-550	-1 348	-2 988	-3 999	-5 307	-6 120	-5 026	-3 407
Lithuania*(29)		-824	-1 775	-3 173	-4 016	-5 409	-6 636	-5 508	-3 942
Luxembourg*	-1 291	-2 094	-2 827	-3 249	-3 517	-3 976	-5 097	-5 097	-4 830
Malta	-776	-988	-863	-1 111	-1 304	-1 491	-1 784	-1 909	-1 900
Netherlands*	5 106	15 488	16 485	37 150	42 323	49 117	53 855	56 443	55 882
Norway	6 268	10 146	21 063	36 644	46 594	54 036	65 388	63 303	62 686
Poland*	2 389	-7 731	-16 659	-13 762	-14 338	-17 973	-26 638	-25 541	-22 991
Portugal*	-8 402	-9 818	-15 456	-19 186	-22 687	-26 174	-30 875	-31 352	-30 448
Romania*	-1 410	-2 225	-2 915	-9 432	-13 533	-20 402	-27 617	-25 955	-20 221
Slovakia*	_	-1 123	-2 015	-2 222	-2 664	-2 659	-2 659	-1 475	-1 167
Slovenia*	_	-921	-1 272	-1 190	-1 131	-1 151	-1 753	-1 560	-1 271
Spain*	-31 291	-13 931	-36 564	-74 670	-95 517	-115 601	-129 814	-113 393	-90 992
Sweden*	3 697	14 299	14 326	20 191	20 759	18 352	16 854	13 724	11 730
Switzerland*	-5 846	1 785	-1 194	5 339	5 951	7 237	11 485	15 031	17 732
United Kingdom*	-36 654	-29 017	-62 090	-115 208	-134 899	-155 131	-169 618	-161 892	-152 374
Developed economies: Oceania	**-2 871**	**-6 533**	**-7 642**	**-23 361**	**-23 351**	**-23 909**	**-21 263**	**-18 672**	**-5 640**
Australia	-3 278	-6 398	-7 079	-19 984	-19 458	-19 882	-17 835	-16 377	-4 724
New Zealand	408	-134	-563	-3 377	-3 894	-4 027	-3 428	-2 295	-916

For sources and notes, see next page.

Percentage of imports (1) Part dans les importations en pourcentage (1)									Régions, pays ou territoires
1989-91	1994-96	1999-01	2003-05	2004-06	2005-07	2006-08	2007-09	2008-10	
-17.60	**-18.06**	**-28.80**	**-37.38**	**-37.95**	**-36.84**	**-34.68**	**-31.95**	**-30.30**	**Économies développées : Amérique**
-90.31	-90.68	-93.58	-93.80	-95.09	-96.84	-97.80	-97.69	-97.51	Bermudes (5)
2.39	12.09	11.88	9.51	8.70	8.11	8.09	3.72	0.93	Canada
-3.41	-18.72	-24.09	-29.14	-33.45	-35.91	-39.73	-43.54	-47.93	Groenland
-65.76	-83.90	-85.05	-86.91	-73.05	-68.42	-68.60	-82.64	-87.55	Saint-Pierre-et-Miquelon
-22.37	-24.57	-36.80	-46.14	-46.64	-45.34	-42.78	-38.88	-36.44	États-Unis (31)
24.49	**25.84**	**21.38**	**18.36**	**15.18**	**12.41**	**8.44**	**6.50**	**5.41**	**Économies développées : Asie**
-30.78	-34.51	-18.95	-10.54	-8.74	-8.25	-8.52	-7.08	-5.81	Israël*
28.54	31.28	25.53	21.06	17.37	14.31	9.98	7.76	6.40	Japon
-3.84	**3.13**	**-0.03**	**0.77**	**-0.38**	**-1.39**	**-2.14**	**-1.47**	**-1.01**	**Économies développées : Europe**
..	-95.19	-95.56	-93.08	-92.22	-92.33	-93.31	-94.80	-95.82	Andorre*
-17.26	-15.44	-6.35	-1.79	-1.10	-0.55	-0.54	-1.84	-3.31	Autriche*
..	8.29	7.12	7.05	5.55	4.65	3.40	3.66	3.95	Belgique*
10.74	-5.49	-27.65	-32.52	-33.94	-36.22	-37.57	-36.09	-29.58	Bulgarie*
-63.79	-66.55	-74.30	-79.34	-80.11	-80.46	-83.08	-84.14	-84.00	Chypre*
0.56									Tchécoslovaquie (anc.) (32)
–	-18.10	-12.72	-2.93	0.85	2.54	2.96	4.85	5.38	République tchèque*(33)
9.66	13.24	12.20	13.84	11.32	8.71	6.80	8.60	11.87	Danemark*(34)
–	-27.83	-24.78	-27.61	-27.14	-27.45	-26.66	-20.93	-12.77	Estonie*(29)
21.08	21.29	-2.02	-13.25	-12.58	-20.98	-19.10	-14.36	-3.74	Îles Féroé
-0.14	31.89	32.62	18.70	14.11	10.98	8.85	6.17	3.43	Finlande*
-9.09	1.71	-0.61	-4.59	-6.86	-9.29	-11.27	-12.96	-13.91	France*
–	13.02	14.41	25.46	24.76	24.13	23.16	22.73	20.63	Allemagne*
-81.93	-72.17	-73.72	-65.03	-63.61	-64.10	-64.79	-64.91	-65.20	Gibraltar (35)
-57.37	-57.37	-64.39	-69.80	-68.88	-68.54	-69.62	-70.67	-69.35	Grèce*
5.20	-19.02	-10.82	-8.10	-5.83	-3.15	-1.47	2.06	4.88	Hongrie*(36)
-6.11	2.13	-19.04	-21.72	-31.01	-34.40	-28.06	-9.75	5.63	Islande
16.76	37.29	55.95	67.20	59.38	51.21	47.81	59.87	76.22	Irlande*
-7.23	15.92	3.67	-0.95	-3.09	-3.71	-3.84	-2.56	-4.40	Italie*
–	-28.92	-41.94	-42.99	-43.61	-44.37	-43.20	-34.81	-25.69	Lettonie*
–	-22.02	-33.96	-25.63	-25.33	-26.95	-26.91	-21.28	-15.01	Lituanie*(29)
-17.35	-22.56	-24.48	-16.94	-15.63	-15.57	-17.61	-17.93	-17.75	Luxembourg*
-42.04	-36.23	-28.88	-31.03	-33.59	-35.09	-37.50	-41.07	-42.49	Malte
4.23	8.83	7.83	11.78	11.58	11.57	10.95	11.32	11.03	Pays-Bas*
24.34	31.27	62.43	75.97	82.34	82.22	83.61	78.43	78.57	Norvège
27.63	-25.23	-34.62	-16.54	-13.70	-13.40	-15.52	-14.15	-12.45	Pologne*
-35.36	-31.24	-38.86	-35.08	-36.40	-36.80	-37.42	-37.95	-37.79	Portugal*
-17.58	-21.94	-21.85	-28.72	-32.04	-36.81	-40.01	-36.27	-28.90	Roumanie*
–	-10.51	-14.59	-7.53	-7.33	-6.13	-4.72	-2.15	-1.58	Slovaquie*
–	-10.23	-12.58	-7.02	-5.67	-4.58	-5.41	-4.57	-3.69	Slovénie*
-37.43	-13.01	-24.53	-29.25	-32.53	-34.40	-34.34	-30.17	-25.81	Espagne*
7.26	22.99	21.01	20.73	18.62	14.43	11.62	9.34	8.10	Suède*
-9.13	2.42	-1.43	4.71	4.69	4.92	6.88	9.03	10.37	Suisse*
-17.45	-11.13	-18.30	-24.93	-25.57	-26.69	-27.43	-27.94	-27.32	Royaume-Uni*
-5.34	**-8.91**	**-9.04**	**-17.95**	**-15.81**	**-13.98**	**-10.98**	**-9.11**	**-2.78**	**Économies développées : Océanie**
-7.40	-10.74	-10.13	-18.74	-15.99	-13.88	-10.92	-9.44	-2.78	Australie
4.90	-0.81	-3.76	-14.27	-15.05	-14.42	-11.37	-7.14	-2.74	Nouvelle-Zélande

Pour les sources et les notes, se reporter à la page suivante.

1.3.1 Value of trade balance, and as percentage of imports of countries and geographical regions

Sources:
- UN DESA Statistics Division, *Yearbook of International Trade Statistics*
- UN DESA Statistics Division, *Monthly Bulletin of Statistics*
- IMF, *International Financial Statistics* on CD-ROM
- IMF, *Direction of Trade Statistics*
- World Trade Organization
- Other international and national sources
- UNCTAD secretariat estimates

Notes:
- (*) Special Trade System.
- (1) Average of three continuous years.
- (2) Excluding exports of gold.
- (3) From 1996 onward, imports f.o.b.
- (4) Prior to 2008, special trade.
- (5) Imports f.o.b.
- (6) Trade with other member countries of CEMAC is excluded. Imports f.o.b.
- (7) Trade with other member countries of CEMAC is excluded.
- (8) Prior to 1995, data refer to fiscal year ending June.
- (9) Prior to 1974, special trade.
- (10) Excluding re-exports (incl for bunkering)
- (11) Excluding re-exports.
- (12) Prior to 2005, special trade.
- (13) Prior to 1986, included in Netherlands Antilles. Including exports and imports of crude oil and oil products. Imports f.o.b.
- (14) From 1990 onwards, trade statistics exclude certain oil and chemical products. Imports f.o.b.
- (15) Prior to 1993, exlcuding free trade processing zones. Imports f.o.b.
- (16) Prior to 1986, including Aruba.
- (17) Prior to 2002, special trade.
- (18) From 1990 onward, including goods for processing. Imports f.o.b.
- (19) Excluding imports of goods financed through foreign aid.
- (20) Excluding military goods, fissionable materials, bunkers, ships and aircraft.
- (21) Inter-trade between the States of Malaysia included. From 1965 onwards, excluding military imports and offshore installations of petroleum industry.
- (22) Including trans-shipments to and from peninsular Malaysia.
- (23) Excluding exports of oil and gas.
- (24) Prior to 2001, special trade.
- (25) Excluding defense imports.
- (26) Data refer to fiscal year ending September.
- (27) Excluding military goods, precious metals and goods procured in foreign ports.
- (28) Prior to 1998, data refer to the Federation of Bosnia and Herzegovina only. The other entity of Bosnia and Herzegovina, Republika Srpska, is not included.
- (29) Prior to 1994, covers only trade with countries outside the CIS.
- (30) Prior to 1994, excluding trade with independent states resulting from the former USSR.
- (31) Prior to 1975, excludes non-monetary gold.
- (32) From 1985 onwards, data are not comparable to those shown for prior periods due to revisions of the koruna-to-US dollar exchange rate.
- (33) From 1995 onward, including goods for processing.
- (34) Prior to 1988, excluding ships.
- (35) Excluding petroleum products.
- (36) Prior to 1996, excluding customs free zones.

Sources :
- ONU DAES Division de statistique, *Annuaire statistique du commerce international*
- ONU DAES Division de statistique, *Bulletin mensuel de statistique*
- FMI, *Statistiques financières internationales* sur CD-ROM
- FMI, *Direction of Trade Statistics*
- Organisation mondiale du commerce
- Autres sources internationales et nationales
- Estimations du secrétariat de la CNUCED

Notes :
(*)   Système du commerce spécial.
(1)   Moyenne de trois années consécutives.
(2)   Non-compris les exportations d'or.
(3)   À partir de 1996, importations f.a.b.
(4)   Avant 2008, commerce spécial.
(5)   Importations f.a.b.
(6)   Non-compris le commerce avec les autres pays membres de la CEMAC. Importations f.a.b.
(7)   Non-compris le commerce avec les autres pays membres de la CEMAC.
(8)   Avant 1995, les données se rapportent à l'exercice budgétaire finissant juin.
(9)   Avant 1974, commerce spécial.
(10)   Non-compris les réexportations (huile pour mise en soute).
(11)   Non-compris les réexportations.
(12)   Avant 2005, commerce spécial.
(13)   Avant 1986 compris dans Antilles néerlandaises. Les données comprennent les exportations et importations de pétrole brut et produits dérivés. Importations f.a.b.
(14)   À partir de 1990, certains produits pétroliers et chimiques ne sont plus inclus dans les statistiques du commerce. Importations f.a.b.
(15)   Avant 1993, non-compris les zones franches douanières. Importations f.a.b.
(16)   Avant 1986, y compris Aruba.
(17)   Avant 2002, commerce spécial.
(18)   À partir de 1990, y compris les biens destinés à subir des transformations. Importations f.a.b.
(19)   Non-compris les biens d'importation financés par l'aide à l'étranger.
(20)   Non-compris les biens à usage militaire, le matériel fissile, le combustible de soute et l'avitaillement des navires et aéronefs.
(21)   Y compris le commerce entre les États de la Malaisie. Non-compris les importations militaires et l'installation près des côtes de l'industrie pétrolière.
(22)   Y compris les transbordements vers et en provenance de la Malaisie péninsulaire.
(23)   Non-compris les exportations de pétrole et le gaz.
(24)   Avant 2001, commerce spécial.
(25)   Non-compris les importations de la défense.
(26)   Les données se rapportent à l'exercice budgétaire finissant septembre.
(27)   Non-compris les biens à usage militaire, les métaux précieux et les biens fournis dans les ports étrangers.
(28)   Avant 1998, les données se réfèrent uniquement à la Fédération de la Bosnie-Herzégovine. L'autre entité de la Bosnie-Herzégovine, Republika Srpska, n'est pas incluse.
(29)   Avant 1994, concerne seulement le commerce avec les pays extérieurs à la CEI.
(30)   Avant 1994, non-compris le commerce avec les républiques indépendantes de l'ancienne URSS.
(31)   Avant 1975, non-compris l'or industriel.
(32)   À partir de 1985, les chiffres ne sont pas comparables à ceux des années antérieures à cause des révisions du taux de change de la couronne par rapport au dollar des États-Unis.
(33)   À partir de 1995, y compris les biens destinés à subir des transformations.
(34)   Avant 1988, non-compris les navires.
(35)   Non-compris les produits pétroliers.
(36)   Avant 1996, non-compris les zones franches douanières.

1.3.2 Value of trade balance, and as percentage of imports of economic groupings

Economic grouping	Trade balance (1) - Balance commerciale (1) Millions of dollars - Millions de dollars								
	1989-91	1994-96	1999-01	2003-05	2004-06	2005-07	2006-08	2007-09	2008-10
DEVELOPING ECONOMIES	**19 118**	**-55 251**	**96 341**	**247 599**	**371 879**	**487 178**	**543 223**	**464 704**	**395 864**
Developing economies excluding China	15 697	-66 643	71 052	194 495	268 070	306 882	297 829	212 632	170 287
Developing economies excluding LDCs	26 151	-45 449	106 921	257 314	376 209	486 924	536 512	467 768	406 088
High-income developing countries	34 097	-4 697	79 494	211 618	278 802	321 103	347 591	317 979	319 020
Middle-income developing countries	-11 324	-43 390	10 832	54 071	116 273	199 459	252 312	231 712	180 518
Low-income developing countries	-3 656	-7 164	6 113	-17 826	-22 884	-33 000	-56 197	-84 458	-103 145
Heavily indebted poor countries (IMF)	-3 377	-6 194	-10 736	-15 669	-18 148	-22 922	-28 864	-33 723	-35 294
Landlocked developing countries	-4 237	-7 446	-6 253	-3 467	2 593	8 829	17 045	11 590	12 342
Small island developing States	-3 659	-4 001	-6 150	-6 771	-6 114	-6 628	-7 323	-9 682	-10 170
Least developed countries	*-7 033*	*-9 802*	*-10 580*	*-9 715*	*-4 330*	*253*	*6 710*	*3 004*	*-10 115*
Africa and Haiti	-2 440	-4 597	-5 014	-1 903	3 573	9 516	18 985	12 370	7 373
Asia	-4 353	-4 960	-5 294	-7 278	-7 240	-8 470	-11 302	-14 354	-16 390
Islands	-240	-246	-272	-535	-664	-792	-973	-1 080	-1 208
Major petroleum and gas exporters	*52 735*	*69 084*	*112 485*	*232 889*	*333 573*	*414 160*	*511 464*	*460 609*	*453 564*
Africa	15 473	13 013	26 070	59 246	86 763	110 228	135 671	116 708	107 173
America	6 471	9 076	10 197	23 694	28 766	28 855	33 470	28 483	29 902
Asia	30 791	46 996	76 218	149 948	218 045	275 078	342 322	315 418	316 488
Major exporters of manufactured goods	*-7 953*	*-33 261*	*53 649*	*108 920*	*162 936*	*245 577*	*292 183*	*309 475*	*288 697*
America	-4 565	-5 395	-15 410	-16 192	-17 732	-20 060	-25 194	-24 758	-22 723
Asia	-3 388	-27 866	69 058	125 112	180 668	265 638	317 377	334 233	311 420
Emerging economies	*6 797*	*-36 329*	*37 329*	*119 144*	*139 732*	*156 421*	*132 778*	*136 611*	*137 679*
America	13 260	-12 819	-15 694	37 088	49 581	54 013	38 517	28 528	19 286
Asia	-6 462	-23 510	53 023	82 056	90 151	102 408	94 261	108 083	118 393
Newly industrialized Asian countries	*-6 136*	*-43 250*	*65 000*	*81 171*	*86 012*	*97 106*	*83 725*	*94 653*	*98 582*
First tier	1 306	-24 331	21 183	51 113	52 749	54 718	33 343	37 049	39 723
Second tier	-7 443	-18 919	43 817	30 058	33 263	42 388	50 381	57 604	58 859
Developing economies: Africa	**4 081**	**-5 783**	**4 033**	**28 159**	**47 952**	**61 037**	**72 194**	**39 600**	**21 789**
Northern Africa excluding Sudan	-3 258	-8 066	-1 715	13 257	24 617	32 078	34 768	13 335	-1 392
Sub-Saharan Africa	7 339	2 282	5 747	14 902	23 335	28 959	37 425	26 266	23 181
Sub-Saharan Africa excluding South Africa	2 806	2 034	4 078	20 678	33 290	41 342	50 693	37 527	33 261
Developing economies: America	**10 504**	**-23 519**	**-30 125**	**29 321**	**41 539**	**37 366**	**15 758**	**-2 656**	**-14 030**
Central America and Greater Caribbean Islands excluding Puerto Rico	-13 458	-15 988	-34 351	-41 597	-48 996	-58 649	-73 914	-74 221	-73 695
Central America and Greater Caribbean Islands excluding Mexico and Puerto Rico	-8 893	-10 594	-18 941	-25 405	-31 264	-38 589	-48 720	-49 463	-50 972
South America and Central America	18 392	-16 211	-17 003	43 499	57 608	56 827	39 485	23 305	13 842
South America excluding Brazil	15 514	-1 466	10 555	43 806	55 771	59 889	61 228	52 506	49 155
Developing economies: Asia	**6 760**	**-24 584**	**124 015**	**193 163**	**285 473**	**392 061**	**459 214**	**432 270**	**393 032**
Eastern and South-Eastern Asia excluding China	-6 263	-47 225	64 006	77 760	83 164	91 864	73 989	81 267	85 764
Southern Asia excluding India	-7 880	-1 479	1 129	-3 937	528	6 952	13 008	8 328	2 957

Sources:
- Data in this table are based on trade figures in table 1.1.1.

Notes:

(1)   Average of three continuous years.

1989-91	1994-96	1999-01	2003-05	2004-06	2005-07	2006-08	2007-09	2008-10	Groupements économiques
2.51	-3.83	5.32	8.42	10.45	12.01	11.51	9.18	7.22	ÉCONOMIES EN DÉVELOPPEMENT
2.32	-5.05	4.41	8.24	9.45	9.58	8.07	5.27	3.90	Économies en développement sans la Chine
3.50	-3.23	6.08	9.02	10.87	12.33	11.70	9.54	7.66	Économies en développement sans les PMA
7.85	-0.66	7.51	13.90	15.54	15.91	14.80	13.08	12.54	Pays en développement à revenu élevé
-4.76	-9.97	2.05	4.90	8.71	13.11	14.39	12.31	8.69	Pays en développement à revenu intermédiaire
-3.61	-4.02	2.92	-4.88	-5.37	-6.10	-7.76	-11.28	-12.65	Pays en développement a revenu faible
-14.87	-20.68	-28.01	-25.30	-24.36	-25.61	-26.08	-28.29	-27.52	Pays pauvres très endettés (FMI)
-28.97	-21.93	-16.66	-6.52	2.17	8.61	13.62	8.24	8.11	Pays en développement sans littoral
-32.64	-29.23	-36.45	-30.41	24.23	21.77	-20.31	-27.61	-29.54	Petits États insulaires en développement
-29.04	-29.68	-24.01	-14.49	-5.98	-0.20	4.61	-1.96	-6.25	*Pays les moins avancés*
-14.81	-22.93	-20.16	-6.03	5.32	13.58	21.42	13.06	6.73	Afrique et Haïti
-57.43	-39.58	-28.17	-27.11	-23.61	-22.84	-24.77	-28.93	-29.48	Asie
-63.90	-53.49	-63.52	-67.80	-71.38	-73.03	-74.35	-75.37	-76.97	Îles
52.78	61.69	73.01	84.57	99.96	104.53	101.47	79.15	72.27	*Principaux exportateurs de pétrole et de gaz*
69.84	56.00	99.58	117.45	144.29	152.53	147.40	106.94	86.54	Afrique
80.79	89.88	60.76	141.56	120.01	92.22	78.86	61.13	68.02	Amérique
44.41	60.20	68.70	72.26	87.75	94.33	92.82	74.29	69.07	Asie
-1.65	-3.88	5.11	6.06	7.53	10.00	10.55	10.97	9.52	*Principaux exportateurs d'articles manufacturés*
-9.43	-6.46	-9.07	-7.86	-7.61	-7.54	-8.38	-8.40	-7.58	Amérique
-0.76	-3.45	7.72	7.91	9.45	12.17	12.82	13.16	11.35	Asie
2.00	-5.30	4.07	11.10	10.94	10.73	8.23	8.43	7.94	*Économies émergentes*
17.39	-7.49	-5.78	11.17	12.56	12.03	7.93	5.55	3.60	Amérique
-2.19	-4.77	10.59	11.17	10.23	10.16	8.42	9.83	10.05	Asie
-1.30	-5.77	8.46	7.45	6.60	6.54	5.21	5.93	5.76	*Économies nouvellement industrialisées d'Asie*
0.76	-4.51	3.82	6.30	5.57	5.14	2.94	3.28	3.24	Première génération
-7.16	-9.03	21.63	10.68	9.46	10.40	11.31	13.09	12.48	Deuxième génération
4.43	-4.97	3.03	11.97	17.64	19.83	18.93	9.09	4.25	Économies en développement : Afrique
-7.08	-18.94	-3.51	17.66	28.54	33.04	29.78	9.97	-1.28	Afrique septentrionale sans le Soudan
12.96	3.02	6.85	9.19	12.74	13.90	14.15	9.06	7.46	Afrique subsaharienne
7.37	3.97	7.65	20.69	29.09	30.94	30.02	19.68	15.84	Afrique subsaharienne sans l'Afrique du Sud
8.76	-9.74	-8.20	6.28	7.56	6.18	2.71	-0.18	-1.56	Économies en développement : Amérique
-20.78	-14.64	-16.11	-15.82	-16.26	-17.09	-18.89	-19.32	-18.81	Amérique centrale et Grandes Antilles sans Porto Rico
-45.73	-39.14	-43.43	-44.95	-47.47	-50.33	-53.51	-53.97	-54.61	Amérique centrale et Grandes Antilles sans le Mexique et Porto Rico
17.77	-7.42	-5.07	10.24	11.43	10.00	6.25	3.37	1.94	Amérique du Sud et Amérique centrale
44.62	-2.28	11.66	40.24	39.53	34.57	28.55	22.06	19.33	Amérique du Sud sans le Brésil
1.32	-2.19	9.72	8.69	10.48	12.59	12.74	11.33	9.50	Économies en développement : Asie
-1.30	-6.15	8.08	6.85	6.12	5.94	4.44	4.85	4.74	Asie orientale et Asie du Sud-Est sans la Chine
-22.53	-3.66	2.60	-4.97	-0.16	6.13	10.83	6.45	1.93	Asie méridionale sans l'Inde

Sources :
- Les données dans ce tableau ont été calculées d'après les chiffres du tableau 1.1.1.

Notes :

(1)   Moyenne de trois années consécutives.

1.4 Intra-trade of trade groups

Trade group	Value of intra-trade (exports in millions of dollars) Valeur du commerce interne au groupement (exportations en millions de dollars)						Intra-trade of groups regional exports Commerce interne des exportations régionales		
	1980	1995	2000	2005	2009	2010	1980	1995	2000
AFRICA									
CEMAC	75	120	96	201	300	383	66.5	40.3	30.3
CEPGL	2	8	10	20	64	81	3.6	6.0	25.0
COMESA	569	1 376	1 518	2 708	6 348	8 286	79.2	44.3	41.1
EAC	337	628	689	1 075	1 572	1 997	64.0	65.4	63.4
ECCAS	89	163	191	274	440	561	49.3	36.3	51.1
ECOWAS	661	1 875	2 728	5 546	7 320	9 105	73.5	77.1	74.7
MRU	13	104	111	251	211	268	2.9	11.6	9.2
SADC	108	4 160	5 709	9 792	12 651	16 556	57.0	61.2	66.7
UMA	109	1 109	1 041	1 878	3 222	3 977	34.0	66.9	68.9
WAEMU	460	560	760	1 412	1 938	2 344	52.9	47.2	47.7
AMERICA									
ANCOM	468	1 788	2 046	4 572	5 788	7 791	8.0	14.8	11.1
CACM	1 174	1 594	2 655	4 311	5 558	6 874	37.2	33.0	24.6
CARICOM	613	878	1 077	2 231	2 708	3 440	7.8	21.0	22.2
FTAA	167 734	525 350	857 711	1 101 823	1 110 067	1 393 458	96.4	99.5	99.0
LAIA	11 192	35 986	44 253	71 727	100 017	129 415	25.4	25.8	17.1
MERCOSUR	3 424	14 199	17 829	21 128	32 699	44 239	31.8	43.1	38.7
NAFTA	102 218	394 472	676 142	824 359	768 771	955 597	79.0	87.4	91.0
OAS	167 067	523 996	855 002	1 099 267	1 107 625	1 387 109	96.3	99.4	98.8
OECS	13	40	37	66	100	127	39.3	22.1	22.4
ASIA									
APTA	783	21 728	37 895	127 340	204 745	278 343	3.6	12.7	15.8
ASEAN	12 413	79 544	98 060	165 458	198 906	267 974	29.0	42.0	39.1
ECO	392	4 746	4 518	12 579	18 534	27 654	17.1	25.5	17.9
GCC	4 632	6 832	8 029	15 408	21 849	28 623	7.2	12.1	7.6
SAARC	768	2 172	2 981	8 830	11 584	16 175	14.9	13.3	13.9
EUROPE									
EFTA	524	925	831	1 252	2 110	2 096	1.4	1.1	0.8
EU	499 570	1 419 198	1 641 252	2 733 936	3 054 707	3 351 711	86.0	91.2	92.4
Euro area	309 150	905 085	980 931	1 639 168	1 808 076	1 961 244	70.6	71.9	70.0
OCEANIA									
MSG	11	18	22	51	78	99	3.7	1.5	1.9
INTERREGIONAL									
ACP	2 366	9 633	13 532	25 824	36 450	46 323	..	..	..
APEC	357 698	1 688 708	2 262 709	3 319 465	3 740 509	4 916 541	..	..	..
BSEC	1 190	25 505	24 736	65 745	74 421	99 223	..	..	..
CIS	—	31 277	28 422	58 113	60 390	68 864	—	..	..

Sources:
- UNCTAD secretariat estimates
- IMF, *Direction of Trade Statistics*

as percentage of of each group du groupement en pourcentage de chaque groupement			Intra-trade of groups as percentage of total exports of each group Commerce interne du groupement en pourcentage des exportations totales de chaque groupement						Groupements commerciaux
2005	2009	2010	1980	1995	2000	2005	2009	2010	
									AFRIQUE
28.6	35.7	36.4	1.6	2.1	1.0	0.9	1.2	1.2	CEMAC
13.7	8.8	5.5	0.1	0.5	0.8	1.2	2.2	1.6	CEPGL
44.3	60.5	60.5	1.8	5.9	4.7	4.5	7.3	7.5	COMESA
58.7	51.8	51.8	15.3	19.5	22.6	18.0	18.9	20.2	CAE
23.7	14.7	12.9	1.4	1.5	1.1	0.6	0.7	0.7	CEEAC
74.7	65.3	64.6	9.6	9.0	7.7	9.4	10.0	9.0	CEDEAO
11.4	6.2	6.5	0.3	1.9	2.1	2.6	1.6	1.9	UFM
78.4	74.6	78.8	0.4	10.5	12.2	11.3	11.2	10.9	SADC
57.4	62.5	62.2	0.3	3.8	2.2	1.9	2.9	3.0	UMA
42.7	40.7	40.9	9.6	10.3	13.5	13.7	13.3	14.8	UEMOA
									AMÉRIQUE
12.5	12.0	13.6	4.1	8.6	7.7	9.0	7.5	8.6	ANCOM
29.0	30.9	20.9	24.4	21.8	19.6	23.2	23.7	14.2	MCAC
15.7	20.3	20.0	5.6	12.0	14.5	12.1	13.7	15.0	CARICOM
98.7	99.1	99.2	43.4	52.5	60.9	60.1	53.8	54.5	ZLEA
19.4	25.5	26.1	13.9	17.3	13.2	13.6	15.7	16.0	ALADI
26.7	38.0	40.2	11.6	20.3	20.0	12.9	15.2	15.7	MERCOSUR
90.7	85.7	85.3	33.6	46.2	55.7	55.7	48.0	48.7	ALENA
98.5	99.0	99.0	43.3	52.4	60.7	60.0	53.7	54.3	OEA
29.2	37.1	39.5	18.0	12.4	11.0	13.1	13.9	21.2	OECO
									ASIE
22.1	23.5	24.4	1.7	6.8	8.0	11.0	11.6	12.1	ACAP
39.5	37.0	36.1	17.3	24.4	23.0	25.3	24.5	24.3	ANASE
21.0	18.7	20.6	6.3	7.9	5.6	6.9	7.2	8.7	ECO
6.8	7.0	6.7	3.0	6.8	4.9	4.4	5.0	4.8	CCG
15.7	11.9	11.8	5.7	4.7	4.7	6.8	5.6	6.0	SAARC
									EUROPE
0.7	1.0	0.9	1.1	0.7	0.6	0.5	0.7	0.6	AELE
91.0	90.0	90.1	62.2	67.2	67.7	67.4	66.5	67.2	UE
69.1	68.3	68.0	51.9	54.1	51.8	51.5	50.2	50.4	Zone euro
									OCÉANIE
2.6	2.8	2.9	0.7	0.4	0.6	0.8	0.8	0.8	MSG
									INTERRÉGIONAUX
..	..	..	4.1	11.0	11.6	12.1	13.6	13.2	ACP
..	..	..	57.8	71.7	73.1	70.9	66.4	67.7	CEAP
..	..	..	5.9	18.1	14.2	16.0	14.0	14.9	CEMN
..	..	..	﹂	28.4	19.8	17.7	14.8	12.9	CEI

Sources :
- Estimations du secrétariat de la CNUCED
- FMI, *Direction of Trade Statistics*

2

INTERNATIONAL **MERCHANDISE** TRADE BY REGION

COMMERCE INTERNATIONAL DES **MARCHANDISES** PAR RÉGIONS

1

2

3

4

5

6

7

8

Destination / Origin / Origine	Year / Année	World (millions of dollars) (1) / Monde (millions de dollars) (1)	Developed economies / Économies développées Total	Europe Total	Europe EU/UE	USA États-Unis	Japan Japon	Other Autres	Transition economies / Économies en transition	Developing economies / Économies en développement Total	Africa Afrique	America Amérique	Eastern, Southern and South-Eastern Asia / Asie orientale, méridionale et du Sud-Est	Western Asia / Asie occidentale	Oceania Océanie
									Percentage / En pourcentage						
Afghanistan	1995	(e)166	25.9	21.9	20.7	3.2	0.6	0.3	49.0	25.0	0.2	0.1	23.9	0.8	0.0
	2005	(e)239	40.2	12.7	12.5	25.8	1.1	0.6	3.2	56.6	1.9	0.8	46.9	7.0	0.0
	2010	(e)493	28.7	12.2	12.0	16.1	0.1	0.4	11.8	59.5	0.6	0.2	54.1	4.7	0.0
Albania - Albanie	1995	202	86.9	82.8	81.8	3.4	0.7	0.0	5.7	7.4	0.1	0.1	1.0	6.2	0.0
	2005	632	94.4	93.4	93.3	1.0	0.0	0.0	2.8	2.7	0.1	0.2	0.7	1.8	0.0
	2010	1 400	85.0	83.3	76.7	1.6	0.0	0.1	3.2	11.7	1.2	0.2	6.0	7.1	0.0
Algeria - Algérie	1995	9 357	87.6	67.8	66.5	16.7	0.7	2.4	1.6	10.8	2.5	2.8	2.0	3.5	0.0
	2005	46 047	84.2	56.2	55.6	23.0	0.0	5.0	0.0	15.7	2.2	7.0	2.6	3.9	0.0
	2010	(e)55 397	77.4	45.7	45.4	24.5	0.7	6.5	0.1	22.5	3.4	5.2	10.0	4.0	0.0
American Samoa - Samoa américaines	1995	(e)272	54.8	0.5	0.5	0.0	27.8	26.5	0.0	45.1	0.0	0.1	30.3	0.0	14.7
	2005	(e)374	52.6	9.1	9.1	0.0	13.0	30.6	0.2	47.1	2.0	0.6	38.5	0.0	6.0
	2010	(e)480	41.2	2.9	2.2	0.0	0.0	38.2	0.3	58.6	2.1	12.9	37.4	0.3	5.8
Andorra - Andorre	1995	49	99.7	99.7	99.7	..	..	0.0	0.0	0.3	0.0	0.0	0.2	0.0	..
	2005	142	98.9	98.7	98.4	0.1	0.1	0.0	0.1	1.0	0.7	0.3	0.0	0.0	..
	2010	54	15.4	15.0	12.9	0.2	0.0	0.2	0.5	84.0	81.5	1.8	0.8	0.0	..
Angola	1995	(e)3 412	85.9	21.6	21.6	63.7	0.4	0.3	0.0	14.1	0.6	3.2	10.3	0.0	0.0
	2005	(e)20 207	56.0	14.7	14.7	39.8	0.1	1.4	0.0	44.0	1.5	7.3	35.2	0.0	0.0
	2010	(e)47 852	36.5	9.7	9.7	23.3	0.2	3.3	0.0	63.5	3.8	2.0	57.8	0.0	0.0
Anguilla	1995	1	8.4	5.6	5.6	1.6	1.0	0.2	..	91.6	0.3	77.0	14.3	..	..
	2005	15	53.7	24.7	24.5	27.7	0.4	0.9	6.5	39.8	1.0	36.5	2.3	..	0.0
	2010	12	76.4	50.7	50.5	20.6	..	5.1	2.3	21.3	0.0	20.4	0.8	0.1	0.0
Antigua and Barbuda - Antigua-et-Barbuda	1995	(e)53	56.9	29.0	25.5	6.1	0.0	21.7	0.0	43.1	1.3	40.6	1.2	0.0	0.0
	2005	(e)83	84.8	82.1	81.6	2.4	0.0	0.3	0.0	15.2	2.3	6.4	6.4	0.0	0.0
	2010	(e)35	42.3	34.9	34.7	6.4	0.1	0.9	5.1	52.6	5.0	37.5	10.1	0.0	0.0
Argentina - Argentine	1995	20 363	32.9	22.5	21.4	7.4	2.1	0.9	0.4	61.2	3.3	46.6	10.3	1.0	0.0
	2005	40 387	31.4	17.7	17.4	11.3	0.8	1.7	1.9	65.1	6.0	40.4	15.9	2.8	0.0
	2010	68 115	27.5	18.0	16.4	5.4	1.3	2.9	1.2	69.6	5.9	42.0	19.7	2.0	0.0
Armenia - Arménie	1995	357	23.4	23.2	22.3	0.2	0.0	0.0	47.5	13.6	2.5	0.0	9.8	1.2	0.0
	2005	974	74.3	50.2	46.6	11.2	0.1	12.7	19.2	6.3	0.0	0.6	4.2	1.4	0.0
	2010	1 041	61.0	49.8	48.1	8.0	0.0	3.3	23.4	14.5	0.1	1.0	12.4	1.0	0.0
Aruba	1995	15	42.5	21.2	21.1	21.3	0.0	0.1	0.0	55.2	0.0	55.1	0.0	0.0	..
	2005	106	49.3	37.9	37.9	11.3	0.0	0.1	0.0	50.5	0.0	50.2	0.3	0.1	0.0
	2010	124	12.3	6.4	6.2	5.9	0.0	0.0	0.0	84.9	0.1	84.1	0.6	0.0	0.0
Australia - Australie	1995	53 061	50.4	12.1	11.4	6.3	23.0	9.0	0.3	46.9	1.4	1.1	39.8	2.1	2.6
	2005	105 222	45.9	11.1	10.8	6.7	20.2	7.9	0.3	52.1	2.5	1.6	42.6	3.5	1.8
	2010	211 814	35.3	8.3	8.1	4.0	18.9	4.1	0.5	63.2	1.6	1.4	56.2	2.7	1.3
Austria - Autriche	1995	57 540	89.1	83.5	77.2	3.0	1.3	1.3	3.0	7.8	1.2	1.0	4.2	1.4	0.0
	2005	125 014	86.0	77.3	71.8	5.8	1.2	1.7	4.7	8.7	1.2	1.0	4.8	1.7	0.0
	2010	148 636	83.7	78.2	73.1	3.5	0.8	1.2	5.6	10.6	1.2	1.6	5.7	2.1	0.0
Azerbaijan - Azerbaïdjan	1995	547	24.9	24.5	19.2	0.2	0.0	0.2	39.4	35.7	0.0	0.0	30.3	5.4	0.0
	2005	4 347	57.4	51.9	51.7	1.0	0.0	4.5	24.9	17.7	0.9	0.0	9.6	7.1	0.0
	2010	21 360	65.5	47.8	47.3	8.0	0.0	9.8	14.9	19.5	1.5	0.0	16.7	1.3	0.0
Bahamas	1995	(e)596	80.4	50.8	40.0	26.0	0.8	2.9	1.4	16.7	3.5	3.8	9.3	0.0	0.0
	2005	(e)2 246	88.6	56.9	55.0	29.4	0.0	2.2	0.1	11.1	0.2	7.8	2.9	0.2	0.0
	2010	(e)2 567	47.5	16.4	14.0	28.9	0.0	2.2	0.2	52.1	1.2	35.0	15.7	0.1	0.0
Bahrain - Bahreïn	1995	4 162	9.9	3.2	3.1	3.1	3.4	0.2	0.0	27.9	0.4	0.1	15.9	11.4	0.0
	2005	(e)15 948	9.1	4.1	3.9	2.6	1.8	0.6	0.0	22.6	6.3	0.0	8.2	8.1	0.0
	2010	(e)29 623	6.4	2.8	2.4	1.4	2.0	0.2	0.0	22.0	4.2	0.3	9.1	8.5	0.0
Bangladesh	1995	3 129	83.5	45.6	45.0	31.9	3.3	2.7	0.8	15.4	2.3	0.7	10.1	2.3	0.1
	2005	8 494	75.2	47.2	46.9	23.6	0.8	3.6	0.2	9.6	0.7	0.4	6.7	1.8	0.0
	2010	14 666	79.8	51.9	51.0	22.1	1.1	4.7	0.6	15.6	1.0	0.9	8.9	4.8	0.0
Barbados - Barbade	1995	240	40.8	20.5	20.3	14.6	0.6	5.0	0.0	43.6	0.0	42.8	0.7	0.0	0.0
	2005	260	38.4	16.9	16.5	18.6	0.0	2.9	0.0	59.5	0.1	58.0	1.2	0.2	0.0
	2010	(e)449	19.1	7.2	6.9	9.0	0.0	2.9	0.1	80.4	0.3	76.8	2.8	0.4	0.0
Belarus - Bélarus	1995	4 641	31.2	29.7	29.4	1.2	0.0	0.2	62.7	6.1	2.2	0.1	2.8	0.9	0.0
	2005	15 976	46.6	44.9	44.6	1.6	0.0	0.1	44.6	8.2	0.6	1.4	5.6	0.6	0.0
	2010	25 214	32.1	31.6	30.2	0.3	0.0	0.2	54.2	12.8	1.0	4.7	5.7	1.4	0.0

For sources and notes, see end of table.

Pour les sources et les notes, se reporter à la fin du tableau.

58

Destination / Origin / Origine	Year / Année	World (millions of dollars) (1) / Monde (millions de dollars) (1)	Developed economies / Économies développées						Transition economies / Économies en transition	Developing economies / Économies en développement					
			Total	Europe		USA États-Unis	Japan Japon	Other Autres		Total	Africa Afrique	America Amérique	Eastern, Southern and South-Eastern Asia / Asie orientale, méridionale et du Sud-Est	Western Asia / Asie occidentale	Oceania Océanie
				Total	EU UE										
									Percentage / En pourcentage						
Belgium - Belgique	1995	(e)175 647	90.0	83.1	81.0	3.5	1.2	2.3	0.8	9.1	1.9	1.2	4.7	1.3	0.0
	2005	334 281	88.1	78.3	76.8	6.4	1.0	2.3	1.2	10.2	1.8	1.1	5.2	2.1	0.0
	2010	402 833	84.7	76.7	74.9	5.3	0.9	1.8	1.6	12.5	2.4	1.5	6.1	2.5	0.0
Belize	1995	162	92.7	51.6	51.3	36.6	0.1	4.4	0.0	7.3	0.0	7.3	0.1	0.0	0.0
	2005	(e)297	75.0	30.7	30.7	31.9	2.5	2.8	0.2	23.9	6.7	13.3	3.5	0.4	0.0
	2010	(e)390	62.3	27.8	27.7	30.3	2.3	1.9	0.0	37.5	9.4	25.5	2.1	0.5	0.0
Benin - Bénin	1995	173	34.0	33.1	31.7	0.8	0.1	0.0	0.0	60.7	17.1	19.4	22.3	1.6	0.2
	2005	300	8.9	8.8	8.1	0.1	0.0	0.0	0.1	91.1	27.0	0.4	61.3	2.4	0.0
	2010	(c)523	7.4	7.1	7.0	0.0	0.4	0.0	0.1	92.5	32.1	0.6	56.3	3.5	0.0
Bermuda - Bermudes	1995	63	55.9	6.2	6.2	49.7	0.0	0.1	0.0	0.0	0.0	0.0	0.0	0.0	0.0
	2005	(e)1 752	92.2	86.4	86.4	4.6	0.3	1.0	0.0	1.3	0.2	1.1	0.0	0.0	0.0
	2010	(e)475	42.8	37.1	29.4	4.4	0.1	1.1	0.1	10.7	2.0	1.8	6.9	0.0	0.0
Bhutan - Bhoutan	1995	(e)103	9.5	9.1	8.0	0.4	..	0.0	0.0	90.5	0.0	1.7	88.4	0.4	0.0
	2005	(e)258	1.4	0.7	0.7	0.5	0.2	0.0	0.0	98.6	0.0	0.2	98.3	0.0	0.0
	2010	(e)641	2.3	0.6	0.6	0.2	1.5	0.0	0.0	97.7	0.0	0.1	97.5	0.0	0.0
Bolivia (Plurinational State of) - Bolivie (État plurinational de)	1995	1 139	62.5	34.0	26.9	27.2	0.3	0.9	0.0	37.2	0.0	36.5	0.4	0.3	0.0
	2005	(e)2 236	23.8	6.9	6.7	12.5	3.3	1.1	0.2	75.6	0.1	72.3	3.1	0.1	0.0
	2010	(e)5 313	27.2	7.6	7.5	11.8	4.9	2.9	0.2	72.2	0.0	64.8	7.1	0.2	0.0
Bosnia and Herzegovina - Bosnie-Herzégovine	1995	(e)52	80.1	71.8	71.2	6.3	0.0	2.0	17.4	2.4	0.7	1.5	0.0	0.2	0.0
	2005	(e)2 175	73.9	70.3	69.8	3.0	0.1	0.5	20.4	5.7	0.5	0.0	4.4	0.7	0.0
	2010	(e)3 306	75.5	74.3	73.3	0.7	0.1	0.3	20.3	4.2	0.9	0.5	0.6	2.2	0.0
Botswana	1995	(e)2 142	86.4	76.7	44.4	6.9	2.5	0.4	0.0	11.9	8.2	0.6	0.9	2.2	0.0
	2005	4 431	86.0	83.5	77.1	2.2	0.0	0.3	0.0	14.0	13.7	0.0	0.2	0.1	0.0
	2010	4 693	78.4	71.9	61.0	1.2	0.0	5.3	0.0	21.6	18.8	0.0	2.7	0.1	0.0
Brazil - Brésil	1995	46 605	57.3	29.9	28.8	18.9	6.7	1.8	1.4	40.4	3.4	22.9	11.7	2.4	0.0
	2005	118 480	46.2	21.8	21.0	19.2	2.9	2.3	2.9	48.9	5.0	25.4	15.4	3.1	0.0
	2010	201 930	37.4	22.6	21.4	9.6	3.5	1.6	2.5	58.0	4.6	23.5	25.4	4.5	0.0
Brunei Darussalam - Brunéi Darussalam	1995	3 388	59.4	0.8	0.8	2.0	55.6	1.1	0.0	40.5	0.0	0.0	40.5	0.0	0.0
	2005	(e)5 633	58.1	1.2	1.1	9.5	36.8	10.5	0.0	41.4	0.0	0.0	41.3	0.0	0.0
	2010	(e)8 305	62.0	0.2	0.1	0.1	44.9	16.8	0.0	37.4	0.1	0.0	37.3	0.0	0.0
Bulgaria - Bulgarie	1995	5 220	49.0	44.0	43.3	3.1	0.3	1.6	28.8	20.4	3.4	1.8	3.9	11.2	0.0
	2005	11 753	65.8	61.5	60.3	3.0	0.1	1.2	10.6	18.2	2.1	1.0	3.3	11.9	0.0
	2010	20 098	67.4	65.3	62.4	1.3	0.1	0.7	12.9	17.8	2.9	0.5	4.5	9.8	0.0
Burkina Faso	1995	164	47.9	44.2	28.5	0.3	3.2	0.1	0.0	51.9	33.3	1.0	17.7	0.0	0.0
	2005	279	64.2	63.4	31.5	0.1	0.6	0.1	0.8	33.2	23.7	0.0	9.5	0.0	0.0
	2010	(e)635	27.0	18.9	18.6	0.3	4.2	3.5	0.0	69.0	13.7	0.0	48.1	7.1	0.0
Burundi	1995	104	49.8	49.6	38.5	0.2	0.0	0.0	0.0	13.0	12.6	0.0	0.1	0.3	0.0
	2005	61	53.6	52.1	18.8	0.5	0.5	0.4	1.2	21.8	11.8	0.0	8.5	1.5	0.0
	2010	(e)77	50.9	46.6	46.0	4.1	0.1	0.1	2.4	30.4	13.2	0.0	15.7	1.4	0.0
Cambodia - Cambodge	1995	(e)357	18.6	15.1	14.6	1.4	1.9	0.3	0.0	81.4	3.4	0.0	77.9	0.1	0.0
	2005	3 014	76.0	17.2	16.8	52.9	2.1	3.7	0.1	23.8	0.0	0.3	23.4	0.1	0.0
	2010	5 571	58.3	17.1	16.7	34.2	1.6	5.4	0.4	41.3	0.1	1.1	39.7	0.4	0.0
Cameroon - Cameroun	1995	1 659	79.9	76.9	76.8	1.8	0.8	0.5	0.0	18.1	8.0	0.9	8.8	0.4	0.0
	2005	(e)3 583	71.8	67.0	66.9	4.3	0.2	0.3	0.1	26.1	10.1	1.7	13.1	1.2	0.0
	2010	(e)4 471	60.9	54.2	54.1	6.3	0.2	0.2	0.2	35.8	14.4	4.1	16.0	1.3	0.0
Canada	1995	190 181	92.1	6.6	6.1	80.4	4.5	0.6	0.1	7.8	0.6	2.0	4.9	0.4	0.0
	2005	360 662	92.9	6.4	5.7	83.8	2.1	0.6	0.2	6.9	0.5	1.9	4.0	0.5	0.0
	2010	387 139	87.5	9.7	8.6	74.9	2.3	0.6	0.4	12.1	0.9	3.1	7.1	0.9	0.0
Cape Verde - Cap-Vert	1995	(e)13	73.2	71.7	71.5	1.4	0.0	0.2	0.0	23.5	7.6	0.2	15.7	0.0	0.0
	2005	18	86.6	76.8	76.8	9.9	0.0	0.0	0.0	13.4	13.3	0.0	0.0	0.0	0.0
	2010	47	95.6	94.1	94.1	1.5	0.0	0.0	0.0	2.6	0.4	1.5	0.7	0.0	0.0
Cayman Islands - Îles Caïmanes	2005	60	89.9	82.7	82.6	6.8	0.1	0.3	0.0	10.1	0.1	9.6	0.4	0.0	..
	2010	16	91.9	88.4	76.9	3.2	0.0	0.3	0.0	8.0	0.2	5.5	2.0	0.4	..
Central African Republic - République centrafricaine	1995	187	57.9	57.4	57.3	0.0	0.0	0.4	0.0	4.8	4.5	0.0	0.3	0.0	..
	2005	(e)114	72.4	66.0	65.9	4.5	1.7	0.2	0.0	27.6	6.6	0.2	14.4	6.3	0.0
	2010	(e)130	44.0	39.2	39.0	4.0	0.7	0.1	0.0	56.0	22.8	0.4	25.8	6.9	0.0

For sources and notes, see end of table.

Pour les sources et les notes, se reporter à la fin du tableau.

2.1 Country trade structure by partner — Exports by main region of destination

2.1 Structure du commerce des pays par partenaires — Exportations par principales régions de destination

Destination / Origin / Origine	Year / Année	World (millions of dollars) (1) / Monde (millions de dollars) (1)	Developed economies / Économies développées — Total	Europe Total	Europe EU / UE	USA / États-Unis	Japan / Japon	Other / Autres	Transition economies / Économies en transition	Developing economies / Économies en développement — Total	Africa / Afrique	America / Amérique	Eastern, Southern and South-Eastern Asia / Asie orientale, méridionale et du Sud-Est	Western Asia / Asie occidentale	Oceania / Océanie
Chad - Tchad	1995	(e)118	87.2	81.7	81.2	2.6	2.9	0.1	0.0	12.8	6.4	0.1	6.1	0.2	0.0
	2005	(e)1 840	82.6	4.5	4.5	78.1	0.0	0.0	0.0	17.4	0.4	0.0	16.9	0.0	0.0
	2010	(e)2 660	82.1	9.9	9.9	72.1	0.0	0.0	0.0	17.9	0.6	0.0	17.3	0.0	0.0
Chile - Chili	1995	16 551	61.1	28.0	27.2	14.5	17.6	1.1	0.0	36.3	0.8	18.8	15.9	0.8	0.1
	2005	39 544	54.0	23.7	23.4	15.8	11.5	3.1	0.4	41.6	0.3	16.8	23.4	1.1	0.0
	2010	70 094	42.0	10.1	17.0	9.0	10.7	0.2	0.0	57.1	0.3	18.3	39.1	0.8	0.0
China - Chine	1995	148 965	52.3	14.2	13.8	16.6	19.1	2.4	1.4	46.3	1.7	2.1	40.5	2.0	0.0
	2005	762 648	55.4	19.5	19.1	21.4	11.0	3.4	2.9	41.6	2.4	3.0	33.3	2.8	0.0
	2010	1 580 400	49.3	20.1	19.7	17.9	7.6	3.6	3.5	46.8	3.8	5.8	33.5	3.7	0.1
China, Hong Kong SAR - Chine (RAS de Hong Kong) (2)	1995	173 556	47.4	16.1	15.3	21.8	6.1	3.3	0.2	52.3	1.4	2.8	46.6	1.4	0.0
	2005	289 628	39.4	15.2	14.6	16.1	5.3	2.9	0.2	60.3	0.5	1.4	57.2	1.1	0.0
	2010	390 348	29.6	11.9	11.2	11.0	4.2	2.5	0.5	69.8	0.6	1.5	66.6	1.1	0.0
China, Macao SAR - Chine (RAS de Macao)	1995	1 992	76.6	32.0	31.5	41.7	1.0	1.8	0.0	23.2	0.1	0.5	22.5	0.1	0.0
	2005	2 476	67.9	17.2	17.1	48.7	0.9	1.1	0.0	28.0	0.0	0.5	27.4	0.1	0.0
	2010	870	19.7	6.0	5.9	11.2	1.6	0.9	0.0	68.7	0.2	1.6	66.9	0.1	0.0
China, Taiwan Province of - Province chinoise de Taiwan	1995	(e)111 939	52.7	13.9	13.4	23.7	11.8	3.3	0.2	46.2	1.5	2.4	40.8	1.6	0.0
	2005	(e)198 535	36.4	11.6	11.3	14.7	7.6	2.5	0.4	62.1	0.8	2.0	57.6	1.7	0.0
	2010	(e)274 721	30.5	10.2	9.9	11.5	6.6	2.2	0.5	67.9	0.7	2.2	63.2	1.8	0.1
Colombia - Colombie	1995	9 859	66.7	26.8	25.9	34.1	3.7	2.1	0.1	32.6	0.4	29.8	2.3	0.2	0.0
	2005	21 191	59.9	14.1	13.3	41.8	1.6	2.4	0.4	37.9	0.2	34.3	2.6	0.7	0.0
	2010	(e)37 021	59.0	15.9	15.3	39.8	1.3	2.0	0.6	39.3	0.6	28.1	9.6	0.9	0.0
Comoros - Comores	1995	(e)11	95.4	71.2	71.1	17.7	2.4	4.1	0.4	4.3	1.1	1.9	1.3	0.0	0.0
	2005	(e)28	58.7	41.3	41.0	4.8	12.4	0.3	0.7	39.3	10.9	0.1	23.5	4.6	0.1
	2010	(e)30	37.5	31.4	31.3	5.5	0.0	0.5	0.9	59.4	1.5	0.1	43.1	14.5	0.2
Congo	1995	842	72.5	49.6	48.9	22.6	0.4	0.0	0.0	23.8	2.5	0.0	21.1	0.2	0.0
	2005	(e)5 428	35.1	6.6	6.2	28.4	0.0	0.1	0.0	64.7	1.9	1.6	60.8	0.3	0.0
	2010	(e)9 811	52.4	18.4	18.3	31.4	0.0	2.5	0.0	47.4	1.2	0.2	45.8	0.2	0.0
Cook Islands - Îles Cook	1995	5	90.5	23.7	23.7	16.6	18.7	31.5	..	9.5	2.2	3.6		..	..
	2005	5	61.8	6.8	6.2	3.0	30.8	21.2	..	38.2	..	..	36.8	0.3	1.0
	2010	5	88.1	5.9	5.9	7.2	71.8	3.2	0.1	11.8	3.5		8.0	0.0	0.0
Costa Rica	1995	2 702	74.7	31.8	31.0	40.1	1.0	1.7	1.2	23.8	0.2	21.0	2.4	0.2	0.0
	2005	7 026	60.7	16.4	16.3	42.6	0.7	1.0	0.3	39.0	0.1	24.8	14.0	0.1	0.0
Côte d'Ivoire	1995	3 729	69.0	63.5	63.4	4.4	0.5	0.6	2.2	28.1	22.6	0.6	4.1	0.7	0.0
	2005	7 253	55.3	40.6	40.0	14.1	0.1	0.5	1.6	42.8	29.8	5.2	7.2	0.6	0.0
	2010	(e)11 004	49.8	35.6	35.2	10.0	0.1	4.0	2.5	42.9	33.9	1.5	6.5	1.0	0.0
Croatia - Croatie	1995	4 633	80.0	77.5	76.1	1.9	0.0	0.5	13.8	6.2	3.3	1.0	1.3	0.6	0.0
	2005	8 774	69.3	64.5	63.4	3.5	0.6	0.8	21.8	8.8	4.3	0.3	0.5	3.7	0.0
	2010	11 616	67.5	62.7	61.1	2.6	0.4	1.7	21.1	8.3	3.1	0.5	1.3	3.5	0.0
Cuba	1995	(e)1 499	56.3	34.8	34.2	0.0	5.7	15.8	13.0	30.7	9.2	6.4	14.1	1.0	0.0
	2005	(e)2 044	66.2	42.2	41.1	0.0	1.4	22.6	4.6	29.2	2.2	15.0	11.8	0.3	0.0
	2010	(e)2 630	40.5	15.8	14.6	0.0	0.5	24.3	4.5	55.0	3.1	22.6	28.9	0.4	0.0
Cyprus - Chypre	1995	1 229	54.6	51.2	49.9	1.2	0.2	2.0	15.1	22.0	5.8	0.2	2.3	13.7	0.0
	2005	1 458	66.8	62.4	61.7	1.6	1.5	1.3	2.4	13.6	2.9	0.2	3.6	7.0	0.0
	2010	1 326	63.5	59.1	58.6	1.6	0.0	2.8	4.1	20.4	4.4	0.3	7.9	7.8	0.0
Czech Republic - République tchèque	1995	17 178	85.1	82.1	80.1	1.8	0.5	0.7	5.8	5.8	1.1	0.6	3.0	1.1	0.0
	2005	78 140	91.1	87.4	85.8	2.6	0.4	0.6	3.9	4.8	0.7	0.6	1.8	1.7	0.0
	2010	132 125	89.3	86.5	84.4	1.7	0.4	0.8	4.6	6.0	1.0	0.6	2.5	1.7	0.0
Dem. Rep. of the Congo - Rép. dém. du Congo	1995	(e)1 533	88.5	65.4	64.2	16.2	4.8	2.2	0.0	11.3	7.7	0.2	3.2	0.1	0.0
	2005	(e)1 442	74.3	57.1	57.0	17.0	0.2	0.1	0.1	25.4	9.0	4.2	12.1	0.0	0.0
	2010	(e)4 718	22.5	11.7	11.7	10.5	0.0	0.3	0.0	77.4	25.9	0.3	51.1	0.1	0.0
Denmark - Danemark	1995	47 500	86.7	76.6	67.9	4.2	4.0	2.0	2.0	11.2	1.9	1.9	5.5	1.8	0.0
	2005	85 083	88.2	77.0	70.1	6.4	2.3	2.5	2.0	8.8	0.9	1.1	5.1	1.6	0.0
	2010	95 066	85.4	74.8	67.6	5.9	1.9	2.8	2.4	12.0	1.2	1.7	6.8	2.3	0.0
Djibouti	1995	(e)95	9.3	9.1	9.0	0.0	0.2	0.0	0.0	90.7	73.8	0.0	3.8	13.2	..
	2005	(e)276	3.3	2.9	2.8	0.3	0.1	0.0	0.0	96.7	88.1	0.2	1.9	6.4	..
	2010	(e)443	4.8	2.7	2.7	0.6	1.5	0.0	0.0	95.2	84.6	0.2	1.4	8.9	..

For sources and notes, see end of table.

Pour les sources et les notes, se reporter à la fin du tableau.

2.1 Country trade structure by partner — Exports by main region of destination
2.1 Structure du commerce des pays par partenaires — Exportations par principales régions de destination

Destination / Origin / Origine	Year / Année	World (millions of dollars) (1) / Monde (millions de dollars) (1)	Developed economies / Économies développées						Transition economies / Économies en transition	Developing economies / Économies en développement					
			Total	Europe Total	Europe EU/UE	USA États-Unis	Japan Japon	Other Autres		Total	Africa Afrique	America Amérique	Eastern, Southern and South-Eastern Asia / Asie orientale, méridionale et du Sud-Est	Western Asia / Asie occidentale	Oceania Océanie
															Percentage / En pourcentage
Dominica - Dominique	1995	47	56.2	48.3	48.3	7.8	0.0	0.0	0.0	41.3	0.0	41.3	0.0	0.0	0.0
	2005	(e)00	37.4	30.0	29.9	4.0	2.0	0.8	0.0	60.2	0.8	45.3	12.7	1.4	0.0
	2010	(e)182	43.1	6.4	6.3	0.8	35.7	0.3	0.5	55.0	12.6	38.9	2.2	1.4	0.0
Dominican Republic - República dominicana	1995	3 438	17.6	5.1	5.1	10.6	0.9	1.0	0.0	2.1	0.0	1.0	1.0	0.0	0.0
	2005	6 146	86.0	7.8	7.6	77.7	0.7	0.7	0.0	7.3	0.0	4.7	2.5	0.1	0.0
	2010	6 599	63.5	10.2	9.9	52.5	0.2	0.7	0.2	29.4	0.1	25.5	3.8	0.1	0.0
Ecuador - Équateur	1995	4 358	66.7	20.3	20.1	42.8	2.7	0.8	1.4	29.5	0.0	21.9	7.5	0.1	0.0
	2005	10 100	64.4	12.8	12.8	50.0	0.7	0.8	3.1	32.4	0.3	30.9	0.6	0.5	0.0
	2010	17 419	50.8	13.1	13.0	34.9	2.3	0.5	3.7	45.1	0.6	40.6	3.3	0.5	0.0
Egypt - Égypte	1995	3 444	70.4	48.7	48.1	15.2	1.3	5.3	1.7	26.1	5.2	0.4	8.7	11.9	0.0
	2005	10 646	44.8	34.2	34.1	9.0	1.1	0.4	0.9	35.7	6.8	0.3	11.3	17.2	0.0
	2010	(e)28 493	41.1	29.9	29.6	7.5	1.5	2.2	1.4	54.4	13.9	1.5	15.2	23.8	0.0
El Salvador	1995	985	51.7	31.2	30.9	17.5	1.5	1.5	0.0	48.2	0.0	47.6	0.6	0.0	0.0
	2005	3 418	59.2	4.5	4.5	53.5	0.5	0.7	0.7	40.0	0.0	38.9	1.0	0.0	0.0
	2010	(e)4 748	51.2	5.1	5.0	43.7	0.5	1.9	0.7	47.5	0.1	44.3	3.1	0.0	0.0
Equatorial Guinea - Guinée équatoriale	1995	(e)124	63.9	26.6	26.6	25.3	12.1	0.0	0.0	36.1	26.8	0.0	9.3	0.0	0.0
	2005	(e)6 195	65.8	30.7	30.2	24.6	3.3	7.3	0.0	34.2	0.1	4.9	29.0	0.1	0.0
	2010	(e)8 290	71.3	34.4	34.4	25.1	3.9	7.8	0.0	28.7	0.1	7.4	21.2	0.0	0.0
Eritrea - Érythrée	1995	(e)86	23.3	19.3	19.0	4.0	..	0.0	0.0	76.7	0.0	0.6	0.0	76.0	..
	2005	(e)11	71.2	57.2	56.4	8.7	0.0	5.4	0.0	28.7	7.4	1.6	10.8	9.0	..
	2010	(e)12	42.4	39.3	39.0	0.8	0.0	2.3	0.1	57.5	30.9	0.5	14.0	12.1	..
Estonia - Estonie	1995	1 840	73.5	70.4	68.1	2.4	0.5	0.2	25.1	1.3	0.4	0.1	0.2	0.6	0.0
	2005	7 695	87.2	82.8	77.8	3.1	0.3	0.9	8.7	3.7	0.6	0.5	1.8	0.9	0.0
	2010	10 675	80.1	77.5	73.5	1.3	0.5	0.8	14.2	4.4	0.6	0.6	1.8	1.5	0.0
Ethiopia - Éthiopie	1995	430	71.9	51.8	51.3	6.3	12.7	1.1	0.1	25.3	11.2	0.0	4.0	10.1	0.0
	2005	782	61.4	43.6	37.1	5.5	8.5	3.8	0.3	37.8	11.7	0.1	14.7	11.3	0.0
	2010	(e)1 789	47.0	34.0	32.0	6.8	2.3	3.9	0.7	38.8	8.9	0.0	17.5	12.3	0.0
Faeroe Islands - Îles Féroé	1995	(e)320	99.6	97.0	90.6	2.3	0.0	0.3	0.0	0.1	0.0	0.1	0.1	0.0	0.0
	2005	(e)546	87.4	85.3	77.6	0.8	0.0	1.3	2.3	9.4	8.9	0.1	0.4	0.0	0.0
	2010	(e)851	81.3	70.7	64.0	9.9	0.0	0.7	2.6	15.3	12.5	0.0	2.8	0.0	0.0
Falkland Islands (Malvinas) - Îles Falkland (Malvinas)	1995	(e)27	99.5	95.4	90.1	1.7	2.5	0.0	0.0	0.5	0.2	0.0	0.3	0.0	..
	2005	(e)154	93.1	86.5	83.7	5.6	0.9	0.1	5.2	1.7	1.2	0.0	0.4	0.1	0.0
	2010	(e)162	92.2	88.4	83.6	3.0	0.7	0.0	6.3	1.5	0.0	0.0	1.4	0.1	0.0
Fiji - Fidji	1995	630	72.9	24.1	24.1	11.3	5.7	31.8	0.0	19.5	0.0	0.0	10.1	0.0	9.3
	2005	(e)892	58.3	13.0	13.0	19.1	5.3	20.8	0.0	20.4	0.0	0.6	2.9	0.1	16.8
	2010	(e)1 263	42.7	4.0	4.0	15.0	5.8	17.9	0.0	28.9	0.3	1.6	3.7	0.2	23.0
Finland - Finlande	1995	39 573	78.5	66.5	62.1	6.7	2.6	2.7	5.3	15.1	1.6	2.6	9.2	1.8	0.0
	2005	65 433	70.3	60.4	56.8	5.9	1.7	2.3	12.2	17.4	2.2	2.2	7.4	5.6	0.0
	2010	68 592	71.1	60.0	55.8	7.0	1.7	2.4	10.0	18.4	2.5	2.4	10.8	2.8	0.0
France (3)	1995	283 159	79.3	69.8	65.5	5.9	2.0	1.6	0.9	17.6	5.7	2.0	7.1	2.5	0.3
	2005	463 031	77.3	66.6	63.2	7.1	1.5	2.0	1.6	19.1	6.3	1.9	6.8	3.7	0.3
	2010	510 767	73.8	65.3	62.0	5.1	1.5	1.9	2.1	23.4	6.8	2.6	9.0	4.7	0.3
French Polynesia - Polynésie française	1995	(e)194	95.4	11.6	11.5	12.4	69.5	1.9	0.1	4.5	1.3	0.6	1.7	0.0	0.9
	2005	(e)210	83.6	49.0	48.8	12.5	20.8	1.3	0.0	16.4	12.9	0.0	2.9	0.0	0.6
	2010	(e)173	58.2	9.4	9.4	16.9	29.7	2.2	0.0	41.8	38.1	0.0	1.9	0.0	1.8
Gabon	1995	(e)2 671	80.5	22.8	20.8	53.0	3.8	0.9	0.0	14.9	3.5	0.6	10.1	0.7	0.0
	2005	(e)5 086	68.7	13.6	12.9	52.8	0.2	2.0	1.4	20.1	4.2	4.0	11.5	0.4	0.0
	2010	(e)6 684	53.4	16.1	15.5	31.0	0.7	5.7	0.9	31.4	3.5	4.5	23.3	0.1	0.0
Gambia - Gambie	1995	28	62.9	59.0	58.8	3.1	0.9	0.0	0.0	37.1	26.8	0.0	10.1	0.3	0.0
	2005	(e)28	31.0	26.4	26.1	1.0	2.3	1.4	0.3	68.7	12.6	0.2	55.3	0.6	0.0
	2010	(e)62	41.5	34.4	34.4	6.1	0.0	1.0	0.1	58.4	8.1	0.8	49.5	0.0	0.0
Georgia - Géorgie	1995	151	13.3	12.8	8.7	0.4	0.0	0.0	62.7	24.0	0.0	0.0	1.4	22.6	0.0
	2005	851	33.5	25.9	25.5	3.1	0.2	4.3	48.1	18.2	0.2	0.4	2.8	14.9	0.0
	2010	1 575	36.3	18.5	18.4	11.5	0.5	5.8	40.9	22.8	1.3	0.8	4.2	16.5	0.0
Germany - Allemagne	1995	509 651	81.5	69.6	63.2	7.5	2.6	1.9	2.4	15.7	2.1	2.5	8.5	2.5	0.0
	2005	977 104	81.2	69.0	64.4	8.8	1.7	1.8	3.6	14.9	1.9	2.2	7.6	3.3	0.0
	2010	1 206 060	76.8	68.7	63.3	5.4	1.1	1.6	4.2	18.5	2.0	2.6	10.2	3.6	0.0

For sources and notes, see end of table.

Pour les sources et les notes, se reporter à la fin du tableau.

2.1 Country trade structure by partner
Exports by main region of destination

2.1 Structure du commerce des pays par partenaires
Exportations par principales régions de destination

Destination / Origin / Origine	Year / Année	World (millions of dollars) (1) / Monde (millions de dollars) (1)	Developed economies / Économies développées						Transition economies / Économies en transition	Developing economies / Économies en développement					
			Total	Europe Total	Europe EU UE	USA États-Unis	Japan Japon	Other Autres		Total	Africa Afrique	America Amérique	Eastern, Southern and South-Eastern Asia / Asie orientale, méridionale et du Sud-Est	Western Asia Asie occidentale	Oceania Océanie
			Percentage / En pourcentage												
Ghana	1995	(e)1 488	77.9	60.4	58.4	12.4	4.3	0.9	0.9	16.5	7.4	0.5	7.5	1.2	0.0
	2005	(e)2 389	58.1	47.3	45.6	6.6	2.9	1.3	4.6	23.0	9.9	1.9	9.4	4.3	0.0
	2010	(e)4 547	50.0	40.8	38.4	5.7	2.8	0.7	9.0	29.0	11.4	1.4	10.0	5.5	0.0
Gibraltar	1995	(e)117	84.1	78.6	38.4	5.2	0.0	0.3	0.4	15.5	6.6	0.5	8.1	0.4	0.0
	2005	(e)200	85.1	82.8	73.1	1.4	0.0	0.9	12.9	2.0	1.5	0.0	0.5	0.1	0.0
Greece - Grèce	1995	10 967	80.9	75.0	72.9	3.2	0.8	2.0	6.1	12.2	2.0	1.0	2.4	0.0	0.0
	2005	17 367	70.3	62.7	61.4	5.2	0.3	2.0	8.5	18.1	4.6	1.0	3.5	9.1	0.0
	2010	21 251	71.0	65.1	63.4	4.0	0.2	1.8	8.8	17.4	5.4	1.2	3.3	7.6	0.0
Greenland - Groenland	1995	364	99.0	93.7	93.3	0.6	4.6	0.0	0.0	0.2	0.0	0.0	0.2	0.0	0.0
	2005	(e)513	88.0	72.5	69.9	3.2	12.2	0.1	0.3	9.3	0.2	0.0	9.1	0.0	0.0
	2010	(e)585	84.3	70.8	67.8	1.3	12.1	0.1	1.1	10.6	0.4	0.0	10.2	0.0	0.0
Grenada - Grenade	1995	23	68.2	37.0	37.0	29.9	0.0	1.2	0.0	31.6	0.0	31.3	0.1	0.1	0.0
	2005	(e)48	44.5	31.4	31.2	11.4	0.0	1.7	0.4	48.4	0.4	47.2	0.7	0.1	0.0
	2010	(e)68	18.7	6.7	6.5	11.2	0.0	0.9	0.2	74.8	16.5	56.8	1.3	0.2	0.0
Guam	1995	(e)85	89.7	0.0	0.0	0.0	88.0	1.7	0.0	10.3	0.0	0.0	10.1	0.0	0.2
	2005	(e)52	68.6	6.6	6.5	0.0	61.4	0.7	0.0	31.4	0.2	0.1	29.7	0.0	1.4
	2010	(e)46	63.2	1.0	1.0	0.0	61.6	0.6	0.0	36.8	0.0	0.2	31.3	0.1	5.3
Guatemala	1995	1 936	51.6	16.2	15.9	31.3	2.8	1.3	0.0	47.1	0.5	39.8	5.5	1.3	0.0
	2005	5 379	58.6	6.3	4.6	50.1	0.7	1.5	0.0	40.5	0.3	37.0	2.1	1.1	0.0
	2010	8 452	48.5	6.1	5.8	38.9	1.7	1.8	0.5	50.8	0.4	43.6	4.3	2.6	0.0
Guinea - Guinée	1995	683	80.5	54.8	52.0	22.0	0.0	3.7	0.0	13.5	4.7	8.8	0.1	0.0	0.0
	2005	(e)1 331	46.2	38.1	38.0	6.1	0.1	1.8	24.7	15.7	2.0	0.2	13.5	0.0	0.0
	2010	(e)2 224	32.3	25.5	25.5	4.6	0.0	2.2	11.4	40.6	3.1	17.6	19.8	0.1	0.0
Guinea-Bissau - Guinée-Bissau	1995	(e)94	56.4	56.0	56.0	0.0	0.5	0.0	0.4	43.1	1.7	0.0	41.5	0.0	0.0
	2005	(e)109	3.7	3.5	3.5	0.2	0.0	0.0	0.0	96.2	18.6	0.0	77.6	0.0	0.0
	2010	(e)171	4.4	3.9	3.9	0.4	0.0	0.0	0.0	95.6	27.2	0.0	68.4	0.0	0.0
Guyana	1995	(e)525	81.6	33.7	33.7	22.3	1.4	24.1	0.1	18.1	0.3	16.5	1.3	0.0	0.0
	2005	(e)643	71.2	31.0	30.8	18.8	0.6	20.7	0.0	28.1	0.5	21.7	5.9	0.0	0.0
	2010	(e)1 152	67.7	17.7	17.7	24.6	0.7	24.8	6.0	25.5	0.5	21.4	3.4	0.2	0.0
Haiti - Haïti	1995	36	99.3	35.4	35.2	60.8	0.7	2.5	0.0	0.4	0.0	0.4	0.0	0.0	0.0
	2005	(e)511	89.9	3.8	3.5	81.6	0.2	4.3	0.0	9.9	0.7	7.8	1.3	0.1	0.0
	2010	(e)643	89.6	5.2	4.8	79.9	0.2	4.2	0.0	10.1	1.3	5.4	3.3	0.1	0.0
Honduras	1995	1 224	74.6	22.6	22.6	48.4	3.2	0.4	0.0	15.5	0.0	15.5	0.0	0.0	0.0
	2005	1 892	69.7	19.7	19.3	48.2	0.9	0.9	0.3	29.8	0.0	27.5	2.2	0.1	0.0
Hungary - Hongrie	1995	12 861	80.5	75.9	74.4	3.2	0.6	0.7	10.9	4.8	0.9	0.4	1.6	1.9	0.0
	2005	62 809	86.6	82.4	80.9	3.0	0.6	0.6	6.1	6.7	1.1	0.5	1.9	3.2	0.0
	2010	95 442	82.1	78.4	77.1	2.1	0.6	1.0	9.4	8.5	1.0	0.7	3.8	3.0	0.0
Iceland - Islande	1995	1 827	95.2	68.4	62.5	12.3	11.4	3.1	1.1	3.3	0.5	0.5	2.3	0.1	0.0
	2005	2 981	94.5	81.6	76.4	8.1	3.3	1.5	1.5	4.0	1.9	0.2	1.7	0.2	0.0
	2010	4 595	92.5	84.3	77.6	4.5	2.5	1.1	2.6	4.8	2.0	0.4	1.9	0.6	0.0
India - Inde	1995	30 539	56.0	28.7	27.6	17.4	7.0	2.9	3.7	36.4	4.8	1.2	22.6	7.8	0.0
	2005	98 212	45.4	23.1	22.4	16.8	2.4	3.1	1.3	53.0	6.7	2.8	30.0	13.4	0.0
	2010	223 179	34.7	19.3	18.7	10.6	2.2	2.6	1.2	62.8	8.1	4.2	31.7	18.8	0.0
Indonesia including East Timor - Indonésie, y compris le Timor oriental	1995	45 479	59.5	15.5	15.3	13.9	27.0	3.1	0.3	35.9	1.2	1.6	30.0	3.0	0.1
Indonesia - Indonésie	2005	85 660	48.4	12.3	12.1	11.5	21.1	3.5	0.5	51.1	1.9	1.5	44.5	3.0	0.1
	2010	157 791	39.9	11.0	10.9	9.1	16.3	3.5	0.8	59.3	2.3	2.2	51.8	2.8	0.1
Iran (Islamic Rep. of) - Iran (Rép. islamique d')	1995	18 360	62.7	43.0	42.2	4.1	15.1	0.5	3.0	33.9	6.0	1.5	17.1	9.3	0.0
	2005	(e)55 219	41.1	23.7	23.6	0.3	17.0	0.1	0.9	42.7	5.3	0.0	28.5	8.9	0.0
	2010	(e)99 817	27.6	17.2	17.1	0.1	10.2	0.2	1.0	55.9	4.6	0.2	41.2	9.9	0.0
Iraq	1995	(e)425	0.6	0.3	0.3	0.0	0.3	0.0	1.7	97.7	0.0	0.1	0.9	96.7	0.0
	2005	(e)17 624	80.6	22.9	22.9	49.8	2.3	5.6	0.0	19.4	0.3	3.0	10.8	5.3	0.0
	2010	(e)46 085	53.5	17.7	17.7	24.9	6.8	4.2	0.0	46.4	0.5	1.6	39.5	4.9	0.0
Ireland - Irlande	1995	43 597	89.5	76.4	73.4	8.4	3.0	1.7	0.9	7.2	1.6	1.0	3.3	1.3	0.0
	2005	109 619	91.0	68.1	63.7	18.5	2.6	1.6	0.4	8.3	0.9	1.1	5.1	1.0	0.0
	2010	112 368	90.9	65.0	60.3	22.1	2.0	1.8	0.6	8.3	0.9	1.1	5.1	1.2	0.0

For sources and notes, see end of table.

Pour les sources et les notes, se reporter à la fin du tableau.

Destination / Origin / Origine	Year / Année	World (millions of dollars) (1) / Monde (millions de dollars) (1)	Developed economies / Économies développées						Transition economies / Économies en transition	Developing economies / Économies en développement					
			Total	Europe Total	EU UE	USA États-Unis	Japan Japon	Other Autres		Total	Africa Afrique	America Amérique	Eastern, Southern and South-Eastern Asia / Asie orientale, méridionale et du Sud-Est	Western Asia / Asie occidentale	Oceania Océanie
										Percentage / En pourcentage					
Israel - Israël	1995	19 027	73.8	35.2	33.3	29.9	6.9	1.8	2.0	17.8	1.5	2.8	12.7	0.0	0.0
	2005	42 515	72.2	31.7	29.4	36.5	1.9	2.2	1.7	22.5	1.5	3.1	15.5	2.4	0.0
	2010	58 416	63.2	28.2	26.3	31.6	1.1	2.3	2.2	30.4	2.2	3.9	21.6	2.6	0.0
Italy - Italie	1995	233 010	70.0	66.0	62.6	7.0	2.0	2.0	2.5	16.2	3.4	3.4	7.4	3.9	0.0
	2005	373 020	77.5	65.7	61.2	8.0	1.5	2.3	4.1	17.5	3.8	2.6	6.4	4.6	0.0
	2010	440 650	72.3	63.2	58.1	5.8	1.2	2.2	4.8	22.1	5.1	3.2	8.0	5.7	0.0
Jamaica - Jamaïque	1995	(e)1 885	83.1	30.6	23.4	43.1	1.8	7.6	1.6	9.3	3.9	5.1	0.4	0.0	0.0
	2005	1 533	83.5	36.7	29.9	25.9	1.0	19.8	1.4	14.4	0.0	5.1	7.5	1.7	0.0
	2010	(e)1 066	74.9	26.2	14.8	31.8	1.6	15.3	5.9	17.9	0.1	15.0	2.8	0.1	0.0
Japan - Japon	1995	443 536	48.2	16.9	16.1	27.5	..	3.8	0.3	51.4	1.6	4.2	43.7	1.8	0.1
	2005	595 138	42.3	15.2	14.6	22.9	..	4.2	0.9	56.7	1.4	3.8	48.8	2.7	0.1
	2010	771 720	31.8	12.5	11.3	15.6	..	3.7	1.2	66.4	1.6	5.4	56.3	3.1	0.1
Jordan - Jordanie	1995	1 444	11.1	7.2	7.2	1.5	1.5	1.0	0.5	73.6	5.7	0.4	25.1	42.4	0.0
	2005	4 301	33.4	3.7	3.6	26.2	0.6	2.9	0.4	57.5	6.4	0.3	12.5	38.2	0.0
	2010	5 939	23.1	4.8	3.7	15.6	1.0	1.8	0.6	74.8	9.4	0.3	20.7	44.5	0.0
Kazakhstan	1995	5 257	32.3	30.6	26.7	0.8	0.9	0.0	54.9	12.8	0.4	1.2	9.9	1.4	0.0
	2005	(e)22 827	58.3	52.2	51.2	4.6	1.3	0.2	17.0	18.0	0.1	0.3	14.7	2.9	0.0
	2010	(e)47 961	49.3	39.8	37.4	3.7	1.2	4.7	11.1	28.5	0.3	0.3	22.7	5.1	0.0
Kenya	1995	1 826	41.8	36.9	35.7	2.7	0.7	1.4	0.1	57.2	45.3	0.1	9.8	2.0	0.0
	2005	(e)3 448	43.5	31.6	30.6	9.7	0.8	1.3	1.0	48.7	36.0	0.3	10.4	2.1	0.0
	2010	(e)5 243	33.4	26.0	24.9	5.6	0.7	1.0	2.1	55.8	41.8	0.2	10.9	3.0	0.0
Kiribati	1995	(e)7	47.4	15.4	15.4	11.9	19.4	0.7	0.0	52.6	0.1	0.5	41.9	0.0	10.1
	2005	(e)4	72.3	23.7	23.7	24.5	15.3	8.8	0.4	27.2	0.0	0.0	17.5	0.0	9.7
	2010	(e)15	34.1	0.7	0.7	6.0	24.6	2.8	0.0	65.8	0.0	0.2	61.3	0.0	4.3
Korea, Dem. People's Rep. of - Corée, Rép. populaire dém. de	1995	(e)829	52.5	15.4	15.3	0.0	36.9	0.2	1.8	45.6	4.5	8.9	25.5	6.6	0.1
	2005	(e)1 252	17.7	7.0	6.9	0.0	9.6	1.1	1.6	80.6	4.7	11.6	55.2	8.9	0.3
	2010	(e)2 306	5.6	5.2	5.2	0.0	0.0	0.3	1.7	92.7	5.0	17.7	58.8	10.8	0.3
Korea, Republic of - Corée, République de	1995	131 360	48.9	14.3	13.6	18.5	13.0	3.1	1.4	44.6	2.3	5.4	33.9	2.9	0.1
	2005	285 484	42.2	15.9	15.5	14.5	8.4	3.3	2.0	54.9	2.8	4.9	43.5	3.6	0.1
	2010	471 071	31.7	12.1	11.4	10.6	6.0	3.0	2.4	63.1	3.3	6.5	48.6	4.3	0.2
Kuwait - Koweït	1995	12 944	0.6	0.2	0.2	0.2	0.1	0.0	0.0	5.0	0.4	0.0	2.5	2.1	0.0
	2005	(e)35 852	42.2	10.3	10.2	11.7	19.3	0.8	0.0	57.8	2.8	0.2	51.7	3.2	0.0
	2010	(e)60 466	31.0	6.2	6.1	8.4	15.5	0.9	0.0	69.0	3.6	0.4	61.1	3.8	0.0
Kyrgyzstan - Kirghizistan	1995	483	21.5	21.1	21.1	0.5	0.0	0.0	73.2	5.3	..	0.0	1.4	3.9	0.0
	2005	634	13.0	8.9	4.4	0.5	0.1	3.6	47.9	39.2	0.0	0.0	8.9	30.2	0.0
	2010	(e)1 100	2.2	1.7	1.7	0.3	0.0	0.1	77.9	19.9	0.0	0.0	12.2	7.6	0.0
Lao People's Dem. Rep. - Rép. dém. populaire lao	1995	311	14.5	11.1	10.9	1.7	1.7	0.0	0.4	59.4	0.0	0.0	59.4	0.0	0.0
	2005	(e)696	23.9	20.4	19.7	0.6	1.0	1.8	0.1	49.2	0.1	0.1	48.8	0.2	0.0
	2010	(e)2 216	13.8	9.3	9.2	2.5	1.5	0.4	0.0	69.7	0.1	0.0	69.5	0.1	0.0
Latvia - Lettonie	1995	1 284	60.8	59.0	56.8	1.3	0.3	0.1	38.1	1.1	0.3	0.1	0.4	0.4	0.0
	2005	5 145	85.1	80.8	76.6	2.7	0.9	0.6	12.3	2.3	0.7	0.7	0.7	0.2	0.0
	2010	9 419	72.9	70.7	67.7	1.3	0.5	0.4	20.2	6.9	2.9	0.3	2.2	1.4	0.0
Lebanon - Liban	1995	(e)716	38.0	32.5	29.3	3.0	1.1	1.4	1.6	57.0	8.4	0.6	2.5	45.5	0.0
	2005	(e)2 171	24.3	19.5	11.4	3.8	0.1	0.8	0.7	74.2	9.4	0.3	5.4	59.0	0.0
	2010	(e)4 021	16.3	13.4	9.2	2.0	0.2	0.8	0.6	82.2	11.5	0.2	5.5	65.0	0.0
Lesotho	1995	(e)160	62.1	18.3	16.5	41.8	0.0	1.9	0.0	37.2	37.1	0.0	0.1	0.0	0.0
	2005	(e)655	97.0	12.8	12.8	81.8	0.1	2.3	0.0	3.0	2.6	0.1	0.2	0.1	0.0
	2010	(e)807	96.3	34.9	34.9	57.9	0.3	3.3	0.0	3.6	2.3	0.4	0.9	0.0	0.0
Liberia - Libéria	1995	(e)955	81.2	80.2	79.8	1.0	0.0	0.0	8.5	10.3	2.7	0.3	6.6	0.7	0.0
	2005	(e)1 071	76.6	67.3	66.8	8.2	0.0	1.0	0.2	23.1	1.6	0.1	20.5	1.0	0.0
	2010	(e)878	56.1	32.8	29.7	19.1	0.1	4.2	1.6	42.3	31.3	0.4	9.8	0.8	0.0
Libyan Arab Jamahiriya - Jamahiriya arabe libyenne	1995	(e)8 510	84.9	84.9	81.8	0.0	0.0	0.0	2.0	13.0	6.1	0.1	2.4	4.4	0.0
	2005	(e)29 015	85.6	79.9	76.5	5.2	0.0	0.5	1.1	13.3	2.2	0.3	3.3	7.5	0.0
	2010	(e)44 398	83.7	78.4	77.4	4.5	0.0	0.8	0.0	16.3	2.4	0.5	11.2	2.2	0.0
Lithuania - Lituanie	1995	2 706	55.2	54.3	51.1	0.7	0.1	0.1	42.3	2.4	0.1	0.3	1.0	1.0	0.0
	2005	11 767	76.4	68.5	65.8	4.7	0.1	3.0	17.8	5.7	0.2	0.4	3.7	1.4	0.0
	2010	20 243	69.8	65.1	62.5	2.7	0.1	1.8	27.2	3.0	0.8	0.2	1.0	1.0	0.0

For sources and notes, see end of table.

Pour les sources et les notes, se reporter à la fin du tableau.

63

Destination / Origin / Origine	Year / Année	World (millions of dollars) (1) / Monde (millions de dollars) (1)	Developed economies / Économies développées						Transition economies / Économies en transition	Developing economies / Économies en développement					
			Total	Europe Total	Europe EU UE	USA États-Unis	Japan Japon	Other Autres		Total	Africa Afrique	America Amérique	Eastern, Southern and South-Eastern Asia / Asie orientale, méridionale et du Sud-Est	Western Asia / Asie occidentale	Oceania / Océanie
			Percentage / En pourcentage												
Luxembourg	1995	(e)7 191	99.0	97.0	95.0	1.8	0.0	0.7	0.3	8.1	1.3	1.7	4.9	1.2	0.0
	2005	18 716	91.0	88.0	86.7	2.1	0.2	0.6	0.7	5.1	0.6	0.9	2.0	1.5	0.0
	2010	19 572	89.9	87.2	83.1	1.8	0.3	0.6	2.0	6.9	1.0	0.8	2.4	2.7	0.0
Madagascar	1995	342	84.5	71.1	68.8	6.8	6.4	0.2	0.0	15.1	9.5	0.1	5.1	0.3	0.0
	2005	(e)940	70.0	51.0	50.5	22.4	0.2	0.0	0.0	10.1	4.1	0.1	11.1	3.8	0.0
	2010	(e)1 118	67.1	52.3	51.4	9.2	1.1	4.4	0.4	22.0	0.7	0.0	11.0	1.7	0.0
Malawi	1995	421	77.4	56.6	52.1	13.5	5.2	2.1	1.2	21.2	17.0	1.4	2.2	0.4	0.2
	2005	(e)595	58.8	33.2	32.4	18.9	5.1	1.6	7.0	33.7	26.0	1.4	3.1	2.7	0.5
	2010	(e)985	47.4	29.1	28.1	7.0	3.5	7.8	10.2	41.8	24.7	0.6	13.9	2.1	0.6
Malaysia - Malaisie	1995	73 728	50.4	14.6	14.4	20.8	12.5	2.6	0.2	48.9	1.1	1.6	43.9	2.3	0.1
	2005	140 980	45.3	12.0	11.8	19.7	9.3	4.3	0.5	54.2	1.4	1.1	48.9	2.6	0.1
	2010	(e)241 938	33.7	10.3	10.1	10.0	8.5	4.8	0.9	65.4	1.8	3.4	57.2	3.0	0.1
Maldives	1995	50	63.7	38.7	38.4	19.2	5.7	0.1	0.0	36.3	0.0	0.0	35.8	0.5	0.0
	2005	99	48.2	24.5	24.5	0.8	22.8	0.1	0.0	51.8	0.0	0.0	51.7	0.0	0.0
	2010	(e)132	37.2	34.1	32.9	1.2	1.1	0.7	0.1	62.7	6.3	0.0	56.2	0.2	0.0
Mali	1995	(e)241	38.6	33.0	32.3	2.2	0.9	2.5	0.1	60.1	8.2	9.1	42.5	0.2	0.1
	2005	(e)253	25.2	21.1	21.0	1.4	0.1	2.7	1.2	68.8	5.3	0.2	62.3	1.1	0.0
	2010	(e)309	14.0	9.9	9.8	1.9	0.0	2.2	0.1	78.2	10.5	0.1	67.0	0.5	0.0
Malta - Malte	1995	1 913	84.1	73.1	71.6	9.6	0.9	0.6	0.3	13.3	3.0	0.3	9.2	0.8	0.0
	2005	2 393	71.0	52.0	51.3	13.7	4.0	1.3	0.6	27.4	7.0	1.2	17.2	1.9	0.0
	2010	1 692	71.0	60.8	58.9	5.7	3.0	1.6	0.5	15.9	8.4	1.0	4.5	2.0	0.0
Marshall Islands - Îles Marshall	1995	23	99.8	14.4	14.4	37.9	47.3	0.1	0.1	0.2	0.0	..	0.0	..	0.2
	2005	25	92.6	85.8	85.8	3.3	3.5	0.0	0.0	7.3	0.0	0.0	7.1	0.1	0.0
	2010	(e)20	57.5	49.5	49.5	4.7	3.2	0.1	0.0	42.5	1.7	4.0	36.8	0.0	0.0
Mauritania - Mauritanie	1995	(e)575	87.0	57.8	57.8	1.2	28.0	0.1	0.1	12.3	11.6	0.1	0.7	0.0	0.0
	2005	(e)958	71.7	59.3	58.4	0.1	12.0	0.4	5.5	21.3	19.7	0.0	1.0	0.6	0.0
	2010	(e)2 151	39.6	31.4	31.0	2.3	6.0	0.0	2.0	57.0	15.0	0.0	41.6	0.5	0.0
Mauritius - Maurice	1995	1 539	91.8	75.2	73.8	14.8	0.6	1.1	0.0	5.7	4.0	0.0	1.7	0.0	0.0
	2005	2 001	78.2	67.3	66.2	9.6	0.9	0.4	0.1	21.6	9.1	0.2	3.2	8.7	0.4
	2010	(e)1 744	72.5	60.0	57.3	10.8	0.6	1.2	1.0	26.5	19.4	0.4	5.6	1.0	0.1
Mayotte	2005	6	58.8	58.7	58.7	0.0	..	0.0	0.7	40.5	40.3	0.0	0.0	0.2	..
Mexico - Mexique	1995	79 557	92.4	5.1	4.3	83.6	1.2	2.6	0.0	7.0	0.0	5.6	1.2	0.1	0.0
	2005	214 233	92.7	4.1	4.0	85.7	0.7	2.2	0.0	6.3	0.1	4.5	1.6	0.1	0.0
	2010	298 473	89.3	4.8	4.5	80.0	0.6	3.9	0.1	10.1	0.1	7.0	3.0	0.1	0.0
Micronesia (Federated States of) - Micronésie (États fédérés de)	1995	39	71.5	0.0	0.0	11.1	60.4	0.0	..	28.5	..	..	28.5	..	..
	2005	13	7.0	0.2	0.2	3.1	3.6	0.0	0.0	93.0	2.6	0.4	90.0	..	..
	2010	(e)27	24.8	0.4	0.4	10.9	13.5	0.0	0.0	75.2	0.6	27.2	47.3	..	0.0
Mongolia - Mongolie	1995	473	46.5	31.2	15.0	5.5	9.9	0.0	30.4	23.0	0.0	0.0	23.0	0.0	0.0
	2005	1 064	40.5	12.8	12.4	14.3	0.5	12.8	4.7	54.8	0.0	0.1	54.5	0.2	0.0
	2010	(e)2 796	13.2	4.0	3.9	0.4	0.8	8.1	3.0	83.7	0.0	0.1	83.4	0.2	0.0
Montenegro - Monténégro	2010	(e)254	87.7	85.6	85.3	1.5	0.4	0.2	4.2	8.1	4.8	0.0	1.1	2.2	0.0
Montserrat	1995	3	88.0	72.4	72.4	15.4	..	0.2	..	12.0	9.2	2.6	0.1	..	..
	2005	1	50.6	17.7	17.7	23.6	..	9.3	..	48.1	..	48.1	..	..	..
	2010	1	59.4	30.7	30.7	28.5	..	0.3	..	15.5	..	15.5	..	..	..
Morocco - Maroc	1995	4 951	72.5	61.1	59.9	3.2	7.3	1.0	0.5	21.1	7.5	2.0	8.5	3.1	0.0
	2005	10 643	75.5	70.3	69.0	2.6	1.1	1.6	1.5	20.6	4.3	3.5	9.9	2.8	0.0
	2010	(e)16 138	65.7	58.3	57.4	4.2	1.4	1.8	2.6	30.5	5.8	6.6	13.9	4.1	0.0
Mozambique	1995	174	62.6	41.1	41.0	5.5	14.2	1.8	0.0	35.0	30.1	0.1	4.7	0.1	0.0
	2005	1 745	67.2	64.5	64.3	2.2	0.5	0.0	0.0	27.3	22.5	0.0	4.7	0.1	0.0
	2010	2 243	62.5	61.4	61.1	0.7	0.2	0.2	0.6	35.1	25.9	0.5	7.7	0.9	0.0
Myanmar	1995	(e)1 198	21.5	6.5	6.1	6.6	7.1	1.3	0.0	68.1	0.9	0.1	66.2	0.9	0.0
	2005	(e)3 702	14.1	8.6	8.5	0.0	5.0	0.6	0.1	78.0	0.4	0.2	76.7	0.7	0.0
	2010	(e)6 437	8.8	3.0	3.0	2.0	5.5	0.3	0.2	85.0	1.6	0.1	82.0	1.2	0.0
Namibia - Namibie	1995	(e)1 416	68.5	60.7	60.4	1.7	0.0	6.1	0.0	30.4	29.1	0.5	0.7	0.1	0.0
	2005	2 504	52.4	37.1	36.7	9.2	1.1	5.0	0.1	47.1	41.5	0.0	4.9	0.7	0.0
	2010	(e)4 247	69.0	48.3	47.5	7.8	3.5	9.4	0.2	30.8	9.0	0.1	21.3	0.4	0.0

For sources and notes, see end of table.

Pour les sources et les notes, se reporter à la fin du tableau.

Destination / Origin / Origine	Year / Année	World (millions of dollars) (1) / Monde (millions de dollars) (1)	Developed economies / Économies développées						Transition economies / Économies en transition	Developing economies / Économies en développement					
			Total	Europe		USA États-Unis	Japan Japon	Other Autres		Total	Africa Afrique	America Amérique	Eastern, Southern and South-Eastern Asia / Asie orientale, méridionale et du Sud-Est	Western Asia / Asie occidentale	Oceania Océanie
				Total	EU UE										
			Percentage / En pourcentage												
Nauru	1995	(e)28	82.4	2.1	2.0	0.0	1.5	78.8	0.1	17.6	0.7	0.6	16.1	0.2	0.0
	2005	(e)4	50.7	19.2	19.2	2.2	5.0	24.3	0.1	49.2	4.3	4.4	40.3	0.2	0.0
	2010	(e)35	37.9	0.2	0.2	0.2	11.8	25.8	0.0	62.0	0.4	0.5	61.0	0.0	0.0
Nepal - Népal	1995	(e)381	88.2	60.0	60.0	80.8	0.5	1.4	0.1	10.7	0.1	0.4	10.2	0.0	0.0
	2005	813	27.4	12.4	11.8	12.9	0.9	1.1	0.0	68.9	0.1	0.1	68.1	0.7	0.0
	2010	(e)744	27.0	14.5	13.7	8.1	1.2	3.2	0.2	69.7	0.5	0.2	66.8	2.2	0.0
Netherlands - Pays-Bas	1995	177 394	88.1	82.3	79.6	3.6	1.1	1.1	1.4	9.8	1.9	1.5	4.7	1.8	0.0
	2005	406 032	88.1	82.0	79.7	4.3	0.7	1.1	2.1	9.0	1.7	1.1	3.9	2.2	0.0
	2010	567 620	85.7	80.3	77.8	3.8	0.7	1.0	2.1	11.3	2.5	1.7	4.7	2.4	0.0
Netherlands Antilles - Antilles néerlandaises	1995	(e)1 431	56.8	32.8	30.5	19.7	0.8	3.4	0.0	37.7	0.8	34.6	2.2	0.1	0.0
	2005	(e)3 230	32.4	4.6	4.6	27.3	0.1	0.4	0.0	63.6	2.7	58.7	2.2	0.0	0.0
	2010	(e)3 809	30.0	4.9	4.6	25.1	0.0	0.1	0.0	63.9	3.3	50.4	10.2	0.0	0.0
New Caledonia - Nouvelle-Calédonie	1995	526	88.7	44.4	44.4	8.5	28.6	7.2	0.0	12.0	0.5	0.0	9.7	0.0	1.8
	2005	(e)996	61.6	34.1	34.1	2.5	21.1	3.9	1.5	36.9	4.4	0.0	30.3	0.0	2.2
	2010	(e)1 392	61.8	29.8	29.8	4.7	19.2	8.0	0.0	38.2	2.6	0.0	32.6	0.0	3.0
New Zealand - Nouvelle-Zélande	1995	13 724	62.8	14.7	14.3	9.9	16.2	22.0	0.9	32.9	1.4	3.1	23.2	2.3	2.9
	2005	21 843	63.4	15.6	15.1	14.0	10.5	23.2	0.7	33.6	2.1	3.4	22.3	2.7	3.2
	2010	31 435	51.8	11.2	10.9	8.6	7.8	24.3	1.0	45.0	3.2	3.3	32.2	3.5	2.8
Nicaragua	1995	466	72.1	31.1	30.2	38.2	1.5	1.3	0.0	25.2	0.0	24.9	0.3	0.0	0.0
	2005	866	53.4	13.0	12.6	35.4	1.2	3.8	1.6	43.4	0.0	41.7	1.6	0.1	0.0
Niger	1995	193	80.2	58.2	57.7	0.2	21.8	0.0	0.0	19.7	19.6	0.0	0.0	0.1	0.0
	2005	(e)297	71.8	49.5	49.3	20.3	0.5	1.5	0.0	28.2	27.1	0.0	0.9	0.1	0.0
	2010	(e)213	15.6	2.1	1.6	11.6	0.0	2.0	0.0	84.4	78.3	0.1	5.9	0.2	0.0
Nigeria - Nigéria	1995	(e)12 248	76.6	34.6	33.3	37.5	1.0	3.5	0.0	22.8	8.8	4.1	9.8	0.1	0.0
	2005	(e)43 541	77.7	22.7	21.7	52.4	2.1	0.5	0.0	21.3	8.8	7.5	4.3	0.6	0.0
	2010	(e)77 654	63.3	22.9	22.6	36.7	0.6	3.0	0.0	35.7	9.6	9.4	15.8	0.8	0.0
Niue - Nioué	1995	0	66.6	8.5	8.5	10.2	..	47.9	35.7	15.5	5.6	2.1	7.8	..	..
	2005	0	45.6	22.0	22.0	8.4	..	15.3	2.8	51.5	26.6	0.4	24.4	0.1	0.1
	2010	(e)0	0.4	0.2	0.2	0.0	0.0	0.1	0.0	99.6	98.3	0.1	1.2	0.0	0.0
Northern Mariana Islands - Îles Mariannes du Nord	2005	651	41.9	24.6	24.5	..	16.7	0.6	1.7	58.1	0.6	24.7	32.6	0.2	..
	2010	(e)10	59.8	47.3	46.0	..	12.1	0.3	0.3	39.9	4.4	3.6	28.7	2.8	0.5
Norway - Norvège	1995	41 069	93.2	80.7	79.6	6.2	1.8	4.5	0.7	6.0	0.6	1.5	3.2	0.7	0.0
	2005	103 785	93.2	81.5	80.8	6.6	1.0	4.1	1.1	5.6	0.6	1.1	3.2	0.6	0.0
	2010	131 400	90.1	81.9	80.9	5.0	1.2	2.0	1.2	8.7	1.0	1.1	5.7	0.8	0.0
Occupied Palestinian territory - Territoire palestinien occupé	1995	(e)394	2.8	2.8	2.8	0.0	..	0.0	0.0	97.2	3.6	3.0	0.0	90.6	..
	2005	(e)335	88.8	68.7	66.7	20.2	0.0	0.0	0.1	11.1	0.2	9.2	0.0	1.7	0.0
	2010	(e)563	30.4	18.7	17.1	11.7	0.0	0.0	0.1	69.5	2.7	0.1	8.2	58.5	0.0
Oman	1995	5 965	33.5	0.9	0.9	3.3	27.7	1.6	0.3	66.3	2.5	0.0	48.7	15.0	0.0
	2005	18 462	18.2	2.5	2.5	2.0	13.5	0.2	0.2	81.5	2.2	0.0	68.2	11.1	0.0
	2010	(e)32 636	17.0	1.6	1.6	2.3	12.6	0.6	0.1	82.8	1.5	0.1	66.4	14.9	0.0
Pakistan	1995	7 992	56.9	31.8	31.1	15.1	6.8	3.2	0.9	37.7	2.9	1.6	22.0	11.1	0.0
	2005	16 053	55.2	27.2	26.6	24.8	0.9	2.3	0.7	43.7	5.7	1.7	22.2	14.0	0.0
	2010	(e)21 623	40.6	21.4	20.8	15.7	1.5	2.1	1.5	56.0	7.3	2.2	29.5	17.0	0.0
Palau - Palaos	1995	(e)13	..	..	..	..	..	..	..	..	..	..	0.0	..	..
	2005	(e)14	95.9	1.2	1.2	0.0	94.7	0.0	0.0	4.1	0.0	0.3	3.8	..	..
	2010	(e)12	96.9	0.8	0.8	0.0	94.5	1.6	0.0	3.1	0.0	0.0	3.1	..	..
Panama	1995	(e)2 062	46.0	28.0	25.8	14.7	2.6	0.7	0.4	52.9	0.1	33.1	18.4	1.3	0.0
	2005	977	70.1	25.3	25.2	44.3	0.3	0.2	0.0	27.0	0.0	18.9	8.1	0.0	0.0
Papua New Guinea - Papouasie-Nouvelle-Guinée	1995	(e)3 132	68.3	16.3	16.3	1.6	21.2	29.2	0.0	15.5	0.0	0.0	15.3	0.0	0.1
	2005	(e)5 237	48.3	8.7	8.7	1.1	8.6	29.9	0.0	13.6	0.0	0.0	13.2	0.0	0.3
	2010	(e)9 929	44.5	7.3	7.3	0.9	9.1	28.1	0.1	16.3	0.0	0.0	16.0	0.0	0.3
Paraguay	1995	919	26.4	19.8	19.4	4.8	0.1	1.6	0.0	73.2	0.6	65.1	7.4	0.1	0.0
	2005	1 688	12.5	7.1	6.1	3.3	1.1	1.1	6.2	71.0	1.1	62.2	6.3	1.4	0.0
	2010	4 534	16.7	12.9	10.7	1.5	0.9	1.5	5.3	76.8	1.0	67.9	5.9	2.0	0.0
Peru - Pérou	1995	5 513	63.8	34.4	30.6	17.3	9.1	3.0	0.4	35.6	0.7	17.1	17.6	0.2	0.0
	2005	17 291	61.9	20.8	16.2	31.2	3.5	6.4	0.2	37.9	0.4	20.4	16.7	0.3	0.0
	2010	(e)30 436	55.8	21.1	20.3	16.0	6.5	12.2	0.2	44.0	0.7	18.9	24.1	0.3	0.0

For sources and notes, see end of table.

Pour les sources et les notes, se reporter à la fin du tableau.

Origin / Origine	Year / Année	World (millions of dollars) (1) — Monde (millions de dollars) (1)	Developed economies — Économies développées						Transition economies — Économies en transition	Developing economies — Économies en développement					
			Total	Europe Total	EU UE	USA États-Unis	Japan Japon	Other Autres		Total	Africa Afrique	America Amérique	Eastern, Southern and South-Eastern Asia / Asie orientale, méridionale et du Sud-Est	Western Asia / Asie occidentale	Oceania Océanie
								Percentage / En pourcentage							
Philippines	1995	17 000	71.6	17.0	17.7	35.0	16.0	2.1	0.0	28.2	0.2	1.1	26.8	1.2	0.1
	2005	41 224	54.5	17.1	17.0	18.0	17.5	1.9	0.1	45.4	0.2	0.7	43.7	0.6	0.1
	2010	(e)59 229	39.6	12.2	12.0	13.0	12.4	1.9	0.4	59.2	0.4	2.3	55.5	0.9	0.1
Poland - Pologne	1995	22 904	82.6	79.2	77.7	2.7	0.2	0.5	10.5	6.7	1.3	1.3	3.2	0.8	0.0
	2000	89 207	84.5	81.0	78.0	2.1	0.2	1.0	9.2	5.0	0.0	0.0	1.0	1.0	0.0
	2010	150 738	85.3	83.0	81.2	1.4	0.3	0.6	8.9	5.7	1.0	0.0	2.2	1.0	0.0
Portugal	1995	23 178	91.1	84.4	81.4	4.5	0.8	1.4	0.3	7.9	3.8	1.7	1.7	0.7	0.0
	2005	38 721	88.1	81.5	80.3	5.3	0.3	0.9	0.4	10.5	4.9	1.3	2.8	1.4	0.0
	2010	48 440	80.9	76.3	74.6	3.4	0.3	0.8	0.5	16.2	9.5	3.4	1.8	1.4	0.0
Qatar	1995	(e)3 681	60.9	1.3	1.3	2.4	53.6	3.5	0.0	36.1	1.1	0.0	28.1	6.9	0.0
	2005	25 332	44.9	2.0	2.0	1.2	40.7	1.0	0.0	44.0	1.3	0.1	37.1	5.5	0.0
	2010	(e)67 808	44.9	13.5	13.3	0.7	29.1	1.6	0.0	46.1	0.3	0.6	43.7	1.5	0.0
Republic of Moldova - République de Moldova	1995	746	34.3	32.6	32.0	1.1	0.0	0.7	62.8	2.4	0.1	0.3	0.4	1.6	0.0
	2005	1 091	45.0	41.3	40.6	3.5	0.0	0.2	50.7	4.0	0.4	0.4	0.1	3.1	0.0
	2010	(e)1 545	47.3	45.5	45.2	0.8	0.6	0.5	39.4	12.4	0.5	3.1	1.6	7.3	0.0
Romania - Roumanie	1995	8 061	65.6	60.6	59.5	2.5	0.4	2.0	6.6	26.9	7.2	2.1	8.9	8.7	0.0
	2005	27 645	76.6	71.6	70.3	3.9	0.3	0.8	5.4	16.5	2.2	0.6	3.2	10.6	0.0
	2010	48 391	77.0	74.5	73.7	1.4	0.4	0.7	7.8	15.0	2.3	0.6	2.9	9.2	0.0
Russian Federation - Fédération de Russie	1995	77 595	63.8	52.2	47.0	6.6	4.1	1.0	18.8	15.6	0.9	1.2	11.0	2.6	0.0
	2005	239 298	68.2	62.8	58.0	3.1	1.6	0.7	13.2	17.7	1.1	0.9	10.4	5.4	0.0
	2010	373 692	59.0	51.7	49.2	3.2	3.3	0.7	7.2	20.3	1.3	1.1	13.4	4.6	0.0
Rwanda	1995	(e)63	63.8	60.9	60.6	2.6	0.1	0.2	0.0	6.5	2.5	0.4	3.6	0.0	0.0
	2005	(e)167	28.7	24.8	24.6	3.7	0.0	0.3	1.2	24.2	6.3	0.3	17.1	0.4	0.0
	2010	(e)385	17.1	11.6	11.5	5.3	0.1	0.2	0.6	81.5	63.2	0.0	17.8	0.4	0.0
Saint Helena - Sainte-Hélène	1995	(e)4	91.8	19.1	19.1	0.0	72.5	0.3	0.0	8.2	0.1	0.3	2.5	5.3	0.0
	2005	(e)20	46.5	16.3	16.1	15.8	13.8	0.6	0.0	53.5	48.3	0.7	4.3	0.1	0.0
	2010	(e)26	46.1	7.5	7.5	23.5	14.7	0.3	0.1	53.9	51.7	0.0	2.2	0.0	0.0
Saint Kitts and Nevis - Saint-Kitts-et-Nevis	1995	(e)40	94.1	34.1	33.8	54.3	0.2	5.6	0.8	5.1	0.0	5.0	0.1	0.0	..
	2005	(e)83	87.2	17.7	17.7	61.3	0.1	8.1	1.2	7.4	3.4	4.0	0.0	0.0	..
	2010	(e)85	78.9	9.5	9.5	59.4	0.1	9.9	0.3	13.9	0.1	9.7	1.1	2.9	..
Saint Lucia - Sainte-Lucie	1995	109	83.3	55.8	55.7	26.4	0.3	0.9	0.0	16.3	1.0	15.1	0.2	0.0	0.0
	2005	(e)163	65.0	46.1	46.1	18.7	0.0	0.3	0.0	34.7	0.0	15.3	19.3	0.0	0.0
	2010	(e)99	39.6	22.0	22.0	17.3	0.0	0.2	0.0	59.8	0.1	55.9	3.7	0.0	0.0
Saint Pierre and Miquelon - Saint-Pierre-et-Miquelon	1995	(e)6	94.1	36.8	35.9	54.5	1.4	1.3	..	5.9	1.6	1.9	2.4	0.0	0.0
	2005	(e)11	75.3	65.3	60.8	9.7	0.0	0.3	0.1	24.6	0.1	0.8	23.8	0.0	0.0
	2010	(e)5	95.4	33.6	33.6	33.0	0.2	28.6	0.0	4.6	0.2	3.0	1.4	0.0	0.0
Saint Vincent and the les Grenadines	1995	45	36.6	23.9	23.9	12.5	0.1	0.1	..	61.9	0.0	61.9	0.0	0.0	0.0
	2005	40	36.7	27.2	27.2	9.2	0.0	0.3	0.0	62.4	0.0	62.2	0.2	0.0	0.0
	2010	(e)128	59.6	58.0	56.8	1.4	0.0	0.2	0.0	40.2	0.2	35.1	1.4	3.6	0.0
Samoa	1995	(e)61	93.4	2.1	2.1	0.9	1.7	88.6	0.0	3.2	0.3	0.0	0.9	0.0	2.0
	2005	234	84.8	0.2	0.2	6.5	0.4	77.7	0.0	14.9	0.0	0.0	0.2	0.0	14.6
	2010	(e)137	35.3	1.1	1.0	2.6	0.2	31.4	0.0	57.5	1.5	0.7	6.9	0.2	48.3
Sao Tome and Principe - Sao Tomé-et-Principe	1995	(e)7	84.0	79.6	73.9	1.4	2.9	0.1	..	16.0	5.3	1.0	9.6	0.0	0.0
	2005	(e)18	83.4	81.2	80.9	1.0	0.6	0.5	0.0	16.6	2.8	3.5	4.5	5.7	0.0
	2010	(e)10	82.2	77.3	77.3	1.8	0.3	2.7	0.0	17.8	9.0	1.2	7.0	0.6	0.0
Saudi Arabia - Arabie saoudite	1995	50 041	55.6	20.4	20.4	16.9	16.2	2.1	0.0	44.2	2.9	2.3	28.5	10.6	0.0
	2005	(e)154 819	52.0	16.5	16.3	17.0	16.8	1.7	0.0	47.9	3.1	1.2	35.8	7.9	0.0
	2010	(e)231 170	36.3	8.2	8.2	12.8	14.1	1.1	0.1	63.6	5.4	1.2	48.7	8.3	0.0
Senegal - Sénégal	1995	609	34.8	33.6	33.3	0.5	0.7	0.0	0.0	56.6	25.8	0.4	29.9	0.5	0.0
	2005	1 443	28.2	26.2	25.9	1.1	0.8	0.1	0.0	60.1	43.1	0.3	16.1	0.5	0.2
	2010	1 949	24.0	23.4	14.9	0.2	0.2	0.2	0.0	67.9	51.2	0.1	12.4	4.0	0.0
Serbia - Serbie	2010	(e)8 754	58.2	56.4	55.6	1.7	0.0	0.1	28.9	4.1	0.8	0.1	1.5	1.6	0.0
Serbia and Montenegro - Serbie-et-Monténégro	1995	(e)66	59.3	59.0	58.7	0.0	0.2	0.1	0.3	40.5	31.5	2.0	0.0	6.9	0.0
	2005	(e)2 715	91.0	87.9	87.2	2.0	0.1	1.0	1.2	7.8	2.1	0.0	1.3	4.4	0.0
Seychelles	1995	25	92.4	86.4	86.3	0.2	5.6	0.3	0.0	6.4	3.3	0.0	3.1	0.1	0.0
	2005	(e)424	87.2	75.0	74.9	1.3	9.7	1.1	0.4	10.6	6.4	0.0	3.7	0.4	0.0
	2010	(e)342	72.8	59.6	58.7	1.3	10.6	1.4	0.3	20.9	8.0	1.2	11.6	0.1	0.0

For sources and notes, see end of table.

Pour les sources et les notes, se reporter à la fin du tableau.

Origin / Origine	Year / Année	World (millions of dollars) (1) / Monde (millions de dollars) (1)	Developed economies / Économies développées						Transition economies / Économies en transition	Developing economies / Économies en développement					
			Total	Europe Total	EU UE	USA États-Unis	Japan Japon	Other Autres		Total	Africa Afrique	America Amérique	Eastern, Southern and South-Eastern Asia / Asie orientale, méridionale et du Sud-Est	Western Asia / Asie occidentale	Oceania Océanie
Sierra Leone	1995	41	50.1	45.0	45.0	5.0	0.2	0.0	0.0	0.0	0.0	0.0	0.0	0.0	0.0
	2005	(e)196	88.9	82.9	82.9	4.6	0.1	1.3	1.0	7.1	3.6	0.1	3.4	0.0	0.0
	2010	(e)305	76.0	63.1	62.8	8.9	1.4	2.6	0.2	20.6	8.6	0.2	8.5	3.3	0.0
Singapore - Singapour (2)	1995	110 866	49.0	14.0	13.9	18.2	7.0	4.2	0.8	49.4	1.3	1.4	49.0	4.9	0.6
	2005	229 708	32.9	12.4	12.0	10.4	6.5	4.6	0.2	66.5	1.0	2.0	60.0	2.2	0.7
	2010	353 644	26.2	10.4	10.0	6.5	4.6	4.7	0.2	72.6	2.0	3.4	65.0	1.6	0.6
Slovakia - Slovaquie	1995	8 579	86.9	85.0	84.0	1.3	0.2	0.5	8.0	5.1	0.9	0.7	2.2	1.3	0.0
	2005	31 795	92.0	88.2	87.2	3.1	0.3	0.4	4.1	3.6	0.6	0.4	1.2	1.5	0.0
	2010	62 084	91.1	90.2	89.0	0.7	0.0	0.2	5.1	3.7	0.4	0.6	1.1	1.6	0.0
Slovenia - Slovénie	1995	8 389	77.9	73.8	72.8	3.1	0.2	0.7	18.7	3.2	0.7	0.4	1.2	0.8	0.0
	2005	19 215	72.3	69.7	68.3	1.9	0.1	0.5	20.4	4.7	1.1	0.4	1.4	1.8	0.0
	2010	29 127	74.3	72.4	71.3	1.3	0.1	0.5	19.0	6.2	1.5	0.5	2.1	2.0	0.0
Solomon Islands - Îles Salomon	1995	(e)203	59.4	10.0	10.0	2.3	44.9	2.2	0.0	35.3	0.3	0.0	33.5	0.0	1.5
	2005	(e)224	16.2	7.8	7.8	0.9	6.0	1.6	0.0	69.1	0.1	0.0	66.6	0.0	2.3
	2010	(e)436	11.1	7.2	7.2	0.3	2.0	1.7	0.0	75.0	0.1	0.0	72.6	0.0	2.3
Somalia - Somalie	1995	(e)172	13.0	13.0	12.9	0.0	0.0	0.0	0.1	86.9	1.3	0.0	3.3	82.3	0.0
	2005	(e)243	1.0	0.6	0.6	0.1	0.2	0.0	0.0	99.0	4.7	0.1	11.2	83.0	0.0
	2010	(e)516	0.4	0.3	0.3	0.0	0.0	0.0	0.0	99.6	4.5	0.1	3.3	91.6	0.0
South Africa - Afrique du Sud	1995	(e)24 515	54.7	34.6	33.5	8.0	8.8	3.3	0.3	29.7	11.1	2.5	15.0	1.1	0.0
	2005	46 991	65.8	38.8	36.0	10.4	11.0	5.6	0.3	33.0	15.3	1.6	13.7	2.4	0.0
	2010	71 484	51.7	29.7	26.1	9.9	9.0	3.1	0.6	47.1	17.2	2.2	25.0	2.7	0.0
Spain - Espagne	1995	91 624	83.3	76.1	74.0	4.2	1.4	1.6	0.6	15.5	3.9	5.5	4.2	1.9	0.0
	2005	192 142	80.4	74.3	71.4	4.1	0.7	1.3	1.1	15.2	4.2	4.9	3.2	2.9	0.0
	2010	241 284	76.6	71.1	68.2	3.3	0.7	1.6	1.5	18.6	5.6	5.1	4.2	3.7	0.0
Sri Lanka	1995	3 801	77.0	33.2	32.4	35.6	5.3	2.9	2.4	18.5	2.4	1.2	9.6	5.2	0.1
	2005	6 384	63.3	26.7	26.0	31.1	2.3	3.2	2.5	31.9	1.3	3.1	20.9	6.5	0.0
	2010	(e)8 323	58.1	32.2	31.0	20.0	2.4	3.5	4.4	31.7	1.4	2.3	19.3	8.7	0.1
Sudan - Soudan	1995	(e)535	45.2	34.7	33.1	4.0	6.5	0.0	0.3	54.3	3.0	0.0	24.6	25.9	0.9
	2005	4 824	16.3	2.7	2.7	0.3	12.0	1.3	0.0	83.4	3.0	0.3	73.8	6.3	0.0
	2010	(e)8 934	14.7	1.2	1.2	0.1	12.5	0.9	0.0	85.1	2.4	0.0	77.7	5.0	0.0
Suriname	1995	482	85.8	58.3	33.6	21.0	6.0	0.5	1.2	13.0	0.2	12.5	0.2	0.0	0.0
	2005	(e)951	80.8	47.3	21.6	16.4	1.1	16.0	0.0	19.2	1.8	8.5	1.6	7.3	0.0
	2010	(e)1 576	79.1	29.7	22.1	12.0	0.4	37.0	0.0	20.9	2.2	7.6	1.4	9.6	0.0
Swaziland	1995	(e)844	37.1	28.6	28.5	6.2	1.9	0.3	0.0	62.7	47.1	1.4	12.0	2.2	0.0
	2005	1 278	51.5	11.4	11.4	4.4	..	35.7	..	48.5	47.9	0.1	0.1	0.4	..
	2010	(e)1 260	54.9	23.6	23.0	18.7	0.3	12.3	0.4	44.8	32.0	5.3	7.3	0.2	0.0
Sweden - Suède	1995	79 638	83.7	69.7	59.9	7.9	2.9	3.2	1.1	12.1	1.6	1.9	7.0	1.7	0.0
	2005	130 915	83.4	68.6	58.7	10.5	1.5	2.7	2.5	13.5	2.3	2.1	6.8	2.3	0.0
	2010	150 041	81.2	71.1	60.1	6.4	1.2	2.5	2.1	16.1	2.9	2.4	7.8	2.9	0.0
Switzerland - Suisse	1995	81 406	80.4	64.9	64.3	8.7	4.0	2.9	0.8	18.7	1.8	2.5	10.8	3.6	0.0
	2005	130 890	80.7	63.3	62.9	10.9	3.6	2.9	1.6	17.6	1.4	2.3	10.2	3.7	0.0
	2010	195 323	75.6	59.0	58.7	10.1	3.3	3.1	2.1	22.3	1.7	2.9	13.5	4.2	0.0
Syrian Arab Republic - République arabe syrienne	1995	3 970	62.6	60.9	60.8	0.9	0.2	0.7	5.1	29.7	5.0	0.1	0.3	24.2	0.0
	2005	(e)9 793	37.7	34.1	34.0	3.3	0.2	0.2	1.5	60.8	4.8	0.6	0.7	54.6	0.0
	2010	(e)15 528	31.1	27.5	27.5	2.6	0.8	0.1	0.6	68.4	5.7	0.4	2.5	59.7	0.0
Tajikistan - Tadjikistan	1995	749	62.6	59.5	53.8	2.0	1.1	0.0	33.6	3.8	0.0	0.1	2.6	1.1	0.0
	2005	909	58.0	58.0	55.0	0.0	0.0	0.0	19.6	22.4	0.0	0.0	6.6	15.8	0.0
	2010	1 195	6.2	6.2	3.7	0.0	0.0	0.0	13.5	80.3	0.1	0.0	48.2	32.0	0.0
Thailand - Thaïlande	1995	60 201	52.2	16.9	16.0	16.7	15.7	2.8	0.1	39.2	1.6	0.9	33.1	3.5	0.1
	2005	110 160	48.1	14.3	13.6	15.4	13.6	4.8	0.4	51.2	2.6	1.8	43.3	3.4	0.2
	2010	195 364	40.4	13.3	11.1	10.4	10.5	6.3	0.5	58.6	3.5	2.9	47.7	4.3	0.2
TFYR of Macedonia - LERY de Macédoine	1995	1 203	71.2	68.0	65.1	3.0	0.1	0.1	14.8	6.9	1.0	0.0	2.4	3.5	..
	2005	2 041	60.2	57.4	57.0	2.2	0.4	0.2	31.6	4.1	0.2	0.2	1.3	2.4	0.0
	2010	3 302	62.6	62.0	61.3	0.4	0.0	0.2	19.2	4.9	0.1	0.1	2.9	1.9	0.0
Timor-Leste	2005	(e)8	3.9	0.3	0.3	3.5	0.0	0.0	0.1	96.0	0.0	0.0	96.0	0.0	..
	2010	(e)17	76.2	76.2	76.2	0.0	0.0	0.0	0.6	23.2	3.6	0.2	19.3	0.0	..

For sources and notes, see end of table. — Pour les sources et les notes, se reporter à la fin du tableau.

Destination / Origin / Origine	Year / Année	World (millions of dollars) (1) / Monde (millions de dollars) (1)	Developed economies / Économies développées Total	Europe Total	Europe EU UE	USA États-Unis	Japan Japon	Other Autres	Transition economies / Économies en transition	Developing economies / Économies en développement Total	Africa Afrique	America Amérique	Eastern, Southern and South-Eastern Asia / Asie orientale, méridionale et du Sud-Est	Western Asia / Asie occidentale	Oceania Océanie
Togo	1995	000	11.0	07.0	06.1	0.1	1.0	13.8	0.0	66.5	17.7	5.6	32.9	0.3	0.0
	2005	364	12.4	9.5	9.3	1.1	0.0	1.8	0.5	85.4	71.9	1.9	11.5	0.1	0.0
	2010	(e)1 025	27.3	26.2	26.1	0.9	0.0	0.3	0.9	71.2	48.6	0.6	21.0	1.0	0.0
Tokelau - Tokélaou	2005	(e)0	50.6	11.7	11.7	37.9	1.0	0.0	0.0	49.3	8.1	3.1	38.0	0.1	0.0
Tonga	1995	10	07.1	0.0	0.0	26.8	17.0	12.1	0.0	1.6	..	..	..	..	1.6
	2005	(e)19	87.1	3.0	3.0	33.3	41.7	9.1	0.0	12.3	0.0	0.3	3.0	0.1	8.8
	2010	(e)13	37.8	4.2	4.2	17.0	5.8	10.9	0.0	60.4	0.0	0.7	34.3	0.4	24.9
Trinidad and Tobago - Trinité-et-Tobago	1995	3 056	49.7	14.8	14.7	33.2	0.0	1.7	0.0	32.3	0.5	31.3	0.6	0.0	0.0
	2005	(e)11 427	73.3	5.1	5.0	66.4	0.0	1.8	0.0	26.0	0.1	25.5	0.3	0.0	0.0
	2010	(e)14 467	61.7	14.0	14.0	44.1	0.4	3.1	0.0	37.1	0.2	32.9	4.0	0.0	0.0
Tunisia - Tunisie	1995	5 785	82.9	81.4	80.4	1.2	0.3	0.1	0.0	14.1	8.1	0.8	3.4	1.8	0.0
	2005	10 094	85.0	83.7	83.2	0.9	0.2	0.1	0.2	14.8	9.4	0.7	2.6	2.2	0.0
	2010	(e)15 489	77.0	73.4	72.9	2.5	0.7	0.5	0.7	22.2	14.3	1.1	4.0	2.9	0.0
Turkey - Turquie	1995	21 650	68.3	58.7	57.3	7.0	0.8	1.8	10.3	21.3	4.9	2.7	6.2	7.5	0.0
	2005	73 592	67.3	57.4	56.2	6.7	0.3	2.9	8.1	19.1	4.9	0.9	3.8	9.5	0.0
	2010	113 966	54.7	48.5	46.2	3.4	0.2	2.6	10.9	31.3	8.1	1.5	7.8	13.9	0.0
Turkmenistan - Turkménistan	1995	1 881	35.6	33.8	27.3	1.7	0.0	0.1	49.4	14.9	0.0	0.1	5.9	8.8	0.0
	2005	(e)4 997	24.5	20.5	20.5	2.7	0.0	1.4	61.7	12.0	0.0	0.1	6.0	5.8	0.0
	2010	(e)3 342	18.3	13.2	13.2	1.4	0.0	3.7	15.3	61.4	0.7	0.1	42.8	17.7	0.0
Turks and Caicos Islands - Îles Turques et Caïques	2005	15	99.7	..	..	99.1	..	0.7	..	0.3	..	0.3	..	..	..
Tuvalu	1995	(e)0	24.4	22.7	22.7	0.0	0.3	1.4	0.0	75.6	53.0	3.8	18.1	0.0	0.6
	2005	(e)0	89.3	85.6	85.5	0.0	0.6	3.1	1.9	8.8	1.5	0.0	0.1	0.0	7.2
	2010	(e)0	53.2	4.4	3.5	0.0	35.5	13.3	3.4	43.4	2.3	0.0	30.2	0.0	10.9
Uganda - Ouganda	1995	(e)529	94.0	87.9	86.0	2.3	1.8	2.0	0.0	5.9	2.4	0.1	2.7	0.7	0.0
	2005	812	45.0	41.2	31.9	2.0	0.6	1.1	0.2	52.5	35.5	0.1	6.4	10.5	0.0
	2010	(e)1 780	30.4	26.5	26.2	3.1	0.3	0.5	1.5	65.1	51.3	0.1	5.0	8.7	0.0
Ukraine	1995	(e)15 104	25.2	21.2	21.0	2.8	0.7	0.4	49.4	16.5	1.6	0.6	8.9	5.4	0.0
	2005	33 968	35.7	31.4	30.1	2.8	0.2	1.2	32.1	31.5	7.0	1.5	11.4	11.5	0.0
	2010	(e)51 655	29.3	26.4	25.5	1.7	0.3	0.9	37.7	31.7	6.1	1.6	11.6	12.5	0.0
United Arab Emirates - Emirats arabes unis	1995	(e)24 089	46.2	4.0	4.0	1.8	38.4	1.9	0.7	38.4	1.6	0.1	28.8	7.9	0.0
	2005	(e)96 331	37.2	11.3	10.8	1.5	23.8	0.7	0.6	48.0	3.2	0.1	37.6	7.1	0.0
	2010	(e)169 489	21.9	3.9	3.5	0.6	15.7	1.6	0.5	62.9	3.3	0.2	51.3	8.1	0.0
United Kingdom - Royaume-Uni	1995	239 435	77.5	59.2	55.9	12.2	2.5	3.6	0.9	17.7	3.1	1.8	9.0	3.8	0.0
	2005	370 301	78.4	57.8	54.0	15.1	1.9	3.7	1.4	18.0	2.8	1.5	8.4	5.3	0.0
	2010	373 539	76.5	60.4	56.9	11.4	1.4	3.2	1.6	18.3	3.4	1.9	8.9	4.1	0.0
United Republic of Tanzania - République-Unie de Tanzanie	1995	(e)697	47.2	34.6	34.0	3.2	8.4	1.0	0.2	49.2	15.4	0.0	28.9	4.9	0.0
	2005	(e)1 495	43.5	27.3	24.6	2.2	4.6	9.5	1.4	48.2	19.1	0.1	24.3	4.7	0.0
	2010	(e)2 389	29.1	20.9	17.8	1.7	5.9	0.5	1.8	60.7	20.7	0.1	33.6	6.2	0.0
United States - États-Unis	1995	583 670	58.8	23.1	21.7	..	11.0	24.7	0.7	40.3	1.7	16.3	19.8	2.4	0.0
	2005	904 431	54.9	22.2	20.7	..	6.1	26.5	0.7	44.3	1.7	21.1	18.5	2.9	0.0
	2010	1 277 630	47.9	20.9	18.8	..	4.7	22.3	0.8	51.2	2.2	23.4	21.8	3.7	0.0
Uruguay	1995	2 121	32.1	22.0	21.3	6.0	0.9	3.2	0.3	66.8	0.9	53.3	11.6	1.1	0.0
	2005	3 403	46.1	18.6	17.2	23.2	0.9	3.4	1.3	49.5	3.8	34.7	9.9	1.0	0.1
	2010	(e)7 936	26.3	21.1	19.7	2.8	0.9	1.5	4.0	67.1	3.1	43.9	17.3	2.8	0.1
Uzbekistan - Ouzbékistan	1995	(e)2 718	35.6	31.2	31.0	0.5	3.7	0.2	55.4	9.0	0.0	4.1	4.3	0.5	0.0
	2005	(e)3 496	24.6	17.4	17.3	2.5	3.2	1.4	46.1	29.4	0.1	0.0	22.4	6.8	0.0
	2010	(e)5 819	14.1	10.2	9.7	1.1	2.7	0.1	40.2	45.7	0.3	0.0	31.9	13.5	0.0
Vanuatu	1995	(e)29	76.6	37.9	37.9	0.0	25.1	13.6	0.4	22.5	7.3	0.1	7.0	0.0	8.1
	2005	(e)227	25.1	13.6	13.6	1.1	7.1	3.3	0.0	74.6	0.3	0.1	63.7	7.9	2.7
	2010	(e)210	31.1	3.4	3.4	0.8	24.9	1.9	0.0	68.4	0.6	0.0	62.2	0.0	5.6
Venezuela (Bolivarian Rep. of) - Venezuela (Rép. bolivarienne du)	1995	19 093	62.6	9.2	9.1	50.5	1.5	1.3	0.2	30.2	0.2	29.6	0.4	0.0	0.0
	2005	55 717	58.3	7.7	7.4	48.4	0.4	1.8	0.1	28.3	0.3	26.5	1.4	0.1	0.0
	2010	65 782	45.7	4.8	4.8	40.2	0.0	0.7	0.0	35.0	0.1	13.6	21.2	0.1	0.0
Viet Nam	1995	5 621	44.4	14.0	12.7	3.0	26.0	1.4	1.6	45.5	0.7	0.9	43.1	0.9	0.0
	2005	32 447	58.8	17.4	17.0	18.3	13.4	9.7	0.9	38.3	1.2	1.7	34.5	1.0	0.0
	2010	(e)70 727	56.6	19.7	15.8	20.4	10.5	6.0	1.8	36.6	1.6	1.7	31.3	2.0	0.0
Wallis and Futuna Islands - Îles Wallis-et-Futuna	2005	(e)0	80.5	80.3	80.3	0.0	..	0.2	0.1	19.4	0.0	0.0	18.4	0.0	1.1

For sources and notes, see end of table.

Pour les sources et les notes, se reporter à la fin du tableau.

Destination / Origin / Origine	Year / Année	World (millions of dollars) (1) / Monde (millions de dollars) (1)	Developed economies / Économies développées Total	Europe Total	Europe EU UE	USA États-Unis	Japan Japon	Other Autres	Transition economies / Économies en transition	Developing economies / Économies en développement Total	Africa Afrique	America Amérique	Eastern, Southern and South-Eastern Asia / Asie orientale, méridionale et du Sud-Est	Western Asia / Asie occidentale	Oceania Océanie
									Percentage / En pourcentage						
Yemen - Yémen	1995	1 945	13.7	1.1	1.1	0.2	12.3	0.1	0.0	85.6	10.4	8.6	61.7	4.8	0.0
	2005	5 611	17.8	6.4	0.9	3.3	6.3	1.8	0.0	81.6	1.7	0.0	71.0	9.0	0.0
	2010	(e)8 049	11.2	4.0	4.0	2.3	4.9	0.0	0.0	88.0	7.5	0.4	69.7	10.3	0.0
Zambia - Zambie	1995	986	42.4	16.8	16.5	9.4	16.0	0.1	0.0	56.8	12.0	0.0	35.8	8.0	0.0
	2005	1 840	55.4	52.8	24.1	0.8	1.6	0.2	0.0	44.6	40.6	0.0	3.9	0.0	0.0
	2010	7 155	55.9	55.7	4.4	0.1	0.1	0.0	0.1	44.0	19.8	0.0	21.2	3.0	0.0
Zimbabwe	1995	1 901	57.1	43.5	42.0	4.7	7.9	1.0	0.4	41.8	32.5	1.0	7.9	0.4	0.0
	2005	1 393	31.2	23.5	16.9	6.9	0.4	0.3	1.2	67.5	58.8	0.0	7.5	1.2	0.0
	2010	(e)1 747	27.8	21.0	20.5	3.1	2.8	0.9	1.1	70.9	48.1	0.6	19.7	2.5	0.0

Sources:
- UNCTAD secretariat calculations
- UN DESA Statistics Division, *COMTRADE* database
- IMF, *Direction of Trade Statistics*

Notes:

(1) Include unspecified destinations.
(2) Exports data include a considerable amount of re-exports.
(3) Estimates. France including French Guiana, Guadeloupe, Martinique, Monaco and Reunion (and excluding intra trade)

Sources :
- Estimations du secrétariat de la CNUCED
- ONU DAES Division de statistique, base de données *COMTRADE*
- FMI, *Direction of Trade Statistics*

Notes :

(1) Y compris des destinations non-spécifiées.
(2) Les données des exportations comprennent une part importante de réexportations.
(3) Estimation. Les données sont dérivées des déclarations rapportées par la France métropolitaine et les départements d'outre-mer par agrégation diminuée des flux intra.

Origin / Origine — Destination	Year / Année	World (millions of dollars) (1) / Monde (millions de dollars) (1)	Developed economies / Économies développées						Transition economies / Économies en transition	Developing economies / Économies en développement					
			Total	Europe Total	EU / UE	USA / États-Unis	Japan / Japon	Other / Autres		Total	Africa / Afrique	America / Amérique	Eastern, Southern and South-Eastern Asia / Asie orientale, méridionale et du Sud-Est	Western Asia / Asie occidentale	Oceania / Océanie
										Percentage / En pourcentage					
Afghanistan	1995	(e)387	46.2	19.4	19.3	1.1	23.8	2.0	9.1	44.7	0.0	0.1	42.3	2.3	0.0
	2005	(e)2 992	28.1	15.0	14.8	9.6	2.8	0.7	13.6	58.3	2.0	0.1	51.6	4.6	0.0
	2010	(e)8 162	43.9	12.1	12.0	29.0	1.3	1.5	15.6	40.5	1.2	0.2	35.4	3.7	0.0
Albania - Albanie	1995	651	90.4	89.9	89.2	0.3	0.0	0.2	3.7	5.5	0.3	0.5	0.4	4.3	0.0
	2005	2 606	71.0	68.7	67.7	1.4	0.4	0.5	11.1	17.9	0.6	1.5	8.0	7.7	0.0
	2010	1 010	72.6	70.1	69.4	1.1	0.5	1.2	6.9	17.0	0.0	1.0	9.1	6.2	0.0
Algeria - Algérie	1995	10 782	83.9	62.2	61.0	13.2	3.4	5.2	1.1	15.0	2.8	3.4	5.2	3.5	0.0
	2005	19 848	68.6	55.9	54.6	6.8	3.9	2.0	5.0	26.3	2.6	6.8	12.5	4.4	0.0
	2010	(e)43 289	58.3	51.6	50.4	3.0	2.4	1.2	9.2	32.5	3.5	5.1	18.3	5.5	0.0
American Samoa - Samoa américaines	1995	(e)416	78.8	0.6	0.4	0.0	25.5	52.8	0.0	21.1	0.0	0.0	6.6	0.0	14.6
	2005	(e)506	79.3	5.1	5.1	0.0	1.7	72.5	0.0	20.7	0.3	0.1	7.3	0.0	13.1
	2010	(e)550	24.8	2.7	2.5	0.0	1.3	20.9	0.0	75.2	0.8	10.6	17.8	0.0	46.0
Andorra - Andorre	1995	1 043	95.6	88.2	86.5	4.0	3.4	0.1	0.1	4.3	0.2	0.2	3.7	0.1	..
	2005	1 802	..	..	..	..	..	..	..	..	..	..	..	..	..
	2010	1 514	61.4	60.2	59.1	1.1	0.1	0.0	..	38.6	35.5	0.1	2.3	0.7	..
Angola	1995	(e)1 891	79.3	62.1	61.0	15.1	1.5	0.5	0.0	20.7	10.2	2.7	7.6	0.1	0.0
	2005	(e)8 221	50.7	35.7	33.4	12.4	1.6	1.0	0.5	48.6	8.5	9.0	30.7	0.5	0.0
	2010	(e)15 373	56.7	45.0	41.5	9.2	0.9	1.5	0.1	43.0	8.0	8.1	25.9	1.0	0.0
Anguilla	1995	53	6.5	1.8	1.8	4.4	0.1	0.2	..	93.5	0.0	93.3	0.2	..	..
	2005	130	60.0	24.3	24.2	32.7	1.7	1.4	0.9	39.1	0.0	38.2	0.4	0.4	0.0
	2010	157	87.9	16.7	16.5	67.6	1.5	2.1	3.6	8.5	0.0	6.1	0.3	2.2	..
Antigua and Barbuda - Antigua-et-Barbuda	1995	(e)346	78.4	40.8	40.0	35.6	0.0	2.1	0.0	21.6	1.6	16.3	3.6	0.0	0.0
	2005	(e)550	54.2	31.6	30.9	20.9	0.0	1.8	0.0	45.8	0.8	12.8	29.6	2.6	0.0
	2010	(e)520	19.2	8.9	8.6	8.6	0.5	1.2	0.0	80.8	0.1	11.9	68.7	0.2	0.0
Argentina - Argentine	1995	19 221	55.6	30.6	29.5	19.1	3.5	2.4	0.5	39.4	0.8	30.9	7.5	0.1	0.0
	2005	28 695	36.1	17.9	17.0	14.1	2.7	1.4	0.9	59.7	0.6	45.0	14.0	0.2	0.0
	2010	56 502	32.8	18.3	17.3	10.8	2.1	1.5	0.9	62.1	0.5	40.8	20.1	0.6	0.0
Armenia - Arménie	1995	696	34.7	18.3	17.2	16.4	0.0	0.0	48.0	16.2	0.4	0.0	13.0	2.8	0.0
	2005	1 802	50.8	36.4	33.8	6.2	1.3	6.9	29.0	20.0	0.2	2.3	12.4	5.1	0.0
	2010	3 749	36.0	29.3	27.4	3.0	2.2	1.5	32.2	31.8	0.7	2.2	21.8	7.0	0.0
Aruba	1995	543	82.0	19.3	18.6	58.6	2.7	1.3	0.0	17.5	0.0	16.1	1.4	0.1	0.0
	2005	1 030	79.8	21.3	20.4	55.9	2.0	0.6	0.0	20.1	0.0	16.9	3.2	0.0	0.0
	2010	1 003	75.9	22.9	21.5	50.8	1.5	0.7	0.0	24.0	0.7	18.9	4.4	0.1	0.0
Australia - Australie	1995	63 234	71.4	27.1	25.6	21.9	15.4	7.0	0.1	28.3	0.6	1.2	22.3	2.3	1.9
	2005	130 974	54.3	24.3	23.2	13.9	11.0	5.0	0.1	45.1	1.2	1.3	39.3	1.8	1.5
	2010	214 164	43.5	19.4	18.1	11.0	8.6	4.5	0.3	51.6	1.6	1.8	44.7	1.9	1.6
Austria - Autriche	1995	66 265	90.4	83.0	78.9	4.2	2.5	0.6	2.3	7.4	1.5	0.8	4.2	0.9	0.0
	2005	127 151	88.8	85.1	80.5	2.2	1.0	0.5	4.0	7.0	0.9	0.5	4.2	1.5	0.0
	2010	157 439	87.2	84.5	78.2	1.6	0.7	0.4	4.2	8.6	1.4	0.3	5.4	1.5	0.0
Azerbaijan - Azerbaïdjan	1995	668	20.9	18.2	17.7	2.0	0.2	0.5	34.1	44.9	0.2	0.0	13.3	31.4	0.0
	2005	4 211	37.1	31.2	29.9	3.4	1.7	0.8	34.4	28.4	1.3	0.4	18.5	8.3	0.0
	2010	6 599	33.8	26.9	25.3	3.1	2.2	1.5	31.9	34.3	0.3	3.6	17.7	12.6	0.0
Bahamas	1995	(e)2 192	73.3	34.1	32.3	33.2	5.1	1.0	10.5	14.8	0.4	9.4	4.7	0.4	0.0
	2005	(e)9 242	46.1	21.7	18.1	21.1	2.6	0.7	3.2	49.1	0.1	23.0	25.0	1.0	0.0
	2010	(e)13 640	47.2	12.6	11.8	26.0	7.3	1.3	2.4	48.4	1.7	12.7	33.2	0.7	0.0
Bahrain - Bahreïn	1995	3 716	38.7	21.0	19.6	8.1	4.0	5.6	0.2	59.1	0.6	2.1	10.7	45.6	0.0
	2005	6 109	44.9	28.7	26.6	6.3	7.7	2.2	0.3	54.1	1.3	2.7	16.1	34.0	0.0
	2010	(e)11 588	40.2	20.1	17.5	11.9	5.6	2.6	0.1	59.2	1.1	5.9	21.5	30.7	0.0
Bangladesh	1995	6 496	31.5	13.9	12.4	6.1	9.2	2.4	1.1	58.2	0.5	2.1	52.0	3.4	0.2
	2005	13 851	19.4	10.4	8.8	2.4	4.1	2.5	3.0	68.5	0.5	1.5	52.7	13.8	0.0
	2010	27 771	18.6	7.8	6.9	1.9	4.2	4.6	4.0	70.7	1.2	2.6	58.4	8.5	0.0
Barbados - Barbade	1995	765	73.0	18.7	17.4	40.9	6.8	6.7	0.0	26.9	0.1	22.9	3.8	0.1	0.0
	2005	1 600	61.7	14.5	12.6	37.2	5.2	4.8	0.0	38.3	0.1	32.1	6.0	0.1	0.0
	2010	(e)2 157	34.0	8.7	8.1	20.3	1.8	3.3	19.3	46.6	0.3	40.6	5.5	0.3	0.0
Belarus - Bélarus	1995	5 505	27.8	24.8	24.4	1.8	0.4	0.7	69.5	2.7	0.3	0.7	1.5	0.2	0.0
	2005	16 708	25.0	22.9	21.6	1.4	0.3	0.4	66.8	5.1	0.2	1.2	3.2	0.5	0.0
	2010	34 868	24.7	22.6	21.6	1.3	0.5	0.4	59.1	12.7	0.4	4.7	6.8	0.9	0.0

For sources and notes, see end of table.

Pour les sources et les notes, se reporter à la fin du tableau.

2.1 Country trade structure by partner
Imports by main region of origin

2.1 Structure du commerce des pays par partenaires
Importations par principales régions d'origine

Origin / Origine — Destination	Year / Année	World (millions of dollars) (1) / Monde (millions de dollars) (1)	Developed economies / Économies développées — Total	Europe — Total	Europe — EU / UE	USA / États-Unis	Japan / Japon	Other / Autres	Transition economies / Économies en transition	Developing economies / Économies en développement — Total	Africa / Afrique	America / Amérique	Eastern, Southern and South-Eastern Asia / Asie orientale, méridionale et du Sud-Est	Western Asia / Asie occidentale	Oceania / Océanie
										Percentage / En pourcentage					
Belgium - Belgique	1995	(e)160 219	90.2	81.1	79.0	5.2	2.4	1.6	1.0	8.8	0.3	1.4	0.7	0.4	0.0
	2005	319 103	84.3	74.4	72.0	5.3	2.7	1.9	1.8	13.5	2.7	1.9	7.3	1.6	0.0
	2010	387 775	81.8	72.7	70.5	5.3	2.2	1.6	2.3	15.9	2.4	2.5	8.7	2.3	0.0
Belize	1995	£50	00.7	11.0	10.7	54.1	1.5	3.3	0.0	30.3	0.0	27.8	2.4	0.0	0.0
	2005	(e)768	50.8	17.3	17.0	31.0	1.5	1.0	8.9	40.3	0.5	32.5	7.3	0.1	0.0
	2010	(e)895	47.6	10.0	8.7	35.6	1.0	0.9	3.1	49.3	0.1	40.5	8.4	0.3	0.0
Benin - Bénin	1995	638	61.3	51.5	50.8	5.6	3.7	0.4	0.0	38.1	18.5	0.7	17.3	1.5	0.1
	2005	893	50.4	46.3	43.1	2.0	1.5	0.5	0.1	49.5	30.3	1.1	15.6	2.5	0.0
	2010	(e)7 107	33.0	25.1	24.6	7.2	0.4	0.2	0.6	66.4	8.9	1.7	53.6	2.3	0.0
Bermuda - Bermudes	1995	693	91.4	11.4	10.9	71.6	3.7	4.5	0.0	8.5	0.1	6.7	1.6	0.0	0.0
	2005	973	92.3	7.9	7.5	78.3	1.7	4.3	0.0	7.5	0.2	6.3	0.9	0.0	0.0
	2010	(e)5 066	50.7	35.7	34.4	13.8	0.2	1.0	6.6	42.6	0.1	0.5	42.1	0.0	0.0
Bhutan - Bhoutan	1995	(e)112	36.6	34.3	32.1	1.8	..	0.5	0.1	63.3	0.1	0.1	61.3	1.8	..
	2005	(e)386	25.6	14.0	12.1	2.1	9.3	0.1	0.0	74.4	0.0	0.0	74.3	0.0	0.0
	2010	(e)855	22.6	8.2	6.5	1.5	8.3	4.8	0.0	77.4	0.2	0.0	77.2	0.0	0.0
Bolivia (Plurinational State of) - Bolivie (État plurinational de)	1995	1 449	56.1	20.0	19.3	21.7	12.4	2.0	0.3	43.5	0.2	38.9	4.4	0.0	0.0
	2005	2 343	30.7	9.9	9.5	13.8	6.1	0.9	0.2	68.9	0.2	60.4	8.3	0.0	0.0
	2010	(e)5 600	21.1	7.9	7.6	10.0	2.1	1.1	0.1	78.7	0.0	73.4	5.1	0.1	0.0
Bosnia and Herzegovina - Bosnie-Herzégovine	1995	(e)950	43.6	40.3	40.0	3.3	0.0	0.1	54.8	1.6	0.8	0.0	0.2	0.6	..
	2005	(e)5 755	69.4	68.9	68.2	0.3	0.1	0.1	27.1	3.5	0.0	0.4	0.6	2.5	..
	2010	(e)6 926	66.5	65.8	64.9	0.4	0.0	0.2	28.6	5.0	0.0	0.3	1.1	3.6	..
Botswana	1995	(e)1 902	13.0	9.5	8.8	2.5	0.1	0.9	0.0	87.5	77.6	0.0	9.9	0.0	0.0
	2005	3 162	9.9	7.0	6.8	1.3	0.7	1.0	0.0	90.1	86.7	0.1	3.1	0.2	..
	2010	5 657	17.5	13.3	13.3	1.3	0.7	2.1	0.1	82.4	75.3	0.0	6.8	0.2	0.0
Brazil - Brésil	1995	54 363	61.4	30.5	28.6	21.2	6.6	3.1	1.2	36.9	2.4	20.7	10.4	3.5	0.0
	2005	80 929	50.8	25.8	23.8	17.5	4.6	2.9	1.5	47.5	9.1	16.2	19.3	2.9	0.0
	2010	199 754	45.2	23.6	21.5	15.0	3.8	2.8	1.7	52.6	6.2	17.0	27.1	2.3	0.0
Brunei Darussalam - Brunéi Darussalam	1995	2 960	39.1	17.2	16.4	8.8	8.8	4.2	0.0	59.8	0.0	0.0	59.6	0.3	0.0
	2005	(e)1 670	22.0	10.0	9.8	3.3	6.9	1.8	0.0	77.8	0.4	0.1	76.9	0.5	0.0
	2010	(e)3 104	21.4	10.1	9.6	4.4	5.3	1.6	0.0	78.4	0.1	0.1	77.8	0.4	0.0
Bulgaria - Bulgarie	1995	5 469	49.0	44.9	43.0	2.2	0.8	1.1	37.4	13.4	2.2	3.5	5.7	2.1	0.0
	2005	18 213	59.1	54.4	53.3	2.6	1.2	1.0	22.2	17.5	0.4	4.0	6.8	6.3	0.0
	2010	25 093	61.8	60.2	59.3	0.7	0.3	0.7	23.9	13.7	0.8	2.9	4.4	5.6	0.0
Burkina Faso	1995	481	58.4	46.0	45.3	4.7	7.1	0.7	0.0	38.3	27.8	2.3	8.0	0.2	0.0
	2005	1 102	39.8	29.7	29.5	4.6	3.7	1.7	3.2	51.8	31.2	1.7	15.9	3.0	0.0
	2010	(e)2 058	35.0	29.8	29.7	2.5	0.8	1.9	1.4	57.6	45.8	1.1	10.1	0.6	0.0
Burundi	1995	233	62.2	51.2	50.6	4.9	5.7	0.3	0.0	23.9	15.0	0.0	8.9	0.0	0.0
	2005	265	45.7	35.6	34.8	2.3	6.9	0.9	0.2	44.9	32.1	0.0	9.1	3.7	0.0
	2010	(e)490	28.6	22.3	22.0	3.2	2.8	0.3	0.0	61.7	31.9	0.0	13.1	16.7	0.0
Cambodia - Cambodge	1995	(e)1 573	15.7	7.1	7.0	1.9	5.4	1.3	0.0	84.3	0.1	0.0	84.2	0.0	0.0
	2005	2 548	15.4	9.3	8.9	1.4	3.9	0.8	0.2	84.3	0.1	0.2	83.9	0.1	0.0
	2010	4 892	12.8	6.5	3.0	2.7	3.2	0.5	0.2	86.9	0.1	0.2	86.5	0.2	0.0
Cameroon - Cameroun	1995	1 199	62.1	54.3	53.4	1.9	4.9	1.1	0.0	28.8	20.8	1.6	6.0	0.5	0.0
	2005	(e)2 520	55.7	48.5	47.9	5.1	0.8	1.3	0.8	43.0	18.8	4.8	17.9	1.5	0.0
	2010	(e)4 482	45.3	39.9	39.1	3.2	0.8	1.2	1.2	53.0	22.8	3.7	24.6	1.9	0.0
Canada	1995	179 628	84.7	11.7	10.3	66.7	5.4	0.8	0.3	13.3	0.8	4.1	8.1	0.3	0.0
	2005	346 014	75.4	14.2	12.1	56.5	3.9	0.8	0.6	23.1	1.8	7.0	13.2	1.0	0.0
	2010	430 295	67.8	13.3	11.9	50.4	3.3	0.8	1.2	30.1	2.5	9.5	16.9	1.2	0.0
Cape Verde - Cap-Vert	1995	(e)260	85.0	81.9	81.5	3.0	0.0	0.1	0.0	11.3	3.4	5.9	2.0	0.0	0.0
	2005	432	75.4	68.7	68.3	3.1	3.2	0.5	0.1	24.5	3.8	9.7	4.0	6.9	0.0
	2010	742	83.3	78.6	78.2	1.8	2.3	0.6	0.0	15.7	1.9	6.3	6.9	0.7	0.0
Cayman Islands - Îles Caïmanes	2005	1 191	82.6	48.5	43.5	31.2	0.8	2.1	0.0	17.4	0.0	12.8	4.6	0.0	..
	2010	991	77.2	30.0	28.3	22.6	23.8	0.9	3.6	19.2	0.0	16.3	1.4	1.5	..
Central African Republic - République centrafricaine	1995	189	76.3	49.4	49.2	2.5	24.3	0.2	0.0	13.0	11.2	0.3	1.2	0.3	0.0
	2005	(e)222	44.6	36.5	36.2	7.3	0.6	0.2	0.0	26.2	16.5	1.2	7.1	1.4	0.0
	2010	(e)583	42.1	39.7	39.5	2.0	0.4	0.1	0.3	36.2	12.8	2.4	20.0	1.0	0.0

For sources and notes, see end of table.

Pour les sources et les notes, se reporter à la fin du tableau.

2.1 Country trade structure by partner
Imports by main region of origin

2.1 Structure du commerce des pays par partenaires
Importations par principales régions d'origine

Origin / Origine / Destination	Year Année	World (millions of dollars) (1) Monde (millions de dollars) (1)	Developed economies Économies développées Total	Europe Total	EU UE	USA États-Unis	Japan Japon	Other Autres	Transition economies Économies en transition	Developing economies Économies en développement Total	Africa Afrique	America Amérique	Eastern, Southern and South-Eastern Asia Asie orientale, méridionale et du Sud-Est	Western Asia Asie occidentale	Oceania Océanie
Chad - Tchad	1995	(e)186	71.8	51.1	50.8	7.1	8.9	9.9	9.9	26.1	15.5	0.1	0.0	0.0	0.0
	2005	(e)479	65.8	51.7	51.2	12.3	0.1	1.6	1.3	32.9	23.1	0.2	4.9	4.6	0.0
	2010	(e)1 187	41.6	32.4	32.2	8.2	0.3	0.8	1.2	57.2	21.2	0.4	32.0	3.6	0.0
Chile - Chili	1995	15 479	56.3	21.7	20.7	24.5	6.5	3.5	0.3	39.0	2.0	26.8	10.1	0.1	0.0
	2005	32 121	36.1	16.1	15.7	14.6	3.2	2.1	0.5	60.7	4.9	33.9	15.9	4.5	0.0
	2010	56 222	39.9	14.2	13.7	17.6	6.0	2.1	0.1	59.3	1.3	29.9	27.6	0.5	0.0
China - Chine	1995	132 164	55.9	17.4	16.5	12.2	21.9	4.3	3.7	38.7	1.1	2.2	33.9	1.4	0.1
	2005	660 224	38.6	12.0	11.2	7.4	15.2	4.0	3.2	49.9	3.2	4.0	39.0	3.6	0.1
	2010	1 393 920	38.7	12.9	12.1	7.3	12.6	5.8	3.0	49.2	4.6	6.5	33.2	4.9	0.1
China, Hong Kong SAR - Chine (RAS de Hong Kong) (2)	1995	192 765	36.8	12.0	10.8	7.7	14.8	2.2	0.3	63.0	0.4	0.6	61.3	0.6	0.0
	2005	300 017	26.6	8.9	7.6	5.1	11.0	1.6	0.2	73.2	0.4	0.7	71.3	0.7	0.0
	2010	433 516	24.9	9.0	7.3	5.4	9.2	1.4	0.2	74.8	0.3	1.0	72.7	0.8	0.0
China, Macao SAR - Chine (RAS de Macao)	1995	2 049	34.6	15.0	14.6	7.3	10.4	1.9	0.3	64.4	0.4	0.1	63.2	0.6	0.0
	2005	3 913	30.4	14.0	13.2	4.1	10.9	1.5	0.2	69.4	0.5	0.4	68.0	0.4	0.0
	2010	5 554	46.6	30.7	22.5	5.9	8.6	1.4	0.1	53.4	0.6	1.0	51.2	0.6	0.0
China, Taiwan Province of - Province chinoise de Taiwan	1995	(e)103 647	70.1	16.3	14.8	20.1	29.2	4.6	1.8	27.6	1.8	2.3	20.3	3.3	0.0
	2005	(e)182 628	51.5	10.7	9.7	11.6	25.2	4.0	1.3	45.7	2.0	1.9	32.9	8.8	0.1
	2010	(e)251 252	44.9	9.3	8.5	10.2	20.7	4.7	1.0	50.9	2.6	2.7	35.2	10.4	0.1
Colombia - Colombie	1995	13 860	70.8	20.9	18.8	39.1	7.5	3.3	0.1	28.6	0.1	25.1	3.3	0.0	0.0
	2005	21 205	49.1	14.9	13.8	28.5	3.3	2.4	1.0	46.3	0.4	31.1	14.6	0.1	0.0
	2010	(e)42 272	49.6	13.0	12.2	31.3	3.2	2.1	0.6	46.5	0.2	27.8	18.3	0.2	0.0
Comoros - Comores	1995	(e)151	72.8	70.5	70.2	0.4	1.8	0.0	0.0	27.2	21.0	0.0	5.8	0.3	0.0
	2005	(e)116	41.2	39.8	39.7	0.3	0.3	0.7	0.3	56.9	23.1	1.8	19.2	12.7	0.0
	2010	(e)212	31.6	30.1	30.0	0.6	0.7	0.2	0.0	66.8	15.8	1.0	37.1	12.8	0.0
Congo	1995	463	71.5	58.5	57.7	9.7	3.2	0.0	0.0	10.5	7.2	0.3	3.0	0.0	0.0
	2005	(e)1 628	55.0	46.7	46.2	7.0	0.4	0.9	0.2	42.3	12.1	5.4	23.4	1.4	0.0
	2010	(e)3 210	57.8	46.8	45.2	8.7	0.4	1.8	0.4	39.9	8.3	2.8	26.8	2.0	0.0
Cook Islands - Îles Cook	1995	49	89.8	23.6	23.6	1.9	2.0	62.3	0.1	10.2	..	0.5	9.7	..	..
	2005	81	91.7	0.3	0.3	1.2	3.4	86.8	0.0	8.3	0.0	0.0	6.6	0.0	1.6
	2010	(e)314	89.8	1.3	1.2	4.4	0.6	83.5	0.0	10.2	0.1	0.4	7.2	2.3	0.3
Costa Rica	1995	3 223	63.1	12.6	12.0	45.1	3.8	1.6	0.4	35.7	0.1	31.1	4.4	0.0	0.0
	2005	9 807	61.7	13.5	12.7	41.3	5.6	1.3	0.8	37.0	0.0	26.8	10.1	0.1	0.0
Côte d'Ivoire	1995	3 038	69.2	58.6	57.4	5.4	4.3	0.9	1.7	29.1	17.3	2.6	8.4	0.7	0.1
	2005	5 871	45.0	41.1	39.9	2.0	1.4	0.4	1.3	53.4	30.3	3.4	18.4	1.4	0.0
	2010	(e)8 301	32.6	29.0	28.1	2.2	0.8	0.6	1.4	57.7	31.3	3.4	21.3	1.8	0.0
Croatia - Croatie	1995	7 510	86.3	82.0	79.1	2.7	1.1	0.5	3.6	10.1	3.5	1.9	3.6	1.0	0.0
	2005	18 560	73.6	69.7	67.9	2.2	1.5	0.3	13.9	12.5	1.0	1.6	7.9	2.0	0.0
	2010	19 987	66.4	62.3	60.2	2.2	1.2	0.7	16.9	16.7	0.8	1.7	10.9	3.2	0.0
Cuba	1995	(e)2 675	49.8	40.9	40.5	0.2	0.8	7.9	10.0	39.5	1.8	27.6	9.8	0.3	0.0
	2005	(e)7 069	40.3	25.3	25.1	5.6	2.8	6.5	2.6	57.2	3.3	40.1	13.8	0.0	0.0
	2010	(e)9 920	28.0	18.8	18.6	4.1	0.4	4.8	2.7	69.2	4.1	48.5	16.4	0.2	0.0
Cyprus - Chypre	1995	3 694	77.0	54.9	53.4	13.0	6.7	2.5	4.8	15.0	1.0	1.3	10.5	2.2	0.0
	2005	6 296	80.7	68.7	67.8	1.6	2.8	7.6	2.9	14.6	1.4	2.3	8.1	2.9	0.0
	2010	8 489	81.2	70.4	69.4	1.3	1.1	8.4	3.4	13.6	1.5	1.0	9.1	1.9	0.0
Czech Republic - République tchèque	1995	22 973	82.8	76.7	74.0	3.7	1.7	0.6	10.2	5.7	0.3	0.9	4.1	0.3	0.0
	2005	76 507	80.2	73.8	71.5	2.6	3.1	0.6	7.9	11.7	0.6	0.9	9.4	0.8	0.0
	2010	125 445	78.6	75.7	74.8	1.3	1.4	0.2	7.6	13.2	0.2	0.2	12.3	0.5	0.0
Dem. Rep. of the Congo - Rép. dém. du Congo	1995	(e)1 351	48.2	38.7	37.8	6.3	0.9	2.3	0.0	51.6	30.8	0.3	20.2	0.3	0.0
	2005	(e)1 685	46.4	39.9	39.1	4.2	1.1	1.2	0.2	53.1	44.8	2.1	6.0	0.3	0.0
	2010	(e)4 187	30.5	26.6	25.9	2.5	0.8	0.6	0.1	69.2	52.4	2.2	14.2	0.4	0.0
Denmark - Danemark	1995	42 231	89.7	80.6	73.1	4.9	2.7	1.5	1.3	8.9	0.8	1.6	6.1	0.4	0.0
	2005	75 522	84.4	79.3	70.9	2.7	1.1	1.3	1.5	13.8	0.4	1.6	9.7	2.1	0.0
	2010	82 902	83.9	79.4	72.3	2.9	0.4	1.3	1.4	14.7	0.6	2.0	10.9	1.2	0.0
Djibouti	1995	(e)440	41.4	33.8	33.3	2.4	4.8	0.4	0.0	55.3	10.6	1.5	35.9	7.3	..
	2005	(e)1 207	21.2	12.4	12.3	4.4	4.2	0.3	1.0	73.7	7.0	0.6	39.9	26.3	..
	2010	(e)2 677	15.0	7.7	7.7	5.1	1.6	0.6	2.0	79.8	5.4	2.3	49.8	22.4	..

For sources and notes, see end of table.

Pour les sources et les notes, se reporter à la fin du tableau.

2.1 Country trade structure by partner
Imports by main region of origin

2.1 Structure du commerce des pays par partenaires
Importations par principales régions d'origine

Origin / Origine (Destination)	Year Année	World (millions of dollars) (1) Monde (millions de dollars) (1)	Developed economies Économies développées						Transition economies Économies en transition	Developing economies Économies en développement					
			Total	Europe Total	EU UE	USA États-Unis	Japan Japon	Other Autres		Total	Africa Afrique	America Amérique	Eastern, Southern and South-Eastern Asia Asie orientale, méridionale et du Sud-Est	Western Asia Asie occidentale	Oceania Océanie
										Percentage / En pourcentage					
Dominica - Dominique	1995	121	68.1	29.5	28.5	32.0	4.4	2.1	0.0	31.0	0.1	29.3	1.5	0.1	0.0
	2005	(e)264	43.0	10.8	9.5	25.5	4.7	2.0	0.0	56.2	0.2	25.2	30.8	0.1	0.0
	2010	(e)591	64.5	4.7	4.5	13.6	45.3	0.9	0.1	34.9	0.0	21.5	13.0	0.4	0.0
Dominican Republic - République dominicaine	1995	5 541	18.5	1.3	1.2	16.0	0.9	0.4	0.0	13.0	0.0	12.0	0.3	0.0	0.0
	2005	10 860	59.2	8.5	8.0	46.1	3.7	0.9	0.2	39.8	0.2	33.1	6.3	0.1	0.0
	2010	16 829	51.9	9.5	8.8	38.6	2.1	1.6	0.1	45.5	0.2	30.7	14.3	0.3	0.1
Ecuador - Équateur	1995	4 193	58.3	16.7	15.7	30.8	8.6	2.1	1.5	36.9	0.7	31.6	4.4	0.2	0.0
	2005	9 549	35.5	10.4	10.3	20.1	3.5	1.4	1.3	62.9	1.5	45.9	14.9	0.7	0.0
	2010	19 294	41.8	9.0	9.0	27.9	3.4	1.5	0.3	56.9	0.9	39.6	16.1	0.3	0.0
Egypt - Égypte	1995	11 739	68.3	44.7	41.9	18.8	2.7	2.1	4.7	21.5	2.4	3.2	11.5	4.3	0.0
	2005	19 812	38.9	25.0	24.0	8.9	2.3	2.6	8.0	38.9	5.4	6.0	12.9	14.6	0.0
	2010	(e)65 666	48.7	32.4	31.1	11.5	2.5	2.3	6.0	44.0	2.3	5.4	23.9	12.4	0.0
El Salvador	1995	2 628	60.3	10.0	9.5	44.2	5.1	1.0	0.1	36.0	0.0	32.4	3.6	0.0	0.0
	2005	6 690	47.4	7.3	6.7	36.9	1.9	1.3	0.7	50.0	0.1	40.9	9.0	0.0	0.0
	2010	(e)8 305	39.9	5.2	5.1	32.3	1.4	1.0	0.1	56.7	0.1	47.4	9.2	0.0	0.0
Equatorial Guinea - Guinée équatoriale	1995	(e)139	76.0	71.1	70.5	4.3	0.3	0.3	0.0	24.0	21.6	0.0	2.4	0.0	0.0
	2005	(e)1 116	83.7	57.1	56.0	24.6	0.6	1.4	0.2	16.2	11.7	0.9	3.1	0.5	0.0
	2010	(e)2 347	60.7	45.4	45.1	12.7	1.1	1.5	0.8	38.5	11.2	2.7	23.0	1.5	0.0
Eritrea - Érythrée	1995	(e)453	64.6	53.7	52.5	10.9	..	0.1	0.2	35.2	0.0	0.2	9.4	25.5	..
	2005	(e)495	62.0	50.1	49.3	11.2	0.0	0.8	5.7	32.3	4.6	3.9	6.7	17.1	..
	2010	(e)690	23.9	21.5	20.9	0.7	0.0	1.7	0.0	76.1	20.9	5.9	28.6	20.7	..
Estonia - Estonie	1995	2 546	78.0	73.3	71.6	2.6	1.9	0.3	18.8	3.2	0.1	0.7	2.2	0.1	0.0
	2005	10 208	81.3	77.5	76.3	1.5	2.0	0.2	11.7	7.1	0.1	0.4	6.2	0.5	0.0
	2010	11 594	87.6	86.1	84.2	0.9	0.4	0.2	6.3	6.1	0.1	0.3	5.2	0.4	0.0
Ethiopia - Éthiopie	1995	1 153	62.2	40.7	39.8	12.8	8.3	0.4	0.2	28.4	6.3	0.1	9.3	12.6	0.0
	2005	4 082	40.8	22.9	22.2	12.4	3.3	2.1	0.6	46.6	4.6	0.7	23.5	17.7	0.0
	2010	(e)8 605	25.5	12.1	11.7	9.8	1.1	2.5	1.6	39.3	4.7	0.6	21.2	12.8	0.0
Faeroe Islands - Îles Féroé	1995	(e)251	98.6	98.4	75.0	0.1	0.0	0.1	0.0	0.5	0.0	0.5	0.0	0.0	0.0
	2005	(e)725	98.2	97.2	71.1	0.4	0.0	0.6	0.0	0.9	0.0	0.6	0.2	0.1	0.0
	2010	(e)741	96.3	95.3	68.8	0.3	0.0	0.7	0.4	1.6	0.0	1.3	0.3	0.0	0.0
Falkland Islands (Malvinas) - Îles Falkland (Malvinas)	1995	(e)48	99.2	98.3	98.3	0.7	0.1	0.1	0.1	0.7	0.4	0.0	0.3	0.0	..
	2005	(e)66	99.5	83.0	82.9	15.2	0.0	1.3	0.0	0.5	0.1	0.0	0.5	0.0	..
	2010	(e)112	99.9	96.6	96.1	2.8	0.1	0.4	0.0	0.1	0.0	0.1	0.0	0.0	..
Fiji - Fidji	1995	892	75.4	5.1	4.8	9.7	7.0	53.7	0.0	23.9	0.1	0.3	23.0	0.0	0.5
	2005	(e)1 451	53.7	4.7	4.6	2.1	3.5	43.3	0.0	45.1	0.3	0.2	44.2	0.0	0.4
	2010	(e)1 632	42.0	2.1	1.9	3.0	2.0	34.9	0.0	56.0	0.7	0.2	54.3	0.1	0.7
Finland - Finlande	1995	28 113	82.8	68.5	62.8	6.5	6.2	1.6	7.5	7.9	0.4	1.6	5.6	0.2	0.0
	2005	58 692	75.8	69.5	66.7	2.8	2.2	1.4	14.4	9.7	0.4	1.7	7.1	0.5	0.0
	2010	68 082	71.4	67.4	64.7	2.0	0.7	1.2	17.9	10.7	0.9	2.0	7.3	0.6	0.0
France (3)	1995	281 272	80.1	67.7	63.8	7.5	3.4	1.5	1.4	14.7	4.1	2.0	7.0	1.6	0.1
	2005	503 950	79.2	71.4	67.4	5.1	1.6	1.2	2.8	17.0	5.0	1.6	7.7	2.6	0.1
	2010	595 973	78.4	73.1	69.6	3.5	1.1	0.8	3.7	17.8	4.9	1.5	9.0	2.4	0.1
French Polynesia - Polynésie française	1995	(e)1 008	94.9	66.9	66.7	10.1	2.5	15.4	0.0	5.1	0.0	0.9	3.4	0.0	0.7
	2005	(e)1 723	78.9	60.3	60.2	6.5	1.6	10.5	0.0	21.1	0.5	0.4	19.0	0.0	1.1
	2010	(e)1 740	71.9	47.3	47.2	8.0	1.6	15.0	0.0	28.1	0.1	0.6	24.9	0.1	2.5
Gabon	1995	(e)930	77.3	65.9	65.4	6.4	4.8	0.2	0.0	16.8	6.4	1.9	8.1	0.4	0.0
	2005	(e)1 688	75.7	65.9	64.6	6.4	2.6	0.7	0.1	22.3	11.9	3.3	6.6	0.6	0.0
	2010	(e)2 705	65.6	52.4	51.6	9.9	2.0	1.3	0.1	32.2	13.2	2.9	15.1	1.1	0.0
Gambia - Gambie	1995	140	57.1	48.0	47.5	5.2	3.5	0.3	0.0	42.3	19.5	2.4	19.9	0.6	0.0
	2005	(e)635	29.8	22.9	22.6	5.3	0.6	1.0	0.5	69.7	23.9	6.2	34.3	5.3	0.0
	2010	(e)888	22.5	18.1	17.7	3.6	0.5	0.2	0.1	77.4	20.4	10.4	39.5	7.2	0.0
Georgia - Géorgie	1995	392	37.3	32.1	31.8	3.8	0.3	1.1	40.5	22.2	0.1	0.2	0.7	21.2	0.0
	2005	2 491	39.5	32.3	31.5	6.0	0.3	0.9	40.3	20.2	0.2	1.7	3.8	14.4	0.0
	2010	5 156	35.5	29.1	28.3	3.4	1.6	1.4	30.8	33.6	0.7	2.1	10.4	20.4	0.0
Germany - Allemagne	1995	443 840	81.5	67.4	61.2	7.1	5.5	1.5	2.7	15.6	2.1	2.4	9.4	1.7	0.1
	2005	776 941	76.9	65.9	59.7	6.6	3.4	0.9	4.4	18.6	2.1	2.1	12.5	1.8	0.0
	2010	1 054 340	76.7	70.3	64.4	3.6	2.0	0.8	4.9	18.4	1.9	1.9	13.2	1.4	0.0

For sources and notes, see end of table.

Pour les sources et les notes, se reporter à la fin du tableau.

2.1 Country trade structure by partner
Imports by main region of origin

2.1 Structure du commerce des pays par partenaires
Importations par principales régions d'origine

Origin / Origine — Destination	Year / Année	World (millions of dollars) (1) / Monde (millions de dollars) (1)	Developed economies / Économies développées — Total	Europe — Total	Europe — EU / UE	USA / États-Unis	Japan / Japon	Other / Autres	Transition economies / Économies en transition	Developing economies / Économies en développement — Total	Africa / Afrique	America / Amérique	Eastern, Southern and South-Eastern Asia / Asie orientale, méridionale et du Sud-Est	Western Asia / Asie occidentale	Oceania / Océanie
										Percentage / En pourcentage					
Ghana	1995	(w)2 507	57.0	45.0	13.8	6.7	4.0	2.1	0.0	41.6	22.3	6.0	12.7	0.6	0.0
	2005	(e)5 921	41.3	29.9	28.9	6.3	1.8	3.3	0.9	56.9	26.0	0.4	24.0	1.6	0.0
	2010	(e)12 859	37.3	24.0	23.5	8.4	1.0	3.9	0.8	61.0	26.2	3.7	29.9	1.1	0.0
Gibraltar	1995	(e)411	88.3	80.8	78.5	2.6	4.3	0.5	1.8	9.9	7.4	0.1	1.9	0.6	0.0
	2005	(e)561	82.6	74.3	73.7	4.6	1.5	2.2	14.6	2.7	1.0	0.1	0.5	1.2	0.0
Greece - Grèce	1995	25 954	82.8	75.9	73.9	3.2	1.6	1.0	0.0	13.0	7.1	1.8	6.6	7.2	0.0
	2005	54 457	66.3	59.9	58.2	3.5	2.1	0.8	10.0	23.3	2.6	1.5	12.7	6.6	0.0
	2010	63 077	57.5	53.7	51.6	2.1	1.2	0.6	13.7	28.4	4.6	2.1	14.9	6.8	0.0
Greenland - Groenland	1995	421	97.5	90.6	83.3	2.4	3.3	1.2	0.1	2.1	0.1	0.2	1.8	0.0	0.0
	2005	(e)728	98.4	95.1	91.8	0.8	0.0	2.5	0.0	1.0	0.0	0.0	1.0	0.0	0.0
	2010	(e)934	98.7	96.0	92.3	1.0	0.0	1.7	0.0	0.4	0.0	0.0	0.4	0.0	0.0
Grenada - Grenade	1995	130	65.4	16.1	15.6	41.5	3.3	4.5	0.0	34.5	0.0	31.5	2.9	0.1	0.0
	2005	(e)344	47.8	14.9	14.5	26.4	3.7	2.8	0.0	43.4	0.1	40.0	3.3	0.0	0.0
	2010	(e)420	27.4	5.3	5.0	18.6	1.4	2.0	0.0	62.1	0.0	59.2	2.9	0.1	0.0
Guam	1995	(e)442	33.4	0.0	0.0	0.0	29.3	4.1	0.0	66.6	0.1	0.2	66.4	0.0	0.0
	2005	(e)533	19.8	3.8	3.8	0.0	13.6	2.4	0.0	80.2	0.0	0.1	80.0	0.0	0.0
	2010	(e)698	19.1	4.6	3.4	0.0	11.9	2.6	0.0	80.9	0.0	0.0	80.7	0.0	0.0
Guatemala	1995	3 293	61.7	11.2	10.6	44.9	3.7	2.0	0.0	37.1	0.1	33.3	3.8	0.0	0.0
	2005	10 432	53.2	10.2	7.3	38.4	2.6	2.0	0.1	45.2	0.0	33.1	12.0	0.1	0.0
	2010	13 837	47.9	7.7	6.9	37.0	2.0	1.2	0.6	50.5	0.4	35.8	14.1	0.3	0.0
Guinea - Guinée	1995	768	60.4	44.3	44.0	7.0	8.7	0.4	0.5	38.7	15.0	6.2	16.7	0.9	0.0
	2005	(e)1 906	35.9	27.1	26.7	7.2	0.8	0.8	1.5	32.1	11.8	1.5	17.0	1.7	0.0
	2010	(e)4 005	22.1	18.3	17.9	2.3	0.5	1.0	0.5	29.9	8.2	1.7	18.4	1.6	0.0
Guinea-Bissau - Guinée-Bissau	1995	(e)138	55.5	48.4	48.0	0.6	6.4	0.1	0.0	41.2	4.5	1.2	35.5	0.0	..
	2005	(e)213	55.3	54.0	53.2	1.1	0.2	0.0	0.1	35.7	23.8	3.6	8.1	0.1	..
	2010	(e)271	38.9	36.8	36.2	1.7	0.3	0.1	0.0	47.4	24.7	10.8	10.8	1.0	..
Guyana	1995	(e)517	56.6	20.3	20.1	30.0	4.0	2.2	0.0	43.4	0.0	38.7	4.6	0.0	0.0
	2005	(e)724	44.6	11.5	11.4	26.6	3.4	3.0	0.1	55.3	0.3	44.3	10.4	0.3	0.0
	2010	(e)1 408	37.8	8.7	8.6	22.7	3.3	3.1	0.0	62.1	0.2	43.8	17.7	0.5	0.0
Haiti - Haïti	1995	(e)976	82.9	14.0	13.4	62.1	4.3	2.5	0.0	16.8	0.2	11.1	5.4	0.0	0.0
	2005	(e)1 708	57.1	9.0	8.8	44.3	1.6	2.2	0.1	42.7	0.3	34.3	7.5	0.5	0.0
	2010	(e)4 415	39.8	6.6	6.4	30.3	1.6	1.3	0.1	60.0	0.2	47.3	11.9	0.5	0.0
Honduras	1995	1 643	56.9	9.7	9.7	42.9	3.6	0.7	0.0	26.9	0.0	26.9	0.0	0.0	0.0
	2005	4 853	48.0	7.4	6.6	37.5	2.3	0.8	0.5	51.3	0.1	46.4	4.7	0.1	0.0
Hungary - Hongrie	1995	15 483	78.0	72.1	69.5	3.1	2.2	0.6	14.7	6.5	0.6	1.4	4.1	0.3	0.0
	2005	66 412	76.0	70.9	69.9	1.6	3.1	0.4	9.6	14.2	0.1	0.5	12.9	0.7	0.0
	2010	88 105	72.4	68.4	67.7	1.5	2.2	0.3	10.0	17.6	0.1	0.5	16.4	0.6	0.0
Iceland - Islande	1995	1 768	90.7	73.5	61.9	8.3	4.4	4.5	2.3	6.3	0.2	0.7	5.3	0.1	0.0
	2005	4 848	87.4	71.6	62.4	9.1	4.7	2.1	0.6	11.9	0.4	1.8	8.8	0.9	0.0
	2010	3 930	75.7	62.7	51.9	8.1	2.3	2.7	0.6	22.8	0.5	12.3	9.5	0.5	0.0
India - Inde	1995	34 490	49.9	29.3	26.9	9.7	6.5	4.4	3.2	41.1	5.0	1.5	15.7	18.8	0.0
	2005	139 888	36.1	22.2	17.4	6.3	2.8	4.8	2.0	32.6	3.3	1.8	21.5	5.9	0.1
	2010	328 731	30.4	18.1	12.0	5.1	2.4	4.9	1.7	66.6	9.2	4.0	30.2	23.1	0.1
Indonesia including East Timor - Indonésie, y compris le Timor oriental	1995	40 630	63.7	21.8	20.6	11.7	22.7	7.5	1.1	34.5	1.0	2.6	27.5	3.4	0.0
Indonesia - Indonésie	2005	57 714	35.6	10.8	10.2	6.7	12.0	6.1	1.4	62.4	2.8	2.0	49.6	7.9	0.1
	2010	135 691	31.7	7.8	7.3	6.9	12.5	4.4	2.0	66.1	1.8	2.5	56.2	5.6	0.0
Iran (Islamic Rep. of) - Iran (Rép. islamique d')	1995	12 313	65.3	46.5	42.4	3.9	7.2	7.7	6.1	28.0	0.9	7.2	13.5	6.5	0.0
	2005	38 904	48.8	44.5	41.3	0.2	3.0	1.0	6.1	44.3	0.5	2.4	19.1	22.2	0.0
	2010	66 395	29.9	26.8	21.4	0.3	2.3	0.5	3.5	65.0	0.4	1.1	22.5	40.9	0.0
Iraq	1995	(e)665	27.4	26.5	19.3	0.0	0.1	0.8	0.0	72.6	0.5	0.0	11.7	60.4	0.0
	2005	(e)12 832	33.1	17.8	17.4	11.8	1.1	2.4	1.8	65.1	0.6	0.6	8.8	55.1	0.0
	2010	(e)27 984	22.5	13.6	13.0	6.5	1.2	1.2	1.7	75.8	2.2	1.2	25.3	47.1	0.0
Ireland - Irlande	1995	32 005	83.2	58.9	56.9	17.9	5.3	1.1	0.2	13.0	1.2	0.7	10.8	0.3	0.0
	2005	68 530	85.2	67.8	64.8	13.8	2.7	1.0	0.2	12.5	0.6	0.8	10.6	0.5	0.0
	2010	59 958	86.4	70.4	65.8	13.7	1.4	0.9	0.4	11.2	1.3	1.1	8.0	0.7	0.0

For sources and notes, see end of table.

Pour les sources et les notes, se reporter à la fin du tableau.

Origin / Origine / Destination	Year / Année	World (millions of dollars) (1) / Monde (millions de dollars) (1)	Developed economies / Économies développées Total	Europe Total	Europe EU UE	USA États-Unis	Japan Japon	Other Autres	Transition economies / Économies en transition	Developing economies / Économies en développement Total	Africa Afrique	America Amérique	Eastern, Southern and South-Eastern Asia / Asie orientale, méridionale et du Sud-Est	Western Asia / Asie occidentale	Oceania / Océanie
Israel - Israël	1995	28 218	82.6	59.5	53.3	18.7	3.3	1.1	1.0	9.8	1.5	0.9	6.6	0.0	0.0
	2005	44 943	61.8	44.6	38.9	13.4	2.8	1.0	3.0	20.8	0.7	2.2	15.1	2.9	0.0
	2010	59 199	55.4	40.1	34.5	11.3	3.0	0.9	1.6	24.9	0.9	1.4	19.3	3.2	0.0
Italy - Italie	1995	205 720	78.3	69.5	64.7	4.9	2.2	1.0	0.0	17.0	0.7	1.0	0.3	2.0	0.0
	2005	384 688	69.5	63.2	59.5	3.5	1.6	1.2	6.3	24.0	8.0	2.4	9.8	3.8	0.0
	2010	476 594	63.9	59.1	55.8	2.7	1.2	0.9	7.1	28.8	8.3	2.7	13.8	4.0	0.0
Jamaica - Jamaïque	1995	(e)2 891	74.9	13.0	12.0	54.1	4.7	3.0	0.0	23.6	0.1	17.6	5.0	0.9	0.0
	2005	5 246	55.9	7.6	6.8	41.5	3.3	3.5	0.1	42.5	0.5	35.9	5.7	0.3	0.0
	2010	(e)5 392	46.7	7.4	6.7	33.7	1.9	3.7	0.0	50.8	0.3	41.7	8.3	0.5	0.1
Japan - Japon	1995	336 254	47.6	16.3	14.7	22.6	..	8.7	1.5	50.8	1.4	3.4	37.4	8.2	0.4
	2005	515 223	32.5	12.7	11.4	12.7	..	7.1	1.3	66.2	1.9	2.8	46.4	14.8	0.2
	2010	694 028	29.4	10.9	9.6	9.9	..	8.6	2.5	68.1	1.7	3.9	46.9	15.4	0.2
Jordan - Jordanie	1995	3 721	51.6	36.8	35.2	9.2	3.9	1.7	1.6	44.4	2.3	2.9	14.8	24.5	0.0
	2005	10 498	36.9	26.0	24.6	5.6	2.8	2.5	4.2	58.7	4.6	1.8	20.2	32.1	0.0
	2010	15 402	31.7	20.7	19.8	5.6	3.1	2.1	3.4	64.8	5.6	2.8	22.7	33.7	0.0
Kazakhstan	1995	3 807	20.8	18.2	16.7	1.7	0.2	0.7	69.7	9.4	0.0	1.0	5.0	3.4	0.0
	2005	(e)20 171	29.5	24.7	24.2	2.9	1.0	0.8	43.1	27.4	0.2	0.5	24.0	2.7	0.0
	2010	(e)29 913	29.0	24.7	23.8	2.7	0.8	0.8	28.9	42.0	0.3	0.7	37.8	3.3	0.0
Kenya	1995	(e)3 249	54.8	40.3	39.0	3.9	9.1	1.6	0.1	45.0	10.9	1.1	22.6	10.4	0.0
	2005	(e)6 874	36.5	20.5	19.8	10.1	4.0	1.9	1.1	61.2	11.5	1.7	23.9	24.2	0.0
	2010	(e)14 878	24.0	15.5	15.0	2.7	4.6	1.2	1.8	73.2	13.4	1.0	38.7	20.0	0.0
Kiribati	1995	(e)34	88.0	61.9	61.8	3.1	2.2	21.6	0.1	11.2	0.0	0.0	2.8	0.0	8.3
	2005	(e)76	62.3	1.1	1.1	3.1	18.1	40.0	0.0	37.7	0.0	1.0	9.5	0.0	27.2
	2010	(e)73	55.3	2.8	2.8	7.7	26.3	18.6	0.0	44.7	0.0	0.2	13.4	0.1	31.0
Korea, Dem. People's Rep. of - Corée, Rép. populaire dém. de	1995	(e)1 549	35.6	16.6	16.2	0.4	18.2	0.4	9.9	54.5	0.2	3.6	49.9	0.5	0.3
	2005	(e)3 312	9.8	7.0	6.8	0.2	2.1	0.6	8.2	82.0	18.1	5.2	51.0	7.7	0.0
	2010	(c)6 006	1.9	1.7	1.0	0.0	0.0	0.2	1.4	96.7	39.9	2.1	52.6	2.1	0.0
Korea, Republic of - Corée, République de	1995	135 110	68.0	15.0	13.7	22.5	24.1	6.4	1.7	29.6	1.7	2.9	17.3	7.4	0.2
	2005	261 238	46.8	11.2	10.5	11.8	18.5	5.3	1.7	51.4	1.3	2.6	31.0	16.4	0.1
	2010	425 265	41.4	10.4	9.1	9.5	15.1	6.3	2.7	55.9	1.5	3.4	34.0	16.9	0.1
Kuwait - Koweït	1995	7 771	68.5	40.2	38.9	16.1	9.4	2.7	0.3	31.2	1.3	1.6	15.3	13.0	0.0
	2005	(e)15 237	63.0	36.7	34.9	14.3	8.5	3.6	0.3	36.7	0.6	1.8	18.2	16.0	0.0
	2010	(e)22 799	47.8	24.6	22.4	13.4	6.8	3.0	0.9	51.2	1.9	2.1	29.3	17.9	0.0
Kyrgyzstan - Kirghizistan	1995	392	3.7	1.6	1.6	0.8	0.5	0.7	68.8	27.5	..	0.7	25.8	0.9	0.0
	2005	1 112	20.2	11.4	10.9	6.0	1.1	1.7	61.1	18.7	1.1	0.7	13.4	3.5	0.0
	2010	(e)7 193	6.1	4.2	4.1	1.2	0.6	0.1	26.7	67.2	0.0	0.1	65.0	2.2	0.0
Lao People's Dem. Rep. - Rép. dém. populaire lao	1995	589	9.8	1.2	1.2	0.3	8.3	0.1	0.5	62.4	0.0	0.0	62.4	0.0	0.0
	2005	(e)1 270	8.4	4.3	4.1	0.8	1.7	1.6	0.9	88.7	0.2	0.0	88.4	0.0	0.0
	2010	(e)3 608	5.8	2.8	2.7	0.4	1.9	0.8	0.7	92.1	0.0	0.0	92.1	0.0	0.0
Latvia - Lettonie	1995	1 810	70.1	66.2	64.5	1.9	0.6	1.4	28.1	1.8	0.1	0.6	0.9	0.2	0.0
	2005	8 662	79.2	77.5	75.2	1.1	0.3	0.4	16.9	3.9	0.1	0.2	2.9	0.7	0.0
	2010	11 641	79.9	78.6	76.2	0.5	0.1	0.7	15.5	4.6	0.2	0.1	3.8	0.5	0.0
Lebanon - Liban	1995	(e)6 769	71.3	57.7	51.6	9.6	2.9	1.2	2.8	23.8	2.2	2.5	11.4	7.8	0.0
	2005	(e)9 695	55.4	47.5	44.7	5.3	1.8	0.8	4.5	38.0	3.5	2.0	11.7	20.8	0.0
	2010	(e)19 708	48.1	35.5	32.7	10.3	1.6	0.6	7.9	42.1	4.5	1.9	14.5	21.2	0.0
Lesotho	1995	(e)886	10.6	9.8	8.6	0.4	0.4	0.0	0.0	89.3	86.7	0.0	2.6	0.0	0.0
	2005	(e)1 361	9.8	7.5	7.5	1.6	0.5	0.2	0.0	93.5	7.7	0.6	85.0	0.3	..
	2010	(e)2 126	19.5	9.3	9.1	9.1	0.6	0.5	0.0	81.0	8.8	0.0	71.5	0.7	..
Liberia - Libéria	1995	(e)5 683	67.8	33.3	32.2	0.8	33.7	0.0	2.7	29.4	0.9	0.8	27.5	0.2	0.0
	2005	(e)5 716	34.3	11.4	9.9	1.4	21.3	0.2	4.8	61.0	2.5	1.0	56.4	1.1	0.0
	2010	(e)17 449	16.6	3.1	3.0	1.2	12.1	0.1	0.3	83.1	0.9	0.6	81.0	0.5	0.0
Libyan Arab Jamahiriya - Jamahiriya arabe libyenne	1995	(e)5 147	72.6	67.4	65.8	0.0	4.0	1.1	0.0	27.4	8.9	1.9	9.3	7.3	0.0
	2005	(e)8 794	61.6	57.8	55.8	1.0	1.7	1.0	3.7	34.5	8.3	3.5	13.3	9.4	0.0
	2010	(e)21 959	49.1	42.5	42.0	3.3	1.7	1.5	3.1	47.7	11.0	3.1	20.9	12.7	0.0
Lithuania - Lituanie	1995	3 649	55.7	52.9	50.5	1.9	0.2	0.7	42.0	2.1	0.2	0.9	0.6	0.4	0.0
	2005	15 490	63.1	60.6	59.4	2.0	0.3	0.2	31.2	5.6	0.2	0.5	4.1	0.7	0.0
	2010	23 166	58.5	57.6	57.1	0.7	0.1	0.1	36.0	5.5	0.6	0.5	3.7	0.7	0.0

For sources and notes, see end of table.

Pour les sources et les notes, se reporter à la fin du tableau.

75

Origin / Origine (Destination)	Year Année	World (millions of dollars) (1) Monde (millions de dollars) (1)	Developed economies Économies développées					Transition economies Économies en transition	Developing economies Économies en développement					
			Total	Europe Total	EU UE	USA États-Unis	Japan Japon	Other Autres		Total	Africa Afrique	America Amérique	Eastern, Southern and South-Eastern Asia Asie orientale, méridionale et du Sud-Est	Western Asia Asie occiden-tale	Oceania Océanie
										Percentage / En pourcentage					
Luxembourg	1995	(e)0.. (1)	97.6	92.0	81.0	3.1	1.1	1.4	0.2	2.2	0.6	0.1	1.4	0.2	0.0
	2005	21 820	79.5	75.2	73.0	3.1	0.8	0.4	0.4	19.0	0.2	0.3	16.7	1.8	0.0
	2010	23 950	86.6	82.1	81.5	3.6	0.6	0.3	0.1	12.9	0.0	1.2	11.5	0.2	0.0
Madagascar	1995	525	64.4	53.8	52.4	3.9	6.1	0.6	0.2	35.1	7.8	1.4	24.4	1.5	0.0
	2005	1 000	20.0	22.1	22.1	2.8	3.8	0.7	0.0	55.4	9.7	1.6	29.4	14.6	0.0
	2010	(e)2 897	28.8	19.7	19.0	4.5	0.5	1.2	0.0	60.6	11.9	1.5	34.0	12.4	0.0
Malawi	1995	500	42.1	33.3	32.4	2.6	5.0	1.2	0.0	57.9	45.3	0.9	11.2	0.6	0.0
	2005	(e)750	19.0	13.5	13.1	4.1	0.8	0.6	0.0	80.3	66.4	0.6	12.8	0.6	0.0
	2010	(e)1 417	18.8	13.5	12.8	2.9	1.7	0.8	0.0	80.5	62.1	0.3	17.9	0.3	0.0
Malaysia - Malaisie	1995	77 646	64.5	17.3	15.4	16.3	27.3	3.6	0.3	34.3	0.5	1.2	31.8	0.7	0.1
	2005	113 619	43.3	12.9	11.8	13.0	14.6	2.7	0.5	56.1	0.6	1.6	50.9	3.0	0.0
	2010	(e)190 936	29.7	8.3	7.8	8.1	10.2	3.2	0.7	69.1	1.1	2.0	63.0	2.8	0.1
Maldives	1995	357	21.0	15.4	14.7	0.4	3.8	1.4	0.0	78.9	0.3	0.0	50.1	28.5	0.0
	2005	745	21.7	15.1	14.2	1.1	1.8	3.7	0.0	78.1	0.4	0.3	58.8	18.6	0.0
	2010	(e)1 245	14.0	7.5	7.3	2.5	0.5	3.5	0.0	85.8	1.2	1.2	62.4	21.0	0.0
Mali	1995	(e)990	39.9	34.8	34.3	2.6	1.5	1.0	0.0	33.3	23.9	0.5	8.5	0.4	0.0
	2005	(e)2 067	29.1	26.2	26.0	1.7	0.3	0.9	1.0	36.7	29.2	0.9	6.0	0.6	0.0
	2010	(e)3 579	26.7	24.0	23.7	1.1	0.6	1.1	1.3	43.5	32.7	0.3	10.1	0.4	0.0
Malta - Malte	1995	2 942	83.6	74.5	73.4	6.0	2.5	0.5	0.5	15.9	3.6	0.8	10.6	0.8	0.0
	2005	3 711	85.2	77.5	75.8	5.4	1.8	0.6	0.2	14.5	0.8	0.7	11.4	1.5	0.0
	2010	4 097	78.7	68.6	65.2	2.8	1.5	5.7	0.4	19.3	1.4	0.9	14.9	2.1	0.0
Marshall Islands - Îles Marshall	1995	75	97.8	62.3	62.3	5.4	29.8	0.3	0.0	2.2	..	..	2.2	..	0.0
	2005	94	31.6	20.7	19.4	3.2	7.5	0.3	0.6	67.8	0.0	0.0	63.4	4.3	0.0
	2010	(e)120	42.0	7.8	7.7	1.5	32.6	0.1	2.0	56.1	0.1	0.2	54.4	1.3	..
Mauritania - Mauritanie	1995	(e)654	69.1	56.5	56.0	7.2	4.9	0.6	0.0	26.0	10.6	0.5	14.3	0.5	0.0
	2005	(e)1 346	61.5	51.1	49.2	7.0	2.4	1.0	1.6	27.2	8.1	4.0	12.6	2.5	0.0
	2010	(e)2 475	50.9	44.5	44.3	3.7	1.4	1.3	0.8	38.1	8.7	5.4	20.7	3.3	0.0
Mauritius - Maurice	1995	1 976	47.5	35.2	32.9	2.6	4.8	4.9	0.0	49.9	14.3	1.9	29.7	4.0	0.0
	2005	3 165	41.7	31.9	30.7	2.1	3.6	4.1	0.1	58.0	12.0	1.8	30.8	13.4	0.0
	2010	(e)4 068	34.1	26.5	25.3	1.1	2.7	3.9	0.1	65.4	14.4	2.0	47.2	1.7	0.0
Mayotte	2005	309	59.8	56.5	56.3	1.3	1.7	0.3	1.8	38.4	17.9	3.8	13.0	3.7	0.0
Mexico - Mexique	1995	79 702	91.7	10.0	9.4	74.5	5.0	2.2	0.0	7.9	0.1	2.7	5.0	0.0	0.0
	2005	244 001	74.4	11.5	11.0	53.4	5.9	3.5	0.4	24.4	0.1	5.8	18.2	0.3	0.0
	2010	331 630	67.3	10.8	10.2	48.1	5.0	3.4	0.4	31.2	0.3	4.3	26.4	0.2	0.0
Micronesia (Federated States of) - Micronésie (États fédérés de)	1995	100	87.1	7.0	7.0	40.5	28.9	10.7	0.0	12.9	..	0.0	12.9	..	..
	2005	130	65.4	1.2	1.2	40.6	14.3	9.4	..	34.6	0.0	2.6	31.4	..	0.5
	2010	(e)155	83.6	0.7	0.6	54.8	19.2	8.8	..	16.4	0.1	0.2	16.1	..	..
Mongolia - Mongolie	1995	415	28.9	14.0	12.5	3.5	10.9	0.6	50.7	20.4	0.0	0.0	20.3	0.1	0.0
	2005	1 175	23.6	10.6	10.4	3.2	6.4	3.5	41.3	35.1	0.0	0.6	34.4	0.0	0.0
	2010	(e)3 842	18.1	8.4	8.4	3.3	4.6	1.8	29.0	52.9	0.0	0.2	51.8	0.9	0.0
Montenegro - Monténégro	2010	(e)1 043	76.7	74.3	72.9	1.5	0.3	0.5	4.8	18.5	0.2	6.9	8.6	2.9	..
Montserrat	1995	30	83.0	67.7	67.6	13.4	1.5	0.3	..	17.0	0.0	16.0	0.9	..	..
	2005	30	74.4	10.7	10.7	56.6	4.8	2.2	..	24.6	0.0	22.3	1.7	0.6	..
	2010	(e)30	..	..	..	..	..	..	..	..	..	..	..	..	..
Morocco - Maroc	1995	9 502	63.4	54.3	53.0	5.9	1.3	2.0	1.9	21.3	5.2	3.7	6.1	6.4	0.0
	2005	20 336	58.5	52.1	50.8	3.4	1.8	1.3	8.0	33.1	5.4	4.3	13.3	10.1	0.0
	2010	(e)34 360	64.8	56.8	55.7	6.2	0.9	0.9	2.5	32.7	5.2	3.6	14.8	9.1	0.0
Mozambique	1995	747	46.0	32.5	31.3	6.7	4.9	1.9	0.0	45.9	35.6	1.3	8.2	0.7	0.0
	2005	2 467	26.9	22.6	21.7	2.6	0.8	0.9	0.0	64.3	47.1	2.2	13.1	1.9	0.0
	2010	3 564	37.0	30.5	30.2	2.1	3.5	0.9	0.4	56.2	38.6	0.8	15.0	1.9	0.0
Myanmar	1995	(e)2 342	17.5	8.7	8.4	0.8	7.4	0.7	0.0	82.4	0.1	0.0	82.3	0.0	0.0
	2005	(e)3 578	7.4	3.3	3.2	0.2	2.8	1.1	0.8	91.7	0.2	0.1	91.2	0.2	0.0
	2010	(e)9 823	5.4	1.3	1.2	0.1	3.0	1.0	0.9	93.6	0.1	0.2	92.9	0.4	0.0
Namibia - Namibie	1995	(e)1 496	13.0	10.3	10.0	2.3	0.0	0.4	0.0	86.8	85.7	0.6	0.5	0.0	0.0
	2005	2 516	10.4	9.2	8.2	0.8	0.2	0.3	0.1	89.3	84.6	0.7	3.6	0.3	0.0
	2010	(e)6 101	46.5	32.4	31.5	10.0	1.3	2.8	0.2	53.3	4.7	20.7	23.9	4.0	..

For sources and notes, see end of table.

Pour les sources et les notes, se reporter à la fin du tableau.

2.1 Country trade structure by partner
Imports by main region of origin

2.1 Structure du commerce des pays par partenaires
Importations par principales régions d'origine

Origin / Origine — Destination	Year / Année	World (millions of dollars) (1) / Monde (millions de dollars) (1)	Developed economies / Économies développées — Total	Europe — Total	Europe — EU / UE	USA / États-Unis	Japan / Japon	Other / Autres	Transition economies / Économies en transition	Developing economies / Économies en développement — Total	Africa / Afrique	America / Amérique	Eastern, Southern and South-Eastern Asia / Asie orientale, méridionale et du Sud-Est	Western Asia / Asie occidentale	Oceania / Océanie
Nauru	1995	(e)28	88.1	9.8	9.7	1.6	4.5	72.2	0.1	11.9	1.4	0.0	7.6	0.0	2.7
	2005	(e)26	49.1	5.4	5.4	6.0	0.6	37.2	0.0	50.9	0.2	0.0	48.4	0.0	2.2
	2010	(e)131	82.3	2.8	2.8	10.9	0.8	67.7	0.0	17.7	0.2	0.3	11.9	0.0	5.3
Nepal - Népal	1995	(e)767	27.1	11.3	9.8	1.4	8.7	5.8	0.0	72.0	0.0	0.0	70.5	1.9	0.0
	2005	2 070	9.3	4.3	4.2	1.2	1.7	2.1	0.9	85.7	0.1	1.3	81.4	2.9	0.0
	2010	(e)3 607	6.9	3.5	3.0	0.9	1.3	1.2	0.1	92.0	0.3	0.0	87.5	4.1	0.0
Netherlands - Pays-Bas	1995	157 683	81.7	67.8	64.4	8.9	3.7	1.3	1.0	17.3	2.2	3.0	9.4	2.6	0.0
	2005	363 230	64.8	52.5	49.4	7.6	3.2	1.4	4.8	30.2	2.7	4.2	19.4	3.9	0.0
	2010	513 130	62.0	50.9	46.9	6.8	2.8	1.5	6.0	31.8	3.4	4.9	21.1	2.3	0.0
Netherlands Antilles - Antilles néerlandaises	1995	(e)1 853	71.7	37.0	30.0	29.9	3.3	1.3	0.0	26.6	0.0	18.9	7.7	0.0	0.0
	2005	(e)11 877	18.6	7.4	7.1	10.5	0.5	0.3	0.0	80.3	0.1	77.9	2.3	0.1	0.0
	2010	(e)6 399	64.4	12.6	12.0	50.1	0.8	0.9	0.7	30.5	0.1	25.3	4.8	0.3	0.0
New Caledonia - Nouvelle-Calédonie	1995	957	87.1	59.6	59.2	4.2	4.3	19.0	0.0	12.2	0.4	0.4	10.6	0.1	0.6
	2005	(e)1 790	74.2	50.6	50.2	2.4	2.2	19.1	0.0	24.6	0.1	0.5	23.5	0.1	0.5
	2010	(e)3 200	64.4	42.0	41.7	3.7	1.5	17.1	0.0	34.3	0.2	0.3	33.2	0.1	0.5
New Zealand - Nouvelle-Zélande	1995	13 796	79.0	22.8	21.7	18.7	13.9	23.5	0.0	20.5	0.6	1.1	15.8	2.2	0.8
	2005	26 134	64.2	19.8	18.9	11.0	11.0	22.4	0.1	35.7	1.7	1.2	28.3	4.2	0.4
	2010	30 695	53.0	15.6	14.8	10.5	7.4	19.6	0.9	45.9	0.8	1.4	37.1	6.3	0.3
Nicaragua	1995	975	46.3	9.8	9.0	29.9	5.2	1.4	0.0	47.7	0.0	45.5	2.1	0.0	0.0
	2005	2 623	32.7	6.8	6.5	20.0	4.5	1.4	1.6	65.5	0.0	55.3	10.1	0.1	0.0
Niger	1995	300	50.6	38.4	38.1	5.6	6.5	0.3	0.0	35.7	27.2	0.7	7.4	0.3	0.0
	2005	(e)832	52.3	39.4	37.6	10.7	0.5	1.7	0.1	47.5	22.2	1.2	14.0	2.6	7.6
Nigeria - Nigéria	1995	(e)5 815	68.3	52.8	50.8	11.4	3.3	0.8	0.4	31.1	4.9	4.9	20.8	0.4	0.0
	2005	(e)24 500	44.9	34.4	33.3	7.3	2.3	0.9	2.0	37.8	6.3	5.3	23.1	3.1	0.0
	2010	(e)47 867	44.2	31.6	29.9	9.3	1.5	1.7	1.2	37.7	5.2	2.6	27.1	2.8	0.0
Niue - Nioué	1995	4	98.8	2.7	2.7	81.3	1.6	13.2	0.1	1.2	..	0.0	1.1		..
	2005	8	97.0	20.5	24.8	3.3	0.6	67.2	..	2.4	0.0	0.2	2.0	0.0	0.2
	2010	(e)5	9.0	0.0	0.0	1.5	0.0	7.4	..	91.0	89.0		2.0	..	0.0
Northern Mariana Islands - Îles Mariannes du Nord	2005	-	16.5	4.5	4.4	..	-	12.0	..	83.5	0.0	0.1	83.2	0.2	0.0
	2010	-	19.2	3.7	3.2	..	-	15.5	..	80.8	0.4	0.0	80.3	..	..
Norway - Norvège	1995	32 525	88.3	75.1	73.5	6.7	3.8	2.6	1.8	9.9	0.9	2.5	6.1	0.3	0.0
	2005	55 481	82.0	70.8	69.6	5.1	3.2	2.9	2.8	15.2	1.3	2.7	10.3	0.9	0.0
	2010	77 270	76.0	64.7	63.3	5.5	2.2	3.6	3.1	20.9	1.7	2.7	15.7	0.9	0.0
Occupied Palestinian territory - Territoire palestinien occupé	1995	(e)1 658	51.0	50.0	46.7	1.0	..	0.0	0.0	48.9	26.7	0.0	0.0	22.2	..
	2005	(e)2 667	64.3	60.6	48.7	3.6	0.0	0.0	0.0	35.7	26.2	0.6	0.0	8.9	..
	2010	(e)4 385	35.8	34.2	26.8	0.7	1.0	0.0	0.3	63.9	28.9	0.5	9.0	25.6	..
Oman	1995	4 253	55.0	29.3	28.3	6.5	15.8	3.5	0.1	44.7	0.4	1.0	14.0	29.3	0.0
	2005	8 827	47.6	23.0	22.0	6.2	15.7	2.7	1.4	51.0	0.7	1.6	16.3	32.4	0.0
	2010	(e)21 933	42.7	18.7	17.5	5.5	15.6	2.9	0.2	57.0	1.2	1.2	21.6	33.0	0.0
Pakistan	1995	11 461	50.7	28.0	24.8	9.3	10.7	2.7	1.4	46.2	2.3	1.7	23.8	18.4	0.0
	2005	25 412	34.6	19.4	17.4	6.0	6.4	2.7	2.7	60.6	3.2	1.7	26.7	29.0	0.0
	2010	(e)43 233	23.2	12.2	11.4	4.8	3.3	2.8	0.8	75.3	2.8	1.2	42.4	29.0	0.0
Palau - Palaos	1995	(e)49	..	..	..	..	..	..	..	100.0	..	..	..	..	..
	2005	(e)108	47.0	7.2	7.2	0.0	29.2	10.7	0.0	53.0	0.0	0.0	53.0	..	..
	2010	(e)113	65.2	2.9	2.9	0.0	57.7	4.6	0.0	34.8	0.0	0.0	34.8	..	..
Panama	1995	2 530	56.5	8.8	8.3	40.6	5.2	1.9	0.0	28.3	0.0	23.4	4.9	0.1	0.0
	2005	4 158	40.0	6.7	6.4	27.5	4.5	1.3	0.2	42.8	0.0	35.5	7.2	0.1	0.0
Papua New Guinea - Papouasie-Nouvelle-Guinée	1995	(e)1 451	73.5	5.2	5.2	3.9	9.2	55.2	0.0	26.0	0.4	0.3	25.0	0.0	0.3
	2005	(e)2 018	68.6	2.3	2.0	3.0	4.3	58.9	0.1	29.8	0.3	0.1	28.8	0.1	0.5
	2010	(e)4 947	61.0	4.5	4.0	4.3	6.6	45.7	0.0	37.7	0.4	0.1	36.7	0.1	0.4
Paraguay	1995	3 077	33.2	11.7	11.2	12.3	8.5	0.7	0.0	66.5	0.9	45.9	19.7	0.0	0.0
	2005	3 577	19.4	10.6	6.3	5.3	2.9	0.6	0.0	78.0	0.3	51.1	26.6	0.0	0.0
	2010	10 340	14.3	6.3	5.3	4.3	3.4	0.2	0.1	85.5	0.1	46.1	39.0	0.3	0.0
Peru - Pérou	1995	8 295	53.6	19.3	18.4	26.7	5.1	2.6	0.5	45.8	0.3	37.6	7.7	0.2	0.0
	2005	13 206	36.5	12.6	11.6	17.9	3.5	2.5	1.0	62.5	3.3	41.8	16.9	0.4	0.0
	2010	(e)30 809	40.7	10.4	9.9	24.1	3.6	2.6	1.0	58.2	3.1	32.9	21.4	0.7	0.0

For sources and notes, see end of table.

Pour les sources et les notes, se reporter à la fin du tableau.

Origin / Origine	Year	World (millions of dollars) (1)	Developed economies / Économies développées						Transition economies / Économies en transition	Developing economies / Économies en développement					
			Total	Europe		USA États-Unis	Japan Japon	Other Autres		Total	Africa Afrique	America Amérique	Eastern, Southern and South-Eastern Asia / Asie orientale, méridionale et du Sud-Est	Western Asia / Asie occidentale	Oceania Océanie
Destination	Année	Monde (millions de dollars) (1)		Total	EU UE										
						Percentage / En pourcentage									
Philippines	1995	28 312	57.7	11.5	10.9	18.5	22.3	5.0	0.3	39.6	0.6	1.7	29.4	7.5	0.4
	2005	47 420	47.3	8.5	7.9	19.2	17.0	2.6	0.9	51.8	0.2	1.3	44.8	6.7	0.3
	2010	(e)77 893	33.5	6.8	6.2	9.7	13.7	3.3	1.0	65.5	0.2	1.8	57.0	6.1	0.4
Poland - Pologne	1995	29 050	80.6	74.2	71.1	3.9	1.6	0.7	9.5	9.9	1.6	1.4	6.5	0.3	0.0
	2005	101 416	80.0	77.5	75.3	1.2	0.9	0.4	11.3	8.5	0.4	1.2	5.8	1.1	0.0
	2010	100 455	78.0	71.0	72.1	1.4	0.8	0.5	10.0	12.0	0.4	0.8	10.0	1.0	0.0
Portugal	1995	33 309	84.1	78.1	75.2	3.3	2.2	0.6	0.9	14.9	5.1	3.3	5.0	1.4	0.0
	2005	63 878	82.9	79.3	77.6	2.1	1.1	0.4	1.4	15.7	6.6	3.5	3.4	2.2	0.0
	2010	75 353	80.2	77.6	76.0	1.3	0.6	0.6	2.5	17.2	6.8	3.5	5.3	1.6	0.0
Qatar	1995	1 929	62.5	35.9	33.7	10.6	13.4	2.7	0.0	34.5	0.6	1.8	15.6	16.5	0.0
	2005	10 060	60.2	35.2	33.7	11.6	11.6	1.8	0.4	39.4	0.9	2.0	20.7	15.7	0.0
	2010	(e)21 301	59.3	35.2	33.1	16.3	5.9	1.9	0.4	40.3	1.9	1.6	17.7	19.1	0.0
Republic of Moldova - République de Moldova	1995	841	30.5	28.2	27.2	1.3	0.2	0.8	67.7	1.2	0.0	0.1	0.3	0.8	0.0
	2005	2 292	49.4	46.2	45.3	1.8	0.9	0.6	39.8	10.7	0.4	0.8	5.3	4.1	0.0
	2010	(e)4 124	54.8	53.2	52.7	1.0	0.2	0.3	35.3	9.8	0.3	1.6	3.7	4.1	0.0
Romania - Roumanie	1995	10 388	66.3	59.3	57.0	4.0	0.7	2.3	15.8	17.8	4.6	2.2	8.0	3.0	0.0
	2005	40 350	69.6	64.3	63.0	2.8	1.4	1.0	14.3	15.2	0.5	1.8	7.9	5.0	0.0
	2010	61 571	76.1	73.9	72.9	1.1	0.5	0.6	9.9	14.0	0.6	0.9	8.7	3.8	0.0
Russian Federation - Fédération de Russie	1995	46 399	60.3	51.4	49.5	5.7	1.6	1.5	29.5	10.1	0.4	2.3	6.1	1.4	0.0
	2005	97 405	58.7	46.8	45.1	4.7	6.0	1.2	18.4	22.5	1.0	4.2	15.4	1.9	0.0
	2010	217 421	55.3	44.7	42.8	4.5	4.7	1.3	9.6	33.1	1.0	3.7	26.1	2.3	0.0
Rwanda	1995	(e)284	53.0	30.0	29.5	14.9	6.6	1.6	0.0	35.6	31.2	0.0	3.1	1.3	..
	2005	(e)524	30.6	20.9	20.7	2.2	2.7	4.7	1.3	43.0	34.1	0.0	5.8	3.1	0.0
	2010	(e)1 022	24.8	19.8	19.1	3.3	0.7	1.0	0.3	73.8	51.6	0.2	11.5	10.5	0.0
Saint Helena - Sainte-Hélène	1995	(e)25	84.7	82.7	82.6	1.3	0.5	0.2	0.0	15.3	14.2	0.2	0.9	0.0	0.0
	2005	(e)61	70.6	64.3	64.2	4.6	0.3	1.5	0.0	29.4	25.3	0.1	2.1	1.9	0.0
	2010	(e)63	65.9	64.6	64.2	0.9	0.0	0.3	0.0	34.1	30.5	0.2	0.3	3.2	0.0
Saint Kitts and Nevis - Saint-Kitts-et-Nevis	1995	(e)176	59.1	16.1	15.8	36.4	3.5	3.1	0.0	40.9	23.1	17.3	0.4	0.0	..
	2005	(e)299	72.0	18.9	18.6	46.4	4.2	2.6	1.6	25.5	0.1	24.1	1.1	0.2	0.0
	2010	(e)461	64.4	20.7	20.3	39.9	1.7	2.1	1.1	33.7	0.0	30.8	2.0	0.8	0.0
Saint Lucia - Sainte-Lucie	1995	307	67.1	19.5	19.3	38.1	4.7	4.8	0.0	32.8	2.4	25.8	4.5	0.1	0.0
	2005	(e)671	59.7	33.1	32.6	22.1	2.7	1.9	0.0	40.2	0.1	38.1	1.9	0.2	0.0
	2010	(e)3 982	13.1	1.3	1.2	11.1	0.3	0.4	1.1	85.9	0.0	85.1	0.7	0.0	0.0
Saint Pierre and Miquelon - Saint-Pierre-et-Miquelon	1995	(e)47	99.2	70.6	70.1	1.2	0.1	27.4	..	0.8	0.0	0.2	0.6	0.0	0.0
	2005	(e)50	95.3	61.0	61.0	2.0	0.2	32.2	0.0	4.7	0.0	0.0	4.6	0.0	0.0
	2010	(e)59	99.8	67.0	66.6	0.0	0.0	32.8	0.0	0.2	0.0	0.1	0.2	0.0	0.0
Saint Vincent and the les Grenadines	1995	136	65.1	22.4	22.1	37.2	2.2	3.3	0.0	34.7	0.1	31.2	3.4	0.0	0.0
	2005	241	57.7	15.4	15.0	33.3	4.2	4.9	0.0	42.2	0.1	35.9	6.1	0.1	0.0
	2010	(e)649	35.4	17.6	15.6	14.5	0.8	2.4	2.3	62.2	0.1	24.6	36.5	1.1	0.0
Samoa	1995	(e)144	82.4	1.8	1.8	5.7	20.7	54.2	0.0	16.6	0.0	0.0	9.1	0.0	7.5
	2005	641	76.1	1.4	1.4	13.5	7.5	53.7	0.0	23.9	0.1	0.8	16.6	0.0	6.5
	2010	(e)463	42.1	1.6	1.6	4.6	7.5	28.3	0.0	56.8	0.2	0.6	37.8	0.0	18.1
Sao Tome and Principe - Sao Tomé-et-Principe	1995	(e)44	87.0	80.6	80.5	4.5	1.6	0.3	0.0	13.0	4.7	2.9	5.4	0.0	0.0
	2005	(e)65	81.7	63.1	63.0	17.2	1.1	0.2	0.8	17.5	5.6	2.0	9.0	0.9	0.0
	2010	(e)104	75.0	71.3	70.6	1.5	2.2	0.1	0.0	25.0	6.3	1.1	17.2	0.5	0.0
Saudi Arabia - Arabie saoudite	1995	27 450	72.8	41.5	36.3	21.4	7.7	2.2	0.9	26.0	3.0	2.4	15.0	5.6	0.0
	2005	59 510	62.0	34.0	31.7	14.8	9.4	4.2	1.7	35.4	3.1	3.7	20.9	7.8	0.0
	2010	(e)103 577	53.0	30.8	29.0	12.3	6.9	3.0	1.1	44.7	2.5	4.0	29.4	8.7	0.0
Senegal - Sénégal	1995	1 256	63.6	52.9	52.3	5.6	3.6	1.4	0.0	34.8	14.0	6.1	14.3	0.4	0.0
	2005	3 217	49.7	42.6	42.0	4.2	1.8	1.2	1.8	47.3	21.2	6.7	16.8	2.6	0.0
	2010	4 372	48.6	42.4	41.2	2.7	2.2	1.4	4.0	47.1	17.7	6.3	19.3	3.7	0.0
Serbia - Serbie	2010	(e)16 518	66.3	65.5	64.2	0.7	0.1	0.0	13.5	7.7	0.4	0.9	4.2	2.2	0.0
Serbia and Montenegro - Serbie-et-Monténégro	1995	(e)383	90.8	90.5	83.2	0.0	0.2	0.1	0.9	8.3	2.6	0.1	0.0	5.6	..
	2005	(e)7 803	87.8	85.5	83.3	1.9	0.1	0.4	0.6	11.6	3.7	0.4	3.8	3.7	0.0
Seychelles	1995	240	44.7	33.6	33.2	3.8	5.6	1.6	0.0	55.3	19.8	0.1	23.3	12.2	0.0
	2005	(e)764	43.3	38.7	38.3	3.0	0.8	0.8	1.4	46.3	16.7	0.1	12.0	17.5	0.0
	2010	(e)1 013	31.0	28.2	27.7	1.2	0.8	0.7	0.2	55.6	14.4	0.8	16.7	23.7	0.0

For sources and notes, see end of table.

Pour les sources et les notes, se reporter à la fin du tableau.

Origin / Origine Destination	Year Année	World (millions of dollars) (1) Monde (millions de dollars) (1)	Developed economies Économies développées						Transition economies Économies en transition	Developing economies Économies en développement					
			Total	Europe		USA États-Unis	Japan Japon	Other Autres		Total	Africa Afrique	America Amérique	Eastern, Southern and South-Eastern Asia Asie orientale, méridionale et du Sud-Est	Western Asia Asie occiden-tale	Oceania Océanie
				Total	EU UE										
			Percentage / En pourcentage												
Sierra Leone	1995	(e)247	62.1	52.7	50.7	8.0	0.9	0.5	0.3	35.0	16.2	1.1	17.3	0.4	0.0
	2005	(e)606	53.4	43.6	43.4	6.9	1.3	1.6	0.7	41.8	19.8	2.2	17.8	2.0	0.0
	2010	(e)1 016	34.1	24.3	24.1	6.6	1.0	2.1	0.2	60.9	25.5	2.1	29.8	3.5	0.0
Singapore - Singapour (2)	1995	124 400	53.7	15.3	13.8	15.1	21.1	2.2	0.3	46.0	0.5	0.9	38.5	6.0	0.0
	2005	200 197	36.8	13.0	11.7	11.7	9.6	2.2	0.5	62.0	0.6	1.0	51.4	9.0	0.0
	2010	310 885	35.4	14.2	12.3	11.5	7.9	1.8	1.3	62.8	0.3	2.3	51.3	8.8	0.0
Slovakia - Slovaquie	1995	9 648	74.8	70.3	68.4	2.5	1.5	0.5	19.3	5.4	0.7	1.1	3.3	0.3	0.0
	2005	34 531	80.5	78.5	77.8	0.8	1.1	0.1	13.1	6.3	0.1	0.2	5.6	0.4	0.0
	2010	64 995	76.5	74.9	74.4	0.4	1.0	0.1	11.1	12.4	0.3	0.1	11.3	0.6	0.0
Slovenia - Slovénie	1995	9 645	84.7	79.1	76.6	3.0	1.6	0.9	9.8	5.5	1.2	0.9	3.0	0.3	0.0
	2005	20 287	83.2	80.8	79.4	0.9	0.8	0.8	9.1	6.9	0.9	1.0	2.9	2.1	0.0
	2010	30 061	72.0	69.3	67.9	1.3	0.4	1.1	11.0	15.5	1.3	1.9	9.0	3.3	0.0
Solomon Islands - Îles Salomon	1995	(e)156	65.7	3.0	3.0	1.9	10.1	50.7	0.0	27.6	0.2	0.0	24.8	0.0	2.6
	2005	(e)210	39.0	3.5	3.5	1.2	3.8	30.6	0.0	47.0	0.6	0.1	38.0	0.0	8.3
	2010	(e)400	40.5	0.9	0.9	1.4	3.3	34.9	0.0	48.3	0.6	0.0	39.2	0.0	8.4
Somalia - Somalie	1995	(e)245	16.1	11.6	11.5	3.6	0.4	0.5	0.0	75.6	36.8	7.1	14.2	17.5	0.0
	2005	(e)616	4.5	2.7	2.6	1.6	0.0	0.2	0.6	81.6	41.1	8.0	14.5	17.9	0.0
	2010	(e)1 284	2.4	2.1	2.1	0.1	0.0	0.2	0.4	84.7	41.3	5.4	21.7	16.3	0.0
South Africa - Afrique du Sud	1995	(e)27 451	70.6	47.1	44.7	10.6	9.6	3.3	0.1	26.1	3.3	2.9	18.6	1.4	0.0
	2005	55 033	57.7	39.6	38.1	7.9	6.8	3.5	0.3	41.2	4.6	4.0	24.9	7.7	0.1
	2010	80 139	49.2	33.6	32.1	7.3	5.3	3.0	0.2	50.4	7.8	3.8	32.2	6.5	0.1
Spain - Espagne	1995	115 502	79.2	68.3	66.2	0.4	3.3	1.3	1.5	18.7	5.7	4.2	6.9	1.8	0.0
	2005	289 130	72.2	66.4	64.1	2.6	2.0	1.1	2.8	24.4	7.5	4.6	9.0	3.3	0.0
	2010	310 998	65.5	60.3	58.2	3.1	1.2	1.0	3.2	31.2	9.0	5.5	12.7	3.9	0.1
Sri Lanka	1995	4 481	40.8	21.8	19.7	3.9	11.1	4.0	0.2	58.7	1.8	2.9	48.7	5.3	0.0
	2005	8 863	23.4	13.2	11.9	2.3	4.3	3.6	0.1	76.4	0.8	1.2	68.3	6.1	0.0
	2010	(e)15 473	21.6	10.2	9.6	1.3	4.0	5.6	1.1	76.7	0.5	1.4	70.5	4.2	0.0
Sudan - Soudan	1995	(e)1 263	44.0	37.2	35.7	3.8	2.6	0.4	0.1	56.0	22.1	0.1	20.1	13.6	0.0
	2005	6 690	29.7	18.1	17.3	1.9	5.1	4.6	2.3	66.7	8.1	2.8	33.1	22.7	0.0
	2010	(e)9 812	21.6	15.1	14.6	1.3	1.0	4.1	3.3	71.3	15.5	1.2	35.5	19.1	0.0
Suriname	1995	586	70.1	25.1	24.3	42.3	2.1	0.5	0.0	29.9	0.6	23.5	5.7	0.0	0.0
	2005	(e)915	65.1	29.4	29.1	29.3	5.2	1.3	0.0	34.9	0.1	22.2	12.2	0.4	0.0
	2010	(e)1 492	58.0	24.8	24.7	26.7	5.5	0.9	0.0	42.0	0.1	27.8	13.9	0.2	0.0
Swaziland	1995	(e)1 054	8.4	6.7	6.6	0.6	1.0	0.1	0.0	91.5	86.5	0.1	4.8	0.1	0.0
	2005	1 656	3.9	2.8	2.8	0.7	0.3	0.1	..	96.1	86.6	0.3	8.8	0.3	..
	2010	(e)1 481	25.2	15.0	14.1	7.1	2.3	0.8	0.7	74.5	49.5	2.7	21.5	0.8	..
Sweden - Suède	1995	64 568	87.3	78.0	68.7	5.4	2.9	0.9	0.8	7.1	0.5	1.2	4.9	0.5	0.0
	2005	111 594	86.0	79.3	70.4	3.6	2.3	0.9	3.7	10.3	0.5	1.4	7.2	1.1	0.0
	2010	146 902	82.4	77.3	67.9	3.1	1.3	0.8	5.2	12.4	0.6	1.4	9.4	0.9	0.0
Switzerland - Suisse	1995	80 051	91.6	81.1	80.7	6.4	3.2	1.0	0.6	7.7	1.3	1.1	4.6	0.7	0.0
	2005	126 522	88.8	80.4	80.2	5.6	1.9	1.0	0.9	10.2	2.3	0.9	5.7	1.2	0.0
	2010	176 163	86.1	77.8	77.6	5.3	2.0	1.0	1.9	12.0	1.2	1.2	8.4	1.2	0.0
Syrian Arab Republic - République arabe syrienne	1995	4 709	52.3	40.9	40.2	6.8	4.4	0.3	9.1	21.6	2.8	2.5	5.7	10.6	0.0
	2005	(e)14 960	30.6	27.0	26.1	1.2	1.9	0.6	8.9	60.5	4.3	2.6	20.5	33.1	0.0
	2010	(e)26 726	22.2	18.7	17.6	2.1	0.9	0.5	8.0	69.7	6.6	3.5	25.2	34.4	0.0
Tajikistan - Tadjikistan	1995	810	38.8	35.0	27.6	3.1	0.0	0.7	59.0	2.2	1.0	0.0	0.7	0.5	0.0
	2005	1 330	17.5	16.1	15.4	0.9	0.4	0.1	66.2	16.3	0.0	2.3	10.5	3.5	0.0
	2010	2 655	14.8	10.1	9.8	3.6	0.1	1.1	59.2	25.9	0.2	2.7	18.6	4.6	0.0
Thailand - Thaïlande	1995	80 478	57.5	17.2	15.7	10.6	26.9	2.8	0.0	28.6	0.8	1.4	23.6	2.8	0.0
	2005	118 143	43.6	10.3	9.1	7.4	22.0	3.9	1.6	53.2	1.4	1.7	37.5	12.4	0.2
	2010	184 613	41.5	10.6	7.6	5.9	20.8	4.2	2.6	54.6	0.9	1.8	40.6	11.1	0.1
TFYR of Macedonia - LERY de Macédoine	1995	1 712	72.6	67.1	66.0	3.4	0.9	1.2	9.7	8.3	0.4	1.5	2.6	3.9	..
	2005	3 225	60.0	56.8	54.8	1.4	0.7	1.1	27.6	12.4	0.3	1.8	6.7	3.6	0.0
	2010	5 451	58.4	55.0	53.1	1.9	0.8	0.7	23.5	17.7	0.6	2.0	10.3	4.8	0.0
Timor-Leste	2005	(e)112	25.1	8.1	8.1	17.0	0.0	0.0	0.0	74.9	0.0	0.0	74.9	0.0	..
	2010	(e)298	0.6	0.1	0.1	0.5	0.0	0.0	0.0	99.4	0.1	0.0	99.3	0.0	..

For sources and notes, see end of table.

Pour les sources et les notes, se reporter à la fin du tableau.

Origin / Origine — Destination	Year / Année	World (millions of dollars) (1) / Monde (millions de dollars) (1)	Developed economies / Économies développées						Transition economies / Économies en transition	Developing economies / Économies en développement					
			Total	Europe Total	Europe EU / UE	USA / États-Unis	Japan / Japon	Other / Autres		Total	Africa / Afrique	America / Amérique	Eastern, Southern and South-Eastern Asia / Asie orientale, méridionale et du Sud-Est	Western Asia / Asie occidentale	Oceania / Océanie
			Percentage / En pourcentage												
Togo	1998	304	60.0	66.6	55.5	5.8	3.8	2.5	0.0	31.0	20.8	1.6	7.9	0.7	0.0
	2005	590	47.8	43.1	42.6	1.2	1.8	1.7	2.7	46.2	17.7	2.9	22.1	0.1	0.0
	2010	(e)3 234	28.2	21.0	20.1	5.8	0.8	0.6	0.4	70.7	6.9	2.5	59.9	1.6	0.0
Tokelau - Tokélaou	2005	(e)0	96.1	44.7	44.7	51.4	0.0	0.0	..	3.9	0.6	0.1	2.4	..	0.8
Tonga	1995	77	82.1	0.1	0.1	10.4	5.8	66.8	0.0	7.5	0.0	0.0	0.0	0.0	7.5
	2005	(e)128	60.2	5.4	5.4	8.4	2.4	11.0	0.0	39.8	0.0	0.0	10.4	0.0	20.3
	2010	(e)209	53.3	1.0	1.0	10.9	11.0	30.4	0.0	46.7	3.2	0.3	9.4	0.1	33.7
Trinidad and Tobago - Trinité-et-Tobago	1995	1 968	70.9	18.3	17.3	44.6	2.8	5.2	0.1	25.8	0.9	19.8	5.0	0.1	0.0
	2005	(e)5 253	54.1	14.3	14.0	30.1	6.0	3.7	0.4	45.4	6.8	31.5	7.0	0.1	0.0
	2010	(e)6 497	52.7	10.1	9.8	32.6	2.8	7.2	1.1	46.1	8.7	26.4	10.6	0.4	0.0
Tunisia - Tunisie	1995	8 032	81.2	73.4	71.9	4.9	1.8	1.1	0.0	12.9	6.2	1.4	2.7	2.7	0.0
	2005	13 327	74.4	70.0	68.9	2.5	1.6	0.3	4.6	18.7	6.3	2.4	5.9	4.1	0.0
	2010	(e)23 809	70.7	67.0	66.0	2.6	0.6	0.5	3.9	24.2	7.5	1.7	10.0	4.9	0.0
Turkey - Turquie	1995	35 766	69.5	52.9	50.4	10.4	3.9	2.2	9.4	20.9	3.9	2.9	9.0	5.1	0.0
	2005	116 579	57.6	48.9	45.1	4.6	2.7	1.3	15.0	26.6	5.2	1.7	17.0	2.7	0.0
	2010	185 545	51.0	41.1	38.9	6.6	1.8	1.5	16.9	31.1	3.5	1.9	22.5	3.2	0.0
Turkmenistan - Turkménistan	1995	1 364	27.0	20.6	19.9	3.9	0.6	2.0	54.6	18.2	0.0	0.0	5.1	13.0	0.0
	2005	(e)2 627	30.8	19.0	17.2	9.9	0.6	1.3	38.0	30.9	0.0	0.1	10.8	20.0	0.0
	2010	(e)5 899	20.4	18.6	16.9	0.7	0.5	0.6	27.4	52.0	0.0	0.1	21.6	30.4	0.0
Turks and Caicos Islands - Îles Turques et Caïques	2005	304	98.3	..	..	98.3	0.0	0.0	0.0	1.7	0.0	1.7	0.0	0.0	..
Tuvalu	1995	(e)6	52.8	10.1	10.1	3.8	2.3	36.5	0.0	47.2	0.0	5.0	2.3	0.0	39.9
	2005	(e)13	41.2	14.7	14.6	0.0	16.3	10.2	0.1	58.7	0.3	0.0	18.4	0.0	40.0
	2010	(e)16	53.9	0.1	0.1	0.5	49.3	4.0	0.0	46.1	0.0	0.0	11.9	0.0	34.2
Uganda - Ouganda	1995	(e)872	41.8	31.3	30.6	2.8	6.6	1.2	0.0	58.2	40.3	0.1	14.9	2.8	0.0
	2005	2 054	33.3	19.4	18.9	3.8	7.1	2.9	0.6	66.1	36.2	1.6	19.0	9.4	0.0
	2010	(e)3 320	28.6	19.1	18.6	3.1	5.9	0.5	1.9	69.5	28.2	0.5	20.3	20.5	0.0
Ukraine	1995	(e)20 077	29.9	28.0	27.5	1.2	0.2	0.5	45.7	3.5	0.5	0.3	1.7	1.0	0.0
	2005	36 154	39.0	34.8	33.7	2.0	1.5	0.7	47.2	13.7	1.2	1.3	9.3	1.8	0.0
	2010	(e)59 642	40.7	36.3	35.0	2.5	1.0	0.9	38.8	19.6	1.5	1.5	14.2	2.4	0.0
United Arab Emirates - Émirats arabes unis	1995	20 984	55.3	34.9	33.4	8.4	9.9	2.1	0.3	42.9	1.2	1.0	33.8	6.9	0.0
	2005	(e)101 359	50.8	34.7	33.3	9.2	5.3	1.7	1.7	46.5	1.7	1.3	35.4	8.2	0.0
	2010	(e)170 831	37.2	22.8	21.2	7.5	4.7	2.2	1.1	60.5	1.9	1.6	48.5	8.5	0.0
United Kingdom - Royaume-Uni	1995	262 511	79.6	58.7	52.8	12.2	5.8	2.9	0.7	15.9	2.1	1.9	10.5	1.3	0.1
	2005	482 622	72.1	57.2	50.8	8.7	3.3	3.0	2.2	23.0	3.3	1.9	14.9	2.8	0.0
	2010	539 063	69.3	59.6	52.5	5.8	1.7	2.2	1.6	24.1	3.0	2.5	16.4	2.3	0.0
United Republic of Tanzania - République-Unie de Tanzanie	1995	(e)1 879	36.4	25.2	24.4	3.9	6.3	1.0	0.0	60.2	25.8	0.4	20.4	13.6	0.0
	2005	(e)3 564	29.3	21.3	20.7	3.0	2.9	2.1	1.6	64.5	23.6	1.4	24.9	14.6	0.0
	2010	(e)8 013	21.2	12.5	12.0	2.2	4.1	2.3	0.9	74.0	17.2	1.1	43.9	11.9	0.0
United States - États-Unis	1995	771 214	56.8	19.6	18.1	..	16.5	20.7	0.7	42.5	2.1	14.0	24.6	1.8	0.0
	2005	1 732 540	46.3	19.7	18.5	..	8.2	18.5	1.2	52.5	3.9	17.4	28.0	3.1	0.0
	2010	1 968 140	40.2	18.0	16.6	..	6.3	15.9	1.7	58.2	4.4	18.7	31.9	3.0	0.0
Uruguay	1995	2 867	36.3	22.4	21.4	9.9	2.6	1.4	0.5	62.8	1.5	52.2	8.1	0.9	0.0
	2005	3 879	19.8	10.9	10.4	6.7	1.1	1.0	8.1	72.1	8.7	51.9	11.4	0.1	0.0
	2010	(e)11 960	24.1	12.9	11.6	9.0	1.0	1.3	0.5	75.3	7.1	48.5	19.4	0.3	0.0
Uzbekistan - Ouzbékistan	1995	(e)3 030	30.1	24.5	24.0	2.3	3.0	0.3	51.8	18.1	0.0	0.2	15.4	2.5	0.0
	2005	(e)3 552	27.5	23.7	22.8	2.3	1.1	0.4	43.1	29.4	0.1	0.2	24.3	4.7	0.0
	2010	(e)8 680	24.3	21.4	20.1	1.3	1.0	0.6	36.7	39.0	0.0	0.3	34.9	3.8	0.0
Vanuatu	1995	(e)151	76.9	7.6	7.5	0.8	40.9	27.6	0.0	22.3	1.1	0.1	14.9	0.0	6.2
	2005	(e)268	58.6	12.2	12.2	3.7	16.6	26.0	0.0	39.4	1.3	0.2	25.4	0.1	12.4
	2010	(e)984	20.4	1.9	1.9	2.1	5.2	11.2	0.0	78.5	0.2	0.0	71.6	0.1	6.6
Venezuela (Bolivarian Rep. of) - Venezuela (Rép. bolivarienne du)	1995	10 796	71.1	19.1	18.1	42.6	4.4	5.0	0.1	28.3	0.3	24.2	3.7	0.2	0.0
	2005	21 855	51.8	14.9	13.8	31.5	3.3	2.1	0.1	46.0	0.2	39.2	6.4	0.2	0.0
	2010	30 744	50.0	15.0	13.5	31.7	1.4	2.0	0.4	48.1	0.1	35.2	12.4	0.4	0.0
Viet Nam	1995	8 359	24.2	10.1	9.2	1.6	11.0	1.6	1.8	64.9	0.1	0.2	64.3	0.3	0.0
	2005	36 761	25.2	9.5	7.0	2.3	11.1	2.2	2.7	71.6	0.5	1.3	68.2	1.6	0.0
	2010	(e)101 268	21.8	6.7	6.1	4.0	8.9	2.3	1.6	75.0	0.2	1.6	72.3	0.9	0.0

For sources and notes, see end of table.

Pour les sources et les notes, se reporter à la fin du tableau.

Origin / Origine	Year Année	World (millions of dollars) (1) Monde (millions de dollars) (1)	Developed economies Économies développées						Transition economies Économies en transition	Developing economies Économies en développement					
			Total	Europe		USA États-Unis	Japan Japon	Other Autres		Total	Africa Afrique	America Amérique	Eastern, Southern and South-Eastern Asia Asie orientale, méridionale et du Sud-Est	Western Asia Asie occiden-tale	Oceania Océanie
				Total	EU UE										
Destination			Percentage / En pourcentage												
Wallis and Futuna Islands - Îles Wallis-et-Futuna	2005	(e)51	64.4	42.9	42.9	1.1		20.4	0.0	35.6	0.0	0.0	0.8	0.0	34.7
Yemen - Yémen	1995	1 587	36.6	24.3	24.1	7.6	3.9	0.7	0.5	61.4	4.6	3.6	20.5	32.7	0.0
	2005	4 800	31.5	23.7	15.1	4.5	2.0	1.3	1.2	66.3	5.4	5.1	15.5	40.3	0.0
	2010	(e)10 657	24.6	14.2	13.6	4.1	3.1	3.1	2.7	71.7	8.1	5.5	29.0	31.1	0.0
Zambia - Zambie	1995	782	34.0	21.5	20.3	3.6	5.8	3.2	0.0	66.0	44.6	0.4	4.7	16.2	0.0
	2005	2 566	28.2	23.1	22.4	1.6	1.6	1.8	0.0	71.8	59.0	0.4	8.5	3.9	0.0
	2010	5 218	13.9	9.6	9.2	1.4	1.6	1.3	0.0	86.1	63.9	0.0	10.6	11.5	0.0
Zimbabwe	1995	2 726	41.0	27.4	25.6	4.5	7.3	1.8	0.1	51.4	42.8	2.4	5.6	0.6	0.0
	2005	2 069	11.3	7.7	7.1	1.4	1.3	0.8	0.0	79.0	66.7	0.2	6.5	5.6	0.0
	2010	(e)4 042	9.4	6.4	6.2	1.8	0.7	0.5	0.2	86.3	69.9	0.3	13.0	3.0	0.0

Sources:
- UNCTAD secretariat calculations
- UN DESA Statistics Division, *COMTRADE* database
- IMF, *Direction of Trade Statistics*

Notes:

(1) Include unspecified destinations.
(2) Imports have considerable amount of re-exports.
(3) Estimates. France including French Guiana, Guadeloupe, Martinique, Monaco and Reunion (and excluding intra trade).

Sources :
- Estimations du secrétariat de la CNUCED
- ONU DAES Division de statistique, base de données *COMTRADE*
- FMI, *Direction of Trade Statistics*

Notes :

(1) Y compris des destinations non-spécifiées.
(2) Les données des importations ont une part importante de réexportations.
(3) Estimation. Les données sont dérivées des déclarations rapportées par la France métropolitaine et les départements d'outre-mer par agrégation diminuée des flux intra.

2

Product group	Year / Année	World (1) / Monde (1)	Developed economies - Économies développées							Transition economies / Économies en transition
			Total	Europe		Canada	USA / États-Unis	Japan / Japon	Other developed countries / Autres économies développées	
				Total	EU / UE					
Millions of dollars										
All products	1995	5 121 450	3 478 681	2 161 628	2 035 835	165 112	754 954	303 487	93 501	90 351
	2005	10 456 609	6 915 919	4 308 410	4 093 426	305 914	1 631 910	487 723	181 962	260 222
	2010	15 147 000	8 725 210	5 600 320	5 279 157	382 049	1 847 750	636 797	268 291	419 753
Share by destination (percentage)										
All products	1995	100.0	67.9	42.2	39.8	3.2	14.7	5.9	1.8	1.9
	2005	100.0	66.1	41.2	39.1	2.9	15.6	4.7	1.7	2.5
	2010	100.0	57.6	36.9	34.9	2.5	12.2	4.2	1.8	2.8
All food items	1995	100.0	67.3	47.1	45.5	2.0	7.5	9.6	1.1	4.4
(SITC 0 + 1 + 22 + 4)	2005	100.0	68.6	48.4	46.9	2.6	9.9	6.4	1.4	4.4
	2010	100.0	59.8	43.2	41.8	2.5	7.9	4.8	1.5	4.8
Agricultural raw materials	1995	100.0	67.8	41.2	39.3	2.1	11.5	12.0	1.0	0.8
(SITC 2 - 22 - 27 - 28)	2005	100.0	61.8	39.4	38.0	2.3	12.9	6.3	0.9	1.8
	2010	100.0	50.3	35.4	34.2	1.6	7.5	4.9	0.9	2.1
Ores, metals, precious stones	1995	100.0	69.0	42.0	37.4	2.5	11.6	10.1	2.7	1.2
and non-monetary gold	2005	100.0	60.3	37.5	33.4	2.3	11.4	6.1	3.0	1.4
(SITC 27 + 28 + 68 + 667 + 971)	2010	100.0	51.4	33.9	28.0	2.2	7.8	5.3	2.2	1.0
Fuels (SITC 3)	1995	100.0	68.5	35.4	33.4	1.3	17.1	13.5	1.2	2.9
	2005	100.0	65.6	33.9	32.3	1.6	19.4	9.4	1.3	1.3
	2010	100.0	56.3	31.1	29.9	1.5	14.4	7.9	1.4	1.2
Manufactured goods	1995	100.0	67.6	41.7	39.2	3.7	15.9	4.4	1.9	1.5
(SITC 5 to 8 less 667 and 68)	2005	100.0	66.0	41.6	39.5	3.3	15.8	3.5	1.8	2.5
	2010	100.0	58.2	37.5	35.5	2.8	12.9	3.2	1.9	3.1
Share by major product group (percentage)										
All products	1995	100.0	100.0	100.0	100.0	100.0	100.0	100.0	100.0	100.0
	2005	100.0	100.0	100.0	100.0	100.0	100.0	100.0	100.0	100.0
	2010	100.0	100.0	100.0	100.0	100.0	100.0	100.0	100.0	100.0
All food items	1995	9.0	8.9	10.0	10.3	5.7	4.6	14.5	5.5	20.3
(SITC 0 + 1 + 22 + 4)	2005	6.5	6.8	7.7	7.8	5.7	4.1	8.9	5.1	11.6
	2010	7.5	7.8	8.8	9.1	7.6	4.9	8.6	6.2	13.1
Agricultural raw materials	1995	2.7	2.7	2.6	2.7	1.7	2.1	5.4	1.5	1.1
(SITC 2 - 22 - 27 - 28)	2005	1.6	1.5	1.5	1.5	1.2	1.3	2.1	0.8	1.1
	2010	1.6	1.4	1.5	1.6	1.0	1.0	1.8	0.8	1.2
Ores, metals, precious stones	1995	4.5	4.6	4.5	4.2	3.5	3.6	7.7	6.8	2.7
and non-monetary gold	2005	4.7	4.2	4.2	4.0	3.7	3.4	6.1	8.0	2.6
(SITC 27 + 28 + 68 + 667 + 971)	2010	6.4	5.7	5.9	5.1	5.5	4.1	8.1	7.9	2.3
Fuels (SITC 3)	1995	7.3	7.4	6.1	6.1	3.0	8.5	16.7	4.9	11.2
	2005	14.1	14.0	11.6	11.6	7.8	17.5	28.3	10.6	7.2
	2010	15.4	15.0	13.0	13.2	9.0	18.2	28.8	12.2	6.9
Manufactured goods	1995	72.7	72.4	71.9	71.8	83.2	78.4	54.0	77.4	56.3
(SITC 5 to 8 less 667 and 68)	2005	70.4	70.2	71.0	71.1	78.6	71.4	52.8	72.1	71.3
	2010	66.2	66.9	67.2	67.5	73.2	70.0	49.8	69.7	74.7

Sources:
- UNCTAD secretariat calculations based on UN DESA Statistics Division's data

Notes:

(1) Includes special category exports, ship stores and bunkers and other exports of minor importance whose destination could not be determined.

(2) It is recognized that the structure of trade and partner distribution for certain countries and years might vary. In this regard, reader should know the coverage and limitations of the main principal data used in this table. For further information, please visit http://comtrade.un.org/db/help/uReadMeFirst.aspx.

2.2.A   Structure des exportations par partenaires et groupes de produits
Monde

Total	Africa / Afrique	America / Amérique	Asia / Asie — Total	Eastern, Southern and South-Eastern Asia / Asie orientale, méridionale et du Sud-Est	China / Chine	Western Asia / Asie occidentale	Oceania (2) / Océanie (2)	Major petroleum exporters and gas exporters / Principaux exportateurs de pétrole et de gaz	Major manufactured goods exporters / Principaux exportateurs d'articles manufacturés	Year / Année	Destinations / Groupes de produits
Millions de dollars											
1 460 186	129 498	245 686	1 080 270	956 250	146 996	124 020	4 732	114 764	856 459	1995	**Total tous produits**
3 227 882	250 641	493 319	2 472 237	2 128 834	594 475	343 403	11 685	312 526	1 911 051	2005	
5 904 482	468 903	862 944	4 552 724	3 952 427	1 274 516	600 298	19 911	575 765	3 345 274	2010	
Parts par destinations (en pourcentage)											
28.5	2.5	4.8	21.1	18.7	2.9	2.4	0.1	2.2	16.7	1995	**Total tous produits**
30.9	2.4	4.7	23.6	20.4	5.7	3.3	0.1	3.0	18.3	2005	
39.0	3.1	5.7	30.1	26.1	8.4	4.0	0.1	3.8	22.1	2010	
25.8	4.4	4.8	16.5	13.0	2.3	3.4	0.1	3.9	10.3	1995	Produits alimentaires
26.2	4.2	5.0	16.8	12.6	2.8	4.2	0.2	4.8	10.2	2005	(CTCI 0 + 1 + 22 + 4)
35.1	5.5	5.7	23.8	18.3	5.1	5.5	0.2	6.5	13.4	2010	
30.4	2.4	3.7	24.2	22.2	5.4	2.0	0.0	1.3	19.2	1995	Matières premières
35.9	2.2	3.9	29.6	27.0	13.5	2.6	0.1	1.4	23.4	2005	d'origine agricole
47.5	2.9	4.3	40.2	36.8	20.3	3.4	0.0	2.0	30.8	2010	(CTCI 2 - 22 - 27 - 28)
27.7	1.3	2.3	24.1	22.2	2.5	2.0	0.0	1.4	18.6	1995	Minerais, métaux, pierres
37.0	1.5	2.6	33.0	29.2	9.8	3.8	0.0	2.8	23.1	2005	précieuses et or (non monétaire)
46.8	1.7	2.3	42.7	38.4	17.3	4.3	0.0	2.9	31.0	2010	(CTCI 27 + 28 + 68 + 667 + 971)
25.7	1.9	4.8	18.8	16.9	1.5	1.9	0.1	0.6	13.6	1995	Combustibles (CTCI 3)
29.5	2.2	4.2	22.9	20.7	4.2	2.2	0.1	1.0	16.9	2005	
39.5	2.8	4.7	31.9	29.6	7.5	2.3	0.1	1.4	23.2	2010	
29.6	2.5	5.0	22.0	19.6	3.1	2.4	0.1	2.3	18.0	1995	Articles manufacturés
31.2	2.3	4.9	23.8	20.5	5.9	3.3	0.1	3.3	19.0	2005	(CTCI 5 à 8 moins 667 et 68)
38.5	3.0	6.2	29.2	25.0	8.0	4.1	0.1	4.2	22.0	2010	
Parts par principaux groupes de produits (en pourcentage)											
100.0	100.0	100.0	100.0	100.0	100.0	100.0	100.0	100.0	100.0	1995	**Total tous produits**
100.0	100.0	100.0	100.0	100.0	100.0	100.0	100.0	100.0	100.0	2005	
100.0	100.0	100.0	100.0	100.0	100.0	100.0	100.0	100.0	100.0	2010	
8.1	15.6	8.9	7.0	6.3	7.1	12.8	14.5	15.7	5.5	1995	Produits alimentaires
5.5	11.5	6.9	4.6	4.0	3.2	8.3	10.3	10.5	3.6	2005	(CTCI 0 + 1 + 22 + 4)
6.8	13.5	7.5	6.0	5.3	4.6	10.4	10.0	12.9	4.6	2010	
2.9	2.6	2.1	3.1	3.2	5.1	2.2	1.0	1.6	3.1	1995	Matières premières
1.8	1.5	1.3	2.0	2.1	3.7	1.3	1.0	0.8	2.0	2005	d'origine agricole
1.9	1.5	1.2	2.1	2.3	3.8	1.4	0.4	0.8	2.2	2010	(CTCI 2 - 22 - 27 - 28)
4.4	2.4	2.1	5.2	5.4	3.9	3.7	0.6	2.8	5.0	1995	Minerais, métaux, pierres
5.6	2.8	2.5	6.5	6.7	8.0	5.3	0.5	4.3	5.9	2005	précieuses et or (non monétaire)
7.7	3.6	2.5	9.1	9.4	13.1	6.9	0.6	4.9	9.0	2010	(CTCI 27 + 28 + 68 + 667 + 971)
6.6	5.6	7.4	6.5	6.6	3.9	5.7	8.5	1.5	6.0	1995	Combustibles (CTCI 3)
13.5	12.8	12.7	13.7	14.3	10.5	9.4	18.6	4.6	13.0	2005	
15.6	13.8	12.6	16.3	17.5	13.8	8.8	14.2	5.5	16.2	2010	
75.5	71.4	76.5	75.7	76.2	77.6	72.0	72.3	74.9	78.1	1995	Articles manufacturés
71.0	68.4	73.6	70.8	70.7	72.5	71.4	63.7	76.6	73.3	2005	(CTCI 5 à 8 moins 667 et 68)
65.5	64.7	72.5	64.2	63.5	62.6	69.1	66.2	73.2	65.9	2010	

Sources :
- Calculs du secrétariat de la CNUCED sur la base des données de ONU DAES Division de statistique

Notes :

(1) Y compris les exportations de catégorie spéciale, approvisionnements des navires et combustibles de soute et autres exportations de moindre importance dont la destination n'a pas pu être déterminée.

(2) Il est reconnu que la structure du commerce et la distribution au niveau partenaire pour certains pays et sur certaines années peuvent varier. À cet égard, le lecteur devrait connaître la couverture ainsi que les limites des données principales utilisées dans ce tableau. Pour de plus amples renseignements, veuillez visiter http://comtrade.un.org/db/help/uReadMeFirst.aspx.

2.2.A Import structure by partner and product group
World

Origin / Product group	Year / Année	World (1) / Monde (1)	Developed economies - Économies développées							Transition economies / Économies en transition
			Total	Europe		Canada	USA / États-Unis	Japan / Japon	Other developed countries / Autres économies développées	
				Total	EU / UE					
Millions of dollars										
All products	1995	5 188 806	3 542 717	2 142 882	2 003 328	197 469	635 273	478 671	88 421	124 513
	2005	10 715 138	6 223 507	4 073 345	3 816 910	362 205	936 790	666 339	184 829	375 414
	2010	15 306 693	8 009 033	5 260 010	4 871 520	399 913	1 235 922	817 735	307 421	604 199
Share by origin (percentage)										
All products	1995	100.0	68.3	41.3	38.6	3.8	12.2	9.2	1.7	2.4
	2005	100.0	58.1	38.0	35.6	3.4	8.7	6.2	1.7	3.5
	2010	100.0	52.3	34.3	31.8	2.5	8.1	5.3	2.0	3.9
All food items	1995	100.0	64.5	42.7	41.0	3.5	13.8	0.5	4.0	2.0
(SITC 0 + 1 + 22 + 4)	2005	100.0	62.0	43.4	41.7	3.6	9.9	0.4	4.6	2.6
	2010	100.0	57.8	40.0	37.9	3.4	10.1	0.5	3.9	2.9
Agricultural raw materials	1995	100.0	65.7	29.7	28.6	12.3	16.6	1.7	5.4	5.3
(SITC 2 - 22 - 27 - 28)	2005	100.0	62.1	33.2	32.5	10.2	12.5	1.8	4.3	6.4
	2010	100.0	56.8	31.4	30.7	6.6	12.4	2.3	4.1	5.8
Ores, metals, precious stones	1995	100.0	60.4	34.7	29.0	6.4	8.5	2.4	8.3	7.5
and non-monetary gold	2005	100.0	52.5	29.8	24.9	4.7	5.6	2.5	10.0	7.7
(SITC 27 + 28 + 68 + 667 + 971)	2010	100.0	48.9	26.1	20.1	3.9	5.1	2.9	10.9	5.5
Fuels (SITC 3)	1995	100.0	30.3	19.4	13.9	4.4	3.2	0.5	2.8	8.9
	2005	100.0	28.7	19.0	14.2	4.9	2.2	0.3	2.3	12.4
	2010	100.0	26.7	16.0	12.7	3.9	3.3	0.6	2.9	14.1
Manufactured goods	1995	100.0	73.0	43.7	41.3	3.2	13.2	12.2	0.7	1.2
(SITC 5 to 8 less 667 and 68)	2005	100.0	63.3	41.5	39.7	2.7	10.0	8.4	0.7	1.4
	2010	100.0	57.2	38.1	36.2	1.8	9.1	7.4	0.7	1.4
Share by major product group (percentage)										
All products	1995	100.0	100.0	100.0	100.0	100.0	100.0	100.0	100.0	100.0
	2005	100.0	100.0	100.0	100.0	100.0	100.0	100.0	100.0	100.0
	2010	100.0	100.0	100.0	100.0	100.0	100.0	100.0	100.0	100.0
All food items	1995	9.1	8.6	9.4	9.7	8.4	10.3	0.5	21.2	7.6
(SITC 0 + 1 + 22 + 4)	2005	6.7	7.2	7.7	7.9	7.1	7.7	0.5	18.0	5.0
	2010	7.6	8.3	8.8	9.0	9.9	9.5	0.6	14.7	5.5
Agricultural raw materials	1995	2.9	2.8	2.1	2.1	9.3	3.9	0.5	9.1	6.4
(SITC 2 - 22 - 27 - 28)	2005	1.7	1.8	1.4	1.5	5.0	2.4	0.5	4.2	3.0
	2010	1.6	1.7	1.5	1.5	4.1	2.5	0.7	3.3	2.3
Ores, metals, precious stones	1995	5.0	4.4	4.2	3.7	8.3	3.4	1.3	24.2	15.5
and non-monetary gold	2005	4.9	4.4	3.8	3.4	6.7	3.2	1.9	28.3	10.8
(SITC 27 + 28 + 68 + 667 + 971)	2010	6.4	6.0	4.9	4.1	9.7	4.1	3.4	34.8	8.9
Fuels (SITC 3)	1995	7.3	3.2	3.4	2.6	8.3	1.9	0.4	12.1	27.0
	2005	13.4	6.6	6.7	5.4	19.3	3.5	0.6	18.3	47.6
	2010	15.4	7.9	7.2	6.2	23.6	6.4	1.6	22.3	55.2
Manufactured goods	1995	72.2	77.2	76.4	77.3	61.3	77.7	95.4	31.3	34.6
(SITC 5 to 8 less 667 and 68)	2005	70.7	77.1	77.2	78.9	57.2	81.2	95.1	28.7	28.4
	2010	66.8	73.0	74.2	76.0	48.2	75.2	92.6	23.5	24.0

Sources:
- UNCTAD secretariat calculations based on UN DESA Statistics Division's data

Notes:

(1) Includes special category exports, ship stores and bunkers and other exports of minor importance whose destination could not be determined.

(2) It is recognized that the structure of trade and partner distribution for certain countries and years might vary. In this regard, reader should know the coverage and limitations of the main principal data used in this table. For further information, please visit
http://comtrade.un.org/db/help/uReadMeFirst.aspx.

2.2.A Structure des importations par partenaires et groupes de produits
Monde

Developing economies - Économies en développement							Oceania (2) Océanie (2)	Major petroleum exporters and gas exporters / Principaux exportateurs de pétrole et de gaz	Major manufactured goods exporters / Principaux exportateurs d'articles manufacturés	Year Année	Origines
			Asia / Asie								
Total	Africa Afrique	America Amérique	Total	Eastern, Southern and South-Eastern Asia / Asie orientale, méridionale et du Sud-Est	China Chine	Western Asia Asie occidentale					Groupes de produits
Millions de dollars											
1 429 741	123 386	245 117	1 056 510	924 754	232 547	131 757	4 727	173 926	851 157	1995	Total tous produits
4 034 325	320 568	624 679	3 081 982	2 604 013	1 073 414	477 969	7 097	616 737	2 395 702	2005	
6 621 706	525 530	957 905	5 127 685	4 321 826	1 968 737	805 859	10 578	1 043 009	3 888 298	2010	
Parts par origines (en pourcentage)											
27.6	2.4	4.7	20.4	17.8	4.5	2.5	0.1	3.4	16.4	1995	Total tous produits
37.7	3.0	5.8	28.8	24.3	10.0	4.5	0.1	5.8	22.4	2005	
43.3	3.4	6.3	33.5	28.2	12.9	5.3	0.1	6.8	25.4	2010	
32.2	4.6	12.5	14.9	13.4	2.7	1.5	0.3	0.7	10.3	1995	Produits alimentaires
35.3	3.9	15.2	16.0	13.6	3.7	2.4	0.2	1.0	9.9	2005	(CTCI 0 + 1 + 22 + 4)
39.2	3.9	16.1	18.9	16.0	3.7	2.9	0.2	1.5	10.9	2010	
28.2	4.3	6.4	17.0	16.4	2.3	0.6	0.5	0.6	12.4	1995	Matières premières
31.4	4.6	7.9	18.5	17.7	3.1	0.8	0.4	0.5	12.1	2005	d'origine agricole
37.3	4.3	8.7	23.8	23.0	3.4	0.8	0.4	0.6	14.0	2010	(CTCI 2 - 22 - 27 - 28)
29.5	6.2	9.9	12.7	11.0	1.9	1.7	0.6	1.7	7.4	1995	Minerais, métaux, pierres
39.2	7.4	12.2	19.4	16.1	3.4	3.3	0.4	3.3	9.1	2005	précieuses et or (non monétaire)
45.0	7.0	14.5	23.0	18.4	3.0	4.7	0.5	4.4	9.8	2010	(CTCI 27 + 28 + 68 + 667 + 971)
57.8	11.7	8.3	37.7	14.7	1.5	22.9	0.2	37.8	8.7	1995	Combustibles (CTCI 3)
56.7	12.4	8.8	35.4	13.3	1.2	22.2	0.1	36.5	8.7	2005	
57.1	12.8	7.7	36.6	14.8	1.1	21.8	0.0	36.5	9.0	2010	
24.5	0.8	3.1	20.6	19.8	5.4	0.8	0.0	0.5	19.2	1995	Articles manufacturés
35.0	0.8	3.9	30.2	28.7	13.2	1.6	0.0	0.8	27.7	2005	(CTCI 5 à 8 moins 667 et 68)
41.2	0.9	4.0	36.3	34.3	18.1	2.0	0.0	1.1	33.0	2010	
Parts par principaux groupes de produits (en pourcentage)											
100.0	100.0	100.0	100.0	100.0	100.0	100.0	100.0	100.0	100.0	1995	Total tous produits
100.0	100.0	100.0	100.0	100.0	100.0	100.0	100.0	100.0	100.0	2005	
100.0	100.0	100.0	100.0	100.0	100.0	100.0	100.0	100.0	100.0	2010	
10.7	17.5	24.1	6.7	6.9	5.5	5.2	25.9	2.0	5.7	1995	Produits alimentaires
6.3	8.9	17.6	3.8	3.8	2.5	3.6	22.8	1.2	3.0	2005	(CTCI 0 + 1 + 22 + 4)
6.9	8.7	19.5	4.3	4.3	2.2	4.2	21.1	1.6	3.3	2010	
3.0	5.2	3.9	2.4	2.7	1.5	0.7	15.3	0.5	2.2	1995	Matières premières
1.4	2.6	2.2	1.1	1.2	0.5	0.3	9.7	0.1	0.9	2005	d'origine agricole
1.4	2.0	2.2	1.1	1.3	0.4	0.2	9.2	0.1	0.9	2010	(CTCI 2 - 22 - 27 - 28)
5.3	13.0	10.4	3.1	3.1	2.1	3.4	30.0	2.5	2.2	1995	Minerais, métaux, pierres
5.1	12.0	10.2	3.3	3.2	1.7	3.6	26.3	2.8	2.0	2005	précieuses et or (non monétaire)
6.7	13.1	14.9	4.4	4.2	1.5	5.7	42.4	4.2	2.5	2010	(CTCI 27 + 28 + 68 + 667 + 971)
15.3	35.7	12.8	13.4	6.0	2.5	65.7	13.7	82.1	3.9	1995	Combustibles (CTCI 3)
20.2	55.5	20.2	16.5	7.3	1.7	66.7	15.5	85.2	5.2	2005	
20.4	57.4	18.9	16.9	8.1	1.3	64.1	10.1	82.7	5.5	2010	
64.3	25.6	46.8	73.1	80.1	87.6	24.2	14.4	11.3	84.5	1995	Articles manufacturés
65.8	20.0	47.8	74.4	83.4	93.1	25.0	23.6	9.7	87.6	2005	(CTCI 5 à 8 moins 667 et 68)
63.7	17.4	43.0	72.4	81.1	94.1	25.5	16.5	10.8	86.8	2010	

Sources :
- Calculs du secrétariat de la CNUCED sur la base des données de ONU DAES Division de statistique

Notes :

(1) Y compris les exportations de catégorie spéciale, approvisionnements des navires et combustibles de soute et autres exportations de moindre importance dont la destination n'a pas pu être déterminée.

(2) Il est reconnu que la structure du commerce et la distribution au niveau partenaire pour certains pays et sur certaines années peuvent varier. À cet égard, le lecteur devrait connaître la couverture ainsi que les limites des données principales utilisées dans ce tableau. Pour de plus amples renseignements, veuillez visiter http://comtrade.un.org/db/help/uReadMeFirst.aspx.

2.2.B Export structure by partner and product group
Developing economies

Product group	Year / Année	World (1) / Monde (1)	Developed economies - Économies développées							Transition economies / Économies en transition
			Total	Europe		Canada	USA / États-Unis	Japan / Japon	Other developed countries / Autres économies développées	
				Total	EU / UE					
Millions of dollars										
All products	1995	1 432 450	802 113	279 009	267 769	16 253	318 960	105 141	22 751	13 462
	2005	3 796 590	1 987 328	712 306	692 057	46 987	822 201	335 950	69 884	48 219
	2010	6 869 625	3 774 316	1 083 101	1 033 481	78 446	1 041 440	446 008	125 221	107 739
Share by destination (percentage)										
All products	1995	100.0	56.0	19.5	18.7	1.1	22.3	11.5	1.6	0.9
	2005	100.0	52.3	18.8	18.2	1.2	21.7	8.8	1.8	1.3
	2010	100.0	43.6	17.0	16.2	1.2	16.4	7.0	2.0	1.7
All food items	1995	100.0	55.5	26.8	25.9	0.9	12.7	13.9	1.1	2.8
(SITC 0 + 1 + 22 + 4)	2005	100.0	51.7	25.1	24.6	1.2	14.7	9.2	1.5	4.0
	2010	100.0	40.9	20.3	19.8	1.2	11.5	6.3	1.5	4.0
Agricultural raw materials	1995	100.0	50.8	23.3	22.7	0.6	11.8	14.0	0.9	0.3
(SITC 2 - 22 - 27 - 28)	2005	100.0	47.1	21.9	21.3	1.0	14.1	9.2	0.9	0.7
	2010	100.0	37.4	18.5	18.3	0.9	10.0	7.0	1.0	1.1
Ores, metals, precious stones	1995	100.0	58.1	26.6	23.2	1.2	12.1	16.5	1.7	0.9
and non-monetary gold	2005	100.0	48.7	24.0	20.9	2.0	11.2	9.1	2.4	0.6
(SITC 27 + 28 + 68 + 667 + 971)	2010	100.0	39.7	19.7	14.3	2.1	7.9	7.6	2.5	0.5
Fuels (SITC 3)	1995	100.0	62.7	19.9	19.5	0.8	19.5	20.9	1.7	0.2
	2005	100.0	56.3	16.9	16.7	1.1	21.7	14.7	1.8	0.1
	2010	100.0	44.4	14.0	13.8	1.0	16.1	11.5	1.9	0.1
Manufactured goods	1995	100.0	54.5	17.5	16.9	1.3	25.5	8.5	1.7	0.9
(SITC 5 to 8 less 667 and 68)	2005	100.0	51.7	18.4	18.0	1.2	23.4	6.8	1.9	1.5
	2010	100.0	44.3	17.3	16.8	1.2	18.2	5.6	2.0	2.1
Share by major product group (percentage)										
All products	1995	100.0	100.0	100.0	100.0	100.0	100.0	100.0	100.0	100.0
	2005	100.0	100.0	100.0	100.0	100.0	100.0	100.0	100.0	100.0
	2010	100.0	100.0	100.0	100.0	100.0	100.0	100.0	100.0	100.0
All food items	1995	10.0	9.9	13.8	13.9	7.8	5.7	12.1	7.2	30.1
(SITC 0 + 1 + 22 + 4)	2005	6.0	5.9	8.0	8.1	5.7	4.1	6.3	4.9	19.0
	2010	6.8	6.4	8.1	8.3	6.7	4.8	6.1	5.2	16.2
Agricultural raw materials	1995	2.7	2.5	3.3	3.3	1.5	1.5	3.3	1.6	0.8
(SITC 2 - 22 - 27 - 28)	2005	1.3	1.2	1.5	1.5	1.1	0.8	1.4	0.7	0.7
	2010	1.4	1.2	1.5	1.6	1.0	0.9	1.4	0.7	0.9
Ores, metals, precious stones	1995	5.2	5.4	7.1	6.4	5.4	2.8	7.4	5.6	4.8
and non-monetary gold	2005	5.1	4.7	6.5	5.8	8.4	2.6	5.2	6.5	2.5
(SITC 27 + 28 + 68 + 667 + 971)	2010	6.9	6.3	8.0	6.1	11.6	3.3	7.5	8.7	2.2
Fuels (SITC 3)	1995	15.0	16.8	15.3	15.7	10.1	13.2	27.2	15.8	3.9
	2005	22.7	24.4	20.5	20.8	20.6	22.7	37.8	22.3	1.2
	2010	21.1	21.5	17.3	17.9	17.7	20.7	34.5	19.9	1.0
Manufactured goods	1995	65.9	64.2	59.4	59.6	74.5	75.6	48.9	69.0	59.7
(SITC 5 to 8 less 667 and 68)	2005	64.1	63.3	62.9	63.2	63.3	69.4	49.0	64.5	76.2
	2010	63.1	64.1	64.3	65.4	61.7	70.0	50.1	64.9	79.5

Sources:
- UNCTAD secretariat calculations based on UN DESA Statistics Division's data

Notes:

(1) Includes special category exports, ship stores and bunkers and other exports of minor importance whose destination could not be determined.

(2) It is recognized that the structure of trade and partner distribution for certain countries and years might vary. In this regard, reader should know the coverage and limitations of the main principal data used in this table. For further information, please visit
http://comtrade.un.org/db/help/uReadMeFirst.aspx.

2.2.B Structure des exportations par partenaires et groupes de produits
Économies en développement

Total	Africa / Afrique	America / Amérique	Asia / Asie — Total	Eastern, Southern and South-Eastern Asia / Asie orientale, méridionale et du Sud-Est	China / Chine	Western Asia / Asie occidentale	Oceania (2) / Océanie (2)	Major petroleum exporters and gas exporters / Principaux exportateurs de pétrole et de gaz	Major manufactured goods exporters / Principaux exportateurs d'articles manufacturés	Year / Année	Destinations / Groupes de produits
Millions de dollars											
609 549	48 258	73 533	486 951	445 789	82 728	41 162	807	37 835	374 499	1995	Total tous produits
1 742 759	109 647	181 697	1 447 083	1 308 501	367 635	138 582	5 342	136 974	1 082 928	2005	
3 472 209	241 050	367 191	2 854 289	2 564 006	766 668	290 104	9 671	310 978	1 996 835	2010	
Parts par destinations (en pourcentage)											
42.6	3.4	5.1	34.0	31.1	5.8	2.9	0.1	2.6	26.1	1995	Total tous produits
45.9	2.9	4.8	38.1	34.5	9.7	3.7	0.1	3.6	28.5	2005	
54.6	3.8	5.8	44.9	40.3	12.0	4.6	0.2	4.9	31.4	2010	
41.1	6.4	6.5	28.2	23.1	4.6	5.1	0.1	5.6	15.6	1995	Produits alimentaires
43.9	6.6	6.4	30.8	23.4	5.1	7.4	0.1	8.5	15.1	2005	(CTCI 0 + 1 + 22 + 4)
54.9	8.0	7.3	39.4	30.3	7.5	9.1	0.1	11.3	18.1	2010	
48.5	3.8	4.9	39.9	37.7	9.4	2.2	0.0	1.9	31.1	1995	Matières premières
51.9	2.7	4.4	44.8	42.1	19.7	2.7	0.0	1.8	33.2	2005	d'origine agricole
61.4	2.6	4.7	54.0	50.6	25.0	3.5	0.0	2.2	38.3	2010	(CTCI 2 - 22 - 27 - 28)
40.5	2.1	3.8	34.6	32.2	5.1	2.4	0.0	2.4	27.2	1995	Minerais, métaux, pierres
50.6	2.1	3.6	44.9	39.4	13.4	5.4	0.0	5.0	31.0	2005	précieuses et or (non monétaire)
59.7	2.4	2.9	54.4	48.8	21.4	5.6	0.0	5.2	38.1	2010	(CTCI 27 + 28 + 68 + 667 + 971)
36.0	3.6	5.4	27.0	25.5	3.5	2.4	0.1	0.3	20.0	1995	Combustibles (CTCI 3)
43.1	2.9	5.0	34.9	32.4	6.4	2.5	0.2	1.0	25.7	2005	
55.3	3.3	4.4	47.4	44.9	11.0	2.5	0.2	1.4	33.5	2010	
44.3	3.2	5.0	36.1	33.3	6.6	2.7	0.1	2.8	28.9	1995	Articles manufacturés
46.6	2.6	4.6	39.3	35.9	10.9	3.5	0.1	3.9	30.7	2005	(CTCI 5 à 8 moins 667 et 68)
53.5	3.6	6.3	43.5	38.8	11.6	4.6	0.1	5.4	31.4	2010	
Parts par principaux groupes de produits (en pourcentage)											
100.0	100.0	100.0	100.0	100.0	100.0	100.0	100.0	100.0	100.0	1995	Total tous produits
100.0	100.0	100.0	100.0	100.0	100.0	100.0	100.0	100.0	100.0	2005	
100.0	100.0	100.0	100.0	100.0	100.0	100.0	100.0	100.0	100.0	2010	
9.7	19.0	12.7	8.3	7.4	7.9	17.7	10.9	21.4	6.0	1995	Produits alimentaires
5.7	13.7	8.0	4.8	4.1	3.2	12.2	5.9	14.0	3.2	2005	(CTCI 0 + 1 + 22 + 4)
6.9	14.4	8.7	6.0	5.1	4.2	13.6	6.5	15.8	3.9	2010	
3.1	3.1	2.6	3.2	3.3	4.4	2.1	0.5	1.9	3.3	1995	Matières premières
1.5	1.2	1.2	1.5	1.6	2.7	1.0	0.2	0.6	1.5	2005	d'origine agricole
1.6	1.0	1.2	1.7	1.8	2.9	1.1	0.2	0.6	1.7	2010	(CTCI 2 - 22 - 27 - 28)
4.9	3.2	3.8	5.3	5.4	4.5	4.4	0.5	4.8	5.4	1995	Minerais, métaux, pierres
5.6	3.7	3.8	6.0	5.8	7.0	7.6	0.2	7.0	5.5	2005	précieuses et or (non monétaire)
7.6	4.4	3.5	8.4	8.4	12.3	8.5	0.3	7.4	8.4	2010	(CTCI 27 + 28 + 68 + 667 + 971)
12.6	11.5	15.7	12.3	12.3	6.4	12.4	15.2	1.5	11.5	1995	Combustibles (CTCI 3)
21.3	22.5	23.9	20.8	21.3	14.9	15.8	31.9	6.4	20.5	2005	
21.4	18.3	16.2	22.3	23.5	19.2	11.7	24.1	6.2	22.5	2010	
68.7	62.5	64.4	69.9	70.6	75.9	63.0	68.5	69.9	72.9	1995	Articles manufacturés
65.1	57.3	61.6	66.2	66.7	72.0	61.2	55.7	69.9	68.9	2005	(CTCI 5 à 8 moins 667 et 68)
61.9	60.5	68.5	61.2	60.9	61.0	64.1	56.3	69.8	63.1	2010	

Sources :
- Calculs du secrétariat de la CNUCED sur la base des données de ONU DAES Division de statistique

Notes :

(1) Y compris les exportations de catégorie spéciale, approvisionnements des navires et combustibles de soute et autres exportations de moindre importance dont la destination n'a pas pu être déterminée.

(2) Il est reconnu que la structure du commerce et la distribution au niveau partenaire pour certains pays et sur certaines années peuvent varier. À cet égard, le lecteur devrait connaître la couverture ainsi que les limites des données principales utilisées dans ce tableau. Pour de plus amples renseignements, veuillez visiter http://comtrade.un.org/db/help/uReadMeFirst.aspx.

Origin Product group	Year Année	World (1) Monde (1)	Developed economies - Économies développées							Transition economies Économies on transition
			Total	Europe		Canada	USA États-Unis	Japan Japon	Other developed countries Autres économies développées	
				Total	EU UE					
						Millions of dollars				
All products	1995	1 499 186	887 616	322 961	299 953	19 486	268 552	242 901	33 716	22 388
	2005	3 396 566	1 517 135	602 607	558 896	31 535	427 108	372 945	82 939	76 916
	2010	6 006 060	2 401 106	094 733	081 117	55 061	610 060	541 000	171 000	140 014
						Share by origin (percentage)				
All products	1995	100.0	59.2	21.5	20.0	1.3	17.9	16.2	2.2	1.5
	2005	100.0	44.7	17.7	16.5	0.9	12.6	11.0	2.4	2.3
	2010	100.0	40.1	16.4	14.7	0.9	10.8	9.0	2.9	2.4
All food items	1995	100.0	53.7	19.8	19.0	3.6	22.6	1.5	6.2	0.8
(SITC 0 + 1 + 22 + 4)	2005	100.0	44.0	15.5	14.6	2.7	17.8	1.2	6.9	2.3
	2010	100.0	41.0	13.9	12.7	3.0	17.3	1.0	5.8	2.3
Agricultural raw materials	1995	100.0	53.0	12.0	11.7	4.5	24.5	4.3	7.7	4.7
(SITC 2 - 22 - 27 - 28)	2005	100.0	51.1	14.7	14.4	4.9	20.9	4.0	6.7	7.4
	2010	100.0	48.1	14.0	13.8	5.3	18.8	3.9	6.0	6.8
Ores, metals, precious stones	1995	100.0	56.0	23.0	17.3	2.8	11.8	6.9	11.4	4.0
and non-monetary gold	2005	100.0	45.3	18.7	13.3	1.6	6.7	5.2	13.0	5.0
(SITC 27 + 28 + 68 + 667 + 971)	2010	100.0	41.8	15.8	9.6	1.2	5.4	4.9	14.6	3.8
Fuels (SITC 3)	1995	100.0	16.6	4.4	4.3	0.7	5.9	1.6	4.0	2.0
	2005	100.0	12.6	3.5	3.0	0.3	4.3	0.7	3.8	4.5
	2010	100.0	14.9	4.1	3.9	0.4	5.4	1.2	3.8	0.0
Manufactured goods	1995	100.0	63.9	23.6	22.1	0.9	18.3	20.2	0.9	1.2
(SITC 5 to 8 less 667 and 68)	2005	100.0	50.1	20.3	19.2	0.7	13.9	14.3	0.8	1.4
	2010	100.0	45.3	19.6	18.2	0.7	11.9	12.5	0.7	1.1
						Share by major product group (percentage)				
All products	1995	100.0	100.0	100.0	100.0	100.0	100.0	100.0	100.0	100.0
	2005	100.0	100.0	100.0	100.0	100.0	100.0	100.0	100.0	100.0
	2010	100.0	100.0	100.0	100.0	100.0	100.0	100.0	100.0	100.0
All food items	1995	8.3	7.5	7.6	7.9	23.1	10.5	0.8	22.7	4.4
(SITC 0 + 1 + 22 + 4)	2005	5.9	5.8	5.2	5.3	17.2	8.3	0.6	16.7	6.0
	2010	6.8	7.0	5.8	5.9	22.3	10.9	0.7	14.0	6.8
Agricultural raw materials	1995	3.0	2.7	1.7	1.8	10.5	4.1	0.8	10.3	9.6
(SITC 2 - 22 - 27 - 28)	2005	1.9	2.2	1.6	1.7	10.0	3.2	0.7	5.3	6.3
	2010	1.9	2.3	1.6	1.8	11.2	3.3	0.8	4.0	5.5
Ores, metals, precious stones	1995	4.9	4.7	5.3	4.3	10.6	3.3	2.1	24.9	13.3
and non-monetary gold	2005	6.3	6.4	6.6	5.1	11.0	3.4	3.0	33.7	14.1
(SITC 27 + 28 + 68 + 667 + 971)	2010	8.7	9.1	8.3	5.7	11.1	4.3	4.7	44.4	13.8
Fuels (SITC 3)	1995	6.6	1.8	1.3	1.4	3.6	2.2	0.7	11.7	8.9
	2005	12.3	3.5	2.4	2.3	4.2	4.2	0.8	19.2	24.6
	2010	15.2	5.7	3.8	4.0	7.4	7.6	2.0	20.3	38.5
Manufactured goods	1995	75.1	81.1	82.5	83.1	50.7	76.7	93.7	29.1	61.9
(SITC 5 to 8 less 667 and 68)	2005	72.0	80.7	82.4	83.9	57.1	79.8	94.0	22.7	43.3
	2010	66.0	74.7	78.7	81.7	47.3	72.6	91.2	16.2	29.7

Sources:
- UNCTAD secretariat calculations based on UN DESA Statistics Division's data

Notes:

(1) Includes special category exports, ship stores and bunkers and other exports of minor importance whose destination could not be determined.

(2) It is recognized that the structure of trade and partner distribution for certain countries and years might vary. In this regard, reader should know the coverage and limitations of the main principal data used in this table. For further information, please visit
http://comtrade.un.org/db/help/uReadMeFirst.aspx.

2.2.B Structure des importations par partenaires et groupes de produits
Économies en développement

			Developing economies - Économies en développement							Origines
				Asia Asie			Oceania (2)	Major petroleum exporters and gas exporters	Major manufactured goods exporters	Year
Total	Africa Afrique	America Amérique	Total	Eastern, Southern and South-Eastern Asia Asie orientale, méridionale et du Sud-Est	China Chine	Western Asia Asie occidentale	Océanie (2)	Principaux exportateurs de pétrole et de gaz	Principaux exportateurs d'articles manufacturés	Année
										Groupes de produits
Millions de dollars										
571 104	39 506	68 347	462 465	405 915	103 297	56 550	876	64 514	361 684	1995	Total tous produits
1 777 519	90 162	179 878	1 496 381	1 263 349	414 128	233 032	2 099	263 792	1 073 273	2005	
3 425 827	223 480	368 882	2 829 693	2 339 795	852 993	489 898	3 771	583 907	1 948 390	2010	
Parts par origines (en pourcentage)										
38.1	2.6	4.6	30.8	27.1	6.9	3.8	0.1	4.3	24.1	1995	Total tous produits
52.3	2.9	5.3	44.1	37.2	12.2	6.9	0.1	7.8	31.6	2005	
57.1	3.7	6.2	47.2	39.0	14.2	8.2	0.1	9.7	32.5	2010	
44.9	6.7	13.7	24.4	21.7	4.2	2.7	0.2	1.6	15.4	1995	Produits alimentaires
53.5	4.7	19.6	28.9	23.5	4.9	5.3	0.3	2.6	13.7	2005	(CTCI 0 + 1 + 22 + 4)
56.6	4.6	20.1	31.7	25.6	4.7	6.1	0.2	3.4	14.1	2010	
41.8	6.0	7.4	27.8	26.9	3.3	0.9	0.6	0.8	20.8	1995	Matières premières
41.3	5.8	7.0	27.7	26.5	2.7	1.2	0.9	0.9	17.4	2005	d'origine agricole
45.0	5.0	7.7	31.6	30.5	2.9	1.1	0.8	0.9	18.1	2010	(CTCI 2 - 22 - 27 - 28)
39.7	6.4	9.8	23.3	19.3	3.3	3.9	0.2	3.0	13.8	1995	Minerais, métaux, pierres
49.5	5.9	12.0	31.4	25.5	4.6	5.9	0.1	5.8	13.3	2005	précieuses et or (non monétaire)
51.3	7.1	14.2	32.8	25.5	3.3	7.3	0.1	7.2	11.6	2010	(CTCI 27 + 28 + 68 + 667 + 971)
80.7	8.3	8.0	64.2	28.0	2.7	36.2	0.1	47.8	17.2	1995	Combustibles (CTCI 3)
82.8	10.7	6.5	65.5	28.2	2.8	37.3	0.0	48.3	16.3	2005	
78.9	12.2	6.7	59.9	26.7	2.4	33.2	0.0	47.5	14.8	2010	
34.0	1.4	2.9	29.7	28.5	8.1	1.2	0.0	1.1	26.8	1995	Articles manufacturés
48.3	1.1	3.4	43.8	41.7	15.5	2.1	0.0	1.7	38.1	2005	(CTCI 5 à 8 moins 667 et 68)
53.5	1.1	3.6	48.7	45.7	20.0	3.1	0.0	2.3	42.1	2010	
Parts par principaux groupes de produits (en pourcentage)										
100.0	100.0	100.0	100.0	100.0	100.0	100.0	100.0	100.0	100.0	1995	Total tous produits
100.0	100.0	100.0	100.0	100.0	100.0	100.0	100.0	100.0	100.0	2005	
100.0	100.0	100.0	100.0	100.0	100.0	100.0	100.0	100.0	100.0	2010	
9.8	21.0	24.9	6.6	6.6	5.0	5.9	27.3	3.2	5.3	1995	Produits alimentaires
6.0	9.5	21.8	3.9	3.7	2.4	4.6	25.5	2.0	2.6	2005	(CTCI 0 + 1 + 22 + 4)
6.8	8.5	22.3	4.6	4.5	2.2	5.1	21.9	2.4	3.0	2010	
3.3	6.9	4.9	2.7	3.0	1.5	0.8	32.4	0.6	2.6	1995	Matières premières
1.5	3.8	2.5	1.2	1.4	0.4	0.3	26.8	0.2	1.1	2005	d'origine agricole
1.5	2.6	2.4	1.3	1.5	0.4	0.3	23.4	0.2	1.1	2010	(CTCI 2 - 22 - 27 - 28)
5.1	12.0	10.6	3.7	3.5	2.4	5.2	19.8	3.4	2.8	1995	Minerais, métaux, pierres
6.0	12.8	14.3	4.5	4.3	2.4	5.4	10.8	4.7	2.7	2005	précieuses et or (non monétaire)
8.3	16.6	20.1	6.0	5.7	2.0	7.7	20.6	6.5	3.1	2010	(CTCI 27 + 28 + 68 + 667 + 971)
14.0	20.9	11.6	13.7	6.8	2.6	63.4	8.2	73.3	4.7	1995	Combustibles (CTCI 3)
19.4	45.1	15.1	18.3	9.3	2.9	66.7	8.1	76.4	6.3	2005	
21.0	49.7	16.7	19.3	10.4	2.5	61.9	10.9	74.4	6.9	2010	
67.0	39.1	47.6	72.3	79.0	88.0	24.5	12.0	19.3	83.5	1995	Articles manufacturés
66.4	26.8	45.6	71.6	80.7	91.6	22.2	28.0	15.3	86.9	2005	(CTCI 5 à 8 moins 667 et 68)
61.7	20.3	38.1	68.1	77.2	92.6	24.9	23.1	15.9	85.4	2010	

Sources :
- Calculs du secrétariat de la CNUCED sur la base des données de ONU DAES Division de statistique

Notes :

(1) Y compris les exportations de catégorie spéciale, approvisionnements des navires et combustibles de soute et autres exportations de moindre importance dont la destination n'a pas pu être déterminée.

(2) Il est reconnu que la structure du commerce et la distribution au niveau partenaire pour certains pays et sur certaines années peuvent varier. À cet égard, le lecteur devrait connaître la couverture ainsi que les limites des données principales utilisées dans ce tableau. Pour de plus amples renseignements, veuillez visiter http://comtrade.un.org/db/help/uReadMeFlrst.aspx.

2.2.C Export structure by partner and product group
Developing economies: Africa

Destination / Product group	Year / Année	World (1) / Monde (1)	Developed economies - Économies développées							Transition economies / Économies en transition
			Total	Europe		Canada	USA / États-Unis	Japan / Japon	Other developed countries / Autres économies développées	
				Total	EU / UE					
Millions of dollars										
All products	1995	113 115	73 250	52 285	49 687	1 030	15 232	3 608	1 094	805
	2005	318 066	215 969	131 290	126 898	5 898	65 374	10 360	3 049	1 591
	2010	402 000	203 363	177 488	150 063	6 000	61 509	11 976	3 461	3 594
Share by destination (percentage)										
All products	1995	100.0	64.8	46.2	43.9	0.9	13.5	3.2	1.0	0.7
	2005	100.0	67.9	41.3	39.9	1.9	20.6	3.3	1.0	0.5
	2010	100.0	58.0	36.0	34.3	2.0	16.8	2.4	0.7	0.7
All food items	1995	100.0	61.3	51.1	49.5	0.6	3.2	5.8	0.7	1.5
(SITC 0 + 1 + 22 + 4)	2005	100.0	65.5	54.2	53.0	1.0	5.6	3.6	1.2	2.8
	2010	100.0	52.1	42.1	41.1	1.0	5.2	2.6	1.1	3.9
Agricultural raw materials	1995	100.0	55.3	45.9	44.7	0.2	2.9	5.7	0.6	0.1
(SITC 2 - 22 - 27 - 28)	2005	100.0	51.1	40.7	39.3	0.2	3.6	6.2	0.4	0.4
	2010	100.0	41.0	34.3	33.5	0.4	3.0	2.9	0.4	1.3
Ores, metals, precious stones	1995	100.0	74.0	51.2	42.2	1.0	10.4	10.1	1.2	0.5
and non-monetary gold	2005	100.0	69.6	47.9	42.0	1.2	10.4	8.9	1.2	1.2
(SITC 27 + 28 + 68 + 667 + 971)	2010	100.0	52.1	34.2	25.5	1.2	7.4	8.6	0.8	1.6
Fuels (SITC 3)	1995	100.0	79.4	49.7	48.0	1.5	26.7	0.6	0.8	0.8
	2005	100.0	70.6	37.5	36.6	2.5	28.4	1.9	0.3	0.0
	2010	100.0	63.6	34.9	34.3	2.8	24.3	1.2	0.4	0.0
Manufactured goods	1995	100.0	44.9	36.2	35.6	0.4	5.6	1.4	1.2	0.4
(SITC 5 to 8 less 667 and 68)	2005	100.0	62.6	45.7	45.2	0.7	9.2	3.8	3.3	0.6
	2010	100.0	51.3	38.5	38.1	0.8	9.0	1.6	1.4	0.6
Share by major product group (percentage)										
All products	1995	100.0	100.0	100.0	100.0	100.0	100.0	100.0	100.0	100.0
	2005	100.0	100.0	100.0	100.0	100.0	100.0	100.0	100.0	100.0
	2010	100.0	100.0	100.0	100.0	100.0	100.0	100.0	100.0	100.0
All food items	1995	16.3	15.4	18.0	18.3	10.0	3.9	29.4	11.7	33.6
(SITC 0 + 1 + 22 + 4)	2005	7.4	7.2	9.8	9.9	3.8	2.0	8.2	8.9	43.3
	2010	9.1	8.1	10.6	10.9	4.5	2.8	9.8	14.2	48.7
Agricultural raw materials	1995	5.2	4.4	5.1	5.3	0.9	1.1	9.2	3.5	1.0
(SITC 2 - 22 - 27 - 28)	2005	2.4	1.8	2.4	2.4	0.3	0.4	4.7	0.9	1.8
	2010	2.4	1.7	2.3	2.3	0.4	0.4	2.8	1.3	4.1
Ores, metals, precious stones	1995	13.0	14.8	14.4	12.5	14.0	10.0	41.2	16.3	8.4
and non-monetary gold	2005	11.2	11.4	13.0	11.8	7.0	5.7	30.5	13.6	28.4
(SITC 27 + 28 + 68 + 667 + 971)	2010	13.7	12.3	13.0	10.2	8.1	6.0	48.7	14.7	29.2
Fuels (SITC 3)	1995	36.8	45.1	39.6	40.2	61.2	72.9	7.4	31.5	40.3
	2005	60.6	63.0	55.0	55.6	82.1	83.9	36.2	16.7	5.7
	2010	56.2	61.6	54.5	56.2	79.3	81.0	26.8	34.2	3.7
Manufactured goods	1995	28.7	19.9	22.5	23.3	13.8	12.0	12.6	37.0	15.5
(SITC 5 to 8 less 667 and 68)	2005	17.5	16.2	19.4	19.8	6.8	7.8	20.3	59.5	20.8
	2010	17.9	15.9	19.2	19.9	7.6	9.6	11.7	35.1	13.6

Sources:
- UNCTAD secretariat calculations based on UN DESA Statistics Division's data

Notes:

(1) Includes special category exports, ship stores and bunkers and other exports of minor importance whose destination could not be determined.

(2) It is recognized that the structure of trade and partner distribution for certain countries and years might vary. In this regard, reader should know the coverage and limitations of the main principal data used in this table. For further information, please visit
http://comtrade.un.org/db/help/uReadMeFirst.aspx.

2.2.C Structure des exportations par partenaires et groupes de produits
Économies en développement : Afrique

Total	Africa / Afrique	America / Amérique	Asia / Asie — Total	Eastern, Southern and South-Eastern Asia / Asie orientale, méridionale et du Sud-Est	China / Chine	Western Asia / Asie occidentale	Oceania (2) / Océanie (2)	Major petroleum exporters and gas exporters / Principaux exportateurs de pétrole et de gaz	Major manufactured goods exporters / Principaux exportateurs d'articles manufacturés	Year / Année	Destinations / Groupes de produits
Millions de dollars											
07 071	23 878	2 385	11 602	9 115	948	2 487	9	2 292	6 065	1995	**Total tous produits**
95 690	28 842	12 322	54 497	44 537	20 089	9 960	28	6 944	30 990	2005	
201 152	58 789	15 940	126 268	106 375	64 839	19 893	154	17 952	80 169	2010	
Parts par destinations (en pourcentage)											
33.5	21.1	2.1	10.3	8.1	0.8	2.2	0.0	2.0	5.4	1995	**Total tous produits**
30.1	9.1	3.9	17.1	14.0	6.3	3.1	0.0	2.2	9.7	2005	
40.8	11.9	3.2	25.6	21.6	13.2	4.0	0.0	3.6	16.3	2010	
36.4	28.2	0.4	7.9	4.4	0.3	3.5	0.0	3.8	2.1	1995	Produits alimentaires
31.1	17.0	0.5	13.5	7.7	1.4	5.8	0.1	6.2	4.0	2005	(CTCI 0 + 1 + 22 + 4)
43.3	22.9	1.0	19.3	9.8	2.1	9.5	0.2	10.1	5.9	2010	
43.9	17.5	2.5	23.9	21.5	4.3	2.4	0.0	1.5	15.5	1995	Matières premières
48.3	9.6	0.5	38.2	35.2	16.8	3.0	0.0	1.3	24.8	2005	d'origine agricole
57.7	9.4	2.4	45.9	41.5	19.0	4.4	0.0	2.7	27.3	2010	(CTCI 2 - 22 - 27 - 28)
24.7	6.5	1.5	16.7	14.6	1.4	2.1	0.0	2.0	11.9	1995	Minerais, métaux, pierres
29.2	6.8	0.7	21.8	17.6	7.2	4.1	0.0	2.6	13.0	2005	précieuses et or (non monétaire)
40.0	8.6	0.9	36.9	30.5	22.2	6.4	0.0	5.5	26.9	2010	(CTCI 27 + 28 + 68 + 667 + 971)
17.7	5.9	3.4	8.3	6.3	0.6	2.0	0.0	0.3	4.1	1995	Combustibles (CTCI 3)
27.8	5.5	5.5	16.8	14.5	7.6	2.3	0.0	0.5	10.2	2005	
35.8	6.4	4.3	25.1	23.3	15.2	1.9	0.0	0.5	17.4	2010	
54.1	43.7	1.6	8.7	7.0	0.6	1.7	0.0	3.4	4.1	1995	Articles manufacturés
36.1	19.4	2.4	14.3	10.0	1.7	4.3	0.0	6.1	6.3	2005	(CTCI 5 à 8 moins 667 et 68)
48.1	27.0	3.1	17.9	11.7	3.1	6.3	0.1	8.9	7.0	2010	
Parts par principaux groupes de produits (en pourcentage)											
100.0	100.0	100.0	100.0	100.0	100.0	100.0	100.0	100.0	100.0	1995	**Total tous produits**
100.0	100.0	100.0	100.0	100.0	100.0	100.0	100.0	100.0	100.0	2005	
100.0	100.0	100.0	100.0	100.0	100.0	100.0	100.0	100.0	100.0	2010	
17.7	21.7	3.0	12.5	8.8	5.0	25.9	31.0	30.8	6.2	1995	Produits alimentaires
7.7	13.9	0.9	5.9	4.1	1.6	13.8	46.3	21.1	3.1	2005	(CTCI 0 + 1 + 22 + 4)
9.6	17.4	2.8	6.8	4.1	1.4	21.2	52.1	25.0	3.3	2010	
6.8	4.3	6.1	12.0	13.8	26.7	5.7	3.2	3.8	14.9	1995	Matières premières
3.9	2.6	0.3	5.4	6.1	6.5	2.4	6.7	1.4	6.2	2005	d'origine agricole
3.3	1.9	1.7	4.2	4.5	3.4	2.6	1.1	1.8	4.0	2010	(CTCI 2 - 22 - 27 - 28)
9.6	4.0	9.2	21.1	23.5	21.6	12.3	7.3	12.5	28.9	1995	Minerais, métaux, pierres
10.8	8.3	1.9	14.2	14.1	12.7	14.8	1.7	13.3	14.9	2005	précieuses et or (non monétaire)
15.6	9.9	3.6	19.7	19.4	23.1	21.6	1.2	20.7	22.7	2010	(CTCI 27 + 28 + 68 + 667 + 971)
19.4	10.3	59.2	29.9	28.9	27.1	33.4	24.7	4.9	28.1	1995	Combustibles (CTCI 3)
56.0	37.0	85.8	59.3	62.6	73.2	44.6	2.5	14.6	63.6	2005	
49.2	30.0	74.3	55.1	60.5	65.1	25.9	5.0	8.3	60.2	2010	
46.5	59.6	22.4	24.5	25.0	19.7	22.7	33.4	48.0	21.9	1995	Articles manufacturés
21.0	37.5	10.7	14.6	12.5	4.7	23.9	42.6	48.7	11.3	2005	(CTCI 5 à 8 moins 667 et 68)
21.1	40.5	17.4	12.5	9.7	4.3	27.8	37.9	43.9	7.7	2010	

Sources :
- Calculs du secrétariat de la CNUCED sur la base des données de ONU DAES Division de statistique

Notes :

(1) Y compris les exportations de catégorie spéciale, approvisionnements des navires et combustibles de soute et autres exportations de moindre importance dont la destination n'a pas pu être déterminée.

(2) Il est reconnu que la structure du commerce et la distribution au niveau partenaire pour certains pays et sur certaines années peuvent varier. À cet égard, le lecteur devrait connaître la couverture ainsi que les limites des données principales utilisées dans ce tableau. Pour de plus amples renseignements, veuillez visiter http://comtrade.un.org/db/help/uReadMeFirst.aspx.

2.2.C Import structure by partner and product group
Developing economies: Africa

Product group	Year / Année	World (1) / Monde (1)	Developed economies - Économies développées — Total	Europe Total	Europe EU / UE	Canada	USA / États-Unis	Japan / Japon	Other developed countries / Autres économies développées	Transition economies / Économies en transition
Millions of dollars										
All products	1995	124 581	75 947	56 234	54 195	1 378	10 835	6 226	1 274	1 525
	2005	261 673	129 604	98 903	95 761	1 716	17 020	8 949	1 917	6 700
	2010	441 799	226 710	172 810	165 974	3 648	31 228	13 003	5 629	10 098
Share by origin (percentage)										
All products	1995	100.0	61.0	45.1	43.5	1.1	8.7	5.0	1.0	1.2
	2005	100.0	49.5	37.8	36.6	0.7	6.5	3.3	1.3	2.6
	2010	100.0	45.9	35.0	33.7	0.7	6.3	2.6	1.1	2.1
All food items	1995	100.0	51.7	32.9	31.6	3.2	14.0	0.2	1.5	0.5
(SITC 0 + 1 + 22 + 4)	2005	100.0	45.4	29.6	28.4	1.9	11.1	0.1	2.7	3.9
	2010	100.0	43.0	28.7	27.4	2.0	9.4	0.2	2.8	4.1
Agricultural raw materials	1995	100.0	54.5	42.0	41.5	1.7	7.7	1.5	1.7	6.0
(SITC 2 - 22 - 27 - 28)	2005	100.0	57.4	45.8	45.1	2.6	6.0	1.4	1.6	7.7
	2010	100.0	62.5	48.4	47.9	3.0	7.5	2.1	1.4	5.4
Ores, metals, precious stones	1995	100.0	64.5	46.5	41.9	3.4	3.1	1.8	9.7	2.7
and non-monetary gold	2005	100.0	38.4	23.7	22.1	0.8	3.6	0.3	10.1	4.7
(SITC 27 + 28 + 68 + 667 + 971)	2010	100.0	40.9	30.1	29.2	1.9	2.9	0.3	5.8	3.1
Fuels (SITC 3)	1995	100.0	23.3	17.8	17.6	0.4	3.7	0.1	1.3	1.7
	2005	100.0	18.9	16.5	15.9	0.2	1.3	0.1	0.7	4.1
	2010	100.0	25.2	21.4	20.7	0.2	3.1	0.0	0.4	3.4
Manufactured goods	1995	100.0	68.4	52.0	50.1	0.5	8.2	7.2	0.5	1.1
(SITC 5 to 8 less 667 and 68)	2005	100.0	58.8	46.1	44.6	0.5	7.2	4.2	0.7	2.0
	2010	100.0	52.1	40.4	38.9	0.5	6.8	3.6	0.7	1.3
Share by major product group (percentage)										
All products	1995	100.0	100.0	100.0	100.0	100.0	100.0	100.0	100.0	100.0
	2005	100.0	100.0	100.0	100.0	100.0	100.0	100.0	100.0	100.0
	2010	100.0	100.0	100.0	100.0	100.0	100.0	100.0	100.0	100.0
All food items	1995	18.5	15.7	13.5	13.5	53.4	29.8	0.6	27.4	7.2
(SITC 0 + 1 + 22 + 4)	2005	12.9	11.8	10.1	10.0	36.6	22.0	0.4	26.8	19.8
	2010	13.3	12.5	10.9	10.8	35.4	19.7	0.8	32.6	26.6
Agricultural raw materials	1995	3.1	2.8	2.9	2.9	4.7	2.7	0.9	5.0	15.2
(SITC 2 - 22 - 27 - 28)	2005	1.6	1.8	1.9	1.9	6.2	1.5	0.7	1.9	4.7
	2010	1.4	2.0	2.0	2.0	5.9	1.7	1.1	1.7	3.8
Ores, metals, precious stones	1995	2.6	2.8	2.7	2.5	8.1	0.9	0.9	24.9	5.9
and non-monetary gold	2005	2.7	2.1	1.7	1.6	3.5	1.5	0.2	21.1	5.1
(SITC 27 + 28 + 68 + 667 + 971)	2010	3.0	2.7	2.6	2.6	7.7	1.4	0.4	15.3	4.5
Fuels (SITC 3)	1995	6.4	2.4	2.5	2.6	2.1	2.7	0.1	8.0	8.9
	2005	11.8	4.5	5.2	5.1	3.8	2.4	0.5	6.1	19.0
	2010	13.0	7.2	8.0	8.0	3.5	6.5	0.1	5.1	21.6
Manufactured goods	1995	67.2	75.4	77.3	77.4	31.2	63.3	97.3	34.5	62.6
(SITC 5 to 8 less 667 and 68)	2005	63.9	75.8	77.9	78.0	49.3	71.1	82.4	36.5	48.9
	2010	64.4	73.1	74.3	74.2	47.4	69.1	88.4	41.9	42.3

Sources:
- UNCTAD secretariat calculations based on UN DESA Statistics Division's data

Notes:

(1) Includes special category exports, ship stores and bunkers and other exports of minor importance whose destination could not be determined.

(2) It is recognized that the structure of trade and partner distribution for certain countries and years might vary. In this regard, reader should know the coverage and limitations of the main principal data used in this table. For further information, please visit
http://comtrade.un.org/db/help/uReadMeFirst.aspx.

2.2.C Structure des importations par partenaires et groupes de produits
Économies en développement : Afrique

			Developing economies - Économies en développement							Origines	
				Asia Asie			Oceania (2) Océanie (2)	Major petroleum exporters and gas exporters Principaux exportateurs de pétrole et de gaz	Major manufactured goods exporters Principaux exportateurs d'articles manufacturés	Year Année	
Total	Africa Afrique	America Amérique	Total	Eastern, Southern and South-Eastern Asia Asie orientale, méridionale et du Sud-Est	China Chine	Western Asia Asie occidentale					Groupes de produits

Millions de dollars

43 507	22 058	3 040	18 398	14 433	2 395	3 965	12	5 678	10 089	1995	Total tous produits
110 951	34 531	9 842	66 491	46 771	17 772	19 720	87	23 273	34 810	2005	
238 744	61 409	21 719	155 311	117 319	59 326	37 992	305	44 104	90 733	2010	

Parts par origines (en pourcentage)

34.9	17.7	2.4	14.8	11.6	1.9	3.2	0.0	4.6	8.1	1995	Total tous produits
42.4	13.2	3.8	25.4	17.9	6.8	7.5	0.0	8.9	13.3	2005	
48.5	12.5	4.4	31.6	23.9	12.1	7.7	0.1	9.0	18.4	2010	
46.9	27.7	7.6	11.5	9.5	1.4	2.0	0.0	0.7	5.7	1995	Produits alimentaires
49.9	16.0	15.9	18.0	14.9	2.1	3.1	0.1	1.4	8.8	2005	(CTCI 0 + 1 + 22 + 4)
52.8	15.8	16.5	20.5	16.7	2.7	3.8	0.0	2.2	10.7	2010	
38.9	26.2	3.2	9.5	6.9	0.3	2.6	0.0	0.7	5.1	1995	Matières premières
34.5	17.7	2.6	14.3	11.3	1.8	3.0	0.0	1.6	7.3	2005	d'origine agricole
31.7	12.9	2.8	16.0	13.4	2.9	2.6	0.0	1.5	8.5	2010	(CTCI 2 - 22 - 27 - 28)
32.7	18.2	4.6	9.9	3.7	0.9	6.2	0.0	4.9	2.7	1995	Minerais, métaux, pierres
52.3	34.2	5.5	12.6	6.5	2.5	6.1	0.0	5.1	4.9	2005	précieuses et or (non monétaire)
55.2	25.1	14.0	16.2	9.9	5.5	6.2	0.0	4.8	7.4	2010	(CTCI 27 + 28 + 68 + 667 + 971)
72.1	32.5	1.5	38.1	19.5	0.2	18.6	0.0	51.1	0.7	1995	Combustibles (CTCI 3)
76.8	32.5	1.6	42.6	11.4	0.4	31.3	0.0	54.9	1.0	2005	
71.0	31.8	1.1	38.1	14.4	0.3	23.7	0.0	47.6	3.4	2010	
29.1	13.7	1.1	14.3	12.2	2.4	2.1	0.0	1.5	10.0	1995	Articles manufacturés
38.1	9.3	1.9	26.9	21.9	9.9	5.0	0.0	3.2	18.1	2005	(CTCI 5 à 8 moins 667 et 68)
46.3	8.2	2.4	35.6	29.6	17.8	6.0	0.1	3.6	24.9	2010	

Parts par principaux groupes de produits (en pourcentage)

100.0	100.0	100.0	100.0	100.0	100.0	100.0	100.0	100.0	100.0	1995	Total tous produits
100.0	100.0	100.0	100.0	100.0	100.0	100.0	100.0	100.0	100.0	2005	
100.0	100.0	100.0	100.0	100.0	100.0	100.0	100.0	100.0	100.0	2010	
24.9	29.1	57.7	14.5	15.3	13.5	11.6	18.2	2.7	13.1	1995	Produits alimentaires
15.1	15.6	54.3	9.1	10.7	3.9	5.3	26.4	2.1	8.5	2005	(CTCI 0 + 1 + 22 + 4)
14.5	16.8	49.7	8.7	9.3	2.9	6.6	1.5	3.3	7.8	2010	
3.4	4.6	4.1	2.0	1.8	0.5	2.5	0.2	0.5	1.9	1995	Matières premières
1.3	2.1	1.1	0.9	1.0	0.4	0.6	0.4	0.3	0.9	2005	d'origine agricole
0.9	1.5	0.9	0.7	0.8	0.3	0.5	0.1	0.2	0.7	2010	(CTCI 2 - 22 - 27 - 28)
2.5	2.7	5.0	1.8	0.8	1.2	5.1	1.0	2.9	0.9	1995	Minerais, métaux, pierres
3.4	7.1	4.0	1.4	1.0	1.0	2.2	0.5	1.6	1.0	2005	précieuses et or (non monétaire)
3.5	6.1	9.6	1.6	1.3	1.4	2.4	0.0	1.6	1.2	2010	(CTCI 27 + 28 + 68 + 667 + 971)
13.1	11.7	3.9	16.4	10.7	0.8	37.2	0.0	71.3	0.6	1995	Combustibles (CTCI 3)
21.3	29.1	5.0	19.8	7.5	0.7	48.9	2.1	72.7	0.9	2005	
19.1	33.2	3.2	15.7	7.9	0.3	40.1	1.8	69.3	2.4	2010	
55.9	52.0	29.2	65.1	71.0	83.7	43.4	79.6	22.6	83.2	1995	Articles manufacturés
57.4	45.2	31.7	67.6	78.2	93.1	42.3	70.6	22.8	86.9	2005	(CTCI 5 à 8 moins 667 et 68)
61.5	42.2	35.0	72.7	79.9	94.9	50.3	96.4	25.5	87.0	2010	

Sources :
- Calculs du secrétariat de la CNUCED sur la base des données de ONU DAES Division de statistique

Notes :

(1) Y compris les exportations de catégorie spéciale, approvisionnements des navires et combustibles de soute et autres exportations de moindre importance dont la destination n'a pas pu être déterminée.

(2) Il est reconnu que la structure du commerce et la distribution au niveau partenaire pour certains pays et sur certaines années peuvent varier. À cet égard, le lecteur devrait connaître la couverture ainsi que les limites des données principales utilisées dans ce tableau. Pour de plus amples renseignements, veuillez visiter http://comtrade.un.org/db/help/uReadMeFirst.aspx.

Product group	Year / Année	World (1) / Monde (1)	Developed economies - Économies développées							Transition Economies / Économies en transition
			Total	Europe		Canada	USA / États-Unis	Japan / Japon	Other developed countries / Autres économies développées	
				Total	EU / UE					
						Millions of dollars				
All products	1995	230 258	162 759	41 235	38 927	4 166	107 180	9 185	994	1 504
	2005	575 862	400 101	76 035	72 958	12 160	297 690	11 988	2 228	5 419
	2010	868 466	522 805	119 725	109 143	23 429	354 340	21 329	3 982	8 528
						Share by destination (percentage)				
All products	1995	100.0	70.7	17.9	16.9	1.8	46.5	4.0	0.4	0.7
	2005	100.0	69.5	13.2	12.7	2.1	51.7	2.1	0.4	0.9
	2010	100.0	60.2	13.8	12.6	2.7	40.8	2.5	0.5	1.0
All food items	1995	100.0	65.2	34.3	33.4	1.1	23.7	5.4	0.8	2.6
(SITC 0 + 1 + 22 + 4)	2005	100.0	57.0	28.1	27.4	1.3	22.8	4.0	0.8	5.1
	2010	100.0	46.4	23.1	22.6	1.5	17.5	3.4	0.8	4.5
Agricultural raw materials	1995	100.0	65.9	30.4	28.9	0.4	24.9	10.0	0.2	0.1
(SITC 2 - 22 - 27 - 28)	2005	100.0	65.7	26.2	25.0	0.9	32.4	5.7	0.6	0.9
	2010	100.0	53.0	25.3	24.8	0.7	21.2	4.9	0.9	1.7
Ores, metals, precious stones	1995	100.0	73.5	33.8	30.1	2.8	20.5	16.1	0.3	0.4
and non-monetary gold	2005	100.0	61.1	26.0	22.8	5.1	19.4	10.4	0.2	0.3
(SITC 27 + 28 + 68 + 667 + 971)	2010	100.0	51.5	23.3	17.1	5.4	13.9	8.4	0.6	0.1
Fuels (SITC 3)	1995	100.0	73.0	8.8	8.8	1.6	60.8	1.6	0.3	0.0
	2005	100.0	73.3	7.6	7.6	1.6	63.9	0.0	0.3	0.0
	2010	100.0	64.2	8.2	8.2	1.3	54.3	0.3	0.2	0.0
Manufactured goods	1995	100.0	72.2	8.6	7.9	2.1	60.0	1.1	0.4	0.1
(SITC 5 to 8 less 667 and 68)	2005	100.0	74.6	7.8	7.6	1.9	64.0	0.5	0.4	0.1
	2010	100.0	67.9	8.2	8.0	2.7	56.0	0.7	0.4	0.2
						Share by major product group (percentage)				
All products	1995	100.0	100.0	100.0	100.0	100.0	100.0	100.0	100.0	100.0
	2005	100.0	100.0	100.0	100.0	100.0	100.0	100.0	100.0	100.0
	2010	100.0	100.0	100.0	100.0	100.0	100.0	100.0	100.0	100.0
All food items	1995	22.3	20.6	42.7	44.0	13.4	11.3	30.1	39.1	87.1
(SITC 0 + 1 + 22 + 4)	2005	16.0	13.1	34.0	34.6	9.9	7.0	30.8	33.0	87.3
	2010	18.7	14.4	31.4	33.7	10.6	8.0	26.3	33.3	85.4
Agricultural raw materials	1995	3.7	3.5	6.3	6.4	0.8	2.0	9.3	1.7	0.3
(SITC 2 - 22 - 27 - 28)	2005	2.0	1.9	4.0	4.0	0.8	1.3	5.5	2.9	1.9
	2010	2.1	1.9	3.9	4.2	0.5	1.1	4.3	4.0	3.8
Ores, metals, precious stones	1995	10.1	10.5	19.1	18.0	15.7	4.5	41.0	6.6	6.7
and non-monetary gold	2005	10.2	8.9	20.0	18.3	24.8	3.8	50.8	4.3	3.6
(SITC 27 + 28 + 68 + 667 + 971)	2010	16.1	13.8	27.2	21.9	32.4	5.5	55.0	19.3	2.2
Fuels (SITC 3)	1995	14.3	14.7	7.0	7.4	12.3	18.6	5.9	9.1	0.6
	2005	21.0	22.2	12.1	12.6	15.9	26.0	0.0	13.6	0.3
	2010	19.6	20.9	11.7	12.8	9.2	26.1	2.3	6.9	0.5
Manufactured goods	1995	49.0	50.1	23.6	23.0	57.5	63.2	13.6	43.2	5.2
(SITC 5 to 8 less 667 and 68)	2005	49.7	53.4	29.4	30.0	45.5	61.5	12.8	46.0	7.0
	2010	42.9	48.5	25.5	27.2	43.4	58.9	12.0	36.4	8.1

Sources:
- UNCTAD secretariat calculations based on UN DESA Statistics Division's data

Notes:

(1) Includes special category exports, ship stores and bunkers and other exports of minor importance whose destination could not be determined.

(2) It is recognized that the structure of trade and partner distribution for certain countries and years might vary. In this regard, reader should know the coverage and limitations of the main principal data used in this table. For further information, please visit
http://comtrade.un.org/db/help/uReadMeFirst.aspx.

2.2.D Structure des exportations par partenaires et groupes de produits
Économies en développement : Amérique

Total	Developing economies - Économies en développement						Oceania (2) Océanie (2)	Major petroleum exporters and gas exporters Principaux exportateurs de pétrole et de gaz	Major manufactured goods exporters Principaux exportateurs d'articles manufacturés	Year Année	Destinations
	Africa Afrique	America Amérique	Asia Asie: Total	Eastern, Southern and South-Eastern Asia — Asie orientale, méridionale et du Sud-Est	China Chine	Western Asia — Asie occidentale					Groupes de produits
Millions de dollars											
65 119	3 025	46 146	15 928	14 017	2 631	1 911	21	5 115	12 197	1995	**Total tous produits**
165 443	9 911	103 802	45 558	43 835	10 927	8 006	81	16 909	16 010	2005	
335 060	15 527	171 392	148 094	134 979	75 565	13 115	48	28 271	119 055	2010	
Parts par destinations (en pourcentage)											
28.3	1.3	20.0	6.9	6.1	1.1	0.8	0.0	2.2	5.3	1995	**Total tous produits**
28.7	1.7	18.4	8.7	7.6	3.5	1.1	0.0	2.7	8.0	2005	
38.6	1.8	19.7	17.1	15.5	8.7	1.5	0.0	3.3	13.7	2010	
31.8	3.3	17.1	11.3	9.4	2.8	1.9	0.0	4.3	6.2	1995	Produits alimentaires
37.6	5.4	14.3	17.8	14.2	6.4	3.7	0.0	6.3	11.4	2005	(CTCI 0 + 1 + 22 + 4)
49.0	6.0	17.1	25.9	21.3	10.0	4.5	0.0	9.7	15.8	2010	
33.6	1.0	15.0	17.5	15.8	3.2	1.7	0.0	2.6	13.5	1995	Matières premières
33.3	0.7	12.4	20.2	18.8	10.6	1.4	0.0	1.6	18.6	2005	d'origine agricole
45.3	1.0	11.4	32.9	30.9	18.9	2.0	0.0	1.8	28.6	2010	(CTCI 2 - 22 - 27 - 28)
25.6	1.1	10.7	13.7	12.8	2.0	1.0	0.0	1.6	12.2	1995	Minerais, métaux, pierres
38.6	1.1	11.0	26.5	25.1	14.3	1.4	0.0	1.7	24.7	2005	précieuses et or (non monétaire)
48.3	0.9	7.8	39.6	37.6	26.6	2.0	0.0	1.7	35.9	2010	(CTCI 27 + 28 + 68 + 667 + 971)
26.4	0.4	24.8	1.3	1.3	0.0	0.0	0.0	0.1	1.0	1995	Combustibles (CTCI 3)
26.5	0.5	22.7	3.3	3.1	0.9	0.2	0.0	0.3	3.0	2005	
35.6	0.3	20.0	15.3	15.0	7.1	0.2	0.0	0.3	10.7	2010	
27.6	0.8	22.4	4.4	3.9	0.4	0.5	0.0	2.0	4.0	1995	Articles manufacturés
26.1	1.1	19.9	4.1	3.5	1.2	0.5	0.0	2.8	5.3	2005	(CTCI 5 à 8 moins 667 et 68)
31.8	1.0	25.8	4.9	4.4	1.7	0.6	0.0	2.4	5.3	2010	
Parts par principaux groupes de produits (en pourcentage)											
100.0	100.0	100.0	100.0	100.0	100.0	100.0	100.0	100.0	100.0	1995	**Total tous produits**
100.0	100.0	100.0	100.0	100.0	100.0	100.0	100.0	100.0	100.0	2005	
100.0	100.0	100.0	100.0	100.0	100.0	100.0	100.0	100.0	100.0	2010	
25.0	56.1	19.0	36.5	34.5	55.2	50.9	38.7	43.6	26.1	1995	Produits alimentaires
20.9	52.5	12.4	32.8	29.7	29.6	55.1	61.9	37.5	22.8	2005	(CTCI 0 + 1 + 22 + 4)
23.8	62.7	16.2	28.4	25.7	21.6	56.2	39.8	56.1	21.6	2010	
4.4	2.8	2.8	9.4	9.7	10.6	7.6	0.4	4.4	9.5	1995	Matières premières
2.4	0.9	1.4	4.7	5.0	6.2	2.6	0.6	1.2	4.7	2005	d'origine agricole
2.5	1.2	1.2	4.1	4.3	4.7	2.8	1.0	1.2	4.5	2010	(CTCI 2 - 22 - 27 - 28)
9.2	8.7	5.4	20.1	21.3	17.9	11.7	0.1	7.3	23.3	1995	Minerais, métaux, pierres
13.7	6.8	6.1	31.1	33.6	42.0	13.4	0.2	6.5	31.5	2005	précieuses et or (non monétaire)
20.2	8.1	6.4	37.4	39.0	49.2	21.3	1.4	8.2	42.1	2010	(CTCI 27 + 28 + 68 + 667 + 971)
13.3	3.8	17.7	2.7	3.0	0.2	0.4	4.2	0.7	4.3	1995	Combustibles (CTCI 3)
19.4	6.3	26.0	7.9	8.6	5.6	3.0	1.5	2.5	7.8	2005	
18.1	3.6	19.9	17.6	18.9	16.1	3.2	0.1	1.9	15.3	2010	
47.9	28.4	54.9	31.3	31.5	16.1	29.4	56.5	44.1	36.7	1995	Articles manufacturés
43.5	33.4	54.0	23.4	23.1	16.6	25.4	35.4	52.1	33.1	2005	(CTCI 5 à 8 moins 667 et 68)
35.4	24.3	56.2	12.4	12.1	8.4	15.9	57.3	32.3	16.5	2010	

Sources :
- Calculs du secrétariat de la CNUCED sur la base des données de ONU DAES Division de statistique

Notes :

(1) Y compris les exportations de catégorie spéciale, approvisionnements des navires et combustibles de soute et autres exportations de moindre importance dont la destination n'a pas pu être déterminée.

(2) Il est reconnu que la structure du commerce et la distribution au niveau partenaire pour certains pays et sur certaines années peuvent varier. À cet égard, le lecteur devrait connaître la couverture ainsi que les limites des données principales utilisées dans ce tableau. Pour de plus amples renseignements, veuillez visiter http://comtrade.un.org/db/help/uReadMeFirst.aspx.

2.2.D Import structure by partner and product group
Developing economies: America

Product group	Year / Année	World (1) / Monde (1)	Developed economies - Économies développées							Transition economies / Économies en transition
			Total	Europe		Canada	USA / États-Unis	Japan / Japon	Other developed countries / Autres économies développées	
				Total	EU / UE					
Millions of dollars										
All products	1995	243 000	173 180	48 340	45 293	5 291	104 306	13 636	1 607	1 182
	2005	516 843	306 095	78 857	74 238	10 323	188 454	24 298	4 162	3 723
	2010	866 203	440 663	131 813	116 533	10 591	265 574	33 330	8 748	7 020
Share by origin (percentage)										
All products	1995	100.0	71.3	19.9	18.6	2.2	42.9	5.6	0.7	0.5
	2005	100.0	59.2	15.3	14.4	2.0	36.5	4.7	0.8	0.7
	2010	100.0	52.0	14.4	13.5	1.9	30.7	4.2	0.8	0.8
All food items	1995	100.0	58.2	15.7	14.5	5.0	35.5	0.1	1.9	0.1
(SITC 0 + 1 + 22 + 4)	2005	100.0	58.2	9.2	8.6	5.0	41.8	0.0	2.2	0.0
	2010	100.0	51.7	8.2	7.5	4.8	37.3	0.0	1.4	0.1
Agricultural raw materials	1995	100.0	60.9	7.6	7.3	3.5	47.3	0.5	2.1	1.7
(SITC 2 - 22 - 27 - 28)	2005	100.0	63.4	8.4	8.2	2.8	50.6	0.6	1.0	0.5
	2010	100.0	58.0	8.5	8.3	2.4	45.6	0.7	0.8	1.1
Ores, metals, precious stones	1995	100.0	53.3	11.1	9.9	5.6	34.1	0.8	1.6	0.3
and non-monetary gold	2005	100.0	43.6	8.0	7.7	3.1	31.3	0.4	0.8	0.8
(SITC 27 + 28 + 68 + 667 + 971)	2010	100.0	41.3	7.3	7.0	3.5	28.5	0.6	1.3	1.2
Fuels (SITC 3)	1995	100.0	30.8	7.0	6.9	1.4	20.3	0.3	1.8	2.4
	2005	100.0	33.0	5.0	4.1	0.7	24.8	0.3	2.1	1.1
	2010	100.0	44.7	6.7	6.2	0.9	34.4	1.1	1.6	1.4
Manufactured goods	1995	100.0	76.6	22.5	21.0	1.7	45.5	6.6	0.4	0.4
(SITC 5 to 8 less 667 and 68)	2005	100.0	64.1	17.8	16.8	1.9	38.0	6.0	0.5	0.7
	2010	100.0	53.6	16.8	15.7	1.7	29.2	5.3	0.6	0.7
Share by major product group (percentage)										
All products	1995	100.0	100.0	100.0	100.0	100.0	100.0	100.0	100.0	100.0
	2005	100.0	100.0	100.0	100.0	100.0	100.0	100.0	100.0	100.0
	2010	100.0	100.0	100.0	100.0	100.0	100.0	100.0	100.0	100.0
All food items	1995	9.5	7.8	7.5	7.4	21.9	7.9	0.1	27.4	1.5
(SITC 0 + 1 + 22 + 4)	2005	7.1	7.0	4.3	4.2	17.6	8.1	0.1	19.3	0.5
	2010	7.7	7.7	4.4	4.3	19.3	9.4	0.1	13.4	0.7
Agricultural raw materials	1995	2.3	2.0	0.9	0.9	3.6	2.5	0.2	7.3	7.8
(SITC 2 - 22 - 27 - 28)	2005	1.4	1.4	0.7	0.8	1.9	1.9	0.2	1.7	0.9
	2010	1.3	1.4	0.7	0.8	1.6	1.9	0.2	1.3	1.8
Ores, metals, precious stones	1995	2.4	1.8	1.3	1.3	6.2	1.9	0.3	6.0	1.3
and non-monetary gold	2005	2.6	1.9	1.3	1.4	4.0	2.2	0.2	2.5	2.9
(SITC 27 + 28 + 68 + 667 + 971)	2010	2.6	2.0	1.3	1.3	4.7	2.4	0.3	4.4	3.9
Fuels (SITC 3)	1995	6.8	2.9	2.4	2.5	4.4	3.2	0.4	18.6	33.3
	2005	11.0	6.1	3.6	3.1	4.0	7.5	0.7	29.2	16.2
	2010	12.7	10.9	5.9	5.8	6.2	14.2	3.2	26.1	21.3
Manufactured goods	1995	76.1	81.7	85.9	85.9	59.6	80.6	89.2	40.6	56.0
(SITC 5 to 8 less 667 and 68)	2005	76.3	82.6	88.8	89.3	72.2	79.5	97.5	45.2	76.7
	2010	74.8	77.0	87.0	87.0	67.1	71.2	95.0	53.6	67.8

Sources:
- UNCTAD secretariat calculations based on UN DESA Statistics Division's data

Notes:

(1) Includes special category exports, ship stores and bunkers and other exports of minor importance whose destination could not be determined.

(2) It is recognized that the structure of trade and partner distribution for certain countries and years might vary. In this regard, reader should know the coverage and limitations of the main principal data used in this table. For further information, please visit
http://comtrade.un.org/db/help/uReadMeFirst.aspx.

2.2.D Structure des importations par partenaires et groupes de produits
Économies en développement : Amérique

			Developing economies - Économies en développement								Origines
				Asia / Asie			Oceania (2) / Océanie (2)	Major petroleum exporters and gas exporters / Principaux exportateurs de pétrole et de gaz	Major manufactured goods exporters / Principaux exportateurs d'articles manufacturés	Year / Année	
Total	Africa / Afrique	America / Amérique	Total	Eastern, Southern and South-Eastern Asia / Asie orientale, méridionale et du Sud-Est	China / Chine	Western Asia / Asie occidentale					Groupes de produits
Millions de dollars											
67 270	2 484	45 492	19 277	17 213	2 843	2 065	16	8 450	20 128	1995	**Total tous produits**
202 170	11 110	108 823	82 206	79 000	35 938	3 206	31	20 290	81 413	2005	
403 922	16 513	178 307	209 045	202 281	118 169	6 763	57	26 698	204 169	2010	
Parts par origines (en pourcentage)											
27.7	1.0	18.7	7.9	7.1	1.2	0.8	0.0	3.5	8.3	1995	**Total tous produits**
39.1	2.1	21.1	15.9	15.3	7.0	0.6	0.0	3.9	15.8	2005	
46.7	1.9	20.6	24.2	23.4	13.7	0.8	0.0	3.1	23.6	2010	
41.2	0.3	38.4	2.5	2.2	0.4	0.4	0.0	1.3	2.2	1995	Produits alimentaires
41.6	0.2	37.7	3.7	3.4	1.1	0.2	0.0	0.7	3.4	2005	(CTCI 0 + 1 + 22 + 4)
47.9	0.4	42.3	5.1	4.9	1.9	0.2	0.1	0.3	4.7	2010	
36.9	2.4	25.5	9.1	9.0	0.4	0.1	0.0	0.7	8.3	1995	Matières premières
36.1	0.6	24.0	11.4	11.2	1.4	0.2	0.1	0.5	8.9	2005	d'origine agricole
40.7	2.1	21.1	17.4	17.3	2.8	0.2	0.1	0.9	11.6	2010	(CTCI 2 - 22 - 27 - 28)
47.7	4.6	41.3	1.8	1.6	0.5	0.2	0.0	4.8	3.0	1995	Minerais, métaux, pierres
55.4	2.0	49.2	4.2	4.0	1.7	0.2	0.0	4.1	3.7	2005	précieuses et or (non monétaire)
57.5	2.8	47.7	7.0	6.3	4.0	0.7	0.0	3.1	9.2	2010	(CTCI 27 + 28 + 68 + 667 + 971)
66.7	8.8	44.3	13.6	3.0	0.0	10.6	0.0	26.1	4.4	1995	Combustibles (CTCI 3)
65.8	16.6	41.4	7.7	3.4	0.9	4.3	0.0	28.4	4.6	2005	
52.5	11.2	31.1	10.2	6.4	0.7	3.8	0.0	20.1	4.6	2010	
22.4	0.3	13.7	8.4	8.3	1.4	0.1	0.0	1.1	9.8	1995	Articles manufacturés
34.9	0.3	15.9	18.7	18.6	8.7	0.1	0.0	0.8	19.1	2005	(CTCI 5 à 8 moins 667 et 68)
45.4	0.5	15.8	29.1	28.7	17.6	0.3	0.0	0.6	29.4	2010	
Parts par principaux groupes de produits (en pourcentage)											
100.0	100.0	100.0	100.0	100.0	100.0	100.0	100.0	100.0	100.0	1995	**Total tous produits**
100.0	100.0	100.0	100.0	100.0	100.0	100.0	100.0	100.0	100.0	2005	
100.0	100.0	100.0	100.0	100.0	100.0	100.0	100.0	100.0	100.0	2010	
14.2	2.6	19.5	3.0	2.9	3.1	4.3	5.7	3.6	2.5	1995	Produits alimentaires
7.6	0.8	12.7	1.6	1.6	1.2	2.6	45.6	1.2	1.5	2005	(CTCI 0 + 1 + 22 + 4)
7.9	1.6	15.9	1.6	1.6	1.1	1.9	70.2	0.8	1.5	2010	
3.1	5.3	3.1	2.6	2.9	0.7	0.2	0.6	0.4	2.3	1995	Matières premières
1.2	0.4	1.5	1.0	1.0	0.3	0.5	12.0	0.2	0.8	2005	d'origine agricole
1.1	1.4	1.3	0.9	0.9	0.3	0.3	20.7	0.4	0.6	2010	(CTCI 2 - 22 - 27 - 28)
4.1	10.8	5.3	0.5	0.5	0.9	0.6	0.0	3.3	0.9	1995	Minerais, métaux, pierres
3.6	2.4	6.0	0.7	0.7	0.6	0.9	4.1	2.6	0.6	2005	précieuses et or (non monétaire)
3.2	3.8	5.9	0.7	0.7	0.7	2.3	0.0	2.6	1.0	2010	(CTCI 27 + 28 + 68 + 667 + 971)
16.4	58.9	16.1	11.7	2.9	5.3	84.9	0.0	68.7	3.6	1995	Combustibles (CTCI 3)
18.6	85.3	21.7	5.4	2.4	1.4	77.3	0.0	79.8	3.2	2005	
14.3	74.1	19.1	5.4	3.5	0.6	61.4	0.2	82.5	2.4	2010	
61.6	22.4	55.5	81.0	89.5	89.5	10.0	93.5	23.4	89.8	1995	Articles manufacturés
68.0	10.8	57.4	89.8	92.7	95.1	18.0	34.8	16.0	92.4	2005	(CTCI 5 à 8 moins 667 et 68)
72.6	18.6	57.4	90.0	91.9	96.4	33.0	8.2	13.5	93.2	2010	

Sources :
- Calculs du secrétariat de la CNUCED sur la base des données de ONU DAES Division de statistique

Notes :

(1) Y compris les exportations de catégorie spéciale, approvisionnements des navires et combustibles de soute et autres exportations de moindre importance dont la destination n'a pas pu être déterminée.

(2) Il est reconnu que la structure du commerce et la distribution au niveau partenaire pour certains pays et sur certaines années peuvent varier. À cet égard, le lecteur devrait connaître la couverture ainsi que les limites des données principales utilisées dans ce tableau. Pour de plus amples renseignements, veuillez visiter http://comtrade.un.org/db/help/uReadMeFirst.aspx.

2.2.E Export structure by partner and product group
Developing economies: Asia

Destination / Product group	Year / Année	World (1) / Monde (1)	Developed economies - Économies développées							Transition economies / Économies en transition
			Total	Europe		Canada	USA / États-Unis	Japan / Japon	Other developed countries / Autres économies développées	
				Total	EU UE					
Millions of dollars										
All products	1995	1 083 576	561 781	184 476	178 145	11 030	196 334	150 448	19 493	11 152
	2005	2 895 766	1 366 583	503 635	490 876	28 906	458 821	312 595	62 626	41 272
	2010	4 333 200	1 333 333	704 433	733 020	43 310	003 773	411 423	114 000	33 007
Share by destination (percentage)										
All products	1995	100.0	51.8	17.0	16.4	1.0	18.1	13.9	1.8	1.0
	2005	100.0	47.2	17.4	17.0	1.0	15.8	10.8	2.2	1.4
	2010	100.0	39.2	15.7	15.1	0.9	12.1	8.2	2.3	1.9
All food items	1995	100.0	46.7	15.0	14.3	0.8	7.4	22.1	1.4	3.4
(SITC 0 + 1 + 22 + 4)	2005	100.0	43.9	16.2	15.9	1.1	9.8	14.8	2.0	3.4
	2010	100.0	34.4	13.8	13.5	1.0	8.4	9.1	2.0	3.8
Agricultural raw materials	1995	100.0	44.0	16.0	15.7	0.8	9.6	16.3	1.2	0.4
(SITC 2 - 22 - 27 - 28)	2005	100.0	39.3	15.6	15.5	1.3	9.9	11.3	1.2	0.8
	2010	100.0	32.0	13.5	13.4	1.1	8.0	8.4	1.1	0.9
Ores, metals, precious stones	1995	100.0	39.8	11.8	10.8	0.2	7.5	18.4	1.8	1.4
and non-monetary gold	2005	100.0	32.8	14.1	12.2	0.5	6.7	8.1	3.3	0.6
(SITC 27 + 28 + 68 + 667 + 971)	2010	100.0	28.0	13.3	9.4	0.3	4.5	6.6	3.3	0.5
Fuels (SITC 3)	1995	100.0	55.3	13.7	13.6	0.4	7.8	31.6	1.9	0.1
	2005	100.0	47.4	11.8	11.7	0.5	10.0	22.5	2.6	0.1
	2010	100.0	34.7	8.6	8.5	0.5	6.2	16.8	2.6	0.1
Manufactured goods	1995	100.0	52.4	18.0	17.4	1.2	21.5	9.9	1.8	1.0
(SITC 5 to 8 less 667 and 68)	2005	100.0	48.2	19.1	18.6	1.1	18.3	7.7	2.0	1.7
	2010	100.0	41.6	17.8	17.2	1.1	14.4	6.2	2.2	2.4
Share by major product group (percentage)										
All products	1995	100.0	100.0	100.0	100.0	100.0	100.0	100.0	100.0	100.0
	2005	100.0	100.0	100.0	100.0	100.0	100.0	100.0	100.0	100.0
	2010	100.0	100.0	100.0	100.0	100.0	100.0	100.0	100.0	100.0
All food items	1995	6.7	6.1	5.9	5.9	5.3	2.7	10.7	5.3	22.1
(SITC 0 + 1 + 22 + 4)	2005	3.8	3.6	3.6	3.6	4.2	2.4	5.2	3.5	9.2
	2010	4.5	3.9	3.9	4.0	5.1	3.1	5.0	3.9	8.8
Agricultural raw materials	1995	2.2	1.9	2.1	2.1	1.8	1.2	2.6	1.5	0.8
(SITC 2 - 22 - 27 - 28)	2005	1.0	0.9	0.9	0.9	1.3	0.6	1.1	0.6	0.6
	2010	1.2	1.0	1.0	1.0	1.4	0.8	1.2	0.5	0.6
Ores, metals, precious stones	1995	3.2	2.5	2.2	2.1	0.8	1.3	4.2	3.3	4.2
and non-monetary gold	2005	3.3	2.3	2.7	2.4	1.8	1.4	2.5	5.1	1.3
(SITC 27 + 28 + 68 + 667 + 971)	2010	4.6	3.3	3.9	2.8	1.6	1.7	3.6	6.6	1.2
Fuels (SITC 3)	1995	12.9	13.7	10.4	10.7	4.5	5.5	29.3	13.5	1.7
	2005	18.9	18.9	12.8	13.0	10.1	11.9	39.4	22.5	1.2
	2010	17.9	15.8	9.8	10.1	9.0	9.2	36.5	19.9	1.0
Manufactured goods	1995	73.7	74.4	78.0	77.9	86.7	87.3	52.3	75.5	70.3
(SITC 5 to 8 less 667 and 68)	2005	72.2	73.8	79.3	79.4	82.3	83.2	51.4	67.1	87.3
	2010	71.2	75.5	80.5	81.2	82.8	84.9	53.3	68.4	88.3

Sources:
- UNCTAD secretariat calculations based on UN DESA Statistics Division's data

Notes:

(1) Includes special category exports, ship stores and bunkers and other exports of minor importance whose destination could not be determined.

(2) It is recognized that the structure of trade and partner distribution for certain countries and years might vary. In this regard, reader should know the coverage and limitations of the main principal data used in this table. For further information, please visit
http://comtrade.un.org/db/help/uReadMeFirst.aspx.

2.2.E   Structure des exportations par partenaires et groupes de produits
Économies en développement : Asie

| | Developing economies - Économies en développement | | | | | | Destinations | | | | |
| | | | | Asia / Asie | | | | | | | |
Total	Africa / Afrique	America / Amérique	Total	Eastern, Southern and South-Eastern Asia / Asie orientale, méridionale et du Sud-Est	China / Chine	Western Asia / Asie occidentale	Oceania (2) / Océanie (2)	Major petroleum exporters and gas exporters / Principaux exportateurs de pétrole et de gaz	Major manufactured goods exporters / Principaux exportateurs d'articles manufacturés	Year / Année	Groupes de produits
Millions de dollars											
505 741	21 349	24 993	458 640	421 880	79 065	36 760	759	30 428	355 574	1995	Total tous produits
1 400 451	71 303	03 231	1 240 030	1 213 001	027 100	122 617	5 010	111 000	1 001 101	2005	
2 933 130	166 681	179 766	2 577 484	2 320 302	624 389	257 182	9 199	264 753	1 795 789	2010	
Parts par destinations (en pourcentage)											
46.7	2.0	2.3	42.3	38.9	7.3	3.4	0.1	2.8	32.8	1995	Total tous produits
51.1	2.5	2.2	46.3	42.1	11.3	4.2	0.2	4.0	34.7	2005	
58.7	3.3	3.6	51.6	46.5	12.5	5.2	0.2	5.3	36.0	2010	
49.2	3.2	0.6	45.3	37.5	7.0	7.8	0.1	7.1	25.6	1995	Produits alimentaires
52.2	5.4	1.1	45.4	34.5	4.9	11.0	0.2	10.8	20.6	2005	(CTCI 0 + 1 + 22 + 4)
61.7	6.6	1.5	53.4	41.0	6.8	12.4	0.2	12.8	22.2	2010	
55.2	1.6	2.0	51.7	49.3	12.9	2.4	0.0	1.7	41.1	1995	Matières premières
59.6	1.7	2.3	55.6	52.4	23.6	3.1	0.0	2.0	40.7	2005	d'origine agricole
66.9	1.8	3.1	62.0	58.2	27.6	3.8	0.0	2.2	43.1	2010	(CTCI 2 - 22 - 27 - 28)
58.3	0.9	0.2	57.1	53.4	8.9	3.7	0.0	3.3	44.5	1995	Minerais, métaux, pierres
66.4	1.0	0.3	65.1	56.6	15.3	8.5	0.0	8.0	42.0	2005	précieuses et or (non monétaire)
71.4	1.5	0.6	69.3	61.7	18.2	7.7	0.0	7.4	43.2	2010	(CTCI 27 + 28 + 68 + 667 + 971)
43.6	2.1	1.4	40.0	36.9	3.0	3.1	0.1	0.3	29.1	1995	Combustibles (CTCI 3)
52.1	2.5	1.0	48.4	45.3	7.1	3.2	0.3	1.3	36.3	2005	
65.1	2.9	1.5	60.5	57.3	10.3	3.2	0.3	1.9	42.9	2010	
46.3	1.9	2.7	41.7	38.6	7.8	3.1	0.1	2.9	33.5	1995	Articles manufacturés
49.9	2.3	2.5	44.8	41.0	12.4	3.9	0.1	4.0	34.8	2005	(CTCI 5 à 8 moins 667 et 68)
55.9	3.3	4.3	48.2	43.1	12.9	5.0	0.1	5.6	34.7	2010	
Parts par principaux groupes de produits (en pourcentage)											
100.0	100.0	100.0	100.0	100.0	100.0	100.0	100.0	100.0	100.0	1995	Total tous produits
100.0	100.0	100.0	100.0	100.0	100.0	100.0	100.0	100.0	100.0	2005	
100.0	100.0	100.0	100.0	100.0	100.0	100.0	100.0	100.0	100.0	2010	
7.1	10.8	1.9	7.2	6.5	6.4	15.4	9.8	17.0	5.2	1995	Produits alimentaires
3.9	8.5	2.0	3.7	3.1	1.7	9.9	3.9	10.5	2.3	2005	(CTCI 0 + 1 + 22 + 4)
4.7	8.9	1.9	4.6	4.0	2.4	10.8	4.5	10.8	2.8	2010	
2.6	1.8	1.9	2.7	2.8	3.9	1.6	0.4	1.4	2.8	1995	Matières premières
1.2	0.7	1.1	1.2	1.3	2.1	0.8	0.1	0.5	1.2	2005	d'origine agricole
1.3	0.6	1.0	1.4	1.5	2.6	0.9	0.1	0.5	1.4	2010	(CTCI 2 - 22 - 27 - 28)
4.0	1.5	0.3	4.3	4.4	3.9	3.5	0.4	3.8	4.3	1995	Minerais, métaux, pierres
4.3	1.4	0.5	4.7	4.5	4.5	6.7	0.2	6.7	4.0	2005	précieuses et or (non monétaire)
5.6	2.1	0.7	6.1	6.1	6.7	6.8	0.2	6.4	5.5	2010	(CTCI 27 + 28 + 68 + 667 + 971)
12.1	13.9	8.1	12.2	12.2	6.3	11.7	15.5	1.3	11.4	1995	Combustibles (CTCI 3)
19.3	18.8	8.4	19.7	20.3	11.9	14.1	32.8	6.4	19.7	2005	
19.8	15.6	7.6	20.9	22.0	14.8	11.0	24.9	6.6	21.3	2010	
73.1	70.6	85.9	72.5	73.0	78.7	67.4	69.6	75.9	75.1	1995	Articles manufacturés
70.4	68.5	84.1	69.9	70.3	79.5	66.0	57.0	73.6	72.3	2005	(CTCI 5 à 8 moins 667 et 68)
67.8	71.0	84.7	66.4	66.1	73.4	69.4	57.0	75.5	68.7	2010	

Sources :
- Calculs du secrétariat de la CNUCED sur la base des données de ONU DAES Division de statistique

Notes :

(1) Y compris les exportations de catégorie spéciale, approvisionnements des navires et combustibles de soute et autres exportations de moindre importance dont la destination n'a pas pu être déterminée.

(2) Il est reconnu que la structure du commerce et la distribution au niveau partenaire pour certains pays et sur certaines années peuvent varier. À cet égard, le lecteur devrait connaître la couverture ainsi que les limites des données principales utilisées dans ce tableau. Pour de plus amples renseignements, veuillez visiter http://comtrade.un.org/db/help/uReadMeFirst.aspx.

2.2.E Import structure by partner and product group
Developing economies: Asia

Product group / Origin	Year / Année	World (1) / Monde (1)	Developed economies - Économies développées							Transition economies / Économies en transition
			Total	Europe Total	EU / UE	Canada	USA / États-Unis	Japan / Japon	Other developed countries / Autres économies développées	
			Millions of dollars							
All products	1995	1 125 010	634 044	217 064	199 154	12 804	153 052	222 232	28 892	19 680
	2005	2 608 447	1 075 705	422 874	386 951	19 465	221 147	339 592	72 628	66 482
	2010	4 624 667	1 719 011	695 130	606 113	31 707	351 000	401 700	154 007	124 000
			Share by origin (percentage)							
All products	1995	100.0	56.4	19.3	17.7	1.1	13.6	19.8	2.6	1.7
	2005	100.0	41.2	16.2	14.8	0.7	8.5	13.0	2.8	2.5
	2010	100.0	37.1	14.8	12.9	0.8	7.6	10.6	3.3	2.7
All food items	1995	100.0	52.6	17.1	16.5	3.4	21.5	2.3	8.3	1.1
(SITC 0 + 1 + 22 + 4)	2005	100.0	39.3	13.6	12.7	2.3	12.7	1.8	8.9	2.5
	2010	100.0	37.6	11.7	10.4	2.8	14.4	1.4	7.3	2.5
Agricultural raw materials	1995	100.0	51.6	9.5	9.2	5.0	22.8	5.2	9.1	5.1
(SITC 2 - 22 - 27 - 28)	2005	100.0	49.0	13.2	12.8	5.3	18.2	4.6	7.8	8.3
	2010	100.0	45.9	12.2	11.9	5.8	16.7	4.4	6.8	7.5
Ores, metals, precious stones	1995	100.0	55.8	22.9	16.8	2.5	10.3	7.8	12.3	4.4
and non-monetary gold	2005	100.0	45.6	19.2	13.3	1.6	5.1	5.7	14.0	5.3
(SITC 27 + 28 + 68 + 667 + 971)	2010	100.0	41.8	15.7	9.1	1.0	4.4	5.2	15.4	3.9
Fuels (SITC 3)	1995	100.0	12.3	2.4	2.3	0.6	2.9	2.1	4.3	2.0
	2005	100.0	8.4	2.0	1.6	0.3	1.0	0.8	4.3	5.2
	2010	100.0	9.0	2.2	2.1	0.4	1.3	1.3	4.3	6.9
Manufactured goods	1995	100.0	60.6	21.1	19.6	0.7	13.5	24.4	0.9	1.4
(SITC 5 to 8 less 667 and 68)	2005	100.0	46.3	18.5	17.4	0.5	9.5	17.0	0.8	1.4
	2010	100.0	42.8	18.0	16.5	0.4	8.7	15.0	0.7	1.1
			Share by major product group (percentage)							
All products	1995	100.0	100.0	100.0	100.0	100.0	100.0	100.0	100.0	100.0
	2005	100.0	100.0	100.0	100.0	100.0	100.0	100.0	100.0	100.0
	2010	100.0	100.0	100.0	100.0	100.0	100.0	100.0	100.0	100.0
All food items	1995	6.9	6.4	6.1	6.4	20.3	10.8	0.8	22.3	4.4
(SITC 0 + 1 + 22 + 4)	2005	4.9	4.7	4.1	4.2	15.3	7.4	0.7	15.7	4.9
	2010	5.9	6.0	4.7	4.8	22.4	11.2	0.8	12.9	5.5
Agricultural raw materials	1995	3.2	2.9	1.6	1.7	13.9	5.3	0.8	11.3	9.2
(SITC 2 - 22 - 27 - 28)	2005	2.1	2.4	1.7	1.8	14.7	4.4	0.7	5.7	6.7
	2010	2.1	2.6	1.7	1.9	16.3	4.6	0.9	4.3	5.9
Ores, metals, precious stones	1995	5.8	5.7	6.8	5.5	12.8	4.4	2.3	27.6	14.6
and non-monetary gold	2005	7.4	8.2	8.8	6.7	15.4	4.5	3.3	37.3	15.6
(SITC 27 + 28 + 68 + 667 + 971)	2010	10.5	11.8	11.1	7.4	14.5	6.1	5.1	48.3	15.1
Fuels (SITC 3)	1995	6.6	1.4	0.8	0.9	3.5	1.4	0.7	11.1	7.5
	2005	12.5	2.5	1.5	1.4	4.4	1.5	0.8	19.5	25.7
	2010	15.9	4.1	2.4	2.6	8.4	2.8	1.9	20.6	40.8
Manufactured goods	1995	75.9	81.7	83.0	84.0	49.0	75.1	93.9	26.4	62.2
(SITC 5 to 8 less 667 and 68)	2005	72.0	80.8	82.2	84.3	49.8	80.8	94.1	19.6	40.9
	2010	64.5	74.3	78.3	82.7	37.8	74.0	91.0	12.8	26.6

Sources:
- UNCTAD secretariat calculations based on UN DESA Statistics Division's data

Notes:

(1) Includes special category exports, ship stores and bunkers and other exports of minor importance whose destination could not be determined.

(2) It is recognized that the structure of trade and partner distribution for certain countries and years might vary. In this regard, reader should know the coverage and limitations of the main principal data used in this table. For further information, please visit
http://comtrade.un.org/db/help/uReadMeFirst.aspx.

2.2.E Structure des importations par partenaires et groupes de produits
Économies en développement : Asie

	Developing economies - Économies en développement									Origines	
			Asia / Asie				Oceania (2)	Major petroleum exporters and gas exporters	Major manufactured goods exporters	Year	
Total	Africa / Afrique	America / Amérique	Total	Eastern, Southern and South-Eastern Asia / Asie orientale, méridionale et du Sud-Est	China / Chine	Western Asia / Asie occidentale	Océanie (2)	Principaux exportateurs de pétrole et de gaz	Principaux exportateurs d'articles manufacturés	Année	Groupes de produits
Millions de dollars											
459 233	14 957	19 782	423 664	373 145	97 989	50 519	829	50 386	330 418	1995	Total tous produits
1 460 556	53 488	61 164	1 344 188	1 134 098	360 074	210 089	1 716	320 327	953 828	2005	
2 777 505	145 478	168 777	2 460 203	2 015 090	674 088	445 112	3 047	513 078	1 648 840	2010	
Parts par origines (en pourcentage)											
40.8	1.3	1.8	37.7	33.2	8.7	4.5	0.1	4.5	29.4	1995	Total tous produits
56.0	2.1	2.3	51.5	43.5	13.8	8.1	0.1	8.4	36.6	2005	
60.1	3.1	3.6	53.2	43.6	14.6	9.6	0.1	11.1	35.7	2010	
45.8	2.4	8.2	34.9	31.3	6.2	3.6	0.3	2.0	22.4	1995	Produits alimentaires
58.1	3.1	15.6	39.1	31.7	6.8	7.5	0.3	3.6	18.0	2005	(CTCI 0 + 1 + 22 + 4)
59.9	3.0	15.6	41.0	32.9	5.7	8.1	0.2	4.4	17.1	2010	
43.0	4.5	5.0	32.7	31.8	4.1	0.9	0.8	0.8	24.4	1995	Matières premières
42.6	5.5	5.2	30.9	29.7	3.0	1.2	1.0	0.9	19.3	2005	d'origine agricole
46.5	4.7	6.6	34.4	33.3	2.9	1.1	0.9	0.9	19.5	2010	(CTCI 2 - 22 - 27 - 28)
39.3	6.0	7.2	25.9	21.7	3.7	4.2	0.3	2.7	15.4	1995	Minerais, métaux, pierres
49.0	5.1	9.7	34.0	27.7	4.9	6.3	0.1	6.0	14.3	2005	précieuses et or (non monétaire)
54.2	6.8	12.7	34.5	26.9	3.2	7.6	0.2	7.5	11.8	2010	(CTCI 27 + 28 + 68 + 667 + 971)
85.0	5.7	0.7	78.5	34.4	3.3	44.1	0.1	50.7	21.7	1995	Combustibles (CTCI 3)
86.3	7.7	0.9	77.6	33.8	3.4	43.8	0.0	51.4	19.4	2005	
83.5	10.7	3.6	69.2	30.6	2.8	38.5	0.1	51.8	17.1	2010	
37.0	0.4	0.7	35.9	34.5	10.1	1.4	0.0	1.1	32.2	1995	Articles manufacturés
52.0	0.5	0.9	50.6	48.3	17.5	2.3	0.0	1.7	43.9	2005	(CTCI 5 à 8 moins 667 et 68)
56.0	0.5	1.0	54.4	51.1	20.7	3.4	0.0	2.6	46.7	2010	
Parts par principaux groupes de produits (en pourcentage)											
100.0	100.0	100.0	100.0	100.0	100.0	100.0	100.0	100.0	100.0	1995	Total tous produits
100.0	100.0	100.0	100.0	100.0	100.0	100.0	100.0	100.0	100.0	2005	
100.0	100.0	100.0	100.0	100.0	100.0	100.0	100.0	100.0	100.0	2010	
7.7	12.1	32.2	6.4	6.5	4.9	5.5	28.2	3.1	5.2	1995	Produits alimentaires
5.1	7.4	32.8	3.7	3.6	2.4	4.6	21.5	2.1	2.4	2005	(CTCI 0 + 1 + 22 + 4)
5.9	5.7	25.4	4.6	4.5	2.3	5.0	19.1	2.4	2.9	2010	
3.4	10.7	9.1	2.8	3.1	1.5	0.6	34.0	0.6	2.7	1995	Matières premières
1.6	5.6	4.5	1.2	1.4	0.4	0.3	32.3	0.2	1.1	2005	d'origine agricole
1.6	3.2	3.8	1.4	1.6	0.4	0.2	28.4	0.2	1.2	2010	(CTCI 2 - 22 - 27 - 28)
5.5	25.8	23.7	4.0	3.8	2.5	5.4	20.8	3.5	3.0	1995	Minerais, métaux, pierres
6.5	18.6	30.8	4.9	4.7	2.6	5.8	12.9	5.3	2.9	2005	précieuses et or (non monétaire)
9.4	22.5	36.4	6.8	6.5	2.3	8.3	25.4	7.1	3.5	2010	(CTCI 27 + 28 + 68 + 667 + 971)
13.7	28.3	2.6	13.7	6.8	2.5	64.6	8.4	74.3	4.8	1995	Combustibles (CTCI 3)
19.3	47.2	4.9	18.9	9.8	3.1	68.3	7.4	76.4	6.6	2005	
22.2	54.0	15.9	20.7	11.2	3.1	63.8	12.2	74.4	7.6	2010	
68.8	23.0	32.0	72.3	78.9	88.0	23.6	8.5	18.3	83.2	1995	Articles manufacturés
66.9	18.3	26.7	70.7	80.1	91.2	20.3	25.8	14.5	86.5	2005	(CTCI 5 à 8 moins 667 et 68)
60.2	11.2	18.2	66.0	75.6	91.8	22.6	14.8	15.1	84.5	2010	

Sources :
- Calculs du secrétariat de la CNUCED sur la base des données de ONU DAES Division de statistique

Notes :

(1) Y compris les exportations de catégorie spéciale, approvisionnements des navires et combustibles de soute et autres exportations de moindre importance dont la destination n'a pas pu être déterminée.

(2) Il est reconnu que la structure du commerce et la distribution au niveau partenaire pour certains pays et sur certaines années peuvent varier. À cet égard, le lecteur devrait connaître la couverture ainsi que les limites des données principales utilisées dans ce tableau. Pour de plus amples renseignements, veuillez visiter http://comtrade.un.org/db/help/uReadMeFirst.aspx.

2.2.F Export structure by partner and product group
Developing economies: Eastern, Southern and South-Eastern Asia

Destination — Product group	Year / Année	World (1) / Monde (1)	Developed economies - Économies développées — Total	Europe — Total	Europe — EU / UE	Canada	USA / États-Unis	Japan / Japon	Other developed countries / Autres économies développées	Transition economies / Économies en transition
Millions of dollars										
All products	1995	949 867	489 248	155 886	150 094	10 540	183 710	121 511	17 602	8 583
	2005	2 381 068	1 110 935	400 585	390 149	25 561	400 982	226 462	57 344	34 069
	2010	4 171 651	1 671 692	608 735	042 040	40 000	547 500	000 000	106 500	91 112
Share by destination (percentage)										
All products	1995	100.0	51.5	16.4	15.8	1.1	19.3	12.8	1.9	0.9
	2005	100.0	46.7	16.8	16.4	1.1	16.8	9.5	2.4	1.4
	2010	100.0	40.1	16.0	15.4	1.0	13.1	7.4	2.6	2.0
All food items	1995	100.0	47.5	13.1	12.5	0.9	7.7	24.4	1.5	2.7
(SITC 0 + 1 + 22 + 4)	2005	100.0	45.5	13.9	13.7	1.2	11.0	17.2	2.1	3.0
	2010	100.0	36.5	13.3	12.9	1.1	9.5	10.5	2.1	3.4
Agricultural raw materials	1995	100.0	43.7	14.8	14.6	0.9	9.9	16.9	1.2	0.4
(SITC 2 - 22 - 27 - 28)	2005	100.0	39.4	14.9	14.8	1.4	10.2	11.7	1.2	0.7
	2010	100.0	32.2	13.2	13.1	1.1	8.2	8.6	1.1	0.8
Ores, metals, precious stones	1995	100.0	41.7	11.2	10.2	0.3	8.5	19.8	2.1	1.4
and non-monetary gold	2005	100.0	34.3	12.5	10.9	0.7	7.6	9.6	4.0	0.5
(SITC 27 + 28 + 68 + 667 + 971)	2010	100.0	31.2	12.6	8.8	0.4	5.6	8.3	4.3	0.4
Fuels (SITC 3)	1995	100.0	48.0	12.6	12.5	0.2	2.6	30.5	2.2	0.3
	2005	100.0	38.8	10.1	10.1	0.1	3.3	19.4	5.9	0.2
	2010	100.0	29.4	8.8	8.7	0.1	2.2	13.2	5.0	0.2
Manufactured goods	1995	100.0	52.6	17.2	16.5	1.2	22.1	10.2	1.9	0.8
(SITC 5 to 8 less 667 and 68)	2005	100.0	48.2	17.8	17.4	1.2	19.0	8.1	2.0	1.5
	2010	100.0	42.2	17.2	16.6	1.1	15.1	6.5	2.2	2.2
Share by major product group (percentage)										
All products	1995	100.0	100.0	100.0	100.0	100.0	100.0	100.0	100.0	100.0
	2005	100.0	100.0	100.0	100.0	100.0	100.0	100.0	100.0	100.0
	2010	100.0	100.0	100.0	100.0	100.0	100.0	100.0	100.0	100.0
All food items	1995	6.9	6.4	5.5	5.4	5.3	2.8	13.1	5.5	20.9
(SITC 0 + 1 + 22 + 4)	2005	4.0	3.8	3.3	3.3	4.5	2.6	7.1	3.4	8.3
	2010	4.6	4.2	3.8	3.9	5.3	3.3	6.6	3.9	8.1
Agricultural raw materials	1995	2.5	2.1	2.2	2.3	1.9	1.3	3.2	1.6	1.0
(SITC 2 - 22 - 27 - 28)	2005	1.2	1.0	1.1	1.1	1.5	0.7	1.5	0.6	0.6
	2010	1.4	1.1	1.1	1.2	1.6	0.9	1.6	0.6	0.6
Ores, metals, precious stones	1995	3.1	2.5	2.1	2.0	0.8	1.4	4.8	3.4	4.9
and non-monetary gold	2005	3.2	2.4	2.4	2.2	2.0	1.5	3.3	5.3	1.0
(SITC 27 + 28 + 68 + 667 + 971)	2010	4.2	3.2	3.3	2.4	1.7	1.8	4.7	7.0	0.9
Fuels (SITC 3)	1995	5.7	5.3	4.3	4.5	1.1	0.7	13.5	6.6	1.7
	2005	8.3	6.9	5.0	5.1	0.5	1.6	16.9	20.5	1.0
	2010	8.8	6.4	4.9	4.9	0.9	1.5	15.7	17.4	0.7
Manufactured goods	1995	80.5	82.2	84.3	84.3	89.9	91.9	64.3	81.8	70.5
(SITC 5 to 8 less 667 and 68)	2005	82.6	85.3	87.6	87.7	91.2	93.3	70.7	69.3	88.9
	2010	80.3	84.5	86.0	86.7	90.5	92.4	71.0	70.7	89.6

Sources:
- UNCTAD secretariat calculations based on UN DESA Statistics Division's data

Notes:

(1) Includes special category exports, ship stores and bunkers and other exports of minor importance whose destination could not be determined.

(2) It is recognized that the structure of trade and partner distribution for certain countries and years might vary. In this regard, reader should know the coverage and limitations of the main principal data used in this table. For further information, please visit http://comtrade.un.org/db/help/uReadMeFirst.aspx.

2.2.F Structure des exportations par partenaires et groupes de produits
Économies en développement : Asie orientale, méridionale et du Sud-Est

Total	Africa / Afrique	America / Amérique	Asia / Asie — Total	Eastern, Southern and South-Eastern Asia / Asie orientale, méridionale et du Sud-Est	China / Chine	Western Asia / Asie occidentale	Oceania (2) / Océanie (2)	Major petroleum exporters and gas exporters / Principaux exportateurs de pétrole et de gaz	Major manufactured goods exporters / Principaux exportateurs d'articles manufacturés	Year / Année	Destinations / Groupes de produits
Millions de dollars											
448 178	17 296	23 190	406 935	383 750	77 150	23 185	758	20 888	329 999	1995	**Total tous produits**
1 232 071	50 736	59 592	1 116 829	1 040 632	302 248	76 196	4 914	73 551	869 261	2005	
2 416 244	130 023	173 189	2 103 953	1 925 372	562 701	178 581	9 079	181 376	1 529 647	2010	
Parts par destinations (en pourcentage)											
47.2	1.8	2.4	42.8	40.4	8.1	2.4	0.1	2.2	34.7	1995	**Total tous produits**
51.7	2.1	2.5	46.9	43.7	12.7	3.2	0.2	3.1	36.5	2005	
57.9	3.1	4.2	50.4	46.2	13.5	4.3	0.2	4.3	36.7	2010	
49.1	2.9	0.6	45.4	40.9	7.7	4.6	0.1	4.1	28.2	1995	Produits alimentaires
51.2	5.2	1.3	44.5	38.6	5.7	5.9	0.2	6.2	23.9	2005	(CTCI 0 + 1 + 22 + 4)
60.1	6.5	1.7	51.7	44.9	7.8	6.8	0.2	7.5	25.4	2010	
55.5	1.2	2.0	52.3	50.4	13.2	1.9	0.0	1.5	42.3	1995	Matières premières
59.7	1.4	2.4	55.9	53.5	24.5	2.3	0.0	1.5	42.1	2005	d'origine agricole
66.8	1.6	3.2	62.0	58.7	28.2	3.3	0.0	1.7	44.0	2010	(CTCI 2 - 22 - 27 - 28)
56.5	0.5	0.2	55.8	54.8	10.2	1.0	0.0	1.0	48.1	1995	Minerais, métaux, pierres
65.1	0.6	0.3	64.2	57.9	18.4	6.2	0.0	6.2	49.0	2005	précieuses et or (non monétaire)
68.4	1.2	0.6	66.6	60.4	22.4	6.2	0.0	6.2	50.2	2010	(CTCI 27 + 28 + 68 + 667 + 971)
49.3	2.8	0.8	45.5	44.1	7.0	1.4	0.2	0.3	37.6	1995	Combustibles (CTCI 3)
60.0	2.2	1.3	55.7	53.0	9.4	2.7	0.8	1.4	38.7	2005	
70.3	3.2	2.7	63.8	59.5	11.5	4.3	0.6	3.2	41.7	2010	
46.4	1.7	2.8	41.8	39.4	8.1	2.4	0.1	2.3	34.5	1995	Articles manufacturés
50.2	2.0	2.7	45.4	42.4	13.0	3.0	0.1	3.0	36.5	2005	(CTCI 5 à 8 moins 667 et 68)
55.6	3.0	4.5	48.0	44.0	13.4	4.0	0.2	4.3	36.1	2010	
Parts par principaux groupes de produits (en pourcentage)											
100.0	100.0	100.0	100.0	100.0	100.0	100.0	100.0	100.0	100.0	1995	**Total tous produits**
100.0	100.0	100.0	100.0	100.0	100.0	100.0	100.0	100.0	100.0	2005	
100.0	100.0	100.0	100.0	100.0	100.0	100.0	100.0	100.0	100.0	2010	
7.2	10.9	1.8	7.3	7.0	6.6	12.9	9.8	12.8	5.6	1995	Produits alimentaires
3.9	9.7	2.0	3.7	3.5	1.8	7.3	4.0	7.9	2.6	2005	(CTCI 0 + 1 + 22 + 4)
4.8	9.6	1.9	4.8	4.5	2.7	7.3	4.5	8.0	3.2	2010	
2.9	1.7	2.1	3.0	3.1	4.0	1.9	0.4	1.6	3.0	1995	Matières premières
1.4	0.8	1.1	1.4	1.5	2.3	0.9	0.1	0.6	1.4	2005	d'origine agricole
1.6	0.7	1.1	1.7	1.7	2.9	1.0	0.1	0.5	1.6	2010	(CTCI 2 - 22 - 27 - 28)
3.7	0.8	0.3	4.0	4.2	3.9	1.3	0.4	1.3	4.3	1995	Minerais, métaux, pierres
4.1	0.9	0.4	4.4	4.3	4.7	6.3	0.2	6.5	4.3	2005	précieuses et or (non monétaire)
4.9	1.6	0.6	5.5	5.4	6.9	6.0	0.2	6.0	5.7	2010	(CTCI 27 + 28 + 68 + 667 + 971)
5.9	8.8	1.8	6.0	6.2	4.8	3.2	15.5	0.9	6.1	1995	Combustibles (CTCI 3)
9.6	8.4	4.2	9.8	10.1	6.2	7.1	33.7	3.7	8.8	2005	
10.7	9.0	5.6	11.1	11.3	7.5	8.8	25.1	6.5	10.0	2010	
79.1	76.3	91.9	78.5	78.4	79.9	79.9	69.6	82.6	79.9	1995	Articles manufacturés
80.1	77.8	88.1	79.9	80.2	84.9	76.3	56.0	79.9	82.5	2005	(CTCI 5 à 8 moins 667 et 68)
77.2	76.8	86.5	76.5	76.6	79.9	75.3	56.7	78.8	79.1	2010	

Sources :
- Calculs du secrétariat de la CNUCED sur la base des données de ONU DAES Division de statistique

Notes :

(1) Y compris les exportations de catégorie spéciale, approvisionnements des navires et combustibles de soute et autres exportations de moindre importance dont la destination n'a pas pu être déterminée.

(2) Il est reconnu que la structure du commerce et la distribution au niveau partenaire pour certains pays et sur certaines années peuvent varier. À cet égard, le lecteur devrait connaître la couverture ainsi que les limites des données principales utilisées dans ce tableau. Pour de plus amples renseignements, veuillez visiter http://comtrade.un.org/db/help/uReadMeFirst.aspx.

2.2.F Import structure by partner and product group
Developing Asia: Eastern, Southern and South-Eastern Asia

Product group	Year / Année	World (1) / Monde (1)	Developed economies - Économies développées							Transition economies / Économies en transition
			Europe			Canada	USA / États-Unis	Japan / Japon	Other developed countries / Autres économies développées	
			Total	Total	EU / UE					
Millions of dollars										
All products	1995	1 001 530	557 868	166 726	152 319	11 825	137 868	213 991	27 459	15 182
	2005	2 244 930	882 164	288 214	261 023	17 594	191 096	320 721	64 539	43 483
	2010	3 071 655	1 428 280	441 771	414 254	30 304	200 020	161 038	145 588	83 814
Share by origin (percentage)										
All products	1995	100.0	55.7	16.6	15.2	1.2	13.8	21.4	2.7	1.5
	2005	100.0	39.3	12.8	11.6	0.8	8.5	14.3	2.9	1.9
	2010	100.0	36.0	12.4	10.4	0.8	7.5	11.7	3.7	2.1
All food items	1995	100.0	53.1	13.6	13.0	4.1	23.2	2.8	9.5	0.7
(SITC 0 + 1 + 22 + 4)	2005	100.0	39.3	10.3	9.4	3.0	14.0	2.4	9.7	2.2
	2010	100.0	39.6	9.4	8.0	3.2	16.9	1.8	8.4	1.9
Agricultural raw materials	1995	100.0	51.3	7.3	7.0	5.2	23.9	5.7	9.3	4.0
(SITC 2 - 22 - 27 - 28)	2005	100.0	48.0	10.9	10.5	5.7	18.2	5.0	8.3	8.1
	2010	100.0	45.4	10.3	10.0	6.3	16.7	4.8	7.4	7.3
Ores, metals, precious stones	1995	100.0	54.9	20.1	15.0	2.5	10.5	8.5	13.3	4.4
and non-monetary gold	2005	100.0	46.2	16.8	12.4	1.7	5.3	6.6	15.8	4.1
(SITC 27 + 28 + 68 + 667 + 971)	2010	100.0	44.4	15.0	8.1	1.2	4.5	6.0	17.7	3.2
Fuels (SITC 3)	1995	100.0	12.2	1.7	1.6	0.7	2.9	2.3	4.7	0.9
	2005	100.0	7.5	1.0	0.8	0.3	1.0	0.9	4.4	3.5
	2010	100.0	8.8	1.3	1.3	0.4	1.2	1.4	4.5	5.4
Manufactured goods	1995	100.0	59.7	18.3	16.9	0.7	13.5	26.2	1.0	1.3
(SITC 5 to 8 less 667 and 68)	2005	100.0	43.8	14.6	13.5	0.5	9.5	18.5	0.7	1.2
	2010	100.0	41.2	15.0	13.6	0.4	8.6	16.5	0.6	0.9
Share by major product group (percentage)										
All products	1995	100.0	100.0	100.0	100.0	100.0	100.0	100.0	100.0	100.0
	2005	100.0	100.0	100.0	100.0	100.0	100.0	100.0	100.0	100.0
	2010	100.0	100.0	100.0	100.0	100.0	100.0	100.0	100.0	100.0
All food items	1995	6.1	5.9	5.0	5.3	21.2	10.3	0.8	21.2	2.9
(SITC 0 + 1 + 22 + 4)	2005	4.2	4.2	3.3	3.4	15.9	6.9	0.7	14.0	4.7
	2010	5.1	5.6	3.9	3.9	21.1	11.5	0.8	11.6	4.6
Agricultural raw materials	1995	3.3	3.0	1.4	1.5	14.4	5.7	0.9	11.2	8.6
(SITC 2 - 22 - 27 - 28)	2005	2.2	2.7	1.8	2.0	15.7	4.6	0.8	6.3	9.1
	2010	2.2	2.8	1.9	2.1	18.2	5.0	0.9	4.5	7.7
Ores, metals, precious stones	1995	5.9	5.8	7.1	5.8	12.6	4.5	2.3	28.5	17.0
and non-monetary gold	2005	7.4	8.7	9.7	7.9	16.1	4.6	3.4	40.8	15.8
(SITC 27 + 28 + 68 + 667 + 971)	2010	10.4	12.9	12.7	8.1	15.7	6.3	5.4	50.3	15.7
Fuels (SITC 3)	1995	6.6	1.5	0.7	0.7	3.7	1.4	0.7	11.3	4.0
	2005	13.1	2.5	1.0	0.9	4.3	1.5	0.8	20.1	24.1
	2010	17.4	4.3	1.9	2.1	8.8	2.7	2.0	21.5	44.5
Manufactured goods	1995	76.4	81.8	83.8	84.8	47.7	75.0	93.7	26.6	64.8
(SITC 5 to 8 less 667 and 68)	2005	72.4	80.7	82.2	84.1	47.7	81.1	93.8	17.2	45.6
	2010	64.1	73.3	77.5	83.2	35.7	73.6	90.6	11.3	27.2

Sources:
- UNCTAD secretariat calculations based on UN DESA Statistics Division's data

Notes:

(1) Includes special category exports, ship stores and bunkers and other exports of minor importance whose destination could not be determined.

(2) It is recognized that the structure of trade and partner distribution for certain countries and years might vary. In this regard, reader should know the coverage and limitations of the main principal data used in this table. For further information, please visit http://comtrade.un.org/db/help/uReadMeFirst.aspx.

2.2.F Structure des importations par partenaires et groupes de produits
Économies en développement : Asie orientale, méridionale et du Sud-Est

			Developing economies - Économies en développement							Origines	
			Asia / Asie				Oceania (2) / Océanie (2)	Major petroleum exporters and gas exporters / Principaux exportateurs de pétrole et de gaz	Major manufactured goods exporters / Principaux exportateurs d'articles manufacturés	Year / Année	
Total	Africa / Afrique	America / Amérique	Total	Eastern, Southern and South-Eastern Asia / Asie orientale, méridionale et du Sud-Est — Total	China / Chine	Western Asia / Asie occidentale					Groupes de produits
Millions de dollars											
421 583	12 016	17 493	391 251	353 157	94 928	38 094	824	39 761	316 666	1995	**Total tous produits**
1 316 009	11 070	59 700	1 217 019	1 066 500	205 017	102 204	1 002	100 051	360 034	2005	
2 457 121	123 892	153 666	2 176 521	1 816 741	605 059	359 780	3 042	452 673	1 523 928	2010	
Parts par origines (en pourcentage)											
42.1	1.2	1.7	39.1	35.3	9.5	3.8	0.1	4.0	31.6	1995	**Total tous produits**
58.6	1.9	2.4	54.2	47.0	15.0	7.2	0.1	8.2	40.1	2005	
61.9	3.1	3.9	54.8	45.7	15.2	9.1	0.1	11.4	38.4	2010	
45.9	1.7	8.5	35.3	34.8	7.5	0.6	0.4	0.5	26.2	1995	Produits alimentaires
58.4	2.2	17.4	38.4	36.9	8.8	1.6	0.4	1.6	22.5	2005	(CTCI 0 + 1 + 22 + 4)
58.5	1.9	17.2	39.1	36.9	7.1	2.2	0.3	2.1	20.8	2010	
44.4	4.4	5.2	34.0	33.4	4.5	0.6	0.9	0.6	25.8	1995	Matières premières
43.8	5.6	5.2	31.9	31.2	3.0	0.7	1.1	0.7	20.3	2005	d'origine agricole
47.3	4.7	6.7	35.0	34.3	2.8	0.7	1.0	0.7	20.0	2010	(CTCI 2 - 22 - 27 - 28)
40.4	5.9	7.5	26.7	23.3	4.1	3.3	0.3	2.1	16.8	1995	Minerais, métaux, pierres
49.6	4.7	10.7	34.0	28.3	5.4	5.7	0.1	5.7	15.5	2005	précieuses et or (non monétaire)
52.3	6.6	14.2	31.4	24.1	3.4	7.3	0.2	7.4	13.0	2010	(CTCI 27 + 28 + 68 + 667 + 971)
00.0	4.0	0.7	00.0	37.2	3.7	43.3	0.1	49.0	24.1	1995	Combustibles (CTCI 3)
88.9	7.4	0.9	80.5	36.2	3.7	44.3	0.0	51.8	21.3	2005	
85.8	10.9	3.8	71.0	31.6	2.9	39.3	0.1	53.0	18.1	2010	
38.4	0.4	0.7	37.3	36.4	10.9	0.9	0.0	0.7	34.3	1995	Articles manufacturés
54.7	0.4	0.9	53.4	52.2	18.8	1.2	0.0	1.2	47.0	2005	(CTCI 5 à 8 moins 667 et 68)
57.9	0.4	1.1	56.4	54.4	21.7	2.1	0.0	2.0	50.3	2010	
Parts par principaux groupes de produits (en pourcentage)											
100.0	100.0	100.0	100.0	100.0	100.0	100.0	100.0	100.0	100.0	1995	**Total tous produits**
100.0	100.0	100.0	100.0	100.0	100.0	100.0	100.0	100.0	100.0	2005	
100.0	100.0	100.0	100.0	100.0	100.0	100.0	100.0	100.0	100.0	2010	
6.7	8.8	29.8	5.5	6.0	4.8	0.9	27.9	0.7	5.1	1995	Produits alimentaires
4.2	4.9	30.4	3.0	3.3	2.4	0.9	21.8	0.8	2.3	2005	(CTCI 0 + 1 + 22 + 4)
4.8	3.0	22.8	3.6	4.1	2.4	1.2	19.1	1.0	2.8	2010	
3.5	12.0	9.7	2.9	3.1	1.5	0.5	34.3	0.5	2.7	1995	Matières premières
1.6	6.5	4.7	1.3	1.4	0.4	0.2	32.7	0.2	1.1	2005	d'origine agricole
1.7	3.3	3.9	1.4	1.7	0.4	0.2	28.4	0.1	1.2	2010	(CTCI 2 - 22 - 27 - 28)
5.6	29.2	25.2	4.0	3.9	2.5	5.1	21.0	3.2	3.1	1995	Minerais, métaux, pierres
6.3	18.8	33.2	4.7	4.5	2.7	5.9	13.0	5.2	2.9	2005	précieuses et or (non monétaire)
8.8	22.0	38.3	6.0	5.5	2.4	8.4	25.4	6.8	3.5	2010	(CTCI 27 + 28 + 68 + 667 + 971)
13.6	26.5	2.8	13.6	7.0	2.6	75.6	8.4	81.6	5.0	1995	Combustibles (CTCI 3)
19.9	52.2	5.1	19.5	10.1	3.3	80.6	7.5	83.3	7.0	2005	
24.1	61.0	17.1	22.5	12.0	3.3	75.5	12.2	80.9	8.2	2010	
69.7	23.4	32.0	72.9	78.9	87.9	17.6	8.4	13.8	83.0	1995	Articles manufacturés
67.6	16.4	26.4	71.3	80.4	90.9	12.2	24.8	10.3	86.3	2005	(CTCI 5 à 8 moins 667 et 68)
60.0	7.8	17.8	66.0	76.1	91.4	14.6	14.7	11.2	84.0	2010	

Sources :
- Calculs du secrétariat de la CNUCED sur la base des données de ONU DAES Division de statistique

Notes :

(1) Y compris les exportations de catégorie spéciale, approvisionnements des navires et combustibles de soute et autres exportations de moindre importance dont la destination n'a pas pu être déterminée.

(2) Il est reconnu que la structure du commerce et la distribution au niveau partenaire pour certains pays et sur certaines années peuvent varier. À cet égard, le lecteur devrait connaître la couverture ainsi que les limites des données principales utilisées dans ce tableau. Pour de plus amples renseignements, veuillez visiter http://comtrade.un.org/db/help/uReadMeFirst.aspx.

2.2.G Export structure by partner and product group
Developing economies: Western Asia

Product group	Year Année	World (1) Monde (1)	Developed economies - Économies développées Total	Europe Total	EU UE	Canada	USA États-Unis	Japan Japon	Other developed countries Autres économies développées	Transition economies Économies en transition
Millions of dollars										
All products	1995	133 709	72 534	28 591	28 052	491	12 624	28 938	1 891	2 569
	2005	514 698	255 648	103 050	100 728	3 345	57 839	86 133	5 282	7 203
	2010	821 556	287 663	115 674	110 980	4 456	56 189	103 325	8 019	14 189
Share by destination (percentage)										
All products	1995	100.0	54.2	21.4	21.0	0.4	9.4	21.6	1.4	1.9
	2005	100.0	49.7	20.0	19.6	0.6	11.2	16.7	1.0	1.4
	2010	100.0	35.0	14.1	13.5	0.5	6.8	12.6	1.0	1.7
All food items	1995	100.0	39.4	32.3	31.1	0.4	4.7	1.0	0.9	9.3
(SITC 0 + 1 + 22 + 4)	2005	100.0	35.2	29.2	28.3	0.4	3.0	1.0	1.5	5.9
	2010	100.0	21.0	17.1	16.7	0.4	1.8	0.5	1.1	6.1
Agricultural raw materials	1995	100.0	51.0	46.3	45.5	0.1	1.7	1.3	1.6	0.5
(SITC 2 - 22 - 27 - 28)	2005	100.0	36.2	32.8	32.4	0.1	1.3	1.0	1.0	1.7
	2010	100.0	25.0	21.9	21.7	0.1	1.0	1.6	0.3	4.4
Ores, metals, precious stones	1995	100.0	29.0	15.6	14.2	0.1	2.1	10.7	0.6	1.0
and non-monetary gold	2005	100.0	26.9	20.5	17.1	0.0	3.2	2.4	0.8	1.0
(SITC 27 + 28 + 68 + 667 + 971)	2010	100.0	18.0	15.7	11.1	0.1	0.9	1.0	0.3	0.6
Fuels (SITC 3)	1995	100.0	59.8	14.3	14.3	0.4	11.0	32.3	1.7	0.1
	2005	100.0	52.2	12.7	12.6	0.8	13.8	24.3	0.7	0.0
	2010	100.0	38.4	8.4	8.4	0.7	9.1	19.4	0.8	0.1
Manufactured goods	1995	100.0	47.5	37.6	36.5	0.3	7.3	1.5	0.9	5.3
(SITC 5 to 8 less 667 and 68)	2005	100.0	48.4	39.4	38.5	0.4	6.3	0.5	1.8	4.7
	2010	100.0	32.9	27.5	26.7	0.3	3.3	0.3	1.5	5.6
Share by major product group (percentage)										
All products	1995	100.0	100.0	100.0	100.0	100.0	100.0	100.0	100.0	100.0
	2005	100.0	100.0	100.0	100.0	100.0	100.0	100.0	100.0	100.0
	2010	100.0	100.0	100.0	100.0	100.0	100.0	100.0	100.0	100.0
All food items	1995	5.4	3.9	8.2	8.0	5.6	2.7	0.3	3.5	26.2
(SITC 0 + 1 + 22 + 4)	2005	3.2	2.3	4.7	4.6	1.8	0.9	0.2	4.7	13.4
	2010	3.8	2.3	4.6	4.6	3.0	1.0	0.2	4.2	13.3
Agricultural raw materials	1995	0.7	0.6	1.4	1.4	0.2	0.1	0.0	0.8	0.2
(SITC 2 - 22 - 27 - 28)	2005	0.2	0.2	0.4	0.4	0.0	0.0	0.0	0.2	0.3
	2010	0.2	0.1	0.3	0.3	0.0	0.0	0.0	0.1	0.5
Ores, metals, precious stones	1995	3.9	2.1	2.8	2.6	0.6	0.9	1.9	1.6	2.1
and non-monetary gold	2005	3.8	2.1	3.9	3.4	0.3	1.1	0.5	3.0	2.7
(SITC 27 + 28 + 68 + 667 + 971)	2010	6.6	3.4	7.4	5.5	0.7	0.9	0.5	2.4	2.4
Fuels (SITC 3)	1995	64.4	70.9	43.1	43.9	75.5	75.3	96.0	77.4	1.8
	2005	67.8	71.3	43.0	43.7	83.3	83.0	98.4	44.9	2.3
	2010	64.0	70.1	38.3	39.6	83.5	84.8	98.5	53.5	2.3
Manufactured goods	1995	25.0	21.9	44.0	43.6	18.0	19.3	1.7	16.4	69.6
(SITC 5 to 8 less 667 and 68)	2005	24.0	23.4	47.4	47.3	14.3	13.4	0.7	43.3	80.0
	2010	24.9	23.4	48.7	49.2	12.5	12.1	0.7	37.6	81.0

Sources:
- UNCTAD secretariat calculations based on UN DESA Statistics Division's data

Notes:

(1) Includes special category exports, ship stores and bunkers and other exports of minor importance whose destination could not be determined.

(2) It is recognized that the structure of trade and partner distribution for certain countries and years might vary. In this regard, reader should know the coverage and limitations of the main principal data used in this table. For further information, please visit
http://comtrade.un.org/db/help/uReadMeFirst.aspx.

			Developing economies - Économies en développement				Oceania (2) / Océanie (2)	Major petroleum exporters and gas exporters / Principaux exportateurs de pétrole et de gaz	Major manufactured goods exporters / Principaux exportateurs d'articles manufacturés	Year / Année	Destinations
				Asia / Asie							
Total	Africa / Afrique	America / Amérique	Total	Eastern, Southern and South-Eastern Asia / Asie orientale, méridionale et du Sud-Est	China / Chine	Western Asia / Asie occidentale					Groupes de produits
Millions de dollars											
57 562	4 053	1 803	51 705	38 131	1 915	13 575	0	9 540	25 576	1995	**Total tous produits**
248 360	20 466	3 699	224 069	177 748	24 939	46 321	126	41 087	135 220	2005	
516 886	36 658	6 577	473 531	394 930	61 689	78 601	120	83 376	266 142	2010	
Parts par destinations (en pourcentage)											
43.1	3.0	1.3	38.7	28.5	1.4	10.2	0.0	7.1	19.1	1995	**Total tous produits**
48.3	4.0	0.7	43.5	34.5	4.8	9.0	0.0	8.0	26.3	2005	
62.9	4.5	0.8	57.6	48.1	7.5	9.6	0.0	10.1	32.4	2010	
50.7	6.0	0.6	44.1	7.3	0.1	36.7	0.0	34.6	2.2	1995	Produits alimentaires
57.9	6.6	0.5	50.8	11.0	0.2	39.8	0.0	37.4	1.6	2005	(CTCI 0 + 1 + 22 + 4)
72.0	7.4	0.5	64.1	16.7	0.4	47.5	0.0	45.7	2.5	2010	
47.8	10.1	0.2	37.4	22.5	3.0	14.9	0.0	9.3	7.9	1995	Matières premières
57.5	9.3	0.4	47.8	25.6	2.8	22.2	0.0	13.8	5.7	2005	d'origine agricole
69.3	8.1	-0.7	61.9	38.0	5.1	24.0	0.0	20.6	12.7	2010	(CTCI 2 - 22 - 27 - 28)
68.3	3.5	0.2	64.7	45.9	1.6	18.8	0.0	16.6	24.1	1995	Minerais, métaux, pierres
71.6	2.8	0.2	68.6	51.3	3.1	17.3	0.0	14.8	14.7	2005	précieuses et or (non monétaire)
81.1	2.6	0.3	78.2	65.9	5.0	12.3	0.0	11.0	21.2	2010	(CTCI 27 + 28 + 68 + 667 + 971)
40.1	1.7	1.9	36.6	32.5	1.4	4.1	0.0	0.3	23.8	1995	Combustibles (CTCI 3)
47.7	2.6	0.8	44.3	40.9	5.9	3.4	0.0	1.3	34.9	2005	
61.6	2.7	0.7	58.1	55.7	9.5	2.4	0.0	1.1	43.7	2010	
45.6	5.6	0.4	39.5	20.8	1.7	18.7	0.0	17.5	10.7	1995	Articles manufacturés
44.5	7.5	0.6	36.3	18.0	3.0	18.3	0.1	20.6	8.0	2005	(CTCI 5 à 8 moins 667 et 68)
60.3	9.0	1.2	50.1	28.6	4.0	21.5	0.0	27.9	11.4	2010	
Parts par principaux groupes de produits (en pourcentage)											
100.0	100.0	100.0	100.0	100.0	100.0	100.0	100.0	100.0	100.0	1995	**Total tous produits**
100.0	100.0	100.0	100.0	100.0	100.0	100.0	100.0	100.0	100.0	2005	
100.0	100.0	100.0	100.0	100.0	100.0	100.0	100.0	100.0	100.0	2010	
6.4	10.7	2.5	6.2	1.4	0.3	19.6	5.4	26.3	0.6	1995	Produits alimentaires
3.8	5.3	2.4	3.7	1.0	0.2	14.1	1.3	15.0	0.2	2005	(CTCI 0 + 1 + 22 + 4)
4.3	6.2	2.3	4.2	1.3	0.2	18.6	1.8	16.9	0.3	2010	
0.7	2.2	0.1	0.6	0.5	1.4	1.0	11.0	0.9	0.3	1995	Matières premières
0.3	0.5	0.1	0.3	0.2	0.1	0.6	0.0	0.4	0.1	2005	d'origine agricole
0.2	0.4	-0.2	0.2	0.2	0.1	0.5	0.0	0.4	0.1	2010	(CTCI 2 - 22 - 27 - 28)
6.2	4.5	0.4	6.5	6.3	4.4	7.2	16.7	9.1	4.9	1995	Minerais, métaux, pierres
5.7	2.7	0.8	6.0	5.7	2.4	7.3	0.1	7.1	2.1	2005	précieuses et or (non monétaire)
8.5	3.9	2.2	9.0	9.1	4.4	8.5	0.3	7.2	4.3	2010	(CTCI 27 + 28 + 68 + 667 + 971)
60.0	36.1	88.8	60.9	73.3	64.6	26.0	0.0	2.4	80.2	1995	Combustibles (CTCI 3)
67.1	44.6	76.1	69.0	80.3	82.0	25.7	0.1	11.4	90.1	2005	
62.6	38.8	57.7	64.5	74.2	81.4	16.1	10.6	6.7	86.3	2010	
26.5	46.4	8.2	25.6	18.3	29.3	46.1	66.9	61.3	14.0	1995	Articles manufacturés
22.2	45.6	19.6	20.0	12.5	14.8	48.9	97.3	62.2	7.3	2005	(CTCI 5 à 8 moins 667 et 68)
23.9	50.2	36.7	21.7	14.8	13.3	56.0	83.5	68.5	8.8	2010	

Sources :
- Calculs du secrétariat de la CNUCED sur la base des données de ONU DAES Division de statistique

Notes :

(1) Y compris les exportations de catégorie spéciale, approvisionnements des navires et combustibles de soute et autres exportations de moindre importance dont la destination n'a pas pu être déterminée.

(2) Il est reconnu que la structure du commerce et la distribution au niveau partenaire pour certains pays et sur certaines années peuvent varier. À cet égard, le lecteur devrait connaître la couverture ainsi que les limites des données principales utilisées dans ce tableau. Pour de plus amples renseignements, veuillez visiter http://comtrade.un.org/db/help/uReadMeFirst.aspx.

2.2.G Import structure by partner and product group
Developing economies: Western Asia

Product group	Year / Année	World (1) / Monde (1)	Developed economies - Économies développées							Transition economies / Économies en transition
			Total	Europe Total	EU / UE	Canada	USA / États-Unis	Japan / Japon	Other developed countries / Autres économies développées	
Millions of dollars										
All products	1995	123 480	76 176	50 338	46 834	979	15 184	8 242	1 432	4 497
	2005	363 517	193 541	134 660	125 927	1 871	30 051	18 871	8 089	22 999
	2010	655 005	289 734	194 100	182 120	4 220	54 474	27 760	9 100	41 066
Share by origin (percentage)										
All products	1995	100.0	61.7	40.8	37.9	0.8	12.3	6.7	1.2	3.6
	2005	100.0	53.2	37.0	34.6	0.5	8.3	5.2	2.2	6.3
	2010	100.0	44.4	29.7	27.9	0.6	8.3	4.3	1.4	6.3
All food items	1995	100.0	50.4	30.8	30.0	0.6	14.8	0.2	4.0	2.7
(SITC 0 + 1 + 22 + 4)	2005	100.0	39.2	22.5	21.6	0.5	9.3	0.1	6.8	3.4
	2010	100.0	32.0	18.4	17.3	1.9	7.2	0.2	4.3	4.3
Agricultural raw materials	1995	100.0	54.9	33.8	33.1	2.7	11.0	0.9	6.5	16.8
(SITC 2 - 22 - 27 - 28)	2005	100.0	58.5	35.8	35.4	2.0	17.7	0.6	2.4	10.5
	2010	100.0	51.2	31.2	30.9	1.2	16.5	1.0	1.3	10.0
Ores, metals, precious stones	1995	100.0	65.2	51.1	34.6	2.5	8.6	0.3	2.6	5.0
and non-monetary gold	2005	100.0	41.7	33.9	18.8	0.6	4.3	0.4	2.6	12.9
(SITC 27 + 28 + 68 + 667 + 971)	2010	100.0	26.6	19.8	14.6	0.3	4.1	0.3	2.2	8.2
Fuels (SITC 3)	1995	100.0	13.3	8.7	8.7	0.1	3.1	0.0	1.3	11.1
	2005	100.0	16.2	10.9	9.7	0.3	1.4	0.1	3.6	20.5
	2010	100.0	20.8	15.2	14.3	0.5	3.7	0.1	1.4	29.4
Manufactured goods	1995	100.0	69.0	45.6	42.9	0.7	13.1	9.2	0.4	2.7
(SITC 5 to 8 less 667 and 68)	2005	100.0	62.0	43.6	42.1	0.5	9.3	7.3	1.2	2.9
	2010	100.0	52.3	35.4	33.8	0.5	9.4	6.2	0.7	2.4
Share by major product group (percentage)										
All products	1995	100.0	100.0	100.0	100.0	100.0	100.0	100.0	100.0	100.0
	2005	100.0	100.0	100.0	100.0	100.0	100.0	100.0	100.0	100.0
	2010	100.0	100.0	100.0	100.0	100.0	100.0	100.0	100.0	100.0
All food items	1995	12.8	10.4	9.7	10.1	10.0	15.4	0.3	44.2	9.3
(SITC 0 + 1 + 22 + 4)	2005	9.6	7.1	5.8	6.0	10.1	10.8	0.2	29.1	5.2
	2010	11.0	7.9	6.8	6.8	32.4	9.5	0.4	33.6	7.5
Agricultural raw materials	1995	2.5	2.2	2.1	2.2	8.6	2.2	0.3	13.9	11.4
(SITC 2 - 22 - 27 - 28)	2005	1.4	1.5	1.3	1.4	5.3	2.9	0.2	1.5	2.3
	2010	1.3	1.6	1.4	1.5	2.6	2.7	0.3	1.3	2.1
Ores, metals, precious stones	1995	4.8	5.0	6.0	4.3	15.1	3.3	0.2	10.6	6.5
and non-monetary gold	2005	7.5	5.9	6.8	4.1	8.9	3.9	0.5	8.7	15.2
(SITC 27 + 28 + 68 + 667 + 971)	2010	10.7	6.4	7.1	5.6	5.7	5.2	0.7	16.6	14.0
Fuels (SITC 3)	1995	6.2	1.3	1.3	1.4	1.1	1.6	0.0	7.2	19.1
	2005	8.8	2.7	2.6	2.5	4.9	1.5	0.1	14.2	28.7
	2010	7.1	3.3	3.6	3.6	5.5	3.1	0.1	7.1	33.2
Manufactured goods	1995	71.8	80.3	80.3	81.1	65.0	76.7	98.7	22.4	53.7
(SITC 5 to 8 less 667 and 68)	2005	69.8	81.3	82.2	84.8	69.9	78.8	98.4	39.0	31.8
	2010	67.3	79.4	80.2	81.6	53.5	76.1	98.0	35.5	25.4

Sources:
- UNCTAD secretariat calculations based on UN DESA Statistics Division's data

Notes:

(1) Includes special category exports, ship stores and bunkers and other exports of minor importance whose destination could not be determined.

(2) It is recognized that the structure of trade and partner distribution for certain countries and years might vary. In this regard, reader should know the coverage and limitations of the main principal data used in this table. For further information, please visit
http://comtrade.un.org/db/help/uReadMeFirst.aspx.

			Developing economies - Économies en développement							Origines	
				Asia Asie				Major petroleum exporters and gas exporters	Major manufactured goods exporters	Year	
Total	Africa Afrique	America Amérique	Total	Eastern, Southern and South-Eastern Asia Asie orientale, méridionale et du Sud-Est	China Chine	Western Asia Asie occidentale	Oceania (2) Océanie (2)	Principaux exportateurs de pétrole et de gaz	Principaux exportateurs d'articles manufacturés	Année	Groupes de produits
Millions de dollars											
37 649	2 941	2 290	32 413	19 989	3 061	12 424	5	10 625	13 752	1995	Total tous produits
145 464	11 616	7 456	126 368	78 533	24 457	47 835	24	36 676	53 145	2005	
320 384	21 586	15 111	283 682	198 349	69 029	85 332	5	60 405	124 913	2010	
Parts par origines (en pourcentage)											
30.5	2.4	1.9	26.2	16.2	2.5	10.1	0.0	8.6	11.1	1995	Total tous produits
40.0	3.2	2.1	34.8	21.6	6.7	13.2	0.0	10.1	14.6	2005	
49.1	3.3	2.3	43.4	30.4	10.6	13.1	0.0	9.3	19.1	2010	
45.3	4.8	7.3	33.2	17.6	1.1	15.6	0.0	8.2	7.6	1995	Produits alimentaires
57.3	5.5	10.8	41.0	17.7	1.5	23.3	0.0	8.8	6.0	2005	(CTCI 0 + 1 + 22 + 4)
63.7	6.3	11.1	46.3	21.3	1.9	25.0	0.0	11.0	6.7	2010	
27.3	5.0	3.4	18.9	14.7	0.5	4.2	0.0	3.4	9.9	1995	Matières premières
30.7	4.8	4.7	21.2	15.6	2.4	5.6	0.0	2.9	10.0	2005	d'origine agricole
38.6	5.0	5.2	28.4	23.2	4.2	5.2	0.0	2.7	13.9	2010	(CTCI 2 - 22 - 27 - 28)
28.8	6.0	4.8	17.9	5.2	0.4	12.7	0.0	8.3	1.5	1995	Minerais, métaux, pierres
45.2	7.6	3.9	33.7	23.9	1.2	9.8	0.0	7.5	7.1	2005	précieuses et or (non monétaire)
65.1	7.9	3.8	53.4	43.8	1.7	9.5	0.0	8.1	4.7	2010	(CTCI 27 + 28 + 68 + 667 + 971)
74.2	13.6	0.1	60.4	10.6	0.3	49.8	0.0	65.2	1.0	1995	Combustibles (CTCI 3)
63.0	10.6	0.7	51.6	12.4	0.9	39.2	0.0	47.9	1.5	2005	
49.8	6.3	1.0	42.5	16.0	1.1	26.5	0.0	33.8	2.7	2010	
25.0	0.7	0.8	23.5	17.6	3.2	5.9	0.0	4.2	13.6	1995	Articles manufacturés
34.6	1.1	0.8	32.6	23.5	9.1	9.0	0.0	5.1	18.9	2005	(CTCI 5 à 8 moins 667 et 68)
45.1	1.5	0.8	42.8	31.9	14.9	10.9	0.0	6.1	25.9	2010	
Parts par principaux groupes de produits (en pourcentage)											
100.0	100.0	100.0	100.0	100.0	100.0	100.0	100.0	100.0	100.0	1995	Total tous produits
100.0	100.0	100.0	100.0	100.0	100.0	100.0	100.0	100.0	100.0	2005	
100.0	100.0	100.0	100.0	100.0	100.0	100.0	100.0	100.0	100.0	2010	
19.0	25.7	50.1	16.2	13.9	5.6	19.8	72.5	12.2	8.7	1995	Produits alimentaires
13.7	16.4	50.5	11.3	7.9	2.1	17.0	2.6	8.4	3.9	2005	(CTCI 0 + 1 + 22 + 4)
14.2	20.8	52.8	11.7	7.7	1.9	21.0	6.4	13.0	3.9	2010	
2.2	5.3	4.6	1.8	2.3	0.5	1.0	0.0	1.0	2.2	1995	Matières premières
1.0	2.0	3.1	0.8	1.0	0.5	0.6	0.0	0.4	0.9	2005	d'origine agricole
1.1	2.0	3.0	0.9	1.0	0.5	0.5	2.8	0.4	1.0	2010	(CTCI 2 - 22 - 27 - 28)
4.5	12.0	12.4	3.2	1.5	0.8	6.0	1.1	4.6	0.6	1995	Minerais, métaux, pierres
8.4	17.8	14.0	7.2	8.3	1.4	5.6	0.3	5.6	3.6	2005	précieuses et or (non monétaire)
14.1	25.4	17.5	13.1	15.4	1.7	7.8	1.9	9.3	2.6	2010	(CTCI 27 + 28 + 68 + 667 + 971)
15.2	35.7	0.4	14.4	4.1	0.8	30.9	0.0	47.3	0.5	1995	Combustibles (CTCI 3)
13.9	29.4	3.1	13.1	5.1	1.1	26.3	0.0	42.0	0.9	2005	
7.2	13.5	3.2	7.0	3.7	0.8	14.4	0.2	26.0	1.0	2010	
58.9	21.4	32.5	64.2	77.8	92.1	42.2	26.4	34.9	87.6	1995	Articles manufacturés
60.3	25.0	28.2	65.4	76.0	94.5	47.9	96.9	35.3	90.1	2005	(CTCI 5 à 8 moins 667 et 68)
61.9	30.9	22.5	66.4	70.7	95.1	56.2	85.0	44.5	91.3	2010	

Sources :
- Calculs du secrétariat de la CNUCED sur la base des données de ONU DAES Division de statistique

Notes :

(1) Y compris les exportations de catégorie spéciale, approvisionnements des navires et combustibles de soute et autres exportations de moindre importance dont la destination n'a pas pu être déterminée.

(2) Il est reconnu que la structure du commerce et la distribution au niveau partenaire pour certains pays et sur certaines années peuvent varier. À cet égard, le lecteur devrait connaître la couverture ainsi que les limites des données principales utilisées dans ce tableau. Pour de plus amples renseignements, veuillez visiter http://comtrade.un.org/db/help/uReadMeFirst.aspx.

2.2.H Export structure by partner and product group
Developing economies: Oceania

Product group	Year / Année	World (1) / Monde (1)	Developed economies - Économies développées							Transition economies / Économies en transition
			Total	Europe Total	EU / UE	Canada	USA / États-Unis	Japan / Japon	Other developed countries / Autres économies développées	
Millions of dollars										
All products	1995	5 500	4 322	1 012	1 009	26	214	1 899	1 171	2
	2005	6 897	4 676	1 345	1 325	23	316	1 007	1 983	24
	2010	9 150	6 273	1 456	1 450	11	356	1 280	3 169	10
Share by destination (percentage)										
All products	1995	100.0	78.6	18.4	18.3	0.5	3.9	34.5	21.3	0.0
	2005	100.0	67.8	19.5	19.2	0.3	4.6	14.6	28.8	0.3
	2010	100.0	68.6	15.9	15.8	0.1	3.9	14.0	34.6	0.1
All food items	1995	100.0	81.4	52.3	52.3	2.1	5.2	13.5	8.3	0.1
(SITC 0 + 1 + 22 + 4)	2005	100.0	79.4	41.2	41.2	0.5	13.8	10.5	13.4	0.3
	2010	100.0	69.5	39.0	39.0	0.3	10.6	7.8	11.8	0.5
Agricultural raw materials	1995	100.0	61.6	1.5	1.5	0.0	0.3	58.2	1.6	0.0
(SITC 2 - 22 - 27 - 28)	2005	100.0	18.6	0.6	0.6	0.1	1.4	12.1	4.4	0.0
	2010	100.0	12.8	0.2	0.2	0.1	0.0	9.6	2.9	0.0
Ores, metals, precious stones	1995	100.0	87.3	15.5	15.4	0.0	2.2	40.3	29.3	0.0
and non-monetary gold	2005	100.0	84.2	15.5	15.4	0.0	1.4	24.6	42.6	0.9
(SITC 27 + 28 + 68 + 667 + 971)	2010	100.0	82.3	9.9	9.8	0.0	0.9	21.2	50.3	0.0
Fuels (SITC 3)	1995	100.0	89.3	0.0	0.0	0.0	3.4	1.9	84.0	0.0
	2005	100.0	78.6	0.0	0.0	0.0	2.6	5.4	70.7	0.0
	2010	100.0	66.0	0.4	0.4	0.0	3.0	2.4	60.2	0.0
Manufactured goods	1995	100.0	85.7	25.4	25.2	0.4	10.3	34.7	14.9	0.1
(SITC 5 to 8 less 667 and 68)	2005	100.0	51.2	25.8	24.9	0.8	3.0	11.2	10.5	0.1
	2010	100.0	58.8	25.8	25.6	0.4	5.5	12.6	14.5	0.1
Share by major product group (percentage)										
All products	1995	100.0	100.0	100.0	100.0	100.0	100.0	100.0	100.0	100.0
	2005	100.0	100.0	100.0	100.0	100.0	100.0	100.0	100.0	100.0
	2010	100.0	100.0	100.0	100.0	100.0	100.0	100.0	100.0	100.0
All food items	1995	18.7	19.3	53.0	53.2	83.5	24.9	7.3	7.3	43.8
(SITC 0 + 1 + 22 + 4)	2005	19.5	22.8	41.1	41.7	31.5	58.7	14.0	9.1	15.5
	2010	19.4	19.7	47.7	47.8	42.4	52.8	10.8	6.6	82.1
Agricultural raw materials	1995	11.8	9.3	1.0	1.0	0.1	0.8	19.9	0.9	0.0
(SITC 2 - 22 - 27 - 28)	2005	8.5	2.3	0.2	0.2	1.3	2.6	7.0	1.3	0.1
	2010	8.3	1.6	0.1	0.1	4.3	0.0	5.7	0.7	0.3
Ores, metals, precious stones	1995	25.0	27.8	21.0	21.0	0.4	14.5	29.2	34.4	0.2
and non-monetary gold	2005	27.9	34.7	22.2	22.4	2.5	8.7	47.1	41.4	75.7
(SITC 27 + 28 + 68 + 667 + 971)	2010	43.9	52.7	27.3	27.3	4.4	10.4	66.4	63.7	0.1
Fuels (SITC 3)	1995	11.5	13.1	0.0	0.0	0.0	10.0	0.6	45.4	0.0
	2005	14.4	16.8	0.0	0.0	0.0	8.2	5.3	35.5	0.1
	2010	12.6	12.1	0.3	0.3	0.2	9.7	2.1	21.9	2.3
Manufactured goods	1995	17.2	18.8	23.8	23.7	15.6	45.6	17.3	12.0	55.7
(SITC 5 to 8 less 667 and 68)	2005	27.4	20.7	36.2	35.4	64.4	17.8	21.0	10.0	8.5
	2010	14.9	12.8	24.2	24.0	48.1	20.9	13.4	6.3	15.2

Sources:
- UNCTAD secretariat calculations based on UN DESA Statistics Division's data

Notes:

(1) Includes special category exports, ship stores and bunkers and other exports of minor importance whose destination could not be determined.

(2) It is recognized that the structure of trade and partner distribution for certain countries and years might vary. In this regard, reader should know the coverage and limitations of the main principal data used in this table. For further information, please visit
http://comtrade.un.org/db/help/uReadMeFirst.aspx.

2.2.H Structure des exportations par partenaires et groupes de produits
Économies en développement : Océanie

Developing economies - Économies en développement								Major petroleum exporters and gas exporters / Principaux exportateurs de pétrole et de gaz	Major manufactured goods exporters / Principaux exportateurs d'articles manufacturés	Year / Année	Destinations
Total	Africa / Afrique	America / Amérique	Asia / Asie Total	Eastern, Southern and South-Eastern Asia / Asie orientale, méridionale et du Sud-Est	China / Chine	Western Asia / Asie occidentale	Oceania (2) / Océanie (2)				Groupes de produits
Millions de dollars											
815	6	9	781	777	84	5	18	1	663	1995	**Total tous produits**
2 195	86	172	1 697	1 687	431	10	240	2	1 407	2005	
2 867	61	93	2 444	2 440	864	4	270	2	1 822	2010	
Parts par destinations (en pourcentage)											
14.8	**0.1**	**0.2**	**14.2**	**14.1**	**1.5**	**0.1**	**0.3**	**0.0**	**12.1**	**1995**	**Total tous produits**
31.8	**1.2**	**2.5**	**24.6**	**24.5**	**6.3**	**0.1**	**3.5**	**0.0**	**20.4**	**2005**	
31.3	**0.7**	**1.0**	**26.7**	**26.7**	**9.4**	**0.0**	**2.9**	**0.0**	**19.9**	**2010**	
18.2	0.1	0.1	17.8	17.5	1.0	0.2	0.3	0.0	15.3	1995	Produits alimentaires
20.3	0.5	0.3	13.1	13.1	0.3	0.0	6.4	0.0	10.5	2005	(CTCI 0 + 1 + 22 + 4)
30.0	0.3	4.5	18.6	18.5	0.4	0.0	6.7	0.0	15.8	2010	
38.4	0.0	0.0	38.2	38.2	4.3	0.0	0.1	0.0	34.1	1995	Matières premières
81.4	0.4	0.8	79.6	79.6	45.1	0.0	0.6	0.0	56.8	2005	d'origine agricole
87.2	0.2	1.1	85.3	85.2	68.1	0.1	0.6	0.0	75.1	2010	(CTCI 2 - 22 - 27 - 28)
12.7	0.0	0.0	12.7	12.7	0.0	0.0	0.0	0.0	8.5	1995	Minerais, métaux, pierres
14.8	0.5	0.0	14.1	14.1	2.5	0.0	0.1	0.0	6.9	2005	précieuses et or (non monétaire)
17.7	0.4	0.0	17.2	17.2	2.2	0.0	0.1	0.0	9.1	2010	(CTCI 27 + 28 + 68 + 667 + 971)
10.7	0.0	0.0	10.3	10.3	7.2	0.0	0.4	0.0	10.3	1995	Combustibles (CTCI 3)
21.2	0.1	0.0	16.4	16.4	3.5	0.0	4.7	0.0	10.9	2005	
34.0	0.1	0.1	31.3	31.3	17.2	0.0	2.5	0.0	25.8	2010	
14.1	0.6	0.9	11.6	11.3	0.0	0.2	1.1	0.0	10.8	1995	Articles manufacturés
48.7	3.5	8.6	32.6	32.0	4.3	0.5	4.0	0.2	36.5	2005	(CTCI 5 à 8 moins 667 et 68)
41.1	2.7	0.3	29.9	29.7	3.8	0.2	8.2	0.1	22.3	2010	
Parts par principaux groupes de produits (en pourcentage)											
100.0	**100.0**	**100.0**	**100.0**	**100.0**	**100.0**	**100.0**	**100.0**	**100.0**	**100.0**	**1995**	**Total tous produits**
100.0	**100.0**	**100.0**	**100.0**	**100.0**	**100.0**	**100.0**	**100.0**	**100.0**	**100.0**	**2005**	
100.0	**100.0**	**100.0**	**100.0**	**100.0**	**100.0**	**100.0**	**100.0**	**100.0**	**100.0**	**2010**	
22.9	9.9	8.6	23.3	23.2	11.7	54.5	14.5	49.4	23.7	1995	Produits alimentaires
12.4	7.4	2.4	10.4	10.4	0.9	1.4	35.7	3.9	10.0	2005	(CTCI 0 + 1 + 22 + 4)
18.6	8.9	85.6	13.5	13.5	0.8	16.1	44.1	30.1	15.4	2010	
30.6	0.1	0.6	31.8	32.0	33.6	0.0	5.1	0.0	33.3	1995	Matières premières
21.7	2.6	2.7	27.4	27.5	61.0	0.0	1.6	0.0	23.6	2005	d'origine agricole
23.2	2.2	9.3	26.7	26.7	60.2	16.4	1.6	1.0	31.5	2010	(CTCI 2 - 22 - 27 - 28)
21.4	0.1	0.1	22.3	22.5	0.0	0.5	1.5	0.0	17.6	1995	Minerais, métaux, pierres
13.0	11.6	0.3	16.0	16.1	11.1	0.5	1.1	0.3	9.4	2005	précieuses et or (non monétaire)
24.8	25.2	0.0	28.3	28.4	10.1	2.1	1.6	0.1	20.1	2010	(CTCI 27 + 28 + 68 + 667 + 971)
8.3	0.0	0.0	8.3	8.4	54.5	0.0	13.3	0.0	9.8	1995	Combustibles (CTCI 3)
9.6	1.2	0.0	9.6	9.7	8.1	0.0	19.5	0.0	7.7	2005	
13.6	2.0	1.1	14.7	14.8	22.9	4.0	10.7	6.2	16.3	2010	
16.4	89.7	90.7	14.0	13.8	0.1	45.0	55.9	50.6	15.4	1995	Articles manufacturés
41.9	77.1	94.2	36.2	35.9	18.9	97.8	31.7	94.9	49.0	2005	(CTCI 5 à 8 moins 667 et 68)
19.5	61.0	3.8	16.7	16.6	6.0	61.3	41.5	62.6	16.7	2010	

Sources :
- Calculs du secrétariat de la CNUCED sur la base des données de ONU DAES Division de statistique

Notes :

(1) Y compris les exportations de catégorie spéciale, approvisionnements des navires et combustibles de soute et autres exportations de moindre importance dont la destination n'a pas pu être déterminée.

(2) Il est reconnu que la structure du commerce et la distribution au niveau partenaire pour certains pays et sur certaines années peuvent varier. À cet égard, le lecteur devrait connaître la couverture ainsi que les limites des données principales utilisées dans ce tableau. Pour de plus amples renseignements, veuillez visiter http://comtrade.un.org/db/help/uReadMeFirst.aspx.

2.2.H Import structure by partner and product group
Developing economies: Oceania

Product group	Year / Année	World (1) / Monde (1)	Developed economies - Économies développées							Transition economies / Économies en transition
			Total	Europe Total	EU / UE	Canada	USA / États-Unis	Japan / Japon	Other developed countries / Autres économies développées	
					Millions of dollars					
All products	1995	6 595	4 446	1 322	1 311	13	360	807	1 943	1
	2005	9 602	5 731	1 974	1 946	30	484	510	2 733	3
	2010	13 300	7 710	2 240	2 196	48	748	639	3 553	10
					Share by origin (percentage)					
All products	1995	100.0	67.4	20.1	19.9	0.2	5.5	12.2	29.5	0.0
	2005	100.0	59.7	20.6	20.3	0.3	5.0	5.3	28.5	0.0
	2010	100.0	57.6	16.7	16.4	0.7	5.6	4.8	29.8	0.1
All food items	1995	100.0	85.7	23.0	22.9	0.2	10.4	5.2	46.9	0.0
(SITC 0 + 1 + 22 + 4)	2005	100.0	71.4	16.9	16.8	0.3	8.7	2.6	42.9	0.0
	2010	100.0	68.3	14.5	14.3	0.5	9.6	1.4	42.4	0.0
Agricultural raw materials	1995	100.0	90.1	6.4	6.4	0.0	27.9	3.2	52.5	0.3
(SITC 2 - 22 - 27 - 28)	2005	100.0	83.5	5.7	5.7	7.3	12.9	0.7	56.9	0.0
	2010	100.0	79.2	4.1	4.1	12.6	9.0	1.1	52.4	0.0
Ores, metals, precious stones	1995	100.0	81.3	27.3	27.3	0.0	3.6	1.8	48.6	0.0
and non-monetary gold	2005	100.0	73.4	30.9	30.7	1.0	2.3	1.9	37.4	0.0
(SITC 27 + 28 + 68 + 667 + 971)	2010	100.0	66.8	18.5	18.4	8.8	2.1	2.7	34.7	0.0
Fuels (SITC 3)	1995	100.0	61.3	0.5	0.5	0.0	1.5	0.0	59.3	0.0
	2005	100.0	20.3	0.3	0.3	0.0	0.3	0.0	19.7	0.0
	2010	100.0	26.3	0.5	0.5	0.0	0.4	0.0	25.4	0.2
Manufactured goods	1995	100.0	77.8	27.1	26.8	0.3	5.2	18.5	26.7	0.0
(SITC 5 to 8 less 667 and 68)	2005	100.0	69.2	29.4	29.0	0.3	5.3	8.1	26.1	0.0
	2010	100.0	66.9	24.7	24.2	0.7	5.9	8.2	27.3	0.1
					Share by major product group (percentage)					
All products	1995	100.0	100.0	100.0	100.0	100.0	100.0	100.0	100.0	100.0
	2005	100.0	100.0	100.0	100.0	100.0	100.0	100.0	100.0	100.0
	2010	100.0	100.0	100.0	100.0	100.0	100.0	100.0	100.0	100.0
All food items	1995	13.9	17.7	15.9	16.0	11.4	26.6	5.9	22.1	8.6
(SITC 0 + 1 + 22 + 4)	2005	17.3	20.7	14.2	14.3	18.6	29.9	8.4	26.1	7.9
	2010	20.1	23.8	17.3	17.5	14.1	34.7	5.7	28.5	7.9
Agricultural raw materials	1995	0.8	1.1	0.3	0.3	0.1	4.3	0.2	1.5	18.0
(SITC 2 - 22 - 27 - 28)	2005	0.9	1.3	0.3	0.3	21.3	2.4	0.1	1.9	0.6
	2010	1.0	1.4	0.2	0.2	17.2	1.6	0.2	1.8	0.2
Ores, metals, precious stones	1995	0.6	0.7	0.8	0.8	0.0	0.4	0.1	1.0	1.5
and non-monetary gold	2005	0.8	1.0	1.2	1.2	2.5	0.4	0.3	1.1	0.0
(SITC 27 + 28 + 68 + 667 + 971)	2010	0.9	1.0	1.0	1.0	10.5	0.3	0.5	1.0	0.0
Fuels (SITC 3)	1995	8.9	8.1	0.2	0.2	0.2	2.4	0.0	17.8	8.4
	2005	20.8	7.1	0.3	0.3	0.1	1.1	0.1	14.4	28.7
	2010	19.8	9.0	0.6	0.5	0.1	1.3	0.1	16.8	41.5
Manufactured goods	1995	60.7	70.1	82.1	82.0	86.6	58.1	91.9	55.0	63.5
(SITC 5 to 8 less 667 and 68)	2005	58.3	67.6	83.5	83.4	56.3	61.5	88.9	53.4	62.4
	2010	53.7	62.3	79.3	79.1	54.4	56.7	92.4	49.2	50.4

Sources:
- UNCTAD secretariat calculations based on UN DESA Statistics Division's data

Notes:

(1) Includes special category exports, ship stores and bunkers and other exports of minor importance whose destination could not be determined.

(2) It is recognized that the structure of trade and partner distribution for certain countries and years might vary. In this regard, reader should know the coverage and limitations of the main principal data used in this table. For further information, please visit
http://comtrade.un.org/db/help/uReadMeFirst.aspx.

2.2.H Structure des importations par partenaires et groupes de produits
Économies en développement : Océanie

Total	Africa / Afrique	America / Amérique	Asia / Asie — Total	Eastern, Southern and South-Eastern Asia / Asie orientale, méridionale et du Sud-Est	China / Chine	Western Asia / Asie occidentale	Oceania (2) / Océanie (2)	Major petroleum exporters and gas exporters / Principaux exportateurs de pétrole et de gaz	Major manufactured goods exporters / Principaux exportateurs d'articles manufacturés	Year / Année	Origines / Groupes de produits
Millions de dollars											
1 184	6	33	1 126	1 125	70	1	19	1	1 049	1995	**Total tous produits**
3 042	23	40	2 768	2 753	274	17	261	3	2 541	2005	
5 656	79	79	5 135	5 105	1 411	30	363	27	4 647	2010	
Parts par origines (en pourcentage)											
18.0	0.1	0.5	17.1	17.1	1.1	0.0	0.3	0.0	15.9	1995	**Total tous produits**
40.0	0.3	0.5	36.4	36.2	3.6	0.2	2.8	0.0	33.4	2005	
42.2	0.6	0.6	38.3	38.1	10.5	0.2	2.7	0.2	34.7	2010	
13.3	0.4	1.4	11.2	11.2	0.7	0.0	0.3	0.0	9.3	1995	Produits alimentaires
27.3	0.9	1.7	16.9	16.8	2.6	0.1	7.7	0.1	14.6	2005	(CTCI 0 + 1 + 22 + 4)
31.6	1.3	1.9	21.0	20.9	9.4	0.1	7.4	0.6	17.5	2010	
9.5	0.1	0.2	7.2	7.1	0.0	0.2	1.9	0.2	6.5	1995	Matières premières
16.5	1.4	0.4	8.8	8.8	1.1	0.0	5.9	0.0	6.4	2005	d'origine agricole
20.8	6.4	0.9	9.0	9.0	1.3	0.0	4.5	5.2	5.6	2010	(CTCI 2 - 22 - 27 - 28)
12.9	1.2	0.1	10.7	10.6	0.1	0.2	0.8	0.0	9.6	1995	Minerais, métaux, pierres
26.6	0.7	0.3	21.2	21.0	2.3	0.2	4.4	0.2	11.2	2005	précieuses et or (non monétaire)
33.2	1.1	0.2	28.4	28.2	6.4	0.3	3.4	0.6	18.6	2010	(CTCI 27 + 28 + 68 + 667 + 971)
38.3	0.2	0.1	37.5	37.5	0.0	0.0	0.4	0.0	30.9	1995	Combustibles (CTCI 3)
79.7	0.0	0.0	77.6	77.6	0.1	0.0	2.1	0.0	76.9	2005	
73.5	0.1	0.0	72.2	72.1	0.5	0.1	1.2	0.0	71.6	2010	
19.9	0.0	0.5	19.1	19.1	1.6	0.0	0.3	0.0	17.8	1995	Articles manufacturés
30.7	0.3	0.4	28.8	28.5	5.2	0.3	1.3	0.0	24.9	2005	(CTCI 5 à 8 moins 667 et 68)
33.0	0.4	0.4	30.5	30.2	11.1	0.3	1.7	0.0	25.9	2010	
Parts par principaux groupes de produits (en pourcentage)											
100.0	100.0	100.0	100.0	100.0	100.0	100.0	100.0	100.0	100.0	1995	**Total tous produits**
100.0	100.0	100.0	100.0	100.0	100.0	100.0	100.0	100.0	100.0	2005	
100.0	100.0	100.0	100.0	100.0	100.0	100.0	100.0	100.0	100.0	2010	
10.3	57.6	39.3	9.2	9.1	9.6	11.1	13.3	16.1	8.1	1995	Produits alimentaires
11.8	48.9	56.6	8.1	8.0	12.5	12.8	48.5	31.5	7.5	2005	(CTCI 0 + 1 + 22 + 4)
15.0	45.4	63.1	11.0	11.0	18.0	10.5	54.7	56.2	10.1	2010	
0.4	0.7	0.4	0.4	0.3	0.0	7.3	5.6	15.5	0.3	1995	Matières premières
0.4	3.8	0.8	0.2	0.2	0.3	0.0	2.0	0.2	0.2	2005	d'origine agricole
0.5	10.8	1.5	0.2	0.2	0.1	0.0	1.7	25.3	0.2	2010	(CTCI 2 - 22 - 27 - 28)
0.4	7.3	0.1	0.4	0.4	0.0	4.9	1.6	1.3	0.3	1995	Minerais, métaux, pierres
0.5	1.6	0.6	0.5	0.5	0.5	0.8	1.3	4.5	0.3	2005	précieuses et or (non monétaire)
0.7	1.6	0.4	0.6	0.6	0.5	1.0	1.1	2.5	0.5	2010	(CTCI 27 + 28 + 68 + 667 + 971)
18.9	20.7	2.3	19.5	19.5	0.1	0.0	13.5	0.0	20.5	1995	Combustibles (CTCI 3)
41.4	0.7	0.1	44.3	44.6	0.6	0.8	15.5	4.1	47.9	2005	
34.5	4.7	0.1	37.3	37.5	0.9	7.5	8.7	4.8	40.9	2010	
67.3	13.7	57.9	68.0	68.0	90.2	76.7	55.5	67.1	68.0	1995	Articles manufacturés
44.7	44.4	41.6	46.1	45.9	84.7	84.5	27.5	59.7	43.4	2005	(CTCI 5 à 8 moins 667 et 68)
41.9	36.5	34.8	42.7	42.5	56.5	79.8	33.3	10.2	40.1	2010	

Sources :
- Calculs du secrétariat de la CNUCED sur la base des données de ONU DAES Division de statistique

Notes :

(1) Y compris les exportations de catégorie spéciale, approvisionnements des navires et combustibles de soute et autres exportations de moindre importance dont la destination n'a pas pu être déterminée.

(2) Il est reconnu que la structure du commerce et la distribution au niveau partenaire pour certains pays et sur certaines années peuvent varier. À cet égard, le lecteur devrait connaître la couverture ainsi que les limites des données principales utilisées dans ce tableau. Pour de plus amples renseignements, veuillez visiter http://comtrade.un.org/db/help/uReadMeFirst.aspx.

2.2.I Export structure by partner and product group
Developing economies: Major petroleum and gas exporters

Product group	Year / Année	World (1) Monde (1)	Developed economies - Économies développées							Transition economies Économies en transition
			Total	Europe Total	Europe EU UE	Canada	USA États-Unis	Japan Japon	Other developed countries Autres économies développées	
Millions of dollars										
All products	1995	171 936	106 422	41 612	40 669	1 508	29 831	31 863	1 609	1 317
	2005	681 725	379 090	138 477	135 795	8 608	128 830	100 004	3 171	2 053
	2010	1 048 490	434 407	163 361	160 124	10 013	127 746	116 861	6 622	3 722
Share by destination (percentage)										
All products	1995	100.0	61.9	24.2	23.7	0.9	17.3	18.5	0.9	0.8
	2005	100.0	55.6	20.3	19.9	1.3	18.9	14.7	0.5	0.3
	2010	100.0	41.4	15.6	15.3	1.0	13.1	11.0	0.6	0.3
All food items (SITC 0 + 1 + 22 + 4)	1995	100.0	27.5	22.1	21.8	0.5	3.0	1.7	0.2	8.7
	2005	100.0	22.1	16.4	16.3	0.6	3.5	1.2	0.4	3.7
	2010	100.0	12.3	9.5	9.1	0.4	1.5	0.7	0.2	2.9
Agricultural raw materials (SITC 2 - 22 - 27 - 28)	1995	100.0	54.0	49.8	48.3	0.2	3.4	0.5	0.0	0.7
	2005	100.0	25.1	23.7	23.4	0.1	0.9	0.1	0.2	1.4
	2010	100.0	29.0	26.0	25.7	0.3	2.1	0.2	0.4	2.0
Ores, metals, precious stones and non-monetary gold (SITC 27 + 28 + 68 + 667 + 971)	1995	100.0	46.4	20.7	19.9	0.4	10.4	14.7	0.0	1.1
	2005	100.0	29.2	20.6	17.8	0.8	4.9	2.9	0.1	0.5
	2010	100.0	13.0	9.3	7.8	0.1	2.5	1.0	0.0	0.1
Fuels (SITC 3)	1995	100.0	67.5	24.8	24.3	1.0	19.0	21.7	1.1	0.3
	2005	100.0	60.0	20.3	20.0	1.4	21.0	17.0	0.4	0.0
	2010	100.0	17.4	16.7	16.5	1.2	15.4	13.4	0.0	0.0
Manufactured goods (SITC 5 to 8 less 667 and 68)	1995	100.0	33.2	20.0	18.8	0.4	10.1	2.3	0.5	2.4
	2005	100.0	30.4	21.5	20.6	0.5	6.8	0.8	0.9	2.2
	2010	100.0	15.9	11.2	10.5	0.2	3.2	0.5	0.8	1.6
Share by major product group (percentage)										
All products	1995	100.0	100.0	100.0	100.0	100.0	100.0	100.0	100.0	100.0
	2005	100.0	100.0	100.0	100.0	100.0	100.0	100.0	100.0	100.0
	2010	100.0	100.0	100.0	100.0	100.0	100.0	100.0	100.0	100.0
All food items (SITC 0 + 1 + 22 + 4)	1995	2.3	1.0	2.1	2.1	1.2	0.4	0.2	0.6	26.3
	2005	1.2	0.5	0.9	1.0	0.5	0.2	0.1	1.1	14.4
	2010	1.6	0.5	1.0	1.0	0.6	0.2	0.1	0.5	18.6
Agricultural raw materials (SITC 2 - 22 - 27 - 28)	1995	0.5	0.4	1.0	1.0	0.1	0.1	0.0	0.0	0.5
	2005	0.1	0.1	0.2	0.2	0.0	0.0	0.0	0.0	0.6
	2010	0.2	0.1	0.3	0.3	0.0	0.0	0.0	0.1	1.3
Ores, metals, precious stones and non-monetary gold (SITC 27 + 28 + 68 + 667 + 971)	1995	2.5	1.9	2.1	2.1	1.2	1.5	2.0	0.1	3.7
	2005	2.7	1.4	2.7	2.4	1.7	0.7	0.5	0.4	4.2
	2010	4.6	1.5	2.8	2.4	0.5	0.9	0.4	0.2	2.4
Fuels (SITC 3)	1995	82.2	89.7	84.2	84.6	92.1	90.2	96.2	92.4	27.5
	2005	85.4	92.2	85.4	85.9	94.0	94.9	98.7	74.1	5.8
	2010	81.6	93.3	87.5	88.3	96.5	95.7	98.9	82.3	8.4
Manufactured goods (SITC 5 to 8 less 667 and 68)	1995	12.1	6.5	10.0	9.6	5.3	7.0	1.5	6.6	38.8
	2005	10.0	5.5	10.6	10.3	3.7	3.6	0.5	18.6	72.8
	2010	11.5	4.4	8.2	7.9	2.3	2.8	0.5	14.4	68.8

Sources:
- UNCTAD secretariat calculations based on UN DESA Statistics Division's data

Notes:

(1) Includes special category exports, ship stores and bunkers and other exports of minor importance whose destination could not be determined.

(2) It is recognized that the structure of trade and partner distribution for certain countries and years might vary. In this regard, reader should know the coverage and limitations of the main principal data used in this table. For further information, please visit
http://comtrade.un.org/db/help/uReadMeFirst.aspx.

2.2.I Structure des exportations par partenaires et groupes de produits
Économies en développement: principaux exportateurs de pétrole et de gaz

Total	Africa / Afrique	America / Amérique	Asia / Asie — Total	Eastern, Southern and South-Eastern Asia / Asie orientale, méridionale et du Sud-Est	China / Chine	Western Asia / Asie occidentale	Oceania (2) / Océanie (2)	Major petroleum exporters and gas exporters / Principaux exportateurs de pétrole et de gaz	Major manufactured goods exporters / Principaux exportateurs d'articles manufacturés	Year / Année	Destinations / Groupes de produits
											Developing economies - Économies en développement
Millions de dollars											
64 178	5 484	8 855	49 838	38 512	1 887	11 326	0	6 385	26 058	1995	**Total tous produits**
298 859	24 310	25 349	249 196	209 721	38 568	39 475	4	26 831	160 703	2005	
611 096	40 008	25 849	545 126	484 026	110 716	61 100	113	54 296	334 621	2010	
Parts par destinations (en pourcentage)											
37.3	3.2	5.2	29.0	22.4	1.1	6.6	0.0	3.7	15.2	1995	**Total tous produits**
43.8	3.6	3.7	36.6	30.8	5.7	5.8	0.0	3.9	23.6	2005	
58.3	3.8	2.5	52.0	46.2	10.6	5.8	0.0	5.2	31.9	2010	
63.7	3.8	10.9	49.0	10.2	0.2	38.8	0.0	35.6	3.5	1995	Produits alimentaires
74.0	6.7	3.0	64.3	23.5	0.4	40.8	0.0	39.1	5.4	2005	(CTCI 0 + 1 + 22 + 4)
83.5	7.9	1.9	73.5	30.0	1.1	43.4	0.3	45.8	6.9	2010	
44.9	3.6	3.8	37.6	22.0	2.8	15.6	0.0	8.6	5.8	1995	Matières premières
72.0	12.1	3.2	56.7	37.1	2.9	19.5	0.0	16.6	6.8	2005	d'origine agricole
68.6	7.0	6.3	55.2	41.6	4.2	13.6	0.1	12.9	12.8	2010	(CTCI 2 - 22 - 27 - 28)
52.4	3.3	6.5	42.7	29.8	1.8	12.9	0.0	10.0	15.2	1995	Minerais, métaux, pierres
70.3	2.5	3.0	64.8	52.9	5.7	11.9	0.0	9.7	16.8	2005	précieuses et or (non monétaire)
86.9	1.5	1.0	84.4	74.0	7.2	10.4	0.0	9.5	26.0	2010	(CTCI 27 + 28 + 68 + 667 + 971)
32.1	2.7	4.4	25.0	21.8	0.8	3.3	0.0	0.3	15.0	1995	Combustibles (CTCI 3)
39.7	2.9	3.7	33.1	30.2	5.8	2.9	0.0	0.6	25.2	2005	
52.6	3.2	2.4	46.9	44.7	11.3	2.2	0.0	0.5	34.5	2010	
64.4	6.5	9.1	48.8	27.4	2.8	21.4	0.0	19.7	15.2	1995	Articles manufacturés
67.2	9.2	4.4	53.6	31.5	5.8	22.1	0.0	24.9	15.0	2005	(CTCI 5 à 8 moins 667 et 68)
82.5	8.3	3.5	70.7	48.1	8.4	22.6	0.0	30.8	20.6	2010	
Parts par principaux groupes de produits (en pourcentage)											
100.0	100.0	100.0	100.0	100.0	100.0	100.0	100.0	100.0	100.0	1995	**Total tous produits**
100.0	100.0	100.0	100.0	100.0	100.0	100.0	100.0	100.0	100.0	2005	
100.0	100.0	100.0	100.0	100.0	100.0	100.0	100.0	100.0	100.0	2010	
3.9	2.7	4.9	3.9	1.1	0.4	13.6	17.3	22.2	0.5	1995	Produits alimentaires
2.0	2.2	0.9	2.1	0.9	0.1	8.2	23.3	11.6	0.3	2005	(CTCI 0 + 1 + 22 + 4)
2.4	3.4	1.3	2.3	1.1	0.2	12.3	46.2	14.6	0.4	2010	
0.6	0.6	0.4	0.7	0.5	1.3	1.2	15.2	1.2	0.2	1995	Matières premières
0.2	0.4	0.1	0.2	0.2	0.1	0.4	0.0	0.5	0.0	2005	d'origine agricole
0.2	0.3	0.4	0.2	0.1	0.1	0.4	1.0	0.4	0.1	2010	(CTCI 2 - 22 - 27 - 28)
3.5	2.6	3.1	3.7	3.3	4.1	4.9	1.3	6.7	2.5	1995	Minerais, métaux, pierres
4.3	1.8	2.2	4.7	4.6	2.7	5.5	2.0	6.6	1.9	2005	précieuses et or (non monétaire)
6.9	1.8	1.9	7.5	7.5	3.2	8.3	0.9	8.5	3.8	2010	(CTCI 27 + 28 + 68 + 667 + 971)
70.8	69.5	70.2	71.1	80.0	63.7	40.8	0.0	5.6	84.6	1995	Combustibles (CTCI 3)
77.3	69.1	84.8	77.3	84.0	86.9	42.1	1.9	12.3	91.3	2005	
73.6	69.4	80.1	73.6	79.1	87.4	30.5	5.7	8.2	88.3	2010	
20.9	24.6	21.4	20.4	14.9	30.5	39.4	66.2	64.2	12.1	1995	Articles manufacturés
15.3	25.8	11.9	14.6	10.2	10.2	38.2	72.8	63.2	6.4	2005	(CTCI 5 à 8 moins 667 et 68)
16.3	25.0	16.3	15.6	12.0	9.1	44.5	42.6	68.2	7.4	2010	

Sources :
- Calculs du secrétariat de la CNUCED sur la base des données de ONU DAES Division de statistique

Notes :

(1) Y compris les exportations de catégorie spéciale, approvisionnements des navires et combustibles de soute et autres exportations de moindre importance dont la destination n'a pas pu être déterminée.

(2) Il est reconnu que la structure du commerce et la distribution au niveau partenaire pour certains pays et sur certaines années peuvent varier. À cet égard, le lecteur devrait connaître la couverture ainsi que les limites des données principales utilisées dans ce tableau. Pour de plus amples renseignements, veuillez visiter http://comtrade.un.org/db/help/uReadMeFirst.aspx.

2.2.I Import structure by partner and product group
Developing economies: Major petroleum and gas importers

Product group	Year Année	World (1) Monde (1)	Developed economies - Économies développées							Transition economies Économies en transition
			Total	Europe		Canada	USA États-Unis	Japan Japon	Other developed countries Autres économies développées	
				Total	EU UE					
Millions of dollars										
All products	1995	115 348	74 483	45 593	42 441	2 244	16 766	8 365	1 515	1 685
	2005	320 428	172 348	111 600	106 061	2 389	35 524	18 019	4 817	7 932
	2010	625 256	279 205	178 928	165 680	4 871	60 283	27 342	7 782	8 834
Share by origin (percentage)										
All products	1995	100.0	64.6	39.5	36.8	1.9	14.5	7.3	1.3	1.5
	2005	100.0	53.8	34.8	33.1	0.7	11.1	5.6	1.5	2.5
	2010	100.0	44.7	28.6	26.5	0.8	9.6	4.4	1.2	1.4
All food items	1995	100.0	54.7	30.5	29.7	5.8	12.3	0.1	5.9	1.0
(SITC 0 + 1 + 22 + 4)	2005	100.0	41.3	25.1	23.6	1.3	10.1	0.1	4.7	2.6
	2010	100.0	35.6	22.5	20.0	2.3	7.2	0.1	3.6	1.8
Agricultural raw materials	1995	100.0	58.2	31.7	31.4	4.5	17.5	3.0	1.5	3.7
(SITC 2 - 22 - 27 - 28)	2005	100.0	55.2	40.2	39.0	3.0	8.6	1.8	1.6	6.8
	2010	100.0	51.6	34.8	33.8	2.3	9.6	2.9	2.0	4.1
Ores, metals, precious stones	1995	100.0	55.5	42.9	21.5	2.4	8.3	0.5	1.3	2.1
and non-monetary gold	2005	100.0	32.7	23.8	17.5	1.0	4.9	0.6	2.4	4.8
(SITC 27 + 28 + 68 + 667 + 971)	2010	100.0	17.8	12.6	9.0	0.4	2.1	0.4	2.3	2.2
Fuels (SITC 3)	1995	100.0	58.2	41.2	41.2	0.7	12.7	0.2	3.4	6.7
	2005	100.0	27.3	23.1	22.9	0.0	3.2	0.2	0.7	7.4
	2010	100.0	36.4	30.5	29.5	0.0	5.4	0.2	0.2	5.9
Manufactured goods	1995	100.0	67.2	41.2	38.9	1.0	15.3	9.5	0.2	1.4
(SITC 5 to 8 less 667 and 68)	2005	100.0	58.3	37.3	35.8	0.7	12.3	7.3	0.8	1.9
	2010	100.0	49.4	31.4	29.5	0.6	10.9	5.8	0.6	1.0
Share by major product group (percentage)										
All products	1995	100.0	100.0	100.0	100.0	100.0	100.0	100.0	100.0	100.0
	2005	100.0	100.0	100.0	100.0	100.0	100.0	100.0	100.0	100.0
	2010	100.0	100.0	100.0	100.0	100.0	100.0	100.0	100.0	100.0
All food items	1995	16.8	14.2	13.0	13.5	50.2	14.3	0.3	75.0	12.0
(SITC 0 + 1 + 22 + 4)	2005	12.8	9.8	9.2	9.1	21.9	11.6	0.3	39.8	13.5
	2010	13.5	10.8	10.6	10.2	39.2	10.1	0.3	39.0	17.7
Agricultural raw materials	1995	1.7	1.5	1.3	1.4	3.8	2.0	0.7	1.8	4.3
(SITC 2 - 22 - 27 - 28)	2005	0.8	0.9	1.0	1.0	3.4	0.7	0.3	0.9	2.3
	2010	0.8	0.9	1.0	1.0	2.4	0.8	0.5	1.3	2.4
Ores, metals, precious stones	1995	3.8	3.3	4.2	2.2	4.8	2.2	0.3	3.8	5.5
and non-monetary gold	2005	5.3	3.2	3.6	2.8	6.9	2.4	0.6	8.5	10.4
(SITC 27 + 28 + 68 + 667 + 971)	2010	8.6	3.4	3.8	2.9	4.2	1.9	0.7	16.2	13.2
Fuels (SITC 3)	1995	1.4	1.3	1.5	1.6	0.5	1.3	0.0	3.8	6.7
	2005	3.6	1.8	2.4	2.5	0.2	1.0	0.1	1.6	10.7
	2010	3.1	2.5	3.3	3.5	0.1	1.8	0.2	0.5	13.1
Manufactured goods	1995	75.5	78.6	78.6	79.7	40.5	79.5	98.4	14.2	71.5
(SITC 5 to 8 less 667 and 68)	2005	75.3	81.7	80.7	81.4	67.0	83.5	97.5	38.0	58.8
	2010	73.2	80.9	80.3	81.4	53.9	82.8	97.8	36.2	50.3

Sources:
- UNCTAD secretariat calculations based on UN DESA Statistics Division's data

Notes:

(1) Includes special category exports, ship stores and bunkers and other exports of minor importance whose destination could not be determined.

(2) It is recognized that the structure of trade and partner distribution for certain countries and years might vary. In this regard, reader should know the coverage and limitations of the main principal data used in this table. For further information, please visit
http://comtrade.un.org/db/help/uReadMeFirst.aspx.

2.2.I Structure des importations par partenaires et groupes de produits
Économies en développement: principaux importateurs de pétrole et de gaz

Total	Africa / Afrique	America / Amérique	Asia / Asie — Total	Eastern, Southern and South-Eastern Asia / Asie orientale, méridionale et du Sud-Est	China / Chine	Western Asia / Asie occidentale	Oceania (2) / Océanie (2)	Major petroleum exporters and gas exporters / Principaux exportateurs de pétrole et de gaz	Major manufactured goods exporters / Principaux exportateurs d'articles manufacturés	Year / Année	Origines / Groupes de produits
Millions de dollars											
35 390	2 518	5 824	27 047	18 997	2 941	8 049	2	5 223	13 904	1995	**Total tous produits**
137 030	7 701	10 050	110 070	71 933	23 353	11 377	21	23 857	52 779	2005	
336 743	19 320	32 631	284 538	192 008	71 896	92 530	255	54 862	131 203	2010	
Parts par origines (en pourcentage)											
30.7	2.2	5.0	23.4	16.5	2.5	7.0	0.0	4.5	12.1	1995	**Total tous produits**
43.0	2.4	5.3	35.3	22.4	7.0	12.9	0.0	7.1	16.3	2005	
53.9	3.1	5.2	45.5	30.7	11.5	14.8	0.0	8.8	21.0	2010	
42.7	4.1	14.3	24.3	13.6	1.1	10.8	0.0	5.6	5.5	1995	Produits alimentaires
55.4	5.0	15.1	35.2	16.4	1.8	18.9	0.0	7.2	6.5	2005	(CTCI 0 + 1 + 22 + 4)
62.5	5.4	16.3	40.8	19.5	2.1	21.3	0.0	9.6	7.7	2010	
37.0	4.5	11.0	21.5	17.0	0.5	4.5	0.0	2.8	13.0	1995	Matières premières
37.5	3.9	7.7	25.9	18.8	2.2	7.2	0.0	4.7	12.8	2005	d'origine agricole
43.9	4.9	7.4	31.6	22.2	3.5	9.4	0.0	5.6	15.8	2010	(CTCI 2 - 22 - 27 - 28)
40.2	7.4	10.3	22.5	7.7	0.6	14.8	0.0	8.4	2.7	1995	Minerais, métaux, pierres
62.3	6.3	5.7	50.3	37.8	1.9	12.5	0.0	9.3	11.5	2005	précieuses et or (non monétaire)
80.0	8.7	3.8	67.6	56.3	2.5	11.3	0.0	9.7	6.5	2010	(CTCI 27 + 28 + 68 + 667 + 971)
31.0	7.1	2.5	21.4	7.0	0.7	14.1	0.0	18.3	2.4	1995	Combustibles (CTCI 3)
64.5	2.9	2.1	59.5	15.8	1.4	43.6	0.0	24.5	4.6	2005	
57.6	2.8	2.5	52.3	18.7	3.3	33.6	0.0	24.2	9.8	2010	
27.6	1.4	2.7	23.5	17.8	3.1	5.7	0.0	3.9	14.3	1995	Articles manufacturés
38.9	1.7	3.8	33.4	23.1	8.7	10.3	0.0	5.9	19.2	2005	(CTCI 5 à 8 moins 667 et 68)
49.6	2.0	3.5	44.0	30.6	14.8	13.4	0.1	8.0	25.9	2010	
Parts par principaux groupes de produits (en pourcentage)											
100.0	100.0	100.0	100.0	100.0	100.0	100.0	100.0	100.0	100.0	1995	**Total tous produits**
100.0	100.0	100.0	100.0	100.0	100.0	100.0	100.0	100.0	100.0	2005	
100.0	100.0	100.0	100.0	100.0	100.0	100.0	100.0	100.0	100.0	2010	
23.3	31.4	47.3	17.4	13.8	7.2	25.9	85.0	20.8	7.6	1995	Produits alimentaires
16.5	26.6	36.8	12.8	9.4	3.3	18.7	53.0	12.9	5.1	2005	(CTCI 0 + 1 + 22 + 4)
15.7	23.6	42.2	12.1	8.6	2.5	19.4	1.0	14.9	4.9	2010	
2.0	3.4	3.6	1.5	1.7	0.3	1.1	0.0	1.0	1.8	1995	Matières premières
0.7	1.4	1.2	0.6	0.7	0.3	0.5	0.5	0.6	0.7	2005	d'origine agricole
0.7	1.3	1.2	0.6	0.6	0.2	0.5	0.0	0.5	0.6	2010	(CTCI 2 - 22 - 27 - 28)
5.0	12.9	7.8	3.7	1.8	1.0	8.1	0.0	7.1	0.9	1995	Minerais, métaux, pierres
7.7	13.9	5.8	7.6	9.0	1.4	5.2	1.3	7.0	3.8	2005	précieuses et or (non monétaire)
12.8	24.2	6.3	12.8	15.8	1.9	6.6	0.0	9.5	2.7	2010	(CTCI 27 + 28 + 68 + 667 + 971)
1.5	4.7	0.7	1.3	0.6	0.4	2.9	0.0	5.9	0.3	1995	Combustibles (CTCI 3)
5.4	4.3	1.5	6.0	2.5	0.7	12.1	4.3	12.2	1.0	2005	
3.3	2.9	1.5	3.6	1.9	0.9	7.1	0.0	8.6	1.4	2010	
68.0	47.5	40.5	75.8	81.6	91.1	61.9	15.0	65.0	89.2	1995	Articles manufacturés
68.2	53.2	54.2	71.3	77.6	93.8	60.3	40.7	62.0	88.8	2005	(CTCI 5 à 8 moins 667 et 68)
67.4	47.9	48.5	70.8	73.0	94.5	66.3	99.0	66.5	90.2	2010	

Sources :
- Calculs du secrétariat de la CNUCED sur la base des données de ONU DAES Division de statistique

Notes :

(1) Y compris les exportations de catégorie spéciale, approvisionnements des navires et combustibles de soute et autres exportations de moindre importance dont la destination n'a pas pu être déterminée.

(2) Il est reconnu que la structure du commerce et la distribution au niveau partenaire pour certains pays et sur certaines années peuvent varier. À cet égard, le lecteur devrait connaître la couverture ainsi que les limites des données principales utilisées dans ce tableau. Pour de plus amples renseignements, veuillez visiter http://comtrade.un.org/db/help/uReadMeFirst.aspx.

Product group	Year / Année	World (1) / Monde (1)	Developed economies - Économies développées							Transition economies / Économies on transition
			Total	Europe Total	Europe EU / UE	Canada	USA / États-Unis	Japan / Japon	Other developed countries / Autres économies développées	
					Millions of dollars					
All products	1995	887 071	476 681	125 187	119 731	11 153	226 636	98 264	15 441	5 997
	2005	2 223 477	1 121 061	333 132	323 899	26 690	532 288	180 170	48 781	30 938
	2010	3 765 962	1 646 111	553 455	512 375	45 983	710 690	247 051	91 643	73 879
				Share by destination (percentage)						
All products	1995	100.0	53.7	14.1	13.5	1.3	25.5	11.1	1.7	0.7
	2005	100.0	50.4	15.0	14.6	1.2	23.9	8.1	2.2	1.4
	2010	100.0	43.7	14.7	14.1	1.2	18.9	6.5	2.4	2.0
All food items	1995	100.0	51.9	8.9	8.3	0.9	15.9	24.6	1.6	1.5
(SITC 0 + 1 + 22 + 4)	2005	100.0	55.8	10.2	10.0	1.4	22.8	19.3	2.1	2.4
	2010	100.0	46.3	9.8	9.6	1.6	19.6	12.8	2.4	2.6
Agricultural raw materials	1995	100.0	44.7	13.2	12.8	0.7	10.4	19.2	1.2	0.2
(SITC 2 - 22 - 27 - 28)	2005	100.0	41.2	14.6	14.6	1.3	11.4	12.7	1.2	0.7
	2010	100.0	34.6	14.1	14.0	1.1	8.5	9.8	1.1	0.8
Ores, metals, precious stones	1995	100.0	38.7	9.1	7.8	0.4	13.0	14.3	1.9	0.4
and non-monetary gold	2005	100.0	37.8	13.1	10.9	0.8	11.2	8.6	4.1	0.6
(SITC 27 + 28 + 68 + 667 + 971)	2010	100.0	37.6	14.6	9.3	0.8	11.9	6.1	4.2	0.4
Fuels (SITC 3)	1995	100.0	46.9	3.8	3.7	0.2	22.0	19.0	1.9	0.3
	2005	100.0	45.0	4.5	4.5	0.6	23.7	10.3	5.9	0.2
	2010	100.0	36.9	4.8	4.7	0.6	18.7	7.3	5.6	0.2
Manufactured goods	1995	100.0	54.9	15.0	14.4	1.4	27.2	9.5	1.7	0.7
(SITC 5 to 8 less 667 and 68)	2005	100.0	51.1	15.9	15.5	1.2	24.6	7.5	1.9	1.5
	2010	100.0	44.5	15.5	15.1	1.3	19.3	6.2	2.2	2.1
				Share by major product group (percentage)						
All products	1995	100.0	100.0	100.0	100.0	100.0	100.0	100.0	100.0	100.0
	2005	100.0	100.0	100.0	100.0	100.0	100.0	100.0	100.0	100.0
	2010	100.0	100.0	100.0	100.0	100.0	100.0	100.0	100.0	100.0
All food items	1995	6.0	5.7	3.7	3.7	4.2	3.7	13.2	5.4	13.6
(SITC 0 + 1 + 22 + 4)	2005	3.2	3.5	2.1	2.2	3.7	3.0	7.5	3.0	5.4
	2010	3.5	3.7	2.3	2.4	4.7	3.6	6.9	3.5	4.6
Agricultural raw materials	1995	2.1	1.7	1.9	2.0	1.1	0.8	3.6	1.5	0.5
(SITC 2 - 22 - 27 - 28)	2005	0.9	0.8	0.9	0.9	1.0	0.4	1.5	0.5	0.4
	2010	0.9	0.7	0.9	0.9	0.8	0.4	1.4	0.4	0.4
Ores, metals, precious stones	1995	2.4	1.7	1.5	1.4	0.7	1.2	3.1	2.7	1.3
and non-monetary gold	2005	2.2	1.7	1.9	1.7	1.4	1.0	2.4	4.1	0.9
(SITC 27 + 28 + 68 + 667 + 971)	2010	3.1	2.7	3.1	2.0	1.9	2.0	2.9	5.4	0.7
Fuels (SITC 3)	1995	3.6	3.2	1.0	1.0	0.7	3.1	6.2	3.8	1.4
	2005	5.7	5.1	1.7	1.7	2.9	5.6	7.3	15.3	0.9
	2010	5.7	4.8	1.8	1.9	2.2	5.7	6.4	13.2	0.5
Manufactured goods	1995	85.3	87.1	90.7	91.0	93.1	90.9	73.5	85.7	82.4
(SITC 5 to 8 less 667 and 68)	2005	87.3	88.5	92.5	92.8	90.8	89.6	80.7	76.1	92.3
	2010	86.0	87.5	90.8	91.8	89.9	88.1	81.8	76.9	93.7

Sources:
- UNCTAD secretariat calculations based on UN DESA Statistics Division's data

Notes:

(1) Includes special category exports, ship stores and bunkers and other exports of minor importance whose destination could not be determined.

(2) It is recognized that the structure of trade and partner distribution for certain countries and years might vary. In this regard, reader should know the coverage and limitations of the main principal data used in this table. For further information, please visit
http://comtrade.un.org/db/help/uReadMeFirst.aspx.

			Asia / Asie				Oceania (2) / Océanie (2)	Major petroleum exporters and gas exporters / Principaux exportateurs de pétrole et de gaz	Major manufactured goods exporters / Principaux exportateurs d'articles manufacturés	Year / Année	Destinations
Total	Africa / Afrique	America / Amérique	Total	Eastern, Southern and South-Eastern Asia / Asie orientale, méridionale et du Sud-Est	China / Chine	Western Asia / Asie occidentale					Groupes de produits
Millions de dollars											
401 818	13 085	25 996	362 025	345 502	73 786	16 523	711	15 495	299 052	1995	**Total tous produits**
1 068 066	37 466	64 923	961 000	910 382	272 531	50 618	4 677	52 470	765 090	2005	
2 044 068	99 265	176 930	1 759 366	1 618 837	404 761	110 528	8 507	123 330	1 322 457	2010	
Parts par destinations (en pourcentage)											
45.3	1.5	2.9	40.8	38.9	8.3	1.9	0.1	1.7	33.7	1995	**Total tous produits**
48.0	1.7	2.9	43.2	40.9	12.3	2.3	0.2	2.4	34.5	2005	
54.3	2.6	4.7	46.7	43.8	13.1	2.9	0.2	3.3	35.1	2010	
46.2	2.2	0.9	43.0	40.6	8.6	2.4	0.1	1.9	29.0	1995	Produits alimentaires
41.6	3.8	1.9	35.7	33.0	5.2	2.7	0.2	3.2	22.8	2005	(CTCI 0 + 1 + 22 + 4)
51.0	5.9	2.6	42.2	39.1	7.4	3.1	0.3	4.1	24.2	2010	
54.8	1.2	2.4	51.2	49.5	14.7	1.7	0.0	1.4	41.6	1995	Matières premières
58.0	1.4	2.5	54.1	52.0	24.2	2.2	0.0	1.4	41.6	2005	d'origine agricole
64.6	1.6	3.6	59.4	56.3	25.0	3.0	0.0	2.1	42.2	2010	(CTCI 2 - 22 - 27 - 28)
60.3	0.5	0.7	59.1	58.7	12.5	0.4	0.0	0.5	51.7	1995	Minerais, métaux, pierres
61.6	0.7	0.9	59.9	55.4	16.5	4.5	0.0	4.7	46.0	2005	précieuses et or (non monétaire)
61.9	1.2	1.4	59.3	57.2	18.9	2.1	0.0	2.4	44.8	2010	(CTCI 27 + 28 + 68 + 667 + 971)
50.1	0.2	1.9	47.6	47.4	8.2	0.1	0.4	0.1	30.1	1995	Combustibles (CTCI 3)
53.2	0.2	3.0	48.7	48.2	5.6	0.5	1.3	0.5	30.7	2005	
62.6	1.2	2.9	57.4	56.6	9.1	0.9	1.1	0.9	35.8	2010	
44.3	1.5	3.1	39.6	37.6	8.0	1.9	0.1	1.9	33.1	1995	Articles manufacturés
47.4	1.7	2.9	42.7	40.3	12.8	2.3	0.1	2.4	34.8	2005	(CTCI 5 à 8 moins 667 et 68)
53.4	2.6	4.8	45.8	42.7	13.4	3.1	0.1	3.5	35.3	2010	
Parts par principaux groupes de produits (en pourcentage)											
100.0	100.0	100.0	100.0	100.0	100.0	100.0	100.0	100.0	100.0	1995	**Total tous produits**
100.0	100.0	100.0	100.0	100.0	100.0	100.0	100.0	100.0	100.0	2005	
100.0	100.0	100.0	100.0	100.0	100.0	100.0	100.0	100.0	100.0	2010	
6.1	8.7	1.9	6.3	6.2	6.2	7.7	9.4	6.6	5.1	1995	Produits alimentaires
2.7	7.2	2.0	2.6	2.6	1.3	3.8	3.1	4.2	2.1	2005	(CTCI 0 + 1 + 22 + 4)
3.3	7.8	2.0	3.2	3.1	2.0	3.7	4.0	4.4	2.4	2010	
2.5	1.7	1.7	2.6	2.6	3.6	1.9	0.3	1.6	2.5	1995	Matières premières
1.1	0.8	0.8	1.2	1.2	1.8	0.9	0.1	0.6	1.1	2005	d'origine agricole
1.1	0.5	0.7	1.2	1.2	1.7	0.9	0.1	0.6	1.1	2010	(CTCI 2 - 22 - 27 - 28)
3.2	0.8	0.6	3.5	3.6	3.6	0.5	0.4	0.7	3.7	1995	Minerais, métaux, pierres
2.8	0.9	0.7	3.1	3.0	3.0	4.4	0.2	4.3	3.0	2005	précieuses et or (non monétaire)
3.5	1.5	0.9	3.9	4.1	4.5	2.3	0.2	2.3	4.0	2010	(CTCI 27 + 28 + 68 + 667 + 971)
4.0	0.5	2.4	4.2	4.4	3.6	0.3	16.0	0.2	4.2	1995	Combustibles (CTCI 3)
6.3	0.8	5.8	6.4	6.7	2.6	1.3	35.4	1.2	5.1	2005	
6.6	2.6	3.5	7.0	7.4	4.0	1.7	26.8	1.5	5.8	2010	
83.4	86.2	91.7	82.7	82.4	82.2	89.1	69.4	90.4	83.8	1995	Articles manufacturés
86.1	87.3	87.0	86.1	86.0	91.0	88.8	55.0	88.7	88.3	2005	(CTCI 5 à 8 moins 667 et 68)
84.6	84.5	88.8	84.3	83.9	87.8	91.1	54.7	91.0	86.4	2010	

Sources :
- Calculs du secrétariat de la CNUCED sur la base des données de ONU DAES Division de statistique

Notes :

(1) Y compris les exportations de catégorie spéciale, approvisionnements des navires et combustibles de soute et autres exportations de moindre importance dont la destination n'a pas pu être déterminée.

(2) Il est reconnu que la structure du commerce et la distribution au niveau partenaire pour certains pays et sur certaines années peuvent varier. À cet égard, le lecteur devrait connaître la couverture ainsi que les limites des données principales utilisées dans ce tableau. Pour de plus amples renseignements, veuillez visiter http://comtrade.un.org/db/help/uReadMeFirst.aspx.

Product group	Year / Année	World (1) / Monde (1)	Developed economies - Économies développées								Transition economies / Économies en transition
			Total	Europe		Canada	USA / États-Unis	Japan / Japon	Other developed countries / Autres économies développées		
				Total	EU / UE						

Millions of dollars

All products	1995	911 557	539 863	136 610	124 433	11 106	176 513	193 664	21 970	11 550
	2005	2 057 264	890 856	234 359	214 957	20 700	282 013	302 726	51 058	32 476
	2010	3 474 157	1 417 714	414 955	363 216	33 533	402 014	433 003	122 002	00 500

Share by origin (percentage)

All products	1995	100.0	59.2	15.0	13.7	1.2	19.4	21.2	2.4	1.3
	2005	100.0	43.3	11.4	10.4	1.0	13.7	14.7	2.5	1.6
	2010	100.0	40.5	11.9	10.5	1.0	11.6	12.5	3.5	2.0
All food items	1995	100.0	61.3	14.3	13.7	4.1	31.3	3.3	8.4	0.8
(SITC 0 + 1 + 22 + 4)	2005	100.0	51.9	9.9	9.3	3.7	26.4	2.7	9.1	1.9
	2010	100.0	50.1	9.2	8.3	3.6	27.4	2.2	7.8	1.6
Agricultural raw materials	1995	100.0	53.2	6.3	6.1	5.3	27.5	5.1	8.9	3.9
(SITC 2 - 22 - 27 - 28)	2005	100.0	52.4	9.8	9.6	6.0	23.2	5.1	8.2	8.1
	2010	100.0	49.7	10.1	9.9	7.0	20.2	4.9	7.5	7.1
Ores, metals, precious stones	1995	100.0	55.2	15.0	10.5	2.7	13.8	9.6	14.2	4.5
and non-monetary gold	2005	100.0	43.9	8.8	6.8	2.1	8.6	8.2	16.2	4.7
(SITC 27 + 28 + 68 + 667 + 971)	2010	100.0	44.7	10.5	7.0	1.5	6.3	7.1	19.3	3.7
Fuels (SITC 3)	1995	100.0	14.7	1.3	1.3	0.9	5.7	2.7	4.1	0.7
	2005	100.0	11.3	1.4	1.1	0.4	4.3	1.0	4.2	3.6
	2010	100.0	13.7	2.0	1.9	0.5	4.5	1.7	5.1	6.2
Manufactured goods	1995	100.0	62.6	16.4	15.1	0.8	19.2	25.4	0.8	1.0
(SITC 5 to 8 less 667 and 68)	2005	100.0	47.6	13.2	12.3	0.8	14.7	18.3	0.6	0.8
	2010	100.0	44.9	14.3	13.1	0.6	12.6	16.8	0.6	0.6

Share by major product group (percentage)

All products	1995	100.0	100.0	100.0	100.0	100.0	100.0	100.0	100.0	100.0
	2005	100.0	100.0	100.0	100.0	100.0	100.0	100.0	100.0	100.0
	2010	100.0	100.0	100.0	100.0	100.0	100.0	100.0	100.0	100.0
All food items	1995	5.4	5.6	5.2	5.4	18.1	8.8	0.8	18.9	3.6
(SITC 0 + 1 + 22 + 4)	2005	3.8	4.5	3.3	3.4	14.0	7.3	0.7	14.0	4.7
	2010	4.6	5.7	3.6	3.7	17.1	10.9	0.8	10.2	3.7
Agricultural raw materials	1995	3.1	2.8	1.3	1.4	13.7	4.5	0.8	11.6	9.5
(SITC 2 - 22 - 27 - 28)	2005	2.0	2.4	1.7	1.9	12.1	3.4	0.7	6.7	10.4
	2010	2.2	2.7	1.8	2.0	15.5	3.8	0.8	4.6	7.8
Ores, metals, precious stones	1995	5.5	5.1	5.5	4.2	12.0	3.9	2.5	32.1	19.2
and non-monetary gold	2005	6.2	6.3	4.8	4.1	12.9	3.9	3.5	40.8	18.6
(SITC 27 + 28 + 68 + 667 + 971)	2010	9.5	10.4	8.3	6.3	14.0	5.2	5.4	51.7	17.9
Fuels (SITC 3)	1995	5.8	1.4	0.5	0.5	4.1	1.7	0.7	9.9	3.4
	2005	11.9	3.1	1.5	1.3	4.3	3.7	0.8	20.2	27.6
	2010	15.3	5.2	2.5	2.7	8.3	5.9	2.1	22.0	48.2
Manufactured goods	1995	78.7	83.2	86.0	87.1	50.6	77.9	94.3	27.0	60.9
(SITC 5 to 8 less 667 and 68)	2005	75.5	82.9	87.6	88.7	56.5	80.9	93.9	17.7	38.4
	2010	67.5	74.8	81.1	84.6	44.2	73.4	90.6	10.8	22.0

Sources:
- UNCTAD secretariat calculations based on UN DESA Statistics Division's data

Notes:

(1) Includes special category exports, ship stores and bunkers and other exports of minor importance whose destination could not be determined.

(2) It is recognized that the structure of trade and partner distribution for certain countries and years might vary. In this regard, reader should know the coverage and limitations of the main principal data used in this table. For further information, please visit
http://comtrade.un.org/db/help/uReadMeFirst.aspx.

2.2.J Structure des importations par partenaires et groupes de produits
Économies en développement: principaux importateurs d'articles manufacturés

| Developing economies - Économies en développement | | | | | | | | | | Origines | |
Total	Africa / Afrique	America / Amérique	Asia / Asie — Total	Eastern, Southern and South-Eastern Asia / Asie orientale, méridionale et du Sud-Est	China / Chine	Western Asia / Asie occidentale	Oceania (2) / Océanie (2)	Major petroleum exporters and gas exporters / Principaux exportateurs de pétrole et de gaz	Major manufactured goods exporters / Principaux exportateurs d'articles manufacturés	Year / Année	Groupes de produits
Millions de dollars											
355 471	9 110	15 310	330 359	303 475	88 607	26 884	692	28 091	274 096	1995	**Total tous produits**
1 130 026	33 398	57 625	1 037 728	915 904	311 248	121 824	1 276	142 765	787 008	2005	
1 995 384	88 562	145 062	1 759 306	1 533 231	537 048	226 075	2 454	291 425	1 299 089	2010	
Parts par origines (en pourcentage)											
39.0	1.0	1.7	36.2	33.3	9.7	2.9	0.1	3.1	30.1	1995	**Total tous produits**
54.9	1.6	2.8	50.4	44.5	15.1	5.9	0.1	6.9	38.3	2005	
57.4	2.5	4.2	50.6	44.1	15.5	6.5	0.1	8.4	37.4	2010	
38.0	1.3	6.9	29.4	29.1	7.9	0.3	0.4	0.3	22.7	1995	Produits alimentaires
46.2	1.3	16.8	27.6	27.3	8.5	0.3	0.4	0.5	18.8	2005	(CTCI 0 + 1 + 22 + 4)
48.3	1.4	18.7	27.9	27.6	6.6	0.3	0.3	0.6	16.9	2010	
42.8	4.2	5.2	32.5	32.3	4.6	0.2	0.9	0.2	24.6	1995	Matières premières
39.5	4.6	6.3	27.6	27.3	2.5	0.2	1.1	0.2	17.9	2005	d'origine agricole
43.2	3.7	7.5	30.9	30.7	2.1	0.2	1.1	0.2	17.8	2010	(CTCI 2 - 22 - 27 - 28)
40.1	6.2	8.4	25.2	23.1	4.4	2.1	0.2	1.4	16.4	1995	Minerais, métaux, pierres
51.3	4.5	13.8	33.0	31.1	6.3	1.9	0.0	2.3	15.9	2005	précieuses et or (non monétaire)
51.5	6.5	17.3	27.6	25.2	3.7	2.4	0.1	2.6	12.3	2010	(CTCI 27 + 28 + 68 + 667 + 971)
83.9	4.1	1.2	78.6	37.5	3.7	41.0	0.1	45.0	23.3	1995	Combustibles (CTCI 3)
85.0	8.1	1.3	75.5	30.9	2.8	44.6	0.0	52.7	15.6	2005	
80.0	9.9	3.6	66.4	29.6	2.7	36.8	0.1	48.7	15.6	2010	
36.0	0.3	0.8	34.9	34.4	11.0	0.5	0.0	0.5	32.6	1995	Articles manufacturés
51.4	0.3	1.3	49.8	49.2	18.5	0.6	0.0	0.6	45.3	2005	(CTCI 5 à 8 moins 667 et 68)
54.4	0.3	1.4	52.7	51.8	21.2	0.9	0.0	1.0	48.1	2010	
Parts par principaux groupes de produits (en pourcentage)											
100.0	100.0	100.0	100.0	100.0	100.0	100.0	100.0	100.0	100.0	1995	**Total tous produits**
100.0	100.0	100.0	100.0	100.0	100.0	100.0	100.0	100.0	100.0	2005	
100.0	100.0	100.0	100.0	100.0	100.0	100.0	100.0	100.0	100.0	2010	
5.3	7.2	22.1	4.4	4.7	4.4	0.6	28.2	0.5	4.1	1995	Produits alimentaires
3.2	3.1	22.8	2.1	2.3	2.1	0.2	25.0	0.3	1.9	2005	(CTCI 0 + 1 + 22 + 4)
3.9	2.6	20.7	2.6	2.9	2.0	0.2	20.9	0.4	2.1	2010	
3.4	13.2	9.8	2.8	3.0	1.5	0.3	36.4	0.2	2.6	1995	Matières premières
1.5	5.7	4.5	1.1	1.2	0.3	0.1	34.5	0.0	0.9	2005	d'origine agricole
1.6	3.2	3.9	1.3	1.5	0.3	0.1	33.5	0.1	1.0	2010	(CTCI 2 - 22 - 27 - 28)
5.6	34.0	27.3	3.8	3.8	2.5	3.8	16.4	2.5	3.0	1995	Minerais, métaux, pierres
5.8	17.2	30.7	4.1	4.4	2.6	2.0	3.7	2.1	2.6	2005	précieuses et or (non monétaire)
8.5	23.9	39.2	5.1	5.4	2.2	3.4	14.6	2.9	3.1	2010	(CTCI 27 + 28 + 68 + 667 + 971)
12.5	23.8	4.0	12.6	6.6	2.2	81.0	10.0	85.0	4.5	1995	Combustibles (CTCI 3)
18.5	59.8	5.5	17.9	8.3	2.2	89.8	7.1	90.6	4.9	2005	
21.3	59.2	13.3	20.0	10.2	2.7	86.5	15.0	88.6	6.4	2010	
72.6	21.7	36.3	75.8	81.3	89.0	14.3	8.9	11.8	85.2	1995	Articles manufacturés
70.7	12.7	35.5	74.5	83.4	92.4	7.9	29.5	7.0	89.3	2005	(CTCI 5 à 8 moins 667 et 68)
63.9	7.1	22.2	70.3	79.2	92.5	9.7	16.0	8.0	86.9	2010	

Sources :
- Calculs du secrétariat de la CNUCED sur la base des données de ONU DAES Division de statistique

Notes :

(1) Y compris les exportations de catégorie spéciale, approvisionnements des navires et combustibles de soute et autres exportations de moindre importance dont la destination n'a pas pu être déterminée.

(2) Il est reconnu que la structure du commerce et la distribution au niveau partenaire pour certains pays et sur certaines années peuvent varier. À cet égard, le lecteur devrait connaître la couverture ainsi que les limites des données principales utilisées dans ce tableau. Pour de plus amples renseignements, veuillez visiter http://comtrade.un.org/db/help/uReadMeFirst.aspx.

2.2.K Export structure by partner and product group
Transition economies

| Product group | Year / Année | World (1) / Monde (1) | Developed economies - Économies développées | | | | | | | Transition economies / Économies en transition |
| | | | Total | Europe | | Canada | USA / États-Unis | Japan / Japon | Other developed countries / Autres économies développées | |
				Total	EU / UE					
Millions of dollars										
All products	1995	117 538	55 170	47 928	43 728	126	4 174	2 568	374	31 070
	2005	360 203	222 145	204 792	186 519	983	9 212	4 186	2 972	69 926
	2010	550 030	024 040	281 107	271 710	4 019	16 967	13 549	5 017	87 316
Share by destination (percentage)										
All products	1995	100.0	46.9	40.8	37.2	0.1	3.6	2.2	0.3	27.1
	2005	100.0	61.7	56.9	51.8	0.3	2.6	1.2	0.8	19.4
	2010	100.0	54.9	48.2	46.0	0.7	2.9	2.3	0.9	14.8
All food items	1995	100.0	32.0	26.7	25.9	0.1	1.8	2.3	1.0	59.2
(SITC 0 + 1 + 22 + 4)	2005	100.0	25.1	21.8	21.1	0.1	0.8	1.3	1.2	53.5
	2010	100.0	20.9	18.1	17.9	0.1	0.5	0.9	1.3	48.0
Agricultural raw materials	1995	100.0	63.7	54.5	52.7	0.0	1.0	8.0	0.1	7.1
(SITC 2 - 22 - 27 - 28)	2005	100.0	48.3	41.4	41.2	0.1	0.6	5.8	0.3	11.4
	2010	100.0	36.0	32.2	31.4	0.1	0.9	2.7	0.2	11.5
Ores, metals, precious stones	1995	100.0	80.5	58.3	50.6	0.0	10.6	11.5	0.1	10.8
and non-monetary gold	2005	100.0	68.9	57.0	46.1	0.2	5.0	5.3	1.4	11.5
(SITC 27 + 28 + 68 + 667 + 971)	2010	100.0	60.5	51.2	42.4	0.3	5.2	2.8	1.0	10.3
Fuels (SITC 3)	1995	100.0	62.3	60.3	54.2	0.0	0.8	0.6	0.5	22.7
	2005	100.0	66.5	63.6	57.6	0.3	1.2	0.7	0.7	8.1
	2010	100.0	66.4	59.0	57.1	1.0	2.5	3.0	1.0	6.1
Manufactured goods	1995	100.0	39.0	31.5	29.5	0.3	6.2	0.8	0.2	30.8
(SITC 5 to 8 less 667 and 68)	2005	100.0	38.0	32.4	31.5	0.4	4.3	0.4	0.5	31.0
	2010	100.0	37.3	32.5	31.3	0.4	3.1	0.8	0.5	32.4
Share by major product group (percentage)										
All products	1995	100.0	100.0	100.0	100.0	100.0	100.0	100.0	100.0	100.0
	2005	100.0	100.0	100.0	100.0	100.0	100.0	100.0	100.0	100.0
	2010	100.0	100.0	100.0	100.0	100.0	100.0	100.0	100.0	100.0
All food items	1995	5.6	3.8	3.7	3.9	4.7	2.8	6.0	17.5	12.2
(SITC 0 + 1 + 22 + 4)	2005	4.0	1.6	1.5	1.6	1.2	1.2	4.4	6.0	11.1
	2010	5.2	2.0	2.0	2.0	0.6	0.9	2.2	8.2	17.0
Agricultural raw materials	1995	5.5	7.5	7.4	7.8	0.6	1.5	20.4	2.4	1.5
(SITC 2 - 22 - 27 - 28)	2005	2.8	2.2	2.1	2.2	1.2	0.7	14.1	0.9	1.7
	2010	2.3	1.5	1.5	1.5	0.3	0.7	2.6	0.4	1.8
Ores, metals, precious stones	1995	10.0	17.2	14.3	13.6	2.3	29.9	52.5	2.7	4.0
and non-monetary gold	2005	7.8	8.7	7.8	6.9	5.1	15.2	35.1	13.2	4.6
(SITC 27 + 28 + 68 + 667 + 971)	2010	7.3	8.0	7.7	6.7	3.3	13.3	9.0	8.4	5.1
Fuels (SITC 3)	1995	32.8	43.5	48.4	47.8	13.3	7.7	9.4	51.8	27.4
	2005	52.9	57.0	59.2	58.9	55.7	24.1	31.3	45.3	22.1
	2010	58.4	70.6	71.4	72.4	81.8	50.8	77.4	65.3	24.0
Manufactured goods	1995	33.3	27.6	25.7	26.4	78.7	58.0	11.7	25.5	37.8
(SITC 5 to 8 less 667 and 68)	2005	26.5	16.3	15.1	16.1	36.4	44.8	9.7	14.9	42.3
	2010	23.3	15.9	15.7	15.9	14.0	25.1	8.4	12.9	51.1

Sources:
- UNCTAD secretariat calculations based on UN DESA Statistics Division's data

Notes:

(1) Includes special category exports, ship stores and bunkers and other exports of minor importance whose destination could not be determined.

(2) It is recognized that the structure of trade and partner distribution for certain countries and years might vary. In this regard, reader should know the coverage and limitations of the main principal data used in this table. For further information, please visit
http://comtrade.un.org/db/help/uReadMeFirst.aspx.

2.2.K Structure des exportations par partenaires et groupes de produits
Économies en transition

Total	Africa Afrique	America Amérique	Asia / Asie Total	Eastern, Southern and South-Eastern Asia Asie orientale, méridionale et du Sud-Est	China Chine	Western Asia Asie occidentale	Oceania (2) Océanie (2)	Major petroleum exporters and gas exporters Principaux exportateurs de pétrole et de gaz	Major manufactured goods exporters Principaux exportateurs d'articles manufacturés	Year Année	Destinations Groupes de produits
Millions de dollars											
17 407	1 001	2 956	13 449	10 416	4 794	3 033	1	1 158	8 209	1995	**Total tous produits**
67 432	5 611	6 706	55 098	35 866	17 501	19 231	17	8 286	24 574	2005	
128 142	9 453	7 184	111 383	81 088	36 337	30 296	122	13 312	57 837	2010	
Parts par destinations (en pourcentage)											
14.8	0.9	2.5	11.4	8.9	4.1	2.6	0.0	1.0	7.0	1995	**Total tous produits**
18.7	1.6	1.9	15.3	10.0	4.9	5.3	0.0	2.3	6.8	2005	
21.7	1.6	1.2	18.9	13.7	6.2	5.1	0.0	2.3	9.8	2010	
6.6	1.2	0.2	5.2	1.5	0.6	3.7	0.0	0.9	1.1	1995	Produits alimentaires
20.7	7.3	0.2	13.2	6.0	1.1	7.2	0.0	5.9	2.4	2005	(CTCI 0 + 1 + 22 + 4)
30.8	8.7	0.3	21.8	12.0	3.3	9.7	0.0	5.8	6.4	2010	
23.5	1.0	1.4	21.1	15.3	6.6	5.8	0.0	0.6	14.0	1995	Matières premières
40.3	2.4	0.1	37.7	33.1	25.1	4.6	0.0	2.1	27.6	2005	d'origine agricole
52.5	3.7	0.3	48.6	41.5	35.0	7.0	0.0	3.0	37.1	2010	(CTCI 2 - 22 - 27 - 28)
7.1	0.1	0.1	6.8	5.4	1.1	1.5	0.0	0.4	4.8	1995	Minerais, métaux, pierres
19.6	0.6	0.3	18.8	11.8	7.1	7.0	0.0	1.5	10.4	2005	précieuses et or (non monétaire)
29.2	0.3	0.4	28.4	17.0	13.6	11.4	0.0	0.9	15.2	2010	(CTCI 27 + 28 + 68 + 667 + 971)
9.7	0.1	5.5	4.1	2.2	0.1	1.9	0.0	0.6	1.3	1995	Combustibles (CTCI 3)
9.5	0.2	2.2	7.1	4.3	2.6	2.8	0.0	0.7	3.3	2005	
14.9	0.4	0.6	13.9	10.9	5.0	3.1	0.0	0.5	9.0	2010	
27.8	2.1	1.8	23.9	20.1	10.6	3.8	0.0	2.0	15.7	1995	Articles manufacturés
30.9	3.6	2.6	24.8	18.0	6.1	6.8	0.0	5.0	10.4	2005	(CTCI 5 à 8 moins 667 et 68)
30.2	2.5	3.6	24.0	17.3	5.2	6.8	0.1	5.0	9.1	2010	
Parts par principaux groupes de produits (en pourcentage)											
100.0	100.0	100.0	100.0	100.0	100.0	100.0	100.0	100.0	100.0	1995	**Total tous produits**
100.0	100.0	100.0	100.0	100.0	100.0	100.0	100.0	100.0	100.0	2005	
100.0	100.0	100.0	100.0	100.0	100.0	100.0	100.0	100.0	100.0	2010	
2.5	7.8	0.5	2.6	1.0	0.8	8.1	13.8	5.2	0.9	1995	Produits alimentaires
4.4	18.9	0.4	3.5	2.4	0.9	5.4	0.2	10.3	1.4	2005	(CTCI 0 + 1 + 22 + 4)
7.4	28.6	1.3	6.0	4.6	2.8	9.9	0.7	13.5	3.4	2010	
8.8	6.5	3.2	10.2	9.6	8.9	12.4	16.3	3.6	11.1	1995	Matières premières
6.1	4.4	0.2	7.0	9.4	14.6	2.4	0.0	2.6	11.5	2005	d'origine agricole
5.5	5.2	0.5	5.8	6.8	12.9	3.1	0.0	3.0	8.5	2010	(CTCI 2 - 22 - 27 - 28)
4.8	1.5	0.4	6.0	6.1	2.8	5.7	0.5	4.2	6.9	1995	Minerais, métaux, pierres
8.1	2.8	1.2	9.5	9.2	11.3	10.2	0.0	5.2	11.8	2005	précieuses et or (non monétaire)
9.8	1.5	2.4	11.0	9.0	16.0	16.2	0.0	2.9	11.3	2010	(CTCI 27 + 28 + 68 + 667 + 971)
21.4	2.4	71.7	11.8	8.1	0.8	24.6	9.9	18.5	6.2	1995	Combustibles (CTCI 3)
26.8	8.3	61.3	24.5	22.9	28.6	27.5	0.3	16.0	25.6	2005	
39.9	14.2	26.4	43.0	46.1	47.5	34.7	0.3	12.2	53.6	2010	
62.5	81.6	24.3	69.4	75.3	86.7	49.2	59.5	68.4	74.9	1995	Articles manufacturés
43.7	60.4	36.8	42.9	47.7	33.4	33.9	99.4	57.5	40.3	2005	(CTCI 5 à 8 moins 667 et 68)
32.5	37.1	68.9	29.7	29.3	19.7	30.8	99.0	52.0	21.6	2010	

Column group header: Developing economies - Économies en développement

Sources :
- Calculs du secrétariat de la CNUCED sur la base des données de ONU DAES Division de statistique

Notes :

(1) Y compris les exportations de catégorie spéciale, approvisionnements des navires et combustibles de soute et autres exportations de moindre importance dont la destination n'a pas pu être déterminée.

(2) Il est reconnu que la structure du commerce et la distribution au niveau partenaire pour certains pays et sur certaines années peuvent varier. À cet égard, le lecteur devrait connaître la couverture ainsi que les limites des données principales utilisées dans ce tableau. Pour de plus amples renseignements, veuillez visiter http://comtrade.un.org/db/help/uReadMeFirst.aspx.

Product group	Year / Année	World (1) / Monde (1)	Developed economies - Économies développées							Transition economies / Économies en transition
			Total	Europe		Canada	USA / États-Unis	Japan / Japon	Other developed countries / Autres économies développées	
				Total	EU UE					
Millions of dollars										
All products	1995	116 242	52 261	45 106	43 744	309	4 610	1 563	672	36 024
	2005	269 784	143 254	125 350	121 558	966	8 216	7 367	1 355	74 723
	2010	490 708	243 347	212 405	201 016	3 089	14 375	13 382	3 216	117 551
Share by origin (percentage)										
All products	1995	100.0	45.0	38.8	37.6	0.3	4.0	1.3	0.6	31.0
	2005	100.0	53.1	46.5	45.1	0.4	3.0	2.7	0.5	27.7
	2010	100.0	50.0	43.3	41.8	0.4	2.9	2.7	0.7	24.0
All food items	1995	100.0	55.1	45.2	44.0	0.3	8.1	0.0	1.5	23.6
(SITC 0 + 1 + 22 + 4)	2005	100.0	42.3	36.4	33.3	0.5	4.4	0.1	0.9	25.7
	2010	100.0	42.1	36.0	32.9	0.9	3.5	0.2	1.6	24.0
Agricultural raw materials	1995	100.0	36.4	33.0	32.3	0.2	2.4	0.3	0.5	54.4
(SITC 2 - 22 - 27 - 28)	2005	100.0	44.5	40.4	40.2	0.3	3.3	0.3	0.0	42.2
	2010	100.0	48.9	42.3	41.9	0.2	4.3	1.1	1.0	29.7
Ores, metals, precious stones	1995	100.0	28.1	21.5	20.5	0.4	2.8	0.0	3.4	49.8
and non-monetary gold	2005	100.0	31.2	25.3	23.7	0.3	1.6	0.2	3.9	49.9
(SITC 27 + 28 + 68 + 667 + 971)	2010	100.0	28.3	22.9	21.2	0.1	0.8	0.1	4.2	50.6
Fuels (SITC 3)	1995	100.0	14.5	13.5	12.7	0.0	0.7	0.2	0.0	81.1
	2005	100.0	9.7	9.3	8.8	0.0	0.2	0.1	0.0	87.9
	2010	100.0	13.4	11.9	11.3	0.0	1.2	0.1	0.1	81.5
Manufactured goods	1995	100.0	63.4	55.6	53.9	0.4	4.5	2.6	0.4	22.3
(SITC 5 to 8 less 667 and 68)	2005	100.0	62.6	54.9	53.6	0.4	3.3	3.8	0.3	17.7
	2010	100.0	57.4	49.8	48.4	0.4	3.1	3.8	0.4	14.5
Share by major commodity group (percentage)										
All products	1995	100.0	100.0	100.0	100.0	100.0	100.0	100.0	100.0	100.0
	2005	100.0	100.0	100.0	100.0	100.0	100.0	100.0	100.0	100.0
	2010	100.0	100.0	100.0	100.0	100.0	100.0	100.0	100.0	100.0
All food items	1995	17.5	21.5	20.4	20.5	18.0	35.7	0.6	45.5	13.3
(SITC 0 + 1 + 22 + 4)	2005	12.3	9.8	9.7	9.1	15.8	17.8	0.4	21.8	11.4
	2010	13.1	11.0	10.9	10.3	27.3	15.6	0.8	31.3	13.2
Agricultural raw materials	1995	1.3	1.0	1.1	1.1	0.8	0.8	0.3	1.1	2.2
(SITC 2 - 22 - 27 - 28)	2005	1.2	1.0	1.0	1.0	1.1	1.3	0.1	0.1	1.8
	2010	1.2	1.2	1.2	1.2	0.6	1.8	0.5	1.8	1.5
Ores, metals, precious stones	1995	2.9	1.8	1.6	1.6	4.0	2.0	0.0	16.7	4.6
and non-monetary gold	2005	3.1	1.8	1.7	1.7	2.5	1.6	0.2	24.3	5.7
(SITC 27 + 28 + 68 + 667 + 971)	2010	2.5	1.4	1.3	1.3	0.8	0.7	0.1	16.2	5.3
Fuels (SITC 3)	1995	11.2	3.6	3.9	3.8	1.0	2.1	1.8	0.5	29.2
	2005	10.7	2.0	2.1	2.1	0.2	0.8	0.4	0.2	34.0
	2010	10.7	2.9	2.9	2.9	1.0	4.5	0.6	1.2	36.3
Manufactured goods	1995	49.2	69.4	70.4	70.5	75.3	55.3	95.2	34.0	35.4
(SITC 5 to 8 less 667 and 68)	2005	71.1	83.9	84.0	84.6	76.5	76.4	98.3	40.8	45.5
	2010	70.6	81.0	81.2	81.8	69.8	74.0	97.4	38.9	42.7

Sources:
- UNCTAD secretariat calculations based on UN DESA Statistics Division's data

Notes:

(1) Includes special category exports, ship stores and bunkers and other exports of minor importance whose destination could not be determined.

(2) It is recognized that the structure of trade and partner distribution for certain countries and years might vary. In this regard, reader should know the coverage and limitations of the main principal data used in this table. For further information, please visit
http://comtrade.un.org/db/help/uReadMeFirst.aspx.

2.2.K Structure des importations par partenaires et groupes de produits
Économies en transition

			Developing economies - Économies en développement								Origines
				Asia / Asie							
Total	Africa / Afrique	America / Amérique	Total	Eastern, Southern and South-Eastern Asia / Asie orientale, méridionale et du Sud-Est	China / Chine	Western Asia / Asie occidentale	Oceania (2) / Océanie (2)	Major petroleum exporters and gas exporters / Principaux exportateurs de pétrole et de gaz	Major manufactured goods exporters / Principaux exportateurs d'articles manufacturés	Year / Année	Groupes de produits
Millions de dollars											
12 590	813	1 932	9 838	7 480	1 822	2 358	6	1 096	5 155	1995	**Total tous produits**
50 030	1 010	6 663	41 327	34 310	16 701	7 003	24	1 667	31 212	2005	
125 947	4 122	13 305	108 509	93 271	63 256	15 237	11	4 088	83 886	2010	
Parts par origines (en pourcentage)											
10.8	0.7	1.7	8.5	6.4	1.6	2.0	0.0	0.9	4.4	1995	**Total tous produits**
18.8	0.7	2.5	15.5	12.9	7.7	2.6	0.0	0.7	11.6	2005	
25.7	0.8	2.7	22.1	19.0	12.9	3.1	0.0	0.8	17.1	2010	
20.3	1.3	7.8	11.2	8.2	2.7	3.0	0.0	1.4	3.8	1995	Produits alimentaires
31.9	2.6	17.4	12.0	9.2	3.0	2.8	0.0	0.8	5.4	2005	(CTCI 0 + 1 + 22 + 4)
33.8	3.4	15.7	14.7	11.1	3.6	3.6	0.0	0.8	5.9	2010	
7.7	0.2	1.3	6.1	5.7	0.9	0.4	0.0	0.1	2.1	1995	Matières premières
13.2	1.1	3.9	8.2	7.5	1.2	0.7	0.0	0.4	5.1	2005	d'origine agricole
21.3	2.7	7.1	11.5	10.1	2.4	1.3	0.0	0.5	5.9	2010	(CTCI 2 - 22 - 27 - 28)
21.2	3.8	5.4	12.0	10.4	1.9	1.6	0.0	1.7	2.6	1995	Minerais, métaux, pierres
18.8	7.1	3.5	8.0	5.7	3.1	2.3	0.2	1.1	3.6	2005	précieuses et or (non monétaire)
21.1	6.9	2.6	11.6	8.6	5.2	3.0	0.0	0.6	6.0	2010	(CTCI 27 + 28 + 68 + 667 + 971)
4.0	2.1	0.2	1.8	1.4	0.3	0.4	0.0	2.8	0.8	1995	Combustibles (CTCI 3)
2.3	0.3	0.1	1.9	1.3	0.8	0.7	0.0	0.4	1.0	2005	
5.2	0.4	2.4	2.4	1.3	0.7	1.0	0.0	2.8	1.0	2010	
12.2	0.2	0.2	11.8	8.9	2.0	2.8	0.0	0.6	7.2	1995	Articles manufacturés
19.3	0.1	0.3	18.9	16.0	10.0	2.9	0.0	0.7	14.9	2005	(CTCI 5 à 8 moins 667 et 68)
28.0	0.2	0.3	27.5	24.1	17.2	3.4	0.0	0.6	22.6	2010	
Parts par principaux groupes de produits (en pourcentage)											
100.0	100.0	100.0	100.0	100.0	100.0	100.0	100.0	100.0	100.0	1995	**Total tous produits**
100.0	100.0	100.0	100.0	100.0	100.0	100.0	100.0	100.0	100.0	2005	
100.0	100.0	100.0	100.0	100.0	100.0	100.0	100.0	100.0	100.0	2010	
32.9	32.7	82.1	23.3	22.4	30.7	26.0	17.5	26.0	14.9	1995	Produits alimentaires
21.0	47.2	84.1	9.5	8.8	4.8	13.2	14.9	14.9	5.7	2005	(CTCI 0 + 1 + 22 + 4)
17.3	52.9	76.0	8.7	7.7	3.7	15.0	93.2	12.9	4.5	2010	
0.9	0.4	1.0	0.9	1.1	0.7	0.2	0.0	0.1	0.6	1995	Matières premières
0.8	1.9	1.8	0.6	0.7	0.2	0.3	0.4	0.7	0.5	2005	d'origine agricole
1.0	3.9	3.1	0.6	0.6	0.2	0.5	0.4	0.7	0.4	2010	(CTCI 2 - 22 - 27 - 28)
5.6	15.7	9.3	4.1	4.7	3.5	2.2	0.0	5.2	1.7	1995	Minerais, métaux, pierres
3.2	33.1	4.3	1.6	1.4	1.3	2.8	78.3	5.1	1.0	2005	précieuses et or (non monétaire)
2.1	20.6	2.4	1.3	1.1	1.0	2.4	0.0	1.9	0.9	2010	(CTCI 27 + 28 + 68 + 667 + 971)
4.1	32.9	1.0	2.4	2.4	1.8	2.3	0.0	30.0	1.9	1995	Combustibles (CTCI 3)
1.3	4.6	0.5	1.3	1.0	1.1	2.9	0.0	6.1	0.9	2005	
2.1	5.2	9.4	1.1	0.8	0.6	3.5	0.1	35.6	0.6	2010	
55.5	16.9	6.0	68.4	68.3	63.3	69.0	81.7	33.4	80.2	1995	Articles manufacturés
73.3	12.5	8.7	86.5	88.0	92.7	79.4	5.7	70.4	91.8	2005	(CTCI 5 à 8 moins 667 et 68)
77.0	16.5	8.7	87.7	89.3	94.1	77.8	6.2	48.0	93.1	2010	

Sources :
- Calculs du secrétariat de la CNUCED sur la base des données de ONU DAES Division de statistique

Notes :

(1) Y compris les exportations de catégorie spéciale, approvisionnements des navires et combustibles de soute et autres exportations de moindre importance dont la destination n'a pas pu être déterminée.

(2) Il est reconnu que la structure du commerce et la distribution au niveau partenaire pour certains pays et sur certaines années peuvent varier. À cet égard, le lecteur devrait connaître la couverture ainsi que les limites des données principales utilisées dans ce tableau. Pour de plus amples renseignements, veuillez visiter http://comtrade.un.org/db/help/uReadMeFirst.aspx.

Product group	Year Année	World (1) Monde (1)	Developed economies - Économies développées								Transition economies Économies en transition
			Total	Europe		Canada	USA États-Unis	Japan Japon	Other developed countries Autres économies développées		
				Total	EU UE						

Millions of dollars

All products	1995	3 571 460	2 621 396	1 834 691	1 724 338	148 733	431 818	135 778	70 376	53 019
	2005	6 299 815	4 706 445	3 391 312	3 214 850	257 944	800 496	147 587	109 105	142 077
	2010	8 190 069	5 626 951	4 222 701	3 979 905	299 604	760 040	177 220	139 063	221 600

Share by destination (percentage)

All products	1995	100.0	73.4	51.4	48.3	4.2	12.1	3.8	2.0	1.5
	2005	100.0	74.7	53.8	51.0	4.1	12.7	2.3	1.7	2.3
	2010	100.0	68.7	51.5	48.5	3.7	9.6	2.2	1.7	2.7
All food items	1995	100.0	73.6	56.9	55.0	2.6	5.2	7.7	1.1	3.9
(SITC 0 + 1 + 22 + 4)	2005	100.0	78.8	61.3	59.3	3.4	7.7	5.1	1.3	3.0
	2010	100.0	73.7	58.9	57.0	3.5	5.9	4.0	1.4	3.4
Agricultural raw materials	1995	100.0	75.3	47.8	45.5	2.9	12.1	11.5	1.1	0.5
(SITC 2 - 22 - 27 - 28)	2005	100.0	70.0	47.5	45.6	3.1	13.5	4.9	0.9	1.3
	2010	100.0	60.0	46.6	44.8	2.2	6.5	3.7	0.9	1.9
Ores, metals, precious stones	1995	100.0	73.6	48.5	43.5	3.4	11.5	6.8	3.5	0.5
and non-monetary gold	2005	100.0	67.8	45.3	41.1	2.7	12.2	3.9	3.6	0.9
(SITC 27 + 28 + 68 + 667 + 971)	2010	100.0	61.2	45.3	39.1	2.4	7.9	3.5	2.0	0.6
Fuels (SITC 3)	1995	100.0	80.8	55.0	51.4	2.7	18.0	4.4	0.7	1.4
	2005	100.0	84.5	55.3	52.7	3.3	23.1	2.3	0.6	0.6
	2010	100.0	75.5	51.9	49.0	2.8	17.3	3.0	0.7	1.0
Manufactured goods	1995	100.0	72.6	50.2	47.1	4.6	12.7	3.0	2.1	1.3
(SITC 5 to 8 less 667 and 68)	2005	100.0	73.7	53.4	50.6	4.4	12.2	1.9	1.8	2.5
	2010	100.0	68.2	51.4	48.5	3.9	9.5	1.6	1.8	3.1

Share by major product group (percentage)

All products	1995	100.0	100.0	100.0	100.0	100.0	100.0	100.0	100.0	100.0
	2005	100.0	100.0	100.0	100.0	100.0	100.0	100.0	100.0	100.0
	2010	100.0	100.0	100.0	100.0	100.0	100.0	100.0	100.0	100.0
All food items	1995	8.7	8.7	9.6	9.9	5.4	3.8	17.5	4.9	22.7
(SITC 0 + 1 + 22 + 4)	2005	7.0	7.4	7.9	8.1	5.7	4.2	15.1	5.3	9.3
	2010	8.3	8.9	9.5	9.7	7.9	5.1	15.1	7.1	10.1
Agricultural raw materials	1995	2.6	2.6	2.4	2.4	1.8	2.6	7.7	1.4	0.9
(SITC 2 - 22 - 27 - 28)	2005	1.7	1.6	1.5	1.5	1.3	1.8	3.5	0.9	1.0
	2010	1.7	1.5	1.5	1.6	1.0	1.1	2.9	0.9	1.2
Ores, metals, precious stones	1995	4.1	4.1	3.8	3.7	3.3	3.9	7.2	7.2	1.5
and non-monetary gold	2005	4.2	3.8	3.5	3.4	2.8	4.0	7.1	8.9	1.7
(SITC 27 + 28 + 68 + 667 + 971)	2010	5.9	5.3	5.2	4.8	3.9	4.9	9.6	7.2	1.4
Fuels (SITC 3)	1995	3.4	3.7	3.6	3.6	2.2	5.0	3.9	1.1	3.2
	2005	6.7	7.5	6.8	6.9	5.3	12.1	6.7	2.1	1.9
	2010	7.9	8.7	7.9	8.0	5.7	14.1	10.9	3.3	3.0
Manufactured goods	1995	76.8	75.9	75.0	74.8	84.2	80.8	61.0	80.3	66.6
(SITC 5 to 8 less 667 and 68)	2005	76.6	75.6	76.1	75.9	81.6	73.8	62.8	78.5	83.8
	2010	71.7	71.2	71.5	71.6	77.0	70.9	52.2	76.2	81.6

Sources:
- UNCTAD secretariat calculations based on UN DESA Statistics Division's data

Notes:

(1) Includes special category exports, ship stores and bunkers and other exports of minor importance whose destination could not be determined.

(2) It is recognized that the structure of trade and partner distribution for certain countries and years might vary. In this regard, reader should know the coverage and limitations of the main principal data used in this table. For further information, please visit
http://comtrade.un.org/db/help/uReadMeFirst.aspx.

2.2.L Structure des exportations par partenaires et groupes de produits
Économies développées

			Developing economies - Économies en développement								Destinations
				Asia / Asie				Major petroleum exporters and gas exporters	Major manufactured goods exporters	Year	
Total	Africa / Afrique	America / Amérique	Total	Eastern, Southern and South-Eastern Asia / Asie orientale, méridionale et du Sud-Est	China / Chine	Western Asia / Asie occidentale	Oceania (2) / Océanie (2)	Principaux exportateurs de pétrole et de gaz	Principaux exportateurs d'articles manufacturés	Année	Groupes de produits

Millions de dollars

Total	Africa	America	Total	Eastern...	China	Western Asia	Oceania	Petroleum	Manufactured	Year	
833 229	80 240	169 197	579 870	500 045	59 474	79 825	3 923	75 771	473 750	1995	Total tous produits
1 416 693	135 383	304 927	970 057	784 467	209 338	185 590	6 326	167 267	000 660	2005	
2 304 131	218 392	488 569	1 587 052	1 307 244	472 521	270 808	10 118	251 475	1 290 602	2010	

Parts par destinations (en pourcentage)

Total	Africa	America	Total	Eastern...	China	Western Asia	Oceania	Petroleum	Manufactured	Year	
23.3	2.2	4.7	16.2	14.0	1.7	2.2	0.1	2.1	13.3	1995	Total tous produits
22.5	2.1	4.8	15.4	12.5	3.3	2.9	0.1	2.7	12.8	2005	
28.1	2.7	6.0	19.4	16.0	5.8	3.4	0.1	3.1	15.8	2010	
19.1	3.5	4.1	11.3	8.6	1.2	2.7	0.2	3.2	8.1	1995	Produits alimentaires
17.2	2.9	4.4	9.6	7.2	1.6	2.4	0.2	2.9	8.0	2005	(CTCI 0 + 1 + 22 + 4)
22.7	3.8	4.8	13.8	10.9	3.6	3.0	0.2	3.5	10.7	2010	
23.1	2.0	3.4	17.7	16.1	3.6	1.6	0.0	1.1	14.5	1995	Matières premières
27.9	2.0	4.1	21.6	19.2	9.5	2.4	0.1	1.2	18.3	2005	d'origine agricole
38.1	3.1	4.4	30.5	27.5	15.9	3.0	0.0	1.7	25.3	2010	(CTCI 2 - 22 - 27 - 28)
22.9	1.0	1.7	20.2	18.4	1.3	1.8	0.0	0.9	15.3	1995	Minerais, métaux, pierres
29.0	1.1	2.1	25.8	23.6	7.5	2.2	0.0	1.3	18.7	2005	précieuses et or (non monétaire)
36.6	1.3	1.8	33.4	30.9	14.0	2.5	0.0	1.0	25.9	2010	(CTCI 27 + 28 + 68 + 667 + 971)
12.6	1.4	3.7	7.3	6.4	0.4	0.9	0.2	0.0	0.2	1995	Combustibles (CTCI 3)
10.8	1.7	3.5	5.5	4.2	0.6	1.2	0.1	1.0	4.9	2005	
19.9	3.0	7.4	9.4	8.0	1.8	1.3	0.1	1.7	9.2	2010	
24.5	2.2	5.1	17.1	14.8	1.7	2.3	0.1	2.1	14.2	1995	Articles manufacturés
23.4	2.2	5.2	15.9	12.7	3.3	3.2	0.1	2.9	13.3	2005	(CTCI 5 à 8 moins 667 et 68)
28.5	2.6	6.3	19.5	15.7	5.5	3.7	0.1	3.4	15.9	2010	

Parts par principaux groupes de produits (en pourcentage)

Total	Africa	America	Total	Eastern...	China	Western Asia	Oceania	Petroleum	Manufactured	Year	
100.0	100.0	100.0	100.0	100.0	100.0	100.0	100.0	100.0	100.0	1995	Total tous produits
100.0	100.0	100.0	100.0	100.0	100.0	100.0	100.0	100.0	100.0	2005	
100.0	100.0	100.0	100.0	100.0	100.0	100.0	100.0	100.0	100.0	2010	
7.1	13.7	7.5	6.0	5.3	6.5	10.4	15.2	13.0	5.3	1995	Produits alimentaires
5.3	9.4	6.4	4.4	4.0	3.3	5.8	14.0	7.5	4.4	2005	(CTCI 0 + 1 + 22 + 4)
6.7	11.8	6.7	5.9	5.6	5.2	7.3	13.5	9.4	5.6	2010	
2.5	2.3	1.8	2.8	3.0	5.6	1.9	1.1	1.4	2.8	1995	Matières premières
2.1	1.6	1.4	2.3	2.6	4.7	1.4	1.6	0.8	2.4	2005	d'origine agricole
2.3	1.9	1.3	2.7	2.9	4.7	1.5	0.7	0.9	2.7	2010	(CTCI 2 - 22 - 27 - 28)
4.0	1.9	1.5	5.1	5.4	3.1	3.3	0.6	1.8	4.7	1995	Minerais, métaux, pierres
5.4	2.1	1.8	7.1	8.0	9.5	3.2	0.6	2.1	6.2	2005	précieuses et or (non monétaire)
7.7	2.8	1.8	10.2	11.5	14.4	4.4	0.9	1.9	9.8	2010	(CTCI 27 + 28 + 68 + 667 + 971)
1.8	2.1	2.6	1.5	1.5	0.7	1.4	7.1	1.2	1.6	1995	Combustibles (CTCI 3)
3.2	5.2	4.9	2.4	2.3	1.1	2.8	7.5	2.6	2.6	2005	
5.6	8.9	9.8	3.8	4.0	2.5	3.1	5.0	4.3	4.6	2010	
80.7	76.6	82.6	80.7	81.2	79.1	77.6	73.1	77.5	82.3	1995	Articles manufacturés
79.6	77.6	81.6	79.3	78.5	76.7	83.0	70.5	83.0	80.1	2005	(CTCI 5 à 8 moins 667 et 68)
72.7	70.5	75.6	72.1	70.7	68.6	78.5	75.2	78.6	72.2	2010	

Sources :
- Calculs du secrétariat de la CNUCED sur la base des données de ONU DAES Division de statistique

Notes :

(1) Y compris les exportations de catégorie spéciale, approvisionnements des navires et combustibles de soute et autres exportations de moindre importance dont la destination n'a pas pu être déterminée.

(2) Il est reconnu que la structure du commerce et la distribution au niveau partenaire pour certains pays et sur certaines années peuvent varier. À cet égard, le lecteur devrait connaître la couverture ainsi que les limites des données principales utilisées dans ce tableau. Pour de plus amples renseignements, veuillez visiter http://comtrade.un.org/db/help/uReadMeFirst.aspx.

Product group	Year / Année	World (1) / Monde (1)	Developed economies - Économies développées							Transition economies / Économies en transition
			Total	Europe Total	Europe EU / UE	Canada	USA / États-Unis	Japan / Japon	Other developed countries / Autres économies développées	
Millions of dollars										
All products	1995	3 573 361	2 602 823	1 774 815	1 659 630	177 674	362 109	234 206	54 019	66 101
	2005	7 048 788	4 563 119	3 345 389	3 136 457	329 703	501 465	286 027	100 535	223 774
	2010	8 822 920	5 002 000	4 000 031	3 786 506	222 760	672 694	262 964	133 137	344 634
Share by origin (percentage)										
All products	1995	100.0	72.8	49.7	46.4	5.0	10.1	6.6	1.5	1.8
	2005	100.0	64.7	47.5	44.5	4.7	7.1	4.1	1.4	3.2
	2010	100.0	60.8	46.0	42.9	3.8	6.5	3.0	1.5	3.9
All food items	1995	100.0	69.2	51.3	49.1	3.7	10.8	0.2	3.3	1.1
(SITC 0 + 1 + 22 + 4)	2005	100.0	70.7	55.3	53.3	4.1	7.1	0.2	3.9	1.1
	2010	100.0	69.3	55.9	53.5	3.8	6.4	0.2	3.0	1.2
Agricultural raw materials	1995	100.0	71.7	37.4	36.0	16.0	13.3	0.5	4.5	4.9
(SITC 2 - 22 - 27 - 28)	2005	100.0	69.1	44.1	43.1	13.7	7.7	0.6	3.0	4.7
	2010	100.0	65.3	47.0	45.9	8.0	6.9	0.8	2.5	3.7
Ores, metals, precious stones	1995	100.0	62.8	39.8	34.0	8.0	7.2	0.6	7.2	8.2
and non-monetary gold	2005	100.0	58.2	37.8	33.2	6.9	5.0	0.5	8.0	8.4
(SITC 27 + 28 + 68 + 667 + 971)	2010	100.0	57.7	38.2	32.4	7.1	4.9	0.6	6.8	6.3
Fuels (SITC 3)	1995	100.0	36.2	25.2	17.5	5.9	2.3	0.1	2.5	8.0
	2005	100.0	36.0	25.7	19.1	6.9	1.5	0.1	1.8	13.5
	2010	100.0	34.8	23.9	18.0	6.3	2.0	0.2	2.4	16.9
Manufactured goods	1995	100.0	77.3	52.2	49.5	4.3	11.1	8.9	0.7	0.6
(SITC 5 to 8 less 667 and 68)	2005	100.0	69.9	51.5	49.3	3.8	8.4	5.6	0.7	0.8
	2010	100.0	65.0	49.8	47.5	2.7	7.6	4.2	0.7	0.9
Share by major product group (percentage)										
All products	1995	100.0	100.0	100.0	100.0	100.0	100.0	100.0	100.0	100.0
	2005	100.0	100.0	100.0	100.0	100.0	100.0	100.0	100.0	100.0
	2010	100.0	100.0	100.0	100.0	100.0	100.0	100.0	100.0	100.0
All food items	1995	9.2	8.7	9.5	9.7	6.8	9.8	0.3	19.9	5.5
(SITC 0 + 1 + 22 + 4)	2005	6.9	7.6	8.1	8.3	6.1	6.9	0.3	19.1	2.5
	2010	7.7	8.8	9.4	9.7	7.8	7.6	0.4	15.2	2.3
Agricultural raw materials	1995	2.9	2.8	2.2	2.2	9.2	3.8	0.2	8.5	7.6
(SITC 2 - 22 - 27 - 28)	2005	1.5	1.7	1.4	1.5	4.5	1.7	0.2	3.3	2.3
	2010	1.4	1.5	1.4	1.5	3.0	1.5	0.4	2.4	1.3
Ores, metals, precious stones	1995	5.0	4.3	4.0	3.7	8.1	3.6	0.5	23.8	22.2
and non-monetary gold	2005	4.3	3.8	3.4	3.2	6.3	3.0	0.6	23.9	11.3
(SITC 27 + 28 + 68 + 667 + 971)	2010	5.1	4.8	4.2	3.8	9.6	3.9	1.0	23.0	8.2
Fuels (SITC 3)	1995	7.4	3.7	3.8	2.8	8.9	1.7	0.1	12.5	32.0
	2005	14.1	7.8	7.6	6.0	20.8	2.9	0.5	17.7	60.0
	2010	15.8	9.1	8.2	6.9	26.5	5.0	1.0	25.4	68.5
Manufactured goods	1995	71.7	76.1	75.4	76.4	62.5	78.7	97.3	32.6	25.0
(SITC 5 to 8 less 667 and 68)	2005	70.1	75.7	76.1	77.7	57.2	82.4	96.4	33.5	17.5
	2010	67.2	71.9	72.8	74.4	48.2	78.2	95.3	32.4	15.3

Sources:
- UNCTAD secretariat calculations based on UN DESA Statistics Division's data

Notes:

(1) Includes special category exports, ship stores and bunkers and other exports of minor importance whose destination could not be determined.

(2) It is recognized that the structure of trade and partner distribution for certain countries and years might vary. In this regard, reader should know the coverage and limitations of the main principal data used in this table. For further information, please visit
http://comtrade.un.org/db/help/uReadMeFirst.aspx.

2.2.L Structure des importations par partenaires et groupes de produits
Économies développées

Total	Africa — Afrique	America — Amérique	Asia — Asie — Total	Eastern, Southern and South-Eastern Asia — Asie orientale, méridionale et du Sud-Est	China — Chine	Western Asia — Asie occidentale	Oceania (2) — Océanie (2)	Major petroleum exporters and gas exporters — Principaux exportateurs de pétrole et de gaz	Major manufactured goods exporters — Principaux exportateurs d'articles manufacturés	Year — Année	Origines — Groupes de produits
— Developing economies - Économies en développement											
Millions de dollars											
845 957	83 067	174 838	584 207	511 358	127 428	72 849	3 845	108 316	484 317	1995	**Total tous produits**
£ £00 1T0	£10 000	40T 000	1 510 071	1 005 717	000 505	007 007	1 071	051 050	1 201 017	2005	
3 069 932	297 936	575 718	2 189 483	1 888 760	1 052 488	300 724	8 795	455 015	1 850 022	2010	
Parts par origines (en pourcentage)											
23.7	2.3	4.9	16.3	14.3	3.6	2.0	0.1	3.0	13.6	1995	**Total tous produits**
31.3	3.1	6.2	21.9	18.5	9.1	3.4	0.1	5.0	18.3	2005	
34.8	3.4	6.5	24.8	21.4	11.9	3.4	0.1	5.2	21.0	2010	
28.2	4.0	12.3	11.6	10.7	2.2	0.9	0.3	0.4	8.7	1995	Produits alimentaires
28.1	3.7	13.2	11.0	9.8	3.2	1.1	0.2	0.4	8.6	2005	(CTCI 0 + 1 + 22 + 4)
29.3	3.6	13.8	11.7	10.7	3.2	0.9	0.2	0.4	9.5	2010	
22.5	3.6	6.0	12.4	11.9	1.9	0.5	0.4	0.5	8.9	1995	Matières premières
26.0	4.0	8.5	13.3	12.8	3.4	0.5	0.1	0.3	9.1	2005	d'origine agricole
30.8	3.8	9.8	17.1	16.6	3.9	0.5	0.1	0.3	10.7	2010	(CTCI 2 - 22 - 27 - 28)
25.4	6.2	10.1	8.4	7.6	1.3	0.8	0.7	1.2	4.8	1995	Minerais, métaux, pierres
32.6	8.4	12.5	11.1	9.6	2.6	1.5	0.5	1.5	6.3	2005	précieuses et or (non monétaire)
34.9	6.9	15.1	12.0	10.3	2.6	1.7	0.8	1.3	7.8	2010	(CTCI 27 + 28 + 68 + 667 + 971)
51.9	13.4	8.8	29.5	10.4	1.2	19.1	0.2	35.0	5.9	1995	Combustibles (CTCI 3)
47.3	13.4	10.0	23.8	7.4	0.6	16.4	0.1	32.6	5.8	2005	
44.8	13.6	8.5	22.6	7.4	0.2	15.2	0.0	30.6	5.5	2010	
20.7	0.6	3.2	16.8	16.2	4.4	0.6	0.0	0.3	16.1	1995	Articles manufacturés
29.1	0.8	4.4	24.0	22.7	12.1	1.3	0.0	0.4	23.0	2005	(CTCI 5 à 8 moins 667 et 68)
33.8	0.8	4.6	28.5	27.3	16.9	1.2	0.0	0.3	27.5	2010	
Parts par principaux groupes de produits (en pourcentage)											
100.0	100.0	100.0	100.0	100.0	100.0	100.0	100.0	100.0	100.0	1995	**Total tous produits**
100.0	100.0	100.0	100.0	100.0	100.0	100.0	100.0	100.0	100.0	2005	
100.0	100.0	100.0	100.0	100.0	100.0	100.0	100.0	100.0	100.0	2010	
10.9	15.7	23.2	6.5	6.8	5.6	4.1	25.6	1.1	5.9	1995	Produits alimentaires
6.2	8.2	14.8	3.5	3.7	2.4	2.4	21.7	0.6	3.3	2005	(CTCI 0 + 1 + 22 + 4)
6.5	8.2	16.4	3.6	3.9	2.1	2.1	20.6	0.5	3.5	2010	
2.7	4.5	3.5	2.2	2.4	1.5	0.7	11.4	0.4	1.9	1995	Matières premières
1.3	2.0	2.1	0.9	1.1	0.6	0.2	2.5	0.1	0.8	2005	d'origine agricole
1.2	1.6	2.1	1.0	1.1	0.5	0.2	1.4	0.1	0.7	2010	(CTCI 2 - 22 - 27 - 28)
5.4	13.4	10.4	2.6	2.7	1.9	2.0	32.4	2.0	1.8	1995	Minerais, métaux, pierres
4.4	11.5	8.6	2.2	2.2	1.2	1.8	32.7	1.3	1.5	2005	précieuses et or (non monétaire)
5.1	10.4	11.8	2.5	2.4	1.1	2.5	54.5	1.3	1.9	2010	(CTCI 27 + 28 + 68 + 667 + 971)
16.3	42.8	13.4	13.4	5.4	2.5	69.5	15.0	87.8	3.2	1995	Combustibles (CTCI 3)
21.3	60.6	22.6	15.3	5.6	0.9	68.5	18.6	92.3	4.4	2005	
20.4	63.8	20.5	14.4	5.5	0.3	70.6	9.7	93.8	4.2	2010	
62.7	19.3	46.9	73.8	81.2	87.7	22.4	14.8	6.4	85.3	1995	Articles manufacturés
65.2	17.0	49.4	76.7	86.0	94.0	26.1	21.9	5.2	88.2	2005	(CTCI 5 à 8 moins 667 et 68)
65.3	15.2	46.9	77.1	85.6	95.2	23.9	12.8	3.9	88.0	2010	

Sources :
- Calculs du secrétariat de la CNUCED sur la base des données de ONU DAES Division de statistique

Notes :

(1) Y compris les exportations de catégorie spéciale, approvisionnements des navires et combustibles de soute et autres exportations de moindre importance dont la destination n'a pas pu être déterminée.

(2) Il est reconnu que la structure du commerce et la distribution au niveau partenaire pour certains pays et sur certaines années peuvent varier. À cet égard, le lecteur devrait connaître la couverture ainsi que les limites des données principales utilisées dans ce tableau. Pour de plus amples renseignements, veuillez visiter http://comtrade.un.org/db/help/uReadMeFirst.aspx.

3

INTERNATIONAL **MERCHANDISE** TRADE BY PRODUCT

COMMERCE INTERNATIONAL DES **MARCHANDISES** PAR PRODUITS

Country or territory / Pays ou territoires	Year / Année	Total value (millions of dollars) / Valeur totale (millions de dollars)	By main SITC Revision 3 product group (percentage) / Par principaux groupes de produits de la CTCI Révision 3 (en pourcentage)					Of which: / dont :		
			All food items / Produits alimentaires	Agricultural raw materials / Matières premières agricoles	Fuels / Combustibles	Ores, metals, precious stones and non monetary gold / Minerais, métaux, pierres précieuses et or (non monétaire)	Manufactured goods / Articles manufacturés	Chemical products / Produits chimiques	Machinery and transport equipment / Machines et matériel de transport	Other manufactured goods / Articles manufacturés divers
			0 1 1 22 + 4	2 (22 + 27 + 28)	3	27 + 28 + 68 + 667 + 971	5 + 6 + 7 + 8 -(667 + 68)	5	7	6 + 8 - (667 + 68)
Afghanistan (1)	1995	(e)166	53.3	26.0	0.1	2.6	16.7	3.1	2.5	11.0
	2005	(e)394	76.6	19.6	0.0	7.5	13.9	2.2	0.0	3.7
	2010	(e)388	31.5	13.8	0.6	7.0	26.9	2.0	8.7	16.2
Albania - Albanie	1995	(e)202	11.2	12.4	2.7	12.3	60.0	1.7	3.4	54.9
	2005	(e)658	5.4	4.7	6.0	8.8	74.0	0.7	5.1	68.2
	2010	(e)1 550	4.1	2.9	15.2	14.7	62.8	0.7	6.0	56.1
Algeria - Algérie	1995	9 357	1.2	0.1	95.2	0.5	3.0	1.2	0.4	1.4
	2005	46 002	0.2	0.0	98.4	0.5	1.0	0.7	0.1	0.2
	2010	57 051	0.6	0.0	98.3	0.3	0.8	0.5	0.0	0.2
American Samoa - Samoa américaines (1)	2005	(e)374	24.8	23.3	0.3	8.3	38.7	4.0	26.4	8.3
	2010	(e)480	35.2	4.8	0.7	4.7	54.4	27.7	18.7	8.1
Andorra - Andorre	1995	48	6.5	1.6	0.2	2.3	89.3	3.6	33.8	52.0
	2005	143	28.9	0.5	0.0	2.2	67.4	3.6	39.7	24.1
	2010	(e)54	0.5	0.0	..	0.0	96.3	0.6	89.0	6.7
Angola	1995	(e)3 723	1.0	0.0	93.9	4.5	0.5	0.0	0.2	0.3
	2005	(e)24 105	0.2	0.0	96.3	3.2	0.2	0.0	0.0	0.0
	2010	(e)49259	0.0	0.0	98.5	1.1	0.3	0.0	0.2	0.1
Anguilla (1)	1995	(e)1	13.8	2.2	3.2	1.8	78.1	16.1	29.2	32.8
	2005	(e)15	25.6	0.1	5.8	0.1	59.5	25.6	15.4	18.6
	2010	(e)12	19.7	0.1	0.0	1.8	74.4	7.9	50.3	16.2
Antigua and Barbuda - Antigua-et-Barbuda (1)	1995	(e)53	18.8	4.2	47.4	4.4	23.2	6.3	11.0	5.8
	2005	(e)83	4.1	0.1	10.4	0.1	84.2	1.5	80.0	2.6
	2010	(e)35	7.8	0.2	1.5	0.6	89.5	7.1	56.0	26.3
Argentina - Argentine	1995	20 963	49.8	4.3	10.3	1.6	33.9	6.4	10.9	16.6
	2005	40 106	46.5	1.4	16.4	3.6	30.6	8.5	10.7	11.4
	2010	68 134	49.7	1.2	7.9	7.2	32.2	8.6	15.9	7.7
Armenia - Arménie	1995	(e)271	12.8	4.9	5.5	22.6	53.0	3.3	27.0	22.7
	2005	(e)937	12.3	0.8	2.5	39.8	43.7	0.4	3.2	40.1
	2010	(e)1 011	16.3	1.3	3.2	51.0	27.0	1.5	3.6	21.9
Aruba (1)	1995	(e)1 347	2.9	0.1	93.6	0.4	2.0	0.9	0.5	0.5
	2005	(e)3 483	2.5	0.0	92.9	0.8	1.5	0.1	1.0	0.4
	2010	(e)266	34.6	0.1	48.4	2.7	8.2	1.3	2.7	4.2
Australia - Australie	1995	53 001	19.6	8.1	16.7	26.4	26.5	4.1	12.8	9.6
	2005	105 751	16.1	3.9	25.6	27.4	20.2	4.6	9.5	6.0
	2010	206 705	10.6	2.5	28.9	40.3	12.8	3.5	5.3	4.0
Austria - Autriche	1995	57 583	3.8	2.9	1.0	3.1	81.6	7.2	36.0	38.3
	2005	117 722	6.2	1.8	4.6	2.9	80.6	8.7	41.1	30.8
	2010	144 882	6.9	1.8	3.2	4.8	79.5	11.5	37.8	30.2
Azerbaijan - Azerbaïdjan	1995	(e)547	10.1	13.0	46.0	3.9	26.9	5.3	12.6	9.0
	2005	(e)7 649	6.2	1.3	76.9	3.7	11.8	2.3	7.1	2.4
	2010	(e)26 476	2.1	0.1	93.7	0.3	2.5	0.5	1.1	0.8
Bahamas	1995	(e)176	20.3	0.8	10.6	6.7	60.2	17.0	36.2	7.0
	2005	(e)549	11.0	0.1	23.5	3.2	58.5	9.3	44.5	4.7
	2010	(e)702	10.8	0.4	38.6	3.3	46.8	14.1	27.8	4.9
Bahrain - Bahreïn	1995	(e)4 113	3.0	0.4	18.4	45.1	32.5	10.7	4.8	17.0
	2005	(e)10 239	1.4	-0.1	43.2	32.3	21.7	5.9	4.2	11.5
	2010	(e)13 647	4.3	0.3	35.0	35.2	24.5	4.7	6.5	13.3
Bangladesh	1995	(e)3 407	9.2	2.6	0.3	0.0	86.9	3.1	1.1	82.7
	2005	(e)9 332	5.8	1.4	0.4	0.2	92.0	1.9	1.3	88.8
	2010	(e)20 305	5.2	2.3	1.0	0.4	91.0	1.5	1.5	88.0
Barbados - Barbade	1995	238	27.3	1.0	14.3	2.2	54.0	12.8	18.9	22.3
	2005	361	20.9	0.2	40.2	0.5	36.9	12.6	10.2	14.1
	2010	(e)429	20.4	0.3	10.6	1.2	66.6	23.6	19.8	23.1

For sources and notes, see end of table.

Pour les sources et les notes, se reporter à la fin du tableau.

3.1 Country trade structure
by product group
Exports

3.1 Structure du commerce des pays
par groupes de produits
Exportations

Country or territory Pays ou territoires	Year Année	Total value (millions of dollars) Valeur totale (millions de dollars)	By main SITC Revision 3 product group (percentage) Par principaux groupes de produits de la CTCI Révision 3 (en pourcentage)					Of which: / dont :		
			All food items Produits alimentaires	Agricultural raw materials Matières premières agricoles	Fuels Combus-tibles	Ores, metals, precious stones and non monetary gold Minerais, métaux, pierres précieuses et or (non monétaire)	Manu-factured goods Articles manu-facturés	Chemical products Produits chimiques	Machinery and transport equipment Machines et matériel de transport	Other manu-factured goods Articles manu-facturés divers
			0 + 1 + 22 + 4	2 - (22 + 27 + 28)	3	27 + 28 + 68 + 667 + 971	5 + 6 +7 + 8 -(667 + 68)	5	7	6 + 8 - (667 + 68)
Belarus - Bélarus	1995	(e)4 804	1.9	5.0	4.6	3.8	32.9	10.8	9.0	13.2
	2005	15 977	8.3	2.5	34.8	0.5	51.9	11.1	18.7	22.2
	2010	25 226	12.6	2.1	28.1	0.7	52.9	14.8	17.2	21.0
Belgium - Belgique	1995	(e)177 831	7.6	0.8	1.8	8.7	53.4	12.7	22.3	18.4
	2005	334 106	8.1	1.2	6.9	7.6	73.9	27.6	25.2	21.1
	2010	411 085	8.8	1.4	8.8	7.9	70.7	30.5	20.3	19.9
Belize	1995	162	78.6	1.5	2.8	0.3	15.5	1.6	3.9	10.0
	2005	208	73.1	1.0	4.5	0.3	20.3	2.3	9.6	8.4
	2010	282	58.2	1.2	33.2	1.3	5.4	0.9	2.7	1.8
Benin - Bénin	1995	420	17.7	71.6	4.7	1.7	5.5	0.6	0.4	4.4
	2005	(e)578	20.7	47.2	17.4	5.8	8.6	0.8	2.2	5.6
	2010	(e)1 388	20.6	41.5	17.9	11.0	9.1	1.6	1.6	6.0
Bermuda - Bermudes (1)	1995	(e)56	7.3	12.9	2.1	0.2	68.3	18.5	45.6	4.2
	2005	(e)49	2.1	0.1	0.6	0.4	89.6	2.6	81.1	6.0
	2010	(e)26	5.1	0.1	18.8	1.3	70.6	4.1	52.1	14.4
Bhutan - Bhoutan (1)	1995	(e)103	20.0	8.5	0.3	1.7	69.2	22.5	7.0	39.8
	2005	(e)258	9.2	0.3	28.9	10.1	51.3	8.1	3.5	39.7
	2010	(e)611	11.6	0.0	10.3	10.0	50.7	10.2	0.0	47.7
Bolivia (Plurinational State of) - Bolivie (État plurinational de)	1995	1 181	19.6	13.3	10.8	40.3	15.7	1.3	2.2	12.2
	2005	2 797	18.2	2.0	53.0	15.1	11.4	1.3	1.6	8.5
	2010	(e)6 179	15.5	1.3	46.6	29.0	7.4	3.1	0.4	4.0
Bosnia and Herzegovina - Bosnie-Herzégovine	1995	(e)152	16.6	20.4	3.8	6.6	51.8	2.6	14.5	34.6
	2005	(e)2 388	5.1	8.4	8.9	23.0	53.7	3.2	16.6	33.9
	2010	(e)4 803	7.9	6.6	10.9	15.7	57.9	5.0	14.4	38.5
Botswana	1995	(e)2 142	7.3	1.0	0.1	54.7	36.9	6.1	18.1	12.8
	2005	4 431	2.3	0.1	0.1	90.4	6.9	0.6	2.8	3.5
	2010	4 693	5.3	0.3	0.6	80.4	13.2	2.5	4.0	6.7
Brazil - Brésil	1995	46 505	28.5	5.2	0.9	11.3	52.8	6.6	19.0	27.2
	2005	118 529	25.7	3.9	6.0	10.5	52.1	6.2	25.8	20.2
	2010	197 356	30.8	4.0	10.1	19.4	35.8	6.2	16.8	12.8
Brunei Darussalam - Brunéi Darussalam	1995	(e)2 379	0.1	0.0	91.1	0.0	8.2	0.1	4.5	3.6
	2005	(e)6 268	0.1	0.1	92.1	0.6	7.2	0.0	1.2	5.9
	2010	(e)9 194	0.2	0.1	97.4	0.3	2.1	0.0	0.9	1.2
Bulgaria - Bulgarie	1995	(e)5 353	18.1	3.0	6.5	9.7	60.1	18.3	12.4	29.4
	2005	11 739	10.3	1.8	10.7	14.3	60.5	8.3	14.2	38.0
	2010	20 608	15.4	1.4	12.2	17.5	50.4	7.3	17.5	25.7
Burkina Faso	1995	(e)276	18.6	60.0	0.7	11.7	8.8	0.4	2.6	5.8
	2005	(e)468	13.7	76.4	0.1	2.0	7.4	0.8	2.2	4.4
	2010	1 288	18.2	35.4	0.0	40.1	6.3	1.7	1.9	2.7
Burundi	1995	(e)106	57.5	3.8	0.0	36.5	2.1	0.2	0.4	1.5
	2005	(e)56	65.8	2.1	0.0	27.2	4.7	0.2	3.0	1.5
	2010	(e)100	72.7	4.5	1.8	13.9	7.0	1.8	2.9	2.3
Cambodia - Cambodge	1995	(e)855	4.0	74.4	0.0	0.3	20.8	0.3	0.7	19.7
	2005	(e)3 019	2.4	3.8	0.0	1.2	92.4	0.1	0.5	91.7
	2010	(e)5 590	2.6	2.9	0.0	3.2	91.2	0.3	3.7	87.2
Cameroon - Cameroun	1995	(e)1 539	26.2	31.1	29.0	7.0	6.6	0.6	0.9	5.1
	2005	(e)2 861	19.4	17.8	49.4	4.7	5.8	0.9	1.1	3.8
	2010	(e)3 878	25.3	17.6	42.6	3.7	10.5	1.3	3.1	6.0
Canada	1995	191 118	7.6	9.2	9.1	7.8	62.0	5.9	38.5	17.6
	2005	360 552	6.7	4.7	20.2	7.0	56.9	7.2	32.8	16.8
	2010	385 816	9.6	3.9	23.7	11.9	47.8	8.6	26.2	13.0

For sources and notes, see end of table.

Pour les sources et les notes, se reporter à la fin du tableau.

Country or territory / Pays ou territoires	Year / Année	Total value (millions of dollars) / Valeur totale (millions de dollars)	By main SITC Revision 3 product group (percentage) / Par principaux groupes de produits de la CTCI Révision 3 (en pourcentage)					Of which: / dont :		
			All food items / Produits alimentaires	Agricultural raw materials / Matières premières agricoles	Fuels / Combustibles	Ores, metals, precious stones and non monetary gold / Minerais, métaux, pierres précieuses et or (non monétaire)	Manu-factured goods / Articles manu-facturés	Chemical products / Produits chimiques	Machinery and transport equipment / Machines et matériel de transport	Other manu-factured goods / Articles manu-facturés divers
			0 + 1 + 22 + 4	2 (22 + 27 + 28)	3	27 + 28 + 68 + 667 + 971	5 + 6 +7 + 8 -(667 + 68)	5	7	6 + 8 - (667 + 68)
Cape Verde - Cap-Vert	1995	9	14.0	0.5	9.1	6.0	68.6	1.8	15.7	51.0
	2005	(e)18	23.2	11.1	32.4	11.5	45.2	0.4	23.9	19.4
	2010	47	76.4	0.1	0.0	1.9	21.4	0.4	3.5	17.5
Central African Republic - République centrafricaine	1995	(e)171	14.3	17.7	0.1	57.0	8.2	0.5	5.3	2.5
	2005	(e)129	1.7	45.8	1.4	44.8	6.1	1.1	2.2	2.9
	2010	(e)139	8.6	45.6	0.8	35.9	9.2	1.0	4.5	3.7
Chad - Tchad	1995	(e)243	1.4	90.3	0.0	0.0	6.0	0.1	5.1	0.8
	2005	(e)3 144	0.1	6.7	90.5	0.1	2.3	0.1	1.9	0.3
	2010	(e)3 411	0.1	3.1	90.7	0.1	5.9	0.4	4.3	1.1
Chile - Chili	1995	15 901	23.7	13.6	0.2	49.5	11.7	3.5	1.8	6.5
	2005	41 266	19.4	6.4	2.0	56.5	12.5	5.1	1.6	5.8
	2010	(e)71 345	15.8	6.1	1.1	65.7	11.3	4.5	2.0	4.8
China - Chine	1995	148 779	8.3	1.8	3.6	2.4	83.6	6.1	21.1	56.4
	2005	761 953	3.2	0.5	2.3	2.0	91.7	4.7	46.2	40.8
	2010	1 577 764	2.8	0.5	1.7	1.5	93.4	5.5	49.5	38.4
China, Hong Kong SAR - Chine (RAS de Hong Kong)	1995	173 871	3.0	1.3	1.0	2.6	91.6	6.2	32.4	53.1
	2005	292 119	0.9	0.6	0.3	4.1	94.0	4.8	52.3	36.9
	2010	400 692	1.5	0.5	0.2	7.7	90.1	4.6	58.6	26.8
China, Macao SAR - Chine (RAS de Macao)	1995	2 025	2.1	1.7	0.0	0.1	95.9	1.2	4.2	90.6
	2005	2 474	1.3	0.3	0.1	2.0	96.2	2.3	8.0	85.8
	2010	870	3.5	0.7	0.2	6.3	70.4	6.3	14.6	49.5
China, Taiwan Province of - Province chinoise de Taiwan	1995	(e)111 343	3.4	1.6	0.7	1.5	92.7	6.8	48.1	37.8
	2005	(e)189 393	1.2	1.2	4.7	1.8	90.7	10.5	49.8	30.4
	2010	(e)274 375	1.1	1.1	5.1	3.4	89.4	13.1	46.2	30.1
Colombia - Colombie	1995	10 201	30.8	5.4	27.2	6.8	29.8	7.9	2.6	19.3
	2005	21 190	17.2	4.5	39.2	4.6	34.4	8.4	6.0	20.0
	2010	39 820	11.2	3.3	56.7	7.2	21.7	7.1	3.2	11.4
Comoros - Comores (1)	1995	11	60.4	0.4	..	0.0	38.6	35.0	1.8	1.8
	2005	(e)12	71.3	1.0	..	1.2	26.3	11.0	12.1	3.3
	2010	(e)13	28.9	0.5	0.0	1.2	69.5	15.3	52.4	1.8
Congo	1995	(e)1 090	1.6	10.7	82.4	1.6	3.4	0.3	0.3	2.7
	2005	(e)4 745	0.9	5.4	87.1	5.7	0.9	0.3	0.2	0.4
	2010	(e)8 192	1.9	4.3	81.9	8.5	1.6	0.3	0.6	0.7
Cook Islands - Îles Cook (1)	1995	(e)5	32.7	5.0	0.5	33.8	24.7	5.4	4.6	14.7
	2005	(e)5	76.8	1.3	..	11.8	8.6	0.6	2.4	5.6
	2010	(e)5	75.1	0.3	..	8.1	15.9	4.9	7.3	3.7
Costa Rica	1995	(e)3 476	56.2	4.6	0.4	1.2	35.3	5.0	4.7	25.6
	2005	7 151	26.4	2.3	0.2	1.1	69.1	5.0	43.7	20.4
	2010	9 045	26.8	2.1	0.4	0.8	69.4	3.6	52.1	13.7
Côte d'Ivoire	1995	3 737	58.7	16.0	9.8	0.8	14.2	4.2	1.4	8.6
	2005	7 248	38.2	8.2	27.7	0.5	24.9	3.6	9.8	11.4
	2010	(e)9 650	42.7	9.6	33.2	0.8	13.8	4.8	3.2	5.8
Croatia - Croatie	1995	4 633	10.8	4.6	8.4	2.3	73.8	17.6	16.8	39.5
	2005	8 773	10.5	3.4	13.9	3.8	68.5	9.9	28.9	29.6
	2010	11 811	11.3	3.7	12.5	4.6	67.9	11.4	31.7	24.9
Cuba	1995	(e)1 625	76.2	0.3	0.3	15.8	7.1	3.8	1.3	2.0
	2005	(e)2 319	28.2	0.6	2.2	32.8	14.4	4.3	3.6	6.4
	2010	(e)3 800	31.7	0.7	3.7	31.0	19.5	7.7	5.1	6.7
Cyprus - Chypre	1995	1 231	45.4	0.7	1.9	2.0	49.2	5.0	20.0	24.2
	2005	1 546	14.7	1.1	12.6	4.5	65.3	13.7	35.6	15.9
	2010	1 516	15.7	1.0	15.6	7.8	57.8	20.8	21.0	15.9

For sources and notes, see end of table.

Pour les sources et les notes, se reporter à la fin du tableau.

Country or territory Pays ou territoires	Year Année	Total value (millions of dollars) Valeur totale (millions de dollars)	By main SITC Revision 3 product group (percentage) Par principaux groupes de produits de la CTCI Révision 3 (en pourcentage)					Of which: / dont :		
			All food items Produits alimentaires	Agricultural raw materials Matières premières agricoles	Fuels Combustibles	Ores, metals, precious stones and non monetary gold Minerais, métaux, pierres précieuses et or (non monétaire)	Manufactured goods Articles manufacturés	Chemical products Produits chimiques	Machinery and transport equipment Machines et matériel de transport	Other manufactured goods Articles manufacturés divers
			0 + 1 + 22 + 4	2 - (22 + 27 + 28)	3	27 + 28 + 68 + 667 + 971	5 + 6 + 7 + 8 -(667 + 68)	5	7	6 + 8 - (667 + 68)
Czech Republic - République tchèque	1995	21 686	6.1	3.9	4.7	3.0	80.8	9.4	28.0	43.4
	2005	78 209	4.1	1.5	3.2	1.7	87.0	6.3	50.3	30.4
	2010	132 141	4.0	1.4	4.0	2.2	84.6	6.1	52.7	25.8
Dem. Rep. of the Congo - Rép. dém. du Congo	1995	1 649	6.7	6.3	10.3	75.4	2.8	0.3	1.0	1.5
	2005	2 403	2.7	6.6	16.4	70.6	2.7	0.3	0.9	1.6
	2010	(e)5 400	0.9	2.4	12.9	77.4	4.7	3.9	0.5	0.3
Denmark - Danemark	1995	48 789	24.0	2.9	2.6	1.2	59.8	9.7	25.1	25.0
	2005	82 415	17.6	2.5	9.4	1.3	65.3	13.2	28.1	24.1
	2010	96 812	18.4	2.9	8.3	1.7	60.3	11.3	24.9	24.0
Djibouti (1)	1995	(e)14	18.7	5.0	10.2	11.6	53.2	7.9	19.0	26.3
	2005	(e)40	21.7	3.6	2.6	12.8	57.7	10.6	34.3	12.7
	2010	(e)70	48.3	2.1	3.8	20.1	18.8	2.8	7.3	8.7
Dominica - Dominique (1)	1995	45	50.3	0.3	0.0	1.3	48.1	42.7	2.7	2.7
	2005	42	33.8	0.1	0.0	6.5	59.6	53.7	4.2	1.7
	2010	34	22.6	0.0	0.1	5.5	71.7	48.4	7.6	15.7
Dominican Republic - République dominicaine	1995	(e)3 780	15.8	0.4	0.0	2.2	79.4	0.9	6.1	72.4
	2005	(e)6 283	14.1	0.4	0.0	2.7	80.3	2.8	14.2	63.3
	2010	(e)6 598	25.0	0.8	2.1	5.3	64.2	5.5	0.3	10.1
Ecuador - Équateur	1995	4 361	51.8	3.0	35.1	2.5	7.6	1.2	2.0	4.4
	2005	9 869	28.2	4.4	59.5	0.6	7.3	1.2	2.2	3.9
	2010	17 490	29.9	4.2	55.3	1.0	9.6	1.6	3.2	4.8
Egypt - Égypte	1995	3 444	9.9	6.1	37.3	6.4	40.3	5.8	0.6	33.8
	2005	10 646	8.8	2.3	51.3	2.9	23.6	5.0	1.2	17.4
	2010	26 332	16.5	2.9	28.7	9.9	41.7	13.4	4.3	24.0
El Salvador	1995	(e)1 651	44.2	1.1	0.2	1.9	52.3	9.0	3.9	39.4
	2005	3 418	18.9	0.4	1.5	1.5	76.7	7.1	5.2	64.4
	2010	4 499	21.4	0.7	2.2	3.5	71.2	6.4	6.2	58.7
Equatorial Guinea - Guinée équatoriale	1995	86	7.5	52.1	33.0	0.0	6.9	0.0	0.5	6.3
	2005	7 064	0.0	1.4	94.0	0.0	4.2	3.7	0.1	0.4
	2010	(e)9 964	0.0	1.4	94.8	0.8	2.7	2.4	0.2	0.1
Eritrea - Érythrée (1)	1995	(e)86	59.1	8.5	..	0.0	30.9	1.4	15.3	14.2
	2005	(e)11	28.4	16.2	0.0	2.5	49.6	3.7	9.6	36.4
	2010	(e)12	30.8	10.7	0.1	3.0	52.0	4.4	10.0	37.6
Estonia - Estonie	1995	1 840	13.9	9.9	10.8	5.2	59.9	8.1	17.8	34.1
	2005	8 247	7.1	6.3	14.0	2.7	65.7	5.0	32.2	28.5
	2010	12 823	9.4	6.2	11.6	4.1	63.8	5.8	30.7	27.3
Ethiopia - Éthiopie	1995	422	72.5	13.4	2.9	0.1	11.2	0.3	0.0	10.8
	2005	926	73.5	15.3	..	5.8	5.1	0.0	0.0	5.0
	2010	2 580	73.1	8.2	0.0	8.9	9.8	0.3	4.0	5.6
Faeroe Islands - Îles Féroé	1995	(e)362	91.1	2.2	..	..	6.7	0.1	4.8	1.8
	2005	602	91.6	1.5	..	0.0	6.9	0.1	5.4	1.4
	2010	(e)817	88.6	3.0	1.9	0.3	5.2	0.2	4.1	0.9
Falkland Islands (Malvinas) - (1) Îles Falkland (Malvinas)	1995	(e)27	68.0	16.3	..	..	16.1	1.0	12.6	2.4
	2005	(e)154	95.0	2.4	..	0.5	0.8	0.1	0.5	0.3
	2010	(e)162	72.5	16.7	0.6	0.0	3.8	1.0	2.2	0.6
Fiji - Fidji	1995	(e)544	50.8	6.6	0.4	8.1	33.7	0.3	1.0	32.5
	2005	(e)702	55.1	4.9	6.8	6.7	23.7	1.8	2.0	19.9
	2010	(e)613	54.0	6.2	4.7	8.3	23.1	3.7	3.4	16.0
Finland - Finlande	1995	40 409	2.4	8.4	1.9	3.1	83.3	6.0	35.4	42.0
	2005	65 238	1.9	5.2	4.4	3.6	84.3	7.6	44.1	32.6
	2010	69 405	2.6	5.9	8.0	5.6	76.3	11.1	32.4	32.8

For sources and notes, see end of table.

Pour les sources et les notes, se reporter à la fin du tableau.

Country or territory / Pays ou territoires	Year / Année	Total value (millions of dollars) / Valeur totale (millions de dollars)	By main SITC Revision 3 product group (percentage) / Par principaux groupes de produits de la CTCI Révision 3 (en pourcentage)					Of which: / dont :		
			All food items / Produits alimentaires	Agricultural raw materials / Matières premières agricoles	Fuels / Combustibles	Ores, metals, precious stones and non monetary gold / Minerais, métaux, pierres précieuses et or (non monétaire)	Manufactured goods / Articles manufacturés	Chemical products / Produits chimiques	Machinery and transport equipment / Machines et matériel de transport	Other manufactured goods / Articles manufacturés divers
			0 + 1 + 22 + 4	2 - (22 + 27 + 28)	3	27 + 28 + 68 + 667 + 971	5 + 6 +7 + 8 -(667 + 68)	5	7	6 + 8 - (667 + 68)
France	1995	277 845	14.3	1.5	2.4	2.7	76.6	12.9	39.4	24.3
	2005	434 354	10.7	0.9	4.1	2.3	80.1	15.9	41.6	22.5
	2010	511 651	12.0	1.0	3.7	2.8	78.2	17.8	39.0	21.3
French Polynesia - Polynésie française	1995	(e)196	2.7	1.0	0.0	61.8	28.6	0.8	20.8	7.1
	2005	210	15.2	1.1	0.0	55.3	26.9	2.8	17.1	7.0
	2010	(e)173	14.6	1.3	0.1	67.1	15.5	1.2	7.8	6.4
Gabon	1995	(e)2 718	0.2	13.1	82.7	2.0	1.9	0.4	0.4	1.1
	2005	5 069	0.9	10.6	78.9	5.6	3.9	0.0	0.9	2.9
	2010	(e)8 374	0.6	10.8	76.5	8.4	3.7	0.2	1.1	2.4
Gambia - Gambie	1995	(e)16	28.4	0.8	0.5	61.5	8.5	2.1	1.7	4.8
	2005	(e)8	66.1	2.1	0.9	3.4	26.7	1.3	18.3	7.0
	2010	(e)15	62.5	4.6	0.1	15.5	17.4	1.2	6.6	9.6
Georgia - Géorgie	1995	(e)158	29.3	3.3	18.8	8.0	40.6	11.1	5.7	23.8
	2005	865	34.9	2.1	3.2	21.1	38.5	6.8	16.9	14.8
	2010	1 583	19.5	0.9	4.4	21.7	53.4	8.0	21.1	24.3
Germany - Allemagne	1995	523 697	5.1	1.1	1.0	2.8	83.4	13.2	46.1	24.2
	2005	977 132	4.5	0.8	2.2	2.7	86.0	13.9	50.2	21.8
	2010	1 271 096	5.2	0.8	1.9	3.7	81.8	14.7	46.0	21.1
Ghana	1995	(e)1 754	41.9	13.2	4.3	34.8	7.1	0.6	0.8	5.7
	2005	(e)3 060	54.4	8.4	8.4	14.0	13.2	0.7	2.3	10.2
	2010	(e)7 960	60.5	7.4	4.1	18.3	9.5	1.4	1.8	6.3
Gibraltar (1)	1995	117	15.0	0.4	0.8	17.0	64.7	3.9	22.2	38.5
	2005	200	0.4	0.4	12.3	5.4	77.9	1.1	62.4	14.4
	2010	(e)264	0.0	0.1	82.8	1.7	13.9	0.2	12.0	1.8
Greece - Grèce	1995	10 955	29.5	4.4	6.5	7.9	49.2	4.9	8.0	36.3
	2005	17 434	22.0	2.4	9.4	8.3	55.3	14.6	12.7	28.0
	2010	21 560	24.3	3.1	11.0	9.5	49.3	14.5	12.0	22.8
Greenland - Groenland	1995	364	94.6	0.3	..	0.0	3.5	0.0	2.5	0.9
	2005	402	89.8	0.5	0.0	5.1	1.7	0.0	0.5	1.2
	2010	(e)382	88.2	0.5	0.0	7.4	3.9	0.0	2.7	1.1
Grenada - Grenade	1995	22	70.2	0.2	1.5	0.4	26.7	2.3	8.0	16.4
	2005	28	64.1	0.2	0.1	0.2	33.9	3.7	16.9	13.4
	2010	(e)24	49.4	0.4	0.1	1.2	48.8	3.9	27.1	17.9
Guam (1)	1995	85	..	..	..	..	..	..	..	..
	2005	(e)52	12.9	2.1	8.1	9.4	19.9	3.5	9.2	7.2
	2010	(e)46	7.9	0.3	0.6	1.8	35.9	0.6	15.8	19.5
Guatemala	1995	1 936	57.3	3.7	1.7	0.4	36.1	8.8	1.8	25.5
	2005	5 381	36.4	3.5	5.7	0.9	53.2	9.2	2.0	42.0
	2010	8 460	45.1	4.4	4.6	4.9	40.6	10.7	2.7	27.2
Guinea - Guinée	1995	(e)702	11.8	2.8	1.0	78.0	6.4	5.4	0.9	0.1
	2005	(e)796	8.4	1.9	6.3	81.6	1.6	0.1	0.5	1.1
	2010	(e)1 568	5.6	2.8	21.2	47.1	23.1	0.6	21.8	0.8
Guinea-Bissau - Guinée-Bissau	1995	(e)24	84.6	5.5	7.5	..	2.5	0.5	0.7	1.4
	2005	(e)89	96.3	1.3	0.3	0.8	1.2	0.0	0.2	0.9
	2010	(e)120	90.3	1.4	6.2	0.9	1.3	0.1	0.5	0.7
Guyana	1995	(e)455	44.9	2.2	0.0	42.1	10.8	0.7	1.1	9.0
	2005	539	45.3	6.6	0.0	38.0	9.1	1.6	1.9	5.6
	2010	937	37.3	6.6	0.1	50.6	5.3	1.0	1.2	3.2
Haiti - Haïti	1995	(e)110	25.4	0.8	0.3	0.3	69.4	7.2	2.8	59.4
	2005	(e)473	6.3	0.6	0.0	0.7	83.6	1.2	2.5	79.9
	2010	(e)583	7.3	1.2	0.0	1.9	76.5	1.8	3.2	71.5

For sources and notes, see end of table.

Pour les sources et les notes, se reporter à la fin du tableau.

Country or territory / Pays ou territoires	Year / Année	Total value (millions of dollars) / Valeur totale (millions de dollars)	By main SITC Revision 3 product group (percentage) / Par principaux groupes de produits de la CTCI Révision 3 (en pourcentage)					Of which: / dont :		
			All food items / Produits alimentaires	Agricultural raw materials / Matières premières agricoles	Fuels / Combustibles	Ores, metals, precious stones and non monetary gold / Minerais, métaux, pierres précieuses et or (non monétaire)	Manufactured goods / Articles manufacturés	Chemical products / Produits chimiques	Machinery and transport equipment / Machines et matériel de transport	Other manufactured goods / Articles manufacturés divers
			0 + 1 + 22 + 4	2 - (22 + 27 + 28)	3	27 + 28 + 68 + 667 + 971	5 + 6 +7 + 8 -(667 + 68)	5	7	6 + 8 - (667 + 68)
Honduras	1995	(e)1 769	52.5	2.3	0.1	0.9	43.7	3.0	1.5	39.2
	2005	(e)5 048	32.5	2.2	0.3	4.0	59.7	2.6	6.7	50.5
	2010	(e)5 742	35.3	1.8	2.4	7.2	53.3	2.9	8.7	41.7
Hungary - Hongrie	1995	12 452	19.3	2.3	3.0	5.0	69.9	11.6	28.8	29.5
	2005	62 272	6.6	0.7	2.8	1.9	85.0	7.8	60.0	17.1
	2010	94 693	7.6	0.7	2.8	1.8	82.3	8.8	57.3	16.1
Iceland - Islande	1995	1 803	75.5	0.5	0.0	12.0	11.6	0.7	5.1	5.8
	2005	3 091	58.5	0.8	1.4	19.0	19.3	3.5	9.3	6.5
	2010	4 600	41.4	0.5	1.0	42.0	14.6	3.2	4.9	6.6
India - Inde	1995	31 699	18.7	1.3	1.7	18.6	58.2	8.1	7.5	42.5
	2005	100 353	9.0	1.3	10.5	19.8	58.4	11.4	10.5	36.4
	2010	(e)237 307	9.9	2.4	15.7	17.4	54.6	11.0	13.6	29.9
Indonesia - Indonésie	2005	85 660	11.7	5.1	27.7	8.7	46.9	5.2	15.9	25.8
	2010	157 779	16.2	6.5	29.6	10.6	37.0	5.2	12.4	19.4
Indonesia including East Timor - Indonésie, y compris le Timor oriental	1995	45 443	11.4	6.7	25.3	6.1	50.5	3.4	8.4	38.7
Iran (Islamic Rep. of) - Iran (Rép. islamique d')	1995	(e)18 360	5.8	1.8	77.3	1.6	13.1	2.3	0.7	10.0
	2005	(e)60 012	2.7	0.4	85.2	2.2	8.1	2.8	1.3	4.1
	2010	(e)100 900	2.5	0.3	81.6	3.7	9.5	5.5	1.1	2.9
Iraq (1)	1995	(e)496	0.1	0.2	95.3	0.0	4.1	0.4	3.4	0.3
	2005	(e)23 697	0.4	0.2	97.1	0.2	0.8	0.7	0.0	0.0
	2010	(e)49 324	0.2	0.1	98.5	0.6	0.6	0.4	0.2	0.0
Ireland - Irlande	1995	43 789	19.4	1.1	0.4	1.2	71.0	18.4	34.5	18.0
	2005	110 003	8.4	0.4	0.7	0.9	85.7	45.6	26.5	13.6
	2010	118 539	9.2	0.5	1.1	1.2	84.2	58.5	12.3	13.4
Israel - Israël	1995	19 047	5.4	1.8	0.0	31.6	58.9	14.7	26.8	17.3
	2005	42 771	2.5	0.7	0.1	38.6	45.2	14.8	18.2	12.2
	2010	58 413	3.1	0.8	0.9	29.8	65.4	26.9	25.1	13.4
Italy - Italie	1995	230 441	6.6	0.7	1.2	1.5	89.2	8.0	37.7	43.6
	2005	372 957	6.5	0.6	3.4	1.7	85.0	10.6	36.8	37.6
	2010	447 455	7.8	0.7	4.9	3.1	81.5	11.5	35.5	34.5
Jamaica - Jamaïque	1995	1 424	21.7	0.3	0.5	49.4	28.1	2.7	3.1	22.4
	2005	1 514	17.2	0.1	7.4	68.5	6.8	3.7	1.1	2.0
	2010	1 328	23.6	0.2	21.2	42.6	11.8	6.3	2.6	2.9
Japan - Japon	1995	442 937	0.5	0.6	0.6	1.2	95.1	6.8	70.3	18.0
	2005	594 941	0.5	0.5	0.7	2.1	91.8	8.8	64.1	18.9
	2010	769 839	0.6	0.7	1.7	3.5	88.3	10.2	59.5	18.6
Jordan - Jordanie	1995	1 769	25.0	1.5	0.2	18.5	54.1	32.6	9.5	12.0
	2005	4 279	13.8	0.3	0.6	10.9	73.5	24.1	11.8	37.7
	2010	7 023	14.8	0.4	1.1	10.1	73.1	34.8	10.5	27.8
Kazakhstan	1995	5 227	9.9	2.8	25.0	24.1	38.1	10.3	6.0	21.9
	2005	27 846	2.4	0.7	70.1	14.7	12.0	1.9	1.2	8.9
	2010	57 244	3.4	0.2	71.7	13.1	11.7	4.4	0.6	6.7
Kenya	1995	1 826	54.7	8.3	5.0	2.7	28.9	6.6	3.2	19.1
	2005	3 420	38.0	12.5	15.5	2.8	31.0	7.0	3.1	20.9
	2010	(e)5 151	41.8	13.2	4.5	4.4	36.0	8.9	5.7	21.5
Kiribati (1)	1995	(e)7	84.3	1.9	..	0.6	5.9	0.1	0.4	5.4
	2005	(e)4	46.9	0.4	0.0	0.9	50.1	2.2	5.5	42.4
	2010	(e)15	80.2	1.7	0.0	0.4	13.4	1.5	9.9	2.0
Korea, Dem. People's Rep. of - (1) Corée, Rép. populaire dém. de	1995	959	15.5	2.7	2.0	9.5	69.3	5.4	27.6	36.2
	2005	1 338	10.9	2.2	9.8	13.2	62.1	7.7	29.6	24.9
	2010	(e)3 000	4.6	1.4	23.9	20.6	49.4	5.4	15.1	29.0

For sources and notes, see end of table.

Pour les sources et les notes, se reporter à la fin du tableau.

3.1 Country trade structure by product group
Exports

3.1 Structure du commerce des pays par groupes de produits
Exportations

Country or territory / Pays ou territoires	Year / Année	Total value (millions of dollars) / Valeur totale (millions de dollars)	By main SITC Revision 3 product group (percentage) / Par principaux groupes de produits de la CTCI Révision 3 (en pourcentage)					Of which: / dont :		
			All food items / Produits alimentaires	Agricultural raw materials / Matières premières agricoles	Fuels / Combustibles	Ores, metals, precious stones and non monetary gold / Minerais, métaux, pierres précieuses et or (non monétaire)	Manufactured goods / Articles manufacturés	Chemical products / Produits chimiques	Machinery and transport equipment / Machines et matériel de transport	Other manufactured goods / Articles manufacturés divers
			0 + 1 + 22 + 4	2 - (22 + 27 + 28)	3	27 + 28 + 68 + 667 + 971	5 + 6 + 7 + 8 -(667 + 68)	5	7	6 + 8 - (667 + 68)
Korea, Republic of - Corée, République de	1995	125 056	2.3	1.3	2.0	3.0	91.5	7.2	52.5	31.8
	2005	284 410	1.1	0.0	5.5	1.0	90.0	9.0	61.0	20.1
	2010	(e)468 856	1.1	0.9	7.3	3.2	87.5	11.3	53.9	22.3
Kuwait - Koweït	1995	12 944	0.5	0.1	89.8	1.1	8.2	3.2	2.6	2.5
	2005	(e)44 909	0.3	0.1	90.6	0.9	8.1	6.4	0.6	1.2
	2010	(e)66 314	0.2	0.2	91.0	0.8	7.7	5.5	1.4	0.9
Kyrgyzstan - Kirghizistan	1995	(e)412	21.4	14.9	13.2	13.6	36.2	7.0	9.7	19.5
	2005	(e)672	12.4	9.3	10.1	34.1	32.5	1.1	8.9	22.5
	2010	(e)1 760	22.0	3.8	12.2	19.4	40.6	7.3	12.4	20.9
Lao People's Dem. Rep. - (1) Rép. dém. populaire lao	1995	311	11.1	42.3	0.3	5.3	40.7	1.6	0.3	38.8
	2005	553	6.6	28.1	11.0	16.8	35.5	0.3	1.5	33.7
	2010	1 746	7.4	10.8	16.9	45.5	19.3	1.4	2.5	15.5
Latvia - Lettonie	1995	1 305	14.4	23.0	1.7	1.0	58.1	6.9	16.3	34.9
	2005	5 303	11.3	17.1	8.9	3.5	55.4	6.0	12.4	37.0
	2010	8 851	16.8	13.2	5.3	3.8	57.6	8.3	18.4	30.9
Lebanon - Liban	1995	(e)656	19.5	1.5	0.1	10.6	68.3	12.5	14.4	41.4
	2005	(e)2 337	16.8	2.3	0.6	16.2	63.0	10.7	14.5	37.7
	2010	(e)5 021	18.9	0.9	0.1	19.7	60.0	10.7	17.8	31.5
Lesotho	1995	(e)160	10.8	4.6	0.0	0.1	84.4	1.0	14.8	68.5
	2005	(e)651	2.7	0.5	0.0	6.8	89.9	0.1	1.4	88.4
	2010	(e)801	0.2	0.0	0.0	32.6	63.4	0.0	0.1	63.2
Liberia - Libéria (1)	1995	(e)820	0.1	1.9	2.1	81.2	14.7	0.4	13.9	0.3
	2005	131	0.4	11.0	0.9	2.7	84.9	0.1	84.4	0.3
	2010	(e)200	2.1	44.8	18.5	18.4	11.3	0.4	9.7	1.2
Libyan Arab Jamahiriya - Jamahiriya arabe libyenne	1995	(e)9 364	0.2	0.2	92.0	0.0	7.4	4.1	0.1	3.2
	2005	(e)30 948	0.1	0.0	95.4	0.6	3.9	2.7	0.1	1.1
	2010	(e)46 310	0.3	0.0	95.8	1.0	2.9	1.8	0.1	1.0
Lithuania - Lituanie	1995	2 706	18.1	7.8	11.4	5.0	57.7	14.3	15.7	27.7
	2005	12 070	12.4	3.3	26.6	1.5	55.5	8.4	21.5	25.5
	2010	20 814	17.3	2.3	23.4	1.4	54.0	12.9	17.7	23.4
Luxembourg	1995	(e)7 244	4.8	0.9	0.8	5.5	57.9	6.2	15.9	35.8
	2005	(e)18 790	6.0	0.6	0.9	5.5	84.4	8.6	29.0	46.8
	2010	(e)19 592	7.5	1.9	2.1	5.8	79.9	8.6	21.8	49.5
Madagascar	1995	(e)507	63.7	4.8	2.6	5.5	22.3	1.7	0.6	20.0
	2005	836	32.2	4.9	2.7	4.8	51.5	1.4	2.7	47.4
	2010	1 082	29.0	5.1	4.4	14.1	45.2	2.7	5.6	36.9
Malawi	1995	433	86.2	2.3	0.1	0.1	11.1	0.3	1.7	9.1
	2005	495	79.8	4.0	0.1	0.3	15.3	0.6	2.4	12.3
	2010	1 066	76.9	4.2	0.2	5.6	13.0	4.7	2.8	5.6
Malaysia - Malaisie	1995	73 778	9.5	6.2	7.0	1.5	74.5	3.0	55.1	16.4
	2005	141 624	6.9	2.5	13.4	1.3	74.5	5.8	54.0	14.7
	2010	198 791	11.9	2.6	15.8	2.2	67.0	6.4	43.9	16.7
Maldives	1995	(e)85	68.7	0.6	..	0.2	30.0	0.3	0.5	29.2
	2005	154	77.7	0.1	6.7	0.9	14.5	1.9	3.8	8.8
	2010	(e)200	91.0	0.2	0.0	2.3	6.5	1.5	3.1	1.9
Mali	1995	(e)443	18.2	58.1	1.0	17.1	5.3	0.3	1.1	3.9
	2005	1 075	5.5	48.3	0.6	37.3	8.0	0.7	4.2	3.1
	2010	1 996	6.1	15.8	0.6	63.3	14.0	9.3	2.2	2.5
Malta - Malte	1995	1 913	2.1	0.1	1.5	0.6	95.6	2.2	66.3	27.1
	2005	2 431	6.2	0.1	1.1	0.3	91.5	4.9	61.1	25.5
	2010	(e)2 573	6.7	0.3	0.6	1.3	91.0	14.6	47.4	29.0

For sources and notes, see end of table.

Pour les sources et les notes, se reporter à la fin du tableau.

Country or territory / Pays ou territoires	Year / Année	Total value (millions of dollars) / Valeur totale (millions de dollars)	By main SITC Revision 3 product group (percentage) / Par principaux groupes de produits de la CTCI Révision 3 (en pourcentage)					Of which: / dont :		
			All food items / Produits alimentaires	Agricultural raw materials / Matières premières agricoles	Fuels / Combustibles	Ores, metals, precious stones and non monetary gold / Minerais, métaux, pierres précieuses et or (non monétaire)	Manufactured goods / Articles manufacturés	Chemical products / Produits chimiques	Machinery and transport equipment / Machines et matériel de transport	Other manufactured goods / Articles manufacturés divers
			0 + 1 + 22 + 4	2 - (22 + 27 + 28)	3	27 + 28 + 68 + 667 + 971	5 + 6 + 7 + 8 - (667 + 68)	5	7	6 + 8 - (667 + 68)
Marshall Islands - Îles Marshall (1)	1995	23	58.6	0.5	..	0.4	17.3	0.0	15.6	1.6
	2005	25	10.9	0.0	0.0	0.0	88.1	0.0	88.0	0.1
	2010	(e)20	25.3	0.0	4.3	0.4	69.7	0.0	68.9	0.8
Mauritania - Mauritanie	1995	(e)509	59.4	0.5	0.3	38.3	1.3	0.0	0.7	0.5
	2005	(e)556	44.4	0.2	0.0	49.6	1.4	0.1	0.8	0.6
	2010	(e)2 044	22.1	0.1	5.9	65.4	0.4	0.0	0.2	0.2
Mauritius - Maurice	1995	1 538	28.9	0.7	0.0	2.0	68.4	0.8	2.3	65.3
	2005	2 144	26.9	0.3	0.1	2.8	63.0	1.4	15.1	46.6
	2010	(e)2 239	30.6	0.8	0.3	3.5	47.4	3.0	2.4	42.0
Mayotte	2005	6	19.4	0.1	0.2	0.1	80.2	15.1	50.4	14.8
	2010	(e)7	7.1	0.0	0.3	0.1	74.2	13.4	49.2	11.7
Mexico - Mexique	1995	79 541	7.7	1.3	10.3	3.1	77.5	5.0	52.3	20.2
	2005	214 207	5.4	0.5	14.9	2.0	77.0	3.7	53.2	20.1
	2010	298 305	5.9	0.4	13.8	4.9	74.5	4.0	55.6	15.0
Micronesia (Federated States of) - (1) Micronésie (États fédérés de)	1995	39	86.3	0.3	..	0.0	8.8	..	0.0	8.8
	2005	13	94.3	0.9	..	1.5	2.9	0.0	0.3	2.6
	2010	(e)27	96.9	0.2	..	0.2	2.2	0.0	0.6	1.5
Mongolia - Mongolie	1995	(e)473	2.2	27.7	0.0	59.9	10.2	0.6	1.7	7.8
	2005	1 064	1.4	8.2	3.9	70.1	16.3	0.1	0.8	15.4
	2010	(e)2 895	1.9	6.9	9.9	77.6	3.7	0.1	0.8	2.8
Montenegro - Monténégro	2010	437	14.0	6.3	10.1	46.8	22.8	3.9	8.2	10.7
Montserrat (1)	1995	(e)3	74.1	0.0	..	0.2	22.6	1.3	17.8	3.5
	2005	(e)1	0.3	0.4	8.1	6.5	79.0	5.9	54.3	18.8
	2010	(e)1	0.3	0.7	..	26.8	63.6	0.1	29.3	34.2
Morocco - Maroc	1995	(e)6 881	27.1	2.9	1.8	9.6	58.4	16.5	7.0	34.9
	2005	11 185	20.8	1.7	5.9	8.1	62.7	11.2	17.9	33.7
	2010	17 765	20.3	1.6	3.9	12.0	61.8	17.7	17.6	26.5
Mozambique	1995	174	64.1	14.2	2.2	5.7	13.2	1.1	3.9	8.1
	2005	1 745	11.6	3.4	14.8	66.9	3.2	0.4	1.7	1.2
	2010	2 243	16.4	4.7	16.7	57.9	2.9	0.3	0.8	1.8
Myanmar	1995	(e)860	41.9	38.5	0.2	7.4	11.9	1.0	0.9	10.0
	2005	(e)4 121	20.8	19.1	33.1	4.2	22.8	0.2	0.7	21.9
	2010	(e)9 455	20.2	19.5	32.7	5.4	22.2	0.3	0.6	21.3
Namibia - Namibie	1995	(e)1 416	38.5	1.4	2.1	33.0	25.0	2.0	7.0	16.0
	2005	(e)2 070	30.5	0.6	1.3	42.1	25.2	10.9	4.5	9.8
	2010	(e)4 111	26.8	0.7	0.9	44.2	27.4	8.6	7.9	10.8
Nauru (1)	1995	28	1.0	0.5	..	70.0	28.0	0.7	25.3	2.0
	2005	4	7.5	1.0	0.6	25.2	62.8	7.4	38.8	16.6
	2010	(e)35	1.4	1.0	10.1	50.7	36.5	0.1	6.3	30.1
Nepal - Népal	1995	(e)359	7.8	1.1	..	0.1	83.7	1.2	0.1	82.4
	2005	(e)888	23.5	1.1	0.0	7.4	68.0	7.8	0.5	59.7
	2010	834	19.1	3.9	0.0	4.7	72.3	4.6	2.4	65.3
Netherlands - Pays-Bas	1995	(e)203 187	20.5	4.1	8.1	3.2	61.4	17.4	24.3	19.7
	2005	(e)406 208	13.1	3.0	12.1	2.7	60.0	15.7	28.2	16.1
	2010	(e)572 808	16.8	3.4	14.3	3.7	61.9	17.6	27.7	16.6
Netherlands Antilles - Antilles néerlandaises	1995	(e)1 522	12.1	0.1	65.9	3.0	14.2	2.0	6.5	5.6
	2005	(e)608	1.9	0.1	76.0	1.0	15.3	3.7	6.2	5.4
	2010	(e)811	3.0	0.5	75.1	4.1	15.1	3.4	7.8	3.8
New Caledonia - Nouvelle-Calédonie	1995	(e)471	2.7	0.3	..	42.1	54.5	0.1	0.7	53.7
	2005	(e)1 114	2.7	0.1	0.9	29.3	66.3	0.2	1.6	64.4
	2010	(e)1 268	2.0	0.3	3.4	37.1	56.7	0.6	1.8	54.3

For sources and notes, see end of table.

Pour les sources et les notes, se reporter à la fin du tableau.

Country or territory / Pays ou territoires	Year / Année	Total value (millions of dollars) / Valeur totale (millions de dollars)	By main SITC Revision 3 product group (percentage) Par principaux groupes de produits de la CTCI Révision 3 (en pourcentage)					Of which: / dont :		
			All food items / Produits alimentaires	Agricultural raw materials / Matières premières agricoles	Fuels / Combustibles	Ores, metals, precious stones and non monetary gold / Minerais, métaux, pierres précieuses et or (non monétaire)	Manufactured goods / Articles manufacturés	Chemical products / Produits chimiques	Machinery and transport equipment / Machines et matériel de transport	Other manufactured goods / Articles manufacturés divers
			0 + 1 + 22 + 4	2 - (22 + 27 + 28)	3	27 + 28 + 68 + 667 + 971	5 + 6 +7 + 8 -(667 + 68)	5	7	6 + 8 - (667 + 68)
New Zealand - Nouvelle-Zélande	1995	13 745	42.4	18.0	1.6	6.3	30.5	7.6	8.6	14.3
	2005	21 723	45.6	10.3	2.5	5.0	31.2	5.8	11.5	13.9
	2010	30 932	53.0	10.3	4.7	5.4	22.9	4.4	8.0	10.5
Nicaragua	1995	509	68.8	2.8	0.6	2.7	24.8	1.6	5.7	17.6
	2005	866	51.3	1.6	0.9	4.0	41.5	2.6	8.9	30.1
	2010	1 848	53.6	0.9	0.8	9.5	34.9	1.0	7.8	26.0
Niger	1995	273	15.9	4.6	4.6	20.9	53.8	40.7	5.9	7.3
	2005	(e)489	19.6	6.0	13.2	19.3	39.9	28.3	6.9	4.7
	2010	(e)1 040	39.8	1.4	3.3	28.8	26.6	18.5	4.5	3.6
Nigeria - Nigéria	1995	(e)12 342	2.8	2.4	92.4	0.3	2.1	0.4	0.2	1.5
	2005	(e)55 995	0.8	0.2	97.4	0.2	1.5	0.1	0.9	0.4
	2010	(e)70 579	2.5	0.8	91.3	1.0	4.1	0.5	0.7	2.9
Niue - Nioué (1)	1995	0	62.1	0.4	2.5	0.2	38.5	5.0	12.7	20.8
	2005	0	6.1	1.4	0.1	25.9	66.5	5.9	28.9	31.7
	2010	(e)0	0.7	0.0	0.0	0.0	99.2	23.9	71.8	3.5
Norway - Norvège	1995	41 740	8.3	1.5	47.3	8.8	26.8	3.1	13.3	10.4
	2005	103 759	5.2	0.5	67.7	6.0	17.1	2.7	8.2	6.2
	2010	131 395	7.2	0.5	63.9	6.4	18.5	3.5	9.4	5.7
Occupied Palestinian territory - (1) Territoire palestinien occupé	1995	394	..	..	..	..	..	..	..	..
	2005	(e)335	19.3	2.7	3.6	3.8	70.7	8.5	5.4	56.7
	2010	(e)563	26.6	0.7	2.9	10.6	59.0	6.8	10.2	42.0
Oman	1995	5 917	4.1	0.0	81.2	2.0	12.3	0.6	7.7	4.1
	2005	18 692	2.8	0.0	84.9	1.0	7.0	2.0	2.0	3.0
	2010	(e)36 601	4.8	0.0	56.9	12.2	25.7	16.2	4.7	4.8
Pakistan	1995	8 158	11.8	3.8	1.0	0.2	83.0	0.7	0.5	81.8
	2005	16 050	12.0	1.5	4.2	0.4	81.8	3.0	1.8	76.9
	2010	21 413	16.5	1.9	5.6	1.6	74.4	3.7	2.6	68.1
Palau - Palaos (1)	1995	13	75.2	1.8	0.0	0.1	22.5	0.1	3.9	18.6
	2005	14	92.5	1.2	..	0.9	3.8	0.0	2.1	1.7
	2010	12	93.9	0.1	..	0.2	4.4	0.0	2.4	2.0
Panama	1995	577	32.6	0.4	2.8	1.8	61.7	5.1	40.3	16.3
	2005	964	25.9	0.4	6.3	2.5	63.1	5.8	35.8	21.4
	2010	(e)832	11.9	2.1	7.3	3.6	74.0	20.3	22.3	31.4
Papua New Guinea - Papouasie-Nouvelle-Guinée	1995	(e)2 654	20.4	18.9	23.7	36.1	0.8	0.1	0.6	0.1
	2005	(e)3 490	19.5	10.3	26.7	39.2	2.6	0.1	1.3	1.1
	2010	(e)6 112	17.2	8.6	17.5	54.5	1.8	0.1	0.9	0.8
Paraguay	1995	919	43.9	36.4	0.2	0.3	19.3	2.6	0.8	15.9
	2005	1 655	76.0	9.0	0.0	1.3	13.8	2.6	0.9	10.2
	2010	4 534	85.5	3.0	0.0	0.8	10.7	2.6	0.7	7.4
Peru - Pérou	1995	5 440	28.8	2.5	4.9	50.2	13.6	2.2	0.6	10.8
	2005	17 114	17.0	1.5	9.3	57.9	14.3	2.4	0.8	11.0
	2010	35 073	15.8	1.1	9.5	62.7	10.9	2.9	0.9	7.1
Philippines	1995	17 447	12.8	1.2	1.5	5.4	40.8	2.0	22.2	16.7
	2005	41 255	6.1	0.5	1.9	2.4	89.0	1.3	74.4	13.3
	2010	51 498	7.3	0.7	2.1	4.8	85.1	3.0	70.1	12.0
Poland - Pologne	1995	22 862	10.4	2.8	8.2	7.3	71.1	7.7	21.1	42.4
	2005	89 378	9.4	1.2	5.1	4.0	78.1	6.7	38.6	32.9
	2010	(e)156 389	10.9	1.1	3.9	4.7	79.3	7.7	40.7	30.9
Portugal	1995	23 370	7.4	4.8	3.2	2.1	81.1	4.9	25.4	50.8
	2005	38 086	8.4	2.7	3.8	2.7	78.9	7.0	33.0	38.9
	2010	48 752	11.5	2.9	6.5	4.2	73.3	8.5	26.6	38.1

For sources and notes, see end of table.

Pour les sources et les notes, se reporter à la fin du tableau.

Country or territory / Pays ou territoires	Year / Année	Total value (millions of dollars) / Valeur totale (millions de dollars)	All food items / Produits alimentaires	Agricultural raw materials / Matières premières agricoles	Fuels / Combustibles	Ores, metals, precious stones and non monetary gold / Minerais, métaux, pierres précieuses et or (non monétaire)	Manufactured goods / Articles manufacturés	Of which: / dont : Chemical products / Produits chimiques	Of which: / dont : Machinery and transport equipment / Machines et matériel de transport	Of which: / dont : Other manufactured goods / Articles manufacturés divers
			0 + 1 + 22 + 4	2 - (22 + 27 + 28)	3	27 + 28 + 68 + 667 + 971	5 + 6 + 7 + 8 - (667 + 68)	5	7	6 + 8 - (667 + 68)
Qatar	1995	(e)3 557	0.3	0.1	81.4	0.8	17.1	9.2	1.3	6.6
	2005	(e)25 762	0.1	0.0	84.7	0.3	10.1	8.3	0.7	1.2
	2010	(e)73 795	0.1	0.0	89.8	0.6	9.2	6.9	0.8	1.5
Republic of Moldova République de Moldova	1995	746	67.0	1.5	0.6	3.0	27.8	1.6	7.7	18.5
	2005	1 091	46.5	2.6	0.1	2.1	48.5	1.7	5.2	41.6
	2010	1 582	42.4	0.7	1.4	2.9	52.4	6.9	10.9	34.7
Romania - Roumanie	1995	7 910	6.6	3.3	7.9	3.5	78.3	10.7	13.1	54.4
	2005	27 730	3.0	2.3	10.7	4.2	79.2	5.7	25.4	48.1
	2010	49 413	8.1	2.0	5.3	4.2	78.5	5.7	41.9	30.8
Russian Federation - Fédération de Russie	1995	(e)78 217	1.8	3.3	43.1	9.9	26.1	5.9	7.0	13.1
	2005	241 452	1.6	2.8	61.8	7.2	18.2	4.2	4.1	9.9
	2010	373 056	2.1	2.3	69.1	6.6	15.1	4.4	3.2	7.5
Rwanda	1995	(e)52	72.7	9.7	0.1	8.3	7.8	1.2	2.5	4.1
	2005	(e)125	45.4	1.1	1.6	38.9	9.8	2.0	5.0	2.9
	2010	(e)297	62.6	1.1	1.1	23.3	11.7	1.4	3.4	6.9
Saint Helena - Sainte-Hélène (1)	1995	(e)4	70.9	0.0	0.0	7.4	25.4	5.1	12.7	7.6
	2005	(e)20	40.0	0.7	0.0	0.1	56.9	6.4	28.8	21.7
	2010	(e)26	60.2	0.0	0.6	0.5	35.3	1.3	24.2	9.0
Saint Kitts and Nevis - Saint-Kitts-et-Nevis	1995	(e)19	38.4	0.2	0.0	0.0	59.4	0.3	52.9	6.1
	2005	(e)34	11.2	1.9	0.0	0.3	82.4	0.1	78.1	4.2
	2010	(e)45	5.4	0.1	0.0	0.5	81.6	0.4	77.3	3.9
Saint Lucia - Sainte-Lucie	1995	109	58.3	0.6	0.0	0.1	37.1	1.0	10.3	25.8
	2005	64	23.8	0.1	52.9	0.7	19.8	1.0	10.2	8.6
	2010	(e)165	31.6	0.1	29.0	2.3	37.0	3.4	14.8	18.8
Saint Pierre and Miquelon - (1) Saint-Pierre-et-Miquelon	1995	6	82.5	1.9	..	0.1	14.2	0.9	4.8	8.5
	2005	(e)11	51.5	5.7	2.8	0.4	39.5	0.6	1.4	37.4
	2010	(e)5	90.9	1.2	..	2.6	5.3	..	1.1	4.2
Saint Vincent and the Grenadines - Saint-Vincent-et-les Grenadines	1995	(e)43	67.0	0.2	0.0	0.2	32.2	0.7	21.4	10.1
	2005	40	20.4	0.2	0.0	0.1	79.2	4.7	70.8	3.6
	2010	42	30.3	0.0	0.3	1.1	68.1	0.7	58.5	8.9
Samoa	1995	(e)9	12.7	1.1	..	2.1	83.5	0.1	72.7	10.7
	2005	87	22.1	0.7	0.5	0.1	75.3	0.3	73.8	1.2
	2010	60	21.0	0.4	0.0	0.3	78.2	0.1	76.4	1.8
Sao Tome and Principe - Sao Tomé-et-Principe	1995	(e)5	58.6	2.2	..	0.1	38.1	5.0	18.4	14.8
	2005	(e)7	66.9	0.8	..	0.4	29.7	0.4	19.0	10.3
	2010	6	44.9	0.5	..	0.4	54.1	1.5	10.7	41.9
Saudi Arabia - Arabie saoudite	1995	(e)49 030	1.1	0.2	83.8	1.0	13.7	9.0	1.8	3.0
	2005	(e)180 737	0.6	0.1	88.3	0.5	10.4	7.7	1.1	1.6
	2010	(e)235 364	1.3	0.1	84.2	0.8	13.5	10.0	1.3	2.2
Senegal - Sénégal	1995	(e)993	39.8	6.7	13.1	11.1	29.0	22.2	1.8	4.9
	2005	(e)1 471	32.5	2.5	19.0	4.4	41.5	23.1	8.3	10.1
	2010	(e)2 161	29.0	1.4	20.6	10.2	32.6	14.5	3.6	14.5
Serbia - Serbie	2010	9 795	22.3	1.7	5.1	9.7	59.7	8.9	16.3	34.5
Serbia and Montenegro - Serbie-et-Monténégro	1995	(e)1 531	28.2	4.0	2.1	14.8	49.0	9.0	12.1	27.9
	2005	(e)5 058	17.5	2.6	3.2	8.2	56.8	9.8	8.8	38.3
Seychelles	1995	53	68.4	0.2	19.2	0.2	10.6	1.3	5.5	3.7
	2005	340	68.9	0.0	10.1	0.3	20.3	2.8	10.9	6.7
	2010	(e)400	83.1	0.2	3.0	1.6	12.1	0.6	4.2	7.2
Sierra Leone (1)	1995	(e)42	52.8	1.0	0.6	30.1	14.6	1.2	3.9	9.6
	2005	(e)159	10.8	0.8	0.7	58.3	29.0	4.0	13.2	11.7
	2010	(e)341	15.0	1.5	1.0	53.4	28.5	4.0	14.0	10.5

For sources and notes, see end of table.

Pour les sources et les notes, se reporter à la fin du tableau.

3.1 Country trade structure by product group
Exports

3.1 Structure du commerce des pays par groupes de produits
Exportations

Country or territory / Pays ou territoires	Year / Année	Total value (millions of dollars) / Valeur totale (millions de dollars)	All food items / Produits alimentaires	Agricultural raw materials / Matières premières agricoles	Fuels / Combustibles	Ores, metals, precious stones and non monetary gold / Minerais, métaux, pierres précieuses et or (non monétaire)	Manufactured goods / Articles manufacturés	Chemical products / Produits chimiques	Machinery and transport equipment / Machines et matériel de transport	Other manufactured goods / Articles manufacturés divers
			0 + 1 + 22 + 4	2 - (22 + 27 + 28)	3	27 + 28 + 68 + 667 + 971	5 + 6 +7 + 8 -(667 + 68)	5	7	6 + 8 - (667 + 68)
Singapore - Singapour	1995	118 263	3.9	1.1	6.8	2.3	83.6	6.0	65.6	12.0
	2005	229 652	1.7	0.3	12.2	2.1	79.9	11.4	58.7	9.8
	2010	351 867	2.0	0.3	16.1	2.5	72.1	11.3	51.1	9.8
Slovakia - Slovaquie	1995	8 374	5.7	3.6	4.1	3.7	82.2	12.3	20.3	49.6
	2005	31 852	4.2	1.6	7.1	2.6	82.4	5.4	44.4	32.6
	2010	64 687	4.0	1.3	5.4	3.0	84.6	4.7	54.0	25.9
Slovenia - Slovénie	1995	8 316	3.9	1.8	1.2	3.4	89.5	10.5	31.4	47.6
	2005	17 896	2.8	1.2	2.1	4.8	89.0	12.9	39.2	36.8
	2010	(e)29 418	3.4	1.4	3.5	4.0	69.8	13.3	32.0	24.5
Solomon Islands - Îles Salomon (1)	1995	(e)168	36.7	61.9	..	0.1	1.2	0.0	0.5	0.8
	2005	(e)103	23.7	73.9	0.1	0.4	1.8	0.3	0.8	0.7
	2010	(e)218	21.6	76.5	0.1	0.5	1.3	0.1	0.4	0.8
Somalia - Somalie (1)	1995	(e)170	90.1	6.8	0.0	0.2	2.6	0.5	0.8	1.3
	2005	(e)251	68.4	11.1	0.7	5.3	2.9	0.7	1.1	1.1
	2010	(e)450	43.8	20.6	0.8	33.2	1.5	0.2	0.4	0.9
South Africa - Afrique du Sud	1995	(e)29 784	15.0	3.0	8.8	21.2	52.0	9.0	20.1	22.9
	2005	(e)56 261	8.5	2.6	10.0	33.9	43.8	7.2	17.3	19.3
	2010	(e)85 700	8.2	2.3	10.6	36.8	39.2	6.8	16.4	16.0
Spain - Espagne	1995	89 616	15.4	1.6	1.7	2.6	77.9	8.5	42.4	27.1
	2005	192 798	14.1	1.2	4.3	2.5	76.3	12.0	40.2	24.2
	2010	(e)241 833	15.5	1.3	3.3	3.4	76.6	13.7	37.6	25.2
Sri Lanka	1995	(e)3 798	18.7	4.3	0.4	6.9	69.0	0.9	3.6	64.5
	2005	6 160	22.2	2.1	0.0	8.6	65.2	1.3	4.5	59.4
	2010	8 304	26.9	3.9	0.2	6.2	61.2	1.2	5.3	54.7
Sudan - Soudan	1995	(e)556	47.7	41.6	0.2	3.1	7.2	0.2	0.9	6.2
	2005	4 506	5.4	4.1	85.5	3.0	1.8	0.2	1.3	0.3
	2010	(e)10 500	3.3	1.4	88.7	5.5	1.1	0.1	0.7	0.3
Suriname	1995	483	18.6	0.7	1.9	73.9	3.8	0.4	1.1	2.2
	2005	997	12.7	0.4	2.6	64.3	5.7	1.0	3.3	1.3
	2010	2 026	6.6	1.5	8.3	51.8	1.8	0.3	0.9	0.6
Swaziland	1995	(e)844	40.0	12.0	1.1	1.5	45.4	15.0	8.6	21.8
	2005	(e)1 774	26.1	7.6	2.3	3.3	60.5	27.2	11.6	21.7
	2010	(e)1 552	29.9	7.7	1.1	3.0	58.3	29.9	12.0	16.4
Sweden - Suède	1995	77 436	2.2	6.5	1.9	3.2	78.6	6.6	42.1	29.9
	2005	130 264	3.5	4.0	5.0	3.3	78.4	10.6	41.8	26.1
	2010	158 079	4.7	4.1	7.0	5.3	73.2	11.4	36.8	25.0
Switzerland - Suisse	1995	81 641	3.0	0.7	0.1	5.3	90.9	26.0	31.4	33.5
	2005	130 930	2.6	0.4	2.1	4.3	90.6	34.7	25.5	30.4
	2010	195 392	3.7	0.3	2.8	5.6	87.6	38.2	20.9	28.5
Syrian Arab Republic - République arabe syrienne	1995	(e)3 563	12.8	9.0	63.4	1.0	13.7	0.6	1.1	12.0
	2005	(e)9 174	22.4	2.6	47.0	2.3	25.0	8.8	3.2	13.0
	2010	(e)13 064	26.5	1.9	36.6	3.6	31.3	6.2	6.2	18.8
Tajikistan - Tadjikistan	1995	(e)749	11.4	44.9	1.3	26.2	16.2	2.5	2.4	11.3
	2005	(e)874	2.8	7.7	7.9	67.1	11.4	0.7	2.2	8.5
	2010	(e)1 184	3.2	23.7	1.4	56.7	8.8	0.5	1.8	6.6
TFYR of Macedonia - LERY de Macédoine	1995	1 204	18.3	5.2	0.4	17.9	58.2	5.5	12.9	39.7
	2005	2 041	16.4	0.8	8.0	3.0	71.6	4.4	5.4	61.8
	2010	(e)3 292	14.7	0.8	2.2	6.5	75.8	4.0	5.8	66.0
Thailand - Thaïlande	1995	56 439	19.3	5.4	0.7	2.9	70.9	4.4	33.7	32.9
	2005	110 110	11.6	4.5	4.3	2.4	75.7	8.1	44.7	22.9
	2010	195 312	12.8	5.2	4.9	5.5	71.6	8.7	42.2	20.7
Timor-Leste (1)	2005	(e)8	5.9	0.6	86.0	0.3	6.9	0.1	3.4	3.4
	2010	(e)17	27.1	0.4	59.9	1.3	11.1	0.5	6.9	3.7

For sources and notes, see end of table.

Pour les sources et les notes, se reporter à la fin du tableau.

Country or territory / Pays ou territoires	Year / Année	Total value (millions of dollars) / Valeur totale (millions de dollars)	All food items / Produits alimentaires	Agricultural raw materials / Matières premières agricoles	Fuels / Combustibles	Ores, metals, precious stones and non monetary gold / Minerais, métaux, pierres précieuses et or (non monétaire)	Manufactured goods / Articles manufacturés	Of which: / dont :		
								Chemical products / Produits chimiques	Machinery and transport equipment / Machines et matériel de transport	Other manufactured goods / Articles manufacturés divers
			0 + 1 + 22 + 4	2 - (22 + 27 + 28)	3	27 + 28 + 68 + 667 + 971	5 + 6 +7 + 8 -(667 + 68)	5	7	6 + 8 - (667 + 68)
Togo	1995	393	16.0	00.1	0.5	3.1	11.4	0.9	3.7	8.8
	2005	(e)659	27.7	11.7	11.2	12.0	37.2	3.9	4.7	28.5
	2010	(e)893	24.9	9.1	11.8	15.1	39.0	3.5	4.3	31.2
Tokelau - Tokélaou (1)	1995	(e)1	11.9	0.1	..	0.9	84.6	0.1	57.3	27.2
	2005	(e)0	1.6	30.9	0.3	3.0	40.3	2.9	9.8	33.6
	2010	(e)0	22.7	2.2	..	3.3	67.8	4.5	23.5	39.8
Tonga	1995	(e)15	84.1	0.5	..	0.5	2.9	0.2	1.1	1.6
	2005	(e)10	54.0	14.2	0.0	2.0	7.7	1.1	3.0	3.6
	2010	(e)8	66.4	5.5	1.2	3.6	21.1	10.4	3.8	6.9
Trinidad and Tobago - Trinité-et-Tobago	1995	2 467	10.3	0.2	43.0	1.5	44.6	26.5	2.4	15.7
	2005	9 611	2.7	0.0	66.8	0.7	28.7	21.6	1.2	5.9
	2010	(e)10 188	2.7	0.0	63.9	2.9	30.6	21.6	1.5	7.5
Tunisia - Tunisie	1995	5 475	9.8	0.6	8.5	1.8	79.3	11.9	9.4	57.9
	2005	10 494	10.4	0.6	12.9	1.2	74.9	9.4	19.2	46.3
	2010	(e)16 422	9.8	0.6	15.2	2.0	72.4	11.1	22.3	39.0
Turkey - Turquie	1995	21 599	19.6	1.5	1.3	3.3	74.3	4.1	11.1	59.1
	2005	73 476	10.5	0.5	3.6	2.7	81.4	3.8	29.3	48.3
	2010	113 979	10.4	0.4	3.9	6.1	77.7	5.4	27.0	44.5
Turkmenistan - Turkménistan	1995	(e)1 939	1.1	20.3	70.3	1.3	6.8	0.5	0.4	5.9
	2005	(e)4 944	0.2	2.5	89.1	0.3	7.7	1.3	0.9	5.4
	2010	(e)6 000	0.3	10.5	73.3	1.0	13.6	3.1	1.7	8.9
Turks and Caicos Islands - Îles Turques et Caïques	1995	(e)5	72.9	0.2	17.6	0.1	7.2	3.7	0.8	2.8
	2005	(e)16	51.7	24.4	0.1	0.1	21.1	0.1	12.4	8.6
	2010	(e)21	21.4	0.7	0.4	2.9	49.6	2.0	34.0	13.6
Tuvalu	1995	(e)0	1.0	1.2	..	1.3	96.4	14.5	31.0	50.9
	2005	(e)0	1.2	0.2	0.1	0.9	97.4	1.7	39.6	56.1
	2010	(e)0	32.8	0.5	2.5	0.9	63.3	0.5	35.5	27.3
Uganda - Ouganda	1995	(e)461	88.7	4.3	0.0	4.5	2.4	0.5	0.8	1.1
	2005	(e)1 016	60.4	12.7	1.9	9.4	14.8	2.2	4.8	7.7
	2010	(e)2 164	58.5	5.6	0.9	5.8	28.8	3.1	10.8	14.8
Ukraine	1995	(e)13 317	19.0	1.0	4.3	8.2	66.4	12.8	14.1	39.4
	2005	34 228	12.4	1.5	9.8	7.2	68.4	9.1	13.1	46.3
	2010	51 430	19.2	1.1	7.1	8.2	63.7	6.7	17.3	39.7
United Arab Emirates - Émirats arabes unis	1995	(e)27 753	3.3	0.3	72.4	5.1	18.0	2.9	6.3	8.8
	2005	(e)115 453	2.9	0.2	61.9	10.2	24.3	3.1	13.1	8.1
	2010	(e)198 362	3.6	0.2	55.6	16.4	23.4	3.0	10.6	9.8
United Kingdom - Royaume-Uni	1995	234 372	7.6	0.7	6.2	4.8	80.0	12.4	43.8	23.8
	2005	384 365	5.2	0.6	9.5	5.3	74.6	14.9	39.6	20.1
	2010	404 737	6.3	0.7	12.7	5.9	68.3	17.9	31.6	18.7
United Republic of Tanzania - République-Unie de Tanzanie	1995	(e)685	65.2	23.1	0.3	3.9	7.1	0.7	1.3	5.0
	2005	1 672	38.8	10.3	4.0	36.4	10.3	1.5	2.3	6.5
	2010	4 051	32.0	7.3	3.1	39.7	17.5	3.9	4.2	9.3
United States - États-Unis	1995	582 965	10.1	3.7	1.8	3.8	77.5	10.6	48.3	18.7
	2005	904 339	6.8	2.3	2.9	4.3	80.4	13.3	48.0	19.1
	2010	1 277 109	8.8	2.4	6.3	6.2	67.4	14.8	35.2	17.4
Uruguay	1995	2 106	44.2	14.9	1.0	0.9	38.7	5.6	6.0	27.1
	2005	3 405	54.5	9.2	4.8	1.9	29.6	5.8	2.9	20.9
	2010	(e)6 668	55.5	13.3	1.6	1.8	27.8	7.5	3.6	16.7
Uzbekistan - Ouzbékistan	1995	3 430	1.3	62.3	15.0	14.1	7.2	3.0	0.8	3.4
	2005	4 749	12.3	25.5	15.5	16.3	28.7	8.7	11.4	8.7
	2010	11 857	10.8	14.0	22.3	13.4	36.1	13.5	11.2	11.4

For sources and notes, see end of table.

Pour les sources et les notes, se reporter à la fin du tableau.

3.1   Country trade structure
by product group
Exports

3.1   Structure du commerce des pays
par groupes de produits
Exportations

Country or territory Pays ou territoires	Year Année	Total value (millions of dollars) Valeur totale (millions de dollars)	By main SITC Revision 3 product group (percentage) Par principaux groupes de produits de la CTCI Révision 3 (en pourcentage)					Of which: / dont :		
			All food items Produits alimentaires	Agricultural raw materials Matières premières agricoles	Fuels Combustibles	Ores, metals, precious stones and non monetary gold Minerais, métaux, pierres précieuses et or (non monétaire)	Manufactured goods Articles manufacturés	Chemical products Produits chimiques	Machinery and transport equipment Machines et matériel de transport	Other manufactured goods Articles manufacturés divers
			0 + 1 + 22 + 4	2 - (22 + 27 + 28)	3	27 + 28 + 68 + 667 + 971	5 + 6 +7 + 8 -(667 + 68)	5	7	6 + 8 - (667 + 68)
Vanuatu	1995	(e)28	82.7	4.8	..	0.0	12.3	0.0	6.1	6.1
	2005	(e)38	64.5	11.3	0.5	0.0	23.0	0.3	22.2	0.4
	2010	(e)49	92.2	1.1	0.0	0.0	5.7	0.6	1.5	1.1
Venezuela (Bolivarian Rep. of) - Venezuela (Rép. bolivarienne du)	1995	19 093	3.1	0.2	72.4	8.1	16.0	5.0	3.1	7.9
	2005	55 413	0.9	0.1	83.5	4.2	11.1	3.1	1.5	6.6
	2010	(e)64 630	0.5	0.1	85.6	4.4	9.3	2.5	1.0	5.8
Viet Nam	1995	(e)5 449	30.2	3.1	18.0	0.8	43.7	1.1	7.0	35.6
	2005	32 447	20.2	3.1	25.8	0.7	49.8	1.6	9.6	38.5
	2010	(e)71 658	20.5	4.8	15.5	2.3	56.9	2.1	12.0	42.8
Wallis and Futuna Islands - Îles Wallis-et-Futuna	1995	(e)1	16.4	..	..	..	83.6	7.9	49.0	26.7
	2005	(e)0	5.2	11.3	0.0	0.8	81.6	8.4	32.6	40.6
	2010	(e)0	0.9	0.5	..	0.0	92.2	11.5	28.3	52.5
Yemen - Yémen	1995	(e)1 917	3.2	0.5	93.5	0.6	2.0	0.4	0.8	0.7
	2005	(e)5 608	5.5	0.3	91.0	1.4	1.7	0.4	1.0	0.4
	2010	(e)8 497	7.0	0.2	87.0	2.6	2.4	0.6	1.2	0.6
Zambia - Zambie	1995	1 055	3.6	0.8	2.3	87.4	5.8	0.3	1.5	4.0
	2005	1 810	12.3	6.4	0.6	68.8	10.9	0.7	1.6	8.6
	2010	7 200	7.0	1.3	0.7	78.9	11.2	2.1	2.5	6.6
Zimbabwe	1995	(e)2 121	41.8	8.9	2.3	15.1	31.4	2.0	2.5	26.9
	2005	(e)1 850	25.0	10.1	0.9	36.9	26.7	1.9	2.3	22.4
	2010	(e)2 500	25.2	14.6	12.4	23.8	26.3	1.5	2.9	21.9

Sources:
- UN DESA Statistics Division, *COMTRADE* database
- UNCTAD secretariat calculations

Notes:

(1)   It is recognized that the structure of trade and partner distribution for certain countries and years might vary. In this regard, reader should know the coverage and limitations of the main principal data used in this table. For further information, please visit http://comtrade.un.org/db/help/uReadMeFirst.aspx.

Sources :
- ONU DAES Division de statistique, base de données *COMTRADE*
- Calculs du secrétariat de la CNUCED

Notes :

(1)   Il est reconnu que la structure du commerce et la distribution au niveau partenaire pour certains pays et sur certaines années peuvent varier. À cet égard, le lecteur devrait connaître la couverture ainsi que les limites des données principales utilisées dans ce tableau. Pour de plus amples renseignements, veuillez visiter http://comtrade.un.org/db/help/uReadMeFirst.aspx.

Country or territory / Pays ou territoires	Year / Année	Total value (millions of dollars) / Valeur totale (millions de dollars)	All food items / Produits alimentaires 0+1+22+4	Agricultural raw materials / Matières premières agricoles 2-(22+27+28)	Fuels / Combustibles 3	Ores, metals, precious stones and non monetary gold / Minerais, métaux, pierres précieuses et or (non monétaire) 27+28+68+667+971	Manufactured goods / Articles manufacturés 5+6+7+8-(667+68)	Chemical products / Produits chimiques 5	Machinery and transport equipment / Machines et matériel de transport 7	Other manufactured goods / Articles manufacturés divers 6+8-(667+68)
Afghanistan (1)	1995	(e)007	23.7	0.8	7.0	0.6	67.4	9.7	19.9	37.8
	2005	(e)2 470	22.1	1.0	17.3	0.4	56.7	6.3	22.3	28.1
	2010	(e)5 154	12.9	0.9	26.1	0.2	39.7	2.4	22.7	14.7
Albania - Albanie	1995	(e)714	55.8	1.5	4.2	1.7	99.6	9.6	37.1	52.9
	2005	(e)2 614	17.7	1.1	7.9	2.4	70.4	8.6	22.7	39.0
	2010	(e)4 603	17.5	1.1	12.8	2.9	65.5	10.4	19.9	35.2
Algeria - Algérie	1995	10 782	29.5	3.2	1.1	1.6	64.7	11.3	30.5	22.9
	2005	20 357	19.3	1.7	1.0	1.5	76.5	12.0	43.0	21.5
	2010	41 000	16.3	1.6	2.1	1.5	78.4	10.9	40.8	26.8
American Samoa - Samoa américaines (1)	2005	(e)506	51.8	2.7	7.1	1.3	32.9	2.2	14.4	16.4
	2010	(e)550	49.3	2.5	1.0	1.3	44.1	8.2	12.5	23.4
Andorra - Andorre	1995	1 025	28.4	0.8	4.3	1.2	65.2	9.5	20.4	35.2
	2010	(e)1 531	20.9	0.8	27.7	0.8	49.4	7.4	16.0	25.9
Angola	1995	(e)1 468	26.2	0.9	0.6	0.4	70.5	6.1	42.4	22.0
	2005	(e)8 353	16.2	0.7	0.7	0.4	80.7	5.0	53.3	22.4
	2010	(e)24 926	17.8	0.8	2.3	0.6	77.4	5.9	40.6	30.9
Anguilla (1)	1995	(e)53	24.8	0.2	67.1	0.1	7.1	0.8	2.8	3.5
	2005	(e)130	20.1	2.0	19.9	1.8	54.0	4.4	28.6	21.0
	2010	(e)157	13.2	2.2	1.5	2.1	78.5	6.6	32.3	39.7
Antigua and Barbuda - Antigua-et-Barbuda (1)	1995	(e)346	15.5	1.8	4.7	0.4	69.9	7.4	46.4	16.1
	2005	(e)525	7.6	0.9	13.3	0.4	62.9	2.5	51.0	9.4
	2010	(e)520	7.7	1.4	8.1	0.6	57.6	2.1	49.4	6.1
Argentina - Argentine	1995	20 122	5.5	2.0	4.2	2.7	85.5	17.8	44.5	23.1
	2005	28 689	2.8	1.5	5.0	3.5	86.4	19.8	46.6	19.9
	2010	56 501	2.7	1.1	7.4	3.3	84.8	18.0	47.9	18.8
Armenia - Arménie	1995	(e)674	32.7	0.2	31.8	1.2	31.4	8.8	10.7	11.9
	2005	(e)1 692	16.9	0.8	12.3	20.2	48.7	7.9	21.1	19.8
	2010	(e)3 782	19.4	0.9	13.8	7.6	56.9	9.4	25.0	22.5
Aruba (1)	1995	(e)1 772	27.9	2.0	14.0	2.9	50.0	6.9	19.6	23.5
	2005	(e)3 462	6.3	0.4	49.5	2.1	29.0	2.8	10.7	15.5
	2010	(e)1 343	20.2	0.8	25.4	1.9	48.9	6.3	20.2	22.5
Australia - Australie	1995	57 423	5.0	1.7	5.0	2.5	85.7	11.0	47.0	27.7
	2005	118 922	4.6	0.9	11.1	3.2	79.9	11.4	44.3	24.2
	2010	188 741	5.2	0.7	13.7	5.3	72.3	10.7	39.2	22.4
Austria - Autriche	1995	66 406	5.7	3.2	4.4	4.3	81.6	10.7	36.8	34.1
	2005	119 950	6.1	2.2	12.2	3.8	74.9	10.7	36.8	27.4
	2010	150 593	7.2	2.3	10.7	6.9	72.5	12.5	32.6	27.4
Azerbaijan - Azerbaïdjan	1995	(e)668	37.2	0.9	6.5	1.0	53.9	10.2	14.1	29.6
	2005	(e)4 211	11.0	1.4	10.3	1.7	74.4	6.2	39.7	28.5
	2010	(e)6 597	15.6	1.8	0.9	1.4	78.7	8.5	37.5	32.7
Bahamas	1995	(e)1 243	18.8	1.9	12.6	0.5	64.5	8.1	25.8	30.6
	2005	(e)2 567	15.6	2.3	19.8	0.6	57.8	8.5	22.1	27.2
	2010	(e)2 863	18.3	2.4	21.7	0.8	56.9	9.9	21.2	25.8
Bahrain - Bahreïn	1995	(e)3 679	10.9	0.5	36.7	4.8	45.1	5.5	17.0	22.6
	2005	(e)9 339	6.7	0.4	32.1	4.9	53.6	4.4	29.3	19.9
	2010	(e)10 143	14.7	0.6	1.5	9.1	72.2	8.5	37.1	26.5
Bangladesh	1995	(e)6 694	16.6	3.4	5.7	2.1	70.9	9.3	18.3	43.3
	2005	(e)12 631	13.1	5.3	12.8	2.7	65.5	11.4	24.5	29.5
	2010	(e)26 341	20.3	6.8	8.2	3.1	61.6	13.0	21.7	27.0
Barbados - Barbade	1995	766	18.5	2.3	8.4	1.3	67.4	11.3	26.8	29.3
	2005	1 672	14.4	1.9	21.7	1.2	59.0	8.2	26.4	24.4
	2010	(e)1 562	23.1	4.9	21.7	2.1	46.9	9.5	14.3	23.1

For sources and notes, see end of table.

Pour les sources et les notes, se reporter à la fin du tableau.

Country or territory / Pays ou territoires	Year / Année	Total value (millions of dollars) / Valeur totale (millions de dollars)	All food items / Produits alimentaires	Agricultural raw materials / Matières premières agricoles	Fuels / Combustibles	Ores, metals, precious stones and non monetary gold / Minerais, métaux, pierres précieuses et or (non monétaire)	Manufactured goods / Articles manufacturés	Chemical products / Produits chimiques	Machinery and transport equipment / Machines et matériel de transport	Other manufactured goods / Articles manufacturés divers
			0 + 1 + 22 + 4	2 - (22 + 27 + 28)	3	27 + 28 + 68 + 667 + 971	5 + 6 +7 + 8 -(667 + 68)	5	7	6 + 8 - (667 + 68)
Belarus - Bélarus	1995	(e)5 563	11.8	0.5	1.1	1.1	32.7	6.1	13.6	13.1
	2005	16 699	9.4	1.7	00.0	3.2	46.3	9.5	18.2	18.6
	2010	34 868	7.9	1.5	34.9	3.4	47.0	10.0	10.1	17.8
Belgium - Belgique	1995	(e)164 590	7.0	1.6	5.2	9.9	48.4	10.6	20.1	17.7
	2005	320 130	7.6	1.2	12.4	8.4	69.7	25.0	25.7	19.0
	2010	390 091	8.4	1.3	13.9	8.2	67.0	25.4	23.2	18.3
Belize	1995	259	16.3	0.7	14.5	0.5	65.6	9.2	28.0	28.4
	2005	593	12.3	0.9	25.6	1.9	56.9	10.8	24.1	22.0
	2010	700	21.4	0.8	15.5	1.4	56.6	11.1	17.4	28.2
Benin - Bénin	1995	719	27.3	2.7	9.4	1.0	59.4	13.7	18.0	27.7
	2005	(e)1 018	26.4	3.7	18.0	0.8	39.3	5.9	10.8	22.6
	2010	(e)2 161	31.5	4.4	20.9	0.8	42.5	7.4	11.0	24.1
Bermuda - Bermudes (1)	1995	(e)550	18.1	0.9	13.9	0.3	60.6	6.3	35.1	19.2
	2005	(e)988	9.1	0.4	5.5	0.3	80.8	3.2	64.1	13.5
	2010	(e)970	3.1	0.1	3.1	0.1	87.1	1.2	81.0	4.9
Bhutan - Bhoutan (1)	1995	(e)113	16.1	1.0	1.7	1.7	60.7	5.3	40.3	15.1
	2005	(e)387	13.6	0.6	11.4	5.0	68.3	6.6	33.8	28.0
	2010	(e)854	10.5	2.0	13.4	8.7	65.2	6.1	37.1	22.0
Bolivia (Plurinational State of) - Bolivie (État plurinational de)	1995	1 396	14.3	1.5	3.7	2.7	77.3	13.7	35.9	27.7
	2005	2 343	10.6	1.4	9.9	1.2	76.5	19.5	29.2	27.8
	2010	(e)5 366	10.0	0.7	14.9	1.1	72.6	18.2	27.9	26.5
Bosnia and Herzegovina - Bosnie-Herzégovine	1995	(e)1 082	37.8	0.9	10.7	1.0	46.4	9.0	12.6	24.8
	2005	(e)7 054	17.7	1.3	12.5	2.1	64.0	11.0	22.7	30.3
	2010	(e)9 223	19.6	1.8	14.3	2.7	61.0	13.3	18.6	29.2
Botswana	1995	(e)1 902	18.1	1.1	3.4	5.0	72.3	7.9	33.2	31.2
	2005	3 162	13.8	0.8	13.7	4.4	64.7	9.2	29.6	25.8
	2010	5 657	11.9	1.4	20.8	7.4	57.1	7.4	24.3	25.4
Brazil - Brésil	1995	53 734	10.7	2.7	12.1	3.4	71.1	15.2	39.2	16.7
	2005	73 600	4.4	1.5	18.3	3.9	71.9	19.9	37.9	14.2
	2010	180 459	4.6	1.3	16.6	3.4	74.0	17.9	39.3	16.8
Brunei Darussalam - Brunéi Darussalam	1995	(e)2 078	13.6	0.6	0.2	3.3	81.8	6.4	39.0	36.5
	2005	(e)1 497	19.9	0.3	1.2	1.6	76.9	9.3	29.8	37.8
	2010	(e)3 373	19.7	0.3	1.7	1.6	76.7	10.5	26.5	39.8
Bulgaria - Bulgarie	1995	(e)5 651	7.6	2.6	33.7	4.4	47.9	11.1	16.0	20.8
	2005	18 162	5.0	1.4	11.1	6.7	67.0	9.9	29.9	27.2
	2010	25 360	10.2	1.1	20.5	9.0	56.1	11.6	22.7	21.8
Burkina Faso	1995	(e)484	17.7	1.7	11.0	1.1	68.0	17.1	24.2	26.7
	2005	(e)1 161	18.6	0.7	12.9	0.6	66.1	18.3	23.4	24.3
	2010	2 048	16.9	1.0	20.7	0.9	59.5	15.9	19.9	23.7
Burundi	1995	(e)234	19.0	4.2	6.2	1.1	68.4	14.1	30.8	23.5
	2005	(e)258	9.9	1.6	9.8	2.4	75.2	14.4	29.8	31.1
	2010	(e)509	13.4	1.9	5.5	0.9	77.5	18.0	25.6	34.0
Cambodia - Cambodge	1995	(e)1 187	23.8	1.6	9.0	7.8	56.3	5.9	34.2	16.2
	2005	(e)3 918	10.1	1.4	10.9	0.9	75.6	6.9	16.3	52.4
	2010	(e)7 400	10.8	1.1	9.9	15.4	62.6	5.5	17.8	39.2
Cameroon - Cameroun	1995	(e)1 079	17.4	2.5	2.4	5.6	72.0	16.5	30.5	24.9
	2005	(e)2 735	18.0	1.8	26.3	3.5	50.0	11.0	20.1	19.0
	2010	(e)5 133	17.6	1.6	27.7	2.0	51.1	10.5	22.6	18.1
Canada	1995	164 371	5.7	1.7	3.6	3.7	82.7	8.1	51.6	23.1
	2005	314 444	5.6	1.2	9.2	3.6	78.9	10.1	45.5	23.2
	2010	391 257	7.1	1.0	10.0	5.5	74.8	10.6	41.1	23.0

For sources and notes, see end of table.

Pour les sources et les notes, se reporter à la fin du tableau.

3.1 Country trade structure
by product group
Imports

3.1 Structure du commerce des pays
par groupes de produits
Importations

Country or territory Pays ou territoires	Year Année	Total value (millions of dollars) Valeur totale (millions de dollars)	By main SITC Revision 3 product group (percentage) Par principaux groupes de produits de la CTCI Révision 3 (en pourcentage)							
			All food items Produits alimentaires	Agricultural raw materials Matières premières agricoles	Fuels Combustibles	Ores, metals, precious stones and non monetary gold Minerais, métaux, pierres précieuses et or (non monétaire)	Manufactured goods Articles manufacturés	Of which: / dont :		
								Chemical products Produits chimiques	Machinery and transport equipment Machines et matériel de transport	Other manufactured goods Articles manufacturés divers
			0 + 1 + 22 + 4	2 - (22 + 27 + 28)	3	27 + 28 + 68 + 667 + 971	5 + 6 +7 + 8 -(667 + 68)	5	7	6 + 8 - (667 + 68)
Cape Verde - Cap-Vert	1995	252	32.0	2.1	14.5	0.4	49.9	5.8	19.6	24.6
	2005	(e)438	28.4	-0.3	10.6	5.7	53.7	6.8	20.8	26.1
	2010	731	27.0	1.1	13.2	1.0	56.6	6.3	26.1	24.3
Central African Republic - République centrafricaine	1995	(e)174	14.2	1.3	0.9	2.0	81.0	12.0	50.3	18.6
	2005	(e)185	19.6	3.6	16.0	1.5	58.2	10.1	28.6	19.5
	2010	(e)341	23.6	1.6	18.0	2.5	54.3	10.7	22.6	21.0
Chad - Tchad	1995	(e)488	17.5	0.5	14.0	0.5	66.8	9.3	31.2	26.3
	2005	(e)949	12.5	1.2	6.9	1.0	78.0	11.1	42.7	24.1
	2010	(e)2 507	15.1	0.7	8.1	1.1	74.7	10.2	42.5	22.0
Chile - Chili	1995	14 903	6.7	1.7	9.0	2.2	79.2	12.2	42.3	24.7
	2005	32 735	5.6	0.9	19.9	3.2	60.4	10.4	32.4	17.6
	2010	(e)59 417	7.5	0.8	22.3	2.7	66.7	11.5	33.9	21.3
China - Chine	1995	132 083	7.0	5.2	3.9	4.6	78.1	12.9	39.8	25.4
	2005	659 953	3.3	3.6	9.7	8.8	74.4	11.8	44.0	18.6
	2010	1 396 002	4.3	3.5	13.5	13.7	63.7	10.7	39.4	13.7
China, Hong Kong SAR - Chine (RAS de Hong Kong)	1995	196 072	5.4	1.6	1.9	5.6	85.1	7.4	36.5	41.3
	2005	300 160	2.9	0.8	2.7	4.9	88.7	6.2	52.1	30.3
	2010	441 300	4.1	0.0	0.5	7.1	84.7	5.3	56.2	23.3
China, Macao SAR - Chine (RAS de Macao)	1995	2 025	18.8	2.6	3.9	1.0	73.2	5.9	20.2	47.2
	2005	3 913	18.3	0.6	7.3	0.7	72.7	4.6	21.3	46.8
	2010	5 629	17.1	0.4	10.7	1.0	66.7	6.7	24.7	35.3
China, Taiwan Province of - Province chinoise de Taiwan	1995	(e)103 506	5.4	4.2	6.9	7.4	74.2	13.3	40.2	20.7
	2005	(e)181 592	3.6	1.6	15.5	6.3	72.1	12.6	41.0	18.4
	2010	(e)252 017	4.2	1.7	20.5	9.2	64.4	14.2	32.6	17.7
Colombia - Colombie	1995	13 883	9.4	2.5	2.8	2.5	78.0	18.1	37.3	22.6
	2005	21 204	8.7	1.6	2.6	2.6	83.7	20.8	40.4	22.5
	2010	40 683	9.7	1.4	5.1	2.0	81.0	18.3	40.0	22.7
Comoros - Comores (1)	1995	62	25.1	1.5	5.0	0.5	67.4	7.4	32.5	27.5
	2005	(e)99	33.6	1.2	9.3	0.4	53.6	3.8	23.2	26.6
	2010	(e)185	34.3	0.9	4.3	0.5	59.9	3.7	31.1	25.1
Congo	1995	(e)670	11.9	0.4	15.6	0.6	70.6	8.8	26.6	35.1
	2005	(e)1 343	20.9	2.2	2.7	1.3	71.8	12.8	29.9	29.1
	2010	(e)2 990	21.0	2.5	2.5	1.7	72.0	10.2	34.7	27.1
Cook Islands - Îles Cook (1)	1995	(e)49	22.7	1.7	11.5	1.2	62.5	5.8	31.0	25.6
	2005	(e)81	28.0	2.6	6.1	0.7	57.4	7.4	20.9	29.1
	2010	(e)305	29.3	3.2	10.8	0.6	55.6	6.0	24.1	25.4
Costa Rica	1995	(e)4 090	9.2	1.3	7.0	2.0	79.1	17.1	26.8	35.2
	2005	9 173	7.0	1.1	9.5	1.9	78.7	14.5	39.1	25.1
	2010	13 920	8.8	1.3	12.0	2.0	73.7	14.5	35.6	23.5
Côte d'Ivoire	1995	2 946	17.5	0.8	16.1	1.3	47.5	10.9	20.5	16.1
	2005	5 865	14.6	0.5	28.0	1.0	54.8	9.4	24.2	21.2
	2010	(e)6 898	24.2	0.6	28.1	1.4	45.6	11.9	17.3	16.5
Croatia - Croatie	1995	7 509	11.8	1.8	11.6	2.5	66.6	10.8	26.7	29.0
	2005	18 560	8.3	1.3	15.1	2.3	72.9	11.1	32.9	28.9
	2010	20 067	10.4	1.1	18.8	2.5	67.2	14.1	25.7	27.5
Cuba	1995	(e)2 805	20.9	1.7	21.4	1.6	53.5	12.3	20.4	20.9
	2005	(e)8 084	19.3	0.7	26.3	1.5	51.0	7.5	24.6	18.9
	2010	(e)11 300	17.2	1.3	24.8	2.1	54.3	10.9	20.0	23.5
Cyprus - Chypre	1995	3 694	20.4	1.3	7.7	2.3	68.3	8.8	27.6	31.9
	2005	6 382	12.4	1.1	16.1	1.3	67.5	8.9	30.9	27.7
	2010	8 570	14.8	0.8	20.3	0.9	61.4	9.8	25.3	26.3

For sources and notes, see end of table.

Pour les sources et les notes, se reporter à la fin du tableau.

Country or territory Pays ou territoires	Year Année	Total value (millions of dollars) Valeur totale (millions de dollars)	By main SITC Revision 3 product group (percentage) Par principaux groupes de produits de la CTCI Révision 3 (en pourcentage)					Of which: / dont :		
			All food items Produits alimentaires	Agricultural raw materials Matières premières agricoles	Fuels Combustibles	Ores, metals, precious stones and non monetary gold Minérais, métaux, pierres précieuses et or (non monétaire)	Manufactured goods Articles manufacturés	Chemical products Produits chimiques	Machinery and transport equipment Machines et matériel de transport	Other manufactured goods Articles manufacturés divers
			0 + 1 + 22 + 4	2 - (22 + 27 + 28)	3	27 + 28 + 68 + 667 + 971	5 + 6 +7 + 8 -(667 + 68)	5	7	6 + 8 - (667 + 68)
Czech Republic - République tchèque	1995	25 303	6.6	2.5	8.6	4.3	76.4	11.6	35.1	29.7
	2005	70 527	6.2	1.5	6.0	3.1	78.2	10.6	41.1	27.5
	2010	125 691	5.8	1.3	8.1	3.8	76.9	10.6	41.4	24.9
Dem. Rep. of the Congo - Rép. dém. du Congo	1995	1 046	21.8	3.3	10.2	1.2	62.2	9.5	20.9	31.9
	2005	2 690	22.9	2.8	13.6	0.9	59.0	11.0	26.3	21.6
	2010	(e)4 500	20.5	2.0	10.8	2.0	62.1	12.8	25.5	23.8
Denmark - Danemark	1995	43 142	12.0	3.0	3.3	2.1	72.7	11.2	32.0	29.5
	2005	74 265	11.3	2.2	6.7	1.8	76.4	10.9	36.3	29.2
	2010	84 468	13.5	2.5	7.5	1.7	72.8	11.6	31.4	29.8
Djibouti (1)	1995	(e)177	28.7	11.3	2.1	0.3	56.8	5.3	15.2	36.3
	2005	(e)277	12.7	3.7	30.6	0.6	51.3	6.8	15.8	28.6
	2010	(e)417	27.9	1.8	3.7	1.0	64.3	9.4	23.9	31.1
Dominica - Dominique (1)	1995	117	26.2	2.0	5.6	0.4	65.7	14.3	24.0	27.5
	2005	165	19.4	1.3	13.3	0.5	65.5	11.4	25.4	28.8
	2010	225	22.5	2.7	17.3	0.4	57.1	8.0	22.7	26.4
Dominican Republic - République dominicaine	1995	(e)5 170	12.4	1.6	11.6	0.7	71.6	7.7	20.5	43.3
	2005	(e)9 862	11.6	1.3	13.3	1.5	70.4	9.4	24.5	36.6
	2010	(e)15 163	14.1	1.1	21.7	1.1	60.0	10.0	23.2	26.8
Ecuador - Équateur	1995	4 195	7.6	2.8	5.9	1.9	81.8	17.6	40.1	24.1
	2005	9 609	8.0	1.3	12.0	1.2	77.4	16.8	36.8	23.9
	2010	20 591	8.3	1.0	21.3	1.2	67.8	15.3	33.2	19.2
Egypt - Égypte	1995	11 739	28.4	7.1	1.2	2.7	60.6	13.2	25.3	22.1
	2005	19 812	20.1	4.1	13.5	3.4	46.2	11.3	18.6	16.3
	2010	53 003	19.1	3.2	13.4	4.3	59.9	11.9	24.4	23.6
El Salvador	1995	(e)3 329	14.3	2.4	7.8	1.4	73.0	15.1	27.4	30.5
	2005	6 690	14.5	1.4	13.0	1.4	66.7	13.9	18.0	34.9
	2010	8 485	17.4	1.9	15.8	1.2	61.8	15.0	16.6	30.1
Equatorial Guinea - Guinée équatoriale	1995	121	25.7	2.6	3.2	0.6	69.0	9.7	27.9	31.4
	2005	1 310	10.3	0.8	9.5	0.4	77.1	2.8	56.3	17.9
	2010	(e)5 680	4.5	0.3	31.4	0.4	62.5	3.1	38.7	20.7
Eritrea - Érythrée (1)	1995	(e)434	12.0	1.5	5.2	0.4	79.2	4.3	46.1	28.8
	2005	(e)487	33.3	0.7	2.3	1.2	59.3	6.5	33.3	19.5
	2010	(e)679	34.4	1.0	6.9	1.8	55.5	9.4	19.9	26.3
Estonia - Estonie	1995	2 546	14.2	2.6	11.5	2.4	68.5	8.9	29.1	30.5
	2005	11 018	8.0	3.4	12.7	1.5	69.2	8.9	35.3	24.9
	2010	13 182	10.9	2.5	15.3	1.6	64.4	10.8	28.6	25.0
Ethiopia - Éthiopie	1995	1 141	13.8	1.9	11.1	0.8	72.4	14.1	35.5	22.7
	2005	4 095	10.6	0.9	15.1	1.2	72.1	12.3	34.7	25.1
	2010	9 692	11.0	0.5	18.5	1.2	68.8	11.5	35.7	21.6
Faeroe Islands - Îles Féroé	1995	(e)314	22.3	3.5	11.7	1.2	57.9	7.3	27.5	23.0
	2005	747	13.2	2.3	16.2	1.1	65.6	6.4	36.8	22.3
	2010	(e)775	19.9	3.0	19.2	1.3	56.6	8.0	20.9	27.6
Falkland Islands (Malvinas) - (1) Îles Falkland (Malvinas)	1995	(e)48	18.1	1.4	4.4	0.1	74.1	2.0	57.9	14.1
	2005	(e)66	1.5	0.1	1.6	0.1	12.1	0.2	5.4	6.5
	2010	(e)112	10.1	0.3	11.3	2.6	63.6	4.9	23.3	35.4
Fiji - Fidji	1995	(e)892	14.1	0.6	13.3	0.9	68.8	6.9	23.6	38.3
	2005	(e)1 607	14.7	0.4	28.8	0.9	54.9	7.7	21.7	25.5
	2010	(e)1 274	17.9	0.4	30.2	1.2	50.5	8.1	18.6	23.7
Finland - Finlande	1995	29 520	6.0	3.6	8.8	5.7	74.3	12.2	38.7	23.3
	2005	58 473	5.2	2.9	13.7	6.5	70.0	11.3	39.2	19.5
	2010	68 246	7.2	2.5	18.4	8.2	60.4	11.5	28.7	20.2

For sources and notes, see end of table.

Pour les sources et les notes, se reporter à la fin du tableau.

3.1 Country trade structure
by product group
Imports

3.1 Structure du commerce des pays
par groupes de produits
Importations

Country or territory Pays ou territoires	Year Année	Total value (millions of dollars) Valeur totale (millions de dollars)	By main SITC Revision 3 product group (percentage) Par principaux groupes de produits de la CTCI Révision 3 (en pourcentage)					Of which: / dont :		
			All food items Produits alimentaires	Agricultural raw materials Matières premières agricoles	Fuels Combustibles	Ores, metals, precious stones and non monetary gold Minerais, métaux, pierres précieuses et or (non monétaire)	Manufactured goods Articles manufacturés	Chemical products Produits chimiques	Machinery and transport equipment Machines et matériel de transport	Other manufactured goods Articles manufacturés divers
			0 + 1 + 22 + 4	2 - (22 + 27 + 28)	3	27 + 28 + 68 + 667 + 971	5 + 6 +7 + 8 -(667 + 68)	5	7	6 + 8 - (667 + 68)
France	1995	275 510	10.7	2.5	6.9	3.0	76.0	12.5	35.4	28.1
	2005	475 857	7.8	1.5	13.4	2.8	74.6	13.3	35.7	25.5
	2010	599 172	8.5	1.4	13.8	3.0	73.3	14.1	34.1	25.0
French Polynesia - Polynésie française	1995	(e)1 019	21.6	1.5	5.5	0.9	70.5	8.5	34.7	27.4
	2005	1 702	19.0	1.3	9.6	0.9	69.2	8.4	35.8	25.0
	2010	(e)1 726	23.5	1.2	13.0	0.8	61.5	9.9	28.0	23.6
Gabon	1995	(e)884	19.1	0.7	3.4	1.1	75.6	10.7	39.3	25.7
	2005	1 472	16.9	0.5	4.1	1.3	76.2	9.1	41.9	25.2
	2010	(e)2 492	17.1	0.9	4.1	1.3	76.5	9.4	42.8	24.3
Gambia - Gambie	1995	(e)182	30.4	1.2	8.8	0.3	57.6	5.5	16.4	35.7
	2005	(e)260	30.7	1.1	13.0	3.4	51.3	5.6	15.4	30.3
	2010	(e)275	33.1	1.4	10.1	0.8	54.6	7.5	13.8	33.3
Georgia - Géorgie	1995	(e)489	31.6	0.2	32.8	0.3	29.5	12.1	8.9	8.4
	2005	2 490	19.7	-0.3	20.1	3.2	55.0	8.9	25.8	20.4
	2010	5 095	19.3	0.3	17.7	3.2	58.4	10.7	23.9	23.9
Germany - Allemagne	1995	464 145	9.8	2.6	6.2	4.4	69.9	9.1	31.8	28.9
	2005	779 819	7.0	1.5	11.5	4.1	71.6	11.7	37.4	22.4
	2010	1 066 817	7.1	1.5	11.4	5.0	67.4	12.0	34.0	20.0
Ghana	1995	(e)1 896	7.9	1.0	5.8	2.6	74.9	9.3	43.7	21.9
	2005	(e)4 878	15.6	1.7	16.4	1.9	63.1	10.2	28.0	24.9
	2010	(e)10 922	15.2	1.6	16.9	1.2	65.1	12.4	30.4	22.3
Gibraltar (1)	1995	411	12.0	0.6	51.9	1.3	33.2	2.8	15.8	14.6
	2005	551	3.7	0.1	67.1	1.2	24.8	1.3	18.2	5.3
	2010	(e)746	2.0	0.0	79.3	0.0	10.5	0.7	8.6	1.1
Greece - Grèce	1995	25 927	16.0	2.5	7.2	3.2	70.6	13.2	27.4	30.0
	2005	54 894	11.2	1.2	17.9	3.1	66.4	14.4	28.9	23.1
	2010	63 321	12.5	1.0	23.5	3.1	59.9	15.2	24.2	20.4
Greenland - Groenland	1995	421	13.7	1.3	6.4	0.4	66.2	5.3	28.3	32.6
	2005	593	18.2	1.3	21.3	0.5	57.3	4.8	27.5	25.0
	2010	(e)777	21.0	1.5	19.9	0.4	57.2	5.4	24.8	27.0
Grenada - Grenade	1995	129	27.5	2.5	7.8	0.4	61.8	8.8	21.3	31.7
	2005	334	16.4	6.2	7.2	0.6	69.6	8.2	23.5	38.0
	2010	(e)317	22.0	2.1	16.2	0.8	58.9	8.3	20.9	29.7
Guam (1)	1995	442	..	..	..	..	..	..	..	..
	2005	(e)533	9.4	0.1	58.0	0.0	31.5	2.0	11.6	17.9
	2010	(e)698	7.9	0.1	55.4	0.2	35.7	1.8	11.7	22.2
Guatemala	1995	3 292	11.9	1.5	12.4	1.2	73.0	17.2	31.5	24.3
	2005	10 500	10.9	1.2	15.5	1.3	71.1	15.8	23.1	32.3
	2010	13 830	13.3	1.3	18.1	1.3	66.0	17.4	21.8	26.7
Guinea - Guinée	1995	(e)819	29.6	1.1	14.4	0.6	53.1	7.5	21.2	24.4
	2005	(e)820	20.3	0.8	12.2	0.5	55.4	9.0	21.0	25.4
	2010	(e)1 405	19.2	1.1	19.9	0.5	59.3	8.6	28.0	22.7
Guinea-Bissau - Guinée-Bissau	1995	(e)133	18.8	0.4	5.4	0.3	74.0	5.7	23.1	45.1
	2005	(e)112	30.6	0.5	36.0	0.1	30.8	5.3	13.2	12.3
	2010	(e)207	37.7	0.5	17.1	3.5	40.9	5.7	15.5	19.7
Guyana	1995	(e)528	14.1	0.4	5.6	0.5	68.7	11.1	34.8	22.8
	2005	778	15.0	0.3	25.2	1.2	54.0	9.2	25.4	19.4
	2010	1 448	13.4	0.3	24.9	2.3	56.9	9.4	25.5	21.9
Haiti - Haïti	1995	(e)654	38.5	1.8	3.8	0.6	48.1	5.6	21.7	20.8
	2005	(e)1 466	40.2	1.6	5.7	0.5	52.1	5.9	15.4	30.8
	2010	(e)3 173	46.1	1.6	5.1	0.5	46.7	5.6	13.7	27.4

For sources and notes, see end of table.

Pour les sources et les notes, se reporter à la fin du tableau.

149

3.1 Country trade structure
by product group
Imports

3.1 Structure du commerce des pays
par groupes de produits
Importations

Country or territory / Pays ou territoires	Year / Année	Total value (millions of dollars) / Valeur totale (millions de dollars)	By main SITC Revision 3 product group (percentage) / Par principaux groupes de produits de la CTCI Révision 3 (en pourcentage)					Of which: / dont :		
			All food items / Produits alimentaires	Agricultural raw materials / Matières premières agricoles	Fuels / Combustibles	Ores, metals, precious stones and non monetary gold / Minerais, métaux, pierres précieuses et or (non monétaire)	Manufactured goods / Articles manufacturés	Chemical products / Produits chimiques	Machinery and transport equipment / Machines et matériel de transport	Other manufactured goods / Articles manufacturés divers
			0 + 1 + 22 + 4	2 - (22 + 27 + 28)	3	27 + 28 + 68 + 667 + 971	5 + 6 +7 + 8 -(667 + 68)	5	7	6 + 8 - (667 + 68)
Honduras	1995	(e)1 728	11.5	1.1	6.0	1.2	77.9	14.2	26.1	37.6
	2005	(e)6 646	12.6	0.0	10.0	0.7	66.7	12.6	16.8	37.3
	2010	(e)8 550	15.2	1.5	15.7	0.7	66.9	13.5	19.4	34.0
Hungary - Hongrie	1995	15 186	5.7	3.0	11.9	4.3	75.2	14.5	30.1	30.6
	2005	65 920	4.1	1.1	10.1	1.9	77.5	9.1	48.9	19.5
	2010	87 356	4.8	1.0	10.6	2.7	71.8	9.9	45.9	16.0
Iceland - Islande	1995	1 751	11.8	1.6	7.2	4.6	74.6	9.3	32.4	32.9
	2005	4 979	7.8	1.3	9.4	4.1	77.3	7.8	41.9	27.6
	2010	3 925	11.0	1.2	13.0	15.9	58.8	10.1	27.2	21.5
India - Inde	1995	36 592	4.6	4.1	14.2	16.7	56.0	15.8	26.4	13.8
	2005	140 862	4.4	2.4	12.5	25.0	53.8	12.0	27.3	14.5
	2010	(e)340 125	3.7	1.5	32.7	22.0	40.1	9.5	20.6	10.0
Indonesia - Indonésie	2005	75 631	6.6	3.0	23.6	3.2	62.3	12.5	33.2	16.6
	2010	135 663	8.3	2.9	19.0	3.4	65.0	12.0	35.8	17.2
Indonesia including East Timor - Indonésie, y compris le Timor oriental	1995	40 645	8.5	5.3	6.4	3.6	75.2	14.0	42.0	19.3
Iran (Islamic Rep. of) - Iran (Rép. islamique d')	1995	(e)13 882	20.9	2.4	1.8	5.1	69.8	13.3	35.6	20.9
	2005	(e)38 675	8.1	1.8	7.9	2.4	73.1	9.6	39.5	24.0
	2010	(e)62 537	11.5	1.7	8.1	3.6	75.1	9.8	35.9	29.3
Iraq (1)	1995	(e)665	63.9	0.2	0.1	0.1	34.8	30.6	1.4	2.8
	2005	(e)23 532	23.0	0.3	9.2	0.6	62.8	9.8	32.9	20.2
	2010	(e)44 203	25.4	0.4	3.8	0.8	67.9	6.9	34.8	26.3
Ireland - Irlande	1995	32 321	8.5	1.2	3.3	2.2	75.7	12.8	42.3	20.7
	2005	70 284	7.9	1.0	6.9	1.4	76.8	12.9	43.9	20.1
	2010	60 337	12.3	0.7	12.2	1.6	66.4	19.1	27.0	20.3
Israel - Israël	1995	28 344	6.6	1.6	5.9	19.3	65.1	9.3	34.0	21.9
	2005	45 032	5.5	1.0	15.0	23.6	54.5	10.2	27.6	16.7
	2010	59 194	7.3	1.2	17.6	15.9	57.4	11.4	28.3	17.7
Italy - Italie	1995	200 320	11.5	5.6	7.3	6.3	66.7	13.1	29.8	23.8
	2005	384 836	8.6	2.6	11.9	5.2	65.7	12.9	30.0	22.7
	2010	486 629	9.1	2.2	18.9	5.9	62.6	13.5	27.2	21.8
Jamaica - Jamaïque	1995	2 773	14.3	1.6	12.7	0.9	67.6	9.9	27.5	30.3
	2005	4 885	14.7	1.4	28.3	0.8	53.3	11.8	19.1	22.4
	2010	5 225	17.7	1.0	30.3	0.5	48.7	13.4	15.2	20.1
Japan - Japon	1995	336 094	16.1	6.2	16.0	8.5	52.0	7.1	22.6	22.3
	2005	515 866	10.4	2.4	25.8	6.6	53.3	7.3	25.7	20.3
	2010	692 621	9.2	1.9	28.7	8.4	50.0	8.8	23.3	17.9
Jordan - Jordanie	1995	3 696	20.6	2.1	12.9	3.4	60.5	12.3	24.5	23.7
	2005	10 455	13.6	1.2	23.1	2.5	57.7	8.8	25.1	23.7
	2010	15 262	16.2	1.3	22.1	2.4	56.3	11.3	23.0	22.0
Kazakhstan	1995	3 805	10.0	2.1	23.5	4.2	59.5	9.9	26.4	23.2
	2005	17 333	6.3	0.9	11.0	1.5	79.6	8.5	36.8	34.3
	2010	24 024	7.8	0.5	8.4	1.0	81.7	10.3	35.7	35.7
Kenya	1995	2 818	11.1	2.5	11.7	1.8	72.4	14.7	34.3	23.3
	2005	5 846	8.6	1.9	20.2	1.8	66.1	13.8	30.5	21.8
	2010	(e)12 085	12.6	1.7	21.8	1.9	62.0	12.9	28.2	20.9
Kiribati (1)	1995	(e)34	33.2	1.8	10.3	0.4	50.7	9.0	15.6	26.1
	2005	(e)74	29.7	1.2	14.1	0.8	45.5	5.3	22.9	17.3
	2010	(e)73	22.7	0.8	14.7	0.7	52.8	5.7	33.2	13.9

For sources and notes, see end of table.

Pour les sources et les notes, se reporter à la fin du tableau.

3.1   Country trade structure
       by product group
       Imports

3.1   Structure du commerce des pays
       par groupes de produits
       Importations

Country or territory / Pays ou territoires	Year / Année	Total value (millions of dollars) / Valeur totale (millions de dollars)	By main SITC Revision 3 product group (percentage) / Par principaux groupes de produits de la CTCI Révision 3 (en pourcentage)					Of which: / dont :		
			All food items / Produits alimentaires	Agricultural raw materials / Matières premières agricoles	Fuels / Combustibles	Ores, metals, precious stones and non monetary gold / Minerais, métaux, pierres précieuses et or (non monétaire)	Manufactured goods / Articles manufacturés	Chemical products / Produits chimiques	Machinery and transport equipment / Machines et matériel de transport	Other manufactured goods / Articles manufacturés divers
			0 + 1 + 22 + 4	2 - (22 + 27 + 28)	3	27 + 28 + 68 + 667 + 971	5 + 6 +7 + 8 -(667 + 68)	5	7	6 + 8 - (667 + 68)
Korea, Dem. People's Rep. of (1) Corée, Rép. populaire dém. de	1995	1 580	14.0	6.4	18.6	3.6	53.9	8.7	18.4	26.7
	2005	2 710	18.4	2.4	28.5	4.1	44.5	6.9	16.7	21.0
	2010	(e)3 000	10.6	2.1	25.9	8.3	52.3	6.4	21.4	24.6
Korea, Republic of - Corée, République de	1995	135 113	5.4	5.5	14.1	8.4	66.6	9.7	36.6	20.3
	2005	261 236	4.4	2.0	25.8	7.1	60.6	9.4	31.6	19.7
	2010	(e)425 526	5.2	1.9	28.6	8.7	55.5	9.0	27.7	18.8
Kuwait - Koweït	1995	7 790	15.5	1.1	0.5	2.0	80.8	7.3	41.2	32.3
	2005	(e)15 807	22.9	0.7	1.5	2.8	72.1	7.2	34.4	30.5
	2010	(e)22 399	16.9	0.7	0.5	3.8	78.1	8.8	36.6	32.7
Kyrgyzstan - Kirghizistan	1995	(e)522	18.3	2.7	35.9	2.6	40.5	6.3	18.4	15.9
	2005	(e)1 108	15.0	1.7	28.9	2.2	52.0	14.2	18.0	19.8
	2010	(e)3 223	16.9	1.2	26.5	0.9	53.9	10.0	21.5	22.3
Lao People's Dem. Rep. - (1) Rép. dém. populaire lao	1995	589	17.6	0.2	7.7	3.8	69.1	6.7	35.1	27.3
	2005	882	14.1	0.6	18.4	2.2	62.3	7.5	30.0	24.8
	2010	2 060	11.5	0.4	19.9	1.4	66.3	6.3	33.1	26.9
Latvia - Lettonie	1995	1 818	10.5	1.7	21.2	1.1	65.6	12.7	25.4	27.5
	2005	8 770	10.8	2.7	15.1	1.5	66.5	10.2	28.7	27.6
	2010	11 143	14.8	1.5	14.7	2.2	60.1	10.2	21.8	24.2
Lebanon - Liban	1995	(e)7 278	20.1	1.9	7.5	6.0	64.2	8.5	25.0	30.7
	2005	(e)9 327	16.2	1.2	20.8	6.0	55.2	11.5	20.0	23.7
	2010	(e)17 970	16.4	1.1	15.7	6.5	59.8	11.5	21.9	26.5
Lesotho	1995	(e)1 107	24.8	1.3	7.6	2.2	64.1	8.9	13.7	41.4
	2005	(e)1 361	5.6	1.1	0.7	1.6	87.9	4.7	14.4	68.8
	2010	(e)2 126	10.4	6.0	0.1	0.8	82.3	3.2	16.1	63.0
Liberia - Libéria (1)	1995	(e)510	1.5	0.1	0.7	0.1	93.1	0.5	92.0	0.6
	2005	324	2.8	0.2	2.6	0.1	80.0	0.6	77.1	2.4
	2010	(e)650	1.8	0.3	4.0	0.0	65.4	0.5	61.5	3.4
Libyan Arab Jamahiriya - Jamahiriya arabe libyenne	1995	(e)5 033	21.6	0.9	4.4	2.0	69.6	8.9	31.1	29.7
	2005	(e)11 188	15.8	0.6	9.7	3.1	67.3	6.0	35.6	25.7
	2010	(e)24 647	16.9	0.7	9.3	3.0	68.9	5.7	36.6	26.6
Lithuania - Lituanie	1995	3 649	13.1	3.9	19.4	3.9	57.8	12.5	21.7	23.6
	2005	15 704	8.0	2.3	24.2	1.5	62.5	11.0	29.7	21.8
	2010	23 378	12.5	1.7	32.0	1.7	49.8	13.4	19.4	17.0
Luxembourg	1995	(e)8 983	8.7	0.9	2.0	5.8	54.2	7.1	28.9	18.3
	2005	(e)21 884	8.9	0.9	9.7	6.1	71.3	8.8	38.1	24.4
	2010	(e)23 960	10.0	1.3	12.5	8.6	63.0	9.5	29.7	23.8
Madagascar	1995	(e)628	14.0	2.0	11.7	0.6	70.4	11.5	26.9	32.0
	2005	1 686	14.6	0.5	16.0	0.4	66.8	7.6	24.7	34.5
	2010	2 546	14.2	0.9	14.2	0.5	69.5	8.5	27.6	33.4
Malawi	1995	500	17.8	0.8	8.4	0.7	71.3	16.7	30.4	24.2
	2005	1 165	19.3	1.0	8.6	0.9	69.3	21.5	22.0	25.8
	2010	2 173	14.0	1.1	10.3	1.1	72.5	23.3	23.1	26.1
Malaysia - Malaisie	1995	77 046	4.8	1.2	2.3	5.9	83.4	7.1	60.0	16.3
	2005	114 290	5.1	1.2	8.1	4.8	79.0	7.8	57.5	13.7
	2010	164 586	7.8	2.0	10.0	6.5	73.2	9.1	49.5	14.6
Maldives	1995	(e)268	24.0	2.1	11.4	1.9	60.7	5.9	26.5	28.4
	2005	745	15.6	3.6	15.5	2.3	63.0	5.3	30.8	26.9
	2010	(e)1 095	17.0	4.2	18.3	2.3	57.9	5.6	25.7	26.6
Mali	1995	(e)774	19.9	0.8	15.6	1.1	62.5	14.9	21.6	26.0
	2005	1 544	16.7	0.5	16.5	0.7	64.7	16.8	23.1	24.8
	2010	2 781	12.5	0.6	23.3	0.9	62.1	14.6	23.1	24.5

For sources and notes, see end of table.

Pour les sources et les notes, se reporter à la fin du tableau.

3.1 Country trade structure
by product group
Imports

3.1 Structure du commerce des pays
par groupes de produits
Importations

Country or territory Pays ou territoires	Year Année	Total value (millions of dollars) Valeur totale (millions de dollars)	By main SITC Revision 3 product group (percentage) Par principaux groupes de produits de la CTCI Révision 3 (en pourcentage)					Of which: / dont :		
			All food items Produits alimentaires	Agricultural raw materials Matières premières agricoles	Fuels Combus- tibles	Ores, metals, precious stones and non monetary gold Minerais, métaux, pierres précieuses et or (non monétaire)	Manu- factured goods Articles manu- facturés	Chemical products Produits chimiques	Machinery and transport equipment Machines et matériel de transport	Other manu- factured goods Articles manu- facturés divers
			0 + 1 + 22 + 4	2 - (22 + 27 + 28)	3	27 + 28 + 68 + 667 + 971	5 + 6 +7 + 8 -(667 + 68)	5	7	6 + 8 - (667 + 68)
Malta - Malte	1995	2 942	8.1	0.7	10.8	1.6	77.5	7.1	49.7	20.8
	2005	3 066	9.9	0.6	14.1	1.1	71.3	7.5	46.3	17.5
	2010	(e)4 086	12.6	0.6	16.2	1.9	68.7	8.3	43.5	16.9
Marshall Islands - Îles Marshall (1)	1995	75	2.1	0.2	0.6	0.5	94.6	0.4	92.5	1.7
	2005	94	0.9	0.1	0.4	0.0	89.0	0.3	88.2	0.6
	2010	(e)120	0.3	0.0	2.3	0.0	78.1	0.2	76.4	1.5
Mauritania - Mauritanie	1995	(e)455	26.6	1.0	10.4	0.4	60.5	7.5	28.0	24.9
	2005	(e)1 342	25.2	0.6	6.2	0.4	66.3	6.7	35.0	24.7
	2010	(e)1 727	28.2	0.5	14.3	0.3	55.5	7.1	26.5	21.9
Mauritius - Maurice	1995	2 000	16.6	3.1	6.9	3.1	70.3	7.7	19.2	43.4
	2005	3 160	16.7	1.9	16.4	3.0	62.0	7.9	28.1	26.0
	2010	(e)4 402	21.0	2.2	19.2	3.1	54.6	9.2	20.2	25.2
Mayotte	2005	309	22.4	1.5	13.4	0.4	62.3	8.5	27.2	26.7
	2010	(e)502	21.1	1.1	2.0	0.6	75.2	10.0	40.5	24.6
Mexico - Mexique	1995	72 453	6.3	2.3	2.1	2.3	80.1	9.8	43.2	27.1
	2005	221 819	6.0	1.4	5.5	2.6	83.4	11.0	48.1	24.2
	2010	301 482	6.5	1.3	8.0	2.8	79.5	11.3	47.2	21.0
Micronesia (Federated States of) - (1) Micronésie (États fédérés de)	1995	100	37.2	2.1	1.0	0.9	52.5	2.7	28.2	21.7
	2005	130	33.8	3.1	1.2	0.5	51.5	3.7	18.8	29.0
	2010	(e)155	36.8	1.8	1.0	0.2	49.6	4.3	21.9	23.4
Mongolia - Mongolie	1995	(e)415	14.3	0.7	19.3	0.7	65.1	5.0	39.7	20.3
	2005	1 183	13.0	0.4	26.6	0.5	59.5	5.0	31.2	23.2
	2010	(e)3 277	12.8	0.4	20.6	0.6	65.6	6.1	29.0	30.5
Montenegro - Monténégro	2010	2 182	24.2	0.8	12.7	4.3	58.1	9.9	20.6	27.7
Montserrat (1)	1995	(e)30	16.0	0.7	4.2	0.1	74.7	3.4	58.7	12.6
	2005	(e)30	16.7	2.2	18.9	2.5	56.7	5.5	27.8	23.5
	2010	(e)30	..	..	..	..	..	..	..	..
Morocco - Maroc	1995	(e)10 023	16.6	5.4	11.7	3.4	48.0	10.2	19.8	18.1
	2005	20 803	10.6	2.8	21.4	3.4	61.8	9.3	26.6	26.0
	2010	35 379	11.5	2.2	23.0	3.3	59.9	9.9	27.9	22.1
Mozambique	1995	727	25.8	1.4	5.8	0.7	65.1	9.7	31.6	23.9
	2005	2 408	15.8	0.9	14.1	0.4	50.9	7.9	23.0	19.9
	2010	3 564	14.5	1.2	18.0	1.0	53.7	8.4	25.0	20.3
Myanmar	1995	(e)1 348	21.7	0.7	4.0	1.8	71.0	9.5	32.8	28.7
	2005	(e)1 977	10.9	0.6	19.2	1.0	68.3	11.6	27.6	29.1
	2010	(e)4 933	12.2	0.7	19.0	1.2	67.0	11.5	26.4	29.1
Namibia - Namibie	1995	(e)1 496	16.8	1.1	3.9	3.7	74.5	9.9	37.1	27.5
	2005	(e)2 516	16.8	0.7	2.0	2.8	76.3	10.6	35.5	30.2
	2010	(e)6 101	8.4	0.7	3.3	34.2	53.3	5.9	28.7	18.6
Nauru (1)	1995	28	24.2	2.3	11.4	0.6	55.7	5.7	28.1	21.9
	2005	26	10.0	1.0	46.8	0.6	21.8	1.2	12.6	8.1
	2010	(e)131	26.7	11.5	2.2	0.1	34.1	6.9	15.1	12.0
Nepal - Népal	1995	(e)1 292	9.8	2.3	9.5	22.3	37.1	8.6	15.0	13.4
	2005	(e)2 243	15.2	3.8	24.6	4.4	51.8	10.0	12.6	29.2
	2010	5 128	12.1	1.4	15.7	14.4	56.5	9.3	24.5	22.7
Netherlands - Pays-Bas	1995	(e)185 240	14.0	2.3	7.2	4.1	70.9	12.1	33.2	25.5
	2005	(e)363 675	8.8	1.5	17.4	3.8	62.5	11.0	32.4	19.2
	2010	(e)516 429	10.7	1.7	19.3	4.5	63.8	12.1	31.2	20.5
Netherlands Antilles - Antilles néerlandaises	1995	(e)1 841	13.6	0.7	32.2	0.6	50.2	3.8	23.0	23.4
	2005	(e)1 950	3.8	0.2	76.5	1.8	16.6	2.5	5.7	8.3
	2010	(e)2 687	6.9	0.3	54.4	2.1	33.3	3.8	12.6	16.9

For sources and notes, see end of table.

Pour les sources et les notes, se reporter à la fin du tableau.

3.1 Country trade structure by product group
Imports

3.1 Structure du commerce des pays par groupes de produits
Importations

Country or territory Pays ou territoires	Year Année	Total value (millions of dollars) Valeur totale (millions de dollars)	By main SITC Revision 3 product group (percentage) Par principaux groupes de produits de la CTCI Révision 3 (en pourcentage)						Of which: / dont :		
			All food items Produits alimentaires	Agricultural raw materials Matières premières agricoles	Fuels Combus-tibles	Ores, metals, precious stones and non monetary gold Minerais, métaux, pierres précieuses et or (non monétaire)	Manu-factured goods Articles manu-facturés	Chemical products Produits chimiques	Machinery and transport equipment Machines et matériel de transport	Other manu-factured goods Articles manu-facturés divers
			0 + 1 + 22 + 4	2 - (22 + 27 + 28)	3	27 + 28 + 68 + 667 + 971	5 + 6 +7 + 8 -(667 + 68)	5	7	6 + 8 - (667 + 68)
New Caledonia - Nouvelle-Calédonie	1995	(e)967	15.4	1.0	11.2	0.8	69.9	9.0	33.7	27.2
	2005	(e)1 774	13.2	0.8	15.8	1.0	68.9	9.2	35.0	24.7
	2010	(e)3 303	11.0	0.7	15.9	1.2	56.6	7.7	27.9	21.0
New Zealand - Nouvelle-Zélande	1995	13 958	7.4	1.2	5.3	3.7	82.4	13.1	42.2	27.1
	2005	26 232	7.7	0.8	12.1	2.5	76.7	11.3	40.7	24.7
	2010	30 158	10.6	0.6	15.3	2.8	70.0	11.7	33.3	25.0
Nicaragua	1995	1 009	17.9	0.9	17.9	0.6	62.6	17.5	23.1	22.0
	2005	2 536	13.2	0.5	18.2	0.4	64.9	17.5	23.0	24.4
	2010	4 191	16.4	0.7	21.7	0.3	60.8	18.1	21.8	20.9
Niger	1995	345	28.2	2.5	8.1	2.6	57.8	10.2	23.5	24.2
	2005	(e)943	26.1	4.2	9.5	1.4	57.9	7.8	25.0	25.1
	2010	(e)2 290	20.8	2.4	12.3	1.4	62.8	8.7	29.5	24.6
Nigeria - Nigéria	1995	(e)8 222	11.6	0.9	5.2	1.0	79.5	17.6	34.9	27.1
	2005	(e)21 314	18.5	0.7	4.1	1.9	74.9	12.6	39.3	22.9
	2010	(e)44 235	13.8	0.7	4.7	1.5	78.5	11.1	43.9	23.5
Niue - Nioué (1)	1995	4	4.0	0.3	0.1	0.1	91.4	3.4	22.8	65.2
	2005	8	13.1	2.1	12.7	5.6	66.3	4.6	29.5	32.2
	2010	(e)5	59.1	0.1	0.5	0.0	31.0	1.7	2.6	27.6
Norway - Norvège	1995	32 706	6.8	2.7	2.9	6.8	79.9	9.6	37.7	32.7
	2005	55 488	6.8	1.9	4.2	7.8	78.9	9.4	39.5	30.1
	2010	77 252	7.9	1.5	6.5	7.9	75.1	9.6	38.5	26.9
Occupied Palestinian territory - (1) Territoire palestinien occupé	2005	(e)2 667	23.3	1.2	31.0	2.7	41.6	8.1	13.6	19.8
	2010	(e)4 385	25.9	0.8	8.7	2.9	61.4	16.9	20.3	24.3
Oman	1995	4 249	18.4	0.7	1.3	4.7	71.9	6.3	42.3	23.3
	2005	8 970	11.4	0.6	3.0	4.2	77.2	7.6	48.8	20.8
	2010	(e)18 160	13.0	0.7	6.5	4.4	74.5	9.7	43.4	21.4
Pakistan	1995	11 704	17.5	5.5	16.1	4.0	56.7	17.0	28.9	10.8
	2005	25 097	10.4	4.2	21.1	5.1	59.0	16.3	29.4	13.3
	2010	37 537	13.0	4.9	30.4	3.3	48.4	15.4	20.5	12.5
Palau - Palaos (1)	1995	49	26.3	3.2	4.2	0.3	59.7	3.8	26.9	29.1
	2005	108	25.8	2.1	2.1	2.4	58.9	5.2	25.9	27.8
	2010	113	36.4	1.3	0.1	0.3	54.5	2.8	33.0	18.7
Panama	1995	2 511	3.2	0.2	4.4	0.7	89.6	5.5	62.0	22.1
	2005	4 155	4.3	0.2	13.9	0.5	74.1	6.7	48.8	18.7
	2010	(e)9 145	3.1	0.1	11.0	0.3	78.0	11.8	46.5	19.7
Papua New Guinea - Papouasie-Nouvelle-Guinée	1995	(e)1 452	14.3	0.8	10.8	0.6	69.8	6.4	39.4	24.0
	2005	(e)1 611	16.7	0.7	26.0	0.8	55.8	7.4	27.4	21.0
	2010	(e)3 619	22.4	0.7	23.2	0.8	52.9	7.7	24.8	20.4
Paraguay	1995	3 136	18.5	0.2	6.5	0.7	74.0	9.0	42.3	22.7
	2005	3 274	8.7	0.8	16.4	1.0	73.1	16.8	32.9	23.4
	2010	10 040	7.5	0.6	11.9	0.6	79.4	13.2	43.0	23.2
Peru - Pérou	1995	7 584	13.5	1.9	8.8	0.8	75.0	13.2	39.2	22.6
	2005	12 502	11.4	1.8	19.8	1.0	66.0	16.1	28.3	21.6
	2010	29 880	10.4	1.7	14.2	1.3	72.5	14.7	35.0	22.8
Philippines	1995	28 487	8.3	2.2	9.2	3.2	57.8	9.2	32.5	16.2
	2005	49 487	6.9	0.9	13.2	2.6	76.4	7.3	57.8	11.3
	2010	58 468	11.0	0.6	16.9	4.6	66.8	9.6	47.1	10.2
Poland - Pologne	1995	29 019	9.6	3.2	9.1	3.3	74.4	14.9	29.9	29.5
	2005	101 539	6.1	1.8	11.4	2.9	75.5	14.0	35.1	26.4
	2010	(e)174 310	7.7	1.8	11.3	3.5	75.6	14.8	33.8	27.0
Portugal	1995	33 565	13.4	3.4	7.2	2.6	72.5	10.0	34.4	28.1
	2005	61 167	11.1	1.5	13.4	3.5	68.7	10.5	33.3	24.9
	2010	75 214	13.5	1.6	13.8	2.8	66.4	12.5	29.3	24.6

For sources and notes, see end of table.

Pour les sources et les notes, se reporter à la fin du tableau.

3.1 Country trade structure
by product group
Imports

3.1 Structure du commerce des pays
par groupes de produits
Importations

Country or territory / Pays ou territoires	Year / Année	Total value (millions of dollars) / Valeur totale (millions de dollars)	By main SITC Revision 3 product group (percentage) / Par principaux groupes de produits de la CTCI Révision 3 (en pourcentage)				Manufactured goods / Articles manufacturés	Of which: / dont :		
			All food items / Produits alimentaires	Agricultural raw materials / Matières premières agricoles	Fuels / Combustibles	Ores, metals, precious stones and non monetary gold / Minerais, métaux, pierres précieuses et or (non monétaire)		Chemical products / Produits chimiques	Machinery and transport equipment / Machines et matériel de transport	Other manufactured goods / Articles manufacturés divers
			0 + 1 + 22 + 4	2 - (22 + 27 + 28)	3	27 + 28 + 68 + 667 + 971	5 + 6 + 7 + 8 -(667 + 68)	5	7	6 + 8 - (667 + 68)
Qatar	1995	(e)3 398	9.4	0.6	0.4	2.5	87.0	5.0	48.3	33.7
	2005	(e)10 001	6.6	0.7	0.2	2.2	89.2	6.6	49.1	11.5
	2010	(e)22 000	7.2	0.6	0.7	3.4	88.1	6.4	51.6	30.1
Republic of Moldova - République de Moldova	1995	841	10.6	2.3	43.4	1.6	41.6	8.5	14.6	18.5
	2005	2 292	12.4	3.4	17.4	7.7	56.6	11.4	18.0	27.2
	2010	3 855	15.8	1.8	14.1	2.9	61.6	13.1	20.9	27.6
Romania - Roumanie	1995	10 278	8.5	2.3	21.4	3.6	63.3	10.6	24.8	28.0
	2005	40 463	6.0	1.0	13.9	2.7	76.0	10.2	33.2	32.6
	2010	62 007	7.7	1.4	10.0	2.8	75.3	12.9	34.4	28.0
Russian Federation - Fédération de Russie	1995	(e)68 863	19.9	0.9	2.3	2.8	48.8	6.7	21.9	20.2
	2005	137 977	15.4	1.0	1.4	2.7	78.0	11.4	40.0	26.5
	2010	273 614	15.2	1.1	1.7	1.8	78.9	12.8	40.6	25.5
Rwanda	1995	(e)241	27.3	2.7	10.0	2.0	56.5	7.5	30.1	18.8
	2005	(e)471	14.6	2.1	10.8	2.3	68.2	14.7	27.7	25.8
	2010	(e)1 431	17.9	2.1	5.9	1.9	71.8	16.9	26.4	28.5
Saint Helena - Sainte-Hélène (1)	1995	(e)25	21.5	1.5	16.8	2.4	61.9	7.0	32.8	22.1
	2005	(e)61	11.9	1.9	15.5	13.6	56.4	3.3	37.7	15.4
	2010	(e)63	15.7	0.7	24.4	18.8	39.6	4.3	15.8	19.5
Saint Kitts and Nevis - Saint-Kitts-et-Nevis	1995	(e)132	21.1	2.5	4.3	0.9	71.2	8.3	27.8	35.1
	2005	(e)210	18.6	1.6	8.8	0.8	70.4	6.0	31.2	32.3
	2010	(e)228	19.2	2.1	7.0	1.0	70.6	7.0	26.4	37.3
Saint Lucia - Sainte-Lucie	1995	306	20.4	1.8	23.6	0.7	51.4	7.7	17.4	26.3
	2005	486	15.1	1.3	41.1	1.0	39.7	4.8	15.4	19.5
	2010	(e)579	5.8	0.5	77.0	0.3	16.5	2.2	5.8	8.4
Saint Pierre and Miquelon - (1) Saint-Pierre-et-Miquelon	1995	47	14.5	1.4	7.8	0.8	69.8	8.4	31.5	29.9
	2005	(e)50	22.5	1.6	2.6	0.3	68.6	8.4	32.3	27.9
	2010	(e)59	21.9	1.5	0.5	0.6	74.5	8.5	38.6	27.5
Saint Vincent and the Grenadines - Saint-Vincent-et-les Grenadines	1995	(e)134	22.5	2.6	6.0	0.5	68.3	12.9	17.7	37.7
	2005	240	21.5	2.4	13.9	0.6	61.7	9.2	22.1	30.4
	2010	379	22.2	1.9	21.9	0.7	53.3	7.2	20.2	26.0
Samoa	1995	(e)95	15.7	0.9	7.4	0.3	74.4	5.1	47.2	22.1
	2005	239	20.3	2.2	14.1	0.7	47.3	5.2	16.5	25.6
	2010	310	23.8	2.0	15.4	1.1	56.3	5.7	29.6	21.0
Sao Tome and Principe - Sao Tomé-et-Principe	1995	(e)29	25.3	0.4	1.9	0.5	71.5	6.6	39.0	25.9
	2005	(e)50	38.5	0.9	20.2	0.2	40.1	4.5	21.3	14.4
	2010	112	29.8	0.8	16.1	1.1	52.0	5.1	27.2	19.7
Saudi Arabia - Arabie saoudite	1995	(e)28 085	16.1	1.2	0.2	7.0	75.0	9.6	35.6	29.7
	2005	(e)59 510	14.6	0.7	0.2	5.4	79.0	9.7	45.2	24.0
	2010	(e)103 635	15.9	0.7	0.2	5.4	77.8	9.4	42.3	26.1
Senegal - Sénégal	1995	(e)1 412	28.2	1.9	8.7	1.4	46.5	12.1	15.7	18.8
	2005	(e)3 498	26.6	1.8	22.4	2.0	46.6	9.1	21.0	16.5
	2010	(e)4 782	21.2	1.6	30.0	1.7	45.1	8.0	19.9	17.2
Serbia - Serbie	2010	16 734	5.9	1.7	17.8	5.8	51.8	12.5	17.9	21.4
Serbia and Montenegro - Serbie-et-Monténégro	1995	(e)2 666	14.2	4.1	13.9	7.1	59.8	14.3	19.4	26.1
	2005	(e)10 461	7.1	1.5	19.4	6.2	65.5	14.0	25.7	25.8
Seychelles	1995	255	21.2	1.4	17.4	0.7	59.1	6.5	27.0	25.5
	2005	675	21.5	1.0	23.5	0.4	48.2	4.3	24.6	19.3
	2010	(e)960	21.9	2.1	24.5	0.7	50.8	4.3	25.4	21.1
Sierra Leone (1)	1995	(e)134	31.1	3.0	10.0	0.9	53.4	7.5	26.9	19.0
	2005	(e)345	21.0	7.0	38.6	1.7	31.7	4.9	13.1	13.7
	2010	(e)773	23.0	7.4	39.5	1.6	28.5	4.5	11.7	12.3

For sources and notes, see end of table.

Pour les sources et les notes, se reporter à la fin du tableau.

Country or territory / Pays ou territoires	Year / Année	Total value (millions of dollars) / Valeur totale (millions de dollars)	By main SITC Revision 3 product group (percentage) / Par principaux groupes de produits de la CTCI Révision 3 (en pourcentage)							
			All food items / Produits alimentaires	Agricultural raw materials / Matières premières agricoles	Fuels / Combustibles	Ores, metals, precious stones and non monetary gold / Minerais, métaux, pierres précieuses et or (non monétaire)	Manu-factured goods / Articles manu-facturés	Of which: / dont :		
								Chemical products / Produits chimiques	Machinery and transport equipment / Machines et matériel de transport	Other manu-factured goods / Articles manu-facturés divers
			0 + 1 + 22 + 4	2 - (22 + 27 + 28)	3	27 + 28 + 68 + 667 + 971	5 + 6 +7 + 8 -(667 + 68)	5	7	6 + 8 - (667 + 68)
Singapore - Singapour	1995	124 503	4.6	0.9	8.1	2.9	82.6	6.5	57.9	18.3
	2005	200 050	2.8	0.4	17.7	3.1	75.1	6.2	55.8	13.1
	2010	310 791	3.2	0.3	26.1	3.0	64.7	6.7	46.3	11.7
Slovakia - Slovaquie	1995	9 225	7.9	2.5	11.2	5.3	61.6	12.8	26.7	22.0
	2005	34 226	6.1	1.3	13.2	3.4	75.3	9.8	37.8	27.7
	2010	65 916	6.4	1.4	12.5	4.0	75.6	8.4	42.7	24.5
Slovenia - Slovénie	1995	9 492	7.8	4.6	6.6	4.4	73.8	12.1	33.8	28.0
	2005	19 626	6.1	2.6	10.6	5.8	74.8	12.8	32.6	29.3
	2010	(e)30 008	7.0	2.8	11.4	5.9	60.6	12.0	26.4	22.2
Solomon Islands - Îles Salomon (1)	1995	(e)154	12.4	0.6	15.4	0.6	67.6	4.1	34.2	29.2
	2005	(e)185	16.3	0.5	23.8	0.8	48.9	5.3	24.4	19.3
	2010	(e)402	21.5	0.7	22.6	0.6	50.3	5.5	25.9	18.9
Somalia - Somalie (1)	1995	(e)268	65.5	2.7	1.3	0.1	31.2	8.3	7.3	15.6
	2005	(e)626	48.3	13.1	0.8	0.1	36.0	6.6	6.7	22.7
	2010	(e)955	70.1	1.6	0.3	0.1	27.8	2.4	9.8	15.5
South Africa - Afrique du Sud	1995	(e)30 979	15.4	3.1	6.3	3.8	71.4	11.9	41.9	17.6
	2005	(e)64 192	3.8	0.9	12.2	3.7	57.6	8.6	33.8	15.3
	2010	(e)96 249	4.0	0.8	16.3	2.6	60.4	9.9	20.5	14.9
Spain - Espagne	1995	113 399	13.6	3.0	8.3	4.3	70.8	12.1	35.6	23.1
	2005	289 611	9.2	1.4	14.0	3.5	71.4	11.6	37.9	22.0
	2010	(e)309 139	10.4	1.4	17.9	4.2	66.2	12.4	31.3	22.4
Sri Lanka	1995	(e)5 185	14.8	1.6	2.2	5.2	73.1	9.2	24.9	38.9
	2005	8 307	12.4	1.2	13.4	7.1	65.8	10.0	20.2	35.6
	2010	12 354	15.2	1.4	16.7	4.8	61.8	11.2	21.4	29.2
Sudan - Soudan	1995	(e)1 185	20.0	1.9	10.4	0.5	66.9	10.7	24.1	32.1
	2005	7 367	11.9	0.6	4.6	0.9	79.4	8.5	43.5	27.4
	2010	(e)9 960	16.4	0.7	1.4	1.2	80.3	8.5	41.8	30.0
Suriname	1995	583	14.0	0.1	11.8	1.2	73.0	16.0	35.7	21.3
	2005	1 050	9.5	0.0	17.2	0.3	41.0	3.9	23.1	13.9
	2010	1 397	15.2	0.1	18.9	1.7	63.7	11.6	28.0	24.1
Swaziland	1995	(e)1 054	21.5	3.4	7.0	2.2	66.0	13.2	24.5	28.2
	2005	(e)1 904	16.8	1.1	11.7	0.9	68.6	20.9	18.8	28.9
	2010	(e)1 703	20.8	1.4	14.5	1.7	61.5	15.5	18.0	28.0
Sweden - Suède	1995	61 647	6.7	2.2	5.8	3.8	80.0	10.7	41.8	27.5
	2005	111 351	7.4	1.6	11.7	3.3	73.3	10.3	38.6	24.3
	2010	148 421	8.8	1.4	13.4	3.7	69.0	10.8	35.8	22.3
Switzerland - Suisse	1995	80 152	6.4	2.0	2.9	5.6	83.1	14.6	33.4	35.0
	2005	126 574	5.4	1.1	7.2	5.8	80.5	21.7	28.5	30.3
	2010	175 933	5.8	1.0	7.4	6.2	79.6	21.6	26.9	31.1
Syrian Arab Republic - République arabe syrienne	1995	(e)4 709	16.7	3.3	1.1	1.3	75.6	10.2	31.6	33.9
	2005	(e)10 862	14.3	2.6	10.8	2.3	67.9	17.2	26.2	24.5
	2010	(e)18 833	15.2	2.4	20.5	3.1	58.7	14.4	21.2	23.1
Tajikistan - Tadjikistan	1995	(e)810	25.4	0.9	14.5	12.1	46.4	7.3	26.5	12.6
	2005	(e)1 330	12.5	1.7	24.2	13.9	43.0	13.1	14.4	15.5
	2010	(e)2 658	17.3	1.2	17.1	8.2	53.9	8.6	13.2	32.1
TFYR of Macedonia - LERY de Macédoine	1995	1 719	17.4	3.3	11.6	3.0	54.2	11.9	19.5	22.8
	2005	3 228	12.7	1.3	19.2	3.2	63.6	10.3	17.4	35.8
	2010	(e)5 462	12.5	1.3	16.2	4.0	66.0	11.0	21.3	33.8
Thailand - Thaïlande	1995	70 781	3.8	4.1	6.7	5.4	78.7	10.5	47.5	20.7
	2005	118 164	4.0	2.0	17.7	6.8	68.2	10.2	38.0	20.0
	2010	182 393	4.7	1.9	17.4	9.6	66.5	10.9	35.3	20.3
Timor-Leste (1)	2005	(e)102	20.0	2.4	26.4	1.6	42.5	5.2	17.6	19.6
	2010	(e)270	25.8	0.3	3.4	0.5	69.4	28.2	14.9	26.3

For sources and notes, see end of table.

Pour les sources et les notes, se reporter à la fin du tableau.

Country or territory / Pays ou territoires	Year / Année	Total value (millions of dollars) / Valeur totale (millions de dollars)	By main SITC Revision 3 product group (percentage) / Par principaux groupes de produits de la CTCI Révision 3 (en pourcentage)					Of which: / dont :		
			All food items / Produits alimentaires	Agricultural raw materials / Matières premières agricoles	Fuels / Combustibles	Ores, metals, precious stones and non monetary gold / Minerais, métaux, pierres précieuses et or (non monétaire)	Manu-factured goods / Articles manu-facturés	Chemical products / Produits chimiques	Machinery and transport equipment / Machines et matériel de transport	Other manu-factured goods / Articles manu-facturés divers
			0 + 1 + 22 + 4	2 - (22 + 27 + 28)	3	27 + 28 + 68 + 667 + 971	5 + 6 +7 + 8 -(667 + 68)	5	7	6 + 8 - (667 + 68)
Togo	1995	556	19.8	2.6	16.5	0.9	59.7	8.0	16.1	35.7
	2005	(e)1 061	16.7	1.2	23.2	1.0	55.5	8.5	15.1	31.9
	2010	(e)1 496	14.2	3.0	28.1	0.7	54.1	7.7	12.3	34.1
Tokelau - Tokélaou (1)	1995	(e)1	4.7	3.4	..	47.5	43.4	3.0	15.3	25.1
	2005	(e)0	1.1	25.7	0.4	0.6	69.0	18.1	32.2	18.7
	2010	(e)0	17.6	0.3	0.0	24.9	54.7	7.2	38.3	9.2
Tonga	1995	(e)77	33.3	3.8	4.3	0.7	53.8	6.6	25.4	21.8
	2005	(e)120	22.5	1.7	18.6	0.4	34.0	3.2	12.6	18.1
	2010	(e)159	37.2	1.5	6.7	0.6	51.5	6.4	26.4	18.7
Trinidad and Tobago - Trinité-et-Tobago	1995	1 724	15.1	0.3	0.5	4.6	59.4	6.5	32.7	20.2
	2005	5 694	9.0	0.6	34.8	4.3	51.2	7.3	26.4	17.4
	2010	(e)6 483	13.2	0.8	21.1	6.3	58.5	9.3	27.7	21.5
Tunisia - Tunisie	1995	7 903	12.5	4.2	7.2	3.3	72.8	9.1	25.9	37.8
	2005	13 174	8.5	2.6	13.7	3.2	72.0	10.5	28.8	32.7
	2010	(e)22 051	8.5	2.1	10.9	4.4	74.2	9.9	31.0	33.3
Turkey - Turquie	1995	35 707	7.0	5.6	12.9	5.9	68.6	15.0	32.2	21.5
	2005	116 774	2.8	2.7	13.5	9.2	66.4	13.8	32.4	20.2
	2010	185 541	4.0	2.9	14.4	9.4	62.5	13.5	29.0	19.9
Turkmenistan - Turkménistan	1995	(e)1 365	29.5	0.5	1.9	1.5	65.0	9.6	27.7	27.7
	2005	(e)2 947	7.2	0.6	0.8	0.7	89.2	7.9	55.3	26.0
	2010	(e)5 600	8.5	1.1	0.9	1.0	86.1	8.9	45.4	31.9
Turks and Caicos Islands - Îles Turques et Caïques	1995	(e)51	11.7	1.7	0.9	0.3	59.7	20.8	16.9	22.0
	2005	(e)304	14.0	2.8	10.3	1.4	68.5	5.0	30.6	32.9
	2010	(e)375	14.4	2.0	8.1	1.6	63.0	4.9	23.8	34.3
Tuvalu	1995	(e)6	31.7	3.1	1.4	..	60.1	2.2	38.3	19.6
	2005	(e)13	18.4	1.2	10.4	0.2	56.7	1.7	45.3	9.8
	2010	(e)16	13.6	1.3	5.3	0.4	75.4	1.7	61.1	12.6
Uganda - Ouganda	1995	(e)1 038	15.3	2.5	4.2	2.2	75.4	11.7	30.7	33.0
	2005	(e)2 054	13.2	1.2	17.2	1.2	66.4	14.6	25.4	26.4
	2010	(e)4 664	9.8	1.2	17.7	1.4	69.2	13.2	31.0	25.0
Ukraine	1995	(e)16 052	7.9	2.4	47.8	3.1	37.9	6.7	17.0	14.2
	2005	36 122	7.2	1.3	29.5	4.3	57.0	11.8	26.4	18.7
	2010	60 737	9.2	1.1	32.3	3.9	52.9	14.2	19.5	19.2
United Arab Emirates - Émirats arabes unis	1995	(e)20 984	10.0	0.9	1.6	2.6	83.6	6.3	36.9	40.3
	2005	(e)80 814	6.3	0.5	3.8	12.7	73.8	5.4	40.6	27.7
	2010	(e)180 726	8.2	0.5	2.3	22.4	65.0	6.0	32.6	26.4
United Kingdom - Royaume-Uni	1995	261 456	10.1	2.4	3.5	5.2	78.1	10.3	41.3	26.6
	2005	515 782	8.5	1.3	8.3	4.1	70.4	10.4	35.8	24.3
	2010	558 647	9.6	1.2	11.3	5.1	67.1	12.1	31.3	23.7
United Republic of Tanzania - République-Unie de Tanzanie	1995	(e)1 653	14.4	1.7	5.0	3.0	75.0	13.7	34.7	26.6
	2005	3 247	10.7	1.3	13.8	2.3	70.3	15.2	29.8	25.4
	2010	8 013	9.9	1.1	21.8	1.3	65.4	13.6	28.9	23.0
United States - États-Unis	1995	770 821	4.8	2.1	8.2	3.8	78.1	5.5	46.4	26.2
	2005	1 732 321	4.2	1.3	17.2	3.4	70.6	7.6	38.3	24.7
	2010	1 966 497	5.0	1.0	18.4	3.9	68.8	9.0	37.0	22.8
Uruguay	1995	2 866	10.4	4.0	10.1	1.2	74.3	15.3	34.5	24.5
	2005	3 879	8.1	3.1	24.3	1.6	62.9	19.4	23.2	20.3
	2010	(e)8 619	9.8	2.4	24.1	1.2	62.5	17.7	26.3	18.5
Uzbekistan - Ouzbékistan	1995	2 900	19.6	0.4	2.3	2.8	73.3	8.9	41.7	22.7
	2005	3 666	7.7	3.2	2.8	2.9	80.9	11.1	43.5	26.3
	2010	8 384	10.8	4.0	9.7	4.5	69.8	10.8	33.0	26.0

For sources and notes, see end of table.

Pour les sources et les notes, se reporter à la fin du tableau.

156

| Country or territory / Pays ou territoires | Year / Année | Total value (millions of dollars) / Valeur totale (millions de dollars) | By main SITC Revision 3 product group (percentage) / Par principaux groupes de produits de la CTCI Révision 3 (en pourcentage) | | | | | Of which: / dont : | | |
			All food items / Produits alimentaires	Agricultural raw materials / Matières premières agricoles	Fuels / Combustibles	Ores, metals, precious stones and non monetary gold / Minerais, métaux, pierres précieuses et or (non monétaire)	Manufactured goods / Articles manufacturés	Chemical products / Produits chimiques	Machinery and transport equipment / Machines et matériel de transport	Other manufactured goods / Articles manufacturés divers
			0 + 1 + 22 + 4	2 - (22 + 27 + 28)	3	27 + 28 + 68 + 667 + 971	5 + 6 +7 + 8 -(667 + 68)	5	7	6 + 8 - (667 + 68)
Vanuatu	1995	(e)55	8.0	0.3	2.3	0.3	80.6	2.9	59.8	17.9
	2005	(o)110	18.0	0.7	17.9	1.0	61.5	6.8	33.8	20.9
	2010	(e)284	20.2	1.0	17.3	0.8	60.6	7.3	29.9	23.5
Venezuela (Bolivarian Rep. of) - Venezuela (Rép. bolivarienne du)	1995	10 791	13.8	4.3	1.3	3.5	75.5	15.2	38.7	21.6
	2005	21 848	10.5	1.1	1.2	1.6	85.0	13.7	48.5	22.7
	2010	(e)36 787	15.6	1.0	2.8	1.6	78.9	14.8	41.1	23.0
Viet Nam	1995	(e)8 155	4.9	2.4	10.3	2.4	75.9	16.7	28.3	30.9
	2005	36 761	6.3	3.7	14.6	5.4	69.7	14.4	25.1	30.2
	2010	(e)83 779	7.3	3.2	11.5	5.7	72.3	13.4	29.0	29.9
Wallis and Futuna Islands - Îles Wallis-et-Futuna	1995	(e)14	32.7	1.2	4.5	0.2	60.8	8.3	38.3	14.2
	2005	(e)51	27.0	0.8	11.2	1.2	55.8	11.1	22.5	22.2
	2010	(e)57	33.0	1.7	3.8	1.1	56.2	12.0	19.2	24.9
Yemen - Yémen	1995	(e)1 582	32.2	1.8	9.9	1.0	54.4	7.3	21.0	26.1
	2005	(e)5 400	24.9	0.7	20.1	1.1	49.7	8.5	19.9	21.3
	2010	(e)9 746	30.2	0.9	16.7	1.0	50.0	7.6	20.4	21.9
Zambia - Zambie	1995	708	10.8	1.9	8.6	2.7	75.4	12.7	39.8	22.9
	2005	2 558	7.4	1.1	10.3	2.9	76.6	19.0	31.7	26.0
	2010	5 321	4.7	0.5	11.7	21.4	61.2	16.7	28.8	16.7
Zimbabwe	1995	(e)2 659	8.2	2.4	6.7	4.6	76.9	17.6	38.9	20.4
	2005	(e)2 350	13.8	1.6	12.6	25.3	46.0	10.8	20.2	15.0
	2010	(e)3 700	19.4	1.6	10.5	14.1	52.6	11.0	21.6	20.0

Sources:
- UN DESA Statistics Division, *COMTRADE* database
- UNCTAD secretariat calculations

Notes:

(1) It is recognized that the structure of trade and partner distribution for certain countries and years might vary. In this regard, reader should know the coverage and limitations of the main principal data used in this table. For further information, please visit http://comtrade.un.org/db/help/uReadMeFirst.aspx.

Sources :
- ONU DAES Division de statistique, base de données *COMTRADE*
- Calculs du secrétariat de la CNUCED

Notes :

(1) Il est reconnu que la structure du commerce et la distribution au niveau partenaire pour certains pays et sur certaines années peuvent varier. À cet égard, le lecteur devrait connaître la couverture ainsi que les limites des données principales utilisées dans ce tableau. Pour de plus amples renseignements, veuillez visiter http://comtrade.un.org/db/help/uReadMeFirst.aspx.

Products ranked by average 2009-2010 values SITC Revision 3 (3-digit level) Produits classés d'après la moyenne des valeurs de 2009-2010 CTCI révision 3 (positions à 3 chiffres)	2000			2010			Growth rates (%) Taux d'accroissement (%) 2000-2010	
	Value (millions of dollars) Valeur (millions de dollars)	% of the country grouping exports En % des exportations du groupe de pays	% of world product exports En % des exportations mondiales des produits	Value (millions of dollars) Valeur (millions de dollars)	% of the country grouping exports En % des exportations du groupe de pays	% of world product exports En % des exportations mondiales des produits	Value Valeur	Difference from world Différence par rapport au monde
All commodity groups	**6 367 875**	**100.00**	**100.00**	**15 147 680**	**100.00**	**100.00**	**10.98**	—
333 Crude petroleum & bituminous oil	374 475	5.88	100.00	1 209 047	7.98	100.00	16.96	—
334 Heavy petroleum & bituminous oil	162 806	2.56	100.00	652 817	4.31	100.00	19.61	—
781 Passenger cars and race cars	304 100	4.70	100.00	500 111	3.72	100.00	6.04	—
776 Valves tubes; diodes, transistors	308 708	4.85	100.00	527 518	3.48	100.00	7.09	—
764 Telecommunicate equipment part nes	223 421	3.51	100.00	453 518	2.99	100.00	9.45	—
542 Medicines including veterinary	76 065	1.19	100.00	319 283	2.11	100.00	15.56	—
752 Computer equipment nes	198 691	3.12	100.00	323 616	2.14	100.00	6.05	—
784 Motor vehicle parts and accessories	142 527	2.24	100.00	302 078	1.99	100.00	8.68	—
343 Natural gas, liquefied or not	68 195	1.07	100.00	229 097	1.51	100.00	15.92	—
759 Office equipment part & accessories	164 256	2.58	100.00	205 710	1.36	100.00	3.43	—
772 Electrical circuit equipment	96 223	1.51	100.00	204 150	1.35	100.00	9.60	—
778 Electrical machinery apparatus nes	103 169	1.62	100.00	201 332	1.33	100.00	8.52	—
793 Ships boats floating structures	40 447	0.64	100.00	159 214	1.05	100.00	16.15	—
874 Measure analyze control device nes	73 283	1.15	100.00	154 063	1.02	100.00	8.77	—
971 Gold non-monetary excluding ores	23 155	0.36	100.00	150 121	0.99	100.00	22.97	—
728 Special industrial machine part nes	74 519	1.17	100.00	157 652	1.04	100.00	10.06	—
541 Pharmaceuticals excluding medicines	31 719	0.50	100.00	137 762	0.91	100.00	16.58	—
792 Aircraft, spacecraft & equipment	100 570	1.58	100.00	135 702	0.90	100.00	4.83	—
821 Furniture part; bedding furnishing	61 406	0.96	100.00	133 002	0.88	100.00	9.27	—
713 Internal combustion engine part nes	69 075	1.08	100.00	139 595	0.92	100.00	8.44	—
845 Articles of apparel nes	65 617	1.03	100.00	124 335	0.82	100.00	7.89	—
699 Base metal manufactures nes	53 147	0.83	100.00	122 483	0.81	100.00	10.92	—
667 Pearls, precious semiprecious stone	55 930	0.88	100.00	125 916	0.83	100.00	9.49	—
682 Copper	32 891	0.52	100.00	131 138	0.87	100.00	18.84	—
893 Articles of plastic nes	53 969	0.85	100.00	116 371	0.77	100.00	9.13	—
641 Paper and paperboard	70 603	1.11	100.00	111 852	0.74	100.00	5.69	—
598 Miscellaneous chemical products nes	38 772	0.61	100.00	107 302	0.71	100.00	12.48	—
743 Gas pump, compressor, fan, filter	41 648	0.65	100.00	106 494	0.70	100.00	11.17	—
515 Organo-inorganic compound acid salt	46 644	0.73	100.00	100 223	0.66	100.00	8.93	—
684 Aluminium	50 234	0.79	100.00	109 544	0.72	100.00	9.97	—
321 Coal excluding non-agglomomerated	17 242	0.27	100.00	106 190	0.70	100.00	21.35	—
782 Goods and service vehicles	57 213	0.90	100.00	107 943	0.71	100.00	8.03	—
761 Television video receive project	28 645	0.45	100.00	99 523	0.66	100.00	15.63	—
741 Heating cooling equipment parts nes	41 380	0.65	100.00	93 928	0.62	100.00	11.20	—
851 Footwear	46 860	0.74	100.00	95 762	0.63	100.00	8.09	—
871 Optical instruments apparatus nes	14 613	0.23	100.00	100 236	0.66	100.00	25.99	—
894 Baby carriage toy game sport good	48 047	0.75	100.00	87 603	0.58	100.00	8.43	—
723 Civil engineering plant & equipment	32 616	0.51	100.00	94 975	0.63	100.00	14.14	—
575 Other plastics, in primary forms	33 872	0.53	100.00	95 116	0.63	100.00	12.42	—
773 Electrical distribute equipment nes	43 090	0.68	100.00	95 315	0.63	100.00	10.34	—
281 Iron ore and concentrates	9 481	0.15	100.00	106 872	0.71	100.00	29.46	—
775 Household equipment nes	36 144	0.57	100.00	85 163	0.56	100.00	9.93	—
582 Plastic sheet film foil & strips	33 336	0.52	100.00	84 993	0.56	100.00	11.27	—
716 Rotating electric plant parts nes	30 988	0.49	100.00	81 564	0.54	100.00	12.09	—
771 Electric power machine part excluding 716	37 042	0.58	100.00	85 130	0.56	100.00	10.86	—
714 Non-electric engines excluding 712, 713, and 718	47 775	0.75	100.00	76 157	0.50	100.00	5.96	—
872 Medical instruments appliances nes	26 728	0.42	100.00	77 910	0.51	100.00	12.10	—
679 Iron steel pipe tube fittings etc	22 290	0.35	100.00	75 600	0.50	100.00	16.85	—
897 Jewellery nes (667)	22 889	0.36	100.00	79 333	0.52	100.00	14.30	—
673 Flat iron non-alloy steel products	30 267	0.48	100.00	83 504	0.55	100.00	14.52	—
842 Female clothing, woven	44 379	0.70	100.00	74 426	0.49	100.00	6.20	—
511 Hydrocarbons nes; derivatives	23 920	0.38	100.00	82 072	0.54	100.00	15.41	—
057 Fruit nut (exc oil), fresh or dried	27 735	0.44	100.00	68 879	0.45	100.00	10.97	—
899 Manufactured articles nes	24 071	0.38	100.00	70 609	0.47	100.00	12.59	—
744 Mechanical handling equipment nes	29 504	0.46	100.00	66 950	0.44	100.00	11.93	—
625 Rubber for wheels, incl inner tube	24 839	0.39	100.00	71 957	0.48	100.00	12.83	—
553 Perfume toilet cosmetics, excluding soap	23 287	0.37	100.00	66 294	0.44	100.00	11.90	—
747 Pipe, boiler, tank & vat appliances	22 985	0.36	100.00	67 155	0.44	100.00	13.36	—
676 Iron steel bar rod section piling	23 305	0.37	100.00	70 404	0.46	100.00	15.73	—
112 Alcoholic beverages	29 255	0.46	100.00	63 250	0.42	100.00	9.17	—

For sources and notes, see end of table.

Pour les sources et les notes, se reporter à la fin du tableau.

Products ranked by average 2009-2010 values SITC Revision 3 (3-digit level) Produits classés d'après la moyenne des valeurs de 2009-2010 CTCI révision 3 (positions à 3 chiffres)	2000			2010			Growth rates (%) Taux d'accroissement (%) 2000-2010	
	Value (millions of dollars) Valeur (millions de dollars)	% of the country grouping exports En % des exportations du groupe de pays	% of world product exports En % des exportations mondiales des produits	Value (millions of dollars) Valeur (millions de dollars)	% of the country grouping exports En % des exportations du groupe de pays	% of world product exports En % des exportations mondiales des produits	Value Valeur	Difference from world Différence par rapport au monde
763 Sound TV recorder or reproducer	27 492	0.43	100.00	62 016	0.41	100.00	9.73	–
012 Meat nes, fresh chilled frozen	23 128	0.36	100.00	62 741	0.41	100.00	11.30	–
841 Male clothing, woven	43 434	0.68	100.00	61 366	0.41	100.00	4.71	–
571 Primary form ethylene polymers	19 784	0.31	100.00	65 742	0.43	100.00	15.29	–
898 Music instrument device recording	34 013	0.53	100.00	60 477	0.40	100.00	7.31	–
081 Animal feed excluding unmilled cereal	20 470	0.32	100.00	60 885	0.40	100.00	12.21	–
054 Vegetable & vegetable products nes	19 788	0.31	100.00	58 846	0.39	100.00	11.69	–
675 Flat rolled products of alloy steel	21 010	0.33	100.00	61 733	0.41	100.00	14.41	–
098 Edible products & preparations nes	17 722	0.28	100.00	51 931	0.34	100.00	12.50	–
222 Oil seed etc for soft oil	13 717	0.22	100.00	53 529	0.35	100.00	15.70	–
642 Cut paper and paperboard articles	28 954	0.45	100.00	51 326	0.34	100.00	7.29	–
034 Fish, fresh live chilled frozen	21 603	0.34	100.00	55 400	0.37	100.00	9.87	–
533 Pigment, paint, varnish & related	24 961	0.39	100.00	53 462	0.35	100.00	9.07	–
562 Manufactured fertilizer excluding crude	12 822	0.20	100.00	55 807	0.37	100.00	19.27	–
742 Liquid pump; liquid elevator parts	19 500	0.31	100.00	51 623	0.34	100.00	11.81	–
892 Printed matter	26 813	0.42	100.00	48 375	0.32	100.00	7.22	–
691 Iron steel aluminium structures nes	13 447	0.21	100.00	45 093	0.30	100.00	17.00	–
751 Office machines	14 304	0.22	100.00	50 002	0.33	100.00	17.91	–
745 Non-electrical machinery tool nes	23 067	0.36	100.00	48 399	0.32	100.00	9.21	–
674 Flat plated iron non-alloy steel	19 294	0.30	100.00	52 616	0.35	100.00	12.82	–
681 Silver, platinum, platinum metals	15 152	0.24	100.00	51 389	0.34	100.00	16.99	–
884 Optical goods fibres nes	19 376	0.30	100.00	48 806	0.32	100.00	11.24	–
651 Textile yarn	33 249	0.52	100.00	50 319	0.33	100.00	4.38	–
574 Polyacetals and polyesters, etc	19 074	0.30	100.00	49 950	0.33	100.00	11.62	–
514 Nitrogen function compounds	19 893	0.31	100.00	46 051	0.30	100.00	9.65	–
512 Alcohols, phenols; derivatives	14 911	0.23	100.00	50 859	0.34	100.00	14.08	–
844 Female clothing, knitted crocheted	18 070	0.28	100.00	45 845	0.30	100.00	10.89	–
522 Inorganic chemical elem oxide salt	16 544	0.26	100.00	47 962	0.32	100.00	13.61	–
658 Made-up textile articles nes	17 249	0.27	100.00	44 071	0.29	100.00	10.89	–
748 Mechanical transmission equipment	16 209	0.25	100.00	44 783	0.30	100.00	12.50	–
513 Carboxylic acid and compounds	16 994	0.27	100.00	46 050	0.30	100.00	11.10	–
283 Copper ores and concentrates	6 762	0.11	100.00	46 757	0.31	100.00	25.66	–
282 Ferrous iron & steel, waste & scrap	7 773	0.12	100.00	46 356	0.31	100.00	22.90	–
785 Motorcycles, mopeds and cycles	21 225	0.33	100.00	41 754	0.28	100.00	8.75	–
342 Liquefied propane and butane	16 855	0.26	100.00	41 994	0.28	100.00	13.22	–
657 Special yarn and textile fabric etc	22 198	0.35	100.00	41 469	0.27	100.00	7.23	–
048 Cereal & preparation flour starch	13 620	0.21	100.00	38 385	0.25	100.00	12.26	–
251 Pulp and waste paper	24 345	0.38	100.00	44 412	0.29	100.00	8.12	–
695 Tools for use in hand or in machine	20 713	0.33	100.00	41 689	0.28	100.00	8.29	–
831 Case bag: storage travel shopping	16 476	0.26	100.00	40 708	0.27	100.00	10.82	–
774 Electrodiagnostic equipment	14 451	0.23	100.00	38 310	0.25	100.00	10.94	–
653 Man-made woven fabrics	31 290	0.49	100.00	36 778	0.24	100.00	2.44	–
292 Crude vegetable materials nes	14 911	0.23	100.00	36 699	0.24	100.00	9.86	–
554 Soaps cleansers polishes	13 074	0.21	100.00	35 448	0.23	100.00	11.49	–
061 Sugar, mollasses and honey	10 200	0.16	100.00	39 048	0.26	100.00	13.17	–
422 Fixed veg fat and oil, excluding "soft"	6 438	0.10	100.00	37 974	0.25	100.00	21.47	–
885 Watches and clocks	19 896	0.31	100.00	36 890	0.24	100.00	7.10	–
041 Wheat meslin, incl spelt, unmilled	14 182	0.22	100.00	32 912	0.22	100.00	11.50	–
664 Glass	16 786	0.26	100.00	34 635	0.23	100.00	8.67	–
351 Electric current	10 052	0.16	100.00	32 928	0.22	100.00	14.46	–
288 Non ferrous base metal waste nes	8 900	0.14	100.00	39 720	0.26	100.00	19.61	–
011 Beef, fresh chilled frozen	14 447	0.23	100.00	34 720	0.23	100.00	10.93	–
022 Milk products, excluding butter & cheese	14 327	0.22	100.00	35 225	0.23	100.00	10.72	–
672 Ingots, Iron steel primary products	11 657	0.18	100.00	38 471	0.25	100.00	15.60	–
248 Wood simply worked, railway sleeper	26 666	0.42	100.00	35 167	0.23	100.00	3.72	–
335 Residual petroleum products nes	9 141	0.14	100.00	36 641	0.24	100.00	17.56	–
516 Other organic chemicals	14 393	0.23	100.00	35 475	0.23	100.00	10.84	–
671 Pig & sponge iron, ferro alloys etc	9 442	0.15	100.00	38 648	0.26	100.00	18.78	–
783 Road motor vehicles nes	16 198	0.25	100.00	33 971	0.22	100.00	10.46	–
634 Veneer, plywood & other wood nes	17 380	0.27	100.00	30 696	0.20	100.00	7.21	–

For sources and notes, see end of table.

Pour les sources et les notes, se reporter à la fin du tableau.

Products ranked by average 2009-2010 values SITC Revision 3 (3-digit level) / Produits classés d'après la moyenne des valeurs de 2009-2010 CTCI révision 3 (positions à 3 chiffres)	2000			2010			Growth rates (%) Taux d'accroissement (%) 2000-2010	
	Value (millions of dollars) Valeur (millions de dollars)	% of the country grouping exports En % des exportations du groupe de pays	% of world product exports En % des exportations mondiales des produits	Value (millions of dollars) Valeur (millions de dollars)	% of the country grouping exports En % des exportations du groupe de pays	% of world product exports En % des exportations mondiales des produits	Value Valeur	Difference from world Différence par rapport au monde
071 Coffee and coffee substitutes	11 461	0.18	100.00	31 081	0.21	100.00	14.18	_
652 Woven cotton fabrics	22 079	0.35	100.00	31 481	0.21	100.00	2.84	_
721 Agricultural machine nes excluding tractor	10 811	0.17	100.00	29 456	0.19	100.00	12.16	_
694 Nails screws nuts bolts rivets	12 537	0.20	100.00	31 312	0.21	100.00	11.46	_
421 Fixed veg fat and oil, "soft"	8 539	0.13	100.00	29 763	0.20	100.00	15.11	_
663 Mineral manufactures nes	13 846	0.22	100.00	29 819	0.20	100.00	9.77	_
746 Ball or roller bearings	12 522	0.20	100.00	29 895	0.20	100.00	10.37	_
813 Lighting fixtures and fittings nes	12 416	0.19	100.00	27 918	0.18	100.00	9.56	_
661 Lime cement construction material	11 072	0.17	100.00	26 522	0.18	100.00	11.33	_
287 Base metal ores & concentrates nes	5 450	0.09	100.00	31 891	0.21	100.00	23.76	_
024 Cheese and curd	9 863	0.15	100.00	27 149	0.18	100.00	11.52	_
122 Manufactured tabacco	16 293	0.26	100.00	24 977	0.16	100.00	5.76	_
056 Vegetables roots tubers nes	9 812	0.15	100.00	26 389	0.17	100.00	11.24	_
655 Knitted or crocheted fabrics nes	15 757	0.25	100.00	27 795	0.18	100.00	6.05	_
731 Machine tools for material removal	18 638	0.29	100.00	27 644	0.18	100.00	6.34	_
036 Crustacean mollusc aquat invertebra	17 558	0.28	100.00	26 884	0.18	100.00	4.26	_
749 Non-electric machinery part nes	15 534	0.24	100.00	25 570	0.17	100.00	6.39	_
697 Base metal household equipment nes	11 965	0.19	100.00	26 188	0.17	100.00	9.02	_
724 Textile leather machinery parts nes	20 188	0.32	100.00	26 916	0.18	100.00	2.93	_
665 Glassware	10 903	0.17	100.00	26 466	0.17	100.00	9.59	_
791 Railway vehicles and equipment	8 336	0.13	100.00	24 534	0.16	100.00	12.99	_
846 Clothing accessory excluding 831, 848, and 851	13 048	0.20	100.00	25 006	0.17	100.00	7.50	_
629 Articles of rubber nes	11 320	0.18	100.00	25 373	0.17	100.00	9.38	_
848 Headgear, non-textile clothing	13 807	0.22	100.00	25 266	0.17	100.00	6.02	_
591 Household and garden chemicals	10 673	0.17	100.00	23 479	0.15	100.00	9.74	_
843 Male clothing, knitted crocheted	11 009	0.17	100.00	24 597	0.16	100.00	9.91	_
786 Trailer caravan transport container	11 074	0.17	100.00	26 610	0.18	100.00	11.61	_
044 Maize unmilled, excluding sweet corn	8 833	0.14	100.00	23 589	0.16	100.00	12.07	_
635 Wood manufactures nes	14 306	0.22	100.00	22 814	0.15	100.00	6.30	_
662 Clay and refractory materials	10 213	0.16	100.00	22 727	0.15	100.00	9.79	_
572 Primary form styrene polymers	12 206	0.19	100.00	24 540	0.16	100.00	8.94	_
551 Essential oils, perfumes & flavours	7 823	0.12	100.00	21 804	0.14	100.00	10.93	_
042 Rice	6 479	0.10	100.00	21 199	0.14	100.00	14.63	_
037 Fish shellfish, prepared preserved	9 462	0.15	100.00	21 277	0.14	100.00	9.91	_
073 Chocolate & cocoa preparations nes	7 004	0.11	100.00	21 068	0.14	100.00	12.40	_
592 Starches, glutenes, glues, etc	8 901	0.14	100.00	21 128	0.14	100.00	9.92	_
737 Metalwork machinery nes excluding tools	9 807	0.15	100.00	20 282	0.13	100.00	10.71	_
611 Leather	16 515	0.26	100.00	22 313	0.15	100.00	2.59	_
072 Cocoa	4 111	0.06	100.00	20 338	0.13	100.00	15.91	_
718 Power generating machinery part nes	6 142	0.10	100.00	20 314	0.13	100.00	14.82	_
231 Natural rubber, latex, gum, etc	3 936	0.06	100.00	24 713	0.16	100.00	21.17	_
001 Live animal excluding fish & crustacean	9 238	0.15	100.00	18 686	0.12	100.00	8.60	_
621 Rubber material e.g. paste tube rod	7 344	0.12	100.00	20 509	0.14	100.00	12.05	_
232 Synthetic & reclaimed rubber; waste	6 386	0.10	100.00	20 955	0.14	100.00	13.83	_
597 Additive e.g. lubricate, antifreeze	6 886	0.11	100.00	19 141	0.13	100.00	12.30	_
523 Inorganic acid metal salt peroxy	7 714	0.12	100.00	18 641	0.12	100.00	10.79	_
581 Plastic tube pipe hose & fittings	6 661	0.10	100.00	18 225	0.12	100.00	12.82	_
683 Nickel	7 471	0.12	100.00	20 315	0.13	100.00	14.60	_
896 Work of art & collections; antiques	10 419	0.16	100.00	18 527	0.12	100.00	8.03	_
692 Metal storage transport container	6 793	0.11	100.00	17 337	0.11	100.00	12.48	_
882 Photo cinematographic supply excluding 883	18 622	0.29	100.00	17 435	0.12	100.00	-0.05	_
722 Tractors	7 831	0.12	100.00	17 073	0.11	100.00	10.99	_
111 Non alcoholic beverage nes	5 229	0.08	100.00	16 865	0.11	100.00	14.08	_
017 Meat offal preserved nes	5 522	0.09	100.00	16 996	0.11	100.00	13.43	_
573 Vinyl chloride etc polymers	8 766	0.14	100.00	17 655	0.12	100.00	8.77	_
525 Radio active & associated materials	5 150	0.08	100.00	16 064	0.11	100.00	15.68	_
058 Fruit preserve preparation excluding juice	5 794	0.09	100.00	15 710	0.10	100.00	11.78	_
263 Cotton	8 023	0.13	100.00	18 740	0.12	100.00	7.23	_
726 Printing bookbinding machines parts	14 217	0.22	100.00	15 279	0.10	100.00	1.94	_
289 Prec metal ore concentrate excluding gold	2 803	0.04	100.00	17 139	0.11	100.00	23.61	_

For sources and notes, see end of table.

Pour les sources et les notes, se reporter à la fin du tableau.

Products ranked by average 2009-2010 values SITC Revision 3 (3-digit level) / Produits classés d'après la moyenne des valeurs de 2009-2010 CTCI révision 3 (positions à 3 chiffres)	2000			2010			Growth rates (%) Taux d'accroissement (%) 2000-2010	
	Value (millions of dollars) / Valeur (millions de dollars)	% of the country grouping exports / En % des exportations du groupe de pays	% of world product exports / En % des exportations mondiales des produits	Value (millions of dollars) / Valeur (millions de dollars)	% of the country grouping exports / En % des exportations du groupe de pays	% of world product exports / En % des exportations mondiales des produits	Value / Valeur	Difference from world / Différence par rapport au monde
762 Radio broadcast receivers	19 337	0.30	100.00	15 758	0.10	100.00	-1.54	_
278 Other crude minerals	7 190	0.11	100.00	10 199	0.11	100.00	0.91	_
059 Fruit & vegetable juice unferment	6 466	0.10	100.00	14 306	0.09	100.00	10.67	_
812 Sanitary plumb heat fixtures nes	6 200	0.10	100.00	13 756	0.09	100.00	10.91	_
659 Floor coverings etc	8 797	0.14	100.00	14 102	0.09	100.00	6.12	_
895 Office and stationery supplies nes	8 331	0.13	100.00	13 648	0.09	100.00	6.29	_
693 Wire products and fencing grills	4 844	0.08	100.00	13 187	0.09	100.00	13.46	_
247 Wood in rough or roughly squared	8 343	0.13	100.00	13 401	0.09	100.00	6.63	_
891 Arms and ammunition	5 348	0.08	100.00	11 998	0.08	100.00	9.79	_
727 Food processing machine excluding domestic	5 657	0.09	100.00	12 344	0.08	100.00	9.95	_
285 Aluminium ore concentrate alumina	6 478	0.10	100.00	13 309	0.09	100.00	10.25	_
735 Machine part accessory for 731 and 733	8 449	0.13	100.00	12 924	0.09	100.00	6.39	_
121 Unmanufactured tabacco and refuse	5 571	0.09	100.00	11 013	0.07	100.00	8.44	_
531 Synthetic organic colour agents	8 933	0.14	100.00	12 361	0.08	100.00	3.41	_
686 Zinc	5 492	0.09	100.00	12 365	0.08	100.00	12.27	_
344 Petroleum and hydrocarbon gas nes	4 537	0.07	100.00	13 813	0.09	100.00	11.47	_
524 Other inorganic chemicals	4 718	0.07	100.00	12 079	0.08	100.00	12.18	_
725 Paper & pulp mill, cut manufacture	6 900	0.11	100.00	10 308	0.07	100.00	5.71	_
654 Other woven textile fabrics nes	9 750	0.15	100.00	10 487	0.07	100.00	1.72	_
733 Metal work tool no material removal	6 488	0.10	100.00	10 170	0.07	100.00	7.52	_
678 Wire of iron or steel	3 825	0.06	100.00	11 090	0.07	100.00	13.54	_
431 Processed animal & veg fats & oils	3 033	0.05	100.00	10 807	0.07	100.00	13.99	_
873 Meters and counters nes	4 085	0.06	100.00	10 019	0.07	100.00	9.92	_
062 Sugar confectionery	4 392	0.07	100.00	9 298	0.06	100.00	8.91	_
273 Stone, sand and gravel	3 952	0.06	100.00	9 125	0.06	100.00	10.59	_
711 Steam generating boilers & parts	2 537	0.04	100.00	8 253	0.05	100.00	15.94	_
696 Cutlery	6 002	0.08	100.00	9 099	0.06	100.00	0.82	_
712 Steam vapour turbines & parts nes	2 539	0.04	100.00	8 378	0.06	100.00	13.54	_
656 Tulle lace embroidery trim etc	5 867	0.09	100.00	9 217	0.06	100.00	5.10	_
284 Nickel ores, concentrates, etc	2 148	0.03	100.00	9 477	0.06	100.00	20.27	_
689 Misc non-ferrous base metals	3 904	0.06	100.00	8 693	0.06	100.00	11.25	_
666 Pottery	5 490	0.09	100.00	7 803	0.05	100.00	3.82	_
881 Photographic device nes	18 808	0.30	100.00	7 725	0.05	100.00	-9.58	_
811 Prefabricated buildings	2 828	0.04	100.00	7 454	0.05	100.00	12.94	_
074 Tea and maté	3 220	0.05	100.00	7 415	0.05	100.00	9.67	_
291 Crude animal materials nes	3 470	0.05	100.00	7 101	0.05	100.00	8.89	_
266 Synthetic fibres for spinning	4 707	0.07	100.00	7 195	0.05	100.00	4.77	_
023 Butter fats oils derived from milk	2 750	0.04	100.00	7 423	0.05	100.00	10.26	_
325 Coke, semi coke, retort carbon	2 203	0.03	100.00	8 175	0.05	100.00	14.71	_
579 Plastic waste, parings and scrap	1 440	0.02	100.00	6 425	0.04	100.00	19.27	_
075 Spices	2 638	0.04	100.00	6 489	0.04	100.00	9.66	_
211 Raw hides & skins, excluding furskins	5 134	0.08	100.00	6 820	0.05	100.00	0.76	_
685 Lead	1 448	0.02	100.00	5 680	0.04	100.00	19.11	_
268 Wool & animal hair, incl wool tops	4 735	0.07	100.00	6 059	0.04	100.00	1.64	_
035 Fish, dried salted smoked	2 757	0.04	100.00	5 508	0.04	100.00	7.64	_
091 Margarine and shortening	1 400	0.02	100.00	5 054	0.03	100.00	16.91	_
043 Barley grain unmilled	2 873	0.05	100.00	5 125	0.03	100.00	9.59	_
687 Tin	1 751	0.03	100.00	5 719	0.04	100.00	16.96	_
025 Eggs, yolks and albumin	1 446	0.02	100.00	4 853	0.03	100.00	14.40	·
246 Wood chips, particles and waste	1 866	0.03	100.00	5 216	0.03	100.00	12.50	_
583 Plastic rod stick & profile shapes	1 867	0.03	100.00	4 863	0.03	100.00	11.35	_
016 Meat offal preserved	1 706	0.03	100.00	4 713	0.03	100.00	11.22	_
411 Animals oils and fats	1 469	0.02	100.00	4 847	0.03	100.00	14.16	_
046 Wheat meal & flour, meslin flour	1 782	0.03	100.00	4 402	0.03	100.00	12.22	_
267 Man made fibre for spinning; waste	2 265	0.04	100.00	4 357	0.03	100.00	7.55	_
677 Iron steel rail railway materials	1 033	0.02	100.00	4 062	0.03	100.00	16.19	_
269 Worn clothing, textile article; rag	1 485	0.02	100.00	3 759	0.02	100.00	10.80	_
272 Crude fertilizer, excluding manufactured	1 324	0.02	100.00	3 590	0.02	100.00	13.65	_
322 Briquettes, lignite and peat	671	0.01	100.00	3 648	0.02	100.00	17.67	_
212 Raw furskins and furskin pieces	1 429	0.02	100.00	3 871	0.03	100.00	9.53	_

For sources and notes, see end of table.

Pour les sources et les notes, se reporter à la fin du tableau.

Products ranked by average 2009-2010 values SITC Revision 3 (3-digit level) Produits classés d'après la moyenne des valeurs de 2009-2010 CTCI révision 3 (positions à 3 chiffres)	2000			2010			Growth rates (%) Taux d'accroissement (%) 2000-2010	
	Value (millions of dollars) Valeur (millions de dollars)	% of the country grouping exports En % des exportations du groupe de pays	% of world product exports En % des exportations mondiales des produits	Value (millions of dollars) Valeur (millions de dollars)	% of the country grouping exports En % des exportations du groupe de pays	% of world product exports En % des exportations mondiales des produits	Value Valeur	Difference from world Différence par rapport au monde
593 Explosives and pyrotechnic products	1 187	0.02	100.00	3 159	0.02	100.00	11.47	–
612 Leather manufactures nes	1 753	0.03	100.00	3 157	0.02	100.00	6.95	–
043 Grain excluding wheat rice barley maize	1 411	0.02	100.00	2 621	0.02	100.00	6.55	–
274 Sulphur and unroasted iron pyrites	773	0.01	100.00	3 420	0.02	100.00	21.10	–
223 Oil seed for non soft oil	749	0.01	100.00	2 422	0.02	100.00	15.19	–
532 Dyeing and tanning extracts	928	0.01	100.00	1 944	0.01	100.00	7.45	–
613 Furskin tanned dressed etc	1 046	0.02	100.00	1 574	0.01	100.00	4.35	–
633 Cork manufactures	1 234	0.02	100.00	1 496	0.01	100.00	2.57	–
277 Natural abrasives nes	1 017	0.02	100.00	1 434	0.01	100.00	3.25	–
245 Fuel wood excluding waste; wood charcoal	335	0.01	100.00	1 154	0.01	100.00	14.27	–
047 Other cereal meals and flours	445	0.01	100.00	1 079	0.01	100.00	11.02	–
286 Uranium & thorium ore concentrates	307	0.00	100.00	708	0.00	100.00	13.90	–
265 Veg textile fibre, excluding cotton jute	600	0.01	100.00	814	0.01	100.00	2.46	–
883 Cinematographic film, developed	380	0.01	100.00	629	0.00	100.00	6.89	–
261 Silk	434	0.01	100.00	529	0.00	100.00	2.25	–
961 Coins, nongold and non currency	719	0.01	100.00	321	0.00	100.00	7.08	–
264 Jute & bast fibre nes, raw & retted	98	0.00	100.00	371	0.00	100.00	14.79	–
244 Natural cork, raw and wastes	248	0.00	100.00	210	0.00	100.00	-1.16	–
345 Coal, water, producer gas etc	4	0.00	100.00	38	0.00	100.00	23.38	–

Sources:
- UN DESA Statistics Division, *COMTRADE* database
- UNCTAD secretariat calculations

Sources :
- ONU DAES Division de statistique, base de données *COMTRADE*
- Calculs du secrétariat de la CNUCED

Products ranked by average 2009-2010 values SITC Revision 3 (3-digit level) Produits classés d'après la moyenne des valeurs de 2009-2010 CTCI révision 3 (positions à 3 chiffres)	2000			2010			Growth rates (%) Taux d'accroissement (%) 2000-2010	
	Value (millions of dollars) Valeur (millions de dollars)	% of the country grouping exports En % des exportations du groupe de pays	% of world product exports En % des exportations mondiales des produits	Value (millions of dollars) Valeur (millions de dollars)	% of the country grouping exports En % des exportations du groupe de pays	% of world product exports En % des exportations mondiales des produits	Value Valeur	Difference from world Différence par rapport au monde
All commodity groups	**2 046 906**	**100.00**	**32.14**	**6 363 625**	**100.00**	**42.01**	**14.32**	**3.34**
333 Crude petroleum & bituminous oil	376 039	10.10	70.71	619 361	13.51	71.09	16.88	-0.08
778 Valves tubes; diodes, transistors	146 943	7.18	47.60	364 666	5.73	69.13	11.57	4.48
764 Telecommunicate equipment part nes	72 385	3.54	32.40	295 483	4.64	65.15	16.97	7.52
334 Heavy petroleum & bituminous oil	79 411	3.88	48.75	293 965	4.62	45.03	18.50	-1.11
752 Computer equipment nes	84 865	4.15	42.71	231 038	3.63	71.39	11.46	5.41
759 Office equipment part & accessories	80 380	3.93	48.94	124 782	1.96	60.66	5.48	2.05
793 Ships boats floating structures	12 989	0.63	32.11	94 273	1.48	59.21	24.51	8.35
343 Natural gas, liquefied or not	24 088	1.18	35.32	95 606	1.50	41.73	18.13	2.21
778 Electrical machinery apparatus nes	30 108	1.47	29.18	98 367	1.55	48.86	14.16	5.64
781 Passenger cars and race cars	34 830	1.70	11.45	97 311	1.53	17.27	11.90	4.96
845 Articles of apparel nes	42 920	2.10	65.41	87 900	1.38	70.70	8.88	0.98
772 Electrical circuit equipment	31 131	1.52	32.35	86 734	1.36	42.49	12.81	3.21
971 Gold non-monetary excluding ores	8 777	0.43	37.91	77 813	1.22	51.83	25.79	2.82
871 Optical instruments apparatus nes	5 494	0.27	37.60	82 975	1.30	82.78	38.13	12.14
784 Motor vehicle parts and accessories	16 601	0.81	11.65	73 378	1.15	24.29	17.86	9.17
682 Copper	13 490	0.66	41.01	69 464	1.09	52.97	21.98	3.14
667 Pearls, precious semiprecious stone	18 732	0.92	33.49	61 522	0.97	48.86	14.09	4.60
821 Furniture part; bedding furnishing	17 771	0.87	28.94	61 076	0.96	45.92	14.51	5.24
851 Footwear	26 268	1.28	56.06	58 956	0.93	61.57	9.21	1.12
761 Television video receive project	15 268	0.75	53.30	57 003	0.90	57.28	15.83	0.20
894 Baby carriage toy game sport good	29 642	1.45	61.69	50 720	0.80	57.90	7.94	-0.50
842 Female clothing, woven	29 486	1.44	66.44	49 620	0.78	66.67	6.03	-0.17
775 Household equipment nes	13 473	0.66	37.28	47 274	0.74	55.51	14.11	4.18
897 Jewellery nes (667)	9 442	0.46	41.25	45 479	0.71	57.33	18.12	3.82
771 Electric power machine part excluding 716	17 840	0.87	48.16	45 626	0.72	53.60	12.19	1.33
841 Male clothing, woven	29 943	1.46	60.94	41 889	0.66	68.26	4.49	-0.21
773 Electrical distribute equipment nes	16 241	0.79	37.69	43 749	0.69	45.90	12.58	2.24
281 Iron ore and concentrates	4 771	0.23	50.32	49 873	0.78	46.67	27.91	-1.55
893 Articles of plastic nes	17 876	0.87	33.12	41 941	0.66	36.04	9.93	0.80
699 Base metal manufactures nes	13 092	0.64	24.63	41 772	0.66	34.10	14.55	3.63
763 Sound TV recorder or reproducer	12 345	0.60	44.91	36 064	0.57	58.15	11.98	2.25
321 Coal excluding non-agglomomerated	5 860	0.29	33.99	36 747	0.58	34.61	19.85	-1.50
057 Fruit nut (exc oil), fresh or dried	12 688	0.62	45.75	33 291	0.52	48.33	11.62	0.65
844 Female clothing, knitted crocheted	12 503	0.61	69.19	35 451	0.56	77.33	12.08	1.20
741 Heating cooling equipment parts nes	8 798	0.43	21.26	34 102	0.54	36.31	16.87	5.68
283 Copper ores and concentrates	5 501	0.27	81.35	37 114	0.58	79.38	25.03	-0.63
658 Made-up textile articles nes	10 817	0.53	62.71	33 089	0.52	75.31	12.98	2.09
422 Fixed veg fat and oil, excluding "soft"	5 604	0.27	87.05	33 753	0.53	88.88	21.69	0.22
684 Aluminium	10 667	0.52	21.24	35 065	0.55	32.01	14.13	4.16
782 Goods and service vehicles	9 321	0.46	16.29	34 489	0.54	31.95	14.74	6.71
511 Hydrocarbons nes; derivatives	6 528	0.32	27.29	34 507	0.54	42.04	20.79	5.38
651 Textile yarn	17 424	0.85	52.41	31 945	0.50	63.48	6.23	1.85
874 Measure analyze control device nes	7 735	0.38	10.55	31 736	0.50	20.60	15.62	6.85
679 Iron steel pipe tube fittings etc	4 670	0.23	20.95	28 290	0.44	37.42	24.73	7.88
728 Special industrial machine part nes	9 047	0.44	12.14	31 668	0.50	20.09	15.33	5.26
751 Office machines	4 902	0.24	34.27	29 209	0.46	58.42	23.31	5.40
342 Liquefied propane and butane	11 519	0.56	68.35	27 950	0.44	66.56	13.36	0.14
743 Gas pump, compressor, fan, filter	7 677	0.38	18.43	29 106	0.46	27.33	15.33	4.16
898 Music instrument device recording	9 069	0.44	26.66	27 876	0.44	46.09	13.53	6.23
716 Rotating electric plant parts nes	10 568	0.52	34.10	28 261	0.44	34.65	11.82	-0.26
081 Animal feed excluding unmilled cereal	7 464	0.36	36.46	26 228	0.41	43.08	14.03	1.82
571 Primary form ethylene polymers	5 712	0.28	28.87	28 207	0.44	42.91	18.99	3.70
713 Internal combustion engine part nes	7 882	0.39	11.41	28 157	0.44	20.17	15.35	6.91
625 Rubber for wheels, incl inner tube	6 163	0.30	24.81	27 706	0.44	38.50	18.35	5.53
575 Other plastics, in primary forms	5 615	0.27	16.58	28 070	0.44	29.51	18.80	6.37
653 Man-made woven fabrics	18 071	0.88	57.75	26 413	0.42	71.82	4.99	2.55
673 Flat iron non-alloy steel products	7 682	0.38	25.38	28 534	0.45	34.17	19.37	4.85
723 Civil engineering plant & equipment	4 288	0.21	13.15	26 546	0.42	27.95	23.29	9.15
831 Case bag: storage travel shopping	11 331	0.55	68.77	26 671	0.42	65.52	10.15	-0.66
061 Sugar, mollasses and honey	5 699	0.28	55.87	27 125	0.43	69.47	14.86	1.69

For sources and notes, see end of table.

Pour les sources et les notes, se reporter à la fin du tableau.

Products ranked by average 2009-2010 values SITC Revision 3 (3-digit level) / Produits classés d'après la moyenne des valeurs de 2009-2010 CTCI révision 3 (positions à 3 chiffres)	2000			2010			Growth rates (%) Taux d'accroissement (%) 2000-2010	
	Value (millions of dollars) / Valeur (millions de dollars)	% of the country grouping exports / En % des exportations du groupe de pays	% of world product exports / En % des exportations mondiales des produits	Value (millions of dollars) / Valeur (millions de dollars)	% of the country grouping exports / En % des exportations du groupe de pays	% of world product exports / En % des exportations mondiales des produits	Value / Valeur	Difference from world / Différence par rapport au monde
512 Alcohols, phenols; derivatives	5 341	0.26	35.82	26 805	0.42	52.70	18.56	4.48
899 Manufactured articles nes	9 879	0.48	41.04	23 090	0.36	32.70	10.23	-2.36
661 Lime, platinum, platinum metal	4 283	0.21	28.27	23 096	0.36	44.94	22.51	5.52
034 Fish, fresh live chilled frozen	8 024	0.12	60.02	22 607	0.37	42.44	10.50	0.70
598 Miscellaneous chemical products nes	5 309	0.26	13.69	23 454	0.37	21.86	18.60	6.11
054 Vegetable & vegetable products nes	6 523	0.32	32.97	22 436	0.35	38.13	13.10	1.41
542 Medicines including veterinary	4 370	0.21	5.74	21 588	0.34	6.76	19.21	3.65
652 Woven cotton fabrics	12 361	0.60	55.98	22 900	0.36	72.74	6.01	3.16
222 Oil seed etc for soft oil	4 688	0.23	34.18	21 747	0.34	40.63	17.00	1.30
513 Carboxylic acid and compounds	4 748	0.23	27.94	23 620	0.37	51.29	17.86	6.75
676 Iron steel bar rod section piling	4 883	0.24	20.95	22 217	0.35	31.56	22.21	6.48
582 Plastic sheet film foil & strips	6 093	0.30	18.28	22 093	0.35	25.99	15.57	4.30
691 Iron steel aluminium structures nes	2 644	0.13	19.66	18 111	0.28	40.16	27.60	10.61
792 Aircraft, spacecraft & equipment	8 198	0.40	8.15	19 782	0.31	14.58	13.09	8.26
884 Optical goods fibres nes	4 051	0.20	20.91	21 029	0.33	43.09	19.49	8.26
843 Male clothing, knitted crocheted	8 561	0.42	77.77	20 583	0.32	83.68	10.92	1.01
785 Motorcycles, mopeds and cycles	7 799	0.38	36.75	21 174	0.33	50.71	12.71	3.96
655 Knitted or crocheted fabrics nes	10 136	0.50	64.33	21 238	0.33	76.41	7.92	1.86
574 Polyacetals and polyesters, etc	5 288	0.26	27.72	20 941	0.33	41.92	16.65	5.03
522 Inorganic chemical elem oxide salt	5 551	0.27	33.55	20 596	0.32	42.94	16.37	2.76
231 Natural rubber, latex, gum, etc	3 774	0.18	95.89	23 575	0.37	95.39	21.15	-0.02
071 Coffee and coffee substitutes	8 278	0.40	72.23	19 571	0.31	62.97	13.08	-1.11
562 Manufactured fertilizer excluding crude	3 351	0.16	26.13	20 266	0.32	36.31	22.31	3.04
641 Paper and paperboard	8 267	0.40	11.71	18 734	0.29	16.75	10.24	4.55
671 Pig & sponge iron, ferro alloys etc	5 452	0.27	57.75	21 683	0.34	56.10	18.71	-0.07
674 Flat plated iron non-alloy steel	4 513	0.22	23.39	21 105	0.33	40.11	19.04	6.21
747 Pipe, boiler, tank & vat appliances	3 816	0.19	16.60	18 377	0.29	27.37	19.24	5.87
042 Rice	4 652	0.23	71.81	16 955	0.27	79.98	16.56	1.93
036 Crustacean mollusc aquat invertebra	11 984	0.59	68.25	17 502	0.28	65.10	3.54	-0.72
848 Headgear, non-textile clothing	9 831	0.48	71.20	17 560	0.28	69.50	5.31	-0.70
287 Base metal ores & concentrates nes	2 506	0.12	45.98	19 620	0.31	61.52	27.10	3.34
657 Special yarn and textile fabric etc	7 718	0.38	34.77	17 231	0.27	41.55	9.45	2.22
515 Organo-inorganic compound acid salt	3 289	0.16	7.05	16 366	0.26	16.33	16.89	7.95
872 Medical instruments appliances nes	4 468	0.22	16.71	16 024	0.25	20.57	14.22	2.12
541 Pharmaceuticals excluding medicines	4 028	0.20	12.70	16 008	0.25	11.62	16.02	-0.55
744 Mechanical handling equipment nes	2 822	0.14	9.57	15 327	0.24	22.89	23.40	11.48
661 Lime cement construction material	4 487	0.22	40.52	15 560	0.24	58.67	15.57	4.24
846 Clothing accessory excluding 831, 848, and 851	6 368	0.31	48.80	15 667	0.25	62.66	10.30	2.80
642 Cut paper and paperboard articles	6 369	0.31	22.00	14 839	0.23	28.91	10.00	2.71
697 Base metal household equipment nes	6 054	0.30	50.60	15 450	0.24	58.99	10.32	1.30
037 Fish shellfish, prepared preserved	5 669	0.28	59.91	14 131	0.22	66.41	11.25	1.33
553 Perfume toilet cosmetics, excluding soap	3 075	0.15	13.20	14 349	0.23	21.64	17.24	5.34
892 Printed matter	4 254	0.21	15.86	13 917	0.22	28.77	14.48	7.26
514 Nitrogen function compounds	3 231	0.16	16.24	14 350	0.23	31.16	18.58	8.93
813 Lighting fixtures and fittings nes	5 410	0.26	43.57	14 481	0.23	51.87	10.94	1.38
675 Flat rolled products of alloy steel	4 717	0.23	22.45	16 141	0.25	26.15	15.91	1.50
012 Meat nes, fresh chilled frozen	3 855	0.19	16.67	13 813	0.22	22.02	13.63	2.34
072 Cocoa	2 637	0.13	64.14	13 146	0.21	64.64	15.96	0.05
572 Primary form styrene polymers	6 307	0.31	51.67	14 450	0.23	58.88	10.41	1.47
098 Edible products & preparations nes	3 736	0.18	21.08	13 228	0.21	25.47	14.31	1.81
335 Residual petroleum products nes	2 981	0.15	32.61	14 118	0.22	38.53	19.69	2.13
885 Watches and clocks	9 391	0.46	47.20	13 521	0.21	36.65	3.89	-3.21
695 Tools for use in hand or in machine	4 415	0.22	21.32	13 907	0.22	33.36	12.60	4.31
634 Veneer, plywood & other wood nes	6 051	0.30	34.82	12 443	0.20	40.54	9.28	2.07
516 Other organic chemicals	3 621	0.18	25.16	12 061	0.19	34.00	14.16	3.33
611 Leather	8 522	0.42	51.60	12 746	0.20	57.13	3.01	0.43
112 Alcoholic beverages	4 102	0.20	14.02	10 861	0.17	17.17	11.55	2.38
745 Non-electrical machinery tool nes	2 510	0.12	10.88	11 063	0.17	22.86	17.94	8.73
714 Non-electric engines excluding 712, 713, and 718	2 164	0.11	4.53	10 208	0.16	13.40	17.61	11.66
694 Nails screws nuts bolts rivets	3 561	0.17	28.41	11 395	0.18	36.39	14.66	3.20

For sources and notes, see end of table.

Pour les sources et les notes, se reporter à la fin du tableau.

Products ranked by average 2009-2010 values SITC Revision 3 (3-digit level) / Produits classés d'après la moyenne des valeurs de 2009-2010 CTCI révision 3 (positions à 3 chiffres)	2000			2010			Growth rates (%) Taux d'accroissement (%) 2000-2010	
	Value (millions of dollars) / Valeur (millions de dollars)	% of the country grouping exports / En % des exportations du groupe de pays	% of world product exports / En % des exportations mondiales des produits	Value (millions of dollars) / Valeur (millions de dollars)	% of the country grouping exports / En % des exportations du groupe de pays	% of world product exports / En % des exportations mondiales des produits	Value / Valeur	Difference from world / Différence par rapport au monde
664 Glass	3 702	0.18	22.06	10 810	0.17	31.21	12.10	3.43
251 Pulp and waste paper	4 150	0.23	19.44	11 409	0.18	26.60	11.25	3.13
665 Glassware	2 506	0.12	22.98	11 312	0.18	42.74	16.78	7.19
292 Crude vegetable materials nes	4 131	0.20	27.70	10 118	0.16	27.57	10.03	0.17
011 Beef, fresh chilled frozen	2 063	0.10	14.28	9 927	0.16	28.59	21.69	10.76
421 Fixed veg fat and oil, "soft"	3 010	0.15	35.25	9 747	0.15	32.75	14.79	-0.32
724 Textile leather machinery parts nes	4 324	0.21	21.42	10 337	0.16	38.41	9.93	7.00
533 Pigment, paint, varnish & related	4 228	0.21	16.94	9 856	0.15	18.44	9.77	0.70
742 Liquid pump; liquid elevator parts	1 762	0.09	9.04	9 995	0.16	19.36	21.44	9.63
554 Soaps cleansers polishes	2 695	0.13	20.61	9 429	0.15	26.60	14.90	3.42
762 Radio broadcast receivers	13 586	0.66	70.26	9 839	0.15	62.44	-2.67	-1.13
672 Ingots, Iron steel primary products	3 802	0.19	32.62	10 590	0.17	27.53	13.39	-2.21
786 Trailer caravan transport container	4 031	0.20	36.40	11 330	0.18	42.58	12.65	1.03
662 Clay and refractory materials	1 613	0.08	15.79	8 940	0.14	39.34	20.15	10.35
749 Non-electric machinery part nes	3 092	0.15	19.90	8 837	0.14	34.56	12.91	6.52
783 Road motor vehicles nes	1 804	0.09	11.13	9 135	0.14	26.89	20.15	9.69
056 Vegetables roots tubers nes	2 629	0.13	26.79	8 578	0.13	32.51	13.58	2.34
748 Mechanical transmission equipment	1 945	0.10	12.00	8 960	0.14	20.01	17.97	5.47
121 Unmanufactured tabacco and refuse	2 976	0.15	53.41	7 337	0.12	66.62	11.14	2.70
635 Wood manufactures nes	4 977	0.24	34.79	7 910	0.12	34.67	5.62	-0.69
248 Wood simply worked, railway sleeper	4 764	0.23	17.87	7 999	0.13	22.75	6.30	2.58
523 Inorganic acid metal salt peroxy	2 129	0.10	27.60	7 713	0.12	41.38	15.92	5.13
288 Non ferrous base metal waste nes	2 053	0.10	23.07	8 975	0.14	22.59	19.45	-0.16
048 Cereal & preparation flour starch	1 899	0.09	13.95	7 513	0.12	19.57	15.76	3.50
263 Cotton	2 982	0.15	37.17	8 503	0.13	45.37	9.90	2.67
058 Fruit preserve preparation excluding juice	2 371	0.12	40.92	7 247	0.11	46.13	12.94	1.16
122 Manufactured tabacco	3 070	0.18	22.53	7 045	0.11	28.21	6.61	0.85
746 Ball or roller bearings	2 490	0.12	19.89	7 865	0.12	26.31	13.25	2.88
044 Maize unmilled, excluding sweet corn	2 367	0.12	26.80	7 654	0.12	32.45	12.17	0.11
344 Petroleum and hydrocarbon gas nes	1 617	0.08	35.64	9 357	0.15	67.74	20.62	9.15
591 Household and garden chemicals	2 106	0.10	19.73	6 523	0.10	27.78	13.52	3.77
278 Other crude minerals	2 404	0.12	33.54	7 264	0.11	44.23	11.54	2.57
659 Floor coverings etc	3 045	0.15	34.61	6 447	0.10	45.72	9.34	3.22
629 Articles of rubber nes	2 012	0.10	17.77	6 350	0.10	25.03	13.82	4.43
621 Rubber material e.g. paste tube rod	1 014	0.05	13.81	6 662	0.10	32.48	22.55	10.50
663 Mineral manufactures nes	1 920	0.09	13.86	6 560	0.10	22.00	14.41	4.64
059 Fruit & vegetable juice unferment	2 540	0.12	39.29	5 892	0.09	41.18	11.88	1.22
017 Meat offal preserved nes	1 523	0.07	27.58	5 682	0.09	33.43	16.24	2.82
592 Starches, glutenes, glues, etc	1 528	0.07	17.17	6 043	0.09	28.60	16.12	6.20
731 Machine tools for material removal	2 463	0.12	13.21	6 658	0.10	24.08	12.65	6.31
656 Tulle lace embroidery trim etc	2 921	0.14	49.78	6 074	0.10	65.91	8.71	3.60
074 Tea and maté	2 630	0.13	81.68	5 613	0.09	75.70	8.72	-0.95
431 Processed animal & veg fats & oils	1 368	0.07	45.10	5 938	0.09	54.95	17.45	3.47
692 Metal storage transport container	1 416	0.07	20.84	5 374	0.08	31.00	17.84	5.36
737 Metalwork machinery nes excluding tools	1 242	0.06	12.66	5 458	0.09	26.91	20.27	9.56
232 Synthetic & reclaimed rubber; waste	1 419	0.07	22.23	6 139	0.10	29.30	17.04	3.21
693 Wire products and fencing grills	1 391	0.07	28.71	5 456	0.09	41.37	18.02	4.56
282 Ferrous iron & steel, waste & scrap	849	0.04	10.93	5 894	0.09	12.71	24.94	2.05
531 Synthetic organic colour agents	2 591	0.13	29.00	5 653	0.09	45.74	8.53	5.12
895 Office and stationery supplies nes	2 880	0.14	34.57	5 196	0.08	38.07	7.41	1.12
711 Steam generating boilers & parts	549	0.03	21.64	4 318	0.07	52.32	27.28	11.34
696 Cutlery	2 292	0.11	45.82	5 220	0.08	53.81	8.77	1.95
075 Spices	2 088	0.10	79.15	5 127	0.08	79.01	9.57	-0.09
666 Pottery	2 683	0.13	48.86	5 041	0.08	64.61	6.65	2.83
285 Aluminium ore concentrate alumina	2 017	0.10	31.13	5 084	0.08	38.20	12.08	1.83
774 Electrodiagnostic equipment	1 011	0.05	7.00	4 740	0.07	12.37	18.46	7.52
284 Nickel ores, concentrates, etc	913	0.04	42.52	5 523	0.09	58.28	25.52	5.25
573 Vinyl chloride etc polymers	2 308	0.11	26.33	4 727	0.07	26.77	10.58	1.81
022 Milk products, excluding butter & cheese	1 453	0.07	10.14	4 622	0.07	13.12	13.29	2.57
654 Other woven textile fabrics nes	3 305	0.16	33.90	4 775	0.08	45.54	4.84	3.11

For sources and notes, see end of table.

Pour les sources et les notes, se reporter à la fin du tableau.

Products ranked by average 2009-2010 values SITC Revision 3 (3-digit level) / Produits classés d'après la moyenne des valeurs de 2009-2010 CTCI révision 3 (positions à 3 chiffres)	2000			2010			Growth rates (%) Taux d'accroissement (%) 2000-2010	
	Value (millions of dollars) Valeur (millions de dollars)	% of the country grouping exports En % des exportations du groupe de pays	% of world product exports En % des exportations mondiales des produits	Value (millions of dollars) Valeur (millions de dollars)	% of the country grouping exports En % des exportations du groupe de pays	% of world product exports En % des exportations mondiales des produits	Value Valeur	Difference from world Différence par rapport au monde
247 Wood in rough or roughly squared	2 643	0.13	31.68	4 565	0.07	34.06	7.76	1.13
687 Tin	1 461	0.07	83.41	4 725	0.07	82.62	17.19	0.23
273 Stone, sand and gravel	1 220	0.06	30.88	4 003	0.06	44.85	15.07	4.49
289 Prec metal ore concentrate excluding gold	959	0.05	34.22	4 036	0.07	27.00	20.00	0.31
351 Electric current	1 116	0.05	11.10	3 483	0.05	10.58	14.78	0.32
581 Plastic tube pipe hose & fittings	811	0.04	12.18	4 149	0.07	22.76	20.89	8.07
881 Photographic device nes	6 605	0.32	35.12	4 140	0.07	53.59	-5.97	3.61
678 Wire of iron or steel	1 022	0.05	26.72	4 520	0.07	40.75	19.19	5.64
266 Synthetic fibres for spinning	2 447	0.12	51.99	4 351	0.07	60.47	6.39	1.62
111 Non alcoholic beverage nes	1 118	0.05	21.39	3 952	0.06	23.43	15.25	1.17
721 Agricultural machine nes excluding tractor	567	0.03	5.24	4 121	0.06	14.13	24.77	12.12
001 Live animal excluding fish & crustacean	1 713	0.08	18.54	3 903	0.06	20.89	8.45	-0.15
686 Zinc	1 811	0.09	32.98	4 260	0.07	34.46	12.58	0.30
062 Sugar confectionery	1 367	0.07	31.12	3 655	0.06	39.31	11.79	2.88
551 Essential oils, perfumes & flavours	1 152	0.06	14.73	3 951	0.06	18.12	11.98	1.04
873 Meters and counters nes	864	0.04	21.15	3 602	0.06	35.96	16.01	6.09
689 Misc non-ferrous base metals	1 119	0.05	28.67	3 906	0.06	44.93	17.31	6.06
812 Sanitary plumb heat fixtures nes	1 255	0.06	20.25	3 087	0.05	22.44	13.29	2.38
882 Photo cinematographic supply excluding 883	2 776	0.14	14.90	3 028	0.05	17.37	0.81	0.86
791 Railway vehicles and equipment	923	0.05	11.08	3 400	0.05	13.86	17.60	4.61
291 Crude animal materials nes	1 454	0.07	41.90	2 840	0.04	40.00	8.70	-0.19
597 Additive e.g. lubricate, antifreeze	759	0.04	11.02	2 880	0.05	15.05	14.93	2.63
683 Nickel	685	0.03	9.16	3 348	0.05	16.48	19.92	5.33
718 Power generating machinery part nes	424	0.02	6.90	2 807	0.04	13.82	25.41	10.59
073 Chocolate & cocoa preparations nes	649	0.03	9.27	2 723	0.04	12.92	16.07	3.67
524 Other inorganic chemicals	746	0.04	15.82	3 028	0.05	25.07	17.03	4.84
272 Crude fertilizer, excluding manufactured	992	0.05	74.88	2 568	0.04	71.53	13.02	-0.64
733 Metal work tool no material removal	994	0.05	15.32	2 654	0.04	26.10	12.87	5.34
722 Tractors	394	0.02	5.03	2 431	0.04	14.24	22.10	11.10
579 Plastic waste, parings and scrap	723	0.04	50.24	2 397	0.04	37.31	15.80	-3.47
811 Prefabricated buildings	213	0.01	7.52	2 226	0.03	29.87	33.52	20.58
041 Wheat meslin, incl spelt, unmilled	1 637	0.08	11.54	2 060	0.03	6.26	4.17	-7.33
735 Machine part accessory for 731 733	731	0.04	8.65	2 460	0.04	19.03	15.06	8.67
268 Wool & animal hair, incl wool tops	1 291	0.06	27.26	2 526	0.04	41.69	5.91	4.28
712 Steam vapour turbines & parts nes	177	0.01	6.97	2 029	0.03	24.21	29.28	15.73
726 Printing bookbinding machines parts	808	0.04	5.69	2 063	0.03	13.50	9.15	7.21
046 Wheat meal & flour, meslin flour	478	0.02	26.84	1 960	0.03	44.52	17.21	5.00
024 Cheese and curd	240	0.01	2.43	1 885	0.03	6.94	26.14	14.62
325 Coke, semi coke, retort carbon	1 015	0.05	46.09	2 759	0.04	33.74	10.00	-4.71
727 Food processing machine excluding domestic	479	0.02	8.47	1 884	0.03	15.26	17.37	7.42
896 Work of art & collections; antiques	435	0.02	4.18	1 829	0.03	9.87	19.38	11.35
091 Margarine and shortening	538	0.03	38.44	1 519	0.02	30.07	14.83	-2.07
267 Man made fibre for spinning; waste	411	0.02	18.17	1 626	0.03	37.32	16.29	8.74
274 Sulphur and unroasted iron pyrites	259	0.01	33.47	1 980	0.03	57.77	26.53	5.37
246 Wood chips, particles and waste	576	0.03	30.87	1 590	0.02	30.48	10.55	-1.95
685 Lead	471	0.02	32.52	1 508	0.02	26.54	16.35	-2.76
891 Arms and ammunition	294	0.01	5.51	1 482	0.02	12.35	17.81	8.01
035 Fish, dried salted smoked	766	0.04	27.80	1 527	0.02	27.73	7.05	-0.59
525 Radio active & associated materials	383	0.02	7.44	1 615	0.03	10.06	15.80	0.11
612 Leather manufactures nes	865	0.04	49.36	1 440	0.02	45.62	6.21	-0.74
725 Paper & pulp mill, cut manufacture	491	0.02	7.11	1 476	0.02	14.32	13.26	7.55
593 Explosives and pyrotechnic products	421	0.02	35.48	1 126	0.02	35.66	11.78	0.31
269 Worn clothing, textile article; rag	387	0.02	26.07	1 094	0.02	29.11	13.09	2.29
277 Natural abrasives nes	417	0.02	40.99	930	0.01	64.83	8.72	5.47
025 Eggs, yolks and albumin	229	0.01	15.85	968	0.02	19.95	16.72	2.32
613 Furskin tanned dressed etc	402	0.02	38.41	901	0.01	57.27	9.78	5.42
211 Raw hides & skins, excluding furskins	835	0.04	16.26	919	0.01	13.47	-1.17	-1.93
411 Animals oils and fats	214	0.01	14.58	808	0.01	16.68	17.94	3.78
677 Iron steel rail railway materials	75	0.00	7.28	665	0.01	16.36	31.18	14.99
223 Oil seed for non soft oil	295	0.01	39.40	729	0.01	30.11	12.11	-3.08

For sources and notes, see end of table.

Pour les sources et les notes, se reporter à la fin du tableau.

Products ranked by average 2009-2010 values SITC Revision 3 (3-digit level) Produits classés d'après la moyenne des valeurs de 2009-2010 CTCI révision 3 (positions à 3 chiffres)	2000			2010			Growth rates (%) Taux d'accroissement (%) 2000-2010	
	Value (millions of dollars) Valeur (millions de dollars)	% of the country grouping exports En % des exportations du groupe de pays	% of world product exports En % des exportations mondiales des produits	Value (millions of dollars) Valeur (millions de dollars)	% of the country grouping exports En % des exportations du groupe de pays	% of world product exports En % des exportations mondiales des produits	Value Valeur	Difference from world Différence par rapport au monde
583 Plastic rod stick & profile shapes	89	0.00	4.78	716	0.01	14.72	25.74	14.39
212 Raw furskins and furskin pieces	333	0.02	25.20	724	0.01	18.60	7.99	-1.54
532 Dyeing and tanning extracts	342	0.02	36.87	752	0.01	38.69	7.35	-0.10
016 Meat offal preserved	42	0.00	2.45	650	0.01	13.79	42.47	31.25
286 Uranium & thorium ore concentrates	58	0.00	18.91	689	0.01	97.37	26.04	12.14
045 Grain, excluding wheat rice barley maize	142	0.01	10.05	565	0.01	21.53	16.08	7.53
245 Fuel wood excluding waste; wood charcoal	206	0.01	61.56	456	0.01	39.48	9.49	-4.78
047 Other cereal meals and flours	152	0.01	34.21	434	0.01	40.23	13.01	2.00
261 Silk	378	0.02	87.08	410	0.01	77.48	1.60	-0.66
023 Butter fats oils derived from milk	121	0.01	4.40	416	0.01	5.61	17.19	6.93
322 Briquettes, lignite and peat	26	0.00	3.88	521	0.01	14.28	29.81	12.14
265 Veg textile fibre, excluding cotton jute	127	0.01	21.11	330	0.01	40.49	10.52	8.07
264 Jute & bast fibre nes, raw & retted	93	0.00	94.79	365	0.01	98.32	15.43	0.64
043 Barley grain unmilled	29	0.00	1.02	293	0.00	5.72	21.09	11.50
883 Cinematographic film, developed	93	0.00	24.51	100	0.00	15.89	2.64	-4.25
633 Cork manufactures	52	0.00	4.18	80	0.00	5.31	5.19	2.62
961 Coins, nongold and non currency	19	0.00	2.64	33	0.00	10.15	13.47	6.39
345 Coal, water, producer gas etc	1	0.00	19.72	30	0.00	78.22	48.06	24.68
244 Natural cork, raw and wastes	42	0.00	16.98	14	0.00	6.45	-9.82	-8.67

Sources:
- UN DESA Statistics Division, *COMTRADE* database
- UNCTAD secretariat calculations

Sources :
- ONU DAES Division de statistique, base de données *COMTRADE*
- Calculs du secrétariat de la CNUCED

3

Products ranked by average 2009-2010 values SITC Revision 3 (3-digit level) / Produits classés d'après la moyenne des valeurs de 2009-2010 CTCI révision 3 (positions à 3 chiffres)	2000			2010			Growth rates (%) Taux d'accroissement (%) 2000-2010	
	Value (millions of dollars) / Valeur (millions de dollars)	% of the country grouping exports / En % des exportations du groupe de pays	% of world product exports / En % des exportations mondiales des produits	Value (millions of dollars) / Valeur (millions de dollars)	% of the country grouping exports / En % des exportations du groupe de pays	% of world product exports / En % des exportations mondiales des produits	Value / Valeur	Difference from world / Différence par rapport au monde
All commodity groups	**4 169 077**	**100.00**	**65.47**	**8 193 959**	**100.00**	**54.09**	**8.68**	**-2.30**
781 Passenger cars and race cars	268 812	6.45	88.39	464 293	5.67	82.41	6.15	-0.79
542 Medicines including veterinary	71 591	1.71	90.06	206 360	2.62	92.82	15.35	-0.21
334 Heavy petroleum & bituminous oil	69 759	1.67	42.82	274 330	0.06	10.02	10.66	0.06
784 Motor vehicle parts and accessories	125 485	3.01	88.04	227 586	2.78	75.34	6.83	-1.85
764 Telecommunicate equipment part nes	150 743	3.62	67.47	157 071	1.92	34.63	2.45	-7.00
776 Valves tubes; diodes, transistors	161 503	3.87	52.32	162 400	1.98	30.79	1.17	-5.92
333 Crude petroleum & bituminous oil	69 299	1.66	18.51	159 859	1.95	13.22	11.91	-5.04
541 Pharmaceuticals excluding medicines	27 515	0.66	86.75	121 573	1.48	88.25	16.72	0.14
792 Aircraft, spacecraft & equipment	91 655	2.20	91.14	115 520	1.41	85.13	4.10	-0.73
874 Measure analyze control device nes	64 901	1.56	88.56	121 083	1.48	78.59	7.64	-1.13
728 Special industrial machine part nes	65 171	1.56	87.46	125 002	1.53	79.29	9.06	-1.00
772 Electrical circuit equipment	64 794	1.55	67.34	116 335	1.42	56.99	7.73	-1.87
713 Internal combustion engine part nes	60 889	1.46	88.15	110 940	1.35	79.47	7.24	-1.20
778 Electrical machinery apparatus nes	72 549	1.74	70.32	101 806	1.24	50.57	5.08	-3.44
752 Computer equipment nes	113 754	2.73	57.25	92 351	1.13	28.54	-0.64	-6.69
641 Paper and paperboard	61 198	1.47	86.68	90 589	1.11	80.99	4.90	-0.79
515 Organo-inorganic compound acid salt	43 080	1.03	92.36	83 041	1.01	82.86	7.94	-0.99
598 Miscellaneous chemical products nes	33 286	0.80	85.85	83 398	1.02	77.72	11.29	-1.19
759 Office equipment part & accessories	83 852	2.01	51.05	80 801	0.99	39.28	1.02	-2.41
343 Natural gas, liquefied or not	26 034	0.62	38.18	81 090	0.99	35.40	14.86	-1.06
699 Base metal manufactures nes	39 338	0.94	74.02	79 024	0.96	64.52	9.43	-1.49
743 Gas pump, compressor, fan, filter	33 700	0.81	80.92	76 599	0.93	71.93	9.96	-1.21
893 Articles of plastic nes	35 900	0.86	66.52	73 412	0.90	63.08	8.61	-0.52
821 Furniture part; bedding furnishing	43 175	1.04	70.31	70 245	0.86	52.82	6.28	-2.99
714 Non-electric engines excluding 712, 713, and 718	45 107	1.08	94.42	63 793	0.78	83.77	4.80	-1.16
782 Goods and service vehicles	47 203	1.13	82.50	71 820	0.88	66.53	5.97	-2.06
723 Civil engineering plant & equipment	28 053	0.67	86.01	67 652	0.83	71.23	11.99	-2.15
971 Gold non-monetary excluding ores	13 850	0.33	59.82	70 759	0.86	47.13	20.78	-2.19
872 Medical instruments appliances nes	22 201	0.53	83.06	61 718	0.75	79.22	11.63	-0.48
575 Other plastics, in primary forms	28 134	0.67	83.06	66 413	0.81	69.82	10.63	-1.79
741 Heating cooling equipment parts nes	32 329	0.78	78.13	59 310	0.72	63.14	9.07	-2.13
684 Aluminium	33 481	0.80	66.65	65 549	0.80	59.84	8.78	-1.19
582 Plastic sheet film foil & strips	27 146	0.65	81.43	62 367	0.76	73.38	10.08	-1.19
793 Ships boats floating structures	25 760	0.62	63.69	61 361	0.75	38.54	9.68	-6.47
667 Pearls, precious semiprecious stone	37 086	0.89	66.31	61 668	0.75	48.98	6.25	-3.24
321 Coal excluding non-agglomomerated	10 010	0.24	58.05	59 218	0.72	55.77	21.69	0.35
716 Rotating electric plant parts nes	20 147	0.48	65.01	52 557	0.64	64.44	12.18	0.10
744 Mechanical handling equipment nes	26 504	0.64	89.83	51 076	0.62	76.29	9.96	-1.97
553 Perfume toilet cosmetics, excluding soap	20 103	0.48	86.33	51 329	0.63	77.43	10.77	-1.13
112 Alcoholic beverages	24 797	0.59	84.76	51 105	0.62	80.80	8.63	-0.54
012 Meat nes, fresh chilled frozen	19 203	0.46	83.04	48 599	0.59	77.46	10.72	-0.57
899 Manufactured articles nes	14 122	0.34	58.67	47 154	0.58	66.78	13.88	1.30
747 Pipe, boiler, tank & vat appliances	18 928	0.45	82.35	48 310	0.59	71.94	11.86	-1.51
682 Copper	17 176	0.41	52.22	52 929	0.65	40.36	15.80	-3.04
773 Electrical distribute equipment nes	26 515	0.64	61.53	49 693	0.61	52.14	8.52	-1.82
679 Iron steel pipe tube fittings etc	16 689	0.40	74.87	44 473	0.54	58.83	13.52	-3.32
761 Television video receive project	13 299	0.32	46.43	41 879	0.51	42.08	15.34	-0.29
281 Iron ore and concentrates	3 941	0.09	41.57	51 473	0.63	48.16	31.70	2.23
533 Pigment, paint, varnish & related	20 494	0.49	82.10	42 823	0.52	80.10	8.78	-0.29
673 Flat iron non-alloy steel products	18 339	0.44	60.59	45 267	0.55	54.21	12.67	-1.85
511 Hydrocarbons nes; derivatives	16 865	0.40	70.50	46 198	0.56	56.29	12.83	-2.58
625 Rubber for wheels, incl inner tube	18 195	0.44	73.25	42 718	0.52	59.37	10.26	-2.56
675 Flat rolled products of alloy steel	16 007	0.38	76.19	44 499	0.54	72.08	13.83	-0.59
742 Liquid pump; liquid elevator parts	17 508	0.42	89.78	41 149	0.50	79.71	10.38	-1.43
098 Edible products & preparations nes	13 842	0.33	78.11	37 873	0.46	72.93	11.82	-0.68
676 Iron steel bar rod section piling	16 379	0.39	70.28	42 366	0.52	60.18	13.33	-2.40
894 Baby carriage toy game sport good	18 352	0.44	38.20	36 584	0.45	41.76	9.11	0.68
775 Household equipment nes	22 413	0.54	62.01	36 821	0.45	43.24	6.38	-3.55
745 Non-electrical machinery tool nes	20 467	0.49	88.73	37 150	0.45	76.76	7.65	-1.56
642 Cut paper and paperboard articles	22 380	0.54	77.30	35 886	0.44	69.92	6.32	-0.97

For sources and notes, see end of table.

Pour les sources et les notes, se reporter à la fin du tableau.

Products ranked by average 2009-2010 values SITC Revision 3 (3-digit level) Produits classés d'après la moyenne des valeurs de 2009-2010 CTCI révision 3 (positions à 3 chiffres)	2000			2010			Growth rates (%) Taux d'accroissement (%) 2000-2010	
	Value (millions of dollars) Valeur (millions de dollars)	% of the country grouping exports En % des exportations du groupe de pays	% of world product exports En % des exportations mondiales des produits	Value (millions of dollars) Valeur (millions de dollars)	% of the country grouping exports En % des exportations du groupe de pays	% of world product exports En % des exportations mondiales des produits	Value Valeur	Difference from world Différence par rapport au monde
771 Electric power machine part excluding 716	19 006	0.46	51.31	38 424	0.47	45.14	9.22	-1.64
845 Articles of apparel nes	22 236	0.53	33.89	35 447	0.43	20.51	5.05	-2.05
851 Footwear	19 997	0.48	42.67	35 403	0.43	36.97	6.50	-1.60
057 Fruit nut (exc oil), fresh or dried	14 761	0.35	53.22	34 037	0.42	49.42	10.08	-0.89
892 Printed matter	22 126	0.53	82.52	33 793	0.41	69.86	5.37	-1.84
748 Mechanical transmission equipment	14 156	0.34	87.33	35 479	0.43	79.22	11.52	-0.98
054 Vegetable & vegetable products nes	13 103	0.31	66.21	35 358	0.43	60.09	10.74	-0.95
571 Primary form ethylene polymers	13 650	0.33	68.99	36 417	0.44	55.39	13.32	-1.96
282 Ferrous iron & steel, waste & scrap	5 805	0.14	74.68	38 323	0.47	82.67	24.05	1.15
774 Electrodiagnostic equipment	13 394	0.32	92.68	33 498	0.41	87.44	10.23	-0.71
898 Music instrument device recording	24 767	0.59	72.82	32 470	0.40	53.69	4.12	-3.19
081 Animal feed excluding unmilled cereal	12 895	0.31	63.00	33 641	0.41	55.25	10.76	-1.45
897 Jewellery nes (667)	13 431	0.32	58.68	33 706	0.41	42.49	10.77	-3.53
048 Cereal & preparation flour starch	11 596	0.28	85.14	30 096	0.37	78.40	11.42	-0.84
514 Nitrogen function compounds	16 588	0.40	83.39	31 411	0.38	68.21	7.06	-2.60
222 Oil seed etc for soft oil	8 655	0.21	63.10	30 508	0.37	56.99	14.62	-1.08
251 Pulp and waste paper	18 994	0.46	78.02	31 795	0.39	71.59	7.23	-0.88
674 Flat plated iron non-alloy steel	14 209	0.34	73.64	30 393	0.37	57.76	10.19	-2.64
034 Fish, fresh live chilled frozen	12 651	0.30	58.56	29 714	0.36	53.63	9.04	-0.83
022 Milk products, excluding butter & cheese	12 636	0.30	88.20	29 498	0.36	83.74	10.14	-0.57
691 Iron steel aluminium structures nes	10 448	0.25	77.70	26 108	0.32	57.90	12.84	-4.16
351 Electric current	8 326	0.20	82.83	27 385	0.33	83.17	14.31	-0.15
041 Wheat meslin, incl spelt, unmilled	11 984	0.29	84.50	26 744	0.33	81.26	11.00	-0.50
574 Polyacetals and polyesters, etc	13 725	0.33	71.96	28 700	0.35	57.46	8.99	-2.64
884 Optical goods fibres nes	15 273	0.37	78.82	27 669	0.34	56.69	7.56	-3.67
695 Tools for use in hand or in machine	15 378	0.37	74.24	27 564	0.34	66.12	7.26	-1.03
763 Sound TV recorder or reproducer	15 142	0.36	55.08	25 910	0.32	41.78	7.23	-2.50
288 Non ferrous base metal waste nes	6 456	0.15	72.54	30 133	0.37	75.86	19.96	0.35
292 Crude vegetable materials nes	10 710	0.26	71.83	26 394	0.32	71.92	9.79	-0.06
554 Soaps cleansers polishes	10 253	0.25	78.43	25 433	0.31	71.75	10.32	-1.16
721 Agricultural machine nes excluding tractor	10 116	0.24	93.57	24 519	0.30	84.10	11.45	-1.20
842 Female clothing, woven	14 163	0.34	31.91	23 655	0.29	31.78	6.57	0.37
681 Silver, platinum, platinum metals	10 661	0.26	70.36	27 927	0.34	54.34	13.39	-3.61
024 Cheese and curd	9 561	0.23	96.93	24 212	0.30	89.18	10.55	-0.97
657 Special yarn and textile fabric etc	14 272	0.34	64.30	23 914	0.29	57.67	6.02	-1.21
522 Inorganic chemical elem oxide salt	10 014	0.24	60.53	24 930	0.30	51.98	11.84	-1.78
664 Glass	12 981	0.31	77.33	23 512	0.29	67.89	7.44	-1.23
011 Beef, fresh chilled frozen	12 176	0.29	84.28	24 240	0.30	69.82	8.21	-2.72
562 Manufactured fertilizer excluding crude	6 838	0.16	53.33	24 112	0.29	43.21	17.08	-2.51
783 Road motor vehicles nes	14 184	0.34	87.57	24 357	0.30	71.70	8.38	-2.08
248 Wood simply worked, railway sleeper	20 581	0.49	77.18	23 279	0.28	66.20	1.93	-1.79
885 Watches and clocks	10 480	0.25	52.68	23 345	0.28	63.28	9.36	2.26
663 Mineral manufactures nes	11 760	0.28	84.93	22 693	0.28	76.10	8.67	-1.10
516 Other organic chemicals	10 629	0.25	73.85	23 060	0.28	65.00	9.44	-1.39
785 Motorcycles, mopeds and cycles	13 377	0.32	63.02	20 548	0.25	49.21	6.10	-2.65
513 Carboxylic acid and compounds	12 067	0.29	71.00	22 007	0.27	47.79	7.03	-4.07
512 Alcohols, phenols; derivatives	9 222	0.22	61.85	23 145	0.28	45.51	10.56	-3.52
751 Office machines	9 395	0.23	65.68	20 748	0.25	41.50	13.41	-4.50
746 Ball or roller bearings	9 790	0.23	78.23	21 685	0.26	72.54	9.64	-0.73
731 Machine tools for material removal	16 056	0.39	86.15	20 891	0.25	75.57	5.07	-1.27
335 Residual petroleum products nes	5 902	0.14	64.56	21 422	0.26	58.47	16.11	-1.45
841 Male clothing, woven	12 864	0.31	29.62	18 525	0.23	30.19	5.14	0.44
791 Railway vehicles and equipment	7 130	0.17	85.53	18 061	0.22	73.62	11.27	-1.72
122 Manufactured tabacco	12 381	0.30	75.99	17 158	0.21	68.69	5.16	-0.60
694 Nails screws nuts bolts rivets	8 907	0.21	71.05	19 626	0.24	62.68	9.88	-1.58
629 Articles of rubber nes	9 232	0.22	81.56	18 843	0.23	74.27	8.23	-1.16
551 Essential oils, perfumes & flavours	6 648	0.16	84.98	17 815	0.22	81.70	10.74	-0.19
056 Vegetables roots tubers nes	7 088	0.17	72.23	17 502	0.21	66.33	10.24	-1.00
591 Household and garden chemicals	8 540	0.20	80.01	16 849	0.21	71.76	8.59	-1.16
073 Chocolate & cocoa preparations nes	6 193	0.15	88.42	17 255	0.21	81.90	11.58	-0.83

For sources and notes, see end of table.

Pour les sources et les notes, se reporter à la fin du tableau.

Products ranked by average 2009-2010 values SITC Revision 3 (3-digit level) Produits classés d'après la moyenne des valeurs de 2009-2010 CTCI révision 3 (positions à 3 chiffres)	2000			2010			Growth rates (%) Taux d'accroissement (%) 2000-2010	
	Value (millions of dollars) Valeur (millions de dollars)	% of the country grouping exports En % des exportations du groupe de pays	% of world product exports En % des exportations mondiales des produits	Value (millions of dollars) Valeur (millions de dollars)	% of the country grouping exports En % des exportations du groupe de pays	% of world product exports En % des exportations mondiales des produits	Value Valeur	Difference from world Différence par rapport au monde
749 Non-electric machinery part nes	12 357	0.30	79.55	16 586	0.20	64.86	4.22	-2.16
634 Veneer, plywood & other wood nes	10 912	0.26	62.79	16 884	0.21	55.00	5.61	-1.60
651 Textile yarn	15 522	0.37	46.08	17 150	0.21	33.00	1.61	-1.76
896 Work of art & collections; antiques	9 971	0.24	95.70	16 686	0.20	90.06	7.28	-0.74
421 Fixed veg fat and oil, "soft"	5 188	0.12	60.76	16 577	0.20	55.70	13.64	-1.47
871 Optical instruments apparatus nes	9 051	0.22	61.94	16 983	0.21	16.94	7.33	-18.66
718 Power generating machinery part nes	5 170	0.12	84.17	15 843	0.19	77.99	14.18	-0.64
597 Additive e.g. lubricate, antifreeze	6 060	0.15	88.00	16 147	0.20	84.36	11.94	-0.36
001 Live animal excluding fish & crustacean	7 500	0.18	81.19	14 616	0.18	78.22	8.54	-0.06
737 Metalwork machinery nes excluding tools	8 366	0.20	85.31	14 527	0.18	71.63	8.68	-2.03
724 Textile leather machinery parts nes	15 799	0.38	78.26	16 532	0.20	61.42	0.22	-2.71
592 Starches, glutenes, glues, etc	7 170	0.17	80.54	14 866	0.18	70.36	8.38	-1.54
044 Maize unmilled, excluding sweet corn	6 412	0.15	72.59	14 696	0.18	62.30	11.13	-0.94
882 Photo cinematographic supply excluding 883	15 838	0.38	85.05	14 392	0.18	82.55	-0.22	-0.17
635 Wood manufactures nes	9 216	0.22	64.42	14 329	0.17	62.81	6.27	-0.03
722 Tractors	7 146	0.17	91.24	13 908	0.17	81.46	9.76	-1.23
786 Trailer caravan transport container	6 937	0.17	62.64	14 992	0.18	56.34	10.91	-0.71
665 Glassware	8 223	0.20	75.42	14 731	0.18	55.66	6.36	-3.23
831 Case bag: storage travel shopping	5 125	0.12	31.11	13 974	0.17	34.33	12.03	1.21
581 Plastic tube pipe hose & fittings	5 799	0.14	87.06	13 837	0.17	75.92	11.12	-1.71
662 Clay and refractory materials	8 390	0.20	82.15	13 306	0.16	58.55	6.19	-3.60
813 Lighting fixtures and fittings nes	6 957	0.17	56.03	13 292	0.16	47.61	8.32	-1.24
726 Printing bookbinding machines parts	13 390	0.32	94.19	13 175	0.16	86.23	1.26	-0.68
621 Rubber material e.g. paste tube rod	6 285	0.15	85.58	13 718	0.17	66.89	9.42	-2.62
111 Non alcoholic beverage nes	4 053	0.10	77.51	12 486	0.15	74.03	13.49	-0.59
672 Ingots, Iron steel primary products	4 334	0.10	37.18	14 363	0.18	37.33	15.33	-0.27
692 Metal storage transport container	5 318	0.13	78.29	11 671	0.14	67.32	10.60	-1.88
342 Liquefied propane and butane	5 138	0.12	30.48	12 917	0.16	30.76	12.16	-1.07
573 Vinyl chloride etc polymers	6 197	0.15	70.70	12 805	0.16	72.53	8.53	-0.24
232 Synthetic & reclaimed rubber; waste	4 642	0.11	72.70	12 750	0.16	60.85	11.85	-1.98
525 Radio active & associated materials	3 392	0.08	65.88	10 949	0.13	68.16	14.76	-0.92
017 Meat offal preserved nes	3 923	0.09	71.04	11 009	0.13	64.77	12.04	-1.39
071 Coffee and coffee substitutes	3 173	0.08	27.68	11 399	0.14	36.68	16.29	2.10
812 Sanitary plumb heat fixtures nes	4 907	0.12	79.15	10 466	0.13	76.08	10.22	-0.69
891 Arms and ammunition	4 560	0.11	85.28	10 392	0.13	86.61	9.79	0.00
658 Made-up textile articles nes	6 293	0.15	36.48	10 553	0.13	23.95	6.34	-4.55
289 Prec metal ore concentrate excluding gold	1 795	0.04	64.01	12 296	0.15	71.75	23.87	0.26
661 Lime cement construction material	6 355	0.15	57.40	10 149	0.12	38.27	6.73	-4.60
653 Man-made woven fabrics	13 141	0.32	42.00	10 284	0.13	27.96	-1.80	-4.24
683 Nickel	5 053	0.12	67.64	11 569	0.14	56.95	13.10	-1.50
727 Food processing machine excluding domestic	5 108	0.12	90.30	10 379	0.13	84.09	9.09	-0.86
697 Base metal household equipment nes	5 795	0.14	48.43	10 314	0.13	39.39	7.28	-1.74
061 Sugar, mollasses and honey	4 351	0.10	42.65	10 917	0.13	27.96	10.08	-3.09
844 Female clothing, knitted crocheted	5 402	0.13	29.90	9 999	0.12	21.81	7.63	-3.25
735 Machine part accessory for 731 733	7 617	0.18	90.15	10 371	0.13	80.24	5.10	-1.30
523 Inorganic acid metal salt peroxy	5 382	0.13	69.77	10 295	0.13	55.23	7.82	-2.97
287 Base metal ores & concentrates nes	2 707	0.06	49.66	11 103	0.14	34.82	19.77	-3.99
572 Primary form styrene polymers	5 844	0.14	47.88	9 953	0.12	40.56	7.11	-1.83
036 Crustacean mollusc aquat invertebra	5 519	0.13	31.43	9 087	0.11	33.80	5.44	1.18
725 Paper & pulp mill, cut manufacture	6 395	0.15	92.68	8 803	0.11	85.40	4.89	-0.82
846 Clothing accessory excluding 831, 848, and 851	6 621	0.16	50.74	8 831	0.11	35.31	3.65	-3.86
611 Leather	7 800	0.19	47.23	9 091	0.11	40.75	1.39	-1.19
895 Office and stationery supplies nes	5 441	0.13	65.31	8 435	0.10	61.80	5.67	-0.62
059 Fruit & vegetable juice unferment	3 864	0.09	59.76	8 197	0.10	57.29	9.78	-0.89
652 Woven cotton fabrics	9 463	0.23	42.86	8 248	0.10	26.20	-2.39	-5.23
058 Fruit preserve preparation excluding juice	3 286	0.08	56.71	7 971	0.10	50.74	10.66	-1.12
278 Other crude minerals	4 523	0.11	63.09	8 268	0.10	50.35	6.89	-2.08
283 Copper ores and concentrates	1 197	0.03	17.70	8 781	0.11	18.78	27.83	2.17
733 Metal work tool no material removal	5 392	0.13	83.11	7 443	0.09	73.18	6.34	-1.18
848 Headgear, non-textile clothing	3 904	0.09	28.28	7 617	0.09	30.14	7.56	1.55

For sources and notes, see end of table.

Pour les sources et les notes, se reporter à la fin du tableau.

Products ranked by average 2009-2010 values SITC Revision 3 (3-digit level) / Produits classés d'après la moyenne des valeurs de 2009-2010 CTCI révision 3 (positions à 3 chiffres)	2000			2010			Growth rates (%) Taux d'accroissement (%) 2000-2010	
	Value (millions of dollars) Valeur (millions de dollars)	% of the country grouping exports En % des exportations du groupe de pays	% of world product exports En % des exportations mondiales des produits	Value (millions of dollars) Valeur (millions de dollars)	% of the country grouping exports En % des exportations du groupe de pays	% of world product exports En % des exportations mondiales des produits	Value Valeur	Difference from world Différence par rapport au monde
659 Floor coverings etc	5 657	0.14	64.31	7 522	0.09	53.34	4.15	-1.97
671 Pig & sponge iron, ferro alloys etc	2 620	0.06	20.70	8 920	0.11	23.08	16.03	-2.76
693 Wire products and fencing grills	3 280	0.08	67.71	7 395	0.09	56.08	11.04	-2.42
037 Fish shellfish, prepared preserved	3 708	0.09	39.19	6 883	0.08	32.35	7.50	-2.41
524 Other inorganic chemicals	3 886	0.09	82.36	7 937	0.10	65.71	9.98	-2.20
285 Aluminium ore concentrate alumina	3 903	0.09	60.25	7 442	0.09	55.92	9.32	-0.93
072 Cocoa	1 473	0.04	35.82	7 172	0.09	35.26	15.78	-0.13
712 Steam vapour turbines & parts nes	2 280	0.05	89.80	6 142	0.07	73.31	11.17	-2.38
263 Cotton	3 494	0.08	43.55	7 752	0.09	41.37	6.56	-0.67
531 Synthetic organic colour agents	6 280	0.15	70.30	6 694	0.08	54.15	0.66	-2.75
655 Knitted or crocheted fabrics nes	5 578	0.13	35.40	6 420	0.08	23.10	1.90	-4.15
686 Zinc	3 259	0.08	59.34	7 190	0.09	58.15	11.96	-0.31
873 Meters and counters nes	3 193	0.08	78.16	6 339	0.08	63.27	7.66	-2.26
247 Wood in rough or roughly squared	4 221	0.10	50.60	6 613	0.08	49.35	5.56	-1.06
023 Butter fats oils derived from milk	2 553	0.06	92.83	6 702	0.08	90.28	9.77	-0.49
762 Radio broadcast receivers	5 748	0.14	29.73	5 898	0.07	37.43	0.64	2.18
654 Other woven textile fabrics nes	6 272	0.15	64.33	5 580	0.07	53.21	-0.02	-1.74
678 Wire of iron or steel	2 685	0.06	70.20	6 188	0.08	55.80	10.56	-2.98
062 Sugar confectionery	2 868	0.07	65.29	5 321	0.06	57.23	7.33	-1.58
811 Prefabricated buildings	2 586	0.06	91.42	5 084	0.06	68.20	8.96	-3.98
211 Raw hides & skins, excluding furskins	4 046	0.10	78.81	5 699	0.07	83.56	1.41	0.65
273 Stone, sand and gravel	2 669	0.06	67.52	4 625	0.06	50.69	7.09	-3.49
431 Processed animal & veg fats & oils	1 649	0.04	54.37	4 738	0.06	43.84	10.56	-3.43
696 Cutlery	2 688	0.06	53.74	4 434	0.05	45.71	4.99	-1.82
291 Crude animal materials nes	1 983	0.05	57.14	4 206	0.05	59.23	9.09	0.20
042 Rice	1 818	0.04	28.06	4 111	0.05	19.39	9.00	-5.64
711 Steam generating boilers & parts	1 803	0.05	74.59	3 762	0.05	45.58	9.98	-5.96
583 Plastic rod stick & profile shapes	1 772	0.04	94.93	4 058	0.05	83.46	9.78	-1.57
843 Male clothing, knitted crocheted	2 403	0.06	21.83	3 882	0.05	15.78	5.76	-4.15
016 Meat offal preserved	1 663	0.04	97.44	4 043	0.05	85.78	9.33	-1.90
025 Eggs, yolks and albumin	1 171	0.03	81.00	3 727	0.05	76.80	13.86	-0.54
579 Plastic waste, parings and scrap	715	0.02	49.68	3 999	0.05	62.25	21.82	2.55
422 Fixed veg fat and oil, excluding "soft"	831	0.02	12.91	4 101	0.05	10.80	19.41	-2.06
411 Animals oils and fats	1 252	0.03	85.22	4 024	0.05	83.02	13.53	-0.63
035 Fish, dried salted smoked	1 975	0.05	71.64	3 913	0.05	71.04	7.68	0.04
121 Unmanufactured tabacco and refuse	2 402	0.06	43.11	3 423	0.04	31.08	4.45	-3.99
043 Barley grain unmilled	2 671	0.06	92.97	3 820	0.05	74.54	7.39	-2.21
325 Coke, semi coke, retort carbon	1 061	0.03	48.15	4 253	0.05	52.02	16.55	1.84
689 Misc non-ferrous base metals	2 395	0.06	61.35	4 127	0.05	47.47	8.07	-3.18
685 Lead	898	0.02	62.02	3 755	0.05	66.10	19.99	0.88
091 Margarine and shortening	838	0.02	59.85	3 277	0.04	64.85	17.26	0.35
881 Photographic device nes	12 195	0.29	64.84	3 579	0.04	46.33	-12.49	-2.91
344 Petroleum and hydrocarbon gas nes	2 835	0.07	62.49	3 851	0.05	27.88	3.60	-7.87
677 Iron steel rail railway materials	857	0.02	82.93	3 129	0.04	77.03	14.89	-1.30
284 Nickel ores, concentrates, etc	1 233	0.03	57.41	3 893	0.05	41.08	15.41	-4.86
246 Wood chips, particles and waste	1 272	0.03	68.18	3 316	0.04	63.59	12.55	0.05
268 Wool & animal hair, incl wool tops	3 421	0.08	72.25	3 484	0.04	57.50	-0.48	-2.11
656 Tulle lace embroidery trim etc	2 939	0.07	50.10	3 095	0.04	33.58	0.48	-4.62
666 Pottery	2 777	0.07	50.58	2 725	0.03	34.92	0.53	-3.28
267 Man made fibre for spinning; waste	1 816	0.04	80.17	2 715	0.03	62.32	4.97	-2.58
269 Worn clothing, textile article; rag	1 092	0.03	73.49	2 654	0.03	70.61	9.97	-0.83
212 Raw furskins and furskin pieces	1 058	0.03	74.05	3 064	0.04	79.16	9.96	0.43
266 Synthetic fibres for spinning	2 099	0.05	44.60	2 590	0.03	36.00	2.62	-2.15
045 Grain, excluding wheat rice barley maize	1 255	0.03	89.00	2 018	0.02	76.90	7.40	-1.15
046 Wheat meal & flour, meslin flour	1 217	0.03	68.30	1 773	0.02	40.27	5.54	-6.68
593 Explosives and pyrotechnic products	705	0.02	59.42	1 944	0.02	61.53	11.67	0.20
074 Tea and maté	575	0.01	17.84	1 718	0.02	23.17	12.49	2.82
223 Oil seed for non soft oil	409	0.01	54.53	1 592	0.02	65.72	16.88	1.69
612 Leather manufactures nes	885	0.02	50.48	1 587	0.02	50.27	6.72	-0.24
322 Briquettes, lignite and peat	628	0.02	93.63	1 401	0.02	38.40	9.44	-8.23

For sources and notes, see end of table.   Pour les sources et les notes, se reporter à la fin du tableau.

3.2.C Export structure by product
Developed economies

3.2.C Structure des exportations par produits
Économies développées

Products ranked by average 2009-2010 values SITC Revision 3 (3-digit level) Produits classés d'après la moyenne des valeurs de 2009-2010 CTCI révision 3 (positions à 3 chiffres)	2000			2010			Growth rates (%) Taux d'accroissement (%) 2000-2010	
	Value (millions of dollars) Valeur (millions de dollars)	% of the country grouping exports En % des exportations du groupe de pays	% of world product exports En % des exportations mondiales des produits	Value (millions of dollars) Valeur (millions de dollars)	% of the country grouping exports En % des exportations du groupe de pays	% of world product exports En % des exportations mondiales des produits	Value Valeur	Difference from world Différence par rapport au monde
633 Cork manufactures	1 182	0.03	95.80	1 416	0.02	94.63	2.43	-0.14
075 Spices	533	0.01	20.19	1 317	0.02	20.29	9.94	0.28
532 Dyeing and tanning extracts	584	0.01	62.97	1 189	0.01	61.18	7.51	0.06
231 Natural rubber, latex, gum, etc	102	0.00	4.10	1 136	0.01	7.54	21.44	0.27
274 Sulphur and unroasted iron pyrites	447	0.01	57.76	1 152	0.01	33.62	15.34	-5.82
687 Tin	277	0.01	15.80	974	0.01	17.04	15.96	-1.00
272 Crude fertilizer, excluding manufactured	179	0.00	13.51	779	0.01	21.70	17.43	3.78
047 Other cereal meals and flours	279	0.01	62.74	601	0.01	55.66	9.40	-1.62
613 Furskin tanned dressed etc	632	0.02	60.45	654	0.01	41.53	-0.30	-4.65
883 Cinematographic film, developed	286	0.01	75.25	524	0.01	83.32	7.61	0.73
245 Fuel wood excluding waste; wood charcoal	118	0.00	35.37	540	0.01	46.76	16.38	2.11
265 Veg textile fibre, excluding cotton jute	467	0.01	77.75	470	0.01	57.74	-0.92	-3.38
277 Natural abrasives nes	599	0.01	58.92	432	0.01	30.14	-4.18	-7.43
961 Coins, nongold and non currency	700	0.02	97.34	288	0.00	89.77	6.83	-0.25
286 Uranium & thorium ore concentrates	249	0.01	81.09	19	0.00	2.63	-3.70	-17.59
244 Natural cork, raw and wastes	206	0.00	83.02	197	0.00	93.55	-0.18	0.98
261 Silk	42	0.00	9.67	40	0.00	7.61	0.71	-1.54
264 Jute & bast fibre nes, raw & retted	5	0.00	5.12	6	0.00	1.66	0.72	-14.08
345 Coal, water, producer gas etc	4	0.00	78.93	4	0.00	9.96	0.43	-22.95

Sources:
- UN DESA Statistics Division, *COMTRADE* database
- UNCTAD secretariat calculations

Sources :
- ONU DAES Division de statistique, base de données *COMTRADE*
- Calculs du secrétariat de la CNUCED

3.2.D Export structure by product
Individual countries and territories

3.2.D Structure des exportations par produits
Pays et territoires individuels

Leading products exported based on average 2009-2010 values SITC Revision 3 (3-digit level) / Principaux produits exportés d'après la moyenne des valeurs de 2009-2010 CTCI révision 3 (positions à 3 chiffres)	Value (f.o.b., thousands of dollars) Valeur (f.a.b., milliers de dollars)	2009-2010 of country total du total du pays	As percentage En pourcentage of ** (1) des ** (1)	of world du monde
Afghanistan (**=Developing)				
All commodity groups	395 962	100.0	0.01	0.00
057 Fruit nut (exc oil), fresh or dried	77 074	19.5	0.24	0.11
263 Cotton	21 699	5.5	0.32	0.15
292 Crude vegetable materials nes	20 445	5.2	0.22	0.06
661 Lime cement construction material	17 412	4.4	0.12	0.07
658 Floor coverings etc	17 310	4.4	0.30	0.13
713 Internal combustion engine part nes	11 844	3.0	0.05	0.01
282 Ferrous iron & steel, waste & scrap	11 573	2.9	0.23	0.03
784 Motor vehicle parts and accessories	8 927	2.3	0.01	0.00
764 Telecommunicate equipment part nes	8 446	2.1	0.00	0.00
054 Vegetable & vegetable products nes	6 245	1.6	0.03	0.01
Remainder	194 988	49.2		
Albania - Albanie (**=Transition)				
All commodity groups	1 318 935	100.0	0.25	0.01
851 Footwear	210 080	15.9	15.96	0.24
333 Crude petroleum & bituminous oil	108 593	8.2	0.07	0.01
841 Male clothing, woven	91 691	7.0	10.47	0.16
287 Base metal ores & concentrates nes	73 578	5.6	7.47	0.29
845 Articles of apparel nes	68 804	5.2	6.87	0.06
699 Base metal manufactures nes	46 280	3.5	2.78	0.04
351 Electric current	38 862	2.9	2.06	0.12
672 Ingots, Iron steel primary products	35 443	2.7	0.31	0.11
842 Female clothing, woven	34 704	2.6	3.20	0.05
844 Female clothing, knitted crocheted	32 133	2.4	8.88	0.08
Remainder	578 768	43.9		
Algeria - Algérie (**=Developing)				
All commodity groups	51 122 447	100.0	0.90	0.37
333 Crude petroleum & bituminous oil	23 031 956	45.1	3.02	2.15
343 Natural gas, liquefied or not	15 958 511	31.2	18.24	7.52
334 Heavy petroleum & bituminous oil	6 620 270	13.0	2.57	1.10
342 Liquefied propane and butane	4 200 128	8.2	16.36	11.04
335 Residual petroleum products nes	436 113	0.9	3.58	1.37
522 Inorganic chemical elem oxide salt	216 796	0.4	1.24	0.52
061 Sugar, mollasses and honey	121 420	0.2	0.53	0.36
272 Crude fertilizer, excl. manufactured	59 903	0.1	2.57	1.80
282 Ferrous iron & steel, waste & scrap	58 350	0.1	1.18	0.15
686 Zinc	49 091	0.1	1.38	0.48
Remainder	360 910	0.7		
American Samoa - Samoa américaines (**=Developing) (2)				
All commodity groups	475 000	100.0	0.01	0.00
081 Animal feed excluding unmilled cereal	65 624	13.8	0.27	0.11
571 Primary form ethylene polymers	60 757	12.8	0.25	0.10
281 Iron ore and concentrates	57 178	12.0	0.15	0.07
034 Fish, fresh live chilled frozen	53 706	11.3	0.26	0.11
728 Special industrial machine part nes	31 925	6.7	0.12	0.02
511 Hydrocarbons nes; derivatives	26 958	5.7	0.10	0.04
743 Gas pump, compressor, fan, filter	25 431	5.4	0.10	0.03
282 Ferrous iron & steel, waste & scrap	22 321	4.7	0.45	0.06
263 Cotton	18 931	4.0	0.28	0.13
411 Animals oils and fats	13 384	2.8	1.80	0.30
Remainder	98 784	20.8		
Andorra - Andorre (**=Developed) (2)				
All commodity groups	58 749	100.0	0.00	0.00
781 Passenger cars and race cars	39 824	67.8	0.01	0.01
061 Sugar, mollasses and honey	2 901	4.9	0.03	0.01
778 Electrical machinery apparatus nes	1 695	2.9	0.00	0.00
898 Music instrument device recording	1 620	2.8	0.01	0.00
763 Sound TV recorder or reproducer	852	1.4	0.00	0.00
896 Work of art & collections; antiques	851	1.4	0.01	0.01
764 Telecommunicate equipment part nes	670	1.1	0.00	0.00
553 Perfume toilet cosmetics, excl. soap	614	1.0	0.00	0.00
899 Manufactured articles nes	503	0.9	0.00	0.00
844 Female clothing, knitted crocheted	436	0.7	0.00	0.00
Remainder	8 784	15.0		

Leading products exported based on average 2009-2010 values SITC Revision 3 (3-digit level) / Principaux produits exportés d'après la moyenne des valeurs de 2009-2010 CTCI révision 3 (positions à 3 chiffres)	Value (f.o.b., thousands of dollars) Valeur (f.a.b., milliers de dollars)	2009-2010 of country total du total du pays	As percentage En pourcentage of ** (1) des ** (1)	of world du monde
Angola (**=Developing) (2)				
All commodity groups	44 069 500	100.0	0.79	0.32
333 Crude petroleum & bituminous oil	43 259 931	98.8	5.66	4.04
667 Pearls, precious semiprecious stone	533 108	1.2	0.97	0.49
334 Heavy petroleum & bituminous oil	395 677	0.9	0.15	0.07
342 Liquefied propane and butane	225 102	0.5	0.88	0.59
781 Passenger cars and race cars	33 852	0.1	0.04	0.01
344 Petroleum and hydrocarbon gas nes	26 100	0.1	0.42	0.26
273 Stone, sand and gravel	25 484	0.1	0.63	0.29
691 Iron steel aluminium structures nes	18 885	0.0	0.10	0.04
036 Crustacean mollusc aquat invertebra	12 157	0.0	0.08	0.05
752 Computer equipment nes	10 624	0.0	0.01	0.00
Remainder	128 581	0.3		
Anguilla (**=Developing) (2)				
All commodity groups	17 749	100.0	0.00	0.00
782 Goods and service vehicles	3 951	22.3	0.01	0.00
112 Alcoholic beverages	2 307	13.0	0.02	0.00
741 Heating cooling equipment parts nes	1 794	10.1	0.01	0.00
845 Articles of apparel nes	587	3.3	0.00	0.00
893 Articles of plastic nes	562	3.2	0.00	0.00
635 Wood manufactures nes	533	3.0	0.01	0.00
697 Base metal household equipment nes	522	2.9	0.00	0.00
744 Mechanical handling equipment nes	438	2.5	0.00	0.00
059 Fruit & vegetable juice unferment	433	2.4	0.01	0.00
772 Electrical circuit equipment	382	2.2	0.00	0.00
Remainder	6 242	35.2		
Antigua and Barbuda - Antigua-et-Barbuda (**=Developing) (2)				
All commodity groups	35 041	100.0	0.00	0.00
793 Ships boats floating structures	5 638	16.1	0.01	0.00
781 Passenger cars and race cars	3 670	10.5	0.00	0.00
702 Goods and service vehicles	2 626	7.5	0.01	0.00
783 Road motor vehicles nes	1 653	4.7	0.02	0.01
634 Veneer, plywood & other wood nes	1 008	2.9	0.01	0.00
699 Base metal manufactures nes	1 000	2.9	0.00	0.00
784 Motor vehicle parts and accessories	813	2.3	0.00	0.00
746 Ball or roller bearings	808	2.3	0.01	0.00
723 Civil engineering plant & equipment	647	1.8	0.00	0.00
091 Margarine and shortening	641	1.8	0.04	0.01
Remainder	16 537	47.2		
Argentina - Argentine (**=Developing)				
All commodity groups	61 903 097	100.0	1.09	0.45
081 Animal feed excluding unmilled cereal	8 704 593	14.1	35.33	15.20
421 Fixed veg fat and oil, "soft"	4 523 062	7.3	49.60	16.48
222 Oil seed etc for soft oil	3 620 315	5.8	18.30	7.28
781 Passenger cars and race cars	3 341 516	5.4	3.99	0.67
333 Crude petroleum & bituminous oil	2 524 174	4.1	0.33	0.24
044 Maize unmilled, excluding sweet corn	2 379 304	3.8	37.08	10.87
782 Goods and service vehicles	1 985 297	3.2	6.86	2.11
334 Heavy petroleum & bituminous oil	1 614 838	2.6	0.63	0.28
971 Gold non-monetary excluding ores	1 525 202	2.5	2.01	1.11
283 Copper ores and concentrates	1 315 526	2.1	4.25	3.36
Remainder	30 369 270	49.1		
Armenia - Arménie (**=Transition)				
All commodity groups	847 707	100.0	0.16	0.01
671 Pig & sponge iron, ferro alloys etc	118 433	14.0	1.76	0.38
283 Copper ores and concentrates	111 706	13.2	15.12	0.29
112 Alcoholic beverages	89 109	10.5	7.12	0.15
682 Copper	76 267	9.0	1.03	0.07
667 Pearls, precious semiprecious stone	72 953	8.6	3.69	0.07
684 Aluminium	72 890	8.6	0.90	0.08
971 Gold non-monetary excluding ores	31 041	3.7	2.26	0.02
287 Base metal ores & concentrates nes	20 086	2.4	2.04	0.08
689 Misc non-ferrous base metals	13 182	1.6	2.32	0.18
661 Lime cement construction material	12 259	1.4	1.49	0.05
Remainder	229 782	27.1		

For sources and notes, see end of table.

Pour les sources et les notes, se reporter à la fin du tableau.

Leading products exported based on average 2009-2010 values SITC Revision 3 (3-digit level) Principaux produits exportés d'après la moyenne des valeurs de 2009-2010 CTCI révision 3 (positions à 3 chiffres)	2009-2010			
	Value (f.o.b., thousands of dollars) Valeur (f.a.b., milliers de dollars)	As percentage En pourcentage		
		of country total du total du pays	of ** (1) des ** (1)	of world du monde

Aruba (**=Developing) (2)

All commodity groups	850 000	100.0	0.01	0.01
334 Heavy petroleum & bituminous oil	642 027	75.5	0.25	0.11
112 Alcoholic beverages	51 134	6.0	0.49	0.08
335 Residual petroleum products nes	29 056	3.4	0.24	0.09
122 Manufactured tabacco	22 635	2.7	0.34	0.09
274 Sulphur and unroasted iron pyrites	15 932	1.9	1.14	0.64
333 Crude petroleum & bituminous oil	11 213	1.3	0.00	0.00
971 Gold non-monetary excluding ores	11 049	1.3	0.01	0.01
713 Internal combustion engine part nes	5 715	0.7	0.02	0.00
716 Rotating electric plant parts nes	3 397	0.4	0.01	0.00
061 Sugar, mollasses and honey	3 367	0.4	0.01	0.01
Remainder	54 446	6.4		

Australia - Australie (**=Developed)

All commodity groups	180 235 847	100.0	2.37	1.30
321 Coal excluding non-agglomomerated	34 755 804	19.3	66.77	36.92
281 Iron ore and concentrates	33 931 747	18.8	84.99	41.28
971 Gold non-monetary excluding ores	12 388 925	6.9	20.70	9.04
333 Crude petroleum & bituminous oil	7 506 896	4.2	5.28	0.70
343 Natural gas, liquefied or not	7 238 628	4.0	9.73	3.41
285 Aluminium ore concentrate alumina	4 253 094	2.4	64.68	36.26
041 Wheat meslin, incl spelt, unmilled	3 742 693	2.1	14.48	11.46
283 Copper ores and concentrates	3 721 907	2.1	49.82	9.50
011 Beef, fresh chilled frozen	3 651 996	2.0	16.44	11.43
684 Aluminium	3 585 848	2.0	6.21	3.78
Remainder	65 458 308	36.3		

Austria - Autriche (**=Developed)

All commodity groups	138 134 625	100.0	1.81	1.00
713 Internal combustion engine part nes	5 296 766	3.8	5.43	4.33
542 Medicines including veterinary	4 882 291	3.5	1.66	1.55
784 Motor vehicle parts and accessories	3 849 677	2.8	1.91	1.45
781 Passenger cars and race cars	3 756 247	2.7	0.90	0.75
641 Paper and paperboard	3 404 992	2.5	3.95	3.22
699 Base metal manufactures nes	3 381 506	2.4	4.57	2.99
728 Special industrial machine part nes	3 257 489	2.4	3.01	2.40
541 Pharmaceuticals excluding medicines	3 009 301	2.2	2.60	2.30
772 Electrical circuit equipment	2 405 563	1.7	2.27	1.31
684 Aluminium	2 069 112	1.5	3.58	2.18
Remainder	102 821 681	74.4		

Azerbaijan - Azerbaïdjan (**=Transition) (2)

All commodity groups	23 786 400	100.0	4.46	0.17
333 Crude petroleum & bituminous oil	20 476 603	86.1	12.47	1.91
334 Heavy petroleum & bituminous oil	1 296 444	5.5	1.79	0.23
343 Natural gas, liquefied or not	205 266	0.9	0.41	0.10
793 Ships boats floating structures	204 047	0.9	7.35	0.14
057 Fruit nut (exc oil), fresh or dried	142 290	0.6	9.49	0.21
061 Sugar, mollasses and honey	121 403	0.5	13.22	0.36
571 Primary form ethylene polymers	55 719	0.2	5.63	0.10
421 Fixed veg fat and oil, "soft"	54 720	0.2	1.76	0.20
431 Processed animal & veg fats & oils	52 329	0.2	47.86	0.56
684 Aluminium	49 699	0.2	0.61	0.05
Remainder	1 127 880	4.7		

Bahamas (**=Developing) (2)

All commodity groups	706 565	100.0	0.01	0.01
334 Heavy petroleum & bituminous oil	286 965	40.6	0.11	0.05
793 Ships boats floating structures	140 743	19.9	0.16	0.09
572 Primary form styrene polymers	51 336	7.3	0.41	0.24
112 Alcoholic beverages	40 121	5.7	0.39	0.07
515 Organo-inorganic compound acid salt	33 059	4.7	0.22	0.03
036 Crustacean mollusc aquat invertebra	27 961	4.0	0.18	0.11
896 Work of art & collections; antiques	16 809	2.4	1.10	0.10
553 Perfume toilet cosmetics, excl. soap	13 543	1.9	0.10	0.02
273 Stone, sand and gravel	10 765	1.5	0.27	0.12
278 Other crude minerals	6 315	0.9	0.11	0.04
Remainder	78 948	11.2		

Bahrain - Bahreïn (**=Developing) (2)

All commodity groups	12 760 372	100.0	0.23	0.09
334 Heavy petroleum & bituminous oil	3 795 425	29.7	1.47	0.66
684 Aluminium	2 728 331	21.4	8.40	2.88
281 Iron ore and concentrates	1 002 051	7.9	2.04	1.22
693 Wire products and fencing grills	333 805	2.6	6.68	2.75
562 Manufactured fertilizer excl. crude	280 919	2.2	1.64	0.58
897 Jewellery nes (807)	262 700	2.1	0.63	0.36
781 Passenger cars and race cars	255 771	2.0	0.31	0.05
335 Residual petroleum products nes	217 299	1.7	1.78	0.68
024 Cheese and curd	209 195	1.6	11.62	0.82
333 Crude petroleum & bituminous oil	206 215	1.6	0.03	0.02
Remainder	3 468 401	27.2		

Bangladesh (**=Developing) (2)

All commodity groups	18 106 521	100.0	0.32	0.13
845 Articles of apparel nes	5 856 274	32.3	7.12	4.95
841 Male clothing, woven	4 072 566	22.5	10.40	6.96
842 Female clothing, woven	1 910 116	10.5	4.09	2.68
843 Male clothing, knitted crocheted	966 464	5.3	5.12	4.25
844 Female clothing, knitted crocheted	948 092	5.2	2.98	2.26
658 Made-up textile articles nes	576 774	3.2	1.86	1.39
036 Crustacean mollusc aquat invertebra	572 393	3.2	3.64	2.34
651 Textile yarn	380 599	2.1	1.38	0.86
611 Leather	264 773	1.5	2.52	1.37
264 Jute & bast fibre nes, raw & retted	220 645	1.2	78.00	76.50
Remainder	2 337 825	12.9		

Barbados - Barbade (**=Developing)

All commodity groups	403 751	100.0	0.01	0.00
542 Medicines including veterinary	33 349	8.3	0.17	0.01
781 Passenger cars and race cars	31 821	7.9	0.04	0.01
333 Crude petroleum & bituminous oil	27 071	6.7	0.00	0.00
112 Alcoholic beverages	24 275	6.0	0.23	0.04
892 Printed matter	11 315	2.8	0.09	0.02
334 Heavy petroleum & bituminous oil	10 905	2.7	0.00	0.00
747 Pipe, boiler, tank & vat appliances	10 810	2.7	0.07	0.02
661 Lime cement construction material	10 575	2.6	0.07	0.04
091 Margarine and shortening	10 345	2.6	0.71	0.21
061 Sugar, mollasses and honey	9 949	2.5	0.04	0.03
Remainder	223 336	55.3		

Belarus - Bélarus (**=Transition)

All commodity groups	23 254 046	100.0	4.36	0.17
334 Heavy petroleum & bituminous oil	6 878 423	29.6	9.51	1.20
562 Manufactured fertilizer excl. crude	2 008 275	8.6	20.35	4.14
333 Crude petroleum & bituminous oil	738 069	3.2	0.45	0.07
782 Goods and service vehicles	651 935	2.8	43.52	0.69
722 Tractors	614 473	2.6	90.27	3.70
022 Milk products, excl. butter & cheese	532 834	2.3	55.00	1.67
024 Cheese and curd	459 622	2.0	49.56	1.81
676 Iron steel bar rod section piling	451 814	1.9	8.76	0.73
011 Beef, fresh chilled frozen	418 482	1.8	82.02	1.31
625 Rubber for wheels, incl inner tube	408 544	1.8	29.12	0.63
Remainder	10 091 574	43.4		

Belgium - Belgique (**=Developed)

All commodity groups	390 517 436	100.0	5.13	2.83
542 Medicines including veterinary	38 308 913	9.8	13.04	12.16
781 Passenger cars and race cars	23 738 525	6.1	5.71	4.74
334 Heavy petroleum & bituminous oil	20 508 466	5.3	8.42	3.58
667 Pearls, precious semiprecious stone	13 808 124	3.5	26.09	12.57
541 Pharmaceuticals excluding medicines	13 504 215	3.5	11.65	10.31
515 Organo-inorganic compound acid salt	12 534 125	3.2	15.41	12.90
575 Other plastics, in primary forms	8 599 399	2.2	14.40	10.17
784 Motor vehicle parts and accessories	6 294 913	1.6	3.12	2.37
571 Primary form ethylene polymers	5 457 823	1.4	16.73	9.41
343 Natural gas, liquefied or not	5 290 449	1.4	7.11	2.49
Remainder	242 472 485	62.1		

For sources and notes, see end of table.

Pour les sources et les notes, se reporter à la fin du tableau.

3.2.D Structure des exportations par produits
Pays et territoires individuels

Leading products exported based on average 2009-2010 values SITC Revision 3 (3-digit level) / Principaux produits exportés d'après la moyenne des valeurs de 2009-2010 CTCI révision 3 (positions à 3 chiffres)	Value (f.o.b., thousands of dollars) Valeur (f.a.b., milliers de dollars)	2009-2010 As percentage En pourcentage of country total du total du pays	of ** (1) des ** (1)	of world du monde
Belize (**=Developing) (2)				
All commodity groups	253 018	100.0	0.00	0.00
333 Crude petroleum & bituminous oil	55 013	21.7	0.01	0.01
057 Fruit nut (exc oil), fresh or dried	38 687	15.3	0.12	0.06
041 Wheat meslin, incl spelt, unmilled	27 687	10.9	1.31	0.08
059 Fruit & vegetable juice unferment	21 911	8.7	0.39	0.16
061 Sugar, mollasses and honey	21 981	8.5	0.09	0.06
036 Crustacean mollusc aquat invertebra	14 103	5.6	0.09	0.06
781 Passenger cars and race cars	9 910	3.9	0.01	0.00
034 Fish, fresh live chilled frozen	6 571	2.6	0.03	0.01
783 Road motor vehicles nes	3 449	1.4	0.04	0.01
054 Vegetable & vegetable products nes	3 159	1.2	0.02	0.01
Remainder	50 947	20.1		
Benin - Bénin (**=Developing) (2)				
All commodity groups	1 306 551	100.0	0.02	0.01
263 Cotton	453 718	34.7	6.77	3.07
334 Heavy petroleum & bituminous oil	204 396	15.6	0.08	0.04
057 Fruit nut (exc oil), fresh or dried	98 756	7.6	0.31	0.15
288 Non ferrous base metal waste nes	92 911	7.1	1.32	0.29
122 Manufactured tabacco	58 513	4.5	0.88	0.23
247 Wood in rough or roughly squared	49 081	3.8	1.21	0.41
282 Ferrous iron & steel, waste & scrap	32 877	2.5	0.67	0.08
661 Lime cement construction material	29 759	2.3	0.20	0.12
223 Oil seed for non soft oil	24 045	1.8	3.59	1.03
342 Liquefied propane and butane	19 493	1.5	0.08	0.05
Remainder	243 002	18.6		
Bermuda - Bermudes (**=Developed) (2)				
All commodity groups	27 500	100.0	0.00	0.00
793 Ships boats floating structures	6 877	25.0	0.01	0.00
342 Liquefied propane and butane	5 410	19.7	0.05	0.01
343 Natural gas, liquefied or not	5 274	19.2	0.01	0.00
112 Alcoholic beverages	2 194	8.0	0.00	0.00
831 Case bag: storage travel shopping	697	2.5	0.01	0.00
896 Work of art & collections; antiques	678	2.5	0.00	0.00
542 Medicines including veterinary	659	2.4	0.00	0.00
334 Heavy petroleum & bituminous oil	657	2.4	0.00	0.00
041 Wheat meslin, incl spelt, unmilled	569	2.1	0.00	0.00
541 Pharmaceuticals excluding medicines	436	1.6	0.00	0.00
Remainder	4 048	14.7		
Bhutan - Bhoutan (**=Developing)				
All commodity groups	568 578	100.0	0.01	0.00
351 Electric current	162 722	28.6	4.14	0.51
671 Pig & sponge iron, ferro alloys etc	118 381	20.8	0.70	0.38
682 Copper	35 837	6.3	0.06	0.03
524 Other inorganic chemicals	30 413	5.3	1.26	0.31
661 Lime cement construction material	27 364	4.8	0.19	0.11
672 Ingots, Iron steel primary products	21 201	3.7	0.25	0.07
278 Other crude minerals	20 806	3.7	0.35	0.15
676 Iron steel bar rod section piling	18 599	3.3	0.09	0.03
273 Stone, sand and gravel	16 650	2.9	0.41	0.19
057 Fruit nut (exc oil), fresh or dried	14 974	2.6	0.05	0.02
Remainder	101 631	17.9		
Bolivia (Plurinational State of) - Bolivie (État plurinational de) (**=Developing)				
All commodity groups	5 738 025	100.0	0.10	0.04
343 Natural gas, liquefied or not	2 392 413	41.7	2.74	1.13
287 Base metal ores & concentrates nes	731 463	12.7	4.71	2.87
289 Prec metal ore concentrate excl. gold	451 887	7.9	11.28	3.16
081 Animal feed excluding unmilled cereal	324 227	5.7	1.32	0.57
687 Tin	247 056	4.3	6.11	5.14
421 Fixed veg fat and oil, "soft"	239 726	4.2	2.63	0.87
333 Crude petroleum & bituminous oil	139 891	2.4	0.02	0.01
057 Fruit nut (exc oil), fresh or dried	102 823	1.8	0.32	0.15
897 Jewellery nes (667)	79 419	1.4	0.19	0.11
061 Sugar, mollasses and honey	77 470	1.4	0.34	0.23
Remainder	951 650	16.6		
Bosnia and Herzegovina - Bosnie-Herzégovine (**=Transition)				
All commodity groups	4 378 514	100.0	0.82	0.03
851 Footwear	351 349	8.0	26.70	0.40
684 Aluminium	327 736	7.5	4.04	0.35
821 Furniture part; bedding furnishing	266 565	6.1	16.60	0.22
351 Electric current	150 569	3.4	7.98	0.47
248 Wood simply worked, railway sleeper	138 215	3.2	3.81	0.43
676 Iron steel bar rod section piling	130 293	3.0	2.53	0.21
325 Coke, semi coke, retort carbon	124 251	2.8	14.08	2.04
743 Gas pump, compressor, fan, filter	108 018	2.5	13.05	0.11
691 Iron steel aluminium structures nes	101 035	2.3	11.34	0.22
285 Aluminium ore concentrate alumina	98 436	2.2	13.38	0.84
Remainder	2 582 048	59.0		
Botswana (**=Developing) (2)				
All commodity groups	4 074 475	100.0	0.07	0.03
667 Pearls, precious semiprecious stone	2 244 202	55.1	4.08	2.04
284 Nickel ores, concentrates, etc	712 337	17.5	16.47	9.62
011 Beef, fresh chilled frozen	144 477	3.5	1.57	0.45
283 Copper ores and concentrates	62 135	1.5	0.20	0.16
971 Gold non-monetary excluding ores	61 055	1.5	0.08	0.04
662 Clay and refractory materials	56 725	1.4	0.69	0.26
842 Female clothing, woven	56 281	1.4	0.12	0.08
523 Inorganic acid metal salt peroxy	41 573	1.0	0.59	0.24
841 Male clothing, woven	34 781	0.9	0.09	0.06
845 Articles of apparel nes	30 696	0.8	0.04	0.03
Remainder	630 212	15.5		
Brazil - Brésil (**=Developing)				
All commodity groups	175 175 590	100.0	3.09	1.27
281 Iron ore and concentrates	21 079 392	12.0	55.53	25.64
333 Crude petroleum & bituminous oil	12 822 224	7.3	1.68	1.20
222 Oil seed etc for soft oil	11 294 298	6.4	57.08	22.72
061 Sugar, mollasses and honey	10 645 414	6.1	46.86	31.86
012 Meat nes, fresh chilled frozen	6 891 782	3.9	54.43	11.72
071 Coffee and coffee substitutes	5 020 870	2.9	29.03	17.94
081 Animal feed excluding unmilled cereal	4 958 893	2.8	20.13	8.66
792 Aircraft, spacecraft & equipment	4 277 269	2.4	22.62	3.27
251 Pulp and waste paper	4 038 462	2.3	42.15	10.69
781 Passenger cars and race cars	3 830 526	2.2	4.58	0.76
Remainder	90 316 469	51.6		
Brunei Darussalam - Brunéi Darussalam (**=Developing) (2)				
All commodity groups	8 211 721	100.0	0.14	0.06
333 Crude petroleum & bituminous oil	4 516 517	55.0	0.59	0.42
343 Natural gas, liquefied or not	3 439 158	41.9	3.93	1.62
334 Heavy petroleum & bituminous oil	34 008	0.4	0.01	0.01
845 Articles of apparel nes	33 810	0.4	0.04	0.03
282 Ferrous iron & steel, waste & scrap	14 263	0.2	0.29	0.04
731 Machine tools for material removal	13 522	0.2	0.25	0.06
897 Jewellery nes (667)	13 484	0.2	0.03	0.02
792 Aircraft, spacecraft & equipment	10 976	0.1	0.06	0.01
844 Female clothing, knitted crocheted	10 301	0.1	0.03	0.02
714 Non-electric engines excl. 712 713 718	8 460	0.1	0.09	0.01
Remainder	117 223	1.4		
Bulgaria - Bulgarie (**=Developed)				
All commodity groups	18 555 263	100.0	0.24	0.13
334 Heavy petroleum & bituminous oil	1 803 511	9.7	0.74	0.31
682 Copper	1 730 663	9.3	3.85	1.58
222 Oil seed etc for soft oil	508 821	2.7	1.78	1.02
842 Female clothing, woven	487 828	2.6	2.06	0.68
542 Medicines including veterinary	422 920	2.3	0.14	0.13
845 Articles of apparel nes	386 963	2.1	1.10	0.33
841 Male clothing, woven	386 482	2.1	2.09	0.66
041 Wheat meslin, incl spelt, unmilled	381 419	2.1	1.48	1.17
773 Electrical distribute equipment nes	306 084	1.6	0.68	0.36
351 Electric current	301 391	1.6	1.15	0.94
Remainder	11 839 179	63.8		

For sources and notes, see end of table.

Pour les sources et les notes, se reporter à la fin du tableau.

175

3.2.D Export structure by product
Individual countries and territories

3.2.D Structure des exportations par produits
Pays et territoires individuels

Leading products exported based on average 2009-2010 values SITC Revision 3 (3-digit level) / Principaux produits exportés d'après la moyenne des valeurs de 2009-2010 CTCI révision 3 (positions à 3 chiffres)	2009-2010 Value (f.o.b., thousands of dollars) Valeur (f.a.b., milliers de dollars)	As percentage En pourcentage — of country total du total du pays	of ** (1) des ** (1)	of world du monde
Burkina Faso (**=Developing) (2)				
All commodity groups	1 094 313	100.0	0.02	0.01
263 Cotton	447 811	40.9	6.67	3.03
971 Gold non-monetary excluding ores	355 140	32.5	0.47	0.26
222 Oil seed etc for soft oil	96 217	8.8	0.49	0.19
223 Oil seed for non soft oil	31 323	2.9	4.68	1.35
001 Live animal excl. fish & crustacean	25 599	2.3	0.71	0.14
057 Fruit nut (exc oil) fresh or dried	15 992	1.5	0.06	0.03
054 Vegetable & vegetable products nes	10 535	1.0	0.05	0.02
287 Base metal ores & concentrates nes	6 666	0.6	0.04	0.03
676 Iron steel bar rod section piling	6 630	0.6	0.03	0.01
661 Lime cement construction material	6 609	0.6	0.05	0.03
Remainder	92 293	8.4		
Burundi (**=Developing) (2)				
All commodity groups	81 245	100.0	0.00	0.00
071 Coffee and coffee substitutes	45 950	56.6	0.27	0.16
074 Tea and maté	9 086	11.2	0.18	0.13
971 Gold non-monetary excluding ores	7 109	8.7	0.01	0.01
287 Base metal ores & concentrates nes	2 519	3.1	0.02	0.01
211 Raw hides & skins, excluding furskins	1 747	2.2	0.23	0.03
334 Heavy petroleum & bituminous oil	1 143	1.4	0.00	0.00
263 Cotton	1 125	1.4	0.02	0.01
554 Soaps cleansers polishes	1 051	1.3	0.01	0.00
061 Sugar, mollasses and honey	943	1.2	0.00	0.00
112 Alcoholic beverages	929	1.1	0.01	0.00
Remainder	9 643	11.9		
Cambodia - Cambodge (**=Developing) (2)				
All commodity groups	4 945 972	100.0	0.09	0.04
845 Articles of apparel nes	1 433 988	29.0	1.74	1.21
844 Female clothing, knitted crocheted	803 263	16.2	2.53	1.92
892 Printed matter	615 908	12.5	4.79	1.32
843 Male clothing, knitted crocheted	360 517	7.3	1.91	1.58
842 Female clothing, woven	346 092	7.0	0.74	0.48
851 Footwear	299 085	6.0	0.57	0.34
841 Male clothing, woven	277 845	5.6	0.71	0.47
971 Gold non-monetary excluding ores	104 315	2.1	0.14	0.08
273 Stone, sand and gravel	103 235	2.1	2.57	1.17
231 Natural rubber, latex, gum, etc	84 826	1.7	0.49	0.46
Remainder	516 898	10.5		
Cameroon - Cameroun (**=Developing) (2)				
All commodity groups	3 715 307	100.0	0.07	0.03
333 Crude petroleum & bituminous oil	1 247 395	33.6	0.16	0.12
072 Cocoa	625 260	16.8	4.98	3.32
334 Heavy petroleum & bituminous oil	310 890	8.4	0.12	0.05
248 Wood simply worked, railway sleeper	286 856	7.7	3.99	0.90
057 Fruit nut (exc oil), fresh or dried	192 646	5.2	0.60	0.29
247 Wood in rough or roughly squared	138 683	3.7	3.42	1.16
231 Natural rubber, latex, gum, etc	92 550	2.5	0.53	0.51
263 Cotton	87 706	2.4	1.31	0.59
684 Aluminium	83 033	2.2	0.29	0.09
071 Coffee and coffee substitutes	57 811	1.6	0.33	0.21
Remainder	592 478	15.9		
Canada (**=Developed)				
All commodity groups	350 545 935	100.0	4.60	2.54
333 Crude petroleum & bituminous oil	44 039 375	12.6	30.97	4.12
781 Passenger cars and race cars	30 121 932	8.6	7.25	6.01
343 Natural gas, liquefied or not	14 348 967	4.1	19.29	6.76
334 Heavy petroleum & bituminous oil	12 437 229	3.5	5.11	2.17
971 Gold non-monetary excluding ores	10 773 561	3.1	18.00	7.86
792 Aircraft, spacecraft & equipment	9 583 802	2.7	8.60	7.33
784 Motor vehicle parts and accessories	7 835 434	2.2	3.89	2.95
641 Paper and paperboard	7 500 120	2.1	8.70	7.09
684 Aluminium	6 506 522	1.9	11.27	6.86
251 Pulp and waste paper	5 852 893	1.7	21.52	15.50
Remainder	201 546 100	57.5		

Leading products exported based on average 2009-2010 values SITC Revision 3 (3-digit level) / Principaux produits exportés d'après la moyenne des valeurs de 2009-2010 CTCI révision 3 (positions à 3 chiffres)	2009-2010 Value (f.o.b., thousands of dollars) Valeur (f.a.b., milliers de dollars)	As percentage En pourcentage — of country total du total du pays	of ** (1) des ** (1)	of world du monde
Cape Verde - Cap-Vert (**=Developing) (2)				
All commodity groups	40 864	100.0	0.00	0.00
037 Fish shellfish, prepared preserved	13 461	32.9	0.10	0.07
034 Fish, fresh live chilled frozen	13 246	32.4	0.00	0.03
851 Footwear	3 409	8.3	0.01	0.00
841 Male clothing, woven	2 920	7.1	0.01	0.00
845 Articles of apparel nes	1 172	2.9	0.00	0.00
843 Male clothing, knitted crocheted	990	2.4	0.01	0.00
541 Pharmaceuticals excluding medicines	636	1.6	0.00	0.00
112 Alcoholic beverages	591	1.4	0.01	0.00
282 Ferrous iron & steel, waste & scrap	546	1.3	0.01	0.00
679 Iron steel pipe tube fittings etc	416	1.0	0.00	0.00
Remainder	3 477	8.5		
Central African Republic - République centrafricaine (**=Developing) (2)				
All commodity groups	131 446	100.0	0.00	0.00
667 Pearls, precious semiprecious stone	32 262	24.5	0.06	0.03
247 Wood in rough or roughly squared	28 074	21.4	0.69	0.24
248 Wood simply worked, railway sleeper	20 537	15.6	0.29	0.06
277 Natural abrasives nes	17 943	13.7	1.98	1.35
263 Cotton	8 334	6.3	0.12	0.06
781 Passenger cars and race cars	3 283	2.5	0.00	0.00
071 Coffee and coffee substitutes	3 264	2.5	0.02	0.01
061 Sugar, mollasses and honey	2 576	2.0	0.01	0.01
782 Goods and service vehicles	905	0.7	0.00	0.00
662 Clay and refractory materials	651	0.5	0.01	0.00
Remainder	13 617	10.4		
Chad - Tchad (**=Developing) (2)				
All commodity groups	3 023 500	100.0	0.05	0.02
333 Crude petroleum & bituminous oil	2 554 631	84.5	0.33	0.24
334 Heavy petroleum & bituminous oil	227 202	7.5	0.09	0.04
751 Office machines	61 260	2.0	0.23	0.13
263 Cotton	54 280	1.8	0.81	0.37
292 Crude vegetable materials nes	28 774	1.0	0.31	0.08
792 Aircraft, spacecraft & equipment	20 895	0.7	0.11	0.02
523 Inorganic acid metal salt peroxy	10 997	0.4	0.16	0.06
764 Telecommunicate equipment part nes	10 897	0.4	0.00	0.00
267 Man made fibre for spinning; waste	9 997	0.3	0.71	0.25
657 Special yarn and textile fabric etc	6 107	0.2	0.04	0.02
Remainder	38 459	1.3		
Chile - Chili (**=Developing)				
All commodity groups	62 538 235	100.0	1.10	0.45
682 Copper	22 939 892	36.7	40.22	20.97
283 Copper ores and concentrates	11 581 101	18.5	37.40	29.56
057 Fruit nut (exc oil), fresh or dried	2 879 119	4.6	8.89	4.27
034 Fish, fresh live chilled frozen	2 768 968	4.4	13.21	5.57
251 Pulp and waste paper	2 318 249	3.7	24.19	6.14
287 Base metal ores & concentrates nes	1 727 240	2.8	11.13	6.78
112 Alcoholic beverages	1 307 192	2.1	12.63	2.15
971 Gold non-monetary excluding ores	958 351	1.5	1.26	0.70
248 Wood simply worked, railway sleeper	769 993	1.2	10.72	2.42
081 Animal feed excluding unmilled cereal	721 410	1.2	2.93	1.26
Remainder	14 566 720	23.3		
China - Chine (**=Developing)				
All commodity groups	1 389 705 254	100.0	24.50	10.06
752 Computer equipment nes	130 346 627	9.4	64.17	44.35
764 Telecommunicate equipment part nes	120 644 629	8.7	44.64	28.76
776 Valves tubes; diodes, transistors	51 625 833	3.7	16.11	11.05
845 Articles of apparel nes	36 620 375	2.6	44.52	30.93
759 Office equipment part & accessories	35 428 354	2.5	31.32	18.59
821 Furniture part; bedding furnishing	34 475 239	2.5	63.53	28.08
793 Ships boats floating structures	34 330 304	2.5	38.12	22.86
778 Electrical machinery apparatus nes	32 943 159	2.4	38.47	18.29
851 Footwear	31 825 059	2.3	60.14	36.06
894 Baby carriage toy game sport good	29 780 179	2.1	59.85	34.60
Remainder	851 685 495	61.3		

For sources and notes, see end of table.

Pour les sources et les notes, se reporter à la fin du tableau.

Leading products exported based on average 2009-2010 values SITC Revision 3 (3-digit level) Principaux produits exportés d'après la moyenne des valeurs de 2009-2010 CTCI révision 3 (positions à 3 chiffres)	2009-2010		
	Value (f.o.b., thousands of dollars) Valeur (f.a.b., milliers de dollars)	As percentage En pourcentage	
		of country total du total du pays	of ** (1) des ** (1)	of world du monde

China, Hong Kong SAR - Chine (RAS de Hong Kong) (**=Developing)			
All commodity groups	365 056 975	100.0	6.44	2.64
776 Valves tubes; diodes, transistors	58 023 964	15.9	18.11	12.42
764 Telecommunicate equipment part nes	51 063 797	14.0	18.89	12.17
759 Office equipment part & accessories	24 496 914	6.7	21.66	12.85
772 Electrical circuit equipment	15 834 233	4.3	20.01	8.66
894 Baby carriage toy game sport good	12 458 561	3.4	25.04	14.48
752 Computer equipment nes	11 925 371	3.3	5.87	4.06
971 Gold non-monetary excluding ores	10 729 768	2.9	14.14	7.83
667 Pearls, precious semiprecious stone	10 692 169	2.9	19.45	9.73
845 Articles of apparel nes	10 185 082	2.8	12.38	8.60
778 Electrical machinery apparatus nes	9 274 417	2.5	10.83	5.15
Remainder	150 372 699	41.2		

China, Macao SAR - Chine (RAS de Macao) (**=Developing)			
All commodity groups	915 220	100.0	0.02	0.01
845 Articles of apparel nes	86 433	9.4	0.11	0.07
842 Female clothing, woven	85 364	9.3	0.18	0.12
897 Jewellery nes (667)	83 844	9.2	0.20	0.12
844 Female clothing, knitted crocheted	36 603	4.0	0.12	0.09
841 Male clothing, woven	36 306	4.0	0.09	0.06
682 Copper	32 303	3.5	0.06	0.03
288 Non ferrous base metal waste nes	27 286	3.0	0.39	0.09
885 Watches and clocks	27 160	3.0	0.23	0.08
579 Plastic waste, parings and scrap	26 345	2.9	1.21	0.45
764 Telecommunicate equipment part nes	22 076	2.4	0.01	0.01
Remainder	451 499	49.3		

China, Taiwan Province of - Province chinoise de Taiwan (**=Developing) (2)			
All commodity groups	238 934 514	100.0	4.21	1.73
776 Valves tubes; diodes, transistors	47 674 776	20.0	14.88	10.21
871 Optical instruments apparatus nes	16 100 861	6.7	22.56	18.65
334 Heavy petroleum & bituminous oil	12 162 874	5.1	4.72	2.12
778 Electrical machinery apparatus nes	11 138 709	4.7	13.01	6.19
764 Telecommunicate equipment part nes	8 756 821	3.7	3.24	2.09
759 Office equipment part & accessories	7 319 985	3.1	6.47	3.84
772 Electrical circuit equipment	7 250 496	3.0	9.53	3.96
898 Music instrument device recording	5 295 246	2.2	20.76	9.22
785 Motorcycles, mopeds and cycles	4 044 065	1.7	21.69	10.50
513 Carboxylic acid and compounds	3 628 499	1.5	18.35	9.11
Remainder	115 562 181	48.4		

Colombia - Colombie (**=Developing)			
All commodity groups	36 336 257	100.0	0.64	0.26
333 Crude petroleum & bituminous oil	10 723 727	29.5	1.40	1.00
321 Coal excluding non-agglomomerated	5 388 894	14.8	16.41	5.73
334 Heavy petroleum & bituminous oil	2 391 920	6.6	0.93	0.42
071 Coffee and coffee substitutes	1 975 728	5.4	11.42	7.06
971 Gold non-monetary excluding ores	1 841 268	5.1	2.43	1.34
292 Crude vegetable materials nes	1 164 203	3.2	12.50	3.43
671 Pig & sponge iron, ferro alloys etc	847 070	2.3	4.98	2.74
057 Fruit nut (exc oil), fresh or dried	838 870	2.3	2.59	1.24
061 Sugar, mollasses and honey	424 014	1.2	1.87	1.27
553 Perfume toilet cosmetics, excl. soap	360 054	1.0	2.75	0.57
Remainder	10 380 509	28.6		

Comoros - Comores (**=Developing) (2)			
All commodity groups	12 422	100.0	0.00	0.00
793 Ships boats floating structures	5 550	44.7	0.01	0.00
075 Spices	3 349	27.0	0.08	0.06
551 Essential oils, perfumes & flavours	1 863	15.0	0.05	0.01
751 Office machines	1 027	8.3	0.00	0.00
971 Gold non-monetary excluding ores	87	0.7	0.00	0.00
673 Flat iron non-alloy steel products	77	0.6	0.00	0.00
034 Fish, fresh live chilled frozen	73	0.6	0.00	0.00
282 Ferrous iron & steel, waste & scrap	40	0.3	0.00	0.00
247 Wood in rough or roughly squared	35	0.3	0.00	0.00
844 Female clothing, knitted crocheted	34	0.3	0.00	0.00
Remainder	287	2.3		

Leading products exported based on average 2009-2010 values SITC Revision 3 (3-digit level) Principaux produits exportés d'après la moyenne des valeurs de 2009-2010 CTCI révision 3 (positions à 3 chiffres)	2009-2010		
	Value (f.o.b., thousands of dollars) Valeur (f.a.b., milliers de dollars)	As percentage En pourcentage	
		of country total du total du pays	of ** (1) des ** (1)	of world du monde

Congo (**=Developing) (2)			
All commodity groups	7 157 119	100.0	0.13	0.05
333 Crude petroleum & bituminous oil	5 636 672	77.4	0.72	0.52
334 Heavy petroleum & bituminous oil	323 489	4.5	0.13	0.06
287 Base metal ores & concentrates nes	183 175	2.6	1.18	0.72
247 Wood in rough or roughly squared	164 659	2.3	4.07	1.38
682 Copper	143 250	2.0	0.25	0.13
282 Ferrous iron & steel, waste & scrap	81 944	1.1	1.66	0.21
342 Liquefied propane and butane	79 434	1.1	0.31	0.21
248 Wood simply worked, railway sleeper	71 223	1.0	0.99	0.22
283 Copper ores and concentrates	56 688	0.8	0.18	0.14
121 Unmanufactured tabacco and refuse	38 673	0.5	0.51	0.34
Remainder	478 012	6.7		

Cook Islands - Îles Cook (**=Developing) (2)			
All commodity groups	3 874	100.0	0.00	0.00
034 Fish, fresh live chilled frozen	2 210	57.0	0.01	0.00
059 Fruit & vegetable juice unferment	287	7.4	0.01	0.00
793 Ships boats floating structures	270	7.0	0.00	0.00
667 Pearls, precious semiprecious stone	242	6.2	0.00	0.00
533 Pigment, paint, varnish & related	124	3.2	0.00	0.00
778 Electrical machinery apparatus nes	77	2.0	0.00	0.00
744 Mechanical handling equipment nes	64	1.7	0.00	0.00
896 Work of art & collections; antiques	61	1.6	0.00	0.00
725 Paper & pulp mill, cut manufacture	41	1.1	0.00	0.00
717 Pipe, boiler, tank & vat appliances	38	1.0	0.00	0.00
Remainder	459	11.8		

Costa Rica (**=Developing)			
All commodity groups	8 940 593	100.0	0.16	0.06
776 Valves tubes; diodes, transistors	2 462 583	27.5	0.77	0.53
759 Office equipment part & accessories	1 641 583	18.4	1.45	0.86
057 Fruit nut (exc oil), fresh or dried	1 274 910	14.3	3.94	1.89
872 Medical instruments appliances nes	415 608	4.6	2.75	0.55
098 Edible products & preparations nes	164 237	1.8	1.34	0.33
071 Coffee and coffee substitutes	154 621	1.7	0.89	0.55
899 Manufactured articles nes	140 073	1.6	0.66	0.21
292 Crude vegetable materials nes	134 101	1.5	1.44	0.40
542 Medicines including veterinary	133 040	1.5	0.66	0.04
772 Electrical circuit equipment	108 743	1.2	0.14	0.06
Remainder	2 311 095	25.8		

Côte d'Ivoire (**=Developing)			
All commodity groups	9 965 217	100.0	0.18	0.07
072 Cocoa	3 330 783	33.4	26.53	17.66
334 Heavy petroleum & bituminous oil	1 509 393	15.1	0.59	0.26
333 Crude petroleum & bituminous oil	1 205 213	12.1	0.16	0.11
231 Natural rubber, latex, gum, etc	446 687	4.5	2.57	2.44
335 Residual petroleum products nes	392 302	3.9	3.22	1.23
057 Fruit nut (exc oil), fresh or dried	279 109	2.8	0.86	0.41
071 Coffee and coffee substitutes	223 919	2.2	1.29	0.80
793 Ships boats floating structures	218 895	2.2	0.24	0.15
553 Perfume toilet cosmetics, excl. soap	163 603	1.6	1.25	0.26
248 Wood simply worked, railway sleeper	152 423	1.5	2.12	0.48
Remainder	2 042 890	20.5		

Croatia - Croatie (**=Transition)			
All commodity groups	11 151 256	100.0	2.09	0.08
793 Ships boats floating structures	1 111 591	10.0	40.03	0.74
334 Heavy petroleum & bituminous oil	992 435	8.9	1.37	0.17
771 Electric power machine part excl. 716	419 304	3.8	35.65	0.55
542 Medicines including veterinary	354 043	3.2	29.13	0.11
821 Furniture part; bedding furnishing	301 297	2.7	18.76	0.25
248 Wood simply worked, railway sleeper	239 087	2.1	6.59	0.75
343 Natural gas, liquefied or not	235 198	2.1	0.47	0.11
562 Manufactured fertilizer excl. crude	207 453	1.9	2.10	0.43
684 Aluminium	192 923	1.7	2.38	0.20
851 Footwear	192 160	1.7	14.60	0.22
Remainder	6 905 765	61.9		

For sources and notes, see end of table.

Pour les sources et les notes, se reporter à la fin du tableau.

177

Leading products exported based on average 2009-2010 values SITC Revision 3 (3-digit level) / Principaux produits exportés d'après la moyenne des valeurs de 2009-2010 CTCI révision 3 (positions à 3 chiffres)	2009-2010			
	Value (f.o.b., thousands of dollars) Valeur (f.a.b., milliers de dollars)	As percentage En pourcentage		
		of country total du total du pays	of ** (1) des ** (1)	of world du monde
Cuba (**=Developing) (2)				
All commodity groups	3 454 704	100.0	0.06	0.02
284 Nickel ores, concentrates, etc	981 927	28.4	22.70	13.26
061 Sugar, molasses and honey	531 471	15.4	2.34	1.59
122 Manufactured tabacco	265 615	7.7	3.97	1.06
542 Medicines including veterinary	172 870	5.0	0.86	0.05
334 Heavy petroleum & bituminous oil	117 293	3.4	0.05	0.02
672 Ingots, iron steel primary products	83 209	2.4	1.00	0.26
036 Crustacean mollusc aquat invertebra	82 298	2.4	0.52	0.34
288 Non ferrous base metal waste nes	75 951	2.2	1.08	0.24
112 Alcoholic beverages	72 066	2.1	0.70	0.12
287 Base metal ores & concentrates nes	67 429	2.0	0.43	0.26
Remainder	1 004 572	29.1		
Cyprus - Chypre (**=Developed)				
All commodity groups	1 433 659	100.0	0.02	0.01
334 Heavy petroleum & bituminous oil	206 529	14.4	0.08	0.04
542 Medicines including veterinary	131 310	9.2	0.04	0.04
776 Valves tubes; diodes, transistors	83 300	5.8	0.06	0.02
899 Manufactured articles nes	53 458	3.7	0.12	0.08
793 Ships boats floating structures	46 538	3.2	0.08	0.03
054 Vegetable & vegetable products nes	42 638	3.0	0.13	0.08
541 Pharmaceuticals excluding medicines	41 714	2.9	0.04	0.03
515 Organo-inorganic compound acid salt	34 912	2.4	0.04	0.04
024 Cheese and curd	34 144	2.4	0.15	0.13
288 Non ferrous base metal waste nes	30 924	2.2	0.13	0.10
Remainder	728 193	50.8		
Czech Republic - République tchèque (**=Developed)				
All commodity groups	122 512 618	100.0	1.61	0.89
781 Passenger cars and race cars	11 747 417	9.6	2.83	2.35
784 Motor vehicle parts and accessories	8 426 164	6.9	4.18	3.17
752 Computer equipment nes	7 230 345	5.9	7.99	2.46
772 Electrical circuit equipment	3 185 051	2.6	3.01	1.74
699 Base metal manufactures nes	2 939 349	2.4	3.97	2.60
761 Television video receive project	2 926 894	2.4	7.17	3.17
778 Electrical machinery apparatus nes	2 871 872	2.3	3.08	1.59
764 Telecommunicate equipment part nes	2 830 568	2.3	1.91	0.67
741 Heating cooling equipment parts nes	2 256 818	1.8	3.80	2.47
821 Furniture part; bedding furnishing	1 996 315	1.6	2.98	1.63
Remainder	76 101 829	62.1		
Dem. Rep. of the Congo - Rép. dém. du Congo (**=Developing) (2)				
All commodity groups	4 450 000	100.0	0.08	0.03
682 Copper	1 171 080	26.3	2.05	1.07
287 Base metal ores & concentrates nes	868 317	19.5	5.59	3.41
283 Copper ores and concentrates	614 352	13.8	1.98	1.57
333 Crude petroleum & bituminous oil	570 939	12.8	0.07	0.05
689 Misc non-ferrous base metals	477 576	10.7	15.30	6.70
667 Pearls, precious semiprecious stone	203 392	4.6	0.37	0.19
522 Inorganic chemical elem oxide salt	109 657	2.5	0.63	0.26
247 Wood in rough or roughly squared	69 085	1.6	1.71	0.58
248 Wood simply worked, railway sleeper	44 873	1.0	0.62	0.14
351 Electric current	34 005	0.8	0.86	0.11
Remainder	286 724	6.4		
Denmark - Danemark (**=Developed)				
All commodity groups	94 822 433	100.0	1.25	0.69
542 Medicines including veterinary	4 285 251	4.5	1.46	1.36
333 Crude petroleum & bituminous oil	4 128 655	4.4	2.90	0.39
012 Meat nes, fresh chilled frozen	3 640 201	3.8	7.94	6.19
716 Rotating electric plant parts nes	2 781 114	2.9	5.44	3.61
334 Heavy petroleum & bituminous oil	2 597 407	2.7	1.07	0.45
541 Pharmaceuticals excluding medicines	2 295 014	2.4	1.98	1.75
821 Furniture part; bedding furnishing	2 086 746	2.2	3.12	1.70
874 Measure analyze control device nes	1 625 606	1.7	1.47	1.17
098 Edible products & preparations nes	1 536 881	1.6	4.15	3.07
741 Heating cooling equipment parts nes	1 392 576	1.5	2.35	1.52
Remainder	68 452 981	72.2		

Leading products exported based on average 2009-2010 values SITC Revision 3 (3-digit level) / Principaux produits exportés d'après la moyenne des valeurs de 2009-2010 CTCI révision 3 (positions à 3 chiffres)	2009-2010			
	Value (f.o.b., thousands of dollars) Valeur (f.a.b., milliers de dollars)	As percentage En pourcentage		
		of country total du total du pays	of ** (1) des ** (1)	of world du monde
Djibouti (**=Developing) (2)				
All commodity groups	73 004	100.0	0.00	0.00
001 Live animal excl. fish & crustacean	16 000	22.1	0.46	0.09
022 Milk products, excl. butter & cheese	15 759	21.3	0.37	0.05
971 Gold non-monetary excluding ores	6 731	9.1	0.01	0.00
098 Edible products & preparations nes	4 530	6.1	0.01	0.01
334 Heavy petroleum & bituminous oil	3 100	4.3	0.00	0.00
071 Coffee and coffee substitutes	2 550	3.5	0.01	0.01
045 Grain, excl. wheat rice barley maize	1 270	1.7	0.27	0.05
061 Sugar, mollasses and honey	1 240	1.7	0.01	0.00
782 Goods and service vehicles	867	1.2	0.00	0.00
723 Civil engineering plant & equipment	846	1.1	0.00	0.00
Remainder	20 568	27.9		
Dominica - Dominique (**=Developing) (2)				
All commodity groups	33 801	100.0	0.00	0.00
554 Soaps cleansers polishes	11 754	34.8	0.13	0.03
057 Fruit nut (exc oil), fresh or dried	7 832	23.2	0.02	0.01
054 Vegetable & vegetable products nes	2 794	8.3	0.01	0.01
533 Pigment, paint, varnish & related	2 470	7.3	0.03	0.01
892 Printed matter	2 281	6.7	0.02	0.01
273 Stone, sand and gravel	2 177	6.4	0.05	0.02
764 Telecommunicate equipment part nes	404	1.2	0.00	0.00
111 Non alcoholic beverage nes	378	1.1	0.01	0.01
551 Essential oils, perfumes & flavours	365	1.1	0.01	0.00
716 Rotating electric plant parts nes	268	0.8	0.00	0.00
Remainder	3 077	9.1		
Dominican Republic - République dominicaine (**=Developing) (2)				
All commodity groups	6 040 500	100.0	0.11	0.04
872 Medical instruments appliances nes	686 547	11.4	4.54	0.91
122 Manufactured tabacco	333 382	5.5	4.99	1.33
772 Electrical circuit equipment	307 452	5.1	0.40	0.17
652 Woven cotton fabrics	305 046	5.1	1.54	1.10
845 Articles of apparel nes	296 489	4.9	0.36	0.25
057 Fruit nut (exc oil), fresh or dried	292 574	4.8	0.90	0.43
893 Articles of plastic nes	232 735	3.9	0.62	0.22
897 Jewellery nes (667)	232 536	3.8	0.55	0.32
851 Footwear	200 462	3.3	0.38	0.23
841 Male clothing, woven	183 959	3.0	0.47	0.31
Remainder	2 969 318	49.2		
Ecuador - Équateur (**=Developing)				
All commodity groups	15 607 103	100.0	0.28	0.11
333 Crude petroleum & bituminous oil	7 618 020	48.8	1.00	0.71
057 Fruit nut (exc oil), fresh or dried	2 084 866	13.4	6.44	3.09
036 Crustacean mollusc aquat invertebra	752 845	4.8	4.79	3.08
334 Heavy petroleum & bituminous oil	636 040	4.1	0.25	0.11
037 Fish shellfish, prepared preserved	617 073	4.0	4.67	3.06
292 Crude vegetable materials nes	563 776	3.6	6.05	1.66
072 Cocoa	397 644	2.5	3.17	2.11
034 Fish, fresh live chilled frozen	234 031	1.5	1.12	0.47
781 Passenger cars and race cars	151 627	1.0	0.18	0.03
071 Coffee and coffee substitutes	150 065	1.0	0.87	0.54
Remainder	2 401 116	15.4		
Egypt - Égypte (**=Developing) (2)				
All commodity groups	25 257 053	100.0	0.45	0.18
334 Heavy petroleum & bituminous oil	2 512 993	9.9	0.98	0.44
343 Natural gas, liquefied or not	2 069 047	8.2	2.37	0.97
333 Crude petroleum & bituminous oil	1 672 898	6.6	0.22	0.16
562 Manufactured fertilizer excl. crude	1 146 209	4.5	6.70	2.36
971 Gold non-monetary excluding ores	970 073	3.8	1.28	0.71
057 Fruit nut (exc oil), fresh or dried	954 968	3.8	2.95	1.42
054 Vegetable & vegetable products nes	803 569	3.2	3.96	1.49
682 Copper	630 598	2.5	1.11	0.58
845 Articles of apparel nes	581 539	2.3	0.71	0.49
773 Electrical distribute equipment nes	520 116	2.1	1.37	0.62
Remainder	13 395 043	53.0		

For sources and notes, see end of table.

Pour les sources et les notes, se reporter à la fin du tableau.

Leading products exported based on average 2009-2010 values SITC Revision 3 (3-digit level) / Principaux produits exportés d'après la moyenne des valeurs de 2009-2010 CTCI révision 3 (positions à 3 chiffres)	Value (f.o.b., thousands of dollars) Valeur (f.a.b., milliers de dollars)	2009-2010 As percentage / En pourcentage		
		of country total / du total du pays	of ** (1) / des ** (1)	of world / du monde
El Salvador (**=Developing)				
All commodity groups	4 148 283	100.0	0.07	0.03
845 Articles of apparel nes	919 854	22.2	1.12	0.78
071 Coffee and coffee substitutes	234 647	5.7	1.36	0.84
843 Male clothing, knitted crocheted	218 187	5.3	1.16	0.96
642 Cut paper and paperboard articles	162 950	3.9	1.18	0.33
061 Sugar, molasses and honey	157 425	3.8	0.69	0.47
893 Articles of plastic nes	152 881	3.7	0.40	0.14
778 Electrical machinery apparatus nes	152 563	3.7	0.18	0.08
844 Female clothing, knitted crocheted	140 518	3.4	0.44	0.34
846 Clothing accessory excl. 831 848 851	130 867	3.2	0.92	0.56
048 Cereal & preparation flour starch	122 676	3.0	1.75	0.32
Remainder	1 755 715	42.3		
Equatorial Guinea - Guinée équatoriale (**=Developing) (2)				
All commodity groups	9 536 000	100.0	0.17	0.07
333 Crude petroleum & bituminous oil	7 455 661	78.2	0.98	0.70
343 Natural gas, liquefied or not	1 345 613	14.1	1.54	0.63
342 Liquefied propane and butane	330 654	3.5	1.29	0.87
512 Alcohols, phenols; derivatives	192 684	2.0	0.88	0.46
247 Wood in rough or roughly squared	73 160	0.8	1.81	0.61
971 Gold non-monetary excluding ores	39 566	0.4	0.05	0.03
511 Hydrocarbons nes; derivatives	20 918	0.2	0.08	0.03
344 Petroleum and hydrocarbon gas nes	16 805	0.2	0.27	0.17
634 Veneer, plywood & other wood nes	7 905	0.1	0.07	0.03
742 Liquid pump; liquid elevator parts	4 438	0.0	0.05	0.01
Remainder	48 608	0.5		
Eritrea - Érythrée (**=Developing) (2)				
All commodity groups	11 133	100.0	0.00	0.00
811 Prefabricated buildings	1 348	12.1	0.06	0.02
001 Live animal excl. fish & crustacean	935	8.4	0.03	0.01
611 Leather	696	6.3	0.01	0.00
651 Textile yarn	542	4.9	0.00	0.00
841 Male clothing, woven	530	4.8	0.00	0.00
211 Raw hides & skins, excluding furskins	443	4.0	0.06	0.01
292 Crude vegetable materials nes	406	3.6	0.00	0.00
061 Sugar, mollasses and honey	404	3.6	0.00	0.00
222 Oil seed etc for soft oil	338	3.0	0.00	0.00
034 Fish, fresh live chilled frozen	302	2.7	0.00	0.00
Remainder	5 189	46.6		
Estonia - Estonie (**=Developed)				
All commodity groups	10 919 004	100.0	0.14	0.08
334 Heavy petroleum & bituminous oil	1 079 290	9.9	0.44	0.19
764 Telecommunicate equipment part nes	758 037	6.9	0.51	0.18
821 Furniture part; bedding furnishing	443 950	4.1	0.66	0.36
781 Passenger cars and race cars	384 191	3.5	0.09	0.08
248 Wood simply worked, railway sleeper	263 631	2.4	1.25	0.83
635 Wood manufactures nes	259 739	2.4	1.87	1.19
773 Electrical distribute equipment nes	240 034	2.2	0.54	0.28
351 Electric current	231 935	2.1	0.88	0.72
772 Electrical circuit equipment	229 793	2.1	0.22	0.13
282 Ferrous iron & steel, waste & scrap	179 958	1.6	0.56	0.46
Remainder	6 848 446	62.7		
Ethiopia - Éthiopie (**=Developing)				
All commodity groups	2 099 109	100.0	0.04	0.02
071 Coffee and coffee substitutes	572 029	27.3	3.31	2.04
054 Vegetable & vegetable products nes	368 027	17.5	1.81	0.68
222 Oil seed etc for soft oil	337 755	16.1	1.71	0.68
292 Crude vegetable materials nes	180 393	8.6	1.94	0.53
971 Gold non-monetary excluding ores	147 235	7.0	0.19	0.11
001 Live animal excl. fish & crustacean	104 340	5.0	2.91	0.58
611 Leather	57 126	2.7	0.54	0.30
223 Oil seed for non soft oil	43 784	2.1	6.54	1.88
012 Meat nes, fresh chilled frozen	38 724	1.8	0.31	0.07
723 Civil engineering plant & equipment	26 189	1.2	0.11	0.03
Remainder	223 508	10.6		
Faeroe Islands - Îles Féroé (**=Developed)				
All commodity groups	789 131	100.0	0.01	0.01
034 Fish, fresh live chilled frozen	556 638	70.5	2.08	1.12
035 Fish, dried salted smoked	79 951	10.1	2.23	1.60
793 Ships boats floating structures	31 177	4.0	0.05	0.02
081 Animal feed excluding unmilled cereal	29 511	3.7	0.09	0.05
036 Crustacean mollusc aquat invertebra	25 583	3.2	0.30	0.10
334 Heavy petroleum & bituminous oil	18 411	2.3	0.01	0.00
291 Crude animal materials nes	14 364	1.8	0.35	0.21
037 Fish shellfish, prepared preserved	3 905	0.5	0.06	0.02
251 Pulp and waste paper	3 792	0.5	0.01	0.01
792 Aircraft, spacecraft & equipment	3 458	0.4	0.00	0.00
Remainder	22 340	2.8		
Falkland Islands (Malvinas) - Îles Falkland (Malvinas) (**=Developing) (2)				
All commodity groups	146 477	100.0	0.00	0.00
036 Crustacean mollusc aquat invertebra	72 500	49.5	0.46	0.30
034 Fish, fresh live chilled frozen	41 313	28.2	0.20	0.08
268 Wool & animal hair, incl wool tops	16 122	11.0	0.82	0.32
012 Meat nes, fresh chilled frozen	3 838	2.6	0.03	0.01
721 Agricultural machine nes excl. tractor	1 071	0.7	0.03	0.03
334 Heavy petroleum & bituminous oil	928	0.6	0.00	0.00
037 Fish shellfish, prepared preserved	640	0.4	0.00	0.00
542 Medicines including veterinary	616	0.4	0.00	0.00
057 Fruit nut (exc oil), fresh or dried	446	0.3	0.00	0.00
713 Internal combustion engine part nes	445	0.3	0.00	0.00
Remainder	8 558	5.8		
Fiji - Fidji (**=Developing) (2)				
All commodity groups	621 002	100.0	0.01	0.00
061 Sugar, mollasses and honey	90 119	14.5	0.40	0.27
034 Fish, fresh live chilled frozen	66 185	10.7	0.32	0.13
111 Non alcoholic beverage nes	56 148	9.0	1.52	0.34
037 Fish shellfish, prepared preserved	43 967	7.1	0.33	0.22
971 Gold non-monetary excluding ores	33 572	5.4	0.04	0.02
048 Cereal & preparation flour starch	31 560	5.1	0.45	0.08
334 Heavy petroleum & bituminous oil	23 937	3.9	0.01	0.00
841 Male clothing, woven	18 930	3.0	0.05	0.03
046 Wheat meal & flour, meslin flour	16 899	2.7	0.93	0.39
845 Articles of apparel nes	15 949	2.6	0.02	0.01
Remainder	223 737	36.0		
Finland - Finlande (**=Developed)				
All commodity groups	66 132 632	100.0	0.87	0.48
641 Paper and paperboard	9 015 800	13.6	10.46	8.52
764 Telecommunicate equipment part nes	4 647 183	7.0	3.14	1.11
334 Heavy petroleum & bituminous oil	4 404 592	6.7	1.81	0.77
675 Flat rolled products of alloy steel	2 424 912	3.7	6.26	4.62
793 Ships boats floating structures	1 851 882	2.8	3.23	1.23
716 Rotating electric plant parts nes	1 763 173	2.7	3.45	2.29
728 Special industrial machine part nes	1 588 225	2.4	1.47	1.17
248 Wood simply worked, railway sleeper	1 443 170	2.2	6.86	4.53
251 Pulp and waste paper	1 225 531	1.9	4.51	3.25
744 Mechanical handling equipment nes	1 184 326	1.8	2.39	1.82
Remainder	36 583 837	55.3		
France (**=Developed)				
All commodity groups	487 881 927	100.0	6.41	3.53
792 Aircraft, spacecraft & equipment	40 459 321	8.3	36.32	30.95
542 Medicines including veterinary	27 944 191	5.7	9.51	8.87
781 Passenger cars and race cars	20 495 311	4.2	4.93	4.09
784 Motor vehicle parts and accessories	16 417 299	3.4	8.15	6.17
553 Perfume toilet cosmetics, excl. soap	12 137 761	2.5	24.67	19.31
112 Alcoholic beverages	11 975 730	2.5	24.39	19.73
334 Heavy petroleum & bituminous oil	11 449 425	2.3	4.70	2.00
714 Non-electric engines excl. 712 713 718	9 576 767	2.0	15.07	12.70
772 Electrical circuit equipment	8 654 450	1.8	8.17	4.73
776 Valves tubes; diodes, transistors	7 989 723	1.6	5.46	1.71
Remainder	320 781 948	65.7		

For sources and notes, see end of table.

Pour les sources et les notes, se reporter à la fin du tableau.

179

Leading products exported based on average 2009-2010 values SITC Revision 3 (3-digit level) Principaux produits exportés d'après la moyenne des valeurs de 2009-2010 CTCI révision 3 (positions à 3 chiffres)	2009-2010			
	Value (f.o.b., thousands of dollars) Valeur (f.a.b., milliers de dollars)	As percentage En pourcentage		
		of country total du total du pays	of ** (1) des ** (1)	of world du monde
French Polynesia - Polynésie française (**=Developing)				
All commodity groups	169 760	100.0	0.00	0.00
667 Pearls, precious semiprecious stone	99 443	58.6	0.18	0.09
694 Nails screws nuts bolts rivets	17 441	10.3	0.18	0.06
034 Fish, fresh live chilled frozen	8 039	4.7	0.04	0.02
058 Fruit preserve preparation excl. juice	6 967	4.1	0.10	0.05
422 Fixed veg fat and oil, excl. "soft"	4 144	2.4	0.01	0.01
897 Jewellery, nes (007)	4 120	2.4	0.01	0.01
793 Ships boats floating structures	4 014	2.4	0.00	0.00
792 Aircraft, spacecraft & equipment	2 906	1.7	0.02	0.00
075 Spices	2 220	1.3	0.05	0.04
291 Crude animal materials nes	1 453	0.9	0.05	0.02
Remainder	19 012	11.2		
Gabon (**=Developing) (2)				
All commodity groups	6 864 989	100.0	0.12	0.05
333 Crude petroleum & bituminous oil	5 066 500	73.8	0.66	0.47
247 Wood in rough or roughly squared	634 536	9.2	15.67	5.32
287 Base metal ores & concentrates nes	520 476	7.6	3.35	2.04
634 Veneer, plywood & other wood nes	154 099	2.2	1.37	0.54
334 Heavy petroleum & bituminous oil	139 267	2.0	0.05	0.02
248 Wood simply worked, railway sleeper	98 929	1.4	1.38	0.31
231 Natural rubber, latex, gum, etc	55 570	0.8	0.32	0.30
122 Manufactured tabacco	16 775	0.2	0.25	0.07
747 Pipe, boiler, tank & vat appliances	14 201	0.2	0.09	0.02
792 Aircraft, spacecraft & equipment	13 845	0.2	0.07	0.01
Remainder	150 791	2.2		
Gambia - Gambie (**=Developing)				
All commodity groups	15 000	100.0	0.00	0.00
057 Fruit nut (exc oil), fresh or dried	5 230	34.9	0.02	0.01
421 Fixed veg fat and oil, "soft"	1 466	9.8	0.02	0.01
653 Man-made woven fabrics	884	5.9	0.00	0.00
287 Base metal ores & concentrates nes	847	5.6	0.01	0.00
282 Ferrous iron & steel, waste & scrap	630	4.2	0.01	0.00
034 Fish, fresh live chilled frozen	549	3.7	0.00	0.00
222 Oil seed etc for soft oil	445	3.0	0.00	0.00
273 Stone, sand and gravel	401	2.7	0.01	0.00
022 Milk products, excl. butter & cheese	320	2.1	0.01	0.00
035 Fish, dried salted smoked	269	1.8	0.02	0.01
Remainder	3 958	26.4		
Georgia - Géorgie (**=Transition) (2)				
All commodity groups	1 358 479	100.0	0.25	0.01
671 Pig & sponge iron, ferro alloys etc	197 010	14.5	2.92	0.64
781 Passenger cars and race cars	152 857	11.3	10.85	0.03
971 Gold non-monetary excluding ores	100 989	7.4	7.35	0.07
112 Alcoholic beverages	92 647	6.8	7.41	0.15
282 Ferrous iron & steel, waste & scrap	86 493	6.4	5.05	0.22
057 Fruit nut (exc oil), fresh or dried	85 559	6.3	5.71	0.13
283 Copper ores and concentrates	66 272	4.9	8.97	0.17
562 Manufactured fertilizer excl. crude	66 164	4.9	0.67	0.14
288 Non ferrous base metal waste nes	41 234	3.0	8.64	0.13
111 Non alcoholic beverage nes	39 467	2.9	9.47	0.24
Remainder	429 789	31.6		
Germany - Allemagne (**=Developed)				
All commodity groups	1 199 468 131	100.0	15.75	8.68
781 Passenger cars and race cars	115 545 614	9.6	27.79	23.07
542 Medicines including veterinary	44 712 272	3.7	15.22	14.19
784 Motor vehicle parts and accessories	39 112 982	3.3	19.41	14.70
792 Aircraft, spacecraft & equipment	31 157 133	2.6	27.97	23.83
772 Electrical circuit equipment	25 291 430	2.1	23.89	13.82
874 Measure analyze control device nes	23 786 919	2.0	21.53	17.09
728 Special industrial machine part nes	21 026 173	1.8	19.40	15.47
541 Pharmaceuticals excluding medicines	20 266 474	1.7	17.48	15.48
713 Internal combustion engine part nes	19 622 270	1.6	20.11	16.02
776 Valves tubes; diodes, transistors	18 108 082	1.5	12.38	3.88
Remainder	840 838 781	70.1		

Leading products exported based on average 2009-2010 values SITC Revision 3 (3-digit level) Principaux produits exportés d'après la moyenne des valeurs de 2009-2010 CTCI révision 3 (positions à 3 chiffres)	2009-2010			
	Value (f.o.b., thousands of dollars) Valeur (f.a.b., milliers de dollars)	As percentage En pourcentage		
		of country total du total du pays	of ** (1) des ** (1)	of world du monde
Ghana (**=Developing) (2)				
All commodity groups	6 899 895	100.0	0.12	0.05
072 Cocoa	3 313 782	48.0	26.40	17.57
287 Base metal ores & concentrates nes	515 334	7.5	3.32	2.02
971 Gold non-monetary excluding ores	488 372	7.1	0.64	0.36
248 Wood simply worked, railway sleeper	233 624	3.4	3.25	0.73
057 Fruit nut (exc oil), fresh or dried	225 650	3.3	0.70	0.33
634 Veneer, plywood & other wood nes	174 309	2.5	1.55	0.61
037 Fish shellfish, prepared preserved	168 783	2.4	1.28	0.84
334 Heavy petroleum & bituminous oil	138 397	2.0	0.05	0.02
351 Electric current	109 827	1.6	2.79	0.34
269 Worn clothing, textile article; rag	86 511	1.3	8.64	2.47
Remainder	1 445 247	20.9		
Gibraltar (**=Developed) (2)				
All commodity groups	264 026	100.0	0.00	0.00
334 Heavy petroleum & bituminous oil	169 487	64.2	0.07	0.03
793 Ships boats floating structures	24 077	9.1	0.04	0.02
716 Rotating electric plant parts nes	19 435	7.4	0.04	0.03
333 Crude petroleum & bituminous oil	11 144	4.2	0.01	0.01
723 Civil engineering plant & equipment	7 232	2.7	0.01	0.01
781 Passenger cars and race cars	5 415	2.1	0.00	0.00
778 Electrical machinery apparatus nes	3 598	1.4	0.00	0.00
022 Milk products, excl. butter & cheese	2 753	1.0	0.01	0.01
792 Aircraft, spacecraft & equipment	2 242	0.8	0.00	0.00
667 Pearls, precious semiprecious stone	2 234	0.8	0.00	0.00
Remainder	16 409	6.2		
Greece - Grèce (**=Developed) (2)				
All commodity groups	20 806 136	100.0	0.27	0.15
334 Heavy petroleum & bituminous oil	1 914 975	9.2	0.79	0.33
542 Medicines including veterinary	1 283 258	6.2	0.44	0.41
684 Aluminium	878 158	4.2	1.52	0.93
057 Fruit nut (exc oil), fresh or dried	765 316	3.7	2.28	1.14
034 Fish, fresh live chilled frozen	594 888	2.9	2.22	1.20
056 Vegetables roots tubers nes	493 836	2.4	2.93	1.98
263 Cotton	472 233	2.3	7.65	3.20
058 Fruit preserve preparation excl. juice	423 867	2.0	5.52	2.85
682 Copper	393 659	1.9	0.88	0.36
792 Aircraft, spacecraft & equipment	391 331	1.9	0.35	0.30
Remainder	13 194 613	63.4		
Greenland - Groenland (**=Developed) (2)				
All commodity groups	370 490	100.0	0.00	0.00
034 Fish, fresh live chilled frozen	118 555	32.0	0.44	0.24
036 Crustacean mollusc aquat invertebra	117 993	31.8	1.39	0.48
037 Fish shellfish, prepared preserved	83 248	22.5	1.25	0.41
289 Prec metal ore concentrate excl. gold	21 207	5.7	0.21	0.15
035 Fish, dried salted smoked	4 923	1.3	0.14	0.10
689 Misc non-ferrous base metals	4 179	1.1	0.12	0.06
793 Ships boats floating structures	3 811	1.0	0.01	0.00
772 Electrical circuit equipment	3 577	1.0	0.00	0.00
273 Stone, sand and gravel	2 016	0.5	0.05	0.02
291 Crude animal materials nes	1 474	0.4	0.04	0.02
Remainder	9 506	2.6		
Grenada - Grenade (**=Developing) (2)				
All commodity groups	26 673	100.0	0.00	0.00
046 Wheat meal & flour, meslin flour	4 756	17.8	0.26	0.11
793 Ships boats floating structures	3 748	14.1	0.00	0.00
034 Fish, fresh live chilled frozen	2 735	10.3	0.01	0.01
075 Spices	2 069	7.8	0.05	0.04
081 Animal feed excluding unmilled cereal	1 807	6.8	0.01	0.00
642 Cut paper and paperboard articles	1 536	5.8	0.01	0.00
072 Cocoa	922	3.5	0.01	0.00
674 Flat plated iron non-alloy steel	778	2.9	0.00	0.00
764 Telecommunicate equipment part nes	754	2.8	0.00	0.00
533 Pigment, paint, varnish & related	627	2.3	0.01	0.00
Remainder	6 941	26.0		

For sources and notes, see end of table.

Pour les sources et les notes, se reporter à la fin du tableau.

Leading products exported based on average 2009-2010 values SITC Revision 3 (3-digit level) / Principaux produits exportés d'après la moyenne des valeurs de 2009-2010 CTCI révision 3 (positions à 3 chiffres)	Value (f.o.b., thousands of dollars) Valeur (f.a.b., milliers de dollars)	of country total du total du pays	of ** (1) des ** (1)	of world du monde
Guam (**=Developing) (2)				
All commodity groups	48 500	100.0	0.00	0.00
793 Ships boats floating structures	6 265	12.9	0.01	0.00
034 Fish, fresh live chilled frozen	5 003	10.3	0.02	0.01
831 Case bag: storage travel shopping	2 492	5.1	0.01	0.01
713 Internal combustion engine part nes	1 986	4.1	0.01	0.00
885 Watches and clocks	1 852	3.8	0.02	0.01
897 Jewellery nes (667)	1 551	3.2	0.00	0.00
282 Ferrous iron & steel, waste & scrap	1 478	3.0	0.03	0.00
781 Passenger cars and race cars	1 038	2.1	0.00	0.00
851 Footwear	714	1.5	0.00	0.00
071 Coffee and coffee substitutes	546	1.1	0.00	0.00
Remainder	25 575	52.7		
Guatemala (**=Developing)				
All commodity groups	7 834 369	100.0	0.14	0.06
061 Sugar, mollasses and honey	726 549	9.3	3.20	2.17
057 Fruit nut (exc oil), fresh or dried	712 777	9.1	2.20	1.06
071 Coffee and coffee substitutes	677 443	8.6	3.92	2.42
845 Articles of apparel nes	432 135	5.5	0.53	0.37
844 Female clothing, knitted crocheted	323 194	4.1	1.02	0.77
075 Spices	285 150	3.6	6.42	4.98
333 Crude petroleum & bituminous oil	206 834	2.6	0.03	0.02
289 Prec metal ore concentrate excl. gold	206 335	2.6	5.15	1.44
842 Female clothing, woven	192 107	2.5	0.41	0.27
054 Vegetable & vegetable products nes	183 027	2.3	0.90	0.34
Remainder	3 889 819	49.0		
Guinea - Guinée (**=Developing) (2)				
All commodity groups	1 343 590	100.0	0.02	0.01
285 Aluminium ore concentrate alumina	645 595	48.1	14.61	5.50
333 Crude petroleum & bituminous oil	187 467	14.0	0.02	0.02
723 Civil engineering plant & equipment	167 573	12.5	0.70	0.20
971 Gold non-monetary excluding ores	62 761	4.7	0.08	0.05
283 Copper ores and concentrates	32 569	2.4	0.11	0.08
071 Coffee and coffee substitutes	29 689	2.2	0.17	0.11
034 Fish, fresh live chilled frozen	26 762	2.0	0.13	0.05
343 Natural gas, liquefied or not	24 235	1.8	0.03	0.01
072 Cocoa	20 959	1.6	0.17	0.11
667 Pearls, precious semiprecious stone	17 670	1.3	0.03	0.02
Remainder	128 310	9.5		
Guinea-Bissau - Guinée-Bissau (**=Developing) (2)				
All commodity groups	120 949	100.0	0.00	0.00
057 Fruit nut (exc oil), fresh or dried	108 299	89.5	0.33	0.16
333 Crude petroleum & bituminous oil	7 226	6.0	0.00	0.00
282 Ferrous iron & steel, waste & scrap	1 057	0.9	0.02	0.00
247 Wood in rough or roughly squared	852	0.7	0.02	0.01
672 Ingots, Iron steel primary products	506	0.4	0.01	0.00
263 Cotton	334	0.3	0.00	0.00
725 Paper & pulp mill, cut manufacture	232	0.2	0.02	0.00
342 Liquefied propane and butane	190	0.2	0.00	0.00
036 Crustacean mollusc aquat invertebra	190	0.2	0.00	0.00
034 Fish, fresh live chilled frozen	186	0.2	0.00	0.00
Remainder	1 878	1.6		
Guyana (**=Developing)				
All commodity groups	862 566	100.0	0.02	0.01
971 Gold non-monetary excluding ores	306 739	35.6	0.40	0.22
042 Rice	119 867	13.9	0.74	0.59
285 Aluminium ore concentrate alumina	109 241	12.7	2.47	0.93
061 Sugar, mollasses and honey	106 925	12.4	0.47	0.32
248 Wood simply worked, railway sleeper	44 696	5.2	0.62	0.14
036 Crustacean mollusc aquat invertebra	33 723	3.9	0.21	0.14
112 Alcoholic beverages	22 931	2.7	0.22	0.04
034 Fish, fresh live chilled frozen	19 763	2.3	0.09	0.04
634 Veneer, plywood & other wood nes	9 714	1.1	0.09	0.03
667 Pearls, precious semiprecious stone	8 647	1.0	0.02	0.01
Remainder	80 320	9.3		

Leading products exported based on average 2009-2010 values SITC Revision 3 (3-digit level) / Principaux produits exportés d'après la moyenne des valeurs de 2009-2010 CTCI révision 3 (positions à 3 chiffres)	Value (f.o.b., thousands of dollars) Valeur (f.a.b., milliers de dollars)	of country total du total du pays	of ** (1) des ** (1)	of world du monde
Haiti - Haïti (**=Developing) (2)				
All commodity groups	581 674	100.0	0.01	0.00
845 Articles of apparel nes	264 052	45.4	0.32	0.22
844 Female clothing, knitted crocheted	40 679	7.0	0.13	0.10
843 Male clothing, knitted crocheted	30 595	5.3	0.16	0.13
841 Male clothing, woven	29 327	5.0	0.07	0.05
846 Clothing accessory excl. 831 848 851	11 050	1.9	0.08	0.05
773 Electrical distribute equipment nes	10 976	1.9	0.03	0.01
071 Coffee and coffee substitutes	10 840	1.9	0.06	0.04
551 Essential oils, perfumes & flavours	9 434	1.6	0.27	0.05
057 Fruit nut (exc oil), fresh or dried	9 194	1.6	0.03	0.01
072 Cocoa	8 731	1.5	0.07	0.05
Remainder	156 797	27.0		
Honduras (**=Developing) (2)				
All commodity groups	5 283 250	100.0	0.09	0.04
845 Articles of apparel nes	1 023 540	19.4	1.24	0.86
071 Coffee and coffee substitutes	656 688	12.4	3.80	2.35
057 Fruit nut (exc oil), fresh or dried	333 600	6.3	1.03	0.49
773 Electrical distribute equipment nes	286 920	5.4	0.75	0.34
843 Male clothing, knitted crocheted	257 831	4.9	1.37	1.13
422 Fixed veg fat and oil, excl. "soft"	186 990	3.5	0.64	0.56
971 Gold non-monetary excluding ores	178 239	3.4	0.23	0.13
036 Crustacean mollusc aquat invertebra	164 004	3.1	1.04	0.67
841 Male clothing, woven	163 505	3.1	0.42	0.28
844 Female clothing, knitted crocheted	148 901	2.8	0.47	0.36
Remainder	1 883 032	35.6		
Hungary - Hongrie (**=Developed) (2)				
All commodity groups	88 632 228	100.0	1.16	0.64
764 Telecommunicate equipment part nes	12 062 042	13.6	8.14	2.88
761 Television video receive project	5 651 722	6.4	13.84	6.12
713 Internal combustion engine part nes	5 320 581	6.0	5.45	4.34
781 Passenger cars and race cars	4 002 488	4.5	0.96	0.80
784 Motor vehicle parts and accessories	3 186 783	3.6	1.58	1.20
752 Computer equipment nes	2 867 803	3.2	3.17	0.98
542 Medicines including veterinary	2 674 421	3.0	0.91	0.85
772 Electrical circuit equipment	2 345 038	2.6	2.21	1.28
778 Electrical machinery apparatus nes	1 904 317	2.1	2.04	1.06
874 Measure analyze control device nes	1 812 852	2.0	1.64	1.30
Remainder	46 804 181	52.8		
Iceland - Islande (**=Developed)				
All commodity groups	4 328 446	100.0	0.06	0.03
684 Aluminium	1 653 442	38.2	2.86	1.74
034 Fish, fresh live chilled frozen	1 066 557	24.6	3.98	2.15
035 Fish, dried salted smoked	374 140	8.6	10.44	7.47
671 Pig & sponge iron, ferro alloys etc	156 019	3.6	2.18	0.50
081 Animal feed excluding unmilled cereal	126 899	2.9	0.40	0.22
792 Aircraft, spacecraft & equipment	121 416	2.8	0.11	0.09
036 Crustacean mollusc aquat invertebra	115 013	2.7	1.35	0.47
542 Medicines including veterinary	110 837	2.6	0.04	0.04
411 Animals oils and fats	76 367	1.8	2.10	1.74
899 Manufactured articles nes	48 513	1.1	0.11	0.07
Remainder	479 243	11.1		
India - Inde (**=Developing)				
All commodity groups	207 035 812	100.0	3.65	1.50
334 Heavy petroleum & bituminous oil	29 460 832	14.2	11.43	5.14
667 Pearls, precious semiprecious stone	19 635 857	9.5	35.72	17.87
897 Jewellery nes (667)	12 733 897	6.2	30.35	17.52
281 Iron ore and concentrates	6 860 902	3.3	18.07	8.35
542 Medicines including veterinary	5 300 429	2.6	26.43	1.68
793 Ships boats floating structures	4 357 126	2.1	4.84	2.90
842 Female clothing, woven	3 842 086	1.9	8.24	5.38
845 Articles of apparel nes	3 294 619	1.6	4.01	2.78
764 Telecommunicate equipment part nes	3 230 123	1.6	1.20	0.77
651 Textile yarn	2 976 464	1.4	10.76	6.72
Remainder	115 343 476	55.7		

For sources and notes, see end of table.

Pour les sources et les notes, se reporter à la fin du tableau.

3

Leading products exported based on average 2009-2010 values SITC Revision 3 (3-digit level) Principaux produits exportés d'après la moyenne des valeurs de 2009-2010 CTCI révision 3 (positions à 3 chiffres)	2009-2010			
	Value (f.o.b., thousands of dollars) Valeur (f.a.b., milliers de dollars)	As percentage En pourcentage		
		of country total du total du pays	of ** (1) des ** (1)	of world du monde
Indonesia - Indonésie (=Developing)**				
All commodity groups	137 144 548	100.0	2.42	0.99
321 Coal excluding non-agglomerated	15 075 775	11.6	18.66	16.97
422 Fixed veg fat and oil, excl. "soft"	13 808 036	10.1	47.00	41.67
343 Natural gas, liquefied or not	11 113 424	8.1	12.71	5.24
333 Crude petroleum & bituminous oil	9 111 562	6.6	1.19	0.85
283 Copper ores and concentrates	5 991 726	4.4	19.35	15.29
231 Natural rubber, latex, gum, etc	5 200 520	3.9	30.00	20.00
641 Paper and paperboard	3 354 339	2.4	19.61	3.17
682 Copper	2 682 656	2.0	4.70	2.45
851 Footwear	2 118 982	1.5	4.00	2.40
845 Articles of apparel nes	1 908 631	1.4	2.32	1.61
Remainder	65 792 897	48.0		
Iran (Islamic Rep. of) - Iran (Rép. islamique d') (=Developing) (2)**				
All commodity groups	89 865 000	100.0	1.58	0.65
333 Crude petroleum & bituminous oil	69 160 385	77.0	9.06	6.46
334 Heavy petroleum & bituminous oil	2 258 101	2.5	0.88	0.39
342 Liquefied propane and butane	1 491 615	1.7	5.81	3.92
511 Hydrocarbons nes; derivatives	1 243 904	1.4	4.49	1.83
057 Fruit nut (exc oil), fresh or dried	1 127 798	1.3	3.48	1.67
512 Alcohols, phenols; derivatives	1 066 829	1.2	4.85	2.52
281 Iron ore and concentrates	876 104	1.0	2.31	1.07
571 Primary form ethylene polymers	860 263	1.0	3.52	1.48
682 Copper	589 862	0.7	1.03	0.54
672 Ingots, Iron steel primary products	563 798	0.6	6.77	1.77
Remainder	10 626 340	11.8		
Iraq (=Developing) (2)**				
All commodity groups	45 626 222	100.0	0.80	0.33
333 Crude petroleum & bituminous oil	44 369 312	97.2	5.81	4.15
334 Heavy petroleum & bituminous oil	348 096	0.8	0.14	0.06
971 Gold non-monetary excluding ores	187 455	0.4	0.25	0.14
511 Hydrocarbons nes; derivatives	121 074	0.3	0.44	0.18
057 Fruit nut (exc oil), fresh or dried	77 584	0.2	0.24	0.12
597 Additive e.g. lubricate, antifreeze	60 899	0.1	2.29	0.35
525 Radio active & associated materials	56 938	0.1	4.28	0.38
274 Sulphur and unroasted iron pyrites	39 336	0.1	2.81	1.59
554 Soaps cleansers polishes	37 301	0.1	0.42	0.11
728 Special industrial machine part nes	31 219	0.1	0.12	0.02
Remainder	297 008	0.7		
Ireland - Irlande (=Developed)**				
All commodity groups	117 716 622	100.0	1.55	0.85
542 Medicines including veterinary	23 158 517	19.7	7.88	7.35
515 Organo-inorganic compound acid salt	22 215 230	18.9	27.32	22.86
541 Pharmaceuticals excluding medicines	7 586 174	6.4	6.54	5.79
551 Essential oils, perfumes & flavours	6 563 017	5.6	38.42	31.91
752 Computer equipment nes	4 509 415	3.8	4.98	1.53
899 Manufactured articles nes	4 417 284	3.8	9.65	6.57
598 Miscellaneous chemical products nes	3 627 625	3.1	4.67	3.68
872 Medical instruments appliances nes	3 398 533	2.9	5.68	4.52
759 Office equipment part & accessories	2 917 181	2.5	3.77	1.53
776 Valves tubes; diodes, transistors	2 844 433	2.4	1.95	0.61
Remainder	36 479 213	31.0		
Israel - Israël (=Developed)**				
All commodity groups	53 173 821	100.0	0.70	0.38
667 Pearls, precious semiprecious stone	14 045 676	26.4	26.54	12.78
542 Medicines including veterinary	5 364 833	10.1	1.83	1.70
776 Valves tubes; diodes, transistors	3 053 853	5.7	2.09	0.65
764 Telecommunicate equipment part nes	2 685 450	5.1	1.81	0.64
598 Miscellaneous chemical products nes	2 227 993	4.2	2.87	2.26
792 Aircraft, spacecraft & equipment	1 724 975	3.2	1.55	1.32
562 Manufactured fertilizer excl. crude	1 454 562	2.7	6.76	3.00
874 Measure analyze control device nes	1 184 992	2.2	1.07	0.85
774 Electrodiagnostic equipment	872 651	1.6	2.73	2.40
778 Electrical machinery apparatus nes	776 798	1.5	0.83	0.43
Remainder	19 782 041	37.2		

Leading products exported based on average 2009-2010 values SITC Revision 3 (3-digit level) Principaux produits exportés d'après la moyenne des valeurs de 2009-2010 CTCI révision 3 (positions à 3 chiffres)	2009-2010			
	Value (f.o.b., thousands of dollars) Valeur (f.a.b., milliers de dollars)	As percentage En pourcentage		
		of country total du total du pays	of ** (1) des ** (1)	of world du monde

Italy - Italie (=Developed)**				
All commodity groups	426 966 933	100.0	5.61	3.09
334 Heavy petroleum & bituminous oil	15 153 082	3.5	6.22	2.64
542 Medicines including veterinary	13 583 426	3.2	4.62	4.31
784 Motor vehicle parts and accessories	11 846 998	2.8	5.88	4.45
728 Special industrial machine part nes	10 829 817	2.5	9.99	7.97
821 Furniture part; bedding furnishing	10 473 273	2.5	15.65	8.53
851 Footwear	8 105 281	2.2	27.61	10.66
699 Base metal manufactures nes	8 910 728	2.1	12.03	7.87
741 Heating cooling equipment parts nes	8 631 640	2.0	14.55	9.45
781 Passenger cars and race cars	8 243 173	1.9	1.98	1.65
745 Non-electrical machinery tool nes	7 024 132	1.6	19.75	15.37
Remainder	322 865 380	75.6		
Jamaica - Jamaïque (=Developing)**				
All commodity groups	1 321 819	100.0	0.02	0.01
285 Aluminium ore concentrate alumina	490 362	37.1	11.10	4.18
334 Heavy petroleum & bituminous oil	247 909	18.8	0.10	0.04
512 Alcohols, phenols; derivatives	109 323	8.3	0.50	0.26
112 Alcoholic beverages	93 764	7.1	0.91	0.15
061 Sugar, mollasses and honey	60 368	4.6	0.27	0.18
071 Coffee and coffee substitutes	28 804	2.2	0.17	0.10
054 Vegetable & vegetable products nes	25 539	1.9	0.13	0.05
098 Edible products & preparations nes	25 345	1.9	0.21	0.05
282 Ferrous iron & steel, waste & scrap	14 373	1.1	0.29	0.04
058 Fruit preserve preparation excl. juice	13 872	1.0	0.21	0.09
Remainder	212 161	16.1		
Japan - Japon (=Developed)**				
All commodity groups	675 279 060	100.0	8.87	4.89
781 Passenger cars and race cars	76 323 837	11.3	18.36	15.24
776 Valves tubes; diodes, transistors	42 018 613	6.2	28.73	9.00
784 Motor vehicle parts and accessories	30 658 553	4.5	15.21	11.53
728 Special industrial machine part nes	24 177 562	3.6	22.31	17.79
793 Ships boats floating structures	24 116 100	3.6	42.06	16.06
778 Electrical machinery apparatus nes	19 384 470	2.9	20.77	10.77
772 Electrical circuit equipment	17 089 111	2.5	16.14	9.34
713 Internal combustion engine part nes	15 867 010	2.3	16.26	12.96
759 Office equipment part & accessories	14 112 053	2.1	18.24	7.40
874 Measure analyze control device nes	13 606 082	2.0	12.32	9.78
Remainder	397 925 670	58.9		
Jordan - Jordanie (=Developing)**				
All commodity groups	6 694 441	100.0	0.12	0.05
562 Manufactured fertilizer excl. crude	967 944	14.5	5.66	2.00
542 Medicines including veterinary	596 190	8.9	2.97	0.19
845 Articles of apparel nes	568 432	8.5	0.69	0.48
272 Crude fertilizer, excl. manufactured	423 383	6.3	18.13	12.70
054 Vegetable & vegetable products nes	362 819	5.4	1.79	0.67
971 Gold non-monetary excluding ores	192 583	2.9	0.25	0.14
773 Electrical distribute equipment nes	144 648	2.2	0.38	0.17
522 Inorganic chemical elem oxide salt	144 256	2.2	0.83	0.34
692 Metal storage transport container	120 398	1.8	2.37	0.71
523 Inorganic acid metal salt peroxy	114 975	1.7	1.63	0.67
Remainder	3 058 812	45.7		
Kazakhstan (=Transition)**				
All commodity groups	50 219 913	100.0	9.41	0.36
333 Crude petroleum & bituminous oil	31 594 583	62.9	19.24	2.95
525 Radio active & associated materials	1 859 229	3.7	60.69	12.26
682 Copper	1 791 770	3.6	24.12	1.64
343 Natural gas, liquefied or not	1 537 511	3.1	3.05	0.72
671 Pig & sponge iron, ferro alloys etc	1 506 953	3.0	22.35	4.88
334 Heavy petroleum & bituminous oil	1 473 267	2.9	2.04	0.26
281 Iron ore and concentrates	1 062 872	2.1	24.61	1.29
673 Flat iron non-alloy steel products	811 595	1.6	9.40	1.13
041 Wheat meslin, incl spelt, unmilled	772 171	1.5	16.39	2.36
971 Gold non-monetary excluding ores	768 776	1.5	55.95	0.56
Remainder	7 041 188	14.0		

3.2.D Export structure by product
Individual countries and territories

3.2.D Structure des exportations par produits
Pays et territoires individuels

Leading products exported based on average 2009-2010 values SITC Revision 3 (3-digit level) Principaux produits exportés d'après la moyenne des valeurs de 2009-2010 CTCI révision 3 (positions à 3 chiffres)	2009-2010			
	Value (f.o.b., thousands of dollars) Valeur (f.a.b., milliers de dollars)	As percentage En pourcentage		
		of country total du total du pays	of ** (1) des ** (1)	of world du monde
Kenya (**=Developing) (2)				
All commodity groups	4 807 054	100.0	0.08	0.03
074 Tea and maté	857 122	17.8	16.57	12.44
292 Crude vegetable materials nes	620 409	12.9	6.66	1.83
054 Vegetable & vegetable products nes	257 353	5.4	1.27	0.48
071 Coffee and coffee substitutes	226 998	4.7	1.31	0.81
334 Heavy petroleum & bituminous oil	199 419	4.1	0.08	0.03
523 Inorganic acid metal salt peroxy	104 848	2.2	1.49	0.61
661 Lime cement construction material	86 111	1.8	0.59	0.34
893 Articles of plastic nes	80 015	1.7	0.21	0.07
122 Manufactured tabacco	79 055	1.6	1.18	0.31
674 Flat plated iron non-alloy steel	78 901	1.6	0.47	0.18
Remainder	2 216 830	46.1		
Kiribati (**=Developing) (2)				
All commodity groups	17 500	100.0	0.00	0.00
034 Fish, fresh live chilled frozen	12 759	72.9	0.06	0.03
793 Ships boats floating structures	2 056	11.7	0.00	0.00
422 Fixed veg fat and oil, excl. "soft"	893	5.1	0.00	0.00
036 Crustacean mollusc aquat invertebra	372	2.1	0.00	0.00
251 Pulp and waste paper	144	0.8	0.00	0.00
035 Fish, dried salted smoked	142	0.8	0.01	0.00
289 Prec metal ore concentrate excl. gold	140	0.8	0.00	0.00
872 Medical instruments appliances nes	127	0.7	0.00	0.00
541 Pharmaceuticals excluding medicines	109	0.6	0.00	0.00
575 Other plastics, in primary forms	107	0.6	0.00	0.00
Remainder	653	3.7		
Korea, Dem. People's Rep. of - Corée, Rép. populaire dém. de (**=Developing) (2)				
All commodity groups	2 497 500	100.0	0.04	0.02
321 Coal excluding non-agglomomerated	497 622	19.9	1.52	0.53
281 Iron ore and concentrates	225 775	9.0	0.59	0.27
841 Male clothing, woven	113 019	4.5	0.29	0.19
842 Female clothing, woven	109 043	4.4	0.23	0.15
671 Pig & sponge iron, ferro alloys etc	99 225	4.0	0.58	0.32
036 Crustacean mollusc aquat invertebra	85 590	3.4	0.54	0.35
686 Zinc	52 856	2.1	1.48	0.51
278 Other crude minerals	51 260	2.1	0.87	0.36
776 Valves tubes; diodes, transistors	46 212	1.9	0.01	0.01
672 Ingots, Iron steel primary products	45 261	1.8	0.54	0.14
Remainder	1 171 638	46.9		
Korea, Republic of - Corée, République de (**=Developing)				
All commodity groups	416 193 778	100.0	7.34	3.01
764 Telecommunicate equipment part nes	40 595 952	9.8	15.02	9.68
793 Ships boats floating structures	39 916 804	9.6	44.32	26.58
776 Valves tubes; diodes, transistors	30 614 164	7.4	9.55	6.55
781 Passenger cars and race cars	28 496 020	6.8	34.05	5.69
334 Heavy petroleum & bituminous oil	27 213 291	6.5	10.56	4.74
871 Optical instruments apparatus nes	26 942 820	6.5	37.75	31.20
784 Motor vehicle parts and accessories	12 943 381	3.1	20.39	4.87
511 Hydrocarbons nes; derivatives	8 304 960	2.0	29.96	12.21
778 Electrical machinery apparatus nes	7 940 941	1.9	9.27	4.41
759 Office equipment part & accessories	7 227 800	1.7	6.39	3.79
Remainder	185 997 644	44.7		
Kuwait - Koweït (**=Developing) (2)				
All commodity groups	59 125 352	100.0	1.04	0.43
333 Crude petroleum & bituminous oil	41 882 904	70.8	5.48	3.91
334 Heavy petroleum & bituminous oil	9 101 983	15.4	3.53	1.59
342 Liquefied propane and butane	2 005 142	3.4	7.81	5.27
571 Primary form ethylene polymers	1 808 055	3.1	7.40	3.12
512 Alcohols, phenols; derivatives	755 646	1.3	3.44	1.79
562 Manufactured fertilizer excl. crude	354 838	0.6	2.07	0.73
781 Passenger cars and race cars	315 989	0.5	0.38	0.06
792 Aircraft, spacecraft & equipment	212 477	0.4	1.12	0.16
575 Other plastics, in primary forms	169 602	0.3	0.70	0.20
274 Sulphur and unroasted iron pyrites	148 602	0.3	10.61	6.01
Remainder	2 370 114	4.0		

Leading products exported based on average 2009-2010 values SITC Revision 3 (3-digit level) Principaux produits exportés d'après la moyenne des valeurs de 2009-2010 CTCI révision 3 (positions à 3 chiffres)	2009-2010			
	Value (f.o.b., thousands of dollars) Valeur (f.a.b., milliers de dollars)	As percentage En pourcentage		
		of country total du total du pays	of ** (1) des ** (1)	of world du monde
Kyrgyzstan - Kirghizistan (**=Transition)				
All commodity groups	1 716 396	100.0	0.32	0.01
971 Gold non-monetary excluding ores	156 062	9.1	11.36	0.11
842 Female clothing, woven	142 698	8.3	13.15	0.20
057 Fruit nut (exc oil), fresh or dried	142 216	8.3	9.49	0.21
054 Vegetable & vegetable products nes	115 856	6.7	11.87	0.21
351 Electric current	76 728	4.5	4.06	0.24
525 Radio active & associated materials	69 565	4.1	2.27	0.46
334 Heavy petroleum & bituminous oil	69 140	4.0	0.10	0.01
778 Electrical machinery apparatus nes	53 676	3.1	4.99	0.03
263 Cotton	41 572	2.4	2.21	0.28
022 Milk products, excl. butter & cheese	35 414	2.1	3.66	0.11
Remainder	813 469	47.4		
Lao People's Dem. Rep. - Rép. dém. populaire lao (**=Developing) (2)				
All commodity groups	1 375 835	100.0	0.02	0.01
682 Copper	330 450	24.0	0.58	0.30
283 Copper ores and concentrates	292 870	21.3	0.95	0.75
351 Electric current	174 632	12.7	4.44	0.54
248 Wood simply worked, railway sleeper	92 839	6.7	1.29	0.29
841 Male clothing, woven	77 853	5.7	0.20	0.13
247 Wood in rough or roughly squared	53 968	3.9	1.33	0.45
845 Articles of apparel nes	45 901	3.3	0.06	0.04
071 Coffee and coffee substitutes	30 833	2.2	0.18	0.11
843 Male clothing, knitted crocheted	29 826	2.2	0.16	0.13
044 Maize unmilled, excluding sweet corn	26 667	1.9	0.42	0.12
Remainder	219 995	16.0		
Latvia - Lettonie (**=Developed)				
All commodity groups	8 011 136	100.0	0.11	0.06
248 Wood simply worked, railway sleeper	470 387	5.9	2.24	1.48
676 Iron steel bar rod section piling	374 540	4.7	1.02	0.61
542 Medicines including veterinary	281 055	3.5	0.10	0.09
634 Veneer, plywood & other wood nes	280 987	3.5	1.75	0.98
781 Passenger cars and race cars	234 637	2.9	0.06	0.05
112 Alcoholic beverages	228 552	2.9	0.47	0.38
041 Wheat meslin, incl spelt, unmilled	224 549	2.8	0.87	0.69
247 Wood in rough or roughly squared	202 489	2.5	3.53	1.70
761 Television video receive project	198 614	2.5	0.49	0.22
334 Heavy petroleum & bituminous oil	193 017	2.4	0.08	0.03
Remainder	5 322 307	66.4		
Lebanon - Liban (**=Developing)				
All commodity groups	4 604 044	100.0	0.08	0.03
971 Gold non-monetary excluding ores	355 813	7.7	0.47	0.26
897 Jewellery nes (667)	230 189	5.0	0.55	0.32
661 Lime cement construction material	212 351	4.6	1.45	0.83
667 Pearls, precious semiprecious stone	200 491	4.4	0.36	0.18
716 Rotating electric plant parts nes	163 810	3.6	0.65	0.21
282 Ferrous iron & steel, waste & scrap	162 708	3.5	3.29	0.42
057 Fruit nut (exc oil), fresh or dried	155 192	3.4	0.48	0.23
562 Manufactured fertilizer excl. crude	152 962	3.3	0.89	0.32
892 Printed matter	142 346	3.1	1.11	0.30
642 Cut paper and paperboard articles	135 334	2.9	0.98	0.27
Remainder	2 692 848	58.5		
Lesotho (**=Developing) (2)				
All commodity groups	763 651	100.0	0.01	0.01
667 Pearls, precious semiprecious stone	231 221	30.3	0.42	0.21
841 Male clothing, woven	185 784	24.3	0.47	0.32
845 Articles of apparel nes	163 119	21.4	0.20	0.14
842 Female clothing, woven	59 367	7.8	0.13	0.08
844 Female clothing, knitted crocheted	44 053	5.8	0.14	0.11
843 Male clothing, knitted crocheted	25 739	3.4	0.14	0.11
652 Woven cotton fabrics	23 514	3.1	0.12	0.08
654 Other woven textile fabrics nes	2 168	0.3	0.05	0.02
846 Clothing accessory excl. 831 848 851	1 911	0.3	0.01	0.01
851 Footwear	602	0.1	0.00	0.00
Remainder	26 173	3.4		

For sources and notes, see end of table.

Pour les sources et les notes, se reporter à la fin du tableau.

Leading products exported based on average 2009-2010 values — SITC Revision 3 (3-digit level)

Principaux produits exportés d'après la moyenne des valeurs de 2009-2010 — CTCI révision 3 (positions à 3 chiffres)

Product	Value (f.o.b., thousands of dollars) / Valeur (f.a.b., milliers de dollars)	of country total / du total du pays	of ** (1) / des ** (1)	of world / du monde
Liberia - Libéria (=Developing) (2)**				
All commodity groups	177 600	100.0	0.00	0.00
792 Ships boats floating structures	62 733	35.3	0.07	0.04
231 Natural rubber, latex, gum, etc	51 756	29.1	0.30	0.28
333 Crude petroleum & bituminous oil	20 934	11.8	0.00	0.00
971 Gold non-monetary excluding ores	12 349	7.0	0.02	0.01
334 Heavy petroleum & bituminous oil	8 190	4.6	0.00	0.00
667 Pearls, precious semiprecious stone	3 102	1.0	0.01	0.00
281 Iron ore and concentrates	3 082	1.7	0.01	0.00
072 Cocoa	2 383	1.3	0.02	0.01
282 Ferrous iron & steel, waste & scrap	1 511	0.9	0.03	0.00
246 Wood chips, particles and waste	813	0.5	0.06	0.02
Remainder	10 688	6.0		
Libyan Arab Jamahiriya - Jamahiriya arabe libyenne (=Developing) (2)**				
All commodity groups	41 682 500	100.0	0.73	0.30
333 Crude petroleum & bituminous oil	32 675 049	78.4	4.28	3.05
343 Natural gas, liquefied or not	3 299 030	7.9	3.77	1.55
334 Heavy petroleum & bituminous oil	3 237 027	7.8	1.26	0.56
342 Liquefied propane and butane	398 057	1.0	1.55	1.05
971 Gold non-monetary excluding ores	344 467	0.8	0.45	0.25
511 Hydrocarbons nes; derivatives	253 553	0.6	0.91	0.37
562 Manufactured fertilizer excl. crude	213 455	0.5	1.25	0.44
344 Petroleum and hydrocarbon gas nes	203 740	0.5	3.25	2.05
512 Alcohols, phenols; derivatives	142 722	0.3	0.65	0.34
673 Flat iron non-alloy steel products	138 338	0.3	0.58	0.19
Remainder	777 064	1.9		
Lithuania - Lituanie (=Developed)**				
All commodity groups	18 655 131	100.0	0.24	0.13
334 Heavy petroleum & bituminous oil	3 864 364	20.7	1.59	0.67
821 Furniture part; bedding furnishing	899 355	4.8	1.34	0.73
562 Manufactured fertilizer excl. crude	757 946	4.1	3.52	1.56
781 Passenger cars and race cars	589 799	3.2	0.14	0.12
574 Polyacetals and polyesters, etc	557 161	3.0	2.18	1.26
893 Articles of plastic nes	337 475	1.8	0.49	0.31
057 Fruit nut (exc oil), fresh or dried	295 655	1.6	0.88	0.44
024 Cheese and curd	268 397	1.4	1.18	1.06
041 Wheat meslin, incl spelt, unmilled	266 388	1.4	1.03	0.82
081 Animal feed excluding unmilled cereal	262 034	1.4	0.83	0.46
Remainder	10 556 557	56.6		
Luxembourg (=Developed)**				
All commodity groups	20 362 853	100.0	0.27	0.15
676 Iron steel bar rod section piling	2 606 499	12.8	7.09	4.23
752 Computer equipment nes	829 369	4.1	0.92	0.28
674 Flat plated iron non-alloy steel	818 490	4.0	3.02	1.82
893 Articles of plastic nes	780 635	3.8	1.12	0.72
625 Rubber for wheels, incl inner tube	708 868	3.5	1.82	1.09
657 Special yarn and textile fabric etc	684 538	3.4	3.05	1.80
684 Aluminium	639 018	3.1	1.11	0.67
641 Paper and paperboard	603 140	3.0	0.70	0.57
582 Plastic sheet film foil & strips	553 324	2.7	0.96	0.71
781 Passenger cars and race cars	475 485	2.3	0.11	0.09
Remainder	11 663 487	57.3		
Madagascar (=Developing)**				
All commodity groups	1 089 025	100.0	0.02	0.01
845 Articles of apparel nes	179 595	16.5	0.22	0.15
075 Spices	95 224	8.7	2.15	1.66
036 Crustacean mollusc aquat invertebra	92 440	8.5	0.59	0.38
842 Female clothing, woven	77 850	7.1	0.17	0.11
841 Male clothing, woven	60 805	5.6	0.16	0.10
287 Base metal ores & concentrates nes	57 460	5.3	0.37	0.23
037 Fish shellfish, prepared preserved	35 289	3.2	0.27	0.18
334 Heavy petroleum & bituminous oil	34 313	3.2	0.01	0.01
971 Gold non-monetary excluding ores	30 660	2.8	0.04	0.02
072 Cocoa	27 606	2.5	0.22	0.15
Remainder	397 784	36.5		

Product	Value (f.o.b., thousands of dollars) / Valeur (f.a.b., milliers de dollars)	of country total / du total du pays	of ** (1) / des ** (1)	of world / du monde
Malawi (=Developing)**				
All commodity groups	1 127 060	100.0	0.02	0.01
121 Unmanufactured tabacco and refuse	657 329	58.3	8.67	5.77
074 Tea and maté	80 566	7.1	1.50	1.17
061 Sugar, mollasses and honey	68 482	6.1	0.30	0.20
054 Vegetable & vegetable products nes	61 095	5.4	0.30	0.11
286 Uranium & thorium ore concentrates	29 083	2.6	4.86	3.33
263 Cotton	20 759	2.1	0.10	0.19
525 Radio active & associated materials	17 241	1.5	1.25	0.11
845 Articles of apparel nes	14 003	1.2	0.02	0.01
222 Oil seed etc for soft oil	13 858	1.2	0.07	0.03
057 Fruit nut (exc oil), fresh or dried	12 482	1.1	0.04	0.02
Remainder	146 163	13.0		
Malaysia - Malaisie (=Developing)**				
All commodity groups	177 992 761	100.0	3.14	1.29
776 Valves tubes; diodes, transistors	28 465 473	16.0	8.88	6.09
422 Fixed veg fat and oil, excl. "soft"	11 628 620	6.5	39.58	35.10
752 Computer equipment nes	10 784 150	6.1	5.31	3.67
759 Office equipment part & accessories	10 443 747	5.9	9.23	5.48
343 Natural gas, liquefied or not	10 354 001	5.8	11.84	4.88
333 Crude petroleum & bituminous oil	8 455 747	4.8	1.11	0.79
334 Heavy petroleum & bituminous oil	6 726 606	3.8	2.61	1.17
764 Telecommunicate equipment part nes	4 611 480	2.6	1.71	1.10
772 Electrical circuit equipment	4 131 220	2.3	5.43	2.26
761 Television video receive project	3 654 056	2.1	7.16	3.96
Remainder	78 737 661	44.2		
Maldives (=Developing) (2)**				
All commodity groups	184 450	100.0	0.00	0.00
034 Fish, fresh live chilled frozen	140 297	76.1	0.67	0.28
037 Fish shellfish, prepared preserved	14 847	8.0	0.11	0.07
035 Fish, dried salted smoked	8 585	4.7	0.63	0.17
282 Ferrous iron & steel, waste & scrap	1 780	1.0	0.04	0.00
288 Non ferrous base metal waste nes	1 521	0.8	0.02	0.00
727 Food processing machine excl. domest	1 210	0.7	0.07	0.01
714 Non-electric engines excl. 712 713 718	1 100	0.6	0.01	0.00
081 Animal feed excluding unmilled cereal	982	0.5	0.00	0.00
598 Miscellaneous chemical products nes	885	0.5	0.00	0.00
515 Organo-inorganic compound acid salt	849	0.5	0.01	0.00
Remainder	12 395	6.7		
Mali (=Developing) (2)**				
All commodity groups	1 855 777	100.0	0.03	0.01
971 Gold non-monetary excluding ores	1 087 888	58.6	1.43	0.79
263 Cotton	383 728	20.7	5.72	2.60
571 Primary form ethylene polymers	64 398	3.5	0.26	0.11
001 Live animal excl. fish & crustacean	59 581	3.2	1.66	0.33
562 Manufactured fertilizer excl. crude	25 425	1.4	0.15	0.05
222 Oil seed etc for soft oil	24 893	1.3	0.13	0.05
057 Fruit nut (exc oil), fresh or dried	16 509	0.9	0.05	0.02
793 Ships boats floating structures	15 059	0.8	0.02	0.01
723 Civil engineering plant & equipment	13 421	0.7	0.06	0.02
611 Leather	11 019	0.6	0.10	0.06
Remainder	153 856	8.3		
Malta - Malte (=Developed)**				
All commodity groups	2 426 635	100.0	0.03	0.02
776 Valves tubes; diodes, transistors	769 212	31.7	0.53	0.16
542 Medicines including veterinary	249 561	10.3	0.08	0.08
772 Electrical circuit equipment	201 530	8.3	0.19	0.11
892 Printed matter	131 815	5.4	0.40	0.28
894 Baby carriage toy game sport good	115 375	4.8	0.32	0.13
893 Articles of plastic nes	58 516	2.4	0.08	0.05
655 Knitted or crocheted fabrics nes	55 995	2.3	0.92	0.23
098 Edible products & preparations nes	51 432	2.1	0.14	0.10
034 Fish, fresh live chilled frozen	51 286	2.1	0.19	0.10
872 Medical instruments appliances nes	47 059	1.9	0.08	0.06
Remainder	694 854	28.6		

For sources and notes, see end of table.

Pour les sources et les notes, se reporter à la fin du tableau.

Leading products exported based on average 2009-2010 values SITC Revision 3 (3-digit level) Principaux produits exportés d'après la moyenne des valeurs de 2009-2010 CTCI révision 3 (positions à 3 chiffres)	2009-2010			
	Value (f.o.b., thousands of dollars) Valeur (f.a.b., milliers de dollars)	As percentage / En pourcentage		
		of country total du total du pays	of ** (1) des ** (1)	of world du monde
Marshall Islands - Îles Marshall (**=Developing) (2)				
All commodity groups	20 500	100.0	0.00	0.00
793 Ships boats floating structures	15 011	73.2	0.02	0.01
034 Fish, fresh live chilled frozen	3 204	15.6	0.02	0.01
334 Heavy petroleum & bituminous oil	1 533	7.5	0.00	0.00
894 Baby carriage toy game sport good	137	0.7	0.00	0.00
422 Fixed veg fat and oil, excl. "soft"	128	0.6	0.00	0.00
037 Fish shellfish, prepared preserved	116	0.6	0.00	0.00
344 Petroleum and hydrocarbon gas nes	63	0.3	0.00	0.00
351 Electric current	54	0.3	0.00	0.00
035 Fish, dried salted smoked	26	0.1	0.00	0.00
667 Pearls, precious semiprecious stone	20	0.1	0.00	0.00
Remainder	207	1.0		
Mauritania - Mauritanie (**=Developing) (2)				
All commodity groups	1 703 899	100.0	0.03	0.01
281 Iron ore and concentrates	775 302	45.5	2.04	0.94
034 Fish, fresh live chilled frozen	223 161	13.1	1.06	0.45
283 Copper ores and concentrates	190 099	11.2	0.61	0.49
036 Crustacean mollusc aquat invertebra	163 045	9.6	1.04	0.67
333 Crude petroleum & bituminous oil	141 262	8.3	0.02	0.01
971 Gold non-monetary excluding ores	62 956	3.7	0.08	0.05
081 Animal feed excluding unmilled cereal	23 609	1.4	0.10	0.04
287 Base metal ores & concentrates nes	6 819	0.4	0.04	0.03
035 Fish, dried salted smoked	3 588	0.2	0.27	0.07
282 Ferrous iron & steel, waste & scrap	3 106	0.2	0.06	0.01
Remainder	110 952	6.5		
Mauritius - Maurice (**=Developing)				
All commodity groups	2 002 451	100.0	0.04	0.01
845 Articles of apparel nes	335 603	16.8	0.41	0.28
061 Sugar, mollasses and honey	245 171	12.2	1.08	0.73
037 Fish shellfish, prepared preserved	235 518	11.8	1.78	1.17
841 Male clothing, woven	193 958	9.7	0.50	0.33
034 Fish, fresh live chilled frozen	66 567	3.3	0.32	0.13
844 Female clothing, knitted crocheted	55 885	2.8	0.18	0.13
842 Female clothing, woven	53 519	2.7	0.11	0.07
897 Jewellery nes (667)	50 080	2.5	0.12	0.07
667 Pearls, precious semiprecious stone	47 843	2.4	0.09	0.04
843 Male clothing, knitted crocheted	43 008	2.1	0.23	0.19
Remainder	675 298	33.7		
Mayotte (**=Developing)				
All commodity groups	6 780	100.0	0.00	0.00
781 Passenger cars and race cars	753	11.1	0.00	0.00
744 Mechanical handling equipment nes	627	9.3	0.00	0.00
034 Fish, fresh live chilled frozen	566	8.3	0.00	0.00
775 Household equipment nes	520	7.7	0.00	0.00
741 Heating cooling equipment parts nes	373	5.5	0.00	0.00
542 Medicines including veterinary	309	4.6	0.00	0.00
551 Essential oils, perfumes & flavours	250	3.7	0.01	0.00
723 Civil engineering plant & equipment	241	3.6	0.00	0.00
699 Base metal manufactures nes	211	3.1	0.00	0.00
728 Special industrial machine part nes	204	3.0	0.00	0.00
Remainder	2 726	40.2		
Mexico - Mexique (**=Developing)				
All commodity groups	264 008 706	100.0	4.66	1.91
333 Crude petroleum & bituminous oil	30 800 470	11.7	4.03	2.88
764 Telecommunicate equipment part nes	19 431 727	7.4	7.19	4.63
761 Television video receive project	19 115 624	7.2	37.45	20.70
781 Passenger cars and race cars	19 097 195	7.2	22.82	3.81
784 Motor vehicle parts and accessories	11 609 658	4.4	18.29	4.36
752 Computer equipment nes	11 045 838	4.2	5.44	3.76
782 Goods and service vehicles	8 527 252	3.2	29.45	9.08
778 Electrical machinery apparatus nes	6 096 987	2.3	7.12	3.39
773 Electrical distribute equipment nes	5 962 148	2.3	15.68	7.06
772 Electrical circuit equipment	5 628 380	2.1	7.40	3.08
Remainder	126 693 428	48.0		
Micronesia (Federated States of) - Micronésie (États fédérés de) (**=Developing) (2)				
All commodity groups	27 000	100.0	0.00	0.00
034 Fish, fresh live chilled frozen	25 546	94.6	0.12	0.05
036 Crustacean mollusc aquat invertebra	284	1.1	0.00	0.00
764 Telecommunicate equipment part nes	221	0.8	0.00	0.00
896 Work of art & collections; antiques	177	0.7	0.01	0.00
035 Fish, dried salted smoked	94	0.3	0.01	0.00
899 Manufactured articles nes	72	0.3	0.00	0.00
657 Special yarn and textile fabric etc	57	0.2	0.00	0.00
037 Fish shellfish, prepared preserved	55	0.2	0.00	0.00
781 Passenger cars and race cars	55	0.2	0.00	0.00
291 Crude animal materials nes	46	0.2	0.00	0.00
Remainder	393	1.5		
Mongolia - Mongolie (**=Developing) (2)				
All commodity groups	2 397 790	100.0	0.04	0.02
283 Copper ores and concentrates	1 065 125	44.4	3.44	2.72
971 Gold non-monetary excluding ores	348 153	14.5	0.46	0.25
287 Base metal ores & concentrates nes	314 777	13.1	2.03	1.23
321 Coal excluding non-agglomerated	186 288	7.8	0.57	0.20
268 Wool & animal hair, incl wool tops	153 177	6.4	7.81	3.05
333 Crude petroleum & bituminous oil	54 679	2.3	0.01	0.01
278 Other crude minerals	44 697	1.9	0.76	0.31
611 Leather	29 599	1.2	0.28	0.15
281 Iron ore and concentrates	29 594	1.2	0.08	0.04
682 Copper	18 231	0.8	0.03	0.02
Remainder	153 469	6.4		
Montenegro - Monténégro (**=Transition) (2)				
All commodity groups	412 058	100.0	0.08	0.00
684 Aluminium	165 338	40.1	2.04	0.17
112 Alcoholic beverages	27 880	6.8	2.23	0.05
351 Electric current	22 513	5.5	1.19	0.07
676 Iron steel bar rod section piling	16 379	4.0	0.32	0.03
672 Ingots, iron steel primary products	15 942	3.9	0.14	0.05
248 Wood simply worked, railway sleeper	15 347	3.7	0.42	0.05
334 Heavy petroleum & bituminous oil	10 721	2.6	0.01	0.00
542 Medicines including veterinary	10 623	2.6	0.87	0.00
288 Non ferrous base metal waste nes	10 394	2.5	2.18	0.03
282 Ferrous iron & steel, waste & scrap	6 857	1.7	0.40	0.02
Remainder	110 064	26.7		
Montserrat (**=Developing)				
All commodity groups	2 124	100.0	0.00	0.00
273 Stone, sand and gravel	673	31.7	0.02	0.01
723 Civil engineering plant & equipment	207	9.8	0.00	0.00
821 Furniture part; bedding furnishing	167	7.8	0.00	0.00
277 Natural abrasives nes	161	7.6	0.02	0.01
714 Non-electric engines excl. 712 713 718	121	5.7	0.00	0.00
764 Telecommunicate equipment part nes	92	4.3	0.00	0.00
112 Alcoholic beverages	88	4.2	0.00	0.00
874 Measure analyze control device nes	63	2.9	0.00	0.00
773 Electrical distribute equipment nes	60	2.8	0.00	0.00
782 Goods and service vehicles	45	2.1	0.00	0.00
Remainder	446	21.0		
Morocco - Maroc (**=Developing)				
All commodity groups	15 916 865	100.0	0.28	0.12
842 Female clothing, woven	1 422 901	8.9	3.05	1.99
773 Electrical distribute equipment nes	1 271 354	8.0	3.34	1.51
522 Inorganic chemical elem oxide salt	1 230 875	7.7	7.07	2.94
562 Manufactured fertilizer excl. crude	1 083 006	6.8	6.33	2.23
272 Crude fertilizer, excl. manufactured	814 585	5.1	34.89	24.44
845 Articles of apparel nes	752 723	4.7	0.92	0.64
054 Vegetable & vegetable products nes	742 012	4.7	3.65	1.38
776 Valves tubes; diodes, transistors	684 647	4.3	0.21	0.15
057 Fruit nut (exc oil), fresh or dried	617 733	3.9	1.91	0.92
037 Fish shellfish, prepared preserved	594 825	3.7	4.50	2.95
Remainder	6 702 204	42.1		

For sources and notes, see end of table.

Pour les sources et les notes, se reporter à la fin du tableau.

3.2.D Export structure by product
Individual countries and territories

3.2.D Structure des exportations par produits
Pays et territoires individuels

Mozambique (**=Developing)

Leading products exported based on average 2009-2010 values SITC Revision 3 (3-digit level) / Principaux produits exportés d'après la moyenne des valeurs de 2009-2010 CTCI révision 3 (positions à 3 chiffres)	Value (f.o.b., thousands of dollars) Valeur (f.a.b., milliers de dollars)	2009-2010 As percentage / En pourcentage		
		of country total du total du pays	of ** (1) des ** (1)	of world du monde
All commodity groups	2 195 119	100.0	0.04	0.02
004 Aluminium	853 551	39.0	2.00	0.00
351 Electric current	219 463	10.0	5.58	0.68
121 Unmanufactured tabacco and refuse	114 424	5.2	1.51	1.00
343 Natural gas, liquefied or not	112 454	5.1	0.13	0.05
334 Heavy petroleum & bituminous oil	72 185	3.3	0.03	0.01
036 Crustacean mollusc aquat invertebra	66 384	3.0	0.42	0.02
061 Sugar, mollasses and honey	50 175	2.3	0.22	0.15
287 Base metal ores & concentrates nes	41 463	1.9	0.27	0.16
222 Oil seed etc for soft oil	33 698	1.5	0.17	0.07
057 Fruit nut (exc oil), fresh or dried	32 678	1.5	0.10	0.05
Remainder	599 645	27.3		

Myanmar (**=Developing) (2)

Product	Value	of country total	of ** (1)	of world
All commodity groups	8 364 383	100.0	0.15	0.06
343 Natural gas, liquefied or not	2 616 495	31.3	2.99	1.23
247 Wood in rough or roughly squared	1 093 365	13.1	27.00	9.16
054 Vegetable & vegetable products nes	786 451	9.4	3.87	1.46
845 Articles of apparel nes	584 888	7.0	0.71	0.49
841 Male clothing, woven	432 640	5.2	1.10	0.74
248 Wood simply worked, railway sleeper	351 754	4.2	4.90	1.10
036 Crustacean mollusc aquat invertebra	329 023	3.9	2.10	1.34
842 Female clothing, woven	302 891	3.6	0.65	0.42
682 Copper	203 518	2.4	0.36	0.19
034 Fish, fresh live chilled frozen	136 153	1.6	0.65	0.27
Remainder	1 527 205	18.3		

Namibia - Namibie (**=Developing) (2)

Product	Value	of country total	of ** (1)	of world
All commodity groups	3 606 100	100.0	0.00	0.03
034 Fish, fresh live chilled frozen	534 675	14.8	2.55	1.08
667 Pearls, precious semiprecious stone	505 748	14.0	0.92	0.46
686 Zinc	352 942	9.8	9.91	3.42
286 Uranium & thorium ore concentrates	338 869	9.4	56.67	38.79
525 Radio active & associated materials	277 575	7.7	20.84	1.83
892 Printed matter	202 720	5.6	1.57	0.43
682 Copper	146 590	4.1	0.26	0.13
112 Alcoholic beverages	72 454	2.0	0.70	0.12
287 Base metal ores & concentrates nes	67 463	1.9	0.43	0.26
121 Unmanufactured tabacco and refuse	66 625	1.8	0.88	0.58
Remainder	1 040 526	28.9		

Nauru (**=Developing) (2)

Product	Value	of country total	of ** (1)	of world
All commodity groups	27 750	100.0	0.00	0.00
272 Crude fertilizer, excl. manufactured	17 781	64.1	0.76	0.53
874 Measure analyze control device nes	4 434	16.0	0.02	0.00
335 Residual petroleum products nes	3 523	12.7	0.03	0.01
744 Mechanical handling equipment nes	441	1.6	0.00	0.00
575 Other plastics, in primary forms	374	1.3	0.00	0.00
842 Female clothing, woven	274	1.0	0.00	0.00
034 Fish, fresh live chilled frozen	248	0.9	0.00	0.00
022 Milk products, excl. butter & cheese	194	0.7	0.00	0.00
251 Pulp and waste paper	185	0.7	0.00	0.00
894 Baby carriage toy game sport good	160	0.6	0.00	0.00
Remainder	136	0.5		

Nepal - Népal (**=Developing) (2)

Product	Value	of country total	of ** (1)	of world
All commodity groups	860 008	100.0	0.02	0.01
674 Flat plated iron non-alloy steel	77 154	9.0	0.46	0.17
659 Floor coverings etc	66 633	7.7	1.14	0.51
054 Vegetable & vegetable products nes	65 427	7.6	0.32	0.12
651 Textile yarn	61 467	7.1	0.22	0.14
653 Man-made woven fabrics	54 114	6.3	0.22	0.16
658 Made-up textile articles nes	34 899	4.1	0.11	0.08
292 Crude vegetable materials nes	25 909	3.0	0.28	0.08
846 Clothing accessory excl. 831 848 851	24 416	2.8	0.17	0.11
075 Spices	23 028	2.7	0.52	0.40
273 Stone, sand and gravel	22 774	2.6	0.57	0.26
Remainder	404 186	47.0		

Netherlands - Pays-Bas (**=Developed) (2)

Product	Value	of country total	of ** (1)	of world
All commodity groups	534 348 498	100.0	7.02	3.87
334 Heavy petroleum & bituminous oil	18 888 818	6.0	18.00	0.00
752 Computer equipment nes	16 705 743	3.1	18.45	5.68
333 Crude petroleum & bituminous oil	16 010 688	3.0	11.26	1.50
764 Telecommunicate equipment part nes	15 527 374	2.9	10.48	3.70
759 Office equipment part & accessories	14 908 646	2.8	10.27	7.82
292 Crude vegetable materials nes	12 004 144	2.4	50.10	50.23
542 Medicines including veterinary	12 407 032	2.3	4.22	3.94
511 Hydrocarbons nes; derivatives	9 388 903	1.8	23.96	13.80
054 Vegetable & vegetable products nes	8 477 634	1.6	25.96	15.71
776 Valves tubes; diodes, transistors	8 168 176	1.5	5.59	1.75
Remainder	373 914 220	70.0		

Netherlands Antilles - Antilles néerlandaises (**=Developing) (2)

Product	Value	of country total	of ** (1)	of world
All commodity groups	810 419	100.0	0.01	0.01
334 Heavy petroleum & bituminous oil	545 449	67.3	0.21	0.10
971 Gold non-monetary excluding ores	26 874	3.3	0.04	0.02
335 Residual petroleum products nes	24 845	3.1	0.20	0.08
781 Passenger cars and race cars	18 865	2.3	0.02	0.00
554 Soaps cleansers polishes	13 153	1.6	0.15	0.04
744 Mechanical handling equipment nes	12 090	1.5	0.08	0.02
846 Clothing accessory excl. 831 848 851	10 638	1.3	0.07	0.05
034 Fish, fresh live chilled frozen	7 700	1.0	0.04	0.02
842 Female clothing, woven	6 838	0.8	0.01	0.01
793 Ships boats floating structures	5 532	0.7	0.01	0.00
Remainder	138 436	17.1		

New Caledonia - Nouvelle-Calédonie (**=Developing) (2)

Product	Value	of country total	of ** (1)	of world
All commodity groups	1 148 084	100.0	0.02	0.01
671 Pig & sponge iron, ferro alloys etc	533 445	46.5	3.13	1.73
284 Nickel ores, concentrates, etc	322 435	28.1	7.45	4.35
281 Iron ore and concentrates	43 366	3.8	0.11	0.05
781 Passenger cars and race cars	23 938	2.1	0.03	0.00
321 Coal excluding non-agglomerated	20 881	1.8	0.06	0.02
782 Goods and service vehicles	19 638	1.7	0.07	0.02
036 Crustacean mollusc aquat invertebra	10 569	0.9	0.07	0.04
334 Heavy petroleum & bituminous oil	7 959	0.7	0.07	0.02
034 Fish, fresh live chilled frozen	7 774	0.7	0.04	0.02
723 Civil engineering plant & equipment	7 763	0.7	0.03	0.01
Remainder	150 316	13.1		

New Zealand - Nouvelle-Zélande (**=Developed)

Product	Value	of country total	of ** (1)	of world
All commodity groups	27 932 239	100.0	0.37	0.20
022 Milk products, excl. butter & cheese	4 023 092	14.4	15.05	12.61
012 Meat nes, fresh chilled frozen	2 173 232	7.8	4.74	3.70
011 Beef, fresh chilled frozen	1 251 310	4.5	5.63	3.92
023 Butter fats oils derived from milk	1 247 504	4.5	22.50	20.28
333 Crude petroleum & bituminous oil	1 231 710	4.4	0.87	0.12
057 Fruit nut (exc oil), fresh or dried	1 010 711	3.6	3.01	1.50
024 Cheese and curd	939 533	3.4	4.14	3.69
098 Edible products & preparations nes	883 361	3.2	2.39	1.76
247 Wood in rough or roughly squared	780 497	2.8	13.60	6.54
112 Alcoholic beverages	772 974	2.8	1.57	1.27
Remainder	13 618 315	48.8		

Nicaragua (**=Developing)

Product	Value	of country total	of ** (1)	of world
All commodity groups	1 620 341	100.0	0.03	0.01
845 Articles of apparel nes	228 820	14.1	0.28	0.19
071 Coffee and coffee substitutes	215 455	13.3	1.25	0.77
011 Beef, fresh chilled frozen	149 844	9.2	1.63	0.47
971 Gold non-monetary excluding ores	107 098	6.6	0.14	0.08
773 Electrical distribute equipment nes	96 861	6.0	0.25	0.11
036 Crustacean mollusc aquat invertebra	82 289	5.1	0.52	0.34
061 Sugar, mollasses and honey	77 959	4.8	0.34	0.23
841 Male clothing, woven	73 753	4.6	0.19	0.13
054 Vegetable & vegetable products nes	52 381	3.2	0.26	0.10
024 Cheese and curd	51 851	3.2	2.88	0.20
Remainder	484 031	29.9		

For sources and notes, see end of table.

Pour les sources et les notes, se reporter à la fin du tableau.

3.2.D Export structure by product
Individual countries and territories

3.2.D Structure des exportations par produits
Pays et territoires individuels

Leading products exported based on average 2009-2010 values SITC Revision 3 (3-digit level) / Principaux produits exportés d'après la moyenne des valeurs de 2009-2010 CTCI révision 3 (positions à 3 chiffres)	Value (f.o.b., thousands of dollars) / Valeur (f.a.b., milliers de dollars)	of country total / du total du pays	of ** (1) / des ** (1)	of world / du monde
Niger (**=Developing) (2)				
All commodity groups	1 018 238	100.0	0.02	0.01
001 Live animal excl. fish & crustacean	259 217	25.5	7.24	1.43
525 Radio active & associated materials	260 240	25.2	19.24	1.69
286 Uranium & thorium ore concentrates	228 354	22.4	38.19	26.14
334 Heavy petroleum & bituminous oil	70 036	6.9	0.03	0.01
054 Vegetable & vegetable products nes	61 206	0.0	0.00	0.11
971 Gold non-monetary excluding ores	38 465	3.8	0.05	0.03
269 Worn clothing, textile article; rag	10 159	1.0	1.01	0.29
652 Woven cotton fabrics	6 782	0.7	0.03	0.02
542 Medicines including veterinary	6 416	0.6	0.03	0.01
720 Civil engineering plant & equipment	5 539	0.5	0.02	0.01
Remainder	75 729	7.4		
Nigeria - Nigéria (**=Developing)				
All commodity groups	60 258 230	100.0	1.06	0.44
333 Crude petroleum & bituminous oil	48 304 683	80.2	6.32	4.51
334 Heavy petroleum & bituminous oil	3 155 948	5.2	1.22	0.55
343 Natural gas, liquefied or not	2 982 998	5.0	3.41	1.41
611 Leather	893 003	1.5	8.50	4.62
072 Cocoa	829 032	1.4	6.60	4.40
342 Liquefied propane and butane	685 108	1.1	2.67	1.80
222 Oil seed etc for soft oil	276 560	0.5	1.40	0.56
344 Petroleum and hydrocarbon gas nes	205 539	0.3	3.28	2.07
231 Natural rubber, latex, gum, etc	190 757	0.3	1.10	1.04
793 Ships boats floating structures	180 856	0.3	0.20	0.12
Remainder	2 553 746	4.2		
Niue - Nioué (**=Developing) (2)				
All commodity groups	20	100.0	0.00	0.00
781 Passenger cars and race cars	5	25.1	0.00	0.00
771 Electric power machine part excl. 716	4	19.9	0.00	0.00
761 Television video receive project	3	16.3	0.00	0.00
718 Power generating machinery part nes	3	13.2	0.00	0.00
513 Carboxylic acid and compounds	2	11.2	0.00	0.00
874 Measure analyze control device nes	0	1.7	0.00	0.00
747 Pipe, boiler, tank & vat appliances	0	1.5	0.00	0.00
661 Lime cement construction material	0	1.2	0.00	0.00
782 Goods and service vehicles	0	1.1	0.00	0.00
699 Base metal manufactures nes	0	0.9	0.00	0.00
Remainder	2	7.8		
Norway - Norvège (**=Developed)				
All commodity groups	123 035 457	100.0	1.62	0.89
333 Crude petroleum & bituminous oil	43 452 159	35.3	30.56	4.06
343 Natural gas, liquefied or not	26 158 245	21.3	35.16	12.32
034 Fish, fresh live chilled frozen	6 729 639	5.5	25.09	13.55
334 Heavy petroleum & bituminous oil	4 981 855	4.0	2.05	0.87
684 Aluminium	3 937 458	3.2	6.82	4.15
342 Liquefied propane and butane	2 544 413	2.1	22.48	6.69
598 Miscellaneous chemical products nes	1 747 861	1.4	2.25	1.77
683 Nickel	1 610 611	1.3	16.15	9.45
793 Ships boats floating structures	1 545 842	1.3	2.70	1.03
874 Measure analyze control device nes	1 367 975	1.1	1.24	0.98
Remainder	28 959 400	23.5		
Occupied Palestinian territory - Territoire palestinien occupé (**=Developing) (2)				
All commodity groups	540 678	100.0	0.01	0.00
661 Lime cement construction material	116 384	21.5	0.79	0.46
821 Furniture part; bedding furnishing	30 528	5.6	0.06	0.02
421 Fixed veg fat and oil, "soft"	29 314	5.4	0.32	0.11
273 Stone, sand and gravel	22 940	4.2	0.57	0.26
893 Articles of plastic nes	20 204	3.7	0.05	0.02
851 Footwear	17 864	3.3	0.03	0.02
122 Manufactured tabacco	16 823	3.1	0.25	0.00
542 Medicines including veterinary	15 474	2.9	0.08	0.00
017 Meat offal preserved nes	14 991	2.8	0.27	0.09
793 Ships boats floating structures	14 709	2.7	0.02	0.01
Remainder	241 447	44.7		
Oman (**=Developing)				
All commodity groups	32 125 966	100.0	0.57	0.23
333 Crude petroleum & bituminous oil	16 259 937	50.6	2.13	1.52
343 Natural gas, liquefied or not	2 489 545	7.7	2.85	1.17
684 Aluminium	2 131 512	6.6	7.34	2.25
334 Heavy petroleum & bituminous oil	1 774 629	5.5	0.69	0.31
562 Manufactured fertilizer excl. crude	1 359 426	4.2	7.94	2.80
512 Alcohols, phenols, derivatives	693 665	2.2	3.16	1.64
511 Hydrocarbons nes; derivatives	458 893	1.4	1.66	0.67
773 Electrical distribute equipment nes	449 583	1.4	1.18	0.53
022 Milk products, excl. butter & cheese	293 137	0.9	6.07	0.92
661 Lime cement construction material	290 323	0.9	1.98	1.14
Remainder	5 925 316	18.4		
Pakistan (**=Developing)				
All commodity groups	19 483 901	100.0	0.34	0.14
658 Made-up textile articles nes	3 081 702	15.8	9.96	7.42
042 Rice	2 025 792	10.4	12.46	9.93
652 Woven cotton fabrics	1 883 308	9.7	9.48	6.76
651 Textile yarn	1 513 818	7.8	5.47	3.42
334 Heavy petroleum & bituminous oil	953 119	4.9	0.37	0.17
841 Male clothing, woven	858 256	4.4	2.19	1.47
843 Male clothing, knitted crocheted	824 769	4.2	4.37	3.62
897 Jewellery nes (667)	530 203	2.7	1.26	0.73
661 Lime cement construction material	505 567	2.6	3.45	1.98
848 Headgear, non-textile clothing	478 166	2.5	3.07	2.08
Remainder	6 829 201	35.1		
Palau - Palaos (**=Developing) (2)				
All commodity groups	11 900	100.0	0.00	0.00
034 Fish, fresh live chilled frozen	10 768	90.5	0.05	0.02
661 Lime cement construction material	497	4.2	0.00	0.00
282 Ferrous iron & steel, waste & scrap	177	1.5	0.00	0.00
793 Ships boats floating structures	149	1.3	0.00	0.00
641 Paper and paperboard	126	1.1	0.00	0.00
112 Alcoholic beverages	107	0.9	0.00	0.00
652 Woven cotton fabrics	94	0.8	0.00	0.00
288 Non ferrous base metal waste nes	93	0.8	0.00	0.00
542 Medicines including veterinary	91	0.8	0.00	0.00
778 Electrical machinery apparatus nes	44	0.4	0.00	0.00
Remainder	-246	-2.1		
Panama (**=Developing) (2)				
All commodity groups	889 872	100.0	0.02	0.01
793 Ships boats floating structures	117 585	13.2	0.13	0.08
541 Pharmaceuticals excluding medicines	80 343	9.0	0.54	0.06
542 Medicines including veterinary	73 651	8.3	0.37	0.02
851 Footwear	52 654	5.9	0.10	0.06
333 Crude petroleum & bituminous oil	30 576	3.4	0.00	0.00
842 Female clothing, woven	29 172	3.3	0.06	0.04
057 Fruit nut (exc oil), fresh or dried	28 019	3.1	0.09	0.04
845 Articles of apparel nes	25 202	2.8	0.03	0.02
334 Heavy petroleum & bituminous oil	24 106	2.7	0.01	0.00
841 Male clothing, woven	22 440	2.5	0.06	0.04
Remainder	406 122	45.6		
Papua New Guinea - Papouasie-Nouvelle-Guinée (**=Developing) (2)				
All commodity groups	5 401 900	100.0	0.10	0.04
971 Gold non-monetary excluding ores	1 527 361	28.3	2.01	1.11
283 Copper ores and concentrates	1 183 393	21.9	3.82	3.02
333 Crude petroleum & bituminous oil	843 557	15.6	0.11	0.08
247 Wood in rough or roughly squared	362 122	6.7	8.94	3.04
422 Fixed veg fat and oil, excl. "soft"	358 902	6.6	1.22	1.08
289 Prec metal ore concentrate excl. gold	174 018	3.2	4.34	1.22
071 Coffee and coffee substitutes	161 806	3.0	0.94	0.58
072 Cocoa	135 565	2.5	1.08	0.72
334 Heavy petroleum & bituminous oil	106 602	2.0	0.04	0.02
034 Fish, fresh live chilled frozen	74 629	1.4	0.36	0.15
Remainder	473 945	8.8		

For sources and notes, see end of table.

Pour les sources et les notes, se reporter à la fin du tableau.

Leading products exported based on average 2009-2010 values SITC Revision 3 (3-digit level) Principaux produits exportés d'après la moyenne des valeurs de 2009-2010 CTCI révision 3 (positions à 3 chiffres)	2009-2010		
	Value (f.o.b., thousands of dollars) Valeur (f.a.b., milliers de dollars)	As percentage En pourcentage	
		of country total du total du pays	of ** (1) des ** (1)

Paraguay (**=Developing)				
All commodity groups	3 850 389	100.0	0.07	0.03
??? Oil seed etc for soft oil	1 280 154	33.2	6.47	2.58
011 Beef, fresh chilled frozen	716 538	18.6	7.77	2.24
081 Animal feed excluding unmilled cereal	361 460	9.4	1.47	0.63
421 Fixed veg fat and oil, "soft"	257 126	6.7	2.82	0.94
044 Maize unmilled, excluding sweet corn	236 802	6.2	3.69	1.08
041 Wheat meslin incl swell, unmilled	200 779	5.4	4.84	0.04
611 Leather	67 625	1.8	0.64	0.35
042 Rice	56 044	1.5	0.34	0.27
248 Wood simply worked, railway sleeper	43 254	1.1	0.60	0.14
893 Articles of plastic nes	40 676	1.1	0.11	0.04
Remainder	580 931	15.1		

Peru - Pérou (**=Developing)				
All commodity groups	30 905 754	100.0	0.54	0.22
971 Gold non-monetary excluding ores	7 233 704	23.4	9.53	5.28
283 Copper ores and concentrates	5 037 627	16.3	16.27	12.86
287 Base metal ores & concentrates nes	2 789 948	9.0	17.98	10.94
682 Copper	2 630 295	8.5	4.61	2.40
334 Heavy petroleum & bituminous oil	1 930 828	6.2	0.75	0.34
081 Animal feed excluding unmilled cereal	1 613 357	5.2	6.55	2.82
071 Coffee and coffee substitutes	737 235	2.4	4.26	2.63
845 Articles of apparel nes	605 231	2.0	0.74	0.51
057 Fruit nut (exc oil), fresh or dried	441 828	1.4	1.37	0.66
333 Crude petroleum & bituminous oil	429 141	1.4	0.06	0.04
Remainder	7 456 559	24.1		

Philippines (**=Developing)				
All commodity groups	44 966 658	100.0	0.79	0.33
776 Valves tubes; diodes, transistors	13 806 505	30.7	4.31	2.96
752 Computer equipment nes	6 980 065	15.5	3.44	2.37
759 Office equipment part & accessories	2 226 736	5.0	1.97	1.17
784 Motor vehicle parts and accessories	1 546 675	3.4	2.44	0.58
778 Electrical machinery apparatus nes	1 440 575	3.2	1.68	0.80
771 Electric power machine part excl. 716	1 098 500	2.4	2.73	1.43
773 Electrical distribute equipment nes	958 716	2.1	2.52	1.14
422 Fixed veg fat and oil, excl. "soft"	932 247	2.1	3.17	2.81
635 Wood manufactures nes	924 571	2.1	12.58	4.24
764 Telecommunicate equipment part nes	887 864	2.0	0.33	0.21
Remainder	14 164 205	31.5		

Poland - Pologne (**=Developed) (2)				
All commodity groups	146 514 904	100.0	1.92	1.06
781 Passenger cars and race cars	9 743 529	6.7	2.34	1.95
821 Furniture part; bedding furnishing	8 246 128	5.6	12.32	6.72
784 Motor vehicle parts and accessories	7 487 973	5.1	3.72	2.82
761 Television video receive project	5 992 381	4.1	14.68	6.49
713 Internal combustion engine part nes	4 464 753	3.0	4.58	3.65
793 Ships boats floating structures	3 190 376	2.2	5.56	2.12
775 Household equipment nes	3 131 945	2.1	8.70	3.92
682 Copper	3 131 600	2.1	6.97	2.86
893 Articles of plastic nes	2 741 887	1.9	3.95	2.53
699 Base metal manufactures nes	2 682 550	1.8	3.62	2.37
Remainder	95 701 780	65.3		

Portugal (**=Developed)				
All commodity groups	46 074 203	100.0	0.60	0.33
334 Heavy petroleum & bituminous oil	2 207 587	4.8	0.91	0.38
784 Motor vehicle parts and accessories	2 036 859	4.4	1.01	0.77
781 Passenger cars and race cars	2 013 370	4.4	0.48	0.40
851 Footwear	1 745 891	3.8	5.13	1.98
845 Articles of apparel nes	1 349 065	2.9	3.84	1.14
641 Paper and paperboard	1 225 939	2.7	1.42	1.16
821 Furniture part; bedding furnishing	1 185 460	2.6	1.77	0.97
112 Alcoholic beverages	1 056 721	2.3	2.15	1.74
633 Cork manufactures	872 600	1.9	64.76	61.27
762 Radio broadcast receivers	842 965	1.8	15.49	5.90
Remainder	31 537 746	68.4		

Qatar (**=Developing) (2)				
All commodity groups	61 634 358	100.0	1.09	0.45
333 Crude petroleum & bituminous oil	25 790 925	41.8	3.38	2.41
343 Natural gas, liquefied or not	18 861 906	30.6	21.55	8.00
342 Liquefied propane and butane	3 822 509	6.2	14.89	10.05
334 Heavy petroleum & bituminous oil	2 880 226	4.7	1.12	0.50
344 Petroleum and hydrocarbon gas nes	2 872 012	4.7	45.84	28.95
571 Primary form ethylene polymers	1 211 592	2.0	4.96	2.09
562 Manufactured fertilizer excl. crude	611 460	1.5	5.11	1.88
511 Hydrocarbons nes; derivatives	570 242	0.9	2.06	0.84
512 Alcohols, phenols; derivatives	367 996	0.6	1.67	0.87
516 Other organic chemicals	312 965	0.5	2.95	0.98
Remainder	4 042 625	6.6		

Republic of Moldova - République de Moldova (***=Transition)				
All commodity groups	1 434 840	100.0	0.27	0.01
112 Alcoholic beverages	146 282	10.2	11.69	0.24
057 Fruit nut (exc oil), fresh or dried	125 654	8.8	8.38	0.19
222 Oil seed etc for soft oil	78 923	5.5	6.12	0.16
676 Iron steel bar rod section piling	75 726	5.3	1.47	0.12
842 Female clothing, woven	64 301	4.5	5.93	0.09
773 Electrical distribute equipment nes	55 853	3.9	3.36	0.07
421 Fixed veg fat and oil, "soft"	49 593	3.5	1.59	0.18
851 Footwear	48 137	3.4	3.66	0.05
845 Articles of apparel nes	46 265	3.2	4.62	0.04
841 Male clothing, woven	45 979	3.2	5.25	0.08
Remainder	698 128	48.7		

Romania - Roumanie (**=Developed)				
All commodity groups	45 017 138	100.0	0.59	0.33
781 Passenger cars and race cars	2 534 391	5.6	0.61	0.51
773 Electrical distribute equipment nes	2 447 904	5.4	5.47	2.90
764 Telecommunicate equipment part nes	2 371 562	5.3	1.60	0.57
784 Motor vehicle parts and accessories	2 352 280	5.2	1.17	0.88
334 Heavy petroleum & bituminous oil	2 044 707	4.5	0.84	0.36
821 Furniture part; bedding furnishing	1 457 211	3.2	2.18	1.19
851 Footwear	1 417 796	3.1	4.17	1.61
793 Ships boats floating structures	1 267 769	2.8	2.21	0.84
772 Electrical circuit equipment	1 092 234	2.4	1.03	0.60
842 Female clothing, woven	1 041 161	2.3	4.40	1.46
Remainder	26 990 122	60.0		

Russian Federation - Fédération de Russie (***=Transition) (2)				
All commodity groups	337 425 852	100.0	63.23	2.44
333 Crude petroleum & bituminous oil	111 347 945	33.0	67.81	10.40
334 Heavy petroleum & bituminous oil	58 220 478	17.3	80.49	10.15
343 Natural gas, liquefied or not	43 405 624	12.9	86.12	20.45
321 Coal excluding non-agglomomerated	8 273 980	2.5	89.54	8.79
562 Manufactured fertilizer excl. crude	6 442 570	1.9	65.28	13.28
684 Aluminium	6 230 638	1.8	76.75	6.57
672 Ingots, Iron steel primary products	6 044 045	1.8	52.70	18.98
683 Nickel	4 510 368	1.3	99.72	26.46
682 Copper	4 203 838	1.2	56.59	3.84
673 Flat iron non-alloy steel products	4 079 680	1.2	47.27	5.66
Remainder	84 666 688	25.1		

Rwanda (**=Developing) (2)				
All commodity groups	244 954	100.0	0.00	0.00
074 Tea and maté	82 870	33.8	1.60	1.20
287 Base metal ores & concentrates nes	57 148	23.3	0.37	0.22
071 Coffee and coffee substitutes	38 117	15.6	0.22	0.14
001 Live animal excl. fish & crustacean	7 517	3.1	0.21	0.04
112 Alcoholic beverages	3 630	1.5	0.04	0.01
111 Non alcoholic beverage nes	3 358	1.4	0.09	0.02
211 Raw hides & skins, excluding furskins	2 874	1.2	0.37	0.05
851 Footwear	2 296	0.9	0.00	0.00
661 Lime cement construction material	2 236	0.9	0.02	0.01
334 Heavy petroleum & bituminous oil	1 889	0.8	0.00	0.00
Remainder	43 018	17.6		

For sources and notes, see end of table.

Pour les sources et les notes, se reporter à la fin du tableau.

188

3.2.D Export structure by product
Individual countries and territories

3.2.D Structure des exportations par produits
Pays et territoires individuels

3

Saint Kitts and Nevis - Saint-Kitts-et-Nevis (**=Developing) (2)

Leading products exported based on average 2009-2010 values SITC Revision 3 (3-digit level) / Principaux produits exportés d'après la moyenne des valeurs de 2009-2010 CTCI révision 3 (positions à 3 chiffres)	Value (f.o.b., thousands of dollars) / Valeur (f.a.b., milliers de dollars)	2009-2010 As percentage / En pourcentage		
		of country total / du total du pays	of ** (1) / des ** (1)	of world / du monde
All commodity groups	44 000	100.0	0.00	0.00
772 Electrical circuit equipment	11 489	26.1	0.02	0.01
761 Telecommunicate equipment part nes	10 388	23.6	0.00	0.00
716 Rotating electric plant parts nes	4 397	10.0	0.02	0.01
771 Electric power machine part excl. 716	2 036	4.6	0.01	0.00
793 Ships boats floating structures	1 413	3.2	0.00	0.00
112 Alcoholic beverages	1 078	2.5	.01	0.00
778 Electrical machinery apparatus nes	898	2.0	0.00	0.00
792 Aircraft, spacecraft & equipment	717	1.6	0.00	0.00
713 Internal combustion engine part nes	443	1.0	0.00	0.00
111 Non alcoholic beverage nes	400	0.9	0.01	0.00
Remainder	10 742	24.4		

Saint Lucia - Sainte-Lucie (**=Developing) (2)

Product	Value	of country total	of ** (1)	of world
All commodity groups	163 635	100.0	0.00	0.00
334 Heavy petroleum & bituminous oil	44 134	27.0	0.02	0.01
057 Fruit nut (exc oil), fresh or dried	31 134	19.0	0.10	0.05
112 Alcoholic beverages	14 315	8.7	0.14	0.02
764 Telecommunicate equipment part nes	5 669	3.5	0.00	0.00
642 Cut paper and paperboard articles	4 838	3.0	0.04	0.01
874 Measure analyze control device nes	3 622	2.2	0.01	0.00
897 Jewellery nes (667)	2 936	1.8	0.01	0.00
885 Watches and clocks	2 839	1.7	0.02	0.01
321 Coal excluding non-agglomomerated	2 697	1.6	0.01	0.00
772 Electrical circuit equipment	2 670	1.6	0.00	0.00
Remainder	48 780	29.8		

Saint Vincent and the Grenadines - Saint-Vincent-et-les Grenadines (**=Developing)

Product	Value	of country total	of ** (1)	of world
All commodity groups	45 290	100.0	0.00	0.00
793 Ships boats floating structures	28 290	62.5	0.03	0.02
046 Wheat meal & flour, meslin flour	2 870	6.3	0.16	0.07
057 Fruit nut (exc oil), fresh or dried	2 225	4.9	0.01	0.00
054 Vegetable & vegetable products nes	1 514	3.3	0.01	0.00
891 Arms and ammunition	1 072	2.4	0.08	0.01
042 Rice	990	2.2	0.01	0.00
111 Non alcoholic beverage nes	881	1.9	0.02	0.01
792 Aircraft, spacecraft & equipment	772	1.7	0.00	0.00
674 Flat plated iron non-alloy steel	595	1.3	0.00	0.00
081 Animal feed excluding unmilled cereal	578	1.3	0.00	0.00
Remainder	5 503	12.2		

Samoa (**=Developing)

Product	Value	of country total	of ** (1)	of world
All commodity groups	52 745	100.0	0.00	0.00
773 Electrical distribute equipment nes	38 135	72.3	0.10	0.05
034 Fish, fresh live chilled frozen	6 347	12.0	0.03	0.01
422 Fixed veg fat and oil, excl. "soft"	1 730	3.3	0.01	0.01
112 Alcoholic beverages	809	1.5	0.01	0.00
059 Fruit & vegetable juice unferment	662	1.3	0.01	0.00
054 Vegetable & vegetable products nes	461	0.9	0.00	0.00
057 Fruit nut (exc oil), fresh or dried	460	0.9	0.00	0.00
111 Non alcoholic beverage nes	458	0.9	0.01	0.00
898 Music instrument device recording	287	0.5	0.00	0.00
269 Worn clothing, textile article; rag	206	0.4	0.02	0.01
Remainder	3 191	6.0		

Sao Tome and Principe - Sao Tomé-et-Principe (**=Developing)

Product	Value	of country total	of ** (1)	of world
All commodity groups	7 249	100.0	0.00	0.00
072 Cocoa	2 876	39.7	0.02	0.02
885 Watches and clocks	1 285	17.7	0.01	0.00
897 Jewellery nes (667)	960	13.2	0.00	0.00
334 Heavy petroleum & bituminous oil	267	3.7	0.00	0.00
773 Electrical distribute equipment nes	232	3.2	0.00	0.00
874 Measure analyze control device nes	216	3.0	0.00	0.00
747 Pipe, boiler, tank & vat appliances	170	2.3	0.00	0.00
792 Aircraft, spacecraft & equipment	142	2.0	0.00	0.00
776 Valves tubes; diodes, transistors	140	1.9	0.00	0.00
699 Base metal manufactures nes	91	1.3	0.00	0.00
Remainder	870	12.0		

Saudi Arabia - Arabie saoudite (**=Developing)

Product	Value	of country total	of ** (1)	of world
All commodity groups	213 839 150	100.0	3.77	1.55
333 Crude petroleum & bituminous oil	158 428 098	74.1	20.74	14.80
334 Heavy petroleum & bituminous oil	14 167 611	6.6	5.50	2.47
571 Primary form ethylene polymers	5 534 361	2.6	22.66	9.54
512 Alcohols, phenols; derivatives	4 712 834	2.2	21.44	11.15
342 Liquefied propane and butane	4 669 958	2.2	18.20	12.27
575 Other plastics, in primary forms	2 680 998	1.3	11.07	3.17
511 Hydrocarbons nes; derivatives	2 444 446	1.1	8.82	3.59
516 Other organic chemicals	1 307 686	0.6	12.33	4.11
562 Manufactured fertilizer excl. crude	1 251 102	0.6	7.31	2.58
343 Natural gas, liquefied or not	1 043 969	0.5	1.19	0.49
Remainder	17 598 087	8.2		

Senegal - Sénégal (**=Developing)

Product	Value	of country total	of ** (1)	of world
All commodity groups	2 089 257	100.0	0.04	0.02
334 Heavy petroleum & bituminous oil	516 940	24.7	0.20	0.09
522 Inorganic chemical elem oxide salt	186 522	8.9	1.07	0.45
034 Fish, fresh live chilled frozen	176 411	8.4	0.84	0.36
661 Lime cement construction material	144 883	6.9	0.99	0.57
971 Gold non-monetary excluding ores	120 745	5.8	0.16	0.09
036 Crustacean mollusc aquat invertebra	81 107	3.9	0.52	0.33
421 Fixed veg fat and oil, "soft"	76 460	3.7	0.84	0.28
122 Manufactured tabacco	45 694	2.2	0.68	0.18
676 Iron steel bar rod section piling	42 338	2.0	0.22	0.07
098 Edible products & preparations nes	41 660	2.0	0.34	0.08
Remainder	656 490	31.4		

Serbia - Serbie (**=Transition)

Product	Value	of country total	of ** (1)	of world
All commodity groups	9 069 809	100.0	1.70	0.07
673 Flat iron non-alloy steel products	541 959	6.0	6.28	0.75
682 Copper	366 154	4.0	4.93	0.33
044 Maize unmilled, excluding sweet corn	311 526	3.4	22.10	1.42
058 Fruit preserve preparation excl. juice	268 546	3.0	55.74	1.81
625 Rubber for wheels, incl inner tube	226 729	2.5	16.16	0.35
351 Electric current	219 128	2.4	11.61	0.68
851 Footwear	201 300	2.2	15.30	0.23
846 Clothing accessory excl. 831 848 851	193 434	2.1	40.82	0.83
893 Articles of plastic nes	186 631	2.1	19.21	0.17
542 Medicines including veterinary	183 906	2.0	15.13	0.06
Remainder	6 370 496	70.2		

Seychelles (**=Developing) (2)

Product	Value	of country total	of ** (1)	of world
All commodity groups	397 723	100.0	0.01	0.00
037 Fish shellfish, prepared preserved	178 073	44.8	1.35	0.88
034 Fish, fresh live chilled frozen	90 898	22.9	0.43	0.18
035 Fish, dried salted smoked	51 060	12.8	3.78	1.02
872 Medical instruments appliances nes	14 087	3.5	0.09	0.02
334 Heavy petroleum & bituminous oil	9 182	2.3	0.00	0.00
899 Manufactured articles nes	5 793	1.5	0.03	0.01
036 Crustacean mollusc aquat invertebra	4 768	1.2	0.03	0.02
411 Animals oils and fats	4 201	1.1	0.56	0.10
752 Computer equipment nes	4 153	1.0	0.00	0.00
282 Ferrous iron & steel, waste & scrap	3 273	0.8	0.07	0.01
Remainder	32 235	8.1		

Sierra Leone (**=Developing) (2)

Product	Value	of country total	of ** (1)	of world
All commodity groups	274 729	100.0	0.00	0.00
667 Pearls, precious semiprecious stone	66 526	24.2	0.12	0.06
285 Aluminium ore concentrate alumina	33 395	12.2	0.76	0.28
287 Base metal ores & concentrates nes	23 985	8.7	0.15	0.09
072 Cocoa	19 373	7.1	0.15	0.10
793 Ships boats floating structures	8 027	2.9	0.01	0.01
723 Civil engineering plant & equipment	7 962	2.9	0.03	0.01
571 Primary form ethylene polymers	6 509	2.4	0.03	0.01
821 Furniture part; bedding furnishing	5 026	1.8	0.01	0.00
061 Sugar, mollasses and honey	4 608	1.7	0.02	0.01
071 Coffee and coffee substitutes	4 340	1.6	0.03	0.02
Remainder	94 978	34.6		

For sources and notes, see end of table.

Pour les sources et les notes, se reporter à la fin du tableau.

Leading products exported based on average 2009-2010 values SITC Revision 3 (3-digit level)

Principaux produits exportés d'après la moyenne des valeurs de 2009-2010 CTCI révision 3 (positions à 3 chiffres)

Columns: Value (f.o.b., thousands of dollars) / Valeur (f.a.b., milliers de dollars) | As percentage — En pourcentage: of country total (du total du pays) | of ** (1) (des ** (1)) | of world (du monde)

Singapore - Singapour (**=Developing)

Product	Value	of country total	of ** (1)	of world
All commodity groups	310 849 814	100.0	5.48	2.25
776 Valve tubes; diodes, transistors	74 106 606	23.8	23.13	15.86
334 Heavy petroleum & bituminous oil	47 580 076	15.3	18.46	8.30
759 Office equipment part & accessories	16 982 188	5.5	15.01	8.91
764 Telecommunicate equipment part nes	8 609 030	2.8	3.19	2.05
752 Computer equipment nes	8 550 808	2.8	4.21	2.91
770 Electrical machinery apparatus nes	6 281 650	1.7	6.17	2.85
772 Electrical circuit equipment	5 075 492	1.6	6.67	2.77
723 Civil engineering plant & equipment	4 883 852	1.6	20.43	5.69
874 Measure analyze control device nes	4 374 172	1.4	15.90	3.14
792 Aircraft, spacecraft & equipment	4 320 263	1.4	22.85	3.30
Remainder	131 085 668	42.2		

Slovakia - Slovaquie (**=Developed) (2)

Product	Value	of country total	of ** (1)	of world
All commodity groups	60 119 794	100.0	0.79	0.44
781 Passenger cars and race cars	8 061 411	13.4	1.94	1.61
761 Television video receive project	7 848 219	13.1	19.22	8.50
784 Motor vehicle parts and accessories	3 631 196	6.0	1.80	1.37
334 Heavy petroleum & bituminous oil	2 454 261	4.1	1.01	0.43
764 Telecommunicate equipment part nes	1 391 647	2.3	0.94	0.33
673 Flat iron non-alloy steel products	1 278 779	2.1	3.24	1.77
773 Electrical distribute equipment nes	1 208 369	2.0	2.70	1.43
821 Furniture part; bedding furnishing	1 083 974	1.8	1.62	0.88
699 Base metal manufactures nes	1 061 415	1.8	1.43	0.94
674 Flat plated iron non-alloy steel	1 060 960	1.8	3.91	2.35
Remainder	31 039 564	51.6		

Slovenia - Slovénie (**=Developed)

Product	Value	of country total	of ** (1)	of world
All commodity groups	27 744 857	100.0	0.36	0.20
781 Passenger cars and race cars	2 574 078	9.3	0.62	0.51
542 Medicines including veterinary	1 989 579	7.2	0.68	0.63
775 Household equipment nes	1 124 916	4.1	3.13	1.41
778 Electrical machinery apparatus nes	724 395	2.6	0.78	0.40
821 Furniture part; bedding furnishing	715 731	2.6	1.07	0.58
784 Motor vehicle parts and accessories	566 373	2.0	0.28	0.21
684 Aluminium	548 459	2.0	0.95	0.58
743 Gas pump, compressor, fan, filter	508 952	1.8	0.71	0.52
641 Paper and paperboard	500 657	1.8	0.58	0.47
699 Base metal manufactures nes	476 483	1.7	0.64	0.42
Remainder	18 015 234	64.9		

Solomon Islands - Îles Salomon (**=Developing) (2)

Product	Value	of country total	of ** (1)	of world
All commodity groups	188 516	100.0	0.00	0.00
247 Wood in rough or roughly squared	136 152	72.2	3.36	1.14
422 Fixed veg fat and oil, excl. "soft"	11 423	6.1	0.04	0.03
034 Fish, fresh live chilled frozen	9 851	5.2	0.05	0.02
037 Fish shellfish, prepared preserved	8 968	4.8	0.07	0.04
072 Cocoa	7 086	3.8	0.06	0.04
223 Oil seed for non soft oil	3 554	1.9	0.53	0.15
248 Wood simply worked, railway sleeper	3 251	1.7	0.05	0.01
035 Fish, dried salted smoked	1 720	0.9	0.13	0.03
971 Gold non-monetary excluding ores	555	0.3	0.00	0.00
291 Crude animal materials nes	550	0.3	0.02	0.01
Remainder	5 408	2.9		

Somalia - Somalie (**=Developing) (2)

Product	Value	of country total	of ** (1)	of world
All commodity groups	436 000	100.0	0.01	0.00
001 Live animal excl. fish & crustacean	137 221	31.5	3.83	0.76
971 Gold non-monetary excluding ores	126 030	28.9	0.17	0.09
245 Fuel wood excl. waste; wood charcoal	71 400	16.4	16.09	6.52
012 Meat nes, fresh chilled frozen	37 634	8.6	0.30	0.06
057 Fruit nut (exc oil), fresh or dried	21 811	5.0	0.07	0.03
211 Raw hides & skins, excluding furskins	6 552	1.5	0.85	0.12
292 Crude vegetable materials nes	5 143	1.2	0.06	0.02
056 Vegetables roots tubers nes	4 840	1.1	0.06	0.02
034 Fish, fresh live chilled frozen	4 689	1.1	0.02	0.01
222 Oil seed etc for soft oil	4 641	1.1	0.02	0.01
Remainder	16 039	3.7		

South Africa - Afrique du Sud (**=Developing)

Product	Value	of country total	of ** (1)	of world
All commodity groups	76 121 100	100.0	1.34	0.55
681 Silver, platinum, platinum metals	9 003 081	11.8	42.49	20.29
321 Coal excluding non-agglomerated	5 556 541	7.6	18.00	8.01
281 Iron ore and concentrates	4 724 557	6.2	12.45	5.75
671 Pig & sponge iron, ferro alloys etc	4 429 147	5.8	26.02	14.33
781 Passenger cars and race cars	3 768 832	5.0	4.50	0.75
667 Pearls, precious semiprecious stone	3 060 636	4.4	6.13	3.07
287 Base metal ores & concentrates nes	3 130 130	4.1	20.17	10.00
057 Fruit nut (exc oil), fresh or dried	2 491 282	3.3	7.70	3.69
971 Gold non-monetary excluding ores	2 437 094	3.2	3.21	1.78
743 Gas pump, compressor, fan, filter	2 014 258	2.6	7.89	2.06
Remainder	34 815 116	45.7		

Spain - Espagne (**=Developed) (2)

Product	Value	of country total	of ** (1)	of world
All commodity groups	232 482 546	100.0	3.05	1.68
781 Passenger cars and race cars	27 138 395	11.7	6.53	5.42
784 Motor vehicle parts and accessories	10 570 127	4.5	5.25	3.97
542 Medicines including veterinary	8 985 137	3.9	3.06	2.85
334 Heavy petroleum & bituminous oil	6 888 025	3.0	2.83	1.20
057 Fruit nut (exc oil), fresh or dried	6 173 621	2.7	18.40	9.16
054 Vegetable & vegetable products nes	5 717 679	2.5	17.51	10.60
782 Goods and service vehicles	5 228 405	2.2	8.24	5.57
676 Iron steel bar rod section piling	3 711 843	1.6	10.10	6.03
792 Aircraft, spacecraft & equipment	3 563 833	1.5	3.20	2.73
716 Rotating electric plant parts nes	3 108 342	1.3	6.08	4.04
Remainder	151 397 138	65.1		

Sri Lanka (**=Developing) (2)

Product	Value	of country total	of ** (1)	of world
All commodity groups	7 712 771	100.0	0.14	0.06
074 Tea and maté	1 281 562	16.6	24.77	18.60
845 Articles of apparel nes	989 890	12.8	1.20	0.84
842 Female clothing, woven	710 990	9.2	1.52	1.00
844 Female clothing, knitted crocheted	654 796	8.5	2.06	1.56
841 Male clothing, woven	498 452	6.5	1.27	0.85
667 Pearls, precious semiprecious stone	402 043	5.2	0.73	0.37
625 Rubber for wheels, incl inner tube	281 039	3.6	1.15	0.43
843 Male clothing, knitted crocheted	189 557	2.5	1.01	0.83
846 Clothing accessory excl. 831 848 851	171 984	2.2	1.21	0.74
848 Headgear, non-textile clothing	162 702	2.1	1.04	0.71
Remainder	2 369 755	30.7		

Sudan - Soudan (**=Developing)

Product	Value	of country total	of ** (1)	of world
All commodity groups	9 166 848	100.0	0.16	0.07
333 Crude petroleum & bituminous oil	7 283 783	79.5	0.95	0.68
334 Heavy petroleum & bituminous oil	737 209	8.0	0.29	0.13
971 Gold non-monetary excluding ores	544 924	5.9	0.72	0.40
222 Oil seed etc for soft oil	131 155	1.4	0.66	0.26
001 Live animal excl. fish & crustacean	117 095	1.3	3.27	0.65
292 Crude vegetable materials nes	67 506	0.7	0.72	0.20
263 Cotton	47 693	0.5	0.71	0.32
061 Sugar, mollasses and honey	30 172	0.3	0.13	0.09
282 Ferrous iron & steel, waste & scrap	16 780	0.2	0.34	0.04
792 Aircraft, spacecraft & equipment	14 687	0.2	0.08	0.01
Remainder	175 844	1.9		

Suriname (**=Developing) (2)

Product	Value	of country total	of ** (1)	of world
All commodity groups	1 709 193	100.0	0.03	0.01
971 Gold non-monetary excluding ores	671 886	39.3	0.89	0.49
285 Aluminium ore concentrate alumina	364 010	21.3	8.24	3.10
334 Heavy petroleum & bituminous oil	106 519	6.2	0.04	0.02
034 Fish, fresh live chilled frozen	47 524	2.8	0.23	0.10
057 Fruit nut (exc oil), fresh or dried	29 039	1.7	0.09	0.04
042 Rice	25 031	1.5	0.15	0.12
036 Crustacean mollusc aquat invertebra	22 667	1.3	0.14	0.09
112 Alcoholic beverages	11 748	0.7	0.11	0.02
288 Non ferrous base metal waste nes	10 145	0.6	0.14	0.03
291 Crude animal materials nes	9 800	0.6	0.36	0.14
Remainder	410 825	24.0		

For sources and notes, see end of table.

Pour les sources et les notes, se reporter à la fin du tableau.

3.2.D Export structure by product
Individual countries and territories

3.2.D Structure des exportations par produits
Pays et territoires individuels

Leading products exported based on average 2009-2010 values SITC Revision 3 (3-digit level) / Principaux produits exportés d'après la moyenne des valeurs de 2009-2010 CTCI révision 3 (positions à 3 chiffres)	Value (f.o.b., thousands of dollars) / Valeur (f.a.b., milliers de dollars)	of country total / du total du pays	of ** (1) / des ** (1)	of world / du monde
Swaziland (=Developing) (2)**				
All commodity groups	1 511 515	100.0	0.03	0.01
061 Sugar, mollasses and honey	305 566	20.2	1.35	0.91
551 Essential oils, perfumes & flavours	245 892	16.3	7.12	1.20
598 Miscellaneous chemical products nes	80 642	5.3	0.39	0.08
251 Pulp and waste paper	78 131	5.2	0.82	0.21
098 Edible products & preparations nes	61 480	4.1	0.50	0.12
845 Articles of apparel nes	58 806	3.9	0.07	0.05
714 Non-electric engines excl. 712 713 718	48 315	3.2	0.49	0.06
842 Female clothing, woven	35 475	2.3	0.08	0.05
541 Pharmaceuticals excluding medicines	34 568	2.3	0.23	0.03
671 Pig & sponge iron, ferro alloys etc	29 689	2.0	0.17	0.10
Remainder	532 950	35.3		
Sweden - Suède (=Developed)**				
All commodity groups	144 597 664	100.0	1.90	1.05
641 Paper and paperboard	9 151 299	6.3	10.61	8.65
764 Telecommunicate equipment part nes	8 529 449	5.9	5.76	2.03
334 Heavy petroleum & bituminous oil	8 112 635	5.6	3.33	1.41
542 Medicines including veterinary	7 594 643	5.3	2.59	2.41
781 Passenger cars and race cars	4 843 896	3.3	1.17	0.97
784 Motor vehicle parts and accessories	4 770 937	3.3	2.37	1.79
248 Wood simply worked, railway sleeper	3 228 694	2.2	15.36	10.14
675 Flat rolled products of alloy steel	2 762 211	1.9	7.14	5.27
251 Pulp and waste paper	2 352 456	1.6	8.65	6.23
744 Mechanical handling equipment nes	2 188 604	1.5	4.41	3.37
Remainder	91 062 840	63.0		
Switzerland - Suisse (=Developed)**				
All commodity groups	183 933 125	100.0	2.42	1.33
542 Medicines including veterinary	26 889 859	14.6	9.15	8.53
541 Pharmaceuticals excluding medicines	20 072 541	11.3	18.00	15.94
885 Watches and clocks	13 850 639	7.5	66.80	41.05
515 Organo-inorganic compound acid salt	7 064 377	3.8	8.69	7.27
899 Manufactured articles nes	6 015 308	3.3	13.14	8.94
897 Jewellery nes (667)	5 537 887	3.0	18.09	7.62
351 Electric current	4 456 901	2.4	16.96	13.88
874 Measure analyze control device nes	4 244 038	2.3	3.84	3.05
728 Special industrial machine part nes	3 994 891	2.2	3.69	2.94
772 Electrical circuit equipment	3 917 195	2.1	3.70	2.14
Remainder	87 089 490	47.3		
Syrian Arab Republic - République arabe syrienne (=Developing) (2)**				
All commodity groups	11 596 835	100.0	0.20	0.08
333 Crude petroleum & bituminous oil	3 091 142	26.7	0.40	0.29
334 Heavy petroleum & bituminous oil	933 119	8.0	0.36	0.16
111 Non alcoholic beverage nes	703 461	6.1	19.07	4.28
054 Vegetable & vegetable products nes	636 983	5.5	3.14	1.18
554 Soaps cleansers polishes	370 392	3.2	4.19	1.09
775 Household equipment nes	357 503	3.1	0.83	0.45
272 Crude fertilizer, excl. manufactured	267 714	2.3	11.47	8.03
773 Electrical distribute equipment nes	265 019	2.3	0.70	0.31
001 Live animal excl. fish & crustacean	234 530	2.0	6.55	1.29
057 Fruit nut (exc oil), fresh or dried	195 657	1.7	0.60	0.29
Remainder	4 541 316	39.2		
Tajikistan - Tadjikistan (=Transition) (2)**				
All commodity groups	1 087 549	100.0	0.20	0.01
684 Aluminium	405 271	37.3	4.99	0.43
263 Cotton	229 580	21.1	12.22	1.56
287 Base metal ores & concentrates nes	132 473	12.2	13.45	0.52
351 Electric current	43 857	4.0	2.32	0.14
845 Articles of apparel nes	28 696	2.6	2.87	0.02
652 Woven cotton fabrics	24 107	2.2	7.87	0.09
971 Gold non-monetary excluding ores	19 553	1.8	1.42	0.01
288 Non ferrous base metal waste nes	17 966	1.7	3.76	0.06
057 Fruit nut (exc oil), fresh or dried	17 823	1.6	1.19	0.03
792 Aircraft, spacecraft & equipment	15 827	1.5	3.92	0.01
Remainder	152 395	14.0		

Leading products exported based on average 2009-2010 values SITC Revision 3 (3-digit level) / Principaux produits exportés d'après la moyenne des valeurs de 2009-2010 CTCI révision 3 (positions à 3 chiffres)	Value (f.o.b., thousands of dollars) / Valeur (f.a.b., milliers de dollars)	of country total / du total du pays	of ** (1) / des ** (1)	of world / du monde
Thailand - Thaïlande (=Developing)**				
All commodity groups	173 904 361	100.0	3.07	1.28
752 Computer equipment nes	12 153 509	7.0	5.98	4.14
776 Valves tubes; diodes, transistors	8 383 386	4.8	2.62	1.79
334 Heavy petroleum & bituminous oil	7 050 191	4.1	2.74	1.23
231 Natural rubber, latex, gum, etc	6 102 015	3.5	35.05	33.36
971 Gold non-monetary excluding ores	6 096 459	3.5	8.04	4.45
781 Passenger cars and race cars	5 559 235	3.2	6.64	1.11
042 Rice	5 193 773	3.0	31.95	25.45
782 Goods and service vehicles	4 707 154	2.7	16.26	5.01
037 Fish shellfish, prepared preserved	3 919 088	2.3	29.66	19.45
764 Telecommunicate equipment part nes	3 657 159	2.1	1.35	0.87
Remainder	111 082 393	63.9		
TFYR of Macedonia - LERY de Macédoine (=Transition) (2)**				
All commodity groups	2 991 579	100.0	0.56	0.02
842 Female clothing, woven	328 119	11.0	30.25	0.46
671 Pig & sponge iron, ferro alloys etc	236 683	7.9	3.51	0.77
841 Male clothing, woven	234 020	7.8	26.72	0.40
673 Flat iron non-alloy steel products	189 857	6.3	2.20	0.26
121 Unmanufactured tabacco and refuse	83 023	2.8	32.62	0.73
679 Iron steel pipe tube fittings etc	78 193	2.6	2.27	0.11
851 Footwear	72 390	2.4	5.50	0.08
845 Articles of apparel nes	69 314	2.3	6.92	0.06
054 Vegetable & vegetable products nes	68 877	2.3	7.05	0.13
674 Flat plated iron non-alloy steel	63 354	2.1	5.76	0.14
Remainder	1 567 750	52.4		
Timor-Leste (=Developing) (2)**				
All commodity groups	12 570	100.0	0.00	0.00
342 Liquefied propane and butane	5 122	40.7	0.02	0.01
333 Crude petroleum & bituminous oil	3 517	28.0	0.00	0.00
071 Coffee and coffee substitutes	2 141	17.0	0.01	0.01
772 Electrical circuit equipment	663	5.3	0.00	0.00
892 Printed matter	158	1.3	0.00	0.00
282 Ferrous iron & steel, waste & scrap	91	0.7	0.00	0.00
699 Base metal manufactures nes	79	0.6	0.00	0.00
061 Sugar, mollasses and honey	68	0.5	0.00	0.00
885 Watches and clocks	47	0.4	0.00	0.00
764 Telecommunicate equipment part nes	45	0.4	0.00	0.00
Remainder	638	5.1		
Togo (=Developing) (2)**				
All commodity groups	898 132	100.0	0.02	0.01
661 Lime cement construction material	117 924	13.1	0.81	0.46
072 Cocoa	102 433	11.4	0.82	0.54
272 Crude fertilizer, excl. manufactured	100 973	11.2	4.32	3.03
334 Heavy petroleum & bituminous oil	91 127	10.1	0.04	0.02
263 Cotton	63 780	7.1	0.95	0.43
657 Special yarn and textile fabric etc	49 877	5.6	0.33	0.13
674 Flat plated iron non-alloy steel	16 828	1.9	0.10	0.04
693 Wire products and fencing grills	16 457	1.8	0.33	0.14
676 Iron steel bar rod section piling	15 831	1.8	0.08	0.03
282 Ferrous iron & steel, waste & scrap	14 660	1.6	0.30	0.04
Remainder	308 242	34.3		
Tokelau - Tokélaou (=Developing) (2)**				
All commodity groups	101	100.0	0.00	0.00
042 Rice	7	7.1	0.00	0.00
059 Fruit & vegetable juice unferment	7	6.5	0.00	0.00
741 Heating cooling equipment parts nes	6	6.0	0.00	0.00
695 Tools for use in hand or in machine	3	2.9	0.00	0.00
057 Fruit nut (exc oil), fresh or dried	3	2.6	0.00	0.00
674 Flat plated iron non-alloy steel	3	2.5	0.00	0.00
845 Articles of apparel nes	2	1.8	0.00	0.00
694 Nails screws nuts bolts rivets	2	1.8	0.00	0.00
659 Floor coverings etc	2	1.7	0.00	0.00
821 Furniture part; bedding furnishing	2	1.7	0.00	0.00
Remainder	66	65.4		

For sources and notes, see end of table.

Pour les sources et les notes, se reporter à la fin du tableau.

Leading products exported based on average 2009-2010 values SITC Revision 3 (3-digit level) Principaux produits exportés d'après la moyenne des valeurs de 2009-2010 CTCI révision 3 (positions à 3 chiffres)	2009-2010		
	Value (f.o.b., thousands of dollars) Valeur (f.a.b., milliers de dollars)	As percentage En pourcentage	
		of country total du total du pays	of ** (1) des ** (1)	of world du monde

Tonga (**=Developing) (2)				
All commodity groups	8 027	100.0	0.00	0.00
036 Crustacean mollusc aquat invertebra	1 000	23.2	0.01	0.01
054 Vegetable & vegetable products nes	1 479	18.4	0.01	0.00
034 Fish, fresh live chilled frozen	994	12.4	0.00	0.00
035 Fish, dried salted smoked	318	4.0	0.02	0.01
533 Pigment, paint, varnish & related	282	3.5	0.00	0.00
057 Fruit nut (exc oil), fresh or dried	241	3.0	0.00	0.00
591 Household and garden chemicals	198	2.5	0.00	0.00
291 Crude animal materials nes	155	1.9	0.01	0.00
292 Crude vegetable materials nes	154	1.9	0.00	0.00
651 Textile yarn	133	1.7	0.00	0.00
Remainder	2 211	27.5		

Trinidad and Tobago - Trinité-et-Tobago (**=Developing)				
All commodity groups	9 657 035	100.0	0.17	0.07
343 Natural gas, liquefied or not	3 158 500	32.7	3.61	1.49
334 Heavy petroleum & bituminous oil	1 883 903	19.5	0.73	0.33
333 Crude petroleum & bituminous oil	1 122 701	11.6	0.15	0.10
522 Inorganic chemical elem oxide salt	798 589	8.3	4.58	1.91
512 Alcohols, phenols; derivatives	784 786	8.1	3.57	1.86
671 Pig & sponge iron, ferro alloys etc	336 923	3.5	1.98	1.09
281 Iron ore and concentrates	209 020	2.2	0.55	0.25
342 Liquefied propane and butane	192 237	2.0	0.75	0.51
562 Manufactured fertilizer excl. crude	145 974	1.5	0.85	0.30
676 Iron steel bar rod section piling	114 643	1.2	0.58	0.19
Remainder	909 758	9.4		

Tunisia - Tunisie (**=Developing)				
All commodity groups	15 433 444	100.0	0.27	0.11
333 Crude petroleum & bituminous oil	1 846 201	12.0	0.24	0.17
845 Articles of apparel nes	1 638 094	10.6	1.99	1.38
773 Electrical distribute equipment nes	966 255	6.3	2.54	1.14
841 Male clothing, woven	845 696	5.5	2.16	1.44
772 Electrical circuit equipment	779 143	5.0	1.02	0.43
562 Manufactured fertilizer excl. crude	755 615	4.9	4.42	1.56
842 Female clothing, woven	576 659	3.7	1.24	0.81
421 Fixed veg fat and oil, "soft"	570 596	3.7	6.26	2.08
851 Footwear	523 712	3.4	0.99	0.59
334 Heavy petroleum & bituminous oil	384 913	2.5	0.15	0.07
Remainder	6 546 560	42.4		

Turkey - Turquie (**=Developing)				
All commodity groups	108 058 989	100.0	1.91	0.78
781 Passenger cars and race cars	6 148 887	5.7	7.35	1.23
676 Iron steel bar rod section piling	5 290 048	4.9	26.87	8.59
845 Articles of apparel nes	4 208 688	3.9	5.12	3.55
334 Heavy petroleum & bituminous oil	3 743 185	3.5	1.45	0.65
971 Gold non-monetary excluding ores	3 357 097	3.1	4.42	2.45
057 Fruit nut (exc oil), fresh or dried	3 204 767	3.0	9.90	4.75
782 Goods and service vehicles	2 934 196	2.7	10.13	3.12
775 Household equipment nes	2 828 875	2.6	6.59	3.54
842 Female clothing, woven	2 451 009	2.3	5.25	3.43
784 Motor vehicle parts and accessories	2 376 624	2.2	3.74	0.89
Remainder	71 515 614	66.2		

Turkmenistan - Turkménistan (**=Transition) (2)				
All commodity groups	6 297 500	100.0	1.18	0.05
343 Natural gas, liquefied or not	2 760 378	43.8	5.48	1.30
334 Heavy petroleum & bituminous oil	1 151 740	18.3	1.59	0.20
263 Cotton	390 943	6.2	20.80	2.65
333 Crude petroleum & bituminous oil	276 237	4.4	0.17	0.03
322 Briquettes, lignite and peat	266 902	4.2	15.93	8.01
651 Textile yarn	187 653	3.0	16.95	0.42
575 Other plastics, in primary forms	126 304	2.0	21.59	0.15
652 Woven cotton fabrics	111 202	1.8	36.29	0.40
351 Electric current	91 811	1.5	4.86	0.29
658 Made-up textile articles nes	42 300	0.7	12.97	0.10
Remainder	892 031	14.2		

Turks and Caicos Islands - Îles Turques et Caïques (**=Developing)				
All commodity groups	20 754	100.0	0.00	0.00
036 Crustacean mollusc aquat invertebra	2 139	10.3	0.01	0.01
037 Fish shellfish, prepared preserved	1 901	9.2	0.01	0.01
723 Civil engineering plant & equipment	1 824	8.8	0.01	0.00
781 Passenger cars and race cars	1 397	6.7	0.00	0.00
961 Coins, nongold and non currency	961	4.6	1.31	0.24
716 Rotating electric plant parts nes	862	4.2	0.00	0.00
792 Aircraft, spacecraft & equipment	859	4.1	0.00	0.00
744 Mechanical handling equipment nes	696	3.4	0.00	0.00
752 Computer equipment nes	422	2.0	0.00	0.00
782 Goods and service vehicles	414	2.0	0.00	0.00
Remainder	9 279	44.7		

Tuvalu (**=Developing) (2)				
All commodity groups	299	100.0	0.00	0.00
793 Ships boats floating structures	64	21.4	0.00	0.00
034 Fish, fresh live chilled frozen	53	17.8	0.00	0.00
684 Aluminium	26	8.7	0.00	0.00
764 Telecommunicate equipment part nes	16	5.3	0.00	0.00
831 Case bag: storage travel shopping	12	4.0	0.00	0.00
894 Baby carriage toy game sport good	11	3.7	0.00	0.00
292 Crude vegetable materials nes	10	3.3	0.00	0.00
693 Wire products and fencing grills	10	3.2	0.00	0.00
874 Measure analyze control device nes	8	2.7	0.00	0.00
653 Man-made woven fabrics	8	2.6	0.00	0.00
Remainder	81	27.2		

Uganda - Ouganda (**=Developing) (2)				
All commodity groups	2 245 265	100.0	0.04	0.02
071 Coffee and coffee substitutes	445 297	19.8	2.57	1.59
034 Fish, fresh live chilled frozen	170 216	7.6	0.81	0.34
121 Unmanufactured tabacco and refuse	119 111	5.3	1.57	1.05
661 Lime cement construction material	106 723	4.8	0.73	0.42
764 Telecommunicate equipment part nes	92 404	4.1	0.03	0.02
074 Tea and maté	82 011	3.7	1.59	1.19
292 Crude vegetable materials nes	81 213	3.6	0.87	0.24
061 Sugar, mollasses and honey	72 143	3.2	0.32	0.22
971 Gold non-monetary excluding ores	61 004	2.7	0.08	0.04
072 Cocoa	49 411	2.2	0.39	0.26
Remainder	965 732	43.0		

Ukraine (**=Transition) (2)				
All commodity groups	45 562 967	100.0	8.54	0.33
672 Ingots, Iron steel primary products	4 702 619	10.3	41.00	14.77
673 Flat iron non-alloy steel products	2 995 352	6.6	34.70	4.15
676 Iron steel bar rod section piling	2 647 075	5.8	51.34	4.30
421 Fixed veg fat and oil, "soft"	2 035 643	4.5	65.44	7.42
281 Iron ore and concentrates	1 849 439	4.1	42.83	2.25
334 Heavy petroleum & bituminous oil	1 699 146	3.7	2.35	0.30
791 Railway vehicles and equipment	1 582 791	3.5	71.57	6.82
671 Pig & sponge iron, ferro alloys etc	1 451 421	3.2	21.52	4.70
679 Iron steel pipe tube fittings etc	1 399 120	3.1	40.62	1.90
041 Wheat meslin, incl spelt, unmilled	1 342 220	2.9	28.50	4.11
Remainder	23 858 142	52.4		

United Arab Emirates - Émirats arabes unis (**=Developing) (2)				
All commodity groups	186 543 500	100.0	3.29	1.35
333 Crude petroleum & bituminous oil	76 959 211	41.3	10.08	7.19
334 Heavy petroleum & bituminous oil	15 153 729	8.1	5.88	2.64
971 Gold non-monetary excluding ores	12 804 565	6.9	16.88	9.34
667 Pearls, precious semiprecious stone	11 731 571	6.3	21.34	10.68
342 Liquefied propane and butane	4 599 679	2.5	17.92	12.09
343 Natural gas, liquefied or not	3 726 528	2.0	4.26	1.76
781 Passenger cars and race cars	3 626 423	1.9	4.33	0.72
764 Telecommunicate equipment part nes	2 914 656	1.6	1.08	0.69
897 Jewellery nes (667)	2 874 885	1.5	6.85	3.95
684 Aluminium	2 251 334	1.2	7.75	2.37
Remainder	49 900 919	26.8		

For sources and notes, see end of table.

Pour les sources et les notes, se reporter à la fin du tableau.

Leading products exported based on average 2009-2010 values SITC Revision 3 (3-digit level) Principaux produits exportés d'après la moyenne des valeurs de 2009-2010 CTCI révision 3 (positions à 3 chiffres)	Value (f.o.b., thousands of dollars) Valeur (f.a.b., milliers de dollars)	2009-2010		
		As percentage En pourcentage		
		of country total du total du pays	of ** (1) des ** (1)	of world du monde
United Kingdom - Royaume-Uni (=Developed)**				
All commodity groups	377 950 065	100.0	4.96	2.73
542 Medicines including veterinary	27 240 570	7.2	0.28	8.66
781 Passenger cars and race cars	22 492 081	6.0	5.41	4.49
333 Crude petroleum & bituminous oil	22 145 050	5.9	15.57	2.07
334 Heavy petroleum & bituminous oil	17 902 212	4.7	7.35	3.12
714 Non electric engines excl. 712 713 718	15 287 020	4.0	24.06	20.27
764 Telecommunicate equipment part nes	8 155 099	2.2	5.50	1.94
874 Measure analyze control device nes	7 861 557	2.1	7.12	5.65
112 Alcoholic beverages	7 639 577	2.0	15.56	12.59
515 Organo-inorganic compound acid salt	7 309 720	1.9	8.99	7.52
667 Pearls, precious semiprecious stone	6 722 306	1.8	12.70	6.12
Remainder	235 195 764	62.2		
United Republic of Tanzania - République-Unie de Tanzanie (=Developing)**				
All commodity groups	3 516 476	100.0	0.06	0.03
971 Gold non-monetary excluding ores	616 225	17.5	0.81	0.45
289 Prec metal ore concentrate excl. gold	404 910	11.5	10.11	2.83
121 Unmanufactured tabacco and refuse	202 126	5.7	2.67	1.77
071 Coffee and coffee substitutes	174 657	5.0	1.01	0.62
034 Fish, fresh live chilled frozen	158 038	4.5	0.75	0.32
057 Fruit nut (exc oil), fresh or dried	147 704	4.2	0.46	0.22
287 Base metal ores & concentrates nes	137 460	3.9	0.89	0.54
054 Vegetable & vegetable products nes	122 781	3.5	0.60	0.23
263 Cotton	122 751	3.5	1.83	0.83
222 Oil seed etc for soft oil	84 190	2.4	0.43	0.17
Remainder	1 345 633	38.3		
United States - États-Unis (=Developed)**				
All commodity groups	1 166 910 620	100.0	15.32	8.44
334 Heavy petroleum & bituminous oil	45 122 560	3.9	18.53	7.87
776 Valves tubes; diodes, transistors	42 782 190	3.7	29.25	9.16
781 Passenger cars and race cars	33 829 054	2.9	8.14	6.75
764 Telecommunicate equipment part nes	31 332 366	2.7	21.14	7.47
784 Motor vehicle parts and accessories	28 533 902	2.4	14.16	10.73
874 Measure analyze control device nes	26 657 101	2.3	24.13	19.16
542 Medicines including veterinary	24 707 369	2.1	8.41	7.84
752 Computer equipment nes	23 162 047	2.0	25.58	7.88
541 Pharmaceuticals excluding medicines	19 532 824	1.7	16.85	14.92
222 Oil seed etc for soft oil	18 186 433	1.6	63.53	36.59
Remainder	873 064 772	74.8		
Uruguay (=Developing)**				
All commodity groups	6 026 799	100.0	0.11	0.04
011 Beef, fresh chilled frozen	1 105 442	18.3	11.99	3.46
042 Rice	447 170	7.4	2.75	2.19
268 Wool & animal hair, incl wool tops	369 192	6.1	18.83	7.36
222 Oil seed etc for soft oil	337 727	5.6	1.71	0.68
022 Milk products, excl. butter & cheese	236 322	3.9	5.62	0.74
611 Leather	221 173	3.7	2.11	1.14
034 Fish, fresh live chilled frozen	200 697	3.3	0.96	0.40
048 Cereal & preparation flour starch	194 728	3.2	2.78	0.51
041 Wheat meslin, incl spelt, unmilled	164 367	2.7	7.75	0.50
893 Articles of plastic nes	160 527	2.7	0.43	0.15
Remainder	2 589 455	43.0		
Uzbekistan - Ouzbékistan (=Transition) (2)**				
All commodity groups	11 295 982	100.0	2.12	0.08
343 Natural gas, liquefied or not	2 251 054	19.9	4.47	1.06
322 Briquettes, lignite and peat	1 305 579	11.6	77.90	39.18
263 Cotton	1 111 857	9.8	59.16	7.53
525 Radio active & associated materials	909 791	8.1	29.70	6.00
781 Passenger cars and race cars	755 114	6.7	53.61	0.15
682 Copper	741 017	6.6	9.98	0.68
057 Fruit nut (exc oil), fresh or dried	602 401	5.3	40.20	0.89
651 Textile yarn	555 184	4.9	50.15	1.25
054 Vegetable & vegetable products nes	305 948	2.7	31.34	0.57
971 Gold non-monetary excluding ores	263 522	2.3	19.18	0.19
Remainder	2 494 513	22.1		
Vanuatu (=Developing) (2)**				
All commodity groups	52 777	100.0	0.00	0.00
034 Fish, fresh live chilled frozen	38 273	72.5	0.18	0.08
793 Ships boats floating structures	6 408	12.1	0.01	0.00
223 Oil seed for non soft oil	1 711	3.2	0.26	0.07
422 Fixed veg fat and oil, excl. "soft"	773	1.5	0.00	0.00
292 Crude vegetable materials nes	717	1.4	0.01	0.00
011 Beef, fresh chilled frozen	689	1.3	0.01	0.00
072 Cocoa	669	1.3	0.01	0.00
054 Vegetable & vegetable products nes	430	0.8	0.00	0.00
344 Petroleum and hydrocarbon gas nes	407	0.8	0.01	0.00
248 Wood simply worked, railway sleeper	245	0.5	0.00	0.00
Remainder	2 455	4.7		
Venezuela (Bolivarian Rep.of)-Venezuela (Rép.bolivarienne du) (=Developing) (2)**				
All commodity groups	60 606 646	100.0	1.07	0.44
333 Crude petroleum & bituminous oil	39 584 592	65.3	5.18	3.70
334 Heavy petroleum & bituminous oil	11 791 179	19.5	4.57	2.06
671 Pig & sponge iron, ferro alloys etc	1 070 314	1.8	6.29	3.46
684 Aluminium	802 567	1.3	2.76	0.85
278 Other crude minerals	554 000	0.9	9.44	3.89
591 Household and garden chemicals	434 305	0.7	7.04	1.90
281 Iron ore and concentrates	433 839	0.7	1.14	0.53
674 Flat plated iron non-alloy steel	403 586	0.7	2.39	0.90
673 Flat iron non-alloy steel products	374 765	0.6	1.56	0.52
335 Residual petroleum products nes	351 168	0.6	2.88	1.10
Remainder	4 806 332	7.9		
Viet Nam (=Developing) (2)**				
All commodity groups	64 377 271	100.0	1.14	0.47
333 Crude petroleum & bituminous oil	7 401 258	11.5	0.97	0.69
851 Footwear	4 758 818	7.4	8.99	5.39
821 Furniture part; bedding furnishing	2 980 680	4.6	5.49	2.43
845 Articles of apparel nes	2 816 774	4.4	3.42	2.38
042 Rice	2 637 317	4.1	16.22	12.92
842 Female clothing, woven	2 268 886	3.5	4.86	3.18
071 Coffee and coffee substitutes	2 227 119	3.5	12.88	7.96
034 Fish, fresh live chilled frozen	2 151 082	3.3	10.26	4.33
841 Male clothing, woven	2 140 231	3.3	5.46	3.66
036 Crustacean mollusc aquat invertebra	2 084 720	3.2	13.27	8.52
Remainder	32 910 385	51.1		
Wallis and Futuna Islands - Îles Wallis-et-Futuna (=Developing) (2)**				
All commodity groups	36	100.0	0.00	0.00
676 Iron steel bar rod section piling	14	37.6	0.00	0.00
772 Electrical circuit equipment	7	19.1	0.00	0.00
759 Office equipment part & accessories	3	8.8	0.00	0.00
598 Miscellaneous chemical products nes	2	6.6	0.00	0.00
728 Special industrial machine part nes	1	4.0	0.00	0.00
764 Telecommunicate equipment part nes	1	3.5	0.00	0.00
592 Starches, glutenes, glues, etc	1	2.4	0.00	0.00
721 Agricultural machine nes excl. tractor	1	2.4	0.00	0.00
821 Furniture part; bedding furnishing	1	1.6	0.00	0.00
572 Primary form styrene polymers	1	1.4	0.00	0.00
Remainder	5	12.6		
Yemen - Yémen (=Developing)**				
All commodity groups	7 377 978	100.0	0.13	0.05
333 Crude petroleum & bituminous oil	5 527 660	74.9	0.72	0.52
334 Heavy petroleum & bituminous oil	468 243	6.3	0.18	0.08
343 Natural gas, liquefied or not	314 098	4.3	0.36	0.15
034 Fish, fresh live chilled frozen	157 582	2.1	0.75	0.32
971 Gold non-monetary excluding ores	154 707	2.1	0.20	0.11
057 Fruit nut (exc oil), fresh or dried	75 376	1.0	0.23	0.11
335 Residual petroleum products nes	63 211	0.9	0.52	0.20
036 Crustacean mollusc aquat invertebra	46 904	0.6	0.30	0.19
781 Passenger cars and race cars	30 993	0.4	0.04	0.01
122 Manufactured tabacco	27 889	0.4	0.42	0.11
Remainder	511 317	6.9		

For sources and notes, see end of table.

Pour les sources et les notes, se reporter à la fin du tableau.

Leading products exported based on average 2009-2010 values SITC Revision 3 (3-digit level) Principaux produits exportés d'après la moyenne des valeurs de 2009-2010 CTCI révision 3 (positions à 3 chiffres)	Value (f.o.b., thousands of dollars) Valeur (f.a.b., milliers de dollars)	2009-2010		
		of country total du total du pays	of ** (1). des ** (1)	of world du monde
Zambia - Zambie (**=Developing)				
All commodity groups	5 756 161	100.0	0.10	0.04
682 Copper	3 108 157	55.1	0.07	0.60
283 Copper ores and concentrates	231 272	4.0	0.76	0.50
699 Base metal manufactures nes	176 380	3.1	0.47	0.16
121 Unmanufactured tabacco and refuse	153 824	2.7	2.03	1.35
061 Sugar, mollasses and honey	123 419	2.1	0.54	0.37
287 Base metal ores & concentrates nes	96 162	1.6	0.02	0.00
661 Lime cement construction material	74 246	1.3	0.51	0.29
689 Misc non-ferrous base metals	65 306	1.1	2.09	0.92
263 Cotton	54 969	1.0	0.82	0.37
288 Non ferrous base metal waste nes	52 046	0.9	0.74	0.16
Remainder	820 180	14.2		

Leading products exported based on average 2009-2010 values SITC Revision 3 (3-digit level) Principaux produits exportés d'après la moyenne des valeurs de 2009-2010 CTCI révision 3 (positions à 3 chiffres)	Value (f.o.b., thousands of dollars) Valeur (f.a.b., milliers de dollars)	2009-2010		
		of country total du total du pays	of ** (1) des ** (1)	of world du monde
Zimbabwe (**=Developing)				
All commodity groups	2 384 449	100.0	0.04	0.02
121 Unmanufactured tabacco and refuse	331 087	13.9	4.37	2.91
325 Coke, semi coke, retort carbon	216 341	9.1	12.19	3.54
263 Cotton	194 616	8.2	2.90	1.32
671 Pig & sponge iron, ferro alloys etc	194 602	8.2	1.14	0.63
284 Nickel ores, concentrates, etc	130 027	5.5	3.49	2.04
061 Sugar, mollasses and honey	120 740	5.1	0.53	0.36
292 Crude vegetable materials nes	101 608	4.3	1.09	0.30
971 Gold non-monetary excluding ores	100 172	4.2	0.13	0.07
122 Manufactured tabacco	86 415	3.6	1.29	0.34
683 Nickel	78 509	3.3	3.08	0.46
Remainder	809 533	34.0		

Sources:
- UN DESA Statistics Division, *COMTRADE* database
- UNCTAD secretariat calculations

Notes:

(1)   The symbol ** indicates the grouping to which the country belongs and the percentage share shown applies. The percentage is the share of exports of each commodity shown by the country in the relevant grouping total exports for that commodity (i.e. "developing", which refers to developing economies; "transition", which refers to transition economies and "developed", which refers to developed economies).

(2)   Data are estimated at least for one of the reference years.

Sources :
- ONU DAES Division de statistique, base de données *COMTRADE*
- Estimations du secrétariat de la CNUCED

Notes :

(1)   Le symbole ** indique le groupement auquel le pays appartient et par rapport auquel est calculé le pourcentage. Ce pourcentage est la part que représentent les exportations du produit par le pays par rapport aux exportations du même produit par le groupement auquel le pays appartient («developing» se réfère aux économies en développement, «transition» aux économies en transition et «developed» aux économies développées).

(2)   Données estimées pour au moins une des années de référence

3.2.E Export structure by product
Major exporters for leading products among developing economies

3.2.E Structure des exportations par produits
Principaux exportateurs de produits majeurs parmi les économies en développement

Leading exporting developing economies (1) based on average 2009-10 exports (2) SITC Rev. 3 (3-digit level) Principales économies en développement exportatrices (1) d'après la moyenne des exportations de 2009-10 (2) CTCI rév. 3 (positions à 3 chiffres)	2009-2010		
	Value (f.o.b., thousands of dollars) Valeur (f.a.b., milliers de dollars)	As percentage En pourcentage	
		of country total du total du pays	of developing economies des économies en déve- loppement	of world du monde

034 - Fish, fresh live chilled frozen			
World	10 677 011	0.00	_ 100.00
Developed economies	26 825 814	0.35	_ 54.00
Transition economies	1 886 669	0.35	_ 3.80
Developing economies	20 965 459	0.27	100.00 42.20
China	5 115 623	0.37	24.40 10.30
Chile	2 768 968	4.43	13.21 5.57
Viet Nam	2 151 082	3.34	10.26 4.33
China, Taiwan Province of	1 315 355	0.55	6.27 2.65
Korea, Republic of	1 031 712	0.25	4.92 2.08
Indonesia	786 719	0.57	3.75 1.58
Thailand	629 311	0.36	3.00 1.27
Argentina	625 063	1.01	2.98 1.26
India	565 259	0.27	2.70 1.14
Namibia	534 675	14.83	2.55 1.08

054 - Vegetable & vegetable products nes			
World	53 947 739	0.39	_ 100.00
Developed economies	32 658 543	0.43	_ 60.54
Transition economies	976 333	0.18	_ 1.81
Developing economies	20 312 863	0.36	100.00 37.65
China	5 115 502	0.37	25.18 9.48
Mexico	4 005 326	1.52	19.72 7.42
Turkey	1 021 845	0.95	5.03 1.89
Thailand	961 810	0.55	4.73 1.78
India	890 696	0.43	4.38 1.65
Egypt	803 569	3.18	3.96 1.49
Myanmar	786 451	9.40	3.87 1.46
Morocco	742 012	4.66	3.65 1.38
Syrian Arab Republic	636 983	5.49	3.14 1.18
Argentina	530 217	0.86	2.61 0.98

057 - Fruit nut (exc oil), fresh or dried			
World	67 425 637	0.49	_ 100.00
Developed economies	33 558 695	0.44	_ 49.77
Transition economies	1 498 693	0.28	_ 2.22
Developing economies	32 368 303	0.57	100.00 48.01
Turkey	3 204 767	2.97	9.90 4.75
Chile	2 879 119	4.60	8.89 4.27
South Africa	2 491 282	3.27	7.70 3.69
China	2 286 572	0.16	7.06 3.39
Mexico	2 152 163	0.82	6.65 3.19
Ecuador	2 084 866	13.36	6.44 3.09
Costa Rica	1 274 910	14.26	3.94 1.89
Iran (Islamic Rep. of)	1 127 798	1.25	3.48 1.67
Argentina	1 120 030	1.81	3.46 1.66
India	1 068 593	0.52	3.30 1.58

061 - Sugar, mollasses and honey			
World	33 417 508	0.24	_ 100.00
Developed economies	9 780 879	0.13	_ 29.27
Transition economies	918 511	0.17	_ 2.75
Developing economies	22 718 118	0.40	100.00 67.98
Brazil	10 645 414	6.08	46.86 31.86
Thailand	2 064 803	1.19	9.09 6.18
India	1 086 547	0.52	4.78 3.25
United Arab Emirates	1 018 863	0.55	4.48 3.05
Mexico	759 854	0.29	3.34 2.27
Guatemala	726 549	9.27	3.20 2.17
China	612 955	0.04	2.70 1.83
Cuba	531 471	15.38	2.34 1.59
Argentina	427 621	0.69	1.88 1.28
Colombia	424 014	1.17	1.87 1.27

Leading exporting developing economies (1) based on average 2009-10 exports (2) SITC Rev. 3 (3-digit level) Principales économies en développement exportatrices (1) d'après la moyenne des exportations de 2009-10 (2) CTCI rév. 3 (positions à 3 chiffres)	2009-2010		
	Value (f.o.b., thousands of dollars) Valeur (f.a.b., milliers de dollars)	As percentage En pourcentage	
		of country total du total du pays	of developing economies des économies en déve- loppement	of world du monde

081 - Animal feed excluding unmilled cereal			
World	57 264 132	0.41	_ 100.00
Developed economies	31 728 722	0.42	_ 55.41
Transition economies	899 270	0.17	_ 1.57
Developing economies	24 636 140	0.43	100.00 43.02
Argentina	8 704 593	14.06	35.33 15.20
Brazil	4 958 883	2.83	20.13 8.66
India	2 506 323	1.21	10.17 4.38
China	1 881 610	0.14	7.64 3.29
Peru	1 613 357	5.22	6.55 2.82
Thailand	896 568	0.52	3.64 1.57
Chile	721 410	1.15	2.93 1.26
Paraguay	361 460	9.39	1.47 0.63
Bolivia (Plurinational State of)	324 227	5.65	1.32 0.57
Indonesia	295 498	0.22	1.20 0.52

222 - Oil seed etc for soft oil			
World	49 701 640	0.36	_ 100.00
Developed economies	28 626 432	0.38	_ 57.60
Transition economies	1 288 578	0.24	_ 2.59
Developing economies	19 786 630	0.35	100.00 39.81
Brazil	11 294 298	6.45	57.08 22.72
Argentina	3 620 315	5.85	18.30 7.28
Paraguay	1 280 154	33.25	6.47 2.58
India	694 894	0.34	3.51 1.40
China	641 735	0.05	3.24 1.29
Ethiopia	337 755	16.09	1.71 0.68
Uruguay	337 727	5.60	1.71 0.68
Nigeria	276 560	0.46	1.40 0.56
Sudan	131 166	1.43	0.00 0.26
United Arab Emirates	106 473	0.06	0.54 0.21

281 - Iron ore and concentrates			
World	82 201 198	0.59	_ 100.00
Developed economies	39 924 730	0.52	_ 48.57
Transition economies	4 318 384	0.81	_ 5.25
Developing economies	37 958 084	0.67	100.00 46.18
Brazil	21 079 392	12.03	55.53 25.64
India	6 860 902	3.31	18.07 8.35
South Africa	4 724 557	6.21	12.45 5.75
Bahrain	1 002 051	7.85	2.64 1.22
Iran (Islamic Rep. of)	876 104	0.97	2.31 1.07
Mauritania	775 302	45.50	2.04 0.94
Chile	572 673	0.92	1.51 0.70
Venezuela (Bolivarian Rep. of)	433 839	0.72	1.14 0.53
Peru	410 480	1.33	1.08 0.50
Korea, Dem. People's Rep. of	225 775	9.04	0.59 0.27

283 - Copper ores and concentrates			
World	39 177 471	0.28	_ 100.00
Developed economies	7 470 624	0.10	_ 19.07
Transition economies	738 575	0.14	_ 1.89
Developing economies	30 968 272	0.55	100.00 79.05
Chile	11 581 101	18.52	37.40 29.56
Indonesia	5 991 726	4.37	19.35 15.29
Peru	5 037 627	16.30	16.27 12.86
Argentina	1 315 526	2.13	4.25 3.36
Papua New Guinea	1 183 393	21.91	3.82 3.02
Mongolia	1 065 125	44.42	3.44 2.72
Brazil	1 020 944	0.58	3.30 2.61
Dem. Rep. of the Congo	614 352	13.81	1.98 1.57
Mexico	510 204	0.19	1.65 1.30
South Africa	424 973	0.56	1.37 1.08

For sources and notes, see end of table.

Pour les sources et les notes, se reporter à la fin du tableau.

3

3.2.E Export structure by product
Major exporters for leading products among developing economies

3.2.E Structure des exportations par produits
Principaux exportateurs de produits majeurs parmi les économies en développement

Left column

Leading exporting developing economies (1) based on average 2009-10 exports (2) SITC Rev. 3 (3-digit level) / Principales économies en dévelopement exportatrices (1) d'après la moyenne des exportations de 2009-10 (2) CTCI rév. 3 (positions à 3 chiffres)	Value (f.o.b., thousands of dollars) Valeur (f.a.b., milliers de dollars)	2009-2010 As percentage / En pourcentage		
		of country total / du total du pays	of developing economies / des économies en développement	of world / du monde
321 - Coal excluding non-agglomerated				
World	94 125 503	0.68	_	100.00
Developed economies	52 051 774	0.68	_	55.30
Transition economies	9 240 997	1.73	_	9.82
Developing economies	32 832 733	0.58	100.00	34.88
Indonesia	10 076 776	11.65	48.66	10.97
South Africa	5 938 941	7.80	18.09	6.31
Colombia	5 388 894	14.83	16.41	5.73
China	2 297 302	0.17	7.00	2.44
Viet Nam	1 625 417	2.52	4.95	1.73
Korea, Dem. People's Rep. of	497 622	19.92	1.52	0.53
Venezuela (Bolivarian Rep. of)	295 302	0.49	0.90	0.31
Mongolia	186 288	7.77	0.57	0.20
Philippines	141 679	0.32	0.43	0.15
India	112 293	0.05	0.34	0.12
333 - Crude petroleum & bituminous oil				
World	1 070 155 668	7.74	_	100.00
Developed economies	142 207 218	1.87	_	13.29
Transition economies	164 207 191	30.77	_	15.34
Developing economies	763 741 259	13.47	100.00	71.37
Saudi Arabia	158 428 098	74.09	20.74	14.80
United Arab Emirates	76 959 211	41.26	10.08	7.19
Iran (Islamic Rep. of)	69 160 385	76.96	9.06	6.46
Nigeria	48 304 683	80.16	6.32	4.51
Iraq	44 369 312	97.25	5.81	4.15
Angola	43 259 931	96.84	5.66	4.04
Kuwait	41 882 904	70.84	5.48	3.91
Venezuela (Bolivarian Rep. of)	39 584 592	65.31	5.18	3.70
Libyan Arab Jamahiriya	32 675 049	78.39	4.28	3.05
Mexico	30 800 470	11.67	4.03	2.88
334 - Heavy petroleum & bituminous oil				
World	573 533 908	4.15	_	100.00
Developed economies	243 465 619	3.20	_	42.45
Transition economies	72 335 552	13.56	_	12.61
Developing economies	257 732 737	4.54	100.00	44.94
Singapore	47 580 076	15.31	18.46	8.30
India	29 460 832	14.23	11.43	5.14
Korea, Republic of	27 213 291	6.54	10.56	4.74
United Arab Emirates	15 153 729	8.12	5.88	2.64
China	14 788 954	1.06	5.74	2.58
Saudi Arabia	14 167 611	6.63	5.50	2.47
China, Taiwan Province of	12 162 874	5.09	4.72	2.12
Venezuela (Bolivarian Rep. of)	11 791 179	19.46	4.57	2.06
Kuwait	9 101 983	15.39	3.53	1.59
Thailand	7 050 191	4.05	2.74	1.23
342 - Liquefied propane and butane				
World	38 053 070	0.28	_	100.00
Developed economies	11 319 023	0.15	_	29.75
Transition economies	1 068 655	0.20	_	2.81
Developing economies	25 665 392	0.45	100.00	67.45
Saudi Arabia	4 669 958	2.18	18.20	12.27
United Arab Emirates	4 599 679	2.47	17.92	12.09
Algeria	4 200 128	8.22	16.36	11.04
Qatar	3 822 509	6.20	14.89	10.05
Kuwait	2 005 142	3.39	7.81	5.27
Iran (Islamic Rep. of)	1 491 615	1.66	5.81	3.92
Nigeria	685 108	1.14	2.67	1.80
China	549 840	0.04	2.14	1.44
Argentina	548 021	0.89	2.14	1.44
Malaysia	525 125	0.30	2.05	1.38

Right column

Leading exporting developing economies (1) based on average 2009-10 exports (2) SITC Rev. 3 (3-digit level) / Principales économies en dévelopement exportatrices (1) d'après la moyenne des exportations de 2009-10 (2) CTCI rév. 3 (positions à 3 chiffres)	Value (f.o.b., thousands of dollars) Valeur (f.a.b., milliers de dollars)	2009-2010 As percentage / En pourcentage		
		of country total / du total du pays	of developing economies / des économies en développement	of world / du monde
343 - Natural gas, liquefied or not				
World	212 169 191	1.84	_	100.00
Developed economies	74 300 711	0.98	_	35.05
Transition economies	50 400 775	9.45	_	23.74
Developing economies	87 468 705	1.54	100.00	41.21
Qatar	18 851 606	30.59	21.55	8.88
Algeria	16 059 611	31.47	18.24	7.57
Indonesia	11 113 424	8.10	12.71	5.24
Malaysia	10 354 001	5.82	11.84	4.88
United Arab Emirates	3 726 528	2.00	4.26	1.76
Brunei Darussalam	3 439 158	41.88	3.93	1.62
Libyan Arab Jamahiriya	3 299 030	7.91	3.77	1.55
Trinidad and Tobago	3 158 500	32.71	3.61	1.49
Nigeria	2 982 998	4.95	3.41	1.41
Myanmar	2 616 495	31.28	2.99	1.23
422 - Fixed veg fat and oil, excl. "soft"				
World	33 133 857	0.24	_	100.00
Developed economies	3 645 895	0.05	_	11.00
Transition economies	106 749	0.02	_	0.32
Developing economies	29 381 212	0.52	100.00	88.67
Indonesia	13 808 036	10.07	47.00	41.67
Malaysia	11 628 620	6.53	39.58	35.10
Philippines	932 247	2.07	3.17	2.81
India	587 563	0.28	2.00	1.77
Papua New Guinea	358 902	6.64	1.22	1.08
Singapore	216 636	0.07	0.74	0.65
Thailand	191 019	0.11	0.65	0.58
Honduras	186 990	3.54	0.64	0.56
United Arab Emirates	182 574	0.10	0.62	0.55
Ecuador	148 416	0.95	0.51	0.45
511 - Hydrocarbons nes; derivatives				
World	68 016 312	0.49	_	100.00
Developed economies	39 178 609	0.51	_	57.60
Transition economies	1 113 309	0.21	_	1.64
Developing economies	27 724 394	0.49	100.00	40.76
Korea, Republic of	8 304 960	2.00	29.96	12.21
China, Taiwan Province of	2 760 335	1.16	9.96	4.06
Saudi Arabia	2 444 446	1.14	8.82	3.59
China	2 184 489	0.16	7.88	3.21
India	2 149 534	1.04	7.75	3.16
Singapore	2 033 614	0.65	7.34	2.99
Thailand	1 269 784	0.73	4.58	1.87
Iran (Islamic Rep. of)	1 243 904	1.38	4.49	1.83
Brazil	879 138	0.50	3.17	1.29
Malaysia	747 382	0.42	2.70	1.10
512 - Alcohols, phenols; derivatives				
World	42 267 726	0.31	_	100.00
Developed economies	19 590 946	0.26	_	46.35
Transition economies	700 226	0.13	_	1.66
Developing economies	21 976 554	0.39	100.00	51.99
Saudi Arabia	4 712 834	2.20	21.44	11.15
China, Taiwan Province of	2 392 379	1.00	10.89	5.66
Singapore	1 579 118	0.51	7.19	3.74
Brazil	1 387 042	0.79	6.31	3.28
Korea, Republic of	1 287 872	0.31	5.86	3.05
Malaysia	1 132 154	0.64	5.15	2.68
China	1 118 521	0.08	5.09	2.65
Iran (Islamic Rep. of)	1 066 829	1.19	4.85	2.52
Trinidad and Tobago	784 786	8.13	3.57	1.86
Kuwait	755 646	1.28	3.44	1.79

For sources and notes, see end of table.

Pour les sources et les notes, se reporter à la fin du tableau.

3.2.E Export structure by product
Major exporters for leading products among developing economies

3.2.E Structure des exportations par produits
Principaux exportateurs de produits majeurs parmi les économies en développement

Leading exporting developing economies (1) based on average 2009-10 exports (2) SITC Rev. 3 (3-digit level) / Principales économies en développement exportatrices (1) d'après la moyenne des exportations de 2009-10 (2) CTCI rév. 3 (positions à 3 chiffres)	2009-2010			
	Value (f.o.b., thousands of dollars) / Valeur (f.a.b., milliers de dollars)	As percentage En pourcentage		
		of country total du total du pays	of developing economies des économies en développement	of world du monde
513 - Carboxylic acid and compounds				
World	39 833 973	0.29	_	100.00
Developed economies	19 729 757	0.26	·	49.53
Transition economies	330 841	0.06		0.83
Developing economies	19 773 375	0.35	100.00	49.64
Korea, Republic of	5 261 081	1.26	26.61	13.21
China	3 882 284	0.28	19.63	9.75
China, Taiwan Province of	3 628 499	1.52	18.35	9.11
Thailand	1 439 715	0.83	7.28	3.61
Singapore	1 252 414	0.40	6.33	3.14
Malaysia	1 063 494	0.60	5.38	2.67
Mexico	904 134	0.34	4.57	2.27
India	592 470	0.29	3.00	1.49
Brazil	346 069	0.20	1.75	0.87
Indonesia	273 688	0.20	1.38	0.69
542 - Medicines including veterinary				
World	315 054 454	2.28	_	100.00
Developed economies	293 783 126	3.86	_	93.25
Transition economies	1 215 211	0.23		0.39
Developing economies	20 056 116	0.35	100.00	6.37
India	5 300 429	2.56	26.43	1.68
Singapore	4 198 193	1.35	20.93	1.33
China, Hong Kong SAR	1 452 210	0.40	7.24	0.46
China	1 342 281	0.10	6.69	0.43
Mexico	1 077 328	0.41	5.37	0.34
Brazil	839 222	0.48	4.18	0.27
Jordan	596 190	8.91	2.97	0.19
Argentina	576 915	0.93	2.88	0.18
Korea, Republic of	536 279	0.13	2.67	0.17
Turkey	427 694	0.40	2.13	0.14
571 - Primary form ethylene polymers				
World	58 026 146	0.42	_	100.00
Developed economies	32 616 007	0.43	_	56.21
Transition economies	989 794	0.19		1.71
Developing economies	24 420 344	0.43	100.00	42.09
Saudi Arabia	5 534 361	2.59	22.66	9.54
Korea, Republic of	3 673 274	0.88	15.04	6.33
Singapore	2 396 995	0.77	9.82	4.13
Kuwait	1 808 055	3.06	7.40	3.12
Thailand	1 490 978	0.86	6.11	2.57
China, Taiwan Province of	1 308 035	0.55	5.36	2.25
United Arab Emirates	1 230 514	0.66	5.04	2.12
Qatar	1 211 592	1.97	4.96	2.09
Brazil	1 036 493	0.59	4.24	1.79
Iran (Islamic Rep. of)	860 263	0.96	3.52	1.48
575 - Other plastics, in primary forms				
World	84 524 302	0.61	_	100.00
Developed economies	59 718 465	0.78	_	70.65
Transition economies	585 148	0.11	_	0.69
Developing economies	24 220 689	0.43	100.00	28.66
Korea, Republic of	4 594 353	1.10	18.97	5.44
Singapore	3 218 945	1.04	13.29	3.81
China, Taiwan Province of	3 068 767	1.28	12.67	3.63
Saudi Arabia	2 680 998	1.25	11.07	3.17
China	2 454 696	0.18	10.13	2.90
China, Hong Kong SAR	2 158 527	0.59	8.91	2.55
Thailand	1 144 921	0.66	4.73	1.35
Brazil	742 979	0.42	3.07	0.88
India	684 835	0.33	2.83	0.81
Malaysia	598 464	0.34	2.47	0.71

Leading exporting developing economies (1) based on average 2009-10 exports (2) SITC Rev. 3 (3-digit level) / Principales économies en développement exportatrices (1) d'après la moyenne des exportations de 2009-10 (2) CTCI rév. 3 (positions à 3 chiffres)	2009-2010			
	Value (f.o.b., thousands of dollars) / Valeur (f.a.b., milliers de dollars)	As percentage En pourcentage		
		of country total du total du pays	of developing economies des économies en développement	of world du monde
598 - Miscellaneous chemical products nes				
World	98 612 372	0.71	_	100.00
Developed economies	77 670 173	1.02	_	78.76
Transition economies	438 322	0.08		0.44
Developing economies	20 503 877	0.36	100.00	20.79
China	6 161 694	0.44	30.05	6.25
China, Taiwan Province of	2 168 134	0.91	10.57	2.20
Korea, Republic of	2 022 201	0.49	9.86	2.05
Singapore	1 855 267	0.60	9.05	1.88
Argentina	1 273 041	2.06	6.21	1.29
China, Hong Kong SAR	1 231 108	0.34	6.00	1.25
Malaysia	1 109 225	0.62	5.41	1.12
Indonesia	614 322	0.45	3.00	0.62
India	597 296	0.29	2.91	0.61
Thailand	502 424	0.29	2.45	0.51
625 - Rubber for wheels, incl inner tube				
World	64 774 797	0.47	_	100.00
Developed economies	39 039 090	0.51	_	60.27
Transition economies	1 403 147	0.26		2.17
Developing economies	24 332 560	0.43	100.00	37.56
China	9 565 611	0.69	39.31	14.77
Korea, Republic of	3 231 182	0.78	13.28	4.99
Thailand	2 285 606	1.31	9.39	3.53
Indonesia	1 299 606	0.95	5.34	2.01
Brazil	1 256 164	0.72	5.16	1.94
India	964 271	0.47	3.96	1.49
United Arab Emirates	953 765	0.51	3.92	1.47
Turkey	911 229	0.84	3.74	1.41
China, Taiwan Province of	900 719	0.37	3.64	1.37
Mexico	479 667	0.18	1.97	0.74
651 - Textile yarn				
World	44 302 780	0.32	_	100.00
Developed economies	15 525 766	0.20	_	35.04
Transition economies	1 107 019	0.21	_	2.50
Developing economies	27 669 995	0.49	100.00	62.46
China	8 380 130	0.60	30.29	18.92
China, Hong Kong SAR	3 030 351	0.83	10.95	6.84
India	2 976 464	1.44	10.76	6.72
China, Taiwan Province of	2 101 712	0.88	7.60	4.74
Indonesia	1 897 077	1.38	6.86	4.28
Pakistan	1 513 818	7.77	5.47	3.42
Korea, Republic of	1 453 404	0.35	5.25	3.28
Turkey	1 175 259	1.09	4.25	2.65
Thailand	946 581	0.54	3.42	2.14
Viet Nam	839 846	1.30	3.04	1.90
652 - Woven cotton fabrics				
World	27 854 732	0.20	_	100.00
Developed economies	7 687 096	0.10	_	27.60
Transition economies	306 415	0.06	_	1.10
Developing economies	19 861 221	0.35	100.00	71.30
China	9 903 762	0.71	49.86	35.56
China, Hong Kong SAR	2 002 224	0.55	10.08	7.19
Pakistan	1 883 308	9.67	9.48	6.76
India	1 407 850	0.68	7.09	5.05
Turkey	968 181	0.90	4.87	3.48
Korea, Republic of	689 133	0.17	3.47	2.47
China, Taiwan Province of	460 263	0.19	2.32	1.65
Thailand	435 288	0.25	2.19	1.56
Dominican Republic	305 046	5.05	1.54	1.10
Indonesia	265 891	0.19	1.34	0.95

For sources and notes, see end of table.

Pour les sources et les notes, se reporter à la fin du tableau.

3.2.E Export structure by product
Major exporters for leading products among developing economies

3.2.E Structure des exportations par produits
Principaux exportateurs de produits majeurs parmi les économies en développement

Leading exporting developing economies (1) based on average 2009-10 exports (2) SITC Rev. 3 (3-digit level) Principales économies en développement exportatrices (1) d'après la moyenne des exportations de 2009-10 (2) CTCI rév. 3 (positions à 3 chiffres)	2009-2010		
	Value (f.o.b., thousands of dollars) Valeur (f.a.b., milliers de dollars)	As percentage En pourcentage		
		of country total du total du pays	of developing economies des économies en développement	of world du monde
653 - Man-made woven fabrics				
World	34 286 524	0.25	_	100.00
Developed economies	10 012 791	0.13	_	29.20
Transition economies	76 081	0.01	_	0.22
Developing economies	24 197 652	0.43	100.00	70.57
China	11 170 800	0.00	40.17	32.50
Korea, Republic of	2 149 320	0.52	8.88	6.27
China, Taiwan Province of	1 996 444	0.84	8.25	5.82
India	1 960 406	0.95	8.10	5.72
United Arab Emirates	1 465 999	0.79	6.06	4.28
Turkey	1 305 869	1.21	5.40	3.81
Indonesia	924 095	0.67	3.82	2.70
China, Hong Kong SAR	886 356	0.24	3.66	2.59
Thailand	611 543	0.35	2.53	1.78
Pakistan	442 372	2.27	1.83	1.29
658 - Made-up textile articles nes				
World	41 554 046	0.30	_	100.00
Developed economies	10 280 751	0.13	_	24.74
Transition economies	326 218	0.06	_	0.79
Developing economies	30 947 077	0.55	100.00	74.47
China	18 122 946	1.30	58.56	43.61
Pakistan	3 081 702	15.82	9.96	7.42
India	2 518 828	1.22	8.14	6.06
Turkey	1 735 603	1.61	5.61	4.18
Mexico	667 356	0.25	2.16	1.61
Bangladesh	576 774	3.19	1.86	1.39
Viet Nam	517 098	0.80	1.67	1.24
Korea, Republic of	402 406	0.10	1.30	0.97
Thailand	335 446	0.19	1.08	0.81
China, Hong Kong SAR	315 677	0.09	1.02	0.76
667 - Pearls, precious semiprecious stone				
World	109 873 383	0.79	_	100.00
Developed economies	52 918 877	0.69	_	48.16
Transition economies	1 979 197	0.37	_	1.80
Developing economies	54 975 308	0.97	100.00	50.04
India	19 635 857	9.48	35.72	17.87
United Arab Emirates	11 731 571	6.29	21.34	10.68
China, Hong Kong SAR	10 692 169	2.93	19.45	9.73
South Africa	3 368 536	4.43	6.13	3.07
Botswana	2 244 202	55.08	4.08	2.04
China	2 065 168	0.15	3.76	1.88
Thailand	1 474 323	0.85	2.68	1.34
Singapore	577 530	0.19	1.05	0.53
Angola	533 108	1.19	0.97	0.49
Namibia	505 748	14.02	0.92	0.46
673 - Flat iron non-alloy steel products				
World	72 095 771	0.52	_	100.00
Developed economies	39 429 276	0.52	_	54.69
Transition economies	8 631 455	1.62	_	11.97
Developing economies	24 035 040	0.42	100.00	33.34
Korea, Republic of	6 791 268	1.63	28.26	9.42
China	6 124 139	0.44	25.48	8.49
China, Taiwan Province of	2 868 177	1.20	11.93	3.98
India	1 250 045	0.60	5.20	1.73
Brazil	1 046 919	0.60	4.36	1.45
Turkey	707 872	0.66	2.95	0.98
South Africa	644 636	0.85	2.68	0.89
Iran (Islamic Rep. of)	492 241	0.55	2.05	0.68
Singapore	444 000	0.14	1.85	0.62
Mexico	428 441	0.16	1.78	0.59

Leading exporting developing economies (1) based on average 2009-10 exports (2) SITC Rev. 3 (3-digit level) Principales économies en développement exportatrices (1) d'après la moyenne des exportations de 2009-10 (2) CTCI rév. 3 (positions à 3 chiffres)	2009-2010		
	Value (f.o.b., thousands of dollars) Valeur (f.a.b., milliers de dollars)	As percentage En pourcentage		
		of country total du total du pays	of developing economies des économies en développement	of world du monde
679 - Iron steel pipe tube fittings etc				
World	73 472 848	0.53	_	100.00
Developed economies	43 294 704	0.57	_	58.93
Transition economies	3 444 725	0.65	_	4.69
Developing economies	26 733 420	0.47	100.00	36.39
China	9 943 030	0.72	37.19	13.53
Korea, Republic of	2 734 870	0.66	10.23	3.72
India	2 511 524	1.21	9.39	3.42
Turkey	1 557 907	1.44	5.83	2.12
Singapore	1 372 097	0.44	5.13	1.87
Mexico	1 235 510	0.47	4.62	1.68
Argentina	1 021 142	1.65	3.82	1.39
China, Taiwan Province of	992 888	0.42	3.71	1.35
Malaysia	950 640	0.53	3.56	1.29
United Arab Emirates	699 211	0.37	2.62	0.95
681 - Silver, platinum, platinum metals				
World	44 371 017	0.32	_	100.00
Developed economies	22 844 038	0.30	_	51.48
Transition economies	340 604	0.06	_	0.77
Developing economies	21 186 375	0.37	100.00	47.75
South Africa	9 003 081	11.83	42.49	20.29
China, Hong Kong SAR	2 407 972	0.66	11.37	5.43
Mexico	1 977 328	0.75	9.33	4.46
United Arab Emirates	1 815 297	0.97	8.57	4.09
India	1 457 681	0.70	6.88	3.29
China	1 372 430	0.10	6.48	3.09
Korea, Republic of	950 117	0.23	4.48	2.14
China, Taiwan Province of	730 733	0.31	3.45	1.65
Chile	404 087	0.65	1.91	0.91
Singapore	221 693	0.07	1.05	0.50
682 - Copper				
World	109 391 231	0.79	_	100.00
Developed economies	44 932 738	0.59	_	41.08
Transition economies	7 428 168	1.39	_	6.79
Developing economies	57 030 324	1.01	100.00	52.13
Chile	22 939 892	36.68	40.22	20.97
Zambia	3 919 367	68.09	6.87	3.58
Korea, Republic of	3 857 805	0.93	6.76	3.53
China	3 670 859	0.26	6.44	3.36
China, Taiwan Province of	3 084 828	1.29	5.41	2.82
Indonesia	2 682 656	1.96	4.70	2.45
Peru	2 630 295	8.51	4.61	2.40
India	2 386 067	1.15	4.18	2.18
China, Hong Kong SAR	1 964 502	0.54	3.44	1.80
Dem. Rep. of the Congo	1 171 080	26.32	2.05	1.07
684 - Aluminium				
World	94 872 631	0.69	_	100.00
Developed economies	57 717 388	0.76	_	60.84
Transition economies	8 118 341	1.52	_	8.56
Developing economies	29 036 902	0.51	100.00	30.61
China	7 090 764	0.51	24.42	7.47
Bahrain	2 728 557	21.38	9.40	2.88
United Arab Emirates	2 251 334	1.21	7.75	2.37
Oman	2 131 512	6.63	7.34	2.25
Korea, Republic of	1 814 224	0.44	6.25	1.91
South Africa	1 720 544	2.26	5.93	1.81
Brazil	1 594 194	0.91	5.49	1.68
Turkey	1 137 162	1.05	3.92	1.20
India	862 563	0.42	2.97	0.91
Mozambique	853 551	38.88	2.94	0.90

For sources and notes, see end of table.

Pour les sources et les notes, se reporter à la fin du tableau.

3.2.E **Export structure by product**
Major exporters for leading products
among developing economies

3.2.E **Structure des exportations par produits**
Principaux exportateurs de produits majeurs
parmi les économies en développement

Leading exporting developing economies (1) based on average 2009-10 exports (2) SITC Rev. 3 (3-digit level) / Principales économies en développement exportatrices (1) d'après la moyenne des exportations de 2009-10 (2) CTCI rév. 3 (positions à 3 chiffres)	Value (f.o.b., thousands of dollars) Valeur (f.a.b., milliers de dollars)	of country total du total du pays	of developing economies des économies en développement	of world du monde
699 - Base metal manufactures nes				
World	113 260 576	0.82	_	100.00
Developed economies	74 071 985	0.97	_	65.40
Transition economies	1 662 335	0.31	_	1.47
Developing economies	37 526 256	0.66	100.00	33.13
China	15 614 095	1.12	41.61	13.79
China, Taiwan Province of	3 305 153	1.38	8.81	2.92
Mexico	2 964 873	1.12	7.90	2.62
Korea, Republic of	2 511 017	0.60	6.69	2.22
India	1 660 993	0.80	4.43	1.47
Thailand	1 655 196	0.95	4.41	1.46
China, Hong Kong SAR	1 645 161	0.45	4.38	1.45
Turkey	1 314 958	1.22	3.50	1.16
Brazil	1 299 628	0.74	3.46	1.15
Singapore	1 067 112	0.34	2.84	0.94
713 - Internal combustion engine part nes				
World	122 462 621	0.89	_	100.00
Developed economies	97 582 271	1.28	_	79.68
Transition economies	516 005	0.10	_	0.42
Developing economies	24 364 345	0.43	100.00	19.90
Mexico	4 687 496	1.78	19.24	3.83
China	4 406 194	0.32	18.08	3.60
Korea, Republic of	3 902 979	0.94	16.02	3.19
Brazil	2 047 747	1.17	8.40	1.67
Singapore	2 041 774	0.66	8.38	1.67
Thailand	2 041 315	1.17	8.38	1.67
Turkey	1 242 224	1.15	5.10	1.01
India	1 059 576	0.51	4.35	0.87
South Africa	530 300	0.70	2.18	0.43
United Arab Emirates	484 960	0.26	1.99	0.40
716 - Rotating electric plant parts nes				
World	76 940 438	0.56	_	100.00
Developed economies	51 145 339	0.67	_	66.47
Transition economies	719 743	0.13	_	0.94
Developing economies	25 075 355	0.44	100.00	32.59
China	10 984 420	0.79	43.81	14.28
Mexico	2 631 512	1.00	10.49	3.42
China, Hong Kong SAR	2 206 901	0.60	8.80	2.87
Korea, Republic of	1 352 183	0.32	5.39	1.76
Singapore	1 278 686	0.41	5.10	1.66
Brazil	1 182 170	0.67	4.71	1.54
India	1 105 908	0.53	4.41	1.44
Thailand	991 360	0.57	3.95	1.29
China, Taiwan Province of	701 515	0.29	2.80	0.91
Viet Nam	544 002	0.85	2.17	0.71
723 - Civil engineering plant & equipment				
World	85 875 337	0.62	_	100.00
Developed economies	61 235 890	0.80	_	71.31
Transition economies	730 814	0.14	_	0.85
Developing economies	23 908 632	0.42	100.00	27.84
China	6 543 611	0.47	27.37	7.62
Singapore	4 883 852	1.57	20.43	5.69
Korea, Republic of	3 768 318	0.91	15.76	4.39
United Arab Emirates	1 323 422	0.71	5.54	1.54
Brazil	1 111 812	0.63	4.65	1.29
Mexico	882 242	0.33	3.69	1.03
China, Hong Kong SAR	779 044	0.21	3.26	0.91
India	582 864	0.28	2.44	0.68
Thailand	529 661	0.30	2.22	0.62
Malaysia	428 289	0.24	1.79	0.50

Leading exporting developing economies (1) based on average 2009-10 exports (2) SITC Rev. 3 (3-digit level) / Principales économies en développement exportatrices (1) d'après la moyenne des exportations de 2009-10 (2) CTCI rév. 3 (positions à 3 chiffres)	Value (f.o.b., thousands of dollars) Valeur (f.a.b., milliers de dollars)	of country total du total du pays	of developing economies des économies en développement	of world du monde
728 - Special industrial machine part nes				
World	135 902 775	0.98	_	100.00
Developed economies	108 383 826	1.42	_	79.75
Transition economies	919 277	0.17	_	0.68
Developing economies	26 599 672	0.47	100.00	19.57
China	7 051 143	0.51	26.51	5.19
Korea, Republic of	5 173 401	1.24	19.45	3.81
Singapore	3 973 857	1.28	14.94	2.92
China, Taiwan Province of	3 218 746	1.35	12.10	2.37
China, Hong Kong SAR	1 634 338	0.45	6.14	1.20
Malaysia	1 049 508	0.59	3.95	0.77
Mexico	752 161	0.28	2.83	0.55
India	735 817	0.36	2.77	0.54
Turkey	559 138	0.52	2.10	0.41
Brazil	467 573	0.27	1.76	0.34
741 - Heating cooling equipment parts nes				
World	91 340 819	0.66	_	100.00
Developed economies	59 335 098	0.78	_	64.96
Transition economies	526 999	0.10	_	0.58
Developing economies	31 478 722	0.56	100.00	34.46
China	13 979 822	1.01	44.41	15.31
Thailand	3 485 957	2.00	11.07	3.82
Korea, Republic of	3 083 483	0.74	9.80	3.38
Mexico	2 887 246	1.09	9.17	3.16
Malaysia	1 367 075	0.77	4.34	1.50
Singapore	920 594	0.30	2.92	1.01
Turkey	801 164	0.74	2.55	0.88
United Arab Emirates	790 698	0.42	2.51	0.87
India	739 835	0.36	2.35	0.81
China, Hong Kong SAR	645 156	0.18	2.05	0.71
743 - Gas pump, compressor, fan, filter				
World	97 869 002	0.71	_	100.00
Developed economies	71 510 685	0.94	_	73.07
Transition economies	827 521	0.16	_	0.85
Developing economies	25 530 796	0.45	100.00	26.09
China	9 548 582	0.69	37.40	9.76
Mexico	2 572 847	0.97	10.08	2.63
South Africa	2 014 258	2.65	7.89	2.06
Korea, Republic of	1 912 516	0.46	7.49	1.95
Thailand	1 778 892	1.02	6.97	1.82
Singapore	1 466 809	0.47	5.75	1.50
Brazil	1 029 188	0.59	4.03	1.05
China, Hong Kong SAR	967 820	0.27	3.79	0.99
China, Taiwan Province of	953 104	0.40	3.73	0.97
India	680 556	0.33	2.67	0.70
751 - Office machines				
World	45 753 078	0.33	_	100.00
Developed economies	19 507 457	0.26	_	42.64
Transition economies	46 986	0.01	_	0.10
Developing economies	26 198 634	0.46	100.00	57.26
China	15 880 924	1.14	60.62	34.71
China, Hong Kong SAR	1 900 531	0.52	7.25	4.15
Singapore	1 728 054	0.56	6.60	3.78
Malaysia	1 312 027	0.74	5.01	2.87
Thailand	1 295 346	0.74	4.94	2.83
Viet Nam	1 179 293	1.83	4.50	2.58
Mexico	1 015 995	0.38	3.88	2.22
Korea, Republic of	923 805	0.22	3.53	2.02
China, Taiwan Province of	288 885	0.12	1.10	0.63
Brazil	157 938	0.09	0.60	0.35

For sources and notes, see end of table.

Pour les sources et les notes, se reporter à la fin du tableau.

3.2.E Export structure by product
Major exporters for leading products
among developing economies

3.2.E Structure des exportations par produits
Principaux exportateurs de produits majeurs
parmi les économies en développement

Leading exporting developing economies (1) based on average 2009-10 exports (2) SITC Rev. 3 (3-digit level) Principales économies en dévelopement exportatrices (1) d'après la moyenne des exportations do 2009-10 (2) CTCI rév. 3 (positions à 3 chiffres)	2009-2010				Leading exporting developing economies (1) based on average 2009-10 exports (2) SITC Rev. 3 (3-digit level) Principales économies en dévelopement exportatrices (1) d'après la moyenne des exportations do 2009-10 (2) CTCI rév. 3 (positions à 3 chiffres)	2009-2010		
	Value (f.o.b., thousands of dollars) Valeur (f.a.b., milliers de dollars)	As percentage En pourcentage				Value (f.o.b., thousands of dollars) Valeur (f.a.b., milliers de dollars)	As percentage En pourcentage	
		of country total du total du pays	of developing economies des économies en déve-loppement	of world du monde			of country total du total du pays	of developing economies des économies en déve-loppement	of world du monde
752 - Computer equipment nes					764 - Telecommunicate equipment part nes				
World	293 917 742	2.13	_	100.00	World	419 539 427	3.04	_	100.00
Developed economies	90 539 768	1.19	_	30.80	Developed economies	148 190 439	1.95	_	35.32
Transition economies	262 314	0.05	_	0.09	Transition economies	1 064 638	0.20	_	0.25
Developing economies	203 115 660	3.58	100.00	69.11	Developing economies	270 284 350	4.77	100.00	64.42
China	130 316 627	8.70	64.17	44.75	China	120 644 670	8.69	44.64	28.76
Thailand	12 153 509	6.99	5.98	4.14	China, Hong Kong SAR	51 063 797	13.99	18.89	12.17
China, Hong Kong SAR	11 925 371	3.27	5.87	4.06	Korea, Republic of	40 595 952	9.75	15.02	9.68
Mexico	11 045 838	4.18	5.44	3.76	Mexico	19 431 727	7.36	7.19	4.63
Malaysia	10 784 150	6.06	5.31	3.67	China, Taiwan Province of	8 756 821	3.66	3.24	2.09
Singapore	8 550 808	2.75	4.21	2.91	Singapore	8 609 030	2.77	3.19	2.05
Philippines	6 980 065	15.52	3.44	2.37	Malaysia	4 611 480	2.59	1.71	1.10
Korea, Republic of	5 978 141	1.44	2.94	2.03	Thailand	3 657 159	2.10	1.35	0.87
China, Taiwan Province of	2 477 413	1.04	1.22	0.84	India	3 230 123	1.56	1.20	0.77
Indonesia	876 949	0.64	0.43	0.30	United Arab Emirates	2 914 656	1.56	1.08	0.69
759 - Office equipment part & accessories					771 - Electric power machine part excl. 716				
World	190 608 981	1.38	_	100.00	World	76 642 934	0.55	_	100.00
Developed economies	77 373 213	1.02	_	40.59	Developed economies	35 252 351	0.46	_	46.00
Transition economies	126 080	0.02	_	0.07	Transition economies	1 176 075	0.22	_	1.53
Developing economies	113 109 689	1.99	100.00	59.34	Developing economies	40 214 508	0.71	100.00	52.47
China	35 428 354	2.55	31.32	18.59	China	17 435 778	1.25	43.36	22.75
China, Hong Kong SAR	24 496 914	6.71	21.66	12.85	China, Hong Kong SAR	8 350 945	2.29	20.77	10.90
Singapore	16 982 188	5.46	15.01	8.91	Korea, Republic of	2 633 466	0.63	6.55	3.44
Malaysia	10 443 747	5.87	9.23	5.48	Mexico	2 090 292	0.79	5.20	2.73
China, Taiwan Province of	7 319 985	3.06	6.47	3.84	China, Taiwan Province of	1 425 327	0.60	3.54	1.86
Korea, Republic of	7 227 800	1.74	6.30	3.70	Singapore	1 414 385	0.46	3.52	1.85
Thailand	3 544 000	2.04	3.13	1.86	Philippines	1 098 500	2.44	2.73	1.43
Philippines	2 226 736	4.95	1.97	1.17	Thailand	1 071 605	0.62	2.66	1.40
Costa Rica	1 641 583	18.36	1.45	0.86	India	1 009 369	0.49	2.51	1.32
Mexico	1 173 893	0.44	1.04	0.62	Turkey	728 583	0.67	1.81	0.95
761 - Television video receive project					772 - Electrical circuit equipment				
World	92 341 281	0.67	_	100.00	World	183 030 914	1.32	_	100.00
Developed economies	40 829 275	0.54	_	44.22	Developed economies	105 888 037	1.39	_	57.85
Transition economies	474 298	0.09	_	0.51	Transition economies	1 040 534	0.19	_	0.57
Developing economies	51 037 708	0.90	100.00	55.27	Developing economies	76 102 343	1.34	100.00	41.58
China	19 253 545	1.39	37.72	20.85	China	23 530 173	1.69	30.92	12.86
Mexico	19 115 624	7.24	37.45	20.70	China, Hong Kong SAR	15 834 233	4.34	20.81	8.65
Malaysia	3 654 056	2.05	7.16	3.96	China, Taiwan Province of	7 250 496	3.03	9.53	3.96
Korea, Republic of	1 793 311	0.43	3.51	1.94	Mexico	5 628 380	2.13	7.40	3.08
Turkey	1 743 938	1.61	3.42	1.89	Korea, Republic of	5 187 469	1.25	6.82	2.83
Thailand	1 305 494	0.75	2.56	1.41	Singapore	5 075 492	1.63	6.67	2.77
China, Taiwan Province of	1 279 143	0.54	2.51	1.39	Malaysia	4 131 220	2.32	5.43	2.26
China, Hong Kong SAR	834 697	0.23	1.64	0.90	Thailand	2 716 166	1.56	3.57	1.48
Singapore	602 170	0.19	1.18	0.65	India	1 054 704	0.51	1.39	0.58
Indonesia	433 021	0.32	0.85	0.47	Turkey	899 710	0.83	1.18	0.49
763 - Sound TV recorder or reproducer					773 - Electrical distribute equipment nes				
World	60 531 204	0.44	_	100.00	World	84 437 776	0.61	_	100.00
Developed economies	24 737 388	0.32	_	40.87	Developed economies	44 755 554	0.59	_	53.00
Transition economies	42 824	0.01	_	0.07	Transition economies	1 664 616	0.31	_	1.97
Developing economies	35 750 992	0.63	100.00	59.06	Developing economies	38 017 606	0.67	100.00	45.02
China	21 280 941	1.53	59.53	35.16	China	11 717 298	0.84	30.82	13.88
China, Hong Kong SAR	5 894 723	1.61	16.49	9.74	Mexico	5 962 148	2.26	15.68	7.06
Indonesia	1 896 954	1.38	5.31	3.13	Korea, Republic of	3 068 961	0.74	8.07	3.63
Thailand	1 518 017	0.87	4.25	2.51	China, Hong Kong SAR	2 366 926	0.65	6.23	2.80
Malaysia	1 455 092	0.82	4.07	2.40	Turkey	1 636 767	1.51	4.31	1.94
Korea, Republic of	1 122 077	0.27	3.14	1.85	Morocco	1 271 354	7.99	3.34	1.51
Singapore	998 191	0.32	2.79	1.65	Viet Nam	1 031 658	1.60	2.71	1.22
China, Taiwan Province of	530 739	0.22	1.48	0.88	Tunisia	966 255	6.26	2.54	1.14
Viet Nam	413 238	0.64	1.16	0.68	Philippines	958 716	2.13	2.52	1.14
Mexico	286 353	0.11	0.80	0.47	Thailand	929 185	0.53	2.44	1.10

For sources and notes, see end of table.

Pour les sources et les notes, se reporter à la fin du tableau.

3.2.E Export structure by product
Major exporters for leading products among developing economies

3.2.E Structure des exportations par produits
Principaux exportateurs de produits majeurs parmi les économies en développement

Leading exporting developing economies (1) based on average 2009-10 exports (2) SITC Rev. 3 (3-digit level) / Principales économies en développement exportatrices (1) d'après la moyenne des exportations de 2009-10 (2) CTCI rév. 3 (positions à 3 chiffres)	2009-2010			
	Value (f.o.b., thousands of dollars) Valeur (f.a.b., milliers de dollars)	As percentage / En pourcentage		
		of country total du total du pays	of developing economies des économies en déve-loppement	of world du monde
775 - Household equipment nes				
World	79 861 582	0.58	_	100.00
Developed economies	35 983 318	0.47	_	45.06
Transition economies	983 174	0.18	_	1.23
Developing economies	42 895 091	0.76	100.00	53.71
China	23 359 190	1.68	54.46	29.25
Mexico	4 181 839	1.58	9.75	5.24
Korea, Republic of	3 128 715	0.75	7.29	3.92
Turkey	2 828 875	2.62	6.59	3.54
Thailand	2 619 352	1.51	6.11	3.28
China, Hong Kong SAR	2 225 736	0.61	5.19	2.79
Malaysia	995 105	0.56	2.32	1.25
Singapore	879 988	0.28	2.05	1.10
United Arab Emirates	471 134	0.25	1.10	0.59
Syrian Arab Republic	357 503	3.08	0.83	0.45
776 - Valves tubes; diodes, transistors				
World	467 112 510	3.38	_	100.00
Developed economies	146 239 113	1.92	_	31.31
Transition economies	439 506	0.08	_	0.09
Developing economies	320 433 891	5.65	100.00	68.60
Singapore	74 106 606	23.84	23.13	15.86
China, Hong Kong SAR	58 023 964	15.89	18.11	12.42
China	51 625 833	3.71	16.11	11.05
China, Taiwan Province of	47 674 776	19.95	14.88	10.21
Korea, Republic of	30 614 164	7.36	9.55	6.55
Malaysia	28 465 473	15.99	8.88	6.09
Philippines	13 806 505	30.70	4.31	2.96
Thailand	8 383 386	4.82	2.62	1.79
Costa Rica	2 462 583	27.54	0.77	0.53
Mexico	1 948 013	0.74	0.61	0.42
778 - Electrical machinery apparatus nes				
World	180 069 084	1.30	_	100.00
Developed economies	93 350 560	1.23	_	51.84
Transition economies	1 076 508	0.20	_	0.60
Developing economies	85 642 016	1.51	100.00	47.56
China	32 943 159	2.37	38.47	18.29
China, Taiwan Province of	11 138 709	4.66	13.01	6.19
China, Hong Kong SAR	9 274 417	2.54	10.83	5.15
Korea, Republic of	7 940 941	1.91	9.27	4.41
Mexico	6 096 987	2.31	7.12	3.39
Singapore	5 281 659	1.70	6.17	2.93
Thailand	2 966 263	1.71	3.46	1.65
Malaysia	2 232 952	1.25	2.61	1.24
Indonesia	1 630 452	1.19	1.90	0.91
Philippines	1 440 575	3.20	1.68	0.80
781 - Passenger cars and race cars				
World	500 805 454	3.62	_	100.00
Developed economies	415 713 641	5.46	_	83.01
Transition economies	1 408 623	0.26	_	0.28
Developing economies	83 683 190	1.48	100.00	16.71
Korea, Republic of	28 496 020	6.85	34.05	5.69
Mexico	19 097 195	7.23	22.82	3.81
Turkey	6 148 887	5.69	7.35	1.23
Thailand	5 559 235	3.20	6.64	1.11
Brazil	3 830 526	2.19	4.58	0.76
South Africa	3 768 832	4.95	4.50	0.75
United Arab Emirates	3 626 423	1.94	4.33	0.72
Argentina	3 341 516	5.40	3.99	0.67
India	2 892 966	1.40	3.46	0.58
China	1 797 261	0.13	2.15	0.36

Leading exporting developing economies (1) based on average 2009-10 exports (2) SITC Rev. 3 (3-digit level) / Principales économies en développement exportatrices (1) d'après la moyenne des exportations de 2009-10 (2) CTCI rév. 3 (positions à 3 chiffres)	2009-2010			
	Value (f.o.b., thousands of dollars) Valeur (f.a.b., milliers de dollars)	As percentage / En pourcentage		
		of country total du total du pays	of developing economies des économies en déve-loppement	of world du monde
782 - Goods and service vehicles				
World	93 928 337	0.68	_	100.00
Developed economies	63 473 975	0.83	_	67.58
Transition economies	1 498 135	0.28	_	1.59
Developing economies	28 956 227	0.51	100.00	30.83
Mexico	8 527 252	3.23	29.45	9.08
Thailand	4 707 154	2.71	16.26	5.01
China	3 117 932	0.22	10.77	3.32
Turkey	2 934 196	2.72	10.13	3.12
Korea, Republic of	2 472 152	0.59	8.54	2.63
Argentina	1 985 297	3.21	6.86	2.11
Brazil	1 342 126	0.77	4.64	1.43
South Africa	1 126 462	1.48	3.89	1.20
United Arab Emirates	790 589	0.42	2.73	0.84
Singapore	400 705	0.13	1.38	0.43
784 - Motor vehicle parts and accessories				
World	265 990 582	1.92	_	100.00
Developed economies	201 502 778	2.65	_	75.76
Transition economies	1 002 225	0.19	_	0.38
Developing economies	63 485 578	1.12	100.00	23.87
China	14 260 937	1.03	22.46	5.36
Korea, Republic of	12 943 381	3.11	20.39	4.87
Mexico	11 609 658	4.40	18.29	4.36
Brazil	3 727 539	2.13	5.87	1.40
Thailand	3 596 231	2.07	5.66	1.35
China, Taiwan Province of	2 705 403	1.13	4.26	1.02
Turkey	2 376 624	2.20	3.74	0.89
Singapore	2 304 731	0.74	3.63	0.87
India	1 636 864	0.79	2.58	0.02
Philippines	1 546 675	3.44	2.44	0.58
793 - Ships boats floating structures				
World	150 177 881	1.09	_	100.00
Developed economies	57 337 897	0.75	_	38.18
Transition economies	2 777 213	0.52	_	1.85
Developing economies	90 062 771	1.59	100.00	59.97
Korea, Republic of	39 916 804	9.59	44.32	26.58
China	34 330 304	2.47	38.12	22.86
India	4 357 126	2.10	4.84	2.90
Singapore	2 336 288	0.75	2.59	1.56
Turkey	1 470 008	1.36	1.63	0.98
China, Taiwan Province of	1 181 856	0.49	1.31	0.79
Indonesia	1 108 569	0.81	1.23	0.74
Malaysia	712 607	0.40	0.79	0.47
United Arab Emirates	661 768	0.35	0.73	0.44
Saudi Arabia	445 603	0.21	0.49	0.30
821 - Furniture part; bedding furnishing				
World	122 789 658	0.89	_	100.00
Developed economies	66 918 281	0.88	_	54.50
Transition economies	1 605 953	0.30	_	1.31
Developing economies	54 265 424	0.96	100.00	44.19
China	34 475 239	2.48	63.53	28.08
Mexico	3 757 828	1.42	6.92	3.06
Viet Nam	2 980 680	4.63	5.49	2.43
Malaysia	2 387 088	1.34	4.40	1.94
Indonesia	1 805 050	1.32	3.33	1.47
Turkey	1 286 965	1.19	2.37	1.05
China, Taiwan Province of	1 255 262	0.53	2.31	1.02
Thailand	1 087 444	0.63	2.00	0.89
Brazil	744 164	0.42	1.37	0.61
Korea, Republic of	741 222	0.18	1.37	0.60

For sources and notes, see end of table.

Pour les sources et les notes, se reporter à la fin du tableau.

3.2.E Export structure by product
Major exporters for leading products among developing economies

3.2.E Structure des exportations par produits
Principaux exportateurs de produits majeurs parmi les économies en développement

Leading exporting developing economies (1) based on average 2009-10 exports (2) SITC Rev. 3 (3-digit level) / Principales économies en dévelopement exportatrices (1) d'après la moyenne des exportations de 2009-10 (2) CTCI rév. 3 (positions à 3 chiffres)	2009-2010			
	Value (f.o.b., thousands of dollars) / Valeur (f.a.b., milliers de dollars)	As percentage En pourcentage		
		of country total / du total du pays	of developing economies / des économies en développement	of world / du monde

821 - Case bags etc travel shopping

	Value	of country total	of developing economies	of world
World	90 838 550	0.27	_	100.00
Developed economies	13 188 782	0.17	_	35.80
Transition economies	59 240	0.01	_	0.16
Developing economies	33 600 520	0.42	100.00	64.04
China	15 510 103	1.12	65.77	42.12
China, Hong Kong SAR	5 145 622	1.41	21.81	13.97
India	774 198	0.37	3.28	2.10
Viet Nam	631 766	0.98	2.68	1.71
Singapore	327 683	0.11	1.39	0.89
Thailand	208 822	0.12	0.89	0.57
United Arab Emirates	142 382	0.08	0.60	0.39
Turkey	125 901	0.12	0.53	0.34
Indonesia	121 702	0.09	0.52	0.33
China, Taiwan Province of	80 526	0.03	0.34	0.22

841 - Male clothing, woven

	Value	of country total	of developing economies	of world
World	58 549 150	0.42	_	100.00
Developed economies	18 502 169	0.24	_	31.60
Transition economies	875 959	0.16	_	1.50
Developing economies	39 171 022	0.69	100.00	66.90
China	16 457 789	1.18	42.02	28.11
Bangladesh	4 072 566	22.49	10.40	6.96
China, Hong Kong SAR	2 682 350	0.73	6.85	4.58
Viet Nam	2 140 231	3.32	5.46	3.66
India	1 824 801	0.88	4.66	3.12
Turkey	1 799 067	1.66	4.59	3.07
Mexico	1 706 539	0.65	4.36	2.91
Indonesia	1 306 189	0.95	3.33	2.23
Pakistan	858 256	4.40	2.19	1.47
Tunisia	845 696	5.48	2.16	1.44

842 - Female clothing, woven

	Value	of country total	of developing economies	of world
World	71 392 152	0.52	_	100.00
Developed economies	23 659 283	0.31	_	33.14
Transition economies	1 084 852	0.20	_	1.52
Developing economies	46 648 016	0.82	100.00	65.34
China	22 100 964	1.59	47.38	30.96
China, Hong Kong SAR	5 204 939	1.43	11.16	7.29
India	3 842 086	1.86	8.24	5.38
Turkey	2 451 009	2.27	5.25	3.43
Viet Nam	2 268 886	3.52	4.86	3.18
Bangladesh	1 910 116	10.55	4.09	2.68
Indonesia	1 515 053	1.10	3.25	2.12
Morocco	1 422 901	8.94	3.05	1.99
Sri Lanka	710 990	9.22	1.52	1.00
Tunisia	576 659	3.74	1.24	0.81

844 - Female clothing, knitted crocheted

	Value	of country total	of developing economies	of world
World	41 917 764	0.30	_	100.00
Developed economies	9 755 476	0.13	_	23.27
Transition economies	361 945	0.07	_	0.86
Developing economies	31 800 343	0.56	100.00	75.86
China	17 229 432	1.24	54.18	41.10
China, Hong Kong SAR	2 640 168	0.72	8.30	6.30
Turkey	1 832 847	1.70	5.76	4.37
India	1 457 583	0.70	4.58	3.48
Viet Nam	1 260 628	1.96	3.96	3.01
Bangladesh	948 092	5.24	2.98	2.26
Cambodia	803 263	16.24	2.53	1.92
Indonesia	781 838	0.57	2.46	1.87
Sri Lanka	654 796	8.49	2.06	1.56
Thailand	436 322	0.25	1.37	1.04

845 - Articles of apparel nes

	Value	of country total	of developing economies	of world
World	118 388 077	0.86	_	100.00
Developed economies	35 127 190	0.46	_	29.67
Transition economies	1 001 571	0.19	_	0.85
Developing economies	82 259 010	1.47	100.00	69.48
China	36 620 375	2.64	44.52	30.93
China, Hong Kong SAR	10 185 082	2.79	12.38	8.60
Bangladesh	5 856 274	32.34	7.12	4.95
Turkey	4 208 688	3.89	5.12	3.55
India	3 294 619	1.59	4.01	2.78
Viet Nam	2 816 774	4.38	3.42	2.38
Indonesia	1 908 631	1.39	2.32	1.61
Tunisia	1 638 094	10.61	1.99	1.38
Cambodia	1 433 988	28.99	1.74	1.21
Thailand	1 391 695	0.80	1.69	1.18

851 - Footwear

	Value	of country total	of developing economies	of world
World	88 267 610	0.64	_	100.00
Developed economies	34 032 132	0.45	_	38.56
Transition economies	1 315 928	0.25	_	1.49
Developing economies	52 919 550	0.93	100.00	59.95
China	31 825 059	2.29	60.14	36.06
China, Hong Kong SAR	5 166 960	1.42	9.76	5.85
Viet Nam	4 758 818	7.39	8.99	5.39
Indonesia	2 118 982	1.55	4.00	2.40
India	1 699 300	0.82	3.21	1.93
Brazil	1 554 287	0.89	2.94	1.76
Thailand	807 458	0.46	1.53	0.91
Tunisia	523 712	3.39	0.99	0.59
Korea, Republic of	489 078	0.12	0.92	0.55
Morocco	389 765	2.45	0.74	0.44

871 - Optical instruments apparatus nes

	Value	of country total	of developing economies	of world
World	86 343 609	0.62	_	100.00
Developed economies	14 747 707	0.19	_	17.08
Transition economies	232 839	0.04	_	0.27
Developing economies	71 363 062	1.26	100.00	82.65
Korea, Republic of	26 942 820	6.47	37.75	31.20
China	24 482 264	1.76	34.31	28.35
China, Taiwan Province of	16 100 861	6.74	22.56	18.65
China, Hong Kong SAR	2 756 144	0.75	3.86	3.19
Singapore	434 457	0.14	0.61	0.50
Thailand	211 916	0.12	0.30	0.25
Malaysia	194 493	0.11	0.27	0.23
Mexico	83 951	0.03	0.12	0.10
India	37 160	0.02	0.05	0.04
South Africa	21 801	0.03	0.03	0.03

874 - Measure analyze control device nes

	Value	of country total	of developing economies	of world
World	139 161 457	1.01	_	100.00
Developed economies	110 482 506	1.45	_	79.39
Transition economies	1 174 096	0.22	_	0.84
Developing economies	27 504 854	0.48	100.00	19.76
China	7 406 428	0.53	26.93	5.32
Singapore	4 374 172	1.41	15.90	3.14
China, Hong Kong SAR	3 679 720	1.01	13.38	2.64
Malaysia	2 985 944	1.68	10.86	2.15
Mexico	2 733 365	1.04	9.94	1.96
Korea, Republic of	1 688 412	0.41	6.14	1.21
China, Taiwan Province of	1 523 432	0.64	5.54	1.09
Thailand	690 038	0.40	2.51	0.50
India	526 432	0.25	1.91	0.38
United Arab Emirates	327 888	0.18	1.19	0.24

For sources and notes, see end of table.

Pour les sources et les notes, se reporter à la fin du tableau.

3.2.E **Export structure by product**
Major exporters for leading products
among developing economies

3.2.E **Structure des exportations par produits**
Principaux exportateurs de produits majeurs
parmi les économies en développement

Leading exporting developing economies (1) based on average 2009-10 exports (2) SITC Rev. 3 (3-digit level) / Principales économies en dévelopement exportatrices (1) d'après la moyenne des exportations de 2009-10 (2) CTCI rév. 3 (positions à 3 chiffres)	Value (f.o.b., thousands of dollars) Valeur (f.a.b., milliers de dollars)	2009-2010		
		As percentage / En pourcentage		
		of country total du total du pays	of developing economies des économies en déve-loppement	of world du monde
893 - Articles of plastic nes				
World	108 198 969	0.78	_	100.00
Developed economies	69 473 810	0.91	_	64.21
Transition economies	971 619	0.18	_	0.90
Developing economies	37 753 540	0.67	100.00	34.89
China	16 545 856	1.19	43.83	15.29
China, Taiwan Province of	2 636 203	1.10	6.98	2.44
China, Hong Kong SAR	2 618 156	0.72	6.93	2.42
Mexico	2 237 056	0.85	5.93	2.07
Korea, Republic of	1 790 671	0.43	4.74	1.65
Thailand	1 688 911	0.97	4.47	1.56
Malaysia	1 578 685	0.89	4.18	1.46
Turkey	1 194 286	1.11	3.16	1.10
Singapore	964 369	0.31	2.55	0.89
India	789 155	0.38	2.09	0.73
894 - Baby carriage toy game sport good				
World	86 060 701	0.62	_	100.00
Developed economies	36 031 691	0.47	_	41.87
Transition economies	268 920	0.05	_	0.31
Developing economies	49 760 090	0.88	100.00	57.82
China	29 780 179	2.14	59.85	34.60
China, Hong Kong SAR	12 458 561	3.41	25.04	14.48
China, Taiwan Province of	1 803 364	0.75	3.62	2.10
Mexico	1 483 012	0.56	2.98	1.72
Thailand	717 716	0.41	1.44	0.83
Singapore	649 742	0.21	1.31	0.75
Korea, Republic of	472 004	0.11	0.95	0.55
Indonesia	398 243	0.29	0.80	0.46
United Arab Emirates	324 879	0.17	0.65	0.38
Viet Nam	294 949	0.46	0.59	0.34
897 - Jewellery nes (667)				
World	72 700 430	0.53	_	100.00
Developed economies	30 616 608	0.40	_	42.11
Transition economies	127 551	0.02	_	0.18
Developing economies	41 956 067	0.74	100.00	57.71
India	12 733 897	6.15	30.35	17.52
China	6 427 361	0.46	15.32	8.84
China, Hong Kong SAR	5 135 085	1.41	12.24	7.06
Thailand	3 088 998	1.78	7.36	4.25
United Arab Emirates	2 874 885	1.54	6.85	3.95
Singapore	2 116 580	0.68	5.04	2.91
Malaysia	1 795 592	1.01	4.28	2.47
Viet Nam	1 739 506	2.70	4.15	2.39
Turkey	1 364 011	1.26	3.25	1.88
Mexico	593 208	0.22	1.41	0.82

Leading exporting developing economies (1) based on average 2009-10 exports (2) SITC Rev. 3 (3-digit level) / Principales économies en dévelopement exportatrices (1) d'après la moyenne des exportations de 2009-10 (2) CTCI rév. 3 (positions à 3 chiffres)	Value (f.o.b., thousands of dollars) Valeur (f.a.b., milliers de dollars)	2009-2010		
		As percentage / En pourcentage		
		of country total du total du pays	of developing economies des économies en déve-loppement	of world du monde
898 - Music instrument device recording				
World	57 426 765	0.42	_	100.00
Developed economies	31 777 328	0.42	_	55.34
Transition economies	138 300	0.03	_	0.24
Developing economies	25 511 137	0.45	100.00	44.42
China	7 058 455	0.51	27.67	12.29
China, Taiwan Province of	5 295 246	2.22	20.76	9.22
Singapore	4 310 532	1.39	16.90	7.51
China, Hong Kong SAR	3 077 043	0.84	12.06	5.36
Korea, Republic of	1 698 460	0.41	6.66	2.96
Malaysia	1 507 598	0.85	5.91	2.63
India	629 024	0.30	2.47	1.10
Mexico	615 340	0.23	2.41	1.07
Indonesia	423 503	0.31	1.66	0.74
Thailand	313 482	0.18	1.23	0.55
899 - Manufactured articles nes				
World	67 259 735	0.49	_	100.00
Developed economies	45 764 412	0.60	_	68.04
Transition economies	267 183	0.05	_	0.40
Developing economies	21 228 139	0.37	100.00	31.56
China	13 026 949	0.94	61.37	19.37
China, Hong Kong SAR	2 069 435	0.57	9.75	3.08
Mexico	904 276	0.34	4.26	1.34
Singapore	853 115	0.27	4.02	1.27
China, Taiwan Province of	506 919	0.21	2.39	0.75
Korea, Republic of	496 665	0.12	2.34	0.74
India	475 789	0.23	2.24	0.71
Indonesia	463 080	0.34	2.18	0.69
Viet Nam	433 359	0.67	2.04	0.64
Thailand	318 714	0.18	1.50	0.47
971 - Gold non-monetary excluding ores				
World	137 081 457	0.99	_	100.00
Developed economies	59 837 120	0.79	_	43.65
Transition economies	1 374 060	0.26	_	1.00
Developing economies	75 870 277	1.34	100.00	55.35
United Arab Emirates	12 804 565	6.86	16.88	9.34
China, Hong Kong SAR	10 729 768	2.94	14.14	7.83
Peru	7 233 704	23.41	9.53	5.28
Thailand	6 096 459	3.51	8.04	4.45
Mexico	4 956 816	1.88	6.53	3.62
Singapore	3 391 919	1.09	4.47	2.47
Turkey	3 357 097	3.11	4.42	2.45
Korea, Republic of	2 855 502	0.69	3.76	2.08
South Africa	2 437 094	3.20	3.21	1.78
Colombia	1 841 268	5.07	2.43	1.34

Sources:
- UN DESA Statistics Division, *COMTRADE* database
- UNCTAD secretariat calculations

Notes:

(1) In addition, are presented for each product group the world total exports, the exports from developed, transition and developing economies.
(2) Commodity groups are selected on the basis of ranking by value.

Sources :
- ONU DAES Division de statistique, base de données *COMTRADE*
- Estimations du secrétariat de la CNUCED

Notes :

(1) Les exportations mondiales totales, les exportations des économies développées, en transition et en développement sont également présentées pour chaque groupe de produits.
(2) Les groupes de produits sont sélectionnés d'après le classement par valeur.

SITC group Revision 3 (3-digit level) ranked according to the concentration index in 2010 / Groupes de la CTCI Révision 3 (positions à 3 chiffres) classés d'après l'indice de concentration en 2010	Concentration index (1) / Indice de concentration (1)			Structural change index (2) / Indice de changement structurel (2) 1995=0	
	2000	2005	2010	2000	2010
264 Jute, other textile bast fibres n.e.s., raw, processed, not spun; waste of	0.882	0.825	0.740	0.133	0.175
261 Silk	0.734	0.738	0.670	0.234	0.309
244 Cork, natural, raw and waste (including natural cork in blocks or sheets)	0.489	0.581	0.616	0.107	0.154
633 Cork manufactures	0.001	0.002	0.592	0.055	0.106
286 Uranium or thorium ores and concentrates	0.747	0.816	0.566	0.221	0.285
422 Fixed vegetable fats and oils, crude, refined or fractionated, other than "soft"	0.442	0.459	0.515	0.191	0.195
666 Pottery	0.280	0.357	0.483	0.167	0.402
883 Cinematographic film, exposed developed, whether or not incorporating soundtrack	0.291	0.495	0.465	0.317	0.551
281 Iron ore and concentrates	0.303	0.371	0.407	0.002	0.202
831 Cases bags(storage hand executive equipment instrument gun travel shopping back)	0.351	0.365	0.450	0.104	0.316
752 Automatic data-processing transcibing machines; magnetic optical readers, n.e.s.	0.213	0.284	0.443	0.199	0.610
885 Watches & clocks	0.394	0.432	0.442	0.080	0.201
871 Optical instruments and apparatus, n.e.s.	0.306	0.379	0.428	0.236	0.639
044 Maize (not including sweet corn), unmilled	0.536	0.443	0.425	0.201	0.348
896 Works of art, collectors' pieces and antiques	0.431	0.441	0.425	0.116	0.179
658 Made-up articles, wholly or chiefly of textile materials, n.e.s.	0.204	0.315	0.423	0.134	0.323
231 Natural rubber, balata, gutta-percha, guayule, chicle, natural gums	0.432	0.444	0.416	0.135	0.190
843 Men's textile, knitted (coat suit trouser short shirt underwear nightwear)	0.173	0.245	0.410	0.200	0.469
844 Women's textiles, knitted (articles as code 841, plus dresses skirts)	0.189	0.235	0.406	0.187	0.495
345 Coal gas, water gas, producer gas, similar gas (exclude other gas hydrocarbons)	0.451	0.685	0.405	0.688	0.635
289 Ores and concentrates of precious metals; waste of (excluding gold)	0.249	0.256	0.400	0.190	0.412
891 Arms and ammunition	0.486	0.401	0.396	0.224	0.302
222 Oil-seed, oleaginous fruit for soft fixed vegetable oils (exclude flours, meals)	0.419	0.380	0.395	0.160	0.268
813 Lighting fixtures and fittings, n.e.s.	0.230	0.277	0.387	0.144	0.356
792 Aircraft, associated equipment; spacecraft, satellites, launch vehicles; parts	0.430	0.422	0.381	0.136	0.470
321 Coal, whether or not pulverized, excluding agglomerated	0.321	0.350	0.381	0.154	0.219
292 Crude vegetable materials, n.e.s.	0.305	0.359	0.374	0.113	0.120
212 Furskins, raw, other than hides and skins of group 211	0.331	0.339	0.373	0.171	0.247
344 Petroleum gases and other gaseous hydrocarbons, n.e.s.	0.330	0.375	0.371	0.358	0.621
751 Office machines	0.278	0.319	0.366	0.141	0.392
846 Clothing accessories of textiles, knitted or crocheted or not (exluding babies)	0.217	0.260	0.363	0.171	0.407
786 Trailers semi-trailers vehicles not mechanically-propelled; transport containers	0.288	0.339	0.361	0.195	0.311
894 Baby carriages, toys, games and sporting goods	0.330	0.345	0.361	0.112	0.332
322 Briquettes, lignites and peat	0.342	0.292	0.360	0.222	0.547
851 Footwear	0.260	0.298	0.360	0.154	0.374
583 Plastic monofilament, cross-section > 1 mm, rods, sticks, profile shapes	0.339	0.359	0.356	0.150	0.229
763 Sound or television image recorder reproducer; prepared unrecorded media	0.362	0.370	0.354	0.207	0.429
697 Household equipment of base metal, n.e.s.	0.200	0.271	0.349	0.137	0.394
263 Cotton	0.261	0.348	0.345	0.220	0.281
652 Cotton fabrics, woven (not including narrow or special fabrics)	0.203	0.260	0.344	0.111	0.322
793 Ships, boats (including hovercraft) and floating structures	0.297	0.274	0.344	0.159	0.386
285 Aluminium ores and concentrates (including alumina)	0.339	0.308	0.342	0.120	0.236
848 Apparel articles accessories other than textile fabrics; headgear (all material)	0.274	0.374	0.339	0.105	0.236
655 Knitted, crocheted fabric (include tubular knit, pile, openwork fabric), n.e.s.	0.258	0.260	0.335	0.120	0.382
431 Animal, vegetable fats, oils, processed; waxes; inedible preparations of, n.e.s.	0.255	0.280	0.331	0.203	0.261
045 Cereals, unmilled (excluding wheat, rice, barley, maize)	0.471	0.366	0.330	0.152	0.292
268 Wool and other animal hair (including wool tops)	0.378	0.344	0.330	0.151	0.295
284 Nickel ores, concentrates; mattes, oxide sinters, intermediate product of	0.303	0.294	0.325	0.124	0.218
653 Fabrics, woven, of man-made textiles (excluding narrow or special fabrics)	0.202	0.253	0.325	0.138	0.398
265 Vegetable textile fibre (exclu cotton, jute), raw, processed, not spun; waste of	0.414	0.370	0.324	0.169	0.285
042 Rice	0.292	0.306	0.315	0.176	0.187
283 Copper ores and concentrates; copper mattes; cement copper	0.378	0.379	0.315	0.201	0.268
774 Electrodiagnostic apparatus, medical surgical dental veterinary radiological	0.348	0.327	0.314	0.130	0.153
711 Steam vapour superheated water boiler, auxiliary plant for use with; parts of	0.200	0.187	0.312	0.211	0.510
696 Cutlery	0.244	0.302	0.311	0.216	0.453
551 Essential oils, perfume and flavour materials	0.263	0.368	0.310	0.178	0.296
687 Tin	0.277	0.302	0.309	0.275	0.283
764 Telecommunications equipment and parts, n.e.s.; accessories within division 76	0.184	0.212	0.309	0.176	0.483
882 Photographic and cinematographic supplies	0.282	0.282	0.308	0.112	0.205
845 Articles of apparel, textile fabrics, knitted or crocheted or not, n.e.s.	0.194	0.243	0.304	0.158	0.366
842 Women's textiles not knitted (articles as code 841, plus dresses skirts)	0.190	0.242	0.304	0.156	0.312
061 Sugar, molasses and honey	0.162	0.209	0.301	0.184	0.440
731 Machine tools working by removing metal or other material	0.340	0.320	0.301	0.061	0.184
775 Household-type electrical and non-electrical equipment, n.e.s.	0.210	0.237	0.300	0.136	0.431

For sources and notes, see end of table 3.3 Imports.

Pour les sources et les notes, se reporter à la fin du tableau 3.3 Importations.

204

SITC group Revision 3 (3-digit level) ranked according to the concentration index in 2010 / Groupes de la CTCI Révision 3 (positions à 3 chiffres) classés d'après l'indice de concentration en 2010	Concentration index (1) / Indice de concentration (1)			Structural change index (2) / Indice de changement structurel (2) 1995=0	
	2000	2005	2010	2000	2010
662 Clay construction materials and refractory construction materials	0.343	0.298	0.298	0.127	0.332
726 Printing and bookbinding machinery, and parts thereof	0.325	0.354	0.298	0.056	0.162
613 Furskin, tanned, dressed, unassembled, assembled (without other materials)	0.230	0.311	0.294	0.219	0.423
025 Eggs, birds', yolks, fresh, dried, preserved, sweetened or not; albumin	0.297	0.285	0.287	0.147	0.249
761 Television receiver, video monitor projector, w wo radio video-record reproduce	0.225	0.223	0.287	0.264	0.562
072 Cocoa	0.297	0.288	0.286	0.136	0.157
821 Furniture and parts; bedding, mattresses, mattress supports, cushions	0.184	0.203	0.286	0.150	0.390
211 Hides and skins (except furskins), raw	0.275	0.267	0.286	0.145	0.204
593 Explosives and pyrotechnic products	0.310	0.306	0.285	0.234	0.277
272 Fertilizers, crude (excluding those of division 56)	0.290	0.299	0.285	0.156	0.305
785 Motor cycles, mopeds, cycles, motorized and non-motorized; invalid carriages	0.332	0.291	0.283	0.118	0.373
525 Radio-actives and associated materials	0.354	0.316	0.281	0.252	0.350
016 Meat, edible meat offal (salted dried); flours, meals	0.313	0.303	0.278	0.107	0.290
654 Other textile fabrics, woven n.e.s.	0.252	0.272	0.275	0.134	0.267
597 Prepared additives: mineral oil; transmission; anti-freeze, de-ice; lubricating	0.298	0.286	0.275	0.101	0.161
656 Tulles, lace, embroidery, ribbons, trimmings and other smallwares	0.199	0.210	0.272	0.145	0.319
841 Men's textile, not knitted (coat suit trouser short shirt underwear nightwear)	0.178	0.217	0.272	0.143	0.305
667 Pearls and precious or semiprecious stones, unworked or worked	0.300	0.264	0.270	0.136	0.326
781 Vehicles to transport less than 10 persons, including station-wagons race cars	0.280	0.273	0.270	0.078	0.179
515 Organo-inorganic and heterocyclic compounds, nucleic acids-salts, sulphonamides	0.312	0.280	0.268	0.235	0.278
267 Other man-made fibres suitable for spinning; waste of man-made fibres	0.370	0.371	0.267	0.090	0.344
961 Coin (other than gold coin), not being legal tender	0.880	0.314	0.267	0.895	0.460
683 Nickel	0.251	0.280	0.266	0.145	0.232
712 Steam turbines and other vapour turbines, and parts thereof, n.e.s.	0.313	0.310	0.266	0.224	0.341
748 Transmission shaft camshaft crankshaft; bearing housing; gearbox speed changer	0.281	0.282	0.265	0.097	0.188
041 Wheat (including spelt) and meslin, unmilled	0.320	0.287	0.263	0.166	0.237
728 Other machinery or specialized industrial equipment; parts thereof, n.e.s.	0.300	0.262	0.262	0.116	0.109
762 Radio-broadcast receivers, with without sound-recording reproducing or clock	0.250	0.249	0.262	0.176	0.423
023 Butter and other fats and oils derived from milk	0.243	0.228	0.261	0.172	0.229
745 Non-electrical machinery, tools and mechanical apparatus, parts thereof, n.e.s.	0.280	0.281	0.259	0.098	0.175
541 Medicinal and pharmaceutical products, excluding medicines of group 542	0.238	0.247	0.258	0.113	0.201
714 Engines, motors, non-electric (exclude group 712, 713 and 718); parts of, n.e.s.	0.371	0.354	0.257	0.091	0.254
872 Instruments and appliances, n.e.s., (medical, surgical, dental or veterinary)	0.271	0.244	0.257	0.109	0.172
771 Electric power machinery parts (excluding rotating electric plant, group 716)	0.199	0.225	0.256	0.144	0.292
776 Thermionic cold cathode photo-cathode valves tubes; diodes, transistors	0.260	0.235	0.254	0.138	0.360
759 Parts, accessories for machines of groups 751, 752	0.213	0.230	0.253	0.188	0.377
874 Measuring, checking, analysing and controlling instruments and apparatus, n.e.s.	0.328	0.274	0.249	0.100	0.185
037 Fish, crustaceans, molluscs, aquatic invertebrates (prepared preserved) n.e.s.	0.230	0.237	0.249	0.176	0.281
899 Miscellaneous manufactured articles, n.e.s.	0.221	0.223	0.248	0.126	0.286
884 Optical goods, n.e.s.	0.281	0.279	0.247	0.167	0.231
251 Pulp and waste paper	0.311	0.262	0.247	0.082	0.201
722 Tractors (excluding headings 714.14 & 744.15)	0.282	0.262	0.246	0.118	0.193
579 Waste, parings and scrap, of plastics	0.293	0.255	0.245	0.201	0.303
724 Textile and leather machinery, and parts thereof, n.e.s.	0.270	0.252	0.243	0.110	0.277
895 Office and stationery supplies, n.e.s.	0.218	0.205	0.242	0.120	0.299
725 Paper mill pulp mill paper-cutting other paper manufacture machines; parts of	0.244	0.252	0.241	0.074	0.189
727 Food-processing machines (excluding domestic); parts thereof	0.243	0.250	0.241	0.084	0.155
122 Tobacco, manufactured (whether or not containing tobacco substitutes)	0.286	0.271	0.240	0.159	0.463
121 Tobacco, unmanufactured; tobacco refuse	0.244	0.241	0.240	0.115	0.342
325 Coke, semi-coke of coal, lignite, peat, agglomerated or not; retort carbon	0.382	0.374	0.239	0.222	0.379
043 Barley, unmilled	0.288	0.263	0.238	0.185	0.343
024 Cheese and curd	0.256	0.240	0.237	0.111	0.200
112 Alcoholic beverages	0.274	0.249	0.236	0.110	0.154
531 Synthetic organic colouring matter and colour lakes, preparations based thereon	0.235	0.232	0.236	0.157	0.325
572 Polymers of styrene, in primary forms	0.215	0.216	0.236	0.139	0.273
074 Tea and maté	0.280	0.240	0.236	0.174	0.195
689 Miscellaneous non-ferrous base metals employed in metallurgy, and cermets	0.177	0.258	0.233	0.194	0.283
694 Nails, screws, nuts, bolts, rivets, of iron, steel, copper or aluminium	0.232	0.224	0.231	0.088	0.184
659 Floor coverings, etc.	0.243	0.234	0.231	0.101	0.285
746 Ball or roller bearings	0.241	0.224	0.231	0.108	0.198
742 Liquid pump, with without a fitted measuring device; liquid elevator; parts for	0.286	0.256	0.231	0.105	0.211
737 Metalworking machinery (other than machine tools), and parts thereof, n.e.s.	0.244	0.222	0.230	0.126	0.221
791 Railway vehicles (including hovertrains) and associated equipment	0.216	0.232	0.230	0.182	0.292
223 Oil-seed, oleaginous fruit to extract other vegetable oil; flour, meal of n.e.s.	0.175	0.280	0.229	0.307	0.417

For sources and notes, see end of table 3.3 Imports.

Pour les sources et les notes, se reporter à la fin du tableau 3.3 Importations.

3.3 Concentration and structural change
indices of product markets
Exports

3.3 Indices de concentration et de changement
structurel des marchés de produits
Exportations

SITC group Revision 3 (3-digit level) ranked according to the concentration index in 2010 / Groupes de la CTCI Révision 3 (positions à 3 chiffres) classés d'après l'indice de concentration en 2010	Concentration index (1) / Indice de concentration (1)			Structural change index (2) / Indice de changement structurel (2) 1995=0	
	2000	2005	2010	2000	2010
721 Agricultural machinery (excluding tractors), and parts thereof	0.266	0.246	0.228	0.072	0.179
573 Polymers of vinyl chloride or of other halogenated olefins, in primary forms	0.177	0.186	0.228	0.188	0.257
723 Civil engineering and contractors' plant and equipment; parts thereof	0.285	0.243	0.228	0.075	0.213
733 Machine tool to work metal sintered metal carbide cermet, not removing material	0.249	0.249	0.228	0.091	0.231
747 Appliances for pipes boiler shells tanks vats; pressure and temperature valves	0.234	0.224	0.227	0.147	0.232
056 Vegetables, roots and tubers (prepared preserved) n.e.s.	0.204	0.203	0.227	0.139	0.180
735 Parts, n.e.s. and accessories for machines of groups 731, 733; tool holder	0.282	0.244	0.226	0.122	0.183
411 Animals oils and fats	0.251	0.206	0.225	0.167	0.208
778 Electrical machinery and apparatus, n.e.s.	0.240	0.200	0.224	0.138	0.294
681 Silver, platinum, other metals of the platinum group	0.280	0.230	0.223	0.116	0.246
232 Synthetic rubber; reclaimed rubber; waste, parings, scrap of unhardened rubber	0.243	0.222	0.222	0.138	0.256
783 Road motor vehicles, n.e.s.	0.252	0.246	0.221	0.172	0.368
081 Feeding stuff for animals (excluding unmilled cereals)	0.234	0.213	0.221	0.146	0.197
657 Special yarns, special textile fabrics and related products	0.201	0.182	0.221	0.104	0.274
553 Perfumery, cosmetic or toilet preparations (excluding soaps)	0.274	0.255	0.220	0.116	0.213
266 Synthetic fibres suitable for spinning	0.247	0.219	0.220	0.131	0.307
718 Power-generating machinery, and parts thereof, n.e.s.	0.213	0.223	0.219	0.232	0.228
343 Natural gas, whether or not liquefied	0.281	0.257	0.219	0.214	0.330
291 Crude animal materials, nes	0.231	0.223	0.219	0.115	0.173
542 Medicines (including veterinary medicines)	0.216	0.230	0.218	0.115	0.197
713 Internal combustion piston engines, and parts thereof, n.e.s.	0.271	0.238	0.217	0.134	0.228
598 Miscellaneous chemical products, n.e.s.	0.253	0.233	0.216	0.109	0.178
524 Other inorganic chemicals; organic and inorganic compounds of precious metals	0.213	0.251	0.216	0.250	0.234
282 Ferrous waste and scrap; remelting scrap ingots of iron or steel	0.192	0.201	0.216	0.214	0.187
672 Ingots, other primary forms of iron or steel; semi-finished products of	0.212	0.209	0.215	0.166	0.332
744 Mechanical handling equipment, and parts thereof, n.e.s.	0.226	0.212	0.215	0.122	0.214
743 Pump (non liquid), air gas compressor, fan ventilation filter; centrifuge; parts	0.238	0.219	0.214	0.106	0.217
612 Manufactures of leather or of composition leather, n.e.s.; saddlery and harness	0.192	0.219	0.214	0.190	0.393
691 Structures and parts of structures, n.e.s., of iron, steel or aluminium	0.172	0.179	0.213	0.196	0.316
523 Metallic salts and peroxysalts, of inorganic acids	0.232	0.213	0.213	0.121	0.271
516 Other organic chemicals	0.201	0.199	0.213	0.117	0.234
741 Heating and cooling equipment, and parts thereof, n.e.s.	0.216	0.193	0.212	0.146	0.302
695 Tools for use in the hand or in machine	0.199	0.211	0.212	0.118	0.199
772 Electrical apparatus to switch protect circuits or make circuit connections	0.220	0.201	0.212	0.146	0.248
075 Spices	0.175	0.163	0.211	0.134	0.286
897 Jewellery, articles of goldsmiths' silversmiths' B2 semiprecious, n.e.s.	0.249	0.206	0.211	0.161	0.312
716 Rotating electric plant, and parts thereof, n.e.s.	0.184	0.189	0.210	0.127	0.262
898 Musical instrument, parts accessory; tape, sound recording (excluding 763 & 883)	0.227	0.208	0.210	0.144	0.371
782 Motor vehicles for the transport of goods and special-purpose motor vehicles	0.246	0.219	0.210	0.154	0.323
812 Sanitary, plumbing and heating fixtures and fittings, n.e.s.	0.222	0.213	0.209	0.144	0.274
012 Other meat and edible meat offal (fresh chilled frozen)	0.215	0.207	0.209	0.159	0.311
511 Hydrocarbons, n.e.s., halogenated, sulphonated, nitrated, nitrosated derivatives	0.218	0.203	0.207	0.116	0.263
611 Leather	0.226	0.224	0.207	0.098	0.192
054 Vegetables and veg products (fresh chilled frozen preserved dried edible) n.e.s.	0.214	0.210	0.207	0.137	0.177
421 Fixed vegetable fats and oils, "soft", crude, refined or fractionated	0.225	0.224	0.206	0.182	0.246
784 Parts and accessories of the motor vehicles of groups 722, 781, 782 and 783	0.267	0.215	0.206	0.087	0.295
663 Mineral manufactures, n.e.s.	0.216	0.200	0.206	0.100	0.210
533 Pigments, paints, varnishes and related materials	0.214	0.208	0.206	0.117	0.149
513 Carboxylic acid, anhydrides, halides, peroxides, peroxyacids; halogenate derivatives	0.202	0.187	0.205	0.158	0.387
664 Glass	0.204	0.182	0.205	0.114	0.230
749 Non-electric parts and accessories of machinery, n.e.s.	0.232	0.203	0.205	0.098	0.244
514 Nitrogen-function compounds	0.214	0.189	0.204	0.099	0.290
581 Tubes, pipes and hoses, and fittings therefor, of plastics	0.221	0.206	0.203	0.166	0.255
073 Chocolate and other food preparations containing cocoa, n.e.s.	0.205	0.199	0.203	0.174	0.197
677 Rails or railway track construction material, of iron or steel	0.200	0.197	0.202	0.196	0.266
071 Coffee and coffee substitutes	0.179	0.207	0.202	0.137	0.291
873 Meters and counters, n.e.s.	0.251	0.219	0.202	0.191	0.372
582 Plates, sheets, film, foil and strip, of plastics	0.215	0.201	0.202	0.094	0.213
682 Copper	0.174	0.189	0.201	0.118	0.241
022 Milk, cream and milk products (excluding butter, cheese)	0.226	0.210	0.200	0.135	0.279
651 Textile yarn	0.153	0.169	0.200	0.122	0.285
011 Meat of bovine animals (fresh chilled frozen)	0.253	0.216	0.200	0.195	0.289
881 Photographic apparatus and equipment, n.e.s.	0.324	0.339	0.198	0.143	0.377
591 Insecticide, rodenticide, fungicide, herbicide, plant-growth reg, disinfectant	0.237	0.210	0.197	0.112	0.239

For sources and notes, see end of table 3.3 Imports.

Pour les sources et les notes, se reporter à la fin du tableau 3.3 Importations.

SITC group Revision 3 (3-digit level) ranked according to the concentration index in 2010 Groupes de la CTCI Révision 3 (positions à 3 chiffres) classés d'après l'indice de concentration en 2010	Concentration index (1) Indice de concentration (1)			Structural change index (2) Indice de changement structurel (2) 1995=0	
	2000	2005	2010	2000	2010
575 Other plastics, in primary forms	0.260	0.230	0.197	0.104	0.224
893 Articles, n.e.s., of plastics	0.195	0.188	0.196	0.147	0.213
592 Starches, inulin and wheat gluten; albuminoidal substances; glues	0.204	0.196	0.196	0.133	0.209
675 Flat-rolled products of alloy steel	0.214	0.189	0.196	0.152	0.258
674 Flat-rolled products of iron or non-alloy steel, clad, plated or coated	0.189	0.180	0.196	0.172	0.335
269 Worn clothing and other worn textile articles; rags	0.226	0.202	0.196	0.138	0.342
665 Glassware	0.181	0.181	0.195	0.120	0.362
035 Fish (dried, salted, in brine, smoked); flours, meals, pellets for human consump	0.220	0.205	0.195	0.160	0.354
699 Manufactures of base metal, n.e.s.	0.210	0.196	0.195	0.131	0.224
621 Materials of rubber (e.g., pastes, plates, sheets, rods, thread, tubes, of rubber)	0.225	0.218	0.194	0.122	0.290
247 Wood in the rough or roughly squared	0.221	0.264	0.193	0.233	0.303
288 Non-ferrous base metal waste and scrap, n.e.s.	0.171	0.185	0.193	0.163	0.221
017 Meat, edible meat offal (prepared preserved) n.e.s.	0.176	0.188	0.193	0.163	0.292
342 Liquefied propane and butane	0.235	0.219	0.191	0.183	0.320
059 Fruit and vegetable juice (unfermented, no added spirit, sweetened or not)	0.209	0.187	0.191	0.151	0.232
629 Articles of rubber, n.e.s.	0.219	0.192	0.190	0.132	0.217
274 Sulphur and unroasted iron pyrites	0.243	0.252	0.190	0.172	0.376
335 Residual petroleum products, n.e.s., related mater.	0.197	0.161	0.190	0.157	0.228
001 Live animals other than animals of division 03	0.210	0.200	0.190	0.163	0.226
892 Printed matter	0.230	0.214	0.189	0.108	0.218
641 Paper and paperboard	0.215	0.201	0.189	0.073	0.176
287 Ores and concentrates of base metals, n.e.s.	0.205	0.210	0.189	0.195	0.236
661 Lime, cement, fabricated construction material (excluding glass, clay material)	0.185	0.175	0.187	0.173	0.380
635 Wood manufactures, n.e.s.	0.164	0.185	0.186	0.157	0.279
625 Rubber tyres, interchangeable tyre treads, tyre flaps, inner tubes for wheels	0.189	0.172	0.186	0.103	0.285
811 Prefabricated buildings	0.170	0.146	0.184	0.169	0.364
693 Wire products (excluding insulated electrical wiring) and fencing grills	0.163	0.167	0.184	0.158	0.273
679 Tubes, pipes and hollow profiles, and tube or pipe fittings, of iron or steel	0.180	0.175	0.183	0.109	0.245
574 Polyacetal, polyether, epoxide resin; polycarbonate, alkyd resin, polyester	0.208	0.188	0.183	0.121	0.230
634 Veneers, plywood, particle board, and other wood, worked, n.e.s.	0.204	0.185	0.182	0.165	0.299
673 Flat-rolled products of iron or non-alloy steel, not clad, plated or coated	0.170	0.157	0.182	0.135	0.214
248 Wood, simply worked, and railway sleepers of wood	0.309	0.251	0.182	0.115	0.303
047 Other cereal meals and flours	0.258	0.190	0.180	0.270	0.320
091 Margarine and shortening	0.155	0.171	0.180	0.273	0.282
642 Paper and paperboard, cut to size or shape, and articles of paper or paperboard	0.179	0.183	0.180	0.125	0.234
562 Fertilizers (excluding group 272)	0.188	0.184	0.180	0.182	0.304
522 Inorganic chemical elements, oxides and halogen salts	0.171	0.173	0.179	0.124	0.216
277 Natural abrasives, n.e.s. (including industrial diamonds)	0.235	0.169	0.179	0.358	0.506
111 Non-alcoholic beverages, n.e.s.	0.197	0.198	0.176	0.173	0.325
046 Meal and flour of wheat and flour of meslin	0.164	0.182	0.174	0.252	0.456
671 Pig-iron, spiegeleisen, sponge iron, iron steel granules, powders, ferro-alloys	0.187	0.187	0.174	0.208	0.317
048 Cereal preparations and preparations of flour or starch of fruits or vegetables	0.195	0.190	0.174	0.121	0.188
571 Polymers of ethylene, in primary forms	0.198	0.179	0.173	0.132	0.259
971 Gold, non-monetary (excluding gold ores and concentrates)	0.262	0.200	0.172	0.221	0.428
333 Petroleum oils and oils obtained from bituminous minerals, crude	0.166	0.181	0.171	0.103	0.193
678 Wire of iron or steel	0.155	0.147	0.171	0.130	0.273
246 Wood in chips or particles and wood waste	0.289	0.227	0.170	0.141	0.393
532 Dyeing and tanning extracts, and synthetic tanning materials	0.187	0.172	0.169	0.140	0.235
773 Equipment for distributing electricity, n.e.s.	0.206	0.169	0.169	0.133	0.332
554 Soaps, cleansing and polishing preparations	0.190	0.182	0.167	0.137	0.186
685 Lead	0.200	0.212	0.166	0.213	0.260
034 Fish, fresh (live dead chilled frozen)	0.149	0.153	0.166	0.135	0.274
278 Other crude minerals	0.199	0.164	0.164	0.118	0.249
058 Fruit, preserved, and fruit preparations (excluding fruit juices)	0.140	0.157	0.163	0.135	0.228
351 Electric current	0.325	0.197	0.162	0.310	0.415
057 Fruits and nuts (excluding oil nuts), fresh or dried	0.173	0.168	0.160	0.116	0.192
686 Zinc	0.180	0.156	0.160	0.185	0.258
512 Alcohol, phenol, phenol-alcohol;halogenate, sulphonate, nitrate, nitrosate deriv	0.175	0.164	0.159	0.157	0.333
692 Metal containers for storage or transport	0.165	0.159	0.159	0.128	0.237
098 Edible products and preparations, n.e.s.	0.190	0.171	0.157	0.197	0.231
334 Petroleum oil, oil from bituminous (excl crude); preparations, n.e.s., > 70% oil	0.120	0.130	0.155	0.146	0.237
036 Crustaceans, mollusks and aquatic invertebrates	0.141	0.135	0.147	0.147	0.237
676 Iron and steel bars, rods, angles, shapes and sections (including sheet piling)	0.150	0.143	0.145	0.125	0.243
273 Stone, sand and gravel	0.144	0.135	0.143	0.165	0.299
684 Aluminium	0.153	0.142	0.138	0.085	0.220
062 Sugar confectionery	0.142	0.139	0.132	0.189	0.275
245 Fuel wood (excluding wood waste) and wood charcoal	0.156	0.099	0.119	0.268	0.390

For sources and notes, see end of table 3.3 Imports.

Pour les sources et les notes, se reporter à la fin du tableau 3.3 Importations.

SITC group Revision 3 (3-digit level) ranked according to the concentration index in 2010 Groupes de la CTCI Révision 3 (positions à 3 chiffres) classés d'après l'indice de concentration en 2010	Concentration index (1) Indice de concentration (1)			Structural change index (2) Indice de changement structurel (2) 1995=0	
	2000	2005	2010	2000	2010
286 Uranium or thorium ores and concentrates	0.683	0.883	0.993	0.299	0.322
871 Optical instruments and apparatus, n.e.s.	0.266	0.596	0.629	0.287	0.703
281 Iron ore and concentrates	0.256	0.431	0.612	0.114	0.535
079 Waste, parings and scrap, of plastic	0.417	0.498	0.606	0.260	0.543
961 Coin (other than gold coin), not being legal tender	0.905	0.174	0.603	0.896	0.352
613 Furskin, tanned, dressed, unassembled, assembled (without other materials)	0.283	0.374	0.493	0.307	0.519
265 Vegetable textile fibre (exclu cotton, jute), raw, processed, not spun; waste of	0.233	0.357	0.448	0.301	0.529
261 Silk	0.328	0.429	0.446	0.199	0.484
883 Cinematographic film, exposed developed, whether or not incorporating soundtrack	0.318	0.612	0.442	0.211	0.360
222 Oil-seed, oleaginous fruit for soft fixed vegetable oils (exclude flours, meals)	0.230	0.305	0.427	0.261	0.522
244 Cork, natural, raw and waste (including natural cork in blocks or sheets)	0.439	0.511	0.419	0.203	0.274
896 Works of art, collectors' pieces and antiques	0.525	0.439	0.409	0.142	0.156
247 Wood in the rough or roughly squared	0.251	0.261	0.386	0.268	0.532
322 Briquettes, lignites and peat	0.253	0.211	0.382	0.242	0.505
212 Furskins, raw, other than hides and skins of group 211	0.322	0.373	0.381	0.186	0.317
268 Wool and other animal hair (including wool tops)	0.285	0.297	0.379	0.183	0.375
246 Wood in chips or particles and wood waste	0.712	0.525	0.369	0.064	0.428
345 Coal gas, water gas, producer gas, similar gas (exclude other gas hydrocarbons)	0.186	0.421	0.363	0.742	0.563
283 Copper ores and concentrates; copper mattes; cement copper	0.355	0.330	0.359	0.212	0.440
287 Ores and concentrates of base metals, n.e.s.	0.168	0.217	0.348	0.129	0.406
288 Non-ferrous base metal waste and scrap, n.e.s.	0.210	0.255	0.345	0.159	0.375
284 Nickel ores, concentrates; mattes, oxide sinters, intermediate product of	0.353	0.295	0.341	0.177	0.367
264 Jute, other textile bast fibres n.e.s., raw, processed, not spun; waste of	0.329	0.345	0.339	0.311	0.360
263 Cotton	0.153	0.291	0.331	0.264	0.461
274 Sulphur and unroasted iron pyrites	0.191	0.344	0.325	0.245	0.403
211 Hides and skins (except furskins), raw	0.265	0.276	0.321	0.166	0.393
016 Meat, edible meat offal (salted dried); flours, meals	0.407	0.380	0.318	0.159	0.298
891 Arms and ammunition	0.230	0.251	0.310	0.273	0.344
043 Barley, unmilled	0.213	0.260	0.306	0.255	0.270
776 Thermionic cold cathode photo-cathode valves tubes; diodes, transistors	0.207	0.250	0.303	0.126	0.379
289 Ores and concentrates of precious metals; waste of (excluding gold)	0.380	0.366	0.302	0.142	0.301
667 Pearls and precious or semiprecious stones, unworked or worked	0.314	0.293	0.295	0.137	0.342
761 Television receiver, video monitor projector, w wo radio video-record reproduce	0.264	0.339	0.291	0.238	0.269
525 Radio-actives and associated materials	0.353	0.317	0.290	0.219	0.251
251 Pulp and waste paper	0.194	0.228	0.287	0.124	0.322
971 Gold, non-monetary (excluding gold ores and concentrates)	0.218	0.244	0.278	0.317	0.555
894 Baby carriages, toys, games and sporting goods	0.361	0.316	0.277	0.091	0.133
658 Made-up articles, wholly or chiefly of textile materials, n.e.s.	0.279	0.299	0.268	0.141	0.195
231 Natural rubber, balata, gutta-percha, guayule, chicle, natural gums	0.230	0.243	0.264	0.157	0.295
572 Polymers of styrene, in primary forms	0.258	0.248	0.262	0.152	0.258
036 Crustaceans, mollusks and aquatic invertebrates	0.368	0.299	0.261	0.127	0.261
881 Photographic apparatus and equipment, n.e.s.	0.261	0.227	0.260	0.148	0.405
843 Men's textile, knitted (coat suit trouser short shirt underwear nightwear)	0.329	0.316	0.259	0.140	0.186
731 Machine tools working by removing metal or other material	0.217	0.199	0.258	0.144	0.336
321 Coal, whether or not pulverized, excluding agglomerated	0.251	0.233	0.249	0.122	0.274
762 Radio-broadcast receivers, with without sound-recording reproducing or clock	0.327	0.278	0.247	0.149	0.203
682 Copper	0.181	0.184	0.245	0.161	0.316
821 Furniture and parts; bedding, mattresses, mattress supports, cushions	0.313	0.303	0.245	0.171	0.193
512 Alcohol, phenol, phenol-alcohol;halogenate, sulphonate, nitrate, nitrosate deriv	0.166	0.208	0.244	0.169	0.318
683 Nickel	0.217	0.202	0.243	0.096	0.301
681 Silver, platinum, other metals of the platinum group	0.337	0.266	0.242	0.201	0.283
845 Articles of apparel, textile fabrics, knitted or crocheted or not, n.e.s.	0.310	0.270	0.242	0.132	0.172
844 Women's textiles, knitted (articles as code 841, plus dresses skirts)	0.303	0.285	0.241	0.146	0.187
515 Organo-inorganic and heterocyclic compounds, nucleic acids-salts, sulphonamides	0.310	0.266	0.240	0.200	0.214
752 Automatic data-processing transcibing machines; magnetic optical readers, n.e.s.	0.263	0.231	0.240	0.092	0.208
633 Cork manufactures	0.255	0.251	0.237	0.126	0.224
848 Apparel articles accessories other than textile fabrics; headgear (all material)	0.341	0.274	0.236	0.147	0.184
333 Petroleum oils and oils obtained from bituminous minerals, crude	0.246	0.241	0.232	0.100	0.195
689 Miscellaneous non-ferrous base metals employed in metallurgy, and cermets	0.252	0.250	0.231	0.102	0.205
897 Jewellery, articles of goldsmiths' silversmiths' B2 semiprecious, n.e.s.	0.316	0.269	0.231	0.154	0.315
045 Cereals, unmilled (excluding wheat, rice, barley, maize)	0.333	0.271	0.229	0.279	0.263
841 Men's textile, not knitted (coat suit trouser short shirt underwear nightwear)	0.326	0.277	0.229	0.117	0.168
611 Leather	0.213	0.227	0.224	0.137	0.225
842 Women's textiles not knitted (articles as code 841, plus dresses skirts)	0.337	0.282	0.224	0.126	0.219

For sources and notes, see end of table.

Pour les sources et les notes, se reporter à la fin du tableau.

SITC group Revision 3 (3-digit level) ranked according to the concentration index in 2010 Groupes de la CTCI Révision 3 (positions à 3 chiffres) classés d'après l'indice de concentration en 2010	Concentration index (1) Indice de concentration (1)			Structural change index (2) Indice de changement structurel (2) 1995=0	
	2000	2005	2010	2000	2010
112 Alcoholic beverages	0.271	0.256	0.224	0.160	0.191
885 Watches & clocks	0.254	0.233	0.223	0.102	0.129
884 Optical goods, n.e.s.	0.237	0.215	0.223	0.119	0.332
831 Cases bags(storage hand executive equipment instrument gun travel shopping back)	0.310	0.267	0.222	0.096	0.223
759 Parts, accessorios for machines of groups 751, 752	0.234	0.205	0.219	0.130	0.320
792 Aircraft, associated equipment; spacecraft, satellites, launch vehicles; parts	0.239	0.217	0.218	0.282	0.376
285 Aluminium ores and concentrates (including alumina)	0.212	0.234	0.217	0.126	0.298
025 Eggs, birds' yolks, fresh, dried, preserved, sweetened or not, albumin	0.180	0.215	0.217	0.184	0.257
511 Hydrocarbons, n.e.s., halogenated, sulphonated, nitrated, nitrosated derivatives	0.167	0.190	0.217	0.152	0.229
342 Liquefied propane and butane	0.303	0.265	0.216	0.134	0.254
851 Footwear	0.301	0.253	0.216	0.109	0.197
751 Office machines	0.221	0.249	0.215	0.116	0.176
072 Cocoa	0.224	0.225	0.214	0.142	0.154
774 Electrodiagnostic apparatus, medical surgical dental veterinary radiological	0.229	0.243	0.212	0.143	0.160
343 Natural gas, whether or not liquefied	0.282	0.259	0.211	0.201	0.329
697 Household equipment of base metal, n.e.s.	0.272	0.267	0.210	0.138	0.166
037 Fish, crustaceans, molluscs, aquatic invertebrates (prepared preserved) n.e.s.	0.293	0.244	0.210	0.110	0.219
344 Petroleum gases and other gaseous hydrocarbons, n.e.s.	0.262	0.231	0.209	0.414	0.525
763 Sound or television image recorder reproducer; prepared unrecorded media	0.381	0.262	0.208	0.140	0.214
017 Meat, edible meat offal (prepared preserved) n.e.s.	0.223	0.229	0.208	0.158	0.246
781 Vehicles to transport less than 10 persons, including station-wagons race cars	0.347	0.259	0.207	0.145	0.232
899 Miscellaneous manufactured articles, n.e.s.	0.208	0.201	0.203	0.102	0.180
273 Stone, sand and gravel	0.164	0.151	0.201	0.202	0.383
714 Engines, motors, non-electric (exclude group 712, 713 and 718); parts of, n.e.s.	0.285	0.226	0.200	0.146	0.237
071 Coffee and coffee substitutes	0.247	0.212	0.200	0.097	0.132
813 Lighting fixtures and fittings, n.e.s.	0.301	0.273	0.198	0.161	0.176
621 Materials of rubber (e.g., pastes, plates, sheets, rods, thread, tubes, of rubber)	0.167	0.155	0.198	0.112	0.313
000 Pottery	0.313	0.251	0.196	0.097	0.223
671 Pig-iron, spiegeleisen, sponge iron, iron steel granules, powders, ferro-alloys	0.215	0.192	0.195	0.155	0.258
635 Wood manufactures, n.e.s.	0.291	0.271	0.192	0.181	0.186
058 Fruit, preserved, and fruit preparations (excluding fruit juices)	0.224	0.217	0.192	0.108	0.220
872 Instruments and appliances, n.e.s., (medical, surgical, dental or veterinary)	0.198	0.208	0.191	0.127	0.149
232 Synthetic rubber; reclaimed rubber; waste, parings, scrap of unhardened rubber	0.162	0.165	0.191	0.138	0.277
282 Ferrous waste and scrap; remelting scrap ingots of iron or steel	0.172	0.178	0.191	0.206	0.285
422 Fixed vegetable fats and oils, crude, refined or fractionated, other than "soft"	0.183	0.174	0.190	0.219	0.290
764 Telecommunications equipment and parts, n.e.s.; accessories within division 76	0.203	0.183	0.190	0.150	0.206
687 Tin	0.203	0.207	0.189	0.124	0.308
728 Other machinery or specialized industrial equipment; parts thereof, n.e.s.	0.170	0.158	0.189	0.164	0.172
612 Manufactures of leather or of composition leather, n.e.s.; saddlery and harness	0.240	0.217	0.188	0.202	0.269
771 Electric power machinery parts (excluding rotating electric plant, group 716)	0.225	0.193	0.187	0.136	0.228
718 Power-generating machinery, and parts thereof, n.e.s.	0.176	0.187	0.187	0.265	0.289
513 Carboxylic acid, anhydrides, halides, peroxides, peroxyacids; halogenate derivatives	0.168	0.216	0.186	0.156	0.265
772 Electrical apparatus to switch protect circuits or make circuit connections	0.179	0.171	0.185	0.121	0.278
724 Textile and leather machinery, and parts thereof, n.e.s.	0.148	0.174	0.184	0.131	0.233
541 Medicinal and pharmaceutical products, excluding medicines of group 542	0.187	0.196	0.184	0.128	0.174
846 Clothing accessories of textiles, knitted or crocheted or not (exluding babies)	0.194	0.194	0.183	0.187	0.228
059 Fruit and vegetable juice (unfermented, no added spirit, sweetened or not)	0.209	0.189	0.182	0.132	0.162
267 Other man-made fibres suitable for spinning; waste of man-made fibres	0.153	0.164	0.182	0.185	0.330
542 Medicines (including veterinary medicines)	0.154	0.202	0.181	0.159	0.208
277 Natural abrasives, n.e.s. (including industrial diamonds)	0.192	0.178	0.180	0.212	0.389
784 Parts and accessories of the motor vehicles of groups 722, 781, 782 and 783	0.236	0.212	0.179	0.111	0.246
793 Ships, boats (including hovercraft) and floating structures	0.150	0.120	0.178	0.399	0.449
035 Fish (dried, salted, in brine, smoked); flours, meals, pellets for human consump	0.222	0.196	0.177	0.140	0.237
873 Meters and counters, n.e.s.	0.250	0.201	0.177	0.123	0.189
335 Residual petroleum products, n.e.s., related mater.	0.155	0.165	0.176	0.193	0.320
325 Coke, semi-coke of coal, lignite, peat, agglomerated or not; retort carbon	0.194	0.193	0.176	0.249	0.393
593 Explosives and pyrotechnic products	0.198	0.221	0.175	0.186	0.294
775 Household-type electrical and non-electrical equipment, n.e.s.	0.194	0.187	0.175	0.130	0.203
874 Measuring, checking, analysing and controlling instruments and apparatus, n.e.s.	0.188	0.171	0.175	0.119	0.183
659 Floor coverings, etc.	0.227	0.220	0.174	0.192	0.237
001 Live animals other than animals of division 03	0.230	0.201	0.172	0.171	0.249
292 Crude vegetable materials, n.e.s.	0.201	0.193	0.172	0.112	0.181
778 Electrical machinery and apparatus, n.e.s.	0.183	0.169	0.172	0.121	0.221
713 Internal combustion piston engines, and parts thereof, n.e.s.	0.245	0.210	0.172	0.132	0.269

For sources and notes, see end of table.

Pour les sources et les notes, se reporter à la fin du tableau.

SITC group Revision 3 (3-digit level) ranked according to the concentration index in 2010 / Groupes de la CTCI Révision 3 (positions à 3 chiffres) classés d'après l'indice de concentration en 2010	Concentration index (1) / Indice de concentration (1)			Structural change index (2) / Indice de changement structurel (2) 1995=0	
	2000	2005	2010	2000	2010
034 Fish, fresh (live dead chilled frozen)	0.281	0.210	0.171	0.114	0.265
024 Cheese and curd	0.206	0.191	0.171	0.150	0.235
514 Nitrogen-function compounds	0.169	0.158	0.171	0.109	0.192
731 Machine tool to work metal sintered metal carbide cermet, not removing material	0.200	0.188	0.171	0.216	0.300
686 Zinc	0.207	0.178	0.169	0.140	0.411
524 Other inorganic chemicals; organic and inorganic compounds of precious metals	0.206	0.169	0.169	0.200	0.208
812 Sanitary, plumbing and heating fixtures and fittings, n.e.s.	0.176	0.181	0.168	0.188	0.221
248 Wood, simply worked, and railway sleepers of wood	0.288	0.283	0.167	0.161	0.294
057 Fruits and nuts (excluding oil nuts), fresh or dried	0.190	0.170	0.166	0.136	0.215
574 Polyacetal, polyether, epoxide resin; polycarbonate, alkyd resin, polyester	0.137	0.144	0.165	0.110	0.204
696 Cutlery	0.220	0.193	0.165	0.140	0.218
748 Transmission shaft camshaft crankshaft; bearing housing; gearbox speed changer	0.203	0.178	0.165	0.110	0.236
291 Crude animal materials, nes	0.218	0.185	0.164	0.143	0.247
044 Maize (not including sweet corn), unmilled	0.188	0.192	0.164	0.194	0.222
351 Electric current	0.262	0.181	0.164	0.320	0.323
122 Tobacco, manufactured (whether or not containing tobacco substitutes)	0.178	0.185	0.164	0.194	0.310
735 Parts, n.e.s. and accessories for machines of groups 731, 733; tool holder	0.201	0.168	0.164	0.092	0.239
895 Office and stationery supplies, n.e.s.	0.198	0.177	0.163	0.111	0.195
571 Polymers of ethylene, in primary forms	0.150	0.160	0.163	0.145	0.264
746 Ball or roller bearings	0.163	0.160	0.162	0.097	0.228
625 Rubber tyres, interchangeable tyre treads, tyre flaps, inner tubes for wheels	0.197	0.187	0.162	0.147	0.188
223 Oil-seed, oleaginous fruit to extract other vegetable oil; flour, meal of n.e.s.	0.179	0.192	0.162	0.234	0.429
575 Other plastics, in primary forms	0.140	0.147	0.161	0.117	0.239
672 Ingots, other primary forms of iron or steel; semi-finished products of	0.213	0.164	0.161	0.258	0.363
522 Inorganic chemical elements, oxides and halogen salts	0.163	0.175	0.160	0.111	0.203
011 Meat of bovine animals (fresh chilled frozen)	0.231	0.202	0.160	0.188	0.273
551 Essential oils, perfume and flavour materials	0.150	0.184	0.159	0.157	0.229
725 Paper mill pulp mill paper-cutting other paper manufacture machines; parts of	0.171	0.139	0.159	0.184	0.245
562 Fertilizers (excluding group 272)	0.142	0.148	0.158	0.195	0.284
516 Other organic chemicals	0.202	0.163	0.156	0.102	0.215
882 Photographic and cinematographic supplies	0.170	0.147	0.156	0.111	0.310
023 Butter and other fats and oils derived from milk	0.213	0.184	0.156	0.175	0.268
893 Articles, n.e.s., of plastics	0.182	0.174	0.155	0.115	0.150
056 Vegetables, roots and tubers (prepared preserved) n.e.s.	0.199	0.183	0.154	0.124	0.187
062 Sugar confectionery	0.186	0.183	0.154	0.172	0.213
685 Lead	0.161	0.159	0.153	0.201	0.267
272 Fertilizers, crude (excluding those of division 56)	0.148	0.176	0.153	0.174	0.316
111 Non-alcoholic beverages, n.e.s.	0.179	0.165	0.153	0.207	0.295
054 Vegetables and veg products (fresh chilled frozen preserved dried edible) n.e.s.	0.195	0.187	0.152	0.136	0.248
694 Nails, screws, nuts, bolts, rivets, of iron, steel, copper or aluminium	0.217	0.194	0.152	0.130	0.233
629 Articles of rubber, n.e.s.	0.180	0.172	0.152	0.133	0.193
747 Appliances for pipes boiler shells tanks vats; pressure and temperature valves	0.202	0.173	0.152	0.139	0.206
266 Synthetic fibres suitable for spinning	0.188	0.186	0.152	0.102	0.263
684 Aluminium	0.181	0.177	0.151	0.110	0.174
722 Tractors (excluding headings 714.14 & 744.15)	0.236	0.212	0.151	0.131	0.243
898 Musical instrument, parts accessory; tape, sound recording (excluding 763 & 883)	0.179	0.172	0.151	0.122	0.262
737 Metalworking machinery (other than machine tools), and parts thereof, n.e.s.	0.163	0.179	0.150	0.167	0.260
773 Equipment for distributing electricity, n.e.s.	0.220	0.185	0.150	0.113	0.223
786 Trailers semi-trailers vehicles not mechanically-propelled; transport containers	0.198	0.163	0.149	0.159	0.207
598 Miscellaneous chemical products, n.e.s.	0.145	0.146	0.148	0.133	0.178
245 Fuel wood (excluding wood waste) and wood charcoal	0.213	0.173	0.148	0.232	0.301
075 Spices	0.192	0.165	0.147	0.118	0.216
791 Railway vehicles (including hovertrains) and associated equipment	0.214	0.139	0.147	0.254	0.381
711 Steam vapour superheated water boiler, auxiliary plant for use with; parts of	0.170	0.124	0.145	0.332	0.403
651 Textile yarn	0.152	0.150	0.145	0.119	0.295
695 Tools for use in the hand or in machine	0.182	0.162	0.144	0.118	0.188
592 Starches, inulin and wheat gluten; albuminoidal substances; glues	0.151	0.142	0.144	0.117	0.216
582 Plates, sheets, film, foil and strip, of plastics	0.144	0.136	0.143	0.119	0.236
012 Other meat and edible meat offal (fresh chilled frozen)	0.224	0.181	0.142	0.157	0.320
712 Steam turbines and other vapour turbines, and parts thereof, n.e.s.	0.174	0.160	0.141	0.451	0.418
742 Liquid pump, with without a fitted measuring device; liquid elevator; parts for	0.156	0.151	0.140	0.128	0.224
411 Animals oils and fats	0.124	0.130	0.140	0.217	0.303
721 Agricultural machinery (excluding tractors), and parts thereof	0.167	0.150	0.139	0.117	0.181
532 Dyeing and tanning extracts, and synthetic tanning materials	0.126	0.138	0.139	0.144	0.251

For sources and notes, see end of table.

Pour les sources et les notes, se reporter à la fin du tableau.

SITC group Revision 3 (3-digit level) ranked according to the concentration index in 2010 Groupes de la CTCI Révision 3 (positions à 3 chiffres) classés d'après l'indice de concentration en 2010	Concentration index (1) Indice de concentration (1)			Structural change index (2) Indice de changement structurel (2) 1995=0	
	2000	2005	2010	2000	2010
745 Non-electrical machinery, tools and mechanical apparatus, parts thereof, n.e.s.	0.163	0.153	0.139	0.118	0.161
663 Mineral manufactures, n.e.s.	0.199	0.163	0.139	0.146	0.158
785 Motor cycles, mopeds, cycles, motorized and non-motorized; invalid carriages	0.214	0.203	0.139	0.205	0.217
675 Flat-rolled products of alloy steel	0.172	0.190	0.138	0.155	0.232
743 Pump (non liquid), air gas compressor, fan ventilation filter; centrifuge; parts	0.170	0.159	0.137	0.110	0.185
749 Non-electric parts and accessories of machinery, n.e.s.	0.154	0.145	0.137	0.127	0.211
655 Knitted, crocheted fabric (include tubular knit, pile, openwork fabric), n.e.s.	0.171	0.163	0.137	0.202	0.391
573 Polymers of vinyl chloride or of other halogenated olefins, in primary forms	0.174	0.150	0.136	0.222	0.337
782 Motor vehicles for the transport of goods and special-purpose motor vehicles	0.250	0.195	0.136	0.169	0.269
073 Chocolate and other food preparations containing cocoa, n.e.s.	0.171	0.154	0.136	0.151	0.215
699 Manufactures of base metal, n.e.s.	0.192	0.169	0.136	0.142	0.176
278 Other crude minerals	0.164	0.142	0.136	0.105	0.174
634 Veneers, plywood, particle board, and other wood, worked, n.e.s.	0.221	0.242	0.135	0.169	0.275
048 Cereal preparations and preparations of flour or starch of fruits or vegetables	0.159	0.152	0.135	0.180	0.231
673 Flat-rolled products of iron or non-alloy steel, not clad, plated or coated	0.149	0.137	0.134	0.172	0.308
334 Petroleum oil, oil from bituminous (excl crude); preparations, n.e.s., > 70% oil	0.171	0.168	0.134	0.151	0.233
046 Meal and flour of wheat and flour of meslin	0.091	0.159	0.133	0.374	0.499
892 Printed matter	0.165	0.155	0.133	0.117	0.151
121 Tobacco, unmanufactured; tobacco refuse	0.147	0.148	0.133	0.185	0.326
664 Glass	0.165	0.147	0.133	0.143	0.214
654 Other textile fabrics, woven n.e.s.	0.151	0.140	0.132	0.180	0.268
642 Paper and paperboard, cut to size or shape, and articles of paper or paperboard	0.155	0.148	0.132	0.118	0.164
716 Rotating electric plant, and parts thereof, n.e.s.	0.185	0.165	0.130	0.167	0.205
074 Tea and maté	0.146	0.133	0.130	0.174	0.240
641 Paper and paperboard	0.183	0.164	0.129	0.103	0.190
583 Plastic monofilament, cross-section > 1 mm, rods, sticks, profile shapes	0.184	0.146	0.127	0.246	0.329
726 Printing and bookbinding machinery, and parts thereof	0.167	0.148	0.126	0.134	0.271
421 Fixed vegetable fats and oils, "soft", crude, refined or fractionated	0.127	0.146	0.125	0.235	0.221
677 Rails or railway track construction material, of iron or steel	0.162	0.138	0.124	0.316	0.340
678 Wire of iron or steel	0.170	0.150	0.124	0.148	0.236
531 Synthetic organic colouring matter and colour lakes, preparations based thereon	0.136	0.128	0.124	0.094	0.225
597 Prepared additives: mineral oil; transmission; anti-freeze, de-ice; lubricating	0.108	0.113	0.124	0.131	0.205
657 Special yarns, special textile fabrics and related products	0.129	0.133	0.124	0.119	0.205
665 Glassware	0.183	0.153	0.123	0.140	0.269
741 Heating and cooling equipment, and parts thereof, n.e.s.	0.130	0.127	0.118	0.159	0.214
783 Road motor vehicles, n.e.s.	0.179	0.136	0.118	0.236	0.311
679 Tubes, pipes and hollow profiles, and tube or pipe fittings, of iron or steel	0.146	0.130	0.116	0.182	0.240
652 Cotton fabrics, woven (not including narrow or special fabrics)	0.147	0.129	0.115	0.153	0.365
553 Perfumery, cosmetic or toilet preparations (excluding soaps)	0.137	0.133	0.115	0.124	0.173
674 Flat-rolled products of iron or non-alloy steel, clad, plated or coated	0.142	0.142	0.114	0.153	0.285
744 Mechanical handling equipment, and parts thereof, n.e.s.	0.188	0.157	0.114	0.204	0.202
081 Feeding stuff for animals (excluding unmilled cereals)	0.127	0.122	0.112	0.121	0.216
723 Civil engineering and contractors' plant and equipment; parts thereof	0.157	0.148	0.112	0.171	0.279
431 Animal, vegetable fats, oils, processed; waxes; inedible preparations of, n.e.s.	0.112	0.123	0.112	0.220	0.259
653 Fabrics, woven, of man-made textiles (excluding narrow or special fabrics)	0.145	0.117	0.112	0.180	0.335
693 Wire products (excluding insulated electrical wiring) and fencing grills	0.164	0.148	0.111	0.155	0.205
656 Tulles, lace, embroidery, ribbons, trimmings and other smallwares	0.144	0.125	0.110	0.185	0.295
042 Rice	0.113	0.088	0.109	0.309	0.334
047 Other cereal meals and flours	0.088	0.116	0.107	0.303	0.396
022 Milk, cream and milk products (excluding butter, cheese)	0.127	0.120	0.104	0.207	0.314
533 Pigments, paints, varnishes and related materials	0.115	0.110	0.103	0.114	0.172
581 Tubes, pipes and hoses, and fittings therefor, of plastics	0.138	0.122	0.102	0.148	0.220
091 Margarine and shortening	0.113	0.115	0.102	0.384	0.388
591 Insecticide, rodenticide, fungicide, herbicide, plant-growth reg, disinfectant	0.124	0.115	0.101	0.120	0.204
661 Lime, cement, fabricated construction material (excluding glass, clay material)	0.220	0.225	0.099	0.246	0.324
691 Structures and parts of structures, n.e.s., of iron, steel or aluminium	0.146	0.123	0.098	0.221	0.283
676 Iron and steel bars, rods, angles, shapes and sections (including sheet piling)	0.164	0.122	0.097	0.199	0.254
811 Prefabricated buildings	0.182	0.124	0.097	0.311	0.438
098 Edible products and preparations, n.e.s.	0.110	0.109	0.097	0.161	0.191
523 Metallic salts and peroxysalts, of inorganic acids	0.120	0.106	0.096	0.109	0.163
554 Soaps, cleansing and polishing preparations	0.112	0.114	0.096	0.118	0.178
692 Metal containers for storage or transport	0.127	0.114	0.095	0.158	0.212
041 Wheat (including spelt) and meslin, unmilled	0.103	0.102	0.092	0.232	0.313
662 Clay construction materials and refractory construction materials	0.168	0.145	0.090	0.202	0.278
727 Food-processing machines (excluding domestic); parts thereof	0.106	0.105	0.090	0.174	0.204
061 Sugar, molasses and honey	0.115	0.108	0.088	0.197	0.267
269 Worn clothing and other worn textile articles; rags	0.080	0.076	0.074	0.281	0.425

For sources and notes, see next page.

Pour les sources et les notes, se reporter à la page suivante.

3

Sources:
- UNCTAD secretariat calculations based on UN DESA Statistics Division, *COMTRADE* database and on IMF, *Direction of Trade Statistics*

Notes:

(1) Concentration index:
The Herfindahl-Hirschmann index is a measure of the degree of market concentration. It has been normalized to obtain values ranking from 0 to 1 (maximum concentration), according to the following formula:

$$H_i = \frac{\sqrt{\sum_{j=1}^{n}(\frac{x_{ij}}{X_i})^2} - \sqrt{\frac{1}{n}}}{1 - \sqrt{\frac{1}{n}}}$$

where

H_i = Value of concentration index for product i

x_{ij} = Value of exports or imports for country j and product i

$$X_i = \sum_{j=1}^{n} x_{ij} \quad \text{and}$$

n = maximum number of individual economies

An index value that is close to 1 indicates a very concentrated market. On the contrary, values closer to 0 reflect a more equal distribution of market shares among exporters or importers.

(2) Structural change index:
This index, ranging from 0 to 1 reveals the structural change in trade for a particular product as compared to the reference year (1995 = 0).

An index value close to 1 indicates a significant change in the composition of exporters (importers). On the contrary, values closer to 0 would demonstrate a higher degree of "traditionality" in the markets over the period concerned.

The value is calculated as follows:

$$I_i = \frac{\sum_{j}\left|S^1_{ij} - S^0_{ij}\right|}{2}$$

where

I_i = Value of structure index for product *i*

S^0_{ij} = Share of trade of product *i* for country *j* in 1995

S^1_{ij} = Share of trade of product *i* for the country *j* in the concerned year

Sources :
- Calculs du secrétariat de la CNUCED basés sur des données de ONU DAES Division de statistique, *COMTRADE* et sur FMI, *Direction of Trade Statistics*

Notes :

(1) Indice de concentration :
L'indice Herfindahl-Hirschmann mesure le degré de concentration des marchés. Il a été normalisé afin d'obtenir des valeurs comprises entre 0 et 1 (concentration maximale), d'après la formule suivante :

$$H_i = \frac{\sqrt{\sum_{j=1}^{n}(\frac{x_{ij}}{X_i})^2} - \sqrt{\frac{1}{n}}}{1 - \sqrt{\frac{1}{n}}}$$

où

H_i = Valeur de l'indice de concentration pour le produit i

x_{ij} = Valeur des exportations ou des importations du pays j pour le produit i

$$X_i = \sum_{j=1}^{n} x_{ij} \quad \text{et}$$

n = nombre maximum d'économies individuelles

Un indice proche de 1 indique une concentration très forte du marché pour ce produit en particulier. En revanche, une valeur proche de 0 démontre une répartition plus homogène du commerce entre les exportateurs ou les importateurs.

(2) Indice de changement structurel :
Cet indice, dont la valeur est comprise entre 0 et 1, représente les changements de structure du commerce par rapport à une année de référence (1995 = 0).

Une valeur proche de 1 indique un important changement structurel du commerce de ce produit, c'est à dire, une grande variation des parts de marché au sein des exportateurs ou importateurs, par rapport à l'année de référence. Plus la valeur de l'indice est proche de 0, plus la structure du commerce de ce produit est stable.

Il est calculé comme suit :

$$I_i = \frac{\sum_{j}\left|S^1_{ij} - S^0_{ij}\right|}{2}$$

où

I_i = Valeur de l'indice de changement structurel, pour le produit *i*

S^0_{ij} = Part du commerce du produit *i* pour le pays *j* par rapport au commerce total de ce produit pour l'année 1995

S^1_{ij} = Part du commerce du produit *i* pour le pays *j*, par rapport au commerce total de ce produit pour l'année concernée

4

INTERNATIONAL **MERCHANDISE** TRADE INDICATORS

INDICATEURS DU COMMERCE INTERNATIONAL DES **MARCHANDISES**

1
2
3
4
5
6
7
8

Region, country or territory	Exports - Exportations					
	2000			2010		
	Number of products exported	Diversification index	Concentration index	Number of products exported	Diversification index	Concentration index
	Nombre de produits exportés	Indice de diversification	Indice de concentration	Nombre de produits exportés	Indice de diversification	Indice de concentration
	(1)	(2)	(3)	(1)	(2)	(3)
WORLD	261	0.000	0.074	260	0.000	0.075
DEVELOPING ECONOMIES	261	0.261	0.129	260	0.212	0.123
TRANSITION ECONOMIES	259	0.378	0.220	260	0.500	0.527
DEVELOPED ECONOMIES	261	0.134	0.071	260	0.180	0.061
Developing economies: Africa	260	0.615	0.333	260	0.562	0.387
Eastern Africa	259	0.696	0.131	260	0.677	0.198
Burundi	14	0.738	0.693	34	0.745	0.539
Comoros	99	0.752	0.760	4	0.749	0.506
Djibouti	181	0.531	0.116	206	0.622	0.300
Eritrea	130	0.629	0.193	176	0.650	0.116
Ethiopia	27	0.570	0.504	131	0.800	0.348
Kenya	252	0.743	0.264	239	0.641	0.186
Madagascar	218	0.758	0.255	231	0.686	0.181
Malawi	73	0.865	0.616	133	0.800	0.519
Mauritius	227	0.831	0.335	229	0.714	0.245
Mayotte	87	0.568	0.443	12	0.579	0.217
Mozambique	214	0.787	0.302	233	0.840	0.511
Rwanda	121	0.723	0.435	87	0.823	0.402
Seychelles	175	0.804	0.635	76	0.815	0.458
Somalia	33	0.800	0.652	27	0.751	0.412
Uganda	207	0.862	0.373	250	0.737	0.188
United Republic of Tanzania	241	0.791	0.219	255	0.746	0.194
Zambia	240	0.847	0.465	251	0.861	0.686
Zimbabwe	196	0.746	0.263	178	0.764	0.198
Middle Africa	243	0.842	0.720	229	0.826	0.818
Angola	45	0.817	0.883	76	0.832	0.970
Cameroon	228	0.806	0.444	240	0.722	0.360
Central African Republic	32	0.836	0.680	51	0.764	0.330
Chad	23	0.773	0.731	51	0.753	0.809
Congo	163	0.795	0.676	120	0.792	0.762
Dem. Rep. of the Congo	185	0.810	0.602	213	0.807	0.368
Equatorial Guinea	16	0.673	0.799	30	0.737	0.819
Gabon	79	0.871	0.735	137	0.841	0.735
Sao Tome and Principe	122	0.676	0.388	4	0.630	0.437
Northern Africa	257	0.723	0.393	256	0.648	0.420
Algeria	101	0.835	0.515	108	0.788	0.523
Egypt	231	0.680	0.314	231	0.587	0.133
Libyan Arab Jamahiriya	82	0.806	0.778	136	0.806	0.795
Morocco	246	0.720	0.177	250	0.664	0.155
Sudan	74	0.820	0.489	140	0.810	0.755
Tunisia	190	0.667	0.207	229	0.544	0.162
Southern Africa	260	0.566	0.134	260	0.578	0.141
Botswana	237	0.870	0.709	186	0.857	0.595
Lesotho	32	0.822	0.396	23	0.881	0.437
Namibia	250	0.811	0.344	219	0.764	0.223
South Africa	260	0.560	0.118	260	0.583	0.151
Swaziland	170	0.759	0.227	190	0.729	0.242
Western Africa	259	0.783	0.635	260	0.717	0.544
Benin	70	0.802	0.572	138	0.752	0.369
Burkina Faso	84	0.743	0.545	118	0.825	0.498
Cape Verde	11	0.697	0.507	16	0.735	0.484
Côte d'Ivoire	229	0.806	0.317	180	0.701	0.349
Gambia	174	0.753	0.359	23	0.690	0.321
Ghana	238	0.801	0.313	228	0.822	0.464
Guinea	51	0.842	0.581	92	0.810	0.439
Guinea-Bissau	60	0.669	0.585	12	0.751	0.887
Liberia	27	0.832	0.565	145	0.687	0.430
Mali	212	0.793	0.624	137	0.870	0.628
Mauritania	138	0.809	0.485	189	0.805	0.484
Niger	64	0.837	0.497	100	0.804	0.378
Nigeria	136	0.885	0.928	185	0.803	0.768

For sources and notes, see end of table.

4.1.1 Indices de concentration et de diversification des exportations et importations des pays et des régions géographiques

Imports - Importations						Régions, pays ou territoires
2000			2010			
Number of products imported	Diversification index	Concentration index	Number of products imported	Diversification index	Concentration index	
Nombre de produits importés	Indice de diversification	Indice de concentration	Nombre de produits importés	Indice de diversification	Indice de concentration	
(1)	(2)	(3)	(1)	(2)	(3)	
261	0.000	0.073	260	0.000	0.076	**MONDE**
261	0.176	0.087	260	0.161	0.089	ÉCONOMIES EN DÉVELOPPEMENT
259	0.307	0.053	260	0.254	0.053	ÉCONOMIES EN TRANSITION
260	0.074	0.077	260	0.106	0.080	ÉCONOMIES DÉVELOPPÉES
260	0.272	0.087	260	0.261	0.060	Economies en développement : Afrique
259	0.402	0.079	260	0.390	0.109	*Afrique orientale*
231	0.524	0.139	243	0.510	0.097	Burundi
219	0.546	0.123	138	0.532	0.111	Comores
219	0.510	0.094	254	0.499	0.094	Djibouti
219	0.552	0.089	247	0.529	0.107	Érythrée
200	0.481	0.169	223	0.499	0.165	Éthiopie
254	0.414	0.112	249	0.385	0.131	Kenya
244	0.484	0.138	250	0.489	0.113	Madagascar
253	0.512	0.100	256	0.511	0.115	Malawi
215	0.472	0.109	222	0.388	0.133	Maurice
237	0.463	0.084	179	0.490	0.105	Mayotte
256	0.439	0.070	256	0.498	0.131	Mozambique
228	0.516	0.117	257	0.489	0.079	Rwanda
233	0.557	0.249	198	0.565	0.238	Seychelles
106	0.690	0.196	138	0.671	0.283	Somalie
255	0.491	0.123	255	0.453	0.147	Ouganda
254	0.442	0.088	259	0.481	0.180	République-Unie de Tanzanie
257	0.463	0.106	260	0.486	0.138	Zambie
259	0.477	0.165	259	0.498	0.105	Zimbabwe
258	0.422	0.066	259	0.422	0.070	*Afrique centrale*
254	0.491	0.071	253	0.503	0.069	Angola
196	0.526	0.179	211	0.485	0.211	Cameroun
202	0.494	0.098	170	0.617	0.154	République centrafricaine
199	0.475	0.099	222	0.486	0.103	Tchad
238	0.435	0.064	250	0.472	0.061	Congo
245	0.508	0.113	254	0.489	0.069	Rép. dém. du Congo
198	0.588	0.227	228	0.558	0.279	Guinée équatoriale
244	0.458	0.074	221	0.464	0.076	Gabon
192	0.577	0.129	118	0.493	0.151	Sao Tomé-et-Principe
258	0.360	0.055	258	0.344	0.056	*Afrique septentrionale*
230	0.478	0.088	232	0.488	0.087	Algérie
251	0.431	0.077	247	0.388	0.071	Égypte
245	0.433	0.077	258	0.443	0.087	Jamahiriya arabe libyenne
238	0.415	0.111	250	0.327	0.090	Maroc
242	0.413	0.073	248	0.451	0.080	Soudan
242	0.404	0.078	247	0.386	0.077	Tunisie
260	0.292	0.159	260	0.286	0.183	*Afrique australe*
259	0.402	0.062	259	0.456	0.143	Botswana
254	0.551	0.112	152	0.790	0.278	Lesotho
258	0.378	0.082	237	0.579	0.263	Namibie
260	0.338	0.190	259	0.308	0.216	Afrique du Sud
229	0.469	0.083	237	0.468	0.086	Swaziland
260	0.397	0.079	260	0.371	0.077	*Afrique occidentale*
157	0.569	0.152	193	0.616	0.173	Bénin
229	0.499	0.164	251	0.536	0.174	Burkina Faso
233	0.430	0.083	250	0.473	0.107	Cap-Vert
245	0.520	0.250	220	0.475	0.247	Côte d'Ivoire
233	0.579	0.116	168	0.576	0.145	Gambie
253	0.416	0.102	241	0.394	0.116	Ghana
241	0.537	0.160	211	0.509	0.173	Guinée
204	0.536	0.108	146	0.574	0.160	Guinée-Bissau
223	0.870	0.856	235	0.810	0.635	Libéria
240	0.525	0.161	245	0.539	0.206	Mali
231	0.447	0.095	248	0.566	0.126	Mauritanie
249	0.545	0.177	193	0.559	0.104	Niger
257	0.461	0.061	257	0.418	0.070	Nigéria

Pour les sources et les notes, se reporter à la fin du tableau.

Region, country or territory	Exports - Exportations					
	2000			2010		
	Number of products exported	Diversification index	Concentration index	Number of products exported	Diversification index	Concentration index
	Nombre de produits exportés	Indice de diversification	Indice de concentration	Nombre de produits exportés	Indice de diversification	Indice de concentration
	(1)	(2)	(3)	(1)	(2)	(3)
Saint Helena	140	0.547	0.309	92	0.628	0.400
Senegal	151	0.757	0.226	190	0.749	0.267
Sierra Leone	10	0.654	0.532	220	0.711	0.265
Togo	216	0.753	0.285	165	0.693	0.206
Developing economies: America	**260**	**0.307**	**0.110**	**259**	**0.355**	**0.126**
Caribbean	*255*	*0.674*	*0.255*	*259*	*0.586*	*0.169*
Anguilla	109	0.558	0.228	156	0.562	0.240
Antigua and Barbuda	210	0.707	0.077	226	0.620	0.140
Aruba	196	0.838	0.810	237	0.753	0.397
Bahamas	223	0.763	0.273	82	0.799	0.419
Barbados	231	0.631	0.171	231	0.570	0.133
Cuba	126	0.849	0.348	242	0.765	0.321
Dominica	20	0.730	0.395	24	0.705	0.407
Dominican Republic	235	0.732	0.224	247	0.685	0.133
Grenada	162	0.660	0.284	25	0.650	0.235
Haiti	137	0.723	0.458	62	0.745	0.491
Jamaica	109	0.810	0.544	221	0.751	0.425
Montserrat	70	0.440	0.161	85	0.568	0.359
Netherlands Antilles	241	0.760	0.693	252	0.762	0.692
Saint Kitts and Nevis	169	0.688	0.343	198	0.685	0.340
Saint Lucia	163	0.694	0.503	100	0.621	0.304
Saint Vincent and the Grenadines	27	0.790	0.386	25	0.782	0.529
Trinidad and Tobago	239	0.779	0.370	201	0.749	0.360
Turks and Caicos Islands	106	0.558	0.269	170	0.572	0.191
Central America	*253*	*0.375*	*0.125*	*259*	*0.382*	*0.133*
Belize	197	0.787	0.290	189	0.756	0.382
Costa Rica	243	0.619	0.270	245	0.683	0.362
El Salvador	243	0.608	0.212	245	0.606	0.215
Guatemala	255	0.700	0.184	253	0.668	0.139
Honduras	239	0.806	0.293	218	0.772	0.224
Mexico	250	0.388	0.137	257	0.410	0.148
Nicaragua	221	0.778	0.251	237	0.818	0.213
Panama	243	0.622	0.162	248	0.586	0.132
South America	*258*	*0.508*	*0.154*	*259*	*0.512*	*0.162*
Argentina	254	0.552	0.137	251	0.587	0.151
Bolivia (Plurinational State of)	221	0.754	0.183	144	0.830	0.431
Brazil	254	0.510	0.088	251	0.519	0.157
Chile	251	0.747	0.289	238	0.758	0.400
Colombia	215	0.637	0.295	233	0.640	0.341
Ecuador	154	0.759	0.450	193	0.718	0.501
Falkland Islands (Malvinas)	81	0.709	0.706	64	0.640	0.442
Guyana	193	0.815	0.326	97	0.828	0.395
Paraguay	99	0.767	0.330	132	0.749	0.390
Peru	194	0.784	0.226	228	0.762	0.278
Suriname	210	0.786	0.530	203	0.787	0.453
Uruguay	166	0.614	0.170	203	0.672	0.191
Venezuela (Bolivarian Rep. of)	225	0.798	0.605	239	0.762	0.663
Developing economies: Asia	**261**	**0.306**	**0.132**	**260**	**0.250**	**0.114**
Eastern Asia	*257*	*0.379*	*0.098*	*257*	*0.395*	*0.108*
China	254	0.456	0.077	255	0.448	0.107
China, Hong Kong SAR	248	0.458	0.110	242	0.530	0.196
China, Macao SAR	226	0.792	0.332	205	0.596	0.203
China, Taiwan Province of	238	0.485	0.170	244	0.465	0.180
Korea, Dem. People's Rep. of	234	0.441	0.107	190	0.583	0.213
Korea, Republic of	240	0.390	0.157	248	0.435	0.148
Mongolia	72	0.839	0.360	127	0.845	0.489
Southern Asia	*259*	*0.608*	*0.235*	*259*	*0.494*	*0.193*
Afghanistan	51	0.816	0.358	224	0.720	0.282
Bangladesh	134	0.840	0.374	213	0.856	0.371
Bhutan	41	0.766	0.418	72	0.786	0.269
India	256	0.571	0.146	254	0.505	0.149
Iran (Islamic Rep. of)	229	0.832	0.801	258	0.751	0.747
Maldives	124	0.751	0.274	38	0.823	0.752

For sources and notes, see end of table.

Imports - Importations						Régions, pays ou territoires
2000			2010			
Number of products imported	Diversification index	Concentration index	Number of products imported	Diversification index	Concentration index	
Nombre de produits importés	Indice de diversification	Indice de concentration	Nombre de produits importés	Indice de diversification	Indice de concentration	
(1)	(2)	(3)	(1)	(2)	(3)	
210	0.556	0.207	203	0.581	0.264	Sainte-Hélène
244	0.444	0.133	253	0.452	0.182	Sénégal
236	0.498	0.226	203	0.633	0.363	Sierra Leone
238	0.568	0.142	206	0.613	0.242	Togo
260	**0.204**	**0.064**	**260**	**0.210**	**0.071**	**Économies en développement : Amérique**
259	*0.358*	*0.127*	*259*	*0.341*	*0.118*	*Caraïbes*
228	0.547	0.200	246	0.516	0.087	Anguilla
253	0.664	0.545	248	0.728	0.475	Antigua-et-Barbuda
244	0.476	0.098	251	0.491	0.206	Aruba
259	0.478	0.086	209	0.517	0.178	Bahamas
256	0.428	0.143	253	0.512	0.149	Barbade
250	0.429	0.159	254	0.436	0.142	Cuba
143	0.454	0.078	154	0.502	0.127	Dominique
253	0.397	0.105	257	0.351	0.100	République dominicaine
157	0.464	0.092	169	0.498	0.128	Grenade
232	0.530	0.123	225	0.601	0.154	Haïti
256	0.398	0.107	246	0.426	0.174	Jamaïque
195	0.393	0.091	..	..	..	Montserrat
246	0.681	0.617	256	0.580	0.439	Antilles néerlandaises
146	0.488	0.082	156	0.475	0.080	Saint-Kitts-et-Nevis
237	0.426	0.107	151	0.658	0.675	Sainte-Lucie
144	0.487	0.079	164	0.474	0.174	Saint-Vincent-et-les Grenadines
222	0.463	0.286	230	0.415	0.165	Trinité-et-Tobago
144	0.478	0.092	153	0.493	0.101	Îles Turques et Caïques
260	*0.275*	*0.087*	*259*	*0.269*	*0.088*	*Amérique centrale*
246	0.474	0.094	250	0.486	0.121	Belize
256	0.352	0.099	258	0.310	0.114	Costa Rica
259	0.398	0.079	257	0.395	0.080	El Salvador
231	0.381	0.081	236	0.412	0.125	Guatemala
252	0.533	0.112	240	0.481	0.124	Honduras
257	0.281	0.097	259	0.298	0.096	Mexique
210	0.433	0.108	217	0.422	0.129	Nicaragua
255	0.531	0.369	257	0.534	0.290	Panama
260	*0.236*	*0.060*	*259*	*0.232*	*0.070*	*Amérique du Sud*
256	0.303	0.069	256	0.334	0.090	Argentine
252	0.403	0.063	257	0.459	0.115	Bolivie (État plurinational de)
253	0.282	0.085	253	0.267	0.079	Brésil
256	0.291	0.101	249	0.289	0.107	Chili
240	0.377	0.053	256	0.340	0.072	Colombie
256	0.435	0.060	256	0.412	0.119	Équateur
186	0.566	0.413	189	0.566	0.182	Îles Falkland (Malvinas)
242	0.480	0.099	252	0.486	0.196	Guyana
212	0.457	0.127	217	0.469	0.126	Paraguay
240	0.354	0.082	242	0.309	0.084	Pérou
212	0.471	0.250	232	0.416	0.151	Suriname
228	0.331	0.090	244	0.324	0.120	Uruguay
259	0.301	0.057	250	0.338	0.053	Venezuela (Rép. bolivarienne du)
261	**0.215**	**0.106**	**260**	**0.204**	**0.106**	**Économies en développement : Asie**
260	*0.265*	*0.109*	*260*	*0.298*	*0.131*	*Asie orientale*
259	0.366	0.099	258	0.360	0.141	Chine
261	0.378	0.107	253	0.460	0.192	Chine (RAS de Hong Kong)
250	0.530	0.132	245	0.451	0.106	Chine (RAS de Macao)
257	0.360	0.160	254	0.352	0.138	Province chinoise de Taiwan
251	0.402	0.104	244	0.398	0.130	Corée, Rép. populaire dém. de
257	0.360	0.169	256	0.321	0.154	Corée, République de
178	0.509	0.158	219	0.487	0.176	Mongolie
259	*0.390*	*0.090*	*260*	*0.377*	*0.172*	*Asie méridionale*
230	0.714	0.157	254	0.589	0.215	Afghanistan
253	0.536	0.089	249	0.543	0.098	Bangladesh
208	0.448	0.097	198	0.517	0.105	Bhoutan
258	0.447	0.148	257	0.452	0.245	Inde
256	0.481	0.065	252	0.396	0.070	Iran (Rép. islamique d')
154	0.502	0.090	179	0.507	0.136	Maldives

Pour les sources et les notes, se reporter à la fin du tableau.

4.1.1 Export and import concentration and diversification indices of countries and geographical regions

Region, country or territory	Exports - Exportations					
	2000			2010		
	Number of products exported	Diversification index	Concentration index	Number of products exported	Diversification index	Concentration index
	Nombre de produits exportés	Indice de diversification	Indice de concentration	Nombre de produits exportés	Indice de diversification	Indice de concentration
	(1)	(2)	(3)	(1)	(2)	(3)
Nepal	89	0.563	0.324	118	0.656	0.140
Pakistan	167	0.797	0.215	221	0.717	0.199
Sri Lanka	172	0.726	0.240	238	0.750	0.212
South-Eastern Asia	**200**	**0.301**	**0.108**	**260**	**0.335**	**0.131**
Brunei Darussalam	92	0.800	0.601	135	0.816	0.674
Cambodia	81	0.832	0.359	137	0.799	0.337
Indonesia including East Timor	243	0.487	0.125	–	–	–
Indonesia	–	–	–	244	0.547	0.155
Lao People's Dem. Rep.	111	0.710	0.006	102	0.766	0.717
Malaysia	257	0.506	0.219	260	0.469	0.165
Myanmar	202	0.790	0.263	178	0.821	0.323
Philippines	219	0.624	0.428	226	0.607	0.326
Singapore	256	0.457	0.270	257	0.491	0.266
Thailand	256	0.403	0.108	251	0.388	0.086
Timor-Leste	–	–	–	8	0.771	0.457
Viet Nam	200	0.570	0.244	245	0.582	0.139
Western Asia	*260*	*0.669*	*0.571*	*260*	*0.563*	*0.487*
Bahrain	232	0.795	0.421	243	0.705	0.341
Iraq	59	0.811	0.966	124	0.876	0.972
Jordan	247	0.582	0.160	251	0.642	0.176
Kuwait	235	0.847	0.644	227	0.807	0.723
Lebanon	246	0.643	0.126	250	0.619	0.098
Occupied Palestinian territory	144	0.597	0.171	103	0.640	0.229
Oman	237	0.785	0.802	218	0.683	0.458
Qatar	237	0.841	0.604	226	0.796	0.486
Saudi Arabia	257	0.824	0.723	253	0.768	0.736
Syrian Arab Republic	239	0.780	0.622	240	0.637	0.264
Turkey	256	0.583	0.098	258	0.457	0.074
United Arab Emirates	258	0.082	0.540	200	0.505	0.435
Yemen	227	0.849	0.851	188	0.773	0.721
Developing economies: Oceania	**250**	**0.732**	**0.172**	**258**	**0.732**	**0.253**
American Samoa	156	0.678	0.201	104	0.705	0.276
Cook Islands	65	0.559	0.777	109	0.642	0.630
Fiji	226	0.782	0.239	253	0.700	0.174
French Polynesia	169	0.797	0.763	172	0.749	0.643
Guam	89	0.715	0.512	131	0.651	0.510
Kiribati	51	0.621	0.585	95	0.718	0.760
Marshall Islands	79	0.616	0.522	94	0.687	0.690
Micronesia (Federated States of)	47	0.587	0.715	65	0.687	0.940
Nauru	12	0.721	0.758	16	0.661	0.524
New Caledonia	61	0.889	0.641	229	0.888	0.586
Niue	83	0.562	0.358	..	0.722	0.504
Palau	49	0.633	0.565	48	0.598	0.912
Papua New Guinea	80	0.841	0.352	132	0.815	0.371
Samoa	9	0.695	0.628	13	0.778	0.744
Solomon Islands	126	0.799	0.581	26	0.862	0.728
Tokelau	96	0.461	0.113	131	0.486	0.126
Tonga	85	0.669	0.415	151	0.690	0.263
Tuvalu	54	0.474	0.163	..	0.589	0.350
Vanuatu	13	0.782	0.506	16	0.822	0.795
Wallis and Futuna Islands	39	0.533	0.395	55	0.530	0.450
Transition economies	**259**	**0.578**	**0.220**	**260**	**0.566**	**0.327**
Albania	227	0.750	0.238	242	0.698	0.191
Armenia	204	0.721	0.292	231	0.744	0.228
Azerbaijan	141	0.786	0.573	223	0.783	0.866
Belarus	251	0.550	0.170	238	0.548	0.250
Bosnia and Herzegovina	243	0.662	0.208	251	0.578	0.108
Croatia	225	0.555	0.139	232	0.450	0.125
Georgia	214	0.703	0.163	160	0.705	0.215
Kazakhstan	188	0.824	0.475	208	0.764	0.628
Kyrgyzstan	138	0.769	0.326	238	0.679	0.157
Montenegro	–	–	–	117	0.670	0.371
Republic of Moldova	217	0.717	0.225	178	0.671	0.136
Russian Federation	253	0.656	0.281	252	0.647	0.380

For sources and notes, see end of table.

	Imports - Importations					Régions, pays ou territoires
	2000			2010		
Number of products imported	Diversification index	Concentration index	Number of products imported	Diversification index	Concentration index	
Nombre de produits importés	Indice de diversification	Indice de concentration	Nombre de produits importés	Indice de diversification	Indice de concentration	
(1)	(2)	(3)	(1)	(2)	(3)	
226	0.564	0.181	228	0.496	0.137	Népal
248	0.530	0.200	248	0.462	0.182	Pakistan
233	0.472	0.096	238	0.437	0.099	Sri Lanka
260	*0.296*	*0.181*	*260*	*0.260*	*0.138*	*Asie du Sud-Est*
197	0.477	0.067	231	0.461	0.066	Brunéi Darussalam
250	0.637	0.177	220	0.606	0.186	Cambodge
259	0.364	0.078				Indonésie y compris le Timor oriental
			259	0.336	0.109	Indonésie
229	0.581	0.131	245	0.463	0.141	Rép. dém. populaire lao
259	0.419	0.274	258	0.331	0.170	Malaisie
245	0.461	0.083	239	0.488	0.123	Myanmar
248	0.419	0.271	249	0.377	0.214	Philippines
257	0.377	0.220	257	0.376	0.236	Singapour
259	0.347	0.141	257	0.315	0.123	Thaïlande
			252	0.589	0.202	Timor-Leste
238	0.457	0.120	255	0.412	0.089	Viet Nam
260	*0.264*	*0.056*	*260*	*0.282*	*0.058*	*Asie occidentale*
253	0.483	0.080	259	0.464	0.080	Bahreïn
226	0.602	0.125	259	0.484	0.063	Iraq
246	0.414	0.136	252	0.321	0.112	Jordanie
205	0.546	0.455	252	0.412	0.092	Koweït
253	0.412	0.113	257	0.421	0.126	Liban
210	0.504	0.117	211	0.570	0.129	Territoire palestinien occupé
257	0.472	0.127	259	0.441	0.117	Oman
214	0.419	0.084	254	0.468	0.088	Qatar
248	0.367	0.072	251	0.345	0.071	Arabie saoudite
252	0.476	0.059	250	0.474	0.150	République arabe syrienne
256	0.265	0.083	257	0.295	0.085	Turquie
259	0.331	0.064	260	0.393	0.123	Émirats arabes unis
243	0.476	0.076	256	0.512	0.150	Yémen
258	*0.441*	*0.160*	*258*	*0.426*	*0.149*	*Économies en développement : Océanie*
184	0.659	0.473	196	0.584	0.131	Samoa américaines
223	0.431	0.059	245	0.515	0.093	Îles Cook
248	0.438	0.088	204	0.487	0.257	Fidji
192	0.366	0.069	202	0.369	0.107	Polynésie française
196	0.687	0.533	209	0.664	0.529	Guam
219	0.503	0.095	237	0.622	0.191	Kiribati
195	0.797	0.780	189	0.825	0.756	Îles Marshall
191	0.533	0.132	189	0.511	0.116	Micronésie (États fédérés de)
174	0.606	0.392	141	0.532	0.229	Nauru
199	0.396	0.120	251	0.448	0.167	Nouvelle-Calédonie
4	0.654	0.376	178	0.687	0.538	Nioué
186	0.536	0.134	166	0.503	0.108	Palaos
249	0.520	0.193	230	0.508	0.185	Papouasie-Nouvelle-Guinée
233	0.540	0.172	244	0.520	0.138	Samoa
210	0.500	0.209	252	0.543	0.206	Îles Salomon
119	0.490	0.161	109	0.553	0.252	Tokélaou
225	0.594	0.271	255	0.524	0.101	Tonga
158	0.500	0.097	223	0.609	0.446	Tuvalu
229	0.545	0.186	180	0.525	0.135	Vanuatu
220	0.465	0.079	236	0.490	0.075	Îles Wallis-et-Futuna
259	*0.307*	*0.053*	*260*	*0.254*	*0.053*	*Économies en transition*
255	0.484	0.064	235	0.444	0.073	Albanie
248	0.539	0.130	255	0.343	0.089	Arménie
250	0.471	0.076	255	0.439	0.062	Azerbaïdjan
256	0.424	0.163	249	0.381	0.189	Bélarus
257	0.439	0.051	258	0.384	0.063	Bosnie-Herzégovine
245	0.320	0.098	248	0.255	0.084	Croatie
250	0.505	0.115	254	0.433	0.118	Géorgie
255	0.413	0.062	256	0.380	0.055	Kazakhstan
197	0.481	0.122	249	0.488	0.195	Kirghizistan
			218	0.450	0.080	Monténégro
255	0.534	0.135	252	0.406	0.091	République de Moldova
259	0.357	0.039	259	0.330	0.061	Fédération de Russie

Pour les sources et les notes, se reporter à la fin du tableau.

Region, country or territory	Exports - Exportations					
	2000			2010		
	Number of products exported	Diversification index	Concentration index	Number of products exported	Diversification index	Concentration index
	Nombre de produits exportés	Indice de diversification	Indice de concentration	Nombre de produits exportés	Indice de diversification	Indice de concentration
	(1)	(2)	(3)	(1)	(2)	(3)
Serbia and Montenegro	210	0.593	0.102	–	–	–
Serbia	–	–	–	254	0.538	0.077
Tajikistan	131	0.764	0.471	64	0.820	0.470
TFYR of Macedonia	236	0.656	0.180	217	0.652	0.186
Turkmenistan	182	0.773	0.569	196	0.753	0.472
Ukraine	246	0.605	0.131	252	0.566	0.130
Uzbekistan	165	0.789	0.374	207	0.720	0.212
Developed economies: America	**259**	**0.207**	**0.084**	**260**	**0.223**	**0.077**
Bermuda	160	0.697	0.366	197	0.744	0.487
Canada	259	0.381	0.133	260	0.359	0.138
Greenland	145	0.806	0.566	29	0.836	0.470
Saint Pierre and Miquelon	68	0.640	0.576	4	0.590	0.500
United States	257	0.263	0.091	260	0.258	0.083
Developed economies: Asia	**257**	**0.362**	**0.129**	**258**	**0.413**	**0.117**
Israel	213	0.564	0.300	230	0.576	0.273
Japan	255	0.376	0.135	254	0.437	0.125
Developed economies: Europe	**261**	**0.161**	**0.067**	**260**	**0.211**	**0.060**
Andorra	169	0.578	0.163	16	0.699	0.838
Austria	255	0.355	0.086	257	0.342	0.059
Belgium	259	0.343	0.092	258	0.362	0.097
Bulgaria	255	0.544	0.117	256	0.449	0.115
Cyprus	242	0.560	0.171	248	0.503	0.162
Czech Republic	260	0.424	0.087	259	0.408	0.108
Denmark	255	0.395	0.077	257	0.422	0.083
Estonia	233	0.600	0.232	253	0.462	0.108
Faeroe Islands	17	0.599	0.599	43	0.765	0.687
Finland	256	0.543	0.239	254	0.461	0.135
France	259	0.262	0.076	259	0.333	0.088
Germany	257	0.287	0.105	258	0.328	0.097
Gibraltar	150	0.669	0.288	128	0.743	0.811
Greece	253	0.537	0.123	254	0.463	0.103
Hungary	255	0.394	0.128	256	0.437	0.142
Iceland	202	0.824	0.381	220	0.827	0.456
Ireland	253	0.559	0.229	252	0.673	0.260
Italy	258	0.378	0.054	259	0.362	0.052
Latvia	206	0.683	0.208	252	0.475	0.081
Lithuania	227	0.552	0.161	253	0.487	0.188
Luxembourg	257	0.541	0.132	257	0.545	0.133
Malta	132	0.687	0.600	177	0.615	0.252
Netherlands	260	0.372	0.134	257	0.314	0.077
Norway	258	0.665	0.474	256	0.628	0.388
Poland	248	0.455	0.077	254	0.426	0.082
Portugal	259	0.454	0.107	259	0.434	0.071
Romania	242	0.549	0.130	250	0.420	0.094
Slovakia	248	0.489	0.144	257	0.445	0.160
Slovenia	224	0.453	0.104	252	0.459	0.176
Spain	259	0.355	0.129	256	0.375	0.100
Sweden	260	0.407	0.152	258	0.370	0.100
Switzerland	236	0.519	0.103	246	0.583	0.168
United Kingdom	255	0.234	0.100	259	0.297	0.106
Developed economies: Oceania	**259**	**0.529**	**0.100**	**258**	**0.633**	**0.224**
Australia	259	0.544	0.116	258	0.654	0.262
New Zealand	251	0.652	0.119	253	0.644	0.161

For sources and notes, see next page.

Imports - Importations						Régions, pays ou territoires
2000			2010			
Number of products imported Nombre de produits importés (1)	Diversification index Indice de diversification (2)	Concentration index Indice de concentration (3)	Number of products imported Nombre de produits importés (1)	Diversification index Indice de diversification (2)	Concentration index Indice de concentration (3)	
242	0.418	0.132	–	–	–	Serbie-et-Monténégro
–	–	–	256	0.359	0.149	Serbie
231	0.714	0.244	246	0.520	0.098	Tadjikistan
251	0.426	0.228	243	0.370	0.085	LERY de Macédoine
248	0.504	0.071	253	0.460	0.079	Turkménistan
247	0.462	0.226	255	0.367	0.145	Ukraine
248	0.483	0.094	249	0.434	0.079	Ouzbékistan
260	**0.151**	**0.099**	**260**	**0.196**	**0.115**	**Économies développées : Amérique**
235	0.645	0.373	254	0.770	0.683	Bermudes
260	0.219	0.089	260	0.220	0.073	Canada
231	0.483	0.193	189	0.519	0.165	Groenland
176	0.449	0.158	213	0.526	0.096	Saint-Pierre-et-Miquelon
259	0.171	0.105	260	0.220	0.127	États-Unis
259	**0.265**	**0.103**	**258**	**0.269**	**0.131**	**Économies développées : Asie**
256	0.259	0.171	254	0.267	0.151	Israël
258	0.284	0.107	258	0.286	0.135	Japon
260	**0.088**	**0.068**	**260**	**0.123**	**0.066**	**Économies développées : Europe**
181	0.518	0.096	241	0.543	0.196	Andorre
258	0.218	0.058	259	0.240	0.055	Autriche
260	0.248	0.078	259	0.274	0.095	Belgique
259	0.337	0.079	259	0.287	0.101	Bulgarie
226	0.360	0.104	250	0.369	0.164	Chypre
259	0.270	0.055	260	0.263	0.073	République tchèque
259	0.254	0.053	258	0.276	0.053	Danemark
258	0.336	0.091	258	0.334	0.109	Estonie
257	0.503	0.186	193	0.521	0.162	Îles Féroé
258	0.196	0.083	257	0.196	0.085	Finlande
258	0.144	0.065	258	0.195	0.071	France
258	0.169	0.106	258	0.177	0.075	Allemagne
229	0.763	0.560	210	0.798	0.778	Gibraltar
257	0.301	0.131	253	0.320	0.153	Grèce
253	0.277	0.089	256	0.331	0.125	Hongrie
222	0.375	0.092	227	0.457	0.158	Islande
258	0.292	0.139	260	0.355	0.095	Irlande
257	0.194	0.078	259	0.211	0.091	Italie
237	0.393	0.063	257	0.380	0.091	Lettonie
256	0.371	0.138	256	0.383	0.206	Lituanie
259	0.336	0.096	258	0.390	0.105	Luxembourg
256	0.502	0.316	233	0.457	0.188	Malte
259	0.216	0.114	257	0.215	0.098	Pays-Bas
258	0.306	0.079	257	0.332	0.064	Norvège
253	0.263	0.067	255	0.227	0.065	Pologne
259	0.210	0.070	259	0.224	0.077	Portugal
250	0.347	0.070	252	0.264	0.066	Roumanie
248	0.333	0.093	255	0.309	0.098	Slovaquie
249	0.301	0.062	255	0.284	0.115	Slovénie
260	0.207	0.092	259	0.181	0.092	Espagne
258	0.167	0.084	259	0.181	0.077	Suède
251	0.268	0.069	253	0.323	0.081	Suisse
256	0.179	0.085	258	0.223	0.077	Royaume-Uni
255	**0.226**	**0.087**	**258**	**0.227**	**0.097**	**Économies développées : Océanie**
258	0.229	0.087	258	0.236	0.099	Australie
245	0.245	0.089	256	0.274	0.096	Nouvelle-Zélande

Pour les sources et les notes, se reporter à la page suivante.

4.1.1 Export and import concentration and diversification indices of countries and geographical regions

Sources:
- UNCTAD secretariat calculations based on ONU DESA Statistics Division, Comtrade database

Notes:

(1) Number of products exported (or imported) at the three-digit SITC, Rev. 2 level; this figure includes only those products that are greater than $100,000 or more than 0.3 per cent of the country's total exports (or imports).
Data for the country groupings are calculated as weighted averages of individual countries data, including those that are estimated and not shown separately.

(2) The diversification index signals whether the structure of exports or imports by product of a given country or group of countries differ from the structure of product of the world. This index that ranges from 0 to 1 reveals the extent of the differences between the structure of trade of the country or country group and the world average. The index value closer to 1 indicates a bigger difference from the world average.

Diversification index is computed by measuring absolute deviation of the country share from world structure, as follows:

$$S_j = \frac{\sum_i \left| h_{ij} - h_i \right|}{2}$$

where h_{ij} = share of product i in total exports or imports of country or country group j
h_i = share of product i in total world exports or imports.

This index is a modified Finger-Kreinin measure of similarity in trade. For more information, please consult the article of Finger, J. M. and M. E. Kreinin (1979), "A measure of 'export similarity' and its possible uses" in the *Economic Journal*, 89: 905-12.

(3) Concentration index, also named Herfindahl-Hirschmann index, is a measure of the degree of market concentration. It has been normalized to obtain values ranking from 0 to 1 (maximum concentration), according to the following formula:

$$H_j = \frac{\sqrt{\sum_{i=1}^{n} \left(\frac{x_{ij}}{X_j} \right)^2} - \sqrt{1/n}}{1 - \sqrt{1/n}}$$

where H_j = country or country group index
Xij = value of exports for country j and product i

$$X_j = \sum_{i=1}^{n} x_{ij}$$

and n = number of products (SITC Revision 3 at 3-digit group level).

Sources :
- Calculs du secrétariat de la CNUCED fondés sur des données de ONU DAES Division de statistique, base de données Comtrade

Notes :

(1) Nombre de produits au niveau de groupes de la CTCI (rév. 2, position à 3 chiffres) exportés (ou importés) par chaque pays ; cependant, seuls les produits ayant une valeur supérieure à 100.000 dollars ou comptant pour plus de 0,3 % des exportations (ou des importations) totales du pays sont inclus.
Les indices de concentration et de diversification calculés au niveau des groupes de pays et du monde sont les moyennes arithmétiques des indices respectifs des pays, pondérées par la valeur de leurs exportations.

(2) L'indice de Diversification indique si la structure par produits des exportations d'un pays ou groupe de pays diverge peu ou beaucoup de la structure par produits des exportations totales dans le monde. Cet indice dont la valeur est comprise entre de 0 à 1, révèle l'ampleur des différences entre la structure des échanges d'un pays ou du groupe de pays et la moyenne mondiale. Plus l'indice est proche de 1, plus la divergence est forte.

L'indice de diversification mesure la déviation absolue de la structure du pays par rapport à la structure mondiale comme ci-dessous :

$$S_j = \frac{\sum_i \left| h_{ij} - h_i \right|}{2}$$

où h_{ij} = part du produit i dans le total des exportations (ou importations) du pays j
h_i = part du produit i dans le total des exportations (ou importations) mondiales.

Cet indice est une variante de l'indicateur de Finger-Kreinin sur la similarité de la structure du commerce. Pour plus d'information, veuillez consulter l'article de Finger, J. M. et M. E. Kreinin (1979), "A measure of 'export similarity' and its possible uses", dans l'*Economic Journal*, 89: 905-12.

(3) L'indice de concentration, aussi appelé indice de Herfindahl-Hirschmann, mesure le degré de concentration des marchés. Il a été normalisé afin d'obtenir des valeurs comprises entre 0 et 1 (concentration maximale), d'après la formule suivante :

$$H_j = \frac{\sqrt{\sum_{i=1}^{n} \left(\frac{x_{ij}}{X_j} \right)^2} - \sqrt{1/n}}{1 - \sqrt{1/n}}$$

où H_j = Indice du pays ou groupe de pays
X_{ij} = valeur des exportations du pays j pour le produit i

$$X_j = \sum_{i=1}^{n} x_{ij}$$

et n = nombre de produits (de la CTCI rév., position à 3 chiffres).

4.1.2 Export and import concentration and diversification indices of economic groupings

Region, country or territory	Exports - Exportations					
	2000			2010		
	Number of products exported	Diversification index	Concentration index	Number of products exported	Diversification index	Concentration index
	Nombre de produits exportés (1)	Indice de diversification (2)	Indice de concentration (3)	Nombre de produits exportés (1)	Indice de diversification (2)	Indice de concentration (3)
DEVELOPING ECONOMIES	**261**	**0.261**	**0.129**	**260**	**0.212**	**0.123**
Developing economies excluding China	261	0.268	0.146	260	0.241	0.161
Developing economies excluding LDCs	261	0.259	0.127	260	0.209	0.118
High-income developing countries	260	0.282	0.146	260	0.266	0.166
Middle-income developing countries	261	0.290	0.081	260	0.275	0.082
Low-income developing countries	260	0.649	0.267	260	0.472	0.212
Heavily indebted poor countries (IMF)	260	0.674	0.150	260	0.607	0.207
Landlocked developing countries	260	0.625	0.174	260	0.630	0.375
Small island developing States	254	0.657	0.171	259	0.627	0.192
Least developed countries	*260*	*0.717*	*0.330*	*260*	*0.673*	*0.435*
Africa and Haiti	260	0.746	0.404	260	0.711	0.574
Asia	256	0.745	0.301	251	0.705	0.237
Islands	202	0.853	0.341	68	0.868	0.450
Major petroleum and gas exporters	*259*	*0.786*	*0.690*	*260*	*0.700*	*0.646*
Africa	196	0.864	0.716	226	0.819	0.733
America	225	0.798	0.605	239	0.762	0.663
Asia	259	0.773	0.699	260	0.678	0.621
Major exporters of manufactured goods	*260*	*0.327*	*0.111*	*260*	*0.325*	*0.105*
America	250	0.388	0.137	257	0.410	0.148
Asia	260	0.358	0.121	260	0.348	0.110
Emerging economies	*260*	*0.273*	*0.126*	*260*	*0.264*	*0.100*
America	258	0.303	0.088	259	0.373	0.098
Asia	260	0.373	0.175	260	0.349	0.141
Newly industrialized Asian countries	*260*	*0.355*	*0.147*	*260*	*0.332*	*0.134*
First tier	259	0.386	0.147	260	0.390	0.161
Second tier	260	0.402	0.160	258	0.380	0.104
Developing economies: Africa	**260**	**0.615**	**0.333**	**260**	**0.562**	**0.387**
Northern Africa excluding Sudan	257	0.726	0.393	255	0.643	0.402
Sub-Saharan Africa	260	0.608	0.317	260	0.580	0.391
Sub-Saharan Africa excluding South Africa	260	0.722	0.490	260	0.674	0.545
Developing economies: America	**260**	**0.307**	**0.110**	**259**	**0.355**	**0.126**
Central America and Greater Caribbean Islands excluding Puerto Rico	254	0.373	0.119	259	0.375	0.127
Central America and Greater Caribbean Islands excluding Mexico and Puerto Rico	260	0.645	0.145	259	0.586	0.115
South America and Central America	260	0.304	0.113	259	0.363	0.129
South America excluding Brazil	257	0.608	0.244	259	0.574	0.219
Developing economies: Asia	**261**	**0.306**	**0.132**	**260**	**0.250**	**0.114**
Eastern and South-Eastern Asia excluding China	260	0.350	0.143	260	0.317	0.127
Southern Asia excluding India	257	0.734	0.436	259	0.677	0.478

For sources and notes, see end of table 4.1.1.

4.1.2 Indices de concentration et de diversification des exportations et importations des groupements économiques

Imports - Importations						Régions, pays ou territoires
2000			2010			
Number of products imported	Diversification index	Concentration index	Number of products imported	Diversification index	Concentration index	
Nombre de produits importés	Indice de diversification	Indice de concentration	Nombre de produits importés	Indice de diversification	Indice de concentration	
(1)	(2)	(3)	(1)	(2)	(3)	
261	0.176	0.087	260	0.161	0.089	ÉCONOMIES EN DÉVELOPPEMENT
261	0.163	0.087	260	0.154	0.083	Économies en développement sans la Chine
261	0.176	0.080	260	0.162	0.091	Économies en développement sans les PMA
260	0.181	0.104	260	0.179	0.095	Pays en développement à revenu élevé
261	0.222	0.091	260	0.222	0.092	Pays en développement à revenu intermédiaire
260	0.328	0.069	260	0.291	0.107	Pays en développement à revenu faible
260	0.393	0.076	260	0.374	0.091	Pays pauvres très endettés (FMI)
260	0.358	0.065	260	0.332	0.068	Pays en développement sans littoral
259	0.342	0.090	259	0.364	0.124	Petits États insulaires en développement
260	0.435	0.073	260	0.394	0.075	Pays les moins avancés
260	0.425	0.079	260	0.398	0.077	Afrique et Haïti
257	0.481	0.079	259	0.460	0.085	Asie
250	0.500	0.124	257	0.476	0.121	Îles
260	0.313	0.051	260	0.339	0.056	Principaux exportateurs de pétrole et de gaz
259	0.406	0.055	259	0.388	0.059	Afrique
259	0.301	0.057	250	0.338	0.053	Amérique
259	0.337	0.058	260	0.357	0.065	Asie
260	0.239	0.122	260	0.246	0.126	Principaux exportateurs d'articles manufacturés
257	0.281	0.097	259	0.298	0.096	Amérique
260	0.263	0.134	260	0.266	0.135	Asie
260	0.230	0.132	260	0.189	0.110	Économies émergentes
259	0.235	0.075	260	0.226	0.076	Amérique
260	0.306	0.176	260	0.265	0.143	Asie
260	0.252	0.145	260	0.238	0.135	Économies nouvellement industrialisées d'Asie
259	0.262	0.136	260	0.272	0.146	Première génération
260	0.314	0.179	260	0.245	0.113	Deuxième génération
260	0.283	0.067	260	0.284	0.068	Économies en développement : Afrique
258	0.361	0.056	258	0.346	0.058	Afrique septentrionale sans le Soudan
260	0.289	0.085	260	0.291	0.086	Afrique subsaharienne
260	0.371	0.065	260	0.353	0.069	Afrique subsaharienne sans l'Afrique du Sud
260	0.204	0.064	260	0.210	0.071	Économies en développement : Amérique
260	0.261	0.081	259	0.260	0.084	Amérique centrale et Grandes Antilles sans Porto Rico
260	0.344	0.080	259	0.320	0.090	Amérique centrale et Grandes Antilles sans le Mexique et Porto Rico
260	0.214	0.066	260	0.214	0.071	Amérique du Sud et Amérique centrale
260	0.247	0.054	260	0.255	0.069	Amérique du Sud sans le Brésil
261	0.215	0.106	260	0.204	0.106	Économies en développement : Asie
260	0.247	0.141	260	0.231	0.129	Asie orientale et Asie du Sud-Est sans la Chine
259	0.433	0.072	259	0.388	0.084	Asie méridionale sans l'Inde

Pour les sources et les notes, se reporter à la fin du tableau 4.1.1.

4.2.1 Volume indices of exports and imports of countries and geographical regions
2000 = 100

Region, country or territory	Exports (1) - Exportations (1)							
	2003	2004	2005	2006	2007	2008	2009	2010
WORLD	**111**	**123**	**130**	**142**	**151**	**154**	**134**	**153**
DEVELOPING ECONOMIES	122	142	155	172	187	193	173	202
TRANSITION ECONOMIES	123	138	139	149	163	162	139	156
DEVELOPED ECONOMIES	105	114	120	130	135	139	118	132
Developing economies: Africa	**107**	**116**	**124**	**124**	**132**	**129**	**115**	**126**
Eastern Africa	*127*	*132*	*134*	*139*	*148*	*153*	*152*	*164*
Burundi	80	88	81	76	75	54	64	85
Comoros	286	214	136	106	117	47	83	78
Djibouti	114	109	105	133	127	126	173	176
Eritrea	37	60	58	59	55	42	43	43
Ethiopia	101	120	141	150	163	174	169	200
Kenya	145	146	157	155	176	185	169	183
Madagascar	127	124	103	119	148	167	115	123
Malawi	151	135	134	162	194	175	209	201
Mauritius	125	120	131	144	130	130	119	142
Mayotte	179	170	216	242	248	228	202	205
Mozambique	287	355	358	402	391	375	387	341
Rwanda	115	143	120	130	144	140	114	128
Seychelles	157	153	163	178	170	204	176	146
Somalia	111	83	107	106	119	123	126	119
Uganda	130	159	186	196	271	291	311	258
United Republic of Tanzania	160	172	178	167	177	210	213	252
Zambia	110	133	126	164	188	203	214	265
Zimbabwe	83	80	73	71	57	44	59	60
Middle Africa	*124*	*141*	*157*	*164*	*186*	*209*	*193*	*181*
Angola	117	128	163	180	227	272	240	214
Cameroon	111	102	93	103	98	89	79	71
Central African Republic	77	72	72	85	88	69	60	70
Chad	309	896	925	826	818	714	665	613
Congo	103	104	105	110	93	101	112	120
Dem. Rep. of the Congo	166	206	190	171	177	207	231	282
Equatorial Guinea	247	313	344	336	381	394	361	342
Gabon	104	106	103	94	96	99	104	103
Sao Tome and Principe	174	137	173	192	150	188	141	106
Northern Africa	*109*	*116*	*120*	*123*	*132*	*130*	*115*	*122*
Algeria	99	104	107	103	106	98	87	95
Egypt	125	131	141	153	169	212	221	230
Libyan Arab Jamahiriya	112	121	130	139	144	145	134	134
Morocco	106	109	122	132	143	121	91	110
Sudan	135	159	148	146	207	201	196	208
Tunisia	135	155	156	167	200	209	173	187
Southern Africa	*101*	*108*	*117*	*116*	*121*	*110*	*92*	*109*
Botswana	104	120	146	135	128	129	99	127
Lesotho	216	321	294	317	360	386	309	365
Namibia	95	127	132	129	127	139	146	172
South Africa	99	103	113	113	119	107	89	106
Swaziland	171	206	157	144	149	112	112	113
Western Africa	*96*	*109*	*127*	*116*	*117*	*108*	*106*	*127*
Benin	125	125	121	139	176	185	211	154
Burkina Faso	138	204	217	253	238	229	320	276
Cape Verde	120	140	137	147	133	212	204	232
Côte d'Ivoire	106	121	117	117	106	100	111	92
Gambia	46	57	43	60	61	57	72	68
Ghana	99	105	109	131	132	131	136	156
Guinea	83	73	69	64	70	71	75	65
Guinea-Bissau	100	101	112	88	118	135	148	160
Liberia	34	31	41	41	45	44	29	25
Mali	138	142	163	193	172	192	161	132
Mauritania	94	118	123	229	223	205	173	251
Niger	114	118	107	102	94	127	142	140
Nigeria	91	110	138	120	123	111	109	145
Saint Helena	278	263	269	266	295	389	340	293
Senegal	134	143	132	119	116	123	129	124
Sierra Leone	744	1 013	1 113	1 500	1 493	1 119	1 159	1 710
Togo	260	199	256	223	213	154	175	175

For sources and notes, see end of table.

		Imports (1) - Importations (1)						Régions, pays ou territoires
2003	2004	2005	2006	2007	2008	2009	2010	
112	125	134	145	155	159	137	156	**MONDE**
119	140	154	170	187	200	180	214	ÉCONOMIES EN DÉVELOPPEMENT
158	188	212	256	325	376	270	312	ÉCONOMIES EN TRANSITION
108	118	124	133	138	138	118	130	ÉCONOMIES DÉVELOPPÉES
119	135	153	167	188	208	202	205	**Économies en développement : Afrique**
121	*138*	*150*	*166*	*181*	*204*	*205*	*220*	*Afrique orientale*
101	104	148	226	154	173	184	225	Burundi
158	176	187	209	232	242	245	250	Comores
107	107	96	106	136	140	123	105	Djibouti
67	90	88	80	71	69	72	78	Érythrée
162	216	261	312	320	410	427	494	Éthiopie
113	123	147	160	182	192	200	205	Kenya
128	147	136	133	172	235	213	171	Madagascar
142	157	182	181	186	248	247	262	Malawi
133	138	146	160	160	158	152	167	Maurice
151	180	181	205	260	282	249	237	Mayotte
144	155	164	185	181	194	204	184	Mozambique
118	118	166	203	248	351	388	429	Rwanda
112	120	144	148	157	174	139	155	Seychelles
147	162	155	178	182	191	159	153	Somalie
86	98	106	122	154	176	184	194	Ouganda
132	153	161	193	221	249	256	288	République-Unie de Tanzanie
169	211	231	264	319	352	303	379	Zambie
84	96	89	76	73	73	85	102	Zimbabwe
166	*173*	*210*	*234*	*297*	*367*	*408*	*357*	*Afrique centrale*
179	180	253	255	369	516	592	422	Angola
141	140	139	145	173	180	165	173	Cameroun
98	119	122	135	152	157	153	166	République centrafricaine
205	204	248	336	407	387	487	548	Tchad
171	169	265	342	394	428	425	435	Congo
219	252	261	298	292	362	314	352	Rép. dém. du Congo
177	194	215	317	403	499	836	828	Guinée équatoriale
107	116	133	151	175	183	165	179	Gabon
131	122	129	172	176	214	219	223	Sao Tomé-et-Principe
110	*128*	*144*	*149*	*170*	*213*	*209*	*215*	*Afrique septentrionale*
140	175	187	187	215	279	294	291	Algérie
72	77	109	106	124	192	196	215	Égypte
110	150	132	123	124	146	175	173	Jamahiriya arabe libyenne
113	127	140	155	183	206	180	177	Maroc
179	234	366	419	429	421	462	456	Soudan
121	131	124	132	154	173	148	155	Tunisie
123	*136*	*148*	*172*	*179*	*168*	*151*	*146*	*Afrique australe*
114	139	127	114	139	159	158	179	Botswana
134	161	152	155	173	180	180	178	Lesotho
125	143	152	160	173	212	251	244	Namibie
123	134	148	177	182	168	147	141	Afrique du Sud
151	165	167	177	165	136	134	132	Swaziland
119	*138*	*170*	*184*	*223*	*226*	*219*	*236*	*Afrique occidentale*
138	123	123	140	213	183	189	180	Bénin
149	187	168	191	193	183	190	209	Burkina Faso
144	164	153	178	222	219	209	204	Cap-Vert
131	168	182	165	175	164	166	151	Côte d'Ivoire
82	109	100	102	109	97	101	90	Gambie
104	123	156	164	187	210	178	218	Ghana
100	97	105	108	132	150	146	132	Guinée
127	139	146	160	191	178	217	209	Guinée-Bissau
29	49	57	75	76	95	57	59	Libéria
154	150	146	160	176	227	184	212	Mali
114	182	267	203	246	256	210	264	Mauritanie
148	163	190	183	203	237	391	446	Niger
122	145	202	238	306	304	303	334	Nigéria
81	91	113	147	185	82	75	82	Sainte-Hélène
148	155	168	165	197	210	179	165	Sénégal
192	157	155	157	163	153	184	241	Sierra Leone
53	56	64	67	67	59	66	63	Togo

Pour les sources et les notes, se reporter à la fin du tableau.

4

4.2.1 Volume indices of exports and imports of countries and geographical regions
2000 = 100

Region, country or territory	Exports (1) (2) - Exportations (1) (2)							
	2003	2004	2005	2006	2007	2008	2009	2010
Developing economies: America	**108**	**118**	**125**	**132**	**135**	**134**	**119**	**132**
Caribbean	*91*	*92*	*92*	*100*	*95*	*85*	*65*	*76*
Anguilla	104	140	322	216	157	182	385	209
Antigua and Barbuda	95	118	173	142	130	107	101	98
Aruba	79	83	72	65	43	45	27	5
Bahamas	77	78	82	97	102	99	91	83
Barbados	88	85	90	100	105	89	73	79
Cuba	84	98	91	91	102	111	..	..
Dominica	73	89	88	84	63	55	40	53
Dominican Republic	96	100	100	103	103	92	80	92
Grenada	52	43	38	32	37	30	29	23
Haiti	109	117	135	139	143	127	138	135
Jamaica	90	93	100	111	99	118	95	77
Montserrat	198	337	110	100	104	223	231	99
Netherlands Antilles	58	31	28	29	28	21	22	18
Saint Kitts and Nevis	181	148	116	134	131	123	136	162
Saint Lucia	139	161	102	133	141	194	229	219
Saint Vincent and the Grenadines	78	72	82	72	81	69	61	47
Trinidad and Tobago	111	115	131	159	154	137	95	97
Turks and Caicos Islands	121	148	177	210	185	262	226	216
Central America	*102*	*108*	*114*	*127*	*129*	*130*	*112*	*136*
Belize	114	111	97	109	104	97	80	87
Costa Rica	112	114	127	148	168	168	162	172
El Salvador	112	113	112	118	120	132	115	132
Guatemala	179	187	185	197	214	218	210	229
Honduras	144	163	166	167	174	173	145	157
Mexico	100	106	112	124	126	127	109	133
Nicaragua	110	130	136	156	175	202	195	242
Panama	103	109	114	120	123	126	97	85
South America	*116*	*132*	*143*	*145*	*150*	*151*	*138*	*146*
Argentina	111	118	136	144	155	157	150	174
Bolivia (Plurinational State of)	129	154	174	179	183	269	204	219
Brazil	138	164	179	185	195	190	170	186
Chile	118	136	141	145	155	154	141	145
Colombia	107	116	131	139	147	156	167	170
Ecuador	139	162	173	186	184	202	193	202
Falkland Islands (Malvinas)	214	188	220	197	220	221	166	184
Guyana	102	108	86	76	88	80	74	74
Paraguay	153	166	178	195	270	363	293	411
Peru	126	151	173	174	178	191	186	190
Suriname	136	142	139	127	138	156	134	115
Uruguay	99	124	140	152	158	171	173	195
Venezuela (Bolivarian Rep. of)	81	93	96	92	84	85	77	71
Developing economies: Asia	**128**	**151**	**167**	**189**	**209**	**219**	**197**	**234**
Eastern Asia	*142*	*174*	*205*	*243*	*281*	*301*	*269*	*334*
China	180	237	301	377	459	507	438	567
China, Hong Kong SAR	118	135	149	161	172	174	151	177
China, Macao SAR	101	108	94	95	93	70	35	30
China, Taiwan Province of	122	136	147	166	180	175	165	199
Korea, Dem. People's Rep. of	162	176	165	168	184	183	185	273
Korea, Republic of	132	161	178	202	224	244	250	288
Mongolia	100	113	119	121	135	142	127	148
Southern Asia	*124*	*137*	*147*	*167*	*177*	*189*	*179*	*197*
Afghanistan	95	183	213	209	224	227	179	167
Bangladesh	111	130	144	183	190	223	216	273
Bhutan	116	129	152	222	359	192	224	215
India	134	155	180	210	224	262	244	275
Iran (Islamic Rep. of)	116	119	109	126	132	125	129	132
Maldives	139	159	127	154	172	218	93	102
Nepal	80	86	91	80	76	75	69	77
Pakistan	137	144	172	177	180	182	168	188
Sri Lanka	97	106	113	117	127	122	104	117
South-Eastern Asia	*115*	*132*	*140*	*155*	*166*	*169*	*151*	*179*
Brunei Darussalam	100	95	85	83	78	75	76	85
Cambodia	149	195	201	251	269	292	269	329
Indonesia	91	89	94	99	101	95	94	109
Lao People's Dem. Rep.	99	102	140	168	169	182	199	246
Malaysia	104	126	134	147	153	157	132	156

For sources and notes, see end of table.

228

Imports (1) (2) - Importations (1) (2)								Régions, pays ou territoires
2003	2004	2005	2006	2007	2008	2009	2010	
95	108	119	135	150	163	133	167	**Économies en développement : Amérique**
93	93	102	113	113	120	97	125	*Caraïbes*
79	98	110	181	188	189	118	107	Anguilla
103	103	117	122	130	108	97	83	Antigua-et-Barbuda
87	92	85	82	56	70	36	23	Aruba
83	85	98	108	105	95	90	88	Bahamas
100	110	112	106	103	97	84	81	Barbade
97	108	142	176	167	163	..	..	Cuba
83	87	91	87	94	106	106	106	Dominique
79	78	93	109	116	123	110	127	République dominicaine
104	96	119	103	116	103	89	84	Grenade
113	115	118	132	122	120	126	186	Haïti
107	99	101	111	123	135	95	84	Jamaïque
126	115	109	105	97	108	106	..	Montserrat
89	54	47	46	47	41	42	39	Antilles néerlandaises
99	84	90	103	105	114	112	102	Saint-Kitts-et-Nevis
115	112	102	114	112	87	100	88	Sainte-Lucie
121	125	122	131	145	146	147	155	Saint-Vincent-et-les Grenadines
114	127	125	128	135	143	122	105	Trinité-et-Tobago
112	135	174	272	295	272	189	179	Îles Turques et Caïques
100	110	117	130	137	142	114	138	*Amérique centrale*
100	86	86	92	86	90	79	79	Belize
123	126	143	163	180	201	165	179	Costa Rica
119	125	126	138	148	155	124	135	El Salvador
159	170	173	184	194	184	164	182	Guatemala
135	153	157	161	183	187	150	163	Honduras
97	107	114	126	132	136	109	134	Mexique
103	112	119	129	147	157	142	161	Nicaragua
91	101	111	123	166	199	183	207	Panama
88	109	126	147	178	204	169	216	*Amérique du Sud*
58	88	108	126	153	178	139	190	Argentine
87	92	110	122	135	187	172	188	Bolivie (État plurinational de)
87	104	109	126	154	182	150	207	Brésil
112	134	162	181	213	245	195	258	Chili
122	138	165	193	231	251	226	263	Colombie
178	208	239	258	270	332	305	386	Équateur
120	131	91	97	125	69	75	138	Îles Falkland (Malvinas)
96	97	102	108	117	125	125	141	Guyana
88	114	132	184	216	303	259	360	Paraguay
113	125	141	161	195	235	185	230	Pérou
129	125	155	140	134	147	157	148	Suriname
68	87	96	107	119	149	127	165	Uruguay
61	93	127	172	226	219	186	178	Venezuela (Rép. bolivarienne du)
127	150	164	180	198	210	191	229	**Économies en développement : Asie**
135	160	170	188	207	208	197	246	*Asie orientale*
184	229	249	282	321	329	323	420	Chine
117	133	143	156	169	171	152	179	Chine (RAS de Hong Kong)
119	144	154	173	193	174	162	187	Chine (RAS de Macao)
106	122	119	125	126	117	103	127	Province chinoise de Taiwan
121	115	118	118	109	101	100	90	Corée, Rép. populaire dém. de
117	130	139	153	166	167	163	192	Corée, République de
124	143	145	169	222	321	218	312	Mongolie
130	146	196	227	249	301	292	312	*Asie méridionale*
177	170	173	171	169	153	181	217	Afghanistan
111	118	124	135	139	143	144	160	Bangladesh
138	214	184	183	204	177	194	259	Bhoutan
130	143	224	280	321	416	413	430	Inde
164	197	205	199	201	219	204	239	Iran (Rép. islamique d')
119	149	157	185	202	222	169	178	Maldives
106	104	105	104	119	114	154	178	Népal
111	136	170	181	179	182	163	171	Pakistan
102	111	112	120	120	125	102	123	Sri Lanka
110	131	141	151	161	175	146	178	*Asie du Sud-Est*
116	117	118	128	148	161	159	207	Brunéi Darussalam
136	154	169	195	207	218	211	238	Cambodge
96	109	132	140	150	174	139	187	Indonésie
84	119	131	148	139	160	179	209	Rép. dém. populaire lao
106	128	133	146	156	154	124	156	Malaisie

Pour les sources et les notes, se reporter à la fin du tableau.

4.2.1 Volume indices of exports and imports of countries and geographical regions
2000 = 100

Region, country or territory	Exports (1) (2) - Exportations (1) (2)							
	2003	2004	2005	2006	2007	2008	2009	2010
Myanmar	137	120	166	171	226	194	217	267
Philippines	116	134	121	137	142	135	110	144
Singapore	129	156	174	192	208	218	196	236
Thailand	118	133	142	160	178	185	159	188
Viet Nam	143	167	178	207	240	260	252	286
Western Asia	*110*	*124*	*125*	*129*	*132*	*137*	*131*	*140*
Bahrain	107	102	108	101	108	110	101	103
Iraq	38	68	62	66	78	92	100	93
Jordan	159	182	173	190	177	157	145	178
Kuwait	103	111	124	132	134	139	122	130
Lebanon	240	264	267	296	342	374	366	418
Occupied Palestinian territory	67	70	72	76	96	95	94	88
Oman	99	91	88	83	87	88	117	124
Qatar	106	120	120	131	161	180	181	200
Saudi Arabia	103	114	113	110	96	102	98	98
Syrian Arab Republic	122	131	131	141	133	134	114	132
Turkey	158	181	199	223	248	265	244	260
United Arab Emirates	130	147	148	159	179	188	171	200
Yemen	90	77	76	76	65	59	72	78
Developing economies: Oceania	**103**	**98**	**92**	**76**	**78**	**67**	**63**	**68**
American Samoa	119	102	87	64	61	57	69	64
Cook Islands	97	76	51	32	..	..	..	..
Fiji	127	124	109	90	98	105	69	68
French Polynesia	63	75	83	90	71	94	59	59
Guam	56	57	49	45	75	76	34	28
Kiribati	91	73	121	159	224	293	248	228
Marshall Islands	186	224	304	236	218	154	149	127
Micronesia (Federated States of)	116	88	73	88	120	130	104	97
Nauru	105	46	12	10	31	44	19	32
New Caledonia	122	115	107	120	143	76	56	68
Niue	36	57	61	342	842	5	6	6
Northern Mariana Islands	77	79	61	44	26	11	0	1
Palau	74	47	101	89	81	72	59	28
Papua New Guinea	105	100	102	82	83	84	95	103
Samoa	630	598	567	393	564	397	263	308
Solomon Islands	95	111	116	123	146	172	155	191
Tokelau	..	..	..	..	..	..	..	..
Tonga	197	148	91	103	78	79	61	65
Vanuatu	109	145	137	157	175	160	137	107
Wallis and Futuna Islands	460	97	77	71	66	51	58	56
Transition economies	**123**	**138**	**139**	**149**	**163**	**162**	**139**	**156**
Albania	170	214	219	253	324	349	301	395
Armenia	228	208	251	225	255	189	139	171
Azerbaijan	144	158	250	356	530	564	594	594
Belarus	132	160	154	176	195	207	168	182
Bosnia and Herzegovina	124	154	178	224	262	285	245	275
Croatia	139	169	170	186	207	203	160	169
Georgia	131	154	188	190	215	212	169	211
Kazakhstan	143	173	175	191	214	240	202	218
Kyrgyzstan	98	109	92	110	151	189	182	173
Republic of Moldova	200	214	253	251	283	289	313	355
Russian Federation	117	128	130	137	145	141	125	141
Serbia and Montenegro	156	206	229	289	359	—	—	—
Tajikistan	95	97	85	104	106	92	89	81
TFYR of Macedonia	103	113	124	140	178	180	127	151
Turkmenistan	121	117	110	122	132	131	99	82
Ukraine	146	171	158	166	187	202	132	165
Uzbekistan	102	124	126	124	166	164	207	189
Developed economies: America	**93**	**99**	**106**	**114**	**120**	**123**	**104**	**118**
Bermuda	120	142	96	46	40	30	50	40
Canada	93	94	100	101	100	97	80	87
Greenland	162	167	166	156	169	175	126	121
Saint Pierre and Miquelon	32	46	67	241	70	61	28	23
United States	93	101	109	120	128	135	115	133
Developed economies: Asia	**108**	**122**	**128**	**143**	**156**	**159**	**120**	**153**
Israel	101	116	119	125	136	132	111	131
Japan	108	123	129	144	157	161	121	155

For sources and notes, see end of table.

4.2.1 Indices du volume des exportations et importations des pays et des régions géographiques
2000 = 100

	Imports (1) (2) - Importations (1) (2)							Régions, pays ou territoires
2003	2004	2005	2006	2007	2008	2009	2010	
84	79	62	77	89	99	114	109	Myanmar
140	155	139	130	133	120	101	122	Philippines
102	124	134	149	158	175	151	177	Singapour
117	140	164	168	175	197	153	193	Thaïlande
156	174	181	203	255	293	280	311	Viet Nam
124	*154*	*171*	*185*	*211*	*239*	*206*	*228*	*Asie occidentale*
116	140	152	146	147	162	115	128	Bahreïn
73	134	146	131	106	173	178	214	Iraq
108	136	154	154	160	165	161	135	Jordanie
150	162	194	203	234	252	187	226	Koweït
113	134	119	111	129	150	164	169	Liban
68	80	79	74	79	72	87	84	Territoire palestinien occupé
147	153	146	160	230	001	251	244	Oman
145	166	268	420	527	621	531	499	Qatar
118	142	170	188	225	256	221	215	Arabie saoudite
129	191	223	219	259	277	263	264	République arabe syrienne
115	139	156	171	190	188	163	198	Turquie
161	206	212	232	275	347	284	329	Émirats arabes unis
152	150	178	185	230	238	244	235	Yémen
131	*129*	*122*	*128*	*138*	*133*	*125*	*125*	*Économies en développement : Océanie*
125	114	89	95	104	86	73	60	Samoa américaines
136	136	136	160	155	198	..	..	Îles Cook
138	150	143	148	135	144	106	103	Fidji
143	125	136	125	131	139	120	112	Polynésie française
124	99	81	68	87	68	84	87	Guam
129	133	153	118	120	102	104	139	Kiribati
157	173	208	184	171	140	111	133	Îles Marshall
110	113	106	109	105	100	105	101	Micronésie (États fédérés de)
85	59	65	76	124	160	261	314	Nauru
164	162	160	182	227	228	201	244	Nouvelle-Calédonie
108	374	355	149	258	256	189	217	Nioué
108	100	77	60	34	15	8	10	Îles Mariannes du Nord
67	75	73	75	65	69	51	58	Palaos
115	126	111	137	161	152	169	140	Papouasie-Nouvelle-Guinée
164	204	205	223	195	182	167	205	Samoa
98	114	153	167	204	176	165	233	Îles Salomon
29	92	57	0	8	0	7	6	Tokélaou
130	127	122	122	122	107	135	131	Tonga
121	137	145	200	193	215	219	196	Vanuatu
110	127	113	121	110	99	104	95	Îles Wallis-et-Futuna
158	*188*	*212*	*256*	*325*	*376*	*270*	*312*	*Économies en transition*
161	185	197	219	280	303	292	280	Albanie
140	138	163	187	260	305	249	273	Arménie
207	253	279	322	324	370	326	346	Azerbaïdjan
125	155	133	160	190	211	187	212	Bélarus
119	134	147	141	173	190	150	149	Bosnie-Herzégovine
175	188	193	209	236	242	185	164	Croatie
152	223	266	361	476	484	389	423	Géorgie
182	240	290	368	474	488	379	309	Kazakhstan
123	144	155	231	305	391	310	305	Kirghizistan
220	235	322	386	485	525	486	566	République de Moldova
166	199	246	312	402	491	335	420	Fédération de Russie
204	275	243	288	392	–	–	–	Serbie-et-Monténégro
117	136	129	147	194	214	192	181	Tadjikistan
105	119	117	127	160	177	140	138	LERY de Macédoine
137	169	145	121	159	226	275	226	Turkménistan
155	172	186	210	265	307	189	242	Ukraine
95	112	114	131	175	232	236	209	Ouzbékistan
106	*117*	*124*	*130*	*132*	*128*	*108*	*122*	*Économies développées : Amérique*
111	125	118	126	126	114	114	98	Bermudes
100	108	119	120	125	128	109	119	Canada
126	137	134	134	135	152	135	138	Groenland
46	60	41	65	34	37	50	41	Saint-Pierre-et-Miquelon
107	118	125	132	133	129	107	123	États-Unis
107	*114*	*116*	*121*	*122*	*122*	*106*	*118*	*Économies développées : Asie*
92	102	104	105	113	114	97	113	Israël
108	115	118	123	124	123	108	119	Japon

Pour les sources et les notes, se reporter à la fin du tableau.

4.2.1 Volume indices of exports and imports of countries and geographical regions
2000 = 100

Region, country or territory	Exports (1) (2) - Exportations (1) (2)							
	2003	2004	2005	2006	2007	2008	2009	2010
Developed economies: Europe	**110**	**120**	**125**	**136**	**141**	**144**	**124**	**137**
Andorra	196	265	286	262	224	157	100	85
Austria	139	160	161	169	189	194	154	165
Belgium	113	121	125	131	135	132	116	126
Bulgaria	139	156	172	194	199	206	185	223
Cyprus	86	90	128	111	108	110	93	97
Czech Republic	130	161	173	201	230	242	207	248
Denmark	107	111	116	121	125	129	116	121
Estonia	85	80	101	131	117	110	91	120
Faeroe Islands	124	123	111	99	123	121	92	89
Finland	109	114	119	134	139	144	108	121
France	102	109	112	118	120	120	104	115
Germany	115	128	136	152	163	165	138	160
Gibraltar	179	166	164	177	202	102	107	163
Greece	85	85	92	105	106	103	90	89
Hungary	125	149	168	199	230	244	213	249
Iceland	127	139	139	138	170	170	172	164
Ireland	104	117	119	119	126	123	119	120
Italy	99	104	104	110	115	110	89	97
Latvia	128	148	181	195	213	225	200	239
Lithuania	192	229	254	286	316	363	288	341
Luxembourg	157	169	189	218	195	201	186	165
Malta	98	99	95	113	123	115	88	99
Netherlands	110	122	131	142	135	158	142	160
Norway	108	107	107	105	107	108	103	100
Poland	144	171	188	219	239	257	235	215
Portugal	129	138	141	158	176	176	144	151
Romania	167	205	221	246	287	310	266	314
Slovakia	181	212	229	290	387	440	367	418
Slovenia	141	170	194	223	271	283	229	249
Spain	113	119	120	126	133	135	124	137
Sweden	106	117	121	130	131	135	109	126
Switzerland	124	138	143	155	170	183	165	180
United Kingdom	99	101	107	120	107	108	95	105
Developed economies: Oceania	**103**	**107**	**109**	**112**	**115**	**120**	**116**	**129**
Australia	102	105	108	111	113	120	114	129
New Zealand	108	115	114	119	128	122	131	132

Sources:
- ECLAC, *CEPALSTAT* external trade deflator
- IMF, *International Financial Statistics* on CD-ROM
- U.S. Bureau of Labor Statistics, external trade prices indices
- Unit value indices of Japan Customs and price indices of Bank of Japan
- UNCTAD, *Commodity Price Statistics*
- UNCTAD, *Merchandise Trade Matrix*
- UNCTAD secretariat estimates

Notes:

(1) Volume or quantum indices: The ratio of the export or import value index to the corresponding unit value index.

Imports (1) (2) - Importations (1) (2)								Régions, pays ou territoires
2003	2004	2005	2006	2007	2008	2009	2010	
109	**119**	**126**	**137**	**144**	**145**	**124**	**135**	**Économies développées : Europe**
147	163	..	..	..	..	..	..	Andorre
133	150	147	149	166	168	140	146	Autriche
110	118	126	132	138	138	121	128	Belgique
152	173	201	232	256	276	203	220	Bulgarie
110	130	136	141	164	180	148	148	Chypre
129	150	154	177	203	212	181	215	République tchèque
106	113	121	132	133	139	118	126	Danemark
127	146	173	216	223	201	142	166	Estonie
137	106	116	116	139	121	104	95	Îles Féroé
108	114	122	133	140	144	110	122	Finlande
103	114	123	126	132	132	117	126	France
110	120	127	142	148	150	135	155	Allemagne
98	91	71	76	87	65	86	71	Gibraltar
98	102	96	107	115	118	95	70	Grèce
122	141	151	173	193	202	167	192	Hongrie
105	118	141	176	174	136	94	94	Islande
95	101	112	115	121	111	91	89	Irlande
103	108	108	113	116	109	94	105	Italie
135	159	182	219	252	227	155	179	Lettonie
180	209	233	271	320	331	228	267	Lituanie
140	157	159	185	179	183	156	145	Luxembourg
90	88	84	97	101	99	84	81	Malte
103	112	126	138	144	158	138	157	Pays-Bas
99	111	122	135	148	155	133	144	Norvège
120	141	148	173	199	218	178	155	Pologne
114	123	126	136	148	148	123	121	Portugal
177	222	252	299	387	409	285	311	Roumanie
171	197	211	258	330	359	290	335	Slovaquie
132	155	164	182	223	233	182	194	Slovénie
115	127	135	148	158	153	126	135	Espagne
00	105	111	118	127	120	107	125	Suède
102	108	117	127	135	134	123	132	Suisse
111	117	124	138	130	127	111	122	Royaume-Uni
121	**138**	**150**	**160**	**178**	**194**	**173**	**188**	**Économies développées : Océanie**
120	138	150	163	181	200	178	195	Australie
124	142	152	151	165	165	149	159	Nouvelle-Zélande

Sources :
- CEPALC, *CEPALSTAT* déflateur du commerce extérieur
- FMI, *Statistiques financières internationales* sur CD-ROM
- Bureau des statistiques du travail des États-Unis (BLS), indices de prix du commerce extérieur
- Indices des valeurs unitaires des douanes japonaises et indices des prix de la Banque du Japon
- CNUCED, *Statistiques de prix des produits de base*
- CNUCED, *Matrice du commerce de marchandises*
- Estimations du secrétariat de la CNUCED

Notes :
(1) Indices du volume ou quantum : représentent le rapport de l'indice de la valeur des exportations ou des importations à l'indice de la valeur unitaire correspondant.

4

4.2.1 Unit value indices of exports and imports of countries and geographical regions
2000 = 100

Region, country or territory	Exports (1) - Exportations (1)							
	2003	2004	2005	2006	2007	2008	2009	2010
WORLD	**106**	**116**	**125**	**132**	**144**	**162**	**145**	**155**
DEVELOPING ECONOMIES	97	106	119	128	137	158	139	154
TRANSITION ECONOMIES	109	132	169	198	219	293	221	255
DEVELOPED ECONOMIES	110	120	125	130	143	155	141	146
Developing economies: Africa	**111**	**134**	**171**	**202**	**221**	**295**	**228**	**269**
Eastern Africa	*94*	*110*	*122*	*140*	*150*	*177*	*164*	*190*
Burundi	94	100	107	154	107	201	104	236
Comoros	69	64	65	72	87	102	105	122
Djibouti	103	111	119	133	145	172	141	153
Eritrea	91	100	102	111	128	141	135	147
Ethiopia	101	117	106	111	101	100	100	204
Kenya	96	106	121	128	134	155	152	163
Madagascar	89	91	94	98	106	116	111	120
Malawi	91	94	99	108	118	132	150	140
Mauritius	84	91	90	89	95	102	90	87
Mayotte	101	105	108	111	114	123	122	120
Mozambique	100	116	134	163	170	194	153	181
Rwanda	103	130	197	214	231	346	317	351
Seychelles	90	98	107	111	109	124	125	142
Somalia	104	115	122	139	151	175	173	196
Uganda	98	106	122	135	146	169	166	186
United Republic of Tanzania	104	117	129	157	171	198	191	219
Zambia	100	132	160	258	275	281	225	304
Zimbabwe	104	122	131	149	188	201	199	217
Middle Africa	*104*	*132*	*183*	*218*	*240*	*326*	*215*	*272*
Angola	103	134	187	224	248	337	216	276
Cameroon	112	132	164	190	209	265	215	262
Central African Republic	103	109	111	116	126	135	129	143
Chad	105	134	186	222	245	331	216	274
Congo	104	132	184	221	244	331	218	274
Dem. Rep. of the Congo	101	109	140	165	179	231	160	213
Equatorial Guinea	103	134	187	223	245	345	223	277
Gabon	104	131	181	214	238	325	220	273
Sao Tome and Principe	141	147	146	149	167	210	214	224
Northern Africa	*110*	*132*	*175*	*207*	*225*	*311*	*228*	*264*
Algeria	113	139	195	240	257	367	234	275
Egypt	105	126	161	192	205	264	223	245
Libyan Arab Jamahiriya	103	133	188	225	248	338	219	273
Morocco	116	127	128	135	149	234	215	223
Sudan	104	131	181	215	237	321	222	280
Tunisia	102	107	115	120	130	158	143	151
Western Sahara	88	91	..	..	..	..	..	..
Southern Africa	*119*	*141*	*150*	*175*	*193*	*236*	*221*	*239*
Botswana	98	106	110	121	143	139	126	134
Lesotho	100	100	100	100	101	104	105	106
Namibia	101	109	119	155	174	174	161	178
South Africa	122	147	156	183	201	252	235	254
Swaziland	98	103	114	127	128	153	162	169
Western Africa	*113*	*139*	*185*	*219*	*243*	*327*	*245*	*300*
Benin	107	116	122	135	151	177	148	196
Burkina Faso	113	114	105	113	127	147	137	185
Cape Verde	100	102	120	132	136	157	171	181
Côte d'Ivoire	140	147	169	187	211	267	243	289
Gambia	111	118	123	127	142	163	140	147
Ghana	140	139	154	170	197	259	258	292
Guinea	110	156	185	243	259	285	209	257
Guinea-Bissau	104	120	128	136	146	153	129	124
Liberia	97	101	98	112	126	161	163	242
Mali	123	126	124	147	166	201	203	271
Mauritania	96	105	143	168	177	246	224	229
Niger	109	131	157	180	245	254	214	234
Nigeria	104	136	190	229	252	346	229	284
Saint Helena	88	90	92	94	94	99	101	107
Senegal	102	115	129	142	155	195	170	190
Sierra Leone	95	105	109	118	126	148	138	153
Togo	63	83	71	75	89	152	128	144

For sources and notes, see end of table.

4.2.1 Indices de la valeur unitaire des exportations et importations des pays et des régions géographiques
2000 = 100

2003	2004	2005	2006	2007	2008	2009	2010	Régions, pays ou territoires
			Imports (1) - Importations (1)					
104	114	121	128	138	155	138	147	**MONDE**
99	108	116	123	131	149	134	145	ÉCONOMIES EN DÉVELOPPEMENT
104	113	122	129	138	154	143	149	ÉCONOMIES EN TRANSITION
107	117	123	130	141	158	139	146	ÉCONOMIES DÉVELOPPÉES
108	121	130	138	151	174	158	169	**Économies en développement : Afrique**
103	113	126	135	147	172	153	164	*Afrique orientale*
106	114	122	129	140	157	148	153	Burundi
102	112	122	127	138	168	160	171	Comores
108	118	140	152	168	199	177	190	Djibouti
106	111	120	131	152	184	174	187	Érythrée
104	113	124	132	144	168	148	156	Éthiopie
106	119	135	147	159	186	165	180	Kenya
104	112	125	132	143	164	149	161	Madagascar
104	112	120	125	139	167	153	156	Malawi
80	91	98	103	110	134	111	119	Maurice
103	113	123	128	139	155	146	153	Mayotte
105	113	126	134	145	178	158	167	Mozambique
103	113	121	127	139	157	145	152	Rwanda
107	120	137	150	160	184	169	186	Seychelles
102	110	117	130	142	173	170	182	Somalie
103	114	127	137	147	167	150	161	Ouganda
106	117	134	144	159	186	161	176	République-Unie de Tanzanie
105	115	124	131	141	162	141	158	Zambie
109	123	140	158	179	209	184	195	Zimbabwe
103	111	117	124	135	151	139	147	*Afrique centrale*
101	106	109	113	122	134	126	129	Angola
104	116	133	147	165	203	180	194	Cameroun
104	109	121	129	140	163	151	162	République centrafricaine
106	114	121	127	139	155	147	151	Tchad
104	112	118	123	134	149	143	153	Congo
105	113	125	132	145	163	151	159	Rép. dém. du Congo
102	112	121	126	136	149	123	137	Guinée équatoriale
103	110	116	120	132	146	140	146	Gabon
105	114	129	139	152	179	168	169	Sao Tomé-et-Principe
107	117	125	132	147	168	154	165	*Afrique septentrionale*
106	114	119	125	140	155	146	151	Algérie
108	119	130	140	156	182	164	176	Égypte
105	114	124	133	147	169	156	164	Jamahiriya arabe libyenne
110	121	129	134	152	179	159	174	Maroc
104	112	119	124	132	143	135	141	Soudan
105	114	124	133	145	166	152	167	Tunisie
96	95	..	..	..	..	..	..	Sahara occidental
112	132	140	149	160	184	164	177	*Afrique australe*
103	112	122	130	140	157	144	152	Botswana
104	110	114	117	124	140	130	153	Lesotho
103	109	113	117	124	138	127	148	Namibie
114	135	143	153	164	190	168	181	Afrique du Sud
104	112	122	129	142	153	147	158	Swaziland
106	116	128	138	150	177	160	170	*Afrique occidentale*
106	119	136	143	156	204	178	198	Bénin
102	111	122	129	142	183	161	170	Burkina Faso
106	114	125	133	147	164	147	159	Cap-Vert
101	113	130	142	154	193	168	184	Côte d'Ivoire
101	113	127	136	149	182	161	177	Gambie
104	111	124	133	144	167	152	166	Ghana
105	116	128	136	147	174	156	169	Guinée
105	116	142	152	168	213	182	194	Guinée-Bissau
88	90	85	93	105	134	147	164	Libéria
103	113	131	141	154	182	164	174	Mali
104	111	118	126	143	167	150	164	Mauritanie
106	116	126	132	143	168	153	162	Niger
102	112	121	129	141	160	148	152	Nigéria
104	113	128	141	149	169	161	181	Sainte-Hélène
105	118	134	143	159	200	170	187	Sénégal
106	122	149	166	184	233	189	215	Sierra Leone
260	281	330	354	383	466	404	465	Togo

Pour les sources et les notes, se reporter à la fin du tableau.

4.2.1 Unit value indices of exports and imports of countries and geographical regions
2000 = 100

Region, country or territory	Exports (1) - Exportations (1)							
	2003	2004	2005	2006	2007	2008	2009	2010
Developing economies: America	99	111	126	143	156	183	157	180
Caribbean	105	120	146	171	188	242	191	176
Anguilla	101	107	115	141	145	156	148	147
Antigua and Barbuda	90	92	91	100	111	139	136	136
Aruba	103	131	191	225	246	324	212	225
Bahamas	96	106	117	126	136	167	136	155
Barbados	104	120	146	161	171	202	190	200
British Virgin Islands	94	102	126	138	149	..	..	..
Cayman Islands	88	116	91	102	113	136	148	164
Cuba	120	142	152	196	233	204	..	..
Dominica	102	111	117	120	128	136	131	132
Dominican Republic	99	103	107	111	121	128	119	125
Grenada	97	97	95	106	118	136	131	140
Haiti	100	106	110	112	115	110	121	130
Jamaica	98	115	115	130	161	160	107	131
Montserrat	100	106	114	117	124	133	122	123
Netherlands Antilles	100	122	169	195	213	274	195	233
Saint Kitts and Nevis	97	97	100	102	105	109	108	108
Saint Lucia	104	114	146	163	174	195	163	173
Saint Vincent and the Grenadines	96	100	97	105	117	149	160	173
Trinidad and Tobago	109	129	171	209	223	318	225	246
Turks and Caicos Islands	92	93	94	95	99	107	104	109
Central America	99	106	114	119	127	135	125	133
Belize	83	88	98	112	112	136	129	148
Costa Rica	93	95	95	95	96	98	92	93
El Salvador	95	99	104	107	113	117	112	116
Guatemala	92	99	107	112	119	131	127	136
Honduras	78	83	91	95	99	107	100	110
Mexico	100	108	115	121	129	138	127	135
Nicaragua	85	90	98	102	106	115	111	119
Panama	98	101	104	106	110	116	113	116
South America	98	114	133	159	177	218	179	216
Argentina	101	111	113	122	137	171	142	149
Bolivia (Plurinational State of)	100	113	130	176	199	213	190	230
Brazil	96	107	120	135	150	189	164	197
Chile	96	125	152	210	227	225	191	248
Colombia	94	108	124	135	155	188	150	179
Ecuador	91	97	119	139	153	189	146	175
Falkland Islands (Malvinas)	80	81	83	85	88	95	93	104
Guyana	101	110	128	155	155	198	207	235
Paraguay	98	108	107	109	120	141	125	127
Peru	103	121	143	195	223	235	205	267
Suriname	108	145	165	213	227	256	240	295
Uruguay	97	103	106	113	124	163	136	150
Venezuela (Bolivarian Rep. of)	100	128	174	214	244	334	223	278
Developing economies: Asia	95	103	113	119	127	143	128	140
Eastern Asia	91	95	97	98	101	106	100	105
China	98	101	102	103	106	113	110	112
China, Hong Kong SAR	94	95	96	97	99	103	105	109
China, Macao SAR	101	102	103	106	108	113	110	116
China, Taiwan Province of	80	86	91	91	93	98	84	93
Korea, Dem. People's Rep. of	93	103	115	123	130	159	152	155
Korea, Republic of	85	92	93	93	96	101	84	94
Mongolia	115	143	168	238	260	333	279	365
Southern Asia	103	118	139	152	170	202	172	202
Afghanistan	110	121	132	142	161	173	164	175
Bangladesh	99	100	101	101	103	108	109	110
Bhutan	111	138	165	181	182	263	215	244
India	104	116	130	137	158	175	159	186
Iran (Islamic Rep. of)	103	132	181	216	238	322	216	269
Maldives	100	105	117	134	122	140	167	181
Nepal	103	112	118	130	142	155	148	154
Pakistan	96	103	103	106	110	123	116	126
Sri Lanka	97	100	103	108	112	123	126	131
South-Eastern Asia	95	100	108	115	121	137	125	136
Brunei Darussalam	113	137	188	235	251	365	242	275
Cambodia	102	103	104	106	109	116	115	120
Indonesia	108	123	140	160	179	225	194	223

For sources and notes, see end of table.

			Imports (1) - Importations (1)					Régions, pays ou territoires
2003	2004	2005	2006	2007	2008	2009	2010	
100	107	114	120	128	144	131	136	**Économies en développement : Amérique**
102	*113*	*127*	*136*	*148*	*175*	*151*	*131*	*Caraïbes*
103	111	124	131	139	152	152	156	Anguilla
101	108	116	125	138	169	164	187	Antigua-et-Barbuda
106	126	158	180	196	232	209	226	Aruba
102	112	126	133	143	163	144	157	Bahamas
103	111	124	133	144	168	151	167	Barbade
100	118	129	137	156	188	159	..	Îles Vierges britanniques
106	116	114	123	138	183	195	219	Îles Caïmanes
99	107	117	119	135	183	..	..	Cuba
104	113	123	129	141	158	143	154	Dominique
101	107	112	117	123	107	118	127	République dominicaine
102	109	117	122	132	147	133	144	Grenade
102	110	119	126	133	192	163	167	Haïti
103	116	134	145	157	190	161	183	Jamaïque
104	115	126	133	142	163	129		Montserrat
102	126	169	197	215	269	216	248	Antilles néerlandaises
103	111	119	124	133	145	137	144	Saint-Kitts-et-Nevis
99	110	133	146	160	212	152	186	Sainte-Lucie
103	112	122	128	140	158	140	151	Saint-Vincent-et-les Grenadines
103	116	138	153	167	202	172	187	Trinité-et-Tobago
101	110	118	123	132	146	133	141	Îles Turques et Caïques
100	*106*	*111*	*116*	*123*	*132*	*124*	*130*	*Amérique centrale*
105	115	132	140	152	178	162	171	Belize
97	103	107	110	113	119	109	118	Costa Rica
98	102	108	112	119	127	118	127	El Salvador
99	108	117	125	136	153	136	147	Guatemala
89	96	104	114	122	140	122	131	Honduras
101	106	111	116	123	131	124	129	Mexique
101	109	120	129	135	153	135	145	Nicaragua
101	106	111	117	122	135	120	132	Panama
98	*106*	*115*	*122*	*130*	*152*	*135*	*142*	*Amérique du Sud*
94	102	105	108	116	128	112	118	Argentine
102	109	117	126	140	148	141	151	Bolivie (État plurinational de)
99	109	121	130	140	171	152	158	Brésil
93	100	109	115	120	137	115	122	Chili
98	105	111	117	125	136	126	134	Colombie
101	106	116	126	135	153	133	143	Équateur
98	102	108	115	122	137	117	121	Îles Falkland (Malvinas)
103	115	132	142	156	181	159	171	Guyana
97	104	110	114	120	132	119	123	Paraguay
101	109	119	128	142	172	159	175	Pérou
103	113	129	137	148	168	157	166	Suriname
93	103	117	128	139	174	141	150	Uruguay
101	108	113	116	121	134	123	129	Venezuela (Rép. bolivarienne du)
98	107	115	122	129	148	132	144	**Économies en développement : Asie**
95	*104*	*112*	*118*	*124*	*143*	*127*	*138*	*Asie orientale*
100	109	118	125	132	153	138	148	Chine
93	96	98	101	102	107	107	114	Chine (RAS de Hong Kong)
102	107	113	117	123	137	127	131	Chine (RAS de Macao)
86	99	109	116	124	147	121	142	Province chinoise de Taiwan
101	117	137	152	167	210	183	197	Corée, Rép. populaire dém. de
96	107	117	126	134	162	123	138	Corée, République de
105	116	133	143	155	183	159	171	Mongolie
107	*127*	*126*	*129*	*144*	*162*	*136*	*159*	*Asie méridionale*
101	109	121	128	142	168	157	165	Afghanistan
106	115	126	134	151	188	171	195	Bangladesh
103	110	120	131	147	174	156	167	Bhoutan
108	135	124	124	138	150	121	146	Inde
106	118	128	135	147	172	163	173	Iran (Rép. islamique d')
102	111	122	129	139	161	147	158	Maldives
105	119	138	153	167	201	181	197	Népal
109	122	138	151	167	214	178	202	Pakistan
104	115	126	137	150	178	159	175	Sri Lanka
98	*103*	*112*	*121*	*127*	*144*	*132*	*142*	*Asie du Sud-Est*
103	110	114	118	128	143	139	147	Brunéi Darussalam
101	110	119	126	136	154	144	158	Cambodge
102	114	131	142	154	181	161	176	Indonésie

Pour les sources et les notes, se reporter à la fin du tableau.

4

Region, country or territory	Exports (1) - Exportations (1)							
	2003	2004	2005	2006	2007	2008	2009	2010
Lao People's Dem. Rep.	103	108	120	159	165	181	153	190
Malaysia	97	102	107	111	117	136	121	130
Myanmar	110	120	140	163	170	217	188	196
Philippines	78	74	83	87	89	92	88	90
Singapore	90	93	96	103	104	113	100	108
Thailand	99	105	113	118	125	138	138	151
Viet Nam	98	108	123	132	139	167	157	171
Western Asia	*108*	*132*	*175*	*204*	*235*	*303*	*218*	*264*
Bahrain	100	119	153	185	200	254	189	215
Iraq	102	133	188	206	250	340	219	279
Jordan	102	114	131	143	170	261	237	201
Kuwait	104	133	186	219	240	322	212	265
Lebanon	106	117	123	133	146	167	160	168
Occupied Palestinian territory	105	111	116	120	133	146	138	147
Oman	104	129	160	191	244	378	212	207
Qatar	110	135	185	227	241	349	230	298
Saudi Arabia	117	143	206	248	313	397	252	335
Syrian Arab Republic	102	124	151	167	187	246	200	229
Turkey	108	126	133	138	155	180	151	158
United Arab Emirates	103	124	159	184	200	256	205	236
Yemen	102	130	181	216	238	316	214	268
Developing economies: Oceania	**103**	**123**	**143**	**199**	**228**	**278**	**221**	**271**
American Samoa	112	126	124	198	211	231	221	245
Cook Islands	98	104	114	121	..	..	..	..
Fiji	99	104	120	141	143	163	170	188
French Polynesia	98	101	104	108	112	118	117	120
Guam	105	125	143	158	165	186	201	220
Kiribati	89	94	99	110	121	143	168	183
Marshall Islands	90	97	91	100	111	143	155	173
Micronesia (Federated States of)	94	95	106	120	107	125	155	166
Nauru	95	113	117	124	171	808	376	391
New Caledonia	106	149	168	186	250	293	284	308
Niue	101	106	113	116	116	125	122	125
Northern Mariana Islands	101	103	105	108	116	131	130	148
Palau	99	108	121	138	122	142	174	187
Papua New Guinea	101	126	157	248	272	329	222	289
Samoa	97	100	108	116	121	128	123	136
Solomon Islands	113	127	131	142	164	178	153	172
Tokelau	108	112	109	113	120	134	129	129
Tonga	103	115	125	122	118	130	131	139
Vanuatu	96	101	106	120	109	136	160	175
Wallis and Futuna Islands	101	121	123	127	137	176	155	160
Transition economies	**109**	**132**	**169**	**198**	**219**	**293**	**221**	**255**
Albania	101	108	115	120	127	148	139	150
Armenia	102	117	129	152	163	190	171	201
Azerbaijan	103	131	175	209	230	311	204	256
Belarus	103	118	141	153	170	214	173	190
Bosnia and Herzegovina	105	117	126	139	148	165	151	164
Croatia	100	107	116	126	135	157	148	157
Georgia	109	130	142	162	179	221	209	233
Kazakhstan	105	135	183	230	256	341	243	298
Kyrgyzstan	117	130	143	158	171	193	179	199
Republic of Moldova	84	97	92	89	101	117	87	92
Russian Federation	110	135	178	210	232	317	231	268
Serbia and Montenegro	103	116	129	146	157	–	–	–
Tajikistan	108	120	133	171	177	194	145	188
TFYR of Macedonia	100	112	124	130	140	165	161	165
Turkmenistan	119	133	179	235	239	363	265	291
Ukraine	109	131	149	159	181	227	206	214
Uzbekistan	111	123	134	161	172	223	184	222
Developed economies: America	**102**	**107**	**113**	**118**	**125**	**134**	**125**	**133**
Bermuda	98	101	100	111	122	158	113	126
Canada	106	117	130	140	150	169	142	160
Greenland	79	84	89	93	93	103	105	116
Saint Pierre and Miquelon	97	100	109	116	105	118	138	158
United States	100	104	107	111	116	123	117	123

For sources and notes, see end of table.

			Imports (1) - Importations (1)					Régions, pays ou territoires
2003	2004	2005	2006	2007	2008	2009	2010	
102	112	126	134	144	164	147	157	Rép. dém. populaire lao
95	100	105	109	115	130	122	129	Malaisie
103	115	129	138	154	181	161	178	Myanmar
82	80	96	112	117	136	122	129	Philippines
99	104	111	119	123	135	121	130	Singapour
105	109	116	124	130	147	142	154	Thaïlande
103	115	128	140	152	176	160	172	Viet Nam
105	*117*	*125*	*134*	*145*	*166*	*152*	*161*	*Asie occidentale*
105	114	133	147	160	189	181	188	Bahreïn
103	113	122	127	140	155	145	150	Iraq
115	130	148	162	184	221	197	243	Jordanie
102	109	111	119	127	138	134	138	Koweït
104	115	130	139	153	179	163	176	Liban
111	124	142	156	166	200	174	181	Territoire palestinien occupé
89	115	121	128	138	150	141	148	Oman
104	111	116	120	129	138	135	136	Qatar
103	111	116	123	133	149	143	150	Arabie saoudite
104	115	128	137	148	172	154	169	République arabe syrienne
111	129	138	150	164	197	159	172	Turquie
102	109	114	123	132	146	141	148	Émirats arabes unis
104	115	130	142	159	189	162	177	Yémen
102	*112*	*126*	*134*	*145*	*173*	*155*	*167*	*Économies en développement : Océanie*
98	105	112	121	124	157	163	180	Samoa américaines
102	110	118	123	135	149	..	..	Îles Cook
103	113	131	142	156	184	158	177	Fidji
103	111	118	123	133	147	135	145	Polynésie française
100	121	156	176	188	226	180	191	Guam
101	113	126	135	148	183	166	181	Kiribati
87	89	82	90	101	131	148	165	Îles Marshall
101	110	115	118	127	145	138	144	Micronésie (États fédérés de)
106	113	146	160	165	201	140	155	Nauru
102	110	120	126	135	152	139	147	Nouvelle-Calédonie
103	110	122	127	137	157	138	120	Nioué
101	109	126	135	144	172	146	156	Îles Mariannes du Nord
104	112	116	120	130	148	160	164	Palaos
103	116	135	146	160	202	179	192	Papouasie-Nouvelle-Guinée
102	114	129	137	151	175	153	167	Samoa
104	116	131	141	153	198	173	184	Îles Salomon
101	105	103	106	116	145	144	146	Tokélaou
104	119	142	153	168	202	171	193	Tonga
101	108	118	125	136	167	153	167	Vanuatu
103	113	122	128	141	158	149	163	Îles Wallis-et-Futuna
104	*113*	*122*	*129*	*138*	*154*	*143*	*149*	*Économies en transition*
106	114	122	128	137	159	143	151	Albanie
104	111	123	133	143	165	150	157	Arménie
108	118	129	140	150	165	160	163	Azerbaïdjan
107	123	145	161	174	216	177	191	Bélarus
104	114	125	133	145	164	150	159	Bosnie-Herzégovine
103	112	122	130	139	161	146	155	Croatie
106	116	132	143	154	177	159	170	Géorgie
104	114	123	130	139	156	149	154	Kazakhstan
105	118	137	150	164	187	176	189	Kirghizistan
82	97	92	90	98	120	87	88	République de Moldova
102	109	114	118	124	133	128	133	Fédération de Russie
105	116	129	141	149	—	—	—	Serbie-et-Monténégro
112	130	153	174	187	227	198	218	Tadjikistan
104	118	132	141	154	185	171	189	LERY de Macédoine
103	110	114	119	127	140	137	139	Turkménistan
107	121	139	154	164	200	172	180	Ukraine
104	113	119	124	134	149	142	149	Ouzbékistan
97	*103*	*111*	*116*	*121*	*134*	*120*	*128*	*Économies développées : Amérique*
104	110	116	121	129	142	130	137	Bermudes
100	106	114	122	127	133	124	134	Canada
100	109	122	129	139	157	142	154	Groenland
102	108	112	114	122	128	127	133	Saint-Pierre-et-Miquelon
97	102	110	115	120	134	119	127	États-Unis

Pour les sources et les notes, se reporter à la fin du tableau.

4

4.2.1 Unit value indices of exports and imports of countries and geographical regions
2000 = 100

Region, country or territory	Exports (1) - Exportations (1)							
	2003	2004	2005	2006	2007	2008	2009	2010
Developed economies: Asia	**91**	**97**	**97**	**95**	**97**	**104**	**103**	**106**
Israel	100	106	114	119	126	147	138	141
Japan	91	96	96	94	95	101	100	104
Developed economies: Europe	**116**	**128**	**132**	**138**	**155**	**168**	**152**	**154**
Andorra	100	101	110	126	125	135	140	141
Austria	104	109	115	120	128	138	131	136
Belgium	120	135	142	149	170	189	168	174
Bulgaria	113	133	142	162	193	224	182	193
Cyprus	102	111	120	126	135	156	142	153
Czech Republic	129	147	156	163	181	208	187	185
Denmark	122	136	143	149	162	176	158	158
Estonia	172	194	199	209	245	273	250	253
Faeroe Islands	101	106	114	137	127	147	174	192
Finland	106	117	120	120	140	145	126	125
France	118	127	126	129	112	150	140	139
Germany	118	129	130	132	147	158	147	144
Gibraltar	90	94	96	108	119	138	111	136
Greece	133	154	160	169	190	217	193	200
Hungary	122	133	134	135	148	158	138	137
Iceland	99	110	117	132	149	166	125	149
Ireland	115	115	119	118	124	132	126	126
Italy	126	142	149	158	181	204	190	192
Latvia	121	145	153	169	209	240	206	213
Lithuania	103	114	131	139	153	183	160	172
Luxembourg	101	115	119	125	137	150	135	142
Malta	102	103	103	101	102	106	103	104
Netherlands	116	126	133	141	175	173	151	153
Norway	104	127	161	193	212	266	194	219
Poland	118	138	150	160	185	209	183	228
Portugal	101	107	111	117	123	134	126	133
Romania	102	111	121	127	136	153	147	152
Slovakia	102	110	117	121	127	136	128	131
Slovenia	103	110	114	119	127	138	130	136
Spain	120	133	140	148	165	180	159	156
Sweden	110	121	124	131	148	156	138	145
Switzerland	105	110	114	119	126	136	130	135
United Kingdom	108	121	126	131	145	149	130	136
Developed economies: Oceania	**110**	**129**	**150**	**168**	**189**	**234**	**199**	**244**
Australia	110	129	153	174	195	244	212	259
New Zealand	111	129	138	139	159	182	137	172

Sources:
- ECLAC, *CEPALSTAT* external trade deflator
- IMF, *International Financial Statistics* on CD-ROM
- U.S. Bureau of Labor Statistics, external trade prices indices
- Unit value indices of Japan Customs and price indices of Bank of Japan
- UNCTAD, *Commodity Price Statistics*
- UNCTAD, *Merchandise Trade Matrix*
- UNCTAD secretariat estimates

Notes:

(1) To improve data coverage, especially for the latest periods, the following procedure was used in the calculation of unit value indices:
- A set of average prices indices at SITC (Revision 3, 3-digit) group level was constructed using UNCTAD, Commodity Price Statistics, international and national sources and UNCTAD secretariat estimates.
- At the country level, unit value indices were calculated using previous year's trade values at the SITC 3-digit level, available in table 3.2 as weights.
In some instances these indices may differ from the estimates published in official sources, since the main aim is to provide tentative estimates for most countries on a comparable basis.

4.2.1 Indices de la valeur unitaire des exportations et importations des pays et des régions géographiques
2000 = 100

| | Imports (1) - Importations (1) | | | | | | | Régions, pays ou territoires |
2003	2004	2005	2006	2007	2008	2009	2010	
94	**105**	**116**	**125**	**133**	**163**	**135**	**153**	**Économies développées : Asie**
104	112	120	127	138	158	134	144	Israël
93	104	115	125	132	164	135	154	Japon
114	**126**	**131**	**138**	**153**	**169**	**149**	**154**	**Économies développées : Europe**
100	105	..	..	..	..	..	..	Andorre
104	111	120	128	136	152	141	150	Autriche
120	136	143	150	168	189	164	172	Belgique
110	128	139	154	180	205	178	177	Bulgarie
102	110	120	127	137	153	137	147	Chypre
123	137	146	156	172	197	170	174	République tchèque
119	132	138	142	161	172	154	148	Danemark
121	134	140	147	165	187	168	176	Estonie
102	111	120	127	137	160	142	154	Îles Féroé
115	131	140	161	169	185	160	163	Finlande
114	121	121	128	142	159	140	142	France
110	120	123	129	143	158	138	139	Allemagne
100	122	161	186	203	263	180	218	Gibraltar
137	155	169	178	199	228	213	216	Grèce
122	134	138	141	155	168	145	143	Hongrie
102	116	124	131	148	175	148	161	Islande
111	120	121	125	136	148	134	131	Irlande
121	138	149	165	184	216	184	194	Italie
122	140	150	166	191	222	198	202	Lettonie
103	113	128	137	146	179	153	168	Lituanie
102	114	122	127	137	153	139	148	Luxembourg
110	121	128	131	138	152	143	152	Malte
117	131	133	138	156	168	147	151	Pays-Bas
116	126	132	139	158	170	151	156	Norvège
116	130	141	150	170	195	171	229	Pologne
103	112	122	130	139	159	145	155	Portugal
104	113	123	131	139	157	145	153	Roumanie
104	113	122	130	137	153	142	148	Slovaquie
104	113	123	131	140	157	143	153	Slovénie
116	131	137	143	158	175	149	149	Espagne
116	131	138	148	166	180	154	163	Suède
119	130	132	135	145	166	153	161	Suisse
104	116	120	126	138	143	125	132	Royaume-Uni
104	**112**	**118**	**121**	**129**	**141**	**129**	**144**	**Économies développées : Océanie**
104	111	117	120	128	140	130	145	Australie
107	116	124	124	134	145	119	136	Nouvelle-Zélande

Sources :
- CEPALC, *CEPALSTAT* déflateur du commerce extérieur
- FMI, *Statistiques financières internationales* sur CD-ROM
- Bureau des statistiques du travail des États-Unis (BLS), indices de prix du commerce extérieur
- Indices des valeurs unitaires des douanes japonaises et indices des prix de la Banque du Japon
- CNUCED, *Statistiques de prix des produits de base*
- CNUCED, *Matrice du commerce de marchandises*
- Estimations du secrétariat de la CNUCED

Notes :

(1) Afin d'améliorer la couverture des données et spécialement pour les années récentes, la méthode suivante a été utilisée pour le calcul des valeurs unitaires :
- Un ensemble d'indices de prix moyens au niveau des groupes de la CTCI (révision 3, position à 3 chiffres) a été construit en utilisant des données de CNUCED, Statistiques des produits de base, des sources internationales et nationales ainsi que des estimations du secrétariat de la CNUCED.
- Au niveau des pays individuels, les indices de la valeur unitaire ont été calculés en utilisant comme pondération les valeurs des exportations et des importations de l'année précédente, disponibles dans la table 3.2.
Dans certains cas ces indices peuvent différer des estimations publiées dans les sources officielles, le but principal étant de fournir des estimations approximatives et comparables pour la plupart des pays.

4.2.1 Terms of trade indices and purchasing power indices of exports of countries and geographical regions
2000 = 100

Region, country or territory	Terms of trade (1) - Termes de l'échange (1)							
	2003	2004	2005	2006	2007	2008	2009	2010
WORLD	101	102	103	103	104	104	105	105
DEVELOPING ECONOMIES	98	98	103	105	105	106	104	107
TRANSITION ECONOMIES	104	117	138	153	159	190	154	171
DEVELOPED ECONOMIES	103	103	101	100	101	98	102	100
Developing economies: Africa	103	112	131	146	146	169	145	159
Eastern Africa	94	97	97	108	108	103	108	116
Burundi	90	93	112	120	119	128	131	154
Comoros	67	57	53	57	63	60	66	71
Djibouti	96	94	85	87	86	87	80	81
Eritrea	89	88	87	85	84	77	78	79
Ethiopia	97	103	109	109	112	113	122	132
Kenya	90	89	90	87	84	83	93	90
Madagascar	86	81	75	74	74	70	74	75
Malawi	87	84	82	86	85	79	46	90
Mauritius	104	101	92	87	86	76	81	73
Mayotte	98	93	88	87	83	79	84	78
Mozambique	95	103	106	122	117	109	96	108
Rwanda	100	115	162	169	166	220	218	230
Seychelles	84	82	78	74	69	68	74	76
Somalia	102	105	104	107	106	101	102	108
Uganda	95	93	96	99	99	101	111	116
United Republic of Tanzania	98	100	96	109	108	106	118	125
Zambia	95	115	129	197	194	173	160	193
Zimbabwe	95	100	93	94	105	96	108	111
Middle Africa	102	120	156	176	178	216	154	185
Angola	102	126	172	198	204	252	172	213
Cameroon	108	114	124	129	127	130	120	135
Central African Republic	99	100	92	90	90	83	85	88
Chad	100	118	154	175	176	213	148	181
Congo	100	118	156	180	182	222	153	179
Dem. Rep. of the Congo	97	97	112	125	123	142	111	134
Equatorial Guinea	101	120	155	176	180	232	181	203
Gabon	102	119	156	179	180	222	156	186
Sao Tome and Principe	135	129	113	107	110	117	135	133
Northern Africa	103	114	140	157	153	185	148	161
Algeria	107	122	164	191	183	237	161	182
Egypt	98	106	124	137	131	145	136	139
Libyan Arab Jamahiriya	98	117	151	169	168	200	140	167
Morocco	105	105	99	100	98	131	136	128
Sudan	100	117	152	174	180	224	164	199
Tunisia	97	94	93	90	90	95	94	90
Western Sahara	91	96	..	..	..	..	..	..
Southern Africa	106	107	107	117	121	129	134	135
Botswana	95	95	90	93	102	88	88	88
Lesotho	96	91	88	85	82	74	80	69
Namibia	98	100	105	132	140	126	127	120
South Africa	107	108	109	119	123	133	139	141
Swaziland	94	91	93	98	90	100	110	107
Western Africa	107	119	144	159	161	185	153	177
Benin	101	97	90	94	97	86	83	99
Burkina Faso	111	103	86	88	89	81	85	109
Cape Verde	95	89	97	99	93	96	116	114
Côte d'Ivoire	139	130	130	132	137	138	144	157
Gambia	110	105	97	93	95	90	87	83
Ghana	135	125	125	128	137	155	169	176
Guinea	105	134	145	179	176	164	134	152
Guinea-Bissau	100	103	90	89	87	71	71	64
Liberia	110	113	115	120	120	120	111	147
Mali	120	112	94	105	108	110	124	156
Mauritania	92	94	122	133	124	147	149	140
Niger	102	112	125	137	171	151	140	144
Nigeria	102	121	157	177	179	217	155	187
Saint Helena	84	80	71	67	63	59	62	59
Senegal	98	98	97	99	98	98	100	102
Sierra Leone	90	86	73	71	68	63	73	71
Togo	24	30	21	21	23	33	32	31

For sources and notes, see end of table.

4.2.1 Indices des termes de l'échange et du pouvoir d'achat des exportations des pays et des régions géographiques
2000 = 100

	Purchasing power (2) - Pouvoir d'achat (2)							Régions, pays ou territoires
2003	2004	2005	2006	2007	2008	2009	2010	
112	125	134	147	157	161	140	161	**MONDE**
120	140	159	180	196	205	180	215	ÉCONOMIES EN DÉVELOPPEMENT
129	161	192	228	259	309	214	266	ÉCONOMIES EN TRANSITION
108	117	121	130	137	136	120	132	ÉCONOMIES DÉVELOPPÉES
110	129	163	180	193	218	167	200	Économies en développement : Afrique
119	*127*	*130*	*151*	*160*	*157*	*164*	*190*	*Afrique orientale*
72	82	91	91	00	69	84	131	Burundi
102	122	72	60	74	28	55	55	Comores
110	102	89	116	109	110	138	142	Djibouti
33	53	50	50	46	32	33	34	Érythrée
98	125	159	162	183	196	225	342	Éthiopie
131	130	141	135	148	154	156	165	Kenya
110	100	78	88	109	118	85	92	Madagascar
132	114	110	140	164	139	204	181	Malawi
130	121	121	125	112	99	96	104	Maurice
176	158	189	209	205	181	169	161	Mayotte
273	365	381	489	456	410	372	369	Mozambique
115	165	194	219	239	307	249	294	Rwanda
132	125	128	131	117	138	131	111	Seychelles
113	87	111	114	126	124	128	128	Somalie
123	148	178	193	268	293	345	299	Ouganda
157	172	171	182	190	222	252	314	République-Unie de Tanzanie
105	154	163	322	366	353	342	510	Zambie
79	80	68	66	60	42	64	67	Zimbabwe
126	*168*	*245*	*288*	*332*	*452*	*298*	*335*	*Afrique centrale*
119	160	281	357	462	684	413	456	Angola
120	117	115	133	124	117	94	96	Cameroun
76	72	66	76	79	57	51	62	République centrafricaine
308	1 056	1 424	1 446	1 438	1 524	982	1 112	Tchad
103	122	163	199	169	225	171	215	Congo
159	198	214	214	218	295	258	376	Rép. dém. du Congo
250	375	533	592	684	913	652	694	Guinée équatoriale
106	126	161	169	173	219	163	192	Gabon
236	176	196	206	165	220	191	140	Sao Tomé-et-Principe
112	*132*	*189*	*192*	*202*	*240*	*170*	*196*	*Afrique septentrionale*
106	128	176	198	194	233	141	173	Algérie
123	138	175	209	222	309	300	321	Égypte
109	142	197	235	242	291	188	223	Jamahiriya arabe libyenne
111	114	121	132	141	158	123	141	Maroc
135	187	225	253	373	451	321	413	Soudan
131	145	145	150	179	199	163	168	Tunisie
..	..	..	..	..	..	..	..	Sahara occidental
107	*115*	*125*	*136*	*146*	*141*	*124*	*147*	*Afrique australe*
99	114	131	126	131	114	87	112	Botswana
208	291	257	271	294	287	249	252	Lesotho
93	127	139	171	178	175	185	207	Namibie
106	112	123	135	146	142	124	149	Afrique du Sud
162	188	147	141	135	112	124	121	Swaziland
102	*131*	*184*	*185*	*190*	*200*	*161*	*224*	*Afrique occidentale*
126	122	109	131	171	160	175	153	Bénin
153	210	187	223	213	185	272	300	Burkina Faso
113	124	132	146	123	203	237	264	Cap-Vert
148	157	152	154	145	138	160	144	Côte d'Ivoire
50	59	42	56	58	51	62	56	Gambie
134	132	135	168	180	203	230	274	Ghana
87	98	99	114	123	116	101	98	Guinée
100	105	102	78	102	97	105	102	Guinée-Bissau
38	35	47	50	54	53	32	37	Libéria
166	158	154	202	185	211	200	206	Mali
86	111	150	305	277	301	258	350	Mauritanie
117	133	134	140	160	192	199	202	Niger
93	132	218	212	220	241	170	272	Nigéria
234	209	192	178	187	228	212	173	Sainte-Hélène
131	139	128	118	113	120	129	126	Sénégal
670	868	814	1 069	1 020	709	842	1 214	Sierra Leone
63	59	55	47	50	50	56	54	Togo

Pour les sources et les notes, se reporter à la fin du tableau.

4

4.2.1 Terms of trade indices and purchasing power indices of exports of countries and geographical regions
2000 = 100

Region, country or territory	Terms of trade (1) - Termes de l'échange (1)							
	2003	2004	2005	2006	2007	2008	2009	2010
Developing economies: America	99	104	110	119	122	127	120	132
Caribbean	102	107	115	126	127	138	126	134
Anguilla	99	96	93	107	104	103	97	94
Antigua and Barbuda	89	86	79	80	81	83	83	73
Aruba	96	104	120	125	126	140	101	100
Bahamas	94	95	93	95	95	102	95	98
Barbados	101	108	118	121	119	120	125	120
British Virgin Islands	94	87	98	101	95	..	..	..
Cayman Islands	87	82	82	83	82	74	76	75
Cuba	121	133	130	164	170	111	..	..
Dominica	99	99	95	93	91	86	92	86
Dominican Republic	98	97	96	95	98	94	101	98
Grenada	06	89	81	87	90	92	98	97
Haiti	95	96	02	89	96	62	80	78
Jamaica	95	99	86	90	100	84	86	71
Montserrat	96	92	90	88	88	82	95	..
Netherlands Antilles	97	96	100	99	99	102	90	94
Saint Kitts and Nevis	94	87	85	82	80	75	79	75
Saint Lucia	104	104	110	112	109	92	108	93
Saint Vincent and the Grenadines	93	90	79	82	84	94	114	114
Trinidad and Tobago	106	112	124	136	134	157	131	132
Turks and Caicos Islands	91	85	80	77	75	73	78	77
Central America	98	101	102	102	103	103	101	102
Belize	79	76	75	80	74	77	80	87
Costa Rica	95	92	88	86	85	82	84	78
El Salvador	98	97	97	95	95	92	95	91
Guatemala	93	92	91	90	88	86	93	93
Honduras	88	87	87	83	82	77	82	83
Mexico	99	102	104	104	105	106	103	104
Nicaragua	84	82	81	79	79	75	82	82
Panama	97	95	94	91	90	86	90	87
South America	99	107	116	131	136	144	133	152
Argentina	107	109	107	113	118	133	127	127
Bolivia (Plurinational State of)	99	104	112	140	142	144	139	152
Brazil	97	98	99	104	107	110	100	125
Chile	103	125	140	183	189	165	167	204
Colombia	95	102	111	115	124	138	119	134
Ecuador	90	91	102	110	113	124	110	122
Falkland Islands (Malvinas)	82	79	76	74	72	70	80	86
Guyana	97	95	96	109	99	109	130	138
Paraguay	101	104	97	96	100	107	105	103
Peru	102	111	119	152	158	137	129	152
Suriname	104	128	128	155	153	152	153	178
Uruguay	103	100	91	89	89	94	97	100
Venezuela (Bolivarian Rep. of)	99	118	154	184	202	249	182	216
Developing economies: Asia	97	96	98	98	98	97	97	97
Eastern Asia	96	92	87	83	81	74	79	76
China	98	92	86	83	80	74	80	76
China, Hong Kong SAR	101	99	98	97	97	96	98	96
China, Macao SAR	99	96	92	90	88	83	87	88
China, Taiwan Province of	93	87	83	78	74	67	69	66
Korea, Dem. People's Rep. of	93	88	84	81	78	76	83	79
Korea, Republic of	89	85	79	74	72	62	68	68
Mongolia	110	124	126	166	167	182	175	213
Southern Asia	96	93	111	118	118	125	127	127
Afghanistan	109	111	108	110	113	103	105	106
Bangladesh	93	87	80	75	68	58	64	57
Bhutan	108	126	138	138	124	151	138	146
India	96	86	105	111	114	117	132	127
Iran (Islamic Rep. of)	97	112	141	160	162	187	133	156
Maldives	99	94	96	104	87	87	113	114
Nepal	98	94	85	85	85	77	82	78
Pakistan	89	85	75	70	66	58	65	62
Sri Lanka	94	87	82	79	75	69	79	75
South-Eastern Asia	97	97	96	95	95	95	95	96
Brunei Darussalam	110	125	165	199	196	256	174	187
Cambodia	101	94	87	84	80	75	80	76

For sources and notes, see end of table.

	Purchasing power (2) - Pouvoir d'achat (2)							Régions, pays ou territoires
2003	2004	2005	2006	2007	2008	2009	2010	
106	123	138	156	165	171	143	175	**Économies en développement : Amérique**
93	*98*	*106*	*125*	*121*	*117*	*81*	*102*	*Caraïbes*
103	135	299	232	164	187	376	197	Anguilla
85	101	136	113	105	89	83	71	Antigua-et-Barbuda
76	86	87	81	54	63	27	5	Aruba
72	74	76	92	98	102	86	82	Bahamas
89	92	106	122	125	106	92	94	Barbade
..	..	..	..	..	..	..	..	Îles Vierges britanniques
..	..	..	..	..	..	..	..	Îles Caïmanes
101	130	118	149	176	123	..	..	Cuba
72	68	63	60	48	47	44	45	Dominique
94	97	96	98	101	86	81	88	République dominicaine
49	38	31	30	33	27	29	22	Grenade
101	112	125	124	123	79	111	105	Haïti
88	93	86	100	102	99	63	55	Jamaïque
152	329	102	88	170	223	218	..	Montserrat
56	30	28	28	27	21	20	17	Antilles néerlandaises
170	130	88	110	105	92	107	121	Saint-Kitts-et-Nevis
145	168	112	148	153	179	247	204	Sainte-Lucie
73	65	65	59	68	65	69	54	Saint-Vincent-et-les Grenadines
118	129	163	216	207	216	124	128	Trinité-et-Tobago
110	126	141	162	139	191	176	167	Îles Turques et Caïques
101	*109*	*116*	*130*	*133*	*134*	*113*	*139*	*Amérique centrale*
89	85	72	87	77	75	64	75	Belize
107	105	112	127	142	137	137	135	Costa Rica
109	110	108	112	114	121	109	121	El Salvador
167	173	169	177	188	186	195	212	Guatemala
127	142	145	139	142	133	119	131	Honduras
99	107	116	130	133	134	111	139	Mexique
93	107	111	124	137	151	161	198	Nicaragua
100	104	107	109	111	108	88	74	Panama
115	*142*	*165*	*190*	*205*	*216*	*184*	*222*	*Amérique du Sud*
119	129	145	164	182	209	190	220	Argentine
128	160	195	250	259	387	284	334	Bolivie (État plurinational de)
134	161	177	193	208	210	183	232	Brésil
121	169	197	266	294	253	236	295	Chili
102	118	145	160	183	216	199	227	Colombie
125	148	177	205	208	250	212	246	Équateur
175	149	168	146	158	154	132	158	Îles Falkland (Malvinas)
99	103	83	83	87	87	95	103	Guyana
155	173	174	186	270	390	307	423	Paraguay
129	168	207	264	280	261	241	289	Pérou
142	182	178	196	211	238	206	204	Suriname
103	124	127	135	140	161	168	194	Uruguay
80	109	148	169	171	212	140	152	Venezuela (Rép. bolivarienne du)
124	145	164	186	205	212	191	227	**Économies en développement : Asie**
136	*160*	*178*	*201*	*227*	*224*	*212*	*254*	*Asie orientale*
176	219	259	311	369	375	349	429	Chine
119	134	146	156	167	168	147	170	Chine (RAS de Hong Kong)
99	104	86	86	81	58	30	26	Chine (RAS de Macao)
113	119	123	130	134	117	114	131	Province chinoise de Taiwan
150	154	138	137	143	139	154	215	Corée, Rép. populaire dém. de
118	137	141	149	161	151	170	196	Corée, République de
110	140	149	201	227	259	223	316	Mongolie
119	*127*	*162*	*197*	*209*	*236*	*227*	*250*	*Asie méridionale*
104	203	230	231	255	234	188	177	Afghanistan
103	113	115	138	129	128	138	154	Bangladesh
125	162	210	307	445	290	308	313	Bhoutan
129	134	190	232	256	307	322	350	Inde
113	132	155	202	213	233	171	206	Iran (Rép. islamique d')
137	150	122	161	151	189	106	116	Maldives
78	81	78	68	65	58	57	60	Népal
122	122	129	124	118	105	109	118	Pakistan
91	92	93	93	95	84	82	87	Sri Lanka
111	*128*	*135*	*148*	*158*	*161*	*143*	*172*	*Asie du Sud-Est*
110	118	140	165	153	192	133	160	Brunéi Darussalam
150	184	175	211	217	219	215	250	Cambodge

Pour les sources et les notes, se reporter à la fin du tableau.

4.2.1 Terms of trade indices and purchasing power indices of exports of countries and geographical regions
2000 = 100

Region, country or territory	Terms of trade (1) - Termes de l'échange (1)							
	2003	2004	2005	2006	2007	2008	2009	2010
Indonesia	105	107	107	112	116	124	120	127
Lao People's Dem. Rep.	101	96	95	119	115	111	104	122
Malaysia	102	102	102	102	102	104	100	101
Myanmar	107	104	108	118	110	120	117	110
Philippines	96	93	86	77	76	68	72	70
Singapore	91	89	87	86	84	83	83	83
Thailand	94	96	97	96	96	94	97	98
Viet Nam	94	94	96	95	92	95	98	100
Western Asia	103	113	140	152	161	182	144	164
Bahrain	98	105	114	126	125	134	105	114
Iraq	99	118	155	177	170	210	151	186
Jordan	88	87	88	88	82	118	120	83
Kuwait	101	122	164	185	189	233	158	191
Lebanon	102	101	94	95	96	93	98	96
Occupied Palestinian territory	94	91	82	77	80	70	79	81
Oman	117	112	156	180	177	239	150	194
Qatar	106	122	160	189	188	252	171	190
Saudi Arabia	114	129	178	202	236	266	176	224
Syrian Arab Republic	98	107	119	122	126	143	130	136
Turkey	97	98	97	92	95	91	95	92
United Arab Emirates	101	114	139	150	152	176	145	160
Yemen	98	114	139	152	149	167	132	151
Developing economies: Oceania	101	110	114	148	157	161	142	163
American Samoa	114	121	111	164	171	147	135	136
Cook Islands	97	95	97	99	..	..	..	..
Fiji	96	92	92	99	92	89	108	106
French Polynesia	95	91	88	87	85	81	87	83
Guam	105	104	92	89	88	82	112	115
Kiribati	88	83	79	81	82	78	101	101
Marshall Islands	103	109	111	111	109	109	105	104
Micronesia (Federated States of)	93	86	92	102	84	86	112	115
Nauru	90	100	80	78	103	401	269	253
New Caledonia	105	135	139	147	184	192	205	209
Niue	98	97	93	92	85	79	88	104
Northern Mariana Islands	100	94	83	80	80	76	89	95
Palau	95	97	104	115	94	96	100	114
Papua New Guinea	98	108	116	170	170	163	124	150
Samoa	95	88	84	85	81	73	80	81
Solomon Islands	109	110	100	101	107	90	88	93
Tokelau	107	106	106	107	104	92	90	89
Tonga	99	97	88	80	70	64	77	72
Vanuatu	96	94	90	96	80	81	104	105
Wallis and Futuna Islands	97	107	101	99	98	112	104	99
Transition economies	104	117	138	153	159	190	154	171
Albania	95	95	94	94	93	94	97	100
Armenia	99	105	105	114	113	116	114	128
Azerbaijan	95	110	136	150	153	188	127	157
Belarus	96	96	97	95	98	99	98	99
Bosnia and Herzegovina	101	102	101	104	103	100	101	103
Croatia	97	96	96	97	97	98	101	101
Georgia	103	112	108	113	116	125	132	137
Kazakhstan	101	119	149	177	184	218	163	193
Kyrgyzstan	111	110	104	106	105	103	102	105
Republic of Moldova	102	100	100	99	103	98	100	105
Russian Federation	107	124	156	178	186	238	180	202
Serbia and Montenegro	98	100	100	104	105	–	–	–
Tajikistan	96	92	87	99	94	86	74	86
TFYR of Macedonia	96	95	94	92	91	89	94	87
Turkmenistan	116	120	157	198	188	259	193	210
Ukraine	102	109	107	103	110	114	120	119
Uzbekistan	106	109	113	129	128	150	130	150
Developed economies: America	104	104	102	102	103	100	104	104
Bermuda	94	92	86	92	94	112	87	92
Canada	106	110	114	114	118	127	115	119
Greenland	79	77	73	72	67	65	74	75
Saint Pierre and Miquelon	95	92	97	102	86	92	108	119
United States	103	101	97	96	97	92	99	97

For sources and notes, see end of table.

	Purchasing power (2) - Pouvoir d'achat (2)							Régions, pays ou territoires
2003	2004	2005	2006	2007	2008	2009	2010	
96	96	101	111	118	118	113	138	Indonésie
99	98	133	199	194	202	207	300	Rép. dém. populaire lao
107	128	137	150	156	164	132	157	Malaisie
146	125	179	202	249	233	254	294	Myanmar
111	124	104	106	108	91	79	100	Philippines
117	139	151	165	176	181	162	196	Singapour
111	128	138	153	171	174	155	184	Thaïlande
135	156	171	196	220	246	247	285	Viet Nam
114	*140*	*175*	*197*	*212*	*250*	*188*	*230*	*Asie occidentale*
102	107	123	127	135	118	106	117	Bahreïn
78	80	96	118	138	201	150	173	Iraq
141	159	153	168	164	185	175	152	Jordanie
104	135	203	243	253	334	100	240	Koweït
245	207	252	283	328	347	360	400	Liban
63	63	59	59	77	67	74	72	Territoire palestinien occupé
116	103	137	149	155	223	176	241	Oman
111	145	192	248	283	348	264	397	Qatar
117	147	201	222	227	271	173	219	Arabie saoudite
119	140	155	172	168	192	148	179	République arabe syrienne
153	177	192	206	235	241	232	238	Turquie
131	167	206	237	272	329	249	320	Émirats arabes unis
88	87	106	115	97	98	95	118	Yémen
104	**108**	**104**	**113**	**122**	**108**	**90**	**110**	**Économies en développement : Océanie**
135	123	96	105	105	85	94	87	Samoa américaines
93	72	49	32	42	31	..	..	Îles Cook
122	115	99	89	90	93	74	72	Fidji
60	69	73	78	60	76	51	49	Polynésie française
58	59	45	41	66	63	38	33	Guam
80	61	95	130	184	229	252	230	Kiribati
191	245	337	262	238	168	156	132	Îles Marshall
108	76	67	89	101	112	117	112	Micronésie (États fédérés de)
95	46	9	8	92	177	52	81	Nauru
128	156	149	176	264	146	115	142	Nouvelle-Calédonie
36	55	56	313	712	4	5	6	Nioué
77	74	51	35	21	9	0	1	Îles Mariannes du Nord
70	46	105	103	76	70	64	32	Palaos
103	109	119	139	142	136	119	155	Papouasie-Nouvelle-Guinée
601	520	474	334	454	289	212	250	Samoa
103	122	116	124	157	154	137	179	Îles Salomon
..	..	..	..	..	..	..	..	Tokélaou
194	144	81	82	54	51	47	47	Tonga
104	136	123	150	140	130	143	112	Vanuatu
448	104	78	70	64	57	60	55	Îles Wallis-et-Futuna
129	**161**	**192**	**228**	**259**	**309**	**214**	**266**	**Économies en transition**
161	203	207	238	300	327	292	394	Albanie
225	219	263	257	289	218	158	219	Arménie
137	175	341	534	810	1 061	754	932	Azerbaïdjan
127	153	150	167	190	206	164	181	Bélarus
126	157	181	233	269	286	247	283	Bosnie-Herzégovine
136	162	163	180	201	198	162	172	Croatie
135	172	203	214	249	264	222	288	Géorgie
144	205	261	338	394	522	330	421	Kazakhstan
109	120	96	116	158	195	186	182	Kirghizistan
204	214	252	248	290	282	314	372	République de Moldova
126	159	202	244	270	336	224	286	Fédération de Russie
153	206	229	300	377	–	–	–	Serbie-et-Monténégro
91	90	74	103	100	79	65	70	Tadjikistan
99	108	117	128	162	160	119	132	LERY de Macédoine
141	140	173	241	248	340	192	173	Turkménistan
148	186	168	171	206	230	158	196	Ukraine
108	135	142	160	213	246	269	283	Ouzbékistan
97	**103**	**108**	**116**	**123**	**124**	**108**	**123**	**Économies développées : Amérique**
113	130	83	42	38	33	44	37	Bermudes
99	104	114	115	118	122	92	104	Canada
129	129	121	113	113	114	93	91	Groenland
30	43	65	246	60	57	31	27	Saint-Pierre-et-Miquelon
96	102	105	115	124	124	114	129	États-Unis

Pour les sources et les notes, se reporter à la fin du tableau.

4.2.1 Terms of trade indices and purchasing power indices of exports of countries and geographical regions
2000 = 100

Region, country or territory	Terms of trade (1) - Termes de l'échange (1)							
	2003	2004	2005	2006	2007	2008	2009	2010
Developed economies: Asia	**97**	**92**	**84**	**76**	**73**	**64**	**76**	**69**
Israel	96	95	95	94	91	93	103	98
Japan	98	92	83	75	72	62	74	68
Developed economies: Europe	**102**	**102**	**101**	**100**	**102**	**99**	**102**	**100**
Andorra	100	96	..	..	..	..	..	..
Austria	100	99	96	94	94	91	93	91
Belgium	101	99	99	99	101	100	103	101
Bulgaria	101	103	102	105	108	109	103	109
Cyprus	100	101	100	99	00	101	103	104
Czech Republic	105	107	106	105	107	106	110	106
Denmark	102	103	104	105	100	102	103	107
Estonia	143	144	143	143	148	146	149	144
Faeroe Islands	100	95	95	100	93	96	123	125
Finland	92	90	86	83	00	74	79	77
France	103	104	104	101	100	98	102	98
Germany	107	107	105	102	103	100	106	104
Gibraltar	91	77	60	58	58	52	62	62
Greece	97	99	95	95	96	95	91	93
Hungary	100	99	97	96	95	94	96	95
Iceland	97	95	94	101	101	95	84	92
Ireland	103	97	99	94	91	89	94	96
Italy	104	103	100	96	98	95	103	99
Latvia	99	104	102	102	109	108	104	105
Lithuania	100	101	103	102	105	102	104	102
Luxembourg	99	101	98	98	100	98	97	96
Malta	92	85	80	77	74	70	72	68
Netherlands	99	96	100	102	112	103	103	102
Norway	90	100	122	139	134	157	129	140
Poland	102	107	107	107	109	107	107	100
Portugal	98	95	91	90	88	84	87	86
Romania	98	98	98	97	98	98	101	99
Slovakia	98	97	96	93	93	89	90	89
Slovenia	100	97	93	91	91	88	91	89
Spain	104	102	102	104	105	103	107	104
Sweden	95	92	90	88	89	87	90	80
Switzerland	88	85	86	88	87	82	85	84
United Kingdom	104	105	105	105	104	105	104	103
Developed economies: Oceania	**106**	**115**	**128**	**139**	**146**	**166**	**154**	**170**
Australia	106	116	131	146	152	175	163	179
New Zealand	104	110	111	112	118	126	115	127

Sources:
- ECLAC, *CEPALSTAT* external trade deflator
- IMF, *International Financial Statistics* on CD-ROM
- U.S. Bureau of Labor Statistics, external trade prices indices
- Unit value indices of Japan Customs and price indices of Bank of Japan
- UNCTAD, *Commodity Price Statistics*
- UNCTAD, *Merchandise Trade Matrix*
- UNCTAD secretariat estimates

Notes:
(1) The "net barter" terms of trade, defined as the ratio of the export unit value index to the import unit value index.
(2) The purchasing power index of exports is the value index of exports deflated by the import unit value index.

4.2.1 Indices des termes de l'échange et du pouvoir d'achat des exportations des pays et des régions géographiques
2000 = 100

	Purchasing power (2) - Pouvoir d'achat (2)							Régions, pays ou territoires
2003	2004	2005	2006	2007	2008	2009	2010	
105	**113**	**108**	**109**	**113**	**101**	**91**	**106**	**Économies développées : Asie**
97	110	114	117	125	123	114	129	Israël
106	114	108	109	113	100	90	104	Japon
113	**122**	**127**	**136**	**143**	**143**	**127**	**137**	**Économies développées : Europe**
196	255	..	..	..	..	..	..	Andorre
139	158	155	158	178	176	143	150	Autriche
113	120	125	130	136	132	120	127	Belgique
143	161	176	204	214	226	190	242	Bulgarie
86	90	128	110	107	112	96	101	Chypre
137	173	184	210	246	256	228	264	République tchèque
109	114	121	127	125	132	119	129	Danemark
122	115	144	172	174	173	140	173	Estonie
124	117	105	107	114	117	113	111	Îles Féroé
100	102	102	111	116	113	85	93	Finlande
105	113	117	119	121	118	105	113	France
123	137	143	156	167	165	147	166	Allemagne
117	127	98	102	117	85	115	95	Gibraltar
83	84	87	99	101	98	82	83	Grèce
124	148	163	190	220	229	204	237	Hongrie
123	132	131	139	170	162	145	151	Islande
108	113	118	112	115	110	111	115	Irlande
103	107	104	105	113	104	92	96	Italie
127	154	184	199	233	244	208	251	Lettonie
191	231	260	291	331	371	301	349	Lituanie
155	171	184	215	196	198	181	158	Luxembourg
91	85	77	87	91	80	64	68	Malte
108	117	132	144	151	163	145	163	Pays-Bas
97	108	130	146	144	169	133	141	Norvège
146	182	201	233	260	275	252	215	Pologne
126	131	129	141	155	148	125	129	Portugal
163	201	217	239	281	304	268	312	Roumanie
178	207	219	270	359	390	330	371	Slovaquie
141	165	179	203	246	248	208	221	Slovénie
117	121	122	130	139	139	133	143	Espagne
101	108	109	114	117	117	98	112	Suède
110	118	124	136	147	150	140	150	Suisse
103	105	113	126	111	113	99	108	Royaume-Uni
109	**123**	**139**	**156**	**169**	**199**	**179**	**218**	**Économies développées : Océanie**
108	122	142	161	173	209	186	230	Australie
112	127	127	133	151	154	151	167	Nouvelle-Zélande

Sources :
- CEPALC, *CEPALSTAT* déflateur du commerce extérieur
- FMI, *Statistiques financières internationales* sur CD-ROM
- Bureau des statistiques du travail des États-Unis (BLS), indices de prix du commerce extérieur
- Indices des valeurs unitaires des douanes japonaises et indices des prix de la Banque du Japon
- CNUCED, *Statistiques de prix des produits de base*
- CNUCED, *Matrice du commerce de marchandises*
- Estimations du secrétariat de la CNUCED

Notes :
(1) Le terme de l'échange, appelé aussi "troc net", est le rapport de l'indice de la valeur unitaire des exportations à l'indice de la valeur unitaire des importations exprimé en pourcentage.
(2) Le pouvoir d'achat des exportations est l'indice de la valeur des exportations corrigé par l'indice de la valeur unitaire des importations.

4.2.2 Volume indices of exports and imports of economic groupings
2000 = 100

Economic grouping	Exports (1) (2) - Exportations (1) (2)							
	2003	2004	2005	2006	2007	2008	2009	2010
DEVELOPING ECONOMIES	**122**	**142**	**155**	**172**	**187**	**193**	**173**	**202**
Developing economies excluding China	114	129	136	146	153	155	141	160
Developing economies excluding LDCs	122	142	156	172	187	193	173	203
High-income developing countries	115	131	139	150	157	159	145	165
Middle-income developing countries	144	175	202	236	271	284	248	303
Low-income developing countries	105	117	127	135	145	152	145	161
Heavily indebted poor countries (IMF)	121	135	133	108	117	140	143	147
Landlocked developing countries	124	144	150	163	189	201	101	188
Small island developing States	108	108	115	123	120	113	89	91
Least developed countries	*124*	*138*	*140*	*160*	*183*	*196*	*191*	*186*
Africa and Haiti	134	154	167	176	208	228	207	200
Asia	109	116	127	144	152	154	157	188
Islands	173	179	175	164	200	195	165	180
Major petroleum and gas exporters	*101*	*113*	*116*	*117*	*119*	*122*	*117*	*124*
Africa	101	111	128	124	133	132	121	133
America	81	93	96	92	84	85	77	71
Asia	104	116	115	120	121	125	121	130
Major exporters of manufactured goods	*130*	*157*	*179*	*208*	*234*	*248*	*220*	*270*
America	100	106	112	124	126	127	109	133
Asia	135	165	190	222	253	269	239	294
Emerging economies	*118*	*137*	*148*	*164*	*175*	*179*	*164*	*192*
America	110	121	130	138	144	142	126	144
Asia	123	145	158	177	193	200	186	220
Newly industrialized Asian countries	*119*	*138*	*149*	*165*	*178*	*182*	*166*	*197*
First tier	125	146	161	179	194	201	187	220
Second tier	106	119	124	136	144	143	126	149
Developing economies: Africa	**107**	**116**	**124**	**124**	**132**	**129**	**115**	**126**
Northern Africa excluding Sudan	108	115	120	122	130	127	112	119
Sub-Saharan Africa	106	117	127	125	133	130	118	130
Sub-Saharan Africa excluding South Africa	110	125	138	134	144	145	136	146
Developing economies: America	**108**	**118**	**125**	**132**	**135**	**134**	**119**	**132**
Central America and Greater Caribbean Islands excluding Puerto Rico	102	108	113	126	128	129	111	135
Central America and Greater Caribbean Islands excluding Mexico and Puerto Rico	115	121	124	132	139	139	125	149
South America and Central America	108	119	127	134	138	137	123	136
South America excluding Brazil	105	117	126	127	130	132	123	127
Developing economies: Asia	**128**	**151**	**167**	**189**	**209**	**219**	**197**	**234**
Eastern and South-Eastern Asia excluding China	119	138	149	165	178	182	167	197
Southern Asia excluding India	116	121	119	134	140	135	131	140

For sources and notes, see end of table 4.2.1 (Volume indices of exports and imports).

4.2.2 Indices du volume des exportations et importations des groupements économiques
2000 = 100

	Imports (1) (2) - Importations (1) (2)							Groupements économiques
2003	2004	2005	2006	2007	2008	2009	2010	
119	**140**	**154**	**170**	**187**	**200**	**180**	**214**	**ÉCONOMIES EN DÉVELOPPEMENT**
111	128	141	155	169	183	161	186	Économies en développement sans la Chine
119	140	153	169	187	199	179	214	Économies en développement sans les PMA
109	126	135	148	161	168	145	170	Pays en développement à revenu élevé
142	170	185	204	228	242	224	279	Pays en développement à revenu intermédiaire
118	136	171	193	216	256	246	268	Pays en développement à revenu faible
128	146	163	177	196	214	205	220	Pays pauvres très endettés (FMI)
132	156	169	193	230	261	241	249	Pays en développement sans littoral
111	116	118	127	133	135	117	110	Petits États insulaires en développement
130	*142*	*159*	*174*	*196*	*217*	*228*	*232*	*Pays les moins avancés*
139	157	182	200	231	266	280	275	Afrique et Haïti
118	123	129	140	152	156	164	178	Asie
131	151	166	188	192	189	182	208	Îles
128	*161*	*182*	*199*	*234*	*276*	*246*	*262*	*Principaux exportateurs de pétrole et de gaz*
134	161	192	203	251	294	312	304	Afrique
61	93	127	172	226	219	186	178	Amérique
137	171	188	203	232	281	241	265	Asie
122	*144*	*154*	*170*	*184*	*188*	*171*	*212*	*Principaux exportateurs d'articles manufacturés*
97	107	114	126	132	136	109	134	Amérique
127	151	162	178	195	199	182	226	Asie
103	*120*	*128*	*140*	*150*	*157*	*134*	*165*	*Économies émergentes*
93	106	116	130	144	158	126	164	Amérique
109	127	134	145	154	158	138	166	Asie
111	*129*	*136*	*147*	*156*	*160*	*139*	*167*	*Économies nouvellement industrialisées d'Asie*
111	128	134	146	156	157	141	167	Première génération
112	132	143	149	157	166	132	168	Deuxième génération
119	**135**	**153**	**167**	**188**	**208**	**202**	**205**	**Économies en développement : Afrique**
107	124	137	140	162	206	201	207	Afrique septentrionale sans le Soudan
126	141	162	182	203	209	204	205	Afrique subsaharienne
129	147	173	188	219	239	243	249	Afrique subsaharienne sans l'Afrique du Sud
95	**108**	**119**	**135**	**150**	**163**	**133**	**167**	**Économies en développement : Amérique**
100	108	117	129	136	142	114	141	Amérique centrale et Grandes Antilles sans Porto Rico
111	115	127	142	153	166	137	172	Amérique centrale et Grandes Antilles sans le Mexique et Porto Rico
95	109	121	137	154	168	137	171	Amérique du Sud et Amérique centrale
89	113	137	161	194	219	182	221	Amérique du Sud sans le Brésil
127	**150**	**164**	**180**	**198**	**210**	**191**	**229**	**Économies en développement : Asie**
112	129	137	148	158	162	142	170	Asie orientale et Asie du Sud-Est sans la Chine
130	150	163	167	169	176	164	186	Asie méridionale sans l'Inde

Pour les sources et les notes, se reporter à la fin du tableau 4.2.1 (Indices du volume des exportations et importations).

4.2.2 Unit value indices of exports and imports of economic groupings
2000 = 100

Economic grouping	Exports (1) - Exportations (1)							
	2003	2004	2005	2006	2007	2008	2009	2010
DEVELOPING ECONOMIES	**97**	**106**	**119**	**128**	**137**	**158**	**139**	**154**
Developing economies excluding China	97	108	124	136	146	173	147	167
Developing economies excluding LDCs	97	106	118	127	136	157	138	152
High-income developing countries	95	105	118	128	137	157	133	149
Middle-income developing countries	99	106	114	121	127	144	134	143
Low-income developing countries	105	121	145	164	182	225	189	222
Heavily indebted poor countries (IMF)	108	123	146	172	190	233	200	240
Landlocked developing countries	106	126	157	192	212	272	212	255
Small Island developing States	102	118	144	178	193	253	191	219
Least developed countries	*103*	*121*	*150*	*178*	*190*	*240*	*191*	*232*
Africa and Haiti	103	126	165	198	217	286	210	261
Asia	102	111	125	136	142	165	150	162
Islands	100	107	112	122	133	148	142	158
Major petroleum and gas exporters	*108*	*134*	*186*	*223*	*253*	*338*	*229*	*285*
Africa	107	137	192	232	254	351	228	281
America	100	128	174	214	244	334	223	278
Asia	109	134	185	221	254	334	230	286
Major exporters of manufactured goods	*93*	*97*	*100*	*102*	*106*	*113*	*106*	*112*
America	100	108	115	121	129	138	127	135
Asia	92	96	98	100	103	110	104	109
Emerging economies	*92*	*99*	*104*	*111*	*116*	*128*	*113*	*125*
America	99	110	121	136	148	169	149	170
Asia	88	94	97	100	104	112	99	108
Newly industrialized Asian countries	*90*	*95*	*99*	*103*	*106*	*115*	*104*	*114*
First tier	88	92	95	97	99	104	94	102
Second tier	97	103	112	119	128	147	136	149
Developing economies: Africa	**111**	**134**	**171**	**202**	**221**	**295**	**228**	**269**
Northern Africa excluding Sudan	110	132	174	206	224	310	228	263
Sub-Saharan Africa	112	135	168	199	219	285	227	270
Sub-Saharan Africa excluding South Africa	107	129	170	201	222	292	218	267
Developing economies: America	**99**	**111**	**126**	**143**	**156**	**183**	**157**	**180**
Central America and Greater Caribbean Islands excluding Puerto Rico	99	107	114	120	128	136	126	132
Central America and Greater Caribbean Islands excluding Mexico and Puerto Rico	94	100	105	111	119	126	118	113
South America and Central America	98	111	125	141	155	180	156	179
South America excluding Brazil	99	118	142	175	196	236	189	227
Developing economies: Asia	**95**	**103**	**113**	**119**	**127**	**143**	**128**	**140**
Eastern and South-Eastern Asia excluding China	91	96	100	104	108	117	106	116
Southern Asia excluding India	101	120	149	170	183	234	182	215

For sources and notes, see end of table 4.2.1 (Unit value indices).

4.2.2 Indices de la valeur unitaire des exportations et importations des groupements économiques
2000 = 100

Imports (1) - Importations (1)								Groupements économiques
2003	2004	2005	2006	2007	2008	2009	2010	
99	**108**	**116**	**123**	**131**	**149**	**134**	**145**	**ÉCONOMIES EN DÉVELOPPEMENT**
99	108	115	122	131	148	133	144	Économies en développement sans la Chine
99	108	116	123	130	149	133	144	Économies en développement sans les PMA
97	105	112	118	125	140	126	136	Pays en développement à revenu élevé
101	110	119	127	135	157	142	151	Pays en développement à revenu intermédiaire
105	121	127	133	147	167	145	163	Pays en développement à revenu faible
104	113	126	134	146	171	164	165	Pays pauvres très endettés (FMI)
103	113	123	131	142	162	149	157	Pays en développement sans littoral
100	111	127	137	148	178	166	170	Petits États insulaires en développement
105	*116*	*125*	*133*	*146*	*172*	*155*	*168*	*Pays les moins avancés*
106	115	125	132	144	167	151	161	Afrique et Haïti
104	114	127	135	150	181	164	182	Asie
102	113	126	134	146	179	161	174	Îles
103	*112*	*118*	*125*	*134*	*150*	*142*	*149*	*Principaux exportateurs de pétrole et de gaz*
104	112	119	126	139	155	144	149	Afrique
101	108	113	116	121	134	123	129	Amérique
103	112	118	125	135	150	144	151	Asie
97	*104*	*112*	*118*	*124*	*141*	*127*	*137*	*Principaux exportateurs d'articles manufacturés*
101	106	111	116	123	131	124	129	Amérique
96	104	112	118	124	142	127	138	Asie
97	*105*	*113*	*120*	*127*	*146*	*128*	*139*	*Économies émergentes*
100	106	113	119	127	142	130	136	Amérique
95	104	113	120	127	147	125	139	Asie
94	*101*	*109*	*116*	*122*	*138*	*123*	*135*	*Économies nouvellement industrialisées d'Asie*
94	101	108	115	120	136	119	131	Première génération
97	102	111	119	126	145	135	145	Deuxième génération
108	**121**	**130**	**138**	**151**	**174**	**158**	**169**	**Économies en développement : Afrique**
107	117	125	133	148	170	155	166	Afrique septentrionale sans le Soudan
108	122	132	141	152	176	159	170	Afrique subsaharienne
104	114	124	132	144	166	151	161	Afrique subsaharienne sans l'Afrique du Sud
100	**107**	**114**	**120**	**128**	**144**	**131**	**136**	**Économies en développement : Amérique**
100	106	112	117	124	133	125	127	Amérique centrale et Grandes Antilles sans Porto Rico
99	106	114	120	128	143	128	121	Amérique centrale et Grandes Antilles sans le Mexique et Porto Rico
100	106	113	119	127	142	130	136	Amérique du Sud et Amérique centrale
98	105	112	117	125	141	125	133	Amérique du Sud sans le Brésil
98	**107**	**115**	**122**	**129**	**148**	**132**	**144**	**Économies en développement : Asie**
95	102	110	117	123	139	125	136	Asie orientale et Asie du Sud-Est sans la Chine
106	118	130	139	153	186	169	185	Asie méridionale sans l'Inde

Pour les sources et les notes, se reporter à la fin du tableau 4.2.1 (Indices de la valeur unitaire).

4

4.2.2 Terms of trade indices and purchasing power indices of exports of economic groupings
2000 = 100

Economic grouping	Terms of trade (1) - Termes de l'échange (1)							
	2003	2004	2005	2006	2007	2008	2009	2010
DEVELOPING ECONOMIES	**98**	**98**	**103**	**105**	**105**	**106**	**104**	**107**
Developing economies excluding China	98	100	107	111	112	117	110	116
Developing economies excluding LDCs	98	98	102	104	104	105	104	106
High-income developing countries	98	100	105	108	109	112	105	110
Middle-income developing countries	98	96	95	95	94	92	94	94
Low-income developing countries	99	100	115	123	124	134	130	136
Heavily indebted poor countries (IMF)	104	100	117	129	130	136	130	145
Landlocked developing countries	102	111	127	147	149	169	147	162
Small island developing States	102	106	114	130	130	142	123	129
Least developed countries	*90*	*116*	*121*	*101*	*133*	*144*	*125*	*138*
Africa and Haiti	97	109	132	150	151	171	149	167
Asia	98	97	99	101	94	91	92	89
Islands	98	95	89	91	91	82	88	91
Major petroleum and gas exporters	*105*	*120*	*158*	*179*	*188*	*226*	*161*	*192*
Africa	103	122	162	185	183	227	158	188
America	99	118	154	184	202	249	182	216
Asia	106	120	157	176	188	222	159	190
Major exporters of manufactured goods	*96*	*93*	*89*	*87*	*85*	*80*	*83*	*82*
America	99	102	104	104	105	106	103	104
Asia	96	92	88	85	83	78	82	79
Emerging economies	*95*	*94*	*92*	*92*	*91*	*88*	*88*	*90*
America	99	104	107	115	117	118	115	125
Asia	93	90	87	83	82	76	79	78
Newly industrialized Asian countries	*96*	*94*	*91*	*88*	*87*	*83*	*85*	*86*
First tier	94	91	87	84	82	77	79	78
Second tier	101	102	101	100	101	102	101	103
Developing economies: Africa	**103**	**112**	**131**	**146**	**146**	**169**	**145**	**159**
Northern Africa excluding Sudan	103	113	139	155	151	182	147	158
Sub-Saharan Africa	103	111	127	141	144	162	143	159
Sub-Saharan Africa excluding South Africa	102	114	136	152	154	176	145	166
Developing economies: America	**99**	**104**	**110**	**119**	**122**	**127**	**120**	**132**
Central America and Greater Caribbean Islands excluding Puerto Rico	99	101	102	102	103	102	101	104
Central America and Greater Caribbean Islands excluding Mexico and Puerto Rico	96	95	93	93	93	88	92	94
South America and Central America	99	104	110	119	122	127	120	131
South America excluding Brazil	101	113	127	149	157	168	151	171
Developing economies: Asia	**97**	**96**	**98**	**98**	**98**	**97**	**97**	**97**
Eastern and South-Eastern Asia excluding China	96	94	91	89	88	84	86	85
Southern Asia excluding India	96	102	115	122	120	126	108	116

For sources and notes, see end of table 4.2.1 (Terms of trade and purchasing power indices).

	Purchasing power (2) - Pouvoir d'achat (2)							Groupements économiques
2003	2004	2005	2006	2007	2008	2009	2010	
120	**140**	**159**	**180**	**196**	**205**	**180**	**215**	**ÉCONOMIES EN DÉVELOPPEMENT**
112	129	145	162	172	181	156	185	Économies en développement sans la Chine
120	140	159	179	195	204	179	215	Économies en développement sans les PMA
113	131	146	161	172	179	152	181	Pays en développement à revenu élevé
141	168	193	224	255	261	234	285	Pays en développement à revenu intermédiaire
105	117	146	166	180	204	189	218	Pays en développement à revenu faible
125	146	156	177	187	201	186	213	Pays pauvres très endettés (FMI)
127	160	191	240	283	338	258	306	Pays en développement sans littoral
110	115	130	161	157	160	110	118	Petits États insulaires en développement
121	*146*	*181*	*214*	*243*	*284*	*226*	*257*	*Pays les moins avancés*
130	168	220	263	315	391	287	324	Afrique et Haïti
107	113	126	145	143	140	144	167	Asie
170	170	155	149	182	160	145	164	Îles
106	*135*	*183*	*210*	*225*	*275*	*188*	*238*	*Principaux exportateurs de pétrole et de gaz*
104	136	207	229	244	299	192	250	Afrique
80	109	148	169	171	212	140	152	Amérique
110	140	181	211	227	277	193	247	Asie
125	*146*	*160*	*180*	*200*	*199*	*183*	*220*	*Principaux exportateurs d'articles manufacturés*
99	107	116	130	133	134	111	139	Amérique
129	152	168	189	211	209	195	233	Asie
112	*128*	*137*	*151*	*160*	*157*	*145*	*173*	*Économies émergentes*
109	126	139	159	108	169	145	180	Amérique
114	130	137	148	157	153	146	171	Asie
114	*129*	*135*	*146*	*155*	*152*	*141*	*166*	*Économies nouvellement industrialisées d'Asie*
117	132	140	150	160	154	147	171	Première génération
106	120	125	136	145	146	127	153	Deuxième génération
110	**129**	**163**	**180**	**193**	**218**	**167**	**200**	**Économies en développement : Afrique**
111	130	167	190	196	232	164	188	Afrique septentrionale sans le Soudan
110	129	162	176	192	211	168	207	Afrique subsaharienne
113	142	188	203	221	254	196	243	Afrique subsaharienne sans l'Afrique du Sud
106	**123**	**138**	**156**	**165**	**171**	**143**	**175**	**Économies en développement : Amérique**
100	108	115	128	132	131	111	140	Amérique centrale et Grandes Antilles sans Porto Rico
110	115	115	123	130	122	115	140	Amérique centrale et Grandes Antilles sans le Mexique et Porto Rico
107	124	140	159	168	175	148	179	Amérique du Sud et Amérique centrale
106	132	160	189	204	222	186	217	Amérique du Sud sans le Brésil
124	**145**	**164**	**186**	**205**	**212**	**191**	**227**	**Économies en développement : Asie**
114	129	136	147	156	153	143	168	Asie orientale et Asie du Sud-Est sans la Chine
111	124	137	164	167	170	142	163	Asie méridionale sans l'Inde

Pour les sources et les notes, se reporter à la fin du tableau 4.2.1 (Indices des termes de l'échange et du pouvoir d'achat).

Market / Marchés	Year / Année	MFN rate - Simple average (2) / Droit NPF - Moyenne simple (2)						MFN rate - Weighted average (3) / Droit NPF - Moyenne pondérée (3)					
		Total of non-agricultural and non-fuel products / Total des produits non-agricoles et non-pétroliers	Ores and metals / Minérais et métaux	Manu-factured products / Produits manu-facturés	Chemical products / Produits chimiques	Machinery and transport equipment / Machines et matériel de transport	Other manu-factured products / Produits manu-facturés divers	Total of non-agricultural and non-fuel products / Total des produits non-agricoles et non-pétroliers	Ores and metals / Minérais et métaux	Manu-factured products / Produits manu-facturés	Chemical products / Produits chimiques	Machinery and transport equipment / Machines et matériel de transport	Other manu-factured products / Produits manu-facturés divers
SITC Rev.3 (1) / CTCI Rév.3 (1)		5+6+7+8 +27+28-667	27+28+68	5+8+7+8 -(667+68)	5	7	6+8 -(667+68)	5+6+7+8 +27+28-667	27+28+68	5+6+7+8 -(667+68)	5	7	6+8 -(667+68)
Afghanistan	2004	4.7	4.2	4.0	4.0	4.7	4.2	4.2	4.5	4.2	3.2	5.3	3.7
	2006	6.1	5.5	6.1	6.1	6.1	6.9	5.6	7.4	5.6	4.0	5.5	6.1
	2007	6.1	5.7	6.1	5.1	5.0	6.9	6.7	6.1	6.2	4.5	6.7	6.2
	2008	6.1	5.4	6.1	5.0	4.8	7.0	6.3	4.8	6.5	7.4	6.9	5.1
Albania - Albanie	2001	11.2	9.2	11.2	8.6	6.1	14.3	11.6	9.5	11.6	8.5	7.2	15.1
	2002	7.7	5.8	7.8	4.7	3.6	10.6	8.6	7.9	8.7	5.2	3.9	11.9
	2005	6.5	3.0	6.6	2.8	2.6	9.4	7.4	0.9	7.6	3.2	4.2	10.7
	2007	5.7	2.8	5.8	2.3	2.5	8.2	6.0	1.4	6.2	2.5	3.6	8.5
	2008	5.4	3.0	5.5	2.2	1.6	8.2	5.1	1.1	5.3	2.6	1.5	8.4
	2009	5.4	1.0	5.6	2.4	1.6	8.2	4.8	0.6	5.0	2.7	1.4	8.0
Algeria - Algérie	2001	21.9	11.9	22.4	14.2	17.2	28.1	17.2	12.7	17.3	9.6	17.0	21.8
	2002	18.8	12.7	19.1	15.7	12.6	23.4	13.1	13.8	13.1	11.7	11.5	16.2
	2003	18.3	12.1	18.6	14.2	12.2	23.2	12.5	10.9	12.5	8.6	11.3	16.5
	2005	18.2	11.9	18.6	14.2	12.1	23.2	11.9	9.3	12.0	8.8	10.5	16.7
	2006	18.2	11.9	18.5	14.2	12.1	23.2	12.1	9.5	12.2	8.4	11.1	15.5
	2007	17.9	11.9	18.2	14.2	11.4	22.9	12.1	9.4	12.1	8.2	11.3	15.2
	2008	17.9	12.0	18.2	14.2	11.3	23.0	11.7	9.7	11.7	8.3	11.1	14.2
	2009	17.9	12.2	18.2	14.2	11.3	22.9	12.0	9.8	12.0	8.3	11.2	14.8
Angola	2002	8.2	7.9	8.2	5.4	3.9	11.0	5.9	6.4	5.8	6.9	4.1	8.8
	2005	6.7	7.9	6.7	5.2	3.1	8.8	5.0	6.5	5.0	7.9	2.8	9.9
	2006	6.7	7.9	6.7	5.2	3.1	8.8	5.0	6.5	5.0	7.9	2.8	9.9
	2008	6.5	7.3	6.5	5.1	2.8	8.6	6.2	8.1	6.2	8.8	3.3	10.9
	2009	6.5	7.3	6.5	5.1	2.8	8.6	5.9	8.0	5.9	8.7	3.2	10.9
Antigua and Barbuda - Antigua-et-Barbuda	2000	12.1	5.4	12.4	8.5	9.7	14.4	15.3	10.0	15.4	16.7	13.6	17.0
	2001	10.1	4.7	10.3	7.1	8.6	11.8	12.4	7.8	12.5	12.5	11.9	13.1
	2002	10.1	4.7	10.3	7.1	8.6	11.8	12.4	7.8	12.5	12.5	11.9	13.1
	2003	10.3	5.1	10.5	7.5	9.0	11.9	13.8	6.4	13.9	12.9	14.5	13.5
	2006	10.3	5.0	10.5	6.7	8.9	12.0	13.4	6.4	13.5	9.3	14.4	13.5
	2007	10.3	5.0	10.5	6.7	8.9	12.0	13.4	6.4	13.5	9.3	14.4	13.5
	2008	10.2	5.2	10.3	6.5	8.7	12.0	14.1	6.0	14.2	11.7	13.3	15.5
	2009	10.3	5.2	10.4	7.2	8.7	12.0	14.4	5.9	14.5	14.2	13.3	15.5
Argentina - Argentine	2000	15.8	9.7	16.2	11.6	14.8	18.6	15.1	8.2	15.3	12.6	15.1	18.0
	2001	13.1	9.0	13.4	11.1	14.7	13.7	14.1	7.3	14.3	12.3	15.4	14.2
	2002	14.6	8.1	15.0	10.0	15.1	17.0	12.7	5.1	13.1	11.0	13.9	15.3
	2003	15.4	6.7	15.8	8.5	14.1	19.6	13.6	4.0	14.1	9.6	16.1	16.3
	2004	12.9	7.9	13.2	9.1	9.0	16.6	12.9	4.8	13.2	9.6	14.2	15.0
	2005	11.8	6.5	12.1	8.1	8.6	15.2	12.5	4.0	12.8	8.7	14.3	13.6
	2006	11.8	6.5	12.1	8.1	8.6	15.2	12.6	4.3	13.0	8.6	14.4	13.8
	2007	11.7	6.5	12.0	8.1	8.5	15.1	12.8	4.7	13.1	8.3	14.7	13.8
	2008	10.3	6.5	10.5	8.1	7.8	13.4	11.1	4.6	11.4	8.1	12.2	12.9
	2009	10.5	6.5	10.8	8.1	8.4	13.7	13.1	3.7	13.5	7.8	16.1	13.4
	2010	13.4	6.5	13.8	8.1	8.5	18.4	13.5	4.4	13.8	8.7	15.2	15.8
Armenia - Arménie	2001	2.7	0.1	2.8	0.1	1.5	4.2	1.9	0.0	2.0	0.0	2.1	2.8
	2006	2.6	0.7	2.7	0.0	2.0	3.9	2.8	0.1	2.9	0.0	3.4	3.8
	2008	2.5	0.7	2.6	0.1	1.8	3.8	2.9	0.1	3.0	0.2	3.2	3.9

For sources and notes, see end of table.

Pour les sources et les notes, se reporter à la fin du tableau.

Market / Marchés	Year / Année	MFN rate - Simple average (2) / Droit NPF - Moyenne simple (2)						MFN rate - Weighted average (3) / Droit NPF - Moyenne pondérée (3)					
		Total of non-agricultural and non-fuel products / Total des produits non-agricoles et non-pétroliers	Ores and metals / Minérais et métaux	Manu-factured products / Produits manu-facturés	Chemical products / Produits chimiques	Machinery and transport equipment / Machines et matériel de transport	Other manu-factured products / Produits manu-facturés divers	Total of non-agricultural and non-fuel products / Total des produits non-agricoles et non-pétroliers	Ores and metals / Minérais et métaux	Manu-factured products / Produits manu-facturés	Chemical products / Produits chimiques	Machinery and transport equipment / Machines et matériel de transport	Other manu-factured products / Produits manu-facturés divers
SITC Rev.3 (1) / CTCI Rév.3 (1)		5+6+7+8 +27+28-667	27+28+68	5+6+7+8 -(667+68)	5	7	6+8 -(667+68)	5+6+7+8 +27+28-667	27+28+68	5+6+7+8 -(667+68)	5	7	6+8 -(667+68)
Australia - Australie	2000	5.2	1.2	5.5	2.0	3.9	7.5	4.7	2.4	4.7	1.8	4.2	7.1
	2001	4.9	1.1	5.1	1.7	3.2	7.2	4.5	2.3	4.5	1.8	3.9	6.9
	2002	4.9	1.1	5.2	1.6	3.2	7.3	4.6	2.2	4.6	1.0	4.0	6.9
	2003	4.9	1.1	5.3	1.0	3.2	7.4	4.7	2.2	4.7	1.8	4.2	6.9
	2004	4.9	1.1	5.2	1.6	3.2	7.4	4.7	2.5	4.7	1.7	4.2	6.9
	2005	4.1	1.1	4.2	1.6	3.0	5.8	3.8	2.6	3.8	1.6	3.4	5.6
	2006	4.0	1.1	4.2	1.5	3.0	5.8	3.8	2.5	3.8	1.6	3.4	5.6
	2007	4.1	1.2	4.3	1.6	3.2	5.8	4.2	2.2	4.2	1.6	4.0	5.7
	2008	4.1	1.2	4.3	1.6	3.2	5.8	4.2	2.2	4.2	1.6	4.0	5.7
	2009	4.1	1.2	4.3	1.6	3.2	5.8	4.1	2.0	4.1	1.5	4.0	5.6
	2010	3.2	1.2	3.3	1.6	2.9	4.2	3.4	2.0	3.4	1.5	3.4	4.3
Azerbaijan - Azerbaïdjan	2002	8.8	5.0	9.0	5.3	5.6	12.2	6.9	3.4	7.0	6.2	4.0	10.6
	2005	9.2	4.9	9.4	5.2	6.2	12.1	5.8	2.1	6.0	5.7	2.9	10.8
	2007	8.6	5.0	8.7	5.2	5.0	12.0	5.5	2.4	5.6	4.8	3.4	10.0
	2008	8.6	5.0	8.7	5.2	5.0	12.0	5.5	2.4	5.6	4.8	3.4	10.0
	2009	8.5	4.4	8.7	5.1	4.8	12.1	5.3	4.0	5.4	5.3	3.2	10.0
Bahamas	2002	31.5	33.4	31.4	32.9	34.8	29.4	30.3	26.9	30.1	25.0	36.7	25.8
	2006	31.1	33.0	31.0	32.8	34.3	28.9	29.7	27.3	29.7	27.1	34.5	26.5
	2010	37.8	41.7	37.6	40.2	38.0	36.6	32.5	29.3	32.6	31.5	32.0	33.5
Bahrain - Bahreïn	2001	7.9	5.3	8.0	5.4	9.5	8.1	9.3	5.3	10.0	6.2	13.0	8.0
	2005	4.9	5.0	4.9	4.8	4.9	5.0	4.9	5.0	4.9	4.3	5.0	5.0
	2006	4.9	4.9	4.9	4.7	4.9	5.0	4.9	5.0	4.9	4.3	5.0	5.0
	2007	4.8	5.0	4.8	4.6	4.6	4.9	4.8	5.0	4.7	4.1	4.8	5.0
	2008	4.8	4.8	4.8	4.6	4.5	4.9	4.6	5.0	4.6	3.5	4.5	4.9
	2009	4.8	4.8	4.8	4.6	4.5	4.9	4.5	5.0	4.5	3.6	4.2	4.9
Bangladesh	2000	21.9	14.9	22.2	17.0	13.6	28.1	18.5	11.7	18.7	11.7	10.8	25.9
	2002	20.6	13.1	21.0	15.2	12.5	27.0	19.1	8.2	19.5	10.8	12.0	27.0
	2003	19.3	13.2	19.6	14.8	13.0	24.4	18.7	11.5	18.9	11.1	12.7	25.4
	2004	18.4	13.7	18.6	14.2	12.5	22.9	16.2	12.1	16.4	9.4	12.4	23.3
	2005	15.2	10.5	15.5	11.5	10.7	19.1	25.5	9.5	26.0	8.7	14.7	43.0
	2006	15.2	10.5	15.5	11.5	10.7	19.1	25.5	9.5	26.0	8.7	14.7	43.0
	2007	14.4	9.7	14.7	10.2	9.8	18.5	12.9	8.7	13.0	6.8	9.4	19.1
	2008	14.3	10.4	14.5	11.1	8.6	18.3	13.9	8.6	14.0	8.0	8.9	20.1
Barbados - Barbade	2000	17.9	18.7	17.9	12.2	16.9	19.1	21.5	18.2	21.5	14.4	26.1	21.1
	2001	10.4	6.5	10.5	7.4	8.3	12.5	14.7	8.9	14.8	14.1	11.3	18.0
	2002	10.3	6.5	10.5	7.3	8.4	12.4	14.2	9.6	14.2	14.3	11.2	17.0
	2003	10.5	6.2	10.6	7.4	8.5	12.6	14.8	9.0	14.8	14.5	12.0	17.6
	2006	11.6	6.1	11.9	6.7	8.3	15.1	15.6	7.1	15.8	12.1	11.4	21.5
	2007	11.6	5.4	11.8	6.7	8.2	15.2	13.8	5.4	14.0	12.0	12.0	16.9
Belarus - Bélarus	2002	11.0	7.5	11.2	6.9	10.4	13.2	10.2	8.1	10.3	8.0	10.6	11.3
	2008	8.9	7.7	8.9	6.7	6.4	11.3	7.8	6.8	7.9	8.6	6.1	9.6
	2009	8.8	7.5	8.9	6.7	6.3	11.3	7.6	5.4	7.7	8.7	5.4	10.2
	2010	7.8	7.0	7.8	6.3	4.7	10.2	6.6	3.8	6.9	8.1	4.2	9.1
Belize	2001	10.3	4.9	10.5	6.7	8.2	12.7	11.2	15.8	11.2	10.2	10.2	12.6
	2002	10.2	4.9	10.4	6.6	8.1	12.7	11.0	15.0	11.0	9.8	10.1	12.3
	2003	10.3	5.1	10.5	6.5	8.2	12.8	10.8	11.8	10.8	9.8	10.7	11.3
	2006	10.1	4.9	10.3	6.6	8.1	12.3	11.9	8.1	11.9	9.3	10.7	13.9
	2007	10.1	4.9	10.2	6.7	8.1	12.3	11.5	8.8	11.5	9.5	10.6	13.1
	2008	10.1	4.9	10.2	6.7	8.1	12.3	11.5	8.8	11.5	9.5	10.6	13.1
	2009	10.0	4.8	10.1	7.0	7.7	12.3	9.3	4.3	9.4	8.0	6.8	13.6
	2010	10.3	4.8	10.4	7.1	7.7	12.7	10.0	4.3	10.1	8.1	6.9	14.6

For sources and notes, see end of table.

Pour les sources et les notes, se reporter à la fin du tableau.

4.3 Average applied import MFN tariff rates on non-agricultural and non-fuel products

4.3 Droits de douane moyens NPF appliqués à l'importation des produits non-agricoles et non-pétroliers

Market / Marchés	Year / Année	MFN rate - Simple average (2) / Droit NPF - Moyenne simple (2)						MFN rate - Weighted average (3) / Droit NPF - Moyenne pondérée (3)					
		Total of non-agricultural and non-fuel products / Total des produits non-agricoles et non-pétroliers	Ores and metals / Minérais et métaux	Manufactured products / Produits manu-facturés	Chemical products / Produits chimiques	Machinery and transport equipment / Machines et matériel de transport	Other manufactured products / Produits manu-facturés divers	Total of non-agricultural and non-fuel products / Total des produits non-agricoles et non-pétroliers	Ores and metals / Minérais et métaux	Manufactured products / Produits manu-facturés	Chemical products / Produits chimiques	Machinery and transport equipment / Machines et matériel de transport	Other manufactured products / Produits manu-facturés divers
SITC Rev.3 (1) / CTCI Rév.3 (1)		5+6+7+8 +27+28-667	27+28+68	5+6+7+8 -(667+68)	5	7	6+8 -(667+68)	5+6+7+8 +27+28-667	27+28+68	5+6+7+8 -(667+68)	5	7	6+8 -(667+68)
Benin - Bénin	2001	13.0	8.9	10.0	7.7	9.3	10.6	12.3	0.0	12.4	5.3	10.3	16.4
	2002	13.0	8.6	13.1	7.5	9.3	16.6	12.4	7.1	12.5	6.6	11.7	16.6
	2003	13.0	7.8	13.1	7.7	9.4	16.6	12.2	6.2	12.4	5.9	10.6	16.2
	2004	13.0	8.6	13.2	7.8	9.4	16.7	12.1	6.5	12.2	5.3	11.0	16.0
	2005	13.2	8.9	13.3	7.9	9.5	16.9	12.7	6.9	12.8	4.6	11.6	15.6
	2006	13.2	8.9	13.3	7.9	9.5	16.8	12.8	6.9	12.9	4.6	11.8	15.6
	2007	13.0	9.1	13.1	8.0	9.1	16.7	12.7	7.0	12.9	4.4	11.9	15.6
	2008	13.0	8.6	13.1	8.0	8.7	16.5	17.6	10.7	17.6	6.8	16.3	19.1
	2009	13.0	8.4	13.1	8.0	8.7	16.5	17.6	10.2	17.6	6.9	16.3	19.0
	2010	12.7	8.4	12.8	7.6	8.6	16.3	17.1	9.1	17.2	6.5	15.4	19.2
Bermuda - Bermudes	2001	19.5	18.4	19.6	17.6	25.1	17.3	26.5	20.2	26.5	2.0	31.0	15.7
	2005	19.5	19.8	19.5	17.8	24.2	17.6	28.2	21.9	28.2	13.8	31.0	14.8
	2007	19.7	20.4	19.7	18.3	24.6	17.7	30.8	21.7	30.8	13.8	31.9	16.3
	2008	19.7	20.9	19.7	17.9	24.9	17.7	31.0	22.2	31.4	13.6	33.4	15.8
	2009	19.6	20.9	19.6	17.9	24.6	17.7	28.8	22.2	28.9	13.6	30.3	15.9
	2010	19.6	20.2	19.6	18.2	24.2	17.8	27.7	21.0	27.7	13.8	29.9	16.8
Bhutan - Bhoutan	2002	16.5	18.4	16.4	18.7	10.7	19.5	15.0	16.3	15.0	26.5	11.2	19.0
	2004	18.0	25.8	17.7	19.6	11.3	21.4	14.7	26.0	14.5	27.0	9.1	21.4
	2005	18.0	25.8	17.7	19.6	11.3	21.4	14.7	26.0	14.5	27.0	9.1	21.4
	2007	16.6	22.5	16.4	15.6	11.0	21.4	16.2	26.2	16.0	6.4	16.0	18.1
Bolivia (Plurinational State of) - Bolivie (État plurinational de)	2000	9.2	9.9	9.1	9.9	6.9	9.9	8.2	10.0	8.2	9.7	6.4	9.7
	2001	9.2	9.9	9.1	9.9	6.8	9.9	8.6	10.0	8.6	9.7	6.8	9.8
	2002	9.7	10.0	9.6	10.7	7.3	10.3	9.0	10.0	9.0	10.3	6.3	10.6
	2004	9.2	10.0	9.2	10.0	6.8	9.9	8.7	10.0	8.7	10.0	6.8	9.8
	2005	8.2	8.5	8.1	7.7	5.7	9.4	8.4	9.5	8.4	9.5	6.6	9.5
	2006	8.1	8.5	8.1	7.6	5.7	9.4	8.1	9.5	8.1	9.4	6.3	9.5
	2007	8.0	8.5	8.0	7.5	5.5	9.3	8.1	9.4	8.1	9.3	6.5	9.5
	2008	8.0	8.5	8.0	7.5	5.5	9.3	8.0	9.4	7.9	9.2	6.3	9.5
	2009	9.8	6.9	10.0	7.0	5.4	13.2	8.0	8.1	8.0	8.2	6.0	10.6
	2010	11.1	6.9	11.3	7.0	5.4	15.6	8.3	8.1	8.3	8.2	6.0	11.4
Bosnia and Herzegovina - Bosnie-Herzégovine	2001	6.8	2.4	7.0	3.2	6.5	8.6	7.8	5.0	7.9	6.6	7.6	8.5
	2006	6.8	2.3	7.0	3.1	6.4	8.6	7.3	3.7	7.6	5.9	7.4	8.3
	2007	6.8	2.3	7.0	3.1	6.4	8.6	7.3	3.7	7.6	6.0	7.5	8.2
	2008	6.5	2.3	6.7	3.1	5.9	8.4	7.2	3.5	7.5	5.9	7.6	8.0
	2009	6.5	2.3	6.7	3.1	5.9	8.3	7.3	4.6	7.5	6.0	7.4	8.2
	2010	6.5	2.2	6.7	3.0	5.9	8.4	7.3	4.3	7.4	5.9	7.4	8.2
Botswana	2001	8.2	1.5	8.7	2.9	3.2	13.2	9.8	0.5	10.1	7.7	9.4	11.3
	2004	11.0	1.7	11.2	4.9	4.2	15.9	11.7	1.1	11.8	1.4	12.6	12.7
	2005	11.5	2.5	11.7	5.2	4.0	16.8	12.0	0.1	13.6	1.0	10.7	22.7
	2006	11.4	2.5	11.6	5.2	4.0	16.8	11.8	0.1	13.4	1.0	10.3	22.7
	2007	10.7	2.0	10.9	6.3	4.1	15.6	13.1	0.7	13.2	1.2	5.2	26.4
	2008	10.8	2.3	11.0	6.0	3.8	15.9	14.3	0.4	14.4	1.4	5.0	26.5
	2009	10.6	2.0	10.9	6.0	3.8	15.6	13.9	0.4	13.9	1.5	7.1	23.1
	2010	10.5	1.1	10.7	4.9	3.6	15.6	8.0	0.2	8.0	0.9	2.5	17.2
Brazil - Brésil	2000	16.4	9.3	16.8	11.6	17.6	18.6	14.7	8.2	15.0	11.1	16.1	16.6
	2001	14.8	8.9	15.2	11.0	12.7	17.9	12.2	7.8	12.4	10.2	12.5	15.0
	2002	14.5	7.9	14.9	10.0	14.7	16.9	11.9	6.8	12.1	8.8	12.8	14.9
	2003	14.1	7.7	14.5	9.9	14.5	16.3	11.4	6.4	11.6	8.5	12.5	14.4
	2004	14.0	7.7	14.4	9.6	14.6	16.3	11.1	6.0	11.3	8.2	12.1	14.4
	2005	13.1	6.1	13.5	8.3	13.9	15.5	10.5	4.7	10.8	7.4	11.5	13.5
	2006	13.0	6.0	13.5	8.2	13.6	15.5	10.5	4.7	10.9	7.4	11.6	13.2
	2007	13.0	6.0	13.4	8.2	13.7	15.4	11.0	4.8	11.5	6.8	13.6	13.2
	2008	14.2	6.0	14.7	8.2	13.7	17.7	11.1	4.2	11.5	6.1	13.9	13.8
	2009	14.8	6.1	15.3	8.1	13.8	18.7	12.2	5.0	12.5	6.9	14.5	14.7
	2010	14.9	6.1	15.4	8.1	13.7	19.0	12.3	5.0	12.6	6.9	14.5	15.1

For sources and notes, see end of table.

Pour les sources et les notes, se reporter à la fin du tableau.

4.3 Average applied import MFN tariff rates on non-agricultural and non-fuel products

4.3 Droits de douane moyens NPF appliqués à l'importation des produits non-agricoles et non-pétroliers

Market / Marchés	Year / Année	MFN rate - Simple average (2) / Droit NPF - Moyenne simple (2)						MFN rate - Weighted average (3) / Droit NPF - Moyenne pondérée (3)					
		Total of non-agricultural and non-fuel products / Total des produits non-agricoles et non-pétroliers	Ores and metals / Minérais et métaux	Manufactured products / Produits manufacturés	Chemical products / Produits chimiques	Machinery and transport equipment / Machines et matériel de transport	Other manufactured products / Produits manufacturés divers	Total of non-agricultural and non-fuel products / Total des produits non-agricoles et non-pétroliers	Ores and metals / Minérais et métaux	Manufactured products / Produits manufacturés	Chemical products / Produits chimiques	Machinery and transport equipment / Machines et matériel de transport	Other manufactured products / Produits manufacturés divers
SITC Rev.3 (1) / CTCI Rév.3 (1)		5+6+7+8 +27+28-667	27+28+68	5+6+7+8 -(667+68)	5	7	6+8 (667+68)	5+6+7+8 +27+28-667	27+28+68	5+6+7+8 (667+68)	5	7	6+8 -(667+68)
Brunei Darussalam - Brunéi Darussalam	2001	3.7	0.0	3.9	0.5	10.0	2.0	10.5	0.0	10.7	1.0	19.0	0.9
	2002	3.7	0.0	3.9	0.5	10.0	2.0	10.5	0.0	10.7	1.0	19.0	0.9
	2003	3.6	0.0	3.8	0.5	9.7	2.0	12.3	0.0	12.5	1.0	27.0	1.0
	2004	3.7	0.0	3.9	0.5	9.9	2.0	6.9	0.0	7.0	1.1	11.4	2.7
	2005	3.7	0.1	3.8	0.5	9.7	2.1	6.5	0.0	6.6	0.9	11.4	2.5
	2006	3.7	0.1	3.8	0.5	9.7	2.1	6.5	0.0	6.6	0.9	11.4	2.5
	2007	3.8	0.1	3.9	0.5	10.0	2.1	6.3	0.0	6.3	1.1	10.0	2.7
	2008	3.5	0.0	3.6	0.5	9.1	2.0	4.2	0.0	4.3	1.1	5.8	2.7
	2010	3.5	0.1	3.6	0.5	9.4	1.9	4.9	0.0	5.0	1.2	7.2	2.9
Bulgaria - Bulgarie (4)	2001	11.6	4.1	12.0	8.2	7.9	15.2	10.3	1.6	11.0	8.5	7.3	15.7
	2003	9.3	3.4	9.5	7.4	5.9	11.9	8.8	1.8	9.4	7.4	6.5	12.8
	2004	9.3	3.4	9.6	7.4	5.9	11.9	8.6	1.6	9.3	6.9	7.1	12.3
	2005	9.3	3.3	9.6	7.5	5.9	11.9	8.2	1.5	8.9	7.2	6.8	12.0
	2006	9.4	3.4	9.7	7.4	6.3	12.0	8.1	1.4	9.0	6.9	7.2	11.9
Burkina Faso	2001	12.8	8.7	12.9	7.3	9.1	16.4	11.4	8.0	11.5	5.6	11.2	15.4
	2002	12.8	8.8	12.9	7.3	9.2	16.3	11.5	8.7	11.5	5.3	12.1	15.5
	2003	12.8	8.4	12.9	7.5	9.2	16.3	12.1	7.9	12.2	5.3	13.4	14.1
	2004	12.7	9.0	12.9	7.4	9.3	16.3	12.6	8.4	12.6	5.9	13.9	14.9
	2005	12.7	8.6	12.9	7.4	9.3	16.3	12.6	8.4	12.6	5.9	13.8	14.8
	2006	12.7	8.6	12.9	7.4	9.3	16.3	12.7	8.4	12.7	5.9	14.0	14.8
	2007	12.6	8.9	12.7	7.5	8.7	16.2	12.6	8.5	12.7	5.1	14.0	14.6
	2008	12.4	8.6	12.5	7.9	8.7	16.2	9.9	8.2	9.9	6.0	9.0	16.1
	2009	12.3	8.7	12.4	7.8	8.7	16.2	9.7	8.3	9.8	5.8	8.8	16.0
	2010	12.5	8.8	12.7	7.6	8.6	16.2	10.5	7.2	10.5	5.0	10.2	14.0
Burundi	2002	23.4	12.8	23.6	15.0	18.2	28.3	20.1	14.6	20.2	14.0	22.8	21.3
	2005	18.6	11.1	18.7	16.0	15.5	21.5	17.9	14.9	18.0	15.8	16.5	21.2
	2006	14.6	5.8	14.8	11.2	10.2	18.2	15.5	5.4	16.2	14.1	15.6	17.7
	2007	14.8	6.0	15.0	11.9	10.3	18.1	14.0	9.2	14.1	14.2	15.0	13.0
	2008	14.7	5.8	14.8	11.9	10.3	17.8	13.6	8.5	13.6	14.5	13.0	13.7
	2009	12.8	10.7	12.9	6.8	7.3	17.7	16.4	16.6	16.4	6.3	8.1	24.1
	2010	12.5	12.0	12.5	6.3	7.3	17.7	14.6	19.3	14.5	5.6	7.5	22.9
Cambodia - Cambodge	2001	16.6	10.4	16.8	10.8	18.4	18.0	16.8	11.4	16.8	6.9	18.9	17.6
	2002	16.4	9.4	16.6	11.0	18.0	17.7	16.7	11.4	16.8	6.4	18.8	17.3
	2003	16.5	8.9	16.7	11.2	18.1	17.8	16.9	9.8	16.9	6.2	18.8	17.5
	2005	14.5	9.3	14.6	9.8	17.4	14.8	10.9	9.9	10.9	6.0	16.4	10.2
	2007	14.3	9.3	14.5	9.8	17.3	14.5	10.9	9.9	10.9	6.0	16.4	10.2
	2008	14.5	8.9	14.6	10.1	17.2	14.8	11.2	11.3	11.2	5.9	16.7	9.1
Cameroon - Cameroun	2001	17.7	10.7	17.9	11.0	14.2	22.2	13.3	10.4	13.5	8.9	14.8	14.2
	2002	17.6	10.8	17.8	11.1	14.2	22.1	13.4	11.0	13.6	9.1	14.5	15.1
	2005	18.0	10.9	18.3	11.3	14.4	22.5	14.8	10.7	15.1	7.8	16.5	17.7
	2007	17.4	11.0	17.7	11.2	13.9	22.0	14.3	10.4	14.6	8.9	16.7	16.1
	2009	17.7	10.7	18.0	11.6	13.9	22.1	15.8	13.9	15.9	8.5	16.0	18.9
Canada	2000	4.7	0.7	5.0	2.9	2.1	7.0	3.1	0.6	3.2	3.3	2.5	4.7
	2001	4.6	0.7	4.8	2.8	2.2	6.8	3.2	0.6	3.3	3.1	2.6	4.7
	2002	4.4	0.7	4.7	2.8	2.2	6.5	3.2	0.7	3.3	3.0	2.8	4.5
	2003	4.3	0.7	4.5	2.7	2.2	6.2	3.2	0.6	3.3	2.8	2.9	4.3
	2004	4.2	0.7	4.4	2.6	2.2	6.1	3.2	0.6	3.2	2.7	2.9	4.2
	2005	4.2	0.7	4.4	2.6	2.2	6.0	3.1	0.6	3.2	2.6	2.8	4.2
	2006	3.9	0.7	4.1	2.5	2.2	5.6	3.1	0.6	3.2	2.7	2.8	4.2
	2007	3.9	0.7	4.1	2.6	2.2	5.5	3.3	0.6	3.4	2.6	3.0	4.4
	2008	3.9	0.7	4.1	2.6	2.3	5.5	3.3	0.6	3.4	2.6	3.0	4.4
	2009	3.8	0.7	4.0	2.6	1.7	5.5	3.1	0.7	3.2	2.3	2.6	4.7
	2010	2.8	0.0	3.0	0.8	1.3	4.5	2.7	0.0	2.8	1.2	2.3	4.3

For sources and notes, see end of table.

Pour les sources et les notes, se reporter à la fin du tableau.

Market / Marchés	Year / Année	MFN rate - Simple average (2) / Droit NPF - Moyenne simple (2)						MFN rate - Weighted average (3) / Droit NPF - Moyenne pondérée (3)					
		Total of non-agricultural and non-fuel products / Total des produits non-agricoles et non-pétroliers	Ores and metals / Minérais et métaux	Manufactured products / Produits manufacturés	Chemical products / Produits chimiques	Machinery and transport equipment / Machines et matériel de transport	Other manufactured products / Produits manufacturés divers	Total of non-agricultural and non-fuel products / Total des produits non-agricoles et non-pétroliers	Ores and metals / Minérais et métaux	Manufactured products / Produits manufacturés	Chemical products / Produits chimiques	Machinery and transport equipment / Machines et matériel de transport	Other manufactured products / Produits manufacturés divers
SITC Rev.3 (1) / CTCI Rév.3 (1)		5+6+7+8 +27+28-667	27+28+68	5+6+7+8 -(667+68)	5	7	6+8 -(667+68)	5+6+7+8 +27+28-667	27+28+68	5+6+7+8 -(667+68)	5	7	6+8 -(667+68)
Cape Verde - Cap-Vert	2005	12.6	1.4	12.9	5.1	0.1	16.4	11.4	1.5	13.5	11.4	12.9	14.6
	2007	11.5	1.2	11.8	4.9	7.9	15.7	9.5	0.1	10.8	11.8	8.4	12.5
	2008	12.0	1.4	12.4	4.9	7.9	16.4	11.6	1.7	11.8	9.6	12.4	11.9
	2009	12.1	1.7	12.4	4.8	7.7	16.5	11.4	2.1	11.6	8.9	10.5	13.4
	2010	11.6	1.7	11.9	4.8	6.7	16.2	10.8	2.1	11.0	8.6	9.8	12.8
Central African Republic - République centrafricaine	2001	17.9	14.4	18.0	13.4	15.7	21.2	15.9	21.0	15.6	9.6	17.1	17.7
	2002	18.2	13.1	18.3	13.3	15.7	21.6	15.1	18.3	15.0	10.0	16.4	16.4
	2005	18.8	13.3	18.9	13.3	15.7	22.1	15.4	22.2	15.2	7.5	15.7	18.9
	2007	17.8	12.7	18.0	12.1	15.0	21.5	13.4	13.3	13.4	7.0	14.2	17.8
Chad - Tchad	2001	17.6	11.2	17.8	12.3	14.4	21.6	12.0	10.4	12.0	9.1	11.5	14.4
	2002	17.4	10.6	17.6	12.6	14.6	21.0	13.5	8.7	13.5	13.9	12.0	15.7
	2005	17.9	13.6	18.0	13.0	14.9	21.7	11.4	14.5	11.3	9.1	10.6	16.0
	2007	17.5	12.7	17.6	12.9	14.4	21.3	12.6	8.9	12.7	8.1	12.2	17.7
	2009	17.4	11.3	17.5	12.5	14.3	21.3	13.8	6.8	13.9	9.2	13.2	17.8
Chile - Chili	2000	9.0	9.0	9.0	9.0	9.0	9.0	9.0	9.0	9.0	9.0	9.0	9.0
	2001	8.0	8.0	8.0	8.0	8.0	8.0	8.0	8.0	8.0	8.0	8.0	8.0
	2002	7.0	7.0	7.0	7.0	6.9	7.0	6.9	7.0	6.9	7.0	6.9	7.0
	2004	6.0	6.0	6.0	6.0	6.0	6.0	6.0	6.0	6.0	6.0	6.0	6.0
	2005	6.0	6.0	6.0	6.0	6.0	6.0	6.0	6.0	6.0	6.0	6.0	6.0
	2006	6.0	6.0	6.0	6.0	6.0	6.0	6.0	6.0	6.0	6.0	5.9	6.0
	2007	6.0	6.0	6.0	6.0	6.0	6.0	6.0	6.0	6.0	6.0	5.9	6.0
	2008	6.0	6.0	6.0	6.0	6.0	6.0	6.0	6.0	6.0	6.0	5.9	6.0
	2009	6.0	6.0	6.0	6.0	5.9	6.0	6.0	6.0	6.0	6.0	5.9	6.0
	2010	6.0	6.0	6.0	6.0	5.9	6.0	6.0	6.0	6.0	6.0	6.0	6.0
China - Chine	2000	15.9	5.3	16.5	11.2	16.2	18.7	13.0	5.2	13.7	13.0	12.6	16.1
	2001	14.8	4.5	15.4	10.3	15.6	17.4	12.4	4.2	13.0	12.5	12.4	14.7
	2003	10.6	3.8	11.1	7.4	10.0	12.9	6.4	2.6	6.7	8.9	5.3	8.4
	2004	9.8	3.7	10.2	7.2	9.4	11.7	5.6	2.0	5.9	8.1	4.5	7.7
	2005	9.2	3.7	9.6	6.9	9.2	10.8	5.0	1.8	5.4	7.3	4.0	7.3
	2006	9.1	3.6	9.5	6.8	9.0	10.7	4.3	1.3	4.7	6.3	3.4	7.0
	2007	9.2	3.7	9.6	6.9	8.9	10.9	5.6	1.5	6.4	6.4	5.5	7.9
	2008	8.9	3.4	9.3	6.6	8.4	10.8	5.1	0.7	6.1	5.9	5.1	7.7
	2009	8.9	3.3	9.3	6.6	8.4	10.7	5.1	0.5	6.3	6.0	5.6	7.6
	2010	9.0	3.3	9.3	6.5	8.6	10.7	5.3	0.4	6.6	5.8	6.2	7.9
China, Taiwan Province of - Province chinoise de Taiwan	2000	6.1	1.6	6.4	3.9	6.0	7.5	2.9	1.4	3.0	3.4	2.5	4.1
	2001	6.1	1.6	6.4	3.9	6.0	7.5	2.9	1.3	3.0	3.6	2.4	4.3
	2002	5.9	1.5	6.2	3.8	5.7	7.4	3.0	1.2	3.1	3.5	2.8	4.0
	2003	5.3	1.2	5.5	3.4	5.2	6.5	2.8	1.1	2.9	2.8	2.8	3.3
	2005	4.5	0.9	4.7	2.8	4.5	5.5	2.3	0.6	2.4	1.9	2.7	2.2
	2006	4.4	0.9	4.6	2.9	4.4	5.4	2.3	0.6	2.4	2.0	2.6	2.2
	2007	4.3	0.9	4.5	2.8	4.1	5.4	1.8	0.5	1.9	1.9	1.7	2.3
	2008	4.3	0.9	4.5	2.8	4.0	5.4	1.7	0.4	1.9	1.8	1.8	2.2
	2009	4.3	0.8	4.6	2.8	4.1	5.5	2.4	0.6	2.7	1.8	3.4	2.6
	2010	4.3	0.9	4.6	2.8	4.1	5.4	2.6	0.5	2.9	2.0	3.8	2.7
Colombia - Colombie	2000	11.9	6.7	12.2	8.1	10.0	14.8	10.5	6.6	10.6	8.0	10.7	13.0
	2001	11.9	6.7	12.2	8.2	10.0	14.8	10.3	7.0	10.4	8.2	9.8	13.2
	2002	12.0	6.6	12.2	8.1	9.9	14.9	10.6	6.9	10.7	8.0	11.0	13.3
	2004	11.9	6.6	12.2	8.1	9.9	14.9	10.9	6.8	11.0	8.0	11.6	13.1
	2005	11.9	6.5	12.2	8.1	9.8	14.9	10.7	6.4	10.9	8.2	10.9	13.2
	2006	11.9	6.5	12.2	8.1	9.9	14.9	11.1	6.2	11.3	8.4	11.7	13.2
	2007	11.9	6.5	12.2	8.1	9.8	14.8	11.8	6.1	12.1	8.5	13.0	13.1
	2008	11.8	6.6	12.1	8.1	9.7	14.8	12.1	6.1	12.4	8.5	14.0	13.1
	2009	11.8	6.5	12.2	8.0	9.8	14.8	10.6	6.8	10.7	7.7	10.7	13.3
	2010	11.9	6.5	12.2	8.0	9.9	14.8	10.5	6.8	10.6	7.5	10.7	13.3

For sources and notes, see end of table.

Pour les sources et les notes, se reporter à la fin du tableau.

Market / Marchés	Year / Année	MFN rate - Simple average (2) / Droit NPF - Moyenne simple (2)						MFN rate - Weighted average (3) / Droit NPF - Moyenne pondérée (3)					
		Total of non-agricultural and non-fuel products / Total des produits non-agricoles et non-pétroliers	of which: / dont :					Total of non-agricultural and non-fuel products / Total des produits non-agricoles et non-pétroliers	of which: / dont :				
			Ores and metals / Minérais et métaux	Manufactured products / Produits manufacturés	Of which: / dont :				Ores and metals / Minérais et métaux	Manufactured products / Produits manufacturés	Of which: / dont :		
					Chemical products / Produits chimiques	Machinery and transport equipment / Machines et matériel de transport	Other manufactured products / Produits manufacturés divers				Chemical products / Produits chimiques	Machinery and transport equipment / Machines et matériel de transport	Other manufactured products / Produits manufacturés divers
SITC Rev.3 (1) / CTCI Rév.3 (1)		5+6+7+8 +27+28-667	27+28+68	5+6+7+8 -(667+68)	5	7	6+8 -(667+68)	5+6+7+8 +27+28-667	27+28+68	5+6+7+8 -(667+68)	5	7	6+8 -(667+68)
Comoros - Comores	2008	11.5	14.5	11.5	11.3	13.3	10.5	11.2	13.0	11.2	7.9	12.4	10.4
	2010	11.4	13.7	11.3	11.5	13.2	10.3	12.2	11.7	12.2	5.5	13.1	11.6
Congo	2001	18.3	11.7	18.4	11.6	14.5	22.6	16.1	10.0	16.1	12.3	13.4	22.2
	2002	18.3	11.0	18.3	11.7	14.5	22.6	16.5	16.4	16.5	11.5	14.4	21.3
	2005	18.4	11.5	18.6	11.7	14.5	22.7	15.9	17.0	15.9	9.4	14.3	20.6
	2007	18.0	11.8	18.2	11.7	14.0	22.3	14.1	14.9	14.1	10.8	12.6	18.3
Costa Rica	2000	4.8	1.6	5.0	1.4	2.2	7.5	3.8	1.6	3.9	3.1	1.9	6.9
	2001	4.7	1.7	4.9	1.4	2.1	7.4	3.7	2.0	3.7	3.2	1.6	7.1
	2002	5.1	1.4	5.2	1.4	2.3	7.9	3.6	1.5	3.6	3.1	2.1	6.3
	2004	5.1	1.3	5.3	1.4	2.5	8.0	3.9	1.3	3.9	3.0	2.7	6.2
	2005	5.1	1.3	5.3	1.4	2.3	8.0	3.6	1.3	3.7	3.0	1.9	6.8
	2007	4.9	1.3	5.1	1.5	2.1	7.8	4.0	0.9	4.1	2.8	3.1	6.0
	2009	4.6	1.3	4.7	1.4	1.8	7.3	3.5	0.9	3.5	2.3	2.0	5.7
Côte d'Ivoire	2001	12.1	7.6	12.3	6.7	8.8	16.1	8.7	7.3	8.8	5.2	9.5	11.7
	2002	12.1	7.6	12.3	6.7	8.8	16.0	8.7	7.4	8.8	5.2	9.5	11.7
	2003	12.1	7.7	12.3	6.8	8.9	16.0	10.9	6.8	11.0	5.1	9.5	15.3
	2004	12.1	8.0	12.3	6.8	8.9	16.0	11.0	6.9	11.1	5.1	9.5	15.5
	2005	12.3	8.2	12.4	6.8	8.9	16.1	10.4	7.0	10.4	5.1	8.2	15.3
	2006	12.3	8.3	12.4	6.8	8.9	16.1	10.5	7.0	10.6	5.4	9.9	14.7
	2007	12.1	8.2	12.2	6.9	8.4	16.0	10.6	7.1	10.7	5.3	10.3	14.6
	2008	12.0	8.1	12.2	6.9	8.3	15.9	9.7	6.8	9.8	5.1	10.9	12.6
	2009	12.0	8.1	12.2	6.9	8.3	15.9	9.7	6.8	9.8	5.1	10.9	12.6
	2010	12.0	8.1	12.2	6.0	8.3	16.0	9.4	7.2	9.5	5.0	10.0	12.6
Croatia - Croatie	2001	10.4	6.1	10.6	7.3	8.9	12.5	10.9	5.9	11.0	10.3	9.5	13.1
	2004	4.1	1.8	4.3	1.4	3.2	5.7	4.0	2.2	4.1	2.7	3.7	5.0
	2005	4.0	1.8	4.2	1.3	3.1	5.6	3.8	2.0	3.9	2.3	3.6	4.9
	2006	4.1	1.7	4.2	1.3	3.3	5.7	4.0	1.7	4.1	2.3	3.7	5.1
	2007	4.2	1.6	4.3	1.4	3.6	5.7	4.2	1.8	4.3	2.3	4.1	5.2
	2008	4.1	1.6	4.3	1.4	3.6	5.7	4.2	1.8	4.3	2.3	4.1	5.2
	2009	4.1	1.6	4.3	1.4	3.5	5.7	4.2	2.1	4.3	2.3	4.1	5.4
	2010	4.1	1.6	4.3	1.3	3.5	5.7	4.2	2.1	4.3	2.2	4.1	5.4
Cuba	2002	11.5	5.6	11.7	9.3	10.0	13.4	10.8	3.7	10.9	7.7	11.1	12.2
	2003	11.6	5.6	11.9	9.3	10.1	13.7	11.0	3.8	11.2	8.5	10.9	12.4
	2004	11.5	6.1	11.8	9.2	10.1	13.5	10.5	4.6	10.6	8.6	10.4	11.8
	2005	11.5	5.6	11.7	9.3	10.1	13.5	9.8	3.9	9.9	8.1	9.3	11.4
	2006	11.5	5.9	11.7	9.1	10.1	13.5	9.8	2.6	10.0	8.2	9.4	11.7
	2007	11.5	5.6	11.7	9.2	10.1	13.5	10.0	3.9	10.1	8.6	9.4	11.6
	2008	11.4	5.9	11.7	9.1	10.1	13.4	9.8	2.6	10.0	8.1	9.4	11.7
	2009	11.3	5.3	11.6	9.3	9.8	13.3	10.0	6.3	10.0	9.4	9.1	11.7
	2010	11.4	5.7	11.6	9.4	9.9	13.3	10.3	6.0	10.4	9.9	9.5	11.6
Cyprus - Chypre (5)	2002	4.4	2.1	4.5	4.8	2.4	5.2	4.6	4.8	4.6	2.9	5.6	4.3
Czech Republic - (5) République tchèque	2002	4.5	1.3	4.7	4.2	3.8	5.3	4.3	1.6	4.4	3.6	3.8	5.6
	2003	4.5	1.3	4.7	4.2	3.8	5.3	4.3	1.7	4.4	3.5	3.9	5.5
Dem. Rep. of the Congo - Rép. dém. du Congo	2003	12.6	9.9	12.6	9.5	8.8	15.6	12.9	13.5	12.9	13.7	8.8	16.4
	2006	12.4	9.8	12.5	9.2	8.6	15.5	11.4	8.4	11.5	14.6	8.0	14.7
	2007	12.4	9.7	12.5	8.9	8.6	15.6	11.3	9.6	11.3	14.0	7.7	15.2
	2008	12.0	8.9	12.2	8.8	8.3	15.3	10.8	6.0	11.1	13.1	7.6	15.2
	2009	12.0	8.9	12.2	8.8	8.3	15.3	10.8	6.0	11.1	13.0	7.6	15.1
Djibouti	2002	32.8	31.7	32.8	30.9	33.4	33.0	32.3	31.8	32.3	27.1	34.5	31.9
	2006	32.1	29.3	32.2	30.4	33.0	32.2	31.3	31.1	31.3	24.9	33.0	31.9
	2009	21.6	22.7	21.5	23.6	20.5	21.4	18.6	21.1	18.6	16.0	18.1	19.9

For sources and notes, see end of table.

Pour les sources et les notes, se reporter à la fin du tableau.

Market / Marchés	Year / Année	MFN rate - Simple average (2) / Droit NPF - Moyenne simple (2)						MFN rate - Weighted average (3) / Droit NPF - Moyenne pondérée (3)					
		Total of non-agricultural and non-fuel products / Total des produits non-agricoles et non-pétroliers	Ores and metals / Minérais et métaux	Manufactured products / Produits manufacturés	Chemical products / Produits chimiques	Machinery and transport equipment / Machines et matériel de transport	Other manufactured products / Produits manufacturés divers	Total of non-agricultural and non-fuel products / Total des produits non-agricoles et non-pétroliers	Ores and metals / Minérais et métaux	Manufactured products / Produits manufacturés	Chemical products / Produits chimiques	Machinery and transport equipment / Machines et matériel de transport	Other manufactured products / Produits manufacturés divers
SITC Rev.3 (1) / CTCI Rév.3 (1)		5+6+7+8 +27+28-667	27+28+68	5+6+7+8 -(667+68)	5	7	6+8 -(667+68)	5+6+7+8 +27+28-667	27+28+68	5+6+7+8 -(667+68)	5	7	6+8 -(667+68)
Dominica - Dominique	2000	14.1	12.0	14.1	10.0	16.1	14.0	16.0	14.4	15.0	10.3	21.8	12.5
	2001	10.1	4.7	10.2	8.7	7.5	11.8	11.2	6.7	11.7	10.6	11.1	12.4
	2002	10.4	4.3	10.5	8.6	7.8	12.2	12.5	5.0	12.5	11.2	10.7	14.4
	2003	10.5	4.3	10.7	9.2	7.7	12.3	12.0	4.8	12.0	10.9	10.3	13.9
	2006	10.5	4.4	10.6	9.3	8.0	12.1	11.9	4.7	11.9	10.0	9.9	14.6
	2007	10.2	4.4	10.4	9.3	7.7	11.8	11.7	4.6	11.7	10.7	10.7	13.0
Dominican Republic - République dominicaine	2000	18.2	10.2	18.5	10.4	13.4	24.1	17.5	13.6	17.6	9.8	17.8	21.3
	2001	8.4	4.3	8.6	4.7	5.6	11.5	8.7	5.1	8.7	4.1	8.6	11.3
	2002	8.3	4.4	8.5	4.6	5.5	11.3	9.3	4.2	9.4	5.0	9.6	11.1
	2003	8.4	4.4	8.6	4.7	5.6	11.5	8.6	5.2	8.7	4.1	8.5	11.3
	2004	8.4	4.4	8.6	4.7	5.6	11.5	8.7	5.3	8.8	4.1	8.5	11.5
	2005	8.1	4.7	8.3	4.9	5.5	10.7	9.1	5.1	9.2	6.2	8.1	10.7
	2006	8.3	5.0	8.4	4.7	5.5	11.1	8.8	5.2	8.8	5.2	8.9	9.9
	2007	6.5	2.7	6.6	2.5	3.2	9.8	7.7	3.1	7.8	3.7	8.3	8.7
	2008	8.1	5.2	8.2	4.9	5.1	10.9	8.7	5.5	8.7	5.3	9.0	9.8
	2010	6.3	2.1	6.5	2.4	3.2	9.4	7.5	6.1	7.5	3.8	7.2	9.2
Ecuador - Équateur	2002	11.7	6.1	11.9	7.5	8.8	15.0	10.8	6.2	10.8	7.2	10.9	13.1
	2004	11.7	6.0	12.0	7.5	8.7	15.1	10.5	6.1	10.6	6.9	10.8	12.9
	2005	11.5	6.0	11.7	7.2	8.3	15.0	10.3	6.6	10.4	7.1	10.5	12.5
	2006	11.5	6.0	11.8	7.2	8.4	15.0	10.3	6.9	10.4	7.2	10.5	12.4
	2007	11.5	6.0	11.8	7.2	8.4	15.0	10.2	6.6	10.2	7.3	10.1	12.5
	2008	10.8	4.4	11.1	4.7	6.2	15.9	8.5	6.1	8.5	5.0	8.6	10.9
	2009	10.1	1.1	10.6	3.1	4.8	16.1	7.3	2.7	7.3	4.6	6.8	10.2
	2010	10.1	1.1	10.6	3.1	4.8	16.1	7.2	2.7	7.3	4.6	6.8	10.2
Egypt - Égypte	2002	20.1	13.8	20.4	13.0	14.3	26.8	16.2	10.9	16.4	11.3	15.9	19.8
	2004	13.4	6.8	13.8	7.3	8.1	18.7	10.9	4.5	11.2	15.7	8.3	13.5
	2005	13.1	5.6	13.5	6.8	8.0	18.5	11.6	2.3	12.1	16.5	10.0	13.0
	2008	10.2	5.1	10.4	6.1	7.0	13.6	9.1	1.8	10.3	10.7	11.5	8.8
	2009	10.0	4.9	10.3	5.9	6.7	13.6	8.9	1.8	10.0	10.1	11.2	8.8
El Salvador	2000	6.7	1.2	7.0	1.6	2.4	11.2	5.4	1.6	5.5	4.6	3.5	8.4
	2001	6.8	1.4	7.0	1.6	2.4	11.2	6.0	1.7	6.0	4.7	3.9	8.8
	2002	6.5	1.3	6.7	1.7	2.3	10.6	6.5	1.3	6.6	5.3	4.8	9.0
	2004	6.9	1.3	7.1	1.7	2.3	11.3	6.4	1.4	6.5	5.2	4.7	8.9
	2005	5.3	1.3	5.5	1.7	2.3	8.3	6.0	1.3	6.1	6.0	4.6	7.5
	2006	6.8	1.4	7.0	1.7	2.1	11.2	7.8	1.3	7.9	10.2	5.0	8.5
	2007	5.2	1.3	5.3	1.7	2.1	8.1	6.8	1.2	6.9	8.4	4.8	7.4
	2008	5.2	1.3	5.3	1.7	2.1	8.1	6.7	1.2	6.8	8.4	4.8	7.2
	2009	5.1	1.4	5.3	1.6	2.0	8.0	6.6	1.8	6.7	5.9	4.0	8.4
	2010	5.1	1.4	5.3	1.7	2.0	8.0	6.6	1.8	6.7	5.9	4.0	8.4
Equatorial Guinea - Guinée équatoriale	2001	18.4	10.4	18.6	13.0	14.8	22.5	12.8	9.8	12.9	15.4	10.4	17.4
	2002	18.3	10.9	18.5	13.2	14.6	22.3	14.0	8.3	14.1	15.9	12.5	17.0
	2005	18.5	12.1	18.7	13.0	14.6	22.4	14.3	9.9	14.3	16.4	12.9	18.3
	2007	18.0	11.0	18.2	12.6	14.3	21.9	14.3	11.5	14.3	14.2	12.1	18.7
Eritrea - Érythrée	2002	8.7	2.2	9.0	3.4	6.5	11.4	7.3	2.1	7.4	3.2	8.3	7.7
	2006	8.7	2.2	9.0	3.4	6.5	11.4	7.3	2.1	7.4	3.2	8.3	7.7
Estonia - Estonie (5)	2000	0.1	0.0	0.1	0.3	0.0	0.0	0.0	0.0	0.0	0.1	0.0	0.0
	2001	0.1	0.0	0.1	0.4	0.0	0.0	0.0	0.0	0.0	0.1	0.0	0.0
	2002	0.1	0.0	0.1	0.3	0.0	0.0	0.0	0.0	0.0	0.1	0.0	0.0
	2003	0.1	0.0	0.1	0.4	0.0	0.0	0.0	0.0	0.0	0.1	0.0	0.0

For sources and notes, see end of table.

Pour les sources et les notes, se reporter à la fin du tableau.

Market / Marchés	Year / Année	MFN rate - Simple average (2) / Droit NPF - Moyenne simple (2)						MFN rate - Weighted average (3) / Droit NPF - Moyenne pondérée (3)					
		Total of non-agricultural and non-fuel products / Total des produits non-agricoles et non-pétroliers	Ores and metals / Minérais et métaux	Manufactured products / Produits manufacturés	Chemical products / Produits chimiques	Machinery and transport equipment / Machines et matériel de transport	Other manufactured products / Produits manufacturés divers	Total of non-agricultural and non-fuel products / Total des produits non-agricoles et non-pétroliers	Ores and metals / Minérais et métaux	Manufactured products / Produits manufacturés	Chemical products / Produits chimiques	Machinery and transport equipment / Machines et matériel de transport	Other manufactured products / Produits manufacturés divers
SITC Rev.3 (1) / CTCI Rév.3 (1)		5+6+7+8 +27+28-667	27+28+68	5+6+7+8 -(667+68)	5	7	6+8 -(667+68)	5+6+7+8 +27+28-667	27+28+68	5+6+7+8 -(667+68)	5	7	6+8 -(667+68)
Ethiopia - Éthiopie	2001	10.2	9.2	19.6	11.1	13.2	25.7	15.0	9.1	15.2	8.9	13.9	19.4
	2002	19.2	8.5	19.6	11.2	13.3	25.7	15.7	8.6	15.8	7.9	14.9	20.4
	2006	17.3	8.5	17.7	10.8	12.1	22.8	13.8	7.0	13.9	7.3	12.9	18.7
	2008	16.9	8.3	17.3	10.7	11.3	22.7	12.7	6.9	12.8	6.5	12.1	17.2
	2009	16.9	8.3	17.3	10.7	11.3	22.7	12.7	6.9	12.8	6.5	12.1	17.2
	2010	16.9	8.3	17.3	10.6	11.3	22.7	13.1	6.7	13.2	6.5	12.1	18.3
EU - UE (6)	2000	4.2	1.6	4.4	4.2	2.3	5.4	3.3	1.8	3.4	2.9	2.3	5.4
	2001	4.3	1.6	4.4	5.0	2.3	5.2	3.5	1.9	3.6	3.5	2.4	5.3
	2002	4.4	1.6	4.6	4.7	2.3	5.6	3.7	1.9	3.8	3.3	2.6	5.6
	2003	4.2	1.6	4.4	4.7	2.3	5.1	3.7	2.0	3.7	3.3	2.8	5.3
	2004	3.9	1.6	4.1	4.5	2.3	4.7	3.4	1.8	3.5	3.0	2.5	5.1
	2005	3.9	1.6	4.1	4.6	2.3	4.7	3.3	1.7	3.4	3.2	2.4	5.0
	2006	3.9	1.6	4.1	4.6	2.2	4.7	3.2	1.6	3.4	3.1	2.5	4.8
	2007	3.7	1.6	3.9	3.7	2.2	4.6	3.3	1.7	3.5	2.2	2.8	4.7
	2008	3.7	1.6	3.9	3.7	2.2	4.6	3.2	1.3	3.4	2.2	2.7	4.7
	2009	3.7	1.6	3.8	3.7	2.2	4.6	3.2	1.3	3.4	2.1	2.7	4.7
	2010	3.9	1.6	4.0	4.6	2.2	4.6	3.2	1.3	3.4	2.9	2.2	5.0
Fiji - Fidji	2008	9.6	5.5	9.8	0.0	7.9	11.7	10.4	5.0	10.5	7.0	9.4	12.9
	2009	10.8	5.3	10.9	7.2	8.7	12.9	12.8	5.0	12.9	7.1	13.9	14.6
	2010	10.5	5.2	10.7	6.9	8.4	12.9	12.0	5.0	12.2	8.2	11.1	14.6
French Polynesia - Polynésie française	2008	11.7	10.0	11.7	10.9	10.1	12.6	11.3	11.1	11.3	13.5	10.6	11.4
	2009	11.7	9.9	11.8	11.1	10.3	12.6	11.7	10.9	11.7	13.8	11.2	11.3
Gabon	2001	18.2	11.3	18.4	11.5	14.7	22.4	15.1	17.9	15.1	11.2	14.4	17.8
	2002	18.1	11.2	18.4	11.6	14.6	22.3	13.5	10.6	13.5	10.1	12.8	16.2
	2005	18.3	11.5	18.5	11.6	14.8	22.5	15.5	16.4	15.5	9.7	15.2	18.2
	2007	17.8	11.0	18.1	11.6	14.2	22.1	14.9	14.8	14.9	11.4	14.4	16.9
	2008	17.9	11.1	18.2	11.8	14.0	22.1	14.2	14.4	14.2	9.8	13.5	17.3
	2009	17.9	11.1	18.1	11.8	14.0	22.0	14.3	14.2	14.3	9.8	13.6	17.4
Gambia - Gambie	2007	19.3	19.0	19.3	18.5	19.1	19.5	17.0	17.7	17.0	12.1	18.1	16.7
	2008	19.3	18.9	19.3	18.6	19.3	19.6	17.4	16.4	17.4	11.7	18.8	17.0
	2009	19.3	18.8	19.3	18.7	19.2	19.6	16.9	15.2	17.0	14.5	18.2	16.6
Georgia - Géorgie	2002	9.8	11.4	9.7	11.4	5.9	11.2	8.5	11.4	8.4	7.3	7.3	10.8
	2003	7.5	8.0	7.5	7.7	4.3	8.9	6.9	9.9	6.8	4.7	5.4	9.3
	2004	7.0	7.1	7.0	6.7	4.0	8.5	6.5	8.8	6.4	4.4	5.2	8.7
	2006	6.5	7.0	6.5	5.9	3.8	7.9	6.0	7.4	6.0	4.6	5.4	7.2
	2007	0.3	3.2	0.2	0.1	0.0	0.3	0.3	3.3	0.2	0.0	0.0	0.6
	2008	0.3	3.2	0.2	0.1	0.0	0.3	0.3	3.3	0.2	0.0	0.0	0.6
	2009	0.3	3.5	0.2	0.1	0.0	0.3	0.3	1.7	0.3	0.0	0.0	0.7
	2010	0.3	3.5	0.2	0.1	0.0	0.3	0.3	1.7	0.3	0.0	0.0	0.7
Ghana	2000	13.8	11.2	13.9	12.1	5.4	18.6	8.9	10.2	8.9	11.4	5.2	13.3
	2004	12.8	11.0	13.0	11.5	6.1	15.9	8.9	11.1	8.8	10.1	5.9	13.4
	2007	12.4	11.0	12.4	11.2	5.9	15.9	8.9	10.2	8.8	10.2	6.4	13.1
	2008	12.3	11.0	12.4	11.2	5.8	15.9	8.8	10.2	8.8	10.2	6.4	13.1
	2009	12.4	11.4	12.4	11.2	5.8	15.9	8.5	10.8	8.5	9.2	5.5	13.0
Grenada - Grenade	2001	17.3	12.5	17.3	13.3	18.3	17.7	16.3	12.4	16.3	14.4	20.3	15.2
	2002	10.5	5.7	10.6	7.7	8.9	12.1	11.3	7.7	11.3	13.3	9.8	11.9
	2003	10.4	6.1	10.5	7.7	8.7	12.0	10.3	6.2	10.4	12.9	9.9	10.3
	2006	10.5	6.4	10.6	7.9	8.5	12.2	11.6	6.5	11.6	13.3	10.3	12.3
	2007	10.2	5.7	10.3	7.7	8.4	11.9	11.1	7.0	11.1	12.8	10.3	11.2
	2008	10.2	5.8	10.4	7.6	8.5	12.0	10.5	8.1	10.5	13.0	11.0	9.7
	2010	10.7	6.3	10.8	9.1	9.1	12.0	11.3	6.9	11.4	12.1	10.8	11.7

For sources and notes, see end of table.

Pour les sources et les notes, se reporter à la fin du tableau.

Market / Marchés	Year / Année	MFN rate - Simple average (2) / Droit NPF - Moyenne simple (2)						MFN rate - Weighted average (3) / Droit NPF - Moyenne pondérée (3)					
		Total of non-agricultural and non-fuel products / Total des produits non-agricoles et non-pétroliers	Ores and metals / Minérais et métaux	Manufactured products / Produits manufacturés	Chemical products / Produits chimiques	Machinery and transport equipment / Machines et matériel de transport	Other manufactured products / Produits manufacturés divers	Total of non-agricultural and non-fuel products / Total des produits non-agricoles et non-pétroliers	Ores and metals / Minérais et métaux	Manufactured products / Produits manufacturés	Chemical products / Produits chimiques	Machinery and transport equipment / Machines et matériel de transport	Other manufactured products / Produits manufacturés divers
SITC Rev.3 (1) / CTCI Rév.3 (1)		5+6+7+8 +27+28-667	27+28+68	5+6+7+8 -(667+68)	5	7	6+8 -(667+68)	5+6+7+8 +27+28-667	27+28+68	5+6+7+8 -(667+68)	5	7	6+8 -(667+68)
Guatemala	2000	6.7	1.4	7.0	1.6	2.6	11.0	5.1	7.0	6.2	3.5	4.7	7.0
	2001	6.4	1.4	6.6	1.6	2.6	10.4	5.8	2.1	5.0	7.9	4.0	7.0
	2002	5.8	1.4	6.0	1.6	2.6	9.3	5.7	2.0	5.7	3.6	5.4	7.7
	2004	5.2	1.3	5.4	1.6	2.6	8.1	5.9	1.4	6.0	3.7	6.0	7.5
	2005	5.2	1.4	5.3	1.6	2.5	8.0	5.9	1.7	6.0	3.2	5.5	7.7
	2007	5.0	1.3	5.2	1.5	2.3	7.8	5.6	1.7	5.7	3.0	5.3	7.3
	2008	5.0	1.3	5.2	1.5	2.3	7.8	5.6	1.7	5.7	3.0	5.3	7.3
	2009	5.0	1.2	5.2	1.6	2.3	7.8	5.4	1.9	5.4	3.1	5.4	6.9
	2010	5.0	1.3	5.2	1.6	2.3	7.8	5.4	2.1	5.5	3.4	5.2	7.1
Guinea - Guinée	2005	12.7	9.8	12.8	7.8	9.2	16.2	11.2	8.8	11.2	4.3	11.8	15.0
	2008	12.6	9.6	12.6	7.5	9.2	16.0	11.2	8.0	11.2	4.1	11.8	15.1
	2009	12.6	10.2	12.7	7.3	8.9	16.0	10.2	9.9	10.2	5.2	8.9	14.7
	2010	12.6	10.2	12.7	7.3	8.9	16.0	10.2	9.9	10.2	5.2	8.9	14.7
Guinea-Bissau - Guinée-Bissau	2001	13.4	9.7	13.5	9.2	10.2	16.6	12.9	9.1	12.9	10.2	10.0	16.2
	2002	13.3	10.7	13.4	9.8	10.1	16.5	13.0	9.4	13.1	8.8	10.9	16.5
	2003	13.7	8.9	13.8	10.5	10.1	16.7	12.9	11.8	12.9	9.4	9.7	16.8
	2004	13.6	12.1	13.7	9.9	10.3	16.6	14.8	10.5	14.9	14.2	11.3	17.3
	2005	13.7	11.0	13.7	9.6	10.0	16.9	13.5	13.4	13.5	10.9	10.2	17.0
	2006	13.7	11.0	13.7	9.6	10.1	16.9	13.5	13.4	13.5	10.9	10.2	17.1
	2007	13.5	10.1	13.6	10.3	9.4	16.9	12.4	7.6	12.4	9.7	9.8	16.5
	2008	13.5	10.7	13.5	9.8	9.4	16.5	13.8	10.8	13.8	11.2	10.3	16.9
	2009	13.4	10.7	13.5	9.8	9.4	16.5	13.8	10.8	13.8	11.5	10.4	16.8
	2010	13.5	10.0	13.6	9.7	9.3	16.6	12.3	11.1	12.3	11.4	8.5	16.2
Guyana	2000	17.7	14.1	17.7	13.6	16.9	18.7	16.1	16.2	16.1	12.2	20.3	14.9
	2001	10.0	5.9	10.1	6.9	8.2	12.1	9.8	6.6	9.8	8.9	9.5	10.5
	2002	10.1	6.0	10.2	7.2	8.3	12.1	10.1	9.2	10.1	9.5	9.7	10.8
	2003	10.1	5.8	10.2	7.3	8.3	12.1	9.7	10.6	9.7	9.9	9.1	10.1
	2006	10.1	5.4	10.2	7.3	8.2	12.2	9.5	7.5	9.5	10.4	8.8	10.1
	2008	9.6	5.8	9.7	7.1	6.7	11.9	9.1	8.1	9.1	10.2	7.8	10.0
	2010	9.5	5.6	9.6	7.3	6.5	11.9	9.5	6.4	9.5	11.1	7.5	11.1
Haiti - Haïti	2007	2.4	0.8	2.4	2.2	0.9	3.3	1.9	0.5	2.0	3.5	1.6	2.0
	2008	2.3	0.8	2.4	2.0	0.9	3.3	5.5	0.0	5.6	3.5	2.4	7.6
	2009	2.4	0.8	2.4	2.1	0.9	3.3	5.8	0.0	5.9	3.6	2.7	7.8
Honduras	2000	7.2	2.1	7.4	2.5	3.6	10.8	6.0	3.8	6.0	2.5	8.0	8.7
	2001	6.8	2.2	7.0	2.4	3.5	10.2	5.4	3.9	5.5	2.3	7.9	7.7
	2002	5.6	1.6	5.8	1.6	2.6	8.7	5.6	3.0	5.6	3.1	5.0	7.9
	2004	5.6	1.3	5.8	1.7	2.6	8.7	4.9	2.9	5.0	2.9	4.0	7.6
	2005	5.3	1.4	5.4	1.6	2.5	8.1	5.3	2.6	5.3	2.7	5.0	7.5
	2007	5.1	1.5	5.2	1.6	2.2	7.9	5.6	2.6	5.7	2.6	5.8	7.7
	2008	5.1	1.5	5.2	1.6	2.2	7.9	5.6	2.6	5.7	2.6	5.8	7.7
	2009	5.1	1.5	5.2	1.6	2.1	7.9	5.4	2.6	5.5	2.6	5.3	7.7
Hungary - Hongrie (5)	2002	7.2	3.0	7.4	5.3	8.8	7.5	8.0	2.8	8.1	4.6	9.0	7.5
Iceland - Islande	2001	3.0	0.0	3.1	1.2	1.4	4.4	2.9	0.0	3.1	3.2	0.8	5.7
	2003	2.9	0.0	3.0	0.9	1.4	4.4	2.8	0.0	3.0	3.0	0.7	5.8
	2006	2.9	0.0	3.0	1.0	1.4	4.4	2.2	0.0	2.4	3.0	0.5	5.4
	2007	2.7	0.0	2.8	0.9	1.2	4.2	2.3	0.0	2.5	3.0	0.5	5.4
	2008	2.7	0.0	2.8	0.9	1.2	4.2	2.3	0.0	2.5	3.0	0.5	5.4
	2009	2.8	0.0	2.9	1.0	1.3	4.2	2.2	0.0	2.6	2.7	0.5	5.4
	2010	2.7	0.0	2.9	0.9	1.2	4.2	2.1	0.0	2.7	2.7	0.6	5.3

For sources and notes, see end of table.

Pour les sources et les notes, se reporter à la fin du tableau.

Market / Marchés	Year / Année	MFN rate - Simple average (2) / Droit NPF - Moyenne simple (2)						MFN rate - Weighted average (3) / Droit NPF - Moyenne pondérée (3)					
		Total of non-agricultural and non-fuel products / Total des produits non-agricoles et non-pétroliers	Ores and metals / Minérais et métaux	Manufactured products / Produits manufacturés	Chemical products / Produits chimiques	Machinery and transport equipment / Machines et matériel de transport	Other manufactured products / Produits manufacturés divers	Total of non-agricultural and non-fuel products / Total des produits non-agricoles et non-pétroliers	Ores and metals / Minérais et métaux	Manufactured products / Produits manufacturés	Chemical products / Produits chimiques	Machinery and transport equipment / Machines et matériel de transport	Other manufactured products / Produits manufacturés divers
SITC Rev.3 (1) / CTCI Rév.3 (1)		5+6+7+8 +27+28-667	27+28+68	5+6+7+8 -(667+68)	5	7	6+8 -(667+68)	5+6+7+8 +27+28-667	27+28+68	5+6+7+8 -(667+68)	5	7	6+8 -(667+68)
India - Inde	2001	31.4	27.2	31.7	34.1	28.1	32.3	26.5	25.1	26.7	30.4	22.7	29.4
	2004	28.2	22.5	28.6	29.4	26.7	29.1	23.9	22.8	24.1	26.3	21.2	27.8
	2005	15.3	14.0	15.4	15.9	15.1	15.3	12.0	13.6	11.8	14.5	9.4	14.9
	2007	13.1	11.8	13.2	13.4	13.3	13.0	11.1	9.6	11.4	11.9	9.7	14.1
	2008	8.6	5.2	8.9	8.5	9.0	9.0	6.9	4.7	7.1	7.0	6.8	7.9
	2009	9.0	5.3	9.3	8.8	9.6	9.3	7.6	6.2	7.8	7.5	7.8	8.1
Indonesia including East Timor - Indonésie, y compris le Timor oriental	2000	8.7	4.8	8.9	6.1	5.4	11.6	6.5	2.9	6.7	5.6	6.1	8.9
	2001	6.8	4.2	7.0	5.1	4.6	8.7	5.3	2.5	5.5	4.3	5.4	7.1
	2002	6.9	4.2	7.0	5.1	4.8	8.8	6.1	3.0	6.2	5.4	5.4	8.4
Indonesia - Indonésie	2003	6.9	4.3	7.1	5.1	4.8	8.9	5.6	3.2	5.7	5.2	4.7	8.5
	2004	7.0	4.3	7.2	5.1	4.8	8.9	6.4	3.5	6.5	5.8	5.6	9.1
	2005	7.0	4.3	7.2	5.2	4.8	8.9	6.4	3.4	6.5	5.8	5.5	9.1
	2006	7.0	4.3	7.2	5.2	4.8	8.9	6.4	3.4	6.5	5.8	5.5	9.1
	2007	6.9	4.3	7.1	5.1	4.5	9.0	6.3	3.5	6.5	5.9	5.5	8.5
	2009	6.8	4.2	7.0	4.9	4.3	8.9	6.3	3.2	6.4	5.5	5.7	8.4
	2010	7.2	4.2	7.4	5.5	6.1	8.7	6.7	3.0	6.8	7.1	6.0	8.1
Iran (Islamic Rep. of) - Iran (Rép. islamique d')	2000	41.8	16.8	43.1	17.0	42.0	60.1	20.1	13.3	28.6	12.7	34.8	28.9
	2002	24.6	9.8	25.4	11.2	16.4	36.2	17.9	9.9	18.1	20.7	18.6	15.6
	2004	20.8	9.2	21.3	11.4	16.2	28.0	14.4	7.5	14.7	14.1	14.9	14.6
	2007	24.0	9.0	24.7	11.2	16.7	35.1	18.3	8.5	18.5	14.0	20.9	17.2
	2008	27.0	8.1	28.0	11.2	16.0	39.8	21.0	9.4	21.2	13.2	20.5	25.1
Israel - Israël	2004	4.7	0.7	4.9	1.8	3.6	6.6	3.8	0.5	3.9	3.0	2.7	6.3
	2005	4.6	0.7	4.8	1.8	3.6	6.5	3.7	0.5	3.8	3.0	2.6	6.4
	2006	4.6	0.7	4.8	1.8	3.6	6.5	3.7	0.7	3.8	3.1	2.6	6.3
	2007	4.5	0.7	4.7	1.7	3.8	6.3	3.9	0.7	4.1	2.9	3.1	6.2
	2008	4.5	0.7	4.7	1.7	3.8	6.2	3.9	0.7	4.0	2.8	3.1	6.0
	2009	4.5	0.7	4.7	1.8	3.8	6.2	4.3	0.8	4.4	3.4	3.3	6.7
Jamaica - Jamaïque	2000	6.1	1.4	6.3	2.5	4.2	8.6	9.9	1.1	10.0	6.9	10.4	10.9
	2001	6.1	1.3	6.3	2.4	4.2	8.7	9.1	0.7	9.2	6.0	9.5	10.3
	2002	6.1	1.4	6.3	2.4	4.1	8.8	9.3	0.7	9.4	6.3	9.1	10.9
	2003	6.1	1.1	6.3	2.4	4.2	8.7	9.5	1.8	9.6	7.0	9.7	10.7
	2006	6.1	1.4	6.3	2.6	4.1	8.7	8.5	2.5	8.6	6.4	8.6	9.6
	2007	6.1	1.6	6.3	2.8	3.9	8.6	9.3	2.4	9.4	9.4	9.9	9.0
	2010	6.1	1.7	6.2	2.8	3.9	8.6	9.9	3.5	9.9	9.1	9.9	10.5
Japan - Japon	2000	2.8	1.2	2.9	2.8	0.1	4.2	2.0	0.1	2.2	1.8	0.1	5.1
	2001	2.7	1.2	2.8	2.8	0.1	4.1	2.0	0.2	2.2	1.9	0.1	5.0
	2002	2.7	1.2	2.8	2.7	0.1	4.0	1.9	0.2	2.1	1.8	0.1	4.8
	2003	2.6	1.2	2.7	2.8	0.1	3.8	1.8	0.2	2.0	1.7	0.1	4.6
	2004	2.5	1.2	2.6	2.8	0.1	3.6	1.7	0.2	1.9	1.8	0.1	4.3
	2005	2.5	1.2	2.6	2.7	0.1	3.6	1.7	0.2	1.8	1.7	0.1	4.1
	2006	2.5	1.2	2.6	2.7	0.1	3.6	1.6	0.1	1.8	1.7	0.1	4.0
	2007	2.5	1.3	2.6	2.8	0.1	3.6	1.9	0.6	2.1	1.8	0.1	4.2
	2008	2.5	1.2	2.6	2.7	0.1	3.6	1.7	0.1	2.0	1.7	0.1	3.9
	2009	2.5	1.2	2.6	2.8	0.1	3.6	1.7	0.1	2.0	1.7	0.1	3.9
	2010	2.5	1.2	2.6	2.8	0.1	3.5	2.0	0.1	2.2	1.6	0.1	4.3
Jordan - Jordanie	2000	22.5	17.9	22.7	18.2	15.4	27.6	19.7	14.2	19.9	14.0	18.7	24.8
	2001	14.7	12.6	14.7	8.1	12.3	18.4	12.7	9.1	12.9	7.4	12.9	15.4
	2002	14.8	12.4	14.9	8.3	12.3	18.6	13.0	8.6	13.2	7.8	12.9	15.9
	2003	12.7	7.3	12.9	3.2	11.0	17.4	10.9	4.8	11.1	4.5	11.4	13.8
	2005	13.3	9.1	13.5	3.0	11.5	18.2	12.1	6.6	12.3	4.2	12.4	15.1
	2006	10.9	7.1	11.0	1.7	9.9	15.0	8.3	6.3	8.4	3.2	8.7	9.9
	2007	10.5	7.4	10.6	1.5	8.8	14.7	8.7	5.9	8.8	2.7	9.9	10.4
	2008	10.0	6.9	10.1	1.3	8.8	14.1	8.0	5.4	8.1	1.5	9.1	10.1
	2009	9.3	6.2	9.4	1.2	8.0	13.2	7.4	5.4	7.5	1.6	7.6	10.2

For sources and notes, see end of table.

Pour les sources et les notes, se reporter à la fin du tableau.

4.3 Average applied import MFN tariff rates on non-agricultural and non-fuel products
4.3 Droits de douane moyens NPF appliqués à l'importation des produits non-agricoles et non-pétroliers

Market / Marchés	Year / Année	MFN rate - Simple average (2) / Droit NPF - Moyenne simple (2)						MFN rate - Weighted average (3) / Droit NPF - Moyenne pondérée (3)					
		Total of non-agricultural and non-fuel products / Total des produits non-agricoles et non-pétroliers	Ores and metals / Minérais et métaux	Manu-factured products / Produits manu-facturés	Chemical products / Produits chimiques	Machinery and transport equipment / Machines et matériel de transport	Other manu-factured products / Produits manu-facturés divers	Total of non-agricultural and non-fuel products / Total des produits non-agricoles et non-pétroliers	Ores and metals / Minérais et métaux	Manu-factured products / Produits manu-facturés	Chemical products / Produits chimiques	Machinery and transport equipment / Machines et matériel de transport	Other manu-factured products / Produits manu-facturés divers
SITC Rev.3 (1) / CTCI Rév.3 (1)		5+6+7+8 +27+28-667	27+28+68	5+6+7+8 -(667+68)	5	7	6+8 -(667+68)	5+6+7+8 +27+28-667	27+28+68	5+6+7+8 -(667+68)	5	7	6+8 -(667+68)
Kazakhstan	2004	2.7	3.8	2.7	4.4	0.5	0.6	1.5	1.7	1.5	1.6	0.2	3.4
	2008	4.6	4.2	4.6	4.6	0.8	6.7	4.0	4.8	4.0	3.9	1.7	7.0
	2010	7.3	5.9	7.4	5.4	4.3	10.1	7.1	3.8	7.2	5.5	3.9	11.7
Kenya	2000	17.6	11.8	17.9	11.6	13.6	23.8	12.9	7.7	13.0	7.2	12.3	19.7
	2001	18.9	10.8	19.2	10.7	11.9	26.1	11.5	6.3	11.6	6.2	9.6	19.9
	2004	15.9	11.2	16.1	9.0	9.8	21.9	10.2	4.0	10.4	3.9	11.2	14.2
	2005	11.9	7.2	12.1	3.4	6.4	18.1	6.9	3.4	7.0	3.4	4.7	13.4
	2006	11.8	6.7	12.0	3.3	6.3	18.0	6.9	3.0	7.1	2.6	5.4	13.6
	2007	11.7	7.0	11.9	3.4	6.3	17.8	7.1	3.8	7.3	2.8	5.5	13.0
	2008	11.4	7.0	11.6	3.6	5.8	17.6	7.2	4.8	7.2	2.5	5.8	12.7
	2009	11.4	7.0	11.6	3.6	5.8	17.5	7.2	4.8	7.2	2.5	5.8	12.7
	2010	11.5	6.8	11.7	3.6	5.7	17.6	7.2	5.0	7.3	2.8	5.8	13.0
Korea, Republic of - Corée, République de	2002	7.9	4.3	8.2	11.0	5.9	8.0	4.8	2.8	5.0	8.5	3.3	6.5
	2004	7.3	4.2	7.5	9.5	6.0	7.4	4.3	2.7	4.5	7.4	3.5	4.9
	2006	7.3	4.2	7.5	9.5	6.0	7.3	4.2	2.5	4.5	7.2	3.5	4.8
	2007	7.3	3.7	7.5	9.7	6.1	7.3	4.6	1.5	5.2	6.8	4.9	4.7
	2009	7.2	3.7	7.5	9.6	6.2	7.2	4.3	1.5	4.9	6.6	4.9	4.0
	2010	7.3	3.7	7.5	9.6	6.1	7.2	4.8	1.5	5.3	6.9	4.9	4.8
Kuwait - Koweït	2002	4.0	4.0	4.0	3.9	4.0	4.0	4.0	4.0	4.0	4.0	4.0	4.0
	2005	4.9	4.8	4.9	4.7	4.9	5.0	4.8	5.0	4.8	3.2	4.8	5.0
	2006	4.9	4.8	4.9	4.6	4.9	5.0	4.8	5.0	4.8	3.2	4.8	5.0
	2007	4.8	4.8	4.8	4.6	4.6	4.9	4.4	5.0	4.4	3.4	4.3	4.9
	2008	4.8	4.8	4.8	4.5	4.6	4.9	4.7	5.0	4.6	3.1	4.7	4.9
	2009	4.8	4.8	4.8	4.5	4.6	4.9	4.7	5.0	4.6	3.2	4.7	4.9
Kyrgyzstan - Kirghizistan	2002	8.3	6.6	8.4	7.2	6.6	9.6	7.1	5.4	7.2	4.9	6.9	9.0
	2003	4.6	2.3	4.7	2.2	4.1	5.7	2.9	3.2	2.9	0.8	3.3	3.9
	2006	4.0	2.1	4.1	2.1	3.2	5.1	1.9	3.0	1.9	0.8	1.4	3.1
	2007	3.9	2.5	4.0	1.9	3.2	5.0	2.1	2.3	2.1	0.8	2.1	2.7
	2008	4.2	1.5	4.3	1.8	3.0	5.5	9.4	0.2	9.5	0.6	4.5	10.0
	2009	4.2	1.5	4.3	1.8	3.0	5.5	9.4	0.2	9.4	0.5	5.0	10.0
	2010	4.1	2.1	4.2	2.2	2.9	5.4	4.1	2.3	4.1	0.4	4.6	5.5
Lao People's Dem. Rep. - Rép. dém. populaire lao	2000	8.3	5.3	8.4	8.3	7.5	9.0	12.6	5.0	12.7	9.7	16.6	8.4
	2001	8.4	5.1	8.5	8.1	7.7	9.1	12.0	5.0	12.0	10.9	14.9	8.3
	2004	8.4	5.3	8.5	8.1	7.9	9.0	11.0	5.1	11.1	11.4	13.6	8.1
	2005	8.4	5.1	8.5	8.0	7.7	9.1	12.3	5.0	12.4	11.7	15.4	8.6
	2006	8.4	5.1	8.5	8.0	7.7	9.1	12.3	5.0	12.4	11.7	15.4	8.6
	2007	8.4	5.5	8.5	8.1	7.8	9.0	13.3	5.0	13.4	12.5	16.8	8.3
	2008	8.3	5.4	8.4	7.9	7.6	8.9	12.7	6.5	12.7	12.5	16.2	8.0
Latvia - Lettonie (5)	2001	2.3	0.5	2.4	0.9	0.3	3.7	1.5	0.5	1.6	0.6	0.1	3.3
Lebanon - Liban	2000	14.6	7.6	14.9	7.9	12.0	18.6	16.1	6.4	16.6	10.7	15.7	19.6
	2001	5.1	2.7	5.3	2.6	4.1	6.7	6.8	2.0	7.0	5.7	5.3	8.7
	2002	4.4	2.8	4.5	2.6	3.8	5.4	6.3	2.0	6.4	5.7	5.1	7.9
	2004	4.5	2.8	4.6	2.8	3.8	5.5	6.1	1.6	6.3	5.6	4.9	7.9
	2005	4.5	2.6	4.6	2.7	3.8	5.5	6.1	1.5	6.3	5.5	4.9	7.9
	2006	4.5	2.7	4.6	2.7	3.8	5.5	6.1	1.6	6.3	5.5	4.9	7.9
	2007	4.2	2.8	4.3	2.9	3.8	5.0	5.8	1.6	6.0	5.6	4.9	7.4
Lesotho	2001	10.0	0.0	10.1	3.6	4.3	14.8	17.6	0.0	17.6	2.0	5.9	21.5
	2004	10.7	3.8	10.8	5.1	4.8	14.7	17.4	4.4	17.4	4.1	7.5	20.2
	2005	10.4	3.5	10.6	4.8	4.1	14.7	17.3	2.4	17.4	2.4	8.0	20.2
	2006	10.4	3.5	10.5	4.8	4.0	14.7	17.3	2.4	17.4	2.4	7.9	20.2
	2007	9.6	2.5	9.7	5.8	4.2	13.9	14.3	0.4	14.3	3.8	4.6	19.9
	2008	10.0	0.4	10.1	5.3	4.0	14.3	17.3	0.0	17.4	1.0	5.8	20.0
	2009	9.9	0.4	10.1	5.5	4.0	14.2	13.7	0.0	13.8	0.9	4.1	20.0
	2010	9.6	2.2	9.7	4.1	4.1	13.7	12.0	4.3	12.0	0.8	5.8	19.0

For sources and notes, see end of table.

Pour les sources et les notes, se reporter à la fin du tableau.

Market / Marchés	Year / Année	MFN rate - Simple average (2) / Droit NPF - Moyenne simple (2)						MFN rate - Weighted average (3) / Droit NPF - Moyenne pondérée (3)					
		Total of non-agricultural and non-fuel products / Total des produits non-agricoles et non-pétroliers	Ores and metals / Minérais et métaux	Manufactured products / Produits manufacturés	Chemical products / Produits chimiques	Machinery and transport equipment / Machines et matériel de transport	Other manufactured products / Produits manufacturés divers	Total of non-agricultural and non-fuel products / Total des produits non-agricoles et non-pétroliers	Ores and metals / Minérais et métaux	Manufactured products / Produits manufacturés	Chemical products / Produits chimiques	Machinery and transport equipment / Machines et matériel de transport	Other manufactured products / Produits manufacturés divers
SITC Rev.3 (1) / CTCI Rév.3 (1)		5+6+7+8 +27+28-667	27+28+68	5+6+7+8 -(667+68)	5	7	6+8 -(667+68)	5+6+7+8 +27+28-667	27+28+68	5+6+7+8 -(667+68)	5	7	6+8 -(667+68)
Libyan Arab Jamahiriya - Jamahiriya arabe libyenne	2002	18.7	8.9	19.1	9.5	20.2	21.2	28.5	7.3	28.7	9.7	38.8	16.2
Lithuania - Lituanie (5)	2002	2.7	0.0	2.9	0.4	0.4	4.7	1.9	0.0	1.9	0.5	0.6	4.4
	2003	2.6	0.0	2.7	0.5	0.4	4.5	1.9	0.0	1.9	0.6	0.7	4.2
Madagascar	2001	5.0	2.0	5.1	0.8	4.5	6.9	4.6	0.7	4.6	0.9	5.3	5.4
	2005	11.1	10.1	11.2	9.8	6.8	13.6	6.1	8.4	6.1	7.9	4.9	6.5
	2006	13.6	9.2	13.8	10.1	11.1	16.2	12.9	7.6	13.0	7.6	11.7	14.9
	2007	12.4	8.2	12.6	7.3	10.9	15.1	11.9	8.4	11.9	6.9	10.9	13.6
	2008	12.5	8.2	12.7	7.3	10.9	15.3	11.9	8.4	11.9	6.9	10.8	13.6
	2010	11.6	8.4	11.7	7.3	8.2	14.7	9.8	7.3	9.9	6.6	7.1	11.9
Malawi	2001	13.8	7.5	14.0	7.0	10.1	18.1	11.6	5.7	11.7	5.6	11.8	14.6
	2006	13.7	7.1	13.9	6.9	10.0	18.0	10.1	2.9	10.2	3.9	10.4	15.0
	2008	13.2	7.4	13.4	7.1	8.9	17.5	7.7	3.2	7.8	2.3	7.1	15.0
	2009	13.1	7.4	13.3	7.1	8.6	17.5	7.6	3.2	7.7	2.3	6.9	15.0
	2010	12.6	10.2	12.6	4.0	7.9	17.9	8.7	6.1	8.7	2.1	9.3	14.4
Malaysia - Malaisie	2001	9.3	2.6	9.7	3.4	7.0	13.4	5.2	4.3	5.2	4.9	4.3	9.0
	2002	9.4	2.8	9.8	3.4	7.0	13.5	5.1	4.6	5.2	4.9	4.3	9.4
	2003	9.3	2.7	9.7	3.5	7.0	13.4	5.1	4.4	5.1	5.0	4.2	9.5
	2005	8.4	2.6	8.8	3.0	5.5	12.5	4.8	4.0	4.9	5.1	2.8	13.3
	2006	8.2	2.5	8.6	2.9	5.1	12.3	4.5	3.7	4.5	4.9	2.2	13.5
	2007	8.2	2.5	8.6	2.9	5.2	12.4	4.7	3.9	4.7	4.8	2.2	14.0
	2008	8.0	2.7	8.3	2.8	4.7	12.1	5.5	3.9	5.6	4.1	3.2	13.4
	2009	8.0	2.7	8.3	2.8	4.7	12.1	5.5	3.9	5.6	4.1	3.2	13.4
Maldives	2000	22.1	23.9	22.0	15.6	24.4	22.4	21.4	19.2	21.5	19.5	23.8	20.0
	2001	21.6	23.3	21.5	14.7	24.2	22.3	21.4	18.3	21.5	20.2	23.8	19.9
	2002	21.7	23.4	21.6	14.6	24.4	22.5	21.5	18.1	21.7	19.8	23.4	20.8
	2003	21.7	23.7	21.6	14.7	24.5	22.3	21.9	19.8	21.9	20.3	24.0	20.4
	2004	21.7	23.4	21.6	14.5	24.9	22.2	21.5	19.7	21.5	20.6	23.8	19.9
	2005	21.7	23.6	21.6	14.8	24.3	22.3	21.9	20.1	22.0	20.3	23.7	20.3
	2006	21.9	23.5	21.8	15.1	24.4	22.4	22.2	20.0	22.3	20.7	24.1	20.7
	2008	22.2	23.6	22.1	15.0	26.0	22.4	22.6	19.9	22.8	20.9	25.3	20.7
	2009	22.2	23.6	22.1	15.0	26.0	22.4	22.6	19.9	22.8	20.9	25.3	20.7
Mali	2001	12.6	9.4	12.7	7.6	9.3	16.2	10.6	8.9	10.6	5.4	9.2	15.5
	2002	12.5	9.6	12.5	7.3	9.0	16.2	10.6	8.8	10.6	5.5	9.7	16.0
	2003	12.5	8.5	12.6	7.5	9.0	16.2	11.2	8.2	11.2	5.0	10.8	16.1
	2004	12.5	8.9	12.6	7.5	9.0	16.2	11.2	8.4	11.2	5.0	10.7	16.2
	2005	12.5	9.0	12.6	7.6	9.0	16.1	10.6	8.1	10.6	5.2	9.7	15.4
	2006	12.4	8.4	12.6	7.4	9.1	16.1	10.7	8.7	10.7	5.2	9.7	15.4
	2007	12.4	8.8	12.5	7.6	8.5	16.1	11.3	8.4	11.3	4.6	10.9	16.2
	2008	12.4	8.6	12.5	7.4	8.5	16.1	10.8	8.1	10.8	5.1	9.3	15.4
	2009	12.4	8.6	12.5	7.4	8.5	16.1	10.8	8.1	10.8	5.1	9.3	15.4
	2010	12.4	8.6	12.5	7.4	8.5	16.1	10.8	8.1	10.8	5.1	9.3	15.4
Malta - Malte (5)	2000	8.0	7.7	8.0	7.1	7.2	8.7	10.3	4.5	10.3	4.3	11.7	8.1
	2002	6.4	3.3	6.5	6.5	4.8	7.3	6.4	5.0	6.4	4.7	6.3	7.2
	2003	6.4	3.4	6.5	6.5	4.8	7.2	6.0	6.0	6.0	4.9	5.6	7.1
Mauritania - Mauritanie	2001	11.8	5.3	11.9	6.4	9.5	14.7	9.9	5.1	9.9	9.7	8.9	12.1
	2006	11.0	5.3	11.2	5.6	9.2	13.7	6.6	5.0	6.6	7.9	5.8	11.6
	2007	12.7	9.0	12.8	8.3	9.8	15.8	11.0	8.2	11.0	6.9	9.5	14.0

For sources and notes, see end of table.

Pour les sources et les notes, se reporter à la fin du tableau.

4.3 Average applied import MFN tariff rates on non-agricultural and non-fuel products

4.3 Droits de douane moyens NPF appliqués à l'importation des produits non-agricoles et non-pétroliers

Market / Marchés	Year / Année	MFN rate - Simple average (2) / Droit NPF - Moyenne simple (2)						MFN rate - Weighted average (3) / Droit NPF - Moyenne pondérée (3)					
		Total of non-agricultural and non-fuel products / Total des produits non-agricoles et non-pétroliers	Ores and metals / Minérais et métaux	Manu-factured products / Produits manu-facturés	Chemical products / Produits chimiques	Machinery and transport equipment / Machines et matériel de transport	Other manu-factured products / Produits manu-facturés divers	Total of non-agricultural and non-fuel products / Total des produits non-agricoles et non-pétroliers	Ores and metals / Minérais et métaux	Manu-factured products / Produits manu-facturés	Chemical products / Produits chimiques	Machinery and transport equipment / Machines et matériel de transport	Other manu-factured products / Produits manu-facturés divers
SITC Rev.3 (1) / CTCI Rév.3 (1)		5+6+7+8 +27+28-667	27+28+68	5+6+7+8 -(667+68)	5	7	6+8 -(667+68)	5+6+7+8 +27+28-667	27+28+68	5+6+7+8 -(667+68)	5	7	6+8 -(667+68)
Mauritius - Maurice	2002	21.2	1.7	21.9	7.5	15.7	29.3	14.7	2.2	14.4	14.4	13.6	15.8
	2005	6.1	1.5	6.3	4.2	5.9	7.3	4.9	1.7	4.9	6.0	3.6	6.1
	2006	2.8	0.4	2.9	1.7	2.8	3.4	1.9	0.3	1.9	3.1	1.2	2.5
	2007	2.7	0.3	2.8	1.7	2.8	3.2	2.7	0.3	2.8	3.4	1.9	3.2
	2008	2.7	0.4	2.8	1.8	2.3	3.3	3.0	0.3	3.0	3.9	1.9	3.5
	2009	1.4	0.1	1.4	0.9	0.8	1.9	1.8	0.5	1.8	2.4	0.5	2.6
	2010	1.4	0.1	1.4	0.9	0.8	1.9	1.8	0.4	1.8	2.5	0.4	2.7
Mayotte	2007	8.9	4.6	9.0	8.6	10.2	8.6	9.5	3.5	9.5	6.0	12.1	6.8
	2008	8.9	4.6	9.0	8.7	10.2	8.6	9.4	3.5	9.5	6.0	12.1	6.8
	2009	8.9	4.6	9.0	8.6	10.1	8.6	9.4	3.5	9.5	6.0	12.1	6.8
	2010	8.9	4.2	9.0	8.8	10.1	8.7	8.1	4.3	8.2	4.6	9.8	7.1
Mexico - Mexique	2000	17.1	12.4	17.4	12.4	14.1	20.7	14.6	11.9	14.7	11.8	13.2	18.4
	2001	17.1	12.4	17.4	12.4	14.0	20.7	14.5	12.2	14.5	11.9	13.0	18.7
	2002	17.2	12.4	17.5	12.4	14.0	20.9	14.6	12.3	14.6	12.1	12.8	19.0
	2003	17.2	12.4	17.5	12.3	14.0	21.0	14.5	12.2	14.5	12.0	12.6	19.2
	2004	16.5	12.5	16.7	12.3	13.5	19.8	12.8	11.8	12.8	11.8	10.8	17.2
	2005	13.6	9.4	13.8	9.3	10.4	17.0	11.8	9.4	11.9	9.0	11.1	14.7
	2006	13.5	9.4	13.7	9.3	10.4	16.9	11.7	9.6	11.8	9.0	11.2	14.1
	2008	11.2	6.5	11.5	6.9	8.8	14.5	10.0	5.6	10.2	6.4	10.8	11.0
	2009	10.0	1.8	10.4	5.3	7.3	13.7	8.4	4.5	8.6	5.2	9.0	9.5
	2010	7.2	0.7	7.7	2.5	4.0	11.2	4.8	1.3	4.0	3.1	4.4	6.9
Mongolia - Mongolie	2005	4.2	5.0	4.2	5.0	2.1	5.0	3.8	5.0	3.7	5.0	2.6	5.0
	2006	4.2	5.0	4.2	5.0	2.1	5.0	3.9	5.0	3.9	5.0	2.8	5.0
	2007	4.9	5.0	4.9	5.0	4.8	5.0	4.9	5.0	4.9	5.0	4.8	5.0
	2008	4.9	5.0	4.9	5.0	4.8	5.0	4.9	5.0	4.9	5.0	4.8	5.0
	2009	4.9	5.0	4.9	5.0	4.8	5.0	4.9	5.0	4.9	5.0	4.8	5.0
Montenegro - Monténégro	2008	4.6	3.4	4.6	2.7	2.5	6.1	5.0	2.5	5.2	4.8	2.9	7.2
	2009	4.6	3.4	4.6	2.7	2.6	6.1	5.0	2.5	5.2	4.8	2.9	7.2
	2010	4.5	3.7	4.6	2.6	2.6	6.0	5.1	2.0	5.3	4.6	2.9	7.2
Morocco - Maroc	2000	28.2	24.1	28.4	26.7	13.2	35.7	25.9	12.8	26.4	26.1	15.5	36.2
	2001	28.0	23.8	28.2	26.5	13.2	35.5	25.7	12.8	26.2	25.8	14.3	36.3
	2002	27.8	24.0	28.0	25.2	13.0	35.5	25.4	12.7	25.9	24.7	15.2	35.6
	2003	27.4	23.5	27.6	23.6	12.9	35.3	24.1	10.7	24.7	21.6	14.5	35.1
	2005	23.7	13.6	24.2	17.6	11.1	32.2	21.2	7.5	21.8	19.4	14.3	30.2
	2006	21.5	13.4	21.9	17.3	11.0	28.2	18.9	8.4	19.5	19.2	14.9	24.6
	2007	20.2	13.3	20.6	15.5	9.0	27.4	17.9	7.9	18.5	17.0	13.4	24.9
	2008	18.0	12.7	18.3	14.5	8.3	24.0	16.3	7.7	16.8	15.5	12.4	22.4
	2009	15.0	10.4	15.3	11.3	8.1	19.9	12.9	3.1	13.9	10.7	11.9	17.6
Mozambique	2001	13.6	5.2	14.0	6.1	9.0	18.9	11.9	6.8	12.0	5.7	8.7	17.7
	2002	12.0	5.0	12.2	5.6	8.4	16.1	9.5	6.7	9.5	9.4	8.2	11.7
	2003	12.0	5.0	12.2	5.6	8.4	16.1	9.5	6.7	9.5	9.4	8.2	11.7
	2005	11.9	4.9	12.2	5.5	8.3	16.2	8.8	6.2	8.8	5.7	8.1	11.1
	2006	11.6	4.8	11.9	5.4	8.2	15.9	8.4	5.9	8.4	5.2	7.6	11.0
	2007	10.1	4.7	10.4	5.1	7.6	13.4	7.9	7.0	7.9	4.7	7.6	9.6
	2009	9.7	4.7	9.9	5.0	6.8	13.1	7.6	2.7	7.9	5.6	6.9	10.2
	2010	9.6	4.7	9.9	5.0	6.9	13.0	7.9	3.5	8.0	5.5	6.2	11.4
Myanmar	2001	4.9	2.9	4.9	2.2	2.9	6.8	4.8	2.9	4.8	2.6	2.8	6.9
	2002	4.8	3.1	4.9	2.2	2.9	6.8	4.7	3.0	4.7	2.5	2.9	6.8
	2003	4.8	3.0	4.9	2.2	2.8	6.7	4.0	2.7	4.0	2.5	2.6	6.2
	2004	4.8	3.0	4.9	2.2	3.0	6.8	4.0	2.5	4.0	2.5	3.1	5.5
	2005	4.9	3.1	5.0	2.2	3.0	6.9	4.1	2.8	4.1	2.6	3.0	5.6
	2006	4.9	3.1	5.0	2.2	3.0	6.9	4.1	2.8	4.1	2.6	3.0	5.6
	2007	4.9	2.9	4.9	2.1	3.0	6.8	4.1	2.6	4.1	2.6	3.2	5.4
	2008	5.0	3.1	5.1	2.2	2.8	7.1	3.9	2.9	3.9	2.7	3.2	5.2

For sources and notes, see end of table.

Pour les sources et les notes, se reporter à la fin du tableau.

Market / Marchés	Year / Année	MFN rate - Simple average (2) / Droit NPF - Moyenne simple (2)						MFN rate - Weighted average (3) / Droit NPF - Moyenne pondérée (3)					
		Total of non-agricultural and non-fuel products / Total des produits non-agricoles et non-pétroliers	Ores and metals / Minérais et métaux	Manufactured products / Produits manufacturés	Chemical products / Produits chimiques	Machinery and transport equipment / Machines et matériel de transport	Other manufactured products / Produits manufacturés divers	Total of non-agricultural and non-fuel products / Total des produits non-agricoles et non-pétroliers	Ores and metals / Minérais et métaux	Manufactured products / Produits manufacturés	Chemical products / Produits chimiques	Machinery and transport equipment / Machines et matériel de transport	Other manufactured products / Produits manufacturés divers
SITC Rev.3 (1) / CTCI Rév.3 (1)		5+6+7+8 +27+28-667	27+28+68	5+6+7+8 -(667+68)	5	7	6+8 -(667+68)	5+6+7+8 +27+28-667	27+28+68	5+6+7+8 -(667+68)	5	7	6+8 -(667+68)
Namibia - Namibie	2001	8.4	1.7	8.8	3.1	3.3	13.2	11.4	0.7	11.6	10.4	10.2	13.9
	2004	8.5	1.6	8.9	2.9	3.1	13.4	10.9	2.3	11.1	6.2	10.2	14.0
	2005	8.6	1.6	9.0	3.1	3.1	13.4	11.0	1.9	11.1	6.0	10.6	13.7
	2006	8.6	1.7	9.0	3.0	3.1	13.4	10.5	1.7	10.6	6.4	9.6	13.4
	2007	8.4	1.7	8.8	3.2	3.1	13.1	10.5	1.5	10.6	6.1	9.3	13.5
	2008	8.4	1.7	8.8	3.1	3.1	13.1	10.3	1.5	10.4	6.1	9.1	13.3
	2009	8.3	1.7	8.6	3.1	3.1	12.9	10.1	1.8	10.2	5.8	9.5	13.0
	2010	8.2	1.1	8.6	2.4	2.9	13.2	10.2	1.2	10.3	5.5	9.2	13.6
Nepal - Népal	2000	13.7	8.0	13.9	12.6	12.3	15.2	19.5	5.4	20.4	12.1	33.2	12.5
	2002	13.9	9.6	14.1	12.8	12.0	15.5	16.8	7.3	17.5	14.2	22.7	15.9
	2003	14.0	9.7	14.2	12.8	12.0	15.7	17.0	7.3	17.7	14.4	23.0	16.1
	2004	14.1	10.0	14.3	13.0	11.4	16.0	16.2	7.2	16.8	14.8	18.8	16.4
	2005	14.1	10.0	14.3	13.0	11.4	16.0	16.4	7.2	17.0	14.8	19.6	16.4
	2006	12.4	9.4	12.6	11.8	10.2	13.9	15.0	7.0	15.5	12.9	17.0	15.6
	2007	12.5	9.2	12.7	11.9	10.4	14.0	15.6	7.0	16.2	13.0	18.8	16.0
	2009	12.8	9.8	12.9	12.6	10.2	14.2	16.5	6.0	16.9	13.1	18.9	16.3
	2010	12.3	9.2	12.4	11.6	9.7	14.0	14.4	6.9	14.9	12.5	18.9	11.7
New Zealand - Nouvelle-Zélande	2000	3.0	0.8	3.1	0.7	3.2	4.1	3.6	1.3	3.7	1.4	3.8	4.6
	2002	3.8	1.0	3.9	0.9	3.9	5.1	4.6	1.8	4.7	2.0	4.8	5.9
	2003	3.7	1.0	3.9	0.9	3.9	5.0	4.6	1.9	4.7	2.0	4.9	5.5
	2004	3.7	1.1	3.8	0.9	4.0	4.9	4.5	2.0	4.5	1.9	4.8	5.3
	2005	3.6	1.0	3.8	0.9	3.9	4.8	4.3	2.2	4.4	1.8	4.6	5.3
	2006	3.5	1.0	3.6	0.9	3.0	4.5	4.1	2.0	4.2	1.9	4.2	5.1
	2007	3.5	1.1	3.6	1.0	4.0	4.5	4.5	2.0	4.6	2.0	5.0	5.3
	2008	2.6	0.8	2.7	0.8	2.9	3.3	3.3	1.5	3.4	1.6	3.7	3.8
	2009	2.4	0.8	2.5	0.7	2.9	3.0	2.8	1.5	2.9	1.6	2.8	3.5
	2010	2.4	0.8	2.5	0.7	2.9	3.0	2.8	1.6	2.9	1.6	2.8	3.5
Nicaragua	2000	3.5	1.3	3.6	1.3	1.7	5.2	3.9	2.3	3.9	3.0	3.5	4.9
	2001	4.5	1.3	4.6	1.6	2.0	6.8	4.5	2.2	4.5	3.9	3.6	5.8
	2002	4.5	1.1	4.6	1.5	2.1	6.8	4.5	2.2	4.5	3.9	3.6	5.6
	2004	4.9	1.5	5.0	1.8	2.4	7.3	5.5	4.5	5.5	3.7	5.2	6.9
	2005	5.4	1.6	5.5	1.8	2.4	8.1	5.4	4.7	5.4	3.6	4.2	7.9
	2007	5.1	1.7	5.2	1.8	2.1	7.9	5.6	3.8	5.6	3.7	4.2	7.9
	2009	5.1	1.7	5.2	1.8	2.1	7.8	5.3	3.8	5.3	3.8	4.3	7.1
	2010	5.1	1.5	5.2	1.8	2.1	7.8	5.0	4.7	5.0	3.6	3.9	7.1
Niger	2001	13.0	8.9	13.2	7.2	9.7	16.5	13.0	5.5	13.3	6.5	12.9	16.8
	2002	12.8	7.9	12.9	7.2	9.5	16.3	12.4	5.4	12.6	6.4	11.5	16.8
	2003	12.8	7.8	13.0	7.5	9.4	16.2	11.3	5.5	11.5	4.7	10.7	15.7
	2004	12.8	8.0	13.0	7.5	9.3	16.2	11.4	5.6	11.5	4.7	10.7	15.7
	2005	12.8	8.1	13.0	7.3	9.5	16.3	11.8	5.6	12.0	5.6	11.0	15.6
	2006	12.8	8.5	12.9	7.4	9.4	16.3	11.3	6.2	11.4	4.9	10.9	15.1
	2007	12.7	7.8	12.8	7.4	9.0	16.2	11.8	5.6	12.0	5.5	11.2	15.4
	2008	12.8	8.5	12.9	7.6	8.8	16.2	9.6	5.4	9.7	3.1	9.3	15.7
	2009	12.8	8.5	12.9	7.6	8.8	16.2	9.6	5.4	9.7	3.1	9.3	15.7
	2010	12.8	8.5	12.9	7.6	8.8	16.2	9.6	5.4	9.7	3.1	9.3	15.7
Nigeria - Nigéria	2000	24.6	17.0	24.9	18.3	16.7	31.9	18.2	15.4	18.2	17.0	17.6	20.5
	2001	24.1	16.8	24.5	18.4	16.7	31.4	18.6	16.9	18.7	17.6	17.5	21.2
	2002	24.7	15.0	25.2	17.0	15.7	33.7	15.7	10.0	15.8	12.6	14.7	20.1
	2005	11.6	7.5	11.8	7.3	6.0	16.3	9.8	10.1	9.8	10.2	6.6	14.8
	2006	10.6	7.3	10.8	7.2	5.6	15.6	8.3	9.1	8.2	6.9	5.4	14.3
	2008	10.8	7.4	11.0	7.2	5.6	16.0	8.7	10.1	8.7	7.7	5.3	15.4
	2009	10.7	6.6	10.9	7.2	5.2	15.0	10.0	11.9	10.0	8.6	8.1	14.7
	2010	10.7	6.8	10.9	7.1	7.4	14.8	10.8	9.6	10.8	8.1	10.0	14.2

For sources and notes, see end of table.

Pour les sources et les notes, se reporter à la fin du tableau.

Market / Marchés	Year / Année	MFN rate - Simple average (2) / Droit NPF - Moyenne simple (2)						MFN rate - Weighted average (3) / Droit NPF - Moyenne pondérée (3)					
		Total of non-agricultural and non-fuel products / Total des produits non-agricoles et non-pétroliers	Ores and metals / Minérais et métaux	Manufactured products / Produits manufacturés	Chemical products / Produits chimiques	Machinery and transport equipment / Machines et matériel de transport	Other manufactured products / Produits manufacturés divers	Total of non-agricultural and non-fuel products / Total des produits non-agricoles et non-pétroliers	Ores and metals / Minérais et métaux	Manufactured products / Produits manufacturés	Chemical products / Produits chimiques	Machinery and transport equipment / Machines et matériel de transport	Other manufactured products / Produits manufacturés divers
SITC Rev.3 (1) / CTCI Rév.3 (1)		5+6+7+8 +27+28-667	27+28+68	5+6+7+8 -(667+68)	5	7	6+8 -(667+68)	5+6+7+8 +27+28-667	27+28+68	5+6+7+8 -(667+68)	5	7	6+8 -(667+68)
Norway - Norvège	2000	2.5	0.3	2.0	1.0	0.3	4.0	1.0	0.3	1.7	0.0	0.2	3.9
	2001	2.3	0.3	2.5	1.2	0.3	3.8	1.5	0.3	1.6	2.2	0.0	7.6
	2002	1.9	0.2	2.0	0.8	0.2	3.2	1.3	0.2	1.4	1.5	0.1	3.0
	2003	0.8	0.0	0.9	0.4	0.0	1.4	0.6	0.0	0.7	0.7	0.0	1.6
	2006	0.7	0.0	0.8	0.4	0.0	1.2	0.4	0.0	0.5	0.5	0.0	1.1
	2007	0.7	0.0	0.8	0.4	0.0	1.2	0.4	0.0	0.5	0.5	0.0	1.1
	2008	0.7	0.0	0.8	0.4	0.0	1.2	0.4	0.0	0.5	0.4	0.0	1.1
	2009	0.6	0.0	0.7	0.4	0.0	1.0	0.5	0.0	0.5	0.4	0.0	1.2
	2010	0.7	0.0	0.7	0.7	0.0	1.0	0.5	0.0	0.5	0.7	0.0	1.2
Oman	2002	7.4	5.5	7.5	5.9	7.1	8.1	6.5	5.2	6.5	7.3	6.1	7.2
	2005	4.9	4.9	4.9	4.8	4.9	5.0	4.7	5.0	4.7	3.8	4.8	5.0
	2006	4.9	4.8	4.9	4.7	4.9	5.0	4.9	5.0	4.9	4.2	5.0	5.0
	2007	4.8	4.8	4.8	4.5	4.6	5.0	4.8	5.0	4.8	4.2	4.7	4.9
	2008	4.8	4.8	4.8	4.5	4.6	5.0	4.8	5.0	4.8	4.2	4.7	4.9
	2009	4.8	4.8	4.8	4.5	4.6	5.0	4.8	5.0	4.8	4.2	4.7	4.9
Pakistan	2001	20.5	13.1	20.9	15.3	19.9	23.9	20.8	9.6	21.3	13.9	25.7	22.7
	2002	17.4	11.4	17.7	14.1	16.6	20.0	17.5	8.9	17.9	13.3	20.5	19.1
	2003	17.1	10.5	17.5	13.8	16.2	19.7	17.2	8.6	17.6	13.1	20.0	18.9
	2004	16.6	10.4	17.0	12.8	15.7	19.4	15.6	8.3	15.9	10.9	18.2	18.6
	2005	14.5	8.9	14.8	9.9	13.7	17.4	14.4	9.4	14.7	8.5	18.0	14.9
	2006	14.6	8.9	14.9	9.8	13.9	17.5	14.3	0.7	14.6	8.7	17.0	15.3
	2007	14.3	8.4	14.6	9.5	12.9	17.5	13.1	8.1	13.4	8.2	15.5	15.3
	2008	13.8	7.3	14.1	9.2	12.4	16.9	12.0	5.5	12.5	6.8	16.1	14.0
	2009	14.0	7.2	14.4	9.6	12.9	17.1	11.8	5.2	12.3	6.9	15.3	14.6
Palau - Palaos	2005	3.2	2.9	3.2	3.9	3.1	3.0	3.2	3.0	3.2	2.6	3.5	3.0
	2006	3.2	2.9	3.2	3.9	3.1	3.0	3.2	3.0	3.2	2.6	3.5	3.0
	2010	3.2	2.8	3.2	4.8	3.0	3.0	3.1	2.9	3.1	4.1	3.0	3.0
Panama	2000	7.2	7.4	7.2	4.2	6.8	8.4	7.7	6.9	7.7	5.0	7.8	8.6
	2001	7.0	6.8	7.0	3.7	6.8	8.3	7.4	6.5	7.4	4.8	7.8	8.2
	2005	6.4	7.0	6.4	2.1	6.6	7.8	6.7	4.3	6.7	2.8	7.5	7.7
	2006	6.4	6.6	6.4	2.1	6.6	7.9	6.7	4.3	6.7	2.9	7.6	7.5
	2007	6.4	6.6	6.4	1.9	6.6	7.9	6.7	4.6	6.8	2.6	7.6	7.5
	2008	6.3	6.8	6.3	1.9	6.5	7.7	7.0	4.9	7.1	2.7	8.1	7.5
	2009	6.2	6.8	6.2	1.8	6.4	7.7	7.0	5.3	7.0	2.9	8.3	7.4
Papua New Guinea - Papouasie-Nouvelle-Guinée	2002	5.2	0.0	5.4	1.8	0.3	9.2	2.5	0.0	2.5	2.6	0.1	5.4
	2003	4.5	0.0	4.6	1.5	0.2	7.9	1.7	0.0	1.8	2.7	0.1	3.7
	2004	4.4	0.0	4.6	1.5	0.3	7.8	1.5	0.0	1.5	1.8	0.1	3.7
	2005	4.5	0.0	4.6	1.5	0.2	7.9	1.7	0.0	1.8	2.7	0.1	3.7
	2006	3.6	0.0	3.7	1.1	0.2	6.3	1.3	0.0	1.3	1.9	0.1	2.9
	2007	3.3	0.1	3.4	1.1	0.2	5.9	1.1	1.3	1.1	1.3	0.0	2.6
	2008	3.4	0.1	3.5	1.4	0.3	5.7	2.2	1.2	2.2	2.1	0.1	5.9
	2010	3.2	0.1	3.4	0.9	0.2	5.7	2.8	0.6	2.8	1.9	0.1	8.1
Paraguay	2000	13.9	9.6	14.0	11.2	9.1	17.3	11.7	8.8	11.7	11.2	10.0	14.1
	2001	13.5	8.8	13.7	10.3	10.1	16.6	11.9	8.5	11.9	10.4	10.8	14.2
	2002	13.4	8.2	13.5	9.8	10.2	16.5	11.3	7.2	11.4	9.8	9.9	14.3
	2003	13.5	8.6	13.6	9.8	10.3	16.5	11.9	7.4	12.0	9.5	11.4	14.7
	2004	12.7	8.7	12.8	9.9	7.0	16.5	12.3	7.6	12.4	9.9	11.5	15.3
	2005	11.4	7.1	11.5	8.2	6.3	15.2	10.1	6.2	10.1	7.4	9.0	13.6
	2006	10.4	6.8	10.5	7.4	5.3	14.2	6.0	4.4	6.0	5.2	4.5	10.1
	2007	11.0	6.4	11.1	7.9	5.7	14.9	6.9	6.8	6.9	5.8	5.2	12.2
	2008	11.0	6.5	11.2	8.1	5.6	15.0	7.1	7.0	7.1	5.4	5.6	11.9
	2009	11.0	6.6	11.1	8.1	5.6	14.9	8.0	6.9	8.0	5.9	6.7	11.0
	2010	11.0	6.6	11.1	8.1	5.2	15.0	8.2	7.0	8.2	6.1	6.8	11.3

For sources and notes, see end of table.

Pour les sources et les notes, se reporter à la fin du tableau.

Market / Marchés	Year / Année	MFN rate - Simple average (2) / Droit NPF - Moyenne simple (2)						MFN rate - Weighted average (3) / Droit NPF - Moyenne pondérée (3)					
		Total of non-agricultural and non-fuel products / Total des produits non-agricoles et non-pétroliers	Ores and metals / Minérais et métaux	Manu-factured products / Produits manu-facturés	Chemical products / Produits chimiques	Machinery and transport equipment / Machines et matériel de transport	Other manu-factured products / Produits manu-facturés divers	Total of non-agricultural and non-fuel products / Total des produits non-agricoles et non-pétroliers	Ores and metals / Minérais et métaux	Manu-factured products / Produits manu-facturés	Chemical products / Produits chimiques	Machinery and transport equipment / Machines et matériel de transport	Other manu-factured products / Produits manu-facturés divers
SITC Rev.3 (1) / CTCI Rév.3 (1)		5+6+7+8 +27+28-667	27+28+68	5+6+7+8 -(667+68)	5	7	6+8 (667+00)	5+6+7+8 +27+28-667	27+28+68	5+6+7+8 (667+68)	5	7	6+8 -(667+68)
Peru - Pérou	2000	13.2	12.0	13.3	12.0	12.3	14.2	12.3	12.0	12.4	12.0	12.2	12.8
	2004	10.2	8.6	10.2	6.7	7.7	12.7	8.9	9.4	8.9	7.3	8.4	10.8
	2005	9.6	8.5	9.7	6.7	6.1	12.4	8.2	9.4	8.1	6.9	7.3	10.2
	2006	9.7	8.3	9.7	6.6	6.2	12.5	7.9	9.2	7.9	7.0	6.6	10.3
	2007	9.6	8.3	9.7	6.6	6.1	12.5	7.6	8.4	7.6	6.6	6.5	10.0
	2008	5.4	3.9	5.5	2.9	1.5	8.3	3.0	5.6	2.9	3.1	1.8	4.5
	2009	5.5	4.0	5.5	2.9	1.5	8.4	3.0	5.6	2.9	3.1	1.9	4.5
	2010	5.4	3.3	5.5	2.8	1.5	8.3	3.3	3.0	3.4	3.6	2.0	5.0
Philippines	2000	7.2	3.4	7.4	3.9	5.1	9.8	3.5	3.4	3.5	5.2	2.1	7.7
	2001	6.9	3.4	7.1	4.0	4.6	9.3	3.2	3.7	3.2	5.1	1.8	7.0
	2002	5.2	2.6	5.3	3.3	3.5	6.9	2.1	2.9	2.1	4.6	1.1	5.4
	2003	4.3	2.6	4.4	3.2	3.2	5.3	2.0	2.9	2.0	4.6	1.2	4.3
	2004	5.8	2.5	6.0	3.4	3.6	8.0	3.1	2.5	3.1	5.3	1.8	6.1
	2005	5.8	2.5	6.0	3.4	3.5	8.1	3.3	2.5	3.3	5.5	2.0	6.2
	2006	5.8	2.5	6.0	3.4	3.5	8.1	3.3	2.5	3.3	5.5	2.0	6.2
	2007	5.8	2.5	6.0	3.4	3.6	8.0	3.8	2.7	3.8	4.7	2.9	6.2
	2008	5.8	2.5	6.0	3.6	3.6	8.0	4.9	2.6	5.0	4.8	4.1	6.5
	2009	5.8	2.5	6.0	3.6	3.6	8.0	5.6	2.9	5.8	5.0	5.0	7.2
	2010	5.8	2.5	6.0	3.6	3.6	8.0	5.6	2.9	5.8	5.0	5.0	7.2
Poland - Pologne (5)	2000	10.5	6.0	10.8	9.0	9.2	12.1	10.0	5.6	10.1	7.8	10.7	10.7
	2001	9.8	5.4	10.1	9.2	8.0	11.3	8.1	5.5	8.2	7.6	6.5	10.3
	2002	9.9	4.9	10.2	8.6	8.7	11.4	10.1	4.7	10.2	7.2	11.4	10.4
	2003	9.9	5.7	10.1	9.4	8.0	11.3	8.2	5.9	8.3	7.5	6.6	10.4
Qatar	2002	4.0	4.0	4.0	4.0	4.0	4.1	4.0	4.0	4.0	4.0	4.0	4.0
	2005	4.9	4.9	4.9	4.8	4.9	5.0	4.9	5.0	4.9	4.2	5.0	5.0
	2006	4.9	4.9	4.9	4.7	4.9	5.0	4.9	5.0	4.9	4.2	5.0	5.0
	2007	4.8	4.9	4.8	4.6	4.6	4.9	4.7	5.0	4.7	4.1	4.6	4.9
	2008	4.8	4.9	4.8	4.5	4.5	4.9	4.4	5.0	4.4	3.8	4.1	4.9
	2009	4.8	4.9	4.8	4.5	4.5	4.9	4.4	5.0	4.3	3.9	4.0	4.9
Republic of Moldova - République de Moldova	2000	4.5	1.9	4.6	3.5	1.7	6.1	2.8	1.8	2.8	1.5	1.2	4.1
	2001	4.4	1.7	4.5	3.4	1.7	6.0	2.9	1.6	2.9	1.8	1.1	4.3
	2006	4.4	1.4	4.5	2.8	1.6	6.4	3.3	0.6	3.3	2.2	1.6	4.7
	2008	4.0	1.1	4.1	2.7	1.7	5.5	2.9	0.1	3.1	2.5	1.8	4.4
	2010	3.9	1.0	4.0	2.8	1.7	5.5	3.2	0.6	3.2	2.1	2.0	4.7
Romania - Roumanie (4)	2001	16.3	7.1	16.8	14.3	13.9	18.9	14.7	3.9	15.1	11.2	12.5	18.1
	2004	16.2	6.8	16.7	14.9	13.2	18.8	14.8	4.4	15.2	12.2	13.8	17.3
	2005	15.5	6.7	16.0	13.9	12.8	18.2	13.9	4.3	14.3	10.1	13.9	15.9
Russian Federation - Fédération de Russie	2001	10.0	7.3	10.2	6.6	10.1	11.9	9.0	6.4	9.2	8.5	8.6	10.7
	2002	9.6	7.5	9.8	6.6	8.8	11.7	8.8	6.8	8.9	8.7	7.9	10.9
	2005	9.5	7.6	9.6	6.6	8.4	11.6	8.4	5.6	8.5	8.9	7.6	10.5
	2007	8.6	7.7	8.7	6.6	6.0	11.1	6.8	3.6	6.9	8.8	5.4	9.5
	2008	8.5	7.3	8.6	6.6	5.7	11.0	6.5	3.8	6.6	8.8	5.2	9.2
	2009	8.5	7.2	8.6	6.5	5.7	11.0	6.7	3.8	6.8	8.8	5.5	9.2
	2010	7.8	6.5	7.8	6.2	4.8	10.1	5.8	3.5	5.9	8.5	3.5	9.2
Rwanda	2001	10.3	7.5	10.3	6.2	8.3	12.8	7.0	5.4	7.1	4.8	8.2	6.9
	2003	10.3	7.9	10.4	6.3	8.0	12.7	8.8	5.5	8.9	4.8	9.1	10.7
	2005	21.6	13.4	21.8	16.4	19.2	24.8	16.2	15.2	16.2	9.8	15.5	22.3
	2006	21.8	11.7	22.1	15.9	20.0	24.6	16.0	6.2	16.4	9.6	16.2	19.6
	2008	21.2	11.4	21.6	16.0	19.1	24.5	17.1	6.8	17.5	10.5	19.5	18.6
	2009	12.4	8.2	12.6	5.2	6.2	17.7	12.9	11.9	12.9	6.1	8.2	20.6
	2010	12.5	7.6	12.7	5.0	6.1	17.8	11.2	11.1	11.3	6.7	7.2	18.7

For sources and notes, see end of table.

Pour les sources et les notes, se reporter à la fin du tableau.

4

Market / Marchés	Year / Année	MFN rate - Simple average (2) / Droit NPF - Moyenne simple (2)						MFN rate - Weighted average (3) / Droit NPF - Moyenne pondérée (3)					
		Total of non-agricultural and non-fuel products / Total des produits non-agricoles et non-pétroliers	Ores and metals / Minérais et métaux	Manufactured products / Produits manufacturés	Chemical products / Produits chimiques	Machinery and transport equipment / Machines et matériel de transport	Other manufactured products / Produits manufacturés divers	Total of non-agricultural and non-fuel products / Total des produits non-agricoles et non-pétroliers	Ores and metals / Minérais et métaux	Manufactured products / Produits manufacturés	Chemical products / Produits chimiques	Machinery and transport equipment / Machines et matériel de transport	Other manufactured products / Produits manufacturés divers
SITC Rev.3 (1) / CTCI Rév.3 (1)		5+6+7+8 +27+28-667	27+28+68	5+6+7+8 -(667+68)	5	7	6+8 -(667+68)	5+6+7+8 +27+28-667	27+28+68	5+6+7+8 -(667+68)	5	7	6+8 -(667+68)
Saint Kitts and Nevis - Saint-Kitts-et-Nevis	2000	11.1	3.8	11.3	7.1	9.0	10.1	12.7	4.4	13.4	10.0	12.5	14.1
	2001	11.3	4.2	11.5	7.5	9.8	13.3	12.1	5.6	12.2	12.7	11.2	12.9
	2002	11.3	3.7	11.5	7.8	9.9	13.1	13.4	2.7	13.6	12.8	11.9	15.2
	2003	11.3	3.8	11.6	7.7	10.0	13.2	13.4	3.9	13.5	12.4	12.2	14.7
	2006	11.1	4.1	11.4	7.4	8.9	13.5	13.7	7.6	13.8	13.1	12.2	15.3
	2007	11.1	4.1	11.4	7.4	8.9	13.5	13.7	7.6	13.8	13.1	12.2	15.3
	2008	11.0	3.9	11.3	7.3	9.1	13.3	13.6	5.3	13.7	14.2	11.9	15.4
	2009	11.0	3.9	11.3	7.3	9.1	13.3	13.6	5.3	13.7	14.2	11.9	15.4
	2010	11.2	4.8	11.4	9.6	8.9	13.1	12.9	5.9	13.0	14.9	10.0	16.0
Saint Lucia - Sainte-Lucie	2000	17.6	13.3	17.6	12.8	18.8	18.1	17.7	13.1	17.7	14.3	24.3	15.6
	2001	9.5	2.2	9.7	7.0	6.6	11.9	11.6	1.5	11.8	13.6	11.5	11.4
	2002	9.7	2.4	9.8	7.0	6.8	11.9	12.3	1.4	12.5	13.6	10.7	13.4
	2003	9.7	2.6	9.9	7.0	6.8	12.0	12.2	1.6	12.4	13.2	10.5	13.8
	2005	9.6	2.7	9.8	7.3	6.3	11.9	13.5	2.8	13.6	13.2	12.8	14.3
	2006	9.6	2.7	9.8	7.3	6.3	11.9	13.5	2.8	13.6	13.2	12.8	14.3
	2007	9.5	2.2	9.7	7.2	6.4	11.8	14.0	3.7	14.1	13.8	14.2	14.1
Saint Vincent and the Grenadines - Saint-Vincent-et-les Grenadines	2000	17.2	12.3	17.2	13.2	17.4	17.8	16.5	14.5	16.6	12.8	22.3	15.5
	2001	10.1	5.2	10.3	7.5	8.4	11.8	12.2	6.9	12.3	10.3	11.4	13.3
	2002	10.2	5.1	10.3	7.5	8.2	11.8	11.3	7.0	11.3	11.6	10.5	11.9
	2003	10.1	5.3	10.3	7.5	8.3	11.8	11.2	5.5	11.2	11.5	10.6	11.6
	2006	1.7	2.3	1.7	5.7	0.8	1.2	3.6	3.5	3.6	8.9	0.5	2.2
	2007	10.1	5.0	10.3	7.6	8.3	11.8	10.8	5.8	10.8	11.8	9.9	11.2
Saudi Arabia - Arabie saoudite	2000	12.1	12.2	12.0	11.8	11.8	12.3	11.3	13.1	11.2	8.5	11.4	12.0
	2003	6.1	5.7	6.1	6.0	5.4	6.5	6.6	7.9	6.5	5.2	5.9	8.1
	2004	6.1	5.7	6.2	6.0	5.4	6.5	6.3	7.5	6.3	5.5	5.6	7.7
	2005	4.9	4.8	4.9	4.8	4.9	5.0	4.7	5.0	4.7	3.4	4.8	5.0
	2006	4.9	4.9	4.9	4.6	4.9	5.0	4.7	5.0	4.7	3.4	4.8	5.0
	2007	4.8	4.8	4.7	4.4	4.6	5.0	4.5	5.0	4.4	3.1	4.4	4.9
	2008	4.7	4.8	4.7	4.5	4.6	4.9	4.5	5.0	4.4	3.1	4.4	4.9
	2009	4.7	4.8	4.7	4.4	4.6	4.9	4.5	5.0	4.4	3.1	4.4	4.9
Senegal - Sénégal	2001	12.5	8.3	12.7	7.0	8.9	16.3	10.3	6.8	10.4	5.8	10.4	13.2
	2002	12.7	9.2	12.8	7.1	9.0	16.2	10.9	8.5	11.0	5.7	12.4	13.4
	2003	12.5	8.2	12.6	7.0	8.9	16.1	10.3	6.4	10.5	5.9	10.4	13.5
	2004	12.4	8.3	12.6	7.0	8.8	16.1	10.3	6.2	10.5	5.6	10.5	13.5
	2005	12.5	8.7	12.7	7.0	8.9	16.2	10.2	6.0	10.4	5.8	10.1	13.6
	2006	12.5	8.6	12.6	6.9	8.9	16.3	10.5	7.7	10.6	5.8	10.2	13.9
	2007	12.3	8.1	12.4	7.0	8.3	16.0	10.7	6.9	10.8	5.9	10.5	13.6
	2008	12.2	8.0	12.4	7.1	8.3	16.0	10.4	5.9	10.6	6.3	9.9	13.7
	2009	12.2	8.0	12.4	7.1	8.3	16.0	10.4	5.9	10.6	6.3	9.9	13.7
	2010	12.3	8.3	12.4	7.1	8.4	16.1	10.4	7.8	10.4	6.2	9.7	13.8
Serbia and Montenegro - Serbie-et-Monténégro	2001	13.7	8.8	14.0	7.7	11.1	17.5	11.6	7.9	11.8	8.7	10.5	15.3
	2002	8.7	3.9	9.0	3.8	6.5	11.9	7.8	3.5	8.0	5.1	7.6	10.2
	2005	6.6	3.6	6.8	3.1	5.2	8.8	6.4	2.3	6.8	4.2	7.2	7.9
Seychelles	2000	25.3	21.2	25.4	32.1	21.4	25.7	18.5	21.3	18.5	23.1	17.3	20.9
	2001	25.4	21.2	25.5	32.1	21.4	25.9	18.5	21.3	18.5	23.1	17.3	20.9
	2005	7.5	2.1	7.7	1.4	8.1	9.1	11.3	1.4	11.3	3.8	17.2	5.6
	2006	5.2	0.0	5.4	1.6	4.4	6.9	6.7	0.0	6.8	2.3	13.5	2.2
	2007	4.6	0.0	4.8	1.6	3.6	6.2	6.4	0.0	6.4	1.9	10.2	2.4
Slovakia - Slovaquie (5)	2002	4.6	1.4	4.7	4.2	3.8	5.3	4.7	1.2	4.9	3.7	4.7	5.6
Slovenia - Slovénie (5)	2001	9.8	3.4	10.2	7.7	9.6	11.4	10.4	4.8	10.8	9.1	10.4	11.9
	2002	9.8	3.5	10.2	7.6	9.5	11.4	10.3	4.9	10.6	9.1	10.1	11.8
	2003	9.8	3.5	10.2	7.6	9.5	11.4	10.3	4.7	10.7	9.1	10.4	11.6

For sources and notes, see end of table.

Pour les sources et les notes, se reporter à la fin du tableau.

4.3 Average applied import MFN tariff rates on non-agricultural and non-fuel products

4.3 Droits de douane moyens NPF appliqués à l'importation des produits non-agricoles et non-pétroliers

Market / Marchés	Year / Année	MFN rate - Simple average (2) / Droit NPF - Moyenne simple (2)						MFN rate - Weighted average (3) / Droit NPF - Moyenne pondérée (3)					
		Total of non-agricultural and non-fuel products / Total des produits non-agricoles et non-pétroliers	Ores and metals / Minérais et métaux	Manufactured products / Produits manufacturés	Chemical products / Produits chimiques	Machinery and transport equipment / Machines et matériel de transport	Other manufactured products / Produits manufacturés divers	Total of non-agricultural and non-fuel products / Total des produits non-agricoles et non-pétroliers	Ores and metals / Minérais et métaux	Manufactured products / Produits manufacturés	Chemical products / Produits chimiques	Machinery and transport equipment / Machines et matériel de transport	Other manufactured products / Produits manufacturés divers
SITC Rev.3 (1) / CTCI Rév.3 (1)		5+6+7+8 +27+28-667	27+28+68	5+6+7+8 -(667+68)	5	7	6+8 -(667+68)	5+6+7+8 +27+28-667	27+28+68	5+6+7+8 -(667+68)	5	7	6+8 -(667+68)
Solomon Islands - Îles Salomon	2006	14.2	10.8	14.2	11.2	13.2	15.5	12.8	14.3	12.8	12.0	12.2	13.6
	2007	9.1	8.2	9.1	8.4	9.1	9.3	7.6	7.8	7.6	8.5	7.0	8.5
	2008	9.1	8.5	9.1	8.5	9.1	9.3	8.6	8.0	8.6	8.7	8.5	8.8
	2010	9.2	8.5	9.2	8.9	9.2	9.3	8.8	7.3	8.8	8.0	8.7	9.0
South Africa - Afrique du Sud	2001	8.0	1.5	8.4	2.6	3.2	13.2	5.9	0.9	6.1	2.7	5.4	9.6
	2004	8.2	1.3	8.6	2.6	3.1	13.3	6.6	0.5	6.9	2.9	6.1	10.9
	2005	8.2	1.3	8.6	2.6	3.0	13.4	7.2	0.6	7.4	3.1	7.0	10.9
	2006	8.1	1.3	8.5	2.6	3.0	13.3	7.1	0.6	7.4	3.2	6.8	11.1
	2007	8.0	1.3	8.4	2.6	3.0	13.0	7.4	0.6	7.8	3.3	7.6	10.8
	2008	8.0	1.3	8.4	2.6	3.0	13.0	7.2	0.6	7.6	3.3	7.4	10.3
	2009	7.9	1.3	8.4	2.6	3.0	13.0	6.4	0.7	6.8	3.0	6.1	10.5
	2010	7.8	0.9	8.3	2.0	2.8	13.1	7.1	0.4	7.3	2.4	6.4	11.8
Sri Lanka	2000	8.0	5.5	8.2	6.4	6.2	9.7	5.7	5.3	5.7	5.4	6.9	5.1
	2001	8.1	5.6	8.2	6.4	6.2	9.7	5.4	6.3	5.3	5.5	6.5	4.8
	2004	8.6	5.7	8.7	5.5	6.9	10.7	6.6	4.2	6.7	5.5	9.3	5.6
	2005	9.7	5.8	9.9	5.3	8.0	12.4	6.8	4.4	7.0	5.0	9.8	5.9
	2006	9.4	5.7	9.6	5.1	7.6	12.2	6.4	4.1	6.6	4.5	9.5	5.5
	2007	9.3	5.6	9.5	5.2	7.2	12.2	6.7	3.9	6.9	4.3	10.8	5.6
	2009	9.0	5.5	9.2	5.1	7.1	11.8	6.3	4.1	6.4	4.0	10.0	5.5
	2010	8.0	4.6	8.2	3.3	4.7	11.7	6.6	2.2	6.7	2.9	10.3	5.7
Sudan - Soudan	2002	22.6	15.3	22.8	17.8	14.5	29.6	19.0	11.2	19.1	15.6	15.7	30.0
	2006	18.8	13.9	19.0	8.6	11.1	26.3	15.0	10.3	15.0	10.1	11.5	23.6
	2008	18.8	16.0	18.9	7.4	10.9	27.1	14.0	12.6	14.0	10.3	11.0	24.4
	2009	19.1	15.2	19.2	7.8	10.9	27.5	10.6	12.7	10.6	10.9	5.8	30.7
	2010	18.0	14.5	18.1	8.4	10.6	25.7	19.1	13.1	19.2	10.7	15.0	26.9
Suriname	2000	10.6	11.5	10.6	9.5	7.1	12.1	11.7	14.1	11.6	9.7	10.9	12.9
	2007	9.9	6.2	10.0	7.8	7.9	11.8	11.7	9.7	11.7	9.6	11.0	12.8
	2010	9.5	5.9	9.7	7.7	7.5	11.3	10.3	9.9	10.3	8.3	10.7	11.2
Swaziland	2001	8.4	1.7	8.8	3.0	3.4	13.2	11.2	3.3	11.4	5.3	10.6	15.0
	2004	11.1	1.5	11.3	4.3	3.9	16.0	12.0	2.1	12.1	1.9	3.9	18.4
	2005	11.2	2.9	11.3	4.7	4.2	16.2	10.1	1.9	10.1	2.1	5.2	16.3
	2006	11.1	2.9	11.3	4.7	4.1	16.1	10.0	1.9	10.1	2.1	5.2	16.2
	2007	10.6	2.1	10.7	5.4	3.8	15.4	9.4	1.0	10.0	3.8	4.2	15.6
	2008	11.1	2.0	11.2	5.6	4.4	16.0	6.8	0.3	7.4	2.8	2.8	16.5
	2009	10.7	1.8	10.8	5.4	4.4	15.4	6.1	0.1	7.6	2.6	2.9	15.3
	2010	11.0	1.3	11.2	3.6	3.8	16.3	14.6	0.0	16.3	0.6	4.7	26.2
Syrian Arab Republic - République arabe syrienne	2002	14.3	5.0	14.7	6.7	16.4	17.5	16.6	5.6	17.1	4.0	30.6	11.3
	2009	13.5	2.3	13.9	4.8	7.2	20.1	12.7	1.3	13.1	6.3	16.1	12.2
	2010	10.0	1.7	10.3	4.5	7.5	15.0	6.8	1.4	7.3	3.4	16.6	4.8
Tajikistan - Tadjikistan	2002	8.2	8.4	8.2	5.3	5.0	10.6	7.4	6.1	8.0	5.1	5.0	11.4
	2006	7.3	7.0	7.3	6.1	5.0	8.7	7.0	5.1	7.4	5.7	5.0	9.8
	2010	7.2	7.9	7.2	6.2	5.0	8.6	8.9	4.2	9.0	6.0	5.0	10.5
Thailand - Thaïlande	2000	15.7	6.7	16.2	11.3	12.2	19.8	10.2	5.4	10.4	10.6	8.8	14.0
	2001	14.7	6.4	15.2	6.5	12.6	19.7	10.7	4.2	11.0	10.3	8.7	17.0
	2003	13.9	4.9	14.5	6.0	12.5	18.6	11.0	3.7	11.3	10.2	10.2	14.7
	2005	10.4	2.5	10.9	4.7	8.1	14.4	6.5	2.0	6.8	7.0	6.1	7.9
	2006	10.3	2.5	10.8	4.7	8.1	14.3	6.3	2.1	6.7	6.9	5.7	8.4
	2007	8.3	1.2	8.8	2.9	7.2	12.3	5.1	1.2	5.5	3.6	5.8	6.2
	2008	8.3	1.2	8.8	3.0	7.2	12.3	5.5	1.1	5.9	3.8	6.4	6.4
	2009	8.4	1.2	8.9	3.0	7.2	12.3	5.9	1.2	6.2	4.1	6.3	7.3

For sources and notes, see end of table.

Pour les sources et les notes, se reporter à la fin du tableau.

4

4.3 Average applied import MFN tariff rates on non-agricultural and non-fuel products
4.3 Droits de douane moyens NPF appliqués à l'importation des produits non-agricoles et non-pétroliers

Market / Marchés	Year / Année	MFN rate - Simple average (2) / Droit NPF - Moyenne simple (2)						MFN rate - Weighted average (3) / Droit NPF - Moyenne pondérée (3)					
		Total of non-agricultural and non-fuel products / Total des produits non-agricoles et non-pétroliers	Ores and metals / Minérais et métaux	Manu-factured products / Produits manu-facturés	Chemical products / Produits chimiques	Machinery and transport equipment / Machines et matériel de transport	Other manu-factured products / Produits manu-facturés divers	Total of non-agricultural and non-fuel products / Total des produits non-agricoles et non-pétroliers	Ores and metals / Minérais et métaux	Manu-factured products / Produits manu-facturés	Chemical products / Produits chimiques	Machinery and transport equipment / Machines et matériel de transport	Other manu-factured products / Produits manu-facturés divers
SITC Rev.3 (1) / CTCI Rév.3 (1)		5+6+7+8 +27+28-667	27+28+68	5+6+7+8 -(667+68)	5	7	6+8 -(667+68)	5+6+7+8 +27+28-667	27+28+68	5+6+7+8 -(667+68)	5	7	6+8 -(667+68)
TFYR of Macedonia - LERY de Macédoine	2001	14.2	8.5	14.5	8.0	11.9	16.0	12.0	9.4	11.1	10.9	11.0	16.7
	2004	9.2	4.5	9.4	3.9	6.8	12.5	7.1	3.3	7.3	6.1	7.1	7.8
	2005	8.4	3.4	8.6	3.6	6.3	11.3	7.0	1.9	7.3	5.7	5.9	8.4
	2006	7.9	3.1	8.2	3.4	6.5	10.5	6.4	1.7	6.7	5.3	6.0	7.5
	2007	7.4	2.6	7.6	3.2	6.5	9.7	5.6	0.7	6.2	4.4	6.4	6.5
	2008	7.4	2.6	7.6	3.1	6.5	9.7	5.6	0.7	6.1	4.2	6.4	6.5
	2009	7.1	2.5	7.3	2.8	5.6	9.6	6.3	2.5	6.4	3.8	6.0	7.5
	2010	6.6	2.5	6.8	2.8	5.6	8.7	5.9	2.5	6.0	3.6	5.5	7.2
Togo	2001	13.2	8.0	13.3	8.1	9.8	16.5	11.1	5.9	11.2	6.2	11.2	12.9
	2002	13.1	8.6	13.2	8.2	9.7	16.5	10.1	5.8	10.3	5.5	9.5	12.5
	2003	13.2	8.1	13.4	8.2	9.8	16.8	11.1	5.6	11.4	5.5	11.0	13.3
	2004	13.2	8.1	13.4	8.2	9.8	16.8	11.2	5.6	11.4	5.5	11.0	13.3
	2005	13.5	9.1	13.6	8.4	9.9	16.8	10.8	5.6	11.0	4.3	10.7	13.1
	2006	13.5	9.1	13.6	8.4	9.9	16.8	10.8	5.6	11.0	4.3	10.8	13.1
	2007	13.3	8.9	13.4	8.5	9.3	16.7	10.8	5.6	11.0	4.1	10.8	13.0
	2008	13.0	9.2	13.1	7.9	8.7	16.6	16.2	8.9	16.2	8.5	13.6	18.6
	2009	13.0	8.7	13.1	7.8	8.7	16.6	16.1	7.9	16.1	8.3	13.6	18.6
	2010	12.7	8.9	12.8	7.4	8.7	16.4	15.1	7.2	15.1	6.7	11.9	18.4
Tonga	2009	10.8	14.0	10.7	12.2	4.8	13.2	9.0	10.8	9.0	9.7	3.2	13.2
	2010	10.9	13.5	10.8	12.0	4.8	13.3	9.0	12.4	9.0	10.8	4.0	12.5
Trinidad and Tobago - Trinité-et-Tobago	2001	6.9	1.7	7.1	2.7	5.5	9.6	4.5	3.2	4.5	6.5	3.3	6.6
	2002	7.0	1.8	7.2	2.7	5.6	9.7	5.4	1.4	5.5	7.3	4.5	6.8
	2003	7.0	1.6	7.3	2.7	5.6	9.9	5.6	0.8	5.9	7.6	4.8	7.1
	2006	6.9	1.8	7.1	2.6	5.5	9.7	6.6	0.6	7.2	6.6	6.9	7.8
	2007	5.9	1.4	6.1	2.5	3.9	8.5	5.0	0.4	5.8	6.4	5.5	6.0
	2008	5.9	1.4	6.1	2.5	3.9	8.5	5.0	0.4	5.8	6.4	5.5	6.0
Tunisia - Tunisie	2002	27.5	24.5	27.7	23.5	18.9	33.1	25.6	22.9	25.6	21.6	18.3	32.9
	2003	22.4	15.1	22.8	14.6	14.9	29.3	22.2	13.8	22.5	13.1	16.9	29.9
	2004	22.7	15.1	23.0	14.3	14.4	30.0	23.2	9.9	23.6	13.0	17.4	32.1
	2005	21.4	15.0	21.7	14.3	14.2	27.7	20.2	9.3	20.7	13.1	16.8	26.5
	2006	21.2	14.4	21.6	14.0	13.8	27.6	19.9	10.1	20.4	13.2	16.6	26.4
	2008	18.7	7.8	19.3	12.0	11.7	25.2	16.9	3.6	18.2	11.4	15.1	23.5
Turkey - Turquie	2003	4.4	1.9	4.5	4.8	2.2	5.4	4.5	1.4	4.7	4.1	4.1	6.2
	2005	4.2	1.9	4.3	4.7	2.2	5.1	4.0	1.5	4.2	4.1	3.9	4.8
	2006	4.3	2.5	4.4	4.9	2.3	5.1	3.7	1.6	3.9	4.6	3.1	4.6
	2007	4.3	2.7	4.3	4.9	2.3	5.0	3.7	1.5	4.0	4.6	3.1	4.6
	2008	4.2	1.9	4.3	4.7	2.3	5.0	3.9	1.3	4.2	4.3	3.6	4.9
	2009	4.2	1.9	4.4	4.7	2.3	5.1	3.9	1.2	4.3	4.0	3.3	5.8
	2010	4.2	1.8	4.4	4.8	2.3	5.1	3.9	1.1	4.3	4.2	3.6	5.3
Turkmenistan - Turkménistan	2002	4.3	2.9	4.4	1.3	1.4	6.7	1.1	2.9	1.1	0.5	0.9	1.6
Uganda - Ouganda	2000	8.6	7.9	8.6	7.3	4.1	11.2	7.0	7.2	7.0	4.9	6.3	8.6
	2001	8.4	7.6	8.4	7.3	4.0	10.8	6.8	7.1	6.8	4.4	5.9	8.9
	2002	8.3	7.6	8.3	7.1	3.8	10.7	6.7	6.9	6.7	4.3	6.2	8.4
	2003	7.7	7.0	7.8	5.7	3.4	10.5	6.2	5.7	6.2	2.9	5.8	8.1
	2004	7.1	6.7	7.2	2.6	3.4	10.5	5.5	5.1	5.5	1.8	4.8	8.0
	2005	12.3	7.7	12.5	4.1	6.6	18.1	11.5	12.5	11.5	6.1	8.1	17.7
	2006	12.3	7.3	12.5	4.0	6.5	18.2	10.5	12.4	10.5	4.2	6.8	18.0
	2007	12.2	8.0	12.3	3.9	6.6	18.1	10.2	11.7	10.2	3.9	6.8	17.8
	2008	11.7	6.9	11.9	4.0	5.8	17.7	10.6	12.7	10.5	3.8	7.6	17.0
	2009	11.7	6.9	11.9	4.0	5.8	17.7	10.6	12.7	10.5	3.8	7.6	17.0
	2010	11.7	6.9	11.9	4.0	5.8	17.7	10.6	12.7	10.6	3.8	7.6	17.1

For sources and notes, see end of table.

Pour les sources et les notes, se reporter à la fin du tableau.

Market / Marchés	Year / Année	MFN rate - Simple average (2) / Droit NPF - Moyenne simple (2)						MFN rate - Weighted average (3) / Droit NPF - Moyenne pondérée (3)					
		Total of non-agricultural and non-fuel products / Total des produits non-agricoles et non-pétroliers	Ores and metals / Minérais et métaux	Manufactured products / Produits manu-facturés	Chemical products / Produits chimiques	Machinery and transport equipment / Machines et matériel de transport	Other manu-factured products / Produits manu-facturés divers	Total of non-agricultural and non-fuel products / Total des produits non-agricoles et non-pétroliers	Ores and metals / Minérais et métaux	Manufactured products / Produits manu-facturés	Chemical products / Produits chimiques	Machinery and transport equipment / Machines et matériel de transport	Other manu-factured products / Produits manu-facturés divers
SITC Rev.3 (1) / CTCI Rév.3 (1)		5+6+7+8 +27+28-667	27+28+68	5+6+7+8 -(667+68)	5	7	6+8 (-667.00)	5+6+7+8 (27+28-667)	27+28+68	5+6+7+8 -(667+68)	5	7	6+8 -(667+68)
Ukraine	2002	7.1	3.6	7.3	5.3	5.9	8.6	6.2	2.2	6.5	5.6	5.6	8.0
	2006	4.6	2.5	4.8	3.2	4.3	5.6	5.7	2.2	5.9	2.2	8.4	4.5
	2008	4.7	2.6	4.8	3.2	4.2	5.6	6.4	1.9	6.7	2.5	9.7	4.5
	2009	4.0	1.9	4.1	3.3	3.1	4.9	3.6	1.3	3.8	2.5	4.6	3.3
	2010	4.0	1.9	4.1	3.3	3.0	4.9	2.9	1.1	3.1	2.3	3.2	3.6
United Arab Emirates - Émirats arabes unis	2003	5.0	4.8	5.0	4.8	4.9	5.1	4.7	4.9	4.7	4.4	4.5	5.0
	2005	4.9	4.8	4.9	4.8	4.9	5.0	4.6	4.8	4.6	4.3	4.5	5.0
	2006	4.9	4.8	4.9	4.6	4.9	5.0	4.6	4.8	4.6	4.3	4.5	5.0
	2007	4.8	4.8	4.8	4.5	4.6	4.9	4.6	3.1	4.7	4.3	4.4	4.9
	2008	4.8	4.8	4.8	4.5	4.5	4.9	4.5	2.4	4.7	4.3	4.5	5.0
	2009	4.8	4.8	4.8	4.5	4.5	4.9	4.5	2.4	4.7	4.3	4.5	5.0
United Republic of Tanzania - République-Unie de Tanzanie	2000	16.5	11.9	16.7	8.7	13.4	21.2	13.0	10.4	13.0	8.9	11.0	18.4
	2003	13.5	7.1	13.8	4.6	9.2	19.5	9.1	7.0	9.1	5.1	7.0	14.7
	2005	11.8	7.5	12.0	3.7	6.4	17.9	8.6	8.5	8.6	4.3	7.8	13.0
	2006	11.8	7.2	12.0	3.6	6.3	17.9	8.3	4.0	8.3	2.9	7.4	13.3
	2007	11.9	7.8	12.0	3.7	6.4	17.9	7.9	4.1	8.0	2.3	8.0	12.1
	2008	11.9	7.1	12.0	4.4	5.9	17.6	11.6	10.5	11.6	4.6	8.1	18.1
	2009	11.8	7.1	12.0	4.3	5.9	17.6	11.6	10.4	11.5	4.4	8.1	18.1
	2010	11.5	7.2	11.7	3.9	5.6	17.6	8.7	7.4	8.7	3.1	7.3	14.3
United States - États-Unis	2000	3.9	1.3	4.0	3.4	1.7	5.3	3.0	1.1	3.0	3.1	1.8	5.2
	2001	3.8	1.3	3.9	3.3	1.6	5.2	3.1	1.1	3.2	2.8	2.0	5.1
	2002	3.7	1.3	3.8	3.2	1.6	5.1	3.1	1.4	3.1	2.6	2.1	5.0
	2003	3.6	1.3	3.7	3.1	1.6	4.9	3.0	1.4	3.0	2.3	2.0	4.8
	2004	3.5	1.3	3.6	3.0	1.6	4.7	2.8	1.3	2.8	2.3	1.9	4.4
	2005	3.5	1.3	3.6	3.1	1.6	4.7	2.8	1.4	2.8	2.3	1.9	4.4
	2006	3.5	1.3	3.6	3.1	1.6	4.7	2.7	1.4	2.7	2.2	1.9	4.3
	2007	3.5	1.3	3.7	3.0	1.7	4.8	2.9	1.3	3.0	2.0	2.1	4.5
	2008	3.5	1.4	3.7	3.0	1.7	4.8	2.7	1.3	2.8	2.0	1.9	4.3
	2009	3.5	1.4	3.7	3.1	1.7	4.8	2.8	1.3	2.9	1.9	1.7	4.7
	2010	3.5	1.4	3.7	3.1	1.7	4.8	2.8	1.3	2.9	1.9	1.7	4.7
Uruguay	2000	14.9	10.5	15.1	11.4	10.9	18.4	14.4	9.6	14.5	12.6	12.8	17.6
	2001	14.8	9.6	15.1	11.1	11.7	18.0	14.1	9.3	14.2	12.5	12.7	17.0
	2002	13.9	8.5	14.1	9.8	11.2	17.0	12.7	6.4	12.8	10.8	11.7	15.6
	2004	14.0	8.3	14.2	9.9	11.3	17.0	12.3	5.4	12.5	10.2	11.6	15.7
	2005	11.8	7.0	12.0	8.4	7.1	15.3	10.5	4.5	10.6	9.2	8.7	14.2
	2006	11.4	6.3	11.7	7.9	6.8	15.1	9.7	2.9	9.9	7.4	8.6	13.7
	2007	11.4	6.3	11.6	7.9	6.8	15.0	9.6	2.8	9.8	7.2	8.7	13.9
	2008	11.4	6.3	11.6	7.9	6.6	15.2	10.0	2.8	10.2	6.7	9.5	14.4
	2009	11.4	6.3	11.6	7.8	6.6	15.1	10.2	3.5	10.3	7.4	8.8	14.9
	2010	11.4	6.3	11.6	7.8	6.6	15.1	10.5	3.5	10.6	7.4	9.4	14.9
Uzbekistan - Ouzbékistan	2001	11.6	10.7	11.7	9.1	4.9	15.9	6.2	7.0	6.2	8.1	3.0	11.0
	2006	15.0	14.8	15.1	9.5	10.9	19.3	11.1	10.2	11.1	11.0	9.8	13.4
	2007	14.7	15.0	14.7	9.3	10.8	19.0	10.4	7.8	10.5	10.3	9.6	12.2
	2008	14.9	15.7	14.9	9.7	10.2	19.3	10.4	10.7	10.4	10.0	10.0	11.0
	2009	14.6	15.6	14.5	9.4	9.1	19.3	10.1	10.7	10.0	9.9	9.4	11.2
Vanuatu	2002	15.5	10.7	15.6	13.1	15.2	16.3	6.9	11.9	6.8	5.7	4.6	16.0
	2006	15.1	11.2	15.1	11.4	15.3	15.8	7.0	10.3	7.0	7.5	4.9	13.2
	2007	15.3	10.1	15.5	12.4	15.1	16.2	9.9	7.0	10.0	9.4	7.4	15.2
	2008	14.8	11.5	14.9	11.4	13.8	16.3	14.3	9.5	14.4	14.5	12.7	16.0
	2009	14.8	11.5	14.9	11.4	13.8	16.3	14.3	9.5	14.4	14.5	12.7	16.0

For sources and notes, see end of table.

Pour les sources et les notes, se reporter à la fin du tableau.

4

4.3 Average applied import MFN tariff rates on non-agricultural and non-fuel products

4.3 Droits de douane moyens NPF appliqués à l'importation des produits non-agricoles et non-pétroliers

Market / Marchés	Year / Année	MFN rate - Simple average (2) / Droit NPF - Moyenne simple (2)						MFN rate - Weighted average (3) / Droit NPF - Moyenne pondérée (3)					
		Total of non-agricultural and non-fuel products / Total des produits non-agricoles et non-pétroliers	of which: / dont :					Total of non-agricultural and non-fuel products / Total des produits non-agricoles et non-pétroliers	of which: / dont :				
			Ores and metals / Minérais et métaux	Manu-factured products / Produits manu-facturés	Of which: / dont :				Ores and metals / Minérais et métaux	Manu-factured products / Produits manu-facturés	Of which: / dont :		
					Chemical products / Produits chimiques	Machinery and transport equipment / Machines et matériel de transport	Other manu-factured products / Produits manu-facturés divers				Chemical products / Produits chimiques	Machinery and transport equipment / Machines et matériel de transport	Other manu-factured products / Produits manu-facturés divers
SITC Rev.3 (1) / CTCI Rév.3 (1)		5+6+7+8 +27+28-667	27+28+68	5+6+7+8 -(667+68)	5	7	6+8 -(667+68)	5+6+7+8 +27+28-667	27+28+68	5+6+7+8 -(667+68)	5	7	6+8 -(667+68)
Venezuela (Bolivarian Rep. of) - Venezuela (Rép. bolivarienne du)	2000	12.1	6.8	12.4	8.4	10.5	11.0	11.1	8.8	10.4	9.6	14.0	14.4
	2002	12.5	7.0	12.8	8.5	10.4	15.5	13.5	8.5	13.6	10.2	13.9	15.5
	2004	12.2	7.1	12.5	8.4	10.5	15.0	12.9	8.3	13.0	9.8	13.8	13.9
	2005	12.1	7.0	12.4	8.4	10.4	14.9	13.5	8.7	13.5	10.1	14.4	13.7
	2006	12.9	7.0	13.2	8.4	10.5	16.3	14.1	8.9	14.2	9.8	14.3	16.6
	2007	12.9	7.0	13.2	8.4	10.5	16.3	14.1	8.9	14.2	9.8	14.3	16.6
	2008	13.1	7.0	13.4	8.3	10.6	16.6	15.5	9.0	15.7	10.1	16.4	16.8
	2009	13.0	7.0	13.4	8.4	10.5	16.5	13.5	8.3	13.7	10.0	12.2	17.6
	2010	13.0	7.0	13.4	8.3	10.5	16.6	12.1	7.8	12.2	9.6	10.4	16.5
Viet Nam	2001	15.3	1.8	16.0	4.2	10.1	23.2	16.1	1.5	16.5	4.1	19.9	19.2
	2002	15.5	2.0	16.2	4.1	9.8	23.6	15.2	1.2	15.5	4.4	16.0	20.0
	2003	15.9	2.1	16.6	4.3	10.2	24.1	13.7	1.3	14.0	4.3	11.8	21.1
	2004	15.8	2.1	16.6	4.3	10.1	24.1	13.8	1.2	14.3	4.1	13.2	19.8
	2005	15.8	1.9	16.6	4.3	10.1	24.2	13.9	1.1	14.3	4.4	13.2	19.8
	2006	15.3	2.0	16.1	4.2	9.8	23.7	11.8	0.9	12.5	3.9	9.5	19.1
	2007	15.3	2.0	16.1	4.1	10.1	23.6	13.0	1.1	13.5	3.9	12.5	19.0
	2008	9.4	1.9	9.9	3.7	7.3	13.5	6.8	0.9	7.2	3.0	7.4	8.9
	2010	8.7	1.9	9.1	3.3	6.7	12.5	6.8	1.0	7.1	2.8	7.9	8.7
Yemen - Yémen	2000	12.5	11.3	12.6	9.8	11.1	14.3	12.5	10.5	12.5	8.5	13.2	13.2
	2006	6.2	6.0	6.2	5.8	4.9	7.0	5.6	5.5	5.6	5.2	4.7	6.7
	2009	6.2	6.8	6.1	5.9	5.0	6.8	5.3	5.6	5.3	5.2	4.6	6.5
Zambia - Zambie	2002	11.7	7.6	11.9	7.1	6.8	16.0	8.3	4.8	8.3	6.0	7.8	10.1
	2003	13.6	9.9	13.8	7.4	10.7	17.6	10.6	4.6	10.8	6.0	10.7	14.1
	2005	13.6	9.5	13.7	7.3	10.6	17.5	9.9	3.6	10.1	3.9	11.2	12.8
	2008	12.8	9.6	12.9	6.9	9.7	16.9	7.9	0.8	9.2	3.7	9.3	13.7
	2009	12.8	9.4	12.9	7.1	9.5	16.6	8.1	3.8	9.0	4.0	8.9	14.2
Zimbabwe	2001	19.4	9.1	19.9	8.4	13.8	27.5	13.9	7.8	14.2	7.6	16.2	18.6
	2002	15.7	8.9	16.1	8.4	12.5	21.6	18.9	7.3	19.4	7.2	26.9	18.6
	2003	15.4	8.5	15.8	8.3	12.1	21.2	14.0	6.2	15.1	8.6	16.8	17.2
	2007	13.1	7.7	13.4	7.9	9.3	18.1	9.7	5.1	14.7	7.5	16.7	16.4

Sources:
- UNCTAD/WITS, *TRAINS (Trade Analysis and Information System)*

Notes:
(1) Product categories are defined in terms of SITC Revision 3, and all corresponding Harmonized System (HS) 6-digit codes have been aggregated for each category.
(2) Simple average for each product group calculated from simple average at HS 6-digit level.
(3) Weighted average for each product group calculated from simple average at HS 6-digit level. Country's own imports at HS 6-digit level for corresponding years are used as weights. Where imports are not reported, mirror imports have been compiled using exports of partner countries.
(4) From 2008 onwards, member of the European Union.
(5) From 2004 onwards, member of the European Union.
(6) For the union, data refer to the composition of the group during that year.

Sources :
- CNUCED/WITS, *TRAINS (Trade Analysis and Information System)*

Notes :
(1) Les catégories de produits sont définies sur la base de la CTCI, révision 3, et pour chaque catégorie, les codes à 6 chiffres du Système harmonisé (SH) correspondants ont été agrégés.
(2) Moyenne arithmétique, pour chaque catégorie de produits, calculée à partir des moyennes arithmétiques au niveau du code à 6 chiffres du SH.
(3) Moyenne arithmétique pondérée, pour chaque catégorie de produits, calculée à partir des moyennes simples au niveau du code à 6 chiffres du SH. Pour chaque année, les coefficients de pondération sont les importations de chaque marché au niveau du code à 6 chiffres du SH. Lorsque les importations n'étaient pas disponibles, elles ont été évaluées par les données miroir basées sur les exportations des pays partenaires.
(4) À partir de 2008, membre de l'Union européenne.
(5) À partir de 2004, membre de l'Union européenne.
(6) Pour une année donnée, les tarifs de l'union se réfèrent à la composition du groupe durant cette année.

5 INTERNATIONAL TRADE IN SERVICES

COMMERCE INTERNATIONAL DES SERVICES

5.1.1 Value of exports and imports of services of countries and geographical regions

Region, country or territory	Exports - Exportations Millions of dollars							
	1980	1990	2000	2006	2007	2008	2009	2010
WORLD	391 365	826 926	1 532 259	2 897 783	3 476 343	3 910 422	3 454 563	3 764 890
DEVELOPING ECONOMIES	73 550	150 468	350 208	734 126	894 961	1 035 763	939 776	1 123 442
TRANSITION ECONOMIES (1)	4 552	6 406	23 535	70 118	89 162	112 567	92 843	100 107
DEVELOPED ECONOMIES	313 263	670 052	1 158 515	2 093 539	2 492 220	2 762 093	2 421 944	2 541 341
Developing economies: Africa	13 559	21 626	33 218	66 841	78 706	89 684	81 892	90 736
Eastern Africa	*1 833*	*3 117*	*5 191*	*9 911*	*12 013*	*14 080*	*13 233*	*15 810*
Burundi	-	17	4	34	31	83	50	79
Comoros	2	17	38	47	55	67	59	61
Djibouti	-	-	162	251	248	297	322	-
Eritrea			61					
Ethiopia	–	–	506	1 174	1 368	1 959	1 895	2 353
Ethiopia (former)	125	305	–	–	–	–	–	–
Kenya	577	1 138	993	2 430	2 931	3 251	2 883	3 675
Madagascar	79	153	364	(e)595	(e)835	(e)866	(e)849	(e)989
Malawi	32	37	34	52	73	75	77	85
Mauritius	140	484	1 070	1 671	2 205	2 544	2 239	2 695
Mozambique	118	103	325	386	459	555	612	647
Rwanda	34	42	59	131	179	408	341	373
Seychelles	91	172	287	430	472	473	404	430
Somalia	66	..	..	..	..	..	..	..
Uganda	10	-	213	526	593	799	967	1 310
United Republic of Tanzania	165	131	627	1 528	1 876	1 999	1 855	2 092
Zambia	151	107	115	228	273	300	241	312
Zimbabwe	169	264	(e)331	(e)292	(e)277	(e)264	(e)300	(e)238
Middle Africa	*1 152*	*1 180*	*1 448*	*2 352*	*2 902*	*3 265*	*3 499*	*3 558*
Angola	-	109	267	200	311	329	623	644
Cameroon	401	382	682	1 017	1 370	1 484	1 249	1 159
Central African Republic	54	69	(e)31	(e)52	(e)61	(e)68	(e)66	(e)65
Chad	0	41	51	158	176	(e)171	(e)150	(e)156
Congo	111	99	137	266	319	351	387	425
Dem. Rep. of the Congo	(e)120	(e)230	71	390	392	(e)522	(e)651	(e)628
Equatorial Guinea	-	5	18	(e)41	(e)47	(e)55	(e)55	(e)65
Gabon	325	242	178	220	218	275	309	404
Sao Tome and Principe	3	4	14	8	7	10	10	-
Northern Africa	*5 175*	*10 455*	*16 761*	*33 517*	*40 355*	*48 532*	*43 116*	*46 437*
Algeria	476	497	(e)958	2 563	2 833	3 490	2 985	(e)3 610
Egypt	2 393	5 971	9 803	16 135	19 943	24 912	21 520	23 807
Libyan Arab Jamahiriya	164	117	172	489	109	208	385	416
Morocco	783	2 009	3 034	9 789	12 165	13 416	12 336	12 545
Sudan	292	173	27	247	384	493	391	254
Tunisia	1 067	1 688	2 767	4 295	4 921	6 014	5 499	5 805
Southern Africa	*2 759*	*3 897*	*5 841*	*13 835*	*15 764*	*14 546*	*13 627*	*15 950*
Botswana	101	210	325	771	849	918	842	807
Lesotho	32	41	24	42	43	43	44	48
Namibia	-	132	174	526	599	555·	521	853
South Africa	2 463	3 407	5 046	12 214	13 818	12 805	12 020	14 004
Swaziland	36	108	273	283	455	225	200	239
Western Africa	*2 640*	*2 976*	*3 977*	*7 226*	*7 672*	*9 261*	*8 416*	*8 975*
Benin	62	126	136	217	302	348	221	346
Burkina Faso	49	69	31	64	91	132	153	119
Cape Verde	10	35	108	382	491	601	486	510
Côte d'Ivoire	564	590	482	845	933	1 025	975	1 002
Gambia	19	59	134	92	128	118	104	88
Ghana	107	86	504	1 383	1 832	1 801	1 770	1 477
Guinea	-	157	68	64	49	103	72	62
Guinea-Bissau	-	7	6	3	33	44	11	(e)19
Liberia	13	..	..	336	346	510	274	158
Mali	58	85	99	313	377	454	354	350
Mauritania	56	27	47	87	81	93	136	(e)160
Niger	41	44	38	91	85	131	128	135
Nigeria	1 127	965	1 833	(b)2 299	1 443	2 264	2 218	3 076
Senegal	337	515	387	807	1 201	1 294	1 162	1 141
Sierra Leone	49	61	42	43	45	61	58	60
Togo	74	149	62	201	236	283	294	272

For sources and notes, see end of table.

Imports - Importations Millions de dollars								Régions, pays ou territoires
1980	1990	2000	2006	2007	2008	2009	2010	
444 244	873 506	1 538 738	2 751 636	3 247 339	3 696 687	3 291 334	3 585 832	**MONDE**
142 723	198 058	422 347	826 491	999 572	1 187 155	1 087 070	1 281 723	ÉCONOMIES EN DÉVELOPPEMENT
5 229	15 041	27 501	82 343	106 495	134 046	109 513	125 525	ÉCONOMIES EN TRANSITION (1)
296 293	660 407	1 088 890	1 842 802	2 141 272	2 375 487	2 094 751	2 178 584	ÉCONOMIES DÉVELOPPÉES
29 353	30 017	41 180	94 209	120 094	152 168	136 334	147 479	Économies en développement : Afrique
3 356	*3 999*	*5 632*	*9 534*	*11 970*	*14 650*	*13 786*	*15 672*	*Afrique orientale*
-	129	43	202	179	259	177	168	Burundi
12	44	23	54	64	80	87	96	Comores
-	-	71	00	108	130	128	-	Djibouti
–	–	28	-	-	-	-	-	Érythrée
–	–	490	1 171	1 752	2 410	2 227	2 537	Éthiopie
208	359	–	–	–	–	–	–	Éthiopie (anc.)
502	700	719	1 402	1 671	1 870	1 812	2 016	Kenya
311	242	522	(e)736	(e)1 174	(e)1 579	(e)1 218	-	Madagascar
179	268	167	265	295	320	363	378	Malawi
174	421	763	1 317	1 569	1 920	1 607	1 984	Maurice
124	206	446	758	856	965	1 062	1 137	Mozambique
133	129	200	243	272	521	519	596	Rwanda
40	80	190	274	303	332	276	332	Seychelles
133	..	..	..	..	..	..	..	Somalie
123	195	459	770	977	1 257	1 423	1 835	Ouganda
295	288	682	1 249	1 414	1 649	1 709	1 850	République-Unie de Tanzanie
651	386	335	588	915	906	705	940	Zambie
394	495	(e)495	(e)380	(e)385	(e)410	(e)430	(e)440	Zimbabwe
3 314	*5 828*	*6 485*	*16 839*	*25 126*	*35 577*	*30 952*	*30 700*	*Afrique centrale*
-	1 807	2 699	7 511	12 643	22 139	19 169	17 337	Angola
717	1 045	1 017	1 475	1 764	2 668	1 780	1 746	Cameroun
142	169	(e)113	(e)120	(e)148	(e)166	(e)156	(e)173	République centrafricaine
24	228	241	1 910	2 127	(e)2 188	(e)2 196	(e)2 371	Tchad
480	769	738	2 426	3 528	2 604	2 425	2 624	Congo
(e)560	(e)758	239	851	1 618	(e)2 146	(e)1 817	(e)2 273	Rép. dém. du Congo
-	36	567	(e)1 159	(e)1 444	(e)1 905	(e)1 851	(e)2 230	Guinée équatoriale
789	1 007	858	1 370	1 836	1 740	1 538	1 918	Gabon
6	9	12	18	19	21	19	-	Sao Tomé-et-Principe
9 733	*9 013*	*14 574*	*28 656*	*34 944*	*45 725*	*43 129*	*44 204*	*Afrique septentrionale*
2 697	1 321	(e)2 408	4 796	6 767	11 082	11 680	(e)11 860	Algérie
2 343	3 788	7 513	11 569	14 342	17 615	13 935	(e)13 530	Égypte
2 303	1 385	895	2 564	2 665	4 344	5 063	5 114	Jamahiriya arabe libyenne
1 436	1 445	1 892	4 473	5 416	6 694	6 899	7 436	Maroc
353	228	(b)648	2 800	2 939	2 620	2 577	2 918	Soudan
600	846	1 218	2 455	2 815	3 370	2 974	3 345	Tunisie
3 998	*4 728*	*7 250*	*16 232*	*18 909*	*19 708*	*17 403*	*21 493*	*Afrique australe*
216	376	547	835	1 027	1 122	1 040	1 229	Botswana
50	81	249	352	380	371	385	516	Lesotho
-	354	320	430	514	589	609	705	Namibie
3 295	3 738	5 823	14 242	16 482	16 976	14 808	18 456	Afrique du Sud
80	179	310	373	507	651	562	586	Swaziland
8 952	*6 450*	*7 238*	*22 948*	*29 144*	*36 506*	*31 063*	*35 411*	*Afrique occidentale*
109	131	192	352	500	510	496	434	Bénin
209	216	140	360	454	605	559	605	Burkina Faso
7	28	100	250	294	359	318	378	Cap-Vert
1 531	1 626	1 227	2 233	2 484	2 660	2 485	2 724	Côte d'Ivoire
43	53	100	94	87	86	83	72	Gambie
270	301	584	1 519	1 994	2 298	2 943	3 003	Ghana
-	367	285	300	295	444	331	396	Guinée
-	20	40	40	68	85	65	(e)53	Guinée-Bissau
73	..	..	1 275	1 249	1 411	1 145	1 080	Libéria
212	374	335	675	777	1 024	826	897	Mali
128	137	168	406	586	769	616	(e)772	Mauritanie
279	227	132	329	369	601	840	1 055	Niger
5 285	1 976	3 300	(b)13 924	18 345	(b)23 755	18 697	22 307	Nigéria
340	676	405	842	1 238	1 415	1 162	1 142	Sénégal
85	74	113	86	98	125	122	144	Sierra Leone
167	244	118	264	305	359	375	350	Togo

Pour les sources et les notes, se reporter à la fin du tableau.

5

Region, country or territory	Exports - Exportations Millions of dollars							
	1980	1990	2000	2006	2007	2008	2009	2010
Developing economies: America	18 615	31 561	62 507	97 945	113 632	129 374	117 245	129 217
Caribbean	3 511	7 474	15 957	23 617	26 348	27 246	25 049	26 079
Anguilla	..	41	65	124	134	117	110	129
Antigua and Barbuda	45	312	415	477	525	563	514	511
Aruba	-	411	1 012	1 309	1 469	1 594	1 517	1 533
Bahamas	746	1 500	1 973	2 436	2 599	2 534	2 266	2 406
Barbados	345	654	1 020	1 453	1 641	1 556	1 416	1 466
Cuba	..	328	9 ???	(e)8 007	(e)8 307	(e)8 842	(e)7 555	(e)7 964
Dominica	6	33	90	100	109	118	110	110
Dominican Republic	309	1 097	3 228	4 567	4 825	4 951	4 946	5 073
Grenada	21	64	153	130	148	149	140	138
Haiti	90	62	172	194	257	343	382	382
Jamaica	401	1 027	2 024	2 049	2 707	2 745	2 061	2 634
Montserrat	-	18	16	15	15	14	12	11
Netherlands Antilles	878	1 161	1 571	1 991	2 098	2 055	2 035	2 203
Saint Kitts and Nevis	8	54	99	177	173	161	132	125
Saint Lucia	41	151	324	344	356	364	353	387
Saint Vincent and the Grenadines	18	45	128	171	161	153	139	139
Trinidad and Tobago	411	329	554	814	924	936	765	861
Central America	6 196	10 793	20 043	27 351	30 537	33 014	29 117	30 748
Belize	-	115	153	363	398	386	344	354
Costa Rica	194	609	1 936	2 972	3 552	4 083	3 593	4 180
El Salvador	139	329	698	1 015	1 134	1 058	863	976
Guatemala	211	356	777	1 519	1 731	1 873	1 925	2 216
Honduras	82	137	507	745	781	885	953	1 022
Mexico	4 591	8 094	13 755	16 392	17 609	18 480	15 423	15 435
Nicaragua	44	60	221	345	374	460	496	472
Panama, excl. Canal Zone (former)	902	–	–	–	–	–	–	–
Panama	–	1 092	1 994	4 000	4 958	5 788	5 519	6 093
South America	8 908	13 294	26 508	46 977	56 747	69 114	63 079	72 390
Argentina	1 876	2 446	4 936	8 023	10 363	12 156	11 058	13 214
Bolivia (Plurinational State of)	88	146	224	477	499	500	515	550
Brazil	1 737	3 762	9 498	19 462	23 954	30 451	27 728	31 821
Chile	1 263	1 848	4 083	7 830	8 962	10 824	8 634	10 797
Colombia	1 342	1 600	2 049	3 377	3 636	4 137	4 202	4 446
Ecuador	367	538	849	1 037	1 200	1 313	1 227	1 367
Guyana	20	-	169	148	173	212	242	273
Paraguay	164	418	595	798	962	1 150	1 406	1 506
Peru	715	798	1 555	2 660	3 152	3 649	3 645	3 956
Suriname	176	37	91	234	245	285	287	241
Uruguay	468	466	1 276	1 387	1 833	2 277	2 129	2 494
Venezuela (Bolivarian Rep. of)	693	1 183	1 182	1 544	1 767	2 162	2 005	1 724
Developing economies: Asia	41 072	96 473	253 511	566 311	699 214	813 074	737 672	900 376
Eastern Asia	15 306	42 380	125 972	261 711	325 941	385 079	340 522	431 593
China	-	5 855	30 431	91 999	122 206	147 112	129 549	171 203
China, Hong Kong SAR	5 790	17 887	40 430	72 735	84 722	92 292	86 411	108 000
China, Macao SAR	379	1 473	3 586	10 459	14 202	17 760	18 821	28 682
China, Taiwan Province of	(e)2 130	7 008	20 010	29 272	31 311	36 829	31 774	40 516
Korea, Republic of	4 915	10 109	31 438	56 761	72 918	90 587	73 553	82 706
Mongolia	-	48	78	486	582	499	415	486
Southern Asia	5 060	7 655	22 075	84 028	102 805	125 044	109 660	144 556
Afghanistan	36	..	..	-	-	-	-	-
Bangladesh	211	392	815	1 334	1 617	1 996	1 976	2 414
Bhutan	-	28	20	52	60	55	58	-
India	2 971	4 625	16 685	69 730	86 929	107 131	93 036	123 762
Iran (Islamic Rep. of)	731	436	1 382	(e)6 713	(e)7 345	(e)7 825	(e)7 007	(e)7 600
Maldives	52	101	348	552	649	721	660	769
Nepal	155	204	506	386	511	724	705	672
Pakistan	652	1 429	1 380	3 506	3 767	4 263	3 983	6 410
Sri Lanka	231	440	939	1 625	1 775	2 002	1 892	2 469
South-Eastern Asia	9 393	29 369	69 086	138 474	176 340	198 423	185 662	221 547
Brunei Darussalam	..	-	(e)363	745	813	867	915	(e)1 061
Cambodia	-	-	428	1 296	1 548	1 645	1 625	1 841
Indonesia including East Timor	381	2 488	5 214	–	–	–	–	–
Indonesia	–	–	–	11 520	12 488	15 247	13 156	16 766
Lao People's Dem. Rep.	-	24	176	223	278	402	391	470
Malaysia	1 135	3 859	13 941	21 681	29 462	30 321	28 769	33 973

For sources and notes, see end of table.

Imports - Importations Millions de dollars								Régions, pays ou territoires
1980	1990	2000	2006	2007	2008	2009	2010	
29 679	37 111	74 553	107 627	127 721	150 608	139 434	166 813	**Économies en développement : Amérique**
2 600	*4 108*	*7 691*	*10 807*	*11 549*	*12 489*	*10 686*	*11 126*	*Caraïbes*
..	15	41	92	103	87	67	68	Anguilla
17	105	156	259	283	273	239	222	Antigua-et-Barbuda
-	135	642	987	915	1 041	768	690	Aruba
226	573	1 026	1 611	1 580	1 403	1 196	1 181	Bahamas
129	250	485	728	816	650	604	755	Barbade
..	600	778	1 263	1 330	2 090	1 375	.	Cuba
6	30	33	52	64	70	64	63	Dominique
399	440	1 373	1 582	1 772	1 989	1 900	2 137	République dominicaine
11	33	89	105	108	113	98	101	Grenade
162	72	200	193	600	746	781	890	Haïti
370	697	1 423	2 021	2 282	2 367	1 881	1 824	Jamaïque
-	12	23	17	19	23	18	17	Montserrat
529	518	668	758	797	871	930	990	Antilles néerlandaises
6	35	76	101	102	120	100	90	Saint-Kitts-et-Nevis
22	81	133	186	206	215	190	202	Sainte-Lucie
11	32	56	88	114	102	94	90	Saint-Vincent-et-les Grenadines
645	479	388	363	377	326	383	431	Trinité-et-Tobago
8 460	*12 652*	*22 700*	*30 828*	*33 214*	*35 582*	*32 133*	*35 755*	*Amérique centrale*
-	60	123	152	168	170	162	162	Belize
286	550	1 273	1 621	1 818	1 882	1 405	1 773	Costa Rica
273	315	933	1 179	1 275	1 271	953	1 070	El Salvador
487	384	825	1 778	2 041	2 149	2 084	2 370	Guatemala
174	220	694	1 036	1 069	1 213	1 103	1 331	Honduras
6 514	10 323	17 360	22 833	24 064	25 535	23 591	25 594	Mexique
104	112	351	502	657	729	644	694	Nicaragua
588	–	–	–	–	–	–	–	Panama, sans la zone du canal (anc.)
–	689	1 141	1 728	2 122	2 633	2 191	2 760	Panama
18 620	*20 351*	*44 162*	*65 993*	*82 959*	*102 537*	*96 615*	*119 932*	*Amérique du Sud*
3 700	3 120	9 219	8 523	10 876	13 440	12 215	14 066	Argentine
259	311	468	827	900	1 017	1 015	1 152	Bolivie (État plurinational de)
4 871	7 523	16 660	29 116	37 173	47 140	46 974	62 628	Brésil
1 583	2 076	4 802	8 462	9 950	11 787	10 078	11 816	Chili
1 170	1 750	3 307	5 496	6 243	7 210	7 030	7 086	Colombie
704	804	1 209	2 341	2 572	2 954	2 607	2 960	Équateur
107	-	193	245	273	323	324	350	Guyana
165	434	420	384	463	592	538	715	Paraguay
880	1 164	2 290	3 397	4 344	5 704	4 789	5 993	Pérou
364	171	216	269	317	398	285	259	Suriname
476	393	882	979	1 130	1 455	1 138	1 427	Uruguay
4 253	2 534	4 435	5 954	8 719	10 516	9 622	10 581	Venezuela (Rép. bolivarienne du)
83 195	130 066	305 242	620 531	746 957	879 350	806 655	961 590	**Économies en développement : Asie**
13 349	*42 681*	*121 995*	*245 207*	*297 694*	*343 160*	*318 348*	*384 289*	*Asie orientale*
-	4 352	36 031	100 833	130 111	158 924	158 947	193 321	Chine
4 370	12 937	24 698	37 060	42 591	47 062	43 939	50 869	Chine (RAS de Hong Kong)
22	238	904	2 974	4 485	5 687	4 931	7 544	Chine (RAS de Macao)
(e)2 960	14 658	26 647	33 661	35 102	34 551	29 783	37 867	Province chinoise de Taiwan
3 738	10 341	33 553	70 156	84 933	96 326	80 190	93 907	Corée, République de
-	155	163	523	472	610	558	780	Mongolie
10 219	*13 697*	*27 333*	*86 537*	*101 836*	*124 418*	*111 257*	*150 538*	*Asie méridionale*
144	..	..	-	-	-	-	-	Afghanistan
481	700	1 620	2 340	2 885	3 664	3 396	4 353	Bangladesh
-	28	46	61	57	93	74	-	Bhoutan
2 981	6 090	19 188	58 696	70 805	88 349	81 049	116 842	Inde
5 223	3 962	2 296	(e)13 257	(o)15 079	(e)17 742	(e)15 802	(e)17 064	Iran (Rép. islamique d')
43	38	110	231	269	351	286	306	Maldives
88	167	200	493	723	852	842	871	Népal
877	2 073	2 252	8 418	8 811	9 717	6 551	7 088	Pakistan
351	639	1 621	2 394	2 602	3 010	2 522	3 122	Sri Lanka
13 748	*29 025*	*88 180*	*157 501*	*183 617*	*212 462*	*188 479*	*227 360*	*Asie du Sud-Est*
..	-	(e)1 043	1 214	1 317	1 403	1 434	-	Brunéi Darussalam
-	-	328	804	915	1 036	1 022	1 166	Cambodge
4 597	6 056	15 637	–	–	–	–	–	Indonésie, y compris le Timor oriental
–	–	–	21 394	24 328	28 245	22 896	26 086	Indonésie
–	26	43	37	44	85	120	126	Rép. dém. populaire lao
2 957	5 485	16 747	23 651	28 668	30 270	27 472	33 695	Malaisie

Pour les sources et les notes, se reporter à la fin du tableau.

Region, country or territory	Exports - Exportations Millions of dollars							
	1980	1990	2000	2006	2007	2008	2009	2010
Myanmar	53	94	478	280	(e)381	(e)356	(e)293	(e)312
Philippines	1 447	3 244	3 377	6 444	9 766	9 717	11 014	13 243
Singapore	4 856	12 811	28 540	66 329	85 155	99 435	93 745	112 308
Thailand	1 490	6 419	13 868	24 822	30 357	33 383	29 941	34 046
Timor-Leste	..			(e)34	(e)63	(e)44	(e)47	(e)68
Viet Nam	..	398	2 702	5 100	6 030	7 006	5 766	7 460
Western Asia	*11 313*	*17 069*	*36 378*	*82 097*	*94 128*	*104 527*	*101 828*	*102 681*
Bahrain	333	359	933	3 322	3 524	3 740	3 653	4 047
Iraq				357	868	1 969	-	-
Jordan	1 003	1 447	1 640	2 907	3 548	4 478	4 663	5 161
Kuwait	1 225	1 279	1 823	8 444	10 169	11 959	11 309	7 716
Lebanon	..	-	-	11 581	12 755	17 574	16 889	15 268
Occupied Palestinian territory	..	-	473	260	369	496	579	609
Oman	0	68	452	1 711	1 603	1 827	1 620	1 761
Qatar	-		363	4 193	3 592	5 420	7 007	7 251
Saudi Arabia	5 191	3 027	4 779	14 202	15 987	(b)9 370	9 749	10 683
Syrian Arab Republic	365	874	1 699	2 924	3 862	4 040	4 798	5 205
Turkey	711	8 016	20 379	25 577	28 988	34 854	33 084	34 357
United Arab Emirates	-	-	2 170	(e)6 470	(e)8 059	(e)9 594	(e)10 155	(e)11 734
Yemen (former Arab Republic)	164							
Yemen (former Democratic)	87							
Yemen		106	211	549	724	1 205	1 237	1 250
Developing economies: Oceania	**305**	**809**	**972**	**3 030**	**3 409**	**3 632**	**2 967**	**3 112**
Fiji	201	417	432	814	855	978	706	-
French Polynesia	..	..	..	1 033	1 201	1 192	1 030	955
Kiribati	4	8	(e)6	(e)9	(e)10	-	-	-
Micronesia (Federated States of)		31	42	41	45	48	39	..
New Caledonia	..	..	..	453	543	583	499	547
Papua New Guinea	43	206	243	322	353	369	187	205
Samoa	8	36	-	133	131	126	148	158
Solomon Islands	12	25	52	53	59	59	72	(e)94
Tonga	9	26	(e)15	26	26	38	35	(e)41
Vanuatu	-	60	130	146	186	(e)233	(e)244	-
Transition economies (1)	**4 552**	**6 406**	**23 535**	**70 118**	**89 162**	**112 567**	**92 843**	**100 107**
Albania	11	32	448	1 504	1 946	2 478	2 483	2 243
Armenia	-	-	137	485	580	645	590	762
Azerbaijan	-	-	260	940	1 248	1 547	1 750	2 065
Belarus	-	-	1 000	2 401	3 264	4 258	3 504	4 504
Bosnia and Herzegovina	-	-	450	1 140	1 458	1 672	1 444	1 284
Croatia	-	-	4 071	10 487	12 499	14 762	11 726	11 021
Georgia	-	-	360	885	1 094	1 260	1 314	1 599
Kazakhstan	-	-	1 053	2 819	3 564	4 426	4 234	4 245
Kyrgyzstan	-	-	62	379	685	896	860	693
Montenegro	-	-	-	-	-	1 099	945	989
Republic of Moldova	-	-	165	466	625	837	669	690
Russian Federation	-	-	9 565	31 102	39 257	51 178	41 594	44 343
Serbia and Montenegro	-	-	624	(e)2 614	4 073			
Serbia	-	-	-	-	-	4 028	3 488	3 532
SFR of Yugoslavia (former)	4 541	6 374	-	-	-	-	-	-
Tajikistan	-	-	(e)62	134	149	181	180	209
TFYR of Macedonia	-	-	317	601	818	1 012	863	916
Ukraine	-	-	3 800	11 290	14 161	17 895	13 859	17 064
Uzbekistan	-	-	543	775	962	(e)1 195	(e)1 036	(e)1 125
Developed economies: America	**54 995**	**165 670**	**335 464**	**474 745**	**550 551**	**597 888**	**557 285**	**614 949**
Bermuda	..	..	..	1 592	1 651	1 580	1 328	1 426
Canada	7 445	19 210	40 230	60 353	65 338	68 359	60 089	69 166
United States	47 550	146 460	295 234	412 800	483 562	527 949	495 867	544 357
Developed economies: Asia	**22 962**	**45 953**	**84 516**	**136 459**	**150 104**	**172 029**	**149 875**	**166 161**
Israel	2 722	4 569	15 402	19 222	21 145	24 306	21 979	24 704
Japan	20 240	41 384	69 114	117 237	128 959	147 722	127 895	141 457
Developed economies: Europe	**230 435**	**445 732**	**714 237**	**1 441 088**	**1 741 664**	**1 937 672**	**1 665 323**	**1 703 008**
Austria	9 423	23 279	23 093	45 634	54 254	63 569	54 673	54 523
Belgium (2)	12 925	28 417	34 429	59 445	74 443	85 940	80 593	83 264
Bulgaria	1 211	837	2 170	5 253	6 515	7 874	6 827	6 996
Cyprus	482	2 004	4 068	7 135	8 765	11 970	9 876	11 549
Czechoslovakia (former)	-	2 673						
Czech Republic	-	-	6 821	13 900	16 835	21 744	20 248	21 654

For sources and notes, see end of table.

			Imports - Importations Millions de dollars					Régions, pays ou territoires
1980	1990	2000	2006	2007	2008	2009	2010	
74	73	328	563	(e)591	(e)615	(e)636	(e)665	Myanmar
1 439	1 761	5 247	6 307	7 517	8 557	8 900	11 297	Philippines
2 912	8 642	30 095	65 175	74 700	87 545	79 504	96 463	Singapour
1 644	6 309	15 460	33 015	38 425	46 263	37 756	45 855	Thaïlande
–	–	–	(e)232	(e)325	(e)488	(e)552	(e)477	Timor-Leste
..	343	3 252	5 108	6 785	7 956	8 187	9 921	Viet Nam
45 879	*44 663*	*67 733*	*131 287*	*163 809*	*199 309*	*188 572*	*199 404*	*Asie occidentale*
474	474	757	1 605	1 701	2 030	1 741	1 905	Bahreïn
–	–	–	5 490	4 866	7 969	–	–	Iraq
1 004	1 268	1 722	2 971	3 517	4 127	3 818	4 271	Jordanie
3 067	3 359	4 921	10 638	13 344	15 777	13 850	13 617	Koweït
..	–	–	8 734	9 988	13 464	14 061	10 000	Liban
		548	560	741	836	861	836	Territoire palestinien occupé
518	719	1 759	3 896	5 095	5 878	5 488	6 525	Oman
–	–	1 640	6 957	7 318	7 222	5 918	6 163	Qatar
30 231	22 384	25 228	49 581	62 677	(b)75 234	74 991	76 772	Arabie saoudite
521	892	1 667	2 520	3 013	3 202	2 866	2 952	République arabe syrienne
569	3 071	9 038	11 979	15 662	17 802	16 845	19 658	Turquie
–	–	8 600	(e)24 500	(e)34 021	(e)43 421	(e)37 428	(e)41 665	Émirats arabes unis
375	–	–	–	–	–	–	–	Yémen (anc. République arabe du)
130	–	–	–	–	–	–	–	Yémen (anc. démocratique)
–	683	809	1 855	1 867	2 348	2 133	2 463	Yémen
495	**863**	**1 372**	**4 124**	**4 800**	**5 031**	**4 647**	**5 839**	**Économies en développement : Océanie**
124	257	329	521	520	597	451	(e)475	Fidji
..	..	..	546	617	719	713	637	Polynésie française
9	19	(e)23	(e)32	(e)47	–	–	–	Kiribati
–	34	60	63	64	72	66	..	Micronésie (États fédérés de)
..	..	..	1 130	1 320	1 390	1 102	1 384	Nouvelle-Calédonie
302	403	772	1 596	1 945	1 843	1 932	2 844	Papouasie-Nouvelle-Guinée
15	25	–	57	71	69	78	87	Samoa
28	79	73	68	87	116	99	(e)184	Îles Salomon
6	23	(e)19	39	43	55	49	(e)45	Tonga
–	24	70	71	76	(e)111	(e)107	(e)129	Vanuatu
5 229	**15 041**	**27 501**	**82 343**	**106 495**	**134 046**	**109 513**	**125 525**	**Économies en transition (1)**
18	29	429	1 585	1 926	2 379	2 231	2 010	Albanie
–	–	193	615	793	973	858	1 004	Arménie
–	–	485	2 863	3 379	3 889	3 358	3 798	Azerbaïdjan
–	–	536	1 663	2 034	2 630	2 116	2 885	Bélarus
–	–	263	467	579	692	647	588	Bosnie-Herzégovine
–	–	1 822	3 102	3 906	4 580	3 853	3 452	Croatie
–	–	295	727	933	1 239	974	1 085	Géorgie
–	–	1 850	8 760	11 730	11 119	10 045	11 298	Kazakhstan
–	–	148	460	604	993	867	924	Kirghizistan
–	–	–	–	–	514	411	398	Monténégro
–	–	202	488	650	839	713	770	République de Moldova
–	–	16 230	44 716	58 145	75 468	61 429	73 540	Fédération de Russie
–	–	293	(e)2 391	3 826	–	–	–	Serbie-et-Monténégro
–	–	–	–	–	4 296	3 456	3 526	Serbie
5 211	15 012	–	–	–	–	–	–	RSF de Yougoslavie (anc.)
–	–	(e)57	394	592	456	291	393	Tadjikistan
–	–	268	573	784	1 001	823	838	L'ERY de Macédoine
–	–	3 004	9 164	11 741	16 154	11 505	12 202	Ukraine
–	–	521	828	390	(e)427	(e)415	(e)600	Ouzbékistan
51 636	**145 353**	**267 305**	**409 072**	**449 568**	**485 445**	**447 967**	**494 291**	**Économies développées : Amérique**
..	..	..	862	1 105	1 042	984	1 007	Bermudes
10 666	28 303	44 118	72 760	82 788	88 791	79 268	91 255	Canada
40 970	117 050	223 187	335 450	365 674	395 613	367 715	402 029	États-Unis
34 670	**89 203**	**128 561**	**150 090**	**167 730**	**188 174**	**165 422**	**175 627**	**Économies développées : Asie**
2 310	4 921	11 901	14 654	17 577	19 909	17 136	18 056	Israël
32 360	84 281	116 660	135 436	150 154	168 264	148 287	157 571	Japon
201 576	**408 755**	**669 634**	**1 243 539**	**1 474 879**	**1 643 837**	**1 431 308**	**1 448 055**	**Économies développées : Europe**
6 204	14 197	16 462	33 442	38 976	42 697	36 823	36 869	Autriche
12 827	26 581	32 350	53 175	68 615	82 957	71 710	78 454	Belgique (2)
549	600	1 666	4 094	4 909	5 927	5 025	4 477	Bulgarie
268	674	1 585	2 932	3 741	4 965	4 124	4 171	Chypre
–	2 472	–	–	–	–	–	–	Tchécoslovaquie (anc.)
–	–	5 408	11 904	14 385	17 877	18 830	18 202	République tchèque

Pour les sources et les notes, se reporter à la fin du tableau.

5.1.1 Value of exports and imports of services of countries and geographical regions

Region, country or territory	Exports - Exportations Millions of dollars							
	1980	1990	2000	2006	2007	2008	2009	2010
Denmark	5 862	12 830	23 940	52 170	61 389	72 570	55 206	59 890
Estonia	–	–	1 501	3 601	4 372	5 145	4 388	4 507
Finland	2 733	4 649	7 684	17 494	23 235	31 922	27 482	24 589
France	43 506	76 457	80 603	128 574	149 234	166 540	142 967	143 712
Germany (former Federal Rep.)	32 817	–	–	–	–	–	–	–
Germany	–	62 662	86 532	194 175	228 299	260 907	230 379	237 574
Greece	3 947	6 560	19 239	35 762	43 080	50 473	37 789	37 465
Hungary	-	2 884	6 084	13 674	17 209	20 161	18 419	19 051
Iceland	380	560	1 041	1 869	2 274	2 181	2 311	2 464
Ireland	1 381	3 445	16 889	71 332	90 085	99 591	92 667	97 109
Italy	19 192	49 666	56 447	98 774	111 031	116 296	95 286	98 313
Latvia	–	–	1 171	2 661	3 705	4 524	3 813	3 673
Lithuania	–	–	1 056	3 612	4 012	4 842	3 691	4 126
Luxembourg	–	–	20 301	60 637	64 820	69 217	60 300	67 481
Malta	481	752	1 094	1 650	2 104	1 870	2 500	2 985
Netherlands	17 150	29 302	52 395	96 620	111 593	125 880	113 808	95 352
Norway	8 615	12 765	17 345	33 271	40 430	45 055	38 481	39 734
Poland	2 018	3 200	10 415	20 519	28 701	35 411	28 725	32 485
Portugal	2 006	5 096	9 057	18 388	23 214	26 169	22 635	23 277
Romania	1 063	610	1 752	6 913	9 434	12 841	9 808	8 574
Slovakia	–	–	2 291	5 412	7 026	8 471	6 282	5 839
Slovenia	–	–	1 879	4 482	5 673	7 387	5 975	5 778
Spain	11 593	27 937	52 582	106 331	127 705	142 728	122 328	124 091
Sweden	7 489	13 726	21 614	49 596	63 209	70 945	59 096	64 376
Switzerland	6 888	19 001	30 707	54 864	65 933	77 298	76 305	83 632
United Kingdom	36 452	56 422	120 041	236 072	287 867	286 206	231 565	237 943
Developed economies: Oceania	**4 871**	**12 698**	**24 299**	**41 247**	**49 901**	**54 504**	**49 463**	**57 223**
Australia	3 862	10 204	19 894	33 088	40 496	45 240	41 589	48 490
New Zealand	1 009	2 494	4 405	8 159	9 406	9 264	7 873	8 733

Sources:
UNCTAD secretariat based on:
IMF, *Balance of Payments Statistics*
- EUROSTAT, online database
- OECD, online database
- IMF, *World Economic Outlook database*
- Economist Intelligence Unit, online database
- National sources

Notes:

(1)   Years 1990, 1991, 1992: the breaks in series result from the data reporting of the former Yugoslavia (SFR) and the countries that succeeded from it, as well as from the inclusion of the figures of the Russian Federation, while the former USSR data are not available.

(2)   Data from 1980 to 1994 inclusive refer to Belgium-Luxembourg Economic Union and from 1995 onwards to Belgium only. Year 2007: break in series

Imports - Importations Millions de dollars								Régions, pays ou territoires
1980	1990	2000	2006	2007	2008	2009	2010	
4 493	10 218	21 064	45 113	53 977	62 442	50 794	50 695	Danemark
		937	2 485	3 072	3 351	2 519	2 772	Estonie
2 555	7 627	9 405	18 594	22 613	30 377	25 636	21 740	Finlande
32 148	61 052	60 802	113 183	129 485	141 367	126 974	129 821	France
45 109								Allemagne (anc. Rép. fédérale d')
_	84 137	141 417	225 740	260 523	290 075	253 950	263 167	Allemagne
1 428	3 000	11 286	16 367	20 270	24 903	20 007	20 187	Grèce
(e)551	2 400	4 948	12 102	15 774	18 804	16 548	15 867	Hongrie
263	556	1 161	2 560	2 964	2 525	1 930	2 183	Islande
1 593	6 170	20 922	80 120	94 549	110 766	104 257	108 394	Irlande
16 249	46 795	55 395	100 361	121 672	129 480	108 978	110 119	Italie
_	_	697	1 989	2 702	3 179	2 258	2 199	Lettonie
..	..	677	2 357	3 381	4 324	2 973	2 829	Lituanie
..	..	13 581	29 813	37 606	40 029	35 567	37 343	Luxembourg
243	514	756	1 761	2 227	2 323	2 139	2 569	Malte
18 148	29 708	53 260	86 809	98 162	112 016	108 348	85 182	Pays-Bas
6 996	12 358	15 434	31 864	39 568	44 775	36 757	42 812	Norvège
2 023	2 847	9 001	19 798	24 031	30 250	23 973	29 004	Pologne
1 525	4 005	7 023	12 093	14 272	16 498	14 323	14 391	Portugal
1 045	787	1 999	6 901	8 875	11 861	10 214	9 418	Roumanie
_	_	1 853	4 747	6 495	9 159	8 013	6 809	Slovaquie
_	_	1 432	3 236	4 240	5 199	4 427	4 380	Slovénie
5 732	16 055	33 207	78 437	96 156	104 432	87 143	87 080	Espagne
7 018	17 058	23 966	39 432	47 488	54 050	45 516	48 458	Suède
4 885	11 202	14 646	26 750	31 747	35 370	38 136	39 612	Suisse
27 933	48 737	99 292	175 204	202 406	201 860	163 418	168 822	Royaume-Uni
8 411	**17 096**	**23 390**	**40 100**	**49 095**	**58 031**	**50 053**	**60 612**	**Économies développées : Océanie**
6 568	13 772	18 934	32 219	39 908	48 338	42 121	51 470	Australie
1 843	3 324	4 456	7 881	9 187	9 692	7 932	9 142	Nouvelle-Zélande

Sources :
Secrétariat de la CNUCED, sur la base de :
- FMI, *Statistiques de la balance des paiements*
- Eurostat, base de données en ligne
- OCDE, base de données en ligne
- FMI, *World Economic Outlook*, base de données
- Economist Intelligence Unit, base de données en ligne
- Sources nationales

Notes :

(1) Années 1990, 1991, 1992 : la rupture de série est due 1) aux chiffres reportés par l'ex Yougoslavie (RSF) et les pays qui lui ont succédé, 2) à l'inclusion des données de la Fédération de Russie, les données de l'ancienne URSS n'étant pas disponibles.
(2) Les données de 1980 à 1994 se réfèrent à l'Union belgo-luxembourgeoise et à partir de 1995 uniquement à la Belgique. Année 2007 : rupture de série.

5

5.1.2 Value of exports and imports of services of economic groupings

Economic grouping	Exports - Exportations Millions of dollars							
	1980	1990	2000	2006	2007	2008	2009	2010
DEVELOPING ECONOMIES	73 550	150 468	350 208	734 126	894 961	1 035 763	939 776	1 123 442
Developing economies excluding China	71 490	144 613	319 778	642 127	772 755	888 651	810 227	952 239
Developing economies excluding LDCs	70 323	146 408	343 099	720 764	878 461	1 015 432	919 885	1 101 475
High-income developing countries	38 948	86 754	205 075	382 815	459 733	522 816	476 783	554 951
Middle-income developing countries	22 396	46 433	106 427	238 491	298 745	345 788	314 676	377 927
Low-income developing countries	12 200	17 281	38 706	112 821	136 483	167 159	148 318	190 564
Heavily indebted poor countries (IMF)	3 637	4 367	6 753	13 937	17 249	20 370	19 492	20 306
Landlocked developing countries	1 408	2 340	6 950	15 459	19 388	23 621	22 126	24 339
Small island developing States	2 643	3 799	6 617	11 419	14 949	16 018	13 835	14 939
Least developed countries	*3 228*	*4 060*	*7 109*	*13 362*	*16 500*	*20 331*	*19 891*	*21 967*
Africa and Haiti	2 413	3 061	4 182	8 682	10 718	13 076	12 677	13 867
Asia	757	850	2 634	4 250	5 271	6 711	6 628	7 419
Islands	57	149	293	430	510	544	586	680
Major petroleum and gas exporters	*11 942*	*9 413*	*15 661*	*48 785*	*54 165*	*54 418*	*52 258*	*53 853*
Africa	1 899	1 688	3 230	5 551	4 695	6 291	6 211	7 746
America	693	1 183	1 182	1 544	1 767	2 162	2 005	1 724
Asia	9 349	6 542	11 249	41 690	47 703	45 965	44 042	44 383
Major exporters of manufactured goods	*26 967*	*72 042*	*192 412*	*379 991*	*473 740*	*548 439*	*489 165*	*598 188*
America	4 591	8 094	13 755	16 392	17 609	18 480	15 423	15 435
Asia	22 376	63 948	178 656	363 599	456 131	529 959	473 742	582 752
Emerging economies	*24 707*	*57 154*	*141 624*	*253 233*	*313 244*	*366 113*	*324 271*	*378 773*
America	10 182	16 948	33 828	54 368	64 041	75 558	66 488	75 224
Asia	14 526	40 206	107 796	198 865	249 203	290 555	257 782	303 549
Newly industrialized Asian countries	*22 143*	*63 825*	*156 817*	*289 564*	*356 178*	*407 811*	*368 362*	*441 558*
First tier	17 691	47 815	120 417	225 096	274 106	319 143	285 483	343 530
Second tier	4 453	16 010	36 400	64 468	82 072	88 668	82 879	98 028
Developing economies: Africa	13 559	21 626	33 218	66 841	78 706	89 684	81 892	90 736
Northern Africa excluding Sudan	4 883	10 283	16 733	33 270	39 971	48 040	42 724	46 184
Sub-Saharan Africa	8 675	11 343	16 484	33 571	38 735	41 644	39 167	44 553
Sub-Saharan Africa excluding South Africa	6 213	7 936	11 439	21 357	24 917	28 839	27 147	30 549
Developing economies: America	18 615	31 561	62 507	97 945	113 632	129 374	117 245	129 217
Central America and Greater Caribbean Islands excluding Puerto Rico	6 996	13 495	28 582	41 428	46 532	49 945	44 651	46 800
Central America and Greater Caribbean Islands excluding Mexico and Puerto Rico	2 405	5 401	14 827	25 036	28 923	31 466	29 227	31 365
South America and Central America	15 104	24 087	46 550	74 328	87 284	102 128	92 196	103 138
South America excluding Brazil	7 171	9 532	17 009	27 514	32 793	38 663	35 351	40 569
Developing economies: Asia	41 072	96 473	253 511	566 311	699 214	813 074	737 672	900 376
Eastern and South-Eastern Asia excluding China	22 639	65 894	164 627	308 186	380 075	436 390	396 635	481 936
Southern Asia excluding India	2 089	3 030	5 390	14 298	15 877	17 913	16 624	20 794

Sources:
UNCTAD secretariat based on:
- IMF, *Balance of Payments Statistics*
- EUROSTAT, online database
- OECD, online database
- IMF, *World Economic Outlook database*
- Economist Intelligence Unit, online database
- National sources

1980	1990	2000	2006	2007	2008	2009	2010	Groupements économiques
			Imports - Importations Millions de dollars					
142 723	**198 058**	**422 347**	**826 491**	**999 572**	**1 187 155**	**1 087 070**	**1 281 723**	**ÉCONOMIES EN DÉVELOPPEMENT**
140 493	193 706	386 316	725 658	869 461	1 028 231	928 123	1 088 402	Économies en développement sans la Chine
135 214	188 005	408 237	792 734	955 201	1 127 125	1 031 993	1 223 619	Économies en développement sans les PMA
76 346	110 340	229 785	410 928	489 706	561 988	509 112	580 869	Pays en développement à revenu élevé
36 168	49 817	119 815	260 188	321 501	387 819	366 047	438 789	Pays en développement à revenu intermédiaire
30 209	37 900	72 746	155 376	188 365	207 040	211 910	262 065	Pays en développement à revenu faible
9 090	10 685	12 377	28 754	35 369	40 456	38 019	41 764	Pays pauvres très endettés (FMI)
3 690	4 932	10 225	30 072	37 324	42 700	44 180	44 703	Pays en développement sans littoral
2 223	3 790	6 454	10 337	11 639	12 113	10 826	12 381	Petits États insulaires en développement
7 509	**10 053**	**14 110**	**33 757**	**44 371**	**60 029**	**55 077**	**58 103**	**Pays les moins avancés**
5 980	8 158	10 508	26 425	35 984	49 752	45 127	46 511	Afrique et Haïti
1 447	1 696	3 374	6 800	7 687	9 334	8 957	10 536	Asie
82	199	227	532	699	943	993	1 056	Îles
62 793	**49 569**	**68 331**	**149 068**	**191 539**	**245 079**	**226 291**	**238 572**	**Principaux exportateurs de pétrole et de gaz**
10 823	6 490	9 303	28 795	40 421	61 320	54 609	56 618	Afrique
4 253	2 534	4 435	5 954	8 719	10 516	9 622	10 581	Amérique
47 716	40 546	54 593	114 319	142 399	173 243	162 060	171 373	Asie
27 325	**73 047**	**200 591**	**386 385**	**458 595**	**526 476**	**481 181**	**577 571**	**Principaux exportateurs d'articles manufacturés**
6 514	10 323	17 360	22 833	24 064	25 535	23 591	25 594	Amérique
20 811	62 724	183 231	363 552	434 531	500 941	457 590	551 077	Asie
31 847	**69 641**	**172 835**	**297 990**	**348 236**	**398 562**	**352 350**	**427 885**	**Économies émergentes**
17 636	24 206	50 332	72 332	86 407	103 607	97 647	120 098	Amérique
14 211	45 435	122 503	225 659	261 829	294 955	254 704	307 787	Asie
24 616	**66 189**	**168 085**	**290 420**	**336 266**	**378 819**	**330 439**	**396 039**	**Économies nouvellement industrialisées d'Asie**
13 980	46 578	114 993	206 053	237 326	265 484	233 416	279 106	Première génération
10 636	19 611	53 092	84 367	98 939	113 335	97 023	116 933	Deuxième génération
29 353	**30 017**	**41 180**	**94 209**	**120 094**	**152 166**	**136 334**	**147 479**	**Économies en développement : Afrique**
9 380	8 785	13 927	25 857	32 005	43 105	40 552	41 286	Afrique septentrionale sans le Soudan
19 974	21 233	27 253	68 353	88 088	109 060	95 782	106 194	Afrique subsaharienne
16 679	17 495	21 430	54 111	71 607	92 085	80 974	87 737	Afrique subsaharienne sans l'Afrique du Sud
29 679	**37 111**	**74 553**	**107 627**	**127 721**	**150 608**	**139 434**	**166 813**	**Économies en développement : Amérique**
9 391	14 462	26 556	36 287	39 278	42 774	38 069	41 981	Amérique centrale et Grandes Antilles sans Porto Rico
2 877	4 139	9 195	13 454	15 213	17 239	14 478	16 387	Amérique centrale et Grandes Antilles sans le Mexique et Porto Rico
27 079	33 003	66 862	96 821	116 173	138 119	128 747	155 687	Amérique du Sud et Amérique centrale
13 749	12 828	27 501	36 877	45 786	55 397	49 641	57 305	Amérique du Sud sans le Brésil
83 195	**130 066**	**305 242**	**620 531**	**746 957**	**879 350**	**806 655**	**961 590**	**Économies en développement : Asie**
24 867	67 354	174 145	301 875	351 200	396 699	347 879	418 328	Asie orientale et Asie du Sud-Est sans la Chine
7 238	7 608	8 145	27 841	31 031	36 070	30 208	33 696	Asie méridionale sans l'Inde

Sources :
Secrétariat de la CNUCED, sur la base de :
- FMI, *Statistiques de la balance des paiements*
- Eurostat, base de données en ligne
- OCDE, base de données en ligne
- FMI, *World Economic Outlook*, base de données
- Economist Intelligence Unit, base de données en ligne
- Sources nationales

5

5.1.3 Value of exports and imports of services of trade groups

Trade group	Exports - Exportations Millions of dollars							
	1980	1990	2000	2006	2007	2008	2009	2010
AFRICA								
CEMAC	897	837	1 096	1 753	2 192	2 404	2 215	2 274
CEPGL	164	289	135	556	602	1 013	1 042	1 081
COMESA	4 489	9 482	14 585	25 540	30 962	37 885	33 914	38 421
EAC	796	1 363	1 897	4 649	5 609	6 540	6 095	7 529
ECCAS	1 196	1 256	1 611	3 617	3 112	3 760	3 890	4 010
ECOWAS	2 584	2 950	3 930	7 139	7 591	9 168	8 200	8 815
MRU	694	809	593	1 287	1 373	1 698	1 380	1 283
SADC	3 877	5 592	8 870	19 014	22 115	21 000	20 620	23 720
UMA	2 547	4 339	6 977	17 222	20 109	23 220	21 341	22 537
WAEMU	1 191	1 585	1 241	2 541	3 258	3 711	3 297	3 383
AMERICA								
ANCOM	2 511	3 082	4 677	7 550	8 488	9 599	9 590	10 319
CACM	670	1 491	4 140	6 596	7 572	8 360	7 830	8 866
CARICOM	2 367	4 442	7 381	9 704	10 430	10 569	9 759	10 045
FTAA	72 538	195 074	392 193	560 993	650 609	713 059	661 973	730 900
LAIA	13 303	21 825	43 117	69 655	82 146	95 939	85 529	95 275
MERCOSUR	4 245	7 092	16 305	29 671	37 113	46 033	42 321	49 035
NAFTA	59 586	173 764	349 219	489 545	566 509	614 787	571 380	628 958
OAS	72 456	195 462	394 800	566 915	658 035	721 016	668 575	737 843
OECS	146	676	1 223	1 414	1 487	1 523	1 407	1 429
ASIA								
APTA	10 401	21 444	80 483	221 672	285 723	349 230	300 398	383 024
ASEAN	9 393	29 369	69 086	138 440	176 278	198 379	185 615	221 479
ECO	2 130	9 881	25 740	43 072	49 640	58 711	54 782	59 911
GCC	7 017	5 876	10 521	37 942	43 014	39 911	38 488	38 192
SAARC	4 329	7 219	20 693	77 315	95 460	117 219	102 653	136 956
EUROPE								
EFTA	15 783	32 325	49 093	90 004	108 637	124 534	117 097	125 830
EU	214 653	413 407	665 144	1 351 084	1 633 027	1 813 139	1 548 226	1 577 177
Euro area	157 635	320 226	470 080	946 715	1 134 152	1 276 021	1 110 829	1 118 409
OCEANIA								
MSG	283	708	857	1 335	1 452	1 639	1 211	1 403
INTERREGIONAL								
ACP	11 648	18 200	31 163	56 072	63 910	67 893	62 901	69 302
APEC	110 921	300 805	648 390	1 077 352	1 282 320	1 445 829	1 307 390	1 508 223
BSEC	6 943	16 055	58 273	120 177	146 928	185 911	153 253	159 690
CIS	–	–	17 266	52 888	67 274	86 255	70 581	78 522

Sources:
UNCTAD secretariat based on:
- IMF, *Balance of Payments Statistics*
- EUROSTAT, online database
- OECD, online database
- IMF, *World Economic Outlook database*
- Economist Intelligence Unit, online database
- National Sources

Imports - Importations Millions de dollars								Groupements commerciaux
1980	1990	2000	2006	2007	2008	2009	2010	
								AFRIQUE
2 209	3 253	3 534	8 459	10 847	11 270	9 946	11 062	CEMAC
723	1 017	482	1 296	2 069	2 926	2 513	3 037	CEPGL
8 444	9 844	14 109	25 684	31 772	39 411	34 970	37 107	COMESA
1 083	1 441	2 103	3 866	4 512	5 556	5 639	6 464	CAE
3 477	6 086	6 728	17 284	25 577	36 357	31 647	31 404	CEEAC
8 825	6 313	7 070	22 542	28 559	35 737	30 447	34 639	CEDEAO
1 887	2 068	1 625	3 894	4 126	4 641	4 083	4 910	UFM
6 503	9 438	13 266	29 425	38 906	50 490	44 543	48 163	SADC
7 164	5 134	6 582	14 694	18 248	26 259	27 233	28 527	UMA
2 863	3 513	2 588	5 094	6 196	7 259	6 808	7 260	UEMOA
								AMÉRIQUE
3 013	4 029	7 335	12 061	14 058	16 886	15 441	18 091	ANCOM
1 325	1 580	4 077	6 115	6 860	7 245	6 189	7 238	MCAC
2 119	2 702	4 720	6 790	7 389	7 301	6 417	6 638	CARICOM
80 721	181 184	339 706	512 720	573 020	630 898	583 260	656 959	ZLEA
24 662	31 032	61 891	89 575	107 763	129 441	120 972	146 293	ALADI
9 300	11 470	27 181	39 002	49 642	62 627	60 865	78 835	MERCOSUR
58 150	155 676	284 665	431 043	472 527	509 938	470 575	518 878	ALENA
80 547	181 565	339 790	512 947	573 281	631 775	583 532	657 002	OEA
82	328	586	000	896	918	802	785	OECO
								ASIE
9 828	22 149	92 056	234 457	291 380	350 358	326 225	411 670	ACAP
13 748	29 025	88 180	157 268	183 291	211 975	187 027	220 883	ANASE
6 813	9 106	17 553	51 154	61 337	69 182	60 430	67 843	ECO
37 879	30 571	42 904	97 177	124 156	149 562	139 415	146 648	CCG
4 996	9 735	25 037	73 280	86 757	106 676	95 454	133 475	SAARC
								EUROPE
12 144	24 116	31 240	61 174	74 278	82 670	76 823	84 638	AELE
189 432	384 639	638 393	1 182 365	1 400 601	1 561 167	1 354 486	1 363 417	UE
144 029	299 521	469 674	863 295	1 022 672	1 150 595	1 014 938	1 013 449	Zone euro
								OCÉANIE
466	763	1 244	2 256	2 638	2 668	2 589	3 632	MSG
								INTERRÉGIONAUX
22 979	25 826	35 473	80 650	101 749	123 827	108 841	120 623	ACP
128 532	331 892	657 220	1 062 325	1 220 637	1 378 137	1 246 150	1 432 145	CEAP
3 609	7 487	44 827	99 499	127 282	165 731	136 614	151 674	CEMN
–	–	24 130	73 499	94 541	119 343	97 119	113 628	CEI

Sources :
Secrétariat de la CNUCED, sur la base de :
- FMI, *Statistiques de la balance des paiements*
- Eurostat, base de données en ligne
- OCDE, base de données en ligne
- FMI, *World Economic Outlook*, base de données
- Economist Intelligence Unit, base de données en ligne
- Sources nationales

5

5.2 Trade in services by category
Leading exporters among
developing economies

5.2 Commerce des services par catégories
Principaux exportateurs parmi les économies
en développement

	2008			2009			2010		
Ranking based on 2009 exports Classement d'après les exportations de 2009	Millions of dollars Millions de dollars	As % of country's total En % du total du pays	Annual change in % Variation annuelle en %	Millions of dollars Millions de dollars	As % of country's total En % du total du pays	Annual change in % Variation annuelle en %	Millions of dollars Millions de dollars	As % of country's total En % du total du pays	Annual change in % Variation annuelle en %
TRANSPORT (1) - TRANSPORTS (1)									
Korea, Republic of - Corée, République de	44 768	49.4	33.4	28 693	39.0	-35.9	38 044	46.0	32.6
Singapore - Singapour	35 340	35.5	21.9	28 592	30.5	-19.1	32 738	29.2	14.5
China, Hong Kong SAR - Chine (RAS de Hong Kong)	28 886	31.3	12.9	23 868	30.1	18.0	32 777	30.3	38.4
China - Chine	38 418	26.1	22.0	23 660	18.2	-38.7	34 211	20.0	45.2
India - Inde	11 565	10.8	28.0	10 978	11.8	-5.1	13 248	10.7	20.7
Turkey - Turquie	7 761	22.3	18.8	7 549	22.8	-2.7	8 584	25.0	13.7
Egypt - Égypte	8 160	32.8	17.4	6 698	31.1	-17.9	7 817	32.8	16.7
China, Taiwan Province of - Province chinoise de Taiwan	9 191	25.0	4.3	6 342	20.0	-31.0	9 705	24.1	54.0
Thailand - Thaïlande	7 282	21.8	14.3	5 665	18.9	-22.2	5 916	17.4	4.4
Chile - Chili	6 503	60.1	24.7	4 774	55.3	-26.6	6 466	59.9	35.4
Malaysia - Malaisie	6 766	22.3	-5.3	4 408	15.3	-34.8	4 698	13.8	6.6
Brazil - Brésil	5 411	17.8	31.4	4 040	14.6	-25.3	4 931	15.5	22.1
Iran (Islamic Rep. of) - Iran (Rép. islamique d')	(e)3 904	(e)49.9	17.4	(e)3 873	(e)55.3	-0.8	..	..	..
Kuwait - Koweït	4 585	38.3	32.6	3 218	28.5	-29.8	3 191	41.4	-0.8
Panama	3 112	53.8	18.8	3 086	55.9	-0.8	3 332	54.7	8.0
Indonesia - Indonésie	2 800	18.4	26.9	2 439	18.5	-12.9	2 665	15.9	9.3
United Arab Emirates - Émirats arabes unis	(e)1 797	(e)18.7	32.0	(e)2 151	(e)21.2	19.7	..	..	..
Morocco - Maroc	2 500	18.6	37.5	2 099	17.0	-16.0	2 152	17.2	2.6
Viet Nam	2 356	33.6	25.4	2 062	35.8	-12.5	..	..	..
Saudi Arabia - Arabie saoudite	2 389	25.5	30.2	1 940	19.9	-18.8	2 031	19.0	4.7
TRAVEL (2) - VOYAGES (2)									
China - Chine	40 843	27.8	9.7	39 675	30.6	-2.9	45 814	26.8	15.5
Turkey - Turquie	21 862	62.7	18.4	21 165	64.0	-3.2	20 807	60.6	-1.7
China, Macao SAR - Chine (RAS de Macao)	16 948	95.4	26.4	18 142	96.4	7.0	27 790	96.9	53.2
China, Hong Kong SAR - Chine (RAS de Hong Kong)	15 307	16.6	11.3	16 408	19.0	7.2	22 766	21.1	38.7
Malaysia - Malaisie	15 293	50.4	8.9	15 798	54.9	3.3	17 855	52.6	13.0
Thailand - Thaïlande	18 163	54.4	9.0	15 665	52.3	-13.8	19 714	57.9	25.8
Mexico - Mexique	13 289	71.9	3.4	11 275	73.1	-15.2	11 872	76.9	5.3
India - Inde	11 832	11.0	10.3	11 136	12.0	-5.9	14 160	11.4	27.2
Egypt - Égypte	10 985	44.1	18.1	10 755	50.0	-2.1	12 453	52.3	15.8
Korea, Republic of - Corée, République de	9 774	10.8	59.2	9 819	13.3	0.5	9 765	11.8	-0.6
Singapore - Singapour	10 711	10.8	17.9	9 383	10.0	-12.4	14 181	12.6	51.1
South Africa - Afrique du Sud	7 956	62.1	-9.4	7 624	63.4	-4.2	9 085	64.9	19.2
United Arab Emirates - Émirats arabes unis	(e)7 162	(e)74.6	18.0	(e)7 352	(e)72.4	2.7	..	..	..
China, Taiwan Province of - Province chinoise de Taiwan	5 937	16.1	13.9	6 816	21.5	14.8	8 721	21.5	27.9
Lebanon - Liban	5 819	33.1	11.6	6 774	40.1	16.4	8 012	52.5	18.3
Morocco - Maroc	7 221	53.8	0.6	6 626	53.7	-8.2	6 702	53.4	1.1
Saudi Arabia - Arabie saoudite	5 909	63.1	-1.0	5 995	61.5	1.4	6 712	62.8	12.0
Indonesia - Indonésie	7 377	48.4	38.0	5 598	42.6	-24.1	6 958	41.5	24.3
Brazil - Brésil	5 785	19.0	16.8	5 305	19.1	-8.3	5 919	18.6	11.6
Dominican Republic - République dominicaine	4 166	84.1	2.5	4 051	81.9	-2.8	4 177	82.3	3.1
COMMUNICATIONS (3)									
Kuwait - Koweït	6 073	50.8	30.1	6 886	60.9	13.4	3 557	46.1	-48.3
India - Inde	2 478	2.3	5.6	1 484	1.6	-40.1	1 411	1.1	-4.9
China - Chine	1 570	1.1	33.6	1 198	0.9	-23.7	1 220	0.7	1.8
Singapore - Singapour	1 212	1.2	27.4	1 056	1.1	-12.8	1 347	1.2	27.6
Indonesia - Indonésie	1 096	7.2	-18.4	1 031	7.8	-6.0	1 126	6.7	9.2
China, Hong Kong SAR - Chine (RAS de Hong Kong)	882	1.0	1.9	894	1.0	1.4	..	..	..
Egypt - Égypte	1 611	6.5	112.8	842	3.9	-47.7	..	..	..
Bahrain - Bahreïn	700	18.7	5.0	740	20.3	5.8	799	19.8	8.0
Korea, Republic of - Corée, République de	724	0.8	32.3	725	1.0	0.2	742	0.9	2.4
Morocco - Maroc	641	4.8	59.5	679	5.5	6.1	713	5.7	4.9
Turkey - Turquie	722	2.1	42.9	630	1.9	-12.7	463	1.3	-26.6
Malaysia - Malaisie	602	2.0	-1.5	560	1.9	-7.0	..	..	..
Lebanon - Liban	329	1.9	31.8	483	2.9	46.5	379	2.5	-21.6
Kenya	437	13.4	32.8	378	13.1	-13.3	360	9.8	-5.0
Thailand - Thaïlande	416	1.2	79.1	365	1.2	-12.2	325	1.0	-11.0
Philippines	404	4.2	-21.9	354	3.2	-12.4	305	2.3	-13.8
Brazil - Brésil	466	1.5	69.1	353	1.3	-24.3	435	1.4	23.3
China, Taiwan Province of - Province chinoise de Taiwan	334	0.9	13.6	343	1.1	2.7	392	1.0	14.3
Argentina - Argentine	363	3.0	15.9	318	2.9	-12.5	335	2.5	5.5
Pakistan	91	2.1	-28.9	284	7.1	>200.0	242	3.8	-14.8

For sources and notes, see end of table.

Pour les sources et les notes, se reporter à la fin du tableau.

	2008			2009			2010		
Ranking based on 2009 exports Classement d'après les exportations de 2009	Millions of dollars Millions de dollars	As % of country's total En % du total du pays	Annual change in % Variation annuelle en %	Millions of dollars Millions de dollars	As % of country's total En % du total du pays	Annual change in % Variation annuelle en %	Millions of dollars Millions de dollars	As % of country's total En % du total du pays	Annual change in % Variation annuelle en %
CONSTRUCTION - BÂTIMENTS ET TRAVAUX PUBLICS									
Korea, Republic of - Corée, République de	13 686	15.1	41.1	14 553	19.8	6.3	11 842	14.3	-18.6
China - Chine	10 329	7.0	92.1	9 463	7.3	-8.4	14 495	8.5	53.2
Turkey - Turquie	1 141	3.2	00.5	1 274	3.9	11.6	1 120	3.3	-12.1
Singapore - Singapour	922	0.9	22.0	928	1.0	0.6	1 049	0.9	13.0
Malaysia - Malaisie	1 212	4.0	-10.8	909	3.2	-25.0	..	..	..
India - Inde	841	0.8	11.6	837	0.9	-0.5	524	0.4	-37.3
Egypt - Égypte	1 345	5.4	36.7	676	3.1	-49.8	..	..	..
Indonesia - Indonésie	667	4.4	45.3	586	4.5	-12.2	520	3.1	-11.2
Thailand - Thaïlande	614	1.8	18.5	472	1.6	-23.1	472	1.4	-0.1
Tunisia - Tunisie	297	4.9	54.4	382	6.9	28.5	479	8.2	25.2
China, Taiwan Province of - Province chinoise de Taiwan	235	0.6	18.1	294	0.9	25.1	355	0.9	20.7
Algeria - Algérie	312	8.9	4.7	185	6.2	-40.7	..	..	..
China, Hong Kong SAR - Chine (RAS de Hong Kong)	203	0.2	-41.4	139	0.2	-31.4	..	..	..
Philippines	90	0.9	-20.4	78	0.7	-13.3	121	0.9	55.1
Morocco - Maroc	61	0.5	..	49	0.4	-19.3	50	0.4	2.4
South Africa - Afrique du Sud	58	0.5	6.6	47	0.4	-19.7	63	0.4	35.0
Netherlands Antilles - Antilles néerlandaises	55	2.7	7.6	43	2.1	-21.0	..	..	..
Papua New Guinea - Papouasie-Nouvelle-Guinée	3	0.8	-62.8	40	21.5	>200.0	..	..	..
Sri Lanka	41	2.0	23.5	40	2.1	-2.0	42	1.7	5.8
New Caledonia - Nouvelle-Calédonie	28	4.8	77.9	35	7.0	24.6	37	6.8	7.1
COMPUTER AND INFORMATION SERVICES - INFORMATIQUE ET INFORMATION									
India - Inde	49 111	45.8	31.0	46 657	50.1	-5.0	56 701	45.8	21.5
China - Chine	6 252	4.2	43.9	6 512	5.0	4.2	9 256	5.4	42.1
Philippines	1 148	11.8	>200.0	1 748	15.9	52.3	2 151	10.2	23.1
Singapore - Singapour	1 552	1.6	54.5	1 585	1.7	2.1	1 790	1.6	12.9
Malaysia - Malaisie	1 025	3.4	20.9	1 454	5.1	41.8	..	..	..
Argentina - Argentine	894	7.4	36.5	1 059	9.6	18.5	1 248	9.4	17.9
Costa Rica	683	16.7	36.8	758	21.1	10.9	1 071	25.6	41.2
China, Hong Kong SAR - Chine (RAS de Hong Kong)	681	0.7	146.2	683	0.8	0.3	..	..	..
Morocco - Maroc	156	1.2	..	248	2.0	59.2	297	2.4	19.9
South Africa - Afrique du Sud	203	1.6	-8.8	245	2.0	20.7	290	2.1	18.3
Sri Lanka	230	11.5	31.3	245	12.9	6.5	265	10.7	8.2
Korea, Republic of - Corée, République de	304	0.3	-10.8	218	0.3	-28.2	235	0.3	7.7
Brazil - Brésil	189	0.6	17.2	209	0.8	10.8	210	0.7	0.3
Pakistan	187	4.4	48.4	182	4.6	-2.7	193	3.0	6.0
Egypt - Égypte	219	0.9	148.9	171	0.8	-22.0	..	..	..
Uruguay	180	7.9	17.0	145	6.8	-19.3	180	7.2	24.0
China, Taiwan Province of - Province chinoise de Taiwan	141	0.4	4.4	129	0.4	-8.5	218	0.5	69.0
Indonesia - Indonésie	178	1.2	26.2	126	1.0	-29.1	114	0.7	-9.3
Chile - Chili	96	0.9	17.1	84	1.0	-12.9	91	0.8	8.4
Tunisia - Tunisie	35	0.6	33.4	41	0.7	14.5	43	0.7	5.0
INSURANCE - ASSURANCES									
Singapore - Singapour	1 836	1.8	20.2	2 403	2.6	30.9	2 837	2.5	18.1
China - Chine	1 383	0.9	53.0	1 596	1.2	15.4	1 727	1.0	8.2
Mexico - Mexique	2 010	10.9	0.6	1 594	10.3	-20.7	1 831	11.9	14.9
India - Inde	1 561	1.5	3.7	1 528	1.6	-2.1	1 782	1.4	16.7
Bahrain - Bahreïn	916	24.5	11.8	851	23.3	-7.0	906	22.4	6.4
Turkey - Turquie	749	2.1	16.3	660	2.0	-11.8	713	2.1	8.0
China, Hong Kong SAR - Chine (RAS de Hong Kong)	547	0.6	17.0	496	0.6	-9.3	..	..	..
China, Taiwan Province of - Province chinoise de Taiwan	350	1.0	-14.4	473	1.5	35.1	430	1.1	-9.1
Malaysia - Malaisie	371	1.2	3.8	379	1.3	2.2	..	..	..
Brazil - Brésil	828	2.7	52.6	373	1.3	-55.0	416	1.3	11.6
Korea, Republic of - Corée, République de	466	0.5	12.4	340	0.5	-27.0	391	0.5	15.0
Saudi Arabia - Arabie saoudite	143	1.5	..	330	3.4	130.4	290	2.7	-12.2
Thailand - Thaïlande	428	1.3	37.0	306	1.0	-28.4	321	0.9	4.8
Peru - Pérou	227	6.2	-21.4	271	7.4	19.3	166	4.2	-38.7
Lebanon - Liban	266	1.5	0.6	242	1.4	-9.2	67	0.4	-72.2
Chile - Chili	258	2.4	15.2	233	2.7	-10.0	286	2.6	22.9
South Africa - Afrique du Sud	251	2.0	17.3	223	1.9	-11.1	273	1.9	22.3
Kuwait - Koweït	63	0.5	-4.9	187	1.7	195.1	57	0.7	-69.2
Morocco - Maroc	112	0.8	56.4	181	1.5	61.5	153	1.2	-15.5
Trinidad and Tobago - Trinité-et-Tobago	225	24.1	61.0	108	14.1	-52.0	..	..	..

For sources and notes, see end of table.

Pour les sources et les notes, se reporter à la fin du tableau.

5.2 Trade in services by category
Leading exporters among developing economies

5.2 Commerce des services par catégories
Principaux exportateurs parmi les économies en développement

	2008			2009			2010		
Ranking based on 2009 exports Classement d'après les exportations de 2009	Millions of dollars Millions de dollars	As % of country's total En % du total du pays	Annual change in % Variation annuelle en %	Millions of dollars Millions de dollars	As % of country's total En % du total du pays	Annual change in % Variation annuelle en %	Millions of dollars Millions de dollars	As % of country's total En % du total du pays	Annual change in % Variation annuelle en %
FINANCIAL SERVICES - SERVICES FINANCIERS									
China, Hong Kong SAR - Chine (RAS de Hong Kong)	11 995	13.0	-3.6	11 286	13.1	-5.9	..	..	..
Singapore - Singapour	10 020	10.1	4.4	9 340	10.0	-6.8	12 182	10.8	30.4
India - Inde	4 291	1.0	27.0	3 662	3.9	-14.7	6 003	4.9	63.9
Korea, Republic of - Corée, République de	3 785	4.2	-5.4	2 280	3.1	-39.8	2 847	6.1	10.0
Brazil - Brésil	1 238	4.1	13.5	1 570	5.7	26.9	2 073	6.5	32.0
Saudi Arabia - Arabie saoudite	432	4.6	..	901	9.2	108.7	951	8.9	5.5
China, Taiwan Province of - Province chinoise de Taiwan	1 116	3.1	-12.0	727	2.3	-36.6	847	2.1	16.5
South Africa - Afrique du Sud	803	6.0	8.1	715	6.0	-11.2	827	5.9	15.7
Turkey - Turquie	838	2.4	112.3	462	1.4	-44.8	482	1.4	4.2
China - Chine	315	0.2	36.6	437	0.3	38.8	1 331	0.8	>200.0
Panama	434	7.5	28.4	303	5.5	-30.1	429	7.0	41.5
Egypt - Égypte	269	1.1	>200.0	196	0.9	-27.3	..	..	..
Algeria - Algérie	143	4.1	62.5	184	6.2	28.7	..	..	..
Indonesia - Indonésie	304	2.0	5.4	178	1.4	-41.5	332	2.0	86.5
Lebanon - Liban	100	0.6	-5.3	115	0.7	15.1	2 114	13.8	>200.0
Kuwait - Koweït	385	3.2	>200.0	105	0.9	-72.8	106	1.4	1.4
Pakistan	55	1.3	-17.9	101	2.5	83.6	50	0.8	-50.5
Malaysia - Malaisie	87	0.3	-1.6	90	0.3	3.9	..	..	..
Uruguay	83	3.6	17.0	89	4.2	7.4	121	4.9	36.0
Syrian Arab Republic - République arabe syrienne	100	2.5	61.3	89	1.9	-11.0	..	..	..
ROYALTIES AND LICENSE FEES - REDEVANCES ET DROITS DE LICENCE									
Korea, Republic of - Corée, République de	2 382	2.6	37.3	3 199	4.3	34.3	3 146	3.8	-1.7
Singapore - Singapour	1 355	1.4	10.9	1 352	1.4	-0.2	1 867	1.7	38.0
Mexico - Mexique	440	2.4	>200.0	656	4.3	49.2	..	..	..
Brazil - Brésil	465	1.5	45.7	434	1.6	-6.8	397	1.2	-8.4
China - Chine	571	0.4	66.5	429	0.3	-24.7	830	0.5	93.4
China, Hong Kong SAR - Chine (RAS de Hong Kong)	380	0.4	6.1	383	0.4	1.0	..	..	..
Paraguay	282	24.5	-1.7	295	21.0	4.6	307	20.4	4.1
Malaysia - Malaisie	199	0.7	>200.0	266	0.9	33.4	..	..	..
China, Taiwan Province of - Province chinoise de Taiwan	191	0.5	-13.2	242	1	26.7	414	1.0	71.1
India - Inde	148	0.1	-9.4	193	0.2	30.3	129	0.1	-33.1
Thailand - Thaïlande	101	0.3	86.1	145	0.5	44.1	153	0.4	5.5
Argentina - Argentine	105	0.9	-1.3	108	1.0	3.4	135	1.0	24.6
Chile - Chili	64	0.6	3.8	59	0.7	-7.0	64	0.6	8.3
South Africa - Afrique du Sud	54	0.4	1.6	48	0.4	-11.2	59	0.4	24.0
Colombia - Colombie	30	0.7	77.1	39	0.9	31.4	56	1.3	44.7
Indonesia - Indonésie	27	0.2	-11.3	38	0.3	40.1	60	0.4	56.2
Yemen - Yémen	9	0.7	..	33	2.7	>200.0	..	..	..
Tunisia - Tunisie	30	0.5	1.2	25	0.5	-15.5	25	0.4	-0.9
Kenya	33	1.0	42.5	19	0.7	-40.7	54	1.5	176.1
Lesotho	20	45.5	-3.7	18	41.8	-6.8	..	..	..
OTHER BUSINESS SERVICES (4) - AUTRES SERVICES AUX ENTREPRISES (4)									
China - Chine	46 349	31.5	14.7	45 623	35.2	-1.6	61 242	35.8	34.2
Singapore - Singapour	36 035	36.2	14.1	38 697	41.3	7.4	43 851	39.0	13.3
China, Hong Kong SAR - Chine (RAS de Hong Kong)	33 079	35.8	9.2	32 230	37.3	-2.6	..	..	..
China, Taiwan Province of - Province chinoise de Taiwan	18 925	51.4	15.8	15 955	50.2	-15.7	19 023	47.0	19.2
India - Inde	24 211	22.6	17.0	15 690	16.9	-35.2	28 985	23.4	84.7
Brazil - Brésil	14 331	47.1	29.5	13 867	50.0	-3.2	15 777	49.6	13.8
Korea, Republic of - Corée, République de	12 965	14.3	-10.1	12 088	16.4	-6.8	13 910	16.8	15.1
Lebanon - Liban	10 545	60.0	66.6	8 878	52.6	-15.8	3 107	20.4	-65.0
Thailand - Thaïlande	6 052	18.1	1.3	7 059	23.6	16.6	6 906	20.3	-2.2
Philippines	4 182	43.0	71.5	5 186	47.1	24.0	6 372	48.1	22.9
Malaysia - Malaisie	3 857	12.7	-4.7	4 218	14.7	9.4	..	..	..
Argentina - Argentine	3 690	30.4	31.0	3 531	31.9	-4.3	3 910	29.6	10.7
Indonesia - Indonésie	2 184	14.3	0.0	2 527	19.2	15.7	4 309	25.7	70.5
Morocco - Maroc	2 016	15.0	0.1	1 920	15.6	-4.8	1 994	15.9	3.9
Egypt - Égypte	1 789	7.2	49.4	1 787	8.3	-0.1	..	..	..
Chile - Chili	1 759	16.3	15.9	1 499	17.4	-14.8	1 865	17.3	24.5
Algeria - Algérie	1 376	39.4	41.0	1 210	40.5	-12.1	..	..	..
South Africa - Afrique du Sud	1 201	9.4	2.1	1 084	9.0	-9.7	1 115	8.0	2.9
Netherlands Antilles - Antilles néerlandaises	612	29.8	-16.1	661	32.5	7.9	..	..	..
Costa Rica	662	16.2	6.8	642	17.9	-3.0	688	16.5	7.2

For sources and notes, see end of table.

Pour les sources et les notes, se reporter à la fin du tableau.

5.2 Trade in services by category
Leading exporters among
developing economies

5.2 Commerce des services par catégories
Principaux exportateurs parmi les économies
en développement

Ranking based on 2009 exports Classement d'après les exportations de 2009	2008			2009			2010		
	Millions of dollars Millions de dollars	As % of country's total En % du total du pays	Annual change in % Variation annuelle en %	Millions of dollars Millions de dollars	As % of country's total En % du total du pays	Annual change in % Variation annuelle en %	Millions of dollars Millions de dollars	As % of country's total En % du total du pays	Annual change in % Variation annuelle en %
PERSONAL, CULTURAL AND RECREATIONAL SERVICES - **SERVICES PERSONNELS, CULTURELS ET RELATIFS AUX LOISIRS**									
Turkey - Turquie	1 219	3.5	25.7	771	2.3	-36.8	912	2.7	18.3
Malaysia - Malaisie	872	2.9	4.7	646	2.2	-25.9	..		
Korea, Republic of - Corée, République de	527	0.6	17.8	523	0.7	-0.8	635	0.8	21.4
India - Inde	707	0.7	39.0	468	0.5	-33.9	335	0.3	-28.5
Argentina - Argentine	486	4.0	54.7	336	3.0	-30.8	356	2.7	5.8
Singapore - Singapour	201	0.2	-14.1	179	0.2	-12.1	219	0.2	22.0
China, Hong Kong SAR - Chine (RAS de Hong Kong)	265	0.3	-2.4	135	0.2	-49.0	..	..	..
Egypt - Égypte	74	0.3	-19.4	103	0.5	38.6	..	..	..
China - Chine	418	0.3	32.1	97	0.1	-76.7	123	0.1	26.4
China, Taiwan Province of - Province chinoise de Taiwan	99	0.3	39.4	87	0.3	-12.1	98	0.2	12.6
Chile - Chili	111	1.0	30.9	82	0.9	-26.0	87	0.8	6.1
Brazil - Brésil	86	0.3	17.8	80	0.3	-6.9	108	0.3	34.6
Mexico - Mexique	87	0.5	-71.8	80	0.5	-8.1	80	0.5	0.0
Indonesia - Indonésie	77	0.5	40.5	75	0.6	-2.4	104	0.6	38.3
South Africa - Afrique du Sud	99	0.8	9.7	73	0.6	-26.5	67	0.5	-8.2
Morocco - Maroc	93	0.7	..	56	0.5	-39.6	37	0.3	-34.7
Ecuador - Équateur	47	3.6	6.7	54	4.4	15.0	..	..	..
Syrian Arab Republic - République arabe syrienne	40	1.0	33.3	43	0.9	7.6	..	..	..
Jamaica - Jamaïque	39	1.4	32.7	34	1.3	-10.7	37	1.4	8.2
Philippines	21	0.2	-4.5	34	0.3	61.9	41	0.3	20.6

Sources:
UNCTAD secretariat, based on:
- IMF, *Balance of Payments Statistics*
- Eurostat, online database
- OECD, Stat.Extracts online database
- IMF, *World Economic Outlook* , database
- Economist Intelligence Unit, online database
- WTO, Statistical database online
- National sources

Notes:

(1) Excludes freight insurance, which is included with insurance services.
(2) Includes goods and services acquired from an economy by non-resident travelers during visits shorter than one year.
(3) Postal, courier and telecommunications services between residents and non-residents.
(4) Includes merchanting and other trade-related services, operational leasing services, and miscellaneous business, professional and technical services.

Sources :
Secrétariat de la CNUCED, sur la base de :
- FMI, *Statistiques de la balance des paiements*
- Eurostat, base de données en ligne
- OCDE, base de données en ligne Stat.Extracts
- FMI, *World Economic Outlook* , base de données
- Economist Intelligence Unit, base de données en ligne
- OMC, base de données en ligne
- Sources nationales

Notes :

(1) Non-compris l'assurance du fret, incluse dans la rubrique des services d'assurance.
(2) Comprend les biens et services acquis dans une économie par les voyageurs non-résidents, au cours d'un séjour inférieur à un an.
(3) Services postaux (y compris les messageries) et services de télécommunication entre résidents et non-résidents.
(4) Y compris le négoce international et les autres services liés au commerce, la location-exploitation et divers services aux entreprises, spécialisés et techniques.

5

5.2 Trade in services by category
Leading importers among
developing economies

5.2 Commerce des services par catégories
Principaux importateurs parmi les économies
en développement

	2008			2009			2010		
Ranking based on 2009 imports Classement d'après les importations de 2009	Millions of dollars Millions de dollars	As % of country's total En % du total du pays	Annual change in % Variation annuelle en %	Millions of dollars Millions de dollars	As % of country's total En % du total du pays	Annual change in % Variation annuelle en %	Millions of dollars Millions de dollars	As % of country's total En % du total du pays	Annual change in % Variation annuelle en %
TRANSPORT (1) - TRANSPORTS (1)									
China - Chine	50 329	31.7	16.3	46 574	29.3	-7.5	63 257	32.7	35.8
India - Inde	42 665	48.3	38.4	35 449	43.7	-16.9	46 422	39.7	31.0
Singapore - Singapour	30 329	34.6	8.7	24 702	31.1	18.0	29 111	29.5	15.0
Korea, Republic of - Corée, République de	36 770	38.2	26.5	23 451	29.2	36.2	28 791	30.7	22.8
United Arab Emirates - Émirats arabes unis	(e)25 479	(e)58.7	33.4	(e)23 042	(e)61.6	-9.6	..	..	..
Thailand - Thaïlande	22 964	49.6	26.3	17 069	45.2	-25.7	22 578	49.2	32.3
China, Hong Kong SAR - Chine (RAS de Hong Kong)	15 651	33.0	10.7	12 247	27.9	-22.6	16 212	31.9	32.4
Saudi Arabia - Arabie saoudite	15 654	20.8	70.0	11 400	16.0	27.7	12 774	16.0	11.0
Malaysia - Malaisie	11 391	37.6	4.1	9 265	33.7	-18.7	11 876	35.2	28.2
Brazil - Brésil	10 405	22.1	22.4	7 966	17.0	-23.4	11 337	18.1	42.3
China, Taiwan Province of - Province chinoise de Taiwan	11 144	32.3	12.6	7 783	26.1	-30.2	9 610	25.4	23.5
Indonesia - Indonésie	13 895	49.2	46.2	6 522	28.5	-53.1	8 673	33.2	33.0
Turkey - Turquie	7 895	44.3	14.5	6 519	38.7	-17.4	8 306	42.3	27.4
Nigeria - Nigéria	(e)6 869	(e)28.9	37.9	6 091	32.6	-11.3	8 717	39.1	43.1
South Africa - Afrique du Sud	7 594	44.7	0.7	5 911	39.9	-22.2	7 088	38.4	19.9
Egypt - Égypte	7 321	41.6	21.7	5 701	40.9	-22.1	(e)6 504	(e)48.1	14.1
Iran (Islamic Rep. of) - Iran (Rép. islamique d')	(e)4 268	(e)24.1	15.4	(e)5 181	(e)32.8	21.4	..	..	..
Chile - Chili	6 765	57.4	28.3	4 892	48.5	-27.7	6 661	56.4	36.2
Kuwait - Koweït	5 562	35.3	56.4	4 570	33.0	-17.8	4 885	35.9	6.9
Viet Nam	4 974	62.5	21.9	4 273	52.2	-14.1	..	..	..
TRAVEL (2) - VOYAGES (2)									
China - Chine	36 157	22.8	21.4	43 702	27.5	20.9	54 880	28.4	25.6
Saudi Arabia - Arabie saoudite	15 129	20.1	-25.0	20 419	27.2	35.0	21 135	27.5	3.5
China, Hong Kong SAR - Chine (RAS de Hong Kong)	16 093	34.2	7.0	15 669	35.7	-2.6	17 803	35.0	13.6
Korea, Republic of - Corée, République de	19 065	19.8	-13.2	15 040	18.8	-21.1	17 669	18.8	17.5
Singapore - Singapour	15 197	17.4	15.3	15 010	18.9	-1.2	16 770	17.4	11.7
Brazil - Brésil	10 962	23.3	33.5	10 898	23.2	-0.6	16 422	26.2	50.7
United Arab Emirates - Émirats arabes unis	(e)13 288	(e)30.6	17.9	(e)10 347	(e)27.6	-22.1	..	..	..
India - Inde	9 606	10.9	16.9	9 310	11.5	-3.1	10 628	9.1	14.2
Iran (Islamic Rep. of) - Iran (Rép. islamique d')	(e)7 643	(e)43.1	12.2	(e)9 108	(e)57.6	19.2	..	..	..
China, Taiwan Province of - Province chinoise de Taiwan	9 116	26.4	0.5	7 800	26.2	-14.4	9 358	24.7	20.0
Mexico - Mexique	8 526	33.4	1.8	7 132	30.2	-16.4	7 283	28.5	2.1
Malaysia - Malaisie	6 709	22.2	19.8	6 508	23.7	-3.0	7 887	23.4	21.2
Kuwait - Koweït	7 570	48.0	14.1	6 443	46.5	-14.9	6 747	49.6	4.7
Indonesia - Indonésie	5 554	19.7	13.3	5 316	23.2	-4.3	6 395	24.5	20.3
Nigeria - Nigéria	(e)9 779	(e)41.2	75.0	5 012	26.8	-48.7	5 587	25.0	11.5
Argentina - Argentine	4 561	33.9	16.3	4 494	36.8	-1.5	4 878	34.7	8.5
Thailand - Thaïlande	5 003	10.8	-2.7	4 343	11.5	-13.2	5 054	11.0	16.4
South Africa - Afrique du Sud	4 404	25.9	12.2	4 151	28.0	-5.7	5 595	30.3	34.8
Turkey - Turquie	3 492	19.6	7.3	4 130	24.5	18.3	4 826	24.5	16.8
Lebanon - Liban	3 564	26.5	14.5	4 012	28.6	12.6	4 734	36.4	18.0
COMMUNICATIONS (3)									
Saudi Arabia - Arabie saoudite	1 269	1.7	58.6	1 857	2.5	46.3	2 197	2.9	18.3
Singapore - Singapour	1 466	1.7	12.5	1 380	1.7	-5.8	1 758	1.8	27.4
India - Inde	1 045	1.2	21.2	1 280	1.6	22.4	1 194	1.0	-6.7
Korea, Republic of - Corée, République de	1 149	1.2	25.8	1 227	1.5	6.8	1 317	1.4	7.3
China - Chine	1 510	1.0	39.6	1 210	0.8	-19.9	1 137	0.6	-6.0
China, Hong Kong SAR - Chine (RAS de Hong Kong)	1 188	2.5	10.0	1 152	2.6	-3.1	..	..	..
Malaysia - Malaisie	817	2.7	-4.7	772	2.8	-5.5	..	..	..
Angola	88	0.4	83.4	608	3.2	>200.0	..	..	..
Egypt - Égypte	785	4.5	66.7	475	3.4	-39.5	..	..	..
Indonesia - Indonésie	776	2.7	21.0	452	2.0	-41.7	547	2.1	20.8
China, Taiwan Province of - Province chinoise de Taiwan	413	1.2	-6.3	431	1.4	4.4	454	1.2	5.3
Argentina - Argentine	438	3.3	20.9	384	3.1	-12.4	381	2.7	-0.9
South Africa - Afrique du Sud	248	1.5	7.7	373	2.5	50.1	397	2.2	6.5
Nigeria - Nigéria	234	1.0	11.4	343	1.8	46.3	286	1.3	-16.8
Venezuela (Bolivarian Rep. of) - Venezuela (Rép. bolivarienne du)	293	2.8	25.8	331	3.4	13.0	369	3.5	11.5
Colombia - Colombie	202	2.8	0.5	279	4.0	37.9	210	2.6	-24.9
Turkey - Turquie	297	1.7	-2.5	246	1.5	-17.1	246	1.3	0.0
Lebanon - Liban	249	1.8	18.3	244	1.7	-2.1	291	2.2	19.4
Honduras	79	6.5	39.8	229	20.8	189.5	220	16.5	-4.2
Thailand - Thaïlande	219	0.5	30.0	219	0.6	0.1	219	0.5	-0.1

For sources and notes, see end of table.

Pour les sources et les notes, se reporter à la fin du tableau.

5.2   Trade in services by category
Leading importers among
developing economies

5.2   Commerce des services par catégories
Principaux importateurs parmi les économies
en développement

	2008			2009			2010		
Ranking based on 2009 imports Classement d'après les importations de 2009	Millions of dollars Millions de dollars	As % of country's total En % du total du pays	Annual change in % Variation annuelle en %	Millions of dollars Millions de dollars	As % of country's total En % du total du pays	Annual change in % Variation annuelle en %	Millions of dollars Millions de dollars	As % of country's total En % du total du pays	Annual change in % Variation annuelle en %
CONSTRUCTION - BÂTIMENTS ET TRAVAUX PUBLICS									
China - Chine	4 363	2.7	49.9	5 868	3.7	34.5	5 072	2.6	-13.6
Angola	5 007	22.6	90.1	4 676	24.4	-6.6	..	..	..
Saudi Arabia - Arabie saoudite	4 491	6.0	-29.0	3 288	4.4	-26.8	3 789	4.9	15.2
Algeria - Algérie	2 658	24.0	80.0	3 023	25.9	13.7	..	..	..
Korea, Republic of - Corée, République de	2 608	2.7	42.6	2 806	3.5	7.6	2 235	2.4	-20.4
Kuwait - Koweït	1 116	7.1	>200.0	1 158	8.4	3.8	47	0.3	-95.9
India - Inde	704	0.8	-3.3	1 079	1.3	53.3	991	0.8	-8.1
Malaysia - Malaisie	1 412	4.7	-16.4	1 034	3.8	-26.8	..	..	..
Indonesia - Indonésie	749	2.7	1.2	798	3.5	6.5	592	2.3	-25.8
Thailand - Thaïlande	786	1.7	22.8	782	2.1	-0.5	713	1.6	-8.8
Singapore - Singapour	347	0.4	35.5	442	0.6	27.5	500	0.5	13.0
Tunisia - Tunisie	329	9.8	22.1	339	11.4	2.8	399	11.9	17.9
Ethiopia - Éthiopie	291	12.1	11.0	288	12.9	-0.8	..	..	..
Yemen - Yémen	349	14.9	>200.0	267	12.5	-23.7	..	..	..
Egypt - Égypte	335	1.9	30.5	262	1.9	-21.8	..	..	..
Papua New Guinea - Papouasie-Nouvelle-Guinée	54	2.9	-2.4	221	11.5	>200.0	..	..	..
Turkey - Turquie	171	1.0	76.7	188	1.1	9.9	261	1.3	38.7
Zambia - Zambie	150	16.6	-46.9	119	16.9	-20.6	156	16.6	30.9
China, Hong Kong SAR - Chine (RAS de Hong Kong)	165	0.4	-44.2	119	0.3	-27.7	..	..	..
Haiti - Haïti	..	..	..	118	15.1				
COMPUTER AND INFORMATION SERVICES - INFORMATIQUE ET INFORMATION									
China - Chine	3 165	2.0	43.3	3 233	2.0	2.1	2 965	1.5	-8.3
Brazil - Brésil	2 787	5.9	22.6	2 795	6.0	0.3	3 505	5.6	25.4
India - Inde	3 787	4.3	5.7	2 266	2.8	-40.1	2 531	2.2	11.7
Malaysia - Malaisie	896	3.0	38.6	1 206	4.4	34.6	..	..	..
Singapore - Singapour	1 069	1.2	60.0	1 090	1.4	1.9	1 230	1.3	12.9
Indonesia - Indonésie	713	2.5	5.1	642	2.8	-10.0	585	2.2	-8.9
China, Hong Kong SAR - Chine (RAS de Hong Kong)	512	1.1	21.1	553	1.3	8.1	..	..	..
Argentina - Argentine	378	2.8	21.8	422	3.5	11.7	463	3.3	9.8
Korea, Republic of - Corée, République de	671	0.0	5.0	401	0.5	-29.9	477	0.5	19.0
China, Taiwan Province of - Province chinoise de Taiwan	284	0.8	10.5	330	1.1	16.2	435	1.1	31.8
Nigeria - Nigéria	222	0.9	11.4	186	1.0	-16.2	124	0.6	-33.3
South Africa - Afrique du Sud	194	1.1	13.7	184	1.2	-5.5	186	1.0	1.5
Peru - Pérou	169	3.0	38.3	153	3.2	-9.6	206	3.4	35.0
Pakistan	113	1.2	-7.4	138	2.1	22.1	168	2.4	21.7
Egypt - Égypte	79	0.4	118.0	134	1.0	70.6	..	..	..
Colombia - Colombie	118	1.6	64.4	109	1.5	-7.9	152	1.9	39.4
Philippines	80	0.9	29.0	91	1.0	13.8	109	1.0	19.8
Algeria - Algérie	80	0.7	37.9	81	0.7	1.3	..	..	..
Venezuela (Bolivarian Rep. of) - Venezuela (Rép. bolivarienne du)	79	0.8	-57.1	79	0.8	0.0	73	0.7	-7.6
Syrian Arab Republic - République arabe syrienne	85	2.7	-22.7	75	2.6	-11.8	..	..	..
INSURANCE - ASSURANCES									
China - Chine	12 743	8.0	19.5	11 309	7.1	-11.3	15 755	8.1	39.3
Mexico - Mexique	12 574	49.2	15.0	10 652	45.2	-15.3	11 210	43.8	5.2
India - Inde	4 332	4.9	35.8	4 021	5.0	-7.2	5 004	4.3	24.4
Singapore - Singapour	2 537	2.9	8.5	2 662	3.3	4.9	3 479	3.6	30.7
Thailand - Thaïlande	2 382	5.1	24.3	1 900	5.0	-20.2	2 418	5.3	27.3
Brazil - Brésil	1 665	3.5	27.3	1 815	3.9	9.0	1 529	2.4	-15.8
Saudi Arabia - Arabie saoudite	1 820	2.4	83.8	1 501	2.0	-17.6	1 669	2.2	11.2
Egypt - Égypte	1 584	9.0	23.6	1 355	9.7	-14.5	..	..	..
Indonesia - Indonésie	683	2.4	2.8	1 318	5.8	93.1	1 149	4.4	-12.9
Turkey - Turquie	1 430	8.0	-7.3	1 195	7.1	-16.4	1 198	6.1	0.2
Chile - Chili	646	5.5	27.9	886	8.8	37.1	510	4.3	-42.4
China, Taiwan Province of - Province chinoise de Taiwan	1 062	3.1	-9.0	881	3.0	-17.0	999	2.6	13.4
Korea, Republic of - Corée, République de	744	0.8	-25.6	735	0.9	-1.2	860	0.9	17.0
Malaysia - Malaisie	728	2.4	6.4	734	2.7	0.9	..	..	..
China, Hong Kong SAR - Chine (RAS de Hong Kong)	726	1.5	2.1	680	1.5	-6.3	..	..	..
Oman	590	10.0	5.1	624	11.4	5.7	715	11.0	14.6
Libyan Arab Jamahiriya - Jamahiriya arabe libyenne	242	5.6	27.4	594	11.7	145.1	..	..	..
Venezuela (Bolivarian Rep. of) - Venezuela (Rép. bolivarienne du)	532	5.1	25.2	448	4.7	-15.8	478	4.5	6.7
Peru - Pérou	379	6.6	21.7	447	9.3	18.0	491	8.2	9.9
Argentina - Argentine	449	3.3	19.8	442	3.6	-1.6	540	3.8	22.3

For sources and notes, see end of table.

Pour les sources et les notes, se reporter à la fin du tableau.

5.2 Trade in services by category
Leading importers among
developing economies

5.2 Commerce des services par catégories
Principaux importateurs parmi les économies
en développement

	2008			2009			2010		
Ranking based on 2009 imports Classement d'après les importations de 2009	Millions of dollars Millions de dollars	As % of country's total En % du total du pays	Annual change in % Variation annuelle en %	Millions of dollars Millions de dollars	As % of country's total En % du total du pays	Annual change in % Variation annuelle en %	Millions of dollars Millions de dollars	As % of country's total En % du total du pays	Annual change in % Variation annuelle en %
FINANCIAL SERVICES - SERVICES FINANCIERS									
India - Inde	3 545	4.0	9.5	3 759	4.6	6.0	6 787	5.8	80.6
China, Hong Kong SAR - Chine (RAS de Hong Kong)	3 137	6.7	11.7	3 305	7.5	5.4	..	..	..
Singapore - Singapour	2 549	2.9	12.1	2 034	2.0	28.2	8 000	3.8	19.5
Brazil - Brésil	1 145	2.4	41.9	1 612	3.4	40.8	1 679	2.7	4.2
Saudi Arabia - Arabie saoudite	1 509	2.0	-40.3	1 188	1.6	-21.3	1 034	1.3	-13.0
Turkey - Turquie	974	5.5	56.5	823	4.9	-15.5	724	3.7	-12.0
China - Chine	666	0.4	1.6	726	0.5	28.3	1 387	0.7	91.2
Korea, Republic of - Corée, République de	691	0.7	-0.8	708	0.9	2.5	860	0.8	21.4
Chile - Chili	536	4.5	45.8	531	5.3	-1.0	459	3.9	-13.5
Angola	537	2.4	>200.0	445	2.3	-17.2	..	..	..
Mexico - Mexique	116	0.5	-57.1	419	1.8	>200.0	548	2.1	30.7
Indonesia - Indonésie	342	1.2	-8.3	405	1.8	18.6	450	1.7	11.2
China, Taiwan Province of - Province chinoise de Taiwan	328	0.9	-58.1	329	1.1	0.3	197	0.5	-40.1
Malaysia - Malaisie	301	1.0	47.5	307	1.1	2.2	..	..	..
Panama	317	12.0	44.0	232	10.6	-26.9	355	12.8	53.0
Papua New Guinea - Papouasie-Nouvelle-Guinée	209	11.3	-10.4	160	8.3	-23.2	..	..	..
Syrian Arab Republic - République arabe syrienne	80	2.5	33.3	148	5.2	85.0	..	..	..
Kuwait - Koweït	171	1.1	>200.0	137	1.0	-20.0	84	0.6	-38.6
Philippines	82	1.0	-61.0	125	1.4	52.4	74	0.7	-40.8
Colombia - Colombie	144	2.0	15.1	124	1.8	-13.6	132	1.7	6.0
ROYALTIES AND LICENSE FEES - REDEVANCES ET DROITS DE LICENCE									
Singapore - Singapour	12 472	14.2	39.2	11 584	14.6	-7.1	15 857	16.4	36.9
China - Chine	10 320	6.5	26.0	11 065	7.0	7.2	13 040	6.7	17.8
Korea, Republic of - Corée, République de	5 656	5.9	10.2	7 188	9.0	27.1	8 965	9.5	24.7
China, Taiwan Province of - Province chinoise de Taiwan	3 015	8.7	17.1	3 424	11.5	13.6	4 943	13.1	44.4
Brazil - Brésil	2 697	5.7	19.4	2 512	5.3	-6.9	2 850	4.6	13.5
Thailand - Thaïlande	2 559	5.5	11.9	2 250	6.0	-12.1	3 084	6.7	37.1
India - Inde	1 529	1.7	31.8	1 860	2.3	21.7	2 438	2.1	31.0
China, Hong Kong SAR - Chine (RAS de Hong Kong)	1 610	3.4	7.0	1 700	3.9	5.5	..	..	..
South Africa - Afrique du Sud	1 676	9.9	5.0	1 658	11	-1.1	1 941	10.5	17.1
Indonesia - Indonésie	1 328	4.7	22.3	1 530	6.7	15.2	1 616	6.2	5.6
Argentina - Argentine	1 463	10.9	40.4	1 454	11.9	-0.7	1 538	10.9	5.8
Malaysia - Malaisie	1 268	4.2	7.0	1 133	4.1	-10.6	..	..	..
Turkey - Turquie	726	4.1	12.4	645	3.8	-11.1	816	4.2	26.4
Chile - Chili	513	4.4	14.7	461	4.6	-10.3	496	4.2	7.8
Philippines	382	4.5	-0.8	421	4.7	10.2	445	3.9	5.7
Venezuela (Bolivarian Rep. of) - Venezuela (Rép. bolivarienne du)	349	3.3	26.4	352	3.7	0.9	340	3.2	-3.4
Colombia - Colombie	263	3.6	40.0	299	4.2	13.5	362	4.5	21.4
Egypt - Égypte	322	1.8	33.7	285	2.0	-11.5	..	..	..
Nigeria - Nigéria	190	0.8	10.2	208	1.1	9.5	224	1.0	7.6
Peru - Pérou	159	2.8	43.3	152	3.2	-4.4	197	3.3	29.1
OTHER BUSINESS SERVICES (4) - AUTRES SERVICES AUX ENTREPRISES (4)									
China - Chine	38 597	24.3	26.8	34 144	21.5	-11.5	34 310	17.7	0.5
Korea, Republic of - Corée, République de	27 245	28.3	24.8	27 094	33.8	-0.6	30 746	32.7	13.5
India - Inde	20 309	23.0	10.4	21 036	26.0	3.6	39 678	34.0	88.6
Singapore - Singapour	21 059	24.1	21.5	19 987	25.1	-5.1	25 418	26.4	27.2
Brazil - Brésil	13 557	28.8	28.1	15 348	32.7	13.2	20 874	33.3	36.0
Thailand - Thaïlande	12 121	26.2	23.2	10 977	29.1	-9.4	11 533	25.2	5.1
China, Hong Kong SAR - Chine (RAS de Hong Kong)	7 517	16.0	14.0	8 293	18.9	10.3	..	..	..
China, Taiwan Province of - Province chinoise de Taiwan	8 368	24.2	-10.3	7 822	26.3	-6.5	10 668	28.2	36.4
Angola	9 197	41.5	55.7	7 680	40.1	-16.5	..	..	..
Lebanon - Liban	7 360	54.7	59.2	7 600	54.1	3.3	4 064	31.2	-46.5
Saudi Arabia - Arabie saoudite	9 700	12.9	63.7	7 383	9.8	-23.9	8 449	11.0	14.4
Indonesia - Indonésie	3 829	13.6	-28.2	5 525	24.1	44.3	5 456	20.9	-1.3
Malaysia - Malaisie	5 363	17.7	13.3	5 400	19.7	0.7	..	..	..
Algeria - Algérie	3 593	32.4	86.0	4 308	36.9	19.9	..	..	..
Nigeria - Nigéria	4 169	17.5	1.2	4 150	22.2	-0.4	4 477	20.1	7.9
China, Macao SAR - Chine (RAS de Macao)	4 159	73.1	33.4	3 365	68.2	-19.1	5 742	76.1	70.6
Egypt - Égypte	2 843	16.1	27.8	1 860	13.3	-34.6	..	..	..
Oman	1 839	31.3	-8.7	1 821	33.2	-1.0	2 107	32.3	15.7
Venezuela (Bolivarian Rep. of) - Venezuela (Rép. bolivarienne du)	1 655	15.7	146.3	1 669	17.3	0.8	2 055	19.4	23.1
Colombia - Colombie	1 171	16.2	17.8	1 596	22.7	36.3	1 706	21.4	6.9

For sources and notes, see end of table.

Pour les sources et les notes, se reporter à la fin du tableau.

5.2 Trade in services by category
Leading importers among developing economies

5.2 Commerce des services par catégories
Principaux importateurs parmi les économies en développement

Ranking based on 2009 imports / Classement d'après les importations de 2009	2008			2009			2010		
	Millions of dollars / Millions de dollars	As % of country's total / En % du total du pays	Annual change in % / Variation annuelle en %	Millions of dollars / Millions de dollars	As % of country's total / En % du total du pays	Annual change in % / Variation annuelle en %	Millions of dollars / Millions de dollars	As % of country's total / En % du total du pays	Annual change in % / Variation annuelle en %
PERSONAL, CULTURAL AND RECREATIONAL SERVICES - SERVICES PERSONNELS, CULTURELS ET RELATIFS AUX LOISIRS									
Brazil - Brésil	869	1.8	33.5	958	2.0	10.2	1 271	2.0	32.7
Malaysia - Malaisie	1 177	3.9	-39.1	897	3.3	-23.8	..		
Korea, Republic of - Corée, République de	901	0.9	-4.1	846	1.1	-5.1	1 016	1.1	20.1
Venezuela (Bolivarian Rep. of) - Venezuela (Rép. bolivarienne du)	452	4.3	37.0	652	6.8	44.2	1 092	10.3	67.5
Singapore - Singapour	291	0.0	-1.1	379	0.5	34.9	462	0.5	21.9
Argentina - Argentine	249	1.9	19.7	289	2.4	15.8	357	2.5	23.5
China - Chine	255	0.2	65.6	278	0.2	9.4	371	0.2	33.2
Mexico - Mexique	227	0.9	-12.3	272	1.2	19.7	272	1.1	0.0
India - Inde	325	0.4	92.4	268	0.3	-17.7	167	0.4	74.4
Turkey - Turquie	180	1.0	62.7	206	1.2	14.3	246	1.3	19.3
China, Taiwan Province of - Province chinoise de Taiwan	184	0.5	-10.2	196	0.7	6.5	215	0.6	9.7
Ecuador - Équateur	137	4.6	9.0	153	5.9	11.9	..	..	..
Angola	121	0.5	22.2	146	0.8	20.9	..	..	..
Indonesia - Indonésie	126	0.4	17.3	126	0.6	0.2	133	0.5	5.3
China, Hong Kong SAR - Chine (RAS de Hong Kong)	140	0.3	109.6	92	0.2	-34.6	..	..	..
Occupied Palestinian territory - Territoire palestinien occupé	67	8.0	28.8	82	9.5	21.3	..	..	..
Egypt - Égypte	80	0.5	172.1	66	0.5	-18.1	..	..	..
Mauritius - Maurice	40	2.1	0.8	55	3.5	40.1	63	3.2	13.1
Chile - Chili	47	0.4	11.6	51	0.5	9.4	55	0.5	7.8
Philippines	26	0.3	18.2	42	0.5	61.5	59	0.5	40.5

Sources:
UNCTAD secretariat, based on:
- IMF, *Balance of Payments Statistics*
- Eurostat, online database
- OECD, Stat.Extracts online database
- IMF, *World Economic Outlook*, database
- Economist Intelligence Unit, online database
- WTO, Statistical database online
- National sources

Notes:

(1) Excludes freight insurance, which is included with insurance services.
(2) Includes goods and services acquired from an economy by non-resident travelers during visits shorter than one year.
(3) Postal, courier and telecommunications services between residents and non-residents.
(4) Includes merchanting and other trade-related services, operational leasing services, and miscellaneous business, professional and technical services.

Sources :
Secrétariat de la CNUCED, sur la base de :
- FMI, *Statistiques de la balance des paiements*
- Eurostat, base de données en ligne
- OCDE, base de données en ligne Stat.Extracts
- FMI, *World Economic Outlook*, base de données
- Economist Intelligence Unit, base de données en ligne
- OMC, base de données en ligne
- Sources nationales

Notes :

(1) Non-compris l'assurance du fret, incluse dans la rubrique des services d'assurance.
(2) Comprend les biens et services acquis dans une économie par les voyageurs non-résidents, au cours d'un séjour inférieur à un an.
(3) Services postaux (y compris les messageries) et services de télécommunication entre résidents et non-résidents.
(4) Y compris le négoce international et les autres services liés au commerce, la location-exploitation et divers services aux entreprises, spécialisés et techniques.

5

5.3 World merchant fleet by flag of registration and type of ship of countries and geographical regions

5.3 Flotte marchande mondiale par pavillons d'immatriculation et par types de navires des pays et des régions géographiques

Region, country or territory / Régions pays ou territoires	Year / Année	Total fleet (thousands of DWT) / Flotte totale (milliers de TPL) (1)	As percentage of world total fleet — Oil tankers / Pétroliers	Bulk carriers / Vraquiers	General cargo / Navires de charge classique (2)	Container ships / Porte-conteneurs	Other types / Autres navires	As percentage of country/region total — Oil tankers / Pétroliers	Bulk carriers / Vraquiers	General cargo / Navires de charge classique (2)	Container ships / Porte-conteneurs	Other types / Autres navires
WORLD - MONDE	1990	629 976.0	100.0	100.0	100.0	100.0	100.0	37.4	35.5	15.9	3.5	7.6
	2000	793 770.8	100.0	100.0	100.0	100.0	100.0	35.7	34.6	12.8	8.0	9.0
	2010	1276 137.2	100.0	100.0	100.0	100.0	100.0	35.3	35.8	8.5	13.3	7.2
	2011	1395 742.7	100.0	100.0	100.0	100.0	100.0	35.0	35.0	7.8	13.3	6.9
DEVELOPING ECONOMIES - (3) ÉCONOMIES EN DÉVELOPPEMENT	1990	334 184.0	52.2	56.5	54.4	43.1	43.1	36.8	37.8	16.4	2.9	6.2
	2000	487 692.9	56.6	68.5	63.7	58.3	53.0	32.9	38.5	13.3	7.6	7.7
	2010	915 129.5	69.1	77.6	70.0	68.4	63.6	34.0	38.7	8.3	12.6	6.4
	2011	1014 955.1	00.0	79.9	70.0	70.0	64.1	33.6	41.0	7.5	12.8	6.1
TRANSITION ECONOMIES - ÉCONOMIES EN TRANSITION	1990	35 090.0	2.9	4.4	12.4	3.2	11.0	19.2	28.4	35.4	2.0	15.0
	2000	13 598.3	0.9	0.9	5.4	0.7	3.8	18.5	18.0	40.2	3.4	19.9
	2010	12 777.5	0.8	0.4	4.5	0.1	2.1	29.6	15.7	38.5	1.3	14.8
	2011	13 038.3	0.8	0.4	4.5	0.1	2.0	29.6	16.9	37.9	1.2	14.4
DEVELOPED ECONOMIES - (3) ÉCONOMIES DÉVELOPPÉES	1990	260 702.0	45.0	39.1	33.2	53.7	45.8	40.7	33.5	12.8	4.6	8.4
	2000	292 479.6	42.5	30.6	30.9	40.9	43.2	41.1	28.7	10.7	8.9	10.5
	2010	342 619.1	29.8	21.8	23.4	31.4	33.3	39.1	29.0	7.4	15.5	9.0
	2011	360 579.5	29.2	21.0	22.9	29.3	32.7	38.4	31.0	6.9	14.9	8.7
Developing economies: Africa - Économies en développement : Afrique	1990	97 139.0	23.1	12.7	6.1	5.4	14.6	56.0	29.3	6.4	1.2	7.2
	2000	91 552.9	14.7	9.7	6.5	9.5	15.1	45.3	29.2	7.2	6.6	11.8
	2010	150 731.7	14.8	8.0	5.4	20.2	8.4	44.1	24.3	3.9	22.6	5.2
	2011	175 681.6	15.0	9.5	6.0	21.7	7.9	40.5	28.7	3.7	22.7	4.3
Eastern Africa - Afrique orientale	1990	482.0	0.0	0.0	0.2	0.1	0.1	22.2	13.7	50.4	6.0	7.5
	2000	437.0	0.0	0.0	0.2	0.2	0.1	6.8	1.2	49.6	30.0	12.5
	2010	1 930.1	0.1	0.1	0.8	0.0	0.3	29.8	13.7	43.3	0.9	12.3
	2011	2 265.6	0.1	0.1	1.0	0.0	0.2	18.9	22.2	48.3	0.8	9.7
Comoros - Comores	1990	3.0	..	..	0.0	..	..	..	..	100.0	..	..
	2000	1.0	..	..	0.0	..	..	..	..	100.0	..	..
	2010	1 211.8	0.1	0.1	0.5	0.0	0.1	27.3	20.5	42.0	1.4	8.8
	2011	1 217.4	0.0	0.1	0.5	0.0	0.1	8.6	37.6	45.4	1.0	7.4
Djibouti	2000	4.9	..	..	0.0	..	0.0	..	..	90.8	..	9.2
	2010	0.7	..	..	..	..	0.0	..	..	..	..	100.0
	2011	0.7	0.0	0.0	0.0	0.0	0.0	0.0	0.0	0.0	0.0	100.0
Eritrea - Érythrée	2010	14.0	0.0	..	0.0	..	0.0	22.7	..	73.3	..	4.0
	2011	14.0	0.0	0.0	0.0	0.0	0.0	22.7	0.0	73.3	0.0	4.0
Ethiopia - Éthiopie	2000	119.7	0.0	..	0.1	..	..	3.0	..	97.0	..	..
	2010	150.0	..	..	0.1	..	..	..	..	100.0	..	..
	2011	146.5	0.0	0.0	0.1	0.0	0.0	0.0	0.0	100.0	0.0	0.0
Ethiopia (former) - Éthiopie (anc.)	1990	94.0	0.0	..	0.1	..	..	2.1	..	96.8	..	..
Kenya	1990	5.0	..	..	..	..	0.0	..	..	..	..	100.0
	2000	19.1	0.0	..	0.0	..	0.0	40.0	..	10.4	..	49.7
	2010	14.0	0.0	..	0.0	..	0.0	54.4	..	3.3	..	42.4
	2011	7.9	0.0	0.0	0.0	0.0	0.0	26.3	0.0	0.0	0.0	73.7
Madagascar	1990	88.0	0.0	..	0.1	..	0.0	8.0	..	80.7	..	11.4
	2000	45.1	0.0	..	0.0	..	0.0	37.5	..	47.5	..	15.0
	2010	30.6	0.0	..	0.0	..	0.0	22.9	..	53.6	..	23.5
	2011	12.2	0.0	0.0	0.0	0.0	0.0	1.5	0.0	65.2	0.0	33.3
Mauritius - Maurice	1990	216.0	0.0	0.0	0.0	0.1	0.0	42.6	30.6	11.1	13.4	2.3
	2000	189.7	..	0.0	0.0	0.2	0.0	..	2.8	21.4	69.0	6.8
	2010	63.8	..	..	0.0	..	0.1	..	..	18.3	..	81.7
	2011	66.3	0.0	0.0	0.0	0.0	0.1	0.8	0.0	17.7	0.0	81.5
Mozambique	1990	27.0	0.0	..	0.0	..	0.0	7.4	..	66.7	..	25.9
	2000	25.2	..	..	0.0	..	0.0	..	..	49.9	..	50.1
	2010	35.0	..	..	0.0	..	0.0	..	..	30.2	..	69.8
	2011	35.5	0.0	0.0	0.0	0.0	0.0	0.0	0.0	29.8	0.0	70.2
Seychelles	1990	2.0	..	..	0.0	..	..	..	..	100.0	..	..
	2000	22.7	..	..	0.0	..	0.0	..	..	50.9	..	49.1
	2010	288.0	0.0	..	0.1	..	0.0	69.6	..	19.4	..	10.9
	2011	286.7	0.0	0.0	0.1	0.0	0.0	69.9	0.0	19.5	0.0	10.5

For sources and notes, see end of table.

Pour les sources et les notes, se reporter à la fin du tableau.

5.3 World merchant fleet by flag of registration and type of ship of countries and geographical regions

5.3 Flotte marchande mondiale par pavillons d'immatriculation et par types de navires des pays et des régions géographiques

Region, country or territory / Régions pays ou territoires	Year / Année	Total fleet (thousands of DWT) / Flotte totale (milliers de TPL) (1)	As percentage of world total fleet / En pourcentage de la flotte mondiale					As percentage of the country or region total fleet / En pourcentage de la flotte totale du pays ou de la région				
			Oil tankers / Pétroliers	Bulk carriers / Vraquiers	General cargo / Navires de charge classique (2)	Container ships / Porte-conteneurs	Other types / Autres navires	Oil tankers / Pétroliers	Bulk carriers / Vraquiers	General cargo / Navires de charge classique (2)	Container ships / Porte-conteneurs	Other types / Autres navires
Somalia - Somalie	1990	14.0	..	..	0.0	..	0.0	..	..	71.4	..	28.6
	2000	6.8	0.0	..	0.0	..	0.0	22.6	..	59.5	..	17.9
	2010	5.5	0.0	..	0.0	..	0.0	27.9	..	25.9	..	46.3
	2011	6.9	0.0	0.0	0.0	0.0	0.0	0.0	0.0	64.0	0.0	36.0
Uganda - Ouganda	1990	1.0	..	..	..	..	0.0	..	..	..	..	100.0
	2000	2.7			0.0	..	..	..	..	100.0	..	..
United Republic of Tanzania - République-Unie de Tanzanie	1990	32.0	0.0	..	0.0	..	0.0	12.5	..	75.0	..	12.5
	2010	116.6	0.0	0.0	0.1	..	0.0	21.3	13.9	60.7	..	4.1
	2011	471.6	0.0	0.0	0.3	0.0	0.0	24.7	9.6	62.5	1.4	1.7
Middle Africa - Afrique centrale	*1000*	*203.0*	*0.0*	*..*	*0.2*	*..*	*0.1*	*0.7*	*..*	*82.8*	*..*	*16.5*
	2000	*143.3*	*0.0*	*..*	*0.1*	*0.0*	*0.1*	*4.9*	*..*	*65.6*	*1.0*	*28.5*
	2010	*132.2*	*0.0*	*0.0*	*0.0*	*..*	*0.1*	*11.7*	*5.2*	*32.7*	*..*	*50.3*
	2011	*145.7*	*0.0*	*0.0*	*0.0*	*0.0*	*0.1*	*18.6*	*4.7*	*28.7*	*0.0*	*48.0*
Angola	1990	122.0	0.0	..	0.1	..	0.0	1.6	..	86.9	..	11.5
	2000	69.7	0.0	..	0.0	..	0.0	6.5	..	69.1	..	24.4
	2010	52.2	0.0	..	0.0	..	0.0	15.7	..	29.3	..	55.0
	2011	58.4	0.0	0.0	0.0	0.0	0.0	17.4	0.0	24.3	0.0	58.3
Cameroon - Cameroun	1990	39.0	..	..	0.0	..	0.0	..	..	92.3	..	7.7
	2000	5.7	..	..	0.0	..	0.0	..	..	5.3	..	94.7
	2010	9.1	..	..	0.0	..	0.0	..	..	28.3	..	71.7
	2011	9.9	0.0	0.0	0.0	0.0	0.0	0.0	0.0	36.1	0.0	63.9
Congo	1990	11.0	..	..	..	..	0.0	..	..	..	..	100.0
	2000	0.7	..	..	..	..	0.0	..	..	..	..	100.0
	2010	0.7	..	..	..	..	0.0	..	..	..	..	100.0
	2011	0.7	0.0	0.0	0.0	0.0	0.0	0.0	0.0	0.0	0.0	100.0
Dem. Rep. of the Congo - Rép. dém. du Congo	1990	76.0	..	..	0.1	..	0.0	..	..	80.3	..	19.7
	2010	16.7	0.0	..	0.0	..	0.0	9.8	..	3.6	..	86.6
	2011	14.3	0.0	0.0	0.0	0.0	0.0	11.5	0.0	4.2	0.0	84.3
Equatorial Guinea - Guinée équatoriale	1990	7.0	..	..	0.0	..	..	..	..	100.0	..	..
	2000	19.4	..	..	0.0	..	0.0	..	..	53.1	..	46.9
	2010	16.9	0.0	..	0.0	..	0.0	23.2	..	13.1	..	63.7
	2011	35.4	0.0	0.0	0.0	0.0	0.0	39.0	0.0	30.7	0.0	30.4
Gabon	1990	29.0	..	..	0.0	..	0.0	..	..	89.7	..	10.3
	2000	11.6	0.0	..	0.0	..	0.0	6.4	..	61.0	..	32.6
	2010	8.9	0.0	..	0.0	..	0.0	8.4	..	50.6	..	41.0
	2011	9.5	0.0	0.0	0.0	0.0	0.0	5.1	0.0	56.7	0.0	38.2
Sao Tome and Principe - Sao Tomé-et-Principe	1990	1.0	..	..	..	..	0.0	..	..	..	..	100.0
	2000	36.3	0.0	..	0.0	0.0	0.0	4.8	..	77.6	4.1	13.5
	2010	27.8	0.0	0.0	0.0	..	0.0	3.6	24.8	64.9	..	6.7
	2011	17.5	0.0	0.0	0.0	0.0	0.0	5.8	39.4	40.8	0.0	14.0
Northern Africa - Afrique septentrionale	*1990*	*5 391.0*	*0.7*	*0.4*	*1.4*	*0.0*	*2.9*	*31.0*	*17.5*	*25.7*	*0.2*	*25.6*
	2000	*4 477.3*	*0.4*	*0.5*	*1.1*	*0.1*	*1.3*	*22.5*	*30.1*	*25.1*	*1.0*	*21.3*
	2010	*4 143.9*	*0.4*	*0.2*	*0.4*	*0.1*	*1.0*	*43.2*	*22.0*	*9.8*	*3.2*	*21.9*
	2011	*4 283.1*	*0.4*	*0.2*	*0.4*	*0.1*	*0.9*	*44.9*	*23.5*	*8.9*	*2.8*	*19.9*
Algeria - Algérie	1990	964.0	0.0	0.1	0.3	..	1.0	4.8	16.2	30.7	..	48.3
	2000	1 110.8	0.0	0.1	0.3	..	0.7	4.7	25.9	26.6	..	42.7
	2010	764.6	0.0	0.0	0.1	..	0.5	3.3	26.7	8.4	..	61.6
	2011	809.5	0.0	0.0	0.1	0.0	0.5	3.7	25.2	8.1	0.0	62.9
Egypt - Égypte	1990	1 796.0	0.2	0.3	0.7	..	0.2	25.9	31.5	37.4	..	5.3
	2000	2 092.6	0.1	0.4	0.5	0.0	0.2	17.4	49.5	26.0	0.8	6.3
	2010	1 517.9	0.1	0.1	0.2	0.0	0.2	24.7	44.7	16.0	4.2	10.4
	2011	1 595.9	0.1	0.1	0.2	0.0	0.2	24.3	48.6	13.1	4.0	10.0
Libyan Arab Jamahiriya - Jamahiriya arabe libyenne	1990	1 463.0	0.5	..	0.1	..	0.6	74.7	..	6.8	..	18.5
	2000	667.1	0.2	..	0.1	..	0.1	80.5	..	13.7	..	5.8
	2010	1 404.9	0.3	..	0.0	..	0.0	95.8	..	2.2	..	2.0
	2011	1 521.8	0.3	0.0	0.0	0.0	0.0	96.0	0.0	2.1	0.0	1.8

For sources and notes, see end of table.

Pour les sources et les notes, se reporter à la fin du tableau.

5.3 World merchant fleet by flag of registration and type of ship of countries and geographical regions

5.3 Flotte marchande mondiale par pavillons d'immatriculation et par types de navires des pays et des régions géographiques

Region, country or territory / Régions pays ou territoires	Year / Année	Total fleet (thousands of DWT) / Flotte totale (milliers de TPL) (1)	As percentage of world total fleet / En pourcentage de la flotte mondiale					As percentage of the country or region total fleet / En pourcentage de la flotte totale du pays ou de la région				
			Oil tankers / Pétroliers	Bulk carriers / Vraquiers	General cargo / Navires de charge classique (2)	Container ships / Porte-conteneurs	Other types / Autres navires	Oil tankers / Pétroliers	Bulk carriers / Vraquiers	General cargo / Navires de charge classique (2)	Container ships / Porte-conteneurs	Other types / Autres navires
Morocco - Maroc	1990	594.0	0.0	0.1	0.1	0.0	0.6	3.2	27.4	21.7	1.7	46.0
	2000	383.8	0.0	..	0.1	0.0	0.3	5.3	..	29.2	6.6	58.9
	2010	332.0	0.0	..	0.0	0.0	0.2	6.0	..	5.8	20.9	67.3
	2011	216.7	0.0	0.0	0.0	0.0	0.1	5.4	0.0	0.1	26.4	68.0
Sudan - Soudan	1990	127.0	0.0	..	0.1	..	0.0	0.8	..	98.4	..	0.8
	2000	53.2	0.0	..	0.1	..	0.0	2.3	..	96.2	..	1.5
	2010	27.6	..	..	0.0	..	0.0	..	..	95.0	..	5.0
	2011	16.4	0.0	0.0	..	..	0.0	0.0	0.0	94.8	0.0	5.2
Tunisia - Tunisie	1990	447.0	0.0	0.0	0.1	..	0.6	10.5	13.2	14.8	..	61.5
	2000	169.9	0.0	0.0	0.0	..	0.1	19.1	15.5	17.9	..	47.5
	2010	96.9	0.0	0.0	0.0	..	0.0	24.8	27.2	21.8	..	26.2
	2011	112.9	0.0	0.0	0.0	0.0	0.0	21.3	23.4	31.3	0.0	24.0
Southern Africa - Afrique australe	*1990*	*352.0*	*0.0*	*..*	*..*	*1.1*	*0.2*	*9.1*	*..*	*..*	*68.2*	*22.7*
	2000	*369.0*	*0.0*	*..*	*0.0*	*0.4*	*0.1*	*1.4*	*..*	*0.0*	*71.1*	*27.4*
	2010	*196.2*	*0.0*	*..*	*0.0*	*0.0*	*0.2*	*4.6*	*..*	*0.9*	*15.1*	*79.4*
	2011	*173.1*	*0.0*	*0.0*	*0.0*	*0.0*	*0.2*	*10.3*	*0.0*	*1.0*	*0.0*	*88.7*
Namibia - Namibie	2010	70.4	..	..	0.0	..	0.1	..	..	2.2	..	97.8
	2011	71.5	0.0	0.0	0.0	0.0	0.1	0.0	0.0	2.2	0.0	97.8
South Africa - Afrique du Sud	1990	352.0	0.0	..	..	1.1	0.2	9.1	..	..	68.2	22.7
	2000	369.0	0.0	..	0.0	0.4	0.1	1.4	..	0.0	71.1	27.4
	2010	125.9	0.0	..	0.0	0.0	0.1	7.1	..	0.1	23.6	69.2
	2011	101.6	0.0	0.0	0.0	0.0	0.1	17.5	0.0	0.1	0.0	82.3
Western Africa - Afrique occidentale	*1990*	*90 629.0*	*22.3*	*12.3*	*4.3*	*4.2*	*11.3*	*58.0*	*30.2*	*4.7*	*1.0*	*6.0*
	2000	*86 126.4*	*14.3*	*9.2*	*5.1*	*8.8*	*13.5*	*47.0*	*29.4*	*6.0*	*6.5*	*11.2*
	2010	*144 329.3*	*14.2*	*7.7*	*4.2*	*20.1*	*7.0*	*44.4*	*24.5*	*3.1*	*23.5*	*4.4*
	2011	*168 814.1*	*14.5*	*9.2*	*4.0*	*21.6*	*6.6*	*40.8*	*29.0*	*3.0*	*23.5*	*3.7*
Benin - Bénin	1990	5.0	..	..	0.0	..	0.0	..	..	80.0	..	20.0
	2000	0.2	..	..	..	..	0.0	..	..	..	..	100.0
	2010	0.4	..	..	..	..	0.0	..	..	..	..	100.0
	2011	0.4	0.0	0.0	0.0	0.0	0.0	0.0	0.0	0.0	0.0	100.0
Cape Verde - Cap-Vert	1990	26.0	..	..	0.0	..	0.0	..	..	92.3	..	7.7
	2000	24.0	0.0	..	0.0	..	0.0	6.4	..	78.4	..	15.3
	2010	23.5	0.0	..	0.0	..	0.0	26.6	..	48.7	..	24.7
	2011	22.2	0.0	0.0	0.0	0.0	0.0	20.4	0.0	52.1	0.0	27.4
Côte d'Ivoire	1990	100.0	..	..	0.1	..	0.0	..	..	85.0	..	15.0
	2000	5.9	0.0	..	..	..	0.0	19.9	..	..	..	80.1
	2010	5.1	0.0	..	..	..	0.0	22.8	..	..	..	77.2
	2011	4.1	0.0	0.0	0.0	0.0	0.0	28.6	0.0	0.0	0.0	71.4
Gambia - Gambie	1990	2.0	..	..	..	..	0.0	..	..	..	..	100.0
	2000	1.9	..	..	..	..	0.0	..	..	..	..	100.0
	2010	11.7	0.0	..	0.0	..	0.0	42.7	..	38.4	..	18.9
	2011	11.4	0.0	0.0	0.0	0.0	0.0	43.8	0.0	39.4	0.0	16.8
Ghana	1990	114.0	0.0	..	0.1	..	0.1	0.9	..	69.3	..	29.8
	2000	92.1	0.0	0.0	0.0	..	0.1	9.3	0.3	19.2	..	71.1
	2010	84.7	0.0	0.0	0.0	..	0.1	5.4	0.3	20.9	..	73.4
	2011	81.1	0.0	0.0	0.0	0.0	0.1	5.6	0.3	26.8	0.0	67.3
Guinea - Guinée	1990	3.0	..	..	..	..	0.0	..	..	..	..	100.0
	2000	4.8	..	..	0.0	..	0.0	..	..	6.0	..	94.0
	2010	11.6	..	..	0.0	..	0.0	..	..	2.5	..	97.5
	2011	12.6	0.0	0.0	0.0	0.0	0.0	0.0	0.0	2.3	0.0	97.7
Guinea-Bissau - Guinée-Bissau	1990	2.0	..	..	..	..	0.0	..	..	..	..	100.0
	2000	2.2	..	..	0.0	..	0.0	..	..	24.7	..	75.3
	2010	2.2	..	..	0.0	..	0.0	..	..	10.2	..	89.8
	2011	2.2	0.0	0.0	0.0	0.0	0.0	0.0	0.0	10.2	0.0	89.8
Liberia - Libéria	1990	89 501.0	22.1	12.3	3.8	4.2	10.9	58.3	30.6	4.2	1.0	5.8
	2000	85 186.9	14.1	9.2	4.9	8.8	13.3	46.8	29.7	5.8	6.6	11.1
	2010	142 121.0	14.0	7.7	3.5	20.0	6.5	44.5	24.8	2.7	23.9	4.2
	2011	166 245.6	14.3	9.1	4.0	21.6	6.1	40.8	29.2	2.6	23.8	3.5

For sources and notes, see end of table.

Pour les sources et les notes, se reporter à la fin du tableau.

Region, country or territory / Régions pays ou territoires	Year / Année	Total fleet (thousands of DWT) / Flotte totale (milliers de TPL) (1)	As percentage of world total fleet / En pourcentage de la flotte mondiale					As percentage of the country or region total fleet / En pourcentage de la flotte totale du pays ou de la région				
			Oil tankers / Pétroliers	Bulk carriers / Vraquiers	General cargo / Navires de charge classique (2)	Container ships / Porte-conteneurs	Other types / Autres navires	Oil tankers / Pétroliers	Bulk carriers / Vraquiers	General cargo / Navires de charge classique (2)	Container ships / Porte-conteneurs	Other types / Autres navires
Mauritania - Mauritanie	1990	22.0	..	..	0.0	..	0.0	..	..	18.2	..	81.8
	2000	22.2	..	..	0.0	..	0.0	..	..	3.2	..	96.8
	2010	24.7	..	..	0.0	..	0.0	..	..	3.5		96.5
	2011	24.5	0.0	0.0	0.0	0.0	0.0	9.8	0.0	3.5	0.0	86.7
Nigeria - Nigéria	1990	737.0	0.2	..	0.3	..	0.1	59.0	..	35.7	..	5.3
	2000	677.0	0.2	..	0.1	..	0.1	70.0	..	17.0	..	8.7
	2010	989.4	0.2	0.0	0.0	..	0.2	76.8	1.3	1.0	..	20.9
	2011	952.0	0.2	0.0	0.0	0.0	0.2	76.6	0.0	1.8	0.0	21.6
Saint Helena - Sainte-Hélène	1990	2.0	..	..	..	..	0.0	..	..	..	..	100.0
	2000	0.5	..	..	..	..	0.0	..	..	..	..	100.0
	2010	0.8	..	..	..	..	0.0	..	..	..	..	100.0
	2011	0.8	0.0	0.0	0.0	0.0	0.0	0.0	0.0	0.0	0.0	100.0
Senegal - Sénégal	1990	36.0	..	..	0.0	..	0.0	..	..	47.2	..	52.8
	2000	22.4	..	..	0.0	..	0.0	..	..	9.1	..	90.9
	2010	19.3	0.0	..	0.0	..	0.0	1.4	..	8.0	..	90.5
	2011	20.7	0.0	0.0	0.0	0.0	0.0	1.4	0.0	14.4	0.0	84.3
Sierra Leone	1990	14.0	0.0	..	0.0	..	0.0	7.1	..	21.4	..	71.4
	2000	11.2	0.0	..	0.0	..	0.0	55.0	..	8.5	..	36.5
	2010	792.2	0.0	0.0	0.5	0.0	0.0	12.9	9.6	70.3	1.4	5.7
	2011	1 089.5	0.0	0.0	0.5	0.0	0.1	19.7	20.6	49.2	3.5	7.0
Togo	1990	65.0	0.0	..	0.0	..	0.1	1.5	..	32.3	..	67.7
	2000	74.4	..	0.0	..	..	0.0	..	99.1	..	..	0.9
	2010	242.8	0.0	0.0	0.1	0.0	0.0	3.3	31.2	57.9	3.4	4.1
	2011	347.0	0.0	0.0	0.2	0.0	0.0	11.6	28.6	47.8	9.2	2.8
Developing economies: America - Économies en développement : Amérique	1990	119 936.0	16.4	20.2	24.0	19.3	16.2	32.2	37.6	20.1	3.6	6.4
	2000	237 755.2	26.8	34.5	31.6	28.8	23.7	31.9	39.8	13.5	7.7	7.1
	2010	395 591.2	24.8	38.9	33.7	25.6	28.6	28.2	45.0	9.2	11.0	6.7
	2011	416 997.8	23.4	37.0	33.8	25.0	27.7	26.6	47.2	8.8	11.0	6.4
Caribbean - Caraïbes	1990	24 104.0	5.1	2.7	4.3	1.1	3.0	49.8	25.2	18.0	1.0	5.9
	2000	62 854.5	9.5	5.3	13.4	6.1	5.4	42.6	23.4	21.7	6.2	6.1
	2010	94 721.4	8.2	4.6	15.1	5.4	12.1	39.1	22.3	17.3	9.6	11.7
	2011	98 548.0	8.1	4.1	15.1	5.3	12.4	39.2	22.1	16.7	9.9	12.1
Anguilla	1990	4.0	..	..	0.0	..	..	..	..	75.0	..	..
	2000	2.0	..	..	0.0	..	..	..	..	100.0	..	..
	2010	0.9	..	..	0.0	..	..	..	..	100.0	..	..
	2011	0.9	0.0	0.0	0.0	0.0	0.0	0.0	0.0	100.0	0.0	0.0
Antigua and Barbuda - Antigua-et-Barbuda	1990	696.0	0.0	0.0	0.5	0.3	0.1	12.2	0.7	70.3	11.2	5.6
	2000	4 677.6	0.0	0.1	1.8	3.9	0.1	0.2	6.7	39.2	53.0	0.9
	2010	13 033.6	0.0	0.3	4.0	4.3	0.1	0.2	9.8	33.1	56.0	0.9
	2011	13 892.3	0.0	0.3	4.4	4.1	0.1	0.2	10.5	34.7	53.6	1.0
Aruba	2010	0.1	..	..	..	..	0.0	..	..	..	..	100.0
	2011	0.1	0.0	0.0	0.0	0.0	0.0	0.0	0.0	0.0	0.0	100.0
Bahamas	1990	19 228.0	4.8	2.2	1.8	0.4	2.2	59.2	25.3	9.6	0.5	5.4
	2000	44 941.4	8.8	3.2	7.3	1.9	3.9	55.4	19.3	16.5	2.7	6.1
	2010	64 109.1	7.4	2.8	6.0	0.9	10.5	52.2	20.1	10.2	2.4	15.1
	2011	67 465.4	7.3	2.7	5.7	1.0	11.0	51.5	20.9	9.2	2.7	15.7
Barbados - Barbade	1990	8.0	..	..	0.0	..	..	..	..	100.0	..	..
	2000	1 162.0	0.2	0.1	0.2	0.0	0.1	55.0	22.7	13.3	1.5	7.4
	2010	1 181.1	0.1	0.1	0.3	..	0.1	23.9	43.4	27.7	..	5.0
	2011	1 881.8	0.1	0.1	0.3	0.1	0.1	35.8	32.8	17.1	11.2	3.1
British Virgin Islands - Îles Vierges britanniques	1990	5.0	..	..	0.0	..	..	..	..	100.0	..	..
	2000	2.1	..	..	0.0	..	0.0	..	..	68.8	..	31.2
	2010	11.0	..	..	0.0	..	0.0	..	..	5.1	..	94.9
	2011	11.4	0.0	0.0	0.0	0.0	0.0	5.3	0.0	4.9	0.0	89.8
Cayman Islands - Îles Caïmanes	1990	566.0	0.0	0.1	0.2	..	0.2	11.0	33.2	38.9	..	17.0
	2000	1 756.2	0.1	0.3	0.4	0.1	0.3	11.9	52.7	22.1	2.2	11.1
	2010	3 960.6	0.5	0.3	0.3	..	0.4	55.0	29.4	7.4	..	8.2
	2011	3 688.4	0.4	0.2	0.4	0.0	0.3	54.9	27.5	10.8	0.0	6.8

For sources and notes, see end of table.

Pour les sources et les notes, se reporter à la fin du tableau.

5

5.3 World merchant fleet by flag of registration and type of ship of countries and geographical regions

5.3 Flotte marchande mondiale par pavillons d'immatriculation et par types de navires des pays et des régions géographiques

Region, country or territory / Régions pays ou territoires	Year / Année	Total fleet (thousands of DWT) / Flotte totale (milliers de TPL) (1)	As percentage of world total fleet / En pourcentage de la flotte mondiale					As percentage of the country or region total fleet / En pourcentage de la flotte totale du pays ou de la région				
			Oil tankers / Pétroliers	Bulk carriers / Vraquiers	General cargo / Navires de charge classique (2)	Container ships / Porte-conteneurs	Other types / Autres navires	Oil tankers / Pétroliers	Bulk carriers / Vraquiers	General cargo / Navires de charge classique (2)	Container ships / Porte-conteneurs	Other types / Autres navires
Cuba	1990	1 198.0	0.0	0.0	0.8	..	0.3	9.8	8.3	68.1	..	13.8
	2000	156.3	0.0	0.0	0.1	..	0.1	3.0	2.0	53.3	..	41.6
	2010	49.4	0.0	0.0	0.0	..	0.0	2.1	7.0	28.8	..	62.1
	2011	49.2	0.0	0.0	0.0	0.0	0.0	2.1	1.8	18.4	0.0	77.7
Dominica - Dominique	1990	5.0	..	..	0.0	..	..	..	..	100.0	..	..
	2000	2.7	..	..	0.0	..	0.0	..	..	79.9	..	20.1
	2010	1 610.4	0.1	0.2	0.1	..	0.0	28.5	62.1	7.1	..	2.3
	2011	1 602.7	0.1	0.2	0.1	0.0	0.0	29.7	60.4	7.2	0.0	2.6
Dominican Republic - République dominicaine	1990	68.0	0.0	0.0	0.0	..	..	2.9	27.9	69.1	..	..
	2000	8.4	..	..	0.0	..	0.0	..	..	85.6	..	14.4
	2010	5.6	..	..	0.0	..	0.0	..	..	89.0	..	11.0
	2011	1.9	0.0	0.0	0.0	0.0	0.0	0.0	0.0	67.2	0.0	32.8
Grenada - Grenade	1990	1.0	..	..	..	..	0.0	..	..	..	..	100.0
	2000	1.0	..	..	0.0	..	..	..	..	100.0	..	..
	2010	1.0	..	..	0.0	..	0.0	..	..	95.5	..	4.5
	2011	1.0	0.0	0.0	0.0	0.0	0.0	0.0	0.0	95.5	0.0	4.5
Haiti - Haïti	2000	1.0	..	..	0.0	..	0.0	..	..	82.3	..	17.7
	2010	1.5	..	..	0.0	..	0.0	..	..	88.9	..	11.1
	2011	0.7	0.0	0.0	0.0	0.0	0.0	0.0	0.0	77.1	0.0	22.9
Jamaica - Jamaïque	1990	21.0	0.0	0.0	0.0	..	0.0	14.3	19.0	38.1	23.8	4.8
	2000	3.3	0.0	..	..	..	0.0	92.9	..	..	..	7.1
	2010	353.3	..	0.1	0.1	0.0	0.0	..	74.4	15.6	9.9	0.2
	2011	232.2	0.0	0.0	0.0	0.0	0.0	0.0	67.0	17.7	15.0	0.3
Montserrat	1990	1.0	..	..	0.0	..	..	..	..	100.0	..	..
Netherlands Antilles - Antilles néerlandaises	2010	1 836.7	0.0	0.0	1.1	0.0	0.3	9.4	8.1	66.7	0.5	15.4
	2011	1 698.3	0.0	0.0	1.0	0.0	0.2	10.1	8.7	67.0	0.5	13.7
Saint Kitts and Nevis - Saint-Kitts-et-Nevis	1990	1.0	..	..	0.0	..	..	..	..	100.0	..	..
	2000	0.6	..	..	0.0	..	..	..	..	100.0	..	..
	2010	1 219.2	0.0	0.1	0.5	0.0	0.1	10.5	39.3	45.0	0.9	4.3
	2011	1 300.2	0.0	0.1	0.5	0.0	0.1	14.4	36.3	42.3	0.8	6.3
Saint Lucia - Sainte-Lucie	1990	2.0	..	..	0.0	..	..	..	..	100.0	..	..
Saint Vincent and the Grenadines - Saint-Vincent-et-les Grenadines	1990	2 282.0	0.2	0.4	0.9	0.3	0.2	15.6	39.7	38.9	2.7	3.2
	2000	10 131.0	0.4	1.6	3.7	0.3	1.0	10.0	44.4	36.8	1.8	7.0
	2010	7 329.2	0.1	0.7	2.8	0.1	0.5	4.3	46.1	40.7	2.1	6.7
	2011	6 701.2	0.1	0.5	2.6	0.1	0.5	5.1	41.8	42.4	3.6	7.0
Trinidad and Tobago - Trinité-et-Tobago	1990	16.0	..	..	0.0	..	0.0	..	..	37.5	..	62.5
	2000	8.9	0.0	..	0.0	..	0.0	16.6	..	28.9	..	54.5
	2010	18.3	0.0	..	..	..	0.0	22.6	..	..	..	77.4
	2011	20.3	0.0	0.0	0.0	0.0	0.0	20.3	0.0	0.0	0.0	79.7
Turks and Caicos Islands - Îles Turques et Caïques	1990	2.0	..	..	0.0	..	0.0	..	..	50.0	..	50.0
	2000	0.2	..	..	0.0	..	..	..	..	100.0	..	..
	2010	0.2	..	..	0.0	..	..	..	..	100.0	..	..
	2011	0.0	0.0	0.0	0.0	0.0	0.0	0.0	0.0	0.0	0.0	100.0
Central America - Amérique centrale	*1990*	*78 245.0*	*8.9*	*14.3*	*16.4*	*17.2*	*10.3*	*27.0*	*40.7*	*21.1*	*4.9*	*6.3*
	2000	*164 753.9*	*15.8*	*27.9*	*17.2*	*22.3*	*16.4*	*27.2*	*46.6*	*10.6*	*8.6*	*7.1*
	2010	*292 694.0*	*15.7*	*34.0*	*17.9*	*20.0*	*14.8*	*24.2*	*53.0*	*6.6*	*11.6*	*4.7*
	2011	*310 079.9*	*14.4*	*32.6*	*18.0*	*19.5*	*13.5*	*22.1*	*55.9*	*6.3*	*11.5*	*4.2*
Belize	2000	3 052.4	0.2	0.1	1.7	0.1	0.6	18.8	10.6	55.5	1.8	13.2
	2010	1 451.1	0.0	0.1	0.8	..	0.3	2.2	20.4	61.4	..	16.0
	2011	1 627.9	0.0	0.1	0.9	0.0	0.2	3.7	24.2	57.9	0.0	14.1
Costa Rica	1990	7.0	..	..	0.0	..	0.0	..	..	42.9	..	57.1
	2000	1.2	..	..	..	..	0.0	..	..	..	..	100.0
	2010	0.4	..	..	..	..	0.0	..	..	..	..	100.0
	2011	0.7	0.0	0.0	0.0	0.0	0.0	0.0	0.0	0.0	0.0	100.0
El Salvador	1990	3.0	..	..	..	..	0.0	..	..	..	..	100.0
	2010	1.7	..	..	..	..	0.0	..	..	..	..	100.0
	2011	1.7	0.0	0.0	0.0	0.0	0.0	0.0	0.0	0.0	0.0	100.0

For sources and notes, see end of table.

Pour les sources et les notes, se reporter à la fin du tableau.

5.3 World merchant fleet by flag of registration and type of ship of countries and geographical regions

5.3 Flotte marchande mondiale par pavillons d'immatriculation et par types de navires des pays et des régions géographiques

Region, country or territory Régions pays ou territoires	Year Année	Total fleet (thousands of DWT) Flotte totale (milliers de TPL) (1)	As percentage of world total fleet En pourcentage de la flotte mondiale					As percentage of the country or region total fleet En pourcentage de la flotte totale du pays ou de la région				
			Oil tankers Pétroliers	Bulk carriers Vraquiers	General cargo Navires de charge classique (2)	Container ships Porte-conteneurs	Other types Autres navires	Oil tankers Pétroliers	Bulk carriers Vraquiers	General cargo Navires de charge classique (2)	Container ships Porte-conteneurs	Other types Autres navires
Guatemala	1990	7.0	..	..	0.0	..	0.0	..	..	85.7	..	14.3
	2000	3.8	..	..	..	..	0.0	..	..	..	..	100.0
	2010	2.8	0.0	..	..	..	0.0	33.4	..			66.6
	2011	2.0	0.0	0.0	0.0	0.0	0.0	33.4	0.0	0.0	0.0	66.6
Honduras	1990	982.0	0.1	0.1	0.6	0.0	0.1	14.1	17.6	62.8	0.9	4.6
	2000	1 520.7	0.1	0.1	0.9	0.0	0.2	16.0	14.0	37.0	0.6	12.1
	2010	702.2	0.0	0.0	0.3	0.0	0.1	26.7	10.1	44.3	0.3	18.5
	2011	550.3	0.0	0.0	0.2	0.0	0.1	26.6	12.2	45.7	0.4	15.1
Mexico - Mexique	1990	1 883.0	0.3	0.2	0.1	0.1	1.4	42.9	18.4	3.3	0.6	34.8
	2000	1 226.6	0.3	..	0.0		0.6	62.2	..	2.0	..	35.8
	2010	1 775.7	0.3	0.0	0.0	..	0.6	63.7	5.2	2.0	..	29.1
	2011	1 862.2	0.2	0.0	0.0	0.0	0.6	56.2	12.3	1.9	0.0	29.7
Nicaragua	1990	3.0	..	..	0.0	..	..	..	..	100.0	..	..
	2000	2.0	..	..	0.0	..	0.0	..	..	59.4	..	40.6
	2010	2.7	0.0	..	0.0	..	0.0	33.9	..	43.4	..	22.7
	2011	2.7	0.0	0.0	0.0	0.0	0.0	33.9	0.0	43.4	0.0	22.7
Panama	1990	75 360.0	8.5	14.0	15.7	17.1	8.8	26.7	41.6	21.0	5.1	5.6
	2000	158 947.3	15.3	27.7	14.6	22.2	15.0	27.2	47.9	9.3	8.9	6.7
	2010	288 757.6	15.4	33.9	16.7	20.0	13.9	24.0	53.6	6.3	11.7	4.4
	2011	306 031.6	14.1	32.4	16.8	19.5	12.6	21.9	56.4	6.0	11.7	4.0
South America - Amérique du Sud	*1990*	*17 587.0*	*2.4*	*3.2*	*3.3*	*1.0*	*2.9*	*31.6*	*40.5*	*18.9*	*1.3*	*7.8*
	2000	*10 146.7*	*1.5*	*1.2*	*1.0*	*0.4*	*1.9*	*42.5*	*32.0*	*10.2*	*2.3*	*13.0*
	2010	*8 175.8*	*0.8*	*0.4*	*0.7*	*0.2*	*1.7*	*46.5*	*19.9*	*9.1*	*5.0*	*19.5*
	2011	*8 360.0*	*0.0*	*0.3*	*0.7*	*0.2*	*1.8*	*46.4*	*18.9*	*8.9*	*4.9*	*20.9*
Argentina - Argentine	1990	2 764.0	0.4	0.4	0.8	0.3	0.5	32.6	29.1	27.6	2.6	8.2
	2000	599.3	0.1	0.0	0.1	..	0.3	30.1	8.7	21.9	..	39.3
	2010	980.9	0.1	0.0	0.1	0.0	0.3	54.7	11.7	7.2	1.9	24.6
	2011	905.0	0.1	0.0	0.1	0.0	0.2	59.4	9.7	6.5	2.0	22.3
Bolivia (Plurinational State of) - Bolivie (État plurinational de)	1990	16.0	..	..	0.0	..	..	..	..	100.0	..	..
	2000	244.5	0.0	0.0	0.1	0.0	0.0	11.4	35.7	44.1	3.4	5.5
	2010	166.0	0.0	0.0	0.1	..	0.0	14.5	28.7	48.1	..	8.7
	2011	193.2	0.0	0.0	0.1	0.0	0.0	6.2	42.8	45.4	0.0	5.7
Brazil - Brésil	1990	10 063.0	1.4	2.3	1.1	0.5	1.1	32.2	50.6	10.9	1.1	5.2
	2000	6 383.6	1.1	0.9	0.4	0.3	0.3	48.0	39.8	6.1	2.6	3.5
	2010	3 406.8	0.3	0.2	0.3	0.2	0.5	42.4	25.3	8.2	10.5	13.6
	2011	3 418.2	0.3	0.1	0.3	0.2	0.5	43.0	23.2	8.8	10.5	14.5
Chile - Chili	1990	870.0	..	0.2	0.2	..	0.3	..	63.4	22.8	..	13.8
	2000	1 012.0	0.1	0.1	0.1	0.1	0.5	16.4	34.5	12.0	5.0	32.1
	2010	1 095.8	0.1	0.1	0.1	0.0	0.2	36.1	34.8	6.9	1.9	20.3
	2011	1 127.2	0.1	0.1	0.1	0.0	0.2	32.2	36.5	7.5	2.6	21.2
Colombia - Colombie	1990	546.0	0.0	0.1	0.4	..	0.0	2.7	28.8	65.0	..	3.5
	2000	119.4	0.0	..	0.1	..	0.0	8.3	..	67.7	..	24.1
	2010	109.0	0.0	..	0.0	..	0.1	7.1	..	49.4	..	43.4
	2011	109.1	0.0	0.0	0.1	0.0	0.0	6.0	0.0	50.1	0.0	43.9
Ecuador - Équateur	1990	531.0	0.1	0.0	0.2	..	0.1	39.4	7.2	47.1	..	6.4
	2000	446.6	0.1	..	0.0	..	0.1	86.3	..	0.8	..	12.9
	2010	400.6	0.1	..	0.0	..	0.1	81.6	..	1.5	..	16.9
	2011	415.8	0.1	0.0	0.0	0.0	0.1	81.4	0.0	1.3	0.0	17.3
Falkland Islands (Malvinas) - Îles Falkland (Malvinas)	1990	4.0	..	..	..	..	0.0	..	..	..	..	100.0
	2000	31.1	..	..	0.0	..	0.0	..	..	2.0	..	98.0
	2010	34.6	..	..	..	..	0.0	..	..	..	..	100.0
	2011	33.7	0.0	0.0	0.0	0.0	0.0	0.0	0.0	0.0	0.0	100.0
Guyana	1990	11.0	..	..	0.0	..	0.0	..	..	45.5	..	54.5
	2000	12.5	..	..	0.0	..	0.0	..	..	53.8	..	46.2
	2010	41.7	0.0	..	0.0	..	0.0	16.4	..	67.1	..	16.5
	2011	44.7	0.0	0.0	0.0	0.0	0.0	20.9	0.0	62.4	0.0	16.6
Paraguay	1990	44.0	0.0	..	0.0	..	0.0	2.3	..	59.1	..	38.6
	2000	48.8	0.0	..	0.0	0.0	0.0	18.2	..	73.3	4.5	4.0
	2010	63.3	0.0	..	0.0	0.0	0.0	10.3	..	73.9	13.4	2.4
	2011	53.0	0.0	0.0	0.0	0.0	0.0	6.9	0.0	74.3	16.0	2.8

For sources and notes, see end of table.　　　　　　　　　　　　　　　Pour les sources et les notes, se reporter à la fin du tableau.

5.3 World merchant fleet by flag of registration and type of ship of countries and geographical regions

5.3 Flotte marchande mondiale par pavillons d'immatriculation et par types de navires des pays et des régions géographiques

Region, country or territory / Régions pays ou territoires	Year / Année	Total fleet (thousands of DWT) / Flotte totale (milliers de TPL) (1)	As percentage of world total fleet / En pourcentage de la flotte mondiale					As percentage of the country or region total fleet / En pourcentage de la flotte totale du pays ou de la région				
			Oil tankers / Pétroliers	Bulk carriers / Vraquiers	General cargo / Navires de charge classique (2)	Container ships / Porte-conteneurs	Other types / Autres navires	Oil tankers / Pétroliers	Bulk carriers / Vraquiers	General cargo / Navires de charge classique (2)	Container ships / Porte-conteneurs	Other types / Autres navires
Peru - Pérou	1990	841.0	0.1	0.1	0.2	..	0.1	40.1	25.7	28.2	..	6.1
	2000	267.0	0.0	0.0	0.1	..	0.1	29.7	9.6	30.4	..	30.4
	2010	317.9	0.0	..	0.0	..	0.1	55.7	..	9.3	..	35.0
	2011	471.1	0.1	0.0	0.0	0.0	0.1	60.1	0.0	8.3	0.0	31.3
Suriname	1990	15.0	0.0	..	0.0	0.0	0.0	13.3	..	66.7	13.3	6.7
	2000	7.2	0.0	..	0.0	..	0.0	42.1	..	43.8	..	14.2
	2010	5.7	0.0	..	0.0	..	0.0	59.7	..	31.3	..	9.0
	2011	5.7	0.0	0.0	0.0	0.0	0.0	60.7	0.0	31.3	0.0	9.0
Uruguay	1990	155.0	0.0	..	0.0	0.2	0.1	60.6	..	1.9	21.9	15.5
	2000	38.1	0.0	..	0.0	..	0.0	22.0	..	3.3	..	74.7
	2010	69.9	0.0	0.0	0.0	..	0.0	22.3	4.6	12.4	..	60.6
	2011	62.6	0.0	0.0	0.0	0.0	0.0	31.0	5.2	12.2	0.0	51.6
Venezuela (Bolivarian Rep. of) - Venezuela (Rép. bolivarienne du)	1990	1 727.0	0.3	0.1	0.4	0.0	0.7	43.9	15.3	21.1	0.2	19.5
	2000	936.7	0.1	0.1	0.1	0.0	0.4	40.1	20.7	8.1	0.1	31.0
	2010	1 483.6	0.2	0.0	0.1	..	0.4	58.0	14.8	4.2	..	22.9
	2011	1 530.5	0.2	0.0	0.0	0.0	0.5	51.5	13.1	2.9	0.0	32.4
Developing economies: Asia - Économies en développement : Asie	**1990**	**115 295.0**	**12.6**	**23.2**	**23.8**	**18.2**	**12.1**	**25.7**	**45.0**	**20.7**	**3.5**	**5.0**
	2000	**156 453.2**	**15.1**	**24.0**	**25.1**	**20.0**	**13.4**	**27.4**	**42.1**	**16.3**	**8.1**	**6.1**
	2010	**285 345.4**	**20.3**	**24.9**	**28.7**	**19.4**	**17.6**	**32.1**	**39.9**	**10.9**	**11.5**	**5.7**
	2011	**318 293.9**	**20.8**	**25.3**	**28.0**	**20.1**	**18.3**	**31.0**	**42.3**	**9.6**	**11.6**	**5.5**
Eastern Asia - Asie orientale	*1990*	*43 401.0*	*2.4*	*10.8*	*9.8*	*9.3*	*3.8*	*12.8*	*55.5*	*22.8*	*4.8*	*4.2*
	2000	*54 642.3*	*2.4*	*11.0*	*9.2*	*9.8*	*3.2*	*12.2*	*55.1*	*17.1*	*11.4*	*4.2*
	2010	*146 890.9*	*7.0*	*17.8*	*11.9*	*10.1*	*4.5*	*21.5*	*55.4*	*8.7*	*11.6*	*2.8*
	2011	*171 184.4*	*7.5*	*18.4*	*11.7*	*10.9*	*4.8*	*20.9*	*57.2*	*7.5*	*11.7*	*2.7*
China - Chine	1990	20 200.0	1.1	3.6	7.7	4.0	1.8	13.2	39.9	38.2	4.5	4.2
	2000	23 701.2	1.2	4.0	6.4	2.6	1.6	14.3	46.8	27.2	7.0	4.7
	2010	45 157.3	2.1	5.0	5.6	3.1	1.7	20.5	51.0	13.4	11.7	3.4
	2011	52 740.5	2.5	5.1	5.2	3.4	2.0	22.2	51.6	10.8	11.8	3.6
China, Hong Kong SAR - Chine (RAS de Hong Kong)	1990	10 337.0	0.6	3.5	0.4	2.1	0.6	13.1	75.2	4.2	4.5	2.8
	2000	13 190.9	0.3	3.6	0.9	2.3	0.1	7.1	73.9	7.2	11.2	0.6
	2010	74 513.5	4.1	9.0	3.5	6.0	1.2	24.9	55.0	5.0	13.6	1.5
	2011	91 732.6	4.5	9.9	3.8	6.6	1.2	23.4	57.7	4.5	13.1	1.3
China, Macao SAR - Chine (RAS de Macao)	2010	2.2	..	..	..	..	0.0	..	..	..	..	100.0
	2011	2.2	0.0	0.0	0.0	0.0	0.0	0.0	0.0	0.0	0.0	100.0
China, Taiwan Province of - Province chinoise de Taiwan	2000	8 248.1	0.6	1.6	0.2	3.4	0.1	18.9	51.8	2.4	26.3	0.7
	2010	3 944.1	0.3	0.4	0.1	0.4	0.1	29.0	46.4	4.1	18.0	2.4
	2011	4 310.0	0.2	0.4	0.1	0.4	0.2	25.8	49.2	3.6	18.0	3.4
Korea, Dem. People's Rep. of - Corée, Rép. populaire dém. de	1990	529.0	0.0	0.0	0.4	..	0.0	3.8	20.6	71.6	..	4.0
	2000	846.6	0.0	0.0	0.7	..	0.1	1.4	10.4	80.7	..	7.6
	2010	1 265.6	0.0	0.0	0.8	0.0	0.1	9.3	12.8	71.1	2.5	4.3
	2011	1 193.9	0.0	0.0	0.8	0.0	0.0	8.0	14.4	71.4	2.6	3.7
Korea, Republic of - Corée, République de	1990	12 335.0	0.6	3.6	1.4	3.2	1.3	12.2	65.8	11.0	5.8	5.2
	2000	8 655.5	0.3	1.8	1.1	1.5	1.3	8.9	56.8	12.3	11.0	11.1
	2010	20 818.6	0.5	3.2	1.6	0.5	1.4	11.7	69.7	8.4	4.1	6.2
	2011	20 155.3	0.3	2.8	1.6	0.5	1.4	7.3	73.0	8.6	4.7	6.5
Mongolia - Mongolie	2010	1 189.6	0.0	0.2	0.2	..	0.0	1.6	75.9	21.0	..	1.5
	2011	1 049.8	0.0	0.1	0.2	0.0	0.0	0.3	75.5	19.0	0.7	4.5
Southern Asia - Asie méridionale	*1990*	*20 524.0*	*3.9*	*3.2*	*3.5*	*..*	*1.4*	*45.3*	*34.6*	*16.9*	*..*	*3.3*
	2000	*18 704.6*	*3.0*	*2.3*	*2.4*	*0.3*	*1.7*	*45.2*	*34.5*	*13.1*	*1.0*	*6.3*
	2010	*18 185.6*	*2.1*	*1.1*	*1.3*	*0.4*	*1.6*	*52.6*	*28.4*	*7.6*	*3.5*	*8.0*
	2011	*18 644.5*	*2.0*	*1.1*	*1.2*	*0.2*	*1.5*	*50.9*	*31.8*	*7.1*	*2.3*	*7.9*
Bangladesh	1990	587.0	0.0	..	0.5	..	0.0	14.1	..	83.5	..	2.4
	2000	518.7	0.0	0.0	0.4	..	0.0	19.6	1.7	74.9	..	3.8
	2010	975.3	0.0	0.1	0.3	0.0	0.0	11.4	47.4	33.7	5.0	2.5
	2011	1 369.1	0.0	0.2	0.3	0.0	0.0	8.3	59.4	27.0	3.5	1.8
India - Inde	1990	10 207.0	1.2	2.3	1.6	..	1.0	28.5	50.9	15.9	..	4.7
	2000	11 209.3	1.7	1.7	0.6	0.2	1.4	43.1	41.3	5.9	1.2	8.6
	2010	14 969.6	2.0	0.9	0.3	0.2	1.3	60.2	27.5	2.4	2.2	7.8
	2011	15 277.7	1.9	0.8	0.3	0.2	1.2	58.3	29.4	2.3	2.1	7.8

For sources and notes, see end of table.

Pour les sources et les notes, se reporter à la fin du tableau.

5.3 World merchant fleet by flag of registration and type of ship of countries and geographical regions

5.3 Flotte marchande mondiale par pavillons d'immatriculation et par types de navires des pays et des régions géographiques

Region, country or territory / Régions pays ou territoires	Year / Année	Total fleet (thousands of DWT) / Flotte totale (milliers de TPL) (1)	As percentage of world total fleet / En pourcentage de la flotte mondiale					As percentage of the country or region total fleet / En pourcentage de la flotte totale du pays ou de la région				
			Oil tankers / Pétroliers	Bulk carriers / Vraquiers	General cargo / Navires de charge classique (2)	Container ships / Porteconteneurs	Other types / Autres navires	Oil tankers / Pétroliers	Bulk carriers / Vraquiers	General cargo / Navires de charge classique (2)	Container ships / Porteconteneurs	Other types / Autres navires
Iran (Islamic Rep. of) - Iran (Rép. islamique d')	1990	8 685.0	2.6	0.8	0.6	..	0.3	71.3	20.4	6.5	..	1.8
	2000	6 097.3	1.2	0.6	0.9	0.0	0.2	55.9	26.4	14.8	0.2	2.6
	2010	1 333.3	0.0	0.1	0.3	0.1	0.2	9.0	34.0	22.3	18.9	15.7
	2011	993.1	0.0	0.1	0.3	0.0	0.2	12.1	34.8	27.9	4.2	21.1
Maldives	1990	148.0	0.0	0.0	0.1	..	0.0	6.8	48.6	43.2	..	1.4
	2000	132.8	0.0	..	0.1	..	0.0	6.5	..	88.5	..	4.9
	2010	107.5	0.0	0.0	0.1	..	0.0	0.4	0.9	80.0	..	4.7
	2011	145.4	0.0	0.0	0.1	0.0	0.0	8.0	1.2	86.1	0.0	4.7
Pakistan	1990	526.0	0.0	..	0.4	..	0.0	17.1	..	80.8	..	2.1
	2000	458.7	0.0	0.0	0.3	0.1	0.0	19.8	11.4	56.8	9.1	2.9
	2010	481.1	0.1	0.0	0.1	..	0.0	58.5	13.7	22.3	..	5.5
	2011	592.5	0.1	0.0	0.1	0.0	0.0	54.4	31.9	9.2	0.0	4.4
Sri Lanka	1990	371.0	0.0	0.0	0.3	..	0.0	4.0	14.8	80.1	..	1.1
	2000	287.6	0.0	0.1	0.1	..	0.0	3.5	52.0	42.2	..	2.4
	2010	238.9	0.0	0.0	0.1	..	0.0	10.9	31.5	51.2	..	6.3
	2011	266.6	0.0	0.0	0.1	0.0	0.0	7.3	28.2	52.1	6.3	6.0
South-Eastern Asia - Asie du Sud-Est	*1990*	*35 050.0*	*2.8*	*7.9*	*6.9*	*6.5*	*4.9*	*19.0*	*50.2*	*19.9*	*4.1*	*6.7*
	2000	*62 945.1*	*7.7*	*7.9*	*9.4*	*8.0*	*6.9*	*34.5*	*34.5*	*15.2*	*8.1*	*7.8*
	2010	*101 728.6*	*9.4*	*5.1*	*12.8*	*7.7*	*10.0*	*41.5*	*23.0*	*13.6*	*12.8*	*9.1*
	2011	*110 366.4*	*9.7*	*4.9*	*12.6*	*7.8*	*10.5*	*41.7*	*23.7*	*12.4*	*13.0*	*9.1*
Brunei Darussalam - Brunéi Darussalam	1990	346.0	..	..	0.0	..	0.7	..	..	0.3	..	99.7
	2000	349.6	0.0	..	0.0	..	0.5	0.1	..	0.7	..	99.2
	2010	448.9	0.0	0.0	0.0	..	0.5	0.1	4.5	0.7	..	94.6
	2011	433.0	0.0	0.0	0.0	0.0	0.4	1.6	0.0	0.7	0.0	97.7
Cambodia - Cambodge	1990	4.0	..	..	0.0	..	0.0	..	..	25.0	..	75.0
	2010	2 517.0	0.0	0.1	1.8	0.0	0.1	2.6	14.6	78.2	0.6	4.0
	2011	2 185.5	0.0	0.1	1.6	0.0	0.1	2.9	13.7	77.5	1.1	4.7
Indonesia including East Timor - Indonésie, y compris le Timor oriental	1990	2 742.0	0.4	0.1	1.2	0.3	0.5	35.2	7.7	45.4	2.7	9.0
	2000	4 153.7	0.5	0.2	1.8	0.1	0.5	32.1	14.8	43.5	1.4	8.2
Indonesia - Indonésie	2010	10 470.7	0.9	0.5	2.7	0.5	0.8	36.9	19.9	28.0	7.9	7.3
	2011	12 104.7	0.9	0.5	2.8	0.5	1.2	36.7	19.9	25.5	8.1	9.9
Lao People's Dem. Rep. - Rép. dém. populaire lao	2010	1.6	..	..	0.0	..	..	..	..	100.0	..	..
	2011	1.6	0.0	0.0	0.0	0.0	0.0	0.0	0.0	100.0	0.0	0.0
Malaysia - Malaisie	1990	2 364.0	0.1	0.3	0.7	1.0	1.1	12.0	26.9	29.6	9.8	21.8
	2000	7 577.5	0.6	1.0	0.8	1.3	2.3	21.6	35.3	11.4	10.5	21.3
	2010	10 224.8	1.2	0.1	0.5	0.5	3.3	51.1	4.9	5.8	8.4	29.8
	2011	10 725.2	1.2	0.1	0.5	0.4	3.2	54.9	3.6	4.8	7.6	29.0
Myanmar	1990	907.0	0.0	0.3	0.2	..	0.1	0.4	72.5	23.5	..	3.5
	2000	792.3	0.0	0.2	0.2	0.0	0.0	0.6	63.7	30.8	3.2	1.7
	2010	210.1	0.0	0.0	0.2	..	0.0	2.2	11.3	79.9	..	6.6
	2011	219.9	0.0	0.0	0.2	0.0	0.0	2.1	10.8	80.8	0.0	6.3
Philippines	1990	15 468.0	0.3	5.5	2.1	0.3	0.3	5.0	79.9	13.7	0.4	1.1
	2000	11 112.0	0.1	3.0	2.0	0.2	0.5	2.1	74.7	18.5	1.4	3.2
	2010	7 032.8	0.2	0.8	1.6	0.2	0.4	11.1	54.6	24.1	5.0	5.2
	2011	6 946.5	0.2	0.7	1.7	0.2	0.4	10.4	52.4	26.8	5.3	5.1
Singapore - Singapour	1990	11 888.0	1.9	1.7	1.7	4.6	2.1	37.6	31.2	14.2	8.6	8.4
	2000	34 635.5	6.2	3.2	2.6	6.1	2.6	50.9	25.0	7.5	11.2	5.4
	2010	61 660.4	6.6	3.2	2.7	6.2	4.4	48.3	23.4	4.7	17.0	6.6
	2011	67 287.1	6.6	3.1	2.9	6.3	4.6	46.6	24.7	4.8	17.3	6.6
Thailand - Thaïlande	1990	805.0	0.1	0.0	0.6	0.2	0.1	16.0	2.1	70.2	6.2	5.5
	2000	3 068.4	0.2	0.3	1.3	0.3	0.2	22.4	25.6	42.7	5.2	4.1
	2010	3 746.8	0.2	0.2	1.2	0.2	0.2	27.7	23.6	34.7	8.4	5.7
	2011	4 563.8	0.4	0.2	0.9	0.2	0.3	43.9	21.3	21.7	7.0	6.2
Timor-Leste	2010	0.3	..	..	..	..	0.0	..	..	..	..	100.0
	2011	0.3	0.0	0.0	0.0	0.0	0.0	0.0	0.0	0.0	0.0	100.0

For sources and notes, see end of table.

Pour les sources et les notes, se reporter à la fin du tableau.

5

5.3 World merchant fleet by flag of registration and type of ship of countries and geographical regions

5.3 Flotte marchande mondiale par pavillons d'immatriculation et par types de navires des pays et des régions géographiques

Region, country or territory / Régions pays ou territoires	Year / Année	Total fleet (thousands of DWT) / Flotte totale (milliers de TPL) (1)	As percentage of world total fleet / En pourcentage de la flotte mondiale					As percentage of the country or region total fleet / En pourcentage de la flotte totale du pays ou de la région				
			Oil tankers / Pétroliers	Bulk carriers / Vraquiers	General cargo / Navires de charge classique (2)	Container ships / Porte-conteneurs	Other types / Autres navires	Oil tankers / Pétroliers	Bulk carriers / Vraquiers	General cargo / Navires de charge classique (2)	Container ships / Porte-conteneurs	Other types / Autres navires
Viet Nam	1990	526.0	0.0	0.0	0.4	..	0.0	6.5	4.6	85.9	..	3.0
	2000	1 256.1	0.1	0.1	0.7	0.0	0.3	13.5	12.0	54.3	1.3	18.9
	2010	8 008.7	0.3	0.3	1.1	0.1	0.1	27.1	11.4	57.7	1.0	4.8
	2011	5 898.9	0.3	0.3	2.0	0.1	0.1	26.1	31.1	37.5	3.0	2.4
Western Asia - Asie occidentale	*1990*	*16 320.0*	*3.5*	*1.4*	*3.5*	*2.4*	*1.9*	*50.2*	*19.0*	*21.8*	*3.3*	*5.7*
	2000	*20 161.2*	*2.1*	*2.8*	*4.1*	*1.9*	*1.7*	*30.1*	*37.5*	*20.5*	*5.9*	*6.0*
	2010	*18 540.3*	*1.8*	*0.8*	*2.7*	*1.3*	*1.6*	*44.0*	*20.8*	*15.9*	*11.6*	*7.8*
	2011	*18 098.6*	*1.5*	*0.9*	*2.4*	*1.2*	*1.5*	*40.5*	*25.4*	*14.7*	*11.7*	*7.7*
Bahrain - Bahreïn	1990	65.0	0.0	0.0	0.0	..	0.0	3.1	30.8	41.5	..	24.6
	2000	369.8	0.0	0.0	0.1	0.2	0.0	26.2	11.9	26.5	27.0	8.3
	2010	613.4	0.0	0.0	0.0	0.2	0.1	25.2	13.9	0.3	44.2	16.4
	2011	621.6	0.0	0.0	0.0	0.1	0.1	30.9	7.1	0.2	43.6	18.3
Iraq	1990	1 813.0	0.7	..	0.1	..	0.3	85.6	..	7.5	..	6.9
	2000	834.7	0.2	..	0.1	..	0.1	79.0	..	12.6	..	8.4
	2010	180.1	0.0	..	0.1	..	0.1	37.7	..	30.2	..	32.1
	2011	29.3	0.0	0.0	0.0	0.0	0.0	91.7	0.0	0.0	0.0	8.3
Jordan - Jordanie	1990	48.0	..	0.0	..	..	0.0	..	91.7	..	..	8.3
	2000	59.3	..	0.0	0.0	0.0	0.0	..	56.3	32.1	11.2	0.4
	2010	369.3	0.1	..	0.1	..	0.0	78.5	..	16.1	..	5.4
	2011	343.3	0.1	..	0.0	0.0	0.0	84.5	0.0	11.9	0.0	3.7
Kuwait - Koweït	1990	2 887.0	0.8	..	0.5	0.7	0.6	65.9	..	18.8	5.1	10.2
	2000	3 884.4	1.0	0.0	0.3	0.4	0.5	76.2	0.7	7.9	5.8	9.4
	2010	3 856.2	0.7	0.0	0.1	0.2	0.3	83.4	1.0	2.0	7.6	6.0
	2011	3 006.3	0.5	0.0	0.1	0.2	0.2	77.5	2.6	2.5	9.7	7.7
Lebanon - Liban	1990	593.0	0.0	0.1	0.4	0.0	0.0	3.9	26.3	68.1	0.5	1.2
	2000	483.2	0.0	0.1	0.2	0.0	0.0	0.3	52.5	44.7	1.5	1.0
	2010	158.6	0.0	0.0	0.1	..	0.0	0.9	33.9	63.2	..	2.0
	2011	129.8	0.0	0.0	0.1	0.0	0.0	0.6	22.9	74.1	0.0	2.4
Oman	1990	13.0	..	..	0.0	..	0.0	..	..	53.8	..	46.2
	2000	10.9	0.0	..	0.0	..	0.0	4.2	..	27.5	..	68.2
	2010	14.3	0.0	..	0.0	..	0.0	15.5	..	11.5	..	73.0
	2011	15.0	0.0	0.0	0.0	0.0	0.0	14.7	0.0	11.0	0.0	74.3
Qatar	1990	459.0	0.1	..	0.2	0.4	0.0	43.8	..	32.9	20.0	3.3
	2000	1 154.0	0.2	0.1	0.2	0.3	0.0	40.4	23.4	17.5	17.1	1.5
	2010	1 363.4	0.1	0.0	0.0	0.2	0.3	40.0	8.5	0.0	29.6	21.8
	2011	1 296.4	0.1	0.0	0.0	0.2	0.3	42.1	8.9	0.0	25.5	23.4
Saudi Arabia - Arabie saoudite	1990	3 535.0	1.0	0.1	0.7	0.3	0.5	63.4	8.8	18.6	2.1	7.0
	2000	1 443.0	0.1	..	0.6	0.3	0.3	28.4	..	39.6	15.0	17.1
	2010	2 319.3	0.3	..	0.3	0.1	0.3	65.1	..	12.7	9.5	12.6
	2011	2 245.7	0.3	0.0	0.2	0.1	0.2	67.6	0.0	12.1	9.8	10.4
Syrian Arab Republic - République arabe syrienne	1990	102.0	..	..	0.1	..	0.0	..	..	97.1	..	2.9
	2000	679.4	..	0.0	0.6	..	0.0	..	6.5	92.1	..	1.4
	2010	344.2	..	0.0	0.2	0.0	0.0	..	22.4	74.9	2.5	0.3
	2011	253.0	0.0	0.0	0.2	0.0	0.0	0.0	33.1	66.8	0.0	0.1
Turkey - Turquie	1990	5 477.0	0.6	1.1	1.3	..	0.2	27.0	46.3	24.6	..	2.2
	2000	10 174.2	0.4	2.5	1.7	0.3	0.4	10.4	67.3	17.2	2.1	3.0
	2010	7 878.0	0.4	0.7	1.9	0.3	0.3	21.5	42.6	25.5	7.3	3.1
	2011	8 745.2	0.4	0.8	1.8	0.3	0.3	20.1	47.6	21.9	7.2	3.2
United Arab Emirates - Émirats arabes unis	1990	1 316.0	0.3	0.0	0.2	1.0	0.2	59.4	2.9	14.6	16.6	6.5
	2000	1 042.5	0.1	0.0	0.2	0.4	0.2	39.3	3.5	22.6	21.8	12.8
	2010	1 412.3	0.1	0.0	0.1	0.2	0.2	46.0	8.5	5.8	26.8	12.9
	2011	1 376.5	0.1	0.0	0.1	0.2	0.2	46.0	6.3	6.2	27.4	14.0
Yemen - Yémen	1990	12.0	0.0	..	0.0	..	0.0	25.0	..	33.3	..	41.7
	2000	25.8	0.0	..	0.0	..	0.0	12.3	..	11.9	..	75.8
	2010	31.2	0.0	..	0.0	..	0.0	69.3	..	10.9	..	19.9
	2011	36.4	0.0	0.0	0.0	0.0	0.0	76.5	0.0	6.4	0.0	17.0

For sources and notes, see end of table.

Pour les sources et les notes, se reporter à la fin du tableau.

5.3 World merchant fleet by flag of registration and type of ship of countries and geographical regions

5.3 Flotte marchande mondiale par pavillons d'immatriculation et par types de navires des pays et des régions géographiques

Region, country or territory / Régions pays ou territoires	Year / Année	Total fleet (thousands of DWT) / Flotte totale (milliers de TPL) (1)	As percentage of world total fleet / En pourcentage de la flotte mondiale					As percentage of the country or region total fleet / En pourcentage de la flotte totale du pays ou de la région				
			Oil tankers / Pétroliers	Bulk carriers / Vraquiers	General cargo / Navires de charge classique (2)	Container ships / Porte-conteneurs	Other types / Autres navires	Oil tankers / Pétroliers	Bulk carriers / Vraquiers	General cargo / Navires de charge classique (2)	Container ships / Porte-conteneurs	Other types / Autres navires
Developing economies: Oceania - (3)	**1990**	**1 814.0**	**0.1**	**0.4**	**0.4**	**0.2**	**0.3**	**15.5**	**48.5**	**24.9**	**2.8**	**8.4**
Économies en développement : Océanie	**2000**	**1 931.6**	**0.0**	**0.3**	**0.5**	**0.1**	**0.7**	**1.2**	**44.4**	**25.4**	**1.8**	**27.2**
	2010	**83 461.2**	**9.2**	**5.7**	**2.2**	**3.2**	**8.9**	**49.6**	**31.2**	**2.9**	**6.4**	**9.9**
	2011	**104 021.9**	**10.6**	**6.5**	**2.2**	**3.7**	**10.2**	**48.5**	**33.3**	**2.3**	**6.6**	**9.4**
Fiji - Fidji	1990	61.0	0.0	..	0.0	..	0.0	10.9	..	71.9	..	17.2
	2000	24.4	0.0	..	0.0	..	0.0	11.0	..	23.0	..	61.6
	2010	17.0	..	..	0.0	..	0.0	..	..	40.0	..	60.0
	2011	16.0	0.0	0.0	0.0	0.0	0.0	0.0	0.0	36.2	0.0	63.8
French Polynesia - Polynésie française	2010	1.1	..	..	0.0	..	..	..	..	100.0	..	..
Kiribati	1990	0.0	..	..	0.0	..	..	..	..	100.0	..	..
	2000	4.1	..	..	0.0	..	0.0	..	..	84.0	..	16.0
	2010	828.8	0.0	0.1	0.3	..	0.1	19.7	41.5	33.3	..	5.6
	2011	814.9	0.0	0.1	0.2	0.0	0.1	18.5	42.7	32.7	0.0	6.0
Marshall Islands - Îles Marshall (4)	2010	77 827.4	8.9	5.2	1.4	3.1	8.0	51.3	30.3	2.0	6.8	9.5
	2011	98 756.9	10.4	6.1	1.4	3.7	9.0	50.2	32.7	1.5	6.9	8.8
Micronesia (Federated States of) - Micronésie (États fédérés de)	2010	9.8	..	0.0	0.0	..	0.0	..	3.8	64.8	..	31.5
	2011	10.5	0.0	0.0	0.0	0.0	0.0	0.0	3.5	60.9	0.0	35.5
Nauru	1990	45.0	..	0.0	0.0	..	0.0	..	60.0	42.2	..	2.2
New Caledonia - Nouvelle-Calédonie	2010	2.7	..	..	0.0	..	..	..	..	100.0	..	..
Papua New Guinea - Papouasie-Nouvelle-Guinée	1990	42.0	0.0	0.0	0.0	..	0.0	4.8	11.9	57.1	..	26.2
	2000	70.9	0.0	..	0.1	..	0.0	3.9	..	77.8	..	18.4
	2010	111.1	0.0	0.0	0.1	..	0.0	2.5	5.7	80.8	..	11.0
	2011	122.2	0.0	0.0	0.1	0.0	0.0	4.9	19.1	65.9	0.0	10.1
Samoa	1990	35.0	..	..	0.0	..	0.0	..	..	97.1	..	2.9
	2010	9.8	..	..	0.0	..	0.0	..	..	93.9	..	6.1
	2011	10.1	0.0	0.0	0.0	0.0	0.0	0.0	0.0	91.9	0.0	8.1
Solomon Islands - Îles Salomon	1990	7.0	..	..	0.0	..	0.0	..	..	71.4	..	28.6
	2000	6.9	..	..	0.0	..	0.0	..	..	35.9	..	64.1
	2010	8.0	..	..	0.0	..	0.0	..	..	24.9	..	75.1
	2011	7.5	0.0	0.0	0.0	0.0	0.0	0.0	0.0	22.4	0.0	77.6
Tonga	1990	43.0	..	..	0.0	0.1	0.0	..	..	27.9	69.8	2.3
	2000	29.3	..	..	0.0	..	0.0	..	..	63.1	..	36.9
	2010	77.5	0.0	0.0	0.1	..	0.0	2.1	8.6	77.5	..	11.8
	2011	58.3	0.0	0.0	0.0	0.0	0.0	2.5	11.4	68.6	0.0	17.4
Tuvalu	1990	1.0	..	..	0.0	..	..	..	..	100.0	..	..
	2000	68.4	..	..	0.0	..	0.1	..	..	37.6	..	62.4
	2010	1 884.1	0.3	0.1	0.1	0.0	0.1	67.3	19.2	7.8	0.8	4.9
	2011	1 202.4	0.1	0.0	0.2	..	0.1	56.8	19.0	15.1	1.3	7.8
Vanuatu	1990	1 574.0	0.1	0.4	0.3	0.1	0.3	17.3	53.9	19.5	1.3	8.0
	2000	1 727.7	0.0	0.3	0.4	0.1	0.6	1.0	49.7	21.9	2.0	25.4
	2010	2 683.7	..	0.4	0.2	0.0	0.7	..	65.2	8.9	1.1	24.9
	2011	3 023.2	0.0	0.3	0.3	0.0	0.9	0.2	59.7	9.1	1.0	30.1
Transition economies -	**1990**	**35 090.0**	**2.9**	**4.4**	**12.4**	**3.2**	**11.0**	**19.2**	**28.4**	**35.4**	**2.0**	**15.0**
Économies en transition	**2000**	**13 598.3**	**0.9**	**0.9**	**5.4**	**0.7**	**3.8**	**18.5**	**18.0**	**40.2**	**3.4**	**19.9**
	2010	**12 777.5**	**0.8**	**0.4**	**4.5**	**0.1**	**2.1**	**29.6**	**15.7**	**38.5**	**1.3**	**14.8**
	2011	**13 038.3**	**0.8**	**0.4**	**4.5**	**0.1**	**2.0**	**29.6**	**16.9**	**37.9**	**1.2**	**14.4**
Albania - Albanie	1990	63.0	..	..	0.1	..	..	..	..	100.0	..	..
	2000	20.1	..	..	0.0	..	0.0	..	..	93.8	..	6.2
	2010	96.8	..	..	0.1	..	0.0	..	..	98.5	..	1.5
	2011	82.4	0.0	0.0	0.1	0.0	0.0	0.0	5.4	92.9	0.0	1.7
Azerbaijan - Azerbaïdjan	2000	507.5	0.1	..	0.1	..	0.2	45.8	..	20.2	..	33.9
	2010	662.6	0.1	..	0.1	..	0.2	53.3	..	18.4	..	28.3
	2011	659.5	0.1	0.0	0.1	0.0	0.2	53.6	0.0	18.5	0.0	28.0
Croatia - Croatie	2000	1 227.7	0.0	0.3	0.2	0.2	0.0	1.1	70.7	17.7	8.0	2.5
	2010	2 277.1	0.3	0.2	0.0	..	0.0	54.4	41.6	2.4	..	1.6
	2011	2 480.1	0.3	0.2	0.0	0.0	0.0	50.1	46.5	2.0	0.0	1.3

For sources and notes, see end of table.

Pour les sources et les notes, se reporter à la fin du tableau.

5.3 World merchant fleet by flag of registration and type of ship of countries and geographical regions

5.3 Flotte marchande mondiale par pavillons d'immatriculation et par types de navires des pays et des régions géographiques

Region, country or territory / Régions pays ou territoires	Year / Année	Total fleet (thousands of DWT) / Flotte totale (milliers de TPL) (1)	As percentage of world total fleet / En pourcentage de la flotte mondiale — Oil tankers / Pétroliers	Bulk carriers / Vraquiers	General cargo / Navires de charge classique (2)	Container ships / Porte-conteneurs	Other types / Autres navires	As percentage of the country or region total fleet / En pourcentage de la flotte totale du pays ou de la région — Oil tankers / Pétroliers	Bulk carriers / Vraquiers	General cargo / Navires de charge classique (2)	Container ships / Porte-conteneurs	Other types / Autres navires
Georgia - Géorgie	2000	183.8	0.0	0.0	0.0	..	0.0	65.3	0.1	24.8	..	9.8
	2010	935.2	0.0	0.0	0.6	0.0	0.0	4.0	22.1	68.2	1.3	4.5
	2011	929.0	0.0	0.0	0.6	0.0	0.0	3.8	22.3	67.7	1.3	4.8
Kazakhstan	2000	4.7	..		0.0	..	0.0	..	..	16.6	..	83.4
	2010	91.3	0.0	..	0.0	..	0.0	69.4	..	2.2	..	28.4
	2011	143.3	0.0	0.0	0.0	0.0	0.0	71.6	0.0	3.5	0.0	24.9
Montenegro - Monténégro	2010	6.1			0.0	..	0.0	..	..	87.7		12.3
	2011	2.7	0.0	0.0	0.0	0.0	0.0	0.0	0.0	65.9	0.0	34.1
Republic of Moldova - République de Moldova	2010	459.8	0.0	0.0	0.3	0.0	0.0	7.1	25.9	64.3	1.2	1.4
	2011	476.5	0.0	0.0	0.3	0.0	0.0	7.9	21.2	69.6	0.0	1.2
Russian Federation - Fédération de Russie	2000	9 950.4	0.7	0.5	4.1	0.5	2.9	20.6	13.2	42.0	3.2	21.0
	2010	7 283.0	0.4	0.1	2.9	0.1	1.5	27.2	8.6	43.5	2.1	18.6
	2011	7 400.2	0.4	0.1	3.0	0.1	1.4	27.1	8.3	44.1	2.0	18.4
SFR of Yugoslavia (former) - RSF de Yougoslavie (anc.)	1990	5 815.0	0.2	1.5	1.8	0.5	0.1	9.1	57.2	30.9	2.0	0.8
Turkmenistan - Turkménistan	2000	36.5	0.0	0.0	0.0	..	0.0	9.3	18.3	41.6	..	30.8
	2010	61.8	0.0	..	0.0	..	0.0	36.4	..	25.1	..	38.5
	2011	75.0	0.0	0.0	0.0	0.0	0.0	45.4	0.0	20.7	0.0	34.0
Ukraine	2000	1 667.5	0.0	0.1	0.9	0.1	0.5	5.4	15.9	52.8	2.7	23.1
	2010	903.9	0.0	0.0	0.5	..	0.2	5.8	12.3	58.2	..	23.6
	2011	789.5	0.0	0.0	0.4	0.0	0.2	5.5	15.0	55.8	0.0	23.8
USSR (former) - URSS (anc.)	1990	29 212.0	2.6	3.0	10.5	2.7	10.9	21.2	22.7	36.2	2.1	17.9
Developed economies: America - (3) Économies développées : Amérique	**1990**	**31 335.0**	**9.0**	**0.9**	**2.0**	**13.0**	**6.7**	**67.6**	**6.3**	**6.5**	**9.3**	**10.2**
	2000	**37 163.0**	**7.3**	**2.4**	**2.0**	**6.8**	**5.1**	**55.4**	**17.8**	**5.4**	**11.7**	**9.7**
	2010	**26 299.5**	**1.6**	**1.6**	**1.1**	**2.7**	**6.6**	**27.5**	**27.8**	**4.5**	**17.2**	**23.1**
	2011	**26 986.2**	**1.5**	**1.4**	**1.1**	**2.3**	**7.1**	**26.6**	**28.2**	**4.4**	**15.6**	**25.2**
Bermuda - Bermudes	1990	7 625.0	2.8	0.1	0.2	0.1	1.0	86.7	3.6	2.8	0.4	6.4
	2000	10 468.5	1.9	1.3	0.3	0.9	0.8	51.0	35.3	3.0	5.3	5.4
	2010	10 106.6	0.5	0.7	0.1	0.4	4.0	22.3	33.0	1.1	7.0	36.5
	2011	10 859.7	0.5	0.7	0.1	0.3	4.5	21.5	32.0	1.1	5.3	40.1
Canada	1990	756.0	0.1	0.2	0.0	0.0	0.1	34.5	53.2	6.3	0.9	5.0
	2000	1 018.4	0.1	0.1	0.1	0.0	0.5	40.1	16.0	11.6	0.2	32.2
	2010	3 401.1	0.2	0.4	0.1	0.0	0.6	29.6	50.8	2.9	0.5	16.2
	2011	3 464.9	0.2	0.4	0.1	0.0	0.6	25.7	54.6	2.9	0.5	16.3
United States - États-Unis (5)	1990	22 954.0	6.1	0.6	1.8	12.8	5.6	62.4	5.7	7.8	12.5	11.7
	2000	25 676.0	5.2	1.0	1.6	5.9	3.8	57.8	10.8	6.2	14.7	10.5
	2010	12 791.8	0.9	0.5	0.9	2.2	2.0	31.1	17.5	7.6	29.6	14.4
	2011	12 661.6	0.8	0.4	0.9	2.0	2.0	31.2	17.6	7.7	28.6	14.9
Developed economies: Asia - Économies développées : Asie	**1990**	**42 943.0**	**6.1**	**7.7**	**6.4**	**7.7**	**6.7**	**33.2**	**40.3**	**15.0**	**4.0**	**7.5**
	2000	**23 554.9**	**3.2**	**2.4**	**2.7**	**2.5**	**5.3**	**38.2**	**27.8**	**11.4**	**6.6**	**16.0**
	2010	**18 193.3**	**1.1**	**1.4**	**2.3**	**0.4**	**3.8**	**27.7**	**36.3**	**13.7**	**3.3**	**19.0**
	2011	**22 543.2**	**1.3**	**1.9**	**2.3**	**0.2**	**3.4**	**27.1**	**45.3**	**11.0**	**2.0**	**14.6**
Israel - Israël	1990	586.0	0.0	0.0	0.1	1.7	0.0	0.2	8.9	24.7	65.9	0.3
	2000	832.1	0.0	..	0.0	1.3	0.0	0.3	..	0.9	98.3	0.5
	2010	486.1	0.0	..	0.0	0.3	0.0	1.1	..	1.1	96.8	1.0
	2011	342.5	0.0	0.0	0.0	0.2	0.0	1.6	0.0	0.8	96.3	1.4
Japan - Japon	1990	42 357.0	6.1	7.7	6.3	6.0	6.7	33.7	40.7	14.8	3.2	7.6
	2000	22 722.9	3.2	2.4	2.6	1.2	5.3	39.6	28.8	11.8	3.3	16.5
	2010	17 707.2	1.1	1.4	2.3	0.1	3.8	28.4	37.3	14.1	0.7	19.5
	2011	22 200.7	1.3	1.9	2.3	0.1	3.4	27.5	46.0	11.1	0.6	14.8
Developed economies: Europe - Économies développées : Europe	**1990**	**182 418.0**	**29.4**	**29.6**	**24.5**	**32.4**	**31.5**	**38.0**	**36.3**	**13.5**	**4.0**	**8.2**
	2000	**228 742.9**	**31.9**	**25.3**	**26.2**	**31.6**	**31.4**	**39.4**	**30.4**	**11.6**	**8.8**	**9.8**
	2010	**295 627.9**	**27.0**	**18.6**	**19.7**	**28.4**	**21.7**	**41.0**	**28.7**	**7.2**	**16.3**	**6.8**
	2011	**308 716.1**	**26.3**	**17.6**	**19.2**	**26.7**	**20.9**	**40.5**	**30.3**	**6.8**	**15.9**	**6.5**
Austria - Autriche	1990	355.0	..	0.1	0.1	..	..	..	69.3	30.7	..	..
	2000	100.3	..	..	0.1	..	..	..	..	100.0	..	..
	2010	11.7	..	..	0.0	..	..	..	..	100.0	..	..
	2011	11.7	0.0	0.0	0.0	0.0	0.0	0.0	0.0	100.0	0.0	0.0

For sources and notes, see end of table.

Pour les sources et les notes, se reporter à la fin du tableau.

5.3 World merchant fleet by flag of registration and type of ship of countries and geographical regions

5.3 Flotte marchande mondiale par pavillons d'immatriculation et par types de navires des pays et des régions géographiques

Region, country or territory / Régions pays ou territoires	Year / Année	Total fleet (thousands of DWT) / Flotte totale (milliers de TPL) (1)	As percentage of world total fleet / En pourcentage de la flotte mondiale					As percentage of the country or region total fleet / En pourcentage de la flotte totale du pays ou de la région				
			Oil tankers / Pétroliers	Bulk carriers / Vraquiers	General cargo / Navires de charge classique (2)	Container ships / Porte-conteneurs	Other types / Autres navires	Oil tankers / Pétroliers	Bulk carriers / Vraquiers	General cargo / Navires de charge classique (2)	Container ships / Porte-conteneurs	Other types / Autres navires
Belgium - Belgique	1990	3 282.0	0.1	0.9	0.1	1.0	1.5	6.3	62.5	3.4	6.6	21.2
	2000	149.5	0.0	..	0.0	..	0.2	4.5		0.4	..	95.1
	2010	6 675.1	0.5	0.6	0.1	0.1	1.5	33.0	41.5	2.3	2.0	21.2
	2011	6 799.9	0.4	0.6	0.1	0.1	1.6	28.5	45.0	1.7	1.8	23.0
Bulgaria - Bulgarie	1990	1 956.0	0.2	0.4	0.4	0.1	0.2	23.6	49.5	22.3	0.9	3.7
	2000	1 501.6	0.1	0.3	0.3	0.1	0.1	18.0	54.1	20.9	1.6	5.7
	2010	606.0	0.0	0.1	0.1	0.0	0.0	3.7	66.6	16.8	9.2	3.8
	2011	597.1	0.0	0.1	0.1	0.0	0.0	2.3	73.5	22.3	0.0	1.9
Cyprus - Chypre	1990	32 699.0	4.7	7.1	4.9	1.9	0.9	33.9	48.5	14.9	1.3	1.3
	2000	36 669.4	2.4	7.2	5.7	4.6	1.7	18.8	54.1	15.9	7.9	3.4
	2010	31 305.2	2.3	3.0	1.6	2.9	0.9	32.4	43.7	5.6	15.6	2.7
	2011	32 321.1	2.0	2.8	1.5	2.7	0.9	30.1	46.6	5.2	15.4	2.7
Czechoslovakia (former) - Tchécoslovaquie (anc.)	1990	279.0	..	0.1	0.1	..	0.0	..	54.8	44.8	..	0.4
Denmark - Danemark	1990	6 926.0	1.2	0.3	0.8	5.5	2.8	42.0	8.7	12.0	17.7	19.6
	2000	7 420.8	0.4	0.3	0.8	5.0	2.0	16.1	11.8	10.8	42.5	18.8
	2010	13 813.8	1.2	0.1	0.3	4.0	1.1	38.1	3.7	2.4	48.5	7.2
	2011	14 739.4	1.2	0.1	0.3	3.9	1.1	38.8	2.9	2.2	48.8	7.3
Estonia - Estonie	2000	363.1	0.0	0.0	0.2	..	0.1	3.7	27.8	51.9	..	16.7
	2010	98.7	0.0	..	0.0	..	0.1	12.9	..	15.6	..	71.6
	2011	96.5	0.0	0.0	0.0	0.0	0.1	13.1	0.0	15.6	0.0	71.3
Finland - Finlande	1990	838.0	0.1	0.1	0.3	..	0.5	21.4	14.8	35.2	..	28.6
	2000	1 239.5	0.2	0.0	0.4	..	0.3	41.0	10.8	31.2	..	17.0
	2010	1 171.3	0.1	0.0	0.4	0.0	0.1	52.0	0.3	34.2	3.2	10.3
	2011	1 156.9	0.1	0.0	0.4	0.0	0.1	52.7	0.3	33.3	3.2	10.5
France	1990	6 653.0	1.6	0.5	0.6	2.6	1.1	57.3	16.3	9.4	8.8	8.2
	2000	7 292.5	1.6	0.4	0.4	0.8	1.4	60.8	14.0	4.9	7.1	13.2
	2010	8 822.3	1.3	0.1	0.1	1.1	1.0	64.0	3.9	1.0	20.3	10.7
	2011	8 335.6	1.1	0.1	0.1	1.1	1.0	59.8	4.2	1.0	23.9	11.1
Germany - Allemagne	1990	6 778.0	0.1	0.5	2.5	9.1	2.0	4.6	14.9	36.9	29.9	13.8
	2000	7 788.3	0.0	0.0	1.0	9.9	0.5	0.1	0.1	13.6	81.2	4.9
	2010	17 570.2	0.1	0.2	0.5	9.0	0.4	3.2	4.7	3.1	86.9	2.1
	2011	17 565.6	0.1	0.2	0.4	8.3	0.4	3.2	4.7	2.6	87.3	2.2
Gibraltar	1990	5 026.0	1.7	0.3	0.2	..	0.1	80.7	14.0	3.9	..	1.4
	2000	728.5	0.2	0.0	0.0	0.1	0.1	76.0	3.7	4.9	8.6	6.8
Greece - Grèce	1990	38 465.0	6.8	8.2	2.9	1.0	2.1	41.6	47.7	7.5	0.6	2.6
	2000	42 532.1	8.9	5.1	0.9	2.2	1.8	58.9	32.7	2.1	3.3	3.0
	2010	67 629.2	9.4	4.7	0.3	1.4	1.2	62.6	31.6	0.5	3.6	1.7
	2011	71 420.3	9.2	4.5	0.3	1.3	1.2	61.4	33.2	0.4	3.3	1.6
Hungary - Hongrie	1990	108.0	..	..	0.1	..	..	..	..	100.0	..	..
	2000	14.9	..	..	0.0	..	..	..	..	100.0	..	..
Iceland - Islande	1990	155.0	0.0	0.0	0.1	..	0.1	0.6	12.3	49.7	..	37.4
	2000	83.6	0.0	0.0	0.0	0.0	0.1	3.2	0.8	3.5	14.8	77.7
	2010	69.4	0.0	0.0	0.0	..	0.1	0.7	0.9	1.0	..	97.4
	2011	66.0	0.0	0.0	0.0	0.0	0.1	0.7	1.0	1.0	0.0	97.3
Ireland - Irlande	1990	178.0	0.0	..	0.1	0.1	0.1	6.2	..	55.1	14.0	24.7
	2000	154.4	0.0	0.0	0.1	0.0	0.0	0.2	7.9	65.5	4.4	22.0
	2010	196.2	0.0	..	0.1	0.0	0.0	9.4	..	73.9	3.8	12.9
	2011	241.5	0.0	0.0	0.2	0.0	0.0	7.6	0.0	78.0	3.1	11.3
Italy - Italie (6)	1990	11 524.0	1.8	1.9	1.2	1.5	2.9	37.7	36.5	10.7	2.9	12.2
	2000	9 768.8	1.0	1.3	0.9	1.0	2.7	28.7	35.8	9.5	6.7	19.4
	2010	17 276.0	1.8	1.1	1.4	0.6	1.6	47.3	29.0	8.8	6.3	8.7
	2011	19 440.2	1.9	1.2	1.5	0.6	1.6	45.3	33.1	8.5	5.4	7.7
Latvia - Lettonie	2000	101.5	0.0	..	0.0	..	0.1	15.1	..	47.0	..	37.9
	2010	180.3	0.0	..	0.0	..	0.1	58.9	..	12.5	..	28.6
	2011	158.5	0.0	0.0	0.0	..	0.1	50.9	0.0	13.4	..	35.7
Lithuania - Lituanie	2000	414.6	0.0	0.1	0.2	..	0.1	1.8	38.6	45.8	..	13.8
	2010	364.2	0.0	..	0.3	0.0	0.1	0.4	..	75.2	3.8	20.6
	2011	350.0	0.0	0.0	0.2	0.0	0.1	0.5	0.0	74.9	3.9	20.7

For sources and notes, see end of table.

Pour les sources et les notes, se reporter à la fin du tableau.

5.3 World merchant fleet by flag of registration and type of ship of countries and geographical regions

5.3 Flotte marchande mondiale par pavillons d'immatriculation et par types de navires des pays et des régions géographiques

Region, country or territory / Régions pays ou territoires	Year / Année	Total fleet (thousands of DWT) / Flotte totale (milliers de TPL) (1)	As percentage of world total fleet / En pourcentage de la flotte mondiale					As percentage of the country or region total fleet / En pourcentage de la flotte totale du pays ou de la région				
			Oil tankers / Pétroliers	Bulk carriers / Vraquiers	General cargo / Navires de charge classique (2)	Container ships / Porte-conteneurs	Other types / Autres navires	Oil tankers / Pétroliers	Bulk carriers / Vraquiers	General cargo / Navires de charge classique (2)	Container ships / Porte-conteneurs	Other types / Autres navires
Luxembourg	1990	6.0	0.0	..	..	..	0.0	50.0	..	..	..	50.0
	2000	1 959.6	0.4	0.1	0.1	0.0	1.0	51.0	8.8	2.9	1.2	36.1
	2010	1 099.8	0.1	0.0	0.1	0.1	0.4	23.2	17.5	10.2	17.1	32.0
	2011	1 135.4	0.0	0.0	0.1	0.1	0.5	17.7	7.5	12.6	20.9	41.2
Malta - Malte	1990	5 691.0	1.1	0.9	1.1	0.0	0.3	43.5	35.2	19.0	0.1	2.2
	2000	46 749.4	7.8	6.2	5.3	1.5	1.7	47.4	36.5	11.5	2.0	2.6
	2010	56 156.1	4.6	6.1	3.4	1.7	1.2	36.8	49.4	6.6	5.1	2.0
	2011	61 204.0	4.6	5.0	0.2	2.2	1.4	37.3	48.2	5.7	6.7	2.1
Netherlands - Pays-Bas	1990	4 557.0	0.2	0.2	1.8	2.3	2.4	12.6	12.0	36.7	11.2	26.6
	2000	6 607.3	0.1	0.0	2.8	2.8	2.3	4.0	1.6	42.4	27.0	25.0
	2010	7 252.5	0.1	0.0	3.3	1.1	1.2	9.0	0.7	49.7	25.6	15.0
	2011	7 036.1	0.1	0.0	3.6	0.7	1.1	9.6	0.7	55.4	18.7	15.6
Norway - Norvège	1990	26 568.0	5.5	3.5	1.7	0.3	8.3	48.9	29.6	6.3	0.2	14.9
	2000	35 388.0	6.2	2.6	3.8	0.2	9.8	49.2	19.9	10.8	0.3	19.7
	2010	20 811.2	2.1	0.9	3.1	0.0	4.4	45.0	19.4	15.9	0.0	19.6
	2011	20 081.2	1.8	0.8	2.9	0.0	4.1	43.2	21.2	15.8	0.0	19.8
Poland - Pologne	1990	4 490.0	0.1	1.2	1.4	0.2	0.5	4.9	57.6	31.6	1.0	4.9
	2000	1 855.4	0.0	0.6	0.1	..	0.2	0.4	88.8	3.8	..	6.9
	2010	130.9	0.0	..	0.0	..	0.1	5.7	..	22.7	..	71.6
	2011	102.6	0.0	0.0	0.0	0.0	0.1	7.3	0.0	19.2	0.0	73.5
Portugal	1990	1 102.0	0.3	0.1	0.1	0.0	0.2	54.8	26.3	9.5	0.9	8.4
	2000	1 630.0	0.3	0.1	0.4	0.1	0.3	44.9	17.6	23.7	2.5	11.3
	2010	1 288.3	0.2	0.0	0.2	0.0	0.2	52.5	11.4	20.1	2.7	13.3
	2011	1 212.1	0.1	0.0	0.2	0.0	0.2	52.1	6.7	22.3	6.0	12.9
Romania - Roumanie	1990	5 711.0	0.4	1.3	1.6	0.1	0.3	18.5	51.1	27.8	0.3	2.3
	2000	1 618.3	0.0	0.2	0.8	0.0	0.2	6.4	32.1	51.3	0.5	9.6
	2010	244.1	0.0	..	0.1	..	0.1	19.3	..	33.6	..	47.1
	2011	64.6	0.0	0.0	0.0	0.0	0.0	12.3	0.0	21.3	0.0	66.4
Slovakia - Slovaquie	2000	19.5	..	..	0.0	..	..	..	..	100.0	..	..
	2010	192.9	..	0.0	0.2	..	0.0	..	7.9	92.0	..	0.1
	2011	73.6	0.0	0.0	0.1	0.0	0.0	0.0	20.6	79.1	0.0	0.3
Slovenia - Slovénie	2000	0.8	..	..	0.0	..	0.0	..	..	29.9	..	70.1
	2010	0.4	..	..	..	..	0.0	..	..	..	..	100.0
	2011	0.4	0.0	0.0	0.0	0.0	0.0	0.0	0.0	0.0	0.0	100.0
Spain - Espagne	1990	6 461.0	1.3	0.8	0.8	0.5	1.6	47.4	27.3	12.0	1.7	11.6
	2000	2 053.0	0.4	0.0	0.3	0.2	0.7	51.1	3.4	14.3	6.6	24.6
	2010	2 554.7	0.2	0.0	0.2	0.1	1.2	40.5	1.4	8.1	6.5	43.5
	2011	2 750.2	0.2	0.0	0.2	0.0	1.4	39.1	1.5	7.8	2.4	49.2
Sweden - Suède	1990	1 995.0	0.1	0.1	0.9	0.3	0.9	14.6	13.7	46.8	3.6	21.3
	2000	1 846.0	0.1	0.0	1.0	..	0.9	8.7	2.4	55.9	..	33.0
	2010	2 206.3	0.1	0.0	1.2	..	0.3	28.0	1.6	57.1	..	13.3
	2011	1 762.4	0.1	0.0	1.0	0.0	0.3	18.5	2.1	63.3	0.0	16.2
Switzerland - Suisse	1990	363.0	..	0.1	0.0	..	0.1	..	83.7	9.4	..	6.9
	2000	779.0	..	0.3	0.0	..	0.1	..	91.7	3.6	..	4.7
	2010	1 023.1	0.0	0.1	0.1	0.1	0.0	8.6	61.3	10.3	19.2	0.5
	2011	1 128.9	0.0	0.1	0.1	0.1	0.0	7.7	68.4	9.4	13.9	0.6
United Kingdom - Royaume-Uni	1990	10 252.0	2.0	1.0	0.7	5.9	2.7	46.1	21.8	6.9	12.8	12.4
	2000	11 913.1	2.0	0.5	0.6	3.0	3.3	46.9	11.8	5.5	16.3	19.6
	2010	36 887.2	2.9	1.5	2.5	6.1	4.3	34.9	18.9	7.4	28.0	10.8
	2011	38 774.3	3.0	1.6	2.6	5.5	3.6	36.3	21.5	7.3	26.1	8.9
Developed economies: Oceania - Économies développées : Océanie	**1990**	**4 006.0**	**0.5**	**0.9**	**0.3**	**0.6**	**0.9**	**30.7**	**48.4**	**7.0**	**3.1**	**10.8**
	2000	**3 018.8**	**0.2**	**0.5**	**0.1**	**0.1**	**1.5**	**17.6**	**44.0**	**2.3**	**1.6**	**34.5**
	2010	**2 498.5**	**0.1**	**0.1**	**0.3**	**0.0**	**1.2**	**19.3**	**24.0**	**11.6**	**0.3**	**44.8**
	2011	**2 334.0**	**0.1**	**0.1**	**0.3**	**0.0**	**1.2**	**12.5**	**23.1**	**13.5**	**0.3**	**50.6**
Australia - Australie	1990	3 707.0	0.5	0.8	0.2	0.5	0.8	29.8	51.1	5.3	3.0	10.8
	2000	2 686.2	0.1	0.5	0.1	0.1	1.2	15.2	48.9	2.2	1.8	32.0
	2010	2 171.1	0.1	0.1	0.1	..	1.2	18.1	26.7	6.1	..	49.1
	2011	1 946.9	0.0	0.1	0.1	0.0	1.2	10.4	24.8	7.4	0.0	57.4

For sources and notes, see end of table.

Pour les sources et les notes, se reporter à la fin du tableau.

5.3 World merchant fleet by flag of registration and type of ship of countries and geographical regions

5.3 Flotte marchande mondiale par pavillons d'immatriculation et par types de navires des pays et des régions géographiques

Region, country or territory / Régions pays ou territoires	Year / Année	Total fleet (thousands of DWT) / Flotte totale (milliers de TPL) (1)	As percentage of world total fleet / En pourcentage de la flotte mondiale					As percentage of the country or region total fleet / En pourcentage de la flotte totale du pays ou de la région				
			Oil tankers / Pétroliers	Bulk carriers / Vraquiers	General cargo / Navires de charge classique (2)	Container ships / Porte-conteneurs	Other types / Autres navires	Oil tankers / Pétroliers	Bulk carriers / Vraquiers	General cargo / Navires de charge classique (2)	Container ships / Porte-conteneurs	Other types / Autres navires
New Zealand - Nouvelle-Zélande	1990	299.0	0.1	0.0	0.1	0.1	0.1	42.1	14.0	27.8	4.7	11.4
	2000	332.7	0.0	0.0	0.0	..	0.3	37.1	5.1	3.2	..	54.6
	2010	327.4	0.0	0.0	0.1	0.0	0.1	27.2	6.2	47.6	2.5	16.5
	2011	387.1	0.0	0.0	0.2	0.0	0.1	22.9	14.5	44.1	2.1	16.4
World n.e.s. - Monde n.d.a.	2010	5 611.0	0.3	0.2	2.1	0.1	1.0	22.5	17.5	40.4	3.5	16.2
	2011	7 129.8	0.2	0.3	2.6	0.1	1.3	16.0	22.8	39.9	3.5	17.0
Major 10 open and international registries - 10 principaux pays de libre immatriculation et de registre international (7)	*1990*	*233 082.0*	*44.2*	*37.0*	*28.9*	*24.4*	*24.4*	*44.7*	*35.5*	*12.4*	*2.3*	*5.0*
	2000	*405 458.6*	*52.3*	*57.2*	*44.0*	*44.6*	*38.4*	*36.5*	*38.7*	*11.0*	*7.0*	*6.7*
	2010	*707 456.7*	*55.5*	*61.3*	*40.0*	*53.6*	*47.7*	*35.3*	*39.6*	*6.1*	*12.8*	*6.2*
	2011	*782 989.9*	*56.0*	*61.2*	*40.1*	*55.2*	*48.2*	*34.0*	*41.6*	*5.6*	*13.0*	*5.9*
Developing economies excluding major open and international registries - Économies en développement sans les principaux pays de libre immatriculation et de registre international	1990	147 117.0	16.5	27.6	31.7	20.8	20.9	26.4	42.0	21.6	3.2	6.8
	2000	183 808.6	18.1	26.6	31.4	21.3	19.9	27.9	39.8	17.3	7.4	7.7
	2010	321 951.6	23.2	27.0	35.6	19.8	24.0	32.5	38.3	12.0	10.4	6.9
	2011	355 902.2	23.5	27.2	35.0	20.6	24.7	31.4	40.6	10.7	10.6	6.7
Developing economies: Africa excluding major open and international registries - Économies en développement : Afrique sans les principaux pays de libre immatriculation et de registre international	1990	7 638.0	1.0	0.5	2.4	1.2	3.6	29.5	13.2	31.0	3.7	22.7
	2000	6 365.9	0.6	0.5	1.6	0.7	1.9	24.9	22.4	25.0	6.9	20.8
	2010	8 610.8	0.7	0.3	1.9	0.1	1.9	37.9	15.6	23.7	2.3	20.4
	2011	9 436.0	0.7	0.3	2.1	0.1	1.8	36.0	19.5	24.2	2.2	18.1
Developing economies: America excluding major open and international registries - Économies en développement : Amérique sans les principaux pays de libre immatriculation et de registre international	1990	22 370.0	2.8	3.6	5.1	1.1	4.9	29.9	35.5	22.9	1.1	10.5
	2000	19 057.9	2.4	1.8	4.2	0.5	3.8	35.4	26.2	22.4	1.8	14.2
	2010	22 361.7	1.9	1.2	4.2	0.3	3.6	37.5	26.3	20.4	2.1	14.7
	2011	22 907.3	1.8	1.1	4.2	0.4	3.5	37.9	24.7	19.9	3.0	14.6
Developed economies excluding major open and international registries - Économies développées sans les principaux pays de libre immatriculation et de registre international (8)	1990	204 435.0	34.4	30.0	26.4	45.7	41.0	39.7	32.8	12.9	5.0	9.6
	2000	186 679.2	28.4	15.3	19.0	31.0	35.7	43.1	22.5	10.3	10.6	13.6
	2010	208 164.0	19.0	10.4	15.7	20.3	22.9	42.4	22.9	8.2	16.5	10.1
	2011	217 330.4	18.9	10.4	15.5	18.5	22.3	41.2	25.5	7.8	15.7	9.8

Sources:
- UNCTAD, Division on Technology and Logistics, Trade Logistics Branch

Notes:

(1) DWT (deadweight ton) is the weight measure of a vessel's carrying capacity. It includes cargo, fuel and stores.
(2) Including passenger/cargo combined.
(3) Year 2002: break in series; from 2002 onwards, ships registered under the flag of the Marshall Islands (developing country) are shown separately; before they were included with the United States of America (developed country).
(4) From 2002 onwards, ships registered under the flag of the Marshall Islands are shown separately; before they were included with the United States of America.
(5) Year 2002: break in series; from 2002 onwards, ships registered under the flag of the Marshall Islands are shown separately; before they were included with the United States of America.
(6) Including San Marino.
(7) UNCTAD has grouped the 10 major open and international registries to include the 10 largest fleets with more than 90 per cent foreign-controlled tonnage. Accordingly, the following 10 economies appear in the group: Antigua and Barbuda, Bahamas, Bermuda, Cyprus, Isle of Man, Liberia, Malta, Marshall Islands, Panama, and Saint Vincent and Grenadines.
From 1995 onwards, the data for this group cover also the fleet of the Isle of Man, included otherwise with figures of the United Kingdom and not shown separately.
(8) Before 1995, Isle of Man is included.

Sources :
- CNUCED, Division de la technologie et de la logistique, Service de la logistique commerciale

Notes :

(1) TPL (Tonne de port en lourd) : c' est une mesure de poids de la capacité de charge d'un navire. Il inclut la cargaison, le carburant et les magasins.
(2) Y compris les cargos mixtes.
(3) Année 2002 : rupture de série ; les navires immatriculés aux Îles Marshall (pays en développement) sont présentés séparément à partir de 2002 ; avant, ils étaient compris dans les chiffres des États-Unis (pays développé).
(4) Les navires immatriculés aux Îles Marshall sont présentés séparément à partir de 2002 ; avant, ils étaient compris dans les chiffres des États-Unis.
(5) Année 2002 : rupture de série ; les navires immatriculés aux Îles Marshall sont présentés séparément à partir de 2002 ; avant, ils étaient compris dans les chiffres des États-Unis.
(6) Y compris Saint-Marin.
(7) La CNUCED a regroupé les pays de libre immatriculation en incluant les 10 plus grandes flottes dont le tonnage, contrôlé par les non-résidents, dépasse 90% du tonnage total du pays. Par conséquent, les 10 pays suivants font partie du groupe : Antigua-et-Barbuda, Bahamas, Bermudes, Chypre, Îles Marshall, Île de Man, Libéria, Malte, Panama et Saint-Vincent-et-les-Grenadines. À partir de 1995, les données de ce groupe comprennent aussi la flotte de l'Île de Man. Avant cette date, les données n'étaient pas présentées séparément car elles étaient comprises dans la flotte du Royaume-Uni.
(8) Y compris l'île de Man avant 1995.

5

6

COMMODITIES

PRODUITS DE BASE

1
2
3
4
5
6
7
8

6.1 Annual and quarterly indices of free-market prices of selected primary commodities
2000 = 100

Primary commodity	Level (1) Niveau (1) 2000	1985	1990	1995	2003	2004	2005	2006	2007	2008	2009	2010
ALL COMMODITIES	–	96.2	124.0	137.6	104.9	125.8	140.4	182.8	206.5	256.0	212.7	251.4
All food	–	103.4	121.8	138.9	106.8	120.8	128.4	149.4	169.2	235.6	215.6	231.6
Food and tropical beverages	–	98.8	123.5	135.5	103.1	116.7	127.0	149.6	162.5	228.2	215.9	227.9
Food	–	89.6	125.4	132.3	104.1	118.6	127.2	151.3	164.1	233.9	219.9	229.6
1. Wheat*	119.6	91.4	88.9	139.4	126.8	114.9	109.2	128.5	209.1	246.0	183.1	210.8
2. Wheat	119.2	110.0	88.8	150.0	126.2	131.8	132.9	168.2	225.9	288.0	197.4	204.0
3. Maize	86.8	..	123.9	142.7	117.9	120.3	103.8	138.6	188.8	237.9	195.9	220.0
4. Maize*	90.0	..	121.9	139.0	118.9	124.9	109.9	136.8	189.0	253.2	191.4	216.8
5. Rice	203.8	106.7	140.9	157.8	97.9	120.6	141.2	149.0	163.1	343.6	289.2	255.8
6. Sugar (2)	8.2	49.6	153.4	102.4	86.7	87.6	120.4	160.0	120.0	166.5	221.9	260.2
7. Beef (2)	87.8	111.2	131.5	98.5	110.2	129.8	135.2	131.9	134.5	138.0	136.3	173.8
8. Bananas (2)	19.0	90.7	123.6	104.7	89.4	125.1	137.4	162.8	161.4	201.1	202.6	210.0
9. Pepper	4 341.6	93.0	41.3	87.3	64.7	59.1	57.1	74.5	109.3	119.9	105.4	139.0
10. Soybean meal	199.7	78.7	107.1	105.5	112.4	128.6	116.5	110.3	160.5	226.2	210.4	196.0
11. Fish meal	413.0	67.8	99.8	119.9	147.9	157.1	172.2	281.9	285.0	274.4	297.7	408.6
Tropical beverages	–	179.1	107.6	163.3	94.1	100.2	125.7	134.1	148.0	178.0	181.5	213.2
12. Coffee (2)	102.6	151.9	94.1	154.3	65.6	82.0	114.0	115.4	123.5	142.1	176.3	218.1
13. Coffee (2)	79.9	190.0	103.7	182.7	63.6	85.4	126.9	128.8	138.6	153.4	139.5	182.5
14. Coffee (2)	85.1	171.1	104.7	175.4	75.3	94.2	134.3	133.9	144.8	162.5	166.5	228.4
15. Coffee (2)	42.1	288.2	130.5	301.0	91.2	88.5	126.7	166.9	209.6	252.4	183.2	199.6
16. Coffee* (2)	63.6	209.8	113.3	217.0	80.6	92.3	131.8	144.8	166.3	192.3	172.0	218.9
17. Cocoa (2)	40.3	254.0	143.2	161.5	197.7	174.5	173.3	179.4	219.9	290.7	325.4	353.0
18. Tea (3)	248.1	..	..	71.1	78.3	79.9	87.2	97.4	85.4	108.6	126.5	125.3
Vegetable oilseeds and oils	–	141.2	107.0	167.1	137.2	155.3	140.6	147.7	225.7	297.8	213.3	261.7
19. Soybeans	211.8	106.3	116.5	122.4	124.6	144.7	129.7	126.8	181.3	246.8	205.9	212.3
20. Soybean oil	338.1	169.2	132.3	184.9	163.8	182.2	161.2	177.1	260.7	372.2	251.0	297.2
21. Sunflower oil	391.8	153.7	124.9	176.9	151.4	174.6	172.9	167.9	260.8	382.5	218.1	274.2
22. Groundnut oil	713.7	126.8	135.0	138.8	174.2	162.7	148.6	135.9	189.4	292.7	165.9	196.7
23. Copra	304.8	126.7	75.7	143.9	98.4	147.7	135.8	132.1	199.3	267.7	157.4	246.0
24. Coconut oil	450.3	131.1	74.8	148.7	103.8	146.7	137.0	134.8	204.1	271.8	161.1	249.5
25. Palm kernel oil	443.5	124.3	75.3	152.8	103.4	146.1	141.4	131.0	200.3	254.7	158.4	267.0
26. Palm oil	310.3	161.3	93.4	202.5	142.9	151.9	136.1	154.2	251.5	305.8	220.1	290.4
Agricultural raw materials	–	94.0	128.2	150.4	110.6	125.4	129.4	146.6	164.2	197.9	163.3	225.7
27. Linseed oil	398.4	157.5	177.9	165.0	170.2	218.5	276.5	168.6	251.3	389.3	246.6	292.0
28. Tobacco	2 988.1	87.4	113.7	88.5	88.6	91.7	93.4	99.4	110.9	120.1	141.8	144.4
29. Cotton (2)	83.8	117.6	112.1	133.8	88.8	97.1	88.0	102.5	..	116.1	105.0	126.9
30. Cotton (2)	65.5	108.9	127.9	159.4	105.9	95.8	89.9	92.8	98.8	111.1	100.4	156.8
31. Cotton (2)	57.3	111.8	138.4	176.0	105.5	107.3	97.6	101.6	111.2	124.7	113.8	180.1
32. Cotton* (2)	51.7	90.7	150.3	161.5	120.7	92.5	101.1	110.9	135.3	..	..	..
33. Cotton* (2)	59.2	101.0	139.5	164.4	107.1	103.6	91.5	97.0	106.8	120.5	105.8	175.0
34. Cotton (2)	108.5	147.9	236.0	..	103.5	109.5	93.2	126.3	114.8	113.8	106.4	156.9
35. Wool	7 335.4	..	..	..	95.7	97.2	92.4	97.6	132.6	132.0	106.1	139.5
36. Wool	2 809.8	..	..	..	234.5	196.9	188.8	192.4	272.2	252.4	217.6	291.7
37. Jute	278.8	204.2	146.5	131.2	86.8	106.3	135.4	136.3	119.6	167.7	201.0	309.9
38. Sisal	782.1	79.2	95.0	97.4	102.1	123.7	128.0	134.2	130.9	145.4	104.5	142.0
39. Sisal	628.7	83.6	113.7	113.0	111.1	139.0	143.3	150.7	152.4	171.3	122.6	160.6
40. Hides (2)	80.2	63.8	115.0	109.9	85.2	83.7	82.0	86.1	90.0	79.8	55.9	89.7
41. Non-coniferous woods*	85.2	..	..	103.6	109.4	111.1	117.4	131.8	145.5	154.0	154.4	160.7
42. Tropical logs (4)	244.6	71.1	140.4	139.4	114.3	136.3	136.7	130.2	155.7	216.8	172.1	175.2
43. Tropical sawnwood* (4)	531.8	51.9	98.6	144.2	102.2	103.4	103.4	103.4	103.4	103.4	103.4	..
44. Plywood* (5)	448.5	47.0	79.1	129.9	97.2	103.6	113.4	132.8	143.9	143.9	125.9	126.9
45. Rubber	726.5	..	119.6	226.9	154.2	185.9	210.9	289.5	319.4	372.7	270.6	492.4

For sources and notes, see end of table.

6.1 Indices annuels et trimestriels des prix d'une sélection de produits de base sur le marché libre
2000 = 100

2008		2009				2010				2011		Produits de base
III	IV	I	II	III	IV	I	II	III	IV	I	II	
270.7	**198.8**	**188.1**	**203.3**	**222.6**	**237.0**	**244.9**	**230.9**	**245.7**	**284.1**	**312.4**	**300.3**	**TOTAL DES PRODUITS**
246.1	**190.6**	**200.2**	**210.7**	**222.6**	**229.0**	**229.0**	**207.4**	**228.3**	**261.5**	**284.1**	**271.8**	**Total des produits alimentaires**
239.0	*191.3*	*201.7*	*208.8*	*223.6*	*229.5*	*228.4*	*204.3*	*224.8*	*254.2*	*274.6*	*263.0*	***Produits alimentaires et boissons tropicales***
244.5	195.5	206.0	212.7	227.9	232.9	231.9	204.7	225.3	256.7	274.3	260.8	*Produits alimentaires*
255.1	178.2	178.7	180.4	186.4	186.7	184.7	185.8	223.2	249.3	285.3	289.5	1. Blé*
279.3	205.0	207.1	217.3	181.5	183.8	173.7	160.8	226.0	266.1	291.7	292.9	2. Blé
258.9	180.5	186.4	206.7	189.0	201.4	192.1	190.6	234.4	290.1	330.5	353.1	3. Maïs
277.7	188.3	189.8	200.4	176.7	198.9	188.2	181.1	222.2	275.5	320.0	347.4	4. Maïs*
369.4	284.3	306.6	272.7	255.5	264.3	282.6	234.0	242.1	263.9	257.3	248.5	5. Riz
172.7	145.8	160.0	100.0	260.6	278.9	287.5	193.4	238.3	321.7	347.7	291.5	6. Sucre (2)
151.1	129.8	126.4	135.9	141.2	141.6	162.5	177.6	171.2	183.8	211.5	210.9	7. Viande de boeuf (2)
185.3	202.9	209.7	209.2	197.0	194.3	191.8	211.7	219.9	216.7	234.9	240.1	8. Bananes (2)
120.4	102.0	93.3	97.1	111.2	119.9	118.5	128.2	144.9	164.5	184.4	205.2	9. Poivre
231.0	175.3	190.8	215.4	221.6	213.7	198.5	178.8	193.0	213.9	221.1	201.0	10. Farine de soja
290.0	247.8	245.4	265.0	309.0	371.6	401.9	439.1	402.7	390.5	421.3	399.0	11. Farine de poisson
191.1	*154.9*	*164.2*	*175.2*	*185.7*	*200.7*	*198.3*	*201.0*	*220.4*	*232.9*	*277.7*	*283.0*	*Boissons tropicales*
148.1	130.4	149.6	198.8	176.6	180.2	204.4	202.0	231.3	234.5	282.8	294.3	12. Café (2)
162.7	126.2	125.0	135.4	138.9	158.7	156.5	159.7	192.7	220.8	293.8	327.5	13. Café (2)
169.5	140.9	150.6	167.2	168.6	179.4	185.0	211.1	250.8	266.8	331.2	342.5	14. Café (2)
265.3	210.9	193.8	181.5	179.8	177.6	175.0	186.0	210.6	227.0	271.5	292.8	15. Café (2)
201.2	164.1	164.9	172.0	172.3	178.8	181.7	202.8	237.5	253.7	311.4	326.1	16. Café* (2)
317.0	254.5	292.3	290.5	333.9	385.0	371.4	361.7	344.6	334.1	376.6	346.2	17. Cacao (2)
125.1	100.9	106.8	114.5	139.7	145.1	128.7	114.1	120.8	137.5	140.9	132.6	18. Thé (3)
305.5	**184.9**	**188.0**	**226.1**	**214.5**	**224.5**	**233.6**	**233.2**	**257.6**	**322.4**	**363.6**	**344.8**	**Graines oléagineuses et huiles végétales**
267.4	178.1	186.0	217.5	213.1	207.2	196.7	192.9	213.4	246.4	266.7	262.8	19. Fèves de soja
400.2	245.5	223.2	255.2	253.3	272.4	271.3	259.0	291.0	367.3	398.9	387.8	20. Huile de soja
356.2	216.4	202.4	228.9	207.0	234.2	243.7	231.6	265.8	355.5	369.0	363.9	21. Huile de tournesol
338.6	248.8	179.8	163.4	168.8	101.4	190.4	189.4	182.4	224.7	241.4	256.4	22. Huile d'arachide
268.0	170.5	146.7	168.2	153.8	161.0	182.6	208.2	252.4	340.6	452.5	440.4	23. Coprah
276.8	171.4	150.4	173.0	158.0	163.1	185.3	212.0	257.3	343.4	460.4	443.3	24. Huile de coprah
251.3	137.3	130.2	172.0	157.8	173.5	208.0	233.1	261.9	365.1	480.5	422.6	25. Huile de palmiste
299.1	165.0	186.1	239.5	218.8	236.1	260.3	262.0	281.9	357.1	403.2	369.7	26. Huile de palme
216.0	**163.3**	**146.0**	**149.5**	**164.4**	**193.1**	**210.1**	**208.6**	**215.9**	**268.3**	**314.9**	**303.4**	**Matières premières d'origine agricole**
446.9	282.9	214.4	232.8	249.0	290.0	265.0	240.9	322.9	339.0	380.5	388.0	27. Huile de lin
123.8	126.2	135.3	141.1	143.1	147.6	145.7	141.7	145.0	144.9	146.6	149.5	28. Tabac
117.2	116.7	109.3	103.9	99.1	107.7	119.4	125.5	140.0	..	..	293.1	29. Coton (2)
117.8	88.9	84.8	94.4	103.8	118.4	118.2	138.5	142.6	228.1	310.4	293.5	30. Coton (2)
132.9	101.0	95.4	105.4	118.8	135.7	143.3	157.1	161.3	258.9	352.5	329.7	31. Coton (2)
..	..	..	..	..	..	..	..	..	..	..	..	32. Coton* (2)
128.8	97.2	92.5	101.4	108.7	120.8	136.9	152.6	157.1	253.4	349.9	309.1	33. Coton* (2)
122.0	120.0	111.8	103.7	97.1	112.8	125.2	136.3	141.6	219.5	257.2	..	34. Coton (2)
131.2	93.0	83.1	99.5	111.5	130.3	135.4	128.6	129.1	164.8	222.0	245.4	35. Laine
257.2	170.7	163.1	204.7	232.0	270.5	297.7	278.2	279.7	311.3	393.4	474.5	36. Laine
182.9	182.3	173.3	202.6	197.3	230.7	316.2	373.6	260.6	289.3	271.4	245.1	37. Jute
153.9	120.8	114.6	..	91.8	107.0	126.2	142.8	148.3	150.9	162.8	166.2	38. Sisal
200.0	143.2	135.2	124.6	106.0	124.6	143.2	157.5	168.9	172.9	186.6	190.9	39. Sisal
85.2	69.0	42.4	39.9	66.9	74.4	83.9	90.5	90.6	93.7	98.0	109.7	40. Peaux (2)
153.8	161.1	162.2	154.1	152.5	149.0	147.6	162.0	166.5	166.7	158.8	157.0	41. Bois non conifères*
224.3	199.2	174.5	161.5	169.7	182.7	176.4	166.5	174.4	183.5	182.3	201.1	42. Grumes tropicales (4)
103.4	103.4	103.4	103.4	..	..	..	..	..	..	..	..	43. Grumes tropicales sciées* (4)
144.7	143.9	127.7	126.1	125.2	124.5	124.2	126.3	127.6	129.4	131.2	134.5	44. Contre-plaqué* (5)
434.9	250.2	208.7	231.7	273.2	368.7	452.6	443.2	459.5	614.4	759.7	679.9	45. Caoutchouc

Pour les sources et les notes, se reporter à la fin du tableau.

6

Primary commodity	Level (1) Niveau (1) 2000	1985	1990	1995	2003	2004	2005	2006	2007	2008	2009	2010
Minerals, ores and metals	_	**81.2**	**127.0**	**128.1**	**97.6**	**137.3**	**173.2**	**277.7**	**313.2**	**332.5**	**231.6**	**309.7**
46. Phosphate rock	43.8	76.6	92.6	80.0	86.9	93.7	96.0	101.1	162.1	789.9	278.1	281.2
47. Manganese ore	186.0	74.5	213.1	109.7	106.7	106.7	175.8	139.7	191.9	758.5	293.8	415.0
48. Iron ore (6)	27.7	96.0	111.3	97.4	112.2	131.7	225.9	268.8	294.4	485.8	348.8	348.8
49. Iron ore* (6)	27.5	96.5	109.8	97.4	109.8	126.2	201.0	256.4	286.1	467.6	396.0	352.7
50. Aluminium	1 549.2	69.8	105.8	116.6	92.4	110.8	122.5	165.9	170.3	166.1	107.4	140.2
51. Copper	1 813.1	78.2	146.8	161.8	98.1	158.0	202.9	370.7	392.6	383.6	282.8	415.6
52. Copper* (2)	86.8	75.6	140.4	158.4	96.6	152.8	198.4	361.2	376.6	366.2	776.4	999.9
53. Nickel*	8 637.7	56.8	102.6	95.3	111.5	160.0	170.6	280.7	430.9	244.3	100.6	262.4
54. Nickel (2)	397.9	56.8	102.3	98.1	111.7	159.4	171.2	276.0	424.8	248.1	174.0	262.3
55. Lead	454.0	86.1	170.6	138.9	113.5	195.2	215.0	283.8	568.2	460.2	378.6	473.2
56. Lead* (2)	43.6	43.8	103.4	96.3	100.4	126.6	140.1	178.0	284.2	276.2	155.4	250.0
57. Zinc	1 128.1	67.0	134.6	91.4	73.4	92.9	122.5	290.3	287.4	166.2	146.7	191.5
58. Zinc* (2)	55.6	72.6	134.1	95.9	73.1	94.4	120.7	285.7	277.6	159.9	139.8	183.4
59. Tin	5 432.8	221.8	114.8	114.3	90.0	156.5	135.8	161.5	267.4	340.5	249.6	375.4
60. Tin*	5 382.0	221.5	113.1	113.1	90.9	157.8	136.7	162.9	269.9	341.6	248.9	377.8
61. Tungsten (7)	44.9	150.9	103.4	141.2	100.0	122.9	271.3	369.7	367.4	366.5	334.0	334.0
62. Gold* (8)	279.0	113.7	137.4	137.7	130.3	146.6	159.4	216.6	249.7	312.4	348.7	439.9
63. Silver* (9)	499.9	122.9	96.4	103.8	98.2	133.3	146.8	231.4	268.3	300.1	294.0	404.1
MEMO ITEM:												
64. Crude petroleum (10)	28.2	95.6	78.1	59.9	102.4	133.8	189.1	227.8	252.1	343.8	219.0	280.2
65. Unit value index of manufactured goods exports	100.0	70.9	110.9	122.3	107.7	116.6	119.5	123.5	132.8	139.3	131.5	134.0

Sources:
- The prices used in the calculation of the indices shown in this table are extracted from *UNCTADstat* Commodity Price Statistics

Notes:
- The group indices include all commodities shown except for those with an asterisk (*).
- The average annual indices are calculated from monthly data and may not correspond to the average from quarterly data.

(1) Dollars per metric ton (unless otherwise specified).
(2) Cents per pound.
(3) Cents per kilogram.
(4) Dollars per cubic meter.
(5) Cents per sheet.
(6) Cents per Fe unit.
(7) Dollars per metric ton unit of WO3.
(8) Dollars per troy ounce.
(9) Cents per troy ounce.
(10) Dollars per barrel.

- For specifications, see next page.

6.1 Indices annuels et trimestriels des prix d'une sélection de produits de base sur le marché libre
2000 = 100

2008		2009				2010				2011		Produits de base
III	IV	I	II	III	IV	I	II	III	IV	I	II	
355.1	**235.8**	**182.3**	**214.0**	**252.4**	**277.8**	**298.9**	**295.9**	**300.6**	**343.6**	**375.6**	**363.5**	**Minéraux, minerais et métaux**
935.3	848.8	441.9	259.0	205.7	205.7	233.4	285.7	285.7	320.0	361.9	417.1	46. Phosphate brut
929.1	817.8	387.6	258.4	232.2	297.0	384.5	438.6	447.0	389.8	376.4	340.6	47. Minerai de manganèse
485.8	485.8	348.8	348.8	348.8	348.8	348.8	348.8	348.8	348.8	..	..	48. Minerai de fer (6)
526.0	526.0	526.0	352.7	352.7	352.7	352.7	352.7	352.7	352.7	..	..	49. Minerai de fer* (6)
179.9	117.6	87.7	95.8	116.9	129.2	139.6	135.3	134.9	151.2	161.3	168.0	50. Aluminium
423.5	215.3	184.2	257.2	323.1	366.7	399.1	387.5	399.5	476.3	532.3	504.7	51. Cuivre
402.2	207.1	185.7	252.4	312.9	354.8	383.6	372.5	385.5	457.9	510.5	484.1	52. Cuivre* (2)
219.4	125.5	121.1	149.5	204.8	202.9	231.0	260.1	245.3	273.3	311.4	281.2	53. Nickel*
224.6	129.6	126.0	151.1	211.3	207.8	240.7	280.0	255.2	273.3	307.3	280.5	54. Nickel (2)
420.8	273.7	254.9	330.5	424.4	504.6	489.4	429.5	447.5	526.2	573.2	503.0	55. Plomb
249.8	205.8	152.5	169.0	221.3	254.7	254.1	249.3	224.3	272.2	278.4	285.0	56. Plomb* (2)
156.9	105.1	103.9	130.6	156.1	196.2	202.9	179.6	178.4	205.1	212.3	199.8	57. Zinc
151.6	103.3	100.9	125.1	147.4	185.7	191.8	171.7	172.4	197.6	205.0	195.9	58. Zinc* (2)
377.3	240.8	202.8	248.4	268.4	278.9	316.5	328.6	378.1	478.5	550.4	532.2	59. Etain
381.2	235.8	202.9	245.2	267.8	279.6	319.5	332.0	379.2	480.3	556.6	540.8	60. Etain*
367.4	363.7	334.0	334.0	334.0	334.0	334.0	334.0	334.0	334.0	334.0	334.0	61. Tungstène (7)
311.6	284.8	325.6	330.3	344.1	394.8	397.4	432.4	439.6	490.1	496.1	539.1	62. Or* (8)
298.9	204.1	253.8	275.3	294.8	351.9	338.6	367.5	380.4	529.8	635.8	770.2	63. Argent* (9)
												POUR MÉMOIRE :
409.2	198.7	156.7	209.7	241.8	267.7	273.1	277.2	267.8	302.8	353.2	390.1	64. Pétrole brut (10)
141.0	130.0	126.0	129.0	134.0	137.0	134.0	130.0	133.0	139.0	142.0	..	65. Valeur unitaire des exportations d'articles manufacturés en dollars

Sources :
- Les prix utilisés pour le calcul des indices présentés dans ce tableau sont extraits des statistiques des prix des produits de base de *UNCTADstat*

Notes:
- Les indices agrégés recouvrent tous les produits présentés à l'exception de ceux munis d'un astérisque (*).
- Les indices moyens annuels sont calculés sur la base de données mensuelles et peuvent ne pas correspondre aux moyennes calculées sur la base de données trimestrielles.

(1) Dollars par tonne métrique (sauf mention spéciale).
(2) Cents par livre.
(3) Cents par kilogramme.
(4) Dollars par mètre cube.
(5) Cents par feuille.
(6) Cents par unité de Fe.
(7) Dollars par tonne métrique d'unité de WO3.
(8) Dollars par once "troy".
(9) Cents par once "troy".
(10) Dollars par baril.

- Pour les spécifications, se reporter à la page suivante.

Specifications

Food

1. Wheat: Argentina, Trigo Pan Upriver, f.o.b.
2. Wheat: United States, no. 2, Hard Red Winter (ordinary), f.o.b. Gulf ports.
3. Maize: Argentina, Rosario, f.o.b.
4. Maize: United States, no. 3 yellow, f.o.b. Gulf ports.
5. Rice: Thailand, white milled, 5 % broken, nominal price quotes, f.o.b. Bangkok.
6. Sugar: Caribbean ports, f.o.b. bulk basis (I.S.A.).
7. Beef: Australia and New-Zealand, frozen and boneless, 85 % visible lean, U.S. import price, f.o.b. port of entry.
8. Bananas: Central America and Ecuador, fresh, U.S. importer's price, f.o.b. U.S. ports.
9. Pepper: Muntok, white, fair average quality (faq) spot. Prior to June 2003, Singapore.
10. Soybean meal: Hamburg, 44/45% protein, f.o.b. ex-mill.
11. Fish meal: Any origin, 64/65% protein, Bremen free carrier price. Prior to March 2006, cost and freight Hamburg.

Tropical beverages

12. Coffee: Colombian mild Arabicas, ex-dock New York (I.C.A.).
13. Coffee: Brazilian and other natural Arabicas, ex-dock New York (I.C.A.).
14. Coffee: Other mild Arabicas, ex-dock New York (I.C.A.).
15. Coffee: Robustas, ex-dock New York (I.C.A.).
16. Coffee: Composite indicator price 1976 (I.C.A.).
17. Cocoa: Average of daily prices, New York/London, 3 months futures (I.C.C.A.).
18. Tea: Best Pekoe Fannings 1, Mombasa auction prices.

Vegetable oils and oilseeds

19. Soybeans: United States, no. 2 yellow, c.i.f. Rotterdam.
20. Soybean oil: Any origin, crude oil, the Netherlands, f.o.b. ex-mill.
21. Sunflower oil: European Union, f.o.b. N.W. European ports.
22. Groundnut oil: Any origin, c.i.f. Rotterdam.
23. Copra: Philippines/Indonesia, bulk, c.i.f. N.W. European ports.
24. Coconut oil: Philippines, c.i.f. Rotterdam.
25. Palm kernel oil: Malaysia, c.i.f. Rotterdam.
26. Palm oil: generally Indonesia, 5% ffa, c.i.f. N.W. European ports.

Agricultural raw materials

27. Linseed oil: Any origin, ex-tank, c.i.f. Rotterdam.
28. Tobacco: Unmanufactured tobacco, US general import price.
29. Cotton: Sudan, Barakat, X4B, CFR Far Eastern quotations. Prior to August 2005, c.i.f. North Europe.
30. Cotton: United States, Memphis/Eastern Midd 1-3/32", c.i.f. North Europe.
31. Cotton: United States; Memphis/Orleans/Texas, Midd 1-3/32", CFR Far Eastern quotations. Prior to June 2005, Memphis/Orleans/Texas, Midd 1-3/32", c.i.f. North Europe.
32. Cotton: Pakistan, Sind/Punjab, Afzal 1-1/32", c.i.f. North Europe.
33. Cotton: Cotton Outlook Index A, Middling 1-3/32", CFR Far Eastern quotations. Prior to August 2004, c.i.f. North Europe.
34. Cotton: Egypt, Giza 88, good + 3/8, CFR Far Eastern quotations. Prior to August 2005, Giza 70, good + 3/8, f.o.b. Alexandria.
35. Wool: fine, 19 micron, Australia.
36. Wool: coarse, 23 micron, Australia.
37. Jute: Bangladesh, Bangladesh White D (BWD), f.o.b. Mongla.
38. Sisal: Tanzania/Kenya, no. 2 & 3 long, f.o.b. Prior to 2007, c.i.f. main European ports.
39. Sisal: Tanzania/Kenya no. 3 & UG, f.o.b. Prior to 2007, c.i.f. main European ports.
40. Hides: US, Chicago packer's heavy native steers over 53lbs., wholesale dealer's price, f.o.b. shipping point.
41. Non-coniferous woods: United Kingdom, import price index 2005=100, dollar equivalent.
42. Tropical logs: Sapele, loyal and marchand, UK import price, f.o.b. plus commission. Prior to June 2000, Cameroun f.o.b.
43. Tropical sawnwood: Malaysia, Dark Red Meranti, select and better, c.i.f. French ports.
44. Plywood: Southeast Asia, Lauan, 3-ply, Extra, 91 cm x 182 cm x 4 mm, wholesale price, spot Tokyo.
45. Rubber: TSR 20 New York.

Spécifications

Produits alimentaires

1. Blé : Argentine, Trigo Pan Upriver, f.a.b.
2. Blé : États-Unis, Hard Red Winter, n° 2 (ordinaire), f.a.b. ports du Golfe.
3. Maïs : Argentine, Rosario, f.a.b.
4. Maïs : États-Unis, jaune n° 3, f.a.b. ports du Golfe.
5. Riz : Thaïlande, blanchi, 5 % brisures, prix nominal, f.a.b. Bangkok.
6. Sucre : Ports des Caraïbes, f.a.b. en vrac (A.I.S.).
7. Viande de boeuf : Australie et Nouvelle-Zélande, désossée et congelée, maigres à 85 % visibles, prix à l'importation aux États-Unis, f.a.b. port d'entrée.
8. Bananes : Amérique centrale et Equateur, fraîches, f.a.b. ports des États-Unis.
9. Poivre : Muntok blanc, fair average quality (faq) au comptant. Avant juin 2003, Singapour.
10. Farine de soja : Hambourg, 44/45 % protéines, f.a.b. départ moulin.
11. Farine de poisson : toutes origines, 64/65 % protéines, Brême, prix franco transporteur. Avant mars 2006, coût et fret Hambourg.

Boissons tropicales

12. Café : Arabicas doux colombiens, ex-dock New York (A.I.C.).
13. Café : Brésilien et autres Arabicas naturels, ex-dock New York (A.I.C.).
14. Café : autres Arabicas doux, ex-dock New York (A.I.C.).
15. Café : Robustas, ex-dock New York (A.I.C.).
16. Café : Prix indicatif composite de 1976 (A.I.C.).
17. Cacao : moyenne des cours quotidiens New York/Londres, 3 mois à terme (A.I.C.C.).
18. Thé : Best Pekoe Fannings 1, cours aux enchères à Mombasa.

Huiles végétales et graines oléagineuses

19. Fèves de soja : États-Unis, n° 2 jaune, c.a.f. Rotterdam.
20. Huile de soja : toutes origines, huile brute, f.a.b. Pays-Bas, départ raffinerie.
21. Huile de tournesol : Union européenne, f.a.b. ports de l'Europe du Nord-Ouest.
22. Huile d'arachide : toutes origines, c.a.f. Rotterdam.
23. Coprah : Philippines/Indonésie, en vrac, c.a.f. ports de l'Europe du Nord-Ouest.
24. Huile de coprah : Philippines, c.a.f. Rotterdam.
25. Huile de palmiste : Malaisie, c.a.f. Rotterdam.
26. Huile de palme : généralement Indonésie, 5 % ffa, c.a.f. ports de l'Europe du Nord-Ouest.

Matières premières d'origine agricole

27. Huile de lin : toutes origines, cours du disponible, c.a.f. Rotterdam.
28. Tabac : tabac non fabriqué, prix général à l'importation aux États-Unis.
29. Coton : Soudan, Barakat, classe X4B, cotations coût et fret Extrême Orient. Avant août 2005, c.a.f. Europe septentrionale.
30. Coton : États-Unis, Memphis, oriental Midd 1-3/32", c.a.f. Europe septentrionale.
31. Coton : États-Unis, Memphis/Orléans/Texas, Midd 1-3/32", cotations coût et fret Extrême Orient. Avant juin 2005, Memphis/Orléans/Texas, Midd 1-3/32", c.a.f. Europe septentrionale.
32. Coton : Pakistan, Sind/Punjab, Afzal 1-1/32", c.a.f. Europe septentrionale.
33. Coton : Indice A de "Cotton Outlook", Middling 1-3/32", cotations coût et fret Extrême Orient. Avant août 2005, c.a.f. Europe septentrionale.
34. Coton : Égypte, Giza 88, good + 3/8, cotations coût et fret Extrême Orient. Avant août 2005, Giza 70, good + 3/8, f.a.b. Alexandrie.
35. Laine fine, 19 microns, Australie.
36. Laine grossière, 23 microns, Australie.
37. Jute : Bengladesh, Bengladesh White D (BWD), f.a.b. Mongla.
38. Sisal : Tanzanie/Kenya, n° 2 et 3 long, f.a.b. Avant 2007 : c.a.f. principaux ports européens.
39. Sisal : Tanzanie/Kenya, n° 3 et UG, f.a.b. Avant 2007 : c.a.f. principaux ports européens.
40. Peaux : États-Unis, lourdes de bouvillons de plus de 24 kgs, abattus à Chicago, prix de gros, f.a.b. point d'expédition.
41. Bois non conifères : Royaume-Uni, indice des prix à l'importation 2005=100, équivalent dollar.
42. Grumes tropicales : Sapelli, loyal et marchand, prix d'importation au Royaume-Uni, f.a.b plus commission. Avant juin 2000, Cameroun, f.a.b.
43. Grumes tropicales sciées : Malaisie, Meranti rouge foncé, select and better, c.a.f. ports français.
44. Contre-plaqué : Asie du Sud-Est, Lauan, 3-feuilles, extra, 91 cm x 182 cm x 4 mm, prix de gros, cours du disponible à Tokyo.
45. Caoutchouc : TSR 20 New York.

Minerals, ores and metals

46. Phosphate rock: Morocco, 70% BPL, contract f.a.s. Casablanca.
47. Manganese ore: Metallurgical 48/50% Mn content, f.o.b. United Kingdom.
48. Iron ore: Brazilian to Europe, fines, Vale, Itabira, f.o.b.
49. Iron ore: Australian to Japan, fines, Hamersley, f.o.b.
50. Aluminium: London Metal Exchange, high grade, cash.
51. Copper: London Metal Exchange, grade A, cash.
52. Copper: United States producer, wire bars, f.o.b. refinery.
53. Nickel: London Metal Exchange, cash.
54. Nickel: New York dealer, 4x4 cathodes, free market.
55. Lead: London Metal Exchange, settlement and cash seller's price in warehouse, excluding duty, range main United Kingdom ports; purity 99.97% Pb.
56. Lead: North America, producer price, refined.
57. Zinc: London Metal Exchange, cash settlement.
58. Zinc: North America, special high grade, daily weighted average, delivered basis.
59. Tin: London Metal Exchange, high grade, cash.
60. Tin: Ex-smelter price, Kuala Lumpur market.
61. Tungsten ore: wolframite and sheelite, c.i.f. European ports, basis minimum 65% WO3. Prior to April 1992, Wolfram.
62. Gold: United Kingdom, 99.5% fine, London afternoon fixing, average of daily rates.
63. Silver: Handy & Harman, 99.9% grade refined, average of daily quotations, New York.

MEMO ITEM:

64. Crude petroleum: Average of United Kingdom Brent, Dubai, and West Texas crude prices, reflecting relatively equal consumption of light, medium and heavy crudes worldwide.
65. Unit value index of manufactured goods exports: Developed economies, sections 5-8 less 68 of the Standard International Trade Classification (SITC), Revision 2.

Minéraux, minerais et métaux

46. Phosphate brut: Maroc, 70 % BPL, f.a.s. Casablanca.
47. Minerai de manganèse: 48/50 % teneur en Mn, f.a.b. Royaume-Uni.
48. Minerai de fer: Brésilien vers l'Europe, minerai fin, Vale, Itabira, f.a.b.
49. Minerai de fer: Australien vers le Japon, minerai fin, Hamersley, f.a.b.
50. Aluminium: Bourse des métaux de Londres, haute qualité, cours au comptant.
51. Cuivre: Bourse des métaux de Londres, grade A, comptant.
52. Cuivre: Producteur États-Unis, barres à fil, f.a.b. sortie affinerie.
53. Nickel: Bourse des métaux de Londres, cours au comptant.
54. Nickel: Prix du négociant à New York, cathodes 4x4, marché libre.
55. Plomb: Bourse des métaux de Londres, prix vendeur, à terme et au comptant, à l'entrepôt, droits non acquittés, principaux ports du Royaume-Uni; pureté: 99,97 % Pb.
56. Plomb: Amérique du Nord, prix des producteurs, raffiné.
57. Zinc: Bourse des métaux de Londres, cours de vente au comptant.
58. Zinc: Amérique du Nord, haute qualité spéciale, moyenne pondérée des prix journaliers à la livraison.
59. Étain: Bourse des métaux de Londres, haute qualité, cours au comptant.
60. Étain: Prix départ fonderie, marché de Kuala Lumpur.
61. Minerai de tungstène: wolframite et scheelite, c.a.f. ports européens, minimum 65 % de WO3. Avant avril 1992, Wolfram.
62. Or: Royaume-Uni, 99,5 % fin, cotation de l'après-midi à Londres, moyenne des taux journaliers.
63. Argent: Handy & Harman, 99,9 % raffiné, moyenne des cotations journalières à New York.

POUR MÉMOIRE :

64. Pétrole brut: moyenne des prix du Brent du Royaume-Uni, de Dubaï et du Texas de l'Ouest, correspondant aux parts relatives de la consommation mondiale du brut léger, moyen et lourd.
65. Valeur unitaire des exportations des produits manufacturés : Économies développées, sections 5 à 8 moins 68 de la Classification type pour le commerce international (CTCI), révision 2.

6

Commodity	Price instability indices (1) Indices d'instabilité des prix (1)			Price trends (2) Tendances des prix (2) In current dollars En dollars courants			In constant dollars (3) En dollars constants (3)			Produits
	81-90	91-00	01-10	81-90	91-00	01-10	81-90	91-00	01-10	
				Annual average rate of change in percentage Taux de variation annuel en pourcentage						
ALL COMMODITIES	11.9	10.2	0.0	0.6	1.3	13.2	-3.8	-1.7	8.3	TOTAL DES PRODUITS
All food	12.1	11.8	7.5	-1.3	-1.0	10.8	-5.7	-1.5	6.8	**Total des produits alimentaires**
Food and tropical beverages	10.6	11.6	7.6	-1.0	-0.7	10.7	-5.1	-1.7	6.8	*Produits alimentaires et boissons tropicales*
Food	16.0	10.4	8.2	-0.5	-1.7	10.7	-4.8	-2.1	6.8	*Produits alimentaires*
Wheat	11.9	15.5	14.8	-2.2	-1.6	8.8	-6.6	-2.1	4.8	Blé
Maize	15.7	14.1	14.2	-3.8	-1.3	9.5	-8.1	-1.8	5.6	Maïs
Rice	20.0	13.8	13.9	-2.4	-2.9	15.0	-6.7	-3.4	11.1	Riz
Sugar	41.0	20.5	19.9	1.6	-2.7	11.5	-2.7	-3.1	7.6	Sucre
Beef	6.1	8.0	6.7	0.6	-4.7	4.2	-3.7	-5.1	0.3	Viande de bœuf
Bananas	14.3	17.0	15.2	2.5	-1.6	7.3	-1.9	-2.1	3.3	Bananes
Pepper	43.8	22.4	16.2	7.0	17.3	11.1	2.7	16.8	7.1	Poivre
Soybean meal	14.1	13.7	14.2	0.1	-1.1	9.5	-4.2	-1.6	5.6	Farine de soja
Fishmeal	17.2	18.5	10.9	0.6	1.1	13.0	-3.7	0.7	9.1	Farine de poisson
Tropical beverages	14.3	22.9	6.4	-4.9	2.9	11.1	-9.2	2.5	7.1	*Boissons tropicales*
Coffee	16.8	30.9	10.5	-3.6	4.1	12.9	-7.9	3.7	9.0	Café
Cocoa	15.5	17.8	14.7	-5.4	0.1	9.5	-9.7	-0.4	5.5	Cacao
Tea	17.9	10.7	9.6	-1.9	3.5	5.9	-6.2	3.1	2.0	Thé
Vegetable oilseeds and oils	17.9	16.5	15.3	-4.0	0.4	11.1	-8.3	-0.1	7.2	**Graines oléagineuses et huiles végétales**
Soybeans	12.5	11.2	13.3	-0.7	-1.1	10.0	-5.0	-1.6	6.1	Fèves de soja
Soybean oil	18.8	18.3	16.8	-2.8	-1.1	11.6	-7.2	-1.5	7.7	Huile de soja
Sunflower oil	18.6	17.1	18.0	-3.9	0.1	9.2	-8.2	-0.4	5.3	Huile de tournesol
Groundnut oil	27.3	15.2	20.8	-1.1	0.4	8.0	-5.4	0.0	4.1	Huile d'arachide
Copra	30.3	17.0	19.5	-4.8	2.3	13.0	-9.1	1.8	9.1	Coprah
Coconut oil	32.2	17.9	18.4	-5.3	2.6	12.5	-9.6	2.2	8.6	Huile de coprah
Palm kernel oil	29.2	18.0	18.9	-5.7	2.6	12.6	-10.0	2.1	8.6	Huile de palmiste
Palm oil	22.6	23.5	17.6	-6.8	1.5	11.8	-11.1	1.1	7.9	Huile de palme
Cotton oil	15.3	11.2	26.3	-1.2	-1.4	8.6	-5.6	-1.9	4.7	Huile de coton
Agricultural raw materials	7.2	10.1	7.6	2.1	-2.3	9.1	-2.3	-2.7	5.2	**Matières premières d'origine agricole**
Linseed oil	23.4	16.8	24.5	0.9	2.0	11.3	-3.5	1.6	7.4	Huile de lin
Tobacco	6.3	8.9	9.5	2.7	-0.3	3.3	-1.6	-0.7	-0.6	Tabac
Cotton	15.1	17.0	14.5	-1.1	-1.7	5.9	-5.4	-2.1	1.9	Coton
Wool	18.5	14.8	11.8	6.2	2.8	5.0	1.8	2.4	1,0	Laine
Jute	26.1	17.8	18.3	0.9	-1.1	11.8	-3.4	-1.5	7.6	Jute
Sisal	5.3	11.8	9.8	0.9	4.6	3.7	-3.5	4.1	-0.4	Sisal
Hides	9.9	7.9	12.0	10.7	-0.2	-3.6	6.3	-0.7	-7.5	Peaux
Non-coniferous woods	9.2	7.2	3.7	4.0	2.4	5.6	-0.3	2.0	1.7	Bois non conifères
Tropical logs	11.6	7.2	10.0	6.9	-4.0	7.4	2.5	-4.4	3.4	Grumes tropicales
Tropical sawnwood	14.7	18.2	5.6	4.0	-0.3	3.7	-0.4	-0.8	-0.3	Grumes tropicales sciées
Plywood	12.1	17.6	8.0	6.3	-0.5	5.1	1.9	-1.0	1.2	Contre-plaqué
Rubber	13.8	28.0	16.2	-0.4	-3.0	17.9	-4.7	-3.4	14.0	Caoutchouc
Minerals, ores and metals	14.4	9.6	20.8	4.7	-1.4	16.4	0.4	-1.9	12.4	**Minéraux, minerais et métaux**
Phosphate rock	12.7	8.7	46.5	-1.1	1.5	17.9	-5.4	1.0	13.9	Phosphate brut
Manganese ore	26.8	12.9	34.3	7.3	-7.8	18.3	2.9	-8.3	14.4	Minerai de manganèse
Iron ore	7.2	5.3	18.1	-1.1	-1.2	17.7	-5.4	-1.7	13.7	Minerai de fer
Aluminium	20.2	11.2	16.9	6.1	1.8	5.7	1.7	1.4	1.8	Aluminium
Copper	18.3	14.4	25.4	6.9	-3.6	19.5	2.5	-4.0	15.6	Cuivre
Nickel	31.6	18.7	35.0	9.3	-0.8	14.5	4.9	-1.3	10.5	Nickel
Lead	21.5	15.2	23.0	3.3	-0.2	20.0	-1.0	-0.7	16.0	Plomb
Zinc	19.7	9.3	33.5	7.9	0.1	12.9	3.5	-0.3	8.9	Zinc
Tin	14.7	6.4	19.2	-9.9	-0.4	18.5	-14.4	-0.8	14.5	Étain
Tungsten ore	14.3	14.8	31.5	-11.1	-1.8	16.6	-15.4	-2.2	12.6	Minerai de tungstène
Gold	10.6	8.2	5.6	-0.4	-3.2	16.9	-4.7	-3.6	13.0	Or
Silver	15.1	8.3	13.1	-7.7	3.0	18.0	-12.0	2.5	14.0	Argent
Crude petroleum	16.7	16.0	20.1	-8.4	2.2	15.1	-12.7	1.7	11.1	Pétrole brut

For sources and notes, see next page.

Pour les sources et les notes, se reporter à la page suivante.

Sources:
- UNCTAD calculations based on *UNCTADstat* Commodity Price Statistics

Notes:

(1) The measure of price instability is

$$1/n \sum_{t=1}^{n} \left[\left(\left| Y(t) - y(t) \right| \right) / y(t) \right] * 100$$

where

    Y(t) is the observed magnitude of the variable
    y(t) is the magnitude estimated by fitting an exponential trend
        to the observed value
    n   is the number of observations

Accordingly, instability is measured as the percentage deviation of the variables concerned from their exponential trend levels for a given period.

(2) The growth rate of each period has been calculated using the formula:

$$\log(p) = a + b(t)$$

where

    p is the price index and *t* is time.

(3) Constant 2000 dollars (current dollars divided by the United Nations unit value index of manufactured goods exported by developed economies).

Sources :
- Calculs du secrétariat de la CNUCED basés sur les statistiques des prix des produits de base de *UNCTADstat*

Notes :

(1) L'indice d'instabilité des prix est calculé selon

$$1/n \sum_{t=1}^{n} \left[\left(\left| Y(t) - y(t) \right| \right) / y(t) \right] * 100$$

où

    Y(t) est la valeur observée de la variable
    y(t) est la valeur estimée par ajustement à la tendance
        exponentielle des valeurs observées
    n   est le nombre d'observations

L'instabilité est le pourcentage de déviation des variables en question par rapport à la ligne de tendance exponentielle pour une période donnée.

(2) Le taux de croissance de chaque période a été calculé selon la formule :

$$\log(p) = a + b(t)$$

où

    p est l'indice de prix et *t* le temps.

(3) Dollars constants 2000 (dollars courants divisés par l'index des Nations Unies de la valeur unitaire des exportations des produits manufacturés par les économies développées).

6

7 | INTERNATIONAL FINANCE

FINANCE INTERNATIONALE

1
2
3
4
5
6
7
8

7.1.1 Balance of payments: Current account net of countries and geographical regions

Region, country or territory	Millions of dollars - Millions de dollars							
	1980	1990	2000	2005	2007	2008	2009	2010
DEVELOPING ECONOMIES	28 412	13 476	97 796	489 377	770 223	772 049	444 817	489 175
TRANSITION ECONOMIES	-2 301	-2 482	46 991	83 022	58 881	85 105	33 917	70 805
DEVELOPED ECONOMIES	-78 720	-103 560	-324 209	-522 063	-546 189	-668 922	-234 287	-256 876
Developing economies: Africa	**6 619**	**3 635**	**16 782**	**60 571**	**59 514**	**50 932**	**-26 889**	**5 896**
Eastern Africa	*-3 829*	*-3 451*	*-2 984*	*-6 396*	*-8 404*	*-15 243*	*-11 900*	*-13 772*
Burundi	80	-69	-50	-6	-108	-259	-164	(e)- 158
Comoros	-9	-10	0	-29	-29	-30	10	14
Djibouti	..	-11	-19	20	-171	-225	71	-
Eritrea	–	–	-105	(e)9	(e)-99	(e)-76	(e)- 105	(e)- 201
Ethiopia	–	–	13	-1 568	-828	-1 806	-2 191	(e)-1 695
Ethiopia (former)	-220	-201	–	–	–	–	–	–
Kenya	-876	-527	-199	-252	-1 032	-1 363	1 001	(e)-1 474
Madagascar	-556	-265	-260	-554	-810	-2 097	(e)-2 216	(e)-2 168
Malawi	-260	-86	-74	(e)- 356	(e)- 143	(e)- 220	(e)- 332	(e)- 510
Mauritius	-117	-119	-37	-324	-434	-976	-655	-800
Mozambique	-367	-415	-764	-761	-785	-1 179	-1 171	-913
Rwanda	-52	-85	-94	-52	-147	-252	-379	(e)- 605
Seychelles	-16	-13	-43	-174	-264	-407	-253	-484
Uganda	-83	-263	-359	-26	-476	-1 314	-451	-1 740
United Republic of Tanzania	-521	-559	-428	-1 105	-1 849	-2 675	-1 934	-1 978
Zambia	-516	-594	-580	-597	-698	-1 039	537	615
Zimbabwe	-149	-140	(e)14	(e)- 622	(e)- 530	(e)- 676	(e)- 807	(e)- 767
Middle Africa	*-460*	*-1 751*	*1 581*	*5 854*	*10 243*	*7 140*	*-15 022*	*-7 337*
Angola	68	-236	796	5 138	10 581	7 194	-7 572	(e)-1 873
Cameroon	-445	-551	-249	-493	286	-450	-1 119	-856
Central African Republic	-43	-89	-13	-88	-106	-206	-155	-175
Chad	12	-46	-213	50	-744	(e)-1 146	(e)-2 305	(e)-2 512
Congo	-167	-251	648	696	-2 181	(e)-1 210	(e)-1 395	(e)596
Dem. Rep. of the Congo	-250	-715	-173	-883	-113	-2 025	-1 166	-898
Equatorial Guinea	-20	-19	-196	-511	546	1 672	-2 093	-3 451
Gabon	384	168	1 001	1 983	2 037	3 403	862	1 905
Sao Tome and Principe	1	-12	-20	-36	-64	-94	-79	(c)- 73
Northern Africa	*5 951*	*4 917*	*12 627*	*36 202*	*55 246*	*61 174*	*-4 004*	*18 548*
Algeria	249	1 420	9 142	21 181	30 631	34 440	402	(e)12 760
Egypt	-436	2 327	-971	2 103	412	-1 415	-3 349	(e)-4 435
Libyan Arab Jamahiriya	8 214	2 201	6 270	14 945	28 510	35 702	9 381	(e)16 164
Morocco	-1 407	-196	-475	1 041	-122	-4 528	-4 971	-3 925
Sudan	-316	-372	-518	-2 768	-3 268	-1 314	-4 232	-1 165
Tunisia	-353	-463	-821	-299	-917	-1 711	-1 234	-
Southern Africa	*2 937*	*1 676*	*349*	*-6 827*	*-17 443*	*-19 420*	*-12 150*	*-11 518*
Botswana	-151	-19	545	1 562	1 796	468	-526	(e)- 341
Lesotho	56	65	-151	-102	99	202	-2	-421
Namibia	..	28	192	333	747	225	120	-
South Africa	3 161	1 552	-191	-8 518	-20 018	-20 083	-11 327	-10 117
Swaziland	-130	51	-46	-103	-66	-231	-414	(e)- 708
Western Africa	*2 020*	*2 244*	*5 209*	*31 738*	*19 872*	*17 282*	*16 187*	*19 975*
Benin	-36	-18	-81	-226	-534	-536	(e)- 552	(e)- 485
Burkina Faso	-49	-77	-319	-634	-1 070	-1 709	(e)- 417	(e)- 373
Cape Verde	4	-4	-58	-41	-198	-205	-239	(e)- 207
Côte d'Ivoire	-1 826	-1 214	-241	40	-139	452	1 670	(e)303
Gambia	-91	24	40	-43	-58	11	63	52
Ghana	30	-223	-387	-1 105	-2 151	-3 543	-1 598	-2 700
Guinea	50	-203	-140	-160	-455	-1 201	-403	-327
Guinea-Bissau	-61	-45	8	-10	-31	-29	27	-52
Mali	-124	-221	-255	-438	-581	-1 066	-655	(e)- 705
Mauritania	-133	-10	-98	-877	-515	-557	-372	-266
Niger	-276	-236	-104	-312	-351	-651	-1 513	-1 715
Nigeria	5 178	4 988	7 427	36 529	27 644	28 646	(e)21 659	(e)28 210
Senegal	-386	-363	-332	-676	-1 312	-1 884	-1 113	(e)-1 102
Sierra Leone	-165	-69	-112	-105	-160	-225	-194	-320
Togo	-95	-84	-140	-204	-216	-219	-177	(e)- 339

For sources and notes, see end of table.

7.1.1 Balance des paiements : compte courant net des pays et des régions géographiques

As percentage of GDP - En pourcentage du PIB (1)								Régions, pays ou territoires
1980	1990	2000	2005	2007	2008	2009	2010	
1.18	0.35	1.41	4.56	5.19	4.48	2.62	2.41	ÉCONOMIES EN DÉVELOPPEMENT
-3.19	-2.84	11.83	7.59	3.21	3.64	1.90	3.38	ÉCONOMIES EN TRANSITION
-0.95	-0.59	-1.30	-1.54	-1.40	-1.61	-0.60	-0.63	ÉCONOMIES DÉVELOPPÉES
1.53	0.74	2.83	6.15	4.63	3.39	-1.89	0.40	**Économies en développement : Afrique**
-7.89	*-5.65*	*-4.49*	*-6.74*	*-6.55*	*-9.84*	*-7.56*	*-8.03*	*Afrique orientale*
-6.26	-4.50	-5.26	-0.53	-8.42	-20.88	-13.08	(e)-11.29	Burundi
-7.21	-4.30	-0.22	-7.37	-6.27	-11.10	-9.12	-6.80	Comores
..	-2.30	-3.43	2.84	-21.61	-26.88	-7.65	-	Djibouti
		-14.82	(e)0.82	(e)-7.49	(e)-5.51	(e)-5.59	(e)-9.40	Érythrée
		0.17	-12.76	-4.32	-6.97	-7.68	(e)-6.35	Éthiopie
-3.84	-2.52							Éthiopie (anc.)
-9.56	-4.78	-1.58	-1.35	-3.80	-6.61	-5.65	(e)-7.24	Kenya
-17.04	-8.60	-6.72	-11.00	-10.92	-21.93	(e)-25.20	(e)-24.67	Madagascar
-15.23	3.57	-3.06	(e)-12.92	(e)-4.00	(e)-5.22	(e)-6.84	(e)-9.81	Malawi
-10.22	-4.61	-0.81	-5.16	-5.77	-10.46	-7.56	-8.41	Maurice
-7.60	-13.99	-17.72	-11.56	-9.77	-11.95	-12.23	-9.97	Mozambique
-3.72	-3.29	-5.33	-2.02	-3.92	-5.35	-7.19	(e)-10.72	Rwanda
-8.62	-2.86	-5.65	-18.76	-25.91	-44.19	-32.11	-51.69	Seychelles
-2.72	-6.52	-5.66	-0.26	-3.52	-7.98	-2.64	-9.47	Ouganda
-7.13	-10.20	-4.11	-7.62	-10.69	-12.55	-8.40	-8.05	République-Unie de Tanzanie
-13.29	-15.88	-17.90	-8.21	-6.03	-7.02	4.22	3.88	Zambie
-2.80	-1.59	(e)0.25	(e)-13.27	(e)-11.99	(e)-17.50	(e)-19.91	..	Zimbabwe
-1.38	*-4.05*	*4.40*	*7.94*	*10.29*	*5.73*	*-13.59*	*-5.59*	*Afrique centrale*
1.26	-2.29	8.71	25.83	35.13	20.66	-21.64	(e)-4.74	Angola
-5.02	-4.65	-2.68	-2.97	1.40	-1.89	-5.04	-3.82	Cameroun
-3.87	-6.19	-1.38	-6.55	-6.19	-10.37	-7.84	-8.71	République centrafricaine
1.34	-2.96	-15.39	0.85	-10.61	(e)-13.72	(e)-33.71	(e)-32.58	Tchad
-9.77	-8.98	20.13	11.65	-28.53	(e)-10.94	(e)-14.01	(e)4.99	Congo
-2.54	-7.79	-3.28	-12.20	-1.13	-17.35	-10.41	-4.53	Rép. dém. du Congo
-37.18	-14.25	-16.68	-7.09	5.10	9.35	-17.64	-24.58	Guinée équatoriale
7.31	2.87	18.20	20.96	17.27	22.86	7.64	14.17	Gabon
0.83	-10.03	-26.18	-27.54	-40.86	-49.57	-37.18	(e)-34.94	Sao Tomé-et-Principe
4.15	*2.59*	*4.81*	*9.76*	*11.13*	*10.07*	*-0.70*	*2.87*	*Afrique septentrionale*
0.59	2.29	16.69	20.52	22.81	20.23	0.29	(e)7.98	Algérie
-1.81	5.91	-0.97	2.14	0.31	-0.86	-1.78	(e)-2.07	Égypte
21.51	7.08	16.30	32.88	45.49	43.87	15.96	(e)22.55	Jamahiriya arabe libyenne
-6.69	-0.68	-1.28	1.75	-0.16	-5.10	-5.48	-4.32	Maroc
-3.52	-2.33	-3.95	-7.87	-5.78	-2.15	-7.67	-1.68	Soudan
-4.04	-3.76	-4.22	-1.03	-2.57	-4.18	-3.12	-	Tunisie
3.55	*1.40*	*0.24*	*-2.54*	*-5.59*	*-6.40*	*-3.90*	*-2.93*	*Afrique australe*
-14.42	-0.52	9.68	15.23	14.51	3.49	-4.53	(e)-2.43	Botswana
14.50	11.79	-20.00	-7.71	6.24	12.64	-0.15	-21.11	Lesotho
..	1.03	4.90	4.59	8.47	2.53	1.29	-	Namibie
3.93	1.39	-0.14	-3.45	-6.99	-7.26	-3.96	-2.80	Afrique du Sud
-18.37	4.87	-3.01	-3.97	-2.14	-7.66	-13.11	(e)-18.04	Swaziland
1.63	*2.89*	*6.18*	*17.92*	*7.95*	*5.54*	*6.00*	*6.20*	*Afrique occidentale*
-2.60	-0.98	-3.42	-5.19	-9.69	-8.07	(e)-8.35	(e)-7.36	Bénin
-2.55	-2.48	-12.18	-11.69	-15.84	-20.91	(e)-5.12	(e)-4.47	Burkina Faso
3.04	-1.24	-10.76	-4.18	-14.89	-13.16	-15.12	(e)-12.59	Cap-Vert
-17.95	-10.21	-2.26	0.24	-0.70	1.93	7.25	(e)1.33	Côte d'Ivoire
-17.92	3.41	5.08	-6.89	-7.10	1.06	6.80	5.36	Gambie
0.93	-3.58	-7.76	-10.29	-14.19	-21.91	-10.69	-15.16	Ghana
3.36	-6.95	-4.39	-5.46	-10.80	-31.63	-8.51	-6.90	Guinée
-12.06	-7.70	2.29	-1.83	-4.42	-3.41	3.22	-6.18	Guinée-Bissau
-8.74	-8.81	-9.58	-7.98	-8.13	-12.20	-7.41	(e)-7.73	Mali
-16.07	-0.92	-9.08	-50.31	-19.29	-16.73	-13.05	-7.46	Mauritanie
-10.22	-8.94	-6.03	-9.25	-8.19	-12.13	-28.85	-30.89	Niger
5.53	14.24	16.01	32.54	16.66	13.36	(e)12.46	(e)12.70	Nigéria
-11.86	-5.86	-7.10	-7.76	-11.63	-14.19	-8.72	(e)-8.58	Sénégal
-11.50	-7.34	-12.13	-7.04	-8.19	-10.46	-8.66	-14.09	Sierra Leone
-8.40	-4.72	-10.79	-9.66	-8.53	-6.92	-5.56	(e)-10.58	Togo

Pour les sources et les notes, se reporter à la fin du tableau.

7.1.1 Balance of payments: Current account net of countries and geographical regions

Region, country or territory	Millions of dollars - Millions de dollars							
	1980	1990	2000	2005	2007	2008	2009	2010
Developing economies: America	**-29 931**	**-4 028**	**-49 385**	**35 651**	**13 696**	**-32 700**	**-20 964**	**-56 145**
Caribbean	*-769*	*-3 226*	*-2 877*	*-135*	*-2 388*	*-6 043*	*-3 911*	*-4 768*
Anguilla	..	-9	-61	-52	-184	-211	-94	-68
Antigua and Barbuda	-19	-31	-42	-188	-380	-354	-262	-113
Aruba	..	-158	204	-197	-88	-165	157	-410
Bahamas	-75	-37	-633	-701	-1 315	-1 164	-861	-900
Barbados	-17	-8	-213	-509	-309	-423	-302	-263
Dominica	-14	-44	-60	-76	-87	-138	-102	-97
Dominican Republic	-720	-280	-1 027	-473	-2 166	-4 519	-2 159	-4 378
Grenada	0	-46	-88	-193	-262	-269	-214	-218
Haiti	-101	-22	-114	7	-86	-289	-232	(e)-1 147
Jamaica	-136	-312	-367	-1 071	-2 038	-2 793	-1 126	(e)-1 250
Montserrat	..	-23	-8	-16	-10	-20	-13	-11
Netherlands Antilles	1	-44	-48	-106	-594	-872	-374	(e)- 600
Saint Kitts and Nevis	-3	-47	-66	-65	-111	-181	-153	-96
Saint Lucia	-33	-57	-95	-129	-345	-347	-133	-150
Saint Vincent and the Grenadines	-9	-24	-24	-99	-191	-228	-198	-206
Trinidad and Tobago	357	459	544	3 594	5 364	8 519	1 614	(e)4 889
Central America	*-12 276*	*-8 372*	*-23 207*	*-10 082*	*-17 042*	*-28 537*	*-8 195*	*-13 204*
Belize	-4	15	-162	-151	-52	-132	-83	-46
Costa Rica	-664	-424	-707	-981	-1 646	-2 752	-537	-1 299
El Salvador	34	-152	-431	-569	-1 183	-1 532	-304	-488
Guatemala	-163	-213	-1 050	-1 241	-1 786	-1 680	-217	-826
Honduras	-317	-51	-508	-304	-1 116	-1 800	-449	-1 002
Mexico	-10 422	-7 451	-18 742	-5 080	-8 851	-16 349	-5 720	-5 626
Nicaragua	-411	-305	-936	-734	-1 001	-1 570	-841	-963
Panama, excl. Canal Zone (former)	-329	—	—	—	—	—	—	—
Panama	—	209	-673	-1 022	-1 407	-2 722	-44	-2 953
South America	*-16 886*	*7 569*	*-23 300*	*45 868*	*33 126*	*1 880*	*-8 858*	*-38 173*
Argentina	-4 774	4 552	-8 981	5 275	7 355	6 755	8 469	3 573
Bolivia (Plurinational State of)	-6	-199	-446	622	1 591	1 993	814	895
Brazil	-12 831	-3 823	24 225	13 985	1 551	-28 192	-24 302	-47 365
Chile	-1 971	-485	-898	1 449	7 458	-3 307	2 570	3 802
Colombia	-206	542	795	-1 886	-5 977	-6 901	-5 001	-8 944
Ecuador	-642	-360	926	347	1 588	1 087	-268	(e)-1 917
Guyana	-129	-161	-82	-96	-112	-192	(e)- 186	(e)- 216
Paraguay	-277	390	-163	16	184	-304	-149	-596
Peru	-101	-1 419	-1 546	1 148	1 460	-5 318	211	-2 315
Suriname	32	67	32	-144	185	353	210	692
Uruguay	-709	186	-566	42	-220	-1 486	215	-160
Venezuela (Bolivarian Rep. of)	4 728	8 279	11 853	25 110	18 063	37 392	8 561	14 378
Developing economies: Asia	**52 060**	**14 067**	**130 126**	**393 205**	**697 677**	**755 513**	**494 509**	**540 034**
Eastern Asia	*-7 379*	*25 654*	*48 591*	*213 642*	*438 567*	*495 436*	*353 898*	*386 535*
China	290	11 997	20 518	160 818	371 833	436 107	261 120	305 374
China, Hong Kong SAR	-1 430	4 764	6 993	20 181	25 532	29 317	17 418	13 936
China, Taiwan Province of	-818	10 923	8 899	17 578	35 154	27 505	42 911	39 899
Korea, Republic of	-5 071	-1 390	12 251	14 981	5 876	3 198	32 791	28 213
Mongolia	-350	-640	-70	84	172	-690	-342	-887
Southern Asia	*-6 444*	*-9 374*	*6 224*	*158*	*15 476*	*-26 771*	*-9 332*	*-36 533*
Afghanistan	54	..	..	-163	76	-166	-261	309
Bangladesh	-702	-398	-306	-176	857	926	3 556	2 502
Bhutan	10	-28	-40	-235	143	-27	-113	-100
India	-1 785	-7 036	-4 601	-10 284	-8 076	-30 953	-25 922	-51 781
Iran (Islamic Rep. of)	-2 438	327	12 481	15 392	32 594	22 903	(e)17 590	(e)16 036
Maldives	-22	10	-51	-273	-438	-647	-403	-463
Nepal	-39	-289	-131	153	6	733	6	-128
Pakistan	-866	-1 661	-85	-3 606	-8 286	-15 655	-3 583	-1 490
Sri Lanka	-655	-298	-1 044	-650	-1 401	-3 885	-215	-1 418
South-Eastern Asia	*-6 768*	*-8 965*	*37 494*	*45 098*	*110 694*	*79 336*	*105 192*	*105 843*
Brunei Darussalam	..	2 531	2 998	4 033	4 828	6 939	3 977	5 573
Cambodia	..	-35	-136	-307	-488	-1 051	-866	(e)-1 004
Indonesia including East Timor	..	-2 988	7 992	—	—	—	—	—
Indonesia	—	—	—	278	10 493	125	10 629	6 294
Lao People's Dem. Rep.	-43	-55	-8	-174	139	115	9	(e)-17
Malaysia	-266	-870	8 488	19 980	29 770	38 914	31 801	(e)28 183
Myanmar	-350	-436	-212	588	(e)1 853	(e)1 208	(e)705	-
Philippines	-1 904	-2 695	-2 225	1 980	7 112	3 627	9 358	8 465

For sources and notes, see end of table.

326

	As percentage of GDP - En pourcentage du PIB (1)							Régions, pays ou territoires
1980	1990	2000	2005	2007	2008	2009	2010	
-4.09	**-0.36**	**-2.33**	**1.32**	**0.37**	**-0.75**	**-0.52**	**-1.15**	**Économies en développement : Amérique**
-3.42	*-5.38*	*-3.18*	*-0.11*	*-1.49*	*-3.46*	*-2.31*	*-4.32*	*Caraïbes*
..	-15.63	-56.44	-30.67	-67.21	-72.73	-43.33	-30.52	Anguilla
-17.09	-7.91	-6.37	-21.68	-32.90	-29.45	-23.11	-10.08	Antigua-et-Barbuda
..	-19.10	10.88	-8.50	-3.44	-6.05	5.99	-15.71	Aruba
-5.57	-1.16	-11.45	-10.76	-18.18	-15.95	-12.16	-12.44	Bahamas
-1.94	-0.45	-8.33	-17.04	-9.07	-11.51	-8.40	-7.19	Barbade
-24.20	-26.03	-22.06	26.42	26.26	-00.57	-20.98	-24.69	Dominique
-8.80	-2.98	-4.34	-1.41	-5.28	-9.93	-4.63	-8.49	République dominicaine
0.36	-20.92	-21.60	-34.89	-42.85	-39.61	-33.65	-32.85	Grenade
-7.29	-0.84	-3.25	0.18	1.60	1.70	0.70	(e)-10.44	Haïti
-4.47	-6.47	-4.11	-9.60	-15.79	-19.96	-9.07	(e)-9.07	Jamaïque
..	-34.13	-22.23	-36.74	-22.51	-39.39	-24.11	..	Montserrat
0.06	-2.21	-1.69	-3.23	-16.26	-22.06	-9.29	(e)-14.15	Antilles néerlandaises
-5.56	-29.50	-20.11	-14.75	-21.85	-31.70	-28.01	-17.45	Saint-Kitts-et-Nevis
24.58	-10.71	-13.40	-14.72	-35.91	-35.08	-14.07	-15.46	Sainte-Lucie
-15.72	-11.89	-7.13	-22.70	-34.38	-39.18	-34.96	-36.74	Saint-Vincent-et-les Grenadines
5.72	9.06	6.67	22.49	25.66	32.80	7.64	(e)22.04	Trinité-et-Tobago
-4.89	*-2.62*	*-3.29*	*-1.07*	*-1.49*	*-2.34*	*-0.81*	*-1.12*	*Amérique centrale*
-1.90	3.79	-19.43	-13.56	-4.08	-9.74	-6.20	-3.31	Belize
-10.81	-5.84	-4.43	-4.91	-6.25	-9.22	-1.83	-3.63	Costa Rica
2.89	-3.16	-3.28	-3.30	-5.81	-6.93	-1.44	-2.25	El Salvador
-2.32	-3.12	-6.10	-4.56	-5.23	-4.29	-0.58	-2.01	Guatemala
-10.35	-1.41	-7.07	-3.12	-9.01	-12.86	-3.11	-6.41	Honduras
-4.58	-2.59	-2.94	-0.60	-0.87	-1.50	-0.66	-0.55	Mexique
-20.74	-11.68	-25.21	-16.09	-18.65	-26.65	-13.15	-14.28	Nicaragua
-8.11								Panama, sans la zone du canal (anc.)
–	3.44	-5.79	-6.61	-7.11	-11.74	-0.18	-10.75	Panama
-3.69	*1.03*	*-1.76*	*2.82*	*1.36*	*0.06*	*-0.31*	*-1.06*	*Amérique du Sud*
6.02	3.22	-3.16	2.88	2.80	2.06	2.74	0.96	Argentine
-0.24	-4.09	-5.32	6.52	12.13	11.95	4.69	4.66	Bolivie (État plurinational de)
-6.71	-0.95	-3.76	1.59	0.11	-1.72	-1.55	-2.30	Brésil
-6.69	-1.45	-1.19	1.23	4.54	-1.94	1.57	1.84	Chili
-0.46	1.01	0.85	-1.30	-2.88	-2.84	-2.18	-3.18	Colombie
-5.19	-3.20	5.81	0.93	3.47	1.00	-0.47	(e)-2.94	Équateur
-13.63	-25.45	-7.23	-7.32	-6.45	-9.97	(e)-9.11	(e)-9.67	Guyana
-7.05	8.39	-2.29	0.21	1.51	-1.80	-1.02	-3.23	Paraguay
-0.60	-4.85	-2.90	1.45	1.36	-4.12	0.16	-1.49	Pérou
3.54	10.87	3.42	-8.05	7.62	11.53	7.06	20.61	Suriname
-6.66	2.01	-2.48	0.24	-0.92	-4.76	0.68	-0.40	Uruguay
6.88	17.76	10.21	17.41	8.04	12.12	2.63	3.69	Venezuela (Rép. bolivarienne du)
4.19	**0.64**	**3.10**	**5.59**	**7.13**	**6.66**	**4.30**	**3.93**	**Économies en développement : Asie**
-1.67	*2.79*	*2.19*	*5.79*	*8.58*	*8.30*	*5.52*	*5.12*	*Asie orientale*
0.09	2.97	1.72	6.98	10.75	9.88	5.24	5.20	Chine
-4.96	6.20	4.13	11.35	12.33	13.61	8.27	6.15	Chine (RAS de Hong Kong)
-1.94	6.62	2.73	4.82	8.94	6.83	11.32	9.23	Province chinoise de Taiwan
-7.88	-0.51	2.30	1.77	0.56	0.34	3.94	2.80	Corée, République de
-61.60	-44.31	-6.42	3.65	4.37	-13.36	-8.11	-15.88	Mongolie
-1.94	*-1.85*	*0.87*	*0.01*	*0.87*	*-1.38*	*-0.47*	*-1.53*	*Asie méridionale*
1.47	..	..	-2.38	0.76	-1.54	-2.03	2.07	Afghanistan
-4.20	-1.41	-0.67	-0.31	1.25	1.16	3.99	2.52	Bangladesh
7.63	-10.01	-9.04	-29.21	12.01	-2.15	-9.08	-6.85	Bhoutan
-0.97	-2.15	-0.98	-1.22	-0.67	-2.42	-2.01	-3.19	Inde
-2.65	0.36	12.00	7.49	10.44	6.20	(e)4.87	(e)4.05	Iran (Rép. islamique d')
-41.40	4.98	-8.25	-36.41	-39.16	-54.51	-31.52	-33.52	Maldives
-1.86	-7.65	-2.28	1.85	0.05	6.23	0.14	-0.79	Népal
-3.01	-3.47	-0.12	-3.30	-5.80	-10.72	-2.24	-0.84	Pakistan
-15.33	-3.64	-6.24	-2.66	-4.33	-9.54	-0.50	-2.81	Sri Lanka
-6.12	*-2.52*	*6.25*	*4.99*	*8.56*	*5.29*	*7.14*	*5.77*	*Asie du Sud-Est*
..	71.91	49.96	42.31	39.42	48.21	37.72	43.55	Brunéi Darussalam
..	-2.47	-3.71	-4.87	-5.65	-9.35	-8.02	(e)-8.84	Cambodge
..	-2.37	4.83						Indonésie, y compris le Timor oriental
			0.10	2.43	0.02	1.97	0.89	Indonésie
-13.32	-6.34	-0.51	-6.34	3.31	2.19	0.17	(e)-0.26	Rép. dém. populaire lao
-1.05	-1.90	9.05	14.48	16.00	17.57	16.62	(e)11.93	Malaisie
-5.93	-8.42	-2.91	4.93	(e)11.61	(e)6.73	(e)3.71	-	Myanmar
-5.87	-6.08	-2.93	2.00	4.94	2.17	5.82	4.49	Philippines

Pour les sources et les notes, se reporter à la fin du tableau.

Region, country or territory	Millions of dollars - Millions de dollars							
	1980	1990	2000	2005	2007	2008	2009	2010
Singapore	-1 563	3 122	10 178	26 666	47 084	36 011	32 628	(e)46 271
Thailand	-2 076	-7 281	9 313	-7 647	15 678	2 211	21 861	14 696
Timor-Leste	–	–	–	261	1 177	2 023	1 363	1 425
Viet Nam	-565	-259	1 106	-560	-6 953	-10 787	-6 274	(e)-5 597
Western Asia	**72 650**	**6 752**	**37 817**	**134 307**	**132 940**	**207 511**	**44 751**	**84 189**
Bahrain	184	70	830	1 474	2 907	2 257	560	770
Jordan	374	-227	27	-2 272	-2 875	-2 179	-1 251	-1 311
Kuwait	15 302	3 886	14 672	30 071	42 175	60 242	28 605	36 822
Lebanon	-139	-1 098	-2 918	-2 748	-1 000	1 103	7 344	-0 797
Occupied Palestinian territory	..	..	-990	1 152	249	535	-737	..
Oman	942	1 106	3 129	5 178	2 463	5 020	-287	(e)1 708
Qatar	8 360	-657	4 128	14 100	20 186	34 577	14 059	24 261
Saudi Arabia	41 500	1 117	14 317	90 061	93 380	132 322	20 955	66 751
Syrian Arab Republic	251	1 702	1 061	000	100	66	-1 161	..
Turkey	-3 408	-2 625	-9 920	-22 197	-38 311	-41 946	-14 410	-47 739
United Arab Emirates	10 090	7 942	12 144	20 870	15 420	21 971	8 227	12 929
Yemen (former Arab Republic)	-685	–	–	–	–	–	–	–
Yemen (former Democratic)	-124	–	–	–	–	–	–	–
Yemen	–	739	1 337	624	-1 508	-1 251	-2 565	(e)-1 802
Developing economies: Oceania	**-336**	**-198**	**273**	**-50**	**-663**	**-1 696**	**-1 839**	**-611**
Fiji	-17	-94	-26	-300	-482	-645	-236	-222
French Polynesia	..	..	..	9	271	-54	205	..
Kiribati	2	-9	-1	-20	-38	-1	-38	-34
New Caledonia	..	..	..	-112	-294	-1 401	-908	..
Papua New Guinea	-289	-76	351	539	56	708	-672	-
Samoa	-13	9	-4	-25	-42	-44	-1	-59
Solomon Islands	-12	-28	-41	-90	-81	-124	-121	-182
Tonga	-7	6	-12	-21	-19	-66	-54	-34
Tuvalu	..	..	..	5	-1	-3	-1	-8
Vanuatu	..	-6	5	-34	-34	-66	-14	-17
Transition economies	**-2 301**	**-2 482**	**46 991**	**83 022**	**58 881**	**85 105**	**33 917**	**70 805**
Albania	16	-118	-156	-571	-1 151	-2 002	-1 875	-1 404
Armenia	–	–	-278	-52	-590	-1 383	-1 369	-1 373
Azerbaijan	–	–	-168	167	9 019	16 454	10 178	15 040
Belarus	–	–	-338	436	-3 032	-5 230	-6 389	-8 493
Bosnia and Herzegovina	–	–	-396	-1 844	-1 648	-2 637	-1 066	-916
Croatia	–	–	-533	-2 555	-4 445	-6 251	-3 356	-1 126
Georgia	–	–	-269	-710	-2 010	-2 912	-1 216	-1 122
Kazakhstan	–	–	366	-1 056	-8 322	6 279	-4 248	4 319
Kyrgyzstan	–	–	-76	-37	-227	-701	-102	-188
Montenegro	–	–	–	–	–	-2 320	-1 245	-1 031
Republic of Moldova	–	–	-98	-226	-674	-987	-469	-523
Russian Federation	–	–	46 839	84 602	77 768	103 530	49 433	70 599
Serbia and Montenegro	–	–	35	-308	-7 798	–	–	–
Serbia	–	–	–	–	–	-10 395	-2 412	-2 819
SFR of Yugoslavia (former)	-2 317	-2 364	–	–	–	–	–	–
Tajikistan	–	–	-62	-19	-495	48	-180	-383
TFYR of Macedonia	–	–	-103	-159	-606	-1 236	-646	-262
Turkmenistan	–	–	412	875	4 037	3 560	-2 981	-2 443
Ukraine	–	–	1 481	2 531	-5 272	-12 763	-1 732	-2 884
Uzbekistan	–	–	335	1 949	4 326	(e)4 050	(e)3 595	(e)5 814
Developed economies: America	**-3 961**	**-98 716**	**-396 752**	**-725 882**	**-704 825**	**-659 602**	**-417 880**	**-519 391**
Bermuda	..	..	..	..	1 267	1 239	579	(e)818
Canada	-6 088	-19 764	19 622	21 714	12 003	8 018	-40 024	-49 307
United States	2 127	-78 952	-416 374	-747 595	-718 095	-668 859	-378 435	-470 902
Developed economies: Asia	**-11 621**	**44 242**	**117 451**	**170 029**	**215 372**	**158 191**	**149 255**	**202 151**
Israel	-871	163	-2 209	4 246	4 882	1 557	7 061	6 396
Japan	-10 750	44 078	119 660	165 783	210 490	156 634	142 194	195 755
Developed economies: Europe	**-57 718**	**-31 684**	**-27 738**	**83 598**	**12 002**	**-108 300**	**81 798**	**98 258**
Austria	-3 865	1 166	-1 339	6 245	13 190	20 127	10 995	10 555
Belgium	(2)-4 931	(2)3 627	9 352	7 703	7 041	-8 342	3 522	4 481
Bulgaria	954	-1 710	-703	-3 347	-11 437	-11 888	-4 258	-578
Cyprus	-258	-154	-488	-971	-1 831	-4 289	-1 745	-1 807
Czechoslovakia (former)	..	-1 227	–	–	–	–	–	–
Czech Republic	–	–	-2 690	-1 577	-5 754	-1 247	-2 147	-7 188
Denmark	-2 389	1 372	2 262	11 104	4 769	9 095	11 222	15 681
Estonia	–	–	-299	-1 386	-3 503	-2 356	741	673

For sources and notes, see end of table.

**7.1.1 Balance des paiements :
compte courant net des pays et des régions
géographiques**

As percentage of GDP - En pourcentage du PIB (1)								Régions, pays ou territoires
1980	1990	2000	2005	2007	2008	2009	2010	
-13.34	8.46	10.98	21.99	27.44	19.13	18.42	(e)21.50	Singapour
-6.42	-8.53	7.59	-4.34	6.34	0.81	8.28	4.60	Thaïlande
			74.71	259.70	355.48	202.70	187.61	Timor-Leste
-23.60	-4.00	3.55	-1.06	-9.79	-11.90	-6.73	(e)-5.64	Viet Nam
20.36	**1.62**	**5.67**	**11.29**	**8.28**	**10.71**	**2.70**	**4.28**	**Asie occidentale**
5.60	1.62	10.34	10.95	15.73	10.19	2.90	3.40	Bahreïn
9.32	-5.65	0.32	-18.05	-16.90	-9.60	-4.98	-4.76	Jordanie
53.33	21.04	38.90	37.22	36.79	40.70	26.13	28.04	Koweït
-3.41	-39.05	-17.49	-12.57	-6.40	-13.71	-20.98	-22.67	Liban
		-20.01	-24.86	5.33	9.01	-12.60	..	Territoire palestinien occupé
15.06	9.57	16.09	16.75	5.88	8.32	-0.54	(e)2.68	Oman
106.66	-8.93	23.24	33.21	25.00	31.23	14.30	18.74	Qatar
25.26	-3.56	7.00	20.74	24.26	27.85	5.68	15.33	Arabie saoudite
1.91	15.81	5.40	1.06	1.14	0.13	-2.15	-	République arabe syrienne
-3.69	-1.30	-3.72	-4.60	-5.92	-5.74	-2.34	-6.39	Turquie
34.06	23.51	17.22	15.12	7.47	8.64	3.30	4.65	Émirats arabes unis
-28.01	-	-	-	-	-	-	-	Yémen (anc. République arabe du)
-20.52	-	-	-	-	-	-	-	Yémen (anc. démocratique)
	15.79	13.31	3.49	-6.36	-4.36	-9.53	(e)-5.39	Yémen
-7.65	**-3.75**	**4.31**	**-0.26**	**-2.64**	**-6.13**	**-6.77**	**-4.07**	**Économies en développement : Océanie**
-1.44	-6.96	-1.48	-9.97	-14.16	-18.05	-7.70	-7.18	Fidji
..	..	..	0.24	6.38	-1.15	4.51	..	Polynésie française
7.00	-22.27	-0.79	-19.10	-29.52	-0.60	-29.11	-22.04	Kiribati
..	..	..	-1.80	-3.27	-15.42	-9.78	-	Nouvelle-Calédonie
-10.23	-2.30	10.02	11.08	0.89	8.84	-8.50	-	Papouasie-Nouvelle-Guinée
-11.52	7.69	-1.81	-5.78	-7.65	-7.99	-0.22	-10.51	Samoa
-8.48	-13.34	-12.11	-21.79	-14.94	-18.51	-16.91	-23.76	Îles Salomon
-11.29	4.94	-6.10	-8.22	-6.26	-19.46	-16.00	-9.18	Tonga
..	..	..	20.71	-1.99	-11.05	-5.24	-23.98	Tuvalu
	-3.45	1.78	-8.38	-6.32	-10.62	-2.13	-2.37	Vanuatu
-3.19	**-2.84**	**11.83**	**7.59**	**3.21**	**3.64**	**1.90**	**3.38**	**Économies en transition**
0.72	-5.32	-4.29	-7.00	-10.77	-15.44	-15.45	-11.82	Albanie
-		-14.56	-1.06	-6.40	-11.86	-16.03	-14.61	Arménie
-		-3.18	1.26	27.29	33.68	23.66	27.64	Azerbaïdjan
-		-3.25	1.44	-6.70	-8.61	-13.03	-15.61	Bélarus
-		-7.19	-16.94	-10.82	-14.25	-6.25	-5.44	Bosnie-Herzégovine
-		-2.50	-5.75	-7.59	-9.02	-5.32	-1.86	Croatie
-		-8.80	-11.07	-19.76	-22.76	-11.32	-9.63	Géorgie
-		2.00	-1.85	-7.94	4.71	-3.89	3.25	Kazakhstan
-		-5.55	-1.52	-5.97	-13.64	-2.23	-4.17	Kirghizistan
-					-51.32	-30.47	-26.11	Monténégro
-		-7.62	-7.56	-15.32	-16.30	-8.68	-9.06	République de Moldova
-		18.03	11.07	5.98	6.21	4.02	4.79	Fédération de Russie
-		0.31	-0.98	-16.34				Serbie-et-Monténégro
-		-	-	-	-19.08	-5.13	-6.37	Serbie
-3.31	-2.78	-	-	-				RSF de Yougoslavie (anc.)
-		-7.20	-0.82	-17.56	1.53	-3.61	-6.78	Tadjikistan
-		-2.87	-2.74	-7.42	-12.57	-6.78	-2.80	LERY de Macédoine
-		9.33	10.08	31.17	22.92	-17.18	-12.14	Turkménistan
-		4.74	2.94	-3.69	-7.09	-1.48	-2.11	Ukraine
-		2.43	14.17	19.35	(e)15.75	(e)10.90	(e)15.22	Ouzbékistan
-0.13	**-1.55**	**-3.71**	**-5.26**	**-4.54**	**-4.13**	**-2.69**	**-3.18**	**Économies développées : Amérique**
..	..	..	..	21.74	20.34	8.81	..	Bermudes
-2.26	-3.39	2.71	1.92	0.84	0.53	-3.00	-3.13	Canada
0.08	-1.36	-4.18	-5.90	-5.09	-4.62	-2.66	-3.19	États-Unis
-1.06	**1.42**	**2.45**	**3.63**	**4.74**	**3.11**	**2.84**	**3.54**	**Économies développées : Asie**
-3.73	0.29	-1.77	3.16	2.92	0.77	3.64	2.97	Israël
-1.00	1.44	2.56	3.64	4.81	3.21	2.81	3.56	Japon
-1.48	**-0.42**	**-0.31**	**0.58**	**0.07**	**-0.56**	**0.47**	**0.57**	**Économies développées : Europe**
-4.74	0.71	-0.70	2.06	3.54	4.85	2.89	2.81	Autriche
-3.94	1.79	4.02	2.05	1.54	-1.65	0.75	0.96	Belgique
5.12	-8.25	-5.45	-11.58	-27.16	-22.94	-8.74	-1.21	Bulgarie
-11.58	-2.67	-5.25	-5.72	-8.39	-16.98	-7.41	-7.82	Chypre
..	-2.34							Tchécoslovaquie (anc.)
-		-4.74	-1.27	-3.30	-0.58	-1.13	-3.74	République tchèque
-3.43	1.01	1.41	4.31	1.53	2.67	3.62	5.03	Danemark
-		-5.26	-9.97	-16.17	-10.00	3.85	3.51	Estonie

Pour les sources et les notes, se reporter à la fin du tableau.

7.1.1 Balance of payments:
Current account net of countries
and geographical regions

Region, country or territory	Millions of dollars - Millions de dollars							
	1980	1990	2000	2005	2007	2008	2009	2010
Faeroe Islands	..	..	99	..	..	..	..	..
Finland	-1 403	-6 962	10 526	6 993	10 610	7 652	5 892	7 477
France	-4 208	-9 944	19 674	-10 260	-26 611	-49 877	-51 858	-44 499
Germany (former Federal Rep.)	-15 622		–	–	–	–	–	–
Germany	–	47 659	-32 279	140 615	254 563	228 115	188 631	188 373
Greece	-2 209	-3 537	-9 820	-18 233	-44 587	-51 313	-35 913	-32 335
Hungary	-1 102	379	-4 004	-8 343	-9 578	-11 116	473	3 049
Iceland	-76	-134	-847	-2 648	-3 195	-4 472	-1 313	-1 235
Ireland	-2 132	-361	-356	-7 150	-13 850	-15 297	-6 488	954
Italy	-10 588	-16 479	5 781	-29 777	-51 574	-78 111	-42 955	-67 942
Latvia	–	–	-371	1 992	-6 425	-4 492	2 284	873
Lithuania	–	–	-675	-1 831	-5 692	-5 812	1 648	667
Luxembourg	..	..	2 562	4 406	5 215	3 147	3 495	4 385
Malta	-39	-50	-480	-524	-606	-469	-600	-415
Netherlands	-855	8 089	7 264	46 618	52 526	67 010	38 893	55 212
Norway	1 079	3 992	25 079	49 003	60 459	79 235	50 122	51 444
Poland	-3 417	3 067	-10 343	-3 716	-26 499	-34 957	-17 155	-20 982
Portugal	-1 064	-181	-12 189	-19 821	-23 517	-31 852	-23 952	-22 605
Romania	-2 420	-3 254	-1 355	-8 504	-23 080	-23 719	-7 298	-6 744
Slovakia	–	–	-694	-4 005	-4 103	-6 185	-2 810	-3 009
Slovenia			-548	-681	-2 298	-3 632	-625	-388
Spain	-5 580	-18 009	-23 185	-83 388	-144 540	-154 529	-80 375	-64 343
Sweden	-4 331	-6 339	9 860	25 526	43 009	45 059	31 460	28 744
Switzerland	-201	6 124	32 830	52 912	40 379	6 468	38 972	70 363
United Kingdom	6 862	-38 811	-38 800	-59 406	-71 079	-41 159	-27 061	-71 604
Developed economies: Oceania	**-5 420**	**-17 401**	**-17 170**	**-49 809**	**-68 738**	**-59 211**	**-47 460**	**-37 893**
Australia	-4 447	-15 948	-14 763	-41 032	-58 032	-47 786	-43 836	-31 991
New Zealand	-973	-1 453	-2 407	-8 777	-10 706	-11 424	-3 624	-5 903

Sources:
- UNCTAD secretariat calculations, based on IMF, *Balance of Payments Statistics*
- IMF, *World Economic Outlook*
- Economist Intelligence Unit, *Country Data*
- OECD, *OECD.Stat Extracts*
- National sources

Notes:

(1) Source of GDP data: table 8.1.1
(2) Refers to Belgium-Luxembourg Economic Union.

7.1.1 Balance des paiements :
compte courant net des pays et des régions
géographiques

As percentage of GDP - En pourcentage du PIB (1)								Régions, pays ou territoires
1980	1990	2000	2005	2007	2008	2009	2010	
..	..	..	..	..	..	..	..	Îles Féroé
-2.65	-5.01	8.65	3.57	4.31	2.83	2.48	3.13	Finlande
-0.61	-0.80	1.48	-0.48	-1.02	-1.74	-1.95	-1.72	France
-1.70								Allemagne (anc. Rép. fédérale d')
–	2.78	-1.70	5.04	7.65	6.28	5.66	5.69	Allemagne
-4.04	-3.75	-7.73	-7.53	-14.44	-14.86	-11.09	-10.70	Grèce
-4.39	1.03	-8.45	-7.58	-6.95	-7.15	0.37	2.36	Hongrie
-2.29	-2.10	-9.74	-16.24	-15.64	-26.61	-10.82	-9.77	Islande
-10.10	0.75	-0.37	-3.54	-5.34	-5.80	-2.93	0.47	Irlande
-2.30	-1.45	-0.53	-1.67	2.11	-3.40	-2.03	-3.31	Italie
–	–	-4.73	-12.42	-22.33	-13.34	8.82	3.64	Lettonie
–	–	-5.90	-7.05	-14.56	-12.29	4.47	1.84	Lituanie
..	..	12.64	11.70	10.16	5.12	6.01	7.99	Luxembourg
3.10	-2.19	-12.34	-8.78	-8.02	-5.58	-7.51	-5.11	Malte
-0.47	2.74	1.89	7.30	6.71	4.35	4.89	7.19	Pays-Bas
1.69	3.39	14.90	16.23	15.60	17.76	13.24	12.43	Norvège
-5.91	4.75	-6.04	-1.22	-6.23	-6.60	-3.98	-4.48	Pologne
-3.28	-0.23	-10.42	-10.37	-10.18	-12.63	-10.26	-9.89	Portugal
-6.99	-8.45	-3.63	-8.57	-13.53	-11.61	-4.53	-4.23	Roumanie
–	–	-3.40	-8.36	-5.46	-6.55	-3.21	-3.45	Slovaquie
–	–	-2.75	-1.90	-4.86	-6.65	-1.27	-0.81	Slovénie
-2.47	-3.46	-3.99	-7.38	-10.02	-9.69	-5.49	-4.57	Espagne
-3.28	-2.59	3.99	6.89	9.30	9.24	7.75	6.26	Suède
-0.18	2.56	13.01	14.07	9.20	1.27	7.85	13.31	Suisse
1.27	-3.83	-2.63	-2.61	-2.53	-1.55	-1.25	-3.19	Royaume-Uni
-2.72	**-4.65**	**-3.70**	**-5.68**	**-6.13**	**-5.01**	**-4.20**	**-2.66**	**Économies développées : Océanie**
-2.53	-4.84	-3.59	-5.37	-5.87	-4.55	-4.32	-2.49	Australie
-4.21	-3.27	-4.52	-7.78	-8.04	-8.80	-3.10	-4.23	Nouvelle-Zélande

Sources :
- Calculs du secrétariat de la CNUCED, sur la base de FMI, *Statistiques de la balance des paiements*
- FMI, *World Economic Outlook*
- Economist Intelligence Unit, *Country Data*
- OCDE, *OECD.Stat Extracts*
- Sources nationales

Notes:
(1)   Source des données du PIB : tableau 8.1.1
(2)   Se réfère à l'Union économique belgo-luxembourgoise.

7.1.2 Balance of payments: Current account net of economic groupings

Economic grouping	Millions of dollars - Millions de dollars							
	1980	1990	2000	2005	2007	2008	2009	2010
DEVELOPING ECONOMIES	**28 412**	**13 476**	**97 796**	**489 377**	**770 223**	**772 049**	**444 817**	**489 175**
Developing economies excluding China	28 122	1 479	77 278	328 559	398 390	335 942	183 697	183 801
Developing economies excluding LDCs	34 943	19 413	102 187	496 873	772 743	785 049	474 810	513 475
High-income developing countries	58 264	30 431	73 761	281 829	337 816	412 772	231 460	277 954
Middle-income developing countries	-20 870	-242	18 190	194 762	425 028	410 404	250 288	264 819
Low-income developing countries	8 063	-16 713	5 845	12 787	7 379	-51 127	-36 931	-53 599
Heavily indebted poor countries (IMF)	-7 950	-8 157	-7 500	-14 023	-20 610	-31 304	-25 395	-24 814
Landlocked developing countries	-2 722	-2 924	-2 214	-1 545	4 826	17 833	-6 021	7 665
Small island developing States	444	-493	-981	1	-564	2 019	-3 187	348
Least developed countries	*-6 531*	*-5 937*	*-4 391*	*-7 495*	*-2 520*	*-13 000*	*-29 993*	*-24 300*
Africa and Haiti	-4 620	-5 378	-4 834	-7 838	-4 488	-15 121	-31 538	-26 630
Asia	-1 880	-502	504	310	1 079	488	484	1 314
Islands	-31	-57	-61	32	889	1 633	1 061	1 016
Major petroleum and gas exporters	*92 196*	*25 111*	*96 359*	*278 574*	*321 647*	*420 409*	*121 580*	*228 147*
Africa	13 708	8 374	23 635	77 793	97 366	105 982	23 870	55 261
America	4 728	8 279	11 853	25 110	18 063	37 392	8 561	14 378
Asia	73 759	8 458	60 871	175 671	206 218	277 035	89 149	158 508
Major exporters of manufactured goods	*-21 356*	*13 814*	*57 898*	*247 477*	*522 076*	*556 913*	*434 810*	*470 945*
America	-10 422	-7 451	-18 742	-5 080	-8 851	-16 349	-5 720	-5 626
Asia	-10 934	21 265	76 640	252 557	530 927	573 262	440 530	476 571
Emerging economies	*-39 893*	*-4 122*	*-5 262*	*88 334*	*142 535*	*61 427*	*143 219*	*109 331*
America	-30 099	-8 626	-54 391	16 776	8 973	-46 411	-18 773	-47 931
Asia	-9 794	4 503	49 129	71 558	133 562	107 839	161 992	157 262
Newly industrialized Asian countries	*-13 128*	*3 585*	*61 889*	*93 996*	*176 698*	*140 908*	*199 397*	*185 957*
First tier	-8 881	17 419	38 321	79 406	113 646	96 030	125 748	128 319
Second tier	-4 246	-13 834	23 568	14 591	63 052	44 877	73 649	57 638
Developing economies: Africa	**6 619**	**3 635**	**16 782**	**60 571**	**59 514**	**50 932**	**-26 889**	**5 896**
Northern Africa excluding Sudan	6 267	5 289	13 145	38 970	58 514	62 487	228	19 713
Sub-Saharan Africa	352	-1 655	3 637	21 601	1 000	-11 555	-27 118	-13 817
Sub-Saharan Africa excluding South Africa	-2 809	-3 206	3 827	30 119	21 018	8 528	-15 791	-3 700
Developing economies: America	**-29 931**	**-4 028**	**-49 385**	**35 651**	**13 696**	**-32 700**	**-20 964**	**-56 145**
Central America and Greater Caribbean Islands excluding Puerto Rico	-13 233	-11 530	-25 495	-11 479	-20 918	-38 730	-11 172	-19 728
Central America and Greater Caribbean Islands excluding Mexico and Puerto Rico	-2 811	-4 079	-6 752	-6 400	-12 068	-22 381	-5 452	-14 102
South America and Central America	-29 162	-802	-46 507	35 786	16 084	-26 657	-17 053	-51 377
South America excluding Brazil	-4 055	11 392	924	31 884	31 575	30 072	15 444	9 192
Developing economies: Asia	**52 060**	**14 067**	**130 126**	**393 205**	**697 677**	**755 513**	**494 509**	**540 034**
Eastern and South-Eastern Asia excluding China	-14 436	4 692	65 567	97 922	177 428	138 665	197 970	187 004
Southern Asia excluding India	-4 659	-2 338	10 825	10 442	23 552	4 182	16 590	15 248

Sources:
For sources and notes, see end of table 7.1.1.

7.1.2 Balance des paiements : compte courant net des groupements économiques

	As percentage of GDP - En pourcentage du PIB (1)							Groupements économiques
1980	1990	2000	2005	2007	2008	2009	2010	
1.18	**0.35**	**1.41**	**4.56**	**5.19**	**4.48**	**2.62**	**2.41**	**ÉCONOMIES EN DÉVELOPPEMENT**
1.34	0.04	1.35	3.89	3.50	2.62	1.53	1.28	Économies en développement sans la Chine
1.52	0.53	1.51	4.76	5.36	4.69	2.88	2.60	Économies en développement sans les PMA
5.97	1.94	2.41	6.70	6.27	6.97	4.45	4.50	Pays en développement à revenu élevé
-2.15	-0.02	0.64	4.09	6.13	4.84	2.80	2.49	Pays en développement à revenu intermédiaire
-1.94	-2.23	0.58	0.72	0.29	-1.81	-1.30	-1.51	Pays en développement à revenu faible
-7.36	-5.94	-5.47	-5.88	-6.32	-8.14	-6.69	-5.91	Pays pauvres très endettés (FMI)
-5.90	-4.35	-1.83	-0.68	1.35	3.97	-1.41	1.73	Pays en développement sans littoral
-2.45	-1.93	-2.39	0.00	-0.78	2.42	4.22	0.43	Petits États insulaires en développement
-5.96	*-3.98*	*-2.51*	*-2.52*	*-0.62*	*-2.71*	*-6.22*	*-4.32*	*Pays les moins avancés*
-5.98	-5.17	-4.85	-4.29	-1.73	-4.87	-10.50	-7.89	Afrique et Haïti
-5.90	-1.13	0.68	0.28	0.75	0.29	0.27	0.60	Asie
-6.23	-6.31	-5.12	1.41	31.06	49.65	30.70	27.18	Îles
15.98	*5.41*	*13.71*	*22.49*	*18.29*	*18.88*	*6.16*	*9.85*	*Principaux exportateurs de pétrole et de gaz*
7.63	6.06	15.89	27.70	24.77	21.16	5.85	11.20	Afrique
6.88	17.76	10.21	17.41	8.04	12.12	2.63	3.69	Amérique
22.45	3.03	13.90	21.60	18.08	19.54	7.19	11.06	Asie
-2.89	*1.01*	*1.83*	*4.98*	*7.75*	*7.20*	*5.50*	*5.05*	*Principaux exportateurs d'articles manufacturés*
-4.58	-2.59	-2.94	-0.60	-0.87	-1.50	-0.66	-0.55	Amérique
-2.14	1.96	3.03	6.12	9.29	8.62	6.26	5.74	Asie
-5.57	*-0.28*	*-0.18*	*2.35*	*2.87*	*1.14*	*2.93*	*1.81*	*Économies émergentes*
-5.57	-0.96	-3.21	0.80	0.31	-1.38	-0.62	-1.25	Amérique
-5.56	0.75	4.20	4.35	6.52	5.35	8.79	7.11	Asie
-5.53	*0.42*	*3.92*	*4.26*	*6.24*	*4.84*	*7.24*	*5.58*	*Économies nouvellement industrialisées d'Asie*
-6.04	3.17	3.42	5.26	6.24	5.53	7.86	6.82	Première génération
-4.71	-4.59	5.15	2.09	6.25	3.83	6.37	3.97	Deuxième génération
1.53	**0.74**	**2.83**	**6.15**	**4.63**	**3.39**	**-1.89**	**0.40**	**Économies en développement : Afrique**
4.66	3.05	5.27	11.61	13.30	11.44	0.04	3.42	Afrique septentrionale sans le Soudan
0.12	-0.52	1.06	3.33	0.12	-1.21	-3.00	-1.21	Afrique subsaharienne
-1.30	-1.56	1.81	7.48	3.75	1.25	-2.55	-0.41	Afrique subsaharienne sans l'Afrique du Sud
-4.09	**-0.36**	**-2.33**	**1.32**	**0.37**	**-0.75**	**-0.52**	**-1.15**	**Économies en développement : Amérique**
-5.01	-3.16	-3.30	-1.11	-1.66	-2.87	-0.99	-1.60	Amérique centrale et Grandes Antilles sans Porto Rico
-7.76	-5.29	-4.95	-3.43	-5.07	-8.54	-2.09	-6.48	Amérique centrale et Grandes Antilles sans le Mexique et Porto Rico
-4.11	-0.08	-2.29	1.39	0.45	-0.64	-0.44	-1.07	Amérique du Sud et Amérique centrale
-1.52	3.39	0.14	4.28	2.96	2.31	1.20	0.59	Amérique du Sud sans le Brésil
4.19	**0.64**	**3.10**	**5.59**	**7.13**	**6.66**	**4.30**	**3.93**	**Économies en développement : Asie**
-5.85	0.54	4.02	4.27	6.02	4.54	6.83	5.33	Asie orientale et Asie du Sud-Est sans la Chine
-3.16	-1.30	4.43	2.53	4.07	0.63	2.44	2.01	Asie méridionale sans l'Inde

Sources :
Pour les sources et les notes, se reporter à la fin du tableau 7.1.1.

Trade group	Millions of dollars - Millions de dollars							
	1980	1990	2000	2005	2007	2008	2009	2010
AFRICA								
CEMAC	-279	-788	978	1 636	-162	2 064	-6 205	-4 494
CEPGL	-382	-869	317	-941	-367	-2 536	-1 709	-1 661
COMESA	4 141	1 015	2 770	8 764	19 706	19 329	-8 577	-1 922
EAC	-1 612	-1 503	-1 131	-1 441	-3 612	-6 483	-4 588	-6 809
ECCAS	-592	-1 905	1 436	5 796	9 988	6 628	-15 564	-8 101
ECOWAS	2 154	2 264	5 307	32 615	20 387	17 839	16 559	20 241
MRU	-1 941	-1 487	-494	-226	-754	-975	1 073	-344
OADO	000	1 202	-939	-6 512	-11 677	-21 423	-25 503	-19 126
UMA	6 570	2 953	14 018	35 991	57 587	63 345	3 206	23 882
WAEMU	-2 853	-2 259	-1 463	-2 460	-4 234	-5 643	-2 728	-4 467
AMERICA								
ANCOM	-955	-1 436	-271	231	-1 337	-9 139	-4 244	-12 281
CACM	-1 522	-1 145	-3 631	-3 829	-6 732	-9 334	-2 348	-4 579
CARICOM	-151	-269	-1 378	162	251	2 345	-2 041	868
FTAA	-33 893	-99 966	-445 444	-689 999	-691 933	-689 681	-439 639	-575 516
LAIA	-27 211	-2 332	-42 772	41 169	24 616	-17 222	-14 063	-44 025
MERCOSUR	-18 591	1 305	-33 934	19 318	8 869	-23 226	-15 768	-44 548
NAFTA	-14 383	-106 167	-415 494	-730 961	-714 942	-677 190	-424 180	-525 836
OAS	-33 576	-102 459	-445 715	-689 555	-690 403	-690 473	-438 651	-574 262
OECS	-78	-271	-383	-767	-1 386	-1 534	-1 074	-891
ASIA								
APTA	-7 966	2 820	26 810	164 515	369 229	405 508	271 339	282 874
ASEAN	-6 768	-8 965	37 494	44 836	109 517	77 313	103 829	104 418
ECO	-6 659	-3 959	3 284	-8 695	-5 589	-5 174	5 597	-10 726
GCC	76 382	8 201	49 220	161 753	176 531	256 389	72 119	143 242
SAARC	-4 006	-9 701	-6 257	-15 234	-17 118	-49 674	-26 922	-52 569
EUROPE								
EFTA	801	9 982	57 062	99 267	97 643	81 231	87 782	120 572
EU	-58 519	-41 666	-84 899	-15 669	-85 641	-189 531	-5 983	-22 314
Euro area	-52 676	4 857	-38 081	36 417	26 125	-109 295	4 849	35 768
OCEANIA								
MSG	-318	-204	289	115	-541	-127	-1 042	-476
INTERREGIONAL								
ACP	-854	-4 924	734	21 761	45	-14 519	-30 539	-16 250
APEC	-46 317	-63 615	-181 745	-268 962	59 959	89 013	180 316	195 364
BSEC	-7 067	-11 244	25 553	33 461	-40 325	-39 324	-11 343	-11 883
CIS	–	–	48 413	89 170	76 538	112 858	45 734	79 484

Sources:
For sources and notes, see end of table 7.1.1.

7.1.3 Balance des paiements : compte courant net des groupements commerciaux

1980	1990	2000	2005	2007	2008	2009	2010	Groupements commerciaux
			As percentage of GDP - En pourcentage du PIB (1)					
								AFRIQUE
-1.56	-3.34	4.55	3.52	-0.27	2.65	-9.68	-6.28	CEMAC
-3.05	-6.54	-3.97	-8.64	-2.45	-14.39	-9.64	-6.18	CEPGL
3.50	0.68	1.32	3.34	5.36	4.34	-1.94	-0.23	COMESA
-7.26	-6.09	-3.52	-3.07	-5.73	-8.79	-6.03	-8.29	CAE
1.65	-4.03	3.71	7.49	9.55	5.08	-13.30	-5.86	CEEAC
1.75	2.94	6.38	18.60	8.24	5.78	6.21	6.35	CEDEAO
-14.82	-9.43	-3.34	-1.09	-2.90	-3.32	3.57	-1.16	UFM
0.00	-0.72	-0.49	-1.92	-2.88	-5.17	-6.05	-3.55	SADC
5.91	2.18	9.30	15.06	18.55	16.46	0.96	6.52	UMA
-12.69	-7.39	-5.55	-5.30	-7.30	-8.10	-3.98	-6.45	UEMOA
								AMÉRIQUE
-1.25	-1.45	-0.16	0.09	-0.36	-2.06	-0.98	-2.36	ANCOM
-7.85	-4.56	-6.35	-4.87	-6.83	-8.41	-2.16	-3.78	MCAC
-0.98	-1.30	-4.01	0.34	0.42	3.46	-3.34	1.37	CARICOM
-0.90	-1.34	-3.49	-4.20	-3.60	-3.41	-2.25	-2.71	ZLEA
-3.98	-0.22	-2.15	1.64	0.70	-0.42	-0.37	-0.96	ALADI
-6.61	0.23	-3.54	1.77	0.53	-1.15	-0.82	-1.79	MERCOSUR
-0.44	-1.59	-3.67	-4.99	-4.32	-3.97	-2.58	-3.03	ALENA
-0.89	-1.37	-3.48	-4.18	-3.59	-3.40	-2.24	-2.71	OEA
-16.05	-16.74	-13.92	-21.79	-33.15	-34.52	26.23	-20.07	OECO
								ASIE
-1.38	0.27	1.19	4.04	6.36	6.00	3.75	3.27	ACAP
-6.12	-2.52	6.25	4.96	8.47	5.16	7.05	5.69	ANASE
-3.07	-1.16	0.68	-0.96	-0.43	-0.35	0.41	-0.67	ECO
31.82	4.27	14.40	26.04	20.84	23.95	8.02	13.51	CCG
-1.67	-2.34	-1.03	-1.45	-1.17	-3.16	-1.67	-2.65	SAARC
								EUROPE
0.45	2.74	13.29	14.29	11.53	8.37	9.89	12.62	AELE
-1.57	-0.57	-1.00	-0.11	-0.50	-1.04	-0.04	-0.14	UE
-1.85	0.09	-0.61	0.36	0.21	-0.81	0.04	0.29	Zone euro
								OCÉANIE
-7.61	-4.05	4.95	1.33	-5.00	-0.99	-8.45	-3.43	MSG
								INTERRÉGIONAUX
-0.26	-1.29	0.17	2.78	0.00	-1.27	-2.81	-1.30	ACP
-0.90	-0.56	-0.92	-1.05	0.20	0.27	0.56	0.55	CEAP
-3.49	-3.14	3.41	1.92	-1.51	-1.18	-0.43	-0.40	CEMN
–	–	13.89	9.04	4.55	5.23	2.82	4.11	CEI

Sources :
Pour les sources et les notes, se reporter à la fin du tableau 7.1.1.

7

7.2.1 Foreign direct investment: Inward and outward flows of countries and geographical regions

Region, country or territory	Inward flows - Flux entrants Millions of dollars							
	1980	1990	2000	2006	2007	2008	2009	2010
WORLD	54 078	207 455	1 402 680	1 461 863	1 970 940	1 744 101	1 185 030	1 243 671
DEVELOPING ECONOMIES	7 479	34 853	257 625	429 459	573 032	658 002	510 578	573 568
TRANSITION ECONOMIES	24	75	7 023	54 516	91 090	120 986	71 618	68 197
DEVELOPED ECONOMIES	46 576	172 526	1 138 032	977 888	1 306 818	965 113	602 835	601 906
Developing economies: Africa	400	2 845	10 967	46 259	63 132	73 413	60 167	55 040
Eastern Africa	797	369	1 488	8 100	8 080	5 375	5 519	5 860
Burundi	5	1	12	0	1	14	10	14
Comoros	..	0	0	1	8	8	9	9
Djibouti	0	0	3	108	195	229	100	27
Eritrea	–	–	28	0	0	0	0	56
Ethiopia	–	–	135	545	222	109	221	104
Ethiopia (former)	1	12	–	–	–	–	–	–
Kenya	79	57	111	51	729	96	141	133
Madagascar	-1	22	83	295	773	1 169	1 066	860
Malawi	9	23	40	72	92	9	60	140
Mauritius	1	41	277	105	339	383	257	430
Mayotte	0	0	0	0	0	0	0	0
Mozambique	4	9	139	154	427	592	893	789
Rwanda	16	8	8	31	82	103	119	42
Seychelles	10	0	24	146	239	179	275	369
Somalia	0	6	0	96	141	87	108	112
Uganda	4	-6	181	644	792	729	816	848
United Republic of Tanzania	5	0	282	597	647	679	645	700
Zambia	62	203	122	616	1 324	939	695	1 041
Zimbabwe	2	12	23	40	69	52	105	105
Middle Africa	353	-345	2 799	12 084	15 698	20 859	16 943	17 844
Angola	37	-335	2 174	9 064	9 796	16 581	11 672	9 942
Cameroon	130	-113	159	309	284	270	337	425
Central African Republic	5	1	1	35	57	117	42	72
Chad	0	9	115	-279	-69	234	462	781
Congo	40	23	162	1 925	2 275	2 483	2 083	2 816
Dem. Rep. of the Congo	110	-14	72	256	1 808	1 727	664	2 939
Equatorial Guinea	..	11	154	470	1 243	-794	1 636	695
Gabon	32	73	-43	268	269	209	33	170
Sao Tome and Principe	..	0	4	38	35	33	14	3
Northern Africa	152	1 155	3 250	23 143	24 775	24 045	18 468	16 926
Algeria	349	40	280	1 795	1 662	2 594	2 761	2 291
Egypt	548	734	1 235	10 043	11 578	9 495	6 712	6 386
Libyan Arab Jamahiriya	-1 089	159	141	2 013	4 689	4 111	2 674	3 833
Morocco	89	165	422	2 449	2 805	2 487	1 952	1 304
Sudan	9	-31	392	3 534	2 426	2 601	2 682	1 600
Tunisia	246	89	779	3 308	1 616	2 758	1 688	1 513
Southern Africa	132	92	1 268	556	7 056	10 416	6 575	3 087
Botswana	112	96	57	486	495	528	579	529
Lesotho	4	16	32	89	97	56	48	55
Namibia	..	30	186	387	733	720	516	858
South Africa	-10	-78	887	-527	5 695	9 006	5 365	1 553
Swaziland	26	28	106	121	37	106	66	93
Western Africa	-434	1 553	2 182	6 976	9 522	12 718	12 662	11 323
Benin	4	62	60	53	255	171	135	111
Burkina Faso	0	0	23	34	344	137	171	37
Cape Verde	0	0	43	131	190	209	119	111
Côte d'Ivoire	95	48	235	319	427	446	381	418
Gambia	0	14	44	71	76	70	47	37
Ghana	16	15	166	636	855	1 220	1 685	2 527
Guinea	1	18	10	125	386	382	141	303
Guinea-Bissau	..	2	1	17	19	6	14	9
Liberia	72	225	21	108	132	395	218	248
Mali	2	6	82	82	65	180	109	148
Mauritania	27	7	40	106	138	338	-38	14
Niger	49	41	8	51	129	566	739	947
Nigeria	-739	1 003	1 310	4 898	6 087	8 249	8 650	6 099
Saint Helena	0	0	-4	0	0	0	0	0
Senegal	14	57	63	210	273	272	208	237
Sierra Leone	-19	32	39	59	97	53	33	36
Togo	43	23	41	77	49	24	50	41

For sources and notes, see end of table.

Outward flows - Flux sortants Millions de dollars								Régions, pays ou territoires
1980	1990	2000	2006	2007	2008	2009	2010	
51 590	241 498	1 232 117	1 405 389	2 174 803	1 910 509	1 170 527	1 323 337	**MONDE**
3 192	11 914	134 194	226 683	294 177	308 891	270 750	327 564	ÉCONOMIES EN DÉVELOPPEMENT
0	0	3 195	23 723	51 581	60 386	48 802	60 584	ÉCONOMIES EN TRANSITION
48 397	229 584	1 094 728	1 154 983	1 829 044	1 541 232	850 975	935 190	ÉCONOMIES DÉVELOPPÉES
1 097	659	1 495	6 943	10 719	9 750	5 627	6 636	**Économies en développement : Afrique**
5	21	28	44	215	141	377	458	*Afrique orientale*
	0	0	0	0	0	0	0	Burundi
0	1	0	0	0	0	0	0	Comores
0	0	0	0	0	0	0	0	Djibouti
–	–	0	0	0	0	0	0	Érythrée
–	–	0	0	0	0	0	0	Éthiopie
0	0		–	–		–	–	Éthiopie (anc.)
1	0	0	24	36	44	46	18	Kenya
0	1	0	0	0	0	0	0	Madagascar
0	0	-1	1	1	25	1	1	Malawi
..	1	13	10	58	52	37	129	Maurice
0	0	0	0	0	0	0	0	Mayotte
0	0	0	0	0	0	-3	1	Mozambique
0	0	0	0	13	0	0	0	Rwanda
4	1	8	8	18	13	5	6	Seychelles
0	0	0	0	0	0	0	0	Somalie
0	0	0	0	0	0	0	0	Ouganda
0	0	0	0	0	0	0	0	République-Unie de Tanzanie
0	0	0	0	86	0	270	289	Zambie
0	17	8	0	3	8	20	15	Zimbabwe
0	52	12	321	986	2 729	126	1 258	*Afrique centrale*
0	1	-21	194	912	2 570	8	1 100	Angola
-8	15	10	-1	-2	2	-9	2	Cameroun
..	4	0	0	0	0	0	0	République centrafricaine
0	0	0	0	0	0	0	0	Tchad
..	3	4	0	0	0	0	0	Congo
0	0	-2	10	14	54	35	7	Rép. dém. du Congo
..	0	-4	0	0	0	0	0	Guinée équatoriale
8	29	25	106	59	96	87	81	Gabon
0	0	0	3	3	7	4	5	Sao Tomé-et-Principe
87	135	223	134	5 545	8 751	2 543	3 384	*Afrique septentrionale*
34	5	14	35	295	318	215	226	Algérie
7	12	51	148	665	1 920	571	1 176	Égypte
47	105	98	-534	3 933	5 888	1 165	1 282	Jamahiriya arabe libyenne
..	13	59	445	622	485	470	576	Maroc
0	0	0	7	11	98	45	51	Soudan
..	0	2	33	20	42	77	74	Tunisie
766	39	285	6 102	2 996	-3 212	1 077	416	*Afrique australe*
2	7	2	50	51	-91	-65	-38	Botswana
0	0	0	0	0	0	0	0	Lesotho
..	1	3	-12	3	5	-3	-4	Namibie
755	27	271	6 063	2 966	-3 134	1 151	450	Afrique du Sud
9	3	10	1	-23	8	-7	8	Swaziland
238	412	947	342	977	1 341	1 504	1 120	*Afrique occidentale*
..	0	4	-2	-6	-4	31	7	Bénin
0	-1	0	1	0	0	1	0	Burkina Faso
0	0	0	0	0	0	0	0	Cap-Vert
0	0	8	-27	0	8	-7	0	Côte d'Ivoire
0	0	0	0	0	0	0	0	Gambie
0	0	0	0	0	9	7	8	Ghana
0	0	..	0	0	126	0	0	Guinée
..	..	0	0	0	0	0	0	Guinée-Bissau
236	6	762	47	65	119	-93	30	Libéria
0	0	4	1	7	3	4	5	Mali
0	0	0	5	4	4	4	4	Mauritanie
-4	0	-1	-1	8	24	10	14	Niger
5	415	169	322	875	1 058	1 542	923	Nigéria
0	0	0	0	0	0	0	0	Sainte-Hélène
2	-10	1	10	25	9	15	154	Sénégal
0	0	0	0	0	0	0	5	Sierra Leone
0	0	0	-14	-1	-16	-10	-31	Togo

Pour les sources et les notes, se reporter à la fin du tableau.

7.2.1 Foreign direct investment: Inward and outward flows of countries and geographical regions

Region, country or territory	Inward flows - Flux entrants Millions of dollars							
	1980	1990	2000	2006	2007	2008	2009	2010
Developing economies: America	**6 416**	**8 926**	**97 688**	**98 459**	**169 514**	**206 733**	**140 997**	**159 171**
Caribbean	*390*	*828*	*20 335*	*28 626*	*60 813*	*80 570*	*65 226*	*48 068*
Anguilla	0	11	43	142	119	99	46	25
Antigua and Barbuda	20	59	67	359	338	174	118	105
Aruba	0	131	-128	565	-127	200	73	161
Bahamas	4	-17	469	1 159	1 164	1 103	657	977
Barbados	2	11	19	218	336	267	160	80
British Virgin Islands	-1	18	9 877	7 549	31 443	51 742	42 100	30 526
Cayman Islands	20	49	7 627	14 963	22 969	18 749	17 878	12 894
Cuba	0	1	-10	26	64	24	24	86
Dominica	..	8	20	26	40	57	41	31
Dominican Republic	93	133	953	1 085	1 667	2 870	2 165	1 626
Grenada	..	13	39	90	152	142	103	89
Haiti	13	8	13	160	75	30	38	150
Jamaica	28	175	469	882	867	1 437	541	201
Montserrat	..	10	2	4	7	13	3	2
Netherlands Antilles	35	8	-1	-22	234	266	117	138
Saint Kitts and Nevis	1	49	99	110	134	178	104	141
Saint Lucia	31	46	58	234	272	161	146	99
Saint Vincent and the Grenadines	1	8	38	109	131	159	106	92
Trinidad and Tobago	143	109	680	883	830	2 801	709	549
Turks and Caicos Islands	0	0	0	58	97	99	95	97
Central America	*2 505*	*3 056*	*20 293*	*25 916*	*37 155*	*34 029*	*20 485*	*24 622*
Belize	..	19	23	109	143	170	109	97
Costa Rica	53	162	409	1 469	1 896	2 078	1 347	1 413
El Salvador	6	2	173	241	1 551	903	366	78
Guatemala	111	59	230	592	745	754	600	687
Honduras	6	44	382	669	928	1 006	523	797
Mexico	2 099	2 633	18 110	20 052	29 734	26 295	15 334	18 679
Nicaragua	13	1	267	287	382	626	434	508
Panama, excl. Canal Zone (former)	219							
Panama	—	136	700	2 498	1 777	2 196	1 773	2 363
South America	*3 521*	*5 042*	*57 060*	*43 916*	*71 546*	*92 134*	*55 287*	*86 481*
Argentina	678	1 836	10 418	5 537	6 473	9 726	4 017	6 337
Bolivia (Plurinational State of)	47	67	736	281	366	513	423	622
Brazil	1 910	989	32 779	18 822	34 585	45 058	25 949	48 438
Chile	213	661	4 860	7 298	12 534	15 150	12 874	15 095
Colombia	157	500	2 436	6 656	9 049	10 596	7 137	6 760
Ecuador	70	126	-23	271	194	1 006	319	164
Falkland Islands (Malvinas)	0	..	45	0	0	0	0	0
Guyana	1	8	67	102	152	178	144	188
Paraguay	30	71	104	173	185	320	209	419
Peru	27	41	810	3 467	5 491	6 924	5 576	7 328
Suriname	18	-77	-148	323	179	209	151	180
Uruguay	290	42	273	1 493	1 329	2 106	1 593	2 355
Venezuela (Bolivarian Rep. of)	80	778	4 701	-508	1 008	349	-3 105	-1 404
Developing economies: Asia	**543**	**22 628**	**148 747**	**283 463**	**339 252**	**375 665**	**307 527**	**357 846**
Eastern Asia	*950*	*8 791*	*116 641*	*131 829*	*151 004*	*185 253*	*161 096*	*188 291*
China	57	3 487	40 715	72 715	83 521	108 312	95 000	105 735
China, Hong Kong SAR	710	3 275	61 938	45 060	54 341	59 621	52 394	68 904
China, Macao SAR	0	0	-1	1 608	2 305	2 591	2 770	2 558
China, Taiwan Province of	166	1 330	4 928	7 424	7 769	5 432	2 805	2 492
Korea, Dem. People's Rep. of	..	-61	3	-105	67	44	2	38
Korea, Republic of	17	759	9 004	4 881	2 628	8 409	7 501	6 873
Mongolia	0	0	54	245	373	845	624	1 691
Southern Asia	*284*	*213*	*4 864*	*27 821*	*34 297*	*51 901*	*42 458*	*31 954*
Afghanistan	9	..	0	238	243	300	185	76
Bangladesh	9	3	579	792	666	1 086	700	913
Bhutan	..	2	0	6	78	28	15	12
India	79	237	3 588	20 328	25 350	42 546	35 649	24 640
Iran (Islamic Rep. of)	81	-362	194	1 647	1 670	1 615	3 016	3 617
Maldives	0	6	22	64	91	135	112	164
Nepal	0	6	0	-7	6	1	39	39
Pakistan	64	278	309	4 273	5 590	5 438	2 338	2 016
Sri Lanka	43	43	173	480	603	752	404	478

For sources and notes, see end of table.

		Outward flows - Flux sortants Millions de dollars						Régions, pays ou territoires
1980	1990	2000	2006	2007	2008	2009	2010	
899	301	49 723	68 129	61 731	80 580	45 544	76 273	**Économies en développement : Amérique**
121	*-1 718*	*42 270*	*24 526*	*38 320*	*43 207*	*32 073*	*29 211*	*Caraïbes*
0	0	0	0	0	0	0	0	Anguilla
0	0	2	0	0	0	0	0	Antigua-et-Barbuda
0	487	0	-13	30	3	1	4	Aruba
115	0	0	0	0	0	0	0	Bahamas
1	1	-1	44	82	3	-80	2	Barbade
..	2 620	34 460	15 090	29 039	29 121	25 742	20 598	Îles Vierges britanniques
5	282	7 649	8 333	8 769	13 333	6 379	8 539	Îles Caïmanes
0	0	0	-2	0	0	0	0	Cuba
0	0	0	0	0	0	0	0	Dominique
0	0	61	61	17	19	22	23	République dominicaine
0	0	0	0	0	0	0	0	Grenade
0	-8	0	0	0	0	0	0	Haïti
..	37	74	85	115	76	61	67	Jamaïque
0	0	0	0	0	0	0	0	Montserrat
1	2	-3	57	-3	-15	-7	17	Antilles néerlandaises
0	0	0	0	0	0	0	0	Saint-Kitts-et-Nevis
0	0	0	0	0	0	0	0	Sainte-Lucie
0	0	0	0	0	0	0	0	Saint-Vincent-et-les Grenadines
0	0	25	370	0	700	0	0	Trinité-et-Tobago
0	0	4	14	5	6	9	7	Îles Turques et Caïques
358	*907*	*-586*	*8 154*	*11 164*	*3 213*	*9 405*	*16 768*	*Amérique centrale*
..	2	0	1	1	3	0	1	Belize
5	2	8	98	263	6	7	9	Costa Rica
0	0	5	26	-95	-80	0	0	El Salvador
2	0	40	40	25	16	26	24	Guatemala
1	-1	-7	1	1	-1	1	-1	Honduras
3	223	363	5 758	8 256	1 157	7 019	14 345	Mexique
0	0	8	21	9	16	16	14	Nicaragua
347								Panama, sans la zone du canal (anc.)
–	681	-1 004	2 209	2 704	2 095	2 336	2 377	Panama
420	*1 112*	*8 038*	*35 449*	*12 247*	*34 161*	*4 066*	*30 294*	*Amérique du Sud*
-110	35	901	2 439	1 504	1 391	712	964	Argentine
1	1	3	0	7	4	-3	-58	Bolivie (État plurinational de)
367	625	2 282	28 202	7 067	20 457	-10 084	11 519	Brésil
44	8	3 987	2 172	2 573	8 041	8 061	8 744	Chili
106	16	325	1 098	913	2 254	3 088	6 504	Colombie
1	3	13	8	-8	8	36	12	Équateur
0	0	0	0	0	0	0	0	Îles Falkland (Malvinas)
0	0	2	0	0	0	0	0	Guyana
0	0	6	7	7	8	8	-4	Paraguay
0	50	0	0	66	736	398	215	Pérou
0	0	0	0	0	0	0	0	Suriname
..	..	-1	-1	89	-11	16	9	Uruguay
12	375	521	1 524	30	1 273	1 834	2 390	Venezuela (Rép. bolivarienne du)
1 179	10 943	82 964	151 566	221 688	218 436	219 500	244 585	**Économies en développement : Asie**
150	*9 574*	*71 229*	*85 402*	*114 391*	*133 173*	*142 941*	*174 283*	*Asie orientale*
..	830	916	21 160	22 469	52 150	56 530	68 000	Chine
82	2 448	59 374	44 979	61 081	50 581	63 991	76 077	Chine (RAS de Hong Kong)
0	0	0	636	3	-102	-708	-269	Chine (RAS de Macao)
42	5 243	6 701	7 399	11 107	10 287	5 877	11 183	Province chinoise de Taiwan
..	1	6	0	0	0	0	0	Corée, Rép. populaire dém. de
26	1 052	4 233	11 175	19 720	20 251	17 197	19 230	Corée, République de
0	0	0	54	13	6	54	62	Mongolie
11	*10*	*551*	*14 812*	*17 709*	*19 897*	*16 405*	*15 079*	*Asie méridionale*
0	0	0	0	0	0	0	0	Afghanistan
..	1	2	4	21	9	29	15	Bangladesh
0	0	0	0	0	0	0	0	Bhoutan
4	6	514	14 285	17 234	19 397	15 929	14 626	Inde
7	0	22	386	302	380	356	346	Iran (Rép. islamique d')
0	0	0	0	0	0	0	0	Maldives
0	0	0	0	0	0	0	0	Népal
0	2	11	109	98	49	71	46	Pakistan
..	1	2	29	55	62	20	46	Sri Lanka

Pour les sources et les notes, se reporter à la fin du tableau.

7

7.2.1 Foreign direct investment: Inward and outward flows of countries and geographical regions

Region, country or territory	Inward flows - Flux entrants Millions of dollars							
	1980	1990	2000	2006	2007	2008	2009	2010
South-Eastern Asia	*2 636*	*12 821*	*23 656*	*56 701*	*75 740*	*46 947*	*37 981*	*79 408*
Brunei Darussalam	-20	7	549	434	260	239	370	496
Cambodia	1	0	149	483	867	815	539	783
Indonesia including East Timor	180	1 092	-4 495	–	–	–	–	–
Indonesia	–	–	–	4 914	6 928	9 318	4 877	13 304
Lao People's Dem. Rep.	0	6	34	187	324	228	319	350
Malaysia	934	2 611	3 788	6 060	8 595	7 172	1 430	9 103
Myanmar	0	225	208	428	715	976	579	756
Philippines	114	550	2 240	2 921	2 916	1 611	1 963	1 713
Singapore	1 236	5 575	16 484	29 348	37 033	8 588	15 279	38 638
Thailand	189	2 575	3 410	9 517	11 355	8 448	4 976	5 813
Timor-Leste	–	–	–	8	9	40	50	280
Viet Nam	2	100	1 298	2 400	6 739	9 579	7 600	8 173
Western Asia	*-3 328*	*804*	*3 586*	*67 112*	*78 211*	*91 564*	*65 993*	*58 193*
Bahrain	-418	-183	364	2 915	1 756	1 794	257	156
Iraq	2	0	-3	383	972	1 856	1 452	1 426
Jordan	34	38	913	3 544	2 622	2 829	2 430	1 704
Kuwait	1	6	16	121	112	-6	1 114	81
Lebanon	-12	6	964	3 132	3 376	4 333	4 804	4 955
Occupied Palestinian territory	0	0	62	19	28	52	265	115
Oman	98	142	83	1 588	3 431	2 528	1 471	2 045
Qatar	11	5	252	3 500	4 700	3 779	8 125	5 534
Saudi Arabia	-3 192	312	183	17 140	22 821	38 151	32 100	28 105
Syrian Arab Republic	0	40	270	659	1 242	1 467	1 434	1 381
Turkey	18	684	982	20 185	22 047	19 504	8 411	9 071
United Arab Emirates	98	-116	-506	12 806	14 187	13 724	4 003	3 948
Yemen (former Arab Republic)	34	–	–	–	–	–	–	–
Yemen	–	-131	6	1 121	917	1 555	129	-329
Developing economies: Oceania	**120**	**454**	**223**	**1 278**	**1 134**	**2 192**	**1 887**	**1 511**
Cook Islands	0	4	-28	3	0	1	1	1
Fiji	36	84	3	370	376	354	114	129
French Polynesia	0	22	2	31	58	14	10	26
Kiribati	0	0	1	1	1	3	3	4
Marshall Islands	–	1	125	6	12	6	8	9
Micronesia (Federated States of)	–	0	0	1	17	6	8	10
Nauru	0	0	0	0	1	1	1	1
New Caledonia	2	31	-41	749	417	1 673	1 146	1 003
Niue	0	0	0	0	0	0	0	0
Northern Mariana Islands	–	124	12	0	0	0	0	0
Pacific Islands, Former (Trust Territory)	-1	–	–	–	–	–	–	–
Palau	–	1	15	1	3	2	2	2
Papua New Guinea	76	155	98	-7	96	-30	423	29
Samoa	0	7	-2	3	3	17	1	2
Solomon Islands	2	10	13	34	64	95	120	238
Tokelau	0	0	0	0	0	0	0	0
Tonga	0	0	5	10	28	6	15	16
Tuvalu	0	0	-1	5	0	2	2	2
Vanuatu	5	13	20	72	57	44	32	39
Wallis and Futuna Islands	0	0	0	0	1	1	1	1
Transition economies	**24**	**75**	**7 023**	**54 516**	**91 090**	**120 986**	**71 618**	**68 197**
Albania	0	0	144	325	656	988	979	1 097
Armenia	–	–	104	453	699	935	778	577
Azerbaijan	–	–	130	-584	-4 749	14	473	563
Belarus	–	–	104	354	1 805	2 180	1 886	1 350
Bosnia and Herzegovina	–	–	146	766	2 080	932	246	63
Croatia	–	–	1 051	3 473	5 035	6 179	2 911	583
Georgia	–	–	131	1 170	1 750	1 564	658	549
Kazakhstan	–	–	1 283	6 278	11 119	14 322	13 771	9 961
Kyrgyzstan	–	–	-2	182	209	377	190	234
Montenegro	–	–	–	–	–	960	1 527	760
Republic of Moldova	–	–	128	240	534	713	128	199
Russian Federation	–	–	2 714	29 701	55 073	75 002	36 500	41 194
Serbia and Montenegro	–	–	52	4 878	4 373	–	–	–
Serbia	–	–	–	–	–	2 955	1 959	1 329
SFR of Yugoslavia (former) (1)	24	71	–	–	–	–	–	–
Tajikistan	–	–	24	339	360	376	16	45
TFYR of Macedonia	–	–	215	433	693	586	201	293
Turkmenistan	–	–	131	731	856	1 277	3 867	2 083

For sources and notes, see end of table.

Outward flows - Flux sortants Millions de dollars								Régions, pays ou territoires
1980	1990	2000	2006	2007	2008	2009	2010	
394	*2 328*	*8 253*	*28 782*	*55 413*	*25 185*	*33 845*	*42 223*	**Asie du Sud-Est**
0	0	30	17	-7	16	9	6	Brunéi Darussalam
0	0	16	12	5	24	18	17	Cambodge
6	-11	150	–	–	–	–	–	Indonésie, y compris le Timor oriental
–	–	–	2 726	4 675	5 900	2 249	2 664	Indonésie
0	0	10	39	1	-75	1	6	Rép. dém. populaire lao
201	129	2 026	6 021	11 314	14 966	7 930	13 329	Malaisie
0	0	0	0	0	0	0	0	Myanmar
86	22	125	103	3 536	259	359	487	Philippines
98	2 034	5 915	18 809	32 702	-256	18 464	19 739	Singapour
0	154	-20	970	3 003	4 053	4 116	5 122	Thaïlande
–	–	–	0	0	0	0	0	Timor-Leste
0	0	0	85	184	300	700	853	Viet Nam
624	*-969*	*2 931*	*22 570*	*34 175*	*40 180*	*26 309*	*12 999*	**Asie occidentale**
..	25	10	980	1 669	1 620	-1 791	334	Bahreïn
0	0	0	305	8	34	116	52	Iraq
3	-31	9	-138	48	13	72	28	Jordanie
407	-239	-303	8 211	9 784	9 091	8 636	2 069	Koweït
2	-16	108	875	848	987	1 126	574	Liban
0	0	213	125	-8	-8	-15	-11	Territoire palestinien occupé
1	0	-2	263	70	481	66	317	Oman
2	2	18	127	5 160	6 029	11 584	1 863	Qatar
211	-638	1 550	-39	-135	3 498	2 177	3 907	Arabie saoudite
0	3	44	-11	2	2	-3	0	République arabe syrienne
0	-16	870	924	2 106	2 549	1 553	1 780	Turquie
-2	-58	424	10 892	14 568	15 820	2 723	2 015	Émirats arabes unis
0								Yémen (anc. République arabe du)
–	0	-9	56	54	66	66	70	Yémen
18	*11*	*12*	*45*	*39*	*125*	*79*	*71*	**Économies en développement : Océanie**
0	0	0	0	0	0	0	0	Îles Cook
2	3	2	1	-6	-8	3	3	Fidji
0	0	0	10	14	30	8	16	Polynésie française
0	0	0	0	0	1	0	0	Kiribati
–	0	2	-8	0	0	0	0	Îles Marshall
–	0	0	0	0	0	0	0	Micronésie (États fédérés de)
0	0	0	0	0	0	0	0	Nauru
0	0	2	31	7	93	58	49	Nouvelle-Calédonie
0	0	5	-2	4	2	0	0	Nioué
–	0	0	0	0	0	0	0	Îles Mariannes du Nord
0			–	–	–	–	–	Îles du Pacifique (anc. Territoire sous tutelle des)
–	0	-1	0	0	0	0	0	Palaos
16	8	1	1	8	0	4	0	Papouasie-Nouvelle-Guinée
0	0	0	2	0	0	0	0	Samoa
0	0	0	7	10	4	3	2	Îles Salomon
0	0	0	0	0	0	0	0	Tokélaou
0	0	0	2	2	2	2	0	Tonga
0	0	0	0	0	0	0	0	Tuvalu
0	0	0	1	1	1	1	1	Vanuatu
0	0	0	0	0	0	0	0	Îles Wallis-et-Futuna
0	*0*	*3 195*	*23 723*	*51 581*	*60 386*	*48 802*	*60 584*	**Économies en transition**
0	0	0	11	28	81	36	-12	Albanie
–	–	-1	3	-2	10	53	8	Arménie
–	–	1	705	286	556	326	232	Azerbaïdjan
–	–	0	3	15	31	102	43	Bélarus
–	–	0	4	28	13	-9	47	Bosnie-Herzégovine
–	–	5	259	289	1 425	1 235	-203	Croatie
–	–	3	-16	76	70	-1	6	Géorgie
–	–	4	-385	3 153	1 204	3 118	7 806	Kazakhstan
–	–	5	0	0	0	0	0	Kirghizistan
–	–				108	46	29	Monténégro
–	–	0	-1	17	16	7	4	République de Moldova
–	–	3 177	23 151	45 916	55 594	43 665	51 697	Fédération de Russie
–	–	2	120	1 104	–	–	–	Serbie-et-Monténégro
–	–	–	–	–	283	52	189	Serbie
0	0							RSF de Yougoslavie (anc.) (1)
–	–	0	0	0	0	0	0	Tadjikistan
–	–	-1	0	-1	-14	11	2	LERY de Macédoine
–	–	0	0	0	0	0	0	Turkménistan

Pour les sources et les notes, se reporter à la fin du tableau.

Region, country or territory	Inward flows - Flux entrants Millions of dollars							
	1980	1990	2000	2006	2007	2008	2009	2010
Ukraine	–	–	595	5 604	9 891	10 913	4 816	6 495
USSR (former) (2)	..	4						
Uzbekistan	–		75	174	705	711	711	822
Developed economies: America	**22 725**	**56 004**	**380 859**	**297 691**	**331 181**	**363 397**	**174 210**	**251 872**
Bermuda	0	0	67	261	577	-146	-88	210
Canada	5 807	7 582	66 795	60 294	114 652	57 177	21 406	23 413
United States	16 918	48 422	313 997	237 136	215 952	306 366	152 892	228 249
Developed economies: Asia	**287**	**1 943**	**15 280**	**8 799**	**31 340**	**35 300**	**16 377**	**3 902**
Israel	9	137	6 957	15 296	8 798	10 875	4 438	5 152
Japan	278	1 806	8 323	-6 507	22 550	24 426	11 939	-1 251
Developed economies: Europe	**21 903**	**104 415**	**724 414**	**676 833**	**806 788**	**314 373**	**387 825**	**313 100**
Austria	239	653	8 840	7 933	31 154	6 858	7 011	6 613
Belgium (3)	1 545	8 047	88 739	58 893	93 429	142 041	23 595	61 714
Bulgaria	0	4	1 016	7 805	12 389	9 855	3 351	2 170
Cyprus	85	127	855	1 864	2 234	4 050	5 725	4 860
Czechoslovakia (former)	0	165		–	–	–	–	–
Czech Republic	–	–	4 985	5 463	10 444	6 451	2 927	6 781
Denmark	104	1 132	33 823	2 691	11 812	2 216	2 966	-1 814
Estonia	–	–	392	1 797	2 725	1 731	1 838	1 539
Finland	28	787	8 834	7 652	12 451	-1 035	-4	4 314
France	3 328	15 629	43 252	71 848	96 221	64 184	34 027	33 905
Germany (former Federal Rep.)	342		–	–	–	–	–	–
Germany	–	2 962	198 277	55 626	80 208	4 218	37 627	46 134
Gibraltar	2	36	138	137	165	159	172	165
Greece	672	1 005	1 108	5 355	2 111	4 499	2 436	2 188
Hungary	0	554	2 764	6 818	3 951	7 384	2 045	2 377
Iceland	22	22	171	3 843	6 824	917	83	2 950
Ireland	286	622	25 779	-5 542	24 707	-16 453	25 960	26 330
Italy	577	6 345	13 375	39 239	40 202	-10 845	20 073	9 498
Latvia	–	–	413	1 663	2 322	1 261	94	349
Lithuania	–	–	370	1 017	2 015	2 045	172	629
Luxembourg	..	..	..	31 843	-28 260	9 785	30 196	20 350
Malta	27	46	618	1 840	1 006	845	760	1 041
Netherlands	2 005	10 516	63 854	13 976	119 383	3 577	34 514	-16 141
Norway	60	1 564	7 090	6 415	5 800	10 781	14 074	11 857
Poland	10	88	9 445	19 603	23 561	14 839	13 698	9 681
Portugal	165	2 902	6 635	10 902	3 055	4 665	2 706	1 452
Romania	..	0	1 057	11 367	9 921	13 910	4 847	3 573
Slovakia	–	–	1 932	4 693	3 581	4 687	-50	526
Slovenia	–	–	137	644	1 514	1 947	-582	834
Spain	1 493	13 294	39 575	30 802	64 264	76 993	9 135	24 547
Sweden	251	1 971	23 430	28 941	27 737	36 771	10 322	5 328
Switzerland	..	5 484	19 255	43 718	32 435	15 149	26 964	-6 561
United Kingdom	10 123	30 461	118 764	156 186	196 390	91 489	71 140	45 908
Developed economies: Oceania	**2 200**	**10 164**	**16 959**	**35 575**	**48 535**	**51 441**	**24 423**	**33 032**
Australia	1 866	8 479	15 612	31 050	45 397	46 843	25 716	32 472
New Zealand	334	1 685	1 347	4 526	3 138	4 598	-1 293	561

Sources:
- UNCTAD, *World Investment Report 2011*

Notes:
- FDI inward flows and outward flows comprise capital provided (either directly or through other related enterprises) by a foreign direct investor to a FDI enterprise, or capital received by a foreign direct investor from a FDI enterprise. FDI includes the three following components: equity capital, reinvested earnings and intra-company loans.

  - Equity capital is the foreign direct investor's purchase of shares of an enterprise in a country other than that of its residence.
  - Reinvested earnings comprise the direct investor's share (in proportion to direct equity participation) of earnings not distributed as dividends by affiliates or earnings not remitted to the direct investor. Such profits, retained by affiliates, are reinvested.

  - Intra-company loans or intra-company debt transactions refer to short- or long-term borrowing and lending of funds between direct investors (parent enterprises) and affiliate enterprises.

  Data on FDI flows are presented on net bases (capital transactions' credits less debits between direct investors and their foreign affiliates). Net decreases in assets or net increases in liabilities are recorded as credits (with a positive sign), while net increases in assets or net decreases in liabilities are recorded as debits (with a negative sign). Hence, FDI flows with a negative sign indicate that at least one of the three components of FDI is negative and not offset by positive amounts of the remaining components. These are called reverse investment or disinvestment.

(1) Data from 1988 to 1991 inclusive refer to Slovenia only, except for the FDI inflows that also cover other Republics of the former SFR Yugoslavia.
(2) Partial data; total USSR territory is not covered.
(3) Data from 1970 to 2001 inclusive refer to Belgium-Luxembourg Economic Union; from 2002 onwards data cover Belgium only.

7.2.1 Investissement étranger direct : flux entrants et sortants des pays et des régions géographiques

		Outward flows - Flux sortants Millions de dollars						Régions, pays ou territoires
1980	1990	2000	2006	2007	2008	2009	2010	
–	–	1	-133	673	1 010	162	736	Ukraine
..	0	–	–	–	–	–	–	URSS (anc.) (2)
–	–	0	0	0	0	0	0	Ouzbékistan
23 328	**36 219**	**187 318**	**271 013**	**452 284**	**388 653**	**324 559**	**368 183**	**Économies développées : Amérique**
0	0	14	579	1 040	563	208	693	Bermudes
4 098	5 237	44 678	46 214	57 726	79 794	41 665	38 585	Canada
19 230	30 982	142 626	224 220	393 518	308 296	282 686	328 905	États-Unis
2 382	**51 036**	**34 892**	**65 727**	**82 152**	**135 229**	**76 394**	**64 224**	**Économies développées : Asie**
-3	261	3 335	15 462	8 604	7 210	1 695	7 960	Israël
2 385	50 775	31 557	50 264	73 548	128 019	74 699	56 263	Japon
11 130	**139 342**	**867 687**	**792 652**	**1 274 118**	**983 284**	**434 171**	**475 763**	**Économies développées : Europe**
101	1 701	5 740	13 670	39 025	29 452	7 381	10 854	Autriche
196	6 314	86 362	50 685	80 127	164 314	-21 667	37 735	Belgique (3)
0	-3	3	177	282	755	-119	238	Bulgarie
0	5	172	902	1 245	4 142	5 052	4 220	Chypre
..	20	–	–	–	–	–	–	Tchécoslovaquie (anc.)
–	–	43	1 468	1 620	4 323	949	1 702	République tchèque
196	1 482	26 549	8 206	20 574	14 142	6 865	3 183	Danemark
–	–	61	1 107	1 746	1 114	1 549	133	Estonie
137	2 708	24 030	4 805	7 203	9 297	3 831	8 385	Finlande
3 137	36 233	177 449	110 673	164 310	155 047	102 949	84 112	France
4 699	–	–	–	–	–	–	–	Allemagne (anc. Rép. fédérale d')
–	24 235	56 557	118 701	170 617	77 142	78 200	104 857	Allemagne
0	0	0	0	0	0	0	0	Gibraltar
..	11	2 137	4 045	5 246	2 418	2 055	1 269	Grèce
0	0	620	3 877	3 621	3 111	2 699	1 546	Hongrie
..	12	390	5 473	10 186	-4 209	2 281	-1 935	Islande
0	364	4 629	15 324	21 146	18 949	26 616	17 802	Irlande
740	7 614	12 316	42 068	90 778	67 002	21 271	21 005	Italie
–	–	12	170	369	243	-62	16	Lettonie
–	–	4	291	597	336	217	128	Lituanie
..	..	..	7 747	73 350	10 171	18 726	18 293	Luxembourg
0	0	21	30	14	305	134	87	Malte
3 847	13 660	75 635	71 174	55 608	67 485	26 927	31 904	Pays-Bas
253	1 583	9 505	21 326	13 588	25 990	28 623	12 195	Norvège
21	5	17	8 864	5 405	4 414	5 219	4 701	Pologne
12	163	8 132	7 139	5 490	2 741	816	-8 608	Portugal
..	18	-13	423	279	277	-86	193	Roumanie
–	–	29	511	600	530	432	328	Slovaquie
–	–	66	862	1 802	1 390	167	151	Slovénie
311	3 349	58 213	104 248	137 052	74 717	9 737	21 598	Espagne
625	14 746	40 964	26 593	38 836	31 326	25 778	30 399	Suède
..	7 176	44 673	75 824	51 020	55 305	33 251	58 253	Suisse
7 881	17 948	233 371	86 271	272 384	161 056	44 381	11 020	Royaume-Uni
531	**2 988**	**4 831**	**25 592**	**20 490**	**34 066**	**15 852**	**27 020**	**Économies développées : Océanie**
460	624	4 221	25 409	16 786	33 604	16 160	26 431	Australie
71	2 363	610	182	3 703	462	-308	589	Nouvelle-Zélande

Sources :
- CNUCED, *World Investment Report 2011*

Notes :

- Les flux entrants et sortants de l'IED comprennent les capitaux fournis par l'investisseur direct (soit directement, soit par l'intermédiaire d'autres entreprises avec lesquelles il est lié) à l'entreprise d'investissement direct ou les capitaux reçus de cette entreprise par l'investisseur. L'IED est composé des trois catégories suivantes : le capital social, les bénéfices réinvestis et les emprunts intra-compagnie.
- Le capital social inclut l'achat des actions d'une entreprise située à l'étranger par l'investisseur direct résident dans l'économie déclarante.
- Les bénéfices réinvestis correspondent à la part qui revient à l'investisseur direct (au prorata de sa participation directe au capital) sur les bénéfices qui ne sont pas distribués sous forme de dividendes par les entreprises apparentées, ainsi que les bénéfices des succursales qui ne sont pas versés à l'investisseur direct. Ces bénéfices retenus par les affiliés sont réinvestis.
- Les emprunts intra-compagnie ou les transactions intra-compagnie concernant les dettes ou les créances se réfèrent aux emprunts et prêts des fonds à court- ou long-terme entre l'investisseur direct (entreprise parente) et les entreprises apparentées (affiliées).

Les données sur l'IED se présentent sur une base nette (les crédits moins les débits des transactions en capital entre l'investisseur direct et son entreprise apparentée). Les augmentations nettes en passifs et les décroissances nettes en actifs se déclarent comme crédits (avec le signe positif), tandis que les augmentations nettes en actifs et les décroissances nettes en passifs se déclarent comme débits (avec le signe négatif). Par conséquent, les flux de l'IED avec un signe négatif indiquent qu'au moins une des trois catégories de l'IED est négative et n'est pas contrebalancée par les valeurs positives des autres catégories. Il s'agit alors de désinvestissements ou de réductions d'investissement.

(1) Les données de 1988 à 1991 se réfèrent seulement à la Slovénie, à l'exception des flux entrants qui comprennent aussi d'autres Républiques de l'ex Yougoslavie (RSF).
(2) Données partielles : elles ne couvrent pas la totalité du territoire de l'URSS.
(3) Les données de 1970 à 2001 se réfèrent à l'Union économique belgo-luxembourgeoise ; à partir de 2002 les données couvrent uniquement la Belgique.

7

7.2.2 Foreign direct investment: Inward and outward flows of economic groupings

Economic grouping	Inward flows - Flux entrants Millions of dollars							
	1980	1990	2000	2006	2007	2008	2009	2010
DEVELOPING ECONOMIES	**7 479**	**34 853**	**257 625**	**429 459**	**573 032**	**658 002**	**510 578**	**573 568**
Developing economies excluding China	7 422	31 366	216 910	356 744	489 511	549 690	415 578	467 833
Developing economies excluding LDCs	6 940	34 281	252 196	408 571	546 948	624 972	484 039	547 178
High-income developing countries	2 235	21 363	156 937	221 205	302 802	312 599	242 843	277 157
Middle-income developing countries	4 714	10 036	92 251	148 841	190 349	230 911	178 028	209 038
Low-income developing countries	530	3 455	8 437	59 413	79 880	114 492	89 707	87 373
Heavily indebted poor countries (IMF)	791	831	4 229	12 704	16 021	19 190	16 756	21 119
Landlocked developing countries	384	603	3 958	11 935	15 736	25 420	26 190	23 022
Small island developing States	260	779	2 007	6 000	6 833	7 968	4 250	4 210
Least developed countries	*538*	*573*	*5 429*	*20 888*	*26 083*	*33 030*	*26 538*	*26 390*
Africa and Haiti	478	431	4 418	17 478	22 090	27 802	23 803	23 214
Asia	53	111	975	3 249	3 816	4 988	2 504	2 600
Islands	7	31	35	160	177	240	231	576
Major petroleum and gas exporters	*-4 264*	*1 632*	*8 824*	*54 447*	*71 134*	*93 530*	*73 931*	*65 518*
Africa	-1 442	867	3 905	17 770	22 233	31 534	25 756	22 165
America	80	778	4 701	-508	1 008	349	-3 105	-1 404
Asia	-2 902	-13	218	37 185	47 892	61 647	51 280	44 757
Major exporters of manufactured goods	*5 408*	*22 245*	*158 376*	*195 058*	*234 977*	*232 277*	*194 718*	*256 237*
America	2 099	2 633	18 110	20 052	29 734	26 295	15 334	18 679
Asia	3 308	19 612	140 267	175 006	205 242	205 982	179 384	237 558
Emerging economies	*7 469*	*19 010*	*104 591*	*112 407*	*156 197*	*141 202*	*95 740*	*158 796*
America	4 928	6 160	66 977	55 170	88 817	103 153	63 749	95 877
Asia	2 541	12 850	37 614	57 230	67 380	38 049	31 990	62 919
Newly industrialized Asian countries	*3 545*	*17 767*	*97 297*	*110 126*	*131 565*	*108 532*	*91 225*	*146 839*
First tier	2 128	10 939	92 354	86 713	101 772	82 050	77 979	116 907
Second tier	1 417	6 828	4 943	23 412	29 794	26 482	13 246	29 933
Developing economies: Africa	**400**	**2 845**	**10 967**	**46 259**	**63 132**	**73 413**	**60 167**	**55 040**
Northern Africa excluding Sudan	144	1 187	2 858	19 609	22 349	21 445	15 786	15 326
Sub-Saharan Africa	257	1 658	8 109	26 650	40 782	51 968	44 381	39 714
Sub-Saharan Africa excluding South Africa	267	1 737	7 222	27 177	35 088	42 962	39 015	38 161
Developing economies: America	**6 416**	**8 926**	**97 688**	**98 459**	**169 514**	**206 733**	**140 997**	**159 171**
Central America and Greater Caribbean Islands excluding Puerto Rico	2 639	3 372	21 718	28 069	39 827	38 390	23 254	26 684
Central America and Greater Caribbean Islands excluding Mexico and Puerto Rico	539	739	3 608	8 017	10 093	12 094	7 920	8 005
South America and Central America	6 026	8 098	77 353	69 833	108 701	126 163	75 772	111 103
South America excluding Brazil	1 610	4 053	24 280	25 094	36 961	47 076	29 338	38 043
Developing economies: Asia	**543**	**22 628**	**148 747**	**283 463**	**339 252**	**375 665**	**307 527**	**357 846**
Eastern and South-Eastern Asia excluding China	3 529	18 125	99 582	115 815	143 223	123 887	104 076	161 964
Southern Asia excluding India	205	-24	1 276	7 493	8 947	9 355	6 809	7 314

Sources:
For sources and notes, see end of table 7.2.1.

7.2.2 Investissement étranger direct : flux entrants et sortants des groupements économiques

Outward flows - Flux sortants Millions de dollars								Groupements économiques
1980	1990	2000	2006	2007	2008	2009	2010	
3 192	**11 914**	**134 194**	**226 683**	**294 177**	**308 891**	**270 750**	**327 564**	**ÉCONOMIES EN DÉVELOPPEMENT**
3 192	11 084	133 278	205 523	271 709	256 741	214 220	259 564	Économies en développement sans la Chine
2 958	11 917	133 431	226 291	292 944	305 841	270 308	325 746	Économies en développement sans les PMA
1 195	8 968	128 976	147 275	224 902	196 848	189 762	209 133	Pays en développement à revenu élevé
1 740	2 497	3 565	61 114	44 903	82 163	59 810	97 331	Pays en développement à revenu intermédiaire
257	450	1 652	18 294	24 372	29 880	21 178	21 100	Pays en développement à revenu faible
227	13	800	72	244	488	319	508	Pays pauvres très endettés (FMI)
8	33	49	476	3 627	1 693	3 809	8 362	Pays en développement sans littoral
137	53	125	526	291	851	42	215	Petits États insulaires en développement
234	*-3*	*763*	*393*	*1 234*	*3 049*	*441*	*1 819*	*Pays les moins avancés*
234	-5	743	269	1 139	3 012	318	1 702	Afrique et Haïti
0	1	19	110	81	25	115	108	Asie
0	1	0	14	14	13	9	8	Îles
724	*-32*	*2 488*	*21 686*	*35 803*	*46 438*	*30 421*	*16 552*	*Principaux exportateurs de pétrole et de gaz*
85	525	259	17	6 015	9 834	2 930	3 593	Afrique
12	375	521	1 524	30	1 273	1 834	2 390	Amérique
626	-932	1 708	20 145	29 758	35 332	25 656	10 569	Asie
455	*12 113*	*79 509*	*116 271*	*169 651*	*153 187*	*181 124*	*227 025*	*Principaux exportateurs d'articles manufacturés*
3	223	363	5 758	8 256	1 157	7 019	14 345	Amérique
452	11 889	79 146	110 512	161 394	152 030	174 105	212 680	Asie
673	*9 551*	*26 388*	*82 945*	*97 311*	*81 081*	*59 689*	*104 389*	*Économies émergentes*
303	940	7 532	38 571	19 466	31 782	6 106	35 786	Amérique
370	8 611	10 056	44 374	77 845	49 299	53 583	68 603	Asie
544	*11 070*	*78 505*	*92 181*	*147 136*	*106 039*	*120 183*	*147 831*	*Économies nouvellement industrialisées d'Asie*
248	10 776	76 224	82 361	124 609	80 862	105 529	126 229	Première génération
296	294	2 281	9 820	22 527	25 176	14 653	21 602	Deuxième génération
1 097	**659**	**1 495**	**6 943**	**10 719**	**9 750**	**5 627**	**6 636**	**Économies en développement : Afrique**
87	135	223	127	5 535	8 653	2 498	3 332	Afrique septentrionale sans le Soudan
1 009	524	1 272	6 816	5 184	1 097	3 129	3 304	Afrique subsaharienne
254	496	1 001	753	2 218	4 231	1 977	2 853	Afrique subsaharienne sans l'Afrique du Sud
899	**301**	**49 723**	**68 129**	**61 731**	**80 580**	**45 544**	**76 273**	**Économies en développement : Amérique**
358	936	-450	8 176	11 262	3 269	9 434	16 812	Amérique centrale et Grandes Antilles sans Porto Rico
354	713	-813	2 418	3 006	2 112	2 415	2 467	Amérique centrale et Grandes Antilles sans le Mexique et Porto Rico
778	2 019	7 453	43 603	23 412	37 374	13 471	47 062	Amérique du Sud et Amérique centrale
54	488	5 756	7 247	5 181	13 704	14 150	18 775	Amérique du Sud sans le Brésil
1 179	**10 943**	**82 964**	**151 566**	**221 688**	**218 438**	**219 500**	**244 585**	**Économies en développement : Asie**
544	11 072	78 567	93 025	147 335	106 208	120 256	148 506	Asie orientale et Asie du Sud-Est sans la Chine
7	4	37	527	476	500	476	453	Asie méridionale sans l'Inde

Sources :
Pour les sources et les notes, se reporter à la fin du tableau 7.2.1.

7

Trade group	Inward flows - Flux entrants Millions of dollars							
	1980	1990	2000	2006	2007	2008	2009	2010
AFRICA								
CEMAC	206	4	549	2 727	4 059	2 519	4 594	4 960
CEPGL	131	-6	92	287	1 891	1 844	792	2 996
COMESA	-208	1 250	2 992	18 621	25 403	22 055	16 671	19 110
EAC	109	60	593	1 323	2 251	1 621	1 730	1 737
ECCAS	374	-336	2 819	12 114	15 781	20 976	17 072	17 900
ECOWAS	-461	1 547	2 146	6 871	9 383	12 379	12 700	11 309
MRU	148	324	304	610	1 041	1 276	773	1 005
SADC	372	31	4 422	11 605	21 797	31 556	21 840	19 543
UMA	-378	459	1 663	9 671	10 910	12 288	9 036	8 954
WAEMU	208	239	514	843	1 561	1 802	1 807	1 948
AMERICA								
ANCOM	301	734	3 959	10 675	15 100	19 038	13 455	14 874
CACM	188	268	1 460	3 258	5 501	5 368	3 270	3 483
CARICOM	262	428	1 916	4 795	4 820	7 078	3 130	2 981
FTAA	29 088	64 703	461 024	372 605	445 312	499 084	254 958	366 905
LAIA	5 601	7 745	75 195	63 569	101 013	118 066	70 349	104 878
MERCOSUR	2 907	2 937	43 575	26 026	42 573	57 209	31 767	57 548
NAFTA	24 825	58 638	398 902	317 482	360 339	389 838	189 632	270 341
OAS	29 082	64 660	460 632	371 961	444 448	498 102	254 459	366 193
OECS	53	191	324	932	1 074	884	621	559
ASIA								
APTA	204	4 536	54 092	99 384	113 093	161 333	139 573	138 989
ASEAN	2 636	12 821	23 656	56 692	75 731	46 907	37 931	79 129
ECO	172	600	3 124	33 462	38 050	43 934	32 978	28 487
GCC	-3 403	166	391	38 070	47 007	59 970	47 069	39 870
SAARC	203	575	4 671	26 175	32 627	50 286	39 442	28 337
EUROPE								
EFTA	82	7 070	26 517	53 976	45 060	26 848	41 121	8 245
EU	21 279	97 309	698 279	581 719	850 528	487 968	346 531	304 689
Euro area	10 791	62 934	502 202	339 366	549 987	301 747	234 969	229 704
OCEANIA								
MSG	119	263	135	469	593	463	689	435
INTERREGIONAL								
ACP	730	2 487	11 219	33 058	47 993	62 472	50 478	45 165
APEC	31 203	92 906	572 515	572 684	726 703	789 412	475 561	627 013
BSEC	690	1 693	8 110	81 621	110 323	140 853	65 336	69 005
CIS	–	–	5 284	43 472	76 502	106 821	63 136	63 523

Sources:
For sources and notes, see end of table 7.2.1.

Outward flows - Flux sortants Millions de dollars								Groupements commerciaux
1980	1990	2000	2006	2007	2008	2009	2010	
								AFRIQUE
-	51	35	105	56	98	78	82	CEMAC
0	0	-2	18	27	54	35	7	CEPGL
67	141	185	-316	4 815	8 110	2 189	2 981	COMESA
1	0	0	24	49	44	46	18	CAE
0	52	12	321	999	2 729	126	1 258	CEEAC
238	412	947	337	973	1 337	1 500	1 116	CEDEAO
236	6	770	19	64	253	-99	36	UFM
770	59	290	6 334	4 088	401	1 451	2 027	SADC
80	123	172	-16	4 874	6 737	1 931	2 161	UMA
-3	-10	16	-32	33	25	44	150	UEMOA
								AMÉRIQUE
108	70	341	1 107	977	3 002	3 519	6 673	ANCOM
8	1	55	186	203	-42	50	45	MCAC
116	32	102	500	198	781	-19	70	CARICOM
24 222	38 268	194 918	314 475	474 835	426 223	337 771	414 598	ZLEA
423	1 335	8 399	41 206	20 504	35 318	11 085	44 639	ALADI
257	660	3 188	30 647	8 667	21 845	-9 348	12 488	MERCOSUR
23 332	36 442	187 667	276 192	459 500	389 247	331 370	381 835	ALENA
24 221	38 269	194 924	314 473	474 834	426 224	337 770	414 599	OEA
0	0	2	0	0	0	0	0	OECO
								ASIE
-	1 889	5 677	46 691	59 499	91 795	89 707	101 922	ACAP
394	2 328	8 253	28 782	55 413	25 185	33 845	42 223	ANASE
7	-14	912	1 739	5 944	4 737	5 424	10 210	ECO
619	-908	1 696	20 435	31 117	36 539	23 393	10 505	CCG
4	9	529	14 427	17 408	19 517	16 050	14 733	SAARC
								EUROPE
-	8 770	54 568	102 622	74 793	77 085	64 155	68 512	AELE
21 902	130 572	813 119	690 030	1 199 325	906 199	370 016	407 251	UE
13 181	96 355	511 549	553 690	855 357	686 215	284 174	354 123	Zone euro
								OCÉANIE
18	11	4	10	12	-3	12	6	MSG
								INTERRÉGIONAUX
1 143	567	1 445	7 258	5 384	1 861	3 091	3 357	ACP
26 851	102 170	310 670	490 815	771 882	774 207	651 470	742 465	CEAP
0	10	6 177	29 289	54 907	63 618	47 703	56 340	CEMN
–	–	3 186	23 344	50 057	58 420	47 433	60 526	CEI

Sources :
Pour les sources et les notes, se reporter à la fin du tableau 7.2.1.

7.3.1 Migrants' remittances:
Receipts of countries and geographical regions

Region, country or territory	Millions of dollars - Millions de dollars							
	1990	1995	2000	2005	2007	2008	2009	2010
WORLD	**79 553**	**101 954**	**134 553**	**275 387**	**387 641**	**447 856**	**421 744**	**443 627**
DEVELOPING ECONOMIES	33 392	54 663	80 169	173 442	245 238	288 376	280 882	297 305
TRANSITION ECONOMIES	9 360	3 730	6 234	16 718	27 343	33 532	28 585	30 288
DEVELOPED ECONOMIES	36 801	43 562	48 149	85 227	115 061	125 948	112 277	116 034
Developing economies: Africa	**8 992**	**10 202**	**11 261**	**22 426**	**36 878**	**41 385**	**38 342**	**39 747**
Eastern Africa	*244*	*578*	*1 100*	*1 658*	*2 912*	*3 456*	*3 333*	*3 606*
Burundi	..	..	..	0	0	4	4	3
Comoros	10	12	12	12	12	12	12	11
Djibouti	..	12	12	26	29	30	32	28
Eritrea	..	..	0	"	..	"	..	..
Ethiopia	–	27	53	174	358	387	262	387
Ethiopia (former)	5	–	–	–	–	–	–	–
Kenya	139	298	538	805	1 588	1 692	1 686	1 758
Madagascar	8	14	11	11	11	11	11	10
Malawi	..	1	1	1	1	1	1	1
Mauritius	..	132	177	146	227	318	297	305
Mozambique	70	59	37	57	99	116	111	117
Rwanda	3	21	7	21	51	68	93	91
Seychelles	8	1	3	12	11	8	12	13
Uganda	..	..	238	322	452	724	750	773
United Republic of Tanzania	..	1	8	19	14	19	23	17
Zambia	..	..	..	53	59	68	41	71
Zimbabwe	1	..	..	..	..	..	..	..
Middle Africa	*25*	*20*	*51*	*108*	*204*	*199*	*182*	*183*
Cameroon	23	11	30	77	167	162	148	148
Central African Republic	0	..	..	..	..	..	..	..
Chad	1	..	..	..	..	..	..	..
Congo	..	4	10	11	15	15	15	13
Equatorial Guinea	..	0	..	..	..	..	..	..
Gabon	1	4	6	11	11	11	11	10
Sao Tome and Principe	0	..	0	2	2	3	3	2
Northern Africa	*7 255*	*7 342*	*7 249*	*14 091*	*20 007*	*22 885*	*20 654*	*21 312*
Algeria	352	1 120	790	2 060	2 120	2 202	2 193	2 031
Egypt	4 284	3 226	2 852	5 017	7 656	8 694	7 150	7 681
Libyan Arab Jamahiriya	..	..	9	15	16	16	16	16
Morocco	2 006	1 970	2 161	4 590	6 730	6 895	6 271	6 447
Sudan	62	346	641	1 016	1 769	3 100	3 059	3 178
Tunisia	551	680	796	1 393	1 716	1 977	1 964	1 960
Southern Africa	*775*	*673*	*689*	*1 229*	*1 506*	*1 479*	*1 511*	*1 790*
Botswana	86	59	26	131	105	114	88	124
Lesotho	428	411	252	327	451	439	414	525
Namibia	13	16	9	18	16	14	14	14
South Africa	136	105	344	658	834	823	902	1 008
Swaziland	113	83	57	95	100	90	93	118
Western Africa	*693*	*1 589*	*2 172*	*5 340*	*12 249*	*13 366*	*12 660*	*12 875*
Benin	101	100	87	173	282	251	266	236
Burkina Faso	140	80	67	50	50	50	49	43
Cape Verde	59	106	87	137	139	155	146	144
Côte d'Ivoire	44	151	119	163	185	199	185	177
Gambia	10	19	14	59	70	67	80	61
Ghana	6	17	32	99	117	126	114	119
Guinea	18	1	1	42	151	82	64	66
Guinea-Bissau	1	2	8	28	29	30	30	27
Liberia	..	..	..	32	62	58	25	57
Mali	107	112	73	177	344	431	405	385
Mauritania	14	5	2	2	2	2	2	2
Niger	14	8	14	66	79	94	79	70
Nigeria	10	804	1 392	3 329	9 221	9 980	9 585	9 975
Senegal	142	146	233	789	1 192	1 476	1 276	1 164
Sierra Leone	0	24	7	2	42	28	47	48
Togo	27	15	34	193	284	337	307	302

For sources and notes, see end of table.

As percentage of GDP En pourcentage du PIB				As percentage of exports of goods and services (1) En pourcentage des exportations des biens et services (1)				Régions, pays ou territoires
1990	2000	2009	2010	1990	2000	2009	2010	
0.40	**0.43**	**0.75**	**0.72**	**2.18**	**1.86**	**2.88**	**2.39**	**MONDE**
0.98	1.24	1.72	1.51	5.27	4.18	5.74	4.65	ÉCONOMIES EN DÉVELOPPEMENT
11.00	1.65	1.65	1.49	45.26	3.02	4.28	3.59	ÉCONOMIES EN TRANSITION
0.22	0.20	0.30	0.29	1.20	0.93	1.25	1.13	ÉCONOMIES DÉVELOPPÉES
2.15	**1.96**	**2.77**	**2.47**	**8.76**	**6.79**	**8.36**	**8.71**	**Économies en développement : Afrique**
0.60	*1.94*	*2.20*	*2.24*	*4.10*	*9.36*	*10.23*	*..*	*Afrique orientale*
"	..	0.31	0.25	..	..	3.29	..	Burundi
4.08	5.94	2.26	2.00	28.55	..	..	..	Comores
..	2.22	3.49	2.79	..	6.36	8.13	..	Djibouti
–	0.47	..	..	–	3.36	..	..	Érythrée
–	0.66	0.92	1.45	–	5.36	7.62	..	Éthiopie
0.04	–	–	–	0.87	–	–	–	Éthiopie (anc.)
1.26	4.27	5.73	5.47	6.25	19.38	22.74	..	Kenya
0.26	0.29	0.12	0.12	1.67	0.95	..	..	Madagascar
..	0.03	0.02	0.02	..	0.17	..	..	Malawi
..	3.86	3.42	3.21	..	6.75	7.10	6.15	Maurice
2.37	0.85	1.16	1.27	30.69	5.34	4.51	4.04	Mozambique
0.10	0.37	1.76	1.61	1.84	5.19	17.35	..	Rwanda
1.66	0.42	1.58	1.43	3.28	0.66	1.49	1.60	Seychelles
..	3.75	4.38	4.21	..	35.91	22.76	22.24	Ouganda
..	0.08	0.10	0.07	..	0.59	0.45	0.27	République-Unie de Tanzanie
..	..	0.32	0.45	..	..	0.90	0.92	Zambie
0.01	..	..	..	0.04	..	..	..	Zimbabwe
0.12	*0.19*	*0.23*	*0.21*	*0.43*	*0.30*	*0.33*	*..*	*Afrique centrale*
0.19	0.32	0.67	0.66	0.92	1.13	2.72	2.63	Cameroun
0.01	..	..	..	0.04	..	..	..	République centrafricaine
0.04	..	..	..	0.22	..	..	..	Tchad
..	0.32	0.15	0.11	..	0.39	..	..	Congo
								Guinée équatoriale
0.01	0.11	0.10	0.08	0.03	0.17	..	..	Gabon
0.26	0.60	1.42	0.93	3.93	2.85	15.27	..	Sao Tomé-et-Principe
4.58	*2.76*	*3.61*	*3.30*	*20.55*	*12.93*	*11.14*	*..*	*Afrique septentrionale*
0.57	1.44	1.56	1.27	2.62	..	4.55	..	Algérie
10.87	2.86	3.80	3.58	43.29	16.91	16.03	..	Égypte
..	0.02	0.03	0.02	..	0.07	0.04	..	Jamahiriya arabe libyenne
6.95	5.84	6.92	7.09	32.16	20.67	23.77	21.40	Maroc
0.39	4.89	5.54	4.57	12.40	34.94	34.51	27.26	Soudan
4.47	4.09	4.97	4.87	10.59	9.25	9.86	..	Tunisie
0.65	*0.48*	*0.48*	*0.46*	*2.49*	*1.60*	*1.69*	*1.52*	*Afrique australe*
2.30	0.47	0.76	0.88	4.27	0.87	2.10	..	Botswana
77.58	33.32	25.67	26.31	427.60	93.83	53.23	58.38	Lesotho
0.50	0.24	0.15	0.12	1.10	0.64	0.34	..	Namibie
0.12	0.26	0.32	0.28	0.50	0.93	1.15	1.01	Afrique du Sud
10.83	3.73	2.96	3.02	17.15	4.59	5.02	..	Swaziland
0.89	*2.58*	*4.68*	*3.98*	*2.82*	*6.68*	*13.12*	*11.61*	*Afrique occidentale*
5.48	3.69	4.04	3.57	27.77	16.48	..	..	Bénin
4.50	2.57	0.60	0.51	40.00	28.41	..	..	Burkina Faso
19.20	16.12	9.23	8.77	104.05	59.57	25.19	..	Cap-Vert
0.37	1.12	0.80	0.78	1.27	2.73	1.62	..	Côte d'Ivoire
1.41	1.79	8.62	6.25	5.77	..	28.67	23.90	Gambie
0.10	0.65	0.77	0.67	0.61	1.33	1.50	1.26	Ghana
0.62	0.04	1.34	1.39	2.17	0.16	5.68	4.28	Guinée
0.17	2.19	3.59	3.24	3.83	..	..	..	Guinée-Bissau
		2.93	6.06			5.53	..	Libéria
4.26	2.76	4.58	4.22	25.47	11.36	19.02	..	Mali
1.31	0.19	0.07	0.05	2.91	..	..	..	Mauritanie
0.53	0.84	1.51	1.26	2.61	4.50	..	..	Niger
0.03	3.00	5.52	4.49	0.07	6.64	16.43	12.99	Nigéria
2.29	4.99	10.00	9.07	9.78	17.87	..	..	Sénégal
0.00	0.77	2.09	2.13	0.01	12.96	14.22	11.44	Sierra Leone
1.51	2.65	9.66	9.41	4.05	8.08	25.64	..	Togo

Pour les sources et les notes, se reporter à la fin du tableau.

Region, country or territory	Millions of dollars - Millions de dollars							
	1990	1995	2000	2005	2007	2008	2009	2010
Developing economies: America	**5 842**	**14 076**	**21 074**	**51 217**	**64 473**	**65 959**	**58 184**	**59 688**
Caribbean	*786*	*2 361*	*4 355*	*6 750*	*8 171*	*8 622*	*8 326*	*8 739*
Anguilla	6	10	13	22	26	25	24	-
Antigua and Barbuda	13	3	21	22	24	26	24	27
Aruba	..	4	8	12	14	15	19	20
Barbados	38	61	115	135	141	168	161	161
Dominica	14	13	18	18	26	28	23	23
Dominican Republic	315	839	1 839	2 719	3 127	3 067	3 407	3 373
Grenada	18	38	46	52	55	55	54	59
Haiti	61	109	578	986	1 222	1 370	1 376	1 499
Jamaica	229	653	892	1 784	2 144	2 181	1 912	2 020
Montserrat	10	11	1	1	1	1	1	..
Netherlands Antilles	5	11	12	11	32	32	37	32
Saint Kitts and Nevis	19	20	27	34	40	44	41	44
Saint Lucia	16	23	26	29	31	31	28	30
Saint Vincent and the Grenadines	16	17	22	26	33	31	30	33
Trinidad and Tobago	3	32	38	92	109	95	103	109
Central America	*3 786*	*6 238*	*10 869*	*32 191*	*39 344*	*39 135*	*33 719*	*34 848*
Belize	18	14	26	46	75	78	80	88
Costa Rica	12	123	136	420	618	605	513	622
El Salvador	366	1 064	1 765	3 030	3 712	3 804	3 482	3 648
Guatemala	119	358	596	3 067	4 236	4 460	4 026	4 255
Honduras	63	124	484	1 821	2 648	2 869	2 520	2 662
Mexico	3 098	4 368	7 525	23 062	27 136	26 304	22 153	22 572
Nicaragua	..	75	320	616	740	818	768	803
Panama	110	112	16	130	180	196	175	198
South America	*1 269*	*5 477*	*5 850*	*12 276*	*16 957*	*18 203*	*16 139*	*16 101*
Argentina	23	64	86	432	606	698	661	682
Bolivia (Plurinational State of)	5	7	127	346	1 065	1 144	1 069	1 064
Brazil	573	3 315	1 649	3 540	4 382	5 089	4 234	4 277
Chile	0	..	13	13	3	3	4	5
Colombia	495	815	1 610	3 346	4 523	4 884	4 180	3 942
Ecuador	51	386	1 322	2 460	3 094	2 828	2 502	2 548
Guyana	..	2	27	201	283	278	266	280
Paraguay	34	287	278	269	484	588	609	573
Peru	87	599	718	1 440	2 131	2 444	2 378	2 494
Suriname	1	0	1	4	140	2	5	2
Uruguay	..	..	..	77	96	108	101	104
Venezuela (Bolivarian Rep. of)	1	2	17	148	151	137	131	129
Developing economies: Asia	**18 451**	**30 275**	**47 692**	**98 333**	**142 203**	**179 260**	**182 706**	**196 038**
Eastern Asia	*1 248*	*2 099*	*6 393*	*26 337*	*40 981*	*52 840*	*53 011*	*55 390*
China	175	878	5 237	24 102	38 791	48 524	48 729	51 000
China, Hong Kong SAR	..	..	136	297	317	355	348	369
China, Macao SAR	..	..	..	588	399	507	725	571
China, Taiwan Province of	36	142	274	323	430	454	455	500
Korea, Republic of	1 037	1 080	735	848	866	2 774	2 555	2 738
Mongolia	..	..	12	180	178	225	200	211
Southern Asia	*6 771*	*11 605*	*17 742*	*34 956*	*55 159*	*72 753*	*76 137*	*83 727*
Bangladesh	779	1 202	1 968	4 315	6 562	8 941	10 523	11 050
Bhutan	..	..	..	..	3	4	5	..
India	2 384	6 223	12 884	22 125	37 217	49 977	49 468	55 000
Iran (Islamic Rep. of)	(e)1 200	1 600	536	1 032	1 115	1 115	1 072	1 141
Maldives	2	2	2	2	3	3	4	3
Nepal	..	57	111	1 212	1 734	2 727	2 986	3 513
Pakistan	2 006	1 712	1 075	4 280	5 998	7 039	8 717	9 407
Sri Lanka	401	809	1 166	1 991	2 527	2 947	3 363	3 612
South-Eastern Asia	*2 946*	*8 537*	*13 054*	*25 785*	*31 893*	*36 930*	*37 423*	*39 547*
Cambodia	..	12	121	200	353	325	338	364
Indonesia including East Timor	166	651	1 190	—	—	—	—	—
Indonesia	—	—	—	5 420	6 174	6 794	6 793	7 139
Lao People's Dem. Rep.	11	22	1	1	1	1	1	1
Malaysia	325	716	981	1 281	1 803	1 920	1 900	1 576
Myanmar	6	81	104	131	125	150	148	154
Philippines	1 465	5 360	6 961	13 566	16 302	18 642	19 766	21 311
Thailand	973	1 695	1 697	1 187	1 635	1 898	1 637	1 788
Viet Nam	..	..	(e)2 000	4 000	5 500	7 200	6 840	7 215

For sources and notes, see end of table.

As percentage of GDP / En pourcentage du PIB				As percentage of exports of goods and services (1) / En pourcentage des exportations des biens et services (1)				Régions, pays ou territoires
1990	2000	2009	2010	1990	2000	2009	2010	
0.53	1.01	1.45	1.19	3.46	4.80	7.03	4.74	Économies en développement : Amérique
1.41	5.12	5.14	6.86	7.65	13.80	20.90	..	Caraïbes
11.56	12.23	11.14	-	15.29	19.04	18.06	-	Anguilla
3.20	3.11	2.16	2.38	3.63	4.17	4.46	4.88	Antigua-et-Barbuda
..	0.42	0.73	0.78	..	0.22	0.65	1.14	Aruba
2.20	4.49	4.47	4.41	4.34	8.88	8.95	..	Barbade
8.32	6.01	6.12	6.35	15.56	11.28	14.94	16.37	Dominique
3.35	7.77	7.44	6.54	17.19	20.51	33.13	..	République dominicaine
8.13	11.37	8.45	8.83	19.31	19.67	30.60	34.66	Grenade
2.33	16.44	21.91	24.11	19.18	114.75	147.47	..	Haïti
4.74	9.96	15.40	14.66	10.32	24.85	47.35	..	Jamaïque
27.01	2.25	2.05	..	64.04	4.60	7.19	-	Montserrat
0.23	0.11	0.93	0.75	0.31	0.60	1.32	..	Antilles néerlandaises
12.11	8.23	7.44	7.97	23.41	18.07	21.84	23.94	Saint-Kitts-et-Nevis
3.87	3.74	2.91	3.05	5.72	7.02	5.08	5.01	Sainte-Lucie
7.89	6.71	5.27	5.85	12.01	13.63	15.54	17.98	Saint-Vincent-et-les Grenadines
0.07	0.47	0.49	0.49	0.15	0.79	1.04	..	Trinité-et-Tobago
1.19	1.54	3.35	2.96	6.41	5.22	11.32	8.80	Amérique centrale
4.55	3.18	6.02	6.37	7.54	6.08	11.05	10.60	Belize
0.17	0.85	1.75	1.74	0.61	1.75	4.11	4.51	Costa Rica
7.63	13.44	16.50	16.81	37.64	48.21	72.66	65.71	El Salvador
1.74	3.47	10.79	10.36	7.57	15.44	43.67	39.47	Guatemala
1.73	6.73	17.49	17.01	6.09	12.57	41.81	..	Honduras
1.08	1.18	2.54	2.20	6.35	4.18	9.04	7.19	Mexique
..	8.62	12.01	11.90	..	29.04	26.63	22.14	Nicaragua
1.81	0.14	0.71	0.72	2.47	0.21	1.05	1.14	Panama
0.17	0.45	0.57	0.45	1.28	3.08	3.33	2.13	Amérique du Sud
0.02	0.03	0.21	0.18	0.15	0.28	0.99	0.84	Argentine
0.09	1.51	6.16	5.54	0.47	8.63	19.67	..	Bolivie (État plurinational de)
0.14	0.26	0.27	0.21	1.63	2.55	2.34	1.83	Brésil
0.00	0.02	0.00	0.00	0.00	0.06	0.01	0.01	Chili
0.92	1.71	1.82	1.40	5.70	10.19	10.93	8.71	Colombie
0.45	8.30	4.37	3.91	1.56	22.39	16.07	..	Équateur
..	2.40	12.98	12.52	..	4.06	..	..	Guyana
0.73	3.92	4.15	3.11	1.34	9.51	8.45	5.84	Paraguay
0.30	1.35	1.85	1.60	2.11	8.43	7.77	6.31	Pérou
0.08	0.13	0.16	0.06	0.06	0.26	0.28	0.09	Suriname
..	..	0.32	0.26	..	..	1.18	0.99	Uruguay
0.00	0.01	0.04	0.03	0.01	0.05	0.22	0.19	Venezuela (Rép. bolivarienne du)
0.98	1.26	1.68	1.50	5.12	3.66	5.09	4.36	Économies en développement : Asie
0.15	0.29	0.82	0.73	0.92	0.83	2.39	1.94	Asie orientale
0.04	0.44	0.98	0.87	0.30	1.87	3.65	2.91	Chine
..	0.08	0.17	0.16	..	0.06	0.09	0.07	Chine (RAS de Hong Kong)
..	..	3.42	2.08	..	..	3.76	..	Chine (RAS de Macao)
0.02	0.08	0.12	0.12	..	..	..	..	Province chinoise de Taiwan
0.38	0.14	0.31	0.27	1.40	0.35	0.59	0.50	Corée, République de
..	1.10	4.74	3.77	..	1.96	8.68	6.21	Mongolie
1.35	2.49	3.89	3.54	12.53	15.41	24.02	20.04	Asie méridionale
2.77	4.33	11.80	11.11	37.74	27.27	61.72	51.03	Bangladesh
..	..	0.39	..	..	..	0.93	..	Bhoutan
0.73	2.75	3.84	3.39	10.40	21.50	18.93	15.75	Inde
(e)1.32	0.52	0.30	0.29	(e)6.08	1.80	..	..	Iran (Rép. islamique d')
0.86	0.35	0.29	0.24	0.95	0.48	0.45	0.35	Maldives
..	1.95	23.35	21.73	..	8.70	193.53	223.22	Népal
4.19	1.51	5.44	5.32	29.35	10.62	39.04	33.75	Pakistan
4.88	6.97	7.87	7.14	17.48	18.28	37.46	33.52	Sri Lanka
0.96	2.60	2.91	2.46	2.86	3.99	6.03	6.48	Asie du Sud-Est
..	3.29	3.13	3.20	..	6.60	5.70	..	Cambodge
0.13	0.72	-	-	0.57	1.69	-	-	Indonésie, y compris le Timor oriental
		1.26	1.01			5.12	4.08	Indonésie
1.26	0.04	0.02	0.02	10.64	0.13	0.07	..	Rép. dém. populaire lao
0.71	1.05	0.99	0.67	0.99	0.87	1.02	..	Malaisie
0.12	1.42	0.78	0.41	1.87	4.84	..	..	Myanmar
3.31	9.17	12.30	11.31	12.82	17.09	40.65	33.34	Philippines
1.14	1.38	0.62	0.56	3.33	2.08	0.91	0.79	Thaïlande
..	(e)6.42	7.34	7.27	..	(e)11.66	10.90	..	Viet Nam

Pour les sources et les notes, se reporter à la fin du tableau.

7

7.3.1 Migrants' remittances: Receipts of countries and geographical regions

Region, country or territory	Millions of dollars - Millions de dollars							
	1990	1995	2000	2005	2007	2008	2009	2010
Western Asia	*7 485*	*8 034*	*10 504*	*11 255*	*14 171*	*16 737*	*16 135*	*17 375*
Jordan	499	1 441	1 845	2 500	3 434	3 794	3 597	3 789
Lebanon	1 818	1 225	1 582	4 924	5 769	7 181	7 558	8 177
Occupied Palestinian territory	..	582	1 010	705	1 085	1 220	1 261	1 307
Oman	39	39	39	39	39	39	39	40
Saudi Arabia	..	..	..	94	124	217	217	233
Syrian Arab Republic	385	339	180	823	1 150	1 400	1 332	1 407
Turkey	3 246	3 327	4 560	887	1 248	1 476	970	950
Yemen	1 400	1 081	1 288	1 283	1 322	1 411	1 160	1 471
Developing economies: Oceania	**108**	**110**	**142**	**1 406**	**1 621**	**1 771**	**1 650**	**1 832**
Fiji	22	33	44	185	160	123	154	128
French Polynesia	..	..	..	557	689	764	728	771
Kiribati	5	7	7	7	7	9	9	9
New Caledonia	..	..	..	512	585	624	509	659
Papua New Guinea	5	16	7	13	13	13	13	14
Samoa	43	41	45	110	120	135	131	142
Solomon Islands	..	..	4	7	2	2	2	-
Tonga	24	..	..	69	101	94	96	99
Vanuatu (2)	8	14	35	5	6	7	7	7
Transition economies	**9 360**	**3 730**	**6 234**	**16 718**	**27 343**	**33 532**	**28 585**	**30 288**
Albania	..	427	598	1 290	1 468	1 495	1 317	1 285
Armenia	–	65	87	498	846	1 062	769	824
Azerbaijan	–	3	57	693	1 287	1 554	1 274	1 472
Belarus	–	29	139	255	354	443	358	387
Bosnia and Herzegovina	–	..	1 607	2 043	2 700	2 735	2 081	2 228
Croatia	–	544	641	1 222	1 394	1 602	1 476	1 545
Georgia	–	..	274	346	695	732	714	824
Kazakhstan	–	116	122	178	223	192	124	131
Kyrgyzstan	–	1	9	322	715	1 232	992	1 037
Montenegro	–	–	–	–	–	298	302	–
Republic of Moldova	–	1	179	920	1 498	1 897	1 211	1 316
Russian Federation (3)	–	2 502	1 275	3 012	4 713	6 033	5 359	5 590
Serbia and Montenegro	–	..	1 132	4 650	4 910	–	–	–
Serbia	–	–	–	–	–	5 538	5 406	5 580
SFR of Yugoslavia (former)	9 360	–	–	–	–	–	–	–
Tajikistan	–	..	..	467	1 691	2 544	1 748	2 065
TFYR of Macedonia	–	41	81	227	345	407	381	414
Ukraine	–	..	33	595	4 503	5 769	5 073	5 289
Developed economies: America	**1 170**	**2 179**	**2 835**	**2 890**	**4 422**	**4 639**	**4 301**	**4 467**
Bermuda	..	..	..	..	1 452	1 594	1 345	-
United States	1 170	2 179	2 835	2 890	2 970	3 045	2 956	3 122
Developed economies: Asia	**1 225**	**1 852**	**1 774**	**1 930**	**2 619**	**3 351**	**3 043**	**3 289**
Israel	812	701	400	850	1 042	1 422	1 267	1 379
Japan	-	1 151	1 374	1 080	1 577	1 929	1 776	1 911
Developed economies: Europe	**31 274**	**36 228**	**41 401**	**76 678**	**103 540**	**112 604**	**100 215**	**103 258**
Austria	635	1 012	1 805	2 608	3 012	3 317	3 286	3 340
Belgium (4)	3 583	(e)4 207	(e)3 426	7 242	9 098	10 288	10 437	10 446
Bulgaria (5)	..	..	58	1 613	1 694	1 874	1 558	1 602
Cyprus	79	49	64	189	172	279	153	146
Czech Republic	–	191	297	1 026	1 332	1 360	1 201	1 263
Denmark	..	523	667	867	819	905	894	952
Estonia	–	1	4	264	426	398	325	342
Faeroe Islands	..	..	43	..	..	..	..	..
Finland	63	74	473	693	762	818	859	872
France	4 035	4 640	8 610	11 945	14 445	16 408	15 550	15 939
Germany	4 876	4 523	3 644	6 933	9 898	10 908	10 879	11 559
Greece	1 817	3 286	2 194	1 220	2 484	2 687	2 020	2 107
Hungary	..	152	281	1 931	2 311	2 520	2 277	2 514
Iceland	62	63	88	88	41	35	23	26
Ireland	286	347	252	513	590	646	581	618
Italy	5 075	2 364	1 937	2 397	3 164	3 139	2 683	3 393
Latvia	–	..	72	381	552	601	599	643
Lithuania	–	1	50	534	1 433	1 468	1 169	1 210
Luxembourg	..	730	579	1 269	1 554	1 723	1 718	1 724
Malta	58	19	20	34	48	46	46	50
Netherlands	709	1 359	1 157	2 197	2 860	3 300	3 712	4 079
Norway	158	239	270	505	613	685	631	657

For sources and notes, see end of table.

As percentage of GDP En pourcentage du PIB				As percentage of exports of goods and services (1) En pourcentage des exportations des biens et services (1)				Régions, pays ou territoires
1990	2000	2009	2010	1990	2000	2009	2010	
3.16	*3.04*	*1.36*	*1.14*	*15.90*	*11.51*	*3.74*	*2.92*	*Asie occidentale*
12.42	21.81	14.34	13.76	19.88	52.14	32.92	31.08	Jordanie
64.66	9.49	21.89	21.07	..	..	34.98	39.44	Liban
..	24.07	21.56	..	..	99.74	102.99	..	Territoire palestinien occupé
0.34	0.20	0.07	0.06	0.70	0.33	0.13	..	Oman
..	..	0.06	0.05	..	..	0.11	0.09	Arabie saoudite
3.45	0.92	2.47	2.37	7.65	2.63	8.50	..	République arabe syrienne
1.60	1.71	0.16	0.13	15.43	9.06	0.68	0.61	Turquie
32.03	12.83	4.31	4.40	100.57	32.13	16.36	..	Yémen
2.11	*2.32*	*6.08*	*..*	*4.52*	*2.52*	*18.06*	*..*	*Économies en développement : Océanie*
1.62	2.55	5.02	4.16	2.64	4.54	11.63	..	Fidji
..	..	16.06	..	..	..	58.82	..	Polynésie française
12.47	10.48	6.66	5.71	46.39	..	..	..	Kiribati
..	..	5.49	..	..	..	35.23	..	Nouvelle-Calédonie
0.17	0.21	0.16	0.15	0.39	0.31	0.28	..	Papouasie-Nouvelle-Guinée
38.26	19.48	25.10	25.37	96.24	..	75.63	72.96	Samoa
..	1.28	0.33	-	..	3.56	1.01	..	Îles Salomon
20.42	..	28.28	26.46	62.59	..	219.92	..	Tonga
4.59	12.35	1.07	0.98	11.11	22.08	..	..	Vanuatu (2)
11.00	*1.65*	*1.65*	*1.49*	*45.26*	*3.02*	*4.28*	*3.59*	*Économies en transition*
..	16.42	10.86	10.82	..	84.98	38.10	33.89	Albanie
–	4.58	9.01	8.76	–	19.58	57.49	42.52	Arménie
–	1.08	2.96	2.71	–	2.70	5.58	5.16	Azerbaïdjan
–	1.34	0.73	0.71	–	1.82	1.44	1.30	Bélarus
–	29.19	12.21	13.24	–	101.74	37.67	35.83	Bosnie-Herzégovine
–	3.00	2.34	2.55	–	7.42	6.53	6.69	Croatie
–	8.94	6.65	7.07	–	41.10	22.27	20.27	Géorgie
–	0.67	0.11	0.10	–	1.18	0.26	0.20	Kazakhstan
–	0.65	21.66	23.02	–	1.54	38.74	41.88	Kirghizistan
–	–	7.39	-	–	–	22.25	-	Monténégro
–	13.86	22.40	22.80	–	27.85	60.67	57.71	République de Moldova
–	0.49	0.44	0.38	–	1.11	1.55	1.26	Fédération de Russie (3)
–	9.87	–	–	–	..	–	–	Serbie-et-Monténégro
–	–	11.51	12.61	–	–	..	..	Serbie
11.00	..	–	–	45.26	..	–	–	RSF de Yougoslavie (anc.)
–	..	35.12	36.58	–	..	143.50	136.55	Tadjikistan
–	2.26	4.00	4.42	–	4.94	10.74	9.82	LERY de Macédoine
–	0.11	4.32	3.87	–	0.17	9.35	7.64	Ukraine
0.02	*0.03*	*0.03*	*0.02*	*0.22*	*0.26*	*0.27*	*0.17*	*Économies développées : Amérique*
..	..	20.47	..	..	..	99.17	..	Bermudes
0.02	0.03	0.02	0.02	0.22	0.26	0.19	0.17	États-Unis
0.04	*0.04*	*0.06*	*0.06*	*0.36*	*0.31*	*0.41*	*0.35*	*Économies développées : Asie*
1.43	0.32	0.65	0.64	4.69	0.86	1.87	1.72	Israël
-	0.03	0.04	0.03	-	0.26	0.26	0.22	Japon
0.43	*0.46*	*0.58*	*0.60*	*1.51*	*1.24*	*1.56*	*1.46*	*Économies développées : Europe*
0.39	0.94	0.86	0.89	1.00	2.06	1.73	1.65	Autriche
1.77	(e)1.47	2.22	2.24	..	..	3.13	2.84	Belgique (4)
..	0.45	3.20	3.35	..	0.83	6.69	5.82	Bulgarie (5)
1.36	0.69	0.65	0.63	2.66	1.28	1.27	1.07	Chypre
–	0.52	0.63	0.66	–	0.83	0.94	0.85	République tchèque
–	0.42	0.29	0.31	..	0.90	0.61	0.61	Danemark
–	0.07	1.68	1.78	–	0.08	2.39	2.11	Estonie
..	..	..	..	..	8.10	..	..	Îles Féroé
0.05	0.39	0.38	0.36	0.20	0.88	0.94	0.92	Finlande
0.32	0.65	0.59	0.62	1.41	2.26	2.51	2.41	France
0.28	0.19	0.33	0.35	1.03	0.58	0.78	0.75	Allemagne
1.93	1.73	0.62	0.70	13.96	7.45	3.42	3.51	Grèce
..	0.59	1.77	1.94	..	0.81	2.27	2.24	Hongrie
0.98	1.01	0.19	0.20	2.90	2.97	0.37	0.36	Islande
0.60	0.26	0.26	0.30	1.07	0.27	0.29	0.30	Irlande
0.45	0.18	0.13	0.17	2.31	0.65	0.53	0.62	Italie
–	0.92	2.31	2.68	–	2.24	5.33	5.06	Lettonie
–	0.44	3.17	3.33	–	0.98	5.79	4.85	Lituanie
..	2.85	3.25	3.14	..	..	2.29	2.04	Luxembourg
2.29	0.51	0.57	0.61	2.99	0.56	0.72	0.71	Malte
0.24	0.30	0.47	0.52	0.45	0.45	0.72	0.70	Pays-Bas
0.13	0.16	0.17	0.16	0.34	0.35	0.41	0.38	Norvège

Pour les sources et les notes, se reporter à la fin du tableau.

Region, country or territory	Millions of dollars - Millions de dollars							
	1990	1995	2000	2005	2007	2008	2009	2010
Poland	..	724	1 496	6 482	10 496	10 447	8 816	9 080
Portugal	4 479	3 953	3 495	3 101	3 941	4 057	3 585	3 664
Romania (6)	..	9	96	(b)4 733	8 542	9 381	4 929	4 517
Slovakia	–	26	18	946	1 483	1 973	1 671	1 651
Slovenia	–	272	205	264	323	347	281	297
Spain	2 186	3 237	4 859	7 961	10 739	11 807	9 904	10 245
Sweden	153	288	510	612	738	780	652	796
Switzerland	924	1 473	1 119	1 828	2 088	2 544	2 524	2 096
United Kingdom	1 000	1 660	1 600	6 000	7 000	7 000	7 000	7 100
Developed economies: Oceania	**3 131**	**3 303**	**2 139**	**3 729**	**4 480**	**5 354**	**4 717**	**5 020**
Australia	2 370	1 651	1 903	2 990	3 826	4 713	4 089	4 335
New Zealand	762	1 652	236	739	654	641	628	685

Sources:
- IMF, *Balance of Payments Statistics*
- World Bank, *Migration and Remittances*
- National sources
- Economist Intelligence Unit, *Country Data*

Notes:

- Migrants' remittances data cover: workers' remittances, compensation of employees and migrants' transfers.
(1) Exports and imports of goods and services data are based on IMF balance-of-payments statistics.
(2) Year 2002: break in series; migrants' transfers data are no longer available starting with 2002.
(3) Workers' remittances and compensation of employees: From 1995 to 2000 (inclusive), data represent compensation of employees only; workers' remittances are available starting from 2001 onwards. Total remittances (including migrants transfers) reflect the same break in series.
(4) Data up to 1994 inclusive refer to Belgium-Luxembourg Economic Union. From 1995, the figures cover Belgium only.
(5) Receipts (credits): Year 2001 - break in series.
(6) Year 2005: break in series; change in classification.

As percentage of GDP En pourcentage du PIB				As percentage of exports of goods and services (1) En pourcentage des exportations des biens et services (1)				Régions, pays ou territoires
1990	2000	2009	2010	1990	2000	2009	2010	
..	0.87	2.05	1.94	..	3.23	5.15	4.66	Pologne
5.77	2.99	1.54	1.60	20.78	10.25	5.31	5.08	Portugal
..	0.26	3.06	2.83	..	0.79	9.76	7.79	Roumanie (6)
—	0.09	1.91	1.89	—	0.13	2.70	2.34	Slovaquie
—	1.03	0.57	0.62	—	1.92	0.98	0.97	Slovénie
0.42	0.84	0.68	0.73	2.61	2.89	2.82	2.72	Espagne
0.06	0.21	0.16	0.17	0.22	0.46	0.34	0.36	Suède
0.39	0.44	0.51	0.40	0.95	0.89	0.90	0.62	Suisse
0.21	0.24	0.33	0.33	0.88	0.89	1.22	1.15	Royaume-Uni
0.84	**0.46**	**0.42**	**0.35**	**5.09**	**2.10**	**2.05**	**1.66**	**Économies développées : Océanie**
0.72	0.46	0.40	0.34	4.75	2.27	2.08	1.66	Australie
1.71	0.44	0.34	0.49	6.52	1.32	1.89	1.69	Nouvelle-Zélande

Sources:
- FMI, *Statistiques de la balance des paiements*
- Banque mondiale, *Migration and Remittances*
- Sources nationales
- Economist Intelligence Unit, *Country Data*

Notes :

-     Les envois de fonds des migrants couvrent : les envois de fonds des travailleurs, la rémunération des employées et les transferts des migrants.
(1)   Les données sur les exportations et importations des biens et services se basent sur les statistiques de la balance des paiements du FMI.
(2)   Année 2002 : rupture de série ; les données sur les transferts des migrants ne sont plus disponibles à partir de 2002.
(3)   L'envoi de fonds des travailleurs et la rémunération des salariés : De 1995 à 2000 (incluses), les données comprennent seulement la rémunération des salariés ; les envois de fonds des travailleurs ne sont disponibles qu'à partir de l'année 2001. Le total des envois de fonds (y compris les transferts des migrants) présentent la même rupture de série.
(4)   Jusqu'à l'année 1994 comprise, les données se réfèrent à l'Union économique belgo-luxembourgeoise. A partir de 1995, les chiffres couvrent uniquement la Belgique.
(5)   Recettes (crédits) : Année 2001 - rupture de série.
(6)   Année 2005 : rupture de série ; changement des méthodes de classification.

7

Economic grouping	Millions of dollars - Millions de dollars							
	1990	1995	2000	2005	2007	2008	2009	2010
DEVELOPING ECONOMIES	**33 392**	**54 663**	**80 169**	**173 442**	**245 238**	**288 376**	**280 882**	**297 305**
Developing economies excluding China	33 217	53 785	74 933	149 341	206 446	239 852	232 152	246 305
Developing economies excluding LDCs	29 821	50 623	74 087	161 528	227 878	265 401	256 745	271 409
High-income developing countries	9 761	11 263	16 357	34 887	41 326	44 626	40 034	41 176
Middle-income developing countries	15 326	29 455	38 183	85 447	119 296	136 412	132 066	138 135
Low-income developing countries	8 006	13 945	25 630	53 109	84 616	107 338	108 781	117 994
Heavily indebted poor countries (IMF)	934	1 495	3 290	7 942	12 571	15 632	14 451	14 924
Landlocked developing countries	945	1 402	1 853	6 730	12 120	16 046	13 646	15 211
Small Island developing States	662	1 333	1 638	2 906	3 407	3 540	3 261	3 387
Least developed countries	*3 571*	*4 040*	*6 083*	*11 914*	*17 360*	*22 975*	*24 136*	*25 897*
Africa and Haiti	1 211	1 512	2 387	4 631	7 113	9 249	8 811	9 170
Asia	2 294	2 454	3 592	7 140	10 099	13 558	15 161	16 553
Islands	66	73	103	143	148	168	164	173
Major petroleum and gas exporters	*1 602*	*3 565*	*2 787*	*6 724*	*12 795*	*13 714*	*13 259*	*13 575*
Africa	362	1 924	2 195	5 411	11 366	12 206	11 800	12 030
America	1	2	17	148	151	137	131	129
Asia	1 239	1 639	575	1 165	1 278	1 371	1 328	1 415
Major exporters of manufactured goods	*5 644*	*8 878*	*16 583*	*51 100*	*70 978*	*82 229*	*77 776*	*80 543*
America	3 098	4 368	7 525	23 062	27 136	26 304	22 153	22 572
Asia	2 546	4 510	9 059	28 037	43 842	55 925	55 624	57 971
Emerging economies	*6 153*	*11 979*	*13 678*	*32 127*	*38 992*	*41 584*	*35 976*	*36 632*
America	3 781	8 346	9 991	28 488	34 258	34 537	29 430	30 030
Asia	2 372	3 633	3 686	3 639	4 734	7 046	6 546	6 602
Newly industrialized Asian countries	*4 003*	*9 644*	*11 973*	*22 921*	*27 527*	*32 838*	*33 453*	*35 421*
First tier	1 073	1 222	1 144	1 467	1 613	3 584	3 357	3 608
Second tier	2 929	8 422	10 829	21 454	25 914	29 254	30 096	31 813
Developing economies: Africa	**8 992**	**10 202**	**11 261**	**22 426**	**36 878**	**41 385**	**38 342**	**39 747**
Northern Africa excluding Sudan	7 193	6 995	6 608	13 075	18 238	19 784	17 595	18 134
Sub-Saharan Africa	1 799	3 207	4 653	9 351	18 640	21 601	20 747	21 612
Sub-Saharan Africa excluding South Africa	1 663	3 101	4 309	8 693	17 807	20 778	19 845	20 604
Developing economies: America	**5 842**	**14 076**	**21 074**	**51 217**	**64 473**	**65 959**	**58 184**	**59 688**
Central America and Greater Caribbean Islands excluding Puerto Rico	4 407	8 354	14 877	38 480	46 982	47 207	41 499	43 023
Central America and Greater Caribbean Islands excluding Mexico and Puerto Rico	1 309	3 986	7 353	15 418	19 846	20 903	19 347	20 451
South America and Central America	5 055	11 715	16 718	44 467	56 302	57 337	49 858	50 949
South America excluding Brazil	696	2 162	4 200	8 736	12 575	13 114	11 905	11 824
Developing economies: Asia	**18 451**	**30 275**	**47 692**	**98 333**	**142 203**	**179 260**	**182 706**	**196 038**
Eastern and South-Eastern Asia excluding China	4 019	9 759	14 210	28 021	34 082	41 246	41 705	43 937
Southern Asia excluding India	4 388	5 382	4 858	12 831	17 942	22 776	26 669	28 727

For sources and notes, see end of table 7.3.1.

As percentage of GDP En pourcentage du PIB				As percentage of exports of goods and services (1) En pourcentage des exportations des biens et services (1)				Groupements économiques
1990	2000	2009	2010	1990	2000	2009	2010	
0.98	**1.24**	**1.72**	**1.51**	**5.27**	**4.18**	**5.74**	**4.65**	**ÉCONOMIES EN DÉVELOPPEMENT**
1.11	1.42	2.05	1.78	5.80	4.60	6.53	5.50	Économies en développement sans la Chine
0.90	1.18	1.62	1.41	4.78	3.94	5.40	4.33	Économies en développement sans les PMA
0.80	0.63	0.88	0.74	3.38	1.56	2.02	1.78	Pays en développement à revenu élevé
1.03	1.34	1.48	1.28	5.76	5.46	6.00	4.24	Pays en développement à revenu intermédiaire
1.20	2.59	3.89	3.42	8.43	10.95	15.44	14.41	Pays en développement à revenu faible
0.89	2.60	4.18	3.99	5.40	10.19	16.31	11.59	Pays pauvres très endettés (FMI)
1.89	2.08	3.90	3.76	8.67	6.08	11.17	9.72	Pays en développement sans littoral
2.82	4.61	4.82	4.64	5.91	0.40	10.04	7.77	Petits États insulaires en développement
3.36	*3.76*	*5.54*	*5.18*	*28.60*	*15.75*	*19.96*	*..*	*Pays les moins avancés*
1.82	2.75	3.30	3.13	14.52	11.37	0.16	10.70	Afrique et Haïti
5.90	4.86	9.16	8.10	57.71	21.16	44.72	..	Asie
9.55	8.65	5.97	5.89	38.60	13.38	31.86	..	Îles
0.65	*0.72*	*0.87*	*0.76*	*2.22*	*1.70*	*2.56*	*2.55*	*Principaux exportateurs de pétrole et de gaz*
0.37	1.48	2.89	2.44	1.29	3.40	6.36	12.99	Afrique
0.00	0.01	0.04	0.03	0.01	0.05	0.22	0.19	Amérique
1.21	0.47	0.17	0.16	4.89	1.39	0.11	0.09	Asie
0.45	*0.54*	*1.01*	*0.88*	*2.32*	*1.47*	*2.78*	*2.35*	*Principaux exportateurs d'articles manufacturés*
1.08	1.18	2.54	2.20	6.35	4.18	9.04	7.19	Amérique
0.26	0.37	0.81	0.72	1.30	0.95	2.17	1.85	Asie
0.42	*0.49*	*0.76*	*0.63*	*2.46*	*1.88*	*2.57*	*2.27*	*Économies émergentes*
0.42	0.59	0.97	0.79	3.34	3.25	5.02	4.00	Amérique
0.42	0.34	0.39	0.33	1.72	0.85	0.76	0.58	Asie
0.54	*0.81*	*1.30*	*1.14*	*2.24*	*1.54*	*2.38*	*2.20*	*Économies nouvellement industrialisées d'Asie*
0.25	0.11	0.24	0.22	1.40	0.19	0.35	0.30	Première génération
0.97	2.37	2.60	2.19	2.85	3.54	5.49	6.48	Deuxième génération
2.15	**1.96**	**2.77**	**2.47**	**8.76**	**6.79**	**8.36**	**8.71**	**Économies en développement : Afrique**
5.05	2.65	3.40	3.14	20.67	12.09	9.97	..	Afrique septentrionale sans le Soudan
0.65	1.43	2.39	2.09	2.65	4.37	7.28	7.06	Afrique subsaharienne
1.02	2.23	3.41	3.07	4.08	6.23	9.91	11.60	Afrique subsaharienne sans l'Afrique du Sud
0.53	**1.01**	**1.45**	**1.19**	**3.46**	**4.80**	**7.03**	**4.74**	**Économies en développement : Amérique**
1.22	1.92	3.66	3.35	6.93	6.40	12.92	..	Amérique centrale et Grandes Antilles sans Porto Rico
1.76	5.39	7.42	8.66	8.86	16.01	26.85	18.49	Amérique centrale et Grandes Antilles sans le Mexique et Porto Rico
0.48	0.83	1.29	1.06	3.19	4.20	6.40	4.73	Amérique du Sud et Amérique centrale
0.21	0.64	0.93	0.76	1.08	3.36	3.93	2.34	Amérique du Sud sans le Brésil
0.98	**1.26**	**1.68**	**1.50**	**5.12**	**3.66**	**5.09**	**4.36**	**Économies en développement : Asie**
0.54	0.93	1.53	1.33	2.25	1.79	2.78	2.21	Asie orientale et Asie du Sud-Est sans la Chine
2.50	1.99	3.99	3.88	14.10	8.80	49.95	43.91	Asie méridionale sans l'Inde

Pour les sources et les notes, se reporter à la fin du tableau 7.3.1.

7

Region, country or territory	Millions of dollars - Millions de dollars							
	1990	1995	2000	2005	2006	2007	2008	2009
WORLD	67 204	100 215	114 306	187 060	215 199	262 233	305 491	290 248
DEVELOPING ECONOMIES	18 835	28 272	33 513	49 473	55 341	64 954	81 308	83 158
TRANSITION ECONOMIES	..	4 504	1 904	10 210	16 227	23 676	31 638	23 451
DEVELOPED ECONOMIES	48 369	67 438	78 889	127 377	143 632	173 603	192 545	183 640
Developing economies: Africa	3 407	2 530	3 091	4 330	4 828	5 296	5 879	5 053
Eastern Africa	*126*	*71*	*657*	*301*	*321*	*..*	*..*	*674*
Burundi	6	5	2	0	0	0	0	1
Comoros	4	4	..	..	..	..	..	..
Djibouti	..	18	2	5	5	5	5	6
Eritrea		..	1	..	..	..	..	..
Ethiopia	–	0	13	16	14	15	21	27
Kenya	7	9	34	56	25	16	64	61
Madagascar	18	11	12	21	21	21	21	..
Malawi	0	1	0	1	1	1	1	..
Mauritius	1	1	1	11	13	12	14	12
Mozambique	25	21	156	21	26	45	57	63
Rwanda	21	1	28	35	47	68	70	71
Seychelles	10	0	10	10	17	21	24	24
Uganda	..	..	353	197	206	236	381	463
United Republic of Tanzania	..	1	20	33	30	46	54	81
Zambia	18	..	24	94	115	124	139	66
Zimbabwe	16	..	..	..	..	..	..	..
Middle Africa	*539*	*358*	*411*	*523*	*771*	*981*	*1 014*	*811*
Angola	150	210	266	215	413	603	669	716
Cameroon	111	22	30	56	92	90	56	94
Central African Republic	36	..	..	..	..	..	..	..
Chad	39	..	..	..	..	..	..	..
Congo	55	27	37	66	81	102	102	..
Gabon	147	99	78	186	186	186	186	..
Sao Tome and Principe	0	..	1	0	1	1	0	1
Northern Africa	*534*	*502*	*556*	*1 028*	*1 140*	*1 011*	*1 281*	*1 690*
Algeria	31	..	..	..	..	..	..	..
Egypt	27	223	32	57	135	180	241	255
Libyan Arab Jamahiriya	446	222	463	914	945	762	964	1 361
Morocco	16	20	29	40	41	52	58	61
Sudan	2	1	4	2	2	2	2	..
Tunisia	13	36	27	16	16	15	16	13
Southern Africa	*1 352*	*919*	*890*	*1 229*	*1 233*	*1 351*	*1 340*	*1 322*
Botswana	119	200	147	129	118	120	145	102
Lesotho	..	75	28	17	11	21	13	35
Namibia	30	11	9	19	20	16	43	16
South Africa	1 199	629	685	1 055	1 068	1 186	1 133	1 158
Swaziland	4	4	21	8	17	8	7	11
Western Africa	*855*	*679*	*577*	*1 048*	*1 163*	*1 343*	*1 390*	*356*
Benin	21	26	9	40	67	115	88	..
Burkina Faso	81	..	45	44	44	44	44	..
Cape Verde	2	5	0	5	6	6	10	12
Côte d'Ivoire	471	457	390	597	660	698	756	20
Gambia	..	..	..	1	1	1	3	8
Ghana	4	5	6	6	6	6	6	..
Guinea	20	10	27	48	48	119	76	45
Guinea-Bissau	12	3	..	5	4	4	17	17
Liberia	..	..	..	0	0	0	0	1
Mali	45	42	26	69	57	83	105	105
Mauritania	31	14	..	..	..	..	..	..
Niger	66	29	12	29	29	18	22	22
Nigeria	9	5	1	68	102	54	58	66
Senegal	79	76	55	98	96	143	144	..
Sierra Leone	0	0	..	2	4	4	3	3
Togo	13	5	7	35	39	47	58	58
Developing economies: America	1 067	1 234	2 239	2 643	3 054	4 038	4 697	4 177
Caribbean	*143*	*200*	*432*	*848*	*891*	*1 005*	*978*	*836*
Anguilla	4	7	9	9	12	19	15	11
Antigua and Barbuda	6	8	2	2	2	2	2	2

For sources and notes, see end of table.

As percentage of GDP En pourcentage du PIB				As percentage of imports of goods and services (1) En pourcentage des importations des biens et services (1)				Régions, pays ou territoires
1990	2000	2008	2009	1990	2000	2008	2009	
0.35	0.38	0.54	0.54	1.95	1.66	1.76	2.13	MONDE
0.72	0.64	0.56	0.58	3.68	2.23	1.64	2.03	ÉCONOMIES EN DÉVELOPPEMENT
..	0.52	1.38	1.35	..	1.61	4.74	5.10	ÉCONOMIES EN TRANSITION
0.29	0.33	0.48	0.48	1.63	1.50	1.65	2.03	ÉCONOMIES DÉVELOPPÉES
0.74	0.59	0.46	0.46	2.90	2.12	1.07	1.26	Économies en développement : Afrique
0.32	1.00	0.37	0.64	1.06	3.58	1.47	1.74	*Afrique orientale*
0.38	0.26	0.02	0.10	1.83	1.64	0.04	0.23	Burundi
1.82	..	..	..	4.97	..	..	..	Comores
	0.32	0.61	0.62	..	0.83	0.73	1.00	Djibouti
_	0.19	..	..	_	0.26	..	..	Érythrée
_	0.15	0.08	0.09	_	0.77	0.22	0.29	Éthiopie
0.07	0.27	0.22	0.21	0.27	0.90	0.51	0.54	Kenya
0.57	0.31	0.22	..	2.16	0.78	..	..	Madagascar
0.00	0.02	0.02	..	0.01	0.07	..	..	Malawi
0.02	0.01	0.15	0.13	0.03	0.02	0.22	0.23	Maurice
0.86	3.62	0.58	0.66	2.55	10.47	1.23	1.46	Mozambique
0.83	1.58	1.49	1.36	6.05	6.62	5.01	4.83	Rwanda
2.16	1.33	2.59	3.03	3.97	2.01	1.78	2.26	Seychelles
..	5.57	2.31	2.71	..	25.06	7.19	8.89	Ouganda
..	0.19	0.26	0.35	..	0.99	0.63	1.07	République-Unie de Tanzanie
0.47	0.74	0.94	0.51	0.92	1.84	2.54	1.59	Zambie
0.19	..	..	..	0.83	..	..	..	Zimbabwe
1.59	1.51	1.20	1.41	5.46	3.69	1.42	1.68	*Afrique centrale*
1.46	2.92	1.92	2.05	4.43	4.64	1.55	1.71	Angola
0.94	0.32	0.24	0.43	4.48	1.20	0.70	1.49	Cameroun
2.50	..	..	..	8.77	..	..	..	République centrafricaine
2.53	..	..	..	7.98	..	..	..	Tchad
1.90	1.13	0.92	..	4.33	3.06	..	..	Congo
2.52	1.41	1.25	..	8.13	4.69	..	..	Gabon
0.07	0.83	0.26	0.26	0.41	1.70	0.43	0.53	Sao Tomé-et-Principe
0.28	0.27	0.29	0.45	1.12	1.07	0.72	1.21	*Afrique septentrionale*
0.05	..	..	..	0.31	..	..	..	Algérie
0.07	0.03	0.15	0.14	0.19	0.14	0.36	0.47	Égypte
1.43	1.20	1.18	2.32	4.97	9.22	3.71	5.03	Jamahiriya arabe libyenne
0.06	0.08	0.06	0.07	0.21	0.23	0.12	0.16	Maroc
0.01	0.03	0.00	..	0.24	0.22	0.02	..	Soudan
0.10	0.14	0.04	0.03	0.21	0.29	0.06	0.06	Tunisie
1.13	0.61	0.44	0.42	5.33	2.25	1.10	1.39	*Afrique australe*
3.20	2.62	1.08	0.88	5.98	6.35	2.62	1.99	Botswana
..	3.63	0.82	2.15	..	2.64	0.69	1.76	Lesotho
1.11	0.23	0.48	0.17	1.88	0.55	0.97	0.31	Namibie
1.07	0.52	0.41	0.41	5.71	2.07	1.05	1.43	Afrique du Sud
0.40	1.36	0.22	0.35	0.54	1.44	0.30	0.47	Swaziland
1.11	0.71	0.45	0.16	4.45	2.28	1.24	0.47	*Afrique occidentale*
1.12	0.38	1.33	..	4.56	1.25	3.68	..	Bénin
2.61	1.70	0.54	..	10.66	6.77	1.54	..	Burkina Faso
0.59	0.09	0.64	0.75	1.23	0.14	0.84	1.09	Cap-Vert
3.96	3.65	3.23	0.08	13.68	10.74	7.77	0.22	Côte d'Ivoire
..	..	0.33	0.91	..	..	0.93	2.46	Gambie
0.06	0.12	0.04	..	0.26	0.18	0.05	..	Ghana
0.70	0.84	1.99	0.95	2.14	3.09	4.18	3.23	Guinée
1.98	..	1.99	2.01	13.18	..	5.90	..	Guinée-Bissau
..	..	0.06	0.12	..	..	0.02	0.06	Libéria
1.81	0.99	1.20	1.19	5.47	2.84	2.79	3.73	Mali
2.97	..	..	..	6.01	..	..	..	Mauritanie
2.52	0.69	0.42	0.43	9.13	2.61	1.14	..	Niger
0.03	0.00	0.03	0.04	0.13	0.01	0.09	0.13	Nigéria
1.28	1.17	1.09	..	4.32	3.15	2.05	..	Sénégal
0.01	..	0.15	0.16	0.03	..	0.54	0.55	Sierra Leone
0.75	0.52	1.82	1.82	1.59	1.12	3.46	3.41	Togo
0.14	0.16	0.15	0.14	1.24	0.93	0.71	0.80	Économies en développement : Amérique
0.78	0.83	1.11	0.96	1.54	1.51	1.93	2.19	*Caraïbes*
8.09	8.25	5.28	5.11	10.15	7.18	4.71	5.11	Anguilla
1.61	0.23	0.20	0.20	1.85	0.31	0.25	0.29	Antigua-et-Barbuda

Pour les sources et les notes, se reporter à la fin du tableau.

Region, country or territory	Millions of dollars - Millions de dollars							
	1990	1995	2000	2005	2006	2007	2008	2009
Aruba	..	9	49	70	80	82	86	77
Bahamas	46	44	73	144	164	171	143	96
Barbados	6	15	19	43	33	54	39	40
Dominica	2	0	0	0	0	0	0	0
Dominican Republic	..	7	19	25	27	28	35	29
Grenada	1	1	3	3	4	4	4	4
Haiti	..	..	11	60	76	96	117	135
Jamaica	27	74	179	410	412	454	419	314
Montserrat	3	2	4	5	4	5	5	5
Netherlands Antilles	11	11	47	59	61	72	54	100
Saint Kitts and Nevis	7	1	7	8	6	6	6	6
Saint Lucia	4	2	3	4	4	4	4	4
Saint Vincent and the Grenadines	3	3	6	6	7	7	7	7
Trinidad and Tobago	33	14	..	..	..	..	..	..
Central America	**45**	**71**	**260**	**384**	**465**	**493**	**550**	**546**
Belize	7	7	11	20	22	22	29	23
Costa Rica	..	36	142	209	246	271	269	239
El Salvador	3	..	20	24	28	29	19	21
Guatemala	14	8	56	42	46	17	26	23
Honduras	..	..	9	0	2	2	9	12
Panama	22	20	22	88	121	151	198	229
South America	**878**	**963**	**1 547**	**1 411**	**1 698**	**2 541**	**3 169**	**2 794**
Argentina	21	195	268	314	356	463	630	755
Bolivia (Plurinational State of)	8	9	37	67	73	79	106	103
Brazil	12	347	366	498	691	896	1 191	1 003
Chile	7	7	16	16	6	6	6	6
Colombia	44	150	219	56	66	95	88	92
Ecuador	2	4	6	54	62	83	66	81
Guyana	..	12	27	55	48	62	77	77
Peru	75	34	275	129	133	141	133	85
Suriname	8	2	2	10	4	65	8	5
Uruguay	..	..	..	2	3	4	5	6
Venezuela (Bolivarian Rep. of)	701	203	331	211	257	649	860	581
Developing economies: Asia	**14 273**	**24 433**	**28 061**	**42 229**	**47 170**	**55 311**	**70 389**	**73 723**
Eastern Asia	**369**	**2 230**	**3 820**	**7 970**	**9 711**	**8 524**	**12 012**	**10 186**
China	5	..	790	2 603	3 025	4 372	5 737	4 444
China, Hong Kong SAR	..	..	225	348	377	388	393	413
China, Macao SAR	..	..	..	229	494	838	961	707
China, Taiwan Province of	..	1 595	1 831	1 413	1 425	1 394	1 640	1 417
Korea, Republic of	364	635	972	3 336	4 314	1 441	3 109	3 120
Mongolia	..	..	3	40	77	90	172	83
Southern Asia	**114**	**476**	**575**	**1 749**	**2 089**	**2 548**	**4 412**	**3 553**
Bangladesh	..	..	4	5	3	3	14	8
Bhutan	..	..	..	..	75	60	61	82
India	106	419	486	1 348	1 562	2 059	3 815	2 893
Maldives	8	27	46	70	84	106	129	116
Nepal	..	9	17	66	79	4	5	12
Pakistan	1	4	2	3	3	2	2	8
Sri Lanka	..	16	20	257	283	314	385	435
South-Eastern Asia	**434**	**1 541**	**3 784**	**7 452**	**7 587**	**8 749**	**9 484**	**9 948**
Brunei Darussalam	..	..	..	376	405	430	420	445
Cambodia	..	52	104	184	173	186	230	215
Indonesia	–	–	–	1 179	1 359	1 654	1 971	2 702
Lao People's Dem. Rep.	..	9	0	1	1	1	1	..
Malaysia (2)	230	(b)1 329	–	5 679	5 597	6 412	6 786	6 529
Myanmar	..	..	14	19	32	32	32	..
Philippines	5	151	21	15	20	35	44	58
Thailand	199	..	..	..	..	..	..	..
Western Asia	**13 356**	**20 187**	**19 881**	**25 057**	**27 784**	**35 489**	**44 482**	**50 037**
Bahrain	332	500	1 013	1 223	1 531	1 483	1 774	1 391
Jordan	71	107	197	349	402	479	472	502
Kuwait	770	1 354	1 734	2 648	3 183	9 764	10 323	9 912
Lebanon	..	..	..	4 012	3 445	2 962	4 366	5 749
Occupied Palestinian territory	..	19	6	8	9	9	9	9
Oman	856	1 537	1 451	2 257	2 788	3 670	5 181	5 313
Saudi Arabia	11 221	16 594	15 390	14 315	15 964	16 447	21 697	26 470
Syrian Arab Republic	..	15	29	40	235	252	212	212

For sources and notes, see end of table.

As percentage of GDP En pourcentage du PIB				As percentage of imports of goods and services (1) En pourcentage des importations des biens et services (1)				Régions, pays ou territoires
1990	2000	2008	2009	1990	2000	2008	2009	
..	2.60	3.14	2.93	..	1.51	1.63	2.86	Aruba
1.47	1.31	1.96	1.36	2.81	2.41	3.11	2.58	Bahamas
0.36	0.75	1.06	1.11	0.71	1.26	1.64	2.11	Barbade
0.97	0.05	0.05	0.05	1.21	0.07	0.06	0.07	Dominique
..	0.08	0.08	0.06	..	0.18	0.19	0.20	République dominicaine
0.58	0.81	0.60	0.57	0.93	1.06	0.90	1.01	Grenade
..	0.31	1.90	2.15	..	0.80	4.10	4.79	Haïti
0.55	2.00	2.99	2.53	1.12	4.05	4.23	4.94	Jamaïque
4.97	11.80	10.13	10.01	6.10	9.85	8.92	12.08	Montserrat
0.53	1.66	2.38	2.63	0.65	2.16	2.38	2.99	Antilles néerlandaises
4.38	2.27	1.13	1.09	5.27	3.01	1.58	1.69	Saint-Kitts-et-Nevis
1.07	0.47	0.45	0.45	1.39	0.75	0.55	0.67	Sainte-Lucie
1.66	1.71	1.22	1.26	2.16	2.06	1.65	1.82	Saint-Vincent-et-les Grenadines
0.43	..	..	..	1.51	..	..	..	Trinité-et-Tobago
0.25	*0.39*	*0.42*	*0.43*	*0.57*	*0.81*	*0.75*	*0.94*	*Amérique centrale*
1.76	1.27	2.16	1.71	2.88	1.75	3.06	2.92	Belize
..	0.85	0.90	0.81	..	1.95	1.63	1.93	Costa Rica
0.06	0.15	0.09	0.10	0.17	0.35	0.18	0.26	El Salvador
0.20	0.32	0.07	0.06	0.75	1.00	0.17	0.18	Guatemala
..	0.13	0.07	0.08	..	0.20	0.08	0.13	Honduras
0.36	0.19	0.85	0.93	0.52	0.27	1.13	1.49	Panama
0.12	*0.12*	*0.11*	*0.10*	*1.27*	*0.85*	*0.59*	*0.65*	*Amérique du Sud*
0.01	0.09	0.19	0.24	0.31	0.81	0.93	1.53	Argentine
0.16	0.44	0.64	0.60	0.71	1.78	1.83	2.01	Bolivie (État plurinational de)
0.00	0.06	0.07	0.06	0.04	0.51	0.54	0.57	Brésil
0.02	0.02	0.00	0.00	0.08	0.07	0.01	0.01	Chili
0.08	0.23	0.04	0.04	0.64	1.52	0.20	0.24	Colombie
0.02	0.04	0.12	0.14	0.08	0.12	0.32	0.48	Équateur
..	2.41	3.99	3.75	..	3.69	5.09	..	Guyana
0.26	0.52	0.10	0.07	1.84	2.85	0.39	0.33	Pérou
1.37	0.19	0.27	0.17	1.00	0.39	0.47	0.32	Surinamе
..	..	0.02	0.02	..	..	0.05	0.07	Uruguay
1.50	0.29	0.28	0.18	7.42	1.55	1.43	1.21	Venezuela (Rép. bolivarienne du)
1.03	**0.85**	**0.70**	**0.72**	**4.62**	**2.55**	**1.88**	**2.33**	**Économies en développement : Asie**
0.05	*0.17*	*0.20*	*0.16*	*0.30*	*0.29*	*0.47*	*0.46*	*Asie orientale*
0.00	0.07	0.13	0.09	0.01	0.31	0.47	0.40	Chine
..	0.13	0.18	0.20	..	0.10	0.09	0.11	Chine (RAS de Hong Kong)
..	..	4.45	3.34	..	..	7.49	6.81	Chine (RAS de Macao)
..	0.56	0.41	0.37	..	..	..	..	Province chinoise de Taiwan
0.13	0.18	0.33	0.37	0.48	0.50	0.59	0.78	Corée, République de
..	0.28	3.33	1.98	..	0.39	4.57	3.17	Mongolie
0.03	*0.09*	*0.28*	*0.22*	*0.29*	*0.55*	*0.93*	*0.88*	*Asie méridionale*
..	0.01	0.02	0.01	..	0.05	0.06	0.03	Bangladesh
..	..	4.90	6.59	..	..	7.98	12.12	Bhoutan
0.03	0.10	0.30	0.22	0.36	0.67	1.00	0.88	Inde
4.16	7.42	10.86	9.08	5.16	10.26	8.20	10.20	Maldives
..	0.29	0.04	0.10	..	0.93	0.12	0.24	Népal
0.00	0.00	0.00	0.00	0.01	0.02	0.00	0.02	Pakistan
..	0.12	0.95	1.02	..	0.24	2.45	3.71	Sri Lanka
0.25	*2.08*	*1.00*	*1.09*	*0.53*	*2.55*	*2.32*	*3.09*	*Asie du Sud-Est*
..	..	2.92	4.22	..	..	9.87	11.97	Brunéi Darussalam
..	2.83	2.05	1.99	..	4.59	3.05	3.12	Cambodge
—	—	0.39	0.50	—	—	1.36	2.42	Indonésie
..	0.03	0.01	..	..	0.08	0.03	..	Rép. dém. populaire lao
0.50	-	3.06	3.41	0.72	-	3.80	4.51	Malaisie (2)
..	0.19	0.18	..	..	0.56	..	..	Myanmar
0.01	0.03	0.03	0.04	0.04	0.04	0.06	0.10	Philippines
0.23	..	..	..	0.55	..	..	..	Thaïlande
8.37	*6.72*	*2.83*	*3.81*	*20.83*	*21.25*	*8.02*	*10.98*	*Asie occidentale*
7.74	12.62	8.01	7.20	8.31	19.73	10.90	12.25	Bahreïn
1.75	2.33	2.08	2.00	1.98	3.41	2.45	3.05	Jordanie
4.17	4.60	6.97	9.06	10.74	15.25	26.66	31.84	Koweït
..	..	14.59	16.65	..	..	14.69	19.20	Liban
..	0.14	0.16	0.16	..	0.18	0.20	0.19	Territoire palestinien occupé
7.40	7.46	8.59	9.89	25.60	22.85	19.48	24.59	Oman
9.62	8.17	4.57	7.17	25.57	29.08	12.28	16.33	Arabie saoudite
..	0.15	0.43	0.39	..	0.54	1.10	1.26	République arabe syrienne

Pour les sources et les notes, se reporter à la fin du tableau.

7.4.1 Migrants' remittances: Payments of countries and geographical regions

Region, country or territory	Millions of dollars - Millions de dollars							
	1990	1995	2000	2005	2006	2007	2008	2009
Turkey	..	..	..	96	107	106	111	141
Yemen	106	61	61	109	120	319	337	337
Developing economies: Oceania	**88**	**76**	**123**	**272**	**288**	**309**	**344**	**205**
Fiji	22	30	26	34	32	31	44	22
French Polynesia	..	..	..	47	51	56	69	64
Kiribati	1	..	..	..	..	..	..	..
New Caledonia	..	..	..	28	50	56	68	92
Papua New Guinea	18	19	18	135	135	135	135	..
Samoa	3	4	..	11	2	13	9	8
Solomon Islands	6	9	6	2	2	4	3	4
Tonga	1	..	..	12	13	13	14	14
Vanuatu (3)	12	18	73	3	3	3	3	..
Transition economies	**..**	**4 504**	**1 004**	**10 810**	**10 007**	**22 679**	**71 679**	**77 461**
Albania	..	..	..	7	27	10	16	10
Armenia	–	..	5	152	154	176	185	145
Azerbaijan	–	9	101	269	301	435	593	652
Belarus	–	12	58	95	93	109	141	118
Bosnia and Herzegovina	–	..	2	40	55	65	70	61
Croatia	–	..	44	62	274	87	117	99
Georgia	–	..	39	29	25	28	47	32
Kazakhstan	–	503	440	2 000	3 033	4 303	3 559	3 138
Kyrgyzstan	–	41	45	125	150	220	196	188
Montenegro							27	26
Republic of Moldova	–	1	46	68	86	87	115	104
Russian Federation (4)	–	3 938	1 099	7 008	11 467	17 763	26 145	18 613
Serbia and Montenegro (5)	–	..	..	162	120	141	–	–
Serbia	–	–	–	–	–	–	140	91
Tajikistan	–	..	..	145	395	184	199	124
TFYR of Macedonia	–	..	14	16	18	25	33	26
Ukraine	–	..	10	34	30	42	54	25
Developed economies: America	**11 850**	**22 181**	**30 961**	**40 635**	**43 791**	**47 174**	**49 011**	**48 495**
Bermuda	..	..	..	..	172	179	182	107
United States	11 850	22 181	30 961	40 635	43 620	46 995	48 829	48 308
Developed economies: Asia	**2 041**	**3 227**	**6 422**	**3 487**	**5 811**	**6 835**	**8 293**	**7 352**
Israel	850	1 407	3 255	2 206	2 334	2 798	3 550	3 283
Japan	-	1 820	3 167	1 281	3 476	4 037	4 743	4 069
Developed economies: Europe	**33 437**	**40 902**	**39 994**	**79 890**	**90 298**	**115 295**	**130 880**	**123 816**
Austria	320	346	1 298	2 567	2 575	3 008	3 505	3 377
Belgium (6)	2 310	(e)1 037	(e)868	2 754	2 698	3 204	4 062	4 278
Bulgaria	..	..	26	35	50	103	162	101
Cyprus	12	48	63	273	279	370	584	409
Czech Republic	–	101	605	1 677	1 481	2 069	2 948	2 562
Denmark	..	209	662	1 488	1 766	3 019	3 994	3 413
Estonia	–	3	3	50	75	96	105	81
Faeroe Islands	..	..	6	5	5	5	5	..
Finland	16	54	100	266	331	391	457	454
France	6 949	4 935	3 769	4 182	5 511	5 998	6 334	5 224
Germany	6 856	11 348	8 734	12 499	12 546	13 882	14 951	15 924
Greece	122	300	545	902	982	1 460	1 912	1 843
Hungary	..	146	86	915	986	1 374	1 536	1 338
Iceland	25	20	31	65	80	100	56	34
Ireland	165	173	181	1 535	1 947	2 625	2 829	2 037
Italy	3 764	1 824	2 582	7 622	8 440	11 284	12 716	12 986
Latvia	–	1	7	20	30	45	58	46
Lithuania	–	1	38	47	426	567	615	620
Luxembourg	..	2 215	2 720	6 627	7 414	9 068	10 832	10 560
Malta	25	13	14	33	46	54	64	53
Netherlands	1 393	2 802	3 122	5 928	6 610	12 635	14 908	14 212
Norway	295	603	1 060	2 174	2 620	3 642	4 776	4 174
Poland	..	262	311	602	802	1 278	1 718	1 330
Portugal	77	527	455	1 306	1 377	1 284	1 410	1 460
Romania (7)	..	2	6	(b)33	57	353	664	310
Slovakia	–	3	8	39	48	73	144	134
Slovenia	–	31	29	94	129	250	380	191
Spain	254	868	2 486	8 136	11 326	15 191	14 755	12 646
Sweden	654	336	545	814	553	741	742	787

For sources and notes, see end of table.

7.4.1 Envois de fonds des migrants : paiements des pays et des régions géographiques

As percentage of GDP En pourcentage du PIB				As percentage of imports of goods and services (1) En pourcentage des importations des biens et services (1)				Régions, pays ou territoires
1990	2000	2008	2009	1990	2000	2008	2009	
..	..	0.02	0.02	..	..	0.05	0.09	Turquie
2.28	0.60	1.17	1.25	4.90	1.84	2.88	3.37	Yémen
1.66	**2.11**	**1.25**	**1.11**	**3.06**	**3.86**	**2.14**	**2.43**	**Économies en développement : Océanie**
1.59	1.48	1.24	0.73	2.40	2.32	1.67	1.27	Fidji
..	..	1.49	1.42	..	..	2.38	2.66	Polynésie française
3.22	..	..	..	2.86			..	Kiribati
..	..	0.76	1.00	..	..	1.53	2.67	Nouvelle-Calédonie
1.30	0.53	1.68	..	2.83	1.04	2.70	..	Papouasie-Nouvelle-Guinée
2.72	..	1.57	1.62	3.21	..	2.67	2.96	Samoa
2.77	1.91	0.38	0.62	3.70	3.92	0.62	1.30	Îles Salomon
1.04	..	3.98	3.99	1.64	..	6.17	7.17	Tonga
0.95	23.07	0.42	..	12.03	49.39	..	..	Vanuatu (3)
..	**0.52**	**1.38**	**1.35**	**..**	**1.61**	**4.74**	**5.10**	**Économies en transition**
..	..	0.12	0.08	..	..	0.22	0.15	Albanie
_	0.26	1.60	1.70	_	0.10	3.00	3.01	Arménie
_	1.91	1.21	1.52	_	4.99	5.17	6.60	Azerbaïdjan
_	0.56	0.23	0.24	_	0.72	0.34	0.39	Bélarus
_	0.04	0.38	0.36	_	0.06	0.54	0.64	Bosnie-Herzégovine
_	0.21	0.17	0.16	_	0.46	0.33	0.40	Croatie
_	1.27	0.37	0.29	_	3.27	0.62	0.60	Géorgie
_	2.41	2.67	2.87	_	4.91	7.18	8.04	Kazakhstan
_	3.31	3.82	4.10	_	6.93	4.14	5.10	Kirghizistan
_	_	0.61	0.63	_	_	0.65	0.94	Monténégro
_	3.57	1.91	1.92	_	4.73	2.02	2.61	République de Moldova
_	0.42	1.57	1.51	_	1.80	7.12	7.35	Fédération de Russie (4)
_	..			_	_	_	_	Serbie-et-Monténégro (5)
_		0.26	0.19	_		_	_	Serbie
_	..	6.40	2.48	_	..	4.79	4.04	Tadjikistan
_	0.40	0.34	0.28	_	0.62	0.44	0.46	LERY de Macédoine
_	0.03	0.03	0.02	_	0.06	0.05	0.04	Ukraine
0.20	**0.31**	**0.34**	**0.34**	**1.92**	**2.14**	**1.93**	**2.48**	**Économies développées : Amérique**
..	..	2.99	2.84	..	..	8.27	9.11	Bermudes
0.20	0.31	0.34	0.34	1.92	2.14	1.92	2.47	États-Unis
0.07	**0.13**	**0.16**	**0.14**	**0.64**	**1.27**	**0.86**	**1.03**	**Économies développées : Asie**
1.49	2.61	1.76	1.69	4.20	6.98	4.21	5.20	Israël
-	0.07	0.10	0.08	-	0.69	0.54	0.63	Japon
0.46	**0.45**	**0.68**	**0.72**	**1.71**	**1.23**	**1.65**	**2.01**	**Économies développées : Europe**
0.19	0.68	0.85	0.89	0.52	1.52	1.57	1.92	Autriche
1.14	(e)0.37	0.80	0.91	..	..	0.94	1.30	Belgique (6)
..	0.20	0.31	0.21	..	0.34	0.39	0.37	Bulgarie
0.21	0.67	2.31	1.74	0.38	1.22	3.59	3.33	Chypre
_	1.07	1.36	1.35	_	1.61	1.87	2.13	République tchèque
..	0.41	1.17	1.10	..	1.03	2.26	2.53	Danemark
_	0.05	0.45	0.42	_	0.06	0.55	0.65	Estonie
..	..	..	..	..	0.94	..	..	Îles Féroé
0.01	0.08	0.17	0.19	0.05	0.25	0.39	0.53	Finlande
0.56	0.28	0.22	0.20	2.45	1.03	0.76	0.78	France
0.40	0.46	0.41	0.48	1.61	1.39	0.98	1.30	Allemagne
0.13	0.43	0.55	0.57	0.62	1.31	1.60	2.19	Grèce
..	0.18	0.99	1.04	..	0.24	1.21	1.43	Hongrie
0.39	0.36	0.34	0.28	1.19	0.87	0.69	0.63	Islande
0.35	0.19	1.07	0.92	0.67	0.23	1.45	1.22	Irlande
0.33	0.24	0.55	0.61	1.72	0.90	1.88	2.52	Italie
_	0.08	0.17	0.18	_	0.17	0.31	0.40	Lettonie
_	0.33	1.30	1.68	_	0.65	1.80	3.00	Lituanie
..	13.42	18.66	19.98	..	..	15.93	19.42	Luxembourg
0.97	0.36	0.76	0.66	1.09	0.35	0.83	0.83	Malte
0.47	0.81	1.71	1.79	0.94	1.31	2.63	3.10	Pays-Bas
0.25	0.63	1.07	1.10	0.76	2.14	3.61	4.01	Norvège
..	0.18	0.32	0.31	..	0.54	0.72	0.76	Pologne
0.10	0.39	0.56	0.63	0.28	0.96	1.30	1.74	Portugal
..	0.02	0.32	0.19	..	0.04	0.74	0.51	Roumanie (7)
_	0.04	0.15	0.15	_	0.05	0.18	0.22	Slovaquie
_	0.15	0.69	0.39	_	0.26	0.98	0.68	Slovénie
0.05	0.43	0.93	0.86	0.25	1.34	2.85	3.37	Espagne
0.27	0.22	0.15	0.19	0.93	0.56	0.33	0.48	Suède

Pour les sources et les notes, se reporter à la fin du tableau.

7.4.1 Migrants' remittances:
Payments of countries and geographical regions

Region, country or territory	Millions of dollars - Millions de dollars							
	1990	1995	2000	2005	2006	2007	2008	2009
Switzerland	8 168	10 114	7 591	13 324	14 377	16 292	19 022	19 562
United Kingdom	2 034	2 581	2 044	3 877	4 732	4 834	4 637	3 670
Developed economies: Oceania	**1 041**	**1 128**	**1 512**	**3 365**	**3 732**	**4 299**	**4 360**	**3 977**
Australia	674	700	1 053	2 375	2 814	3 024	3 049	3 000
New Zealand	367	427	459	991	918	1 275	1 312	977

Sources:
- IMF, *Balance of Payments Statistics*
  World Bank, *Migration and Remittances*
- National sources
- Economist Intelligence Unit, *Country Data*

Notes:

-    Migrants' remittances data cover: workers' remittances, compensation of employees and migrants' transfers.
- (1)   Exports and imports of goods and services data are based on IMF balance-of-payments statistics.
- (2)   Payments (debits), breaks in series: for years 1985-1994 and 1999-2001 inclusive, data include compensation of employees only; workers' remittances were not available. Migrants' transfers are not available after 1994 neither.
- (3)   Year 2002: break in series; migrants' transfers data are no longer available starting with 2002.
- (4)   Workers' remittances and compensation of employees: From 1995 to 2000 (inclusive), data represent compensation of employees only; workers' remittances are available starting from 2001 onwards. Total remittances (including migrants transfers) reflect the same break in series.
- (5)   Covers Serbia only.
- (6)   Data up to 1994 inclusive refer to Belgium-Luxembourg Economic Union. From 1995, the figures cover Belgium only.
- (7)   Year 2005: break in series; change in classification.

7.4.1 Envois de fonds des migrants :
paiements des pays et des régions géographiques

As percentage of GDP En pourcentage du PIB				As percentage of imports of goods and services (1) En pourcentage des importations des biens et services (1)				Régions, pays ou territoires
1990	2000	2008	2009	1990	2000	2008	2009	
3.41	3.01	3.75	3.94	8.47	7.07	7.20	8.02	Suisse
0.20	0.14	0.17	0.17	0.77	0.47	0.55	0.56	Royaume-Uni
0.28	**0.33**	**0.37**	**0.35**	**1.61**	**1.44**	**1.53**	**1.71**	**Économies développées : Océanie**
0.20	0.26	0.29	0.30	1.27	1.20	1.26	1.49	Australie
0.83	0.86	1.01	0.84	3.13	2.65	3.08	3.06	Nouvelle-Zélande

Sources :
- FMI, *Statistiques de la balance des paiements*
- Banque mondiale, *Migration and Remittances*
- Sources nationales
- Economist Intelligence Unit, *Country Data*

Notes :

- Les envois de fonds des migrants couvrent : les envois de fonds des travailleurs, la rémunération des employées et les transferts des migrants.

(1) Les données sur les exportations et importations des biens et services se basent sur les statistiques de la balance des paiements du FMI.

(2) Paiements (débits), ruptures de série : pour les années 1985-1994 et 1999-2001, incluses, les données comprennent seulement la rémunération des salariés ; les envois de fonds des travailleurs ne sont pas disponibles. Les transferts des migrants ne sont également pas disponibles après 1994.

(3) Année 2002 : rupture de série ; les données sur les transferts des migrants ne sont plus disponibles à partir de 2002.

(4) L'envoi de fonds des travailleurs et la rémunération des salariés : De 1995 à 2000 (incluses), les données comprennent seulement la rémunération des salariés ; les envois de fonds des travailleurs ne sont disponibles qu'à partir de l'année 2001. Le total des envois de fonds (y compris les transferts des migrants) présentent la même rupture de série.

(5) Couvre uniquement la Serbie.

(6) Jusqu'à l'année 1994 comprise, les données se réfèrent à l'Union économique belgo-luxembourgoise. A partir de 1995, les chiffres couvrent uniquement la Belgique.

(7) Année 2005 : rupture de série ; changement des méthodes de classification.

7.4.2 Migrants' remittances: Payments of economic groupings

Economic grouping	Millions of dollars - Millions de dollars							
	1990	1995	2000	2005	2006	2007	2008	2009
DEVELOPING ECONOMIES	**18 835**	**28 272**	**33 513**	**49 473**	**55 341**	**64 954**	**81 308**	**83 158**
Developing economies excluding China	18 830	28 272	32 723	46 870	52 316	60 582	75 572	78 714
Developing economies excluding LDCs	18 017	27 556	32 132	47 983	53 493	62 468	78 501	80 569
High-income developing countries	15 068	24 320	27 703	38 027	41 927	48 036	60 051	65 082
Middle-income developing countries	2 197	2 310	3 503	6 426	7 503	9 581	11 349	9 492
Low-income developing countries	1 570	1 618	2 308	5 020	5 911	7 336	9 909	8 584
Heavily indebted poor countries (IMF)	1 188	825	1 388	1 826	2 041	2 493	2 734	1 660
Landlocked developing countries	460	939	1 407	3 589	5 100	6 402	6 174	5 561
Small island developing States	230	277	474	614	808	1 011	1 010	888
Least developed countries	*818*	*716*	*1 381*	*1 490*	*1 848*	*2 486*	*2 807*	*2 589*
Africa and Haiti	684	550	1 101	1 089	1 357	1 862	2 113	1 922
Asia	106	131	200	384	484	604	680	654
Islands	27	35	80	16	8	20	14	13
Major petroleum and gas exporters	*14 184*	*20 124*	*19 637*	*20 628*	*23 652*	*31 948*	*39 752*	*44 419*
Africa	636	436	730	1 197	1 459	1 419	1 692	2 143
America	701	203	331	211	257	649	860	581
Asia	12 847	19 485	18 576	19 220	21 936	29 880	37 200	41 695
Major exporters of manufactured goods	*798*	*3 559*	*7 462*	*13 380*	*14 737*	*14 007*	*17 664*	*15 923*
Asia	798	3 559	7 462	13 380	14 737	14 007	17 664	15 923
Emerging economies	*908*	*4 142*	*7 371*	*11 385*	*12 520*	*10 752*	*13 494*	*12 915*
America	115	583	925	957	1 185	1 505	1 960	1 849
Asia	793	3 559	6 447	10 429	11 335	9 247	11 534	11 066
Newly industrialized Asian countries	*798*	*3 710*	*6 693*	*11 971*	*13 091*	*11 324*	*13 943*	*14 239*
First tier	364	2 230	3 028	5 097	6 115	3 223	5 142	4 950
Second tier	434	1 480	3 665	6 873	6 976	8 101	8 801	9 288
Developing economies: Africa	**3 407**	**2 530**	**3 091**	**4 330**	**4 828**	**5 296**	**5 879**	**5 053**
Northern Africa excluding Sudan	532	501	551	1 027	1 137	1 009	1 279	1 690
Sub-Saharan Africa	2 874	2 028	2 539	3 303	3 691	4 287	4 600	3 363
Sub-Saharan Africa excluding South Africa	1 675	1 399	1 854	2 248	2 624	3 101	3 467	2 205
Developing economies: America	**1 067**	**1 234**	**2 239**	**2 643**	**3 054**	**4 038**	**4 697**	**4 177**
Central America and Greater Caribbean Islands excluding Puerto Rico	72	152	469	878	979	1 071	1 121	1 024
Central America and Greater Caribbean Islands excluding Mexico and Puerto Rico	72	152	469	878	979	1 071	1 121	1 024
South America and Central America	924	1 034	1 807	1 795	2 163	3 034	3 719	3 340
South America excluding Brazil	866	616	1 181	913	1 007	1 645	1 978	1 791
Developing economies: Asia	**14 273**	**24 433**	**28 061**	**42 229**	**47 170**	**55 311**	**70 389**	**73 723**
Eastern and South-Eastern Asia excluding China	798	3 771	6 814	12 820	14 272	12 901	15 759	15 689
Southern Asia excluding India	9	56	89	401	527	489	596	660

For sources and notes, see end of table 7.4.1.

As percentage of GDP En pourcentage du PIB				As percentage of imports of goods and services En pourcentage des importations des biens et services				Groupements économiques
1990	2000	2008	2009	1990	2000	2008	2009	
0.72	0.64	0.56	0.58	3.68	2.23	1.64	2.03	ÉCONOMIES EN DÉVELOPPEMENT
0.85	0.81	0.75	0.83	4.05	2.65	2.04	2.65	Économies en développement sans la Chine
0.71	0.63	0.56	0.57	3.66	2.21	1.64	2.03	Économies en développement sans les PMA
2.06	1.44	1.41	1.71	7.25	3.70	3.02	4.04	Pays en développement à revenu élevé
0.16	0.14	0.15	0.12	0.98	0.63	0.54	0.54	Pays en développement à revenu intermédiaire
0.29	0.29	0.37	0.34	1.96	1.42	1.14	1.23	Pays en développement à revenu faible
1.23	1.12	0.80	0.77	4.98	3.53	2.03	2.02	Pays pauvres très endettés (FMI)
1.15	1.63	1.69	1.76	3.78	4.20	4.26	4.91	Pays en développement sans littoral
0.90	1.47	1.79	1.54	1.83	2.63	2.56	2.66	Petits États insulaires en développement
1.09	0.85	0.66	0.83	4.09	2.88	1.60	1.90	*Pays les moins avancés*
0.99	1.26	0.79	1.14	3.95	4.00	1.74	2.14	Afrique et Haïti
2.28	0.27	0.44	0.46	4.90	0.99	1.27	1.43	Asie
3.00	11.46	0.70	0.93	5.30	22.81	1.38	1.85	Îles
4.28	4.31	3.01	3.95	15.22	17.11	9.13	11.65	*Principaux exportateurs de pétrole et de gaz*
0.46	0.78	0.51	0.80	2.17	3.21	1.27	1.81	Afrique
1.50	0.29	0.28	0.18	7.42	1.55	1.43	1.21	Amérique
8.76	7.56	5.44	7.83	23.62	26.29	15.37	19.41	Asie
0.10	0.32	0.29	0.24	0.42	0.73	0.68	0.71	*Principaux exportateurs d'articles manufacturés*
0.10	0.32	0.29	0.24	0.42	0.73	0.68	0.71	Asie
0.09	0.37	0.35	0.36	0.47	1.31	1.08	1.36	*Économies émergentes*
0.02	0.09	0.09	0.09	0.24	0.67	0.50	0.62	Amérique
0.20	0.68	0.74	0.79	0.55	1.61	1.40	1.77	Asie
0.18	0.56	0.57	0.62	0.50	0.85	0.91	1.16	*Économies nouvellement industrialisées d'Asie*
0.13	0.29	0.33	0.35	0.48	0.28	0.36	0.45	Première génération
0.25	2.16	0.98	1.04	0.53	2.56	2.24	2.98	Deuxième génération
0.74	0.59	0.46	0.46	2.98	2.12	1.07	1.25	Économies en développement : Afrique
0.31	0.28	0.34	0.45	1.13	1.11	0.77	1.21	Afrique septentrionale sans le Soudan
1.01	0.78	0.51	0.46	4.28	2.64	1.22	1.27	Afrique subsaharienne
0.96	0.96	0.55	0.49	3.63	2.93	1.29	1.20	Afrique subsaharienne sans l'Afrique du Sud
0.14	0.16	0.15	0.14	1.24	0.93	0.71	0.80	Économies en développement : Amérique
0.31	0.46	0.57	0.53	0.70	0.97	1.08	1.26	Amérique centrale et Grandes Antilles sans Porto Rico
0.31	0.46	0.57	0.53	0.70	0.97	1.08	1.26	Amérique centrale et Grandes Antilles sans le Mexique et Porto Rico
0.12	0.13	0.12	0.11	1.20	0.85	0.61	0.69	Amérique du Sud et Amérique centrale
0.27	0.18	0.15	0.14	2.12	1.09	0.62	0.71	Amérique du Sud sans le Brésil
1.03	0.85	0.70	0.72	4.62	2.55	1.88	2.33	Économies en développement : Asie
0.18	0.56	0.62	0.66	0.50	0.86	1.02	1.26	Asie orientale et Asie du Sud-Est sans la Chine
0.02	0.06	0.21	0.21	0.09	0.28	0.62	0.86	Asie méridionale sans l'Inde

Pour les sources et les notes, se reporter à la fin du tableau 7.4.1.

7

Region, country or territory	Total reserves including gold (1) - Réserves totales, y compris l'or (1) Millions of dollars - Millions de dollars							
	1980	1990	2000	2005	2007	2008	2009	2010
DEVELOPING ECONOMIES	177 117	330 903	1 056 881	2 694 521	4 500 557	5 153 837	5 958 165	6 802 993
Developing economies: Africa	**36 550**	**27 978**	**79 915**	**220 397**	**399 304**	**457 282**	**474 626**	**494 399**
Eastern Africa	*1 788*	*2 326*	*6 017*	*10 735*	*16 632*	*15 914*	*21 604*	*23 418*
Burundi	95	106	34	100	176	266	322	331
Comoros	6	30	43	86	117	112	150	145
Djibouti	-	94	68	89	132	175	242	249
Eritrea			27	28	34	58	-	
Ethiopia			316	1 043	1 290	871	1 781	(e)1 631
Ethiopia (former)	94	25						
Kenya	495	209	898	1 799	3 355	2 879	3 849	4 320
Madagascar	9	92	285	481	847	982	1 135	1 172
Malawi	69	138	244	160	217	243	150	-
Mauritius	92	741	900	1 343	1 784	1 746	2 186	2 449
Mozambique	-	232	726	1 059	1 450	1 583	2 103	2 163
Rwanda	196	44	191	406	553	596	743	813
Seychelles	18	17	44	56	41	64	191	236
Somalia	26	..	..		..	..	..	
Uganda	3	44	808	1 344	2 560	2 301	2 994	2 960
United Republic of Tanzania	20	193	974	2 049	2 886	2 863	3 470	3 905
Zambia	88	194	245	560	1 090	1 096	1 892	2 094
Zimbabwe	229	168	214	(e)133	(e)100	(e)80	(e)291	(e)312
Middle Africa	*2 344*	*2 401*	*2 187*	*8 176*	*22 613*	*32 791*	*28 319*	*39 022*
Angola	-	-	1 198	3 197	11 197	17 869	13 664	19 665
Cameroon	190	27	213	951	2 908	3 088	3 677	(e)4 084
Central African Republic	55	119	134	140	83	122	211	(e)246
Chad	6	128	111	226	956	1 346	617	-
Congo	86	6	223	732	2 175	3 872	3 807	-
Dem. Rep. of the Congo	217	224	83	131	181	78	1 035	1 300
Equatorial Guinea	-	1	23	2 102	3 846	4 431	3 252	(e)3 786
Gabon	108	274	191	669	1 228	1 924	1 994	(e)2 632
Sao Tome and Principe	1	0	12	27	39	-	-	-
Northern Africa	*19 482*	*12 721*	*44 993*	*139 591*	*254 012*	*300 856*	*316 012*	*330 046*
Algeria	4 022	981	12 278	56 582	110 626	143 544	149 347	162 915
Egypt	1 155	2 005	13 220	20 731	30 322	32 347	32 386	33 743
Libyan Arab Jamahiriya	13 228	6 018	12 672	39 739	79 660	92 563	99 279	99 895
Morocco	430	2 102	4 855	16 223	24 162	22 142	22 836	22 651
Sudan	49	11	138	1 869	1 378	1 399	1 094	-
Tunisia	598	804	1 821	4 448	7 863	8 861	11 069	9 471
Southern Africa	*1 811*	*4 912*	*13 700*	*26 163*	*42 227*	*42 961*	*48 159*	*49 676*
Botswana	334	3 331	6 318	6 309	9 790	9 119	8 704	7 885
Lesotho	50	72	418	519	(e)958	(e)998	(e)988	(e)948
Namibia	..	80	260	312	896	1 293	2 051	1 696
South Africa	1 268	1 212	6 352	18 779	29 810	30 800	35 458	38 392
Swaziland	159	216	352	244	774	752	959	756
Western Africa	*11 125*	*5 618*	*13 019*	*35 732*	*63 820*	*64 760*	*60 532*	*52 236*
Benin	9	65	459	657	1 209	1 263	1 230	(e)1 246
Burkina Faso	69	301	244	438	1 029	928	1 296	(e)1 718
Cape Verde	42	77	28	165	364	361	366	(e)392
Côte d'Ivoire	22	6	674	1 367	2 519	2 253	3 267	(e)3 590
Gambia	6	55	109	98	143	117	224	202
Ghana	192	231	245	1 767	-	-	-	-
Guinea	-	-	151	95	85	-	-	-
Guinea-Bissau	-	18	67	80	113	125	169	-
Liberia	5	-	0	25	119	161	372	-
Mali	15	191	382	855	1 087	1 072	1 604	(e)1 810
Mauritania	140	55	47	65	198	189	226	(e)280
Niger	126	223	81	251	593	705	656	(e)764
Nigeria	10 265	3 899	9 942	28 314	51 372	53 039	44 800	34 956
Senegal	9	12	388	1 191	1 660	1 602	2 123	(e)2 200
Sierra Leone	31	5	49	171	217	220	405	(e)354
Togo	78	354	152	195	438	582	703	(e)700
Developing economies: America	**40 316**	**49 202**	**157 762**	**258 926**	**451 167**	**502 850**	**553 941**	**638 433**
Caribbean	*3 445*	*1 712*	*5 471*	*14 475*	*19 599*	*21 526*	*23 725*	*25 996*
Anguilla	..	7	20	40	45	41	37	40
Antigua and Barbuda	8	28	64	127	144	138	128	137
Aruba	..	103	213	279	378	610	584	574
Bahamas	92	158	350	586	464	568	1 010	1 044
Barbados	79	118	473	603	839	739	875	834
Cuba	..	(e)198	(e)543	(e)2 747	(e)4 947	(e)4 047	(e)4 647	(e)4 847
Dominica	5	14	29	49	61	55	75	76
Dominican Republic	208	62	628	1 844	2 547	2 273	2 886	3 477
Grenada	13	18	58	94	111	105	129	119

For sources and notes, see end of table.

Annual change in reserves (millions of dollars) Variations annuelles des réserves (millions de dollars)				Number of months of imports (2) Nombre de mois d'importations (2)								Régions, pays ou territoires
2007	2008	2009	2010	1980	1990	2000	2005	2007	2008	2009	2010	
1 139 727	653 281	804 328	844 828	4.4	5.0	6.6	9.5	11.5	10.9	15.5	13.8	ÉCONOMIES EN DÉVELOPPEMENT
94 127	57 978	17 344	19 773	4.6	3.6	7.4	10.3	13.0	11.7	13.8	13.2	Économies en développement : Afrique
4 369	-718	5 690	1 814	2.0	2.2	4.4	4.1	4.6	3.3	5.0	4.7	Afrique orientale
46	89	56	9	6.8	5.5	2.7	4.5	6.6	7.9	9.6	7.8	Burundi
24	-5	38	-5	2.6	6.9	12.0	10.4	10.2	7.7	10.6	9.4	Comores
12	43	00	7	-	5.2	3.9	3.9	3.4	3.7	6.4	7.2	Djibouti
9	24	-	-			0.7	0.7	0.8	1.2	-	-	Érythrée
422	-419	910	(e)50	_	_	3.0	3.1	2.7	1.2	2.7	(e)2.3	Éthiopie
				1.6	0.3	_	_	_	_	_	_	Éthiopie (anc.)
939	-476	970	471	2.8	1.1	3.5	3.5	4.5	3.1	4.5	4.5	Kenya
203	136	153	36	0.1	2.0	3.4	3.4	4.2	3.1	4.3	5.1	Madagascar
83	26	03	-	1.0	2.9	5.5	1.0	1.9	1.3	0.9	-	Malawi
511	-38	440	263	1.8	5.5	4.9	5.1	5.5	4.5	7.0	6.7	Maurice
289	133	521	60	-	3.2	7.5	5.3	5.7	4.7	6.7	7.3	Mozambique
113	43	146	70	9.0	1.9	10.7	11.3	9.0	6.1	7.4	7.0	Rwanda
-72	23	127	45	2.2	1.1	1.5	1.0	0.6	0.7	2.8	2.9	Seychelles
..	..	..	..	0.7	..	..	..	..	..	..	..	Somalie
749	-259	694	-34	0.1	1.8	6.3	7.9	8.8	6.1	8.5	7.4	Ouganda
627	-23	608	434	0.2	1.7	7.7	7.5	6.5	4.9	6.6	6.1	République-Unie de Tanzanie
370	6	796	202	1.0	1.9	3.3	2.6	3.3	2.6	6.0	4.7	Zambie
(e)-17	(e)-20	(e)212	(e)21	2.0	1.1	1.4	(e)0.7	(e)0.5	(e)0.3	(e)1.2	(e)1.0	Zimbabwe
5 334	10 178	-4 473	10 704	4.8	4.1	3.4	5.2	8.9	9.3	7.8	11.7	Afrique centrale
2 598	6 673	-4 205	6 001	-	-	4.7	4.6	9.8	10.2	7.2	14.2	Angola
1 191	180	589	(e)407	1.4	0.2	1.7	4.2	8.3	6.8	10.0	(e)9.9	Cameroun
-43	39	89	(e)35	8.2	9.3	13.7	9.7	4.0	4.9	9.4	(e)9.4	République centrafricaine
330	390	-729	-	0.9	3.1	4.2	2.9	6.4	8.5	3.3	-	Tchad
333	1 697	-66	-	1.8	0.1	5.6	5.9	10.3	15.2	15.7	-	Congo
26	-103	958	264	1.7	1.5	1.4	0.7	0.7	0.2	3.8	4.0	Rép. dém. du Congo
779	585	-1 179	(e)534	-	0.1	0.5	19.3	16.7	14.2	7.5	(e)8.0	Guinée équatoriale
114	696	70	(e)638	1.9	3.6	2.4	5.5	6.7	9.1	10.9	(e)12.6	Gabon
5	-	-	-	0.7	0.0	4.7	6.4	6.0	-	-	-	Sao Tomé-et-Principe
62 860	46 844	15 157	14 034	7.4	4.1	11.1	19.3	25.1	20.8	24.3	23.1	Afrique septentrionale
32 419	32 918	5 803	13 568	4.6	1.2	16.1	33.4	48.0	43.6	45.7	48.6	Algérie
5 733	2 025	39	1 357	2.9	3.7	11.4	12.6	13.4	8.0	8.7	7.7	Égypte
20 128	12 902	6 717	615	23.4	13.5	41.1	78.7	141.6	121.8	117.4	114.2	Jamahiriya arabe libyenne
3 784	-2 020	694	-185	1.2	3.6	5.1	9.4	9.1	6.3	8.3	7.7	Maroc
-282	21	-305	-	0.4	0.2	1.1	3.3	1.9	1.8	1.4	-	Soudan
1 078	998	2 208	-1 598	2.0	1.8	2.6	4.1	4.9	4.3	6.9	5.1	Tunisie
9 487	734	5 199	1 517	1.0	2.6	4.6	4.3	5.0	4.7	6.5	6.5	Afrique australe
1 797	-671	-415	-819	5.8	20.5	36.4	23.4	28.9	21.0	22.1	16.7	Botswana
(e)299	(e)40	(e)-10	(e)-40	1.4	1.3	6.2	4.4	(e)6.6	(e)5.9	(e)6.2	(e)5.2	Lesotho
446	397	758	-355	..	0.8	2.0	1.4	3.2	3.4	5.0	3.6	Namibie
6 542	990	4 658	2 934	0.8	0.8	2.5	3.5	4.0	3.8	5.7	6.0	Afrique du Sud
402	-22	207	-203	3.0	3.9	4.0	1.4	3.8	4.1	5.6	4.1	Swaziland
12 078	941	-4 229	-8 295	5.2	4.7	7.4	9.3	10.8	9.2	9.8	7.4	Afrique occidentale
297	54	-34	(e)16	0.3	3.0	9.0	7.7	7.1	6.6	7.1	(e)6.8	Bénin
474	-102	368	(e)422	2.3	6.7	4.8	4.2	7.4	5.5	8.3	(e)9.5	Burkina Faso
120	-3	5	(e)25	7.5	6.8	1.5	4.5	5.8	5.3	6.2	(e)6.3	Cap-Vert
721	-266	1 014	(e)323	0.1	0.0	3.3	2.8	4.5	3.4	5.6	(e)6.2	Côte d'Ivoire
22	-26	108	-23	0.4	3.5	7.0	5.0	5.6	4.2	8.9	8.1	Gambie
-	-	-	-	2.0	2.3	1.0	3.7	-	-	-	-	Ghana
-12	-	-	-	-	-	3.0	1.4	0.9	-	-	-	Guinée
31	12	44	-	-	2.6	13.5	7.8	7.1	6.6	8.6	-	Guinée-Bissau
47	42	212	-	0.1	-	0.0	0.9	2.7	2.3	7.9	-	Libéria
118	-16	533	(e)206	0.4	3.8	5.7	6.6	6.0	3.9	7.9	(e)7.3	Mali
11	-9	37	(e)54	5.9	3.0	1.2	0.5	1.5	1.2	1.9	(e)1.7	Mauritanie
222	112	-50	(e)108	2.6	6.9	2.5	3.2	6.2	5.4	3.3	(e)3.2	Niger
9 037	1 667	-8 238	-9 844	7.4	8.3	13.7	15.9	16.4	15.0	13.8	9.5	Nigéria
326	-58	521	(e)77	0.1	0.1	3.0	4.1	4.1	2.9	5.4	(e)5.5	Sénégal
33	4	185	(e)-51	0.9	0.4	4.0	5.9	5.8	5.0	9.3	(e)5.5	Sierra Leone
64	144	121	(e)-3	1.7	7.3	3.3	2.0	3.6	4.5	5.6	(e)5.1	Togo
136 172	51 683	51 091	84 492	4.1	4.6	4.8	5.8	7.2	6.5	9.7	8.6	Économies en développement : Amérique
1 953	1 927	2 199	2 271	2.0	1.1	2.0	4.2	4.4	3.8	6.0	5.9	Caraïbes
3	-4	-4	2	..	..	2.6	3.7	2.2	1.8	2.7	3.0	Anguilla
1	-6	-10	9	1.1	1.3	1.9	2.8	2.4	2.2	2.4	2.6	Antigua-et-Barbuda
35	233	-27	-10	..	2.1	1.0	1.0	1.6	1.7	3.6	5.1	Aruba
3	103	442	34	0.1	1.7	2.0	2.7	1.8	2.1	4.5	4.4	Bahamas
203	-101	136	-41	1.8	2.0	4.9	4.5	5.9	4.7	7.1	6.4	Barbade
(e)1 200	(e)- 900	(e)600	(e)200	..	(e)0.4	(e)1.3	(e)4.1	(e)5.5	(e)3.2	(e)5.8	(e)5.1	Cuba
-3	-5	20	1	1.3	1.5	2.4	3.6	3.7	2.7	4.0	3.8	Dominique
431	-275	614	591	1.3	0.2	0.8	2.2	2.2	1.7	2.8	2.7	République dominicaine
11	-5	24	-10	3.1	2.0	2.9	3.4	3.6	3.5	5.5	5.0	Grenade

Pour les sources et les notes, se reporter à la fin du tableau.

Region, country or territory	Total reserves including gold (1) - Réserves totales, y compris l'or (1) Millions of dollars - Millions de dollars							
	1980	1990	2000	2005	2007	2008	2009	2010
Haiti	17	4	182	133	452	541	789	1 294
Jamaica	105	(e)168	1 054	2 170	1 879	1 773	2 080	2 501
Montserrat	..	10	10	14	14	12	14	17
Netherlands Antilles	119	242	280	566	684	842	890	-
Saint Kitts and Nevis	..	16	45	72	96	110	136	169
Saint Lucia	8	45	79	116	154	143	175	206
Saint Vincent and the Grenadines	7	26	55	70	87	84	88	113
Trinidad and Tobago	2 783	495	1 389	4 964	6 697	9 446	9 181	(e)9 659
Central America	*4 116*	*11 728*	*43 037*	*86 124*	*103 171*	*112 070*	*118 431*	*140 538*
Belize	13	70	123	71	109	166	214	218
Costa Rica	149	521	1 318	2 313	4 114	3 799	4 066	4 627
El Salvador	101	438	1 794	1 739	2 123	2 456	2 882	2 582
Guatemala	468	292	1 756	3 675	4 142	4 474	4 976	5 649
Honduras	151	41	1 314	2 328	2 529	2 475	2 088	2 672
Mexico	3 052	9 905	35 328	74 000	87 110	95 107	90 991	120 070
Nicaragua	65	113	489	728	1 103	1 141	1 573	1 799
Panama, excl. Canal Zone (former)	117	_	_			_	_	
Panama	_	344	723	1 211	1 935	2 424	3 028	2 714
South America	*32 756*	*35 762*	*109 254*	*158 327*	*328 397*	*369 254*	*411 786*	*471 899*
Argentina (3)	6 915	4 803	25 148	27 267	44 779	44 950	46 190	49 829
Bolivia (Plurinational State of)	140	211	969	1 373	4 604	6 976	7 634	8 195
Brazil	5 853	7 668	32 531	53 299	179 493	192 902	237 424	287 114
Chile	3 199	6 161	15 038	16 930	16 837	23 073	25 284	27 817
Colombia	4 955	4 659	8 931	14 803	20 779	23 491	24 760	27 778
Ecuador	1 031	861	985	1 757	2 863	3 784	2 920	1 480
Guyana	13	29	305	252	313	356	631	782
Paraguay	763	663	764	1 297	2 461	2 846	3 840	4 138
Peru	2 042	1 150	8 424	13 655	26 918	30 332	32 074	42 708
Suriname	192	24	75	127	403	476	662	642
Uruguay	537	643	2 528	3 074	4 115	6 353	8 029	7 645
Venezuela (Bolivarian Rep. of)	7 116	8 891	13 555	24 493	24 830	33 716	22 339	13 771
Developing economies: Asia	**99 596**	**252 901**	**818 230**	**2 213 821**	**3 647 062**	**4 191 030**	**4 925 855**	**5 665 611**
Eastern Asia	*13 441*	*143 242*	*483 419*	*1 418 060*	*2 231 274*	*2 642 887*	*3 312 233*	*3 836 728*
China	3 117	30 219	168 857	822 479	1 531 349	1 950 305	2 417 911	2 867 905
China, Hong Kong SAR	(e)5 041	24 579	107 545	124 247	152 641	182 473	255 772	268 641
China, Macao SAR	..	521	3 323	6 689	13 230	15 930	18 350	23 726
China, Taiwan Province of	2 345	73 115	107 360	253 971	271 063	292 442	348 946	382 739
Korea, Republic of	2 938	14 809	96 150	210 340	262 176	201 170	269 958	291 515
Mongolia	..	..	183	333	815	567	1 296	2 200
Southern Asia	*19 546*	*9 587*	*56 683*	*197 283*	*377 922*	*367 124*	*382 272*	*392 258*
Afghanistan	414	314	-	-	-	-	-	-
Bangladesh	302	633	1 491	2 773	5 190	5 695	10 225	10 588
Bhutan	-	89	318	467	699	765	891	-
India	7 327	2 053	38 427	132 500	267 625	248 039	266 166	276 243
Iran (Islamic Rep. of)	10 417	5 351	12 426	(e)45 459	(e)82 059	(e)96 559	(e)81 309	(e)75 060
Maldives	1	24	123	189	308	244	276	364
Nepal	190	303	952	1 505	-	-	-	-
Pakistan	577	393	1 609	10 138	14 160	7 308	11 434	14 457
Sri Lanka	248	426	1 054	2 658	3 389	2 478	4 653	6 728
South-Eastern Asia	*21 461*	*60 508*	*187 458*	*298 069*	*464 014*	*488 599*	*546 870*	*676 342*
Brunei Darussalam	..	..	408	492	667	751	1 357	-
Cambodia	..	..	520	973	1 829	2 313	2 873	3 277
Indonesia including East Timor	5 499	7 614	28 643	_	_	_	_	_
Indonesia	_	_	_	33 296	55 106	49 723	63 692	93 035
Lao People's Dem. Rep.	..	2	139	234	533	629	703	796
Malaysia	4 491	9 871	28 383	69 916	101 084	91 212	95 496	104 947
Myanmar	272	325	234	782	(e)2 312	(e)3 412	(e)3 561	(e)3 762
Philippines	2 932	1 068	13 420	16 174	30 445	33 460	39 056	55 630
Singapore	6 567	27 790	80 170	116 172	162 957	174 192	187 803	225 714
Thailand	1 671	13 428	32 124	50 826	85 371	108 807	135 631	167 703
Timor-Leste	_	_	_	153	230	210	250	406
Viet Nam	-	409	3 417	9 051	23 479	23 890	16 447	-
Western Asia	*45 147*	*39 564*	*90 671*	*300 408*	*573 852*	*692 419*	*684 481*	*760 284*
Bahrain	960	1 242	1 571	-	-	-	-	-
Iraq	-	-	-	12 114	31 308	50 053	46 266	50 387
Jordan (4)	1 188	886	3 350	5 271	7 567	8 584	11 712	13 079
Kuwait	4 042	2 078	7 198	8 990	16 800	17 250	20 407	21 373
Lebanon	2 000	1 119	6 364	12 348	13 420	20 742	29 609	32 011
Oman	591	1 687	2 393	4 358	9 524	11 582	12 203	13 024
Qatar	365	673	1 159	4 543	9 438	9 671	18 392	30 642
Saudi Arabia (5)	23 640	11 897	19 795	(b)155 259	305 709	442 809	410 263	445 281
Syrian Arab Republic (6)	374	1 730	2 805	(b)17 388	17 059	17 107	17 443	19 510
Turkey	1 245	6 253	22 659	50 766	73 590	70 629	71 078	80 914
United Arab Emirates	2 040	4 624	13 541	21 010	77 239	31 694	36 104	42 785

For sources and notes, see end of table.

Annual change in reserves (millions of dollars) Variations annuelles des réserves (millions de dollars)				Number of months of imports (2) Nombre de mois d'importations (2)								Régions, pays ou territoires
2007	2008	2009	2010	1980	1990	2000	2005	2007	2008	2009	2010	
199	89	247	505	0.5	0.1	2.1	1.1	3.2	2.7	4.4	4.8	Haïti
-440	-106	308	421	1.1	(e)1.0	3.8	5.8	3.5	2.5	4.9	6.0	Jamaïque
0	-3	3	3	..	2.5	5.8	5.6	5.9	3.7	5.8	6.7	Montserrat
167	157	49	-	0.3	1.4	1.2	3.0	2.9	3.2	4.1	-	Antilles néerlandaises
7	15	26	32		1.8	2.8	4.1	4.2	4.1	5.4	7.0	Saint-Kitts-et-Nevis
19	-11	32	31	0.8	2.0	2.7	2.9	2.9	2.6	3.9	4.3	Sainte-Lucie
8	-3	4	25	1.5	2.3	4.1	3.5	3.2	2.7	3.2	3.6	Saint-Vincent-et-les Grenadines
108	2 749	-265	(e)478	10.5	5.4	5.0	10.4	10.8	11.8	15.8	(e)17.9	Trinité-et-Tobago
13 027	*8 900*	*6 360*	*22 108*	*1.7*	*2.7*	*2.5*	*3.8*	*3.5*	*3.5*	*4.8*	*4.5*	**Amérique centrale**
-5	58	48	4	1.0	4.0	2.8	1.4	1.9	2.4	3.8	3.7	Belize
999	-315	268	561	1.2	3.1	2.5	2.8	3.8	3.0	4.3	4.1	Costa Rica
296	333	426	-299	1.3	4.2	4.4	3.1	2.9	3.0	4.8	3.7	El Salvador
216	332	502	673	3.5	2.1	4.1	4.2	3.7	3.7	5.2	4.9	Guatemala
-100	-55	-307	684	1.8	0.6	4.0	4.3	3.4	2.8	3.4	3.8	Honduras
10 840	8 021	4 467	20 672	1.7	2.7	2.3	3.8	3.5	3.5	4.9	4.6	Mexique
181	38	432	226	0.9	2.1	3.3	3.4	3.7	3.2	5.5	5.1	Nicaragua
				1.0								Panama, sans la zone du canal (anc.)
800	489	604	-314		2.7	2.6	3.5	3.4	3.2	4.7	3.5	Panama
121 193	*40 856*	*42 532*	*60 113*	*5.9*	*7.5*	*8.7*	*8.7*	*11.3*	*9.5*	*14.4*	*12.3*	**Amérique du Sud**
13 783	170	1 240	3 639	7.9	14.1	12.0	11.4	12.0	9.4	14.2	10.6	Argentine (3)
1 942	2 372	657	561	2.5	3.7	6.4	7.0	16.0	16.5	20.7	19.0	Bolivie (État plurinational de)
94 280	13 409	44 522	49 690	2.8	4.1	6.7	8.2	17.0	12.7	21.3	18.0	Brésil
-2 555	6 236	2 211	2 533	6.6	9.3	9.8	6.2	4.3	4.5	7.3	5.8	Chili
5 472	2 711	1 269	3 018	12.5	10.0	9.3	8.4	7.5	7.2	9.0	8.2	Colombie
1 329	921	-864	-1 439	5.5	5.5	3.2	2.0	2.5	2.4	2.3	0.9	Équateur
33	43	275	151	0.4	1.1	6.3	3.8	3.5	3.3	6.5	6.7	Guyana
759	384	994	298	14.9	5.9	4.1	4.8	5.0	3.8	6.6	4.9	Paraguay
10 126	3 413	1 742	10 634	9.8	4.0	13.6	13.1	15.8	12.2	17.6	17.2	Pérou
186	73	186	-20	4.6	0.6	1.7	1.5	4.6	4.4	6.1	5.9	Suriname
1 029	2 238	1 676	-384	3.8	5.7	8.8	9.5	8.6	8.5	15.5	10.6	Uruguay
-5 191	8 885	-11 376	-8 569	7.2	14.5	9.6	12.2	6.5	8.2	7.0	4.3	Venezuela (Rép. bolivarienne du)
908 502	*543 968*	*734 825*	*739 756*	*4.4*	*5.4*	*7.1*	*10.2*	*12.3*	*11.7*	*16.9*	*14.9*	**Économies en développement : Asie**
513 099	*411 613*	*669 345*	*524 495*	*1.9*	*6.6*	*7.8*	*12.1*	*14.0*	*14.4*	*21.4*	*18.3*	**Asie orientale**
461 841	418 956	467 606	449 994	1.9	6.8	9.0	14.9	19.2	20.7	28.9	24.7	Chine
19 469	29 832	73 299	12 870	(e)2.7	3.6	6.1	5.0	5.0	5.6	8.8	7.4	Chine (RAS de Hong Kong)
4 098	2 700	2 420	5 376	..	4.1	17.7	20.5	29.6	35.6	47.6	51.5	Chine (RAS de Macao)
4 199	21 378	56 504	33 793	1.4	16.0	9.2	16.7	14.8	14.6	24.0	18.3	Province chinoise de Taiwan
23 271	-61 006	68 788	21 558	1.6	2.5	7.2	9.7	8.8	5.5	10.0	8.2	Corée, République de
220	-248	729	904	..	..	3.6	3.4	4.6	1.9	7.3	8.1	Mongolie
125 374	*-10 798*	*15 147*	*9 986*	*5.9*	*2.0*	*7.1*	*10.0*	*13.2*	*9.4*	*12.1*	*9.9*	**Asie méridionale**
-	-	-	-	5.9	4.0	-	-	-	-	-	-	Afghanistan
1 378	506	4 530	363	1.4	2.1	2.0	2.4	3.3	2.9	5.6	4.6	Bangladesh
154	66	126	-	-	13.1	21.8	14.5	16.0	17.0	20.2	-	Bhoutan
96 281	-19 586	18 127	10 077	5.9	1.0	8.9	11.1	14.0	9.3	12.4	10.2	Inde
(e)23 600	(e)14 500	(e)-15 250	(e)-6 249	9.3	3.5	9.8	(e)13.6	(e)21.9	(e)20.2	(e)19.3	(e)14.4	Iran (Rép. islamique d')
77	-65	32	89	0.4	2.1	3.8	3.0	3.4	2.1	3.4	4.0	Maldives
-	-	-	-	6.6	5.8	7.3	7.9	-	-	-	-	Népal
2 507	-6 853	4 126	3 024	1.3	0.6	1.8	4.8	5.2	2.1	4.3	4.6	Pakistan
654	-911	2 175	2 075	1.5	1.9	2.0	3.6	3.6	2.1	5.5	6.0	Sri Lanka
101 894	*24 586*	*58 270*	*129 472*	*4.0*	*4.5*	*6.0*	*6.0*	*7.2*	*6.2*	*9.1*	*8.5*	**Asie du Sud-Est**
154	84	606	-	..	..	4.4	4.0	3.8	3.5	6.6	-	Brunéi Darussalam
651	484	560	404	..	..	3.2	3.0	4.0	4.3	5.9	5.4	Cambodge
				6.1	4.2	8.5						Indonésie, y compris le Timor oriental
13 880	-5 383	13 969	29 342				5.8	7.1	4.7	8.5	8.4	Indonésie
204	96	74	93	..	0.1	3.1	3.2	6.0	5.4	6.0	5.5	Rép. dém. populaire lao
18 890	-9 872	4 284	9 451	5.0	4.0	4.2	7.3	8.3	6.7	9.3	7.6	Malaisie
(e)1 064	(e)1 100	(e)149	(e)201	9.1	14.3	1.2	4.9	(e)8.5	(e)9.5	(e)9.7	(e)9.7	Myanmar
10 176	3 015	5 597	16 573	4.2	1.0	4.3	3.9	6.3	6.6	10.2	11.5	Philippines
26 697	11 235	13 611	37 912	3.3	5.5	7.2	7.0	7.4	6.5	9.2	8.7	Singapour
19 937	23 436	26 825	32 072	2.2	4.9	6.2	5.2	7.3	7.3	12.1	10.9	Thaïlande
147	-20	40	156				16.4	15.7	9.4	10.2	11.1	Timor-Leste
10 095	411	-7 443	-	-	1.8	2.6	3.0	4.6	3.6	2.8	-	Viet Nam
168 135	*118 567*	*-7 938*	*75 803*	*6.6*	*5.6*	*6.4*	*9.9*	*13.1*	*12.2*	*15.4*	*14.5*	**Asie occidentale**
-	-	-	-	3.3	4.0	4.1	-	-	-	-	-	Bahreïn
11 366	18 745	-3 787	4 121	-	-	-	6.2	19.2	16.9	16.3	14.2	Iraq
824	1 016	3 128	1 367	5.9	4.1	8.7	6.0	6.7	6.1	9.7	10.4	Jordanie (4)
4 101	449	3 157	967	7.4	6.3	12.1	6.8	9.5	8.3	13.7	11.4	Koweït
-442	7 322	8 867	2 402	6.6	5.3	12.3	15.4	13.1	14.9	21.4	20.8	Liban
4 509	2 058	621	821	4.1	7.5	5.7	5.9	7.2	6.1	8.2	8.6	Oman
4 055	233	8 721	12 251	3.0	4.8	4.3	5.4	5.1	4.2	9.5	16.7	Qatar
79 432	137 100	-32 546	35 018	9.4	5.9	7.9	(b)31.3	40.7	46.2	51.5	55.0	Arabie saoudite (5)
548	48	337	2 067	1.1	8.7	8.8	(b)19.2	14.0	11.3	13.6	13.8	République arabe syrienne (6)
12 502	-2 961	449	9 836	1.9	3.4	5.0	5.2	5.2	4.2	6.1	5.2	Turquie
49 621	-45 544	4 410	6 681	2.8	5.0	4.6	3.0	7.3	2.1	3.1	3.0	Émirats arabes unis

Pour les sources et les notes, se reporter à la fin du tableau.

Region, country or territory	Total reserves including gold (1) - Réserves totales, y compris l'or (1) Millions of dollars - Millions de dollars							
	1980	1990	2000	2005	2007	2008	2009	2010
Yemen (former Arab Republic)	1 283	–	–	–	–	–	–	–
Yemen (former Democratic)	236	–	–	–	–	–	–	–
Yemen	–	425	2 903	6 118	7 718	8 114	6 938	5 871
Developing economies: Oceania	**655**	**823**	**974**	**1 378**	**3 024**	**2 676**	**3 743**	**4 550**
Fiji	168	261	412	315	519	317	567	716
Micronesia (Federated States of)	–	..	113	50	48	40	56	56
Papua New Guinea	426	406	290	721	2 057	1 957	2 564	3 037
Samoa	3	69	64	82	95	87	166	209
Solomon Islands	30	18	32	95	119	90	146	266
Tonga	14	31	25	47	65	70	96	105
Vanuatu	-	38	39	67	120	115	149	161

Sources:
- IMF, *International Financial Statistics*
- IMF, *World Economic Outlook*
- World Bank, *Global Development Finance*
- EIU, online database
- National sources

Notes:

(1)   End of year position, including gold.

(2)   Reserve stock of the year, divided by the average monthly imports of the current year. Data on imports are based on figures shown in table 1.1.1.

(3)   Year 1985, break in series.

(4)   Year 1993, break in series.

(5)   Year 1996, break in seris. Year 2005, break in series: prior to 2005, data exclude Saudi Arabian Monetary Agency investments and deposits abroad.

(6)   Year 2005, break in series.

7.5.1 Réserves internationales des économies en développement par pays et régions géographiques

Annual change in reserves (millions of dollars) Variations annuelles des réserves (millions de dollars)				Number of months of imports (2) Nombre de mois d'importations (2)								Régions, pays ou territoires
2007	2008	2009	2010	1980	1990	2000	2005	2007	2008	2009	2010	
–	–	–	–	8.3	–	–	–	–	–	–	–	Yémen (anc. République arabe du)
				1.9								Yémen (anc. démocratique)
204	396	-1 176	-1 067	–	3.2	15.0	13.7	10.9	9.3	9.1	7.3	Yémen
926	**-349**	**1 067**	**807**	**3.9**	**4.5**	**4.8**	**4.0**	**6.2**	**4.6**	**7.5**	**9.1**	**Économies en développement : Océanie**
209	-202	250	149	3.6	4.2	5.8	2.4	3.5	1.7	4.7	5.5	Fidji
2	-8	16	0	–	..	12.7	4.6	4.1	3.1	4.3	4.3	Micronésie (États fédérés de)
653	-100	607	473	4.3	4.4	3.0	5.0	8.4	6.6	8.8	11.8	Papouasie-Nouvelle-Guinée
15	-8	79	44	0.5	10.3	8.5	4.1	4.3	3.6	8.6	8.1	Samoa
15	-30	56	120	4.0	2.3	4.2	6.2	5.0	3.4	6.7	8.1	Îles Salomon
17	5	26	9	4.4	6.1	4.3	4.7	5.5	5.6	7.2	7.2	Tonga
15	-4	33	13	-	4.7	5.4	5.4	6.3	4.4	6.1	6.8	Vanuatu

Sources :
- FMI, *Statistiques financières internationales*
- FMI, *World Economic Outlook*
- Banque mondiale, *Global Development Finance*
- EIU, base de données en ligne
- Sources nationales

Notes :

(1) Position en fin d'année, y compris l'or.
(2) Montant des réserves de l'année, divisé par la moyenne mensuelle des importations de l'année en cours. Les données des importations se basent sur les chiffres présentés dans le tableau 1.1.1.
(3) Année 1985, rupture de série.
(4) Année 1993, rupture de série.
(5) Année 1996, rupture de série. Année 2005, rupture de série : avant 2005 les données ne comprennent pas les investissements et les dépôts en devises de l'Agence monétaire de l'Arabie Saudite à l étranger.
(6) Année 2005, rupture de série.

7

7.5.2 International reserves of developing economies by economic grouping

Economic grouping	Total reserves including gold (1) - Réserves totales, y compris l'or (1) Millions of dollars - Millions de dollars							
	1980	1990	2000	2005	2007	2008	2009	2010
DEVELOPING ECONOMIES	**177 117**	**330 903**	**1 056 881**	**2 694 521**	**4 500 557**	**5 153 837**	**5 958 165**	**6 802 993**
Developing economies excluding China	174 000	300 685	888 024	1 872 042	2 969 207	3 203 532	3 540 254	3 935 088
Developing economies excluding LDCs	170 672	323 911	1 041 519	2 659 808	4 439 886	5 081 144	5 879 080	6 713 498
High-income developing countries	93 588	218 442	606 789	1 238 747	1 748 872	1 883 465	2 101 069	2 311 551
Middle-income developing countries	44 607	83 068	342 373	1 189 852	2 236 181	2 756 070	3 312 592	3 893 863
Low-income developing countries	38 921	29 393	107 719	265 923	515 504	514 302	544 504	597 579
Heavily indebted poor countries (IMF)	3 104	3 970	11 640	25 626	43 658	48 383	59 336	68 479
Landlocked developing countries	3 166	6 884	20 435	37 492	82 503	94 197	104 301	115 575
Small island developing States	2 017	2 797	5 710	13 348	16 430	18 622	21 000	22 440
Least developed countries	*6 445*	*6 992*	*15 362*	*34 713*	*60 671*	*72 693*	*79 085*	*89 495*
Africa and Haiti	3 624	4 748	8 334	19 756	37 178	45 055	45 654	55 147
Asia	2 766	2 091	6 839	14 447	22 772	26 965	32 510	33 110
Islands	54	154	190	510	721	674	921	1 238
Major petroleum and gas exporters	*84 569*	*54 668*	*113 092*	*404 058*	*809 763*	*1 000 348*	*954 374*	*1 009 755*
Africa	29 175	12 518	36 091	127 832	252 856	307 015	307 091	317 431
America	7 116	8 891	13 555	24 493	24 830	33 716	22 339	13 771
Asia	48 279	33 260	63 446	251 733	532 077	659 618	624 943	678 554
Major exporters of manufactured goods	*29 222*	*203 720*	*656 111*	*1 722 011*	*2 653 757*	*3 095 737*	*3 811 121*	*4 429 442*
America	3 052	9 909	35 520	74 060	87 116	95 137	99 604	120 276
Asia	26 170	193 811	620 590	1 647 952	2 566 641	3 000 600	3 711 516	4 309 165
Emerging economies	*39 073*	*168 704*	*460 849*	*886 436*	*1 237 794*	*1 254 215*	*1 478 409*	*1 700 363*
America	21 061	29 691	116 661	185 211	355 143	386 393	440 575	527 744
Asia	18 012	139 013	344 188	701 225	882 651	867 822	1 037 834	1 172 619
Newly industrialized Asian countries	*31 483*	*172 275*	*493 796*	*874 942*	*1 120 843*	*1 133 478*	*1 396 354*	*1 589 925*
First tier	16 891	140 293	391 226	704 730	848 837	850 277	1 062 478	1 168 610
Second tier	14 593	31 982	102 570	170 212	272 006	283 202	333 876	421 314
Developing economies: Africa	**36 550**	**27 978**	**79 915**	**220 397**	**399 304**	**457 282**	**474 626**	**494 399**
Northern Africa excluding Sudan	19 433	12 710	44 855	137 723	252 634	299 457	314 918	328 675
Sub-Saharan Africa	17 117	15 268	35 060	82 674	146 670	157 825	159 708	165 725
Sub-Saharan Africa excluding South Africa	15 849	14 056	28 708	63 895	116 860	127 026	124 250	127 333
Developing economies: America	**40 316**	**49 202**	**157 762**	**258 926**	**451 167**	**502 850**	**553 941**	**638 433**
Central America and Greater Caribbean Islands excluding Puerto Rico	4 446	12 160	45 444	93 018	112 996	120 704	128 833	152 657
Central America and Greater Caribbean Islands excluding Mexico and Puerto Rico	1 394	2 252	9 924	18 959	25 880	25 567	29 229	32 380
South America and Central America	36 872	47 490	152 291	244 452	431 568	481 324	530 217	612 437
South America excluding Brazil	26 903	28 094	76 724	105 028	148 905	176 352	174 362	184 785
Developing economies: Asia	**99 596**	**252 901**	**818 230**	**2 213 821**	**3 647 062**	**4 191 030**	**4 925 855**	**5 665 611**
Eastern and South-Eastern Asia excluding China	31 785	173 531	502 019	893 650	1 163 939	1 181 182	1 441 192	1 645 164
Southern Asia excluding India	12 219	7 533	18 256	64 783	110 297	119 085	116 106	116 015

Sources:
- IMF, *International Financial Statistics*
- IMF, *World Economic Outlook*
- World Bank, *Global Development Finance*
- EIU, online database
- National sources

Notes:
(1) End of year position, including gold.
(2) Reserve stock of the year, divided by the average monthly imports of the current year. Data on imports are based on figures shown in table 1.1.1.

7.5.2 Réserves internationales des économies en développement par groupements économiques

Annual change in reserves (millions of dollars) Variations annuelles des réserves (millions de dollars)				Number of months of imports (2) Nombre de mois d'importations (2)								Groupements économiques
2007	2008	2009	2010	1980	1990	2000	2005	2007	2008	2009	2010	
1 139 727	653 281	804 328	844 828	4.4	5.0	6.6	9.5	11.5	10.9	15.5	13.8	ÉCONOMIES EN DÉVELOPPEMENT
677 886	234 325	336 722	394 833	4.5	4.9	6.3	8.2	9.6	8.4	11.8	10.4	Économies en développement sans la Chine
1 126 606	641 258	797 936	834 418	4.4	5.1	6.7	9.6	11.7	11.0	15.9	14.0	Économies en développement sans les PMA
292 258	134 592	217 604	210 483	4.7	5.8	6.3	8.6	9.1	8.3	12.0	10.4	Pays en développement à revenu élevé
687 501	519 889	556 523	581 271	3.5	4.2	7.3	11.6	15.5	15.5	22.2	19.7	Pays en développement à revenu intermédiaire
159 968	-1 200	30 201	53 074	5.0	3.4	6.5	7.4	9.8	7.2	9.2	8.2	Pays en développement à revenu faible
10 708	4 725	10 953	9 144	1.5	2.0	3.8	4.1	5.0	4.3	6.1	6.2	Pays pauvres très endettés (FMI)
19 573	11 694	10 105	11 274	3.7	5.6	6.7	5.9	8.3	7.3	9.5	9.7	Pays en développement sans littoral
1 055	2 193	2 466	2 350	3.0	3.3	4.0	5.7	5.8	5.4	8.1	8.7	Petits États insulaires en développement
13 121	12 023	6 392	10 410	3.1	3.3	4.3	4.8	5.9	5.4	6.2	6.4	*Pays les moins avancés*
8 523	7 877	600	9 492	2.6	3.3	4.2	4.4	5.7	5.1	5.4	6.3	Afrique et Haïti
4 378	4 193	5 545	601	4.4	3.4	4.3	5.6	6.3	6.0	7.7	6.4	Asie
220	-47	248	317	2.4	5.4	6.6	7.3	7.4	5.5	8.2	8.6	Îles
235 675	190 585	-45 975	55 381	8.6	6.7	9.0	15.0	20.6	19.3	21.7	20.7	*Principaux exportateurs de pétrole et de gaz*
64 182	54 159	76	10 340	9.9	6.7	17.6	27.4	35.4	32.9	33.2	34.2	Afrique
-5 191	8 885	-11 376	-8 569	7.2	14.5	9.6	12.2	6.5	8.2	7.0	4.3	Amérique
176 685	127 541	-34 674	53 610	8.2	5.8	7.0	12.5	18.7	17.2	19.8	18.7	Asie
585 145	441 980	715 383	618 321	2.3	5.7	6.6	10.0	11.6	11.7	17.6	15.3	*Principaux exportateurs d'articles manufacturés*
10 840	8 021	4 467	20 672	1.7	2.7	2.3	3.8	3.5	3.5	4.9	4.6	Amérique
574 305	433 959	710 916	597 649	2.4	6.1	7.3	10.8	12.6	12.6	18.9	16.3	Asie
219 469	16 421	224 193	221 954	3.1	6.1	6.3	8.4	8.9	7.5	12.0	10.3	*Économies émergentes*
126 474	31 249	54 182	87 169	3.8	4.4	4.8	5.8	8.0	7.1	11.0	9.7	Amérique
92 994	-14 829	170 011	134 785	2.5	6.7	7.1	9.6	9.4	7.8	12.4	10.5	Asie
136 519	12 635	262 076	193 571	3.0	5.7	6.8	8.1	8.2	7.1	11.3	9.7	*Économies nouvellement industrialisées d'Asie*
73 637	1 439	212 202	106 132	2.3	6.3	7.2	9.0	8.4	7.4	11.7	9.9	Première génération
62 883	11 196	50 674	87 439	4.5	4.0	5.6	5.8	7.4	6.4	10.2	9.4	Deuxième génération
94 127	57 978	17 344	19 773	4.6	3.6	7.4	10.3	13.0	11.7	13.8	13.2	Économies en développement : Afrique
63 142	46 822	15 461	13 757	7.8	4.1	11.5	20.6	26.9	21.9	25.8	24.4	Afrique septentrionale sans le Soudan
30 986	11 156	1 883	6 017	3.1	3.2	5.1	5.6	6.9	6.2	7.2	6.9	Afrique subsaharienne
24 443	10 166	-2 775	3 083	4.2	4.3	6.6	6.8	8.5	7.3	7.7	7.3	Afrique subsaharienne sans l'Afrique du Sud
136 172	51 683	51 091	84 492	4.1	4.6	4.8	5.8	7.2	6.5	9.7	8.6	Économies en développement : Amérique
14 416	7 709	8 129	23 824	1.6	2.3	2.4	3.8	3.5	3.4	4.8	4.5	Amérique centrale et Grandes Antilles sans Porto Rico
3 576	-313	3 661	3 151	1.5	1.3	2.7	3.5	3.5	2.9	4.5	4.2	Amérique centrale et Grandes Antilles sans le Mexique et Porto Rico
134 219	49 756	48 892	82 221	4.6	5.2	5.1	6.0	7.4	6.8	10.0	8.8	Amérique du Sud et Amérique centrale
26 913	27 447	-1 989	10 423	7.8	9.8	10.0	9.0	8.0	7.5	10.0	8.2	Amérique du Sud sans le Brésil
908 502	543 968	734 825	739 756	4.4	5.4	7.1	10.2	12.3	11.7	16.9	14.9	Économies en développement : Asie
153 152	17 243	260 010	203 972	2.9	5.6	6.7	8.0	8.1	7.0	11.0	9.5	Asie orientale et Asie du Sud-Est sans la Chine
29 093	8 788	-2 979	-91	5.9	2.7	4.9	8.3	11.5	9.8	11.3	9.1	Asie méridionale sans l'Inde

Sources :
- FMI, *Statistiques financières internationales*
- FMI, *World Economic Outlook*
- Banque mondiale, *Global Development Finance*
- EIU, base de données en ligne
- Sources nationales

Notes :

(1) Position en fin d'année, y compris l'or.
(2) Montant des réserves de l'année, divisé par la moyenne mensuelle des importations de l'année en cours. Les données des importations se basent sur les chiffres présentés dans le tableau 1.1.1.

7

Region, country or territory / Régions, pays ou territoires	Year / Année	Total official net (1) / Total secteur officiel net (1)	Total ODA Net (2) / APD totale nette (2)			Total OOF Net (3) / Flux AASP nets (3)		
			Total donors (4) / Tous donneurs (4)	of which: / dont :		Total donors / Tous donneurs	of which: / dont :	
				DAC bilateral donors / Donneurs bilatéraux du CAD	Multilateral donors / Donneurs multilatéraux		DAC bilateral donors / Donneurs bilatéraux du CAD	Multilateral donors / Donneurs multilatéraux
			Millions of dollars / Millions de dollars					
WORLD - MONDE	1990	76 036.7	56 943.6	38 474.0	12 608.8	18 093.1	7 958.7	10 146.8
	1995	72 198.9	58 974.7	40 552.4	17 732.7	13 224.2	5 616.8	7 607.4
	2000	53 280.6	49 526.3	36 195.3	12 679.7	3 754.3	-4 995.0	8 749.3
	2009	166 000.9	126 639.0	83 074.1	38 012.0	39 361.9	8 045.3	31 327.6
DEVELOPING ECONOMIES - ÉCONOMIES EN DÉVELOPPEMENT (5)	1990	73 492.9	55 307.7	36 874.1	12 578.6	18 185.2	8 065.1	10 128.2
	1995	67 970.8	56 860.1	39 005.0	16 409.6	12 351.4	9 449.1	2 897.7
	2000	47 918.8	44 870.2	33 422.6	10 902.8	3 048.6	-5 196.4	8 245.0
	2009	155 944.7	120 081.9	79 752.5	35 233.1	35 862.8	8 380.6	27 457.2
TRANSITION ECONOMIES - ÉCONOMIES EN TRANSITION	1990	72.3	177.9	165.5	12.4	-105.6	-83.7	-17.2
	1995	3 785.0	2 918.4	1 584.5	1 270.1	866.6	382.9	495.2
	2000	5 242.2	4 574.1	2 750.9	1 715.8	668.1	203.3	464.8
	2009	10 056.3	6 557.2	3 321.6	2 778.9	3 499.1	-335.3	3 870.4
DEVELOPED ECONOMIES - ÉCONOMIES DÉVELOPPÉES	1990	1 471.4	1 458.1	1 434.3	17.8	13.4	-22.8	35.9
	1995	443.1	416.9	362.9	58.0	26.2	25.9	0.3
	2000	119.5	82.1	21.9	61.1	37.5	-1.9	39.4
Developing economies: Africa - Économies en développement : Afrique	1990	28 027.2	25 076.3	15 826.4	6 126.3	2 950.9	850.9	1 950.3
	1995	25 154.0	21 781.1	13 238.3	8 410.6	3 372.9	3 577.0	-203.6
	2000	14 106.0	15 380.9	10 396.8	4 708.5	-1 274.8	-343.5	-931.4
	2009	52 233.3	47 609.9	28 155.8	19 161.2	4 623.4	1 224.8	3 373.6
Eastern Africa - Afrique orientale	1990	8 338.0	8 185.1	5 169.2	2 708.0	152.9	137.0	11.9
	1995	8 939.9	9 233.3	4 796.0	4 419.6	-293.4	-41.7	-251.7
	2000	6 572.9	6 676.8	4 296.4	2 326.6	-103.9	-38.1	-65.8
	2009	19 801.1	18 780.1	10 815.9	7 890.0	1 021.0	760.5	260.5
Burundi	1990	259.1	262.6	157.0	104.7	3.4	1.0	-4.4
	1995	285.2	287.0	108.5	181.3	-1.8	0.2	-2.0
	2000	93.1	93.1	40.9	52.2	0.0	0.0	0.0
	2009	548.8	548.8	260.9	287.8	0.0	0.0	0.0
Comoros - Comores	1990	44.9	44.8	30.6	14.0	0.1	0.1	0.0
	1995	41.5	41.6	21.8	19.8	-0.1	-0.1	0.0
	2000	18.7	18.7	10.8	7.7	0.0	0.0	0.0
	2009	49.6	50.6	28.1	21.6	-1.0	-1.0	0.0
Djibouti	1990	193.6	193.7	88.3	17.3	-0.1	-0.1	0.0
	1995	104.9	104.7	79.6	21.9	0.2	0.2	0.0
	2000	71.4	71.4	42.2	19.7	0.0	0.0	0.0
	2009	277.7	162.2	97.7	53.7	115.5	35.3	80.3
Eritrea - Érythrée	1995	148.2	148.2	94.7	48.3	0.0	0.0	0.0
	2000	175.8	175.8	112.0	54.7	0.0	0.0	0.0
	2009	144.8	144.8	43.4	86.6	0.0	0.0	0.0
Ethiopia - Éthiopie	1995	899.0	876.5	526.0	350.4	22.5	5.5	17.1
	2000	667.2	686.1	380.0	291.5	-18.8	-1.0	-17.9
	2009	3 808.7	3 820.0	1 816.6	1 983.9	-11.3	1.2	-12.5
Ethiopia (former) - Éthiopie (anc.)	1990	1 007.2	1 009.2	509.8	431.7	-1.9	-2.3	0.3
Kenya	1990	1 141.3	1 181.3	735.2	441.6	-40.0	15.4	-55.4
	1995	629.7	731.4	462.1	267.5	-101.7	-16.4	-85.3
	2000	475.4	509.2	292.4	211.4	-33.8	-4.9	-29.0
	2009	1 866.9	1 778.0	1 224.0	548.6	88.9	94.8	-6.0
Madagascar	1990	411.9	397.0	268.2	129.9	14.9	11.2	3.2
	1995	299.7	299.4	195.0	104.4	0.3	4.8	-4.5
	2000	314.7	320.2	138.7	182.6	-5.5	1.4	-6.9
	2009	1 123.0	445.5	241.6	202.4	677.5	636.8	40.7
Malawi	1990	486.3	500.4	216.2	283.6	-14.1	-5.8	-8.3
	1995	416.2	434.1	221.0	210.5	-18.0	-1.0	-17.0
	2000	443.7	446.1	269.3	170.7	-2.4	-0.1	-2.3
	2009	773.9	772.4	435.2	333.4	1.5	-0.4	1.9

For sources and notes, see end of table.

Pour les sources et les notes, se reporter à la fin du tableau.

Region, country or territory / Régions, pays ou territoires	Year / Année	Total official net (1) / Total secteur officiel net (1)	Total ODA Net (2) / APD totale nette (2)			Total OOF Net (3) / Flux AASP nets (3)		
			Total donors (4) / Tous donneurs (4)	of which: / dont :		Total donors / Tous donneurs	of which: / dont :	
				DAC bilateral donors / Donneurs bilatéraux du CAD	Multilateral donors / Donneurs multilatéraux		DAC bilateral donors / Donneurs bilatéraux du CAD	Multilateral donors / Donneurs multilatéraux
		Millions of dollars / Millions de dollars						
Mauritius - Maurice	1990	107.2	88.3	75.7	11.0	18.0	16.2	2.7
	1995	3.7	23.1	11.1	13.5	-19.5	-1.2	-18.3
	2000	-18.1	20.2	12.4	7.2	-38.3	-20.7	-17.5
	2009	292.5	155.6	63.6	93.8	136.9	8.3	129.6
Mayotte	1990	60.5	60.5	58.5	2.0	0.0	0.0	0.0
	1995	107.8	107.8	106.2	1.5	0.0	0.0	0.0
	2000	103.2	103.2	103.0	0.2	0.0	0.0	0.0
	2009	535.1	544.3	543.1	1.2	-9.2	-9.2	0.0
Mozambique	1990	999.4	997.3	750.3	246.9	2.1	3.3	-1.5
	1995	1 035.6	1 062.4	698.4	361.9	-26.8	-23.4	-3.4
	2000	1 072.6	906.2	623.6	282.7	166.5	105.2	61.2
	2009	1 998.2	2 013.3	1 287.7	723.9	-15.1	-4.2	-10.9
Rwanda	1990	286.9	287.9	183.2	94.5	-1.0	-0.1	-0.9
	1995	695.0	694.7	339.3	355.7	0.3	0.1	0.2
	2000	323.5	321.5	175.4	145.9	2.1	2.2	-0.2
	2009	944.9	934.4	519.8	411.8	10.5	0.0	10.5
Seychelles	1990	37.4	35.6	32.7	3.0	1.9	-0.8	-0.4
	1995	16.3	12.8	11.0	2.3	3.4	-0.4	3.9
	2000	14.3	18.1	3.3	8.2	-3.8	-0.7	-3.1
	2009	22.1	23.2	11.8	11.4	-1.1	0.0	-1.1
Somalia - Somalie	1990	490.2	491.4	269.6	139.8	-1.2	0.8	0.4
	1995	188.0	187.8	119.2	68.6	0.2	0.2	0.0
	2000	101.0	101.0	56.4	44.4	0.0	0.0	0.0
	2009	661.7	661.7	499.5	152.5	0.0	0.0	0.0
Uganda - Ouganda	1990	665.2	663.1	244.4	376.1	2.1	9.4	-7.3
	1995	817.2	832.9	427.7	308.0	-15.7	-5.7	-9.9
	2000	809.4	853.0	578.2	269.2	-43.6	-46.3	2.8
	2009	1 888.6	1 785.9	1 013.3	768.8	102.7	17.6	85.1
United Republic of Tanzania - République-Unie de Tanzanie	1990	1 163.1	1 163.2	844.1	315.8	-0.1	28.2	-28.2
	1995	837.3	869.1	587.0	278.0	-31.9	-9.0	-22.9
	2000	1 089.9	1 062.8	779.0	286.7	27.1	32.0	-4.9
	2009	2 946.4	2 934.2	1 408.8	1 526.8	12.2	13.1	-0.9
Zambia - Zambie	1990	540.8	474.8	408.9	65.9	66.0	47.2	18.8
	1995	1 963.6	2 030.7	439.7	1 591.0	-67.1	3.7	-70.8
	2000	674.5	794.7	486.3	308.1	-120.1	-104.4	-15.8
	2009	1 181.3	1 268.7	700.6	566.0	-87.4	-33.3	-54.1
Zimbabwe	1990	443.0	334.3	295.9	29.3	108.7	14.9	93.8
	1995	451.3	489.1	347.8	144.9	-37.8	1.0	-38.8
	2000	142.4	175.6	192.7	-16.3	-33.2	-0.9	-32.3
	2009	737.3	736.8	620.4	115.9	0.5	1.5	-1.0
Middle Africa - Afrique centrale	*1990*	*3 591.1*	*2 628.2*	*1 821.6*	*725.4*	*963.0*	*678.6*	*284.4*
	1995	*2 435.8*	*1 842.7*	*1 279.0*	*559.4*	*593.1*	*670.4*	*-77.3*
	2000	*968.8*	*1 161.4*	*667.9*	*498.5*	*-192.6*	*-52.5*	*-140.2*
	2009	*4 164.8*	*4 463.3*	*2 275.9*	*2 173.2*	*-298.5*	*-204.0*	*-94.5*
Angola	1990	343.5	265.8	163.2	100.8	77.7	76.2	1.5
	1995	489.6	416.4	241.9	174.5	73.1	73.1	0.0
	2000	256.3	302.2	197.7	107.1	-45.9	-23.3	-22.6
	2009	225.4	239.5	131.5	98.4	-14.1	-13.6	-0.4
Cameroon - Cameroun	1990	607.2	444.4	339.1	107.9	162.8	75.1	87.7
	1995	578.2	442.8	345.8	95.8	135.4	235.2	-99.8
	2000	306.1	376.7	213.7	165.9	-70.6	9.4	-80.0
	2009	724.5	649.4	267.7	380.7	75.1	10.4	64.8
Central African Republic - République centrafricaine	1990	251.6	248.9	99.9	146.7	2.8	3.9	-1.1
	1995	170.0	167.8	122.4	42.0	2.2	2.2	0.0
	2000	74.0	75.3	53.1	22.4	-1.3	-1.3	0.0
	2009	235.6	236.9	98.6	137.7	-1.3	-1.3	0.0

For sources and notes, see end of table.

Pour les sources et les notes, se reporter à la fin du tableau.

7.6.1   Official financial flows from
        bilateral and multilateral sources
        by country and geographical region

7.6.1   Flux financiers publics bilatéraux
        et multilatéraux par pays et régions
        géographiques

Region, country or territory / Régions, pays ou territoires	Year / Année	Total official net (1) / Total secteur officiel net (1)	Total ODA Net (2) / APD totale nette (2)			Total OOF Net (3) / Flux AASP nets (3)		
			Total donors (4) / Tous donneurs (4)	of which: / dont :		Total donors / Tous donneurs	of which: / dont :	
				DAC bilateral donors / Donneurs bilatéraux du CAD	Multilateral donors / Donneurs multilatéraux		DAC bilateral donors / Donneurs bilatéraux du CAD	Multilateral donors / Donneurs multilatéraux
				Millions of dollars / Millions de dollars				
Chad - Tchad	1990	310.8	310.8	181.1	120.0	-0.1	-0.1	0.0
	1995	237.2	235.0	127.1	107.4	2.2	2.2	0.0
	2000	129.2	130.2	53.5	76.1	-0.9	-0.9	0.0
	2009	556.6	561.2	355.5	205.8	-4.6	-3.6	-1.0
Congo	1990	226.3	217.2	202.0	15.2	9.1	13.2	-4.1
	1995	394.0	124.9	105.1	19.8	269.2	287.2	-18.0
	2000	16.4	32.0	23.0	9.0	-15.6	-12.4	-3.2
	2009	171.0	283.0	226.1	56.4	-111.9	-100.4	-11.5
Dem. Rep. of the Congo - Rép. dém. du Congo	1990	1 419.7	895.8	632.7	185.9	523.9	380.6	143.3
	1995	188.5	194.8	117.8	76.9	-6.3	-5.1	-1.2
	2000	173.7	177.1	102.7	74.3	-3.4	0.0	-3.4
	2009	2 179.3	2 353.6	1 099.3	1 251.6	-174.2	-1.0	-173.3
Equatorial Guinea - Guinée équatoriale	1990	60.8	60.2	43.6	16.5	0.6	0.0	0.6
	1995	35.2	33.4	21.7	11.7	1.8	1.8	0.0
	2000	20.2	21.3	18.2	3.3	-1.1	-0.7	-0.4
	2009	24.3	31.6	25.1	6.5	-7.3	-7.3	0.0
Gabon	1990	317.5	131.2	126.9	4.4	186.3	129.7	56.5
	1995	284.9	143.5	135.7	8.7	141.4	99.7	41.7
	2000	-42.1	11.7	-11.6	23.3	-53.7	-23.2	-30.5
	2009	17.3	77.6	52.5	25.0	-60.3	-87.2	26.9
Sao Tome and Principe - Sao Tomé-et-Principe	1990	54.1	54.1	31.0	23.1	0.0	0.0	0.0
	1995	58.3	84.1	61.6	22.5	-25.8	-25.8	0.0
	2000	34.9	34.9	17.7	17.2	0.0	0.0	0.0
	2009	30.7	30.7	19.7	11.0	0.0	0.0	0.0
Northern Africa - Afrique septentrionale	*1990*	*7 994.0*	*7 817.1*	*4 501.3*	*653.2*	*176.9*	*-949.7*	*977.3*
	1995	*6 305.0*	*3 114.3*	*2 506.3*	*504.2*	*3 190.7*	*2 709.3*	*481.9*
	2000	*2 017.3*	*2 387.3*	*1 750.9*	*428.0*	*-370.0*	*91.4*	*-461.4*
	2009	*6 096.5*	*4 958.1*	*3 777.9*	*1 088.6*	*1 138.4*	*-187.6*	*1 301.0*
Algeria - Algérie	1990	675.6	131.7	102.2	21.5	543.9	114.2	283.3
	1995	1 986.1	293.9	275.4	30.7	1 692.2	1 325.6	366.6
	2000	-41.8	199.6	65.7	62.7	-241.4	-143.4	-98.0
	2009	115.8	319.3	200.3	107.3	-203.5	-137.7	-65.9
Egypt - Égypte	1990	4 153.9	5 425.1	3 163.1	76.2	-1 271.1	-1 234.0	-37.6
	1995	2 648.5	2 010.5	1 691.5	202.4	638.0	775.7	-137.7
	2000	1 366.9	1 327.0	1 139.6	134.2	39.9	220.0	-180.0
	2009	1 594.1	925.1	580.0	222.8	669.0	19.0	650.0
Libyan Arab Jamahiriya - Jamahiriya arabe libyenne	1990	8.3	8.3	7.7	0.7	0.0	0.0	0.0
	1995	5.8	5.8	3.2	2.6	0.0	0.0	0.0
	2009	39.4	39.4	32.4	6.0	0.0	0.0	0.0
Morocco - Maroc	1990	1 696.0	1 048.0	595.4	91.5	648.1	164.5	486.2
	1995	485.7	492.6	347.9	125.4	-6.9	-163.6	156.7
	2000	275.8	418.8	293.1	129.8	-143.0	-47.3	-95.7
	2009	1 295.1	911.6	704.7	305.1	383.5	-54.6	438.1
Sudan - Soudan	1990	810.6	813.1	420.0	385.2	-2.6	2.7	-5.2
	1995	250.7	237.0	131.7	102.8	13.7	-4.3	18.1
	2000	210.9	220.4	90.3	30.7	-9.5	-9.1	-0.4
	2009	2 317.1	2 288.9	1 911.0	317.2	28.2	3.0	0.2
Tunisia - Tunisie	1990	649.6	391.0	212.9	78.1	258.5	2.9	250.7
	1995	928.2	74.4	56.7	40.4	853.7	775.9	78.3
	2000	205.5	221.5	162.3	70.6	-16.0	71.2	-87.2
	2009	735.0	473.9	349.5	130.2	261.2	-17.4	278.6
Southern Africa - Afrique australe	*1990*	*460.8*	*457.6*	*281.9*	*177.8*	*3.2*	*-2.2*	*5.4*
	1995	*1 165.2*	*836.5*	*620.6*	*210.3*	*328.7*	*359.7*	*-30.9*
	2000	*842.3*	*719.1*	*500.4*	*219.5*	*123.2*	*-83.6*	*206.8*
	2009	*4 391.5*	*1 861.8*	*1 420.4*	*433.9*	*2 529.7*	*720.1*	*1 809.6*

For sources and notes, see end of table.

Pour les sources et les notes, se reporter à la fin du tableau.

Region, country or territory / Régions, pays ou territoires	Year / Année	Total official net (1) / Total secteur officiel net (1)	Total ODA Net (2) / APD totale nette (2)			Total OOF Net (3) / Flux AASP nets (3)		
			Total donors (4) / Tous donneurs (4)	of which: / dont :		Total donors / Tous donneurs	of which: / dont :	
				DAC bilateral donors / Donneurs bilatéraux du CAD	Multilateral donors / Donneurs multilatéraux		DAC bilateral donors / Donneurs bilatéraux du CAD	Multilateral donors / Donneurs multilatéraux
				Millions of dollars / Millions de dollars				
Botswana	1990	167.4	145.2	121.2	25.8	22.2	4.6	17.6
	1995	68.6	89.5	54.5	34.6	-20.9	18.5	-39.4
	2000	34.2	30.6	23.5	8.0	3.6	23.1	-19.5
	2009	1 246.5	279.6	223.4	56.6	966.9	0.0	966.9
Lesotho	1990	139.7	139.1	85.2	54.3	0.5	-1.5	2.0
	1995	134.1	112.7	61.8	51.0	21.5	12.6	8.9
	2000	47.1	36.7	21.8	16.1	10.4	-8.2	18.6
	2009	121.0	123.0	70.7	47.7	-2.1	0.0	-2.1
Namibia - Namibie	1990	119.6	119.6	39.4	80.3	0.0	0.0	0.0
	1995	192.5	190.4	147.8	42.5	2.1	2.1	0.0
	2000	154.0	152.3	96.8	54.5	1.6	-0.5	2.1
	2009	353.4	326.2	246.5	78.4	27.2	0.5	26.7
South Africa - Afrique du Sud	1995	712.7	386.2	318.5	64.7	326.6	326.6	0.0
	2000	591.2	486.4	355.5	130.8	104.8	-94.5	199.3
	2009	2 627.3	1 075.0	861.3	211.1	1 552.2	719.6	832.6
Swaziland	1990	34.1	53.6	36.1	17.4	-19.5	-5.3	-14.2
	1995	57.3	57.8	37.9	17.4	-0.5	0.0	-0.5
	2000	15.9	13.1	2.8	10.2	2.8	-3.5	6.2
	2009	43.4	58.0	18.5	40.1	-14.6	0.0	-14.6
Western Africa - Afrique occidentale	*1990*	*6 724.0*	*5 085.5*	*3 212.0*	*1 808.8*	*1 638.5*	*981.3*	*660.7*
	1995	*5 287.4*	*5 768.1*	*3 213.9*	*2 553.3*	*-480.6*	*-151.6*	*-329.0*
	2000	*2 672.4*	*3 405.0*	*2 333.6*	*1 065.1*	*-732.6*	*-267.6*	*-465.0*
	2009	*12 148.4*	*12 294.7*	*6 813.2*	*5 436.6*	*-146.4*	*-27.4*	*-118.9*
Benin - Bénin	1990	294.8	266.9	125.7	141.5	27.9	26.2	1.7
	1995	282.2	280.1	177.5	95.9	2.2	2.9	-0.8
	2000	232.5	243.5	190.5	54.0	-11.0	-11.0	0.0
	2009	683.7	682.9	325.7	353.8	0.8	0.8	0.0
Burkina Faso	1990	328.0	326.5	238.7	76.5	1.4	1.3	0.1
	1995	487.6	490.0	252.5	229.9	-2.4	0.1	-2.5
	2000	174.2	179.7	227.8	-51.8	-5.5	-3.5	-2.0
	2009	1 077.6	1 083.9	452.9	629.3	-6.3	-0.3	-6.0
Cape Verde - Cap-Vert	1990	103.9	105.3	75.9	29.0	-1.4	-0.2	-1.1
	1995	115.8	115.7	76.9	38.7	0.1	0.4	-0.3
	2000	92.2	93.7	69.7	24.4	-1.6	-0.1	-1.4
	2009	222.8	195.9	161.9	34.5	26.9	0.0	26.9
Côte d'Ivoire	1990	1 121.9	686.4	530.6	155.8	435.5	134.2	301.3
	1995	1 147.3	1 211.8	727.1	484.7	-64.5	31.6	-96.1
	2000	275.6	350.5	250.1	99.9	-74.9	17.8	-92.7
	2009	1 629.7	2 366.3	1 722.6	641.4	-736.6	-290.2	-446.4
Gambia - Gambie	1990	105.3	97.3	56.9	39.9	8.0	8.5	-0.5
	1995	43.1	45.4	25.2	21.8	-2.3	-0.4	-1.9
	2000	48.9	49.6	14.6	32.6	-0.7	0.0	-0.7
	2009	137.2	128.0	21.9	105.1	9.2	0.0	9.2
Ghana	1990	716.4	559.7	264.9	293.7	156.6	26.4	130.2
	1995	579.1	648.4	358.8	295.8	-69.3	10.7	-80.0
	2000	580.8	597.5	375.6	219.2	-16.8	8.6	-25.3
	2009	1 870.4	1 582.8	820.5	756.1	287.7	16.0	271.7
Guinea - Guinée	1990	300.4	291.5	139.0	148.4	8.8	19.6	-10.8
	1995	432.7	415.9	220.4	189.7	16.8	-2.3	19.1
	2000	141.5	152.9	92.8	57.5	-11.4	-1.4	-10.0
	2009	199.9	214.7	171.0	47.5	-14.8	-12.2	-2.6
Guinea-Bissau - Guinée-Bissau	1990	125.0	126.4	75.4	51.0	-1.3	0.0	-1.3
	1995	114.3	117.6	76.9	37.7	-3.3	0.0	-3.3
	2000	81.1	81.1	41.6	39.5	0.0	0.1	-0.1
	2009	145.5	145.5	50.6	93.9	0.0	0.0	0.0

For sources and notes, see end of table.

Pour les sources et les notes, se reporter à la fin du tableau.

7.6.1   Official financial flows from
        bilateral and multilateral sources
        by country and geographical region

7.6.1   Flux financiers publics bilatéraux
        et multilatéraux par pays et régions
        géographiques

Region, country or territory / Régions, pays ou territoires	Year / Année	Total official net (1) Total secteur officiel net (1)	Total ODA Net (2) APD totale nette (2)			Total OOF Net (3) Flux AASP nets (3)		
			Total donors (4) Tous donneurs (4)	DAC bilateral donors Donneurs bilatéraux du CAD	Multilateral donors Donneurs multilatéraux	Total donors Tous donneurs	DAC bilateral donors Donneurs bilatéraux du CAD	Multilateral donors Donneurs multilatéraux
				Millions of dollars / Millions de dollars				
Liberia - Libéria	1990	111.5	113.7	43.3	80.3	-17.1	12.0	-30.8
	1995	119.7	123.1	31.1	90.7	-3.4	-3.1	-0.4
	2000	69.1	67.4	23.8	43.6	1.6	-1.9	3.5
	2009	530.6	505.0	340.8	163.3	25.5	25.5	0.0
Mali	1990	480.1	479.0	312.5	151.1	1.1	1.9	-0.8
	1995	584.8	539.8	285.2	268.2	45.0	21.3	23.8
	2000	271.4	287.8	299.8	-10.6	-16.4	-6.9	-9.5
	2009	997.1	985.1	574.6	408.9	12.0	0.0	12.0
Mauritania - Mauritanie	1990	224.8	236.1	106.4	105.1	-11.3	0.8	-12.1
	1995	218.4	229.8	126.3	119.7	-11.4	-9.0	-2.4
	2000	216.8	220.9	82.5	138.3	-4.2	6.8	-11.0
	2009	275.7	286.7	122.2	143.8	-11.0	-2.9	-8.1
Niger	1990	392.9	387.6	254.6	129.4	5.3	6.7	-1.4
	1995	198.5	271.0	194.2	76.2	-72.6	-71.3	-1.2
	2000	184.2	208.4	105.8	102.6	-24.3	-24.3	0.0
	2009	456.6	470.0	255.3	212.7	-13.5	-16.4	2.9
Nigeria - Nigéria	1990	1 307.7	255.1	181.7	73.4	1 052.6	739.4	313.2
	1995	-67.2	210.9	72.1	138.8	-278.1	-125.3	-152.8
	2000	-390.6	173.7	84.4	89.1	-564.3	-260.5	-303.8
	2009	1 705.5	1 659.1	687.5	969.4	46.3	12.0	34.3
Saint Helena - Sainte-Hélène	1990	24.7	24.7	23.3	1.4	0.0	0.0	0.0
	1995	12.6	12.6	12.4	0.2	0.0	0.0	0.0
	2000	18.7	18.7	18.4	0.3	0.0	0.0	0.0
	2009	34.8	34.8	33.3	1.5	0.0	0.0	0.0
Senegal - Sénégal	1990	823.7	811.7	589.2	220.1	12.0	31.1	-15.6
	1995	632.8	659.3	399.6	247.3	-26.5	-0.4	-26.1
	2000	423.3	429.3	288.5	145.6	-6.0	9.2	-15.2
	2009	1 104.5	1 017.6	514.4	498.7	86.8	99.6	-12.8
Sierra Leone	1990	55.1	59.3	39.9	19.3	-4.3	-3.4	-0.9
	1995	200.4	205.3	59.7	145.1	-4.9	-1.4	-3.5
	2000	178.8	180.6	115.6	65.0	-1.8	-0.9	-0.9
	2009	436.3	437.3	196.3	240.5	-1.0	0.0	-1.0
Togo	1990	252.8	258.2	155.0	103.9	-5.4	1.3	-6.7
	1995	185.3	191.3	117.9	73.2	-6.0	-5.4	-0.6
	2000	74.0	69.6	52.0	16.2	4.5	0.4	4.1
	2009	640.7	499.0	361.8	136.2	141.7	140.7	1.0
Developing economies: Africa n.e.s. - Économies en développement : Afrique n.d.a. (6)	1990	(e)919.3	(e)902.8	(e)840.4	(e)53.1	16.5	5.8	10.6
	1995	(e)1 020.7	(e)986.4	(e)822.6	(e)163.8	34.3	30.9	3.5
	2000	(e)1 032.5	(e)1 031.4	(e)847.7	(e)170.9	1.1	6.9	-5.8
	2009	(e)5 630.9	(e)5 251.8	(e)3 052.5	(e)2 139.0	379.1	163.1	216.0
Developing economies: America - Économies en développement : Amérique	1990	13 525.1	5 189.4	4 146.4	1 032.0	8 335.7	3 729.7	4 634.3
	1995	8 022.0	6 386.5	4 813.1	1 543.2	1 635.6	78.1	1 557.5
	2000	10 364.7	4 837.6	3 858.4	940.8	5 527.0	-1 012.2	6 539.2
	2009	25 489.6	9 089.3	6 572.7	2 496.1	16 400.2	2 493.3	13 906.9
Caribbean - Caraïbes	1990	1 015.6	808.2	624.6	180.0	207.4	93.9	130.5
	1995	1 421.8	1 321.8	858.0	456.5	100.1	-75.9	176.0
	2000	570.5	418.7	279.2	121.1	151.8	-88.9	240.6
	2009	2 466.2	1 738.2	921.4	812.8	727.9	-101.1	829.0
Anguilla	1990	3.9	3.8	2.4	1.4	0.1	0.0	0.1
	1995	3.5	3.4	2.5	0.8	0.1	0.0	0.1
	2000	7.7	3.5	3.8	-0.3	4.2	0.0	4.2
	2009	0.4	1.4	1.5	-0.1	-1.0	0.0	-1.0
Antigua and Barbuda - Antigua-et-Barbuda	1990	-2.7	4.6	2.9	1.7	-7.3	-7.3	0.0
	1995	-0.8	2.3	0.9	0.7	-3.1	-3.1	0.0
	2000	9.9	9.8	3.7	1.1	0.1	0.0	0.1
	2009	16.2	5.9	2.8	3.1	10.3	0.0	10.3

For sources and notes, see end of table.

Pour les sources et les notes, se reporter à la fin du tableau.

Region, country or territory / Régions, pays ou territoires	Year / Année	Total official net (1) / Total secteur officiel net (1)	Total ODA Net (2) / APD totale nette (2)			Total OOF Net (3) / Flux AASP nets (3)		
			Total donors (4) / Tous donneurs (4)	DAC bilateral donors / Donneurs bilatéraux du CAD	Multilateral donors / Donneurs multilatéraux	Total donors / Tous donneurs	DAC bilateral donors / Donneurs bilatéraux du CAD	Multilateral donors / Donneurs multilatéraux
		Millions of dollars / Millions de dollars						
Aruba	1990	30.0	30.0	28.9	1.1	0.0	0.0	0.0
	1995	29.7	25.8	18.0	7.8	3.9	4.0	-0.1
Bahamas	1990	00.0	?.?	0.4	1.8	27.4	-0.6	28.0
	1995	6.7	4.3	1.3	2.2	2.4	-4.6	7.0
Barbados - Barbade	1990	21.4	2.6	1.4	1.2	18.8	10.7	8.1
	1995	8.2	-1.2	0.1	-1.3	9.4	-3.0	12.3
	2000	13.1	0.2	1.0	-0.8	12.8	3.1	9.7
	2009	16.3	12.2	2.9	9.3	4.1	-17.5	21.6
British Virgin Islands - Îles Vierges britanniques	1990	9.4	5.6	3.0	2.5	3.9	1.6	2.3
	1995	2.6	1.4	0.3	1.1	1.2	0.0	1.2
Cayman Islands - Îles Caïmanes	1990	11.9	3.0	2.1	0.9	8.9	2.4	6.5
	1995	-0.1	-0.6	-0.6	0.0	0.5	0.7	-0.3
Cuba	1990	60.1	50.8	33.6	17.2	9.3	8.3	0.0
	1995	56.2	63.2	33.7	29.5	-7.1	-7.1	0.0
	2000	47.5	44.0	30.8	12.8	3.5	3.5	0.0
	2009	115.3	116.4	86.7	29.1	-1.1	-1.1	0.0
Dominica - Dominique	1990	19.4	19.6	10.8	8.4	-0.3	-0.4	0.1
	1995	24.3	25.0	9.5	14.4	-0.8	-1.2	0.4
	2000	18.5	15.2	5.9	6.4	3.3	-0.1	3.4
	2009	00.0	36.2	5.2	30.0	-2.3	0.0	-2.3
Dominican Republic - République dominicaine	1990	136.4	101.7	72.7	27.8	34.7	1.4	33.3
	1995	165.4	119.4	81.3	36.8	46.0	-12.1	58.1
	2000	72.9	56.0	44.7	11.3	16.9	-36.3	53.1
	2009	758.9	119.8	52.1	67.6	639.1	-16.6	655.7
Grenada - Grenade	1990	12.9	13.8	5.0	8.7	-0.9	-1.1	0.2
	1995	8.3	10.8	5.6	4.5	-2.5	-0.6	-1.9
	2000	19.9	16.5	9.9	3.2	3.4	-0.2	3.6
	2009	51.1	48.2	3.3	40.2	2.9	-0.1	3.0
Haiti - Haïti	1990	166.9	167.4	117.1	50.1	-0.5	-0.1	-0.4
	1995	716.2	722.2	510.1	212.1	-6.0	-6.0	0.0
	2000	206.7	207.8	153.9	53.9	-1.1	-1.1	0.0
	2009	1 110.9	1 119.7	704.2	415.5	-8.8	-15.8	7.0
Jamaica - Jamaïque	1990	325.3	270.6	251.9	18.9	54.7	55.4	17.3
	1995	87.6	107.7	67.6	40.5	-20.1	-8.7	-11.5
	2000	128.8	8.6	-26.3	28.5	120.2	-19.9	140.1
	2009	265.7	149.6	6.4	143.8	116.1	-44.5	160.6
Montserrat	1990	8.3	8.4	7.8	0.5	-0.1	0.0	-0.1
	1995	9.8	9.5	9.1	0.4	0.3	0.0	0.3
	2000	30.9	30.9	30.9	0.1	-0.1	0.0	-0.1
	2009	44.1	44.1	38.6	5.5	0.0	0.0	0.0
Netherlands Antilles - Antilles néerlandaises	1990	50.1	58.0	53.0	5.0	-7.9	-10.9	3.0
	1995	97.0	98.4	94.0	4.4	-1.4	0.0	-1.4
Saint Kitts and Nevis - Saint-Kitts-et-Nevis	1990	8.2	8.1	5.0	2.9	0.1	0.0	0.1
	1995	5.6	3.9	1.7	0.6	1.7	0.2	1.5
	2000	6.0	3.9	0.1	4.1	2.1	-1.3	3.3
	2009	6.5	5.5	1.6	4.9	1.0	-0.4	1.4
Saint Lucia - Sainte-Lucie	1990	15.8	12.3	6.2	5.8	3.5	-0.4	3.9
	1995	52.8	48.2	12.7	34.6	4.6	0.1	4.5
	2000	13.5	11.0	7.1	4.4	2.5	0.0	2.5
	2009	47.3	41.1	6.7	34.7	6.2	-0.3	6.5
Saint Vincent and the Grenadines - Saint-Vincent-et-les Grenadines	1990	15.4	15.4	5.2	9.7	0.0	0.0	0.0
	1995	48.2	47.6	6.3	40.7	0.6	0.4	0.2
	2000	9.7	6.2	3.8	1.1	3.5	0.0	3.5
	2009	43.6	31.1	5.0	26.9	12.5	0.0	12.5

For sources and notes, see end of table.

Pour les sources et les notes, se reporter à la fin du tableau.

Region, country or territory / Régions, pays ou territoires	Year / Année	Total official net (1) / Total secteur officiel net (1)	Total ODA Net (2) / APD totale nette (2)			Total OOF Net (3) / Flux AASP nets (3)		
			Total donors (4) / Tous donneurs (4)	of which: / dont :		Total donors / Tous donneurs	of which: / dont :	
				DAC bilateral donors / Donneurs bilatéraux du CAD	Multilateral donors / Donneurs multilatéraux		DAC bilateral donors / Donneurs bilatéraux du CAD	Multilateral donors / Donneurs multilatéraux
		Millions of dollars / Millions de dollars						
Trinidad and Tobago - Trinité et Tobago	1990	80.8	17.8	6.1	11.7	63.0	34.8	28.2
	1995	95.1	24.9	-1.7	26.6	70.2	-35.1	105.4
	2000	-21.6	-1.5	4.4	-5.9	-20.1	-36.7	16.5
	2009	-44.1	6.9	4.4	2.4	-51.0	-4.8	-46.2
Turks and Caicos Islands	1990	11.6	11.6	8.9	2.8	0.0	0.0	0.0
Îles Turques et Caïques	1995	5.7	5.6	5.5	0.0	0.1	0.0	0.1
	2000	7.3	6.7	5.6	1.1	0.6	0.0	0.6
Central America - Amérique centrale	*1990*	*6 613.6*	*1 839.6*	*1 599.5*	*234.1*	*4 774.0*	*2 028.6*	*2 751.0*
	1995	*2 379.3*	*2 027.7*	*1 555.1*	*450.8*	*351.6*	*-836.1*	*1 187.7*
	2000	*1 723.2*	*1 433.3*	*1 011.4*	*414.7*	*289.9*	*-740.0*	*1 029.9*
	2009	*10 563.3*	*2 272.2*	*1 701.8*	*564.9*	*8 291.1*	*489.9*	*7 801.2*
Belize	1990	38.5	30.3	18.8	11.3	8.1	4.1	4.1
	1995	23.4	18.2	8.9	6.3	5.2	-2.0	7.2
	2000	31.8	14.7	2.9	11.2	17.2	3.5	13.7
	2009	39.8	27.9	7.1	20.1	11.9	-1.8	13.7
Costa Rica	1990	237.7	227.0	206.6	19.1	10.8	21.1	-10.3
	1995	79.6	29.7	16.7	0.1	49.9	-28.2	78.1
	2000	-39.6	9.6	17.4	-8.4	-49.2	-26.9	-22.3
	2009	134.6	109.3	98.7	10.2	25.3	14.4	10.9
El Salvador	1990	308.3	347.3	312.0	34.3	-39.0	-0.9	-38.1
	1995	381.6	296.0	243.9	51.2	85.7	0.1	85.6
	2000	283.4	179.7	172.4	6.8	103.7	-13.5	117.2
	2009	685.9	276.7	259.7	10.5	409.2	23.0	386.2
Guatemala	1990	221.5	201.4	149.5	50.5	20.1	6.2	13.9
	1995	206.0	208.4	161.8	45.1	-2.4	11.6	-14.0
	2000	321.2	263.1	230.4	32.3	58.0	6.7	51.4
	2009	1 008.8	376.2	341.4	34.2	632.6	-1.3	633.8
Honduras	1990	433.3	448.5	383.5	64.0	-15.2	-0.7	-14.6
	1995	394.0	402.4	233.0	168.1	-8.4	25.4	-33.9
	2000	396.1	448.3	310.7	133.1	-52.2	19.5	-71.7
	2009	489.9	457.1	304.7	152.8	32.8	10.6	22.2
Mexico - Mexique	1990	5 024.2	156.3	144.8	11.5	4 868.0	2 035.6	2 837.9
	1995	407.8	384.1	365.1	19.0	23.7	-990.9	1 014.6
	2000	74.1	-57.8	-68.3	10.0	131.9	-710.7	842.6
	2009	7 004.4	185.5	158.7	25.5	6 818.9	421.8	6 397.2
Nicaragua	1990	326.6	329.6	288.5	41.1	-2.9	-1.8	-1.1
	1995	823.0	649.1	492.2	155.9	173.9	165.1	8.8
	2000	552.1	560.4	326.1	234.1	-8.3	-6.2	-2.0
	2009	794.0	774.0	472.9	298.8	20.0	-1.9	21.9
Panama	1990	23.5	99.3	96.0	2.4	-75.8	-35.0	-40.8
	1995	63.9	39.8	33.6	5.1	24.2	-17.2	41.3
	2000	104.0	15.4	19.8	-4.5	88.7	-12.4	101.1
	2009	405.9	65.5	58.6	6.8	340.4	25.0	315.4
South America - Amérique du Sud	*1990*	*5 246.4*	*2 030.9*	*1 569.5*	*460.0*	*3 215.5*	*1 607.5*	*1 613.8*
	1995	*3 590.5*	*2 457.0*	*1 911.9*	*544.9*	*1 133.5*	*862.2*	*271.4*
	2000	*6 917.8*	*1 868.5*	*1 565.0*	*290.6*	*5 049.3*	*-184.8*	*5 234.2*
	2009	*10 884.0*	*3 578.7*	*2 782.8*	*787.0*	*7 305.3*	*1 967.6*	*5 337.7*
Argentina - Argentine	1990	903.8	168.7	166.2	2.6	735.1	411.9	323.2
	1995	2 529.4	142.6	110.3	32.2	2 386.9	719.7	1 667.1
	2000	677.1	52.4	43.5	1.4	624.6	-553.4	1 178.0
	2009	1 359.6	127.7	78.9	47.5	1 231.9	-195.4	1 427.3
Bolivia (Plurinational State of) -	1990	576.2	545.4	364.7	180.7	30.8	10.4	20.4
Bolivie (État plurinational de)	1995	712.4	711.5	518.3	193.2	0.9	-18.8	19.7
	2000	445.9	481.7	336.3	145.4	-35.8	-25.4	-10.4
	2009	642.0	725.8	485.0	240.6	-83.9	-29.2	-54.7

For sources and notes, see end of table.

Pour les sources et les notes, se reporter à la fin du tableau.

7.6.1 Official financial flows from bilateral and multilateral sources by country and geographical region

7.6.1 Flux financiers publics bilatéraux et multilatéraux par pays et régions géographiques

Region, country or territory / Régions, pays ou territoires	Year / Année	Total official net (1) / Total secteur officiel net (1)	Total ODA Net (2) / APD totale nette (2) Total donors (4) / Tous donneurs (4)	Total ODA Net (2) — of which: / dont : DAC bilateral donors / Donneurs bilatéraux du CAD	Total ODA Net (2) — of which: / dont : Multilateral donors / Donneurs multilatéraux	Total OOF Net (3) / Flux AASP nets (3) Total donors / Tous donneurs	Total OOF Net (3) — of which: / dont : DAC bilateral donors / Donneurs bilatéraux du CAD	Total OOF Net (3) — of which: / dont : Multilateral donors / Donneurs multilatéraux
				Millions of dollars / Millions de dollars				
Brazil - Brésil	1990	526.5	151.1	142.1	9.0	375.5	715.7	224.5
	1995	-40.3	271.3	204.1	70.6	-311.6	-33.0	-278.6
	2000	4 097.7	231.4	222.5	7.3	3 866.3	430.9	3 435.4
	2009	2 165.0	338.5	309.2	27.5	1 826.5	1 090.1	736.4
Chile - Chili	1990	787.2	103.5	83.4	20.2	683.7	207.9	475.8
	1995	-1 627.4	156.6	143.3	13.2	-1 783.9	-98.2	-1 685.8
	2000	-207.6	48.9	41.0	7.3	-256.5	-175.6	-80.8
	2009	845.4	79.7	59.7	19.1	765.8	849.7	-84.0
Colombia - Colombie	1990	-1.5	88.5	86.7	1.9	-90.0	-93.2	3.2
	1995	71.5	168.9	160.9	8.0	-97.4	131.3	-228.7
	2000	-24.9	185.9	178.5	6.8	-210.9	-276.9	66.0
	2009	2 841.0	1 060.2	998.5	60.7	1 780.8	-38.5	1 819.3
Ecuador - Équateur	1990	352.6	159.3	122.2	36.7	193.3	112.7	80.6
	1995	632.9	222.9	160.9	61.3	410.1	85.3	324.8
	2000	226.4	146.1	137.9	7.9	80.3	-28.4	108.7
	2009	264.6	208.6	147.2	60.7	56.0	-6.3	62.3
Falkland Islands (Malvinas) - Îles Falkland (Malvinas)	1990	1.8	1.8	1.8	..	0.0	0.0	..
	1995	1.7	1.7	0.1	1.6	0.0	0.0	0.0
Guyana	1990	221.5	168.3	35.8	132.5	53.2	72.0	-18.8
	1995	81.1	85.7	23.3	62.4	-4.6	11.3	-15.8
	2000	103.9	115.8	51.9	64.0	-11.9	-0.7	-11.2
	2009	177.8	173.5	40.6	132.9	4.3	0.0	4.3
Paraguay	1990	29.4	57.2	47.6	8.6	-27.8	1.6	-29.4
	1995	153.5	139.3	106.3	30.1	14.1	-20.1	34.2
	2000	202.0	81.6	73.1	8.2	120.5	8.3	112.2
	2009	237.0	148.3	121.4	26.6	88.7	-2.5	91.2
Peru - Pérou	1990	398.3	397.1	350.4	46.7	1.2	-2.0	3.2
	1995	817.8	370.9	327.4	43.6	446.9	65.4	381.5
	2000	1 111.9	396.8	374.5	21.7	715.1	513.2	201.9
	2009	1 246.4	441.9	338.7	101.4	804.5	334.1	470.5
Suriname	1990	64.3	61.1	51.2	10.0	3.1	-0.9	4.0
	1995	74.9	76.7	70.4	6.4	-1.8	-1.1	-0.7
	2000	36.2	34.3	29.2	5.2	1.8	0.0	1.8
	2009	175.0	157.1	124.3	32.8	17.9	10.1	7.8
Uruguay	1990	86.6	52.4	41.7	10.7	34.2	1.1	33.1
	1995	52.6	65.7	57.5	8.1	-13.0	-2.6	-10.4
	2000	198.7	17.4	15.4	1.3	181.3	2.0	179.2
	2009	734.9	50.6	32.4	17.6	684.2	-8.8	693.0
Venezuela (Bolivarian Rep. of) - Venezuela (Rép. bolivarienne du)	1990	1 299.5	76.4	75.8	0.6	1 223.2	170.3	1 052.9
	1995	130.2	43.3	29.0	14.3	86.9	22.9	64.0
	2000	50.6	76.1	61.3	14.1	-25.5	-78.8	53.3
	2009	195.3	66.8	46.9	19.6	128.5	-35.7	164.3
Developing economies: America n.e.s. - Économies en développement : (6) Amérique n.d.a.	1990	(e)649.5	(e)510.7	(e)352.8	(e)157.9	138.8	-0.2	139.1
	1995	(e)630.4	(e)580.0	(e)488.1	(e)91.0	50.4	127.9	-77.6
	2000	(e)1 153.2	(e)1 117.1	(e)1 002.7	(e)114.4	36.1	1.5	34.5
	2009	(e)1 576.1	(e)1 500.2	(e)1 166.7	(e)331.3	76.0	137.0	-61.0
Developing economies: Asia - Économies en développement : Asie	1990	24 239.3	17 827.0	10 546.2	4 600.1	6 412.3	3 072.7	3 481.1
	1995	24 178.8	17 377.6	11 788.3	5 193.1	6 801.2	5 252.2	1 555.2
	2000	13 347.9	14 888.8	10 383.9	4 146.7	-1 541.0	-4 175.8	2 634.8
	2009	46 174.6	37 050.4	22 744.0	10 478.4	9 124.1	-837.9	9 962.0
Eastern Asia - Asie orientale	1990	2 879.4	2 177.9	1 553.4	605.2	701.6	662.3	39.3
	1995	6 909.4	3 764.0	2 699.0	1 044.0	3 145.4	1 869.6	1 275.8
	2000	1 451.7	2 002.0	1 450.0	546.7	-550.3	-2 189.4	1 639.1
	2009	1 908.7	1 570.7	1 410.5	113.1	338.0	-1 190.6	1 528.6

For sources and notes, see end of table.

Pour les sources et les notes, se reporter à la fin du tableau.

7

Region, country or territory Régions, pays ou territoires	Year Année	Total official net (1) Total secteur officiel net (1)	Total ODA Net (2) APD totale nette (2)			Total OOF Net (3) Flux AASP nets (3)		
			Total donors (4) Tous donneurs (4)	of which: / dont :		Total donors Tous donneurs	of which: / dont :	
				DAC bilateral donors Donneurs bilatéraux du CAD	Multilateral donors Donneurs multilatéraux		DAC bilateral donors Donneurs bilatéraux du CAD	Multilateral donors Donneurs multilatéraux
				Millions of dollars / Millions de dollars				
China - Chine	1990	3 294.5	2 030.4	1 465.5	570.1	1 264.1	835.9	428.2
	1995	7 041.6	3 470.6	2 482.5	952.5	3 571.0	1 943.0	1 627.9
	2000	1 160.6	1 711.8	1 270.8	440.3	-551.2	-2 190.2	1 639.1
	2009	1 429.4	1 131.8	1 156.9	-50.5	297.7	-1 192.8	1 490.4
China, Hong Kong SAR - Chine (RAS de Hong Kong)	1990	31.4	38.2	19.5	18.7	-6.8	-6.8	0.0
	1995	2.3	17.7	11.0	0.0	15.5	15.5	0.0
China, Macao SAR - Chine (RAS de Macao)	1990	0.2	0.2	0.1	0.1	0.0	0.0	0.0
	1995	-4.0	-4.0	0.1	-4.1	0.0	0.0	0.0
China, Taiwan Province of - Province chinoise de Taiwan	1990	24.6	36.3	6.4	..	-11.7	-3.1	-8.6
	1995	10.1	0.2	11.1	..	9.9	9.9	..
Korea, Dem. People's Rep. of - Corée, Rép. populaire dém. de	1990	6.9	7.7	0.9	6.9	-0.9	-0.9	0.0
	1995	17.0	13.5	1.5	11.9	3.5	3.5	0.0
	2000	74.2	73.3	26.9	46.4	0.9	0.9	0.0
	2009	70.4	66.8	46.4	20.7	3.7	3.7	0.0
Korea, Republic of - Corée, République de	1990	-491.2	52.0	54.8	2.7	-543.2	-162.9	-380.3
	1995	-354.1	57.0	60.4	0.5	-411.1	-59.0	-352.1
Mongolia - Mongolie	1990	13.1	13.1	6.4	6.7	0.0	0.0	0.0
	1995	196.6	209.0	131.9	77.1	-12.4	-12.4	0.0
	2000	217.0	217.0	152.3	60.1	0.0	0.0	0.0
	2009	408.8	372.2	207.2	142.9	36.7	-1.5	38.2
Southern Asia - Asie méridionale	*1990*	*7 890.8*	*6 062.9*	*3 318.8*	*2 741.1*	*1 827.9*	*174.5*	*1 654.6*
	1995	*5 997.0*	*5 341.8*	*3 144.0*	*2 298.0*	*655.2*	*469.5*	*185.6*
	2000	*3 367.3*	*4 243.4*	*2 480.3*	*1 744.6*	*-876.1*	*-662.2*	*-213.9*
	2009	*18 549.2*	*14 554.7*	*9 733.7*	*4 373.1*	*3 994.4*	*123.7*	*3 870.7*
Afghanistan	1990	121.7	121.7	100.4	22.7	0.0	0.0	0.0
	1995	212.5	212.5	106.1	106.4	0.0	0.0	0.0
	2000	136.0	136.0	87.5	47.8	0.0	0.0	0.0
	2009	6 277.6	6 235.3	5 089.3	953.5	42.3	29.1	13.2
Bangladesh	1990	2 112.4	2 092.8	1 103.3	999.8	19.7	21.9	-2.2
	1995	1 272.8	1 281.5	728.4	563.2	-8.8	-3.3	-5.5
	2000	1 171.0	1 171.7	623.0	519.9	-0.7	-5.3	4.6
	2009	1 903.1	1 226.9	717.6	500.3	676.1	-34.7	710.8
Bhutan - Bhoutan	1990	46.0	46.0	20.1	26.7	0.0	0.0	0.0
	1995	71.2	71.2	55.5	15.6	0.0	0.0	0.0
	2000	53.0	53.1	33.8	19.8	-0.1	-0.1	0.0
	2009	136.8	125.4	55.3	69.2	11.3	3.3	8.1
India - Inde	1990	2 900.2	1 398.9	751.9	644.6	1 501.2	252.9	1 248.3
	1995	1 769.6	1 729.0	1 060.8	695.1	40.6	41.4	-0.8
	2000	1 153.2	1 372.7	650.5	734.0	-219.4	51.6	-271.0
	2009	5 694.0	2 502.2	1 577.8	921.8	3 191.8	515.6	2 676.2
Iran (Islamic Rep. of) - Iran (Rép. islamique d')	1990	-96.1	104.8	34.8	35.7	-200.9	-133.9	-67.0
	1995	395.5	186.5	158.9	27.6	209.0	129.6	79.4
	2000	-586.5	129.9	112.8	16.9	-716.4	-756.8	40.4
	2009	-212.6	92.7	65.8	11.4	-305.3	-383.5	78.1
Maldives	1990	24.9	20.9	11.6	9.9	4.1	4.1	0.0
	1995	59.1	57.8	30.5	21.3	1.3	1.3	0.0
	2000	16.2	19.2	13.3	7.1	-3.0	-1.8	-1.2
	2009	71.1	33.3	18.5	16.2	37.9	-2.5	40.4
Nepal - Népal	1990	432.1	422.8	239.0	181.5	9.3	0.0	9.2
	1995	428.3	428.6	266.9	163.0	-0.3	0.7	-1.0
	2000	409.0	386.0	233.6	151.3	23.0	2.7	20.2
	2009	844.5	854.6	504.8	349.4	-10.1	0.5	-10.6
Pakistan	1990	1 631.1	1 126.6	653.8	492.3	504.5	31.2	474.7
	1995	1 241.8	820.9	360.4	525.5	421.0	299.9	121.1
	2000	763.6	700.4	475.5	224.3	63.3	74.7	-11.4
	2009	3 102.8	2 780.6	1 330.6	1 230.6	322.2	-7.0	329.2

For sources and notes, see end of table.

Pour les sources et les notes, se reporter à la fin du tableau.

Region, country or territory / Régions, pays ou territoires	Year / Année	Total official net (1) / Total secteur officiel net (1)	Total ODA Net (2) / APD totale nette (2)			Total OOF Net (3) / Flux AASP nets (3)		
			Total donors (4) / Tous donneurs (4)	DAC bilateral donors / Donneurs bilatéraux du CAD	Multilateral donors / Donneurs multilatéraux	Total donors / Tous donneurs	DAC bilateral donors / Donneurs bilatéraux du CAD	Multilateral donors / Donneurs multilatéraux
				of which: / dont :			of which: / dont :	
		Millions of dollars / Millions de dollars						
Sri Lanka	1990	718.3	728.3	404.0	328.0	-10.0	-1.0	8.6
	1995	546.2	553.8	376.4	180.2	-7.6	-0.1	-7.6
	2000	251.7	274.5	250.4	23.5	-22.8	-27.2	4.4
	2009	732.0	703.8	373.9	320.0	28.2	0.0	25.3
South-Eastern Asia - Asie du Sud-Est	*1990*	*7 777.3*	*4 782.1*	*4 086.8*	*677.7*	*2 995.1*	*1 561.3*	*1 456.8*
	1995	*7 567.2*	*5 012.2*	*4 109.2*	*909.7*	*2 555.0*	*2 066.3*	*488.8*
	2000	*4 307.9*	*5 658.9*	*4 767.5*	*894.6*	*-1 351.0*	*-1 685.8*	*334.8*
	2009	*9 126.1*	*6 886.9*	*3 844.2*	*2 993.3*	*2 239.2*	*-284.7*	*2 523.9*
Brunei Darussalam - Brunéi Darussalam	1990	-4.5	3.9	3.7	0.1	-8.4	-8.4	0.0
	1995	4.3	4.3	4.2	0.1	0.0	0.0	0.0
Cambodia - Cambodge	1990	41.3	41.3	28.5	12.8	0.0	0.0	0.0
	1995	554.0	551.0	341.2	209.8	3.0	3.0	0.0
	2000	395.3	395.7	248.6	147.0	-0.4	-0.4	0.0
	2009	710.3	722.3	473.7	239.9	-12.0	-7.7	-4.4
Indonesia including East Timor - Indonésie, y compris le Timor oriental	1990	3 255.5	1 716.0	1 520.7	171.4	1 539.6	534.3	1 029.3
	1995	2 705.3	1 301.2	1 218.4	96.2	1 404.1	858.9	545.2
	2000	2 963.6	1 882.0	1 760.1	121.4	1 081.6	360.4	721.2
Indonesia - Indonésie	2009	984.3	1 049.5	332.9	716.7	-65.1	-815.8	750.7
Lao People's Dom. Rep. - Rép. dém. populaire lao	1990	149.1	148.1	51.2	96.9	1.0	0.0	0.0
	1995	307.0	306.9	170.1	136.8	0.1	0.1	0.0
	2000	280.3	280.6	195.5	84.9	-0.4	-0.5	0.2
	2009	428.4	420.1	260.0	138.0	8.3	10.9	-2.6
Malaysia - Malaisie	1990	538.5	468.5	458.7	13.3	70.1	-6.3	76.4
	1995	399.9	108.1	106.9	7.3	291.8	412.8	-121.0
	2000	-117.6	45.4	43.5	3.3	163.0	-89.1	-73.9
	2009	354.7	143.6	132.9	10.6	211.1	302.3	-91.2
Myanmar	1990	184.0	160.8	83.1	77.7	23.2	23.6	-0.4
	1995	154.4	150.2	128.2	22.0	4.2	5.1	-0.9
	2000	125.8	105.6	68.9	36.6	20.2	20.2	0.0
	2009	345.2	357.0	234.0	115.0	-11.8	-11.8	0.0
Philippines	1990	2 176.9	1 270.6	1 102.2	167.3	906.3	411.7	494.6
	1995	675.3	902.1	765.4	128.8	-226.8	-169.5	-57.2
	2000	353.3	571.7	505.1	66.3	-218.4	-20.3	-198.1
	2009	1 106.7	310.0	244.4	64.8	796.7	-376.4	1 173.1
Singapore - Singapour	1990	152.1	-3.1	-3.2	0.1	155.2	193.2	-38.1
	1995	-49.0	16.7	13.9	2.8	-65.6	-65.6	0.0
Thailand - Thaïlande	1990	1 103.8	795.6	734.0	65.7	308.2	413.2	-104.9
	1995	1 765.7	837.0	807.9	35.1	928.7	821.8	106.9
	2000	-1 246.7	696.5	683.6	15.8	-1 943.2	-1 783.5	-159.7
	2009	74.6	-76.6	-92.5	15.0	151.1	168.9	-17.8
Timor-Leste	2009	218.5	216.7	183.0	33.5	1.8	1.8	0.0
Viet Nam	1990	180.6	180.6	107.9	72.5	0.0	0.2	-0.1
	1995	1 050.4	834.8	553.0	270.9	215.6	199.8	15.8
	2000	1 553.9	1 681.4	1 262.2	419.1	-127.5	-172.5	45.1
	2009	4 903.5	3 744.3	2 075.9	1 659.8	1 159.2	443.2	716.0
Western Asia - Asie occidentale	*1990*	*4 597.0*	*3 709.2*	*1 349.8*	*203.4*	*887.7*	*674.6*	*330.4*
	1995	*2 986.1*	*2 526.8*	*1 364.9*	*680.2*	*459.3*	*846.8*	*-381.4*
	2000	*3 587.4*	*2 351.7*	*1 254.6*	*834.1*	*1 235.7*	*352.7*	*883.0*
	2009	*11 836.6*	*9 537.6*	*6 121.7*	*2 618.7*	*2 299.0*	*240.7*	*2 058.4*
Bahrain - Bahreïn	1990	136.1	136.9	1.9	2.3	-0.8	-0.8	0.0
	1995	47.3	49.1	1.8	0.4	-1.8	-1.8	0.0
	2000	48.8	49.1	1.6	-0.1	-0.2	-0.2	0.0
Iraq	1990	700.0	63.1	-8.6	16.3	636.9	642.3	-5.4
	1995	322.3	332.8	239.0	81.7	-10.5	-10.5	0.0
	2000	99.6	99.6	84.1	15.4	0.0	0.0	0.0
	2009	2 828.9	2 791.5	2 628.7	108.1	37.4	23.4	14.0

For sources and notes, see end of table.

Pour les sources et les notes, se reporter à la fin du tableau.

Region, country or territory / Régions, pays ou territoires	Year / Année	Total official net (1) / Total secteur officiel net (1)	Total ODA Net (2) / APD totale nette (2)			Total OOF Net (3) / Flux AASP nets (3)		
			Total donors (4) / Tous donneurs (4)	of which: / dont :		Total donors / Tous donneurs	of which: / dont :	
				DAC bilateral donors / Donneurs bilatéraux du CAD	Multilateral donors / Donneurs multilatéraux		DAC bilateral donors / Donneurs bilatéraux du CAD	Multilateral donors / Donneurs multilatéraux
			Millions of dollars / Millions de dollars					
Jordan - Jordanie	1990	1 080.0	886.0	136.0	25.0	194.1	126.1	75.5
	1995	1 031.8	539.1	395.1	144.1	492.7	410.0	82.7
	2000	552.0	552.2	385.0	167.7	-0.2	-21.4	21.2
	2009	1 200.5	760.6	486.3	232.9	440.0	130.3	310.0
Kuwait - Koweït	1990	9.7	5.7	2.2	3.5	0.0	0.0	0.0
	1995	19.6	3.1	2.1	1.0	16.5	16.5	0.0
Lebanon - Liban	1990	229.6	252.1	64.9	39.0	-22.5	-13.6	-8.9
	1995	309.4	186.1	57.2	72.2	123.4	2.2	121.2
	2000	268.1	199.3	93.7	90.9	68.8	2.8	66.0
	2009	460.9	641.0	389.0	203.1	-180.1	-86.2	-93.9
Occupied Palestinian territory - Territoire palestinien occupé	1995	498.4	498.4	183.4	262.6	0.0	0.0	0.0
	2000	682.6	637.3	306.8	226.1	45.3	-0.1	45.4
	2009	3 041.5	3 026.1	1 737.6	1 014.0	15.4	0.4	15.0
Oman	1990	57.6	61.1	11.4	2.2	-3.5	6.0	-9.6
	1995	51.7	58.3	11.9	2.1	-6.6	-10.8	4.1
	2000	50.0	45.0	9.2	1.7	5.0	9.7	-4.7
	2009	483.7	212.0	8.4	1.8	271.7	276.7	-5.0
Qatar	1990	1.5	1.5	1.3	0.2	0.0	0.0	0.0
	1995	618.0	2.3	2.1	0.2	615.7	615.7	0.0
Saudi Arabia - Arabie saoudite	1990	14.0	14.6	12.8	1.7	-0.6	-0.6	0.0
	1995	6.4	16.9	14.5	1.9	-10.6	-10.6	0.0
	2000	48.0	21.9	18.0	2.1	20.1	20.1	0.0
Syrian Arab Republic - République arabe syrienne	1990	673.7	682.6	69.4	34.2	-8.9	0.5	-10.3
	1995	322.5	355.7	158.9	69.5	-33.2	-5.1	-21.9
	2000	485.8	157.9	97.4	38.1	327.9	342.1	-14.2
	2009	419.3	244.7	61.2	137.2	174.6	2.3	172.4
Turkey - Turquie	1990	1 292.3	1 202.3	587.9	-16.2	90.0	-88.5	289.1
	1995	-329.0	312.7	185.3	-12.7	-641.8	-74.2	-567.5
	2000	1 082.2	326.7	99.1	190.3	755.5	-6.2	761.6
	2009	2 786.1	1 362.2	558.1	799.7	1 423.9	-192.4	1 616.3
United Arab Emirates - Émirats arabes unis	1990	3.8	3.5	2.8	0.7	0.3	0.3	0.0
	1995	-77.6	5.4	4.9	0.4	-83.0	-83.0	0.0
Yemen - Yémen	1990	402.7	399.9	168.8	94.5	2.8	2.8	0.0
	1995	165.4	166.9	108.8	56.8	-1.6	-1.6	0.0
	2000	270.4	262.8	159.7	101.9	7.6	0.0	7.7
	2009	615.7	499.7	252.4	122.0	116.0	87.1	28.9
Developing economies: Asia n.e.s. - Économies en développement : Asie n.d.a. (6)	1990	(e)1 094.9	(e)1 094.9	(e)237.5	(e)372.6	0.0	0.0	0.0
	1995	(e)719.1	(e)732.7	(e)471.3	(e)261.2	-13.7	0.0	-13.7
	2000	(e)633.6	(e)632.8	(e)431.4	(e)126.7	0.7	8.9	-8.2
	2009	(e)4 754.0	(e)4 500.5	(e)1 633.9	(e)380.2	253.4	273.0	-19.6
Developing economies: Oceania - Économies en développement : Océanie	**1990**	**1 495.0**	**1 372.5**	**1 215.0**	**154.6**	**122.5**	**60.0**	**62.5**
	1995	**1 974.0**	**1 865.7**	**1 712.3**	**150.3**	**108.3**	**119.6**	**-11.3**
	2000	**886.8**	**815.9**	**712.5**	**102.2**	**70.9**	**68.4**	**2.4**
	2009	**2 049.9**	**1 647.2**	**1 351.6**	**294.9**	**402.7**	**345.1**	**57.5**
Cook Islands - Îles Cook	1990	11.4	12.1	10.1	2.0	-0.8	-0.8	0.0
	1995	13.0	13.0	10.4	2.6	0.0	0.0	0.0
	2000	4.2	4.3	3.4	0.9	-0.2	-0.2	0.0
	2009	7.1	7.6	5.8	1.9	-0.6	-0.6	0.0
Fiji - Fidji	1990	34.9	49.6	43.5	5.6	-14.7	-0.4	-14.3
	1995	41.9	44.4	39.6	4.0	-2.5	3.6	-6.0
	2000	22.8	29.1	28.9	0.2	-6.3	-0.1	-6.2
	2009	73.6	71.1	49.7	21.3	2.5	3.1	-0.6
French Polynesia - Polynésie française	1990	304.0	259.7	258.0	1.7	44.3	44.7	-0.4
	1995	434.3	450.9	444.4	6.5	-16.6	-16.1	-0.5

For sources and notes, see end of table.

Pour les sources et les notes, se reporter à la fin du tableau.

Region, country or territory / Régions, pays ou territoires	Year / Année	Total official net (1) / Total secteur officiel net (1)	Total ODA Net (2) / APD totale nette (2)			Total OOF Net (3) / Flux AASP nets (3)		
			Total donors (4) / Tous donneurs (4)	of which: / dont :		Total donors / Tous donneurs	of which: / dont :	
				DAC bilateral donors / Donneurs bilatéraux du CAD	Multilateral donors / Donneurs multilatéraux		DAC bilateral donors / Donneurs bilatéraux du CAD	Multilateral donors / Donneurs multilatéraux
				Millions of dollars / Millions de dollars				
Kiribati	1990	20.2	20.2	17.7	2.5	0.0	0.0	0.0
	1995	15.3	15.3	11.5	3.9	0.0	0.0	0.0
	2000	17.9	17.9	14.8	3.1	0.0	0.0	0.0
	2009	27.6	27.2	22.5	4.7	0.4	0.1	0.0
Marshall Islands - Îles Marshall	1995	38.9	38.9	32.1	6.7	0.0	0.0	0.0
	2000	57.2	57.2	47.1	10.1	0.0	0.0	0.0
	2009	58.4	58.8	59.3	-0.7	-0.4	0.0	-0.4
Micronesia (Federated States of) - Micronésie (États fédérés de)	1995	78.2	77.2	71.8	5.3	1.0	1.0	0.0
	2000	101.4	101.5	96.6	4.9	-0.1	-0.1	0.0
	2009	121.5	121.0	119.3	1.7	0.5	0.4	0.0
Nauru	1990	0.2	0.2	0.2	..	0.0	0.0	..
	1995	2.7	2.7	2.2	..	0.0	0.0	..
	2000	4.0	4.0	3.9	0.1	0.0	0.0	0.0
	2009	24.4	24.1	22.5	1.5	0.3	0.4	-0.1
New Caledonia - Nouvelle-Calédonie	1990	325.8	302.4	300.2	2.2	23.4	24.0	-0.6
	1995	548.8	451.2	442.3	8.9	97.6	98.7	-1.1
Niue - Nioué	1990	7.2	7.2	7.0	0.2	0.0	0.0	0.0
	1995	8.2	8.2	8.1	0.2	0.0	0.0	0.0
	2000	3.2	3.2	3.0	0.2	0.0	0.0	0.0
	2009	9.0	9.0	6.9	2.1	0.0	0.0	0.0
Northern Mariana Islands - Îles Mariannes du Nord	1990	63.1	63.1	61.9	1.2	0.0	0.0	0.0
	1995	18.8	-0.7	-0.2	-0.5	19.5	19.5	0.0
Palau - Palaos	1995	156.3	142.3	141.7	0.1	14.0	14.0	0.0
	2000	37.7	39.1	39.0	0.2	-1.5	-1.5	0.0
	2009	35.4	35.4	34.0	1.4	0.0	0.0	0.0
Papua New Guinea - Papouasie-Nouvelle-Guinée	1990	474.9	412.4	320.2	90.8	62.5	-15.3	77.8
	1995	365.3	370.3	300.8	68.9	-5.0	-1.3	-3.7
	2000	357.0	275.2	270.4	4.9	81.9	72.7	9.2
	2009	797.4	413.7	322.2	91.5	383.7	325.2	58.6
Samoa	1990	47.4	47.6	27.8	19.5	-0.1	-0.1	0.0
	1995	43.2	43.2	31.4	12.1	0.0	0.0	0.0
	2000	27.5	27.1	18.2	9.0	0.4	0.3	0.1
	2009	77.9	77.4	46.5	30.9	0.5	0.5	0.0
Solomon Islands - Îles Salomon	1990	46.2	45.7	31.1	14.2	0.5	0.5	0.0
	1995	47.0	47.7	36.8	10.1	-0.7	-0.7	0.0
	2000	69.5	68.3	20.8	46.2	1.2	1.2	0.0
	2009	214.7	205.9	202.3	4.1	8.8	8.8	0.0
Tokelau - Tokélaou	1990	4.8	4.8	4.4	0.4	0.0	0.0	0.0
	1995	3.7	3.7	3.5	0.3	0.0	0.0	0.0
	2000	3.5	3.5	3.4	0.1	0.0	0.0	0.0
	2009	9.8	9.8	9.7	0.2	0.0	0.0	0.0
Tonga	1990	29.6	29.8	24.2	5.4	-0.2	-0.2	0.0
	1995	38.8	38.8	28.9	9.9	0.0	0.0	0.0
	2000	18.9	18.8	14.9	4.0	0.0	0.0	0.0
	2009	39.9	39.5	34.6	4.9	0.4	0.4	0.0
Tuvalu	1990	5.1	5.1	4.8	0.3	0.0	0.0	0.0
	1995	7.9	7.9	6.3	1.5	0.0	0.0	0.0
	2000	4.0	4.0	3.8	0.2	0.0	0.0	0.0
	2009	17.5	17.5	14.8	2.7	0.0	0.0	0.0
Vanuatu	1990	54.1	49.5	42.1	7.5	4.6	4.6	0.0
	1995	45.1	45.6	39.6	6.0	-0.5	-0.5	0.0
	2000	45.2	45.8	28.3	17.5	-0.7	0.0	-0.7
	2009	105.1	103.3	98.1	5.2	1.8	1.8	0.0
Wallis and Futuna Islands - Îles Wallis-et-Futuna	1990	3.9	0.9	0.0	0.9	3.0	3.0	0.0
	1995	0.5	1.0	0.1	0.8	-0.4	-0.4	0.0
	2000	53.3	52.1	52.1	0.0	1.2	1.2	0.0
	2009	116.1	117.7	117.5	0.2	-1.5	-1.5	0.0

For sources and notes, see end of table.

Pour les sources et les notes, se reporter à la fin du tableau.

Region, country or territory / Régions, pays ou territoires	Year / Année	Total official net (1) / Total secteur officiel net (1) / Tous donneurs	Total ODA Net (2) / APD totale nette (2) — Total donors (4) / Tous donneurs (4)	of which: / dont : DAC bilateral donors / Donneurs bilatéraux du CAD	of which: / dont : Multilateral donors / Donneurs multilatéraux	Total OOF Net (3) / Flux AASP nets (3) — Total donors / Tous donneurs	of which: / dont : DAC bilateral donors / Donneurs bilatéraux du CAD	of which: / dont : Multilateral donors / Donneurs multilatéraux
		Millions of dollars / Millions de dollars						
Developing economies: Oceania n.e.s. - Économies en développement . Océanie n.d.a. (6)	1990	(e)62.4	(e)62.4	(e)61.9	(e)0.1	0.0	0.0	0.0
	1995	(e)65.9	(e)64.0	(e)61.1	(e)3.0	1.9	1.9	0.0
	2000	(e)59.5	(e)64.7	(e)64.0	(e)0.7	-5.2	-5.2	0.0
	2009	(e)314.6	(e)308.3	(e)186.2	(e)121.3	6.3	6.3	0.0
Developing economies n.e.s. Économies en développement n.d.a.	1990	(e)6 706.4	(e)6 013.1	(e)5 148.0	(e)865.6	363.9	351.9	0.0
	1995	(e)8 642.1	(e)8 228.6	(e)7 053.0	(e)1 107.4	413.5	413.5	0.0
	2000	(e)9 213.5	(e)8 946.9	(e)8 071.0	(e)1 004.5	266.6	266.6	0.0
	2009	(e)29 997.4	(e)24 685	(e)20 928.5	(e)2 802.5	5 312.4	5 155.3	157.1
Transition economies - □ Économies en transition	**1990**	**72.3**	**177.9**	**165.5**	**12.4**	**-105.6**	**-83.7**	**-17.2**
	1995	**3 785.0**	**2 918.4**	**1 584.5**	**1 270.1**	**866.6**	**382.9**	**495.2**
	2000	**5 242.2**	**4 574.1**	**2 750.9**	**1 715.8**	**668.1**	**203.3**	**464.8**
	2009	**10 056.3**	**6 557.2**	**3 321.6**	**2 778.9**	**3 499.1**	**-335.3**	**3 870.4**
Albania - Albanie	1990	11.1	11.1	9.0	2.0	0.0	0.0	0.0
	1995	208.1	180.2	74.8	100.0	27.9	3.4	24.4
	2000	316.0	317.4	141.9	175.0	-1.5	-1.1	-0.4
	2009	418.3	357.9	245.6	100.4	60.3	5.4	56.7
Armenia - Arménie	1995	245.4	217.6	90.7	126.9	27.8	0.0	27.8
	2000	232.8	215.9	139.4	75.6	16.9	2.5	14.4
	2009	640.3	527.6	235.0	290.2	112.7	24.1	88.7
Azerbaijan - Azerbaïdjan	1995	131.0	118.6	31.7	76.8	12.3	0.0	1.1
	2000	204.8	139.1	70.7	60.2	65.7	42.4	23.3
	2009	402.5	232.3	124.0	71.7	170.2	-79.3	258.0
Belarus - Bélarus	2009	351.3	98.1	61.2	16.8	253.3	0.4	252.8
Bosnia and Herzegovina - Bosnie-Herzégovine	1995	924.6	924.5	734.0	156.7	0.1	0.1	0.0
	2000	774.8	736.9	452.6	266.2	37.9	18.5	19.5
	2009	474.0	415.2	276.4	102.2	58.8	-3.6	62.4
Croatia - Croatie	1995	99.6	53.3	42.1	11.1	46.3	-1.2	47.5
	2000	154.9	65.5	42.5	22.7	89.4	-18.1	107.5
	2009	434.5	169.4	30.7	133.8	265.1	20.4	244.8
Georgia - Géorgie	1995	213.0	209.1	81.6	127.0	4.0	0.0	4.0
	2000	230.9	169.2	120.4	42.9	61.8	2.5	59.3
	2009	1 247.1	907.9	435.9	431.5	339.2	13.4	331.6
Kazakhstan	1995	435.6	64.6	30.7	27.0	371.0	158.7	193.2
	2000	277.2	188.7	160.6	14.4	88.5	-12.1	100.6
	2009	1 039.2	297.9	172.3	36.6	741.3	-5.3	759.7
Kyrgyzstan - Kirghizistan	1995	338.3	284.7	96.9	186.0	53.7	0.0	46.5
	2000	211.5	214.7	91.9	111.6	-3.2	0.0	-3.2
	2009	318.3	314.7	139.6	108.6	3.6	-0.7	4.3
Montenegro - Monténégro	2009	143.7	75.4	46.8	23.7	68.3	30.8	37.5
Republic of Moldova - République de Moldova	2000	121.3	122.5	61.6	51.1	-1.2	-2.4	1.2
	2009	220.5	245.1	96.1	138.1	-24.6	-2.3	-21.9
Serbia and Montenegro - Serbie-et-Monténégro	1995	71.8	95.1	86.2	8.9	-23.3	0.0	-23.3
	2000	1 131.8	1 133.6	592.9	540.2	-1.8	-1.8	0.0
Serbia - Serbie	2009	849.3	608.5	272.5	325.7	240.8	17.0	223.9
Tajikistan - Tadjikistan	1995	69.0	65.1	39.2	25.3	3.9	0.0	0.0
	2000	124.2	123.5	38.2	84.8	0.7	0.0	0.7
	2009	423.5	408.9	140.3	257.8	14.6	0.0	17.1
TFYR of Macedonia - LERY de Macédoine	1995	93.0	78.8	25.4	53.4	14.2	0.0	14.2
	2000	269.4	250.1	110.9	138.7	19.2	-5.9	25.1
	2009	173.2	193.4	133.3	52.2	-20.2	-2.6	-17.6
Turkmenistan - Turkménistan	1995	33.0	27.9	17.1	9.0	5.1	11.7	1.0
	2000	193.0	31.5	9.9	5.7	161.6	138.0	23.6
	2009	-45.6	39.9	13.4	13.1	-85.5	-81.5	-4.0
Ukraine	2009	1 654.8	668.0	396.9	232.0	986.8	-177.5	1 164.3

For sources and notes, see end of table.

Pour les sources et les notes, se reporter à la fin du tableau.

Region, country or territory Régions, pays ou territoires	Year Année	Total official net (1) Total secteur officiel net (1)	Total ODA Net (2) / APD totale nette (2)			Total OOF Net (3) / Flux AASP nets (3)		
			Total donors (4) Tous donneurs (4)	of which: / dont :		Total donors Tous donneurs	of which: / dont :	
				DAC bilateral donors Donneurs bilatéraux du CAD	Multilateral donors Donneurs multilatéraux		DAC bilateral donors Donneurs bilatéraux du CAD	Multilateral donors Donneurs multilatéraux
			Millions of dollars / Millions de dollars					
Uzbekistan - Ôuzbékistan	1995	287.2	63.7	66.0	11.6	203.4	53.2	195.5
	2000	324.2	185.8	152.2	16.9	138.5	40.0	98.4
	2009	157.0	190.3	77.5	90.0	-33.3	-97.9	68.5
Transition economies n.e.s. - (6) Économies en transition n.d.a.	1990	(e)61.3	(e)166.8	(e)156.5	(6)10.3	-105.6	-88.7	-17.2
	1995	(e)635.5	(e)515.3	(e)167.8	(e)347.6	120.2	157.0	-36.8
	2000	(e)675.3	(e)679.7	(e)565.3	(e)110.0	-4.4	0.8	-5.2
	2009	(e)1 154.4	(e)806.8	(e)424.1	(e)354.8	347.6	3.9	343.7
Developed economies: America - **Économies développées : Amérique**	**1990**	**51.0**	**42.2**	**42.1**	**0.1**	**8.8**	**8.8**	**0.0**
	1995	**27.4**	**-2.1**	**-2.1**	**..**	**29.5**	**29.5**	**..**
Bermuda - Bermudes	1990	51.0	42.2	42.1	0.1	8.8	8.8	0.0
	1995	27.4	-2.1	-2.1	..	29.5	29.5	..
Developed economies: Asia - **Économies développées : Asie**	**1990**	**1 351.1**	**1 371.9**	**1 370.7**	**1.2**	**-20.8**	**-47.1**	**26.2**
	1995	**317.5**	**335.6**	**330.9**	**4.7**	**-18.1**	**-3.2**	**-14.9**
Israel - Israël	1990	1 351.1	1 371.9	1 370.7	1.2	-20.8	-47.1	26.2
	1995	317.5	335.6	330.9	4.7	-18.1	-3.2	-14.9
Developed economies: Europe - **Économies développées : Europe**	**1990**	**69.4**	**44.0**	**21.6**	**16.5**	**25.4**	**15.4**	**9.7**
	1995	**98.2**	**83.4**	**34.1**	**53.3**	**14.8**	**-0.4**	**15.2**
	2000	**119.5**	**82.1**	**21.9**	**61.1**	**37.5**	**-1.9**	**39.4**
Cyprus - Chypre	1990	42.4	38.1	18.5	14.8	4.3	3.1	1.0
	1995	-42.6	21.4	8.0	12.0	-64.1	0.2	-64.2
Gibraltar	1990	-0.8	0.6	0.6	..	-1.3	-1.3	..
	1995	0.2	0.2	0.2	..	0.0	0.0	..
Malta - Malte	1990	27.7	5.3	2.5	1.8	22.4	13.7	8.7
	1995	-27.4	9.2	8.9	5.9	-36.6	-5.1	-31.0
	2000	19.6	21.2	21.2	0.9	1.6	-0.6	-1.1
Slovenia - Slovénie	1995	168.0	52.5	17.1	35.5	115.5	4.5	111.0
	2000	99.9	60.8	0.6	60.1	39.1	-1.4	40.5

For sources and notes, see next page.

Pour les sources et les notes, se reporter à la page suivante.

7

Sources:
- OECD, *OLISnet* online statistical database⁻

Notes:

(1) Sum of "Total ODA Net; total donors" and "Total OOF Net; total donors". It represents the total net disbursements by the official sector at large to the recipient country.

(2) Total ODA Net; total donors:
The Total Official Development Assistance (ODA) includes grants and loans to countries and territories on the "DAC List of ODA Recipients" which are:
- undertaken by the official sector;
- with promotion of economic development and welfare as the main objective;
- at concessional financial terms (if a loan, have a grant element of at least 25 per cent).

(3) Total OOF Net; total donors:
The Other Official Flows (OOF) are transactions by the official sector whose main objective is other than development motivated, or if development motivated, whose grant element is below the 25% threshold which would make them eligible to be recorded as ODA. The main classes of transactions included here are official export credits, official sector equity and portfolio investment, and debt reorganisation undertaken by the official sector at non-concessional terms (irrespective of the nature or the identity of the original creditor).

(4) Total Donors is the sum of the three following donor types:
- DAC Bilateral Donors: The Development Assistance Committee (DAC) is the Committee of the OECD which deals with development co-operation matters. It consists of 23 Member countries.
- Multilateral Donors (i.e. AfDB, IBRD, IMF, UNDP).
- Other Donors: the Non-DAC Bilateral Donors (i.e. Hungary, Lithuania, Turkey).

(5) Developing economies is the sum of:
- Developing economies: Africa
- Developing economies: America
- Developing economies: Asia
- Developing economies: Oceania
- Developing economies n.e.s.

(6) "n.e.s." refers to Unallocated or Unspecified economies, i.e. a group of recipient economies and not an individual recipient economy.

Sources :
- OCDE, base de données en ligne *OLISnet*

Notes :

(1) Somme de "APD totale nette ; tous donneurs" et de "Flux AASP nets ; tous donneurs". Cet agrégat correspond aux versements nets effectués par le secteur public dans son ensemble aux pays bénéficiaires considérés.

(2) APD totale nette ; tous donneurs :
Par aide publique au développement (APD), on entend l'ensemble des apports de ressources qui sont fournis aux pays qui figurent sur la "Liste des bénéficiaires de l'APD établie par le CAD" et qui répondent aux critères suivants :
a) être dispensés dans le but essentiel de favoriser le développement économique et l'amélioration du niveau de vie dans les pays en développement ; et
b) revêtir un caractère de faveur et comporter un élément de libéralité d'au moins 25 pour cent.

(3) Flux AASP nets ; tous donneurs :
Autres apports du secteur public (AASP) : il s'agit des opérations du secteur public dont le but essentiel est autre que le développement ou dont l'élément de libéralité, en visant à favoriser le développement, sont assorties d'un élément de libéralité inférieur au seuil de 25 pour cent à partir duquel elles auraient pu être notifiées comme de l'APD. Les principales catégories d'opérations couvertes dans les AASP sont les crédits publics à l'exportation, les prises de participation et les investissements de portefeuille du secteur public et le réaménagement de la dette effectué par le secteur public aux conditions du marché (et ce, quelle que soit la nature ou l'identité du créancier initial).

(4) "Tous Donneurs" est la somme des 3 types de donneurs suivants :
- Donneurs Bilatéraux du CAD : Le Comité d'aide au développement (CAD) est la principale instance chargée, à l'OCDE, des questions relatives à la coopération avec les pays en développement. Le CAD regroupe 23 pays membres.
- Donneurs Multilatéraux (i.e. BAfD, BIRD, FMI, PNUD).
- Autres Donneurs : les Donneurs Bilatéraux non-membres du CAD (i.e. Hongrie, Lituanie, Turquie).

(5) Économies en développement est la somme de :
- Économies en développement : Afrique
- Économies en développement : Amérique
- Économies en développement : Asie
- Économies en développement : Océanie
- Économies en développement n.d.a.

(6) "n.d.a." se réfère à des économies "Non ventilées" ou "Non spécifiées", c-à-d un groupe d'économies bénéficiaires et non pas une économie bénéficiaire individuelle

7.6.2 Official financial flows from bilateral and multilateral sources to developing economies by economic grouping
7.6.2 Flux financiers publics bilatéraux et multilatéraux à destination des économies en développement par groupements économiques

Economic grouping / Groupements économiques	Year / Année	Total official net (1) / Total secteur officiel net (1)	Total ODA Net (2) / APD totale nette (2) — Total donors (4) / Tous donneurs (4)	of which / dont : DAC bilateral donors / Donneurs bilatéraux du CAD	of which / dont : Multilateral donors / Donneurs multilatéraux	Total OOF Net (3) / Flux AASP nets (3) — Total donors / Tous donneurs	of which / dont : DAC bilateral donors / Donneurs bilatéraux du CAD	of which / dont : Multilateral donors / Donneurs multilatéraux
			Millions of dollars / Millions de dollars					
DEVELOPING ECONOMIES - ÉCONOMIES EN DÉVELOPPEMENT (5)	1990	73 492.9	55 307.7	36 874.1	12 578.6	18 185.2	8 065.1	10 128.2
	1995	67 970.8	55 639.4	38 605.0	16 404.6	12 331.4	9 440.4	2 897.7
	2000	47 918.8	44 870.2	33 422.6	10 902.8	3 048.6	-5 196.4	8 245.0
	2009	155 944.7	120 081.9	79 752.5	35 233.1	35 862.8	8 380.6	27 457.2
Developing economies excluding China - Économies en développement sans la Chine	1990	61 266.0	44 864.0	28 776.1	10 759.1	16 402.0	6 871.7	9 550.3
	1995	49 851.1	41 577.1	27 226.4	13 825.8	8 274.0	6 923.2	1 357.6
	2000	34 666.0	31 365.5	21 734.9	9 045.3	3 300.5	-3 284.9	6 585.4
	2009	112 242.2	82 704.3	51 627.9	29 509.3	29 537.9	3 838.7	25 674.2
Developing economies excluding LDCs - Économies en développement sans les PMA	1990	47 343.1	30 398.6	20 440.9	5 209.5	16 944.5	7 020.1	9 942.9
	1995	40 057.8	28 078.1	20 457.9	7 085.0	11 979.7	8 906.3	3 080.1
	2000	23 717.4	20 895.5	15 332.6	5 151.2	2 821.9	-5 404.3	8 226.2
	2009	71 915.4	43 763.5	28 474.7	14 246.3	28 151.9	1 695.7	26 456.2
High-income developing countries - Pays en développement à revenu élevé	1990	11 429.9	3 977.3	2 794.4	199.8	7 452.7	2 853.9	4 711.7
	1995	3 781.5	3 000.4	2 436.3	279.3	781.2	436.0	345.2
	2000	2 278.9	984.4	499.0	330.5	1 294.5	-1 638.1	2 932.6
	2009	14 583.6	3 241.5	1 738.2	1 243.8	11 342.1	1 315.6	10 026.6
Middle-income developing countries - Pays en développement à revenu intermédiaire	1990	20 972.3	17 645.9	11 681.5	2 274.8	3 326.5	1 650.3	1 556.3
	1995	24 409.1	15 019.4	11 319.4	3 362.5	9 389.7	6 779.3	2 617.2
	2000	12 204.4	10 745.3	8 330.3	2 157.8	1 459.2	-3 916.9	5 376.1
	2009	28 725.5	16 767.1	12 000.1	4 310.8	11 958.4	55.1	11 903.3
Low-income developing countries - Pays en développement à revenu faible	1990	32 097.7	25 210.8	15 707.2	8 852.6	6 887.0	3 203.5	3 710.5
	1995	28 594.3	26 920.2	15 847.0	11 134.9	1 674.1	1 651.0	23.2
	2000	21 240.0	21 244.3	14 073.4	6 997.0	-4.3	79.9	-84.2
	2009	69 827.5	63 283.2	38 503.5	23 903.1	6 544.3	1 284.5	5 234.8
Heavily indebted poor countries (IMF) - Pays pauvres très endettés (FMI)	1990	17 168.6	15 756.8	10 011.9	5 387.8	1 411.8	000.5	525.9
	1995	18 007.0	17 747.7	9 821.8	7 895.0	259.4	617.1	364.8
	2000	11 733.9	12 109.2	7 723.6	4 233.0	-375.4	-46.2	-329.2
	2009	42 280.1	41 988.7	25 400.1	16 159.6	291.4	489.6	-223.2
Landlocked developing countries - Pays en développement sans littoral	1990	7 160.4	6 977.1	4 176.8	2 635.9	183.4	87.9	94.4
	1995	11 179.4	10 628.4	5 298.7	5 299.6	551.0	162.3	400.1
	2000	7 785.8	7 439.6	4 858.1	2 470.5	346.2	11.6	334.6
	2009	26 921.6	24 996.4	15 270.6	9 184.6	1 925.2	-269.8	2 223.5
Small island developing States - Petits États insulaires en développement	1990	1 612.1	1 376.9	1 064.1	307.6	235.2	99.5	150.5
	1995	1 511.1	1 482.9	1 059.6	410.1	28.2	-65.3	93.5
	2000	1 118.9	962.7	723.4	214.3	156.2	-5.8	162.0
	2009	2 937.1	2 237.6	1 550.4	686.6	699.5	280.0	419.6
Least developed countries - Pays les moins avancés	*1990*	*17 217.4*	*16 495.8*	*9 800.7*	*6 119.8*	*721.6*	*687.6*	*35.6*
	1995	*16 834.9*	*16 969.6*	*9 251.0*	*7 693.3*	*-134.7*	*-40.1*	*-94.6*
	2000	*12 109.2*	*12 181.7*	*7 673.1*	*4 334.3*	*-72.5*	*-70.8*	*-1.7*
	2009	*41 756.3*	*40 072.5*	*24 310.1*	*15 212.5*	*1 683.7*	*950.2*	*708.5*
Africa and Haiti - Afrique et Haïti	1990	13 456.2	12 795.5	7 821.2	4 526.1	660.6	634.4	28.9
	1995	13 411.1	13 515.4	7 137.0	6 343.9	-104.4	-17.0	-87.3
	2000	9 050.7	9 173.4	5 908.2	3 124.2	-122.7	-88.9	-33.8
	2009	29 753.2	28 901.8	16 108.2	12 611.5	851.4	861.3	-35.0
Asia - Asie	1990	3 489.3	3 433.3	1 794.4	1 512.6	56.0	48.2	6.7
	1995	3 165.6	3 168.9	1 905.2	1 273.5	-3.3	4.0	-7.3
	2000	2 840.8	2 791.6	1 650.6	1 109.2	49.2	16.5	32.7
	2009	11 261.5	10 441.3	7 587.1	2 487.3	820.1	76.7	743.4
Islands - Îles	1990	272.0	267.0	185.1	81.1	5.0	5.0	0.0
	1995	258.3	285.4	208.9	75.9	-27.1	-27.1	0.0
	2000	217.6	216.7	114.3	100.9	0.9	1.5	-0.6
	2009	741.6	729.4	614.9	113.7	12.2	12.2	0.0

For sources and notes, see end of table.

Pour les sources et les notes, se reporter à la fin du tableau.

7.6.2 Official financial flows from bilateral and multilateral sources to developing economies by economic grouping

7.6.2 Flux financiers publics bilatéraux et multilatéraux à destination des économies en développement par groupements économiques

Economic grouping / Groupements économiques	Year / Année	Total official net (1) / Total secteur officiel net (1)	Total ODA Net (2) / APD totale nette (2)			Total OOF Net (3) / Flux AASP nets (3)		
			Total donors (4) / Tous donneurs (4)	of which: / dont :		Total donors / Tous donneurs	of which: / dont :	
				DAC bilateral donors / Donneurs bilatéraux du CAD	Multilateral donors / Donneurs multilatéraux		DAC bilateral donors / Donneurs bilatéraux du CAD	Multilateral donors / Donneurs multilatéraux
					Millions of dollars / Millions de dollars			
Major petroleum and gas exporters - Principaux exportateurs de pétrole et de gaz	1990	4 921.3	991.6	587.2	257.2	3 329.6	1 614.4	1 568.9
	1995	3 880.4	1 575.8	1 054.9	475.8	2 304.6	1 943.3	361.3
	2000	-514.5	1 047.9	633.2	309.0	-1 562.4	-1 226.9	-335.4
	2009	5 381.4	5 420.3	3 801.3	1 322.0	-38.9	-258.4	219.5
Africa - Afrique	1990	2 335.1	660.8	454.8	106.3	1 674.2	929.9	597.9
	1995	2 414.3	927.1	332.0	040.0	1 107.0	1 274.6	711.8
	2000	-176.1	675.5	347.7	258.8	-851.6	-427.2	-424.4
	2009	2 086.1	2 257.3	1 051.6	1 181.1	-171.2	-139.3	-31.9
America - Amérique	1990	1 299.5	76.4	75.8	0.6	1 223.2	170.3	1 052.9
	1995	130.2	43.3	29.0	14.3	86.9	22.9	64.0
	2000	50.6	76.1	61.3	14.1	-25.5	-78.8	53.3
	2009	195.3	66.8	46.9	19.6	128.5	-35.7	164.3
Asia - Asie	1990	686.6	254.3	56.7	60.3	432.2	514.2	-82.0
	1995	1 335.8	605.4	433.3	114.9	730.5	647.0	83.5
	2000	-389.0	296.3	224.1	36.1	-685.3	-721.0	35.7
	2009	3 100.0	3 096.2	2 702.8	121.3	3.8	-83.3	87.1
Major exporters of manufactured goods - Principaux exportateurs d'articles manufacturés	1990	9 677.9	3 574.1	2 880.3	682.1	6 103.9	3 298.9	2 810.5
	1995	9 224.3	4 891.5	3 859.3	1 023.3	4 332.8	2 056.5	2 276.3
	2000	-129.6	2 395.9	1 929.6	469.4	-2 525.5	-4 773.5	2 248.1
	2009	8 863.1	1 384.3	1 356.1	0.6	7 478.9	-299.8	7 778.7
America - Amérique	1990	5 024.2	156.3	144.8	11.5	4 868.0	2 035.6	2 837.9
	1995	407.8	384.1	365.1	19.0	23.7	-990.9	1 014.6
	2000	74.1	-57.8	-68.3	10.0	131.9	-710.7	842.6
	2000	7 004.4	185.5	158.7	25.5	6 818.9	421.8	6 397.2
Asia - Asie	1990	4 653.7	3 417.8	2 735.5	670.6	1 235.9	1 263.3	-27.4
	1995	8 816.4	4 507.3	3 494.2	1 004.3	4 309.1	3 047.4	1 261.7
	2000	-203.7	2 453.6	1 997.9	459.4	-2 657.3	-4 062.8	1 405.5
	2009	1 858.7	1 198.8	1 197.3	-24.9	659.9	-721.6	1 381.5
Emerging economies - Économies émergentes	1990	8 967.9	2 326.0	2 137.4	171.6	6 642.0	3 803.2	2 850.1
	1995	3 860.1	2 344.5	2 150.4	224.3	1 515.5	782.9	732.7
	2000	4 388.9	1 413.6	1 340.3	66.9	2 975.3	-2 368.3	5 343.6
	2009	13 050.2	1 240.3	985.6	246.6	11 809.9	2 971.4	8 838.5
America - Amérique	1990	7 640.1	976.7	886.8	89.9	6 663.4	3 369.1	3 305.7
	1995	2 087.4	1 325.5	1 150.2	178.6	761.9	-337.0	1 098.9
	2000	5 753.2	671.7	613.2	47.8	5 081.4	-495.7	5 577.1
	2009	12 620.9	1 173.3	945.2	221.0	11 447.6	2 500.2	8 947.4
Asia - Asie	1990	1 327.8	1 349.3	1 250.6	81.7	-21.5	434.1	-455.6
	1995	1 772.6	1 019.0	1 000.2	45.6	753.6	1 119.9	-366.3
	2000	-1 364.3	741.9	727.1	19.2	-2 106.2	-1 872.6	-233.6
	2009	429.3	67.0	40.4	25.5	362.3	471.2	-108.9
Newly industrialized Asian countries - Économies nouvellement industrialisées d'Asie	1990	6 791.6	4 374.1	3 893.0	439.1	2 417.6	1 373.3	1 068.3
	1995	5 155.5	3 240.0	2 995.5	276.8	1 915.5	1 793.8	121.7
	2000	1 952.6	3 195.6	2 992.2	206.9	-1 243.0	-1 532.5	289.5
	2009	2 520.3	1 426.5	617.7	807.0	1 093.8	-721.0	1 814.8
First tier - Première génération	1990	-283.1	123.4	77.5	21.5	-406.5	20.5	-427.0
	1995	-390.7	91.6	96.9	9.4	-482.3	-130.2	-352.1
Second tier - Deuxième génération	1990	7 074.8	4 250.7	3 815.5	417.7	2 824.1	1 352.8	1 495.3
	1995	5 546.2	3 148.4	2 898.6	267.4	2 397.8	1 924.0	473.8
	2000	1 952.6	3 195.6	2 992.2	206.9	-1 243.0	-1 532.5	289.5
	2009	2 520.3	1 426.5	617.7	807.0	1 093.8	-721.0	1 814.8

For sources and notes, see end of table.

Pour les sources et les notes, se reporter à la fin du tableau.

7.6.2   Official financial flows from bilateral and multilateral sources to developing economies by economic grouping

7.6.2   Flux financiers publics bilatéraux et multilatéraux à destination des économies en développement par groupements économiques

Economic grouping / Groupements économiques	Year / Année	Total official net (1) / Total secteur officiel net (1)	Total ODA Net (2) / APD totale nette (2)			Total OOF Net (3) / Flux AASP nets (3)		
			Total donors (4) / Tous donneurs (4)	of which: / dont :		Total donors / Tous donneurs	of which: / dont :	
				DAC bilateral donors / Donneurs bilatéraux du CAD	Multilateral donors / Donneurs multilatéraux		DAC bilateral donors / Donneurs bilatéraux du CAD	Multilateral donors / Donneurs multilatéraux
				Millions of dollars / Millions de dollars				
Developing economies: Africa -	**1990**	**28 027.2**	**25 076.3**	**15 826.4**	**6 126.3**	**2 950.9**	**850.9**	**1 950.3**
Économies en développement : Afrique	**1995**	**25 154.0**	**21 781.1**	**13 238.3**	**8 410.6**	**3 372.9**	**3 577.0**	**-203.6**
	2000	**14 106.0**	**15 380.9**	**10 396.8**	**4 708.5**	**-1 274.8**	**-343.5**	**-931.4**
	2009	**53 233.3**	**47 609.9**	**28 155.8**	**19 161.2**	**4 623.4**	**1 224.8**	**3 373.6**
Northern Africa excluding Sudan -	1990	7 183.5	7 004.0	4 081.3	268.0	179.4	-952.3	902.5
Afrique septentrionale sans le Soudan	1995	6 054.2	2 877.2	2 374.6	401.4	3 177.0	2 713.7	463.9
	2000	1 806.4	2 166.9	1 660.6	397.3	-360.5	100.5	-461.0
	2009	3 779.4	2 669.2	1 866.9	771.4	1 110.2	-190.6	1 300.8
Sub-Saharan Africa - Afrique subsaharienne	1990	19 924.4	17 169.4	10 904.7	5 805.2	2 755.0	1 797.4	957.1
	1995	18 079.1	17 917.5	10 041.1	7 845.4	161.6	832.5	-670.9
	2000	11 267.2	12 182.6	7 888.5	4 140.3	-915.4	-450.8	-464.6
	2009	42 822.9	39 688.8	23 236.5	16 250.9	3 134.1	1 252.3	1 856.8
Sub-Saharan Africa excluding South Africa -	1990	19 924.4	17 169.4	10 904.7	5 805.2	2 755.0	1 797.4	957.1
Afrique subsaharienne sans l'Afrique du Sud	1995	17 366.3	17 531.4	9 722.6	7 780.8	-165.0	505.9	-670.9
	2000	10 676.0	11 696.2	7 533.0	4 009.5	-1 020.2	-356.2	-663.9
	2009	40 195.7	38 613.8	22 375.2	16 039.7	1 581.9	532.6	1 024.2
Developing economies: America -	**1990**	**13 525.1**	**5 189.4**	**4 146.4**	**1 032.0**	**8 335.7**	**3 729.7**	**4 634.3**
Économies en développement : Amérique	**1995**	**8 022.0**	**6 386.5**	**4 813.1**	**1 543.2**	**1 635.6**	**78.1**	**1 557.5**
	2000	**10 364.7**	**4 837.6**	**3 858.4**	**940.8**	**5 527.0**	**-1 012.2**	**6 539.2**
	2009	**25 489.6**	**9 089.3**	**6 572.7**	**2 496.1**	**16 400.2**	**2 493.3**	**13 906.9**
Central America and Greater Caribbean Islands	1990	7 302.3	2 430.1	2 074.9	348.1	4 872.2	2 093.5	2 801.2
excluding Puerto Rico - Amérique centrale et	1995	3 404.7	3 040.2	2 247.7	769.7	364.5	-869.9	1 234.4
Grandes Antilles sans Porto Rico	2000	2 179.0	1 749.7	1 214.4	521.3	429.4	-793.8	1 223.1
	2009	12 814.1	3 777.8	2 551.2	1 220.9	9 036.3	411.9	8 624.4
Central America and Greater Caribbean Islands	1990	2 278.0	2 273.8	1 930.2	336.6	4.2	57.9	-36.7
excluding Mexico and Puerto Rico -	1995	2 996.9	2 656.1	1 882.6	750.7	340.8	121.0	219.8
Amérique centrale et Grandes Antilles sans le	2000	2 104.0	1 807.4	1 282.7	511.3	297.5	-83.1	380.5
Mexique et Porto Rico	2009	5 809.7	3 592.3	2 392.4	1 195.4	2 217.4	-9.9	2 227.3
South America and Central America -	1990	11 860.0	3 870.5	3 169.0	694.1	7 989.5	3 636.0	4 364.7
Amérique du Sud et Amérique centrale	1995	5 969.8	4 484.7	3 466.9	995.7	1 485.1	26.1	1 459.0
	2000	8 641.0	3 301.8	2 576.4	705.3	5 339.2	-924.9	6 264.1
	2009	21 447.3	5 850.9	4 484.6	1 351.9	15 596.4	2 457.4	13 138.9
South America excluding Brazil -	1990	4 719.9	1 879.9	1 427.4	451.0	2 840.0	891.8	1 948.2
Amérique du Sud sans le Brésil	1995	3 630.8	2 185.7	1 707.8	474.3	1 445.1	895.2	550.0
	2000	2 820.1	1 637.1	1 342.5	283.3	1 183.0	-615.7	1 798.7
	2009	8 719.0	3 240.2	2 473.6	759.6	5 478.8	877.5	4 601.3
Developing economies: Asia -	**1990**	**24 239.3**	**17 827.0**	**10 546.2**	**4 600.1**	**6 412.3**	**3 072.7**	**3 481.1**
Économies en développement : Asie	**1995**	**24 178.8**	**17 377.6**	**11 788.3**	**5 193.1**	**6 801.2**	**5 252.2**	**1 555.2**
	2000	**13 347.9**	**14 888.8**	**10 383.9**	**4 146.7**	**-1 541.0**	**-4 175.8**	**2 634.8**
	2009	**46 174.6**	**37 050.4**	**22 744.0**	**10 478.4**	**9 124.1**	**-837.9**	**9 962.0**
Eastern and South-Eastern Asia excluding China -	1990	7 362.2	4 929.6	4 174.8	712.8	2 432.6	1 387.7	1 067.9
Asie orientale et Asie du Sud-Est sans la Chine	1995	7 435.1	5 305.7	4 325.7	1 001.3	2 129.4	1 992.8	136.6
	2000	4 599.0	5 949.2	4 946.7	1 001.0	-1 350.2	-1 684.9	334.8
	2009	9 605.4	7 325.8	4 097.8	3 156.9	2 279.6	-282.6	2 562.1
Southern Asia excluding India -	1990	4 990.6	4 664.0	2 566.9	2 096.5	326.6	-78.4	406.3
Asie méridionale sans l'Inde	1995	4 227.4	3 612.8	2 083.1	1 602.9	614.6	428.2	186.4
	2000	2 214.1	2 870.7	1 829.9	1 010.6	-656.7	-713.8	57.1
	2009	12 855.2	12 052.6	8 155.8	3 451.3	802.6	-391.9	1 194.5

For sources and notes, see end of table.   Pour les sources et les notes, se reporter à la fin du tableau.

7

7.6.2 Official financial flows from bilateral and multilateral sources to developing economies by economic grouping

7.6.2 Flux financiers publics bilatéraux et multilatéraux à destination des économies en développement par groupements économiques

Sources:
- OECD, *OLISnet* online statistical database

Notes:

- The groupings presented in this table do not include "n.e.s." recipient countries.

(1) Sum of "Total ODA Net; total donors" and "Total OOF Net; total donors". It represents the total net disbursements by the official sector at large to the recipient country.

(2) Total ODA Net; total donors:
The Total Official Development Assistance (ODA) includes grants and loans to countries and territories on the "DAC List of ODA Recipients" which are:
- undertaken by the official sector;
- with promotion of economic development and welfare as the main objective;
- at concessional financial terms (if a loan, have a grant element of at least 25 per cent).

(3) Total OOF Net; total donors:
The Other Official Flows (OOF) are transactions by the official sector whose main objective is other than development motivated, or, if development motivated, whose grant element is below the 25% threshold which would make them eligible to be recorded as ODA. The main classes of transactions included here are official export credits, official sector equity and portfolio investment, and debt reorganisation - undertaken by the official sector at non-concessional terms (irrespective of the nature or the identity of the original creditor).

(4) Total Donors is the sum of the three following donor types:
- DAC Bilateral Donors: The Development Assistance Committee (DAC) is the Committee of the OECD which deals with development co-operation matters. It consists of 23 member countries.
- Multilateral Donors (i.e. African Development Bank, International Bank for Reconstruction and Development, International Monetary Fund, United Nations Development Programme).
- Other Donors: the Non-DAC Bilateral Donors (i.e. Hungary, Lithuania, Turkey).

(5) Developing economies is the sum of:
- Developing economies: Africa
- Developing economies: America
- Developing economies: Asia
- Developing economies: Oceania
- Developing economies n.e.s.

Sources :
- OCDE, base de données en ligne *OLISnet*

Notes :

- Les groupements présentés dans ce tableau n'incluent pas les pays bénéficiaires "n.d.a.".

(1) Somme de "APD totale nette ; tous donneurs" et de "Flux AASP nets ; tous donneurs". Cet agrégat correspond aux versements nets effectués par le secteur public dans son ensemble aux pays bénéficiaires considérés.

(2) APD totale nette ; tous donneurs :
Par aide publique au développement (APD), on entend l'ensemble des apports de ressources qui sont fournis aux pays qui figurent sur la "Liste des bénéficiaires de l'APD établie par le CAD" et qui répondent aux critères suivants :
a) être dispensés dans le but essentiel de favoriser le développement économique et l'amélioration du niveau de vie dans les pays en développement ; et
b) revêtir un caractère de faveur et comporter un élément de libéralité d'au moins 25 pour cent.

(3) Flux AASP nets ; tous donneurs :
Autres apports du secteur public (AASP) : il s'agit des opérations du secteur public dont le but essentiel est autre que le développement ou qui, tout en visant à favoriser le développement, sont assorties d'un élément de libéralité inférieur au seuil de 25 pour cent à partir duquel elles auraient pu être notifiées comme de l'APD. Les principales catégories d'opérations couvertes dans les AASP sont les crédits publics à l'exportation, les prises de participation et les investissements de portefeuille du secteur public et le réaménagement de la dette effectué par le secteur public aux conditions du marché (et ce, quelle que soit la nature ou l'identité du créancier initial).

(4) Tous Donneurs est la somme des 3 types de donneurs suivants :
- Donneurs Bilatéraux du CAD : Le Comité d'aide au développement (CAD) est la principale instance chargée, à l'OCDE, des questions relatives à la coopération avec les pays en développement. Le CAD regroupe 23 pays membres.
- Donneurs Multilatéraux (i.e. Banque africaine de développement, Banque internationale pour la reconstruction et le développement, Fonds monétaire international, Programme des Nations Unies pour le développement).
- Autres Donneurs : les Donneurs Bilatéraux non-membres du CAD (i.e. Hongrie, Lituanie, Turquie).

(5) Économies en développement est la somme de :
- Économies en développement : Afrique
- Économies en développement : Amérique
- Économies en développement : Asie
- Économies en développement : Océanie
- Économies en développement n.d.a.

7.7.A External long-term debt by lending source
Developing economies

7.7.A Dette extérieure à long terme par catégories de prêt
Économies en développement

	Total long-term debt (1) / Dette totale à long terme (1)	Public and publicly guaranteed debt (2) / Dette publique et garantie par l'état (2)									Private non-guaranteed debt (5) / Dette privée non garantie (5)
		Total creditors / Total créanciers	Official creditors (3) / Créanciers publics (3)					Private creditors (4) / Créanciers (4)			
			Total	Bilateral / Bilatéraux			Multilateral / Multilatéraux	Total	Bonds / Obligations	Commercial banks / Banques commerciales	
				Total	DAC / CAD	OPEC / OPEP					
	Millions of dollars / Millions de dollars										
1990											
Debt outstanding	961 787	905 658	505 210	308 920	209 326	18 380	196 290	400 448	97 364	196 392	56 129
Disbursments (6)	95 678	79 625	45 284	19 141	16 206	670	20 140	84 540	7 002	13 507	16 053
Debt service (7)	105 496	95 232	39 018	17 759	13 423	1 123	21 259	56 214	8 389	29 113	10 264
Principal repayments	60 772	54 704	21 827	10 562	7 544	871	11 265	32 876	4 367	15 145	6 069
Interest payments	44 724	40 529	17 191	7 197	5 879	253	9 994	23 337	4 022	13 969	4 195
Net transfers on debt (8)	-9 818	-15 608	6 266	1 382	2 883	-551	4 884	-21 874	-4 527	-15 607	5 789
1993											
Dette totale	1 334 158	1 125 823	684 064	414 238	307 450	13 897	269 826	441 759	213 046	128 888	208 335
Décaissements (6)	174 052	120 668	60 484	32 124	26 182	535	28 360	60 184	22 001	21 916	53 384
Service de la dette (7)	171 703	134 428	66 484	34 696	26 209	944	31 788	67 944	24 241	22 619	37 275
Remboursement du principal	107 789	81 578	41 088	22 140	15 501	735	18 948	40 490	10 039	15 272	26 211
Paiement des intérêts	63 914	52 850	25 396	12 555	10 708	209	12 840	27 454	14 202	7 347	11 064
Transfers nets (8)	2 350	-13 760	-6 000	-2 572	-27	-409	-3 428	-7 760	-2 240	-703	16 110
2000											
Debt outstanding	1 575 902	1 125 365	649 169	346 361	252 167	13 909	302 808	476 196	295 186	120 382	450 537
Disbursments (6)	211 995	127 780	47 855	16 477	13 859	456	31 377	79 925	54 995	16 992	84 215
Debt service (7)	298 409	176 438	71 372	36 206	28 421	969	35 166	105 065	55 970	33 841	121 971
Principal repayments	212 287	118 854	47 731	26 596	20 544	802	21 135	71 122	33 649	25 463	93 434
Interest payments	86 121	57 584	23 641	9 610	7 877	166	14 031	33 943	22 321	8 378	28 537
Net transfers on debt (8)	-86 413	-48 658	-23 518	-19 729	-14 563	-513	-3 789	-25 140	-975	-16 849	-37 756
2005											
Dette totale	1 616 513	1 132 393	640 637	297 621	243 484	13 163	343 016	491 757	346 550	106 904	484 119
Décaissements (6)	271 338	121 572	41 845	10 991	7 672	826	30 854	79 727	56 009	20 229	149 766
Service de la dette (7)	308 019	171 634	72 192	39 056	32 601	873	33 136	99 442	64 699	25 808	136 385
Remboursement du principal	237 188	118 857	51 714	28 166	22 999	736	23 548	67 143	38 129	21 370	118 331
Paiement des intérêts	70 831	52 777	20 478	10 890	9 603	137	9 588	32 299	26 570	4 438	18 054
Transfers nets (8)	-36 681	-50 062	-30 347	-28 065	-24 930	-47	-2 282	-19 715	-8 689	-5 579	13 381
2006											
Debt outstanding	1 650 372	1 073 010	584 792	269 064	211 397	13 105	315 728	488 218	350 236	104 403	577 362
Disbursments (6)	327 058	118 930	50 541	13 693	7 325	1 485	36 848	68 389	48 396	15 348	208 128
Debt service (7)	356 907	203 054	84 764	40 531	36 242	907	44 233	118 290	82 346	25 958	153 852
Principal repayments	280 737	154 894	68 055	34 316	31 159	755	33 739	86 839	57 281	20 885	125 844
Interest payments	76 169	48 160	16 709	6 215	5 083	152	10 494	31 451	25 065	5 073	28 009
Net transfers on debt (8)	-29 849	-84 124	-34 223	-26 838	-28 917	578	-7 385	-49 901	-33 950	-10 610	54 275
2007											
Dette totale	1 843 651	1 129 765	612 597	273 912	211 404	14 131	338 686	517 167	375 168	112 296	713 886
Décaissements (6)	419 524	127 256	52 990	13 000	7 487	1 301	39 991	74 265	49 780	21 144	292 268
Service de la dette (7)	360 673	163 953	68 125	32 957	25 499	881	35 168	95 827	65 095	23 063	196 721
Remboursement du principal	276 133	112 089	49 918	26 254	20 265	717	23 663	62 171	38 148	17 961	164 044
Paiement des intérêts	84 541	51 864	18 207	6 703	5 234	165	11 505	33 657	26 946	5 103	32 677
Transfers nets (8)	58 851	-36 697	-15 135	-19 958	-18 013	420	4 823	-21 562	-15 315	-1 920	95 547
2008											
Debt outstanding	1 973 753	1 171 800	651 423	292 785	222 873	15 474	358 638	520 377	379 222	115 499	801 953
Disbursments (6)	388 389	143 244	60 983	18 120	10 244	2 149	42 863	82 261	59 035	20 920	245 145
Debt service (7)	359 727	164 378	62 538	27 667	23 608	848	34 870	101 841	74 242	19 491	195 349
Principal repayments	274 529	114 874	45 523	21 623	18 568	671	23 901	69 350	47 888	14 881	150 656
Interest payments	85 198	49 504	17 014	6 044	5 041	178	10 970	32 490	26 353	4 611	35 694
Net transfers on debt (8)	28 661	28 661	-21 134	-1 554	-9 547	-13 364	7 993	-19 580	-15 207	1 429	49 796
2009											
Dette totale	2 039 305	1 224 695	699 431	302 972	218 830	16 110	396 458	525 264	387 729	108 705	814 611
Décaissements (6)	353 090	163 672	83 409	23 970	10 786	1 431	59 438	80 263	57 531	17 017	189 419
Service de la dette (7)	351 911	141 454	57 628	25 647	21 473	925	31 981	83 826	50 790	25 002	210 456
Remboursement du principal	272 860	95 705	42 310	19 691	16 764	709	22 619	53 396	25 647	20 818	177 154
Paiement des intérêts	79 051	45 749	15 318	5 956	4 708	216	9 363	30 431	25 143	4 185	33 302
Transfers nets (8)	1 179	22 217	25 781	-1 676	-10 687	506	27 457	-3 564	6 742	-7 985	-21 038

For sources and notes, see end of table 7.7.G.

Pour les sources et les notes, se reporter à la fin du tableau 7.7.G.

7

7.7.B **External long-term debt by lending source**
Developing economies:
Africa

7.7.B **Dette extérieure à long terme par catégories de prêt**
Économies en développement :
Afrique

	Total long-term debt (1) / Dette totale à long terme (1)	Public and publicly guaranteed debt (2) / Dette publique et garantie par l'état (2)									Private non-guaranteed debt (5) / Dette privée non garantie (5)
		Total creditors / Total créanciers	Official creditors (3) / Créanciers publics (3)					Private creditors (4) / Créanciers (4)			
			Total	Bilateral / Bilatéraux			Multilateral / Multilatéraux	Total	Bonds / Obligations	Commercial banks / Banques commerciales	
				Total	DAC / CAD	OPEC / OPEP					
								Millions of dollars / Millions de dollars			
1990											
Debt outstanding	235 385	228 691	157 999	107 383	77 559	11 464	50 616	70 692	1 721	24 622	6 694
Disbursments (6)	21 528	20 809	12 158	5 502	4 701	204	6 656	8 651	0	1 032	719
Debt service (7)	23 034	21 957	9 982	5 725	4 755	294	4 257	11 975	231	3 782	1 078
Principal repayments	14 680	14 038	5 402	3 013	2 521	210	2 389	8 636	108	2 517	643
Interest payments	8 354	7 919	4 580	2 712	2 234	84	1 868	3 339	123	1 265	435
Net transfers on debt (8)	-1 507	-1 148	2 176	-223	-54	-90	2 399	-3 324	-231	-2 750	-359
1995											
Dette totale	281 328	268 778	206 964	133 600	106 612	8 502	73 364	61 814	5 319	22 067	12 550
Décaissements (6)	19 081	18 200	10 250	3 232	2 936	140	7 018	7 950	1 129	2 156	881
Service de la dette (7)	22 234	20 323	11 736	5 524	4 783	318	6 212	8 587	667	2 753	1 910
Remboursement du principal	13 405	12 033	6 480	2 707	2 162	246	3 773	5 553	318	1 728	1 372
Paiement des intérêts	8 828	8 290	5 256	2 817	2 621	72	2 440	3 034	348	1 025	538
Transfers nets (8)	-3 153	-2 123	-1 487	-2 292	-1 847	-178	805	-637	463	-597	-1 029
2000											
Debt outstanding	250 251	235 669	195 972	123 662	78 486	9 393	72 309	39 697	10 630	15 351	14 582
Disbursments (6)	14 549	11 265	6 501	1 724	1 298	271	4 777	4 764	765	2 514	3 284
Debt service (7)	23 087	21 000	12 114	7 000	4 782	351	5 114	8 886	1 555	4 156	2 087
Principal repayments	16 156	14 572	7 738	4 490	2 817	266	3 247	6 834	881	3 425	1 585
Interest payments	6 931	6 428	4 376	2 510	1 965	84	1 867	2 052	674	730	502
Net transfers on debt (8)	-8 538	-9 735	-5 613	-5 276	-3 483	-79	-337	-4 122	-789	-1 641	1 197
2005											
Dette totale	250 741	236 343	191 999	100 475	81 623	8 796	91 524	44 344	14 363	21 687	14 399
Décaissements (6)	23 646	18 996	10 025	2 249	1 065	400	7 776	8 071	1 199	6 843	4 650
Service de la dette (7)	31 350	29 490	21 488	15 540	13 974	497	5 948	8 002	971	5 026	1 860
Remboursement du principal	21 266	19 957	13 646	9 237	7 891	422	4 409	6 312	178	4 455	1 309
Paiement des intérêts	10 084	9 533	7 842	6 304	6 084	76	1 539	1 691	793	571	551
Transfers nets (8)	-7 704	-10 494	-11 463	-13 291	-12 909	-31	1 829	968	528	1 817	2 790
2006											
Debt outstanding	191 753	176 660	136 521	75 164	55 837	9 080	61 357	40 140	15 022	18 221	15 093
Disbursments (6)	18 426	14 040	9 902	2 976	1 124	597	6 926	4 138	2 328	1 254	4 386
Debt service (7)	41 739	37 110	26 039	18 772	17 655	515	7 267	11 070	2 937	5 810	4 629
Principal repayments	35 735	31 773	22 908	17 128	16 219	427	5 780	8 866	2 043	4 863	3 961
Interest payments	6 004	5 336	3 132	1 644	1 436	88	1 487	2 205	894	948	668
Net transfers on debt (8)	-23 313	-23 070	-16 137	-15 796	-16 531	82	-341	-6 933	-609	-4 557	-243
2007											
Dette totale	213 122	190 771	147 197	77 259	57 127	9 617	69 939	43 573	18 765	18 937	22 352
Décaissements (6)	32 792	23 760	13 061	3 843	1 348	598	9 219	10 698	4 423	5 963	9 032
Service de la dette (7)	28 128	23 223	13 334	7 704	5 569	398	5 629	9 889	2 338	5 677	4 905
Remboursement du principal	21 737	17 590	9 718	5 951	4 171	304	3 767	7 873	1 472	4 780	4 147
Paiement des intérêts	6 390	5 633	3 616	1 753	1 398	93	1 863	2 017	866	897	757
Transfers nets (8)	4 664	537	-272	-3 861	-4 221	201	3 589	809	2 084	285	4 128
2008											
Debt outstanding	214 126	193 784	149 911	77 573	55 090	9 926	72 337	43 874	18 009	20 747	20 342
Disbursments (6)	20 375	17 286	12 393	4 691	2 048	660	7 702	4 894	0	4 457	3 089
Debt service (7)	22 582	17 779	11 354	5 560	4 336	418	5 793	6 426	1 649	3 488	4 802
Principal repayments	16 562	12 536	8 024	4 087	3 182	321	3 938	4 511	640	2 798	4 026
Interest payments	6 020	5 244	3 329	1 473	1 154	96	1 856	1 914	1 009	691	776
Net transfers on debt (8)	-2 207	-493	1 039	-869	-2 287	242	1 908	-1 532	-1 649	969	-1 713
2009											
Dette totale	229 713	207 008	160 789	81 088	56 178	9 980	79 701	46 219	19 027	21 384	22 704
Décaissements (6)	30 662	25 503	17 068	5 748	1 980	504	11 320	8 435	2 200	4 919	5 159
Service de la dette (7)	21 775	17 340	10 380	5 252	3 807	450	5 128	6 960	1 594	4 458	4 435
Remboursement du principal	16 255	12 621	7 304	3 879	2 841	347	3 425	5 317	615	3 938	3 634
Paiement des intérêts	5 520	4 720	3 077	1 374	966	104	1 703	1 643	978	520	801
Transfers nets (8)	8 887	8 163	6 688	496	-1 827	53	6 192	1 475	606	460	724

For sources and notes, see end of table 7.7.G.

Pour les sources et les notes, se reporter à la fin du tableau 7.7.G.

7.7.C External long-term debt by lending source
Developing economies:
America

7.7.C Dette extérieure à long terme par catégories de prêt
Économies en développement :
Amérique

	Total long-term debt (1) / Dette totale à long terme (1)	Total creditors / Total créanciers	Public and publicly guaranteed debt (2) / Dette publique et garantie par l'état (2)								Private non-guaranteed debt (5) / Dette privée non garantie (5)
			Official creditors (3) / Créanciers publics (3)					Private creditors (4) / Créanciers (4)			
			Total	Bilateral / Bilatéraux			Multilateral / Multilatéraux	Total	Bonds / Obligations	Commercial banks / Banques commerciales	
				Total	DAC / CAD	OPEC / OPEP					
				Millions of dollars / Millions de dollars							
1990											
Debt outstanding	352 866	327 848	121 469	61 499	48 108	1 742	59 970	206 378	75 976	101 883	25 018
Disbursments (6)	27 731	23 033	13 183	4 198	3 245	211	8 986	9 850	1 938	4 803	4 698
Debt service (7)	36 600	32 124	11 950	3 075	2 368	182	8 875	20 174	4 406	11 917	4 476
Principal repayments	18 470	16 255	6 453	1 702	1 215	133	4 751	9 803	2 008	5 219	2 215
Interest payments	18 130	15 869	5 498	1 373	1 153	49	4 124	10 371	2 398	6 698	2 261
Net transfers on debt (8)	-8 869	-9 091	1 233	1 123	876	29	110	-10 324	-2 468	-7 113	222
1995											
Dette totale	461 600	374 206	160 181	87 407	76 752	1 327	72 775	214 025	165 484	35 374	87 394
Décaissements (6)	74 094	46 564	23 720	13 699	13 405	95	10 021	22 844	13 694	7 417	27 530
Service de la dette (7)	69 190	50 630	23 555	10 329	9 624	286	13 226	27 075	17 128	5 963	18 560
Remboursement du principal	40 583	27 859	14 628	6 290	5 777	230	8 338	13 231	5 839	4 333	12 724
Paiement des intérêts	28 607	22 771	8 927	4 039	3 847	56	4 888	13 844	11 289	1 630	5 836
Transfers nets (8)	4 904	-4 066	166	3 370	3 781	-191	-3 205	-4 231	-3 434	1 454	8 970
2000											
Debt outstanding	631 276	389 554	139 655	47 002	36 397	833	92 653	249 900	210 023	31 416	241 722
Disbursements (6)	116 345	58 443	16 176	2 879	2 209	39	13 297	42 267	35 022	6 499	57 903
Debt service (7)	157 440	81 392	25 536	9 398	8 291	129	16 138	55 857	43 769	9 658	76 048
Principal repayments	110 166	52 143	17 004	7 189	6 548	96	9 815	35 139	26 575	6 943	58 024
Interest payments	47 274	29 250	8 532	2 209	1 744	34	6 323	20 718	17 194	2 715	18 024
Net transfers on debt (8)	-41 095	-22 950	-9 360	-6 519	-6 082	-60	2 840	13 590	-8 747	-3 159	-18 145
2005											
Dette totale	623 822	410 018	134 217	30 966	25 105	430	103 251	275 801	232 945	38 471	213 804
Décaissements (6)	106 499	54 835	12 897	2 369	1 937	140	10 528	41 938	35 298	6 144	51 664
Service de la dette (7)	128 542	68 408	22 397	7 006	5 972	47	15 391	46 011	36 081	8 941	60 133
Remboursement du principal	94 239	44 267	16 806	5 867	5 175	39	10 939	27 461	19 360	7 312	49 972
Paiement des intérêts	34 302	24 141	5 591	1 139	797	8	4 452	18 550	16 721	1 629	10 161
Transfers nets (8)	-22 042	-13 573	-9 500	-4 637	-4 035	94	-4 863	-4 074	-783	-2 796	-8 469
2006											
Debt outstanding	634 444	393 079	123 759	27 887	21 574	931	95 872	269 320	226 707	39 476	241 365
Disbursements (6)	134 862	49 416	16 747	2 072	1 196	561	14 674	32 669	24 854	7 219	85 447
Debt service (7)	178 235	103 668	30 565	6 339	5 653	27	24 226	73 103	59 725	12 051	74 567
Principal repayments	137 616	79 067	24 570	5 329	4 933	21	19 240	54 497	43 228	10 118	58 549
Interest payments	40 619	24 601	5 995	1 010	720	6	4 985	18 606	16 496	1 934	16 018
Net transfers on debt (8)	-43 373	-54 252	-13 818	-4 267	-4 457	534	-9 551	-40 434	-34 871	-4 833	10 879
2007											
Dette totale	698 541	405 866	121 360	26 013	21 016	1 361	95 347	284 506	237 076	43 335	292 675
Décaissements (6)	152 358	45 729	14 774	1 713	1 015	487	13 060	30 955	24 473	6 148	106 629
Service de la dette (7)	148 501	74 041	22 888	7 050	6 002	104	15 838	51 154	41 880	8 189	74 460
Remboursement du principal	106 855	48 755	16 890	6 073	5 315	98	10 817	31 865	24 603	6 481	58 100
Paiement des intérêts	41 646	25 287	5 998	977	687	6	5 020	19 289	17 276	1 708	16 359
Transfers nets (8)	3 857	-28 312	-8 114	-5 337	-4 988	383	-2 777	-20 199	-17 407	-2 041	32 169
2008											
Debt outstanding	748 783	418 965	130 602	29 260	22 192	2 323	101 343	288 363	242 381	42 613	329 818
Disbursements (6)	164 386	63 370	19 335	3 590	1 207	1 041	15 745	44 035	36 092	7 784	101 015
Debt service (7)	151 413	71 209	18 340	3 185	2 617	54	15 155	52 869	44 231	7 749	80 203
Principal repayments	109 523	47 507	12 876	2 379	1 995	37	10 497	34 632	27 882	6 119	62 015
Interest payments	41 890	23 702	5 465	806	621	18	4 659	18 237	16 350	1 630	18 188
Net transfers on debt (8)	12 973	-7 839	995	405	-1 410	987	590	-8 833	-8 140	36	20 812
2009											
Dette totale	771 968	430 982	149 072	33 982	22 633	2 798	115 090	281 910	241 735	36 006	340 986
Décaissements (6)	155 639	68 397	31 028	6 726	2 102	551	24 302	37 368	32 530	4 173	87 242
Service de la dette (7)	143 760	59 390	18 502	4 648	3 840	159	13 854	40 888	28 927	10 475	84 370
Remboursement du principal	103 922	37 298	13 468	3 698	3 160	118	9 770	23 831	13 926	8 716	66 624
Paiement des intérêts	39 838	22 092	5 034	950	681	40	4 084	17 057	15 001	1 759	17 746
Transfers nets (8)	11 879	9 007	12 527	2 079	-1 738	393	10 448	-3 519	3 603	-6 302	2 872

For sources and notes, see end of table 7.7.G.

Pour les sources et les notes, se reporter à la fin du tableau 7.7.G.

7.7.D **External long-term debt by lending source**
Developing economies:
Asia

7.7.D **Dette extérieure à long terme par catégories de prêt**
Économies en développement :
Asie

	Total long-term debt (1) / Dette totale à long terme (1)	Public and publicly guaranteed debt (2) / Dette publique et garantie par l'état (2)									Private non-guaranteed debt (5) / Dette privée non garantie (5)
		Total creditors / Total créanciers	Official creditors (3) / Créanciers publics (3)					Private creditors (4) / Créanciers (4)			
			Total	Bilateral / Bilatéraux			Multilateral / Multilatéraux	Total	Bonds / Obligations	Commercial banks / Banques commerciales	
				Total	DAC / CAD	OPEC / OPEP					
1990											
Debt outstanding	370 418	347 034	224 149	139 592	83 247	5 164	84 557	122 885	19 628	69 557	23 384
Disbursments (6)	45 737	35 458	19 665	9 382	8 304	157	10 282	15 793	1 923	7 651	10 279
Debt service (7)	45 197	40 786	16 923	8 913	6 256	646	8 010	23 862	3 749	13 239	4 411
Principal repayments	27 149	24 160	9 874	5 822	3 783	527	4 053	14 285	2 251	7 271	2 989
Interest payments	18 048	16 626	7 049	3 091	2 473	119	3 958	9 577	1 498	5 968	1 422
Net transfers on debt (8)	540	-5 327	2 742	469	2 048	-490	2 272	-8 069	-1 826	-5 588	5 868
1995											
Dette totale	588 199	480 634	314 951	192 660	123 545	4 058	122 291	165 683	42 243	71 290	107 564
Décaissements (6)	80 639	55 722	26 350	15 124	9 775	300	11 226	29 372	7 178	12 329	24 916
Service de la dette (7)	79 593	63 135	30 996	18 782	11 743	338	12 214	32 139	6 412	13 830	16 458
Remboursement du principal	53 244	41 442	19 860	13 103	7 523	257	6 757	21 582	3 850	9 147	11 802
Paiement des intérêts	26 349	21 693	11 136	5 679	4 220	81	5 457	10 557	2 562	4 683	4 656
Transfers nets (8)	1 046	-7 413	-4 646	-3 658	-1 968	-38	-988	-2 767	766	-1 501	8 459
2000											
Debt outstanding	691 571	498 119	311 584	175 000	136 719	3 673	136 583	186 536	74 533	73 561	193 452
Disbursments (6)	80 809	57 816	24 935	11 730	10 217	143	13 205	32 882	19 208	7 966	22 993
Debt service (7)	117 554	73 834	33 536	19 735	15 286	488	13 801	40 298	10 646	20 014	43 720
Principal repayments	85 735	51 994	22 864	14 865	11 135	439	7 999	29 130	6 192	15 085	33 742
Interest payments	31 819	21 840	10 672	4 870	4 152	48	5 802	11 168	4 454	4 929	9 978
Net transfers on debt (8)	-36 745	-16 018	-8 602	-8 006	-5 069	-344	-596	-7 417	8 562	-12 048	-20 727
2005											
Dette totale	739 646	484 122	312 562	165 645	136 350	3 929	146 917	171 560	99 241	46 738	255 524
Décaissements (6)	140 823	47 661	18 844	6 370	4 666	220	12 474	28 817	19 212	7 242	93 162
Service de la dette (7)	147 850	73 549	28 147	16 442	12 596	328	11 704	45 403	27 647	11 825	74 300
Remboursement du principal	121 472	54 495	21 148	13 012	9 888	275	8 136	33 347	18 591	9 588	66 977
Paiement des intérêts	26 378	19 054	6 998	3 430	2 708	53	3 568	12 056	9 056	2 237	7 324
Transfers nets (8)	-7 026	-25 888	-9 303	-10 073	-7 929	-108	770	-16 585	-8 435	-4 583	18 862
2006											
Debt outstanding	821 699	501 253	322 691	165 517	133 612	3 087	157 174	178 562	108 356	46 702	320 446
Disbursments (6)	173 325	55 245	23 817	8 641	5 006	327	15 175	31 428	21 064	6 875	118 080
Debt service (7)	136 586	62 087	27 980	15 375	12 896	365	12 606	34 107	19 685	8 091	74 499
Principal repayments	107 096	43 913	20 446	11 827	9 980	307	8 619	23 467	12 010	5 900	63 183
Interest payments	29 490	18 174	7 535	3 548	2 916	58	3 987	10 639	7 675	2 191	11 316
Net transfers on debt (8)	36 739	-6 842	-4 164	-6 733	-7 890	-38	2 569	-2 678	1 379	-1 216	43 581
2007											
Dette totale	929 777	531 157	342 260	170 154	132 907	3 148	172 106	188 897	119 178	50 019	398 620
Décaissements (6)	233 696	57 684	25 072	7 431	5 123	216	17 641	32 612	20 885	9 033	176 012
Service de la dette (7)	182 988	66 425	31 658	18 151	13 885	376	13 507	34 767	20 866	9 197	116 563
Remboursement du principal	146 562	45 542	23 115	14 193	10 746	312	8 922	22 428	12 073	6 699	101 019
Paiement des intérêts	36 426	20 882	8 543	3 958	3 139	64	4 585	12 339	8 794	2 498	15 544
Transfers nets (8)	50 708	-8 741	-6 585	-10 720	-8 762	-160	4 134	-2 155	18	-163	59 449
2008											
Debt outstanding	1 008 528	557 105	369 160	185 464	145 270	3 222	183 695	187 946	118 682	52 135	451 422
Disbursments (6)	202 619	62 504	29 172	9 799	6 988	449	19 374	33 331	22 943	8 679	140 115
Debt service (7)	184 705	75 138	32 609	18 802	16 546	375	13 807	42 529	28 352	8 254	109 566
Principal repayments	147 481	54 636	24 435	15 053	13 292	311	9 382	30 201	19 366	5 964	92 845
Interest payments	37 223	20 502	8 174	3 749	3 253	63	4 425	12 328	8 985	2 290	16 721
Net transfers on debt (8)	17 914	-12 634	-3 437	-9 004	-9 557	74	5 567	-9 197	-5 408	425	30 548
2009											
Dette totale	1 035 245	584 744	387 796	187 390	139 723	3 330	200 406	196 947	126 816	51 311	450 501
Décaissements (6)	166 190	69 669	35 211	11 443	6 702	376	23 768	34 458	22 801	7 925	96 521
Service de la dette (7)	185 783	64 591	28 631	15 708	13 795	315	12 923	35 960	20 259	10 068	121 192
Remboursement du principal	152 140	45 696	21 455	12 088	10 741	244	9 367	24 241	11 106	8 163	106 444
Paiement des intérêts	33 643	18 895	7 176	3 620	3 054	72	3 555	11 719	9 153	1 906	14 748
Transfers nets (8)	-19 593	5 078	6 580	-4 265	-7 093	61	10 845	-1 502	2 542	-2 143	-24 671

For sources and notes, see end of table 7.7.G.

Pour les sources et les notes, se reporter à la fin du tableau 7.7.G.

7.7.E **External long-term debt by lending source**
Developing economies:
Oceania

7.7.E **Dette extérieure à long terme par catégories de prêt**
Économies en développement :
Océanie

	Total long-term debt (1) / Dette totale à long terme (1)	Total creditors / Total créanciers	Public and publicly guaranteed debt (2) / Dette publique et garantie par l'état (2)								Private non-guaranteed debt (5) / Dette privée non garantie (5)
			Official creditors (3) / Créanciers publics (3)					Private creditors (4) / Créanciers (4)			
			Total	Bilateral / Bilatéraux			Multilateral / Multilatéraux	Total	Bonds / Obligations	Commercial banks / Banques commerciales	
				Total	DAC / CAD	OPEC / OPEP					
	Millions of dollars / Millions de dollars										
1990											
Debt outstanding	3 118	2 085	1 593	447	412	10	1 146	493	39	330	1 033
Disbursments (6)	682	325	270	50	67	0	218	46	0	24	358
Debt service (7)	665	366	163	47	44	0	116	203	3	175	299
Principal repayments	473	251	99	26	25	0	73	152	0	137	222
Interest payments	193	115	65	21	19	0	44	50	3	38	77
Net transfers on debt (8)	17	-42	115	12	13	0	103	-157	-3	-155	59
1995											
Dette totale	3 032	2 205	1 967	571	541	11	1 396	237	0	157	828
Décaissements (6)	238	182	164	69	67	0	95	18	0	13	57
Service de la dette (7)	686	340	196	61	59	1	136	143	35	73	347
Remboursement du principal	556	243	120	40	39	1	80	124	32	63	313
Paiement des intérêts	130	96	77	21	20	0	56	19	2	9	34
Transfers nets (8)	-448	-158	-33	8	8	-1	-41	-125	-35	-59	-290
2000											
Debt outstanding	2 804	2 023	1 959	697	564	10	1 263	64	0	54	781
Disbursments (6)	291	256	243	145	134	2	98	13	0	13	35
Debt service (7)	328	211	186	73	62	1	113	25	0	13	116
Principal repayments	229	146	126	52	45	1	74	20	0	10	84
Interest payments	98	66	61	21	17	0	40	5	0	3	33
Net transfers on debt (8)	-36	45	56	72	72	1	-16	-11	0	0	-81
2005											
Dette totale	2 304	1 911	1 859	535	400	7	1 324	52	0	8	393
Décaissements (6)	369	80	79	3	3	0	75	1	0	0	290
Service de la dette (7)	277	186	160	67	59	1	93	26	0	17	91
Remboursement du principal	211	137	114	50	45	1	64	23	0	15	73
Paiement des intérêts	67	49	47	17	14	0	29	2	0	1	18
Transfers nets (8)	92	-106	-82	-64	-56	-1	-18	-25	0	-17	199
2006											
Debt outstanding	2 476	2 018	1 822	497	373	7	1 325	196	150	4	458
Disbursments (6)	445	229	75	3	0	0	72	154	150	0	216
Debt service (7)	347	190	179	45	39	1	134	11	0	5	157
Principal repayments	291	141	132	32	28	1	100	9	0	4	150
Interest payments	57	49	48	13	11	0	34	1	0	0	8
Net transfers on debt (8)	98	40	-104	-42	-39	-1	-62	144	150	-5	58
2007											
Dette totale	2 211	1 972	1 779	485	353	5	1 294	192	150	4	239
Décaissements (6)	678	83	83	13	0	0	70	0	0	0	595
Service de la dette (7)	1 057	263	246	52	43	4	194	17	10	1	794
Remboursement du principal	979	201	195	38	32	2	157	6	0	0	777
Paiement des intérêts	78	62	51	14	10	2	37	11	10	0	16
Transfers nets (8)	-379	-180	-164	-40	-43	-4	-124	-17	-10	-1	-199
2008											
Debt outstanding	2 316	1 945	1 751	488	320	3	1 262	195	150	4	371
Disbursments (6)	1 009	83	83	41	0	0	42	0	0	0	926
Debt service (7)	1 029	252	234	119	110	2	115	17	10	1	777
Principal repayments	963	194	188	103	98	2	85	6	0	0	709
Interest payments	65	57	46	16	12	0	30	11	10	0	8
Net transfers on debt (8)	-19	-168	-151	-78	-110	-2	-72	-17	-10	-1	149
2009											
Dette totale	2 380	1 961	1 773	512	296	2	1 261	188	150	3	419
Décaissements (6)	599	102	102	53	1	0	49	1	0	0	497
Service de la dette (7)	593	133	115	38	30	1	77	18	10	0	460
Remboursement du principal	543	90	83	26	22	1	57	7	0	0	452
Paiement des intérêts	50	43	32	12	8	0	20	11	10	0	7
Transfers nets (8)	6	-31	-13	15	-29	-1	-28	-17	-10	0	37

For sources and notes, see end of table 7.7.G.

Pour les sources et les notes, se reporter à la fin du tableau 7.7.G.

7

7.7.F **External long-term debt by lending source**
Developing economies:
Major petroleum and gas exporters

7.7.F **Dette extérieure à long terme par catégories de prêt**
Économies en développement :
Principaux exportateurs de pétrole et de gaz

	Total long-term debt (1) / Dette totale à long terme (1)	Public and publicly guaranteed debt (2) / Dette publique et garantie par l'état (2)									Private non-guaranteed debt (5) / Dette privée non garantie (5)
		Total creditors / Total créanciers	Official creditors (3) / Créanciers publics (3)					Private creditors (4) / Créanciers (4)			
			Total	Bilateral / Bilatéraux			Multilateral / Multilatéraux	Total	Bonds / Obligations	Commercial banks / Banques commerciales	
				Total	DAC CAD	OPEC OPEP					
	Millions of dollars / Millions de dollars										
1990											
Debt outstanding	98 584	94 543	27 197	19 493	16 065	238	7 704	67 346	21 064	14 847	4 041
Disbursments (6)	11 296	11 296	3 814	1 569	1 255	14	2 245	7 482	599	249	0
Debt service (7)	17 859	17 267	3 918	2 700	2 265	36	1 125	13 349	509	6 043	592
Principal repayments	10 653	10 464	2 188	1 328	1 348	27	669	8 276	769	2 803	100
Interest payments	7 206	6 803	1 730	1 273	917	9	456	5 073	240	3 240	403
Net transfers on debt (8)	-6 563	-5 971	-104	-1 224	-1 010	-22	1 120	-5 867	90	-5 794	-592
1995											
Dette totale	120 189	114 963	55 126	42 195	27 987	460	12 931	59 837	22 796	8 035	5 227
Décaissements (6)	7 999	7 604	3 187	1 343	1 225	61	1 843	4 417	349	1 336	395
Service de la dette (7)	16 816	15 602	7 355	5 320	931	48	2 036	8 247	2 770	1 010	1 214
Remboursement du principal	10 560	9 667	5 085	3 892	300	39	1 192	4 583	1 095	553	893
Paiement des intérêts	6 256	5 935	2 271	1 427	631	9	843	3 664	1 674	457	321
Transfers nets (8)	-8 817	-7 999	-4 169	-3 976	294	13	-192	-3 830	-2 420	326	-818
2000											
Debt outstanding	100 428	94 080	54 717	43 274	16 841	500	11 443	39 363	18 268	9 667	6 347
Disbursments (6)	6 224	6 224	2 245	1 198	619	10	1 047	3 979	462	1 946	0
Debt service (7)	15 890	14 614	6 892	4 826	1 888	81	2 065	7 723	2 545	2 524	1 276
Principal repayments	10 672	9 981	4 676	3 429	1 024	49	1 247	5 305	1 119	2 027	690
Interest payments	5 219	4 633	2 216	1 398	864	32	818	2 417	1 426	497	586
Net transfers on debt (8)	-9 666	-8 390	-4 647	-3 629	-1 268	-71	-1 018	-3 743	-2 083	-578	-1 276
2005											
Dette totale	91 360	86 792	39 103	30 586	27 632	609	8 517	47 689	24 988	13 324	4 568
Décaissements (6)	15 251	14 788	2 174	1 064	232	24	1 110	12 014	6 143	4 009	463
Service de la dette (7)	24 289	22 999	14 070	11 353	10 619	113	2 717	8 928	2 563	3 807	1 290
Remboursement du principal	15 132	14 216	8 267	6 016	5 395	102	2 251	5 949	646	3 158	916
Paiement des intérêts	9 157	8 783	5 803	5 337	5 224	11	466	2 979	1 917	649	374
Transfers nets (8)	-9 038	-8 210	-11 896	-10 289	-10 387	-89	-1 607	3 686	3 580	1 192	-827
2006											
Debt outstanding	59 289	53 251	13 807	6 994	3 335	571	6 812	39 444	19 478	11 377	6 038
Disbursments (6)	6 294	5 743	2 891	1 361	421	27	1 530	2 852	0	1 700	551
Debt service (7)	36 025	34 805	19 208	15 362	14 944	82	3 846	15 597	7 711	4 857	1 221
Principal repayments	30 974	30 244	17 994	14 560	14 275	65	3 434	12 251	5 734	3 990	729
Interest payments	5 052	4 560	1 214	802	669	17	412	3 346	1 977	867	491
Net transfers on debt (8)	-29 731	-29 062	-16 317	-14 001	-14 523	-56	-2 316	-12 745	-7 711	-3 157	-669
2007											
Dette totale	59 469	55 360	14 626	7 983	3 375	575	6 643	40 735	20 675	12 692	4 108
Décaissements (6)	9 792	9 488	2 384	1 445	321	48	939	7 104	1 250	5 352	304
Service de la dette (7)	14 102	12 969	2 823	1 234	766	80	1 589	10 146	1 960	5 565	1 133
Remboursement du principal	10 081	9 276	2 163	888	608	63	1 275	7 113	209	4 683	806
Paiement des intérêts	4 021	3 694	661	346	158	17	314	3 033	1 751	881	327
Transfers nets (8)	-4 310	-3 481	-439	211	-445	-33	-650	-3 042	-710	-212	-829
2008											
Debt outstanding	63 226	58 472	15 557	8 675	3 117	532	6 882	42 916	23 353	14 102	4 754
Disbursments (6)	12 057	10 999	2 585	1 481	213	47	1 104	8 415	4 000	4 026	1 057
Debt service (7)	11 489	10 664	2 402	1 267	556	98	1 135	8 262	3 305	2 861	825
Principal repayments	7 438	6 994	1 827	957	436	91	870	5 167	1 299	2 122	444
Interest payments	4 051	3 669	575	311	120	7	264	3 094	2 006	739	382
Net transfers on debt (8)	568	336	183	214	-343	-51	-31	153	695	1 164	232
2009											
Dette totale	67 515	63 223	16 911	9 112	2 914	509	7 799	46 313	28 360	13 445	4 292
Décaissements (6)	11 330	11 207	2 945	1 509	119	13	1 436	8 262	4 992	3 091	123
Service de la dette (7)	10 857	9 962	2 090	1 282	511	42	808	7 873	2 024	4 427	895
Remboursement du principal	7 219	6 697	1 584	980	429	36	604	5 114	0	3 869	522
Paiement des intérêts	3 638	3 265	506	302	81	6	204	2 759	2 024	558	373
Transfers nets (8)	474	1 245	855	227	-392	-28	629	389	2 968	-1 336	-771

For sources and notes, see end of table 7.7.G.

Pour les sources et les notes, se reporter à la fin du tableau 7.7.G.

7.7.G External long-term debt by lending source
Developing economies:
Major manufactured goods exporters

7.7.G Dette extérieure à long terme par catégories de prêt
Économies en développement :
Principaux exportateurs d'articles manufacturés

	Total long-term debt (1) Dette totale à long terme (1)	Public and publicly guaranteed debt (2) / Dette publique et garantie par l'état (2)									Private non-guaranteed debt (5) Dette privée non garantie (5)
		Total creditors Total créanciers	Official creditors (3) / Créanciers publics (3)					Private creditors (4) / Créanciers (4)			
			Total	Bilateral / Bilatéraux			Multilateral Multilatéraux	Total	Bonds Obligations	Commercial banks Banques commerciales	
				Total	DAC CAD	OPEC OPEP					
	Millions of dollars / Millions de dollars										
1990											
Debt outstanding	160 518	145 541	49 609	23 667	20 974	305	25 942	95 932	50 354	25 561	14 976
Disbursments (6)	27 963	21 726	9 655	1 315	0 000	0	9 340	12 071	1 252	5 908	6 237
Debt service (7)	22 974	20 613	5 873	2 303	2 067	41	3 571	14 740	4 054	6 560	2 360
Principal repayments	12 291	11 034	3 290	1 379	1 241	28	1 911	7 744	2 115	2 981	1 257
Interest payments	10 683	9 580	2 583	924	826	13	1 659	6 996	1 938	3 579	1 103
Net transfers on debt (8)	4 989	1 113	3 782	2 012	1 491	-33	1 769	-2 669	-2 802	-594	3 877
1995											
Dette totale	291 027	221 426	92 656	52 868	42 056	207	39 788	128 770	63 606	36 386	69 601
Décaissements (6)	70 880	51 749	24 753	18 759	13 927	0	5 994	26 996	10 624	8 969	19 131
Service de la dette (7)	48 181	34 336	10 375	5 363	4 798	33	5 012	23 961	9 172	7 182	13 845
Remboursement du principal	32 082	21 794	5 623	2 869	2 681	24	2 755	16 171	5 324	5 118	10 288
Paiement des intérêts	16 099	12 542	4 752	2 494	2 117	8	2 257	7 790	3 848	2 065	3 557
Transfers nets (8)	22 700	17 413	14 379	13 396	9 129	-32	982	3 035	1 452	1 787	5 286
2000											
Debt outstanding	363 678	225 026	96 994	47 301	41 965	204	49 693	128 032	76 700	23 308	138 652
Disbursments (6)	59 559	27 670	12 247	5 599	4 639	59	6 649	15 422	9 277	2 354	31 889
Debt service (7)	101 447	51 005	15 359	8 008	6 853	102	7 351	35 646	18 144	10 399	50 441
Principal repayments	77 626	36 420	10 153	6 044	5 129	91	4 109	26 267	12 079	8 758	41 205
Interest payments	23 821	14 585	5 206	1 964	1 724	11	3 242	9 379	6 065	1 641	9 236
Net transfers on debt (8)	-41 888	-23 335	-3 111	-2 409	-2 214	-43	-702	-20 224	-8 867	-8 016	18 552
2005											
Dette totale	366 093	230 690	85 389	40 743	31 347	79	44 646	145 300	101 470	27 329	135 404
Décaissements (6)	85 306	28 970	5 894	1 858	1 601	1	4 036	23 077	16 391	5 177	56 335
Service de la dette (7)	95 299	40 475	10 159	4 749	4 388	6	5 410	30 315	19 570	7 080	54 824
Remboursement du principal	79 394	29 810	7 389	3 530	3 352	3	3 859	22 420	12 747	6 437	49 585
Paiement des intérêts	15 905	10 665	2 770	1 219	1 036	3	1 551	7 895	6 823	643	5 240
Transfers nets (8)	-9 993	-11 504	-4 266	-2 892	-2 787	-6	-1 374	-7 239	-3 180	-1 903	1 511
2006											
Debt outstanding	375 447	219 388	79 224	41 845	29 308	59	37 379	140 164	96 299	28 758	156 059
Disbursments (6)	79 295	23 981	6 774	2 446	968	0	4 328	17 207	9 269	5 161	55 313
Debt service (7)	98 640	53 742	18 410	4 423	3 826	24	13 987	35 333	23 764	6 936	44 897
Principal repayments	80 797	43 336	15 655	3 510	3 144	21	12 145	27 681	17 232	6 227	37 461
Interest payments	17 842	10 406	2 755	913	681	3	1 843	7 651	6 533	709	7 436
Net transfers on debt (8)	-19 345	-29 761	-11 636	-1 976	-2 858	-24	-9 660	-18 125	-14 495	-1 774	10 416
2007											
Dette totale	404 385	222 464	80 054	40 924	24 843	42	39 130	142 410	100 155	30 425	181 922
Décaissements (6)	96 819	23 310	5 481	1 293	873	0	4 188	17 829	13 493	2 158	73 509
Service de la dette (7)	96 689	36 141	9 917	5 320	4 182	8	4 597	26 224	19 420	3 870	60 548
Remboursement du principal	77 044	24 901	7 357	4 354	3 551	5	3 002	17 544	12 174	3 112	52 143
Paiement des intérêts	19 645	11 240	2 560	965	632	2	1 595	8 680	7 246	759	8 405
Transfers nets (8)	130	-12 832	-4 437	-4 027	-3 310	-8	-410	-8 395	-5 927	-1 713	12 962
2008											
Debt outstanding	444 633	236 279	87 657	45 690	26 493	28	41 967	148 622	105 886	31 633	208 355
Disbursments (6)	100 533	33 735	6 826	1 328	303	0	5 498	26 909	18 748	6 536	66 798
Debt service (7)	95 261	35 527	8 391	4 189	3 962	16	4 202	27 136	18 846	4 094	59 734
Principal repayments	77 378	25 800	6 278	3 508	3 304	14	2 770	19 523	12 587	3 470	51 578
Interest payments	17 883	9 726	2 113	682	659	2	1 432	7 613	6 260	625	8 157
Net transfers on debt (8)	5 272	-1 792	-1 565	-2 861	-3 659	-16	1 297	-227	-98	2 441	7 063
2009											
Dette totale	430 222	225 095	99 900	48 950	25 334	17	50 950	125 195	84 786	26 485	205 127
Décaissements (6)	73 187	34 049	12 153	1 904	1 250	0	10 249	21 896	15 397	3 335	39 139
Service de la dette (7)	100 596	33 114	7 784	3 689	3 618	11	4 095	25 330	13 616	6 917	67 483
Remboursement du principal	83 769	24 879	5 906	3 023	2 971	10	2 883	18 973	8 624	6 043	58 890
Paiement des intérêts	16 828	8 235	1 877	665	647	1	1 212	6 357	4 992	875	8 593
Transfers nets (8)	-27 409	935	4 369	-1 785	-2 367	-11	6 154	-3 434	1 781	-3 582	-28 344

For sources and notes, see next page.

Pour les sources et les notes, se reporter à la page suivante.

7.7.G External long-term debt by lending source
Developing economies:
Major manufactured goods exporters

7.7.G Dette extérieure à long terme par catégories de prêt
Économies en développement :
Principaux exportateurs d'articles manufacturés

Sources:
- World Bank, *Global Development Finance*

Notes:

(1) Long-term debt is defined as debt that has an original or extended maturity of more than one year and that is owed to nonresidents and repayable in foreign currency, goods, or services.
Long-term debt has three components:
-"Public debt";
-"Publicly guaranteed debt";
-"Private nonguaranteed debt".
In this table, "Public debt" and "Publicly guaranteed debt" are aggregated.
Outstanding long-term debt at year end is the sum of long-term debt outstanding and long-term debt disbursed.

(2) "Public debt" is an obligation of a public debtor, including the national government, a political subdivision (or an agency of either), and autonomous public bodies.
"Publicly guaranteed debt" is an external obligation of a private debtor that is guaranteed for repayment by a public entity.
In this table, "Public debt" and "Publicly guaranteed debt" are aggregated.
Data of " Public and publicly guaranteed debt" is shown by type of creditor: official creditors and private creditors.

(3) "Public and publicly guaranteed debt" from official creditors includes loans from governments (referred to as bilateral creditors) and loans from international organizations (referred to as multilateral creditors).
Government loans include loans from governments and their agencies (including central banks), loans from autonomous bodies, and direct loans from official export credit agencies.
Loans from international organizations include loans and credits from the World Bank, regional development banks, and other multilateral and intergovernmental agencies. Excluded are loans from funds administered by an international organization on behalf of a single donor government; these are classified as loans from governments.

(4) "Public and publicly guaranteed debt" from private creditors includes:
- "Bonds" that are either publicly issued or privately placed;
- "Commercial bank loans" from private banks and other private financial institutions;
- "Other private credits" from manufacturers, exporters, and other suppliers of goods, and bank credits covered by a guarantee of an export credit agency.

(5) Private nonguaranteed long-term debt outstanding and disbursed is an obligation of a private debtor that is not guaranteed for repayment by a public entity.

(6) Disbursements on long-term debt are drawings on loan commitments during the year specified.

(7) Long-term debt service payments are the sum of principal repayments and interest payments in the year specified.

(8) Net transfers on long-term debt are "disbursements" minus "debt service payments".

Sources :
- Banque mondiale, *Global Development Finance*

Notes :

(1) La dette à long terme a une durée de remboursement (d'origine ou différée) supérieure à une année, et son amortissement est dû, en monnaies convertibles ou en nature, à des créanciers non-résidents.
La dette à long terme a trois composantes :
- "Dette publique" ;
- "Dette garantie par l'État" ;
- "Dette du secteur privé non garantie".
Dans ce tableau, la "dette publique" et la "dette garantie par l'État" sont agrégées.

(2) La "dette publique" est une dette contractée par le secteur public, y compris le gouvernement, une entité politique et d'autres organismes publics autonomes.
La "dette garantie par l'État" est une dette contractée par le secteur privé, dont l'amortissement est garanti par une entité publique.
Dans ce tableau, "dette publique" et "dette garantie par l'État" sont agrégées.
Les données de la "dette publique et garantie par l'État" sont indiquées par types de créanciers : créanciers publics et créanciers privés.

(3) La "dette publique et garantie par l'État" octroyée par les créanciers publics inclut les prêts des gouvernements (appelés créditeurs bilatéraux) et les prêts des organisations internationales (appelées créditeurs multilatéraux).
Les prêts des gouvernements incluent les prêts des gouvernements et des organismes publics (y compris les banques centrales), les prêts provenant d'entités autonomes et les prêts octroyés directement par des organismes publics de crédits à l'exportation.
Les prêts des organisations internationales incluent les prêts et les crédits de la Banque mondiale, des banques régionales de développement, et d'autres organismes multilatéraux et intergouvernementaux.Ne sont pas compris les prêts provenant des fonds administrés par une organisation internationale, pour le compte d'un gouvernement ; ceux-ci sont classés sous la rubrique des prêts des gouvernements.

(4) La "dette publique et garantie par l'État" octroyée par les créanciers privés comprend :
- "Obligations" qui sont soit des émissions publiques, soit des placements privés ;
- "Prêts des banques commerciales" octroyés par des banques privées et par d'autres entités financières ;
- "Autres crédits privés" provenant du secteur manufacturier, du secteur des exportations, et d'autres fournisseurs de biens, ainsi que des crédits bancaires couverts par un organisme de crédits à l'exportation.

(5) La dette du secteur privé non-garantie encourue et décaissée, est une dette contractée par le secteur privé, dont l'amortissement n'est pas garanti par une entité publique.

(6) Les décaissements de la dette à long terme sont les tirages sur les engagements de la dette effectués au cours de l'année spécifiée.

(7) Les paiements du service de la dette à long terme sont la somme du remboursement du principal et du paiement des intérêts, effectués au cours de l'année spécifiée.

(8) Les transferts nets sont les "décaissements" moins les "paiements du service de la dette".

8 DEVELOPMENT INDICATORS

INDICATEURS DU DÉVELOPPEMENT

1

2

3

4

5

6

7

8

8.1.1 Nominal gross domestic product: Total and per capita of countries and geographical regions

Region, country or territory	Total gross domestic product / Produit intérieur brut total (1) Millions of dollars / Millions de dollars							
	1980	1990	2000	2006	2007	2008	2009	2010 (e)
WORLD	11 864 690	22 205 664	32 244 443	49 536 231	55 755 969	61 146 661	58 068 608	63 150 553
DEVELOPING ECONOMIES	2 539 911	3 850 600	6 972 864	12 553 209	14 897 180	17 289 154	17 059 105	20 362 432
TRANSITION ECONOMIES	1 012 216	864 522	397 174	1 399 520	1 832 086	2 340 280	1 786 718	2 094 417
DEVELOPED ECONOMIES	8 312 564	17 490 542	24 874 405	35 583 502	39 026 703	41 517 227	39 222 785	40 693 705
Developing economies: Africa	435 535	492 979	596 384	1 126 028	1 289 758	1 505 808	1 424 905	1 656 132
Eastern Africa	*49 424*	*62 036*	*68 517*	*111 204*	*130 833*	*157 531*	*159 421*	*161 920*
Burundi	1 278	1 542	955	1 217	1 284	1 242	1 251	1 400
Comoros	124	244	202	403	465	530	530	536
Djibouti	301	457	553	750	793	838	930	1 010
Eritrea	–		700	1 211	1 010	1 000	1 073	2 126
Ethiopia			8 111	15 134	19 165	25 897	28 538	26 680
Ethiopia (former)	5 889	11 658		–	–	–	–	
Kenya	9 165	11 035	12 604	22 504	27 165	29 983	29 412	32 152
Madagascar	3 265	3 080	3 878	5 515	7 417	9 559	8 790	8 790
Malawi	1 705	2 414	2 402	3 136	3 574	4 220	4 860	5 196
Mauritius	1 146	2 588	4 583	6 507	7 521	9 326	8 668	9 512
Mozambique	4 826	2 969	4 310	7 096	8 036	9 867	9 579	9 159
Rwanda	1 401	2 574	1 772	3 111	3 741	4 716	5 265	5 645
Seychelles	181	453	760	1 015	1 018	921	788	935
Somalia	573	994	2 052	2 390	2 483	2 600	2 012	..
Uganda	3 038	4 039	6 341	11 011	13 549	16 472	17 110	18 372
United Republic of Tanzania	7 310	5 480	10 424	14 739	17 299	21 318	23 016	24 568
Zambia	3 885	3 742	3 239	10 886	11 582	14 798	12 748	15 834
Zimbabwe	5 339	8 767	5 627	4 580	4 424	3 864	4 056	..
Middle Africa	*33 267*	*43 212*	*35 958*	*85 276*	*99 538*	*124 573*	*110 504*	*131 184*
Angola	5 415	10 295	9 133	24 347	30 122	34 817	34 991	39 545
Cameroon	8 869	11 846	9 287	17 953	20 432	23 735	22 181	22 423
Central African Republic	1 112	1 441	914	1 477	1 712	1 982	1 980	2 013
Chad	919	1 542	1 385	6 300	7 008	8 354	6 839	7 711
Congo	1 706	2 799	3 220	7 731	7 646	11 060	9 958	11 957
Dem. Rep. of the Congo	9 860	9 187	5 265	8 785	9 963	11 668	11 204	..
Equatorial Guinea	54	133	1 177	8 526	10 703	17 884	11 864	14 042
Gabon	5 251	5 850	5 498	10 015	11 795	14 884	11 276	13 443
Sao Tome and Principe	82	120	77	143	158	189	212	209
Northern Africa	*143 352*	*189 491*	*262 419*	*426 709*	*496 531*	*607 383*	*572 751*	*646 658*
Algeria	42 348	61 891	54 790	117 288	134 304	170 228	140 601	159 914
Egypt	24 057	39 393	99 601	112 152	132 165	164 844	187 981	214 406
Libyan Arab Jamahiriya	38 186	31 088	38 471	55 077	62 668	81 376	58 762	71 670
Morocco (2)	21 030	28 855	37 022	65 640	75 223	88 879	90 660	90 913
Sudan	8 989	15 949	13 092	45 460	56 554	61 118	55 186	69 494
Tunisia	8 743	12 314	19 444	31 092	35 617	40 937	39 562	40 259
Southern Africa	*84 994*	*120 002*	*144 699*	*284 612*	*312 137*	*303 355*	*311 686*	*393 080*
Botswana	1 047	3 715	5 633	11 256	12 379	13 426	11 620	14 015
Lesotho	389	552	757	1 420	1 579	1 595	1 613	1 997
Namibia	2 308	2 679	3 909	7 979	8 815	8 863	9 310	11 865
South Africa	80 544	112 014	132 878	261 007	286 302	276 451	285 983	361 276
Swaziland	706	1 042	1 523	2 951	3 062	3 020	3 161	3 927
Western Africa	*124 498*	*78 240*	*84 792*	*218 226*	*250 719*	*312 967*	*270 537*	*323 284*
Benin	1 374	1 845	2 359	4 705	5 512	6 643	6 602	6 594
Burkina Faso	1 913	3 101	2 617	5 771	6 757	8 174	8 145	8 341
Cape Verde	142	308	539	1 108	1 331	1 561	1 583	1 643
Côte d'Ivoire	10 176	11 893	10 682	18 144	19 794	23 414	23 042	22 769
Gambia	506	710	783	691	823	1 026	925	977
Ghana	3 253	6 229	4 983	12 736	15 160	16 169	14 947	17 814
Guinea	1 489	2 920	3 192	2 821	4 209	3 799	4 737	4 737
Guinea-Bissau	506	588	366	579	691	843	833	835
Liberia	765	487	528	671	653	830	856	949
Mali	1 423	2 510	2 655	6 123	7 145	8 738	8 838	9 121
Mauritania	829	1 050	1 075	2 579	2 671	3 332	2 850	3 572
Niger	2 697	2 638	1 727	3 647	4 291	5 369	5 244	5 550
Nigeria	93 606	35 026	46 386	145 428	165 921	214 473	173 766	222 070
Senegal	3 254	6 205	4 680	9 359	11 277	13 274	12 756	12 834
Sierra Leone	1 433	946	926	1 646	1 954	2 156	2 237	2 273
Togo	1 131	1 785	1 294	2 219	2 531	3 168	3 175	3 205

For sources and notes, see end of table.

404

Per capita gross domestic product / Produit intérieur brut par habitant Dollars								Régions, pays ou territoires
1980	1990	2000	2006	2007	2008	2009	2010 (e)	
2 675	**4 201**	**5 286**	**7 551**	**8 400**	**9 105**	**8 548**	**9 275**	**MONDE**
772	947	1 444	2 388	2 796	3 202	3 118	3 715	ÉCONOMIES EN DÉVELOPPEMENT
3 496	2 743	1 302	4 640	6 071	7 748	5 907	6 916	ÉCONOMIES EN TRANSITION
9 710	19 303	25 711	35 518	38 727	40 961	38 482	39 723	ÉCONOMIES DÉVELOPPÉES
903	**777**	**736**	**1 210**	**1 354**	**1 545**	**1 428**	**1 658**	**Économies en développement : Afrique**
346	*323*	*273*	*381*	*437*	*513*	*506*	*538*	*Afrique orientale*
309	275	150	163	167	156	153	167	Burundi
376	557	359	610	685	761	741	730	Comores
885	813	755	910	945	900	1 000	1 136	Djibouti
–	–	193	261	275	279	367	407	Érythrée
		124	199	247	326	352	322	Éthiopie
155	226	–	–	–	–	–	–	Éthiopie (anc.)
563	471	403	616	725	780	745	794	Kenya
379	273	252	299	391	489	437	424	Madagascar
273	257	214	238	263	301	337	349	Malawi
1 189	2 442	3 832	5 137	5 896	7 264	6 711	7 322	Maurice
397	219	237	333	368	442	419	392	Mozambique
271	362	219	330	385	471	511	531	Rwanda
2 885	6 380	9 658	12 037	11 984	10 763	9 155	10 811	Seychelles
89	151	277	280	284	291	221	..	Somalie
240	228	262	375	447	526	529	550	Ouganda
391	215	306	369	421	504	529	548	République-Unie de Tanzanie
673	476	317	926	961	1 195	1 002	1 210	Zambie
732	837	450	366	354	310	325	..	Zimbabwe
623	*603*	*374*	*748*	*850*	*1 036*	*895*	*1 035*	*Afrique centrale*
709	996	656	1 431	1 719	1 930	1 886	2 072	Angola
974	972	592	1 000	1 113	1 265	1 157	1 144	Cameroun
489	491	247	361	411	468	450	457	République centrafricaine
202	256	168	625	676	784	625	687	Tchad
949	1 172	1 027	2 131	2 049	2 883	2 526	2 958	Congo
365	252	106	149	164	187	175	..	Rép. dém. du Congo
244	356	2 263	13 624	16 622	27 002	17 419	20 049	Guinée équatoriale
7 692	6 297	4 451	7 168	8 285	10 263	7 631	8 930	Gabon
868	1 034	544	921	1 001	1 180	1 303	1 263	Sao Tomé-et-Principe
1 269	*1 298*	*1 492*	*2 189*	*2 503*	*3 009*	*2 788*	*3 095*	*Afrique septentrionale*
2 251	2 446	1 794	3 512	3 961	4 944	4 023	4 509	Algérie
535	693	1 472	1 484	1 718	2 105	2 358	2 643	Égypte
12 467	7 172	7 354	9 345	10 405	13 233	9 383	11 278	Jamahiriya arabe libyenne
1 075	1 164	1 286	2 138	2 426	2 838	2 866	2 845	Maroc (2)
448	602	383	1 155	1 401	1 476	1 299	1 596	Soudan
1 354	1 499	2 056	3 104	3 516	3 995	3 817	3 841	Tunisie
2 576	*2 851*	*2 813*	*5 123*	*5 557*	*5 345*	*5 440*	*6 803*	*Afrique australe*
1 051	2 688	3 204	5 921	6 422	6 868	5 864	6 983	Botswana
297	336	385	681	750	750	750	920	Lesotho
2 279	1 894	2 062	3 766	4 083	4 028	4 152	5 196	Namibie
2 770	3 044	2 969	5 400	5 862	5 605	5 748	7 206	Afrique du Sud
1 170	1 207	1 432	2 640	2 702	2 625	2 706	3 311	Swaziland
891	*429*	*360*	*795*	*890*	*1 083*	*912*	*1 063*	*Afrique occidentale*
381	387	362	598	679	795	768	745	Bénin
265	333	213	395	449	527	510	506	Burkina Faso
474	885	1 233	2 316	2 756	3 203	3 220	3 313	Cap-Vert
1 197	950	644	990	1 062	1 233	1 191	1 154	Côte d'Ivoire
803	734	604	446	517	627	550	565	Gambie
298	421	260	574	667	695	627	730	Ghana
338	507	383	307	449	397	485	475	Guinée
607	578	295	415	485	580	561	551	Guinée-Bissau
398	229	185	203	188	227	223	237	Libéria
196	289	235	450	510	604	593	593	Mali
546	526	407	824	831	1 011	844	1 033	Mauritanie
459	339	158	271	308	372	350	358	Niger
1 239	359	375	1 015	1 129	1 424	1 125	1 402	Nigéria
601	857	492	838	983	1 126	1 054	1 032	Sénégal
453	238	223	309	357	384	390	387	Sierra Leone
424	487	270	401	448	548	538	532	Togo

Pour les sources et les notes, se reporter à la fin du tableau.

Region, country or territory	Total gross domestic product / Produit intérieur brut total (1) Millions of dollars / Millions de dollars							
	1980	1990	2000	2006	2007	2008	2009	2010 (e)
Developing economies: America	751 854	1 118 337	2 124 118	3 175 836	3 740 844	4 345 328	4 035 274	4 904 547
Caribbean	*43 148*	*60 955*	*93 628*	*148 021*	*165 604*	*180 348*	*174 691*	..
Anguilla	9	54	108	219	274	290	216	224
Antigua and Barbuda	110	392	664	1 003	1 155	1 203	1 132	1 118
Aruba	493	828	1 873	2 421	2 563	2 724	2 623	2 611
Bahamas	1 352	3 166	5 528	6 876	7 234	7 298	7 077	7 232
Barbados	865	1 720	2 559	3 191	3 409	3 670	3 595	3 658
British Virgin Islands	20	105	759	1 041	1 134	1 215	1 328	..
Cayman Islands	154	831	2 036	2 867	3 172	3 355	3 370	..
Cuba	19 913	28 645	30 565	52 742	58 604	00 000	60 017	..
Dominica	59	167	271	316	344	372	378	392
Dominican Republic	8 178	9 385	23 655	35 660	41 013	45 523	46 598	51 570
Grenada	73	221	408	564	610	678	636	664
Haiti	1 384	2 614	3 515	4 679	5 727	6 146	6 279	6 218
Jamaica	3 045	4 822	8 949	11 957	12 908	13 995	12 414	13 776
Montserrat	24	67	35	45	46	50	53	..
Netherlands Antilles	948	1 990	2 856	3 438	3 652	3 954	4 022	4 242
Saint Kitts and Nevis	48	159	329	487	509	570	545	550
Saint Lucia	135	416	708	933	960	988	948	973
Saint Vincent and the Grenadines	59	198	335	489	555	582	567	561
Trinidad and Tobago	6 236	5 068	8 154	18 369	20 904	25 968	21 125	22 181
Turks and Caicos Islands	32	106	319	722	829	976	1 161	..
Central America	*251 294*	*319 621*	*706 359*	*1 055 068*	*1 142 472*	*1 221 964*	*1 006 649*	*1 175 561*
Belize	195	405	832	1 214	1 277	1 359	1 336	1 381
Costa Rica	6 139	7 254	15 947	22 526	26 322	29 848	29 284	35 810
El Salvador	1 173	4 801	13 134	18 749	20 377	22 107	21 101	21 701
Guatemala	7 024	6 820	17 196	30 231	34 113	39 139	37 322	41 079
Honduras	3 061	3 637	7 187	10 918	12 392	13 993	14 408	15 649
Mexico	227 664	288 013	636 731	949 326	1 022 831	1 086 442	872 088	1 025 713
Nicaragua	1 984	2 614	3 711	4 967	5 366	5 892	6 398	6 748
Panama, excl. Canal Zone (former) (3)	4 054							
Panama	—	6 077	11 621	17 137	19 794	23 184	24 711	27 480
South America	*457 412*	*737 761*	*1 324 132*	*1 972 746*	*2 432 768*	*2 943 016*	*2 853 934*	*3 613 018*
Argentina	75 492	141 353	284 346	214 267	262 451	328 468	308 740	370 470
Bolivia (Plurinational State of)	2 696	4 868	8 398	11 452	13 120	16 674	17 340	19 208
Brazil	191 125	402 137	644 729	1 089 254	1 366 854	1 638 639	1 571 957	2 061 352
Chile	29 479	33 507	75 197	146 774	164 317	170 850	163 305	206 258
Colombia	44 452	53 606	94 053	162 347	207 786	243 105	229 693	280 992
Ecuador	12 351	11 248	15 934	41 763	45 789	54 686	57 303	65 142
Guyana	943	632	1 137	1 458	1 740	1 923	2 046	2 234
Paraguay	3 931	4 652	7 095	9 275	12 222	16 873	14 692	18 460
Peru	16 738	29 281	53 336	92 319	107 524	129 107	128 416	155 397
Suriname	891	615	946	2 136	2 425	3 061	2 966	3 358
Uruguay	10 642	9 239	22 823	19 802	23 952	31 178	31 511	40 496
Venezuela (Bolivarian Rep. of)	68 672	46 623	116 139	181 898	224 587	308 452	325 965	389 650
Developing economies: Asia	1 345 629	2 228 712	4 239 606	8 229 407	9 840 688	11 409 484	11 570 871	13 786 743
Eastern Asia	*453 377*	*936 144*	*2 239 303*	*4 329 073*	*5 144 739*	*6 005 671*	*6 443 912*	*7 571 155*
China	306 520	404 494	1 192 836	2 779 871	3 458 333	4 416 104	4 984 426	5 871 798
China, Hong Kong SAR	28 818	76 890	169 121	189 932	207 069	215 354	210 570	226 484
China, Macao SAR	981	3 235	6 102	14 211	18 684	21 617	21 188	27 430
China, Taiwan Province of	42 225	164 974	326 162	376 334	393 111	402 690	378 969	432 301
Korea, Dem. People's Rep. of	9 879	14 702	10 608	13 764	14 375	13 337	12 035	..
Korea, Republic of	64 385	270 405	533 385	951 773	1 049 239	931 405	832 512	1 007 561
Mongolia	568	1 443	1 089	3 188	3 928	5 164	4 212	5 582
Southern Asia	*332 328*	*509 988*	*715 635*	*1 423 230*	*1 775 886*	*1 941 893*	*1 968 451*	*2 380 525*
Afghanistan	3 642	3 622	..	8 166	10 120	10 789	12 853	—
Bangladesh	16 729	28 137	45 470	60 309	68 599	79 568	89 159	99 428
Bhutan	131	279	439	873	1 194	1 245	1 243	1 461
India	184 761	326 796	467 788	945 544	1 196 622	1 281 330	1 287 292	1 623 804
Iran (Islamic Rep. of)	91 892	91 036	104 016	243 672	312 141	369 227	360 840	395 910
Maldives	54	198	624	915	1 118	1 187	1 278	—
Nepal	2 089	3 780	5 730	8 990	10 948	11 766	12 784	16 167
Pakistan	28 757	47 937	71 319	126 481	142 793	146 068	160 257	176 888
Sri Lanka	4 273	8 204	16 717	28 280	32 350	40 713	42 745	50 561

For sources and notes, see end of table.

Per capita gross domestic product / Produit intérieur brut par habitant Dollars								Régions, pays ou territoires
1980	1990	2000	2006	2007	2008	2009	2010 (e)	
2 098	2 550	4 112	5 683	6 615	7 596	6 974	8 548	**Économies en développement : Amérique**
1 676	*2 044*	*2 778*	*4 140*	*4 593*	*4 961*	*4 768*	..	*Caraïbes*
1 304	6 536	9 760	15 600	19 021	19 709	14 355	14 586	Anguilla
1 567	6 295	8 553	11 812	13 438	13 850	12 890	12 602	Antigua-et-Barbuda
8 195	13 322	20 754	23 574	24 592	25 814	24 605	24 288	Aruba
6 421	12 360	18 573	21 217	21 997	21 872	20 916	21 091	Bahamas
3 478	6 628	9 565	11 772	12 551	13 485	13 181	13 382	Barbade
2 519	6 356	36 985	46 726	50 313	53 302	57 626	..	Îles Vierges britanniques
9 142	31 917	50 654	53 383	58 015	60 379	55 194	..	Îles Caïmanes
2 029	2 710	2 753	4 682	5 201	5 397	5 409	..	Cuba
785	2 358	3 892	4 595	5 032	5 461	5 561	5 789	Dominique
1 111	1 004	2 793	3 794	4 303	4 710	4 756	5 195	République dominicaine
841	2 298	4 017	5 478	5 904	6 541	6 107	6 358	Grenade
243	367	407	494	596	631	637	622	Haïti
1 428	2 039	3 466	4 435	4 765	5 145	4 546	5 026	Jamaïque
2 034	6 265	7 052	7 837	7 921	8 519	8 941		Montserrat
5 471	10 445	15 890	18 220	19 043	20 276	20 311	21 135	Antilles néerlandaises
1 109	3 909	7 144	9 782	10 093	11 161	10 534	10 498	Saint-Kitts-et-Nevis
1 151	3 014	4 503	5 588	5 687	5 792	5 496	5 586	Sainte-Lucie
589	1 844	3 107	4 493	5 092	5 328	5 186	5 128	Saint-Vincent-et-les Grenadines
5 784	4 169	6 311	13 912	15 769	19 510	15 808	16 535	Trinité-et-Tobago
4 276	9 171	16 926	22 151	24 084	27 141	31 162	..	Îles Turques et Caïques
2 738	*2 822*	*5 211*	*7 157*	*7 642*	*8 060*	*6 547*	*7 541*	*Amérique centrale*
1 354	2 131	3 320	4 228	4 356	4 541	4 376	4 432	Belize
2 620	2 363	4 069	5 141	5 912	6 600	6 379	7 686	Costa Rica
252	900	2 211	3 087	3 340	3 607	3 425	3 504	El Salvador
998	764	1 530	2 319	2 554	2 859	2 659	2 855	Guatemala
844	744	1 156	1 556	1 731	1 916	1 934	2 059	Honduras
3 310	3 416	6 370	8 803	9 365	9 821	7 784	9 043	Mexique
612	634	731	904	965	1 046	1 121	1 166	Nicaragua
2 076								Panama, sans la zone du canal (anc.) (3)
–	–	–	–	–	–	–	–	
	2 515	3 931	5 202	5 907	6 806	7 138	7 814	Panama
1 900	*2 497*	*3 813*	*5 251*	*6 403*	*7 662*	*7 351*	*9 209*	*Amérique du Sud*
2 684	4 330	7 699	5 491	6 667	8 271	7 706	9 167	Argentine
504	731	1 011	1 231	1 386	1 734	1 774	1 934	Bolivie (État plurinational de)
1 570	2 687	3 696	5 795	7 202	8 555	8 134	10 574	Brésil
2 637	2 541	4 877	8 912	9 879	10 172	9 631	12 052	Chili
1 654	1 614	2 365	3 715	4 685	5 402	5 031	6 070	Colombie
1 552	1 096	1 291	3 062	3 306	3 890	4 018	4 503	Équateur
1 214	872	1 550	1 949	2 320	2 558	2 717	2 961	Guyana
1 230	1 096	1 328	1 544	1 997	2 708	2 317	2 860	Paraguay
968	1 350	2 062	3 313	3 817	4 536	4 464	5 344	Pérou
2 435	1 511	2 026	4 231	4 754	5 943	5 705	6 401	Suriname
3 651	2 972	6 876	5 951	7 181	9 318	9 386	12 021	Uruguay
4 567	2 368	4 770	6 705	8 139	10 994	11 429	13 446	Venezuela (Rép. bolivarienne du)
551	747	1 214	2 190	2 589	2 968	2 977	3 535	**Économies en développement : Asie**
434	*769*	*1 662*	*3 102*	*3 667*	*4 259*	*4 546*	*5 408*	*Asie orientale*
317	360	957	2 152	2 663	3 383	3 800	4 454	Chine
5 703	13 271	24 932	27 796	30 129	31 092	30 133	32 111	Chine (RAS de Hong Kong)
3 986	8 995	14 129	28 810	36 947	41 695	39 888	50 455	Chine (RAS de Macao)
2 393	8 135	14 702	16 495	17 165	17 505	16 418	18 681	Province chinoise de Taiwan
573	730	463	576	599	553	497	..	Corée, Rép. populaire dém. de
1 719	6 291	11 598	20 136	22 090	19 512	17 357	20 911	Corée, République de
336	658	452	1 234	1 497	1 936	1 553	2 025	Mongolie
352	*426*	*490*	*885*	*1 088*	*1 172*	*1 172*	*1 397*	*Asie méridionale*
257	278	155	287	347	362	420	-	Afghanistan
207	267	351	424	477	547	606	669	Bangladesh
304	499	769	1 295	1 734	1 775	1 742	2 012	Bhoutan
264	374	444	817	1 019	1 076	1 066	1 326	Inde
2 382	1 659	1 592	3 452	4 370	5 108	4 934	5 352	Iran (Rép. islamique d')
342	901	2 285	3 057	3 684	3 860	4 100	-	Maldives
139	198	235	323	386	407	434	540	Népal
357	429	493	783	868	872	940	1 019	Pakistan
283	473	892	1 410	1 596	1 989	2 068	2 424	Sri Lanka

Pour les sources et les notes, se reporter à la fin du tableau.

8

8.1.1 Nominal gross domestic product: Total and per capita of countries and geographical regions

Region, country or territory	Total gross domestic product / Produit intérieur brut total (1) Millions of dollars / Millions de dollars							
	1980	1990	2000	2006	2007	2008	2009	2010 (e)
South-Eastern Asia	*196 391*	*355 590*	*600 251*	*1 083 665*	*1 293 572*	*1 500 194*	*1 473 107*	*1 835 769*
Brunei Darussalam	5 587	3 520	6 001	11 470	12 247	14 394	10 546	12 797
Cambodia	594	1 404	3 667	7 275	8 639	11 243	10 798	11 362
Indonesia including East Timor	79 636	125 866	165 337			—		
Indonesia	—	—	—	364 571	432 217	510 504	540 277	708 396
Lao People's dem. Rep.	322	866	1 653	3 325	4 214	5 285	5 585	6 457
Malaysia	25 429	45 716	93 790	156 601	186 113	221 437	191 356	236 261
Myanmar	5 905	5 172	7 275	13 852	15 956	17 948	18 989	..
Philippines	32 460	44 312	75 912	117 534	144 043	167 479	160 676	188 402
Singapore	11 718	36 901	92 717	140 544	171 564	188 261	177 132	213 100
Thailand	32 354	85 361	122 725	207 228	247 111	272 429	263 889	310 203
Timor-Leste	—	—	—	353	453	569	673	760
Viet Nam	2 396	6 472	31 173	60 914	71 016	90 645	93 188	99 312
Western Asia	*303 333*	*180 000*	*544 418*	*1 191 818*	*1 070 431*	*1 001 726*	*1 646 409*	*1 999 283*
Bahrain	3 292	4 293	8 028	15 852	18 472	22 151	19 319	22 661
Iraq	5 689	7 766	16 900	20 660	21 544	24 277	25 531	32 172
Jordan	4 013	4 020	8 461	14 638	17 006	22 698	25 092	27 543
Kuwait	28 691	18 471	37 718	101 559	114 653	148 001	109 457	131 300
Lebanon	4 074	2 812	16 679	22 438	25 057	29 933	34 528	38 801
Occupied Palestinian territory	1 074	1 936	4 195	4 619	4 672	5 937	5 848	..
Oman	6 256	11 556	19 450	36 804	41 908	60 299	53 709	63 748
Qatar	7 838	7 360	17 760	60 496	80 751	110 712	98 313	129 486
Saudi Arabia	164 306	116 622	188 442	356 630	384 942	475 094	369 178	435 331
Syrian Arab Republic	13 146	11 150	19 666	32 698	40 212	49 197	53 945	59 403
Turkey	92 477	202 546	266 560	530 917	647 140	730 325	614 619	747 420
United Arab Emirates	29 626	33 780	70 522	175 222	206 406	254 394	248 958	277 970
Yemen (former Arab Republic)	2 446	—	—	—	—	—	—	—
Yemen (former Democratic)	606	—	—	—	—	—	—	—
Yemen	—	4 677	10 039	20 903	23 727	28 707	26 903	33 459
Developing economies: Oceania	**6 892**	**10 572**	**12 755**	**21 938**	**25 891**	**28 533**	**28 056**	**..**
Cook Islands	22	59	81	180	202	203	193	..
Fiji	1 215	1 351	1 723	3 102	3 405	3 572	3 061	3 086
French Polynesia	1 014	2 322	2 445	3 803	4 251	4 671	4 535	..
Kiribati	35	41	67	107	127	136	131	155
Marshall Islands	—	79	108	145	156	166	171	..
Micronesia (Federated States of)	—	153	223	243	249	254	270	..
Nauru	36	49	27	25	23	42	54	..
New Caledonia	1 182	2 529	3 412	6 973	9 000	9 089	9 283	..
Pacific Islands, Former (Trust Territory)	115							
Palau	—	77	120	158	170	187	204	..
Papua New Guinea	2 823	3 286	3 499	5 528	6 339	8 009	7 906	9 319
Samoa	112	112	231	449	544	546	523	561
Solomon Islands	144	208	338	457	542	672	715	768
Tonga	60	117	189	293	310	339	339	374
Tuvalu	4	10	12	23	27	28	27	32
Vanuatu	129	179	281	451	545	619	644	717
Transition economies	**1 012 216**	**864 522**	**397 174**	**1 399 520**	**1 832 086**	**2 340 280**	**1 786 718**	**2 094 417**
Albania	2 219	2 222	3 640	8 993	10 690	12 967	12 135	11 875
Armenia	—	—	1 912	6 384	9 206	11 662	8 541	9 401
Azerbaijan	—	—	5 273	20 982	33 049	48 851	43 020	54 407
Belarus	—	—	10 418	36 962	45 276	60 752	49 038	54 406
Bosnia and Herzegovina	—	—	5 506	12 348	15 227	18 500	17 043	16 827
Croatia	—	—	21 345	49 050	58 574	69 333	63 033	60 649
Georgia	—	—	3 058	7 745	10 173	12 795	10 745	11 648
Kazakhstan	—	—	18 292	81 004	104 850	133 442	109 157	133 042
Kyrgyzstan	—	—	1 370	2 834	3 803	5 140	4 578	4 504
Montenegro						4 520	4 086	3 948
Republic of Moldova	—	—	1 288	3 408	4 401	6 055	5 405	5 771
Russian Federation	—	—	259 718	989 428	1 300 119	1 667 600	1 230 724	1 473 835
Serbia and Montenegro	—	—	11 468	35 835	47 715			
Serbia	—	—	—	—	—	54 483	46 982	44 262
SFR of Yugoslavia (former)	69 959	85 129						
Tajikistan	—	—	861	2 546	2 819	3 107	4 978	5 644
TFYR of Macedonia	—	—	3 587	6 558	8 160	9 834	9 523	9 365
Turkmenistan	—	—	4 418	10 612	12 950	15 536	17 356	20 125
Ukraine	—	—	31 262	107 753	142 719	179 992	117 404	136 509
USSR (former)	940 038	777 171	—	—	—	—	—	—
Uzbekistan	—	—	13 759	17 077	22 355	25 712	32 971	38 197

For sources and notes, see end of table.

Per capita gross domestic product / Produit intérieur brut par habitant Dollars								Régions, pays ou territoires
1980	1990	2000	2006	2007	2008	2009	2010 (e)	
547	*798*	*1 146*	*1 912*	*2 256*	*2 586*	*2 510*	*3 094*	*Asie du Sud-Est*
28 943	13 698	17 996	30 390	31 824	36 692	26 385	31 439	Brunéi Darussalam
91	147	295	538	632	813	772	804	Cambodge
526	680	772						Indonésie, y compris le Timor oriental
–	–	–	1 586	1 859	2 173	2 276	2 953	Indonésie
100	206	311	569	710	878	914	1 041	Rép. dém. populaire lao
1 838	2 511	4 006	5 890	6 880	8 052	6 847	8 319	Malaisie
180	132	162	297	340	380	399	..	Myanmar
689	719	982	1 349	1 625	1 857	1 752	2 020	Philippines
4 050	12 233	23 656	31 870	37 419	39 449	35 816	42 302	Singapour
681	1 496	1 943	3 080	3 645	3 991	3 841	4 619	Thaïlande
–	–	–	339	427	527	611	676	Timor-Leste
44	90	390	729	836	1 055	1 072	1 130	Viet Nam
3 799	*3 300*	*4 238*	*7 462*	*8 481*	*9 962*	*8 344*	*9 858*	*Asie occidentale*
9 197	8 710	12 579	19 536	19 954	21 049	16 518	17 959	Bahreïn
414	447	708	734	744	814	831	1 016	Iraq
1 746	1 177	1 753	2 664	3 001	3 881	4 164	4 452	Jordanie
20 836	8 848	19 434	43 190	46 839	58 077	41 362	47 977	Koweït
1 458	954	4 457	5 476	6 060	7 183	8 227	9 178	Liban
711	930	1 311	1 270	1 253	1 551	1 488		Territoire palestinien occupé
5 296	6 186	8 590	14 777	16 363	22 867	19 803	22 911	Oman
35 371	15 537	30 053	61 836	68 538	79 303	61 532	73 622	Qatar
16 763	7 226	9 401	14 381	15 093	18 156	13 771	15 860	Arabie saoudite
1 476	905	1 230	1 728	2 081	2 498	2 690	2 910	République arabe syrienne
2 097	3 742	4 189	7 687	9 246	10 297	8 555	10 273	Turquie
29 153	18 677	23 248	37 579	38 184	40 988	35 879	37 005	Émirats arabes unis
409	–	–	–	–	–	–	–	Yémen (anc. République arabe du)
252	–	–	–	–	–	–	–	Yémen (anc. démocratique)
–	391	566	982	1 081	1 269	1 153	1 391	Yémen
1 390	*1 696*	*1 632*	*2 474*	*2 860*	*3 087*	*2 973*	*..*	*Économies en développement : Océanie*
1 276	3 330	4 591	9 159	10 159	10 158	9 581	..	Îles Cook
1 913	1 854	2 122	3 747	4 076	4 234	3 591	3 586	Fidji
6 712	11 886	10 290	14 734	16 267	17 657	16 943	..	Polynésie française
631	574	795	1 143	1 341	1 404	1 336	1 553	Kiribati
–	1 666	2 067	2 784	2 975	3 140	3 196	..	Îles Marshall
–	1 586	2 080	2 212	2 264	2 207	2 430	..	Micronésie (États fédérés de)
4 793	5 377	2 701	2 506	2 276	4 081	5 312	..	Nauru
8 302	14 906	16 095	29 675	37 670	37 415	37 599	..	Nouvelle-Calédonie
863							–	Îles du Pacifique (anc. Territoire sous tutelle d
–	5 096	6 252	7 880	8 457	9 252	10 008	..	Palaos
878	790	651	885	991	1 223	1 179	1 359	Papouasie-Nouvelle-Guinée
723	695	1 308	2 486	3 002	3 004	2 869	3 062	Samoa
627	664	814	940	1 087	1 316	1 366	1 433	Îles Salomon
648	1 233	1 926	2 887	3 031	3 298	3 273	3 590	Tonga
534	1 059	1 302	2 394	2 732	2 896	2 783	3 264	Tuvalu
1 119	1 220	1 517	2 080	2 449	2 716	2 756	2 991	Vanuatu
3 496	*2 743*	*1 302*	*4 640*	*6 071*	*7 748*	*5 907*	*6 916*	*Économies en transition*
831	675	1 185	2 849	3 373	4 076	3 801	3 706	Albanie
–	–	621	2 080	2 995	3 787	2 769	3 040	Arménie
–	–	650	2 411	3 747	5 462	4 745	5 922	Azerbaïdjan
–	–	1 036	3 781	4 654	6 276	5 089	5 670	Bélarus
–	–	1 491	3 265	4 029	4 902	4 523	4 475	Bosnie-Herzégovine
–	–	4 738	11 063	13 234	15 692	14 290	13 773	Croatie
–	–	644	1 743	2 304	2 912	2 457	2 676	Géorgie
–	–	1 223	5 290	6 775	8 524	6 891	8 301	Kazakhstan
–	–	277	557	740	988	869	844	Kirghizistan
–	–	–	–	–	7 184	6 481	6 252	Monténégro
–	–	314	917	1 199	1 666	1 500	1 615	République de Moldova
–	–	1 770	6 894	9 073	11 648	8 603	10 310	Fédération de Russie
–	–	1 065	3 425	4 561				Serbie-et-Monténégro
–	–	–	–	–	5 536	4 769	4 491	Serbie
3 263	3 727		–	–	–	–	–	RSF de Yougoslavie (anc.)
–	–	139	390	427	464	734	821	Tadjikistan
–	–	1 785	3 210	3 984	4 791	4 630	4 545	LERY de Macédoine
–	–	982	2 210	2 665	3 159	3 485	3 992	Turkménistan
–	–	639	2 313	3 084	3 914	2 568	3 004	Ukraine
3 542	2 689							URSS (anc.)
–	–	555	651	843	959	1 215	1 392	Ouzbékistan

Pour les sources et les notes, se reporter à la fin du tableau.

8

Region, country or territory	Total gross domestic product / Produit intérieur brut total (1) Millions of dollars / Millions de dollars							
	1980	1990	2000	2006	2007	2008	2009	2010 (e)
Developed economies: America	**3 055 140**	**6 372 838**	**10 697 508**	**14 710 308**	**15 535 754**	**15 972 064**	**15 561 723**	**16 336 235**
Bermuda	919	1 997	3 518	5 356	5 828	6 093	6 574	..
Canada	268 889	582 735	724 914	1 278 607	1 424 067	1 499 108	1 336 067	1 574 059
Greenland	476	1 019	1 068	1 739	2 133	1 755	1 268	..
United States	2 784 856	5 787 087	9 968 008	13 424 605	14 103 726	14 465 108	14 217 814	14 762 176
Developed economies: Asia	**1 094 366**	**3 114 961**	**4 792 195**	**4 508 422**	**4 544 952**	**5 089 053**	**5 263 012**	**5 715 067**
Israel	23 369	56 923	124 747	145 844	166 991	202 101	194 015	215 686
Japan	1 070 997	3 058 038	4 667 448	1 000 070	1 077 000	4 886 007	5 000 997	5 400 381
Developed economies: Europe	**3 963 888**	**7 628 709**	**8 920 481**	**15 433 815**	**17 823 932**	**19 275 099**	**17 267 353**	**17 219 013**
Andorra	446	1 029	1 134	2 824	3 245	3 712	3 743	..
Austria	81 464	164 851	191 200	322 340	372 292	414 671	381 084	375 946
Belgium	125 201	202 669	232 371	000 114	160 620	505 374	471 161	403 004
Bulgaria	18 620	20 726	12 904	33 210	42 115	51 824	48 722	47 865
Cyprus	2 230	5 777	9 293	18 410	21 810	25 265	23 542	23 121
Czechoslovakia (former)	47 822	52 522	–	–	–	–	–	–
Czech Republic	–	–	56 717	142 611	174 215	216 089	190 204	192 034
Denmark	69 709	135 839	160 082	274 377	310 721	340 801	310 093	311 936
Estonia	–	–	5 680	16 808	21 659	23 565	19 265	19 195
Finland	52 984	138 852	121 715	207 796	245 952	270 479	237 989	238 833
France	692 536	1 246 900	1 330 611	2 270 801	2 599 989	2 860 812	2 655 498	2 584 865
Germany (former Federal Rep.) (4)	919 651	–	–	–	–	–	–	–
Germany	–	1 714 447	1 900 220	2 918 556	3 329 147	3 634 527	3 330 030	3 310 847
Greece	54 702	94 203	127 088	263 341	308 689	345 229	323 745	302 135
Hungary	25 089	36 618	47 377	112 791	137 897	155 444	128 764	129 452
Iceland	3 331	6 373	8 697	16 651	20 428	16 805	12 138	12 640
Ireland	21 103	47 846	96 755	222 474	259 189	263 653	221 778	203 775
Italy	459 811	1 133 465	1 097 343	1 863 381	2 116 203	2 296 630	2 112 779	2 051 831
Latvia	–	–	7 833	19 935	28 766	33 668	25 878	23 989
Lithuania	–	–	11 434	30 082	39 097	47 297	36 846	36 283
Luxembourg	5 969	12 670	20 270	42 552	51 312	58 065	52 851	54 879
Malta	1 250	2 547	3 893	6 462	7 548	8 413	7 987	8 125
Netherlands	180 777	294 869	385 074	677 692	782 567	873 368	794 588	781 837
Norway	63 714	117 624	168 288	336 732	387 536	446 241	378 592	413 897
Poland	57 828	64 550	171 276	341 597	425 129	529 391	430 640	468 542
Portugal	32 421	77 584	117 014	201 060	230 945	252 102	233 489	228 574
Romania	34 599	38 511	37 305	122 696	170 617	204 339	161 109	159 338
San Marino	229	565	774	1 469	1 688	1 844	1 697	1 575
Slovakia	–	–	20 403	55 876	75 094	94 500	87 589	87 244
Slovenia	–	–	19 890	38 952	47 312	54 645	49 156	47 735
Spain	225 984	520 938	580 673	1 234 768	1 441 942	1 593 913	1 464 088	1 406 601
Sweden	131 879	244 459	247 259	399 076	462 513	487 576	406 072	459 040
Switzerland	112 622	239 641	252 396	395 233	438 721	507 377	496 750	528 716
United Kingdom	541 917	1 012 617	1 477 512	2 444 150	2 810 974	2 657 481	2 169 485	2 242 283
Developed economies: Oceania	**199 170**	**374 033**	**464 221**	**930 957**	**1 122 065**	**1 181 012**	**1 130 698**	**1 423 388**
Australia	176 088	329 607	410 991	821 799	988 852	1 051 119	1 013 862	1 283 732
New Zealand	23 082	44 426	53 229	109 158	133 213	129 893	116 835	139 656

Sources:
- UN DESA Statistics Division

Notes:

(1)   GDP by expenditure, in current prices and current exchange rates.
(2)   Including Western Sahara.
(3)   Data refer to Panama from 1970 to 1980.
(4)   Data refer to Germany from 1970 to 1989.

Per capita gross domestic product / Produit intérieur brut par habitant Dollars								Régions, pays ou territoires
1980	1990	2000	2006	2007	2008	2009	2010 (e)	
11 853	**22 378**	**33 724**	**43 755**	**45 793**	**46 660**	**45 061**	**46 908**	**Économies développées : Amérique**
16 391	33 400	55 995	83 268	90 349	94 237	101 441	..	Bermudes
10 968	21 037	23 638	39 187	43 183	44 980	39 675	46 273	Canada
9 482	18 343	19 005	30 360	37 223	30 620	22 123	..	Groenland
11 946	22 520	34 802	44 240	46 067	46 834	45 636	46 977	États-Unis
9 146	**24 575**	**36 377**	**33 842**	**34 061**	**38 081**	**39 331**	**42 664**	**Économies développées : Asie**
6 239	12 650	20 739	21 590	24 131	28 496	26 720	29 074	Israël
9 240	25 014	37 126	31 106	34 004	38 618	40 055	43 461	Japon
8 602	**16 091**	**18 003**	**30 412**	**34 969**	**37 658**	**33 603**	**33 397**	**Économies développées : Europe**
11 958	19 498	17 539	35 340	00 070	44 000	44 726	..	Andorre
10 792	21 492	23 886	38 962	44 802	49 710	45 532	44 789	Autriche
12 714	20 373	22 836	38 102	43 517	47 667	44 195	43 492	Belgique
2 101	2 350	1 612	4 319	5 512	6 827	6 460	6 387	Bulgarie
3 253	7 535	9 852	17 562	20 517	23 459	21 589	20 949	Chypre
3 111	3 373	–	–	–	–	–	–	Tchécoslovaquie (anc.)
–	–	5 537	13 901	16 892	20 823	18 219	18 301	République tchèque
13 607	26 423	29 981	50 412	56 814	61 994	56 127	56 203	Danemark
–	–	4 144	12 506	16 129	17 558	14 359	14 313	Estonie
11 086	27 846	23 527	39 460	46 490	50 877	44 554	44 521	Finlande
12 560	21 419	21 885	35 887	40 840	44 674	41 232	39 911	France
11 747								Allemagne (anc. Rép. fédérale d') (4)
–	21 675	23 075	35 361	40 345	44 068	40 410	40 228	Allemagne
5 673	9 271	11 567	23 472	27 425	30 573	28 583	26 598	Grèce
2 345	3 529	4 640	11 207	13 731	15 510	12 874	12 966	Hongrie
14 601	25 012	30 928	55 318	66 819	54 092	38 468	39 483	Islande
6 174	13 549	25 436	52 639	60 399	60 570	50 265	45 588	Irlande
8 179	19 944	19 256	31 539	35 569	38 347	35 068	33 886	Italie
–	–	3 284	8 694	12 607	14 824	11 444	10 652	Lettonie
–	–	3 267	8 853	11 570	14 077	11 028	10 917	Lituanie
16 301	33 230	48 544	91 395	107 864	119 284	106 205	108 146	Luxembourg
3 827	6 931	9 796	15 719	18 293	20 324	19 237	19 508	Malte
12 832	19 801	24 275	41 378	47 591	52 921	47 984	47 062	Pays-Bas
15 595	27 732	37 473	72 124	82 070	93 376	78 319	84 761	Norvège
1 625	1 696	4 472	8 949	11 132	13 852	11 259	12 241	Pologne
3 313	7 817	11 321	19 008	21 771	23 706	21 909	21 411	Portugal
1 558	1 659	1 681	5 653	7 883	9 465	7 480	7 416	Roumanie
10 703	23 392	28 698	47 817	54 425	59 113	54 102	49 943	Saint-Marin
–	–	3 775	10 305	13 827	17 367	16 066	15 973	Slovaquie
–	–	10 018	19 409	23 511	27 076	24 286	23 519	Slovénie
6 027	13 395	14 413	28 052	32 327	35 306	32 080	30 527	Espagne
15 869	28 562	27 907	43 899	50 485	52 786	43 612	48 940	Suède
17 796	35 753	35 051	52 674	58 056	66 684	64 875	68 661	Suisse
9 592	17 634	25 002	40 221	45 985	43 208	35 055	36 008	Royaume-Uni
11 154	**18 251**	**20 164**	**37 344**	**44 259**	**45 791**	**43 115**	**53 437**	**Économies développées : Océanie**
11 971	19 280	21 446	39 616	46 821	48 858	46 290	57 648	Australie
7 334	13 074	13 797	26 084	31 474	30 364	27 029	31 971	Nouvelle-Zélande

Sources :
- ONU DAES Division de statistique

Notes :

(1) PIB par dépenses, aux prix et taux de change courants.
(2) Y compris le Sahara occidental.
(3) Les données se réfèrent au Panama de 1970 à 1980.
(4) Les données se réfèrent à l'Allemagne de 1970 à 1989.

8

8.1.2 Nominal gross domestic product: Total and per capita of economic groupings

Economic grouping	Total gross domestic product / Produit intérieur brut total (1) Millions of dollars / Millions de dollars							
	1980	1990	2000	2006	2007	2008	2009	2010 (e)
DEVELOPING ECONOMIES	**2 539 911**	**3 850 600**	**6 972 864**	**12 553 209**	**14 897 180**	**17 289 154**	**17 059 105**	**20 362 432**
Developing economies excluding China	2 233 390	3 446 106	5 780 028	9 773 338	11 438 847	12 873 050	12 074 679	14 490 634
Developing economies excluding LDCs	2 427 905	3 696 307	6 791 668	12 209 132	14 488 801	16 805 492	16 574 210	19 799 233
High-income developing countries	984 981	1 576 637	3 076 013	4 792 723	5 415 672	5 947 885	5 233 779	6 202 549
Middle-income developing countries	995 382	1 497 793	2 855 227	5 657 437	6 936 113	8 477 898	8 946 944	10 630 352
Low income developing countries	559 549	776 170	1 041 624	2 103 049	2 545 395	2 863 372	2 878 382	3 529 532
Heavily indebted poor countries (IMF)	109 289	142 510	144 347	270 862	329 120	388 195	382 222	421 023
Landlocked developing countries	46 119	70 785	124 354	284 693	358 592	449 001	425 506	488 520
Small island developing States	18 387	25 901	41 508	65 612	73 091	84 179	76 192	81 092
Least developed countries	*112 006*	*154 293*	*181 196*	*344 077*	*408 379*	*483 662*	*484 895*	*563 199*
Africa and Haiti	78 912	105 444	102 183	217 999	262 122	313 821	303 126	338 639
Asia	32 464	47 936	77 806	123 692	143 397	166 552	178 314	220 823
Islands	630	914	1 208	2 386	2 860	3 289	3 455	3 737
Major petroleum and gas exporters	*582 523*	*471 515*	*719 727*	*1 519 081*	*1 779 948*	*2 251 351*	*2 000 072*	*2 348 766*
Africa	179 554	138 300	148 780	342 139	393 014	500 894	408 120	493 200
America	68 672	46 623	116 139	181 898	224 587	308 452	325 965	389 650
Asia	334 297	286 592	454 808	995 044	1 162 346	1 442 004	1 265 987	1 465 916
Major exporters of manufactured goods	*739 113*	*1 372 754*	*3 167 467*	*5 751 609*	*6 735 370*	*7 734 122*	*7 910 941*	*9 334 576*
America	227 664	288 013	636 731	949 326	1 022 831	1 086 442	872 088	1 025 713
Asia	511 449	1 084 741	2 530 736	4 802 283	5 712 539	6 647 680	7 038 853	8 308 863
Emerging economies	*716 610*	*1 497 649*	*2 863 117*	*4 324 420*	*4 971 114*	*5 369 729*	*4 888 363*	*6 029 771*
America	540 499	894 291	1 694 338	2 491 940	2 923 976	3 353 507	3 044 506	3 819 190
Asia	176 111	603 357	1 168 779	1 832 480	2 047 138	2 016 222	1 843 857	2 210 581
Newly industrialized Asian countries	*317 016*	*850 425*	*1 579 149*	*2 504 516*	*2 830 466*	*2 909 559*	*2 755 380*	*3 333 863*
First tier	147 146	549 170	1 121 385	1 658 583	1 820 982	1 737 711	1 599 182	1 881 511
Second tier	169 869	301 255	457 764	845 933	1 009 484	1 171 848	1 156 198	1 452 352
Developing economies: Africa	**435 535**	**492 979**	**596 384**	**1 126 028**	**1 289 758**	**1 505 808**	**1 424 905**	**1 656 132**
Northern Africa excluding Sudan	134 363	173 542	249 327	381 249	439 978	546 265	517 566	577 163
Sub-Saharan Africa	301 172	319 438	347 057	744 779	849 781	959 544	907 339	1 078 968
Sub-Saharan Africa excluding South Africa	220 628	207 424	214 180	483 772	563 479	683 093	621 357	717 692
Developing economies: America	**751 854**	**1 118 337**	**2 124 118**	**3 175 836**	**3 740 844**	**4 345 328**	**4 035 274**	**4 904 547**
Central America and Greater Caribbean Islands excluding Puerto Rico	283 814	365 087	773 043	1 160 107	1 260 724	1 348 434	1 132 857	1 247 124
Central America and Greater Caribbean Islands excluding Mexico and Puerto Rico	56 151	77 074	136 312	210 781	237 894	261 991	260 768	221 411
South America and Central America	708 706	1 057 383	2 030 490	3 027 815	3 575 240	4 164 980	3 860 582	4 788 578
South America excluding Brazil	266 287	335 624	679 403	883 492	1 065 914	1 304 377	1 281 977	1 551 666
Developing economies: Asia	**1 345 629**	**2 228 712**	**4 239 606**	**8 229 407**	**9 840 688**	**11 409 484**	**11 570 871**	**13 786 743**
Eastern and South-Eastern Asia excluding China	343 248	887 240	1 646 717	2 632 867	2 979 978	3 089 761	2 932 593	3 535 126
Southern Asia excluding India	147 567	183 193	247 847	477 686	579 264	660 563	681 159	756 721

Sources:
- UN DESA Statistics Division

Notes:

(1) GDP by expenditure, in current prices and current exchange rates.

Per capita gross domestic product / Produit intérieur brut par habitant Dollars								Groupements économiques
1980	1990	2000	2006	2007	2008	2009	2010 (e)	
772	**947**	**1 444**	**2 388**	**2 796**	**3 202**	**3 118**	**3 715**	**ÉCONOMIES EN DÉVELOPPEMENT**
961	1 172	1 614	2 465	2 839	3 144	2 903	3 480	Économies en développement sans la Chine
838	1 040	1 630	2 717	3 185	3 651	3 559	4 250	Économies en développement sans les PMA
3 622	4 716	7 854	11 251	12 522	13 545	11 746	13 753	Pays en développement à revenu élevé
677	849	1 424	2 670	3 246	3 936	4 121	4 893	Pays en développement à revenu intermédiaire
362	395	428	776	923	1 020	1 008	1 235	Pays en développement à revenu faible
391	391	296	490	562	646	620	675	Pays pauvres très endettés (FMI)
303	357	375	755	932	1 142	1 060	1 228	Pays en développement sans littoral
1 719	2 037	2 761	3 743	4 107	4 660	4 156	4 405	Petits États insulaires en développement
285	*303*	*274*	*451*	*524*	*607*	*596*	*684*	*Pays les moins avancés*
341	345	254	461	540	629	592	655	Afrique et Haïti
201	236	302	432	493	565	597	728	Asie
639	727	767	840	985	1 110	1 142	1 208	Îles
3 132	*1 872*	*2 286*	*4 211*	*4 817*	*5 950*	*5 164*	*5 928*	*Principaux exportateurs de pétrole et de gaz*
1 709	1 006	858	1 714	1 923	2 393	1 905	2 249	Afrique
4 567	2 368	4 770	6 705	8 139	10 994	11 429	13 446	Amérique
5 071	3 029	3 885	7 425	8 454	10 222	8 757	9 913	Asie
638	*1 012*	*2 094*	*3 652*	*4 251*	*4 852*	*4 934*	*5 789*	*Principaux exportateurs d'articles manufacturés*
3 310	3 416	6 370	8 803	9 365	9 821	7 784	9 043	Amérique
469	853	1 792	3 274	3 872	4 481	4 719	5 542	Asie
1 050	*3 380*	*5 600*	*7 898*	*8 989*	*9 616*	*8 672*	*10 599*	*Économies émergentes*
2 188	2 966	4 805	6 572	7 631	8 662	7 785	9 670	Amérique
1 482	4 262	7 366	10 885	12 054	11 771	10 680	12 709	Asie
983	*2 158*	*3 456*	*5 088*	*5 686*	*5 781*	*5 416*	*6 485*	*Économies nouvellement industrialisées d'Asie*
2 352	7 620	14 217	20 394	22 245	21 079	19 272	22 543	Première génération
654	936	1 211	2 059	2 427	2 784	2 716	3 372	Deuxième génération
903	**777**	**736**	**1 210**	**1 354**	**1 545**	**1 428**	**1 658**	**Économies en développement : Afrique**
1 447	1 453	1 760	2 451	2 784	3 404	3 177	3 490	Afrique septentrionale sans le Soudan
774	620	519	961	1 069	1 178	1 087	1 295	Afrique subsaharienne
613	434	344	665	756	893	792	916	Afrique subsaharienne sans l'Afrique du Sud
2 098	**2 550**	**4 112**	**5 683**	**6 615**	**7 596**	**6 974**	**8 548**	**Économies en développement : Amérique**
2 464	2 598	4 644	6 436	6 904	7 289	6 045	6 985	Amérique centrale et Grandes Antilles sans Porto Rico
1 209	1 371	2 049	2 910	3 241	3 523	3 460	3 400	Amérique centrale et Grandes Antilles sans le Mexique et Porto Rico
2 131	2 587	4 205	5 788	6 753	7 775	7 123	8 735	Amérique du Sud et Amérique centrale
2 236	2 302	3 931	4 706	5 606	6 774	6 575	7 862	Amérique du Sud sans le Brésil
551	**747**	**1 214**	**2 190**	**2 589**	**2 968**	**2 977**	**3 535**	**Économies en développement : Asie**
783	1 652	2 637	3 926	4 396	4 510	4 236	5 236	Asie orientale et Asie du Sud-Est sans la Chine
603	569	610	1 057	1 263	1 419	1 442	1 578	Asie méridionale sans l'Inde

Sources :
- ONU DAES Division de statistique

Notes :

(1) PIB par dépenses, aux prix et taux de change courants.

413

8.2.1 Annual average growth rates of total and per capita real gross domestic product of countries and geographical regions

Region, country or territory	Total real gross domestic product (1) / Produit intérieur brut réel total (1) Percentage / En pourcentage										
	80 -89	92 -00	92 -10 (e)	95 -10 (e)	00 -10 (e)	2005	2006	2007	2008	2009	2010 (e)
WORLD	3.3	3.1	3.0	3.0	2.8	3.6	4.1	4.0	1.7	-2.0	3.9
DEVELOPING ECONOMIES	3.6	4.7	5.2	5.4	6.1	6.9	7.6	8.0	5.3	2.5	7.4
TRANSITION ECONOMIES	3.5	-2.5	3.4	5.1	5.7	6.5	8.0	8.3	5.5	-6.6	4.1
DEVELOPED ECONOMIES	3.2	2.9	2.3	2.2	1.7	2.5	2.8	2.6	0.3	-3.5	2.6
Developing economies: Africa	1.8	3.2	4.3	4.6	5.3	5.5	6.1	5.9	5.1	1.6	4.5
Eastern Africa	2.3	3.3	1.3	4.8	5.4	6.3	6.3	6.8	5.6	4.7	5.5
Burundi	4.3	-2.9	0.8	2.0	3.1	0.9	5.4	3.2	4.3	3.5	3.9
Comoros	3.0	1.1	1.8	2.0	1.8	4.2	1.2	0.5	1.0	1.1	2.1
Djibouti	0.4	1.0	2.5	2.9	4.0	3.2	4.8	4.8	5.8	5.1	4.5
Eritrea	—	5.7	1.6	0.3	0.2	2.6	-1.0	1.4	-9.8	3.6	2.2
Ethiopia	—	5.3	6.3	6.8	8.0	11.0	11.8	11.1	11.0	8.0	8.0
Ethiopia (former)	1.7	—	—	—	—	—	—	—	—	—	—
Kenya	4.3	2.5	3.3	3.5	4.4	5.9	6.3	7.0	1.5	2.6	5.0
Madagascar	0.8	2.8	3.0	3.1	3.2	4.6	5.0	6.3	7.1	-5.0	-2.0
Malawi	2.0	3.8	4.2	4.5	6.3	3.3	7.7	8.6	9.0	7.5	6.6
Mauritius	6.2	5.1	4.4	4.2	3.7	1.2	3.9	5.5	5.1	1.7	4.0
Mozambique	-1.5	8.7	8.2	8.1	7.7	8.4	8.7	7.3	6.7	4.3	7.0
Rwanda	2.1	3.0	6.8	8.2	8.0	9.3	9.0	7.7	11.6	6.0	6.5
Seychelles	3.7	4.8	2.7	2.5	2.5	6.7	9.5	9.6	-1.3	0.7	6.2
Somalia	1.7	-1.6	1.7	2.7	2.9	3.0	2.4	2.6	2.6	2.6	2.6
Uganda	3.1	7.6	6.9	6.8	7.2	10.0	7.0	8.1	9.2	7.1	5.2
United Republic of Tanzania	2.4	4.0	5.8	6.3	7.0	7.3	6.7	7.1	7.4	6.2	6.2
Zambia	1.0	0.8	3.5	4.3	5.3	5.2	6.2	6.3	6.0	3.4	5.7
Zimbabwe	3.3	1.7	-2.8	-4.0	-4.7	-4.0	-5.4	-6.1	-14.5	4.0	6.0
Middle Africa	2.3	2.7	5.2	5.8	7.3	9.0	7.6	10.2	7.9	1.4	3.3
Angola	3.6	5.1	8.5	9.4	12.3	20.6	18.6	20.3	13.2	-0.4	1.6
Cameroon	1.5	3.6	3.7	3.7	3.2	2.3	3.2	3.3	2.9	2.0	3.0
Central African Republic	1.1	4.1	3.8	3.7	3.8	0.9	7.9	8.7	5.5	1.7	3.3
Chad	6.6	3.0	6.5	7.3	7.8	7.9	0.2	0.1	0.3	-1.6	5.1
Congo	4.0	1.2	3.2	3.7	4.4	7.7	6.2	-1.6	5.6	7.6	9.1
Dem. Rep. of the Congo	2.1	-3.6	0.9	2.2	5.5	7.0	5.6	6.3	6.2	2.8	7.2
Equatorial Guinea	2.3	28.5	24.1	22.9	16.6	8.9	5.3	23.2	15.2	5.3	-0.8
Gabon	0.5	2.1	1.3	1.0	2.2	3.5	1.2	5.3	2.7	-1.4	5.7
Sao Tome and Principe	-1.2	1.7	4.2	4.8	6.2	4.2	10.3	5.2	5.8	4.0	4.5
Northern Africa	2.6	3.5	4.3	4.5	4.9	5.8	5.8	5.3	4.4	1.6	4.1
Algeria	2.9	2.5	3.5	3.8	3.9	5.1	2.0	3.0	3.0	2.0	3.3
Egypt	7.3	4.9	5.0	5.0	5.5	6.8	7.1	7.2	4.7	5.0	5.1
Libyan Arab Jamahiriya	-3.4	0.8	3.1	3.8	5.2	10.3	6.7	5.1	2.7	-0.7	4.2
Morocco (2)	4.2	2.9	3.7	4.0	3.9	3.0	7.8	2.7	5.6	-5.9	3.2
Sudan	-0.2	7.8	7.4	7.2	7.1	6.1	9.4	10.2	6.8	4.5	5.1
Tunisia	3.2	4.7	4.8	4.9	4.8	4.0	5.5	6.3	4.6	3.0	3.7
Southern Africa	1.6	2.9	3.5	3.6	3.9	5.0	5.6	5.4	3.6	-1.8	3.0
Botswana	11.0	7.2	5.9	5.6	4.3	1.6	5.1	4.8	3.1	-3.7	8.6
Lesotho	3.4	3.9	3.2	3.0	3.1	1.4	6.6	2.3	4.4	1.4	2.4
Namibia	2.2	2.9	4.0	4.3	4.9	2.5	7.1	5.5	3.3	-0.7	4.4
South Africa	1.4	2.7	3.4	3.5	3.9	5.3	5.6	5.5	3.7	-1.8	2.8
Swaziland	7.5	3.3	2.7	2.5	2.5	2.3	3.2	4.0	0.5	1.2	2.0
Western Africa	0.1	3.0	5.4	6.1	7.4	3.8	6.4	5.8	7.4	4.8	7.0
Benin	3.4	4.9	4.4	4.3	3.8	2.9	3.8	4.6	5.0	2.7	2.5
Burkina Faso	2.6	6.0	5.7	5.6	5.4	7.1	5.5	3.6	4.5	3.2	5.8
Cape Verde	5.6	7.9	7.0	6.8	6.3	6.5	10.1	8.6	5.9	4.1	5.4
Côte d'Ivoire	3.3	4.1	1.7	1.1	1.2	1.8	1.2	1.5	2.3	3.8	2.6
Gambia	3.4	3.1	3.6	3.8	3.7	2.1	6.7	6.3	6.1	4.6	5.7
Ghana	2.6	4.2	4.9	5.1	5.7	5.9	6.4	6.2	6.7	4.7	5.7
Guinea	3.0	4.6	3.6	3.4	2.9	2.4	1.0	1.8	4.7	4.9	1.9
Guinea-Bissau	2.3	-0.5	1.0	1.1	2.1	5.0	2.2	0.3	3.5	3.0	3.5
Liberia	-0.4	16.5	8.2	7.7	0.9	5.3	7.8	9.4	7.1	4.6	5.1
Mali	3.8	4.4	4.9	5.0	5.2	6.1	5.3	4.3	5.0	4.4	4.5
Mauritania	1.5	3.0	4.8	5.2	6.8	5.4	29.4	1.0	3.7	-1.1	4.7
Niger	-1.9	4.0	4.0	4.0	4.3	8.4	5.8	3.3	5.9	-0.9	7.5
Nigeria	-1.7	2.3	6.5	7.7	9.8	3.4	7.5	6.9	9.1	5.6	8.4
Senegal	3.2	4.1	4.2	4.3	4.2	5.6	2.5	4.9	3.3	2.2	4.2
Sierra Leone	2.5	-9.5	2.4	5.4	8.6	7.5	7.5	6.4	4.3	4.4	4.9
Togo	1.3	3.1	2.0	1.7	2.3	1.2	3.9	2.1	2.4	3.3	3.4

For sources and notes, see end of table.

414

Per capita real gross domestic product (1) / Produit intérieur brut réel par habitant (1) Percentage / En pourcentage											Régions, pays ou territoires
80 -89	92 -00	92 -10 (e)	95 -10 (e)	00 -10 (e)	2005	2006	2007	2008	2009	2010 (e)	
1.5	1.7	1.7	1.7	1.6	2.3	2.9	2.8	0.5	-3.1	2.8	**MONDE**
1.4	3.0	3.7	3.9	4.7	5.5	6.2	6.5	3.9	1.2	6.0	ÉCONOMIES EN DÉVELOPPEMENT
2.5	-2.4	3.5	5.3	5.7	6.6	8.1	8.3	5.4	-6.7	4.0	ÉCONOMIES EN TRANSITION
2.6	2.3	1.7	1.6	1.1	1.9	2.2	2.0	-0.3	-4.0	2.0	ÉCONOMIES DÉVELOPPÉES
-0.9	0.7	1.9	2.2	2.9	3.1	3.6	3.5	2.7	-0.7	2.1	Économies en développement : Afrique
-0.5	0.8	1.6	1.9	2.7	3.6	3.7	4.2	2.0	0.1	2.0	*Afrique orientale*
1.0	-3.8	-1.2	-0.3	0.2	-2.0	2.3	0.1	1.2	0.6	1.2	Burundi
0.1	-1.5	-0.8	-0.7	-0.9	1.5	-1.5	-2.2	-1.7	-1.5	-0.5	Comores
-4.5	-1.7	0.1	0.6	2.0	1.3	2.0	3.0	0.0	3.1	2.6	Djibouti
_	3.8	-1.5	-3.2	-3.4	-1.3	-4.4	-1.8	12.5	0.0	-0.8	Érythrée
_	2.2	3.8	4.2	6.3	9.2	8.3	8.7	8.9	7.5	5.7	Éthiopie
-1.4	_	_	_	_	_	_	_	_	_	_	Éthiopie (anc.)
0.5	-0.3	0.6	0.8	1.7	3.2	3.6	4.4	-1.0	0.0	2.3	Kenya
-1.8	-0.4	-0.1	0.0	0.1	1.5	1.9	3.2	4.0	-7.8	-4.8	Madagascar
-2.2	1.8	1.6	1.7	3.3	0.5	4.7	5.5	5.8	4.3	3.3	Malawi
5.3	3.9	3.3	3.3	2.9	0.3	3.1	4.8	4.4	1.1	3.4	Maurice
-2.5	5.5	5.3	5.4	5.0	5.7	6.0	4.7	4.2	1.9	4.6	Mozambique
-1.6	-0.7	2.9	3.9	5.3	7.0	6.2	4.7	8.3	2.8	3.4	Rwanda
2.4	3.7	1.7	1.5	1.5	5.6	8.5	8.7	-1.9	0.1	5.7	Seychelles
1.8	-3.2	-0.6	0.3	0.5	0.7	0.2	0.4	0.4	0.4	0.3	Somalie
-0.3	4.3	3.6	3.5	3.8	6.5	3.6	4.6	5.7	3.7	1.9	Ouganda
-0.7	1.2	3.0	3.5	4.1	4.4	3.8	4.2	4.3	3.2	3.1	République-Unie de Tanzanie
-2.1	-1.8	0.9	1.8	2.7	2.7	3.6	3.6	3.2	0.6	2.8	Zambie
-0.5	0.1	-3.4	-4.3	-4.6	-3.7	-5.1	-5.7	-14.3	3.8	5.2	Zimbabwe
-0.6	-0.1	2.3	3.0	4.3	6.0	4.7	7.3	5.1	-1.2	0.7	*Afrique centrale*
0.4	2.0	5.2	6.0	8.8	16.7	14.9	16.7	10.0	-3.2	-1.2	Angola
-1.4	1.1	1.3	1.4	0.9	0.0	1.0	1.0	0.6	-0.3	0.8	Cameroun
-1.5	1.8	1.8	1.9	2.0	-0.7	6.1	6.7	3.6	-0.2	1.4	République centrafricaine
3.7	-0.2	3.1	3.8	4.5	4.5	-2.8	-2.6	-2.3	-4.1	2.3	Tchad
1.0	-1.6	0.5	1.1	1.7	5.0	3.4	-4.3	2.7	4.7	6.4	Congo
-0.8	-6.3	-1.8	-0.6	2.5	4.8	2.6	3.3	3.3	0.0	4.4	Rép. dém. du Congo
-3.4	24.4	20.2	19.2	13.2	5.7	2.3	19.7	12.0	2.4	-3.5	Guinée équatoriale
-2.6	-0.7	-1.0	-1.2	0.2	1.5	-0.7	3.3	0.8	-3.2	3.7	Gabon
-3.2	0.2	2.4	3.1	4.5	2.7	8.6	3.6	4.2	2.3	2.7	Sao Tomé-et-Principe
0.0	1.7	2.5	2.7	3.1	4.0	4.0	3.5	2.5	-0.2	2.4	*Afrique septentrionale*
-0.1	0.7	1.9	2.2	2.3	3.5	0.5	1.4	1.4	0.5	1.8	Algérie
4.8	3.2	3.1	3.2	3.6	4.9	5.2	5.3	2.8	3.2	3.3	Égypte
-6.9	-1.0	1.2	1.8	3.1	8.1	4.5	2.8	0.6	-2.5	2.6	Jamahiriya arabe libyenne
1.7	1.4	2.5	2.8	2.9	1.9	6.7	1.7	4.5	-6.8	2.1	Maroc (2)
-3.0	5.1	4.8	4.6	4.5	3.6	6.7	7.4	4.2	1.9	2.5	Soudan
0.7	3.4	3.6	3.8	3.7	3.0	4.4	5.2	3.4	1.8	2.5	Tunisie
-0.9	1.0	2.0	2.2	2.7	3.8	4.4	4.3	2.6	-2.7	2.2	*Afrique australe*
7.4	4.7	4.1	4.0	2.9	0.4	3.7	3.4	1.7	-5.0	7.2	Botswana
1.0	2.0	1.9	1.7	2.1	0.5	5.6	1.3	3.3	0.4	1.4	Lesotho
-1.2	0.1	1.7	2.1	3.0	0.7	5.1	3.5	1.4	-2.6	2.5	Namibie
-1.0	0.9	1.9	2.2	2.7	4.0	4.4	4.4	2.7	-2.6	2.0	Afrique du Sud
3.6	1.3	1.3	1.3	1.4	1.4	2.1	2.6	-1.1	-0.4	0.5	Swaziland
-2.6	0.5	2.8	3.4	4.7	1.2	3.7	3.1	4.7	2.2	4.3	*Afrique occidentale*
0.6	1.8	1.3	1.2	0.7	-0.3	0.6	1.5	2.0	-0.2	-0.4	Bénin
0.0	3.1	2.7	2.6	2.3	4.0	2.5	0.6	1.4	0.2	2.7	Burkina Faso
4.0	5.5	5.2	5.2	5.0	5.1	8.9	7.6	5.0	3.2	4.5	Cap-Vert
-0.6	1.4	-0.4	-0.8	-0.6	0.2	-0.5	-0.2	0.5	1.8	0.6	Côte d'Ivoire
-1.0	0.3	0.7	0.9	0.8	-0.8	3.7	3.3	3.2	1.7	2.9	Gambie
-0.5	1.7	2.4	2.6	3.2	3.3	3.9	3.6	4.1	2.2	3.3	Ghana
0.5	1.5	1.5	1.6	1.1	0.6	-0.8	-0.1	2.7	2.7	-0.3	Guinée
0.3	-2.4	-1.0	-0.9	0.1	3.0	0.2	-1.7	1.4	0.9	1.3	Guinée-Bissau
-1.7	11.3	4.0	3.6	-2.5	2.3	3.5	4.3	1.8	-0.3	1.0	Libéria
2.0	1.6	1.9	1.9	2.0	2.9	2.0	1.1	1.8	1.3	1.3	Mali
-1.2	0.1	1.9	2.3	3.9	2.6	26.0	-1.6	1.1	-3.5	2.2	Mauritanie
-4.6	0.4	0.4	0.4	0.7	4.7	2.1	-0.3	2.2	-4.4	3.8	Niger
-4.1	-0.1	4.0	5.1	7.1	0.9	4.9	4.3	6.5	3.0	5.7	Nigéria
0.2	1.4	1.5	1.6	1.4	2.8	-0.3	2.1	0.6	-0.5	1.5	Sénégal
0.0	-9.9	-0.3	2.1	4.8	3.3	4.0	3.4	1.8	2.1	2.7	Sierra Leone
-2.0	0.2	-0.6	-0.9	0.0	-1.0	1.6	-0.1	0.2	1.1	1.2	Togo

Pour les sources et les notes, se reporter à la fin du tableau.

8.2.1 Annual average growth rates of total and per capita real gross domestic product of countries and geographical regions

Region, country or territory	Total real gross domestic product (1) / Produit intérieur brut réel total (1) Percentage / En pourcentage										
	80 -89	92 -00	92 -10 (e)	95 -10 (e)	00 -10 (e)	2005	2006	2007	2008	2009	2010 (e)
Developing economies: America	**1.8**	**3.1**	**3.1**	**3.2**	**3.6**	**4.6**	**5.5**	**5.6**	**4.0**	**-2.1**	**5.9**
Caribbean	*2.5*	*3.6*	*4.2*	*4.4*	*4.7*	*7.6*	*9.4*	*6.0*	*3.1*	*0.3*	*2.7*
Anguilla	7.7	5.2	6.0	6.4	7.3	8.3	26.2	18.3	1.3	-25.5	2.6
Antigua and Barbuda	6.8	3.6	4.0	4.2	4.4	4.7	12.6	10.0	2.5	-11.5	-4.1
Aruba	11.0	4.7	1.6	0.7	-1.1	1.0	0.6	0.4	-2.5	-19.2	-2.5
Bahamas	4.5	4.6	2.3	1.8	0.7	3.3	4.6	2.8	-1.7	-5.0	0.5
Barbados	1.7	3.4	1.9	1.5	1.1	3.2	3.4	0.5	0.2	-5.3	-0.5
British Virgin Islands	5.0	18.1	7.3	4.2	2.4	9.7	2.5	1.8	2.5	2.3	2.3
Cayman Islands	8.9	8.1	4.4	3.7	2.1	6.9	4.0	1.1	1.1	6.6	1.0
Cuba	4.0	2.2	4.5	5.3	6.1	11.2	12.1	7.3	4.1	1.4	1.9
Dominica	5.2	2.0	1.7	1.8	2.8	3.4	6.3	4.9	2.9	-0.2	1.0
Dominican Republic	3.0	6.3	5.5	5.5	5.6	9.3	10.7	8.5	5.3	3.5	7.8
Grenada	0.1	5.1	3.4	3.1	1.3	12.0	-1.9	4.5	0.9	-6.8	-1.4
Haiti	0.1	0.9	0.7	0.7	0.6	1.8	2.3	3.0	0.8	2.9	-5.1
Jamaica	1.5	0.3	0.9	0.9	1.0	1.1	3.0	1.4	-0.9	-3.0	-1.1
Montserrat	2.8	-11.2	-4.3	-2.6	1.1	0.4	-5.9	1.5	6.7	3.6	1.0
Netherlands Antilles	-0.9	0.8	0.9	0.8	1.8	1.7	2.4	3.7	2.1	-0.2	2.6
Saint Kitts and Nevis	6.3	4.7	3.4	3.1	2.7	5.6	5.5	2.0	4.6	-8.0	-1.5
Saint Lucia	7.7	2.7	2.1	2.1	2.4	6.2	3.5	1.9	0.8	-3.8	0.8
Saint Vincent and the Grenadines	8.6	3.3	3.6	3.8	4.1	2.0	9.7	10.3	0.9	-2.5	-2.3
Trinidad and Tobago	-3.7	5.9	6.9	7.3	6.8	6.2	13.5	4.6	2.3	-0.9	0.0
Turks and Caicos Islands	10.7	9.2	9.6	9.8	11.8	14.4	17.9	11.2	12.9	13.6	13.6
Central America	*0.8*	*3.3*	*2.9*	*3.0*	*2.3*	*3.4*	*5.0*	*3.8*	*1.8*	*-5.9*	*5.2*
Belize	3.8	4.6	5.1	5.2	3.9	3.1	5.6	0.3	3.8	0.0	2.0
Costa Rica	2.8	5.0	4.7	4.8	4.9	5.9	8.8	7.9	2.8	-1.1	4.2
El Salvador	0.3	4.2	2.9	2.5	2.3	3.3	4.2	4.3	2.4	-3.5	0.7
Guatemala	0.4	4.1	3.7	3.6	3.6	3.3	5.4	6.3	3.3	0.6	2.6
Honduras	2.7	2.9	3.8	4.1	4.6	6.1	6.6	6.3	4.2	-2.1	2.8
Mexico	0.8	3.3	2.8	2.9	2.1	3.3	4.8	3.4	1.5	-6.5	5.4
Nicaragua	-1.7	4.4	3.9	3.8	3.4	4.8	4.1	3.5	3.2	2.6	4.5
Panama	_	4.2	5.1	5.6	7.0	7.2	8.5	12.1	10.7	2.4	7.5
South America	*2.2*	*2.9*	*3.1*	*3.1*	*4.2*	*5.1*	*5.5*	*6.7*	*5.3*	*-0.3*	*6.5*
Argentina	-0.2	3.0	2.9	3.2	5.6	9.2	8.5	8.7	6.8	0.9	9.2
Bolivia (Plurinational State of)	-0.7	4.0	3.6	3.5	4.1	4.4	4.8	4.6	6.1	3.4	4.2
Brazil	3.1	2.9	3.0	3.0	3.7	3.2	4.0	6.1	5.1	-0.2	7.5
Chile	2.5	5.7	4.3	3.8	4.0	5.6	4.6	4.6	3.7	-1.5	5.2
Colombia	3.5	2.4	3.2	3.3	4.6	5.7	6.9	7.5	2.4	0.4	4.3
Ecuador	1.9	1.7	3.2	3.5	4.5	6.0	3.9	2.5	6.5	0.4	3.6
Guyana	-3.2	4.6	2.6	2.0	2.4	-2.0	5.1	7.0	2.0	3.3	3.6
Paraguay	2.5	1.7	2.1	2.2	3.8	2.9	4.3	6.8	5.8	-4.5	15.3
Peru	0.4	4.8	4.6	4.5	6.1	6.8	7.7	8.9	9.8	0.9	8.8
Suriname	1.0	1.4	3.4	4.0	5.0	3.9	4.5	5.4	6.0	2.5	4.4
Uruguay	0.7	2.8	2.0	2.0	3.9	7.5	4.3	7.5	8.5	2.9	8.5
Venezuela (Bolivarian Rep. of)	0.6	0.9	2.2	2.7	4.5	10.3	9.9	8.2	4.8	-3.3	-1.4
Developing economies: Asia	**5.5**	**5.9**	**6.3**	**6.4**	**7.2**	**8.1**	**8.7**	**9.1**	**5.8**	**4.3**	**8.4**
Eastern Asia	*9.7*	*7.6*	*7.7*	*7.7*	*8.3*	*8.6*	*10.0*	*11.1*	*7.0*	*5.9*	*9.5*
China	10.8	9.9	9.9	9.9	10.8	11.3	12.7	14.2	9.6	9.1	10.3
China, Hong Kong SAR	7.3	2.8	3.6	3.8	4.6	7.1	7.0	6.4	2.4	-2.8	7.0
China, Macao SAR	7.5	0.6	7.8	9.8	14.9	6.9	16.5	26.0	12.9	1.3	26.2
China, Taiwan Province of	7.8	5.7	4.5	4.1	4.1	4.7	5.4	6.0	0.7	-1.9	10.9
Korea, Dem. People's Rep. of	2.7	-2.3	0.4	1.1	1.2	3.8	-1.0	-1.2	3.1	-0.9	-0.9
Korea, Republic of	10.1	5.8	5.0	4.6	4.1	4.0	5.2	5.1	2.3	0.2	6.2
Mongolia	6.3	3.0	5.1	5.7	7.2	7.3	8.6	10.2	8.9	-1.6	6.1
Southern Asia	*4.6*	*5.3*	*6.1*	*6.3*	*7.1*	*8.2*	*8.4*	*8.9*	*4.5*	*6.3*	*7.0*
Afghanistan	-1.0	-0.4	9.2	11.2	15.9	14.5	11.2	16.2	2.3	22.5	8.2
Bangladesh	3.7	4.9	5.5	5.6	5.9	6.0	6.6	6.4	6.2	6.0	6.0
Bhutan	10.4	6.1	7.4	7.8	8.3	7.0	6.4	19.7	5.0	6.3	6.7
India	5.7	6.3	6.8	6.9	7.9	9.3	9.4	9.6	5.1	7.7	8.5
Iran (Islamic Rep. of)	1.5	3.3	4.6	5.0	5.3	5.3	6.1	8.3	2.3	1.8	1.0
Maldives	11.9	8.2	7.1	6.9	6.7	-5.0	22.5	6.1	6.3	-3.9	8.0
Nepal	4.6	4.9	4.2	4.1	3.9	3.1	3.7	3.2	4.7	6.5	4.6
Pakistan	6.4	3.4	4.2	4.4	5.2	7.7	6.2	5.7	2.0	3.7	4.8
Sri Lanka	4.1	5.3	5.0	5.0	5.7	6.2	7.7	6.8	6.0	3.5	9.1

For sources and notes, see end of table.

Per capita real gross domestic product (1) / Produit intérieur brut réel par habitant (1) Percentage / En pourcentage											Régions, pays ou territoires
80-89	92-00	92-10 (e)	95-10 (e)	00-10 (e)	2005	2006	2007	2008	2009	2010 (e)	
-0.3	1.4	1.6	1.8	2.3	3.3	4.2	4.4	2.8	-3.2	4.7	Économies en développement : Amérique
1.0	2.4	3.1	3.4	3.7	6.6	8.5	5.1	2.3	-0.5	1.9	Caraïbes
5.7	2.6	2.7	3.0	3.8	4.4	22.3	15.2	-1.0	-27.1	0.6	Anguilla
8.4	1.0	2.1	2.5	3.0	3.3	11.2	8.7	1.4	-12.4	-5.1	Antigua-et-Barbuda
10.8	1.3	-0.8	-1.3	-2.8	-1.0	-1.1	-1.0	-3.7	-20.0	-3.3	Aruba
2.4	3.1	0.9	0.4	-0.7	1.8	3.1	1.3	-3.1	-6.3	-0.8	Bahamas
1.3	3.1	1.6	1.3	0.9	3.0	3.2	0.3	0.0	-5.5	-0.7	Barbade
1.5	15.6	5.5	2.6	1.1	8.4	1.3	0.6	1.4	1.2	1.2	Îles Vierges britanniques
4.4	3.7	0.2	-0.3	-1.2	2.4	1.8	2.5	0.0	-7.4	0.2	Îles Caïmanes
3.3	1.8	4.2	5.0	5.9	11.0	12.0	7.2	4.1	1.4	1.9	Cuba
5.9	2.3	2.1	2.2	3.1	3.6	6.6	5.3	3.4	0.1	1.3	Dominique
0.8	4.5	3.9	3.9	4.1	7.7	9.1	7.0	3.8	2.1	6.3	République dominicaine
4.9	4.5	3.0	2.8	1.1	11.7	-2.2	4.2	0.6	-7.1	-1.8	Grenade
-2.2	-1.0	-1.0	-0.9	-0.9	0.3	0.8	2.0	-0.5	1.6	-6.3	Haïti
0.4	-0.7	0.1	0.2	0.4	0.4	2.4	1.0	-1.3	-3.4	-1.5	Jamaïque
4.0	-1.5	-0.4	0.0	-1.6	-4.5	-8.6	0.0	6.1	3.3	0.3	Montserrat
-1.9	1.7	0.7	0.4	0.6	0.4	0.9	2.0	0.4	-1.7	1.2	Antilles néerlandaises
7.0	3.3	2.1	1.7	1.4	4.3	4.2	0.7	3.3	-9.2	-2.7	Saint-Kitts-et-Nevis
6.0	1.3	0.9	0.9	1.3	5.1	2.5	0.9	-0.2	-4.9	-0.2	Sainte-Lucie
7.9	3.3	3.5	3.7	3.9	1.8	9.6	10.2	0.8	-2.6	-2.3	Saint-Vincent-et-les Grenadines
-5.0	5.3	6.5	6.8	6.4	5.8	13.1	4.2	1.9	-1.3	-0.3	Trinité-et-Tobago
6.0	4.7	2.6	2.4	4.0	5.6	10.4	5.4	8.0	9.6	10.3	Îles Turques et Caïques
-1.3	1.5	1.4	1.5	0.9	2.0	3.5	2.4	0.4	-7.2	3.8	Amérique centrale
0.9	1.8	2.6	2.8	1.7	0.8	3.4	-1.8	1.7	-2.1	0.0	Belize
0.0	2.5	2.6	2.8	3.1	4.1	7.0	6.2	1.2	-2.5	2.6	Costa Rica
-1.0	3.3	2.3	2.1	1.9	3.0	3.8	3.9	2.0	-4.0	0.2	El Salvador
-2.0	1.8	1.3	1.1	1.1	0.7	2.8	3.7	0.8	-1.9	0.1	Guatemala
-0.4	0.5	1.7	2.0	2.6	4.0	4.5	4.2	2.1	-4.0	0.7	Honduras
-1.2	1.5	1.3	1.5	0.8	2.0	3.5	2.1	0.2	-7.7	4.1	Mexique
-4.0	2.4	2.3	2.3	2.1	3.5	2.8	2.2	1.9	1.2	0.1	Nicaragua
–	2.1	3.2	3.7	5.1	5.3	6.7	10.2	8.9	0.8	5.8	Panama
0.1	1.3	1.7	1.8	3.0	3.8	4.3	5.5	4.1	-1.3	5.3	Amérique du Sud
-1.7	1.7	1.8	2.2	4.6	8.2	7.5	7.7	5.8	0.0	8.2	Argentine
-2.9	1.8	1.6	1.6	2.2	2.6	3.0	2.8	4.4	1.7	2.5	Bolivie (État plurinational de)
0.9	1.3	1.7	1.7	2.6	2.0	2.9	5.1	4.2	-1.1	6.6	Brésil
0.9	4.1	3.0	2.6	2.9	4.5	3.5	3.6	2.7	-2.5	4.2	Chili
1.3	0.6	1.5	1.6	3.0	4.1	5.3	6.0	0.9	-1.1	2.9	Colombie
-0.7	0.0	1.5	1.8	2.9	4.3	2.3	0.9	4.9	-1.1	2.1	Équateur
-2.4	4.4	2.3	1.7	2.1	-2.3	4.8	6.8	1.8	3.1	3.4	Guyana
-0.4	-0.6	0.1	0.2	1.8	0.9	2.4	4.8	3.9	-6.2	13.3	Paraguay
-1.9	3.0	3.2	3.2	4.9	5.6	6.6	7.7	8.6	-0.1	7.6	Pérou
0.0	0.0	2.1	2.7	3.8	2.7	3.3	4.3	5.0	1.6	3.5	Suriname
0.1	2.1	1.6	1.8	3.8	7.4	4.2	7.2	8.2	2.5	8.1	Uruguay
-2.1	-1.2	0.3	0.8	2.7	8.4	8.0	6.3	3.0	-4.9	-3.0	Venezuela (Rép. bolivarienne du)
3.4	4.3	4.9	5.1	6.0	6.8	7.4	7.9	4.7	3.2	7.2	Économies en développement : Asie
8.0	6.6	6.9	7.0	7.7	8.1	9.4	10.5	6.4	5.3	9.0	Asie orientale
9.1	8.9	9.1	9.2	10.2	10.7	12.1	13.6	9.0	8.6	9.8	Chine
5.9	1.0	2.7	3.1	4.3	7.0	6.7	5.8	1.6	-3.6	6.0	Chine (RAS de Hong Kong)
3.2	-1.0	5.7	7.5	12.2	4.4	13.7	22.9	10.1	-1.1	23.3	Chine (RAS de Macao)
6.3	4.8	3.8	3.6	3.6	4.3	5.0	5.6	0.3	-2.2	10.6	Province chinoise de Taiwan
1.1	-3.5	-0.5	0.4	0.5	3.1	-1.6	-1.7	2.6	-1.4	-1.3	Corée, Rép. populaire dém. de
8.6	5.1	4.4	4.1	3.6	3.5	4.7	4.6	1.8	-0.3	5.7	Corée, République de
3.4	2.2	3.9	4.4	5.7	5.9	7.0	8.5	7.2	-3.2	4.4	Mongolie
2.2	3.3	4.3	4.5	5.5	6.6	6.8	7.3	3.0	4.8	5.5	Asie méridionale
0.9	-4.9	5.4	7.7	12.3	10.7	8.0	13.3	-0.1	19.6	5.4	Afghanistan
1.0	2.8	3.7	4.0	4.5	4.5	5.3	5.2	5.1	4.9	4.8	Bangladesh
7.3	5.4	5.2	5.1	5.7	4.3	3.9	17.3	3.0	4.5	4.9	Bhoutan
3.3	4.4	5.0	5.2	6.2	7.7	7.8	8.1	3.6	6.2	7.0	Inde
-2.1	1.6	3.1	3.5	4.0	4.0	4.8	7.0	1.1	0.6	-0.1	Iran (Rép. islamique d')
8.1	6.0	5.3	5.2	5.2	-6.4	20.8	4.7	4.9	-5.1	6.6	Maldives
2.1	2.3	1.9	1.8	1.8	1.0	1.7	1.2	2.8	4.6	2.7	Népal
2.9	0.7	2.0	2.4	3.3	5.8	4.3	3.8	0.2	1.9	2.9	Pakistan
2.6	4.6	4.1	4.0	4.5	5.0	6.5	5.7	4.9	2.5	8.1	Sri Lanka

Pour les sources et les notes, se reporter à la fin du tableau.

8

8.2.1 Annual average growth rates of total and per capita real gross domestic product of countries and geographical regions

Region, country or territory	Total real gross domestic product (1) / Produit intérieur brut réel total (1) Percentage / En pourcentage									
	80 -89	92 -00	92 -10 (e)	95 -10 (e)	00 -10 (e)	2005	2006	2007	2008	2009	2010 (e)
South-Eastern Asia	*4.7*	*4.2*	*4.5*	*4.3*	*5.3*	*5.8*	*6.2*	*6.6*	*4.3*	*1.0*	*7.8*
Brunei Darussalam	-2.5	1.7	1.8	1.7	1.4	0.4	4.4	0.2	-1.9	-0.5	4.1
Cambodia	6.5	6.5	8.0	8.4	8.4	13.3	10.8	10.2	6.7	-2.7	6.0
Indonesia including East Timor	5.7	2.9	–	–	–						
Indonesia	–	–				5.7	5.5	6.3	6.0	4.5	6.1
Lao People's Dem. Rep.	5.0	6.5	7.2	7.4	8.5	7.3	8.3	18.2	7.8	7.5	7.7
Malaysia	4.9	6.1	5.1	4.6	4.9	5.3	5.8	6.2	4.6	-1.7	7.2
Myanmar	0.9	7.4	10.4	11.2	11.6	13.6	13.1	12.0	10.1	4.8	5.3
Philippines	0.5	3.9	4.3	4.4	4.9	5.0	5.3	7.1	3.8	0.9	7.3
Singapore	8.3	7.3	5.8	5.3	5.7	7.6	8.7	8.2	1.4	-2.0	14.5
Thailand	7.0	2.8	3.5	3.4	4.5	4.6	5.1	4.9	2.5	-2.3	7.8
Timor-Leste	–	–	–	–	–	2.3	-3.4	16.2	6.8	7.4	6.0
Viet Nam	5.6	7.8	7.3	7.2	7.4	8.4	8.2	8.5	6.3	5.0	0.0
Western Asia	*1.3*	*3.6*	*4.3*	*4.6*	*5.4*	*7.8*	*6.7*	*5.2*	*4.8*	*-0.7*	*6.3*
Bahrain	-0.7	3.7	5.2	5.6	6.3	7.9	6.6	8.4	6.3	3.1	4.1
Iraq	0.9	3.6	3.5	4.3	4.3	4.4	10.2	1.4	10.3	4.2	0.8
Jordan	2.0	3.8	5.3	5.7	6.7	8.1	8.1	8.9	7.1	2.3	3.1
Kuwait	1.1	3.1	4.6	4.9	6.6	10.2	5.2	4.4	6.4	-2.7	2.0
Lebanon	1.6	3.4	3.7	3.6	4.9	1.0	0.6	7.5	9.3	8.0	7.5
Occupied Palestinian territory	2.8	8.1	3.4	2.4	3.3	8.6	-5.2	4.9	2.3	5.5	4.8
Oman	8.2	3.7	4.0	4.0	4.9	4.0	5.5	6.8	12.8	3.4	4.2
Qatar	1.4	8.9	10.9	12.0	14.4	6.1	18.6	26.8	25.4	8.6	16.3
Saudi Arabia	-2.1	1.8	2.8	3.1	3.6	5.6	3.2	2.0	4.3	0.1	3.7
Syrian Arab Republic	0.9	5.3	4.5	4.2	5.1	6.2	5.0	5.7	4.3	5.9	3.2
Turkey	5.3	3.8	3.9	3.9	4.7	8.4	6.9	4.7	0.7	-4.7	8.9
United Arab Emirates	-2.9	6.2	7.5	7.9	8.9	13.1	13.0	6.2	7.4	1.3	3.2
Yemen (former Arab Republic)	5.1	–	–	–	–	–	–	–	–	–	–
Yemen (former Democratic)	2.4	–	–	–	–	–	–	–	–	–	–
Yemen	–	8.9	6.1	5.2	4.7	5.9	3.8	4.4	4.7	3.9	8.0
Developing economies: Oceania	*3.7*	*1.9*	*1.7*	*1.7*	*2.0*	*2.1*	*1.5*	*2.8*	*2.6*	*1.4*	*2.9*
Cook Islands	9.6	0.7	3.0	3.6	3.0	0.0	0.7	9.5	-1.2	0.3	0.3
Fiji	1.3	2.7	2.0	1.7	1.2	0.7	1.9	-0.5	-0.1	-2.5	0.1
French Polynesia	6.2	2.2	2.3	2.4	2.1	2.3	1.1	2.1	2.5	2.1	2.1
Kiribati	0.8	4.2	2.6	2.3	1.4	0.0	3.2	-0.5	3.4	-0.7	1.8
Marshall Islands	–	-1.0	1.3	1.5	2.4	2.0	0.9	1.3	1.4	0.0	0.0
Micronesia (Federated States of)	–	0.2	0.3	0.2	-0.3	3.0	-0.4	-0.1	-2.9	-1.0	-1.0
Nauru	-1.1	-8.4	-6.6	-6.2	-6.9	-9.8	-20.3	-10.8	95.6	-18.2	-18.2
New Caledonia	4.6	1.4	0.8	0.5	0.6	0.8	0.5	0.5	0.6	0.6	1.5
Palau	–	3.2	1.7	1.1	1.9	5.5	3.0	2.1	-1.0	2.9	2.9
Papua New Guinea	2.3	2.0	2.3	2.4	3.9	3.9	2.3	7.2	6.7	4.5	7.0
Samoa	1.1	3.4	3.8	3.7	2.9	5.4	1.0	6.4	-3.0	-1.8	0.0
Solomon Islands	1.8	1.7	1.2	1.1	4.7	5.4	6.9	11.8	7.3	-2.2	5.6
Tonga	4.6	2.1	1.8	1.6	0.9	-1.0	0.5	-1.2	2.0	-0.4	0.3
Tuvalu	6.2	3.9	3.9	4.1	2.4	2.0	1.0	2.0	2.0	2.0	0.2
Vanuatu	6.0	2.9	2.8	2.9	4.2	5.1	7.2	6.7	6.3	5.6	2.2
Transition economies	*3.5*	*-2.5*	*3.4*	*5.1*	*5.7*	*6.5*	*8.0*	*8.3*	*5.5*	*-6.6*	*4.1*
Albania	1.9	6.3	6.1	5.8	5.6	5.8	5.4	6.0	7.8	2.8	3.5
Armenia	–	4.4	7.9	8.7	9.2	13.9	13.2	13.7	6.9	-14.2	2.6
Azerbaijan	–	-2.1	9.7	13.8	17.1	26.4	34.5	25.1	10.8	9.3	5.0
Belarus	–	0.6	5.5	7.3	8.0	9.4	10.0	8.6	10.2	0.2	7.6
Bosnia and Herzegovina	–	22.2	12.6	10.3	8.5	6.4	10.3	12.0	13.5	4.3	0.8
Croatia	–	3.5	3.5	3.3	3.3	4.2	4.7	5.5	2.4	-5.8	-1.2
Georgia	–	1.2	5.0	6.2	6.9	9.6	9.4	12.3	2.3	-3.9	6.4
Kazakhstan	–	-2.5	5.2	7.5	8.3	9.7	10.6	8.7	3.3	1.2	7.0
Kyrgyzstan	–	-0.8	3.1	4.5	4.4	-0.2	3.1	8.5	8.4	2.3	-1.4
Montenegro	–									-7.0	1.1
Republic of Moldova	–	-6.4	1.3	3.5	5.2	7.5	4.8	3.0	7.8	-6.5	6.9
Russian Federation	–	-2.6	3.2	4.9	5.3	6.4	7.7	8.1	5.6	-7.9	4.0
Serbia and Montenegro	–	-0.2	–	–	–	5.3	5.3	7.0	–	–	–
Serbia	–	–	–	–	–	–	–	·	–	-2.2	2.1
SFR of Yugoslavia (former)	1.0	–	–	–	–	–	–	–	–	–	–
Tajikistan	–	-6.8	3.7	7.1	8.0	6.7	6.7	7.6	7.9	3.4	6.5
TFYR of Macedonia	–	1.3	2.2	2.6	3.1	4.1	4.0	6.1	5.0	-0.7	0.7
Turkmenistan	–	-1.0	4.6	6.6	7.8	13.0	11.4	11.6	10.5	4.1	9.2
Ukraine	–	-7.9	1.3	4.1	4.8	2.7	7.3	7.9	2.1	-15.1	4.2
USSR (former)	3.8	–	–	–	–	–	–	–	–	–	–
Uzbekistan	–	1.6	4.8	5.9	7.1	7.1	7.4	9.6	9.0	7.0	8.5

For sources and notes, see end of table.

8.2.1 Taux de croissance annuels moyens du produit intérieur brut réel total et par habitant des pays et des régions géographiques

	Per capita real gross domestic product (1) / Produit intérieur brut réel par habitant (1) Percentage / En pourcentage										Régions, pays ou territoires
80-89	92-00	92-10 (e)	95-10 (e)	00-10 (e)	2005	2006	2007	2008	2009	2010 (e)	
2.5	2.6	3.0	3.0	4.0	4.5	4.9	5.3	3.1	-0.1	6.6	*Asie du Sud-Est*
-5.3	-0.8	-0.4	-0.5	-0.6	-1.6	2.4	-1.8	-3.8	-2.3	2.2	Brunéi Darussalam
2.3	3.9	6.1	6.7	7.1	11.9	9.5	9.0	5.5	-3.8	4.8	Cambodge
3.5	1.4	–	–	–						–	Indonésie, y compris le Timor oriental
					4.4	4.3	5.2	4.9	3.5	5.0	Indonésie
2.3	4.2	5.2	5.6	6.8	5.7	6.7	16.4	6.2	5.9	6.2	Rép. dém. populaire lao
2.0	3.5	2.8	2.4	2.9	3.3	3.9	4.4	2.9	-3.3	5.5	Malaisie
-0.9	5.9	9.4	10.3	10.9	13.0	12.4	11.3	9.4	4.1	4.5	Myanmar
-2.2	1.6	2.2	2.4	3.0	3.0	3.4	5.2	2.1	-0.8	5.5	Philippines
4.0	4.6	3.3	2.9	2.8	5.0	5.1	4.1	-2.6	-5.5	11.3	Singapour
5.0	1.7	2.5	2.4	3.5	3.6	4.2	4.1	1.8	-2.9	7.2	Thaïlande
					-1.4	-6.0	13.8	4.9	5.4	3.7	Timor-Leste
3.3	6.2	6.1	6.0	6.3	7.3	7.1	7.3	5.0	4.2	5.6	Viet Nam
-1.6	1.2	1.9	2.1	2.8	5.1	3.9	2.4	2.1	-3.2	3.8	*Asie occidentale*
-3.7	1.0	0.7	0.5	-1.4	0.0	-4.7	-5.0	-6.5	-7.2	-3.5	Bahreïn
-1.4	0.2	0.5	1.3	1.4	1.6	7.1	-1.5	7.1	1.1	-2.2	Iraq
-1.9	0.9	2.8	3.4	4.0	5.5	5.1	5.6	3.7	-0.7	0.4	Jordanie
-3.6	2.6	1.8	1.2	3.0	6.5	1.3	0.3	2.2	-6.3	-1.4	Koweït
1.2	1.1	2.0	2.2	3.6	-0.4	-0.5	6.5	8.5	7.2	6.7	Liban
-0.3	3.5	0.2	-0.3	1.0	6.4	-7.3	2.4	-0.3	2.7	1.9	Territoire palestinien occupé
3.3	2.5	2.5	2.6	2.6	1.8	2.9	3.9	9.6	0.5	1.6	Oman
-6.6	6.2	3.5	3.0	1.5	-7.6	-0.5	5.3	5.9	-5.1	5.6	Qatar
-7.1	0.0	0.1	0.2	0.3	1.9	0.0	-0.8	1.7	-2.3	1.3	Arabie saoudite
-2.4	2.7	1.9	1.6	2.5	3.5	2.6	3.5	2.3	4.0	1.4	République arabe syrienne
3.1	2.2	2.4	2.5	3.3	7.0	5.5	3.3	-0.7	-5.9	7.5	Turquie
-8.2	0.8	0.3	0.0	-1.3	1.7	-1.4	-8.4	-6.4	-9.4	-4.6	Émirats arabes unis
2.2	–	–	–	–	–	–	–	–	–	–	Yémen (anc. République arabe du)
-3.5	–	–	–	–	–	–	–	–	–	–	Yémen (anc. démocratique)
–	5.0	2.7	2.1	1.5	2.7	0.7	1.2	1.5	0.7	4.8	Yémen
1.3	-0.4	-0.4	-0.5	-0.1	0.0	-0.6	0.7	0.5	-0.7	0.9	*Économies en développement : Océanie*
9.5	0.8	2.3	2.7	1.6	-1.7	-0.6	8.4	-1.9	-0.4	-0.4	Îles Cook
-0.2	1.5	1.3	1.1	0.7	0.3	1.2	-1.4	-1.1	-3.5	-0.9	Fidji
3.5	0.2	0.7	0.9	0.8	0.9	-0.1	0.8	1.2	0.9	0.9	Polynésie française
-2.0	2.6	0.9	0.6	-0.3	-1.7	1.5	-2.0	1.8	-2.2	0.2	Kiribati
–	-1.7	0.9	1.3	2.1	1.9	0.5	0.8	0.7	-1.0	-1.2	Îles Marshall
–	-0.4	-0.1	0.0	-0.7	2.5	-0.7	-0.3	-3.1	-1.3	-1.3	Micronésie (États fédérés de)
-3.0	-9.0	-6.9	-6.4	-7.0	-10.0	-20.5	-10.9	95.1	-18.4	-18.5	Nauru
2.9	-0.9	-1.1	-1.2	-1.1	-0.9	-1.1	-1.1	-1.1	-1.0	-0.1	Nouvelle-Calédonie
–	0.8	0.3	0.1	1.3	5.0	2.5	1.6	-1.5	2.3	2.3	Palaos
-0.4	-0.6	-0.2	-0.1	1.4	1.4	-0.2	4.6	4.2	2.1	4.6	Papouasie-Nouvelle-Guinée
0.8	2.4	3.1	3.2	2.6	5.1	0.7	6.1	-3.3	-2.1	-0.4	Samoa
-1.4	-1.1	-1.5	-1.5	2.1	2.7	4.3	9.0	4.7	-4.5	3.1	Îles Salomon
4.4	1.8	1.3	1.1	0.2	-1.6	-0.1	-1.8	1.4	-1.0	-0.2	Tonga
4.9	3.4	3.4	3.6	1.9	1.5	0.6	1.7	1.7	1.8	0.0	Tuvalu
3.6	0.7	0.4	0.5	1.5	2.3	4.4	4.0	3.7	3.0	-0.3	Vanuatu
2.5	-2.4	3.5	5.3	5.7	6.6	8.1	8.3	5.4	-6.7	4.0	*Économies en transition*
-0.4	7.2	6.1	5.6	5.1	5.2	4.9	5.6	7.4	2.4	3.1	Albanie
	5.9	8.4	8.9	9.1	13.7	13.1	13.6	6.8	-14.3	2.4	Arménie
–	-3.1	8.5	12.5	15.6	24.9	32.7	23.4	9.2	7.8	3.6	Azerbaïdjan
–	0.9	5.9	7.8	8.5	10.0	10.5	9.1	10.8	0.7	8.1	Bélarus
–	22.8	12.0	9.3	8.4	6.4	10.3	12.1	13.7	4.5	1.0	Bosnie-Herzégovine
–	3.8	3.8	3.8	3.5	4.4	4.9	5.7	2.5	-5.7	-1.0	Croatie
–	2.7	6.2	7.4	7.8	10.6	10.2	13.0	2.8	-3.5	6.9	Géorgie
–	-1.2	5.4	7.4	8.8	9.6	7.5	2.1	0.0	5.8		Kazakhstan
–	-2.1	2.1	3.6	3.6	-0.7	2.3	7.4	7.0	1.0	-2.5	Kirghizistan
									-7.2	0.9	Monténégro
–	-5.6	2.6	5.0	6.7	9.2	6.2	4.2	8.9	-5.7	7.8	République de Moldova
–	-2.5	3.5	5.2	5.6	6.7	7.9	8.2	5.7	-7.8	4.0	Fédération de Russie
–	-0.5	–	–	–	5.7	5.5	7.0	–	–	–	Serbie-et-Monténégro
–	–	–	–	–	–	–	–	–	-2.3	2.0	Serbie
0.4	–	–	–	–	–	–	–	–	–	–	RSF de Yougoslavie (anc.)
–	-8.1	2.5	5.9	6.9	5.7	5.5	6.3	6.5	2.0	5.0	Tadjikistan
–	0.8	1.8	2.3	2.8	3.8	3.7	5.9	4.7	-1.0	0.5	LERY de Macédoine
–	-2.8	3.2	5.3	6.6	11.8	10.2	10.3	9.2	2.9	7.9	Turkménistan
–	-7.2	2.1	5.0	5.5	3.5	8.1	8.7	2.7	-14.6	4.8	Ukraine
2.8	–	–	–	–	–	–	–	–	–	–	URSS (anc.)
–	-0.2	3.5	4.7	6.1	6.1	6.3	8.4	7.7	5.8	7.2	Ouzbékistan

Pour les sources et les notes, se reporter à la fin du tableau.

8

8.2.1 Annual average growth rates of total and per capita real gross domestic product of countries and geographical regions

Region, country or territory	Total real gross domestic product (1) / Produit intérieur brut réel total (1) Percentage / En pourcentage										
	80 -89	92 -00	92 -10 (e)	95 -10 (e)	00 -10 (e)	2005	2006	2007	2008	2009	2010 (e)
Developed economies: America	**3.7**	**3.9**	**2.9**	**2.6**	**1.9**	**3.0**	**2.7**	**2.1**	**0.4**	**-2.6**	**2.9**
Bermuda	1.6	4.1	3.8	3.7	3.8	5.2	5.7	4.2	0.7	3.9	2.0
Canada	3.3	3.7	3.0	2.8	2.0	3.0	2.8	2.2	0.5	-2.5	3.1
Greenland	2.4	3.2	2.2	2.0	1.1	2.0	4.6	6.0	1.0	-6.5	-6.5
United States	3.7	3.9	2.9	2.6	1.9	3.0	2.6	2.1	0.4	-2.6	2.8
Developed economies: Asia	**4.4**	**1.1**	**1.1**	**1.0**	**1.0**	**2.0**	**2.1**	**2.4**	**-1.1**	**-5.0**	**4.0**
Israel	3.4	5.6	4.0	3.7	3.5	5.1	5.3	5.2	4.0	0.5	4.7
Japan	4.5	0.9	1.0	0.9	1.0	1.9	2.0	2.4	-1.2	-5.2	4.0
Developed economies: Europe	**2.4**	**2.6**	**2.2**	**2.0**	**1.5**	**2.0**	**3.2**	**3.0**	**0.5**	**-4.1**	**1.8**
Andorra	2.9	3.9	5.1	5.4	5.2	5.9	6.8	1.4	3.6	3.0	3.0
Austria	1.0	2.6	2.3	2.1	1.0	2.5	3.6	3.7	2.2	-3.9	2.0
Belgium	1.9	2.5	2.1	2.0	1.6	1.8	2.7	2.9	1.0	-2.8	2.2
Bulgaria	4.1	-0.6	3.2	4.1	4.8	6.4	6.5	6.4	6.2	-4.9	0.1
Cyprus	6.1	4.5	3.8	3.5	3.1	3.9	4.1	5.1	3.6	-1.7	1.0
Czechoslovakia (former)	2.1	–	–	–	–	–	–	–	–	–	–
Czech Republic	–	–	–	3.1	3.8	6.3	6.8	6.1	2.5	-4.1	2.3
Denmark	2.6	3.0	1.8	1.5	1.0	2.4	3.4	1.7	-0.9	-4.7	2.1
Estonia	–	4.5	5.5	5.8	4.5	9.4	10.6	6.9	-5.1	-13.9	3.1
Finland	3.3	4.1	3.2	3.0	2.2	2.9	4.4	5.3	0.9	-8.0	3.1
France	2.3	2.2	2.0	1.9	1.3	1.9	2.2	2.4	0.2	-2.6	1.6
Germany (former Federal Rep.) (4)	2.0	–	–	–	–	–	–	–	–	–	–
Germany	–	1.8	1.4	1.3	0.9	0.8	3.4	2.7	1.0	-4.7	3.6
Greece	0.7	2.6	3.2	3.4	2.8	2.3	4.5	4.3	1.3	-2.3	-4.5
Hungary	1.6	2.8	3.0	3.0	2.1	3.2	3.6	0.8	0.8	-6.7	1.2
Iceland	3.2	3.8	3.7	3.7	3.1	7.5	4.6	6.0	1.0	-6.8	-3.5
Ireland	2.8	8.7	6.1	5.4	3.0	6.0	5.3	5.6	-3.5	-7.6	-1.0
Italy	2.5	1.7	1.2	1.0	0.4	0.7	2.0	1.5	-1.3	-5.0	1.3
Latvia	–	2.4	5.0	5.7	4.8	10.6	12.2	10.0	-4.2	-18.0	-0.3
Lithuania	–	1.3	4.5	5.4	5.3	7.8	7.8	9.8	2.9	-14.7	1.3
Luxembourg	5.0	4.7	4.4	4.4	3.4	5.4	5.0	6.6	1.4	-3.7	3.5
Malta	3.2	5.1	3.0	2.5	2.0	4.0	3.6	3.7	2.6	-2.1	3.7
Netherlands	2.3	3.6	2.5	2.2	1.0	2.0	3.4	3.9	1.9	-3.9	1.8
Norway	3.1	4.0	2.6	2.3	1.8	2.7	2.3	2.7	0.8	-1.4	0.3
Poland	2.3	5.7	4.5	4.2	4.3	3.6	6.2	6.8	5.1	1.7	3.8
Portugal	2.9	3.4	2.0	1.7	0.7	0.8	1.4	2.4	0.0	-2.6	1.3
Romania	2.0	0.5	3.0	3.4	4.8	4.2	7.9	6.3	7.3	-7.1	-1.3
San Marino	4.2	6.3	3.8	3.1	1.8	2.3	3.9	3.5	-1.1	-5.0	-5.0
Slovakia	–	–	–	4.5	5.5	6.7	8.5	10.5	5.8	-4.8	4.0
Slovenia	–	4.3	3.8	3.7	3.3	4.5	5.9	6.9	3.7	-8.1	1.2
Spain	2.9	3.2	3.2	3.2	2.4	3.6	4.0	3.6	0.9	-3.7	-0.1
Sweden	2.6	3.1	2.8	2.8	2.2	3.2	4.3	3.3	-0.4	-5.1	5.5
Switzerland	2.0	1.5	1.7	1.9	1.9	2.7	3.7	3.7	1.8	-1.9	2.5
United Kingdom	3.3	3.3	2.6	2.3	1.6	2.2	2.8	2.7	-0.1	-5.0	1.3
Developed economies: Oceania	**3.4**	**4.1**	**3.4**	**3.3**	**3.0**	**3.1**	**3.4**	**3.6**	**0.8**	**2.0**	**2.6**
Australia	3.5	4.2	3.5	3.3	3.1	3.1	3.8	3.7	1.1	2.4	2.7
New Zealand	2.3	3.4	2.9	2.7	2.3	3.2	0.9	2.9	-1.4	-0.4	1.5
World n.e.s.	..	..	..	..	..	..	..	..	..	..	..

Sources:
- UN DESA Statistics Division

Notes:

(1) Growth rates are based on gross domestic product at constant 2005 US dollars.
(2) Including Western Sahara.
(3) Data refer to Panama from 1970 to 1980.
(4) Data refer to Germany from 1970 to 1989.

8.2.1 Taux de croissance annuels moyens du produit intérieur brut réel total et par habitant des pays et des régions géographiques

Per capita real gross domestic product (1) / Produit intérieur brut réel par habitant (1) Percentage / En pourcentage											Régions, pays ou territoires
80 -89	92 -00	92 -10 (e)	95 -10 (e)	00 -10 (e)	2005	2006	2007	2008	2009	2010 (e)	
2.6	**2.8**	**1.8**	**1.6**	**1.0**	**2.1**	**1.7**	**1.2**	**-0.5**	**-3.5**	**2.0**	**Économies développées : Amérique**
0.9	3.6	3.3	3.3	3.4	4.9	5.4	4.0	0.4	3.6	1.8	Bermudes
2.1	2.7	1.9	1.8	0.9	1.9	1.7	1.1	-0.5	-3.5	2.0	Canada
1.2	3.1	2.0	1.8	0.9	1.7	4.4	5.9	1.0	-6.5	-6.5	Groenland
2.7	2.8	1.8	1.6	1.0	2.1	1.7	1.2	-0.5	-3.5	2.0	États-Unis
3.8	**0.7**	**0.8**	**0.8**	**0.9**	**1.8**	**2.0**	**2.3**	**-1.2**	**-5.2**	**3.9**	**Économies développées : Asie**
1.7	2.7	1.7	1.5	1.3	3.0	2.9	2.7	1.6	1.9	2.5	Israël
3.9	0.7	0.8	0.8	0.9	1.9	2.0	2.3	-1.3	-5.2	4.0	Japon
2.2	**2.4**	**1.8**	**1.7**	**1.1**	**1.6**	**2.8**	**2.5**	**0.1**	**-4.5**	**1.4**	**Économies développées : Europe**
-0.7	2.8	3.0	3.1	2.3	2.4	4.1	-0.5	2.1	1.7	1.6	Andorre
1.8	2.2	1.8	1.7	1.4	1.9	3.1	3.3	1.8	-4.2	1.7	Autriche
1.8	2.3	1.7	1.5	1.1	1.2	2.1	2.3	0.4	-3.3	1.7	Belgique
4.0	0.4	4.0	4.9	5.5	7.0	7.2	7.1	6.9	-4.3	0.8	Bulgarie
5.1	2.4	1.9	1.7	1.5	2.2	2.6	3.7	2.3	-3.0	-0.2	Chypre
1.9	–	–	–	–	–	–	–	–	–	–	Tchécoslovaquie (anc.)
			3.0	3.5	6.1	6.4	5.6	1.8	-4.7	1.8	République tchèque
2.6	2.5	1.5	1.2	0.6	2.1	3.0	1.2	-1.4	-5.2	1.6	Danemark
–	5.9	6.2	6.2	4.7	9.6	10.7	7.0	-5.0	-13.9	3.1	Estonie
2.9	3.8	2.9	2.7	1.8	2.6	4.0	4.8	0.4	-8.5	2.7	Finlande
1.7	1.8	1.4	1.3	0.7	1.2	1.6	1.8	-0.4	-3.2	1.0	France
2.0	–	–	–	–	–	–	–	–	–	–	Allemagne (anc. Rép. fédérale d') (4)
–	1.5	1.3	1.2	0.9	0.7	3.4	2.7	1.0	-4.6	3.7	Allemagne
0.3	1.9	2.7	3.0	2.5	2.0	4.2	3.9	0.9	-2.6	-4.8	Grèce
2.0	3.0	3.2	3.3	2.3	3.4	3.9	1.0	1.0	-6.5	1.4	Hongrie
2.1	2.8	2.5	2.5	1.8	6.1	3.1	4.3	-0.6	-8.2	-4.9	Islande
2.5	7.8	4.6	3.8	1.3	4.2	3.6	4.0	-4.9	-8.8	-2.3	Irlande
2.4	1.7	0.8	0.5	-0.3	0.0	1.3	0.8	-2.0	-5.6	0.8	Italie
–	3.6	5.8	6.4	5.4	11.3	12.8	10.5	-3.8	-17.6	0.1	Lettonie
–	1.9	5.1	6.0	5.8	8.3	8.4	10.5	3.5	-14.3	1.9	Lituanie
4.7	3.2	3.0	3.0	1.8	4.0	3.1	4.3	-0.9	-5.8	1.5	Luxembourg
1.9	4.3	2.4	2.0	1.5	3.5	3.2	3.3	2.2	-2.4	3.3	Malte
1.7	2.9	1.9	1.7	1.1	1.5	2.9	3.5	1.5	-4.2	1.5	Pays-Bas
2.7	3.4	1.9	1.5	1.0	1.9	1.3	1.6	-0.4	-2.6	-0.7	Norvège
1.5	5.7	4.5	4.2	4.3	3.0	6.2	6.7	5.0	1.6	3.7	Pologne
2.7	3.0	1.6	1.3	0.4	0.4	1.1	2.1	-0.2	-2.8	1.1	Portugal
1.6	1.0	3.4	3.7	5.2	4.5	8.2	6.6	7.6	-6.9	-1.0	Roumanie
3.0	5.3	2.3	1.5	0.1	0.4	2.4	2.5	-1.7	-5.5	-5.6	Saint-Marin
–	–	–	4.4	5.4	6.6	8.4	10.3	5.6	-5.0	3.8	Slovaquie
–	4.0	3.6	3.5	3.1	4.3	5.6	6.6	3.4	-8.4	0.9	Slovénie
2.5	2.9	2.1	2.0	1.0	2.0	2.5	2.2	-0.4	-4.8	-1.1	Espagne
2.3	2.9	2.4	2.4	1.6	2.6	3.6	2.5	-1.2	-5.9	4.8	Suède
1.4	0.8	1.1	1.2	1.2	1.9	2.9	3.0	1.1	-2.5	1.9	Suisse
3.1	3.0	2.1	1.9	1.1	1.6	2.2	2.1	-0.7	-5.6	0.6	Royaume-Uni
1.9	**2.9**	**2.1**	**1.9**	**1.5**	**1.6**	**1.8**	**1.9**	**-0.9**	**0.3**	**1.0**	**Économies développées : Océanie**
2.0	3.0	2.2	2.0	1.5	1.6	2.1	1.9	-0.8	0.6	1.1	Australie
1.5	2.2	1.7	1.5	1.0	1.8	-0.4	1.8	-2.4	-1.5	0.5	Nouvelle-Zélande
..	..	..	..	..	..	..	..	..	..	..	Monde n.d.a.

Sources :
- ONU DAES Division de statistique

Notes :

(1) Les taux de croissance sont basés sur le produit intérieur brut aux prix constants en dollars des États-Unis de 2005.
(2) Y compris le Sahara occidental.
(3) Les données se réfèrent au Panama de 1970 à 1980.
(4) Les données se réfèrent à l'Allemagne de 1970 à 1989.

8

8.2.2 Annual average growth rates of total and per capita real gross domestic product of economic groupings

Region, country or territory	Total real gross domestic product (1) / Produit intérieur brut réel total (1) Percentage / En pourcentage										
	80 - 89	92 - 00	92 - 10 (e)	95 - 10 (e)	00 - 10 (e)	2005	2006	2007	2008	2009	2010 (e)
DEVELOPING ECONOMIES	**3.6**	**4.7**	**5.2**	**5.4**	**6.1**	**6.9**	**7.6**	**8.0**	**5.3**	**2.5**	**7.4**
Developing economies excluding China	3.0	3.9	4.2	4.3	4.8	5.8	6.2	6.2	4.0	0.4	6.4
Developing economies excluding LDCs	3.6	4.7	5.2	5.4	6.1	6.9	7.6	8.0	5.3	2.5	7.5
High-income developing countries	2.7	4.0	4.0	4.0	4.3	5.8	6.1	5.4	3.1	-2.0	6.7
Middle-income developing countries	4.4	5.5	6.3	6.4	7.5	7.7	8.9	10.2	7.1	4.9	8.2
Low-income developing countries	4.1	4.7	5.6	5.8	6.9	7.6	7.9	8.1	5.6	6.0	7.1
Heavily indebted poor countries (IMF)	1.5	3.7	4.6	4.9	5.4	5.9	6.1	6.2	5.6	4.4	4.8
Landlocked developing countries	2.5	1.2	5.0	6.1	7.2	8.3	9.1	9.0	5.8	3.6	6.5
Small island developing States	1.4	2.3	0.1	0.3	3.0	3.5	6.6	4.0	1.8	-1.4	1.3
Least developed countries	*2.2*	*4.7*	*5.9*	*6.3*	*6.9*	*7.7*	*7.7*	*8.6*	*7.0*	*4.6*	*5.1*
Africa and Haiti	1.7	4.2	5.7	6.2	7.0	8.0	8.0	9.1	7.6	3.7	4.3
Asia	3.4	5.6	6.3	6.5	6.9	7.4	7.2	7.7	6.1	6.2	6.3
Islands	2.4	2.3	3.9	4.3	5.6	4.3	3.2	7.5	3.8	1.9	3.3
Major petroleum and gas exporters	*-0.3*	*2.6*	*4.3*	*4.9*	*5.9*	*7.2*	*7.0*	*6.4*	*6.2*	*1.2*	*3.6*
Africa	0.1	2.2	4.9	5.7	7.0	6.2	6.1	6.3	6.4	2.9	5.5
America	0.6	0.9	2.2	2.7	4.5	10.3	9.9	8.2	4.8	-3.3	-1.4
Asia	-0.6	3.2	4.6	5.0	5.9	7.0	6.8	6.1	6.4	1.4	3.9
Major exporters of manufactured goods	*6.1*	*6.4*	*6.5*	*6.5*	*7.0*	*7.4*	*8.8*	*9.4*	*5.8*	*3.4*	*8.9*
America	0.8	3.3	2.8	2.9	2.1	3.3	4.8	3.4	1.5	-6.5	5.4
Asia	9.3	7.4	7.4	7.3	8.0	8.3	9.6	10.6	6.6	5.1	9.5
Emerging economies	*3.5*	*4.1*	*3.7*	*3.6*	*3.8*	*4.2*	*5.2*	*5.4*	*3.1*	*-1.8*	*7.4*
America	1.7	3.2	3.0	3.1	3.4	4.0	4.9	5.3	4.0	-2.6	6.8
Asia	8.5	5.6	4.8	4.4	4.3	4.6	5.5	5.6	2.1	-0.9	8.1
Newly industrialized Asian countries	*7.3*	*4.9*	*4.5*	*4.3*	*4.5*	*4.9*	*5.7*	*5.8*	*2.7*	*-0.2*	*7.7*
First tier	8.8	5.5	4.7	4.4	4.3	4.8	5.7	5.7	1.9	-0.8	8.1
Second tier	4.7	3.6	4.0	3.9	5.0	5.2	5.5	6.1	4.5	1.1	6.9
Developing economies: Africa	**1.8**	**3.2**	**4.3**	**4.6**	**5.3**	**5.5**	**6.1**	**5.9**	**5.1**	**1.6**	**4.5**
Northern Africa excluding Sudan	2.9	3.2	4.0	4.3	4.6	5.8	5.5	4.8	4.1	1.2	4.0
Sub-Saharan Africa	1.4	3.2	4.5	4.8	5.6	5.4	6.4	6.5	5.6	1.8	4.7
Sub-Saharan Africa excluding South Africa	1.4	3.5	5.2	5.7	6.7	5.4	6.8	7.2	6.8	3.8	5.7
Developing economies: America	**1.8**	**3.1**	**3.1**	**3.2**	**3.6**	**4.6**	**5.5**	**5.6**	**4.0**	**-2.1**	**5.9**
Central America and Greater Caribbean Islands excluding Puerto Rico	1.0	3.3	3.0	3.1	2.6	3.9	5.4	4.1	2.0	-5.1	5.0
Central America and Greater Caribbean Islands excluding Mexico and Puerto Rico	2.2	3.7	4.1	4.3	4.7	6.7	8.2	7.0	4.1	0.7	3.6
South America and Central America	1.7	3.1	3.0	3.1	3.6	4.5	5.3	5.6	4.0	-2.2	6.0
South America excluding Brazil	1.1	2.9	3.2	3.3	4.8	7.5	7.3	7.3	5.4	-0.4	5.3
Developing economies: Asia	**5.5**	**5.9**	**6.3**	**6.4**	**7.2**	**8.1**	**8.7**	**9.1**	**5.8**	**4.3**	**8.4**
Eastern and South-Eastern Asia excluding China	7.0	4.8	4.6	4.4	4.6	5.1	5.8	6.0	2.9	0.0	7.7
Southern Asia excluding India	3.1	3.7	4.7	5.0	5.5	6.1	6.4	7.3	3.0	3.5	3.5

Sources:
- UN DESA Statistics Division

Notes:

(1) Growth rates are based on gross domestic product at constant 2005 U.S. dollars.

8.2.2 Taux de croissance annuels moyens du produit intérieur brut réel total et par habitant des groupements économiques

80 - 89	92 - 00	92 - 10 (e)	95 - 10 (e)	00 - 10 (e)	2005	2006	2007	2008	2009	2010 (e)	Régions, pays ou territoires
1.4	3.0	3.7	3.9	4.7	5.5	6.2	6.5	3.9	1.2	6.0	**ÉCONOMIES EN DÉVELOPPEMENT**
0.6	1.9	2.4	2.5	3.1	4.1	4.5	4.5	2.4	-1.2	4.8	Économies en développement sans la Chine
1.5	3.2	3.8	4.0	4.8	5.6	6.3	6.7	4.0	1.3	6.3	Économies en développement sans les PMA
0.6	2.5	2.5	2.5	2.8	4.3	4.6	3.8	1.6	-3.5	5.2	Pays en développement à revenu élevé
2.5	4.2	5.2	5.4	6.5	6.8	7.9	9.3	6.2	4.1	7.3	Pays en développement à revenu intermédiaire
1.6	2.5	3.6	3.9	5.0	5.7	0.0	0.2	0.0	1.2	6.2	Pays en développement à revenu faible
-1.1	0.9	1.9	2.1	2.7	3.1	3.4	3.5	2.9	1.8	2.2	Pays pauvres très endettés (FMI)
-0.1	-1.1	3.7	3.5	4.0	0.0	0.0	0.7	2.6	1.1	1.3	Pays en développement sans littoral
-0.4	1.6	1.3	1.3	1.2	1.8	4.9	2.4	0.3	-2.8	-0.2	Petits États insulaires en développement
-0.4	*2.0*	*3.4*	*3.8*	*4.5*	*5.3*	*5.3*	*6.2*	*4.7*	*2.3*	*2.8*	*Pays les moins avancés*
-1.1	1.4	2.9	3.3	4.1	5.1	5.2	6.2	4.8	0.9	1.6	Afrique et Haïti
1.1	3.2	4.3	4.6	5.2	5.7	5.6	6.2	4.7	4.7	4.8	Asie
-0.1	0.0	-1.9	-2.3	-1.7	1.4	0.7	5.2	1.7	-0.2	1.0	Îles
-3.3	*0.4*	*2.0*	*2.5*	*3.5*	*4.8*	*4.5*	*3.9*	*3.7*	*-1.2*	*1.3*	*Principaux exportateurs de pétrole et de gaz*
-2.6	-0.1	2.5	3.3	4.5	3.7	3.7	3.8	3.9	0.5	3.0	Afrique
-2.1	-1.2	0.3	0.8	2.7	8.4	8.0	6.3	3.0	-4.9	-3.0	Amérique
-4.3	1.1	2.3	2.7	3.4	4.5	4.1	3.4	3.7	-1.1	1.5	Asie
4.4	*5.3*	*5.6*	*5.7*	*6.3*	*6.8*	*8.1*	*8.7*	*5.1*	*2.8*	*8.3*	*Principaux exportateurs d'articles manufacturés*
-1.2	1.5	1.3	1.5	0.8	2.0	3.5	2.1	0.2	-7.7	4.1	Amérique
7.6	6.3	6.6	6.6	7.3	7.7	9.0	9.9	6.0	4.6	8.9	Asie
1.5	*2.7*	*2.5*	*2.4*	*2.7*	*3.1*	*4.1*	*4.4*	*2.1*	*-2.7*	*6.4*	*Économies émergentes*
-0.3	1.7	1.7	1.8	2.2	2.8	3.7	4.2	2.9	-3.5	5.8	Amérique
6.5	4.4	3.7	3.4	3.4	3.6	4.6	4.7	1.2	-1.6	7.3	Asie
5.1	*3.3*	*3.1*	*2.9*	*3.3*	*3.7*	*4.4*	*4.6*	*1.6*	*-1.3*	*6.6*	*Économies nouvellement industrialisées d'Asie*
7.2	4.6	4.0	3.8	3.7	4.3	5.1	5.0	1.1	-1.5	7.5	Première génération
2.5	1.9	2.5	2.4	3.6	3.8	4.1	4.8	3.3	0.0	5.7	Deuxième génération
-0.9	*0.7*	*1.9*	*2.2*	*2.9*	*3.1*	*3.6*	*3.5*	*2.7*	*-0.7*	*2.1*	*Économies en développement : Afrique*
0.2	1.5	2.4	2.7	3.0	4.2	3.8	3.1	2.5	-0.3	2.5	Afrique septentrionale sans le Soudan
-1.4	0.6	1.9	2.3	3.0	2.8	3.8	4.0	3.1	-0.7	2.2	Afrique subsaharienne
-1.5	0.9	2.5	3.0	4.0	2.8	4.1	4.5	4.1	1.2	3.1	Afrique subsaharienne sans l'Afrique du Sud
-0.3	*1.4*	*1.6*	*1.8*	*2.3*	*3.3*	*4.2*	*4.4*	*2.8*	*-3.2*	*4.7*	*Économies en développement : Amérique*
-0.9	1.6	1.6	1.7	1.3	2.5	4.1	2.8	0.7	-6.3	3.7	Amérique centrale et Grandes Antilles sans Porto Rico
0.3	2.0	2.6	2.8	3.2	5.2	6.7	5.6	2.8	-0.6	2.3	Amérique centrale et Grandes Antilles sans le Mexique et Porto Rico
-0.4	1.4	1.6	1.7	2.3	3.2	4.0	4.4	2.8	-3.4	4.8	Amérique du Sud et Amérique centrale
-0.9	1.2	1.7	1.9	3.5	6.1	5.9	6.0	4.1	-1.6	4.0	Amérique du Sud sans le Brésil
3.4	*4.3*	*4.9*	*5.1*	*6.0*	*6.8*	*7.4*	*7.9*	*4.7*	*3.2*	*7.2*	*Économies en développement : Asie*
4.8	3.3	3.2	3.1	3.5	3.9	4.6	4.9	1.8	-1.1	6.6	Asie orientale et Asie du Sud-Est sans la Chine
0.3	1.4	2.7	3.1	3.8	4.4	4.7	5.7	1.5	2.0	1.9	Asie méridionale sans l'Inde

Sources :
- ONU DAES Division de statistique

Notes :
(1) Les taux de croissance sont basés sur le produit intérieur brut aux prix constants en dollars des États-Unis de 2005.

423

8

8.3.1 Nominal gross domestic product by type of expenditure and by kind of economic activity of countries and geographical regions

8.3.1 Produit intérieur brut nominal par catégories de dépenses et par branches d'activité économique des pays et des régions géographiques

Region, country or territory / Régions, pays ou territoires	Year / Année	Total GDP / PIB total	GDP by type of expenditure (1) / PIB par catégories de dépense (1)					GDP by kind of economic activity (2) / PIB par branches d'activité économique (2)			
			Final consumption / Consommation finale		Gross capital formation / Formation brute de capital	Exports / Exportations	Less imports / Moins les importations	Agriculture (3)	Industry (4) / Industrie (4)		Services (5)
			Government / Administration publique	Household / Ménages		Of goods and services / Des biens et services			Total	Manufacturing / Activités de fabrication	
			Percentage / En pourcentage								
WORLD - MONDE	**1990**	**100.0**	**17.3**	**59.2**	**23.5**	**19.6**	**19.9**	**5.4**	**32.8**	**21.7**	**61.9**
	1995	**100.0**	**16.8**	**60.0**	**22.7**	**21.6**	**21.2**	**4.3**	**30.6**	**20.4**	**65.1**
	2000	**100.0**	**16.3**	**61.2**	**22.4**	**24.8**	**24.7**	**3.6**	**29.1**	**19.2**	**67.2**
	2009	**100.0**	**18.3**	**59.7**	**21.1**	**28.3**	**27.3**	**4.0**	**29.0**	**17.6**	**67.0**
DEVELOPING ECONOMIES - ÉCONOMIES EN DÉVELOPPEMENT	1990	100.0	13.8	59.3	25.2	25.9	24.9	14.2	35.6	21.7	50.3
	1995	100.0	13.7	59.0	27.4	29.7	30.0	11.9	35.2	22.5	52.9
	2000	100.0	14.1	58.4	24.9	34.8	32.3	10.3	36.3	22.6	53.4
	2009	100.0	14.3	53.3	30.1	38.0	34.5	9.7	39.2	24.3	51.1
TRANSITION ECONOMIES - ÉCONOMIES EN TRANSITION	1990	100.0	20.9	49.1	28.1	22.7	24.7	17.7	38.0	28.6	44.3
	1995	100.0	19.5	55.9	24.5	32.0	31.8	10.7	38.7	21.5	50.6
	2000	100.0	16.1	52.8	19.2	45.0	33.1	10.3	37.6	21.5	52.1
	2009	100.0	19.1	56.5	20.3	32.3	27.8	6.4	33.4	15.4	60.3
DEVELOPED ECONOMIES - ÉCONOMIES DÉVELOPPÉES	1990	100.0	17.9	59.7	22.9	18.0	18.6	2.8	31.9	21.4	65.4
	1995	100.0	17.6	60.3	21.5	19.4	18.7	2.2	29.3	19.8	68.5
	2000	100.0	16.9	62.1	21.8	21.7	22.5	1.7	27.0	18.2	71.3
	2009	100.0	19.9	62.7	17.3	23.9	24.2	1.4	24.3	14.7	74.3
Developing economies: Africa - Économies en développement : Afrique	**1990**	**100.0**	**16.4**	**63.9**	**20.3**	**26.3**	**25.7**	**18.3**	**35.2**	**15.0**	**46.7**
	1995	**100.0**	**16.2**	**66.4**	**19.0**	**26.3**	**28.3**	**17.0**	**32.9**	**14.8**	**50.2**
	2000	**100.0**	**15.2**	**63.0**	**17.6**	**31.7**	**27.4**	**15.4**	**35.3**	**12.6**	**49.3**
	2009	**100.0**	**14.9**	**62.8**	**22.5**	**33.2**	**33.2**	**16.8**	**37.9**	**10.1**	**45.2**
Eastern Africa - Afrique orientale	*1990*	*100.0*	*17.7*	*71.3*	*19.1*	*17.9*	*25.5*	*32.1*	*23.0*	*15.3*	*45.6*
	1995	*100.0*	*14.3*	*76.1*	*18.6*	*24.5*	*33.4*	*32.8*	*19.2*	*11.2*	*48.6*
	2000	*100.0*	*14.2*	*76.6*	*19.1*	*21.0*	*30.2*	*30.9*	*18.5*	*10.3*	*50.7*
	2009	*100.0*	*13.5*	*78.8*	*22.5*	*22.9*	*35.8*	*29.3*	*20.5*	*9.3*	*50.1*
Burundi	1990	100.0	13.5	89.8	12.3	4.5	19.6	61.9	14.9	10.2	23.2
	1995	100.0	7.4	97.3	10.2	9.6	22.7	55.6	15.5	9.8	28.9
	2000	100.0	8.1	96.8	8.3	5.8	17.6	45.5	15.2	10.4	39.3
	2009	100.0	10.6	88.5	14.8	4.6	18.5	45.5	14.5	9.7	40.0
Comoros - Comores	1990	100.0	25.7	79.7	20.2	11.7	37.3	40.4	8.1	4.1	51.5
	1995	100.0	22.3	83.1	19.5	19.8	44.6	39.9	11.7	4.1	48.5
	2000	100.0	11.7	94.0	10.1	16.7	32.5	47.7	11.3	4.5	41.0
	2009	100.0	15.7	100.8	13.4	14.9	44.9	48.2	10.5	4.1	41.4
Djibouti	1990	100.0	33.6	67.2	27.1	81.4	109.3	3.1	22.0	3.6	74.9
	1995	100.0	35.4	62.6	18.7	39.2	55.8	3.2	15.4	2.9	81.3
	2000	100.0	25.8	81.6	12.2	44.0	63.6	3.5	15.4	2.6	81.1
	2009	100.0	19.9	68.4	16.0	50.7	53.9	3.7	17.9	2.7	78.4
Eritrea - Érythrée	1995	100.0	38.4	96.1	22.3	21.0	77.8	20.9	16.8	9.0	62.3
	2000	100.0	54.8	71.7	22.0	9.7	58.2	15.1	23.0	11.2	61.9
	2009	100.0	20.0	86.9	9.1	4.5	20.5	24.2	18.9	5.8	56.9
Ethiopia - Éthiopie	1995	100.0	7.9	85.5	12.7	10.3	19.0	56.7	9.9	4.7	33.4
	2000	100.0	17.9	73.1	20.3	12.0	23.9	49.4	12.2	5.5	38.4
	2009	100.0	8.2	90.8	22.4	10.5	28.6	46.7	12.6	4.4	40.7
Ethiopia (former) - Éthiopie (anc.)	1990	100.0	19.2	72.9	12.5	7.7	12.2	41.1	16.4	11.1	42.5
Kenya	1990	100.0	18.3	68.8	18.0	20.2	24.7	29.9	20.9	13.9	49.2
	1995	100.0	14.5	76.6	16.2	25.4	30.4	32.6	17.8	11.9	49.6
	2000	100.0	15.3	78.1	17.6	22.3	30.5	32.8	17.3	11.5	49.9
	2009	100.0	16.3	80.0	20.9	25.3	38.0	27.1	18.4	10.4	54.4
Madagascar	1990	100.0	8.0	86.0	17.0	15.9	26.9	31.8	14.0	12.2	54.1
	1995	100.0	6.7	89.9	10.9	24.1	31.7	32.3	14.8	11.9	52.8
	2000	100.0	7.9	83.5	16.2	31.1	38.7	28.9	15.9	12.2	55.2
	2009	100.0	11.0	84.2	23.5	23.8	41.9	26.8	19.5	14.5	53.7

For sources and notes, see end of table.

Pour les sources et les notes, se reporter à la fin du tableau.

8.3.1 Nominal gross domestic product by type of expenditure and by kind of economic activity of countries and geographical regions

8.3.1 Produit intérieur brut nominal par catégories de dépenses et par branches d'activité économique des pays et des régions géographiques

Region, country or territory / Régions, pays ou territoires	Year / Année	Total GDP / PIB total	GDP by type of expenditure (1) / PIB par catégories de dépense (1)					GDP by kind of economic activity (2) / PIB par branches d'activité économique (2)			
			Final consumption / Consommation finale		Gross capital formation / Formation brute de capital	Exports / Exportations	Less imports / Moins les importations	Agriculture (3)	Industry (4) / Industrie (4)		Services (5)
			Government / Administration publique	Household / Ménages		Of goods and services / Des biens et services			Total	Manufacturing / Activités de fabrication	
			Percentage / En pourcentage								
Malawi	1990	100.0	9.4	75.1	23.7	22.0	29.5	41.6	30.1	19.5	28.3
	1995	100.0	12.7	70.0	16.4	28.0	31.1	27.4	19.9	12.9	52.7
	2000	100.0	8.5	78.6	20.0	21.8	28.8	35.2	18.3	11.4	49.4
	2009	100.0	14.5	89.3	25.3	22.5	46.8	29.1	16.1	10.0	54.8
Mauritius - Maurice	1990	100.0	12.7	64.6	30.3	66.8	74.3	12.1	33.8	26.0	54.0
	1995	100.0	13.1	63.7	25.6	58.6	61.1	10.0	30.9	22.2	59.1
	2000	100.0	14.1	60.3	26.1	61.4	61.9	6.6	29.3	22.2	64.1
	2009	100.0	14.4	74.2	21.8	47.1	57.4	4.0	27.0	18.4	69.0
Mozambique	1990	100.0	11.0	104.9	17.2	6.4	37.2	37.1	18.4	12.7	44.5
	1995	100.0	9.7	99.4	30.6	12.6	52.4	33.9	14.2	7.4	51.9
	2000	100.0	11.5	80.1	33.5	12.7	37.8	23.6	24.1	12.0	52.3
	2009	100.0	13.1	79.3	20.3	21.1	32.5	27.9	24.6	14.7	47.4
Rwanda	1990	100.0	20.0	77.8	10.9	5.5	13.2	43.1	18.6	12.1	38.3
	1995	100.0	18.1	92.8	10.6	5.7	27.2	43.3	12.3	7.7	44.4
	2000	100.0	17.6	83.1	14.2	6.1	21.8	39.2	15.2	7.4	45.6
	2009	100.0	14.5	81.3	21.6	11.6	29.0	36.1	15.3	6.8	48.6
Seychelles	1990	100.0	27.7	52.0	24.6	62.5	66.7	5.3	7.7	4.0	87.0
	1995	100.0	27.7	51.0	30.1	60.5	75.2	4.7	11.1	5.1	84.2
	2000	100.0	27.1	39.4	36.2	62.5	65.1	4.0	16.3	9.6	79.7
	2009	100.0	13.7	67.2	33.8	116.0	130.8	2.6	16.4	8.9	81.0
Somalia - Somalie	1990	100.0	10.3	71.0	23.6	0.9	5.7	69.3	6.0	2.0	24.7
	1995	100.0	8.5	72.2	20.7	0.3	1.7	60.1	7.3	2.5	32.6
	2000	100.0	8.6	72.3	20.5	0.3	1.7	60.2	7.3	2.5	32.5
	2009	100.0	8.7	72.6	20.0	0.3	1.7	60.2	7.4	2.5	32.5
Uganda - Ouganda	1990	100.0	9.9	80.1	14.1	6.2	16.1	42.5	14.2	5.3	43.3
	1995	100.0	11.9	76.0	16.1	9.9	17.8	36.6	18.1	6.4	45.3
	2000	100.0	14.0	79.2	18.1	9.7	21.6	28.9	22.5	7.5	48.6
	2009	100.0	10.3	83.7	21.4	19.5	34.7	23.0	24.9	7.5	52.1
United Republic of Tanzania - République-Unie de Tanzanie	1990	100.0	29.1	53.7	41.4	10.2	27.5	33.1	19.4	12.0	54.6
	1995	100.0	22.7	73.1	24.3	21.9	36.5	36.9	19.3	10.1	49.7
	2000	100.0	11.7	78.3	16.7	13.4	20.1	33.0	18.9	9.2	48.1
	2009	100.0	16.4	68.0	27.5	24.2	36.3	30.2	22.6	8.4	47.2
Zambia - Zambie	1990	100.0	19.0	63.2	17.3	35.9	36.6	20.6	51.3	36.1	28.1
	1995	100.0	15.5	72.3	15.9	36.1	39.8	17.3	33.6	10.6	49.1
	2000	100.0	9.5	82.1	18.7	21.1	31.4	21.0	23.8	10.8	55.2
	2009	100.0	21.4	54.9	24.1	35.2	32.4	20.9	32.8	9.3	46.3
Zimbabwe	1990	100.0	19.4	63.1	17.4	22.9	22.8	16.1	32.4	22.3	51.5
	1995	100.0	17.9	59.3	25.4	38.0	40.7	14.9	28.5	21.4	56.6
	2000	100.0	17.3	74.4	13.1	32.7	32.9	20.2	16.5	11.7	63.3
	2009	100.0	5.1	81.3	17.0	28.4	31.9	17.5	20.8	15.9	61.8
Middle Africa - Afrique centrale	*1990*	*100.0*	*20.7*	*60.6*	*14.1*	*32.5*	*26.6*	*22.1*	*33.7*	*10.6*	*44.2*
	1995	*100.0*	*20.8*	*55.1*	*18.7*	*40.8*	*36.6*	*25.7*	*37.6*	*9.7*	*36.6*
	2000	*100.0*	*19.6*	*47.9*	*15.5*	*53.7*	*37.5*	*19.4*	*50.1*	*8.1*	*30.5*
	2009	*100.0*	*17.6*	*50.2*	*19.8*	*51.7*	*38.4*	*14.8*	*58.5*	*5.2*	*26.8*
Angola	1990	100.0	28.6	44.8	11.7	39.0	23.7	18.0	40.8	4.9	41.2
	1995	100.0	52.3	21.9	27.9	76.2	78.2	7.4	67.4	4.0	25.2
	2000	100.0	42.5	15.6	12.7	89.6	62.8	5.8	72.8	3.0	21.4
	2009	100.0	26.1	44.9	17.5	53.1	41.5	8.6	70.9	0.9	20.5
Cameroon - Cameroun	1990	100.0	12.8	68.9	17.9	20.5	20.1	21.7	30.5	19.8	47.8
	1995	100.0	9.0	70.9	14.5	23.5	17.8	23.7	29.8	19.9	46.5
	2000	100.0	9.5	70.2	16.7	23.3	19.7	22.0	35.8	20.7	42.3
	2009	100.0	13.9	73.8	16.6	24.0	28.4	22.2	31.0	16.0	46.8

For sources and notes, see end of table.

Pour les sources et les notes, se reporter à la fin du tableau.

8

8.3.1 Nominal gross domestic product by type of expenditure and by kind of economic activity of countries and geographical regions

8.3.1 Produit intérieur brut nominal par catégories de dépenses et par branches d'activité économique des pays et des régions géographiques

Region, country or territory / Régions, pays ou territoires	Year / Année	Total GDP / PIB total	GDP by type of expenditure (1) / PIB par catégories de dépense (1)					GDP by kind of economic activity (2) / PIB par branches d'activité économique (2)			
			Final consumption / Consommation finale		Gross capital formation / Formation brute de capital	Exports / Exportations / Of goods and services / Des biens et services	Less imports / Moins les importations	Agriculture (3)	Industry (4) / Industrie (4)		Services (5)
			Government / Administration publique	Household / Ménages					Total	Manufacturing / Activités de fabrication	
			Percentage / En pourcentage								
Central African Republic - République centrafricaine	1990	100.0	15.4	80.7	12.7	17.1	25.9	47.6	19.7	11.3	32.7
	1995	100.0	14.0	73.2	16.9	17.2	18.5	58.1	17.2	7.1	24.7
	2000	100.0	16.3	77.6	11.1	20.4	25.3	59.3	16.7	7.0	24.0
	2009	100.0	9.6	89.4	11.8	11.5	22.3	58.4	15.2	7.0	26.4
Chad - Tchad	1990	100.0	47.3	51.7	7.2	19.0	24.8	39.2	17.0	14.6	43.8
	1995	100.0	50.1	54.8	9.7	22.8	37.2	37.0	13.9	11.9	49.1
	2000	100.0	39.4	65.8	17.5	20.0	42.7	42.3	11.3	9.1	46.4
	2009	100.0	29.4	35.4	20.2	44.0	28.9	20.6	53.6	5.8	25.8
Congo	1990	100.0	20.4	52.7	15.9	50.2	39.1	12.9	40.6	8.3	46.5
	1995	100.0	17.9	50.4	41.5	55.7	65.5	10.9	46.9	8.5	42.2
	2000	100.0	11.1	27.7	19.7	81.8	40.3	5.4	73.9	3.6	20.7
	2009	100.0	12.3	45.4	24.9	67.6	50.2	4.3	73.7	3.9	22.0
Dem. Rep. of the Congo - Rép. dém. du Congo	1990	100.0	13.6	81.8	9.1	31.8	31.8	31.8	27.3	9.1	40.9
	1995	100.0	4.9	81.0	9.4	28.5	23.7	57.0	17.0	4.9	26.0
	2000	100.0	6.5	88.3	3.5	22.4	20.7	50.0	20.3	4.8	29.7
	2009	100.0	12.1	87.2	19.4	45.2	63.9	41.9	27.5	5.7	30.5
Equatorial Guinea - Guinée équatoriale	1990	100.0	11.4	69.2	54.4	31.8	66.8	61.9	10.6	1.6	27.6
	1995	100.0	13.0	41.2	79.2	55.9	89.3	55.3	28.2	1.0	16.5
	2000	100.0	4.9	19.0	61.9	105.2	90.9	8.3	88.1	0.2	3.7
	2009	100.0	2.8	7.4	25.7	97.4	33.3	3.2	92.6	0.2	4.2
Gabon	1990	100.0	28.3	38.3	18.5	45.9	29.7	7.3	43.0	5.6	49.7
	1995	100.0	22.6	30.7	17.8	53.4	32.7	8.1	52.5	4.5	39.4
	2000	100.0	14.5	33.4	17.2	62.3	28.5	6.4	58.0	3.7	35.7
	2009	100.0	17.8	33.9	23.1	58.8	25.1	4.6	61.5	4.4	33.9
Sao Tome and Principe - Sao Tomé-et-Principe	1990	100.0	27.6	100.8	29.5	14.5	72.5	27.6	17.9	7.1	54.5
	1995	100.0	27.6	83.8	68.1	20.6	100.1	26.4	19.6	7.8	53.9
	2000	100.0	31.6	92.4	35.8	35.1	95.0	20.0	17.3	6.9	62.6
	2009	100.0	38.5	85.1	65.0	25.3	113.9	16.7	21.0	6.4	62.4
Northern Africa - Afrique septentrionale	*1990*	*100.0*	*14.8*	*61.8*	*25.6*	*27.1*	*28.9*	*15.7*	*37.1*	*13.4*	*47.2*
	1995	*100.0*	*14.7*	*66.8*	*21.5*	*24.9*	*28.6*	*15.6*	*34.3*	*14.0*	*50.2*
	2000	*100.0*	*14.1*	*62.1*	*19.8*	*29.2*	*25.1*	*13.1*	*37.3*	*12.3*	*49.5*
	2009	*100.0*	*14.2*	*58.1*	*28.5*	*33.0*	*33.9*	*12.2*	*45.2*	*11.0*	*42.6*
Algeria - Algérie	1990	100.0	16.2	56.6	28.9	23.4	25.1	11.9	48.3	11.6	39.8
	1995	100.0	17.0	55.6	31.6	26.6	30.7	10.3	47.9	8.9	41.8
	2000	100.0	13.6	41.6	23.5	42.1	20.7	8.8	56.7	6.0	34.5
	2009	100.0	16.1	35.7	49.2	34.1	35.0	8.0	61.7	4.4	30.3
Egypt - Égypte	1990	100.0	8.6	71.5	28.3	27.4	33.8	16.2	34.0	18.6	49.8
	1995	100.0	10.4	76.9	16.6	20.8	26.6	17.3	31.6	17.7	51.1
	2000	100.0	11.1	76.8	17.7	19.1	24.7	14.7	29.9	15.9	55.4
	2009	100.0	11.4	76.1	19.2	25.0	31.6	13.6	37.6	16.6	48.8
Libyan Arab Jamahiriya - Jamahiriya arabe libyenne	1990	100.0	24.4	48.4	18.6	39.7	31.1	6.6	39.7	6.6	53.7
	1995	100.0	22.3	58.8	12.2	29.2	22.4	6.7	40.3	7.2	53.0
	2000	100.0	20.6	46.4	13.0	35.2	15.3	6.5	47.6	5.4	45.9
	2009	100.0	12.6	36.6	9.7	68.1	27.0	2.6	72.5	6.0	24.9
Morocco - Maroc (6)	1990	100.0	14.4	61.1	29.6	26.5	30.9	20.0	28.6	18.6	51.4
	1995	100.0	16.4	64.7	24.3	24.7	30.5	16.2	27.2	18.2	56.6
	2000	100.0	18.4	61.4	25.5	28.0	33.4	14.2	27.7	17.5	58.1
	2009	100.0	17.9	60.9	32.6	28.3	39.7	14.3	26.8	14.3	58.8
Sudan - Soudan	1990	100.0	5.8	84.5	11.2	4.0	7.1	40.6	15.3	8.7	44.2
	1995	100.0	6.3	78.3	22.1	6.3	13.0	47.0	12.1	6.3	40.9
	2000	100.0	5.5	86.0	11.5	14.6	17.6	36.7	17.1	5.6	45.2
	2009	100.0	14.4	68.4	22.7	16.0	22.2	28.8	29.3	6.4	41.9

For sources and notes, see end of table.

Pour les sources et les notes, se reporter à la fin du tableau.

8.3.1 Nominal gross domestic product by type of expenditure and by kind of economic activity of countries and geographical regions

8.3.1 Produit intérieur brut nominal par catégories de dépenses et par branches d'activité économique des pays et des régions géographiques

Region, country or territory / Régions, pays ou territoires	Year / Année	Total GDP / PIB total	Final consumption / Consommation finale — Government / Administration publique	Final consumption — Household / Ménages	Gross capital formation / Formation brute de capital	Exports / Exportations — Of goods and services / Des biens et services	Less imports / Moins les importations — Of goods and services / Des biens et services	Agriculture / Agriculture (3)	Industry (4) / Industrie (4) — Total	Industry (4) — Manufacturing / Activités de fabrication	Services (5)
						Percentage / En pourcentage					
Tunisia Tunisie	1990	100.0	16.4	62.6	27.1	40.6	60.0	17.2	32.1	20.2	50.7
	1995	100.0	16.3	62.9	24.7	44.9	48.8	12.6	32.5	22.0	54.9
	2000	100.0	15.6	60.7	27.3	44.5	48.2	13.8	31.9	20.4	54.3
	2009	100.0	14.4	62.8	26.2	49.9	53.3	10.6	34.0	17.1	55.4
Southern Africa / *Afrique australe*	*1990*	*100.0*	*19.9*	*60.6*	*18.8*	*25.9*	*21.8*	*4.9*	*40.6*	*23.0*	*54.4*
	1995	*100.0*	*18.8*	*62.3*	*18.7*	*24.5*	*24.6*	*4.2*	*35.2*	*20.7*	*60.6*
	2000	*100.0*	*18.7*	*62.6*	*16.5*	*29.7*	*27.3*	*3.6*	*32.6*	*18.4*	*63.8*
	2009	*100.0*	*21.1*	*60.6*	*19.6*	*28.8*	*30.5*	*3.3*	*31.7*	*14.9*	*65.0*
Botswana	1990	100.0	24.4	36.1	37.0	53.5	51.9	4.3	59.5	5.2	36.2
	1995	100.0	28.9	37.7	27.1	50.7	43.7	4.9	48.8	5.2	46.4
	2000	100.0	25.4	33.4	31.8	53.3	41.2	2.7	52.6	4.5	44.7
	2009	100.0	24.2	43.7	24.0	37.7	43.2	3.1	40.0	4.2	56.8
Lesotho	1990	100.0	27.4	153.7	55.7	15.8	155.1	18.6	19.0	9.6	62.4
	1995	100.0	34.9	128.8	63.8	20.0	151.8	13.2	26.5	9.4	60.3
	2000	100.0	36.1	123.5	43.8	35.5	137.8	12.0	30.8	13.7	57.2
	2009	100.0	50.2	86.3	30.2	50.3	117.8	8.5	34.4	19.8	57.2
Namibia - Namibie	1990	100.0	25.1	50.5	29.6	46.7	59.0	13.3	39.5	16.8	47.1
	1995	100.0	24.6	56.7	19.0	44.3	48.6	13.6	29.3	15.0	57.1
	2000	100.0	23.5	60.8	17.1	40.9	44.5	11.6	27.5	12.6	60.9
	2009	100.0	22.6	63.3	24.1	55.6	64.0	9.9	32.8	14.5	57.3
South Africa - Afrique du Sud	1990	100.0	19.7	61.0	17.7	24.2	18.8	4.6	40.1	23.6	55.3
	1995	100.0	18.3	62.6	18.2	22.8	22.1	3.9	34.8	21.2	61.3
	2000	100.0	18.1	63.4	15.7	27.9	24.9	3.3	31.8	19.0	64.9
	2009	100.0	20.8	60.8	19.3	27.1	28.0	3.0	31.1	15.1	65.8
Swaziland	1990	100.0	15.3	84.4	16.2	59.5	72.8	9.8	43.4	36.7	46.8
	1995	100.0	16.1	85.0	16.7	60.6	76.5	12.0	46.2	39.3	41.8
	2000	100.0	18.3	77.3	18.1	74.4	88.1	11.9	43.3	37.6	44.8
	2009	100.0	13.7	88.2	10.3	55.5	67.7	7.7	45.2	41.4	47.1
Western Africa - / *Afrique occidentale*	*1990*	*100.0*	*11.4*	*69.9*	*14.0*	*28.3*	*23.3*	*31.8*	*32.0*	*9.6*	*36.2*
	1995	*100.0*	*14.0*	*70.9*	*13.4*	*30.2*	*28.2*	*32.0*	*32.9*	*9.2*	*35.1*
	2000	*100.0*	*11.6*	*61.8*	*12.4*	*42.2*	*27.8*	*28.1*	*39.7*	*7.7*	*32.2*
	2009	*100.0*	*8.8*	*71.3*	*14.3*	*37.1*	*31.5*	*35.3*	*30.5*	*5.2*	*34.2*
Benin - Bénin	1990	100.0	13.2	80.4	14.2	20.4	28.2	35.4	12.7	7.5	51.9
	1995	100.0	14.5	73.2	21.4	27.4	36.4	35.4	14.3	8.6	50.3
	2000	100.0	12.6	73.1	18.7	25.4	29.7	37.8	14.0	8.9	48.2
	2009	100.0	12.6	72.1	24.6	17.2	26.5	35.0	14.0	8.1	51.0
Burkina Faso	1990	100.0	21.1	73.5	18.9	11.0	24.5	28.8	21.0	14.3	50.3
	1995	100.0	25.2	63.3	23.9	14.1	26.6	35.4	21.3	13.6	43.3
	2000	100.0	20.8	76.9	17.9	9.6	25.1	32.6	21.1	13.1	46.3
	2009	100.0	20.2	71.8	22.7	11.3	26.0	34.6	23.5	12.0	41.9
Cape Verde - Cap-Vert	1990	100.0	18.9	88.9	43.6	17.1	68.6	15.2	22.6	7.9	62.3
	1995	100.0	22.8	86.3	40.8	16.6	66.5	14.6	20.4	7.3	65.1
	2000	100.0	18.9	82.8	30.7	24.8	57.3	14.0	16.3	5.4	69.7
	2009	100.0	22.2	75.9	44.4	15.7	58.8	8.2	17.4	3.3	74.4
Côte d'Ivoire	1990	100.0	20.7	69.1	6.1	28.8	24.6	29.7	24.0	19.8	46.3
	1995	100.0	16.9	64.1	14.1	37.0	32.1	26.7	22.4	18.2	50.9
	2000	100.0	15.5	67.2	11.3	39.8	33.8	24.8	27.4	22.5	47.8
	2009	100.0	8.7	69.2	10.2	48.9	37.0	26.2	28.4	17.0	45.4
Gambia - Gambie	1990	100.0	18.8	69.9	29.7	10.0	40.3	15.4	13.1	7.6	71.4
	1995	100.0	12.6	67.8	55.6	6.2	29.5	20.6	14.3	7.9	65.1
	2000	100.0	12.2	72.9	36.7	6.6	29.0	23.8	14.4	6.6	61.7
	2009	100.0	10.5	83.2	37.1	2.6	28.3	27.7	16.6	5.8	55.7

For sources and notes, see end of table.

Pour les sources et les notes, se reporter à la fin du tableau.

8

8.3.1 Nominal gross domestic product by type of expenditure and by kind of economic activity of countries and geographical regions

8.3.1 Produit intérieur brut nominal par catégories de dépenses et par branches d'activité économique des pays et des régions géographiques

Region, country or territory / Régions, pays ou territoires	Year / Année	Total GDP / PIB total	GDP by type of expenditure (1) / PIB par catégories de dépense (1)					GDP by kind of economic activity (2) / PIB par branches d'activité économique (2)			
			Final consumption / Consommation finale		Gross capital formation / Formation brute de capital	Exports / Exportations	Less imports / Moins les importations	Agriculture (3)	Industry (4) / Industrie (4)		Services (5)
			Government / Administration publique	Household / Ménages	Formation brute de capital	Of goods and services / Des biens et services	Of goods and services / Des biens et services		Total	Manufacturing / Activités de fabrication	
			Percentage / En pourcentage								
Ghana	1990	100.0	10.9	85.5	12.3	15.4	24.0	43.7	17.3	10.1	39.0
	1995	100.0	12.1	75.1	21.1	22.7	31.1	42.7	20.7	10.3	30.6
	2000	100.0	16.9	77.6	24.0	49.0	67.5	39.4	28.4	10.1	32.2
	2009	100.0	19.5	69.5	30.1	50.3	69.6	35.7	27.7	8.0	36.6
Guinea - Guinée	1990	100.0	14.0	57.0	34.9	26.9	24.8	19.5	33.3	3.0	47.1
	1995	100.0	12.2	65.8	24.6	17.1	19.3	25.7	27.2	2.9	47.1
	2000	100.0	10.2	59.1	36.7	17.9	18.6	22.7	32.7	3.0	44.6
	2009	100.0	9.5	70.6	24.9	31.3	36.2	24.7	40.8	7.1	34.4
Guinea-Bissau - Guinée-Bissau	1990	100.0	11.4	100.9	14.7	12.0	39.0	44.6	18.2	7.4	37.2
	1995	100.0	6.4	94.8	22.3	11.7	35.1	55.1	12.2	9.2	32.7
	2000	100.0	14.0	94.6	11.3	31.8	51.6	58.1	12.5	9.7	29.4
	2009	100.0	11.8	94.5	10.3	16.0	34.1	44.9	13.6	11.9	41.6
Liberia - Libéria	1990	100.0	13.0	69.8	10.8	34.2	27.8	53.4	16.5	11.2	30.0
	1995	100.0	13.0	69.6	10.8	35.7	29.0	80.5	5.2	2.7	14.3
	2000	100.0	13.5	80.6	7.5	26.5	28.1	72.6	0.7	0.3	26.8
	2009	100.0	15.1	184.4	20.0	29.3	148.9	63.7	12.7	7.2	23.6
Mali	1990	100.0	15.2	79.0	22.2	17.3	33.7	47.8	13.5	8.1	38.8
	1995	100.0	18.2	77.6	18.8	19.6	34.7	37.7	19.0	9.6	43.2
	2000	100.0	16.4	73.4	20.2	22.8	32.7	36.3	20.9	7.2	42.9
	2009	100.0	17.6	62.4	22.1	22.8	24.9	39.2	20.4	5.6	40.4
Mauritania - Mauritanie	1990	100.0	16.6	78.3	19.5	43.4	57.8	37.0	23.6	8.9	39.4
	1995	100.0	23.3	72.5	9.8	37.1	42.6	36.4	25.7	8.1	38.0
	2000	100.0	27.6	74.2	18.6	35.6	56.0	27.1	29.1	7.4	43.8
	2009	100.0	16.3	83.0	24.9	51.6	79.2	18.4	37.6	5.4	44.0
Niger	1990	100.0	19.4	72.9	15.2	20.1	27.4	34.0	17.4	6.4	48.6
	1995	100.0	17.2	75.1	15.2	18.7	26.1	35.9	14.3	6.5	49.7
	2000	100.0	18.3	74.2	15.6	18.6	26.4	41.1	12.7	6.4	46.1
	2009	100.0	17.2	74.3	29.1	19.8	40.5	43.6	16.0	5.5	40.4
Nigeria - Nigéria	1990	100.0	5.0	62.9	14.4	35.3	17.7	31.5	45.3	5.5	23.2
	1995	100.0	12.1	69.1	7.1	35.8	24.0	32.1	46.0	5.4	21.9
	2000	100.0	8.3	52.5	7.0	51.7	19.7	26.0	52.2	3.7	21.8
	2009	100.0	5.6	70.3	9.6	39.5	25.0	37.2	33.9	2.5	28.9
Senegal - Sénégal	1990	100.0	16.7	77.8	8.8	22.4	24.8	19.1	23.4	17.3	57.5
	1995	100.0	14.0	80.4	10.6	28.4	32.9	19.4	24.7	17.7	55.9
	2000	100.0	12.6	76.2	20.5	27.9	37.2	19.1	23.2	14.7	57.6
	2009	100.0	14.2	78.6	27.1	23.2	43.1	18.5	21.4	13.0	60.1
Sierra Leone	1990	100.0	7.8	83.5	9.6	22.4	23.8	46.9	19.2	4.6	33.9
	1995	100.0	8.8	86.3	5.6	19.8	20.4	42.9	38.7	9.3	18.4
	2000	100.0	14.3	98.9	8.0	18.1	39.4	58.4	28.4	3.5	13.3
	2009	100.0	14.4	70.8	40.1	13.1	38.3	58.2	5.2	1.8	36.6
Togo	1990	100.0	13.0	89.3	15.7	28.7	46.7	37.9	25.3	10.5	36.9
	1995	100.0	11.3	84.5	13.9	29.8	39.5	41.9	24.6	10.2	33.4
	2000	100.0	14.5	83.5	15.8	32.7	46.5	37.8	19.7	9.2	42.4
	2009	100.0	13.6	84.8	18.4	33.7	50.6	47.2	18.9	8.8	34.0
Developing economies: America - Économies en développement : Amérique	**1990**	**100.0**	**13.9**	**63.6**	**20.4**	**16.3**	**14.6**	**7.2**	**32.8**	**20.6**	**60.0**
	1995	**100.0**	**15.8**	**65.0**	**20.3**	**15.9**	**16.9**	**6.7**	**30.1**	**18.6**	**63.1**
	2000	**100.0**	**14.6**	**65.5**	**21.2**	**20.6**	**21.6**	**5.7**	**31.7**	**18.4**	**62.6**
	2009	**100.0**	**16.4**	**63.9**	**19.7**	**20.5**	**20.7**	**5.7**	**32.8**	**16.4**	**61.5**
Caribbean - Caraïbes	*1990*	*100.0*	*20.7*	*61.1*	*23.3*	*40.5*	*45.8*	*11.4*	*24.8*	*11.9*	*63.8*
	1995	*100.0*	*16.7*	*70.8*	*15.5*	*33.3*	*36.4*	*8.2*	*26.2*	*14.8*	*65.6*
	2000	*100.0*	*17.9*	*66.6*	*20.1*	*35.3*	*39.9*	*6.8*	*28.3*	*15.7*	*64.9*
	2009	*100.0*	*19.9*	*66.3*	*16.6*	*32.4*	*35.7*	*5.0*	*27.1*	*14.0*	*67.9*

For sources and notes, see end of table.

Pour les sources et les notes, se reporter à la fin du tableau.

8.3.1 Nominal gross domestic product by type of expenditure and by kind of economic activity of countries and geographical regions

8.3.1 Produit intérieur brut nominal par catégories de dépenses et par branches d'activité économique des pays et des régions géographiques

Region, country or territory / Régions, pays ou territoires	Year / Année	Total GDP / PIB total	GDP by type of expenditure (1) / PIB par catégories de dépense (1)					GDP by kind of economic activity (2) / PIB par branches d'activité économique (2)			
			Final consumption / Consommation finale		Gross capital formation / Formation brute de capital	Exports / Exportations	Less imports / Moins les impor-tations	Agri-culture (3)	Industry (4) / Industrie (4)		Services (5)
			Government / Administra-tion publique	Household / Ménages		Of goods and services / Des biens et services			Total	Manu-facturing / Activités de fabrication	
			Percentage / En pourcentage								
Anguilla	1990	100.0	13.4	51.6	40.8	75.6	79.7	4.9	21.0	0.7	74.1
	1995	100.0	17.6	77.5	29.0	76.0	100.1	3.5	16.5	0.7	80.0
	2000	100.0	17.1	90.2	43.4	64.2	114.9	2.4	19.0	1.2	78.5
	2009	100.0	20.1	80.9	39.1	48.3	88.3	1.8	23.1	1.6	75.1
Antigua and Barbuda - Antigua-et-Barbuda	1990	100.0	18.0	47.6	32.4	89.0	87.0	4.0	19.0	3.2	77.0
	1995	100.0	21.4	49.3	36.9	81.4	90.1	3.6	17.2	2.2	79.2
	2000	100.0	22.3	34.4	48.1	70.3	74.8	3.6	18.3	2.1	78.1
	2009	100.0	19.4	25.5	75.8	47.5	68.2	3.3	25.7	1.6	71.1
Aruba	1990	100.0	18.6	50.2	30.0	83.2	81.9	0.5	15.9	2.1	83.6
	1995	100.0	20.0	50.5	31.1	84.9	86.5	0.5	15.6	2.7	83.9
	2000	100.0	21.4	49.4	25.5	74.4	70.7	0.4	16.3	4.0	83.3
	2009	100.0	21.7	55.3	29.0	65.0	71.0	0.4	20.2	3.9	79.4
Bahamas	1990	100.0	12.9	62.8	29.4	54.2	56.0	2.3	14.6	3.9	83.1
	1995	100.0	13.9	68.1	27.7	49.5	54.9	2.8	13.8	3.5	83.4
	2000	100.0	12.3	60.7	35.5	43.3	51.9	2.0	19.3	5.4	78.7
	2009	100.0	12.4	68.9	38.2	38.6	65.5	1.7	18.0	4.5	80.3
Barbados - Barbade	1990	100.0	20.2	63.6	18.8	49.1	51.7	5.4	18.3	8.0	76.3
	1995	100.0	20.1	61.6	15.2	58.2	55.0	6.3	15.6	6.7	78.2
	2000	100.0	21.2	61.8	22.7	52.1	57.8	4.3	16.3	6.4	79.4
	2009	100.0	19.5	49.4	28.9	66.9	64.6	3.0	17.0	6.2	80.0
British Virgin Islands - Îles Vierges britanniques	1990	100.0	14.0	45.4	25.7	101.0	86.2	3.2	10.6	2.5	86.1
	1995	100.0	13.9	49.9	25.4	92.2	81.4	1.8	13.3	3.6	84.9
	2000	100.0	10.5	40.4	23.2	104.5	78.7	1.2	11.8	3.5	87.0
	2009	100.0	9.0	36.5	22.3	109.6	77.5	0.9	10.7	2.6	88.4
Cayman Islands - Îles Caïmanes	1990	100.0	14.2	62.5	21.4	64.1	58.5	0.3	9.7	1.0	89.9
	1995	100.0	14.6	63.2	22.2	62.0	60.2	0.3	9.3	0.9	90.4
	2000	100.0	14.6	63.3	22.4	61.9	61.1	0.3	9.3	0.9	90.4
	2009	100.0	14.6	63.4	22.4	61.9	61.3	0.3	9.1	0.9	90.5
Cuba	1990	100.0	31.0	53.9	24.8	30.2	40.9	14.0	18.6	7.7	67.4
	1995	100.0	24.4	70.5	7.0	13.4	15.9	8.8	22.9	14.6	68.4
	2000	100.0	29.6	60.7	12.5	14.1	16.9	8.4	27.9	17.7	63.7
	2009	100.0	35.8	52.2	12.3	19.9	20.2	4.8	20.5	10.1	74.7
Dominica - Dominique	1990	100.0	20.3	64.1	40.8	50.1	75.3	24.1	17.1	6.6	58.8
	1995	100.0	20.8	63.8	31.5	50.9	67.0	17.3	20.1	6.8	62.7
	2000	100.0	22.5	63.7	28.1	53.3	67.5	16.6	21.6	8.1	61.8
	2009	100.0	18.1	79.6	29.5	38.4	65.5	17.9	21.3	3.9	60.8
Dominican Republic - République dominicaine	1990	100.0	2.8	80.0	20.3	42.6	45.6	12.9	36.9	28.3	50.2
	1995	100.0	4.6	81.3	17.7	35.8	39.3	9.9	35.3	25.2	54.8
	2000	100.0	7.8	77.8	23.3	37.0	45.9	7.0	34.6	25.2	58.4
	2009	100.0	7.8	85.3	14.8	22.2	30.3	6.0	31.4	23.7	62.6
Grenada - Grenade	1990	100.0	20.5	64.9	42.0	44.4	71.8	12.6	17.0	6.2	70.4
	1995	100.0	16.5	67.6	32.0	44.7	60.7	9.6	19.0	6.2	71.4
	2000	100.0	15.0	59.3	44.0	57.8	76.0	6.8	20.7	6.1	72.5
	2009	100.0	18.7	101.4	28.2	25.2	68.2	6.0	16.0	4.4	78.0
Haiti - Haïti	1990	100.0	8.0	81.3	14.3	18.1	21.7	35.8	22.6	15.5	41.6
	1995	100.0	7.8	100.5	13.8	10.9	33.0	33.2	18.0	7.5	48.8
	2000	100.0	8.8	97.1	12.9	13.8	31.7	29.9	22.1	7.2	48.0
	2009	100.0	10.5	105.5	12.9	15.5	41.7	26.8	23.6	7.3	49.6
Jamaica - Jamaïque	1990	100.0	12.5	64.7	24.4	49.5	51.4	6.2	33.7	15.3	60.1
	1995	100.0	9.9	73.1	25.3	48.6	56.1	8.9	29.3	12.9	61.7
	2000	100.0	14.3	74.2	23.5	39.0	51.0	6.7	24.4	10.1	68.9
	2009	100.0	15.7	81.6	21.1	34.3	52.7	6.0	20.9	8.6	73.1

For sources and notes, see end of table.

Pour les sources et les notes, se reporter à la fin du tableau.

8.3.1 Nominal gross domestic product by type of expenditure and by kind of economic activity of countries and geographical regions

8.3.1 Produit intérieur brut nominal par catégories de dépenses et par branches d'activité économique des pays et des régions géographiques

Region, country or territory / Régions, pays ou territoires	Year / Année	Total GDP / PIB total	GDP by type of expenditure (1) / PIB par catégories de dépense (1)					GDP by kind of economic activity (2) / PIB par branches d'activité économique (2)			
			Final consumption / Consommation finale		Gross capital formation / Formation brute de capital	Exports / Exportations	Less imports / Moins les importations	Agriculture (3) / Agriculture (3)	Industry (4) / Industrie (4)		Services (5)
			Government / Administration publique	Household / Ménages		Of goods and services / Des biens et services			Total	Manufacturing / Activités de fabrication	
			Percentage / En pourcentage								
Montserrat	1990	100.0	17.7	61.6	73.4	28.6	81.4	2.4	37.6	2.3	60.0
	1995	100.0	22.7	61.0	66.1	61.0	61.1	5.5	19.0	3.0	61.0
	2000	100.0	49.6	73.8	46.6	49.8	119.8	1.3	20.6	0.7	78.0
	2009	100.0	55.4	84.7	32.0	32.4	104.6	1.6	17.5	0.7	80.9
Netherlands Antilles - Antilles néerlandaises	1990	100.0	23.8	56.6	29.7	82.4	92.3	0.8	17.1	7.5	82.1
	1995	100.0	25.2	62.6	24.1	76.3	89.6	0.9	18.4	7.7	80.7
	2000	100.0	23.2	53.2	27.3	73.2	76.8	0.7	16.3	6.9	83.0
	2009	100.0	18.8	59.2	29.0	77.1	84.1	0.7	16.2	6.4	83.1
Saint Kitts and Nevis - Saint-Kitts-et-Nevis	1990	100.0	18.0	57.9	55.4	51.7	83.1	6.1	27.4	12.1	66.5
	1995	100.0	20.4	56.5	46.5	51.5	74.9	5.0	23.5	10.0	71.6
	2000	100.0	21.1	59.3	49.6	45.6	75.6	2.6	27.1	9.8	70.3
	2009	100.0	19.6	63.1	39.6	42.4	65.3	2.5	20.2	7.5	77.3
Saint Lucia - Sainte-Lucie	1990	100.0	15.2	69.8	24.6	68.5	78.1	13.7	16.8	7.7	69.5
	1995	100.0	17.4	58.7	24.6	69.6	70.3	8.9	17.9	6.5	73.3
	2000	100.0	18.5	65.6	25.7	53.3	63.0	6.3	16.8	4.4	76.9
	2009	100.0	21.9	70.2	23.6	49.7	65.0	4.4	16.0	5.5	79.5
Saint Vincent and the Grenadines - Saint-Vincent-et-les Grenadines	1990	100.0	20.9	68.4	31.0	65.8	76.8	20.0	21.7	8.1	58.3
	1995	100.0	20.2	64.0	30.2	51.6	66.1	13.3	23.6	8.0	63.1
	2000	100.0	19.4	59.3	27.3	53.6	59.7	10.1	22.6	5.7	67.3
	2009	100.0	20.7	80.6	30.8	32.8	63.5	7.1	23.2	4.2	69.8
Trinidad and Tobago - Trinité-et-Tobago	1990	100.0	16.2	54.8	13.8	49.1	33.5	2.6	46.4	13.8	51.0
	1995	100.0	15.9	48.8	20.8	53.8	39.2	1.9	41.7	16.5	56.3
	2000	100.0	12.0	57.4	16.8	59.2	45.3	1.2	44.8	16.9	53.9
	2009	100.0	10.1	52.5	10.3	61.9	36.4	0.4	51.0	19.6	48.7
Turks and Caicos Islands - Îles Turques et Caïques	1990	100.0	27.6	51.0	30.8	62.2	71.9	1.3	16.4	4.4	82.3
	1995	100.0	25.7	57.0	32.9	64.1	79.7	1.3	16.4	4.3	82.3
	2000	100.0	15.2	30.8	26.3	78.5	50.8	1.5	15.6	3.5	82.9
	2009	100.0	18.1	53.8	46.1	62.2	80.3	1.0	22.0	1.9	76.9
Central America - Amérique centrale	*1990*	*100.0*	*8.6*	*68.6*	*25.0*	*19.1*	*20.4*	*8.3*	*35.0*	*20.2*	*56.7*
	1995	*100.0*	*10.1*	*66.4*	*21.9*	*29.8*	*28.6*	*6.5*	*31.8*	*19.7*	*61.6*
	2000	*100.0*	*10.8*	*66.1*	*26.0*	*29.7*	*32.1*	*5.0*	*34.2*	*21.0*	*60.7*
	2009	*100.0*	*11.9*	*67.8*	*21.6*	*29.6*	*31.6*	*4.3*	*34.7*	*18.6*	*61.0*
Belize	1990	100.0	14.4	60.4	26.1	60.3	61.3	20.7	25.4	14.9	53.8
	1995	100.0	15.9	65.1	22.0	51.3	54.3	18.7	22.2	12.5	59.1
	2000	100.0	12.9	74.0	31.7	53.0	73.7	16.4	20.7	10.6	63.0
	2009	100.0	15.7	64.8	27.5	62.3	70.3	11.9	19.7	12.8	68.4
Costa Rica	1990	100.0	15.0	74.5	19.6	29.9	39.0	12.1	29.3	22.1	58.6
	1995	100.0	13.5	71.1	18.2	37.6	40.4	13.3	28.7	21.3	58.0
	2000	100.0	13.3	67.0	16.9	48.6	45.8	9.1	31.0	24.6	59.9
	2009	100.0	16.7	67.7	15.0	42.6	42.0	6.7	25.7	18.1	67.7
El Salvador	1990	100.0	9.9	88.9	13.9	18.6	31.2	17.1	26.8	21.8	56.1
	1995	100.0	8.6	87.4	20.0	21.6	37.8	14.0	28.7	22.3	57.3
	2000	100.0	10.2	87.9	16.9	27.4	42.4	10.0	30.3	23.6	59.7
	2009	100.0	10.5	91.8	13.1	22.2	37.5	12.3	27.4	21.1	60.3
Guatemala	1990	100.0	9.0	82.2	15.0	29.6	33.9	25.9	19.8	15.1	54.3
	1995	100.0	7.4	84.1	16.6	28.9	36.3	24.2	19.7	14.1	56.2
	2000	100.0	9.3	82.5	19.7	30.3	41.3	22.8	19.8	13.2	57.4
	2009	100.0	10.5	85.1	13.6	23.3	32.6	12.0	27.6	19.2	60.4
Honduras	1990	100.0	13.8	67.0	21.2	48.6	48.1	21.2	26.4	18.2	52.5
	1995	100.0	10.0	63.6	29.1	57.0	57.8	20.6	30.1	20.1	49.3
	2000	100.0	13.4	70.8	28.3	54.0	66.4	15.2	31.1	21.7	53.7
	2009	100.0	18.2	78.9	22.6	42.3	62.0	11.5	25.6	17.8	62.8

For sources and notes, see end of table.

Pour les sources et les notes, se reporter à la fin du tableau.

8.3.1 Nominal gross domestic product by type of expenditure and by kind of economic activity of countries and geographical regions

8.3.1 Produit intérieur brut nominal par catégories de dépenses et par branches d'activité économique des pays et des régions géographiques

Region, country or territory / Régions, pays ou territoires	Year / Année	Total GDP / PIB total	GDP by type of expenditure (1) / PIB par catégories de dépense (1)					GDP by kind of economic activity (2) / PIB par branches d'activité économique (2)			
			Final consumption / Consommation finale		Gross capital formation / Formation brute de capital	Exports / Exportations	Less imports / Moins les importations	Agriculture (3)	Industry (4) / Industrie (4)		Services (5)
			Government / Administration publique	Household / Ménages		Of goods and services / Des biens et services			Total	Manufacturing / Activités de fabrication	
			Percentage / En pourcentage								
Mexico - Mexique	1990	100.0	8.0	68.0	25.8	17.0	17.9	7.4	36.1	20.4	56.4
	1995	100.0	10.0	65.0	22.1	27.7	25.3	5.1	32.9	20.0	62.1
	2000	100.0	10.6	65.1	26.6	28.2	30.0	4.1	35.2	21.3	60.7
	2009	100.0	11.7	66.7	22.2	27.9	29.4	3.5	36.1	18.9	60.4
Nicaragua	1990	100.0	31.9	60.5	17.5	14.2	25.8	21.2	25.8	18.7	53.0
	1995	100.0	14.9	79.8	21.3	17.5	33.5	22.3	26.6	18.3	51.0
	2000	100.0	16.8	78.5	34.4	23.0	52.7	19.8	27.2	16.1	53.0
	2009	100.0	19.3	81.9	31.4	33.0	65.6	17.7	28.7	18.2	53.6
Panama	1990	100.0	15.7	63.3	14.7	77.9	70.5	9.0	17.7	13.2	73.3
	1995	100.0	13.1	57.4	26.5	90.5	87.8	7.4	19.8	12.5	72.8
	2000	100.0	13.2	59.9	24.1	72.6	69.8	7.0	18.5	9.7	74.5
	2009	100.0	10.5	48.8	24.8	77.0	61.1	5.8	16.4	6.6	77.8
South America - Amérique du Sud	*1990*	*100.0*	*15.6*	*61.6*	*18.2*	*13.0*	*9.5*	*6.3*	*32.5*	*21.5*	*61.2*
	1995	*100.0*	*17.3*	*64.3*	*20.1*	*11.3*	*12.9*	*6.7*	*29.8*	*18.4*	*63.5*
	2000	*100.0*	*16.4*	*65.1*	*18.7*	*14.6*	*14.8*	*6.0*	*30.5*	*17.2*	*63.5*
	2009	*100.0*	*17.8*	*62.4*	*19.2*	*16.6*	*16.0*	*6.3*	*32.4*	*15.7*	*61.2*
Argentina - Argentine	1990	100.0	12.9	66.8	14.6	10.3	4.6	8.0	35.6	26.5	56.4
	1995	100.0	13.3	68.8	18.5	9.7	10.1	5.7	28.0	18.4	66.3
	2000	100.0	13.8	69.3	17.5	11.0	11.6	5.0	27.6	17.5	67.4
	2009	100.0	15.2	58.3	21.2	21.4	16.0	7.5	31.8	21.2	60.7
Bolivia (Plurinational State of) - Bolivie (État plurinational de)	1990	100.0	11.8	76.9	12.5	22.8	23.9	16.4	34.2	18.2	49.4
	1995	100.0	13.6	75.8	15.2	22.6	27.2	16.4	32.1	18.4	51.5
	2000	100.0	14.5	76.4	18.1	18.3	27.3	14.3	28.3	14.6	57.4
	2009	100.0	14.7	65.5	17.0	35.7	32.9	13.3	34.8	13.8	51.9
Brazil - Brésil	1990	100.0	18.1	59.5	18.5	7.4	5.6	4.1	27.9	20.0	68.1
	1995	100.0	21.0	62.5	18.0	7.3	8.8	5.8	27.5	18.6	66.7
	2000	100.0	19.2	64.3	18.3	10.0	11.7	5.6	27.7	17.2	66.7
	2009	100.0	20.8	62.8	16.5	11.3	11.3	6.1	25.4	15.5	68.5
Chile - Chili	1990	100.0	10.4	60.2	25.6	33.1	29.4	7.1	41.2	18.0	51.7
	1995	100.0	10.4	60.8	26.3	29.2	26.9	6.1	40.8	19.0	53.1
	2000	100.0	12.5	63.8	21.9	31.6	29.7	5.9	37.0	18.7	57.1
	2009	100.0	13.4	59.8	19.0	38.1	30.4	3.3	42.1	12.7	54.6
Colombia - Colombie	1990	100.0	10.1	67.7	25.4	15.0	15.6	14.0	33.6	18.3	52.4
	1995	100.0	13.3	69.8	29.5	11.8	20.4	11.0	30.6	15.4	58.4
	2000	100.0	18.9	66.9	15.7	17.4	18.9	10.4	30.0	15.6	59.7
	2009	100.0	17.2	62.2	24.2	16.4	20.0	9.2	35.6	15.3	55.2
Ecuador - Équateur	1990	100.0	13.1	67.4	17.0	31.4	28.6	13.9	39.5	20.1	46.6
	1995	100.0	12.5	68.5	21.6	25.7	28.3	17.6	26.2	11.9	56.2
	2000	100.0	9.8	64.0	20.1	37.1	31.0	11.5	37.6	5.5	50.9
	2009	100.0	12.4	64.2	26.4	26.7	29.7	6.9	38.1	1.6	55.0
Guyana	1990	100.0	8.5	75.8	26.5	34.5	49.2	31.5	26.7	10.1	41.8
	1995	100.0	10.0	57.7	28.5	50.0	53.2	37.6	32.6	8.0	29.8
	2000	100.0	17.3	62.0	24.1	40.0	51.5	28.1	31.5	6.7	40.4
	2009	100.0	16.2	81.8	26.6	46.0	70.6	19.8	33.1	7.4	47.1
Paraguay	1990	100.0	9.2	66.0	27.1	52.4	50.4	26.4	25.9	19.3	47.7
	1995	100.0	10.0	75.8	26.0	59.4	71.3	22.8	25.7	18.0	51.5
	2000	100.0	12.7	79.2	18.8	38.1	48.8	18.5	24.8	17.2	56.7
	2009	100.0	11.4	74.0	18.3	45.6	49.4	24.2	22.3	14.3	53.6
Peru - Pérou	1990	100.0	11.5	71.2	18.1	15.1	14.5	7.7	30.4	19.4	61.9
	1995	100.0	9.8	71.2	24.8	12.5	18.2	8.8	31.0	16.8	60.2
	2000	100.0	10.6	71.2	20.2	16.0	18.0	8.5	29.9	15.8	61.6
	2009	100.0	10.2	64.6	21.0	23.7	19.9	7.1	36.7	16.0	56.2

For sources and notes, see end of table.

Pour les sources et les notes, se reporter à la fin du tableau.

8.3.1 Nominal gross domestic product by type of expenditure and by kind of economic activity of countries and geographical regions

8.3.1 Produit intérieur brut nominal par catégories de dépenses et par branches d'activité économique des pays et des régions géographiques

Region, country or territory / Régions, pays ou territoires	Year / Année	Total GDP / PIB total	GDP by type of expenditure (1) / PIB par catégories de dépense (1)					GDP by kind of economic activity (2) / PIB par branches d'activité économique (2)			
			Final consumption / Consommation finale		Gross capital formation / Formation brute de capital	Exports / Exportations	Less imports / Moins les importations	Agriculture (3)	Industry (4) / Industrie (4)		Services (5)
			Government / Administration publique	Household / Ménages	Formation brute de capital	Of goods and services / Des biens et services			Total	Manufacturing / Activités de fabrication	
			Percentage / En pourcentage								
Suriname	1990	100.0	20.0	44.0	17.0	22.4	21.7	9.9	27.6	11.7	62.4
	1995	100.0	14.5	12.1	38.8	73.1	63.6	18.3	30.3	10.0	40.4
	2000	100.0	4.6	16.0	56.2	51.2	46.2	11.9	30.9	17.7	57.2
	2009	100.0	4.5	15.7	76.7	64.5	59.7	5.8	44.3	22.4	49.9
Uruguay	1990	100.0	12.4	71.5	12.1	22.2	19.8	10.7	28.3	22.5	61.0
	1995	100.0	10.6	75.4	17.1	16.1	18.8	8.2	26.3	17.0	65.5
	2000	100.0	12.4	76.5	14.5	16.7	20.0	6.4	23.6	13.4	70.0
	2009	100.0	12.9	68.2	17.9	26.5	25.5	9.1	25.5	15.4	65.3
Venezuela (Bolivarian Rep. of) - Venezuela (Rép. bolivarienne du)	1990	100.0	16.8	46.6	13.4	40.6	20.4	5.9	57.3	27.1	36.8
	1995	100.0	14.8	54.1	23.8	27.9	22.1	5.9	47.1	23.4	47.0
	2000	100.0	12.4	51.7	24.2	29.7	18.1	4.1	48.4	19.3	47.5
	2009	100.0	13.3	64.2	24.8	18.3	20.5	3.9	55.6	15.6	40.4
Developing economies: Asia - Économies en développement : Asie	1990	100.0	13.1	56.1	28.7	30.7	29.8	17.0	37.2	23.8	45.8
	1995	100.0	12.2	54.8	32.4	37.3	37.0	13.8	38.1	25.7	48.1
	2000	100.0	13.6	54.2	27.8	42.4	38.2	11.7	38.7	26.1	49.6
	2009	100.0	13.5	48.3	34.7	44.8	39.4	10.2	41.5	28.7	48.3
Eastern Asia - Asie orientale	1990	100.0	13.0	50.2	32.7	35.2	32.5	15.3	38.9	31.1	45.7
	1995	100.0	12.4	50.4	36.4	38.4	37.7	11.4	40.0	31.5	48.6
	2000	100.0	14.0	50.9	31.9	40.5	37.8	9.8	39.7	33.0	50.4
	2009	100.0	13.6	41.2	40.4	47.1	39.1	9.0	44.2	37.9	46.7
China - Chine	1990	100.0	13.6	48.8	34.9	18.4	15.0	26.0	39.7	35.5	34.3
	1995	100.0	13.3	44.9	40.3	22.2	20.1	19.7	46.6	40.6	33.7
	2000	100.0	15.9	46.4	35.3	23.4	21.0	15.1	46.0	40.5	38.9
	2009	100.0	13.6	36.8	45.6	39.2	30.6	11.0	48.0	42.1	41.1
China, Hong Kong SAR - Chine (RAS de Hong Kong)	1990	100.0	7.2	57.1	27.0	130.6	122.0	0.2	24.4	16.7	75.4
	1995	100.0	8.4	62.0	34.1	143.2	147.6	0.1	15.2	7.7	84.7
	2000	100.0	9.1	59.0	27.5	143.3	138.8	0.1	13.4	5.4	86.5
	2009	100.0	8.7	61.5	22.6	193.8	186.7	0.1	8.2	2.8	91.8
China, Macao SAR - Chine (RAS de Macao)	1990	100.0	8.9	37.0	25.4	96.9	68.0	..	23.8	16.5	76.2
	1995	100.0	8.4	33.6	29.5	74.2	45.7	..	15.6	7.6	84.4
	2000	100.0	12.3	40.2	11.6	100.4	64.6	..	14.8	9.5	85.2
	2009	100.0	8.1	24.6	18.5	91.9	43.2	..	17.0	2.8	83.0
China, Taiwan Province of - Province chinoise de Taiwan	1990	100.0	17.4	53.9	24.4	45.7	41.4	4.2	40.2	32.7	55.6
	1995	100.0	14.6	57.2	26.7	47.0	45.5	3.5	34.3	26.5	62.2
	2000	100.0	13.4	58.8	25.7	52.9	50.8	2.1	30.1	24.6	67.9
	2009	100.0	12.8	60.8	17.2	62.5	53.4	1.6	30.6	25.4	67.8
Korea, Dem. People's Rep. of - Corée, Rép. populaire dém. de	1990	100.0	..	..	..	7.5	11.8	27.4	54.6	31.8	18.0
	1995	100.0	..	..	..	3.8	5.7	27.6	42.0	22.5	30.3
	2000	100.0	..	..	..	4.2	10.0	30.4	37.1	17.7	32.4
	2009	100.0	..	..	..	5.8	11.2	20.9	46.9	22.1	32.1
Korea, Republic of - Corée, République de	1990	100.0	11.8	50.7	38.1	27.6	28.3	8.7	40.5	27.3	50.8
	1995	100.0	11.2	52.3	36.9	28.5	29.0	6.2	40.2	27.6	53.6
	2000	100.0	12.0	54.8	30.6	38.6	35.7	4.6	39.5	29.7	55.9
	2009	100.0	16.0	54.3	25.9	49.9	46.0	2.6	36.7	27.7	60.7
Mongolia - Mongolie	1990	100.0	22.8	65.6	33.0	16.5	34.9	16.0	28.2	9.5	55.8
	1995	100.0	11.6	66.8	25.4	41.7	42.8	38.8	24.8	11.1	36.4
	2000	100.0	15.4	75.7	29.0	56.4	70.9	31.9	19.8	4.5	48.2
	2009	100.0	14.1	46.9	48.0	55.3	62.1	22.9	31.8	4.5	45.4
Southern Asia - Asie méridionale	1990	100.0	11.4	66.4	27.4	9.4	13.6	27.5	27.0	15.6	45.6
	1995	100.0	11.2	62.7	27.5	13.9	14.1	25.1	28.3	16.2	46.6
	2000	100.0	11.9	63.8	24.7	15.4	16.3	22.3	27.5	15.3	50.2
	2009	100.0	11.7	59.9	32.5	20.6	24.9	16.2	30.9	15.2	52.9

For sources and notes, see end of table.   Pour les sources et les notes, se reporter à la fin du tableau.

8.3.1 Nominal gross domestic product by type of expenditure and by kind of economic activity of countries and geographical regions

8.3.1 Produit intérieur brut nominal par catégories de dépenses et par branches d'activité économique des pays et des régions géographiques

Region, country or territory / Régions, pays ou territoires	Year / Année	Total GDP / PIB total	GDP by type of expenditure (1) / PIB par catégories de dépense (1)					GDP by kind of economic activity (2) / PIB par branches d'activité économique (2)			
			Final consumption / Consommation finale		Gross capital formation / Formation brute de capital	Exports / Exportations / Of goods and services / Des biens et services	Less imports / Moins les importations / Des biens et services	Agriculture (3)	Industry (4) / Industrie (4)		Services (5)
			Government / Administration publique	Household / Ménages					Total	Manufacturing / Activités de fabrication	
			Percentage / En pourcentage								
Afghanistan	1990	100.0	6.2	83.3	13.4	11.5	14.4	35.7	23.7	20.3	40.6
	1995	100.0	7.5	100.5	13.8	23.5	45.4	65.7	10.5	5.4	23.8
	2000	100.0	8.8	117.7	14.3	35.6	76.4	57.0	23.2	16.9	19.8
	2009	100.0	9.1	91.6	24.6	16.6	43.9	37.3	26.9	17.0	35.8
Bangladesh	1990	100.0	4.5	84.6	18.3	6.3	14.0	31.5	21.4	13.4	47.2
	1995	100.0	4.6	82.0	19.1	10.9	17.3	26.4	24.6	15.3	49.1
	2000	100.0	4.6	77.5	23.0	14.0	19.2	25.5	25.3	15.2	49.2
	2009	100.0	5.2	74.8	24.2	20.9	30.5	18.6	28.6	17.9	52.8
Bhutan - Bhoutan	1990	100.0	17.5	54.2	36.3	28.9	33.0	39.0	28.0	8.4	33.0
	1995	100.0	18.6	41.6	48.6	38.9	43.9	34.0	34.8	10.9	31.2
	2000	100.0	21.9	47.7	48.2	29.0	53.5	27.4	36.0	8.4	36.6
	2009	100.0	18.2	39.8	37.9	65.2	78.5	20.6	41.8	8.4	37.6
India - Inde	1990	100.0	11.8	65.9	27.8	7.1	8.5	30.0	27.6	17.2	42.4
	1995	100.0	10.8	62.8	29.3	10.9	12.1	26.8	28.0	18.0	45.2
	2000	100.0	12.6	63.7	24.2	13.2	14.2	23.2	26.4	15.8	50.4
	2009	100.0	12.3	57.3	35.0	20.6	25.3	17.1	28.2	15.9	54.6
Iran (Islamic Rep. of) Iran (Rép. islamique d')	1990	100.0	12.1	57.5	34.2	14.7	27.2	17.8	28.0	10.5	54.1
	1995	100.0	15.9	46.0	30.0	21.2	12.8	18.3	33.8	11.7	47.9
	2000	100.0	13.8	46.4	33.4	22.1	17.0	13.4	36.2	13.2	50.5
	2009	100.0	10.9	54.3	32.2	23.1	20.6	9.4	43.6	11.2	47.0
Maldives	1990	100.0	17.2	35.9	31.5	92.0	76.5	14.3	12.3	8.8	73.4
	1995	100.0	16.8	36.5	31.3	92.7	77.2	11.0	13.0	7.6	76.0
	2000	100.0	22.9	32.9	26.3	89.5	71.6	8.4	14.5	7.7	77.1
	2009	100.0	40.0	24.6	57.5	77.3	99.3	4.9	16.8	6.6	78.4
Nepal - Népal	1990	100.0	7.2	87.8	17.1	10.6	22.3	48.4	12.3	6.0	39.3
	1995	100.0	7.7	79.9	23.3	24.5	36.6	38.9	17.7	9.3	43.4
	2000	100.0	7.4	79.8	22.5	23.5	34.3	37.7	17.3	9.2	45.0
	2009	100.0	10.7	79.5	31.9	12.4	34.6	32.6	15.8	6.8	51.6
Pakistan	1990	100.0	11.7	72.3	20.4	12.2	16.6	25.2	25.3	16.7	49.4
	1995	100.0	9.1	73.3	20.0	13.7	15.9	25.4	23.7	15.6	51.0
	2000	100.0	8.6	75.4	17.2	13.4	14.7	25.9	23.3	14.7	50.7
	2009	100.0	10.7	79.4	19.7	14.1	24.0	20.8	24.3	17.7	54.9
Sri Lanka	1990	100.0	12.7	75.3	20.6	29.5	37.3	25.6	29.2	18.5	45.2
	1995	100.0	14.2	71.2	25.4	34.7	44.0	20.6	29.7	18.4	49.7
	2000	100.0	13.7	70.9	25.6	38.2	48.4	17.6	29.9	19.5	52.5
	2009	100.0	14.7	66.0	25.3	22.4	28.4	13.8	31.7	19.3	54.5
South-Eastern Asia - Asie du Sud-Est	*1990*	*100.0*	*9.8*	*56.4*	*31.4*	*49.5*	*50.2*	*16.4*	*36.7*	*23.3*	*47.1*
	1995	*100.0*	*9.3*	*55.8*	*33.8*	*59.7*	*61.2*	*13.9*	*38.1*	*25.5*	*48.0*
	2000	*100.0*	*9.8*	*56.0*	*24.8*	*84.8*	*74.7*	*11.8*	*40.7*	*27.4*	*47.5*
	2009	*100.0*	*11.0*	*57.3*	*25.0*	*67.3*	*59.7*	*12.8*	*40.9*	*25.3*	*46.3*
Brunei Darussalam - Brunéi Darussalam	1990	100.0	22.0	26.5	18.7	61.8	37.3	2.3	53.6	8.8	44.1
	1995	100.0	26.8	36.6	36.7	59.7	55.8	2.5	42.8	11.7	54.7
	2000	100.0	25.8	24.8	13.1	67.3	35.8	1.0	63.7	15.4	35.3
	2009	100.0	19.3	19.2	12.4	72.6	26.9	0.7	72.9	11.6	26.5
Cambodia - Cambodge	1990	100.0	7.2	90.4	8.3	2.4	8.4	56.5	11.3	5.3	32.2
	1995	100.0	5.1	90.9	13.4	32.7	43.9	51.4	12.9	7.4	35.7
	2000	100.0	5.2	88.8	17.5	49.8	61.8	37.8	23.0	16.9	39.1
	2009	100.0	3.4	95.2	16.0	49.0	63.8	32.7	26.1	18.2	41.2
Indonesia including East Timor - Indonésie, y compris le Timor oriental	1990	100.0	8.1	53.0	27.9	24.1	21.6	17.6	39.0	23.0	43.5
	1995	100.0	7.1	56.8	29.0	25.0	25.1	15.4	41.6	26.6	43.0
	2000	100.0	6.6	61.7	22.3	41.0	30.5	15.6	45.9	27.7	38.5
Indonesia - Indonésie	2009	100.0	9.6	58.6	31.0	24.1	21.3	15.3	47.6	26.4	37.1

For sources and notes, see end of table.

Pour les sources et les notes, se reporter à la fin du tableau.

8

8.3.1 Nominal gross domestic product by type of expenditure and by kind of economic activity of countries and geographical regions

8.3.1 Produit intérieur brut nominal par catégories de dépenses et par branches d'activité économique des pays et des régions géographiques

Region, country or territory / Régions, pays ou territoires	Year / Année	Total GDP / PIB total	GDP by type of expenditure (1) / PIB par catégories de dépense (1)					GDP by kind of economic activity (2) / PIB par branches d'activité économique (2)			
			Final consumption / Consommation finale		Gross capital formation / Formation brute de capital	Exports / Exportations	Less imports / Moins les importations	Agriculture (3) / Agriculture (3)	Industry (4) / Industrie (4)		Services (5)
			Government / Administration publique	Household / Ménages		Of goods and services / Des biens et services			Total	Manufacturing / Activités de fabrication	
			Percentage / En pourcentage								
Lao People's Dem. Rep. - RDP lao démocratique pop	1990	100.0	0.5	92.0	11.5	11.3	24.5	61.2	14.6	10.0	24.0
	1995	100.0	9.7	93.0	11.3	23.2	37.3	44.5	12.1	6.2	43.5
	2000	100.0	8.1	77.7	28.3	30.0	44.1	44.4	16.1	7.8	39.5
	2009	100.0	9.4	72.7	31.1	25.8	38.1	31.6	25.4	10.5	43.0
Malaysia - Malaisie	1990	100.0	13.5	53.5	31.8	71.7	69.7	14.8	40.2	22.9	45.6
	1995	100.0	12.1	49.5	42.9	90.6	94.4	12.5	39.1	24.8	48.5
	2000	100.0	10.2	43.8	26.9	119.8	100.6	8.3	46.8	29.9	44.9
	2009	100.0	14.3	50.2	14.0	96.9	75.4	9.4	43.6	25.1	47.0
Myanmar	1990	100.0	13.6	74.7	13.4	1.9	3.6	57.3	10.5	7.8	32.2
	1995	100.0	8.2	78.4	14.2	0.8	1.7	60.0	9.9	6.9	30.1
	2000	100.0	9.4	78.3	12.4	0.5	0.6	57.2	9.7	7.2	33.1
	2009	100.0	4.3	79.1	15.1	0.1	0.1	48.0	16.5	11.8	35.6
Philippines	1990	100.0	10.1	71.2	24.2	27.5	33.3	21.9	34.5	24.8	43.6
	1995	100.0	11.4	74.1	22.5	36.4	44.2	21.6	32.1	23.0	46.3
	2000	100.0	13.1	69.6	21.2	55.4	53.5	15.8	32.3	22.2	52.0
	2009	100.0	10.5	73.9	14.6	31.7	30.8	14.8	30.2	21.4	55.0
Singapore - Singapour	1990	100.0	10.1	46.1	36.4	182.9	176.0	0.2	34.4	26.6	65.4
	1995	100.0	8.5	41.3	34.2	187.8	172.2	0.1	35.5	26.1	64.4
	2000	100.0	10.8	42.2	33.3	195.6	182.0	0.1	33.7	26.1	66.3
	2009	100.0	11.4	41.4	27.6	202.0	182.2	0.0	25.8	18.2	74.1
Thailand - Thaïlande	1990	100.0	9.4	56.5	41.3	34.1	41.6	14.4	35.9	24.9	49.7
	1995	100.0	9.9	53.2	42.1	41.8	48.6	10.8	40.2	28.6	49.0
	2000	100.0	11.3	56.1	22.8	66.8	58.1	9.0	42.0	33.6	49.0
	2009	100.0	13.3	55.0	21.9	68.5	57.9	11.6	43.3	34.1	45.1
Timor-Leste	2009	100.0	58.3	91.6	24.0	11.5	85.5	30.5	13.6	2.5	56.0
Viet Nam	1990	100.0	7.5	89.6	14.4	26.4	35.7	38.7	22.7	12.3	38.6
	1995	100.0	8.2	73.6	27.1	32.8	41.9	27.2	28.8	15.0	44.1
	2000	100.0	6.4	66.5	29.6	55.0	57.5	24.5	36.7	18.6	38.7
	2009	100.0	6.4	67.0	38.4	76.2	88.6	20.7	40.2	20.9	39.1
Western Asia - Asie occidentale	*1990*	*100.0*	*18.0*	*56.6*	*19.4*	*30.4*	*26.5*	*9.3*	*45.4*	*17.5*	*45.3*
	1995	*100.0*	*16.4*	*58.6*	*22.8*	*31.6*	*29.7*	*8.6*	*43.2*	*18.1*	*48.2*
	2000	*100.0*	*17.6*	*53.0*	*19.9*	*39.8*	*30.4*	*7.1*	*44.6*	*13.6*	*48.3*
	2009	*100.0*	*17.6*	*54.0*	*23.9*	*44.3*	*39.7*	*5.1*	*44.0*	*12.1*	*50.8*
Bahrain - Bahreïn	1990	100.0	23.6	55.6	16.9	91.9	90.3	0.8	36.7	11.1	62.5
	1995	100.0	20.7	52.6	16.7	81.5	70.0	0.8	36.0	16.3	63.2
	2000	100.0	17.4	44.5	12.6	89.5	63.9	0.7	40.0	10.5	59.3
	2009	100.0	15.5	34.8	27.2	81.3	58.8	0.4	40.9	13.6	58.7
Iraq	1990	100.0	12.1	21.3	17.1	118.6	69.1	6.4	79.3	0.5	14.3
	1995	100.0	21.6	66.3	4.9	24.1	16.8	6.2	79.8	0.4	14.0
	2000	100.0	14.7	16.8	36.2	93.9	61.6	4.6	84.6	0.9	10.8
	2009	100.0	26.5	54.8	26.1	42.6	41.3	4.8	60.8	1.6	34.3
Jordan - Jordanie	1990	100.0	24.9	74.1	31.9	61.9	92.7	7.5	30.9	17.0	61.7
	1995	100.0	23.6	64.6	33.0	51.7	72.9	4.3	27.5	13.9	68.3
	2000	100.0	23.7	80.6	22.4	41.8	68.5	2.3	24.4	14.8	73.3
	2009	100.0	16.4	72.1	27.1	42.9	64.9	2.7	30.1	18.7	67.2
Kuwait - Koweït	1990	100.0	38.6	58.6	15.9	44.8	57.8	0.9	51.7	11.5	47.4
	1995	100.0	33.0	41.3	15.1	53.6	43.0	0.4	52.8	11.1	46.7
	2000	100.0	21.5	41.5	10.7	56.5	30.1	0.3	57.2	6.7	42.5
	2009	100.0	20.5	37.2	13.9	56.4	28.0	0.2	51.7	5.1	48.1
Lebanon - Liban	1990	100.0	25.1	123.3	28.7	22.2	99.2	8.8	21.2	12.6	70.0
	1995	100.0	9.9	107.7	36.3	11.0	64.9	12.4	26.6	11.3	61.0
	2000	100.0	17.6	85.6	20.3	13.6	37.1	6.4	20.9	12.0	72.7
	2009	100.0	16.5	77.9	30.2	22.8	49.0	5.9	17.8	9.1	76.2

For sources and notes, see end of table.

Pour les sources et les notes, se reporter à la fin du tableau.

8.3.1 Nominal gross domestic product by type of expenditure and by kind of economic activity of countries and geographical regions

8.3.1 Produit intérieur brut nominal par catégories de dépenses et par branches d'activité économique des pays et des régions géographiques

Region, country or territory / Régions, pays ou territoires	Year / Année	Total GDP / PIB total	GDP by type of expenditure (1) / PIB par catégories de dépense (1)					GDP by kind of economic activity (2) / PIB par branches d'activité économique (2)				
			Final consumption / Consommation finale		Gross capital formation / Formation brute de capital	Exports / Exportations	Less imports / Moins les importations	Agriculture (3)	Industry (4) / Industrie (4)			Services (5)
			Government / Administration publique	Household / Ménages		Of goods and services / Des biens et services			Total	Manufacturing / Activités de fabrication	
			Percentage / En pourcentage								
Occupied Palestinian territory - Territoire palestinien occupé	1990	100.0	22.2	102.1	36.8	14.6	72.0	13.5	30.9	18.5	55.6
	1995	100.0	18.5	98.2	35.4	15.5	67.6	12.9	31.3	19.5	55.8
	2000	100.0	26.5	94.5	33.8	16.6	71.4	11.3	25.7	13.1	63.0
	2009	100.0	22.4	114.5	21.7	13.1	71.7	7.1	25.3	13.1	67.6
Oman	1990	100.0	27.4	33.6	17.6	37.4	22.8	2.7	56.9	2.9	40.5
	1995	100.0	28.3	39.7	21.3	34.9	29.4	2.9	49.7	4.7	47.4
	2000	100.0	21.5	35.2	15.4	53.9	26.0	2.0	58.5	5.7	39.4
	2009	100.0	17.0	39.4	28.3	48.3	34.2	1.2	63.2	10.6	35.6
Qatar	1990	100.0	32.9	27.8	18.0	53.5	32.1	0.8	55.7	12.7	43.6
	1995	100.0	31.9	32.1	35.1	44.3	43.3	1.0	52.1	8.2	46.9
	2000	100.0	19.7	15.2	20.2	67.3	22.3	0.4	69.5	5.3	30.1
	2009	100.0	24.2	18.0	46.8	43.5	31.6	0.1	61.3	7.8	38.6
Saudi Arabia - Arabie saoudite	1990	100.0	29.2	46.7	15.1	40.6	31.6	5.7	48.6	8.6	45.7
	1995	100.0	23.6	46.9	19.8	37.6	27.9	5.9	48.6	9.6	45.5
	2000	100.0	26.0	36.5	18.7	43.7	24.9	4.9	53.6	9.6	41.5
	2009	100.0	25.9	38.6	25.5	52.7	42.6	3.0	59.1	10.6	37.9
Syrian Arab Republic - République arabe syrienne	1990	100.0	14.3	68.7	16.5	28.3	28.0	28.3	24.2	5.5	47.6
	1995	100.0	13.4	66.2	27.2	31.0	37.9	20.2	10.1	6.2	63.7
	2000	100.0	12.4	63.4	17.3	36.1	29.2	24.7	33.3	1.5	41.9
	2009	100.0	11.4	69.3	24.0	31.7	36.4	21.0	33.9	4.6	45.1
Turkey - Turquie	1990	100.0	8.8	65.9	22.3	11.6	12.7	13.4	38.9	29.1	47.6
	1995	100.0	8.7	67.6	23.3	17.4	17.6	11.9	38.4	29.4	49.8
	2000	100.0	11.7	70.5	20.8	20.1	23.1	10.8	30.0	21.4	59.2
	2009	100.0	14.7	71.5	14.9	23.2	24.4	9.1	25.1	16.6	65.7
United Arab Emirates - Émirats arabes unis	1990	100.0	16.3	38.6	20.4	65.4	40.8	1.6	62.2	7.2	36.2
	1995	100.0	16.4	47.9	29.7	69.0	63.0	2.8	51.0	10.2	46.1
	2000	100.0	15.4	43.5	23.2	73.7	55.8	3.5	54.8	13.3	41.8
	2009	100.0	9.6	47.4	36.5	84.2	77.7	1.1	55.0	12.4	43.9
Yemen - Yémen	1990	100.0	16.2	84.3	8.2	13.2	18.5	23.7	24.3	7.8	52.0
	1995	100.0	13.6	97.1	11.8	20.6	39.7	18.3	29.0	11.9	52.7
	2000	100.0	13.0	64.3	15.8	39.7	32.8	12.9	44.5	5.6	42.6
	2009	100.0	13.6	74.4	21.3	25.1	35.6	10.0	42.4	7.5	47.6
Developing economies: Oceania - Économies en développement : Océanie	**1990**	**100.0**	**25.0**	**64.9**	**24.9**	**33.3**	**48.1**	**15.5**	**22.8**	**7.9**	**61.6**
	1995	**100.0**	**21.0**	**63.6**	**21.3**	**38.0**	**43.9**	**17.4**	**22.6**	**7.9**	**60.0**
	2000	**100.0**	**20.6**	**65.9**	**22.2**	**40.9**	**49.6**	**16.2**	**25.4**	**10.0**	**58.5**
	2009	**100.0**	**18.2**	**73.6**	**27.0**	**38.4**	**57.3**	**14.7**	**27.3**	**10.5**	**58.1**
Cook Islands - Îles Cook	1990	100.0	55.5	52.5	17.1	81.2	106.3	11.3	8.2	4.2	80.5
	1995	100.0	47.6	39.1	12.7	61.0	60.5	9.5	7.6	2.9	83.0
	2000	100.0	38.8	38.0	12.4	95.0	84.2	13.0	8.1	3.4	78.9
	2009	100.0	35.4	43.3	14.1	90.3	83.1	8.8	9.5	3.6	81.7
Fiji - Fidji	1990	100.0	17.3	68.6	19.5	61.0	66.4	19.1	20.0	10.9	60.9
	1995	100.0	15.8	73.8	14.4	53.6	57.6	18.4	19.5	14.1	62.1
	2000	100.0	16.9	72.8	18.1	56.1	63.8	16.3	19.2	14.7	64.5
	2009	100.0	15.3	88.6	17.1	51.4	74.4	13.4	19.8	15.2	66.8
French Polynesia - Polynésie française	1990	100.0	13.5	85.7	25.6	15.2	40.0	4.4	15.0	7.2	80.5
	1995	100.0	13.5	80.9	21.4	19.2	35.0	4.1	13.3	6.4	82.6
	2000	100.0	11.6	87.9	21.8	24.8	46.1	4.0	14.5	6.6	81.5
	2009	100.0	10.7	102.3	25.5	18.0	56.5	2.5	12.9	5.6	84.6
Kiribati	1990	100.0	52.8	74.3	93.1	11.6	147.2	28.0	14.0	9.6	58.0
	1995	100.0	46.4	59.6	54.3	11.6	71.9	29.0	8.8	6.1	62.1
	2000	100.0	40.5	52.1	48.3	7.0	47.8	22.0	11.6	4.9	66.4
	2009	100.0	69.7	89.7	83.3	16.9	159.6	27.1	9.6	5.8	63.3

For sources and notes, see end of table.

Pour les sources et les notes, se reporter à la fin du tableau.

8

8.3.1 Nominal gross domestic product by type of expenditure and by kind of economic activity of countries and geographical regions

8.3.1 Produit intérieur brut nominal par catégories de dépenses et par branches d'activité économique des pays et des régions géographiques

Region, country or territory / Régions, pays ou territoires	Year / Année	Total GDP / PIB total	GDP by type of expenditure (1) / PIB par catégories de dépense (1)					GDP by kind of economic activity (2) / PIB par branches d'activité économique (2)			
			Final consumption / Consommation finale		Gross capital formation / Formation brute de capital	Exports / Exportations	Less imports / Moins les importations	Agriculture (3)	Industry (4) / Industrie (4)		Services (5)
			Government / Administration publique	Household / Ménages		Of goods and services / Des biens et services			Total	Manufacturing / Activités de fabrication	
			Percentage / En pourcentage								
Marshall Islands - Îles Marshall	1990	100.0	50.2	97.6	88.4	11.0	147.2	13.9	12.9	1.0	73.2
	1995	100.0	54.2	91.0	56.3	12.5	114.0	14.9	15.0	2.6	70.0
	2000	100.0	54.1	91.1	56.8	12.4	114.5	10.0	19.2	4.6	70.9
	2009	100.0	54.1	91.1	56.8	12.4	114.5	10.0	19.2	4.4	70.7
Micronesia (Federated States of) - Micronésie (États fédérés de)	1990	100.0	52.6	75.8	34.1	17.7	80.2	19.1	4.0	1.4	76.9
	1995	100.0	50.4	72.5	32.6	17.9	73.5	19.1	4.0	1.4	76.9
	2000	100.0	50.9	73.3	33.0	17.2	74.5	19.1	4.0	1.4	76.9
	2009	100.0	52.0	74.8	33.6	17.3	77.7	19.1	4.0	1.4	76.9
Nauru	1990	100.0	52.8	89.6	93.1	11.6	147.2	6.6	16.2	3.9	77.2
	1995	100.0	51.7	79.0	60.5	17.5	108.6	7.0	11.1	4.3	81.9
	2000	100.0	42.5	65.2	50.7	10.1	68.4	5.7	26.9	3.6	67.5
	2009	100.0	65.1	99.9	77.8	16.9	159.6	4.1	51.1	24.9	44.8
New Caledonia - Nouvelle-Calédonie	1990	100.0	32.6	57.3	23.3	22.0	35.4	2.0	25.2	6.4	72.8
	1995	100.0	28.3	69.2	21.8	17.5	36.8	1.8	22.2	6.0	76.0
	2000	100.0	26.8	65.1	22.9	22.8	37.6	2.4	26.0	14.9	71.6
	2009	100.0	24.2	59.9	39.0	23.4	46.3	1.8	28.7	17.4	69.4
Palau - Palaos	1990	100.0	33.2	44.2	38.3	35.8	47.5	25.9	15.5	0.7	58.6
	1995	100.0	41.5	88.0	19.4	14.6	63.5	5.9	9.4	0.9	84.7
	2000	100.0	41.9	125.5	29.0	9.6	106.1	3.9	15.3	1.4	80.8
	2009	100.0	35.0	49.4	21.8	72.3	78.5	3.2	20.3	0.4	76.4
Papua New Guinea - Papouasie-Nouvelle-Guinée	1990	100.0	26.3	51.8	24.0	43.0	45.4	29.7	31.2	9.2	39.0
	1995	100.0	17.1	42.7	21.9	59.3	41.1	35.1	33.3	8.3	31.6
	2000	100.0	16.6	44.6	21.9	66.2	49.2	35.2	40.7	7.4	24.1
	2009	100.0	10.7	66.4	18.5	63.6	59.2	34.5	42.1	6.5	23.4
Samoa	1990	100.0	27.7	82.6	22.9	28.0	61.2	20.5	28.8	19.2	50.6
	1995	100.0	23.8	80.5	19.6	31.8	55.7	18.4	29.4	19.2	52.2
	2000	100.0	24.0	85.2	14.2	30.6	53.9	16.7	26.8	15.0	56.6
	2009	100.0	21.1	92.5	9.2	31.1	53.9	11.7	26.0	8.4	62.3
Solomon Islands - Îles Salomon	1990	100.0	31.1	57.4	20.1	46.5	56.8	45.5	7.9	3.7	46.6
	1995	100.0	32.9	48.9	19.2	57.7	58.8	38.3	9.9	6.3	51.8
	2000	100.0	31.8	48.5	19.6	59.1	59.1	38.5	10.0	6.3	51.4
	2009	100.0	36.8	74.0	13.9	34.8	54.4	35.6	7.5	5.3	56.9
Tonga	1990	100.0	18.7	93.7	18.1	33.2	63.8	34.7	13.6	6.0	51.7
	1995	100.0	18.3	107.4	19.6	18.7	64.0	22.2	22.1	9.0	55.7
	2000	100.0	21.5	96.5	18.7	15.0	51.7	22.2	20.7	10.2	57.0
	2009	100.0	19.7	99.7	26.1	13.2	58.5	19.1	17.9	7.9	63.0
Tuvalu	1990	100.0	54.7	40.7	53.0	2.6	51.0	25.6	14.5	3.1	59.8
	1995	100.0	49.9	55.3	57.7	2.2	65.1	24.0	14.0	3.9	62.0
	2000	100.0	147.1	-25.8	52.0	2.3	75.6	17.3	13.1	3.2	69.7
	2009	100.0	71.3	101.5	8.2	1.9	82.8	17.5	13.6	3.6	68.9
Vanuatu	1990	100.0	30.1	75.2	31.4	48.1	78.3	22.5	9.5	5.2	67.9
	1995	100.0	27.1	56.0	23.2	45.8	54.8	28.9	8.8	4.7	62.3
	2000	100.0	15.0	64.3	25.0	38.3	46.2	24.3	11.9	4.8	63.8
	2009	100.0	14.8	61.6	27.1	48.3	55.4	21.3	8.9	3.9	69.8
Transition economies - Économies en transition	**1990**	**100.0**	**20.9**	**49.1**	**28.1**	**22.7**	**24.7**	**17.7**	**38.0**	**28.6**	**44.3**
	1995	**100.0**	**19.5**	**55.9**	**24.5**	**32.0**	**31.8**	**10.7**	**38.7**	**21.5**	**50.6**
	2000	**100.0**	**16.1**	**52.8**	**19.2**	**45.0**	**33.1**	**10.3**	**37.6**	**21.5**	**52.1**
	2009	**100.0**	**19.1**	**56.5**	**20.3**	**32.3**	**27.8**	**6.4**	**33.4**	**15.4**	**60.3**
Albania - Albanie	1990	100.0	10.2	72.7	24.4	14.9	22.2	40.2	43.8	..	16.0
	1995	100.0	13.3	88.4	20.5	12.2	33.8	54.6	22.0	..	23.4
	2000	100.0	9.5	76.6	34.2	17.9	38.1	25.5	16.1	4.8	58.5
	2009	100.0	9.1	81.9	33.1	28.0	52.8	18.9	24.4	8.0	56.6

For sources and notes, see end of table.

Pour les sources et les notes, se reporter à la fin du tableau.

8.3.1 Nominal gross domestic product by type of expenditure and by kind of economic activity of countries and geographical regions

8.3.1 Produit intérieur brut nominal par catégories de dépenses et par branches d'activité économique des pays et des régions géographiques

Region, country or territory / Régions, pays ou territoires	Year / Année	Total GDP / PIB total	GDP by type of expenditure (1) / PIB par catégories de dépense (1)					GDP by kind of economic activity (2) / PIB par branches d'activité économique (2)			
			Final consumption / Consommation finale		Gross capital formation / Formation brute de capital	Exports / Exportations / Of goods and services / Des biens et services	Less imports / Moins les importations	Agriculture (3)	Industry (4) / Industrie (4)		Services (5)
			Government / Administration publique	Household / Ménages					Total	Manufacturing / Activités de fabrication	
			Percentage / En pourcentage								
Armenia - Arménie	1995	100.0	11.2	106.3	18.4	23.9	62.2	42.3	28.6	19.3	29.1
	2000	100.0	11.8	97.1	18.6	23.4	50.5	25.1	38.3	18.2	36.5
	2009	100.0	12.6	81.3	33.8	15.5	43.4	18.2	34.5	9.7	47.3
Azerbaijan - Azerbaïdjan	1995	100.0	12.8	84.3	23.8	32.5	53.4	26.9	32.9	12.2	40.3
	2000	100.0	15.2	64.4	20.7	40.2	38.4	17.0	45.1	5.6	37.9
	2009	100.0	12.9	43.2	18.3	53.2	27.5	7.1	61.0	4.3	31.9
Belarus - Bélarus	1995	100.0	20.6	59.1	24.8	49.7	54.1	16.8	37.7	29.9	45.5
	2000	100.0	19.5	56.9	25.4	64.7	68.2	13.9	40.4	31.0	45.8
	2009	100.0	16.7	55.8	38.3	50.7	62.1	9.3	42.9	29.1	47.8
Bosnia and Herzegovina - Bosnie-Herzégovine	1995	100.0	25.3	106.9	20.0	20.4	71.5	22.0	31.8	14.1	46.2
	2000	100.0	24.5	103.3	21.2	29.6	77.9	11.6	26.1	10.9	62.3
	2009	100.0	24.0	90.7	23.0	31.9	55.3	8.8	26.2	12.4	65.0
Croatia - Croatie	1995	100.0	24.5	67.7	16.3	33.4	42.2	9.7	31.6	22.5	58.6
	2000	100.0	21.7	62.8	18.7	42.0	45.3	8.4	28.4	20.3	63.2
	2009	100.0	19.7	56.9	26.7	36.1	39.4	6.7	27.1	15.4	66.1
Georgia - Géorgie	1995	100.0	8.0	83.2	24.0	14.0	28.5	44.4	14.3	10.2	41.3
	2000	100.0	8.5	90.5	26.6	23.0	39.7	21.7	22.1	12.9	56.1
	2009	100.0	24.4	82.7	12.1	29.5	49.0	9.5	21.0	11.4	69.5
Kazakhstan	1995	100.0	13.6	71.1	23.3	39.0	43.5	12.8	42.8	19.2	44.4
	2000	100.0	12.1	61.9	18.1	56.6	49.1	8.6	40.1	17.5	51.3
	2009	100.0	12.3	46.1	29.6	44.4	35.7	6.3	38.1	11.4	55.6
Kyrgyzstan - Kirghizistan	1995	100.0	19.5	75.0	18.3	29.5	42.4	43.1	21.7	12.5	35.2
	2000	100.0	20.0	65.7	20.0	41.8	47.6	36.6	31.3	19.4	32.1
	2009	100.0	19.2	91.0	19.0	56.2	80.6	23.9	22.3	13.6	53.8
Montenegro - Monténégro	2009	100.0	20.6	94.0	18.0	33.3	66.0	9.5	20.8	7.6	69.7
Republic of Moldova - République de Moldova	1995	100.0	25.9	57.0	24.9	60.1	67.9	32.2	31.4	25.1	36.4
	2000	100.0	14.7	88.4	23.9	49.6	76.6	28.3	21.2	15.8	50.6
	2009	100.0	24.1	88.7	23.8	36.8	73.4	9.8	19.2	12.3	71.0
Russian Federation - Fédération de Russie	1995	100.0	19.1	52.1	25.4	29.3	25.9	7.6	39.5	20.1	53.0
	2000	100.0	15.1	46.2	18.7	44.1	24.0	6.7	39.8	22.7	53.5
	2009	100.0	20.1	54.6	18.8	27.8	20.4	4.7	32.9	15.0	62.4
Serbia and Montenegro - Serbie-et-Monténégro	1995	100.0	24.8	76.8	14.6	18.7	35.0	19.6	31.4	20.1	49.0
	2000	100.0	21.9	80.5	12.0	14.1	28.7	22.3	30.3	21.8	47.3
Serbia - Serbie	2009	100.0	19.5	76.4	22.7	26.9	45.5	11.1	27.7	17.0	61.2
SFR of Yugoslavia (former) - RSF de Yougoslavie (anc.)	1990	100.0	17.6	66.1	22.1	23.7	29.4	12.9	43.3	31.2	43.9
Tajikistan - Tadjikistan	1995	100.0	10.9	60.5	28.7	112.0	121.2	35.9	38.6	33.6	25.5
	2000	100.0	11.6	87.7	9.4	92.4	100.2	27.3	43.3	36.4	29.4
	2009	100.0	9.7	105.5	25.0	16.4	56.7	28.0	38.8	29.3	33.1
TFYR of Macedonia - LERY de Macédoine	1995	100.0	18.6	70.4	20.8	33.0	42.8	12.4	32.0	20.3	55.6
	2000	100.0	18.2	74.4	22.3	48.6	63.5	11.7	32.9	20.2	55.4
	2009	100.0	17.9	78.6	23.4	43.4	63.2	11.4	29.8	19.4	58.8
Turkmenistan - Turkménistan	1995	100.0	8.4	60.6	33.6	142.5	145.0	16.9	65.3	59.2	17.9
	2000	100.0	14.2	36.5	34.7	95.5	80.9	22.9	41.8	35.0	35.2
	2009	100.0	9.1	54.0	4.5	72.1	39.8	16.3	42.7	35.6	41.0
Ukraine (6)	1995	100.0	21.3	55.1	26.7	47.1	50.2	15.0	43.1	34.1	41.9
	2000	100.0	18.6	56.6	19.7	62.4	57.4	16.8	37.6	21.3	45.5
	2009	100.0	19.2	65.5	17.1	46.3	48.0	7.7	27.6	17.1	64.7
USSR (former) - URSS (anc.)	1990	100.0	21.2	47.1	28.7	22.6	24.2	18.1	37.5	28.5	44.4

For sources and notes, see end of table.

Pour les sources et les notes, se reporter à la fin du tableau.

8

8.3.1 Nominal gross domestic product by type of expenditure and by kind of economic activity of countries and geographical regions

8.3.1 Produit intérieur brut nominal par catégories de dépenses et par branches d'activité économique des pays et des régions géographiques

Region, country or territory / Régions, pays ou territoires	Year / Année	Total GDP / PIB total	GDP by type of expenditure (1) / PIB par catégories de dépense (1)					GDP by kind of economic activity (2) / PIB par branches d'activité économique (2)			
			Final consumption / Consommation finale		Gross capital formation / Formation brute de capital	Exports / Exportations	Less imports / Moins les importations	Agriculture (3)	Industry (4) / Industrie (4)		Services (5)
			Government / Administration publique	Household / Ménages		Of goods and services / Des biens et services			Total	Manufacturing / Activités de fabrication	
			Percentage / En pourcentage								
Uzbekistan - Ouzbékistan	1995	100.0	22.3	50.6	24.2	31.6	28.7	31.4	30.9	19.3	37.7
	2000	100.0	10.7	91.9	19.0	20.5	20.7	34.0	22.0	19.1	12.0
	2009	100.0	17.4	53.7	20.5	40.7	32.3	25.6	31.0	21.1	43.4
Developed economies: America - Économies développées : Amérique	**1990**	**100.0**	**17.5**	**65.7**	**17.9**	**11.4**	**12.6**	**2.0**	**27.8**	**18.2**	**70.2**
	1995	**100.0**	**15.8**	**66.9**	**18.1**	**13.3**	**14.1**	**1.6**	**26.2**	**17.8**	**72.2**
	2000	**100.0**	**14.6**	**68.0**	**20.5**	**13.8**	**16.9**	**1.1**	**24.2**	**16.2**	**74.7**
	2009	**100.0**	**17.6**	**69.9**	**14.3**	**13.1**	**15.6**	**1.1**	**22.3**	**13.0**	**76.6**
Bermuda - Bermudes	1990	100.0	12.5	69.1	16.4	47.5	43.7	0.8	10.3	2.4	88.9
	1995	100.0	11.8	64.3	14.0	45.5	36.0	0.8	10.4	2.4	88.8
	2000	100.0	10.9	51.5	20.1	47.4	41.1	0.7	11.0	2.4	88.4
	2009	100.0	19.8	74.7	19.8	42.1	56.4	0.8	8.8	1.5	90.4
Canada	1990	100.0	22.3	56.7	20.9	25.8	25.7	2.9	31.3	16.9	65.8
	1995	100.0	21.3	56.9	18.8	37.3	34.1	2.9	30.7	18.4	66.4
	2000	100.0	18.6	55.4	20.2	45.6	39.8	2.3	33.2	19.2	64.5
	2009	100.0	21.9	58.8	21.0	28.7	30.4	1.5	28.2	11.3	70.3
Greenland - Groenland	1990	100.0	53.4	27.0	19.0	44.3	43.7	7.7	21.5	12.3	70.7
	1995	100.0	54.0	34.8	16.3	30.7	35.9	7.7	21.6	12.4	70.6
	2000	100.0	52.4	32.9	23.2	25.5	34.1	7.3	21.0	11.2	71.7
	2009	100.0	53.0	32.2	24.9	23.7	33.9	5.4	19.2	9.1	75.3
United States - États-Unis	1990	100.0	17.0	66.6	17.7	10.0	11.3	1.9	27.5	18.3	70.6
	1995	100.0	15.4	67.7	18.1	11.4	12.5	1.5	25.8	17.8	72.6
	2000	100.0	14.3	68.9	20.6	11.5	15.2	1.0	23.6	16.0	75.4
	2009	100.0	17.2	70.9	13.6	11.6	14.2	1.1	21.7	13.1	77.2
Developed economies: Asia - Économies développées : Asie	**1990**	**100.0**	**13.6**	**53.0**	**32.5**	**10.7**	**9.9**	**2.5**	**38.2**	**25.9**	**59.3**
	1995	**100.0**	**15.4**	**55.1**	**28.3**	**9.5**	**8.3**	**1.9**	**33.1**	**22.3**	**65.0**
	2000	**100.0**	**17.1**	**56.2**	**25.3**	**11.7**	**10.3**	**1.7**	**31.0**	**21.2**	**67.3**
	2009	**100.0**	**19.9**	**58.2**	**20.5**	**13.4**	**13.0**	**1.4**	**28.0**	**20.0**	**70.6**
Israel - Israël	1990	100.0	28.6	55.0	19.8	31.0	34.9	3.0	25.6	18.5	71.5
	1995	100.0	28.0	55.2	25.1	29.1	37.3	2.1	26.1	16.9	71.8
	2000	100.0	25.9	54.0	20.4	37.1	37.4	1.7	25.2	18.0	73.0
	2009	100.0	24.3	57.2	16.3	34.5	32.3	1.8	22.6	15.9	75.6
Japan - Japon	1990	100.0	13.3	53.0	32.7	10.4	9.4	2.5	38.4	26.0	59.1
	1995	100.0	15.2	55.1	28.3	9.1	7.7	1.9	33.2	22.4	64.9
	2000	100.0	16.9	56.2	25.4	11.0	9.5	1.7	31.1	21.3	67.2
	2009	100.0	19.7	58.3	20.7	12.5	12.2	1.4	28.2	20.2	70.4
Developed economies: Europe - Économies développées : Europe	**1990**	**100.0**	**19.9**	**57.5**	**23.1**	**26.5**	**27.2**	**3.5**	**32.8**	**22.6**	**63.7**
	1995	**100.0**	**20.2**	**57.8**	**20.4**	**29.9**	**28.3**	**2.9**	**29.8**	**20.3**	**67.3**
	2000	**100.0**	**19.5**	**58.4**	**21.3**	**36.4**	**35.7**	**2.4**	**28.2**	**19.3**	**69.4**
	2009	**100.0**	**22.1**	**58.0**	**18.3**	**37.1**	**35.6**	**1.6**	**24.7**	**14.9**	**73.6**
Andorra - Andorre	1990	100.0	16.7	60.4	26.1	16.1	19.4	0.6	16.4	3.2	83.0
	1995	100.0	18.1	60.0	21.9	22.4	22.4	0.7	16.8	3.3	82.6
	2000	100.0	17.2	59.7	26.3	29.0	32.2	0.7	14.9	3.1	84.4
	2009	100.0	21.1	56.6	24.4	23.4	25.5	0.6	15.7	3.0	83.7
Austria - Autriche	1990	100.0	18.8	56.4	25.1	37.1	36.9	3.7	32.2	21.7	64.1
	1995	100.0	20.5	55.5	24.8	34.9	35.8	2.6	30.8	19.6	66.6
	2000	100.0	19.1	54.8	24.5	46.4	44.7	2.0	30.8	20.6	67.2
	2009	100.0	19.9	54.3	21.2	50.5	46.0	1.5	29.2	18.6	69.3
Belgium - Belgique	1990	100.0	19.7	55.3	22.4	69.5	67.5	2.3	30.9	22.5	66.8
	1995	100.0	21.4	54.1	20.6	65.4	61.5	1.5	28.4	20.3	70.1
	2000	100.0	21.3	53.3	22.5	78.2	75.3	1.4	27.0	19.3	71.6
	2009	100.0	24.7	52.4	20.2	73.0	70.2	0.7	21.7	14.0	77.6

For sources and notes, see end of table.

Pour les sources et les notes, se reporter à la fin du tableau.

Region, country or territory — Régions, pays ou territoires	Year — Année	Total GDP — PIB total	GDP by type of expenditure (1) — PIB par catégories de dépense (1)					GDP by kind of economic activity (2) — PIB par branches d'activité économique (2)			
			Final consumption — Consommation finale		Gross capital formation — Formation brute de capital	Exports — Exportations	Less imports — Moins les impor-tations	Agri-culture (3)	Industry (4) — Industrie (4)		Services (5)
			Government — Administra-tion publique	Household — Ménages		Of goods and services — Des biens et services			Total	Manu-facturing — Activités de fabrication	
			Percentage / En pourcentage								
Bulgaria - Bulgarie	1990	100.0	7.2	68.0	30.4	33.1	37.6	18.3	50.9	33.2	30.8
	1995	100.0	15.3	70.7	15.7	44.7	46.3	13.4	32.4	20.2	54.3
	2000	100.0	19.0	68.4	18.0	50.5	55.8	13.9	30.1	17.8	56.0
	2009	100.0	16.3	66.0	25.6	47.8	55.8	5.6	30.3	15.1	64.1
Cyprus - Chypre	1990	100.0	14.7	60.1	26.8	55.5	57.6	6.9	25.9	14.3	67.2
	1995	100.0	13.7	64.8	21.8	50.2	50.5	5.1	22.8	12.1	72.0
	2000	100.0	16.0	64.8	18.3	55.4	54.5	3.6	19.1	9.9	77.3
	2009	100.0	19.9	68.7	17.2	39.4	45.2	2.1	18.7	7.2	79.3
Czechoslovakia (former) - Tchécoslovaquie (anc.)	1990	100.0	23.9	50.4	26.0	-2.9	38.8	7.6	44.0	34.9	48.4
Czech Republic - République tchèque	1995	100.0	20.9	50.9	32.6	50.7	55.1	5.0	38.3	24.3	56.7
	2000	100.0	21.1	52.5	29.5	63.4	66.4	3.9	38.1	26.8	58.0
	2009	100.0	22.0	50.7	21.7	69.1	63.6	2.3	37.7	23.6	60.0
Denmark - Danemark	1990	100.0	25.1	50.3	19.9	37.2	32.6	4.0	25.6	17.4	70.4
	1995	100.0	25.2	51.2	19.5	37.6	33.5	3.5	25.1	17.1	71.5
	2000	100.0	25.1	47.7	21.2	46.6	40.5	2.6	26.8	16.2	70.6
	2009	100.0	29.9	49.2	17.4	47.2	43.7	1.1	22.2	13.0	76.7
Estonia - Estonie	1995	100.0	25.5	54.4	28.2	68.1	75.7	5.8	32.0	21.0	61.2
	2000	100.0	19.8	55.5	28.4	84.6	88.2	4.8	27.5	17.7	67.6
	2009	100.0	22.0	51.9	18.7	64.7	58.6	2.6	26.5	14.3	71.0
Finland - Finlande	1990	100.0	21.7	51.0	28.5	22.5	24.1	6.3	33.6	22.7	60.1
	1995	100.0	22.7	52.1	10.2	36.5	29.0	4.5	33.3	25.4	62.2
	2000	100.0	20.5	49.4	20.9	43.6	34.5	3.5	34.7	26.5	61.8
	2009	100.0	25.1	54.9	18.3	37.4	34.9	2.7	28.2	18.2	69.2
France	1990	100.0	21.7	57.1	22.5	21.2	22.6	3.8	26.6	17.9	69.6
	1995	100.0	23.7	56.6	18.6	22.8	21.6	3.3	24.6	16.4	72.1
	2000	100.0	22.9	55.7	20.5	28.6	27.7	2.8	22.9	16.0	74.3
	2009	100.0	24.6	58.3	19.0	23.0	25.0	1.7	18.8	10.6	79.5
Germany - Allemagne	1990	100.0	19.3	57.8	23.2	24.8	24.9	1.5	37.3	28.0	61.2
	1995	100.0	19.6	57.7	22.2	24.0	23.5	1.3	32.1	22.6	66.6
	2000	100.0	19.0	58.9	21.8	33.4	33.0	1.3	30.3	22.9	68.5
	2009	100.0	19.7	58.9	16.5	40.8	35.9	0.8	26.5	19.1	72.7
Greece - Grèce	1990	100.0	15.2	75.2	22.6	17.5	29.6	9.3	25.9	14.5	64.8
	1995	100.0	15.5	76.7	18.4	17.1	26.5	8.9	21.5	12.0	69.6
	2000	100.0	17.8	72.4	23.3	24.9	38.4	6.6	21.0	11.1	72.5
	2009	100.0	19.5	74.8	16.5	19.0	29.8	3.2	17.9	10.3	78.9
Hungary - Hongrie	1990	100.0	21.7	49.0	24.3	28.5	24.7	12.5	34.0	20.5	53.5
	1995	100.0	23.3	54.4	22.0	45.1	44.8	8.0	29.3	21.3	62.6
	2000	100.0	21.0	53.0	29.4	73.0	76.4	5.4	31.7	23.0	62.9
	2009	100.0	22.2	53.4	19.2	77.4	72.2	3.3	29.4	21.3	67.3
Iceland - Islande	1990	100.0	19.9	59.8	19.0	33.6	32.3	11.7	30.8	16.9	57.4
	1995	100.0	22.1	58.0	16.3	35.5	31.9	11.6	28.9	16.6	59.5
	2000	100.0	23.4	60.6	23.2	33.8	40.9	9.1	26.1	13.9	64.8
	2009	100.0	26.4	51.0	13.8	53.0	44.2	6.2	26.7	11.7	67.2
Ireland - Irlande	1990	100.0	16.3	59.4	20.7	56.7	51.8	8.9	35.1	28.1	56.0
	1995	100.0	16.3	54.4	18.1	76.3	64.6	7.0	38.0	30.2	55.0
	2000	100.0	13.6	48.8	24.0	98.1	84.7	3.2	41.8	32.7	55.0
	2009	100.0	19.5	50.7	14.1	90.7	75.4	1.0	31.9	24.2	67.1
Italy - Italie	1990	100.0	20.1	57.3	22.3	19.2	19.0	3.5	32.1	23.3	64.4
	1995	100.0	18.0	58.4	19.8	25.7	21.9	3.3	30.3	22.2	66.4
	2000	100.0	18.4	59.9	20.7	27.1	26.1	2.8	28.4	21.0	68.8
	2009	100.0	21.6	59.9	18.9	24.0	24.4	1.9	25.5	16.5	72.7

For sources and notes, see end of table.

Pour les sources et les notes, se reporter à la fin du tableau.

8

8.3.1 Nominal gross domestic product by type of expenditure and by kind of economic activity of countries and geographical regions

8.3.1 Produit intérieur brut nominal par catégories de dépenses et par branches d'activité économique des pays et des régions géographiques

Region, country or territory / Régions, pays ou territoires	Year / Année	Total GDP / PIB total	GDP by type of expenditure (1) / PIB par catégories de dépense (1)					GDP by kind of economic activity (2) / PIB par branches d'activité économique (2)			
			Final consumption / Consommation finale		Gross capital formation / Formation brute de capital	Exports / Exportations	Less imports / Moins les importations	Agriculture (3) / Agriculture (3)	Industry (4) / Industrie (4)		Services (5)
			Government / Administration publique	Household / Ménages		Of goods and services / Des biens et services			Total	Manufacturing / Activités de fabrication	
			Percentage / En pourcentage								
Latvia - Lettonie	1995	100.0	24.5	62.9	15.0	41.9	44.3	9.1	30.4	20.7	60.6
	2000	100.0	20.8	62.5	23.7	41.6	48.7	4.6	23.6	13.7	71.8
	2009	100.0	19.6	61.6	20.3	43.9	45.4	3.3	20.6	9.9	70.1
Lithuania - Lituanie	1995	100.0	24.5	63.5	22.6	47.5	58.1	11.0	31.5	19.1	57.5
	2000	100.0	22.8	64.6	18.9	44.7	51.0	6.3	29.8	19.3	63.9
	2009	100.0	21.9	68.8	10.6	54.6	56.1	3.4	26.9	16.4	69.7
Luxembourg	1990	100.0	15.8	47.0	23.7	101.5	88.2	1.5	28.7	20.1	69.8
	1995	100.0	15.9	43.3	19.6	106.4	85.2	1.0	21.7	13.7	77.2
	2000	100.0	15.1	40.7	23.2	150.0	129.0	0.7	18.4	11.3	81.0
	2009	100.0	16.7	34.1	16.4	167.6	134.7	0.3	13.1	6.5	86.6
Malta - Malte	1990	100.0	16.2	64.0	30.6	75.8	88.7	3.5	31.4	24.0	65.2
	1995	100.0	18.9	62.3	29.3	83.4	96.3	2.8	28.3	21.6	68.9
	2000	100.0	18.5	65.9	26.2	92.1	102.7	2.3	28.5	22.4	69.1
	2009	100.0	21.7	63.2	14.5	74.2	73.7	1.8	19.4	13.6	78.8
Netherlands - Pays-Bas	1990	100.0	23.0	49.7	23.5	56.5	52.6	4.4	29.4	18.6	66.2
	1995	100.0	23.8	49.5	21.0	59.4	53.7	3.5	27.4	17.4	69.2
	2000	100.0	22.0	50.4	22.0	70.1	64.5	2.6	24.9	15.6	72.4
	2009	100.0	28.4	45.9	18.4	69.2	62.0	1.7	23.9	12.6	74.4
Norway - Norvège	1990	100.0	21.2	49.8	22.7	40.1	33.8	3.4	34.0	12.3	62.6
	1995	100.0	21.6	49.9	22.3	38.0	31.8	3.1	34.2	13.2	62.8
	2000	100.0	19.3	43.2	20.4	46.5	29.4	2.1	42.0	10.6	56.0
	2009	100.0	22.4	42.6	20.2	42.4	27.6	1.2	40.4	9.6	58.4
Poland - Pologne	1990	100.0	20.8	48.0	24.3	26.2	19.7	9.2	46.0	29.2	44.8
	1995	100.0	18.7	60.4	18.7	23.2	21.0	8.0	35.2	21.1	56.8
	2000	100.0	17.4	64.1	24.8	27.1	33.5	5.0	31.7	18.5	63.3
	2009	100.0	18.4	61.1	20.4	39.5	39.4	3.6	31.8	18.6	64.6
Portugal	1990	100.0	15.1	64.4	27.5	29.6	36.7	8.9	28.2	19.2	62.9
	1995	100.0	17.4	65.3	24.0	27.2	33.9	5.6	28.4	18.5	66.0
	2000	100.0	18.8	63.8	28.5	29.0	40.0	3.7	28.0	17.5	68.3
	2009	100.0	21.3	66.6	19.7	27.9	35.5	2.3	22.8	13.0	74.8
Romania - Roumanie	1990	100.0	13.6	65.7	29.9	16.4	24.8	23.6	47.6	36.9	28.8
	1995	100.0	14.0	67.5	24.0	26.5	32.6	21.0	40.4	26.1	38.6
	2000	100.0	17.5	68.5	19.4	32.8	38.1	12.1	34.4	23.4	53.6
	2009	100.0	18.1	62.8	25.1	31.2	37.2	7.0	37.3	22.7	55.7
San Marino - Saint-Marin	1990	100.0	20.1	57.3	22.3	19.2	19.0	3.5	32.1	23.3	64.4
	1995	100.0	9.5	68.5	18.0	236.7	232.7	3.3	30.3	22.2	66.4
	2000	100.0	12.5	42.9	50.4	193.7	199.4	2.8	28.4	21.0	68.8
	2009	100.0	10.0	37.1	46.9	207.2	201.2	1.9	25.5	16.5	72.7
Slovakia - Slovaquie	1995	100.0	21.7	51.8	24.3	57.8	55.5	5.9	37.8	26.8	56.3
	2000	100.0	20.1	56.5	26.0	70.4	73.0	4.5	36.2	24.7	59.3
	2009	100.0	20.0	60.9	19.5	70.6	71.0	3.9	35.2	19.6	60.9
Slovenia - Slovénie	1995	100.0	18.6	60.0	23.4	49.8	51.7	4.3	35.4	25.9	60.2
	2000	100.0	18.8	57.4	27.3	53.9	57.4	3.3	35.8	25.8	60.9
	2009	100.0	20.3	55.4	23.0	58.1	56.8	2.4	31.1	19.6	66.5
Spain - Espagne	1990	100.0	16.7	60.4	26.1	16.1	19.4	5.5	33.0	20.7	61.5
	1995	100.0	18.1	60.0	21.9	22.4	22.4	4.5	29.4	18.5	66.1
	2000	100.0	17.2	59.7	26.3	29.0	32.2	4.4	29.2	18.6	66.4
	2009	100.0	21.1	56.6	24.4	23.4	25.5	2.6	26.1	12.7	71.3
Sweden - Suède	1990	100.0	26.9	49.3	23.5	30.5	29.8	4.1	31.1	20.8	64.8
	1995	100.0	26.6	49.4	17.2	39.7	32.9	3.0	30.5	22.4	66.5
	2000	100.0	25.8	49.2	18.6	46.5	40.2	2.1	28.8	22.0	69.1
	2009	100.0	27.8	48.8	16.6	48.5	41.6	1.7	25.1	16.1	73.1

For sources and notes, see end of table.

Pour les sources et les notes, se reporter à la fin du tableau.

8.3.1 Nominal gross domestic product by type of expenditure and by kind of economic activity of countries and geographical regions

8.3.1 Produit intérieur brut nominal par catégories de dépenses et par branches d'activité économique des pays et des régions géographiques

Region, country or territory / Régions, pays ou territoires	Year / Année	Total GDP / PIB total	GDP by type of expenditure (1) / PIB par catégories de dépense (1)					GDP by kind of economic activity (2) / PIB par branches d'activité économique (2)			
			Final consumption / Consommation finale		Gross capital formation / Formation brute de capital	Exports / Exportations	Less imports / Moins les importations	Agriculture (3)	Industry (4) / Industrie (4)		Services (5)
			Government / Administration publique	Household / Ménages		Of goods and services / Des biens et services			Total	Manufacturing / Activités de fabrication	
			Percentage / En pourcentage								
Switzerland - Suisse	1990	100.0	11.0	59.9	30.7	30.4	34.7	2.9	31.9	21.1	66.9
	1995	100.0	11.8	59.7	23.4	35.9	30.8	2.1	30.3	20.4	67.6
	2000	100.0	11.1	59.9	23.2	46.5	40.7	1.6	27.3	19.0	71.1
	2009	100.0	11.3	58.0	19.7	51.7	40.7	1.2	26.8	19.0	72.0
United Kingdom - Royaume-Uni	1990	100.0	19.7	62.2	20.2	24.0	26.1	1.8	34.1	22.5	64.1
	1995	100.0	19.5	63.5	17.1	28.2	28.4	1.8	31.0	21.2	67.2
	2000	100.0	18.6	65.5	17.7	27.6	29.5	1.0	27.3	17.4	71.7
	2009	100.0	23.5	65.2	13.6	27.7	30.1	0.7	21.1	11.1	78.2
Developed economies: Oceania - Économies développées : Océanie	**1990**	**100.0**	**17.8**	**58.3**	**23.3**	**17.0**	**17.2**	**3.8**	**29.7**	**14.4**	**66.5**
	1995	**100.0**	**17.6**	**58.8**	**23.9**	**20.1**	**20.4**	**4.1**	**28.1**	**14.7**	**67.8**
	2000	**100.0**	**17.5**	**59.2**	**23.0**	**23.5**	**23.1**	**4.4**	**25.7**	**12.7**	**69.9**
	2009	**100.0**	**18.3**	**56.1**	**27.3**	**20.4**	**20.7**	**2.8**	**27.0**	**10.5**	**70.2**
Australia - Australie	1990	100.0	17.7	57.9	23.7	15.8	16.0	3.4	30.1	13.9	66.5
	1995	100.0	17.6	58.8	24.0	18.8	19.2	3.6	28.4	14.2	68.0
	2000	100.0	17.5	59.1	23.2	22.0	21.8	3.9	25.9	12.2	70.2
	2009	100.0	18.0	55.7	28.3	19.5	20.0	2.4	27.3	9.9	70.2
New Zealand - Nouvelle-Zélande	1990	100.0	18.9	61.1	19.8	26.5	26.3	6.7	26.8	18.0	66.6
	1995	100.0	17.3	58.9	23.0	28.7	27.9	7.2	25.9	17.9	66.9
	2000	100.0	17.3	59.7	21.3	35.1	33.5	8.6	24.4	16.3	66.9
	2009	100.0	20.6	59.1	18.2	28.3	26.6	5.5	24.3	14.9	70.2

Sources:
- UN DESA Statistics Division

Notes:

- Data in this table are shown as percentage of GDP / Value added at current prices in US dollars.

- For countries' notes on GDP / Value added breakdown, see: http://unstats.un.org/unsd/snaama/downloads/Download-GDPcurrent-USD-countries.xls

(1) The breakdown in shares by type of expenditure is shown as percentage of GDP. The breakdown in shares of GDP might not add-up to 100 percent due to statistical discrepancies.

(2) The breakdown in shares by kind of economic activity is shown as percentage of total value added.

(3) Includes agriculture, hunting, forestry and fishing (ISIC Revision 3 divisions 01-05).

(4) Includes mining and quarrying, manufacturing, electricity, gas and water supply, and construction (ISIC Revision 3 divisions 10-45).

(5) Include all other economic activities (ISIC Revision 3 divisions 50-99).

(6) Including Western Sahara.

Sources :
- ONU DAES Division de statistique

Notes :

- Les données de ce tableau sont indiquées en pourcentage du PIB / Valeur ajoutée aux prix courants en dollars des États-Unis.

- Pour les notes des pays sur la ventilation du PIB / Valeur ajoutée, se référer à: http://unstats.un.org/unsd/snaama/downloads/Download-GDPcurrent-USD-countries.xls

(1) La ventilation par catégories de dépense est calculée en pourcentage du PIB. La somme des pourcentages du PIB ventilé peut ne pas être égale à 100 à cause des écarts statistiques.

(2) La ventilation par branches d'activité économique est calculée en pourcentage de la valeur ajoutée totale.

(3) Inclut l'agriculture, la chasse, la sylviculture et la pêche (CITI Révision 3 divisions 01-05).

(4) Inclut les activités extractives, les activités de fabrication, la production et distribution d'électricité, de gaz et d'eau et la construction (CITI Révision 3 divisions 10-45).

(5) Incluent toutes les autres activités économiques (CITI Révision 3 divisions 50-99).

(6) Y compris le Sahara occidental.

8

8.3.2 Nominal gross domestic product by type of expenditure and by kind of economic activity of economic groupings

8.3.2 Produit intérieur brut nominal par catégories de dépenses et par branches d'activité économique des groupements économiques

Economic grouping / Groupements économiques	Year / Année	Total GDP / PIB total	Final consumption / Consommation finale — Government / Administration publique	Final consumption / Consommation finale — Household / Ménages	Gross capital formation / Formation brute de capital	Exports / Exportations — Of goods and services / Des biens et services	Less imports / Moins les importations — Of goods and services / Des biens et services	Agriculture (3)	Industry (4) / Industrie (4) — Total	Industry (4) / Industrie (4) — Manufacturing / Activités de fabrication	Services (5)
			Percentage / En pourcentage								
DEVELOPING ECONOMIES - ÉCONOMIES EN DÉVELOPPEMENT	1990	100.0	13.8	59.3	25.2	25.9	24.9	14.2	35.6	21.7	50.3
	1995	100.0	13.7	59.0	27.4	29.7	30.0	11.9	35.2	22.6	52.9
	2000	100.0	14.1	58.4	24.9	34.8	32.3	10.3	36.3	22.6	53.4
	2009	100.0	14.3	53.3	30.1	38.0	34.5	9.7	39.2	24.3	51.1
Developing economies excluding China - Économies en développement sans la Chine	1990	100.0	13.8	60.5	24.1	26.8	26.1	12.7	35.1	20.0	52.2
	1995	100.0	13.7	61.1	25.5	30.8	31.5	10.7	33.4	19.8	55.9
	2000	100.0	13.7	60.8	22.7	37.2	34.6	9.2	34.2	18.7	56.6
	2009	100.0	14.6	60.0	23.7	37.6	36.1	9.2	35.5	16.8	55.3
Developing economies excluding LDCs - Économies en développement sans les PMA	1990	100.0	13.8	58.6	25.6	26.4	25.1	13.3	36.1	22.1	50.5
	1995	100.0	13.7	58.5	27.6	30.0	30.1	11.3	35.6	22.9	53.2
	2000	100.0	14.1	57.9	25.0	35.2	32.3	9.7	36.6	23.0	53.7
	2009	100.0	14.4	52.7	30.3	38.4	34.5	9.2	39.5	24.8	51.3
High-income developing countries - Pays en développement à revenu élevé	1990	100.0	13.6	57.6	25.0	37.5	34.3	7.3	39.6	22.6	53.1
	1995	100.0	12.8	58.1	27.6	44.2	42.8	5.7	36.1	21.3	58.2
	2000	100.0	13.2	58.0	24.6	48.1	43.7	4.4	36.1	20.3	59.4
	2009	100.0	14.6	56.8	22.6	54.8	49.0	3.7	38.7	17.7	57.6
Middle-income developing countries - Pays en développement à revenu intermédiaire	1990	100.0	15.1	58.1	26.8	19.2	19.6	14.5	34.0	23.4	51.5
	1995	100.0	15.9	57.6	28.0	20.0	21.4	13.0	35.9	25.5	51.2
	2000	100.0	16.2	56.4	26.5	24.4	23.4	11.7	38.0	27.7	50.3
	2009	100.0	15.1	48.0	34.8	32.4	27.9	9.9	41.5	30.9	48.6
Low-income developing countries - Pays en développement à revenu faible	1990	100.0	11.4	65.0	22.7	15.4	16.1	28.0	30.3	16.4	41.7
	1995	100.0	10.1	65.3	25.0	18.2	20.2	25.5	30.9	17.9	43.6
	2000	100.0	10.9	64.9	21.5	24.4	22.7	23.6	31.9	15.9	44.4
	2009	100.0	11.3	63.0	29.2	25.1	28.7	20.2	33.1	16.1	46.7
Heavily indebted poor countries (IMF) - Pays pauvres très endettés (FMI)	1990	100.0	15.0	75.3	15.1	18.6	23.6	32.8	22.8	13.5	44.7
	1995	100.0	12.7	76.2	18.0	22.5	29.3	35.8	21.0	10.9	43.4
	2000	100.0	12.9	77.0	18.2	24.4	32.5	31.3	23.9	11.4	44.8
	2009	100.0	14.1	74.8	22.0	27.3	37.8	28.7	26.9	9.8	44.4
Landlocked developing countries - Pays en développement sans littoral	1990	100.0	16.5	72.2	17.8	20.6	27.0	31.4	26.1	15.0	42.5
	1995	100.0	15.6	71.1	21.3	34.3	42.1	27.7	29.2	15.6	43.2
	2000	100.0	15.3	70.9	20.2	35.0	41.1	25.6	28.0	13.4	46.5
	2009	100.0	13.8	62.1	23.6	36.9	37.3	18.9	33.8	11.9	47.3
Small island developing States - Petits États insulaires en développement	1990	100.0	17.6	61.4	24.3	51.4	54.2	10.9	29.3	11.8	59.8
	1995	100.0	16.1	61.1	24.2	53.3	54.1	12.6	27.1	11.6	60.3
	2000	100.0	15.8	62.0	25.0	51.6	54.4	8.5	28.2	11.4	63.3
	2009	100.0	15.2	66.6	22.4	50.2	55.5	8.1	31.4	11.8	60.5
Least developed countries - Pays les moins avancés	*1990*	*100.0*	*13.5*	*77.3*	*15.9*	*14.7*	*20.9*	*34.8*	*21.6*	*11.0*	*43.8*
	1995	*100.0*	*11.6*	*79.4*	*18.3*	*18.0*	*27.3*	*36.3*	*20.7*	*9.7*	*43.3*
	2000	*100.0*	*11.6*	*75.6*	*19.0*	*22.6*	*29.0*	*31.3*	*25.0*	*9.7*	*43.7*
	2009	*100.0*	*12.4*	*72.6*	*22.7*	*25.2*	*33.9*	*26.3*	*30.8*	*9.5*	*42.8*
Africa and Haiti - Afrique et Haïti	1990	100.0	16.3	74.4	15.7	17.9	23.7	34.0	22.7	10.7	43.7
	1995	100.0	15.1	76.1	18.6	20.8	30.6	37.6	20.6	7.8	42.3
	2000	100.0	15.2	73.7	17.7	24.6	31.2	32.2	24.8	7.4	43.0
	2009	100.0	15.3	69.5	22.4	27.9	34.7	27.7	32.6	6.6	39.7
Asia - Asie	1990	100.0	7.2	83.8	16.0	7.4	14.1	36.6	19.5	11.8	43.9
	1995	100.0	6.4	84.2	17.6	13.7	22.2	34.5	21.1	12.4	44.4
	2000	100.0	6.7	78.3	20.7	19.8	25.7	30.2	25.4	12.7	44.4
	2009	100.0	7.2	77.7	23.2	20.6	31.9	24.0	28.3	14.4	47.7
Islands - Îles	1990	100.0	29.8	76.2	27.6	29.0	62.4	33.0	12.6	6.8	54.4
	1995	100.0	28.5	65.3	26.3	38.2	58.9	31.8	14.0	7.7	54.2
	2000	100.0	24.7	69.0	21.2	36.7	52.5	30.4	14.6	7.3	55.0
	2009	100.0	32.9	83.5	23.3	27.7	67.0	28.9	13.2	4.8	57.9

For sources and notes, see end of table.

Pour les sources et les notes, se reporter à la fin du tableau.

Economic grouping / Groupements économiques	Year / Année	Total GDP / PIB total	GDP by type of expenditure (1) / PIB par catégories de dépense (1)					GDP by kind of economic activity (2) / PIB par branches d'activité économique (2)			
			Final consumption / Consommation finale		Gross capital formation / Formation brute de capital	Exports / Exportations	Less imports / Moins les importations	Agriculture (3)	Industry (4) / Industrie (4)		Services (5)
			Government / Administration publique	Household / Ménages		Of goods and services / Des biens et services			Total	Manufacturing / Activité de fabrication	
			Percentage / En pourcentage								
Major petroleum and gas exporters - Principaux exportateurs de pétrole et de gaz	*1990*	*100.0*	*20.0*	*50.2*	*21.1*	*36.2*	*29.6*	*10.3*	*46.8*	*10.4*	*42.9*
	1995	*100.0*	*19.9*	*49.6*	*23.1*	*35.0*	*27.9*	*9.6*	*45.8*	*11.3*	*44.6*
	2000	*100.0*	*18.1*	*42.0*	*21.3*	*44.5*	*26.1*	*7.1*	*52.1*	*10.4*	*40.8*
	2009	*100.0*	*15.7*	*48.5*	*28.1*	*43.2*	*35.3*	*7.0*	*53.8*	*9.7*	*39.2*
Africa - Afrique	1990	100.0	16.1	55.5	21.6	31.2	24.5	15.8	44.8	8.4	39.4
	1995	100.0	18.7	58.7	19.2	32.3	28.8	15.1	46.0	7.2	38.9
	2000	100.0	15.5	44.7	15.0	46.2	21.6	13.2	53.8	5.0	33.0
	2009	100.0	12.0	51.4	23.9	42.9	30.2	19.1	53.0	3.6	27.9
America - Amérique	1990	100.0	16.8	46.6	13.4	40.6	20.4	5.9	57.3	27.1	36.8
	1995	100.0	14.8	54.1	23.8	27.9	22.1	5.9	47.1	23.4	47.0
	2000	100.0	12.4	51.7	24.2	29.7	18.1	4.1	48.4	19.3	47.5
	2009	100.0	13.3	64.2	24.8	18.3	20.5	3.9	55.6	15.6	40.4
Asia - Asie	1990	100.0	22.4	48.2	22.0	37.9	33.6	8.4	46.1	8.7	45.5
	1995	100.0	21.4	45.9	24.1	37.3	28.9	8.7	45.4	10.0	45.9
	2000	100.0	20.3	38.7	22.7	47.7	29.6	5.9	52.5	10.0	41.7
	2009	100.0	17.5	43.5	30.3	49.7	40.7	3.9	53.6	10.2	42.4
Major exporters of manufactured goods - Principaux exportateurs d'articles manufacturés	*1990*	*100.0*	*11.8*	*54.9*	*32.3*	*36.7*	*35.2*	*13.0*	*37.9*	*28.0*	*49.1*
	1995	*100.0*	*11.8*	*52.3*	*35.2*	*44.5*	*43.8*	*10.1*	*38.8*	*29.3*	*51.1*
	2000	*100.0*	*13.0*	*53.7*	*30.5*	*46.0*	*43.2*	*8.2*	*39.0*	*30.4*	*52.8*
	2009	*100.0*	*13.4*	*44.8*	*37.0*	*50.3*	*42.7*	*8.3*	*42.9*	*35.0*	*48.8*
America - Amérique	1990	100.0	8.0	60.0	25.8	17.0	17.9	7.4	36.1	20.4	56.4
	1995	100.0	10.0	65.0	22.1	27.7	26.3	5.1	32.9	20.0	62.1
	2000	100.0	10.6	65.1	26.6	28.2	30.0	4.1	35.2	21.3	60.7
	2009	100.0	11.7	66.7	22.2	27.9	29.4	3.5	36.1	18.9	60.4
Asia - Asie	1990	100.0	12.8	51.4	34.0	41.9	39.8	14.6	38.5	30.2	47.0
	1995	100.0	12.0	50.4	37.2	47.1	46.7	10.9	39.8	30.9	49.2
	2000	100.0	13.7	50.8	31.5	50.4	46.5	9.3	40.0	32.8	50.7
	2009	100.0	13.6	42.1	38.8	53.1	44.4	8.9	43.7	37.0	47.3
Emerging economies - Économies émergentes	*1990*	*100.0*	*13.3*	*59.2*	*26.0*	*25.9*	*24.8*	*6.8*	*35.0*	*23.7*	*58.2*
	1995	*100.0*	*14.3*	*59.2*	*26.6*	*30.1*	*30.4*	*5.9*	*33.5*	*22.5*	*60.6*
	2000	*100.0*	*13.5*	*61.0*	*24.3*	*37.1*	*35.7*	*4.7*	*33.7*	*22.8*	*61.6*
	2009	*100.0*	*15.9*	*59.9*	*20.3*	*40.0*	*36.1*	*4.9*	*32.9*	*20.9*	*62.3*
America - Amérique	1990	100.0	13.5	63.8	20.5	12.1	10.6	6.0	32.3	21.0	61.7
	1995	100.0	16.4	64.3	19.6	13.3	13.8	5.7	29.7	18.9	64.6
	2000	100.0	14.5	65.7	21.5	18.2	19.6	5.0	31.2	18.9	63.8
	2009	100.0	16.8	63.4	18.9	19.0	18.4	5.3	30.8	17.0	63.9
Asia - Asie	1990	100.0	13.0	52.3	34.2	46.3	45.9	8.1	39.4	28.1	52.5
	1995	100.0	11.7	52.6	35.5	51.5	51.5	6.2	38.3	27.1	55.5
	2000	100.0	12.1	54.2	28.3	64.5	59.1	4.3	37.2	28.4	58.4
	2009	100.0	14.3	54.1	22.5	74.7	65.4	4.2	36.1	26.9	59.7
Newly industrialized Asian countries - Économies nouvellement industrialisées d'Asie	*1990*	*100.0*	*11.6*	*53.8*	*32.1*	*49.7*	*48.6*	*9.7*	*37.7*	*26.1*	*52.7*
	1995	*100.0*	*10.7*	*55.0*	*33.9*	*55.4*	*56.2*	*7.8*	*36.4*	*25.1*	*55.8*
	2000	*100.0*	*11.2*	*56.2*	*27.2*	*70.0*	*64.4*	*5.7*	*35.4*	*25.6*	*58.9*
	2009	*100.0*	*12.8*	*56.7*	*23.7*	*71.4*	*64.0*	*6.8*	*36.0*	*24.7*	*57.2*
First tier - Première génération	1990	100.0	12.7	52.2	32.3	57.9	55.3	5.5	37.7	27.4	56.8
	1995	100.0	11.5	54.1	33.6	62.3	61.5	4.1	34.6	24.4	61.3
	2000	100.0	11.8	55.5	28.9	71.5	67.7	2.8	32.1	24.1	65.1
	2009	100.0	13.8	55.4	23.6	88.8	81.4	1.7	30.1	22.7	68.2
Second tier - Deuxième génération	1990	100.0	9.6	56.8	31.8	34.7	36.3	17.0	37.7	23.7	45.4
	1995	100.0	9.4	56.8	34.4	42.5	46.2	14.5	39.5	26.3	46.1
	2000	100.0	9.7	57.8	23.2	66.4	56.1	12.4	42.8	28.8	44.8
	2009	100.0	11.4	58.5	23.8	47.3	39.9	13.4	43.6	27.2	43.0

For sources and notes, see end of table.

Pour les sources et les notes, se reporter à la fin du tableau.

8

8.3.2 Nominal gross domestic product by type of expenditure and by kind of economic activity of economic groupings

8.3.2 Produit intérieur brut nominal par catégories de dépenses et par branches d'activité économique des groupements économiques

Economic grouping / Groupements économiques	Year / Année	Total GDP / PIB total	Final consumption / Consommation finale — Government / Administration publique	Final consumption — Household / Ménages	Gross capital formation / Formation brute de capital	Exports / Exportations — Of goods and services / Des biens et services	Less imports / Moins les importations — Of goods and services / Des biens et services	Agriculture / Agriculture (3)	Industry (4) / Industrie (4) — Total	Industry — Manufacturing / Activités de fabrication	Services (5)
			Percentage / En pourcentage								
Developing economies: Africa - Économies en développement : Afrique	1990	100.0	16.4	63.9	20.3	26.3	25.7	18.3	35.2	15.0	46.7
	1995	100.0	16.2	66.4	19.0	26.3	28.3	17.0	32.9	14.8	50.2
	2000	100.0	15.2	63.0	17.6	31.7	27.4	15.4	35.3	12.6	49.3
	2009	100.0	14.9	62.8	22.5	33.2	33.2	16.8	37.9	10.1	45.2
Northern Africa excluding Sudan - Afrique septentrionale sans le Soudan	1990	100.0	15.7	59.8	26.9	29.2	30.9	13.4	39.1	13.9	47.5
	1995	100.0	15.2	66.0	21.4	26.2	29.7	13.4	35.8	14.5	50.8
	2000	100.0	14.5	60.9	20.2	29.9	25.5	11.9	38.4	12.6	49.7
	2009	100.0	14.2	57.0	29.1	34.8	35.1	10.5	46.8	11.5	42.7
Sub-Saharan Africa - Afrique subsaharienne	1990	100.0	16.8	66.1	16.6	24.8	22.8	21.0	32.9	15.7	46.2
	1995	100.0	16.7	66.6	17.7	26.4	27.5	19.1	31.1	14.9	49.9
	2000	100.0	15.7	64.5	15.7	33.0	28.7	18.1	32.9	12.5	49.0
	2009	100.0	15.3	66.2	18.7	32.2	32.2	20.6	32.6	9.2	46.8
Sub-Saharan Africa excluding South Africa - Afrique subsaharienne sans l'Afrique du Sud	1990	100.0	15.2	68.9	16.1	25.0	25.0	29.6	29.1	11.5	41.5
	1995	100.0	15.3	69.8	17.3	29.3	31.9	31.1	28.2	10.0	40.9
	2000	100.0	14.1	65.3	15.8	36.1	31.0	26.9	33.5	8.7	39.5
	2009	100.0	12.7	68.7	18.5	34.6	34.1	28.3	33.3	6.6	38.4
Developing economies: America - Économies en développement : Amérique	1990	100.0	13.9	63.6	20.4	16.3	14.6	7.2	32.8	20.6	60.0
	1995	100.0	15.8	65.0	20.3	15.9	16.9	6.7	30.1	18.6	63.1
	2000	100.0	14.6	65.5	21.2	20.6	21.6	5.7	31.7	18.4	62.6
	2009	100.0	16.4	63.9	19.7	20.5	20.7	5.7	32.8	16.4	61.5
Central America and Greater Caribbean Islands excluding Puerto Rico - Amérique centrale et Grandes Antilles sans Porto Rico	1990	100.0	10.3	67.8	24.7	21.0	23.1	9.0	33.8	19.4	57.2
	1995	100.0	10.9	67.5	20.7	29.0	28.5	6.9	31.4	19.4	61.7
	2000	100.0	11.4	66.4	25.3	29.4	32.1	5.3	33.9	20.8	60.8
	2009	100.0	13.0	68.0	20.8	28.7	31.2	4.6	33.7	18.3	61.8
Central America and Greater Caribbean Islands excluding Mexico and Puerto Rico - Amérique centrale et Grandes Antilles sans le Mexique et Porto Rico	1990	100.0	18.8	66.9	20.6	36.0	42.3	15.4	24.1	15.2	60.4
	1995	100.0	13.6	75.0	16.5	32.9	38.0	13.5	26.0	17.5	60.5
	2000	100.0	15.2	72.6	19.5	34.6	41.9	11.4	27.4	18.5	61.1
	2009	100.0	17.6	72.4	16.0	31.3	37.2	8.4	24.9	16.0	66.7
South America and Central America - Amérique du Sud et Amérique centrale	1990	100.0	13.5	63.7	20.2	14.9	12.8	7.0	33.2	21.1	59.8
	1995	100.0	15.8	64.8	20.5	15.2	16.1	6.7	30.3	18.7	63.0
	2000	100.0	14.4	65.4	21.3	19.9	20.8	5.7	31.9	18.6	62.5
	2009	100.0	16.2	63.8	19.8	19.9	20.1	5.8	33.1	16.5	61.2
South America excluding Brazil - Amérique du Sud sans le Brésil	1990	100.0	12.6	64.1	17.8	19.8	14.2	9.2	38.3	23.4	52.6
	1995	100.0	12.7	66.7	22.6	16.4	17.9	7.8	32.4	18.1	59.8
	2000	100.0	13.7	65.7	19.1	19.0	17.6	6.4	32.9	17.1	60.7
	2009	100.0	14.1	62.0	22.6	23.0	21.7	6.6	40.5	15.9	52.9
Developing economies: Asia - Économies en développement : Asie	1990	100.0	13.1	56.1	28.7	30.7	29.8	17.0	37.2	23.8	45.8
	1995	100.0	12.2	54.8	32.4	37.3	37.0	13.8	38.1	25.7	48.1
	2000	100.0	13.6	54.2	27.8	42.4	38.2	11.7	38.7	26.1	49.6
	2009	100.0	13.5	48.3	34.7	44.8	39.4	10.2	41.5	28.7	48.3
Eastern and South-Eastern Asia excluding China - Asie orientale et Asie du Sud-Est sans la Chine	1990	100.0	11.4	53.3	31.2	48.6	47.5	10.6	37.6	25.7	51.9
	1995	100.0	10.7	55.2	33.5	54.7	55.5	8.5	36.0	24.7	55.5
	2000	100.0	11.1	56.1	26.9	69.0	63.5	6.6	35.3	25.1	58.1
	2009	100.0	12.4	56.7	24.0	70.7	63.8	7.7	36.0	24.2	56.3
Southern Asia excluding India - Asie méridionale sans l'Inde	1990	100.0	10.7	67.4	26.7	13.4	22.5	23.1	25.9	12.9	50.9
	1995	100.0	11.8	62.5	24.7	18.3	17.2	22.7	28.7	13.6	48.6
	2000	100.0	10.4	63.9	25.8	19.6	20.3	20.6	29.5	14.3	49.9
	2009	100.0	10.4	64.7	27.7	20.5	24.1	14.4	35.7	14.0	49.9

For sources and notes, see next page.

Pour les sources et les notes, se reporter à la page suivante.

8.3.2 Nominal gross domestic product by type of expenditure and by kind of economic activity of economic groupings

8.3.2 Produit intérieur brut nominal par catégories de dépenses et par branches d'activité économique des groupements économiques

Sources:
- UN DESA Statistics Division

Notes:

- Data in this table are shown as percentage of GDP / Value added at current prices in US dollars.

(1) The breakdown in shares by type of expenditure is shown as percentage of GDP.
The breakdown in shares might not add-up to 100 percent due to statistical discrepancies.

(2) The breakdown in shares by kind of economic activity is shown as percentage of total value added.

(3) Includes agriculture, hunting, forestry and fishing (ISIC Revision 3 divisions 01-05).

(4) Includes mining and quarrying, manufacturing, electricity, gas and water supply, and construction (ISIC Revision 3 divisions 10-45).

(5) Include all other economic activities (ISIC Revision 3 divisions 50-99).

Sources :
- ONU DAES Division de statistique

Notes :

- Les données de ce tableau sont indiquées en pourcentage du PIB /Valeur ajoutée aux prix courants en dollars des États-Unis.

(1) La ventilation par catégories de dépense est calculée en pourcentage du PIB.
La somme des pourcentages du PIB peut ne pas être égale à 100 à cause des écarts statistiques.

(2) La ventilation par branches d'activité économique est calculée en pourcentage de la valeur ajoutée totale.

(3) Inclut l'agriculture, la chasse, la sylviculture et la pêche (CITI Révision 3, divisions 01 05).

(4) Inclut les activités extractives, les activités de fabrication, la production et distribution d'électricité, de gaz et d'eau et la construction (CITI Révision 3, divisions 10-45).

(5) Incluent toutes les autres activités économiques (CITI Révision 3, divisions 50-99).

8

Region, country or territory / Régions, pays ou territoires	Year / Année	Population		Total labour force / Main-d'œuvre totale		Agriculture labour force / Main-d'œuvre dans l'agriculture	
		Total (thousands) / Total (milliers)	Urban population (% of total population) / Population urbaine (en % de la population totale)	Total (thousands) / Total (milliers)	Female labour (% of total labour force) / Main-d'œuvre féminine (en % de la main-d'œuvre totale)	Total (thousands) / Total (milliers)	Female labour (% of total agriculture labour force) / Main-d'œuvre féminine (en % de la main-d'œuvre totale dans l'agriculture)
		(1)	(2)	(3)	(4)	(5)	(6)
WORLD - MONDE	1990	5 306 425	42.9	2 375 048	39.3	1 138 466	41.6
	2000	6 122 770	46.8	2 796 254	39.9	1 236 175	42.1
	2005	6 506 649	48.8	3 036 678	40.3	1 275 959	42.4
	2010	6 895 889	50.9	3 276 145	40.6	1 307 071	42.6
DEVELOPING ECONOMIES - ÉCONOMIES EN DÉVELOPPEMENT	1990	4 064 796	34.5	1 768 550	37.9	1 078 442	41.7
	2000	4 828 147	39.9	2 160 039	38.5	1 192 669	42.3
	2005	5 186 172	42.9	2 394 747	38.9	1 237 626	42.6
	2010	5 545 097	45.2	2 566 384	38.4	1 272 876	42.9
TRANSITION ECONOMIES - ÉCONOMIES EN TRANSITION	1990	315 195	64.0	153 486	47.4	29 375	40.2
	2000	305 154	63.4	144 092	47.5	21 316	35.8
	2005	301 738	63.1	146 413	47.8	19 542	34.5
	2010	302 849	62.9	151 578	47.5	18 235	33.2
DEVELOPED ECONOMIES - ÉCONOMIES DÉVELOPPÉES	1990	906 210	71.8	438 945	42.4	30 649	38.8
	2000	967 546	74.3	479 082	44.1	22 190	37.5
	2005	996 021	75.7	495 980	44.6	18 791	36.7
	2010	1 024 733	76.8	512 669	45.2	15 960	36.3
Developing economies: Africa - Économies en développement : Afrique	1990	634 675	32.3	227 627	39.9	145 387	45.9
	2000	810 362	36.3	302 119	41.5	177 263	47.1
	2005	910 325	38.3	347 343	42.2	195 315	47.9
	2010	1 021 388	40.4	397 233	42.5	214 508	48.4
Eastern Africa - Afrique orientale	1990	192 189	17.8	83 428	47.9	68 611	50.3
	2000	250 845	20.7	110 102	48.0	88 608	51.0
	2005	284 918	22.1	128 361	48.4	100 236	51.3
	2010	323 198	23.6	148 140	48.5	112 616	51.3
Burundi	1990	5 602	6.4	2 809	52.5	2 582	55.7
	2000	6 374	8.4	2 915	53.2	2 754	56.5
	2005	7 251	9.7	3 517	52.6	3 225	56.3
	2010	8 383	11.2	4 314	52.1	3 741	56.0
Comoros - Comores	1990	438	27.9	126	25.6	163	50.3
	2000	562	27.6	179	28.0	171	50.9
	2005	643	26.7	210	29.1	195	51.3
	2010	735	26.5	243	30.2	222	51.8
Djibouti	1990	562	75.4	147	29.5	181	46.4
	2000	732	75.8	209	32.4	233	46.4
	2005	808	75.7	248	33.7	257	46.3
	2010	889	75.4	292	34.9	285	46.3
Eritrea - Érythrée	2000	3 668	17.7	1 661	47.3	1 090	44.0
	2005	4 486	19.4	2 178	48.4	1 354	43.9
	2010	5 254	21.5	2 596	48.6	1 547	43.6
Ethiopia - Éthiopie	2000	65 578	14.9	28 972	45.2	24 049	44.3
	2005	74 264	16.0	34 898	46.9	27 952	45.4
	2010	82 950	17.1	40 787	47.2	31 657	45.5
Ethiopia (former) - Éthiopie (anc.)	1990	51 492	12.8	22 957	45.2	18 071	42.3
Kenya	1990	23 447	18.2	8 997	47.2	7 842	49.4
	2000	31 254	19.8	11 857	46.8	10 757	49.4
	2005	35 615	20.9	13 237	46.5	12 053	49.0
	2010	40 513	22.4	15 461	46.5	13 220	48.7
Madagascar	1990	11 281	23.5	5 373	48.4	4 026	54.2
	2000	15 364	27.0	7 299	48.7	5 243	53.7
	2005	17 886	28.1	8 586	48.9	6 318	53.9
	2010	20 714	29.4	10 147	48.9	7 255	53.5
Malawi	1990	9 381	11.6	3 945	50.7	3 403	55.7
	2000	11 229	16.0	4 816	49.7	3 907	57.1
	2005	12 823	18.5	5 717	48.5	4 294	58.0
	2010	14 901	20.8	6 710	51.5	4 909	58.9

For sources and notes, see end of table.

Pour les sources et les notes, se reporter à la fin du tableau.

Region, country or territory Régions, pays ou territoires	Year Année	Population		Total labour force Main-d'œuvre totale		Agriculture labour force Main-d'œuvre dans l'agriculture	
		Total (thousands) Total (milliers) (1)	Urban population (% of total population) Population urbaine (en % de la population totale) (2)	Total (thousands) Total (milliers) (3)	Female labour (% of total labour force) Main-d'œuvre féminine (en % de la main-d'œuvre totale) (4)	Total (thousands) Total (milliers) (5)	Female labour (% of total agriculture labour force) Main-d'œuvre féminine (en % de la main-d'œuvre totale dans l'agriculture) (6)
Mauritius - Maurice	1990	1 060	43.8	444	31.8	75	28.0
	2000	1 196	42.6	532	34.5	63	25.4
	2005	1 257	42.0	556	35.9	55	25.6
	2010	1 299	41.8	603	37.7	48	25.0
Mayotte	1990	92	36.0	..	..	..	..
	2000	149	47.7	..	..	..	..
	2005	175	50.2	..	..	..	..
	2010	204	48.8	..	..	..	..
Mozambique	1990	13 547	21.1	6 019	55.5	5 207	62.2
	2000	18 201	30.8	8 726	55.1	7 092	64.3
	2005	20 770	34.6	9 881	54.3	7 868	65.0
	2010	23 391	38.5	11 078	53.5	8.674	65.2
Rwanda	1990	7 110	5.4	3 222	51.1	2 843	54.8
	2000	8 098	13.5	3 799	52.3	3 242	55.9
	2005	9 202	17.1	4 495	52.2	3 768	56.3
	2010	10 624	18.2	5 228	51.8	4 360	56.4
Seychelles	1990	71	50.0	..	..	26	50.0
	2000	79	52.6	..	..	28	50.0
	2005	84	52.3	..	..	29	51.7
	2010	87	54.1	..	..	30	50.0
Somalia - Somalie	1990	6 599	29.6	2 060	31.9	1 874	44.5
	2000	7 399	33.2	2 348	32.8	2 048	45.3
	2005	8 360	35.2	2 639	33.1	2 247	45.7
	2010	9 331	37.6	2 926	33.6	2 440	45.9
Uganda - Ouganda	1990	17 700	11.1	7 550	50.8	6 677	49.0
	2000	24 213	12.2	10 133	50.0	8 420	50.1
	2005	28 431	12.7	11 447	49.5	9 592	49.9
	2010	33 425	13.4	13 419	49.3	11 016	49.6
United Republic of Tanzania - République-Unie de Tanzanie	1990	25 479	18.9	12 246	49.8	10 544	54.0
	2000	34 038	22.4	16 709	49.7	13 557	54.3
	2005	38 831	24.3	19 288	50.0	14 970	54.8
	2010	44 841	26.5	22 137	49.8	16 879	54.9
Zambia - Zambie	1990	7 860	39.7	3 402	46.8	2 229	47.5
	2000	10 202	35.7	4 475	47.2	2 685	47.1
	2005	11 462	35.8	4 950	46.4	2 884	47.1
	2010	13 089	36.2	5 579	46.1	3 215	46.3
Zimbabwe	1990	10 469	29.0	4 131	46.3	2 868	54.8
	2000	12 509	33.6	5 470	46.4	3 269	54.4
	2005	12 571	35.6	6 515	48.8	3 175	53.4
	2010	12 571	38.5	6 620	49.3	3 118	52.4
Middle Africa - Afrique centrale	*1990*	*71 676*	*33.1*	*27 167*	*46.8*	*19 897*	*50.5*
	2000	*96 187*	*37.9*	*36 817*	*48.3*	*23 998*	*49.7*
	2005	*110 931*	*40.8*	*42 697*	*48.1*	*26 526*	*50.4*
	2010	*126 689*	*43.9*	*49 787*	*47.9*	*28 772*	*50.7*
Angola	1990	10 335	38.3	3 844	47.0	3 428	53.2
	2000	13 926	50.2	5 199	48.4	4 337	53.1
	2005	16 489	54.4	6 063	46.9	5 078	53.7
	2010	19 082	58.2	7 109	45.9	5 878	54.8
Cameroon - Cameroun	1990	12 181	40.9	4 493	41.8	3 099	48.1
	2000	15 678	50.5	6 199	45.1	3 482	48.1
	2005	17 554	55.1	7 142	45.4	3 559	47.9
	2010	19 599	59.5	8 211	45.6	3 569	47.4
Central African Republic - République centrafricaine	1990	2 935	36.7	1 301	45.7	1 036	50.0
	2000	3 702	38.1	1 679	46.4	1 189	50.4
	2005	4 018	38.9	1 840	46.8	1 208	50.1
	2010	4 401	39.9	2 064	47.1	1 254	49.8

For sources and notes, see end of table.

Pour les sources et les notes, se reporter à la fin du tableau.

8

Region, country or territory / Régions, pays ou territoires	Year / Année	Population		Total labour force / Main-d'œuvre totale		Agriculture labour force / Main-d'œuvre dans l'agriculture	
		Total (thousands) / Total (milliers)	Urban population (% of total population) / Population urbaine (en % de la population totale)	Total (thousands) / Total (milliers)	Female labour (% of total labour force) / Main-d'œuvre féminine (en % de la main-d'œuvre totale)	Total (thousands) / Total (milliers)	Female labour (% of total agriculture labour force) / Main-d'œuvre féminine (en % de la main-d'œuvre totale dans l'agriculture)
		(1)	(2)	(3)	(4)	(5)	(6)
Chad - Tchad	1990	6 011	21.1	2 363	45.3	1 918	45.8
	2000	8 222	23.9	3 215	45.5	2 418	51.6
	2005	9 786	25.9	3 827	45.4	2 779	55.7
	2010	11 227	28.3	4 425	45.2	2 962	56.9
Congo	1990	2 389	55.6	851	16.0	469	54.0
	2000	3 136	56.5	1 251	48.0	501	58.7
	2005	3 533	58.2	1 441	48.8	510	57.6
	2010	4 043	57.8	1 693	48.6	524	56.3
Dem. Rep. of the Congo - Rép. dém. du Congo	1990	36 406	28.3	13 694	48.7	9 618	51.0
	2000	49 626	30.6	18 525	50.1	11 694	48.2
	2005	57 421	33.0	21 513	50.1	13 004	48.6
	2010	65 966	36.2	25 270	49.9	14 194	48.6
Equatorial Guinea - Guinée équatoriale	1990	374	35.2	201	45.1	109	40.4
	2000	520	39.4	260	44.3	142	41.5
	2005	608	39.0	313	44.5	161	42.2
	2010	700	39.3	369	44.7	176	42.0
Gabon	1990	929	68.9	344	45.1	207	49.8
	2000	1 235	80.0	444	45.6	207	48.3
	2005	1 371	83.5	506	46.1	197	47.7
	2010	1 505	85.8	587	46.4	183	45.4
Sao Tome and Principe - Sao Tomé-et-Principe	1990	116	43.6	35	33.4	24	41.7
	2000	141	53.1	45	35.2	28	42.9
	2005	153	58.1	52	36.2	30	46.7
	2010	165	62.2	59	37.2	32	50.0
Northern Africa - Afrique septentrionale	*1990*	*146 188*	*45.0*	*42 285*	*23.5*	*17 868*	*35.7*
	2000	*176 166*	*48.6*	*54 479*	*22.9*	*19 564*	*39.5*
	2005	*192 017*	*50.2*	*62 527*	*23.3*	*20 287*	*41.4*
	2010	*209 459*	*52.0*	*70 050*	*24.7*	*20 886*	*42.9*
Algeria - Algérie	1990	25 299	52.1	6 032	11.8	1 906	49.7
	2000	30 534	59.8	8 802	13.7	2 718	51.6
	2005	32 888	63.3	9 986	15.0	2 999	51.9
	2010	35 468	66.4	11 207	16.9	3 175	52.7
Egypt - Égypte	1990	56 843	44.2	16 842	26.5	6 605	37.4
	2000	67 648	44.4	20 085	21.4	6 339	36.2
	2005	74 203	44.7	23 923	21.5	6 576	39.1
	2010	81 121	45.2	27 076	24.2	6 620	40.4
Libyan Arab Jamahiriya - Jamahiriya arabe libyenne	1990	4 334	76.2	1 166	17.7	128	41.4
	2000	5 231	78.1	1 801	26.1	103	60.2
	2005	5 770	79.1	2 129	27.9	86	65.1
	2010	6 355	80.2	2 381	28.0	71	70.4
Morocco - Maroc	1990	24 781	48.4	7 867	25.3	3 267	35.6
	2000	28 793	53.4	10 206	27.9	3 372	43.2
	2005	30 392	55.4	10 990	27.7	3 208	45.3
	2010	31 951	59.0	11 375	27.1	3 009	47.7
Sudan - Soudan	1990	26 494	27.2	7 863	26.0	5 267	28.7
	2000	34 188	34.1	10 326	27.8	6 223	35.8
	2005	38 410	36.8	11 930	28.3	6 566	37.3
	2010	43 552	39.8	13 991	28.7	7 124	39.5
Tunisia - Tunisie	1990	8 215	57.9	2 448	21.6	653	34.0
	2000	9 456	63.4	3 151	24.9	756	34.7
	2005	9 912	65.1	3 400	26.4	781	34.4
	2010	10 481	66.6	3 801	26.9	805	33.0
Western Sahara - Sahara occidental	1990	221	86.1	68	14.6	42	47.6
	2000	315	83.9	109	17.8	53	50.9
	2005	440	80.8	169	20.6	71	52.1
	2010	531	81.8	219	23.3	82	53.7

For sources and notes, see end of table.

Pour les sources et les notes, se reporter à la fin du tableau.

Region, country or territory Régions, pays ou territoires	Year Année	Population		Total labour force Main-d'œuvre totale		Agriculture labour force Main-d'œuvre dans l'agriculture	
		Total (thousands) Total (milliers)	Urban population (% of total population) Population urbaine (en % de la population totale)	Total (thousands) Total (milliers)	Female labour (% of total labour force) Main-d'œuvre féminine (en % de la main-d'œuvre totale)	Total (thousands) Total (milliers)	Female labour (% of total agriculture labour force) Main-d'œuvre féminine (en % de la main-d'œuvre totale dans l'agriculture)
		(1)	(2)	(3)	(4)	(5)	(6)
Southern Africa - *Afrique australe*	*1990*	*42 093*	*48.7*	*12 816*	*36.7*	*2 466*	*40.6*
	2000	*51 442*	*53.8*	*18 132*	*43.6*	*2 512*	*41.4*
	2005	*54 919*	*56.4*	*20 344*	*44.0*	*2 383*	*42.0*
	2010	*57 780*	*58.9*	*21 481*	*43.2*	*2 272*	*42.2*
Botswana	1990	1 382	41.0	561	46.6	201	46.3
	2000	1 758	52.1	817	46.9	281	53.0
	2005	1 876	56.2	925	46.7	289	55.7
	2010	2 007	60.2	1 036	46.3	317	56.5
Lesotho	1990	1 639	13.7	682	49.6	295	68.1
	2000	1 964	19.2	848	49.1	348	67.0
	2005	2 066	22.5	850	47.5	357	66.7
	2010	2 171	25.8	894	46.0	362	65.7
Namibia - Namibie	1990	1 415	27.7	444	44.5	219	48.9
	2000	1 896	31.1	639	44.4	253	45.5
	2005	2 080	33.9	781	45.8	255	45.5
	2010	2 283	36.8	929	46.3	267	43.8
South Africa - Afrique du Sud	1990	36 794	52.0	10 878	35.0	1 612	31.6
	2000	44 760	57.0	15 497	43.1	1 482	30.7
	2005	47 793	59.6	17 426	43.7	1 341	30.3
	2010	50 133	62.1	18 208	42.8	1 188	29.4
Swaziland	1990	863	22.9	251	41.7	139	64.7
	2000	1 064	23.0	331	40.3	148	58.8
	2005	1 105	22.3	361	39.9	141	56.7
	2010	1 186	21.7	414	39.6	138	54.3
Western Africa - *Afrique occidentale*	*1990*	*182 529*	*33.2*	*61 930*	*37.9*	*36 545*	*40.0*
	2000	*235 722*	*39.1*	*82 588*	*41.6*	*42 581*	*41.3*
	2005	*267 540*	*42.2*	*93 414*	*43.1*	*45 883*	*42.2*
	2010	*304 261*	*45.1*	*107 773*	*43.0*	*49 962*	*43.2*
Benin - Bénin	1990	4 773	34.6	1 850	42.5	1 106	39.9
	2000	6 518	39.2	2 559	46.5	1 384	42.2
	2005	7 634	41.2	3 051	47.5	1 502	41.2
	2010	8 850	43.8	3 616	47.6	1 601	40.7
Burkina Faso	1990	9 324	13.1	4 084	48.5	3 538	48.2
	2000	12 294	16.9	5 500	48.2	4 982	48.2
	2005	14 198	20.9	6 431	47.8	5 861	48.0
	2010	16 469	25.4	7 548	47.6	6 909	48.1
Cape Verde - Cap-Vert	1990	348	44.9	117	36.9	35	40.0
	2000	437	53.6	163	38.1	35	37.1
	2005	473	58.0	194	38.3	34	38.2
	2010	496	63.1	225	38.4	32	40.6
Côte d'Ivoire	1990	12 518	40.0	4 607	30.1	2 706	35.6
	2000	16 582	45.4	6 384	35.1	2 946	36.5
	2005	18 021	50.0	6 987	36.2	2 860	36.3
	2010	19 738	55.3	7 792	37.4	2 814	36.1
Gambia - Gambie	1990	966	35.5	399	44.8	328	51.2
	2000	1 297	49.3	544	47.0	461	51.6
	2005	1 504	54.7	640	47.5	527	52.4
	2010	1 728	58.9	752	47.9	605	53.6
Ghana	1990	14 793	36.9	5 899	48.4	3 627	45.4
	2000	19 165	44.8	8 426	48.1	4 785	43.9
	2005	21 640	48.4	9 118	47.9	5 345	44.5
	2010	24 392	51.3	10 372	47.6	6 075	44.1
Guinea - Guinée	1990	5 759	29.9	2 282	45.1	2 531	49.6
	2000	8 344	31.2	3 294	44.6	3 320	49.6
	2005	9 041	33.6	3 618	44.7	3 536	49.6
	2010	9 982	36.6	4 090	45.2	3 832	49.7

For sources and notes, see end of table.

Pour les sources et les notes, se reporter à la fin du tableau.

8

Region, country or territory / Régions, pays ou territoires	Year Année	Population		Total labour force Main-d'œuvre totale		Agriculture labour force Main-d'œuvre dans l'agriculture	
		Total (thousands) Total (milliers) (1)	Urban population (% of total population) Population urbaine (en % de la population totale) (2)	Total (thousands) Total (milliers) (3)	Female labour (% of total labour force) Main-d'œuvre féminine (en % de la main-d'œuvre totale) (4)	Total (thousands) Total (milliers) (5)	Female labour (% of total agriculture labour force) Main-d'œuvre féminine (en % de la main-d'œuvre totale dans l'agriculture) (6)
Guinea-Bissau - Guinée-Bissau	1990	1 017	28.3	396	44.5	340	40.0
	2000	1 241	31.2	498	45.5	391	45.5
	2005	1 368	31.9	568	46.6	417	45.6
	2010	1 515	32.6	649	47.3	447	45.4
Liberia - Libéria	1990	2 127	41.7	807	47.7	570	46.0
	2000	2 847	44.0	963	49.1	712	44.9
	2005	3 183	48.2	1 088	48.7	765	44.6
	2010	3 994	49.1	1 375	47.7	913	44.0
Mali	1990	8 673	23.3	2 328	38.8	1 953	35.8
	2000	11 295	26.4	3 058	37.5	2 376	36.3
	2005	13 177	28.7	3 608	36.1	2 700	36.9
	2010	15 370	31.1	4 296	35.4	3 049	37.2
Mauritania - Mauritanie	1990	1 996	39.5	521	19.9	434	47.7
	2000	2 643	39.4	761	23.3	570	50.9
	2005	3 047	39.6	934	25.1	656	52.6
	2010	3 460	40.3	1 116	26.6	745	54.2
Niger	1990	7 788	15.6	2 285	22.6	2 280	36.5
	2000	10 922	16.3	3 526	30.9	3 099	35.4
	2005	12 994	16.8	4 282	30.9	3 612	35.9
	2010	15 512	17.5	5 114	31.2	4 237	36.4
Nigeria - Nigéria	1990	97 552	35.2	30 564	34.5	12 613	34.7
	2000	123 689	42.9	39 254	40.1	12 443	35.2
	2005	139 823	46.5	43 766	43.3	12 315	36.9
	2010	158 423	49.8	50 245	42.9	12 267	39.2
Saint Helena - Sainte-Hélène	1990	6	41.6	..	..	1	0.0
	2000	5	39.8	..	..	1	0.0
	2005	5	40.7	..	..	1	0.0
	2010	4	42.5	..	..	1	0.0
Senegal - Sénégal	1990	7 242	40.5	2 897	41.5	2 391	45.4
	2000	9 506	42.0	3 948	43.0	2 929	46.1
	2005	10 872	42.7	4 615	43.4	3 328	46.6
	2010	12 434	43.8	5 384	43.9	3 821	47.4
Sierra Leone	1990	3 982	33.8	1 516	50.3	1 112	59.4
	2000	4 143	36.2	1 560	53.2	1 041	57.7
	2005	5 153	36.5	1 976	51.2	1 225	60.7
	2010	5 868	38.2	2 262	50.7	1 326	61.6
Togo	1990	3 666	32.2	1 490	45.1	974	38.0
	2000	4 794	40.0	2 150	49.0	1 106	39.4
	2005	5 408	44.3	2 537	50.5	1 199	40.4
	2010	6 028	48.9	2 938	50.5	1 288	41.2
Developing economies: America - Économies en développement : Amérique	**1990**	**438 537**	**70.1**	**170 320**	**33.7**	**42 395**	**16.8**
	2000	**516 529**	**75.3**	**225 581**	**38.3**	**43 453**	**19.5**
	2005	**552 101**	**77.5**	**253 417**	**40.1**	**42 991**	**20.4**
	2010	**585 126**	**79.2**	**279 453**	**41.2**	**41 502**	**20.9**
Caribbean - Caraïbes	*1990*	*29 827*	*53.2*	*11 955*	*37.4*	*3 664*	*23.9*
	2000	*33 706*	*57.0*	*13 747*	*39.6*	*3 657*	*24.0*
	2005	*35 442*	*60.2*	*14 959*	*40.8*	*3 669*	*24.0*
	2010	*36 922*	*63.4*	*16 408*	*41.8*	*3 667*	*24.4*
Anguilla	1990	8	100.0	..	..	1	0.0
	2000	11	100.0	..	..	1	0.0
	2005	14	100.0	..	..	1	0.0
	2010	15	100.0	..	..	1	0.0
Antigua and Barbuda - Antigua-et-Barbuda	1990	62	35.3	..	..	7	28.6
	2000	78	31.9	..	..	7	28.6
	2005	84	30.6	..	..	8	25.0
	2010	89	30.3	..	..	8	25.0

For sources and notes, see end of table.

Pour les sources et les notes, se reporter à la fin du tableau.

Region, country or territory Régions, pays ou territoires	Year Année	Population		Total labour force Main-d'œuvre totale		Agriculture labour force Main-d'œuvre dans l'agriculture	
		Total (thousands) Total (milliers)	Urban population (% of total population) Population urbaine (en % de la population totale)	Total (thousands) Total (milliers)	Female labour (% of total labour force) Main-d'œuvre féminine (en % de la main-d'œuvre totale)	Total (thousands) Total (milliers)	Female labour (% of total agriculture labour force) Main-d'œuvre féminine (en % de la main-d'œuvre totale dans l'agriculture)
		(1)	(2)	(3)	(4)	(5)	(6)
Aruba	1990	62	51.2	..	..	7	28.6
	2000	90	46.9	..	..	9	22.2
	2005	101	46.6	..	..	9	22.2
	2010	107	46.8	..	..	9	22.2
Bahamas	1990	256	79.7	125	45.9	6	16.7
	2000	298	84.0	148	48.8	5	20.0
	2005	319	84.7	173	48.4	5	0.0
	2010	343	84.8	197	48.3	5	0.0
Barbados - Barbade	1990	260	32.7	136	46.8	9	44.4
	2000	268	36.1	145	46.5	7	42.9
	2005	271	38.7	153	46.7	5	40.0
	2010	273	41.7	159	46.7	4	50.0
British Virgin Islands - Îles Vierges britanniques	1990	17	..	..	..	2	0.0
	2000	21	..	..	..	2	0.0
	2005	22	..	..	..	2	0.0
	2010	23	..	..	..	2	50.0
Cayman Islands - Îles Caïmanes	1990	26	100.0	..	..	3	33.3
	2000	40	100.0	..	..	4	25.0
	2005	52	100.0	..	..	5	20.0
	2010	56	100.0	..	..	5	20.0
Cuba	1990	10 570	73.5	4 363	32.6	833	14.9
	2000	11 104	75.5	4 697	35.0	733	17.6
	2005	11 254	75.2	4 807	36.5	658	17.8
	2010	11 258	74.9	5 270	38.0	586	17.7
Dominica - Dominique	1990	71	65.7	..	..	7	28.6
	2000	70	65.6	..	..	7	28.6
	2005	69	65.5	..	..	6	33.3
	2010	68	66.0	..	..	6	16.7
Dominican Republic - République dominicaine	1990	7 195	56.6	2 848	34.0	637	8.9
	2000	8 592	63.5	3 537	36.6	547	19.7
	2005	9 264	67.6	4 012	37.9	507	25.2
	2010	9 927	71.3	4 432	39.4	457	31.3
Grenada - Grenade	1990	96	33.4	..	..	10	30.0
	2000	102	36.0	..	..	10	20.0
	2005	103	37.3	..	..	9	22.2
	2010	104	39.2	..	..	9	22.2
Haiti - Haïti	1990	7 125	28.4	2 713	44.0	1 783	32.9
	2000	8 645	35.6	3 242	46.5	1 994	27.1
	2005	9 347	44.4	3 694	46.8	2 139	25.4
	2010	9 993	53.1	4 163	47.0	2 277	24.6
Jamaica - Jamaïque	1990	2 365	49.4	1 133	46.3	275	27.3
	2000	2 582	51.5	1 187	44.3	248	27.4
	2005	2 682	51.8	1 230	44.3	229	27.5
	2010	2 741	51.8	1 240	45.1	214	27.6
Montserrat	1990	11	12.6	..	..	1	0.0
	2000	5	11.1	..	..	0	..
	2005	6	13.6	..	..	1	0.0
	2010	6	14.3	..	..	1	0.0
Netherlands Antilles - Antilles néerlandaises	1990	191	85.6	83	43.8	1	0.0
	2000	180	90.6	83	48.4	0	..
	2005	186	92.2	88	50.1	0	..
	2010	201	93.2	100	49.7	0	..
Saint Kitts and Nevis - Saint-Kitts-et-Nevis	1990	41	34.6	..	..	4	25.0
	2000	46	32.8	..	..	4	25.0
	2005	49	32.2	..	..	5	20.0
	2010	52	32.4	..	..	5	20.0

For sources and notes, see end of table.

Pour les sources et les notes, se reporter à la fin du tableau.

Region, country or territory Régions, pays ou territoires	Year Année	Population		Total labour force Main-d'œuvre totale		Agriculture labour force Main-d'œuvre dans l'agriculture	
		Total (thousands) Total (milliers) (1)	Urban population (% of total population) Population urbaine (en % de la population totale) (2)	Total (thousands) Total (milliers) (3)	Female labour (% of total labour force) Main-d'œuvre féminine (en % de la main-d'œuvre totale) (4)	Total (thousands) Total (milliers) (5)	Female labour (% of total agriculture labour force) Main-d'œuvre féminine (en % de la main-d'œuvre totale dans l'agriculture) (6)
Saint Lucia - Sainte Lucie	1990	138	29.4	58	45.0	15	26.7
	2000	157	28.0	73	47.0	16	25.0
	2005	165	27.6	83	46.8	17	23.5
	2010	174	27.9	91	47.2	17	23.5
Saint Vincent and the Grenadines - Saint-Vincent-et-les Grenadines	1990	107	41.4	42	36.0	12	25.0
	2000	108	45.2	48	38.4	11	27.3
	2005	109	47.1	52	39.8	11	27.3
	2010	109	49.3	54	41.0	11	27.3
Trinidad and Tobago - Trinité-et-Tobago	1990	1 215	8.6	455	35.2	50	18.0
	2000	1 292	10.9	586	39.9	50	18.0
	2005	1 315	12.3	669	43.2	49	18.4
	2010	1 341	13.9	701	43.3	47	17.0
Turks and Caicos Islands - Îles Turques et Caïques	1990	12	74.3	..	..	1	0.0
	2000	19	84.5	..	..	2	0.0
	2005	31	89.6	..	..	3	33.3
	2010	38	80.2	..	..	3	33.3
Central America - Amérique centrale	*1990*	*113 249*	*64.4*	*40 464*	*30.2*	*12 126*	*11.5*
	2000	*135 555*	*68.6*	*53 574*	*33.4*	*12 545*	*11.6*
	2005	*145 384*	*69.9*	*59 507*	*35.1*	*12 541*	*11.8*
	2010	*155 881*	*70.7*	*67 215*	*36.8*	*12 173*	*11.9*
Belize	1990	190	47.4	63	31.2	19	5.3
	2000	251	48.0	91	32.6	25	4.0
	2005	281	50.4	108	35.8	28	3.6
	2010	312	52.5	131	37.5	31	3.2
Costa Rica	1990	3 070	50.8	1 158	27.6	308	7.1
	2000	3 919	59.2	1 600	30.8	326	9.8
	2005	4 309	62.0	1 940	34.8	327	11.3
	2010	4 659	64.2	2 192	36.3	322	12.7
El Salvador	1990	5 333	49.2	1 890	35.4	655	9.0
	2000	5 940	59.0	2 218	39.6	661	8.3
	2005	6 051	61.7	2 329	40.3	626	8.6
	2010	6 193	64.3	2 594	41.5	590	9.3
Guatemala	1990	8 923	41.1	3 133	31.6	1 487	7.2
	2000	11 237	45.1	3 969	34.6	1 492	7.2
	2005	12 717	47.2	4 709	36.3	1 889	9.7
	2010	14 389	49.4	5 680	38.1	2 061	9.9
Honduras	1990	4 889	40.6	1 590	28.1	674	18.1
	2000	6 218	45.5	2 363	34.2	735	21.6
	2005	6 879	48.7	2 539	32.8	678	19.8
	2010	7 601	51.7	2 988	34.1	665	20.8
Mexico - Mexique	1990	84 307	70.7	30 395	29.9	8 344	12.5
	2000	99 960	74.4	40 256	33.0	8 658	12.3
	2005	106 484	75.5	44 344	34.7	8 365	12.3
	2010	113 423	75.9	49 605	36.5	7 905	12.3
Nicaragua	1990	4 121	52.6	1 308	30.3	392	9.9
	2000	5 074	55.0	1 797	32.5	390	7.7
	2005	5 424	56.3	2 079	36.1	371	7.5
	2010	5 788	57.7	2 376	37.9	351	7.7
Panama	1990	2 416	53.8	926	32.6	247	3.6
	2000	2 956	65.7	1 281	35.4	258	3.9
	2005	3 238	70.7	1 459	37.0	257	3.5
	2010	3 517	74.6	1 649	37.3	248	3.6

For sources and notes, see end of table.

Pour les sources et les notes, se reporter à la fin du tableau.

Region, country or territory Régions, pays ou territoires	Year Année	Population		Total labour force Main-d'œuvre totale		Agriculture labour force Main-d'œuvre dans l'agriculture	
		Total (thousands) Total (milliers)	Urban population (% of total population) Population urbaine (en % de la population totale)	Total (thousands) Total (milliers)	Female labour (% of total labour force) Main-d'œuvre féminine (en % de la main-d'œuvre totale)	Total (thousands) Total (milliers)	Female labour (% of total agriculture labour force) Main-d'œuvre féminine (en % de la main-d'œuvre totale dans l'agriculture)
		(1)	(2)	(3)	(4)	(5)	(6)
South America - *Amérique du Sud*	*1990*	*295 460*	*74.1*	*117 901*	*34.5*	*26 605*	*18.2*
	2000	*347 268*	*79.7*	*158 259*	*39.9*	*27 251*	*22.5*
	2005	*371 275*	*82.1*	*178 951*	*41.8*	*26 781*	*23.9*
	2010	*392 324*	*84.1*	*195 830*	*42.6*	*25 662*	*24.6*
Argentina - Argentine	1990	32 642	86.6	13 304	36.1	1 454	6.7
	2000	36 931	90.1	15 408	38.1	1 458	9.9
	2005	38 681	91.5	17 723	40.6	1 442	10.5
	2010	40 412	93.0	18 366	40.2	1 405	10.7
Bolivia (Plurinational State of) - Bolivie (État plurinational de)	1990	6 658	55.7	2 600	39.0	1 193	34.8
	2000	8 307	61.9	3 529	43.2	1 560	40.7
	2005	9 147	64.5	4 015	43.8	1 762	42.2
	2010	9 930	67.2	4 585	44.8	*1 973	41.9
Brazil - Brésil	1990	149 650	73.9	62 657	35.1	14 056	18.5
	2000	174 425	81.1	83 762	41.2	13 325	23.4
	2005	185 987	84.3	94 565	43.0	12 424	24.1
	2010	194 946	86.7	101 601	43.6	11 049	24.5
Chile - Chili	1990	13 188	83.3	4 999	30.5	935	9.7
	2000	15 420	85.9	6 087	33.1	962	11.5
	2005	16 302	87.6	6 765	35.3	977	12.9
	2010	17 114	89.1	8 032	39.6	964	14.2
Colombia - Colombie	1990	33 203	68.3	11 362	30.0	3 343	18.5
	2000	39 764	72.1	17 269	38.7	3 584	22.6
	2005	43 041	73.6	19 836	41.0	3 568	24.0
	2010	46 295	75.1	22 143	42.4	3 529	24.8
Ecuador - Équateur	1990	10 261	55.2	3 862	31.9	1 110	14.7
	2000	12 345	60.1	5 391	37.4	1 210	20.2
	2005	13 426	61.9	6 355	39.7	1 237	23.0
	2010	14 465	63.8	6 857	39.7	1 228	24.8
Falkland Islands (Malvinas) - Îles Falkland (Malvinas)	1990	2	75.3	..	..	0	..
	2000	3	68.1	..	..	0	..
	2005	3	71.3	..	..	0	..
	2010	3	74.1	..	..	0	..
Guyana	1990	725	30.6	281	31.4	59	11.9
	2000	733	29.6	285	32.6	55	10.9
	2005	746	29.0	283	33.1	53	9.4
	2010	754	28.9	302	34.7	50	8.0
Paraguay	1990	4 244	48.8	1 802	36.7	577	8.3
	2000	5 344	55.4	2 281	36.7	715	8.1
	2005	5 898	58.5	2 661	38.6	776	8.1
	2010	6 455	61.5	3 088	39.7	831	7.7
Peru - Pérou	1990	21 686	69.2	8 273	37.4	2 785	26.1
	2000	25 862	73.4	11 968	41.2	3 344	28.2
	2005	27 559	75.8	12 799	42.3	3 547	30.6
	2010	29 077	78.0	15 481	44.5	3 692	31.3
Suriname	1990	407	60.0	157	37.3	29	27.6
	2000	467	64.9	166	35.1	30	26.7
	2005	499	67.2	184	35.9	32	25.0
	2010	525	69.3	204	37.1	33	24.2
Uruguay	1990	3 109	89.0	1 392	39.0	185	10.8
	2000	3 319	91.4	1 586	43.1	197	12.7
	2005	3 323	92.0	1 593	44.1	191	13.1
	2010	3 369	92.6	1 708	44.5	186	14.0
Venezuela (Bolivarian Rep. of) - Venezuela (Rép. bolivarienne du)	1990	19 685	84.5	7 213	31.5	870	4.1
	2000	24 348	90.1	10 527	37.2	811	5.4
	2005	26 664	92.1	12 171	38.8	772	6.1
	2010	28 980	93.6	13 463	39.4	722	6.4

For sources and notes, see end of table.

Pour les sources et les notes, se reporter à la fin du tableau.

8

Region, country or territory / Régions, pays ou territoires	Year / Année	Population		Total labour force Main-d'œuvre totale		Agriculture labour force Main-d'œuvre dans l'agriculture	
		Total (thousands) Total (milliers) (1)	Urban population (% of total population) Population urbaine (en % de la population totale) (2)	Total (thousands) Total (milliers) (3)	Female labour (% of total labour force) Main-d'œuvre féminine (en % de la main-d'œuvre totale) (4)	Total (thousands) Total (milliers) (5)	Female labour (% of total agriculture labour force) Main-d'œuvre féminine (en % de la main-d'œuvre totale dans l'agriculture) (6)
Developing economies: Asia - Économies en développement : Asie	1990	2 985 108	29.8	1 368 136	38.1	888 878	13.3
	2000	3 493 142	35.5	1 629 114	37.9	960 780	42.4
	2005	3 714 747	38.9	1 790 313	38.0	996 962	42.5
	2010	3 928 628	41.5	1 885 572	37.1	1 014 276	42.6
Eastern Asia - Asie orientale	1990	1 216 665	29.0	681 487	44.4	490 174	47.7
	2000	1 347 625	38.0	773 268	44.7	510 620	47.8
	2005	1 388 222	44.6	816 923	44.6	510 797	48.0
	2010	1 424 218	49.1	851 089	44.4	505 536	47.9
China - Chine (7)(8)	1990	1 124 916	26.8	649 073	44.6	472 838	47.3
	2000	1 246 932	36.3	728 129	45.0	504 849	47.9
	2005	1 284 863	43.4	769 342	44.8	505 637	48.0
	2010	1 318 194	48.2	801 588	44.6	500 977	48.0
China, Hong Kong SAR - Chine (RAS de Hong Kong)	1990	5 794	98.0	2 892	36.5	..	..
	2000	6 783	98.3	3 410	41.9	..	..
	2005	6 810	100.0	3 557	44.8	..	..
	2010	7 053	100.0	3 689	46.0	..	..
China, Macao SAR - Chine (RAS de Macao)	1990	360	100.0	155	40.5	..	..
	2000	432	100.0	217	45.3	..	..
	2005	481	100.0	264	47.0	..	..
	2010	544	100.0	337	48.8	..	..
China, Taiwan Province of - (9) Province chinoise de Taiwan	1990	20 279	..	3 220	18.4	..	..
	2000	22 185	..	4 825	20.2	..	..
	2005	22 730	..	5 221	17.0	..	..
	2010	23 141	..	5 452	15.2	..	..
Korea, Dem. People's Rep. of - Corée, Rép. populaire dém. de	1990	20 143	58.4	12 192	48.1	3 618	45.2
	2000	22 894	59.3	13 565	47.5	3 328	45.3
	2005	23 746	59.3	14 039	47.6	3 233	46.2
	2010	24 346	59.3	14 575	47.7	3 065	46.4
Korea, Republic of - Corée, République de	1990	42 980	73.8	19 207	39.7	3 470	44.1
	2000	45 988	80.4	22 175	40.5	2 206	44.0
	2005	47 044	82.2	23 420	41.2	1 699	44.3
	2010	48 184	83.5	24 265	41.3	1 274	43.4
Mongolia - Mongolie	1990	2 193	57.6	748	46.6	248	43.5
	2000	2 411	56.3	946	46.8	237	45.1
	2005	2 547	59.5	1 080	46.9	228	46.9
	2010	2 756	60.8	1 183	46.4	220	47.7
Southern Asia - Asie méridionale	1990	1 195 985	26.6	441 093	27.5	275 192	33.2
	2000	1 460 201	29.1	554 268	27.9	313 156	33.5
	2005	1 584 702	30.4	638 357	29.4	335 403	34.1
	2010	1 704 146	32.0	663 247	26.8	355 387	34.8
Afghanistan	1990	13 032	17.5	3 459	14.9	2 707	28.6
	2000	22 856	18.1	5 745	13.3	4 485	29.0
	2005	27 615	18.9	7 012	13.8	5 337	30.7
	2010	31 412	20.9	8 270	15.2	6 046	32.1
Bangladesh	1990	105 256	21.8	45 675	39.4	33 784	45.3
	2000	129 592	25.6	57 288	37.5	31 757	45.0
	2005	140 588	28.0	65 212	38.5	32 663	47.7
	2010	148 692	31.0	72 274	39.9	32 100	50.9
Bhutan - Bhoutan	1990	559	16.1	206	37.1	163	22.7
	2000	571	25.0	228	39.5	169	23.1
	2005	659	30.5	311	41.4	250	30.0
	2010	726	33.9	365	42.5	311	34.4
India - Inde	1990	873 785	25.2	330 509	27.4	207 371	32.4
	2000	1 053 898	27.4	409 206	27.9	239 959	32.4
	2005	1 140 043	28.5	467 692	29.4	255 029	32.4
	2010	1 224 614	29.8	472 580	25.3	269 740	32.4

For sources and notes, see end of table.

Pour les sources et les notes, se reporter à la fin du tableau.

Region, country or territory / Régions, pays ou territoires	Year / Année	Population		Total labour force / Main-d'œuvre totale		Agriculture labour force / Main-d'œuvre dans l'agriculture	
		Total (thousands) / Total (milliers)	Urban population (% of total population) / Population urbaine (en % de la population totale)	Total (thousands) / Total (milliers)	Female labour (% of total labour force) / Main-d'œuvre féminine (en % de la main-d'œuvre totale)	Total (thousands) / Total (milliers)	Female labour (% of total agriculture labour force) / Main-d'œuvre féminine (en % de la main-d'œuvre totale dans l'agriculture)
		(1)	(2)	(3)	(4)	(5)	(6)
Iran (Islamic Rep. of) - Iran (Rép. islamique d')	1990	54 871	58.2	13 329	10.8	5 257	26.5
	2000	65 342	65.7	18 491	16.0	5 761	39.2
	2005	69 732	68.6	24 367	20.2	6 288	42.4
	2010	73 974	71.8	25 226	17.9	6 553	46.5
Maldives	1990	219	25.4	58	19.4	19	15.8
	2000	273	27.6	89	33.8	21	28.6
	2005	295	33.4	124	40.1	23	34.8
	2010	316	39.9	153	41.8	23	39.1
Nepal - Népal	1990	19 081	8.9	9 379	46.9	6 665	39.2
	2000	24 401	13.4	12 352	49.0	8 677	44.1
	2005	27 282	15.9	14 021	49.2	10 352	46.7
	2010	29 959	18.6	16 034	49.2	12 066	48.1
Pakistan	1990	111 845	31.7	31 717	12.8	15 659	16.0
	2000	144 522	34.0	43 036	15.3	18 712	22.9
	2005	158 645	36.0	51 465	18.1	21 643	26.5
	2010	173 593	38.2	59 739	20.7	24 520	30.1
Sri Lanka	1990	17 337	18.6	6 761	31.5	3 567	38.0
	2000	18 745	15.8	7 833	33.1	3 615	34.1
	2005	19 843	14.5	8 153	31.8	3 818	36.0
	2010	20 860	14.0	8 607	32.2	4 028	37.2
South-Eastern Asia - Asie du Sud-Est	*1990*	*445 366*	*31.2*	*200 525*	*42.8*	*118 114*	*43.0*
	2000	*523 838*	*37.7*	*252 071*	*42.0*	*131 986*	*42.5*
	2005	*559 888*	*39.4*	*278 196*	*42.1*	*136 937*	*42.5*
	2010	*593 423*	*41.6*	*302 270*	*42.4*	*139 939*	*42.4*
Brunei Darussalam - Brunéi Darussalam	1990	257	65.8	105	31.7	2	50.0
	2000	333	71.1	154	40.7	1	0.0
	2005	370	74.3	175	41.6	1	0.0
	2010	407	77.0	195	42.0	1	0.0
Cambodia - Cambodge	1990	9 532	12.8	4 321	52.6	3 190	55.7
	2000	12 447	17.3	5 773	51.2	4 028	53.5
	2005	13 358	19.5	6 903	49.3	4 554	52.2
	2010	14 138	21.4	7 973	49.8	4 966	51.3
Indonesia including East Timor - Indonésie, y compris le Timor oriental	1990	185 089	29.4	77 054	38.6	41 565	39.3
	2000	214 226	40.3	99 931	37.6	48 669	39.1
Indonesia - Indonésie	2005	227 303	41.5	109 286	37.3	49 307	39.2
	2010	239 871	42.9	118 023	38.2	49 513	39.4
Lao People's Dem. Rep. - Rép. dém. populaire lao	1990	4 192	15.5	1 924	49.7	1 491	51.3
	2000	5 317	22.3	2 459	49.9	1 865	52.0
	2005	5 753	28.0	2 767	50.2	2 088	52.6
	2010	6 201	34.4	3 169	49.8	2 368	52.3
Malaysia - Malaisie	1990	18 209	49.5	7 124	34.3	1 921	32.1
	2000	23 415	61.6	9 890	34.7	1 849	26.3
	2005	26 100	66.4	10 957	35.2	1 746	23.3
	2010	28 401	70.9	11 977	35.8	1 612	21.0
Myanmar	1990	39 288	25.7	19 003	48.4	15 452	45.9
	2000	44 958	28.8	24 151	48.3	17 125	47.3
	2005	46 321	31.7	26 005	48.8	17 948	47.6
	2010	47 963	35.4	27 971	48.9	18 788	47.8
Philippines	1990	61 629	49.2	23 724	36.6	10 973	24.5
	2000	77 310	48.2	30 971	37.4	12 405	24.1
	2005	85 546	48.1	34 845	38.6	12 913	24.4
	2010	93 261	49.1	38 719	38.8	13 404	24.2

For sources and notes, see end of table.

Pour les sources et les notes, se reporter à la fin du tableau.

Region, country or territory Régions, pays ou territoires	Year Année	Population		Total labour force Main-d'œuvre totale		Agriculture labour force Main-d'œuvre dans l'agriculture	
		Total (thousands) Total (milliers)	Urban population (% of total population) Population urbaine (en % de la population totale)	Total (thousands) Total (milliers)	Female labour (% of total labour force) Main-d'œuvre féminine (en % de la main-d'œuvre totale)	Total (thousands) Total (milliers)	Female labour (% of total agriculture labour force) Main-d'œuvre féminine (en % de la main-d'œuvre totale dans l'agriculture)
		(1)	(2)	(3)	(4)	(5)	(6)
Singapore - Singapour	1990	3 017	100.0	1 388	38.1	0	16.7
	2000	3 919	100.0	2 012	40.7	3	0.0
	2005	4 266	100.0	2 244	40.9	2	0.0
	2010	5 086	95.1	2 809	42.3	2	0.0
Thailand - Thaïlande	1990	57 072	29.7	32 100	47.4	21 170	17.0
	2000	63 155	30.7	34 824	46.1	20 089	46.4
	2005	66 698	31.9	37 886	46.2	20 191	46.0
	2010	69 122	33.5	39 404	45.7	19 302	45.1
Timor-Leste	2005	1 010	25.6	312	33.0	309	44.3
	2010	1 124	29.3	343	33.3	352	44.9
Viet Nam	1990	67 102	20.0	33 244	49.6	22 388	51.0
	2000	78 758	24.5	41 906	49.1	25 952	50.1
	2005	83 161	27.6	46 816	48.8	27 878	49.7
	2010	87 848	30.8	51 687	48.5	29 631	49.1
Western Asia - Asie occidentale	*1990*	*127 092*	*62.2*	*39 031*	*22.7*	*15 390*	*41.1*
	2000	*161 478*	*66.1*	*49 508*	*22.0*	*14 018*	*43.5*
	2005	*181 935*	*67.2*	*56 838*	*20.9*	*13 825*	*45.6*
	2010	*206 841*	*67.0*	*68 966*	*22.1*	*13 414*	*47.9*
Bahrain - Bahreïn	1990	493	88.2	214	17.0	4	0.0
	2000	638	90.0	302	21.4	3	0.0
	2005	725	88.8	340	22.4	3	0.0
	2010	1 262	56.7	711	19.3	4	0.0
Iraq	1990	17 374	72.6	3 712	14.2	655	34.2
	2000	23 857	70.1	5 437	15.9	535	42.8
	2005	27 359	69.0	6 266	16.9	479	47.0
	2010	31 672	65.7	7 452	17.6	436	50.7
Jordan - Jordanie	1990	3 416	68.8	708	10.7	97	38.1
	2000	4 827	78.7	1 212	14.3	118	50.0
	2005	5 342	81.6	1 369	14.3	115	56.5
	2010	6 187	82.1	1 589	18.1	114	61.4
Kuwait - Koweït	1990	2 088	100.0	786	26.9	10	0.0
	2000	1 941	100.0	962	25.1	11	0.0
	2005	2 264	100.0	1 165	24.6	12	0.0
	2010	2 737	100.0	1 357	23.9	14	0.0
Lebanon - Liban	1990	2 948	83.9	786	21.1	70	31.4
	2000	3 742	86.7	1 140	22.9	48	33.3
	2005	4 052	87.2	1 313	24.5	37	32.4
	2010	4 228	87.8	1 454	25.5	28	32.1
Occupied Palestinian territory - Territoire palestinien occupé	1990	2 081	70.2	425	12.5	132	61.4
	2000	3 199	70.9	656	13.4	125	66.4
	2005	3 556	77.3	789	17.2	117	69.2
	2010	4 039	80.9	947	17.9	110	72.7
Oman	1990	1 868	65.2	558	12.9	254	6.3
	2000	2 264	75.9	787	17.1	293	6.8
	2005	2 430	77.4	897	19.9	282	7.4
	2010	2 782	76.3	1 216	17.9	318	6.9
Qatar	1990	474	91.0	274	14.4	7	0.0
	2000	591	99.1	332	15.6	4	0.0
	2005	821	100.0	524	16.1	5	0.0
	2010	1 759	82.2	1 315	12.4	8	0.0
Saudi Arabia - Arabie saoudite	1990	16 139	77.2	4 998	10.7	966	7.0
	2000	20 045	82.9	5 963	14.8	659	6.5
	2005	24 041	79.5	8 119	14.3	624	5.8
	2010	27 448	78.5	9 557	14.8	515	5.6

For sources and notes, see end of table.

Pour les sources et les notes, se reporter à la fin du tableau.

Region, country or territory / Régions, pays ou territoires	Year / Année	Population		Total labour force / Main-d'œuvre totale		Agriculture labour force / Main-d'œuvre dans l'agriculture	
		Total (thousands) / Total (milliers)	Urban population (% of total population) / Population urbaine (en % de la population totale)	Total (thousands) / Total (milliers)	Female labour (% of total labour force) / Main-d'œuvre féminine (en % de la main-d'œuvre totale)	Total (thousands) / Total (milliers)	Female labour (% of total agriculture labour force) / Main-d'œuvre féminine (en % de la main-d'œuvre totale dans l'agriculture)
		(1)	(2)	(3)	(4)	(5)	(6)
Syrian Arab Republic - République arabe syrienne	1990	12 324	50.5	3 220	18.4	985	41.6
	2000	15 989	53.6	4 825	20.2	1 116	49.1
	2005	18 484	55.6	5 221	17.0	1 263	51.0
	2010	20 411	61.5	5 452	15.2	1 337	60.7
Turkey - Turquie	1990	54 130	61.3	19 951	30.0	10 734	47.4
	2000	63 628	67.6	21 960	26.9	9 131	48.7
	2005	68 143	70.3	23 069	25.4	8 644	50.1
	2010	72 752	72.5	26 531	28.7	8 067	52.6
United Arab Emirates - Émirats arabes unis	1990	1 809	81.6	905	9.7	75	0.0
	2000	3 033	85.7	1 718	12.0	87	0.0
	2005	4 069	82.7	2 534	13.4	99	0.0
	2010	7 512	52.7	4 927	14.8	148	0.0
Yemen - Yémen	1990	11 948	21.6	2 497	18.9	1 401	27.3
	2000	17 723	26.9	4 212	24.0	1 888	34.3
	2005	20 649	29.5	5 232	25.1	2 145	39.2
	2010	24 053	32.1	6 459	25.9	2 315	40.3
Developing economies: Oceania - Économies en développement : Océanie	1990	6 477	24.3	2 468	43.8	1 790	47.6
	2000	8 114	23.5	3 225	45.3	2 173	50.3
	2005	8 999	23.1	3 674	45.4	2 358	51.1
	2010	9 954	23.0	4 127	45.4	2 590	51.9
American Samoa - Samoa américaines	1990	47	81.0	..	..	7	28.6
	2000	58	88.9	..	..	8	37.5
	2005	63	91.0	..	..	8	37.5
	2010	68	93.1	..	..	8	37.5
Cook Islands - Îles Cook	1990	18	58.2	..	..	3	33.3
	2000	18	64.2	..	..	2	50.0
	2005	19	69.9	..	..	2	50.0
	2010	20	74.0	..	..	2	50.0
Fiji - Fidji	1990	728	41.3	253	25.5	115	16.5
	2000	812	47.3	311	32.9	125	20.8
	2005	823	50.2	342	32.6	124	21.0
	2010	861	51.5	365	32.4	126	21.4
French Polynesia - Polynésie française	1990	195	55.9	78	37.4	33	36.4
	2000	238	52.0	94	39.4	34	35.3
	2005	255	51.9	107	40.4	34	35.3
	2010	271	51.8	117	40.5	33	36.4
Guam	1990	134	90.8	61	35.4	20	25.0
	2000	155	93.1	68	38.5	19	26.3
	2005	169	93.1	74	38.6	20	25.0
	2010	180	93.2	79	38.6	20	25.0
Kiribati	1990	72	35.0	..	..	10	30.0
	2000	84	43.0	..	..	10	30.0
	2005	92	43.6	..	..	11	27.3
	2010	100	43.9	..	..	11	27.3
Marshall Islands - Îles Marshall	1990	47	65.1	..	..	..	..
	2000	52	68.4	..	..	6	33.3
	2005	52	76.3	..	..	6	33.3
	2010	54	84.2	..	..	6	33.3
Micronesia (Federated States of) - Micronésie (États fédérés de)	1990	96	25.8	..	..	..	..
	2000	107	22.3	..	..	13	23.1
	2005	109	22.3	..	..	13	23.1
	2010	111	22.7	..	..	12	25.0
Nauru	1990	9	99.9	..	..	1	0.0
	2000	10	100.0	..	..	1	0.0
	2005	10	100.0	..	..	1	0.0
	2010	10	100.0	..	..	1	0.0

For sources and notes, see end of table.

Pour les sources et les notes, se reporter à la fin du tableau.

8

Region, country or territory Régions, pays ou territoires	Year Année	Population		Total labour force Main-d'œuvre totale		Agriculture labour force Main-d'œuvre dans l'agriculture	
		Total (thousands) Total (milliers)	Urban population (% of total population) Population urbaine (en % de la population totale)	Total (thousands) Total (milliers)	Female labour (% of total labour force) Main-d'œuvre féminine (en % de la main-d'œuvre totale)	Total (thousands) Total (milliers)	Female labour (% of total agriculture labour force) Main-d'œuvre féminine (en % de la main-d'œuvre totale dans l'agriculture)
		(1)	(2)	(3)	(4)	(5)	(6)
New Caledonia - Nouvelle-Calédonie	1990	170	60.0	68	37.6	30	40.0
	2000	212	60.1	90	40.1	32	40.6
	2005	231	58.9	99	40.5	32	40.6
	2010	251	58.0	108	40.9	32	40.6
Niue - Nioué	1990	2	00.0	..	..	0	..
	2000	2	32.8	..	..	0	..
	2005	2	34.3	..	..	0	..
	2010	1	36.8	..	..	0	..
Northern Mariana Islands - Îles Mariannes du Nord	1990	44	89.3	..	..	..	..
	2000	68	90.9	..	..	8	25.0
	2005	67	100.0	..	..	8	25.0
	2010	61	100.0	..	..	7	28.6
Palau - Palaos	1990	15	68.9	..	..	..	..
	2000	19	70.3	..	..	2	50.0
	2005	20	78.6	..	..	2	50.0
	2010	20	83.6	..	..	2	50.0
Papua New Guinea - Papouasie-Nouvelle-Guinée	1990	4 158	14.9	1 740	48.1	1 410	51.8
	2000	5 379	13.2	2 319	48.5	1 725	54.4
	2005	6 095	12.6	2 666	48.4	1 895	55.1
	2010	6 858	12.6	3 025	48.3	2 110	55.5
Samoa	1990	161	21.2	56	31.9	24	29.2
	2000	177	22.0	65	33.0	22	31.8
	2005	180	21.1	67	33.7	19	31.6
	2010	183	19.8	69	34.3	18	33.3
Solomon Islands - Îles Salomon	1990	314	13.7	110	39.2	91	46.2
	2000	416	15.7	158	38.9	118	45.8
	2005	474	16.9	186	38.9	133	45.9
	2010	536	18.4	217	38.5	151	46.4
Tokelau - Tokélaou	1990	2	..	..	..	0	..
	2000	2	..	..	..	0	..
	2005	1	..	..	..	0	..
	2010	1	..	..	..	0	..
Tonga	1990	95	22.6	32	32.3	12	25.0
	2000	98	23.2	37	40.1	12	41.7
	2005	101	23.4	40	42.3	12	41.7
	2010	104	23.5	42	42.7	11	45.5
Tuvalu	1990	9	40.2	..	..	1	0.0
	2000	9	46.6	..	..	1	0.0
	2005	10	48.4	..	..	1	0.0
	2010	10	51.1	..	..	1	0.0
Vanuatu	1990	147	19.1	69	46.2	31	48.4
	2000	185	22.2	83	44.7	33	48.5
	2005	211	24.0	93	43.8	35	48.6
	2010	240	26.2	105	42.9	38	47.4
Wallis and Futuna Islands - Îles Wallis-et-Futuna	1990	14	..	..	..	2	50.0
	2000	14	..	..	..	2	50.0
	2005	14	..	..	..	2	50.0
	2010	14	..	..	..	1	100.0

For sources and notes, see end of table.

Pour les sources et les notes, se reporter à la fin du tableau.

Region, country or territory Régions, pays ou territoires	Year Année	Population		Total labour force Main-d'œuvre totale		Agriculture labour force Main-d'œuvre dans l'agriculture	
		Total (thousands) Total (milliers)	Urban population (% of total population) Population urbaine (en % de la population totale)	Total (thousands) Total (milliers)	Female labour (% of total labour force) Main-d'œuvre féminine (en % de la main-d'œuvre totale)	Total (thousands) Total (milliers)	Female labour (% of total agriculture labour force) Main-d'œuvre féminine (en % de la main-d'œuvre totale dans l'agriculture)
		(1)	(2)	(3)	(4)	(5)	(6)
Transition economies - Économies en transition	1990	315 195	64.0	153 486	47.4	29 375	40.2
	2000	305 154	63.4	144 092	47.5	21 316	35.8
	2005	301 738	63.1	146 413	47.8	19 513	34.0
	2010	302 849	62.9	151 578	47.5	18 235	33.2
Albania - Albanie	1990	3 289	36.4	1 415	40.4	921	47.6
	2000	3 072	41.7	1 331	41.7	620	44.4
	2005	3 142	46.3	1 406	41.7	630	43.3
	2010	3 204	51.3	1 496	41.6	614	42.5
Armenia - Arménie	2000	3 076	64.7	1 472	48.8	174	23.0
	2005	3 066	64.1	1 438	47.7	159	19.5
	2010	3 092	64.2	1 438	46.5	148	16.2
Azerbaijan - Azerbaïdjan	2000	8 111	51.3	3 573	47.0	972	54.4
	2005	8 588	50.7	4 129	48.4	1 026	54.1
	2010	9 188	50.5	4 676	49.0	1 085	53.4
Belarus - Bélarus	2000	10 058	69.9	4 768	48.9	636	25.3
	2005	9 825	72.1	4 677	49.0	529	21.9
	2010	9 595	74.6	4 530	48.9	434	18.7
Bosnia and Herzegovina - Bosnie-Herzégovine	2000	3 694	43.2	1 332	39.0	100	60.0
	2005	3 781	45.8	1 384	38.8	67	59.7
	2010	3 760	48.6	1 478	40.0	44	59.1
Croatia - Croatie	2000	4 506	55.6	2 005	44.2	170	35.3
	2005	4 442	56.5	1 998	45.5	120	32.5
	2010	4 403	57.8	1 964	46.0	84	29.8
Georgia - Géorgie	2000	4 746	52.6	2 357	46.2	472	39.6
	2005	4 477	52.3	2 324	46.9	401	38.4
	2010	4 352	51.1	2 322	47.0	354	36.2
Kazakhstan	2000	14 957	56.3	7 585	49.1	1 321	29.1
	2005	15 172	57.2	7 965	49.5	1 225	26.7
	2010	16 026	57.5	8 625	49.4	1 192	24.2
Kyrgyzstan - Kirghizistan	2000	4 955	35.2	2 090	44.7	543	35.2
	2005	5 042	36.3	2 243	42.8	514	31.9
	2010	5 334	35.9	2 476	42.7	510	29.8
Montenegro - Monténégro	2010	631	60.9	..	..	39	38.5
Republic of Moldova - République de Moldova	2000	4 107	44.5	1 857	49.7	390	34.4
	2005	3 767	43.1	1 489	51.1	268	32.5
	2010	3 573	47.0	1 221	49.2	200	30.0
Russian Federation - Fédération de Russie	2000	146 758	73.3	73 524	48.6	7 648	28.9
	2005	143 843	72.6	73 773	49.2	6 879	26.9
	2010	142 958	71.8	76 185	48.8	6 251	24.6
Serbia and Montenegro - Serbie-et-Monténégro	2000	10 766	53.5	4 758	45.0	1 007	44.0
	2005	10 483	54.9	4 760	44.8	811	41.1
Serbia - Serbie	2010	9 856	56.1	4 433	43.2	617	38.1
SFR of Yugoslavia (former) - RSF de Yougoslavie (anc.)	1990	22 839	49.5	10 231	43.9	911	49.0
Tajikistan - Tadjikistan	2000	6 173	26.5	2 374	44.1	610	52.8
	2005	6 453	26.7	2 536	45.0	679	53.3
	2010	6 879	27.1	2 847	45.2	773	53.2
TFYR of Macedonia - LERY de Macédoine	2000	2 009	59.4	831	38.8	107	36.4
	2005	2 038	59.0	865	39.9	85	35.3
	2010	2 061	58.8	946	38.5	68	32.4
Turkmenistan - Turkménistan	2000	4 501	45.8	1 735	40.6	627	52.2
	2005	4 748	48.3	1 934	39.9	660	52.6
	2010	5 042	50.8	2 164	39.3	705	53.2

For sources and notes, see end of table.

Pour les sources et les notes, se reporter à la fin du tableau.

8

Region, country or territory Régions, pays ou territoires	Year Année	Population		Total labour force Main-d'œuvre totale		Agriculture labour force Main-d'œuvre dans l'agriculture	
		Total (thousands) Total (milliers)	Urban population (% of total population) Population urbaine (en % de la population totale)	Total (thousands) Total (milliers)	Female labour (% of total labour force) Main-d'œuvre féminine (en % de la main-d'œuvre totale)	Total (thousands) Total (milliers)	Female labour (% of total agriculture labour force) Main-d'œuvre féminine (en % de la main-d'œuvre totale dans l'agriculture)
		(1)	(2)	(3)	(4)	(5)	(6)
Ukraine	2000	48 892	67.1	23 259	49.2	3 295	33.0
	2005	46 924	67.8	23 118	49.0	2 831	29.9
	2010	45 448	68.8	22 999	49.3	2 412	27.4
USSR (former) - URSS (anc.)	1990	289 067	65.4	141 840	47.8	27 543	39.6
Uzbekistan - Ouzbékistan	2000	24 776	37.4	9 243	40.6	2 624	45.5
	2005	25 947	37.2	10 373	40.4	2 658	44.5
	2010	27 445	36.7	11 780	39.8	2 705	43.5
Developed economies: America - **Économies développées : Amérique**	**1990**	**284 794**	**75.8**	**145 823**	**44.6**	**4 299**	**22.4**
	2000	**317 212**	**80.7**	**164 928**	**45.8**	**3 515**	**25.8**
	2005	**333 123**	**82.4**	**172 930**	**45.9**	**3 165**	**27.3**
	2010	**348 387**	**84.1**	**178 230**	**46.2**	**2 867**	**28.9**
Bermuda - Bermudes	1990	60	100.0	..	..	1	0.0
	2000	63	100.0	..	..	1	0.0
	2005	64	100.0	..	..	1	0.0
	2010	65	100.0	..	..	1	0.0
Canada	1990	27 701	76.6	14 669	44.1	495	32.1
	2000	30 667	79.5	16 206	45.7	382	41.9
	2005	32 283	80.2	17 738	46.4	354	47.2
	2010	34 017	80.3	18 930	47.1	332	52.4
Greenland - Groenland	1990	56	79.7	..	..	1	0.0
	2000	56	81.6	..	..	1	0.0
	2005	57	82.8	..	..	1	0.0
	2010	57	84.2	..	..	0	..
Saint Pierre and Miquelon - Saint-Pierre-et-Miquelon	1990	6	89.0	..	..	0	..
	2000	6	89.2	..	..	0	..
	2005	6	90.0	..	..	0	..
	2010	6	90.5	..	..	0	..
United States - États-Unis	1990	256 971	75.7	131 154	44.6	3 802	21.1
	2000	286 419	80.8	148 723	45.8	3 131	23.9
	2005	300 712	82.6	155 191	45.8	2 809	24.8
	2010	314 242	84.5	159 300	46.1	2 534	25.8
Developed economies: Asia - **Économies développées : Asie**	**1990**	**126 751**	**64.5**	**64 860**	**40.7**	**4 713**	**46.2**
	2000	**131 735**	**66.9**	**69 349**	**40.8**	**2 773**	**42.3**
	2005	**132 998**	**67.8**	**68 531**	**41.5**	**2 036**	**41.0**
	2010	**133 954**	**68.4**	**69 284**	**42.6**	**1 469**	**39.7**
Israel - Israël	1990	4 500	90.6	1 603	40.4	65	23.1
	2000	6 015	92.5	2 343	45.8	61	23.0
	2005	6 605	92.9	2 632	46.6	56	23.2
	2010	7 418	90.2	3 094	47.1	51	21.6
Japan - Japon	1990	122 251	63.6	63 257	40.7	4 648	46.5
	2000	125 720	65.7	67 006	40.6	2 712	42.7
	2005	126 393	66.5	65 899	41.3	1 980	41.5
	2010	126 536	67.1	66 190	42.4	1 418	40.3
Developed economies: Europe - **Économies développées : Europe**	**1990**	**474 171**	**70.7**	**218 096**	**41.6**	**20 996**	**40.8**
	2000	**495 577**	**71.6**	**233 242**	**43.8**	**15 285**	**39.3**
	2005	**505 363**	**72.7**	**241 773**	**44.5**	**12 960**	**38.2**
	2010	**515 755**	**73.6**	**250 983**	**45.1**	**10 981**	**37.5**
Andorra - Andorre	1990	53	94.7	..	..	3	33.3
	2000	65	94.9	..	..	2	50.0
	2005	78	92.5	..	..	3	33.3
	2010	85	89.9	..	..	2	50.0
Austria - Autriche	1990	7 671	65.8	3 524	40.9	274	47.1
	2000	8 005	65.8	3 860	43.5	199	46.7
	2005	8 232	66.5	4 079	45.1	171	46.2
	2010	8 394	67.5	4 337	45.9	144	45.8

For sources and notes, see end of table.   Pour les sources et les notes, se reporter à la fin du tableau.

Region, country or territory / Régions, pays ou territoires	Year / Année	Population		Total labour force / Main-d'œuvre totale		Agriculture labour force / Main-d'œuvre dans l'agriculture	
		Total (thousands) / Total (milliers)	Urban population (% of total population) / Population urbaine (en % de la population totale)	Total (thousands) / Total (milliers)	Female labour (% of total labour force) / Main-d'œuvre féminine (en % de la main-d'œuvre totale)	Total (thousands) / Total (milliers)	Female labour (% of total agriculture labour force) / Main-d'œuvre féminine (en % de la main-d'œuvre totale dans l'agriculture)
		(1)	(2)	(3)	(4)	(5)	(6)
Belgium - Belgique	1990	9 949	96.2	3 924	39.0	..	..
	2000	10 176	97.3	4 402	43.0	79	29.1
	2005	10 414	97.3	4 624	44.1	68	30.9
	2010	10 712	97.3	4 810	45.3	59	32.2
Bulgaria - Bulgarie	1990	8 819	66.4	4 128	47.9	572	47.0
	2000	8 006	68.9	3 535	47.1	228	37.7
	2005	7 739	70.2	3 371	46.2	173	34.1
	2010	7 494	71.5	3 491	46.8	124	30.6
Cyprus - Chypre (10)(11)	1990	767	59.3	344	38.1	44	43.2
	2000	943	57.2	445	40.7	38	42.1
	2005	1 033	56.2	524	42.0	35	40.0
	2010	1 104	56.1	584	43.6	30	36.7
Czechoslovakia (former) - Tchécoslovaquie (anc.)	1990	15 573	68.8	7 467	45.2	984	36.7
Czech Republic - République tchèque	2000	10 243	73.9	5 155	44.4	431	29.0
	2005	10 221	73.3	5 167	44.2	372	25.8
	2010	10 493	73.0	5 277	43.3	327	23.2
Denmark - Danemark	1990	5 141	84.8	2 912	46.1	162	24.1
	2000	5 340	85.0	2 863	46.6	108	24.1
	2005	5 419	85.8	2 901	46.8	90	23.3
	2010	5 550	85.8	2 941	47.1	75	24.0
Estonia - Estonie	2000	1 371	69.4	657	48.7	76	30.3
	2005	1 346	69.5	672	49.9	68	29.4
	2010	1 341	69.4	699	50.4	61	26.2
Faeroe Islands - Îles Féroé	1990	48	30.5	..	..	1	0.0
	2000	46	30.2	..	..	1	0.0
	2005	48	40.1	..	..	1	0.0
	2010	49	41.5	..	..	1	0.0
Finland - Finlande	1990	4 986	79.4	2 615	47.1	218	35.3
	2000	5 173	82.2	2 613	47.4	143	35.0
	2005	5 244	83.7	2 640	48.0	117	35.9
	2010	5 365	84.8	2 696	47.8	98	35.7
France	1990	58 214	74.5	25 716	43.3	1 416	34.8
	2000	60 799	77.4	27 220	45.6	913	34.2
	2005	62 872	81.9	28 717	46.5	750	33.9
	2010	64 767	85.3	29 752	47.1	598	32.9
Germany - Allemagne	1990	79 098	73.4	37 155	40.7	1 564	41.6
	2000	82 349	72.8	40 445	43.7	1 016	39.7
	2005	82 541	73.2	41 394	44.6	821	38.1
	2010	82 302	73.6	42 465	45.6	661	36.9
Gibraltar	1990	27	100.0	..	..	2	50.0
	2000	27	100.0	..	..	1	0.0
	2005	29	100.0	..	..	1	0.0
	2010	29	100.0	..	..	1	0.0
Greece - Grèce	1990	10 161	58.8	4 185	36.1	963	45.4
	2000	10 987	59.5	4 897	39.2	826	49.6
	2005	11 183	59.7	5 116	40.4	731	51.3
	2010	11 359	60.5	5 293	41.5	637	52.7
Holy See - Saint-Siège	1990	1	100.0	..	..	0	..
	2000	1	100.0	..	..	0	..
	2005	0	100.0	..	..	0	..
	2010	0	100.0	..	..	0	..
Hungary - Hongrie	1990	10 376	65.8	4 540	44.5	700	31.0
	2000	10 211	64.6	4 178	44.7	452	26.3
	2005	10 087	66.2	4 271	45.6	384	24.7
	2010	9 984	68.0	4 312	46.0	322	22.7

For sources and notes, see end of table.

Pour les sources et les notes, se reporter à la fin du tableau.

Region, country or territory / Régions, pays ou territoires	Year / Année	Population		Total labour force / Main-d'œuvre totale		Agriculture labour force / Main-d'œuvre dans l'agriculture	
		Total (thousands) / Total (milliers)	Urban population (% of total population) / Population urbaine (en % de la population totale)	Total (thousands) / Total (milliers)	Female labour (% of total labour force) / Main-d'œuvre féminine (en % de la main-d'œuvre totale)	Total (thousands) / Total (milliers)	Female labour (% of total agriculture labour force) / Main-d'œuvre féminine (en % de la main-d'œuvre totale dans l'agriculture)
		(1)	(2)	(3)	(4)	(5)	(6)
Iceland - Islande	1990	255	90.8	143	45.4	13	16.6
	2000	281	92.3	166	46.8	13	15.4
	2005	297	92.6	175	46.8	12	16.7
	2010	320	96.1	189	47.3	12	16.7
Ireland - Irlande	1990	3 531	56.6	1 360	34.2	180	8.1
	2000	3 804	59.1	1 757	40.6	166	8.4
	2005	4 158	60.9	2 052	42.2	160	8.1
	2010	4 470	63.6	2 124	43.7	149	7.4
Italy - Italie	1990	56 832	66.9	23 830	36.4	2 073	39.0
	2000	56 986	67.4	23 312	38.6	1 250	40.9
	2005	58 671	67.6	24 674	40.0	1 025	42.8
	2010	60 551	67.8	25 151	40.3	845	45.0
Latvia - Lettonie	2000	2 385	67.7	1 095	48.1	132	31.8
	2005	2 306	67.6	1 138	48.3	122	27.9
	2010	2 252	67.4	1 163	50.0	113	25.7
Lithuania - Lituanie	2000	3 500	67.0	1 685	49.5	204	28.9
	2005	3 416	66.7	1 608	49.1	159	25.2
	2010	3 324	65.6	1 648	50.3	126	23.0
Luxembourg	1990	381	81.1	160	34.7	..	..
	2000	435	84.0	189	39.7	4	25.0
	2005	457	85.2	204	42.3	3	33.3
	2010	507	82.6	238	43.4	3	33.3
Malta - Malte	1990	368	88.6	143	26.7	3	0.0
	2000	397	90.4	159	30.4	3	0.0
	2005	409	92.1	167	31.3	2	0.0
	2010	417	93.2	181	34.7	2	0.0
Netherlands - Pays-Bas	1990	14 892	69.0	6 860	38.9	316	28.5
	2000	15 863	77.1	8 131	43.1	269	33.1
	2005	16 305	80.3	8 580	44.8	239	35.1
	2010	16 613	83.1	8 860	45.7	213	36.6
Norway - Norvège	1990	4 241	72.0	2 169	44.6	139	27.3
	2000	4 491	76.0	2 376	46.4	110	33.6
	2005	4 623	77.7	2 428	46.9	97	37.1
	2010	4 883	79.0	2 613	46.9	88	39.8
Poland - Pologne	1990	38 056	61.4	18 069	45.5	4 963	45.5
	2000	38 302	61.9	17 302	45.8	3 763	41.3
	2005	38 165	61.5	17 437	45.3	3 364	38.4
	2010	38 277	60.6	18 230	45.1	2 960	36.2
Portugal	1990	9 925	48.2	4 782	42.8	861	50.6
	2000	10 336	53.8	5 277	45.4	678	58.0
	2005	10 544	57.6	5 525	46.6	602	61.3
	2010	10 676	61.0	5 614	47.4	515	63.7
Romania - Roumanie	1990	23 207	53.2	10 529	44.7	2 603	53.7
	2000	22 192	52.9	11 704	46.6	1 739	48.8
	2005	21 772	54.3	10 106	45.2	1 176	45.2
	2010	21 486	56.7	10 208	44.7	868	43.3
San Marino - Saint-Marin	1990	24	90.5	..	..	1	100.0
	2000	27	93.4	..	..	1	0.0
	2005	30	93.8	..	..	1	0.0
	2010	32	94.1	..	..	1	0.0
Slovakia - Slovaquie	2000	5 405	56.0	2 598	45.6	240	28.3
	2005	5 415	55.3	2 674	44.8	217	24.4
	2010	5 462	54.5	2 742	44.6	197	21.8

For sources and notes, see end of table.

Pour les sources et les notes, se reporter à la fin du tableau.

Region, country or territory / Régions, pays ou territoires	Year / Année	Population		Total labour force / Main-d'œuvre totale		Agriculture labour force / Main-d'œuvre dans l'agriculture	
		Total (thousands) Total (milliers)	Urban population (% of total population) Population urbaine (en % de la population totale)	Total (thousands) Total (milliers)	Female labour (% of total labour force) Main-d'œuvre féminine (en % de la main-d'œuvre totale)	Total (thousands) Total (milliers)	Female labour (% of total agriculture labour force) Main-d'œuvre féminine (en % de la main-d'œuvre totale dans l'agriculture)
		(1)	(2)	(3)	(4)	(5)	(6)
Slovenia - Slovénie	1990	–	–	–	–	–	–
	2000	1 985	50.8	960	46.3	19	47.4
	2005	2 002	50.2	1 017	46.0	12	41.7
	2010	2 030	49.4	1 031	46.4	7	42.9
Spain - Espagne	1990	38 889	75.3	15 825	34.4	1 888	30.2
	2000	40 288	76.2	18 209	39.5	1 339	34.8
	2005	43 395	76.1	21 017	41.3	1 205	36.3
	2010	46 077	76.1	23 235	44.3	1 015	37.6
Sweden - Suède	1990	8 559	83.1	4 687	47.7	209	28.7
	2000	8 860	84.0	4 545	47.1	146	31.5
	2005	9 029	84.7	4 749	47.3	129	34.1
	2010	9 380	83.9	4 990	47.0	115	35.7
Switzerland - Suisse	1990	6 703	73.4	3 756	42.8	197	31.0
	2000	7 201	73.2	3 990	44.3	167	38.3
	2005	7 450	73.3	4 160	45.7	151	41.1
	2010	7 700	72.7	4 404	45.8	137	43.1
United Kingdom - Royaume-Uni	1990	57 425	78.0	29 273	43.3	639	20.3
	2000	59 096	78.5	29 517	45.3	529	22.9
	2005	60 431	79.0	30 588	45.8	499	24.0
	2010	62 272	79.3	31 707	45.9	475	24.8
Developed economies: Oceania - Économies développées : Océanie	1990	20 494	85.2	10 166	41.6	641	29.3
	2000	23 022	87.0	11 562	44.0	617	35.7
	2005	24 538	87.7	12 745	45.1	630	38.9
	2010	26 637	85.9	14 172	45.5	643	41.8
Australia - Australie	1990	17 096	85.4	8 505	41.3	470	28.0
	2000	19 164	87.2	9 631	43.8	442	36.7
	2005	20 404	88.2	10 563	44.9	446	40.8
	2010	22 268	86.1	11 822	45.3	457	44.6
New Zealand - Nouvelle-Zélande	1990	3 398	84.4	1 660	43.2	171	30.4
	2000	3 858	85.9	1 932	45.2	175	33.1
	2005	4 134	85.6	2 183	46.2	184	34.2
	2010	4 368	84.9	2 350	46.8	186	34.9

For sources and notes, see next page.

Pour les sources et les notes, se reporter à la page suivante.

8

Sources:
- UN DESA Population Division, *World Population Prospects: The 2010 Revision*
- UN DESA Population Division, *World Population Prospects: The 2009 Revision*
- ILO, *LABORSTA* online database
- FAO, *FAOSTAT* online database
- National sources

Labour force data are derived from activity rates that were based on population estimates and projections of *World Population Prospects: The 2010 Revision*.
The figures for certain groups might be different from those published by the sources, when the UNCTAD definitions for those groups are different.
- Estimates.

Notes:

(1) Total population: de facto population in a country, area or region as of 1 July of the year indicated. Figures are presented in thousands.
(2) Urban population as percentage of total population: population living in areas classified as urban according to the criteria used by each area or country. Data refer to 1st July of the year indicated.
(3) Total labour force: comprises all persons (both sexes) of age 15 and above.
(4) Female labour force as percentage of total labour force: comprises all persons of feminine sex of age 15 and above.
(5) Total labour force in agriculture: is that part (male and female) of the total labour force engaged in or seeking work agriculture, hunting, fishing or forestry.
(6) Female labour force as percentage of total agriculture labour force: is that part (female) of the total labour force engaged or seeking work in agriculture, hunting, fishing or forestry.
(7) Agriculture labour force: includes Hong Kong, Macao and Taiwan; Total labour force: includes Taiwan only.
(8) From 1961, excluding Taiwan.
(9) National source.
(10) Labour data refer to Cyprus Island.
(11) Between 1974 and 2009 data refer to Republic of Cyprus; Between 1950 and 1973 and between 2010 and 2050 data refer to Cyprus Island.

Sources :
- ONU DAES Division de la population, *World Population Prospects: The Revision 2010*
- ONU DAES Division de la population, *World Population Prospects: The Revision 2009*
- BIT, *LABORSTA* base de données en ligne
- FAO, *FAOSTAT* base de données en ligne
- Sources nationales

Les données de la main-d'œuvre sont dérivées des taux d'activité qui sont basés sur des estimations et projections du *World Population Prospects: The 2010 Revision*.
Les chiffres pour certains groupes peuvent être différents de ceux publiés par les sources, lorsque les définitions de la CNUCED de ces groupes sont différentes.
- Estimations.

Notes :

(1) Population totale : de facto la population dans un pays ou région au 1er juillet de l'année indiquée. Les chiffres sont présentés en milliers.
(2) Population urbaine en pourcentage de la population totale : la population au 1er juillet vivant dans une région classée comme urbaine selon les critères définis par une région ou un pays.
(3) Main-d'œuvre totale : toutes les personnes (hommes et femmes) de 15 ans et plus.
(4) Main-d'œuvre féminine en pourcentage de la main d'œuvre totale : toutes les personnes de sexe féminin de 15 ans et plus.
(5) Main-d'œuvre totale dans l'agriculture : la part (hommes et femmes) du total de la main d'œuvre qui travaille ou cherche du travail dans l'agriculture, la chasse, la pêche ou la sylviculture.
(6) Main-d'œuvre totale féminine en pourcentage du total de la main-d'œuvre dans l'agriculture : la part (femmes) du total de la main-d'œuvre qui travaille ou cherche du travail dans l'agriculture, la chasse, la pêche ou la sylviculture.
(7) La main-d'œuvre agricole inclut Hong Kong, Macao et Taiwan. La main-d'œuvre totale inclut uniquement Taiwan.
(8) Taiwan est exclu à partir de 1961.
(9) Source nationale.
(10) Les données de la main-d'œuvre se réfèrent à l'île de Chypre.
(11) Entre 1974 et 2009 les données se réfèrent à la République de Chypre; entre 1950 et 1973 et entre 2010 et 2050 les données se réfèrent à l'île de Chypre.

Economic grouping / Groupements économiques	Year / Année	Population Total (thousands) / Total (milliers) (1)	Population Urban population (% of total population) / Population urbaine (en % de la population totale) (2)	Total labour force / Main-d'œuvre totale Total (thousands) / Total (milliers) (3)	Total labour force / Main-d'œuvre totale Female labour (% of total labour force) / Main-d'œuvre féminine (en % de la main-d'œuvre totale) (4)	Agriculture labour force / Main-d'œuvre agricole Total (thousands) / Total (milliers) (5)	Agriculture labour force / Main-d'œuvre agricole Female labour (% of total agriculture labour force) / Main-d'œuvre féminine (en % de la main-d'œuvre agricole totale) (6)
DEVELOPING ECONOMIES - ÉCONOMIES EN DÉVELOPPEMENT	1990	4 064 796	34.5	1 768 550	37.9	1 078 442	41.7
	2000	4 828 147	39.9	2 160 039	38.5	1 192 669	42.3
	2005	5 186 172	42.9	2 394 747	38.0	1 237 020	42.6
	2010	5 545 097	45.2	2 566 384	38.4	1 272 876	42.9
Developing economies excluding China - Économies en développement sans la Chine	1990	2 939 880	37.4	1 119 478	34.0	605 604	37.4
	2000	3 581 215	41.1	1 431 909	35.1	687 820	38.2
	2005	3 901 309	42.7	1 625 405	36.0	731 909	38.9
	2010	4 226 903	44.3	1 764 796	35.5	771 899	39.5
Developing economies excluding LDCs - Économies en développement sans les PMA	1990	3 555 429	36.4	1 558 555	37.1	914 591	40.9
	2000	4 166 974	42.2	1 883 579	37.7	997 256	41.3
	2005	4 440 877	45.5	2 075 143	38.1	1 020 207	41.4
	2010	4 712 770	48.0	2 200 196	37.3	1 034 113	41.4
High-income developing countries - Pays en développement à revenu élevé	1990	334 550	68.2	123 601	31.4	30 078	29.3
	2000	391 941	73.3	154 660	32.9	27 192	28.0
	2005	420 014	74.9	172 223	33.6	25 720	27.9
	2010	451 991	75.6	193 460	34.3	23 983	28.2
Middle-income developing countries - Pays en développement à revenu intermédiaire	1990	1 763 763	37.2	884 015	41.6	558 516	44.9
	2000	2 004 830	45.1	1 033 202	42.3	592 965	45.7
	2005	2 100 962	50.5	1 114 787	42.4	595 209	46.0
	2010	2 187 840	54.3	1 177 417	42.3	589 582	46.1
Low-income developing countries - Pays en développement à revenu faible	1990	1 966 171	26.4	760 866	34.7	489 806	38.9
	2000	2 430 911	30.1	972 068	35.2	572 459	39.4
	2005	2 664 581	31.8	1 107 569	36.1	616 626	40.0
	2010	2 904 532	33.7	1 195 288	35.1	659 229	40.5
Heavily indebted poor countries (IMF) - Pays pauvres très endettés (FMI)	1990	364 193	24.9	143 551	43.8	109 743	46.4
	2000	487 999	28.5	195 498	44.5	139 657	47.0
	2005	556 723	30.6	226 870	44.8	156 710	47.7
	2010	632 739	32.8	263 341	44.9	175 108	47.9
Landlocked developing countries - Pays en développement sans littoral	1990	198 187	18.2	81 990	44.6	63 077	44.8
	2000	331 296	26.0	137 856	44.6	88 243	45.6
	2005	368 946	26.8	158 502	44.9	99 904	46.4
	2010	410 363	28.0	181 313	45.0	112 445	46.6
Small island developing States - Petits États insulaires en développement	1990	12 715	29.9	4 989	41.9	2 432	43.8
	2000	15 035	30.0	6 169	43.0	2 779	46.7
	2005	17 257	29.7	7 200	43.2	3 271	47.6
	2010	18 604	30.0	7 890	43.5	3 552	48.6
Least developed countries - Pays les moins avancés	*1990*	*509 368*	*21.6*	*209 995*	*43.9*	*163 851*	*46.5*
	2000	*661 173*	*25.2*	*276 460*	*43.8*	*195 413*	*47.3*
	2005	*745 295*	*27.4*	*319 605*	*44.1*	*217 419*	*48.3*
	2010	*832 327*	*29.9*	*366 188*	*44.4*	*238 763*	*49.0*
Africa and Haiti - Afrique et Haïti	1990	305 243	22.3	123 134	45.6	98 654	47.9
	2000	401 734	26.0	163 721	46.2	125 036	48.7
	2005	460 298	28.1	191 222	46.4	141 349	49.2
	2010	526 091	30.4	222 638	46.4	158 978	49.5
Asia - Asie	1990	202 869	20.5	86 464	41.5	64 853	44.3
	2000	257 865	24.0	112 209	40.3	69 994	44.8
	2005	282 225	26.2	127 462	40.7	75 337	46.5
	2010	303 144	29.2	142 514	41.4	78 960	48.0
Islands - Îles	1990	1 256	24.4	397	34.5	344	46.2
	2000	1 574	26.4	530	35.1	383	46.7
	2005	2 773	26.4	920	34.6	733	46.1
	2010	3 092	28.2	1 035	34.9	825	46.8

For sources and notes, see end of table.   Pour les sources et les notes, se reporter à la fin du tableau.

8

Economic grouping / Groupements économiques	Year / Année	Population		Total labour force / Main-d'œuvre totale		Agriculture labour force / Main-d'œuvre agricole	
		Total (thousands) / Total (milliers)	Urban population (% of total population) / Population urbaine (en % de la population totale)	Total (thousands) / Total (milliers)	Female labour (% of total labour force) / Main-d'œuvre féminine (en % de la main-d'œuvre totale)	Total (thousands) / Total (milliers)	Female labour (% of total agriculture labour force) / Main-d'œuvre féminine (en % de la main-d'œuvre agricole totale)
		(1)	(2)	(3)	(4)	(5)	(6)
Major petroleum and gas exporters -	*1990*	*251 827*	*53.1*	*73 379*	*25.2*	*26 169*	*34.2*
Principaux exportateurs de pétrole et de gaz	*2000*	*314 803*	*59.6*	*99 273*	*29.4*	*27 762*	*38.7*
	2005	*352 351*	*62.0*	*117 986*	*31.1*	*29 039*	*40.9*
	2010	*396 191*	*63.5*	*135 453*	*30.5*	*30 105*	*43.6*
Africa - Afrique	1990	137 521	39.8	41 606	31.9	18 075	39.9
	2000	173 380	47.5	55 056	36.2	19 601	41.5
	2005	194 971	51.0	61 944	38.5	20 478	43.4
	2010	219 328	54.1	70 941	38.6	21 391	45.6
America - Amérique	1990	19 685	84.5	7 213	31.5	870	4.1
	2000	24 348	90.1	10 527	37.2	811	5.4
	2005	26 664	92.1	12 171	38.8	772	6.1
	2010	28 980	93.6	13 463	39.4	722	6.4
Asia - Asie	1990	94 622	65.8	24 560	11.9	7 224	23.5
	2000	117 074	71.2	33 690	15.8	7 350	34.7
	2005	130 716	72.4	43 871	18.3	7 789	37.8
	2010	147 883	71.7	51 049	17.0	7 992	41.5
Major exporters of manufactured goods -	*1990*	*1 356 573*	*31.5*	*745 935*	*43.8*	*507 705*	*46.6*
Principaux exportateurs d'articles manufacturés	*2000*	*1 512 337*	*40.3*	*845 522*	*44.1*	*537 654*	*47.1*
	2005	*1 564 996*	*46.4*	*896 971*	*44.0*	*537 640*	*47.3*
	2010	*1 612 605*	*50.7*	*938 790*	*43.9*	*531 072*	*47.2*
America - Amérique	1990	84 307	70.7	30 395	29.9	8 344	12.5
	2000	99 960	74.4	40 256	33.0	8 658	12.3
	2005	106 484	75.5	44 344	34.7	8 365	12.3
	2010	113 423	75.9	49 605	36.5	7 905	12.3
Asia - Asie	1990	1 272 267	28.9	715 540	44.4	499 361	47.2
	2000	1 412 377	37.8	805 266	44.6	528 996	47.7
	2005	1 458 512	44.3	852 627	44.5	529 275	47.8
	2010	1 499 182	48.8	889 185	44.3	523 167	47.8
Emerging economies - Économies émergentes	*1990*	*443 029*	*64.3*	*183 203*	*36.6*	*54 097*	*31.1*
	2000	*511 259*	*69.7*	*231 207*	*39.3*	*51 894*	*31.1*
	2005	*541 851*	*71.8*	*255 923*	*40.6*	*50 393*	*31.4*
	2010	*568 907*	*73.7*	*276 993*	*41.3*	*47 205*	*31.2*
America - Amérique	1990	301 473	74.4	119 628	33.8	27 574	16.5
	2000	352 597	79.8	157 481	38.5	27 747	19.4
	2005	375 012	82.0	176 196	40.3	26 755	20.1
	2010	394 972	83.7	193 086	41.4	25 015	20.5
Asia - Asie	1990	141 557	42.7	63 575	41.9	26 523	46.2
	2000	158 661	47.2	73 726	41.0	24 147	44.6
	2005	166 839	48.9	79 728	41.1	23 638	44.2
	2010	173 934	50.8	83 907	40.9	22 190	43.2
Newly industrialized Asian countries -	*1990*	*394 068*	*38.3*	*167 247*	*39.5*	*79 061*	*39.6*
Économies nouvellement industrialisées d'Asie	*2000*	*456 980*	*44.9*	*208 039*	*38.9*	*85 221*	*38.5*
	2005	*486 498*	*46.0*	*227 416*	*39.0*	*85 858*	*38.3*
	2010	*514 119*	*47.5*	*244 339*	*39.4*	*85 107*	*38.0*
First tier - Première génération	1990	72 070	56.1	26 858	36.7	3 476	44.1
	2000	78 875	60.4	32 422	37.6	2 209	44.0
	2005	80 850	61.6	34 442	37.9	1 701	44.2
	2010	83 464	62.5	36 215	37.9	1 276	43.3
Second tier - Deuxième génération	1990	321 998	34.3	140 388	40.1	75 585	39.4
	2000	378 105	41.7	175 616	39.1	83 012	38.3
	2005	405 648	42.9	192 974	39.2	84 157	38.2
	2010	430 655	44.6	208 124	39.6	83 831	37.9

For sources and notes, see end of table.

Pour les sources et les notes, se reporter à la fin du tableau.

Economic grouping / Groupements économiques	Year / Année	Population Total (thousands) / Total (milliers) (1)	Population Urban population (% of total population) / Population urbaine (en % de la population totale) (2)	Total labour force Total (thousands) / Total (milliers) (3)	Total labour force Female labour (% of total labour force) / Main-d'œuvre féminine (en % de la main-d'œuvre totale) (4)	Agriculture labour force Total (thousands) / Total (milliers) (5)	Agriculture labour force Female labour (% of total agriculture labour force) / Main-d'œuvre féminine (en % de la main-d'œuvre agricole totale) (6)
Developing economies: Africa - Économies en développement : Afrique	1990	634 675	32.3	227 627	39.9	145 387	45.9
	2000	810 362	36.3	302 119	41.5	177 263	47.1
	2005	910 325	38.3	347 343	42.2	195 715	47.0
	2010	1 021 388	40.4	397 233	42.5	214 508	48.4
Northern Africa excluding Sudan - Afrique septentrionale sans le Soudan	1990	119 473	48.8	34 354	23.0	12 559	38.7
	2000	141 663	52.0	44 045	21.8	13 288	41.2
	2005	153 166	53.4	50 428	22.1	13 650	43.3
	2010	165 377	55.1	55 840	23.7	13 680	44.6
Sub-Saharan Africa - Afrique subsaharienne	1990	514 981	28.4	193 204	42.9	132 786	46.6
	2000	668 384	32.9	257 965	44.9	163 922	47.6
	2005	756 719	35.2	296 746	45.6	181 594	48.3
	2010	855 481	37.5	341 173	45.5	200 746	48.7
Sub-Saharan Africa excluding South Africa - Afrique subsaharienne sans l'Afrique du Sud	1990	478 408	26.6	182 395	43.4	131 216	46.8
	2000	623 939	31.2	242 576	45.0	162 493	47.7
	2005	709 366	33.6	279 489	45.7	180 324	48.4
	2010	805 879	36.0	323 185	45.7	199 640	48.8
Developing economies: America - Économies en développement : Amérique	1990	438 537	70.1	170 320	33.7	42 395	16.8
	2000	516 529	75.3	225 581	38.3	43 453	19.5
	2005	552 101	77.5	253 417	40.1	42 991	20.4
	2010	585 126	79.2	279 453	41.2	41 502	20.9
Central America and Greater Caribbean Islands excluding Puerto Rico - Amérique centrale et Grandes Antilles sans Porto Rico	1990	140 504	62.6	51 521	31.7	15 654	14.3
	2000	166 478	66.8	66 238	34.5	16 067	14.3
	2005	177 931	68.5	73 249	36.1	16 074	14.5
	2010	189 801	69.8	82 321	37.7	15 707	14.7
Central America and Greater Caribbean Islands excluding Mexico and Puerto Rico - Amérique centrale et Grandes Antilles sans le Mexique et Porto Rico	1990	50 197	50.6	21 126	34.3	7 310	16.4
	2000	66 518	55.4	25 982	36.9	7 409	16.7
	2005	71 447	58.1	28 906	38.2	7 709	16.8
	2010	76 378	60.7	32 716	39.4	7 802	17.2
South America and Central America - Amérique du Sud et Amérique centrale	1990	408 709	71.4	158 365	33.4	38 731	16.1
	2000	482 823	76.5	211 834	38.2	39 796	19.1
	2005	516 659	78.7	238 458	40.1	39 322	20.0
	2010	548 205	80.3	263 045	41.1	37 835	20.5
South America excluding Brazil - Amérique du Sud sans le Brésil	1990	145 810	74.2	55 244	33.8	12 549	17.8
	2000	172 843	78.2	74 497	38.4	13 926	21.7
	2005	185 288	79.9	84 385	40.3	14 357	23.7
	2010	197 377	81.5	94 228	41.5	14 613	24.6
Developing economies: Asia - Économies en développement : Asie	1990	2 985 108	29.8	1 368 136	38.1	888 870	42.2
	2000	3 493 142	35.5	1 629 114	37.9	969 780	42.4
	2005	3 714 747	38.9	1 790 313	38.0	996 962	42.5
	2010	3 928 628	41.5	1 885 572	37.1	1 014 276	42.6
Eastern and South-Eastern Asia excluding China - Asie orientale et Asie du Sud-Est sans la Chine	1990	537 115	35.3	238 939	42.4	125 450	43.1
	2000	624 531	41.1	297 209	41.8	137 757	42.6
	2005	663 247	42.6	325 776	41.9	142 097	42.6
	2010	699 447	44.4	351 771	42.2	144 498	42.5
Southern Asia excluding India - Asie méridionale sans l'Inde	1990	322 200	30.3	110 584	27.7	67 821	35.4
	2000	406 303	33.4	145 063	27.9	73 197	37.2
	2005	444 659	35.3	170 665	29.3	80 374	39.7
	2010	479 532	37.7	190 667	30.3	85 647	42.2

For sources and notes, see next page.   Pour les sources et les notes, se reporter à la page suivante.

8

Sources:
- UN DESA Population Division, *World Population Prospects: The 2010 Revision*
- UN DESA Population Division, *World Population Prospects: The 2009 Revision*
- ILO, *LABORSTA* online database
- FAO, *FAOSTAT* online database
- National sources

Labour force data are derived from activity rates that were based on population estimates and projections of *World Population Prospects: The 2010 Revision*.
The figures for certain groups might be different from those published by the sources, when the UNCTAD definitions for those groups are different.
- Estimates.

Sources :
- ONU DAES Division de la population, *World Population Prospects: The Revision 2010*
- ONU DAES Division de la population, *World Population Prospects: The Revision 2009*
- BIT, *LABORSTA* base de données en ligne
- FAO, *FAOSTAT* base de données en ligne
- Sources nationales

Les données de la main-d'œuvre sont dérivées des taux d'activité qui sont basés sur des estimations et projections du *World Population Prospects: The 2010 Revision*.
Les chiffres pour certains groupes peuvent être différents de ceux publiés par les sources, lorsque les définitions de la CNUCED de ces groupes sont différentes.
- Estimations.

Notes:

(1)   Total population: de facto population in a country, area or region as of 1 July of the year indicated. Figures are presented in thousands.

(2)   Urban population as percentage of total population: population living in areas classified as urban according to the criteria used by each area or country. Data refer to 1st July of the year indicated.

(3)   Total labour force: comprises all persons (both sexes) of age 15 and above.

(4)   Female labour force as percentage of total labour force: comprises all persons of feminine sex of age 15 and above.

(5)   Total labour force in agriculture: is that part (male and female) of the total labour force engaged in or seeking work agriculture, hunting, fishing or forestry.

(6)   Female labour force as percentage of total agriculture labour force: is that part (female) of the total labour force engaged or seeking work in agriculture, hunting, fishing or forestry.

Notes :

(1)   Population totale : de facto la population dans un pays ou région au 1er juillet de l'année indiquée. Les chiffres sont présentés en milliers.

(2)   Population urbaine en pourcentage de la population totale : la population au 1er juillet vivant dans une région classée comme urbaine selon les critères définis par une région ou un pays.

(3)   Main-d'œuvre totale : toutes les personnes (hommes et femmes) de 15 ans et plus.

(4)   Main-d'œuvre féminine en pourcentage de la main d'œuvre totale : toutes les personnes de sexe féminin de 15 ans et plus.

(5)   Main-d'œuvre totale dans l'agriculture : la part (hommes et femmes) du total de la main-d'œuvre qui travaille ou cherche du travail dans l'agriculture, la chasse, la pêche ou la sylviculture.

(6)   Main-d'œuvre totale féminine en pourcentage du total de la main-d'œuvre dans l'agriculture : la part (femmes) du total de la main-d'œuvre qui travaille ou cherche du travail dans l'agriculture, la chasse, la pêche ou la sylviculture.

FEEDBACK QUESTIONNAIRE

In order to keep improving its products, the UNCTAD secretariat seeks feedback about its publications. Please take a few minutes to fill in and return, by fax or by mail, this short questionnaire on the *Handbook of Statistics*. Thank you in advance.

-   **For what main purposes do you use this statistical publication?** (*one or more answers*)
    Analysis and research ☐   Education and training ☐
    Policy formulation and management ☐   Legislation ☐
    Other (*please specify*)
    _____

-   **How do you rate this publication as regards its quality?**

(*one box in each case*)	Very good	Adequate	Poor
Presentation and readability	☐	☐	☐
Comprehensiveness	☐	☐	☐
Up-to-date information	☐	☐	☐
Technical and analytical value	☐	☐	☐
CD-ROM version only			
Availability of full historical time series	☐	☐	☐
Multiple dimensions of statistics	☐	☐	☐
Ease of data manipulation and extraction	☐	☐	☐
Ease of creation of charts	☐	☐	☐

-   **In the context of your specific needs and the availability of a PC, what version of the *Handbook of Statistics* would you most likely use?**
    Printed version ☐   CD-ROM ☐

-   **With regard to your area of work and interest, which data sets from the *Handbook* do you use most?**
    (*one or more answers*)

    ☐ Trade in goods   ☐ Commodity price indices
    ☐ Structure of international trade by region   ☐ Balance of payments
    ☐ Structure of international trade by product ☐ Foreign direct investment
    ☐ International merchandise trade indicators   ☐ Official financial flows
    ☐ Import tariffs   ☐ External debt
    ☐ Trade in services   ☐ National accounts
    ☐ Maritime transport   ☐ Demographic indicators

-   **What other statistics or analytical indicators would you like to find in the *Handbook of Statistics*? Please use an extra sheet for suggestions, if necessary**.
    _____
    _____
    _____

-   **Finally, in order to help gauge the level and structure of demand and to ensure appropriate distribution policies, please tell us something about yourself** (*this information will, of course, remain confidential*).

    Name and address:
    _____
    _____
    _____

    Professional title or status and area of work (*e.g. governmental, private enterprise, academic institution, media, NGO*):
    _____
    _____

-   **Would you like to receive regularly the updated versions of the *UNCTAD Handbook of Statistics*?**
    Yes ☐   No ☐

Your response would be in our mutual interest and greatly appreciated. Please return the questionnaire to:
Head, Development Statistics and Information Branch
UNCTAD, Palais des Nations
1211 Geneva 10 (Switzerland)
Fax: (+ 41 22) 917 00 48
e-mail: statistics@unctad.org

QUESTIONNAIRE D'ÉVALUATION

En vue de continuer à améliorer ses produits, le secrétariat de la CNUCED aimerait avoir vos commentaires sur ses publications. Prenez, s'il vous plaît, quelques minutes pour remplir et nous renvoyer, par fax ou par courrier, ce bref questionnaire concernant le *Manuel de statistiques*. Merci d'avance.

- **À quelles fins principales utilisez-vous cette publication ?** *(une ou plusieurs réponses)*

  Analyse et recherche ☐   Enseignement et formation ☐
  Gestion et prise de décisions ☐   Législation ☐
  Autres *(veuillez préciser)*

  _____

- **Comment jugez-vous cette publication en ce qui concerne sa qualité ?** *(cochez une réponse par critère d'évaluation)*

	Très bien	Convenable	Médiocre
Présentation et lisibilité	☐	☐	☐
Couverture et étendue	☐	☐	☐
Actualité des informations	☐	☐	☐
Valeur technique et analytique	☐	☐	☐
Seulement pour la version CD-ROM			
Disponibilité de la série historique complète de données	☐	☐	☐
Présentation multi-critères des statistiques	☐	☐	☐
Facilité de traitement et d'extraction des données	☐	☐	☐
Facilité de création de graphiques	☐	☐	☐

- **En fonction de vos besoins spécifiques et de la disponibilité d'un ordinateur, quelle version du *Manuel de statistiques* souhaiteriez-vous utiliser ?**

  Version imprimée ☐   CD-ROM ☐

- **Eu égard à votre travail et vos intérêts, quelles sont les données du *Manuel* que vous utilisez le plus ?**
  (une ou plusieurs réponses)

  ☐ Commerce des biens   ☐ Indices des prix des produits de base
  ☐ Structure du commerce international par régions   ☐ Données de la balance des paiements
  ☐ Structure du commerce international par produits   ☐ Investissement direct étranger
  ☐ Indicateurs du commerce international des marchandises   ☐ Flux financiers officiels
  ☐ Droits de douane aux importations   ☐ Dette externe
  ☐ Commerce des services   ☐ Comptes nationaux
  ☐ Transport maritime   ☐ Indicateurs démographiques

- **Quels autres indicateurs analytiques ou statistiques voudriez-vous trouver dans le *Manuel de statistiques* ? Veuillez utiliser une feuille supplémentaire pour vos suggestions, si besoin est.**

  _____

  _____

  _____

- **Enfin, pour nous permettre de déterminer le niveau et la nature de la demande et d'assurer une bonne politique de distribution, veuillez nous donner quelques informations à votre sujet** *(cette information demeurera bien sûr confidentielle).*

  Nom et adresse :

  _____

  _____

  Titre professionnel (ou statut) et domaine d'activité *(ex. administration, entreprise privée, université, médias, ONG)* :

  _____

  _____

- **Souhaiteriez-vous recevoir régulièrement les versions du *Manuel de statistiques de la CNUCED* mises à jour ?**

  Oui ☐   Non ☐

Votre réponse est d'un intérêt mutuel et très appréciée. Veuillez retourner le questionnaire rempli au :
Chef, Service de la documentation et des statistiques du développement
CNUCED, Palais des Nations
1211 Genève 10 (Suisse)
Fax : (+ 41 22) 917 00 48
Adresse électronique : statistics@unctad.org